21st Century Estate Planning:
Practical Applications
2005 Edition

BY

ROY M. ADAMS
SONNENSCHEIN NATH & ROSENTHAL LLP

2005

SONNENSCHEIN NATH & ROSENTHAL LLP
CANNON FINANCIAL INSTITUTE, INC.

1221 AVENUE OF THE AMERICAS
NEW YORK, NEW YORK 10020-1089
(212) 768-6726 (TELEPHONE)
(212) 768-6800 (FACSIMILE)

8000 SEARS TOWER
CHICAGO, ILLINOIS 60606-6404
(312) 876-7424 (TELEPHONE)
(312) 876-7934 (FACSIMILE)

WWW.SONNENSCHEIN.COM
WWW.CANNONFINANCIAL.COM

21st Century Estate Planning:
Practical Applications
2005 Edition

BY

ROY M. ADAMS
Sonnenschein Nath & Rosenthal LLP

Editors and Contributing Authors:

Carole M. Bass, Sonnenschein Nath & Rosenthal LLP
Richard M. Brown, Sonnenschein Nath & Rosenthal LLP
J. Phillips Buchanan, Jr., Cannon Financial Institute, Inc.
Keith A. Davidson, Sonnenschein Nath & Rosenthal LLP
Lawrence T. Divers, Cannon Financial Institute, Inc.
Scott T. Filmore, Sonnenschein Nath & Rosenthal LLP
Susan M. Hughes, Sonnenschein Nath & Rosenthal LLP
Kevin C. Lane, Sonnenschein Nath & Rosenthal LLP
Wendy Byers Marvin, Sonnenschein Nath & Rosenthal LLP
Thomas G. Opferman, Sonnenschein Nath & Rosenthal LLP
Abraham D. Piontnica, Sonnenschein Nath & Rosenthal LLP
Charles A. Redd, Sonnenschein Nath & Rosenthal LLP
Daniel A. Smith, Cannon Financial Institute, Inc.
Eileen B. Trost, Sonnenschein Nath & Rosenthal LLP

Editorial Consulting Staff

Ted R. Ridlehuber, CEO, Cannon Financial Institute, Inc.
J. Phillips Buchanan, Jr., Cannon Financial Institute, Inc.
Lawrence T. Divers, Cannon Financial Institute, Inc.
Daniel A. Smith, Cannon Financial Institute, Inc.
Milton F. Eisenberg, II, Cannon Financial Institute, Inc.

The materials in this volume are current through March 31, 2005.

These materials are intended to stimulate thought and discussion and to provide the reader with useful ideas and guidance in the areas of estate planning and administration. The materials do not constitute, and should not be treated as, legal advice regarding the use of any particular estate planning or other technique, device, or suggestion, or any of the tax or other consequences associated with them. Although we have made every effort to ensure the accuracy of these materials, neither the authors, nor Sonnenschein Nath & Rosenthal LLP and Cannon Financial Institute, Inc. assumes any responsibility for any individual's reliance on the written information presented during these materials. The reader should verify independently all statements made in the materials before applying them to a particular fact pattern and should determine independently the tax and other consequences of using any particular device, technique, or suggestions before recommending the same to a client or implementing the same on a client's or his or her own behalf.

Roy M. Adams (NY)
Senior Chairman of the
Trusts & Estates Practice Group

N. Todd Angkatavanich
(NJ) 973-912-7104
Carole M. Bass
(NY) 212-768-6949
Richard M. Brown
(CH) 312-876-2855
Patricia N. Chock
(LA) 213-892-5008
Robert W. Cockren
(NJ) 973-912-7101
Keith A. Davidson
(LA) 213-892-5067
Arlene G. Dubin
(NY) 212-398-5765
Ralph M. Engel
(NY) 212-768-6919
Scott T. Filmore
(SL) 314-259-5835
Brit L. Geiger
(NY) 212-398-8793

Elga A. Goodman
(NJ) 212-398-8703
Susan M. Hughes
(CH) 312-876-3176
Ralph B. Kelley
(NY) 212-768-6908
Azniv Ksachikyan
(LA) 213-892-2924
Kevin C. Lane
(CH) 312-876-7466
Arthur S. Levine
(LA) 213-892-5081
Wendy Byers Marvin
(KC) 816-460-2494
Edward J. McCaffery
(LA) 213-892-5112
Thomas G. Opferman
(CH) 312-876-7481
Barbara L. Pedersen
(NY) 212-398-8706

Abraham D. Piontnica
(NY) 212-768-6818
Charles A. Redd
(SL) 314-259-5819
Martin Rosen
(NY) 212-768-6912
Mitchell D. Schepps
(FL) 561-868-7317
Joseph D. Serrano
(KC) 816-460-2497
Susan B. Slater-Jansen
(NY) 212-768-6920
Jadene M.W. Tamura
(LA) 213-892-5026
Eileen B. Trost
(CH) 312-876-8149
Michael J. Weinberger
(NY) 212-398-5270
Alan T. Yoshitake
(LA) 213-892-5011

Ted R. Ridlehuber
Chief Executive Officer
Cannon Financial Institute, Inc.

Roy M. Adams
David C. Bell
Clark D. Brown
J. Phillips Buchanan, Jr.
Fran M. DeMaris

Lawrence T. Divers
Milton F. Eisenberg, II
Duane E. Lee, II
Donna G. Schumell
Daniel A. Smith

ISBN 0-9702186-6-4
Copyright © 2005 Sonnenschein Nath & Rosenthal LLP and Cannon Financial Institute, Inc.
All Rights Reserved

ROY M. ADAMS

ROY M. ADAMS is Senior Chairman of the Trusts & Estates Practice Group at the National Law Firm of SONNENSCHEIN NATH & ROSENTHAL LLP with offices in Chicago, IL, New York City, NY, Short Hills, NJ, Los Angeles, CA, San Francisco, CA, Washington, DC, St. Louis, MO, Kansas City, MO, and West Palm Beach, FL. Mr. Adams is an Adjunct Professor of Estate Planning and Taxation at Northwestern University School of Law, where for over 25 years he has taught estate planning and taxation. He has been presented Northwestern University's Alumni Merit Award for outstanding professional achievement. Mr. Adams is a member of the distinguished teaching faculty of Cannon Financial Institute and is also a Senior Consultant to Cannon's Management. He contributes extensively to Internet publications through a joint venture with Cannon, and conducts special Professional Education Seminars and monthly telephone conferences, web-casts and satellite broadcasts on sophisticated and practical planning techniques. Mr. Adams is a Fellow of the American College of Trusts and Estates Counsel. He is Special Consultant to TRUSTS & ESTATES magazine, for which he writes a bimonthly column entitled "*Wit, Wisdom and the Fiduciary Professions*," and a highly acclaimed quarterly column on tax fundamentals entitled, "*Back-To-School*." Additionally, he was a member of the Editorial Board and Contributing Author of The Chase Journal, which was published by J.P. Morgan-Chase Bank, and distributed to over 4,000 Trust & Estates tax specialists around the world before it ceased publication. Mr. Adams also contributes a monthly column on estate planning, principally for the brokerage community, in the REGISTERED REPRESENTATIVE magazine, and a quarterly article on estate planning in the FINANCIAL ADVISOR magazine, mainly for investment advisors. One of Mr. Adams' newest books, 21ˢᵗ CENTURY ESTATE PLANNING: PRACTICAL APPLICATIONS, was published by Cannon Financial Institute in 2002, revised and updated in 2003, 2004 and 2005; reviews of this work have reflected very high acclaim, particularly for innovation, creativity and practical advice, notwithstanding possible transfer tax repeal. He has been the co-author of a two-volume text, ILLINOIS ESTATE PLANNING, WILL DRAFTING AND ESTATE ADMINISTRATION (2nd Edition) published in 1994, and revised, and he is a contributing editor to UNDERSTANDING LIVING TRUSTS (5th Edition) published in October, 1994, and annually revised. Another of Mr. Adams' publications, published by Primedia in 2002, is his book entitled, WIT & WISDOM - THE BEST OF ROY ADAMS, which contains essays and commentaries upon a variety of non-technical but extremely entertaining and meaningful topics of interest to estate planning professionals and their clients. He conducts an extensive national and international practice in the areas of estate and tax planning, advising wealthy families, private foundations, public charities, as well as individuals whose assets often include substantial business interests. He lectures nationally and internationally in his areas of expertise and is a much sought-after speaker. Mr. Adams has been recognized in several countries for his humanitarian work, and he actively pursues charitable activities throughout the world. He is admitted to practice in the States of New York and Illinois. Mr. Adams serves as a member of the Tax Advisory Boards of the Museum of Modern Art and Lincoln Center for the Performing Arts, and is listed in "Best Lawyers in America."

Preface

From the Internal Revenue Serice Circular 230 through the Twilight Zone of the Year 2010, change…change…change. Thus, the 4th Edition of this book. My hope is that each of you with whom I have the privilege of sharing thoughts and concepts in this book will find the ideas contained in the chapters of this book clearly presented and useful in your daily professional life. My colleagues at Sonnenschein Nath & Rosenthal LLP and I have tried to explain the transfer tax rules cogently and concisely without omitting details or nuances that may be needed to assist you and your clients to plan for and minimize or eliminate the unduly heavy burden of the federal gift, estate and generation-skipping transfer taxes, not to mention the income taxation of trusts and estates. Add to this the entry of the States in to the transfer tax system and there is much to consider. While the initial chapters in the book contain an explanation of the important transfer tax and income tax rules that you need to know, most of the chapters are devoted to planning strategies to help you assist your clients keep the assets that they have worked so hard to accumulate, including their interests in family businesses that are a central and increasing part of the American way of life.

Virtually all of the chapters in this book have been completely updated to reflect the latest legal and tax developments and to offer you more planning ideas and examples. This book is my sixth major publication venture done in conjunction with Cannon Financial Institute, Inc.. The leadership and technical expertise of Ted Ridlehuber, CEO of Cannon, in the financial services and educational fields are unparalleled in the industry. The teaching faculty at Cannon Financial Institute, Inc. is superb, and this book could not have been produced without the excellent editorial assistance of the entire Cannon faculty. My thanks for your wonderful professional insights and continuing support.

Several years ago, I joined the national law firm of Sonnenschein Nath & Rosenthal LLP and am resident in our New York and Chicago offices. The firm has a preeminent and rapidly expanding practice in the area of tax and estate planning, and I am honored to serve as Senior Chairman of Sonnenschein's Trusts & Estates Practice Group. I owe an enormous debt of gratitude to my partners and colleagues at Sonnenschein for the tremendous support and responsive assistance they have given me in producing this book written in its entirety after I joined the firm. While I cannot mention all of those to whom I am indebted at Sonnenschein, I do want to thank a number of my colleagues whose hard work and extraordinary legal skills have especially assisted me in producing this work.

In particular, I appreciate the insight, dedication and skill that my partner Clary Redd (resident in our St. Louis office) brought to the discussion of the tax planning ideas discussed in detail. Clary was ably assisted by Scott Filmore. Eileen Trost (resident in our Chicago office), one of the leading lawyers in the country in advising clients regarding retirement benefits and IRAs, has shared her wisdom with me and assisted in writing and editing the chapter on planning for retirement benefits. Tom Opferman's major supervisory duties in our group did not prevent his significant contributions to this work with many brilliant insights throughout joined by our colleagues every step of the way. I have never worked more able professionals in my entire career.

I am most indebted, however, to you, the readers and users of these materials, for your kind words of support and loyalty over the years that we have worked together to further the interests of our clients, to reduce or eliminate their transfer tax burdens, as well as to reduce the personal burdens they often carry.

Roy M. Adams

New York, New York
April 5, 2005

Dedication

This book is dedicated to my son, Daniel Adams, my grandson, Roy Adams (affectionately known as "Little Roy"), and my granddaughters, Danniela and Janai. They bring special joy with their zest for life and pleasure in all that our great country has to offer, besides the unnumbered ice cream cones and visits to Disney World rightfully demanded as an offset to the time writing a book such as this requires of anyone to be away from his or her family.

Roy M. Adams

New York, New York
April 5, 2005

TABLE OF CONTENTS

21st Century Estate Planning:
Practical Applications
2005 Edition

©*2005 Sonnenschein Nath & Rosenthal LLP*
and Cannon Financial Institute, Inc.

iii

21st Century Estate Planning:
Practical Applications
2005 Edition

©*2005 Sonnenschein Nath & Rosenthal LLP*
and Cannon Financial Institute, Inc.

vii

21st Century Estate Planning:
Practical Applications
2005 Edition

©2005 Sonnenschein Nath & Rosenthal LLP
and Cannon Financial Institute, Inc.

viii

21st Century Estate Planning:
Practical Applications
2005 Edition

©2005 Sonnenschein Nath & Rosenthal LLP
and Cannon Financial Institute, Inc.

xii

21st Century Estate Planning:
Practical Applications
2005 Edition

©2005 Sonnenschein Nath & Rosenthal LLP
and Cannon Financial Institute, Inc.

xiii

21st Century Estate Planning:
Practical Applications
2005 Edition

©2005 Sonnenschein Nath & Rosenthal LLP
and Cannon Financial Institute, Inc.

xiv

21st Century Estate Planning:
Practical Applications
2005 Edition

©2005 Sonnenschein Nath & Rosenthal LLP
and Cannon Financial Institute, Inc.

xvi

21st Century Estate Planning:
Practical Applications
2005 Edition

©2005 Sonnenschein Nath & Rosenthal LLP
and Cannon Financial Institute, Inc.

xvii

APPENDICES

21st Century Estate Planning:
Practical Applications
2005 Edition

©2005 Sonnenschein Nath & Rosenthal LLP
and Cannon Financial Institute, Inc.

xviii

I.   INTRODUCTION TO FEDERAL TRANSFER TAXES

A. Introduction

The federal transfer tax system is comprised of three separate transfer taxes: (1) the federal estate tax, (2) the federal gift tax, and (3) the federal generation-skipping transfer ("GST") tax. Each of these transfer taxes is imposed on the *privilege* of being able to *transfer* property rather than a tax on the transferred property itself. The federal estate tax covers transfers at death; the federal gift tax addresses lifetime transfers; and the federal GST tax catches transfers to grandchildren and others that would otherwise escape taxation through a loophole in the transfer tax system. The tax rules governing these transfers are highly technical and extremely complex, and the enactment of the Economic Growth and Tax Relief Reconciliation Act of 2001 (the "Act"), discussed below, has complicated an already difficult set of tax rules.

B. Marginal Rates

Without proper estate planning, the unified transfer tax system can result in a significant loss of an individual's assets, including ownership of a family business interest. The marginal tax rates for federal gift and estate tax purposes in effect for 2005 as adjusted by the Act are shown in the following chart:

Taxable Amount	Tax Rate
$10,000 or less	18%
$10,001 to $20,000	20%
$20,001 to $40,000	22%
$40,001 to $60,000	24%
$60,001 to $80,000	26%
$80,001 to $100,000	28%
$100,001 to $150,000	30%
$150,001 to $250,000	32%
$250,001 to $500,000	34%
$500,001 to $750,000	37%
$750,001 to $1,000,000	39%
$1,000,001 to $1,250,000	41%
$1,250,001 to $1,500,000	43%
$1,500,001 to $2,000,000	45%
$2,000,001 or more	47%

C. Unified Transfer Tax System

Like most bodies of law, the transfer tax laws have evolved significantly since their inception. Since the Tax Reform Act of 1976, however, lifetime transfers by gift and transfers at death have been taxed under a unified transfer tax system. The purpose of this unified system is to equalize the treatment of lifetime and testamentary transfers.

Under the unified system, which is still in effect today, a single tax rate schedule applies to transfers for both gift tax and estate tax purposes. The applicable tax rates are progressive, based on an individual's aggregate lifetime transfers and transfers at death. Under current law as shown in the chart above, the maximum tax rate ranges from 18% for transfers of $10,000 or less to 47% for transfers over $2,000,000. In addition to the unified tax rate, a cumulative "unified credit" ("applicable credit amount") applies against an individual's transfer tax liability for transfers by gift and at death. For 2005, the applicable credit amount for estate tax purposes is $555,800 ($345,800 for gift tax purposes), and the applicable exclusion amount (the amount of transferred property exempt from tax by the applicable credit amount) for estate tax purposes is $1,500,000 ($1,000,000 for gift tax purposes). The applicable credit amount and the applicable exclusion amount are scheduled to increase in stages over the next several years for estate tax purposes and remain frozen for gift tax purposes.

The GST tax was enacted to close a loophole in the unified transfer tax system by approximating the transfer taxes that would have been due if property had been transferred at each generation level. Unlike the estate and gift tax rates, which increase with the value of the property transferred, the GST tax rate is a flat rate based on the maximum estate tax rate (47% for 2005). The GST tax is imposed *in addition to* the estate tax and the gift tax with respect to certain transfers, making it an extremely expensive tax.

Because of the number of tax exclusions, deductions, exemptions and credits available under the transfer tax system, only significant transfers of property are subject to transfer tax. Therefore, it is incumbent on the practitioner to be aware of what exclusions, deductions, exemptions and credits are available to reduce or even eliminate a client's transfer tax liability.

D. Economic Growth and Tax Relief Reconciliation Act of 2001

The Act is comprised of applicable rules for three time periods: (1) pre-repeal of the estate tax and the GST tax in 2010, (2) repeal of the estate tax and GST tax in 2010, and (3) post-2010 when the "sunset" provisions of the Act repeal the changes made to the transfer tax system by the Act. Some of the major changes the Act made to the transfer tax system include the following. These changes are discussed in detail in subsequent chapters in this book.

1.   De-Unification of the Unified Credit

Since 2004, the unified credit against estate tax and gift tax has no longer been unified because the Act has increased the applicable exclusion amount for estate tax purposes (referred to here as the "estate tax exemption") while the applicable exclusion amount for gift tax purposes (referred to here as the "gift tax exemption") has remained at $1,000,000. The increase in the estate tax exemption is as follows:

Year of Transfer	Estate Tax Exemption	Gift Tax Exemption	Maximum Estate & Gift Tax Rate
2005	$1,500,000	$1,000,000	47%
2006	$2,000,000	$1,000,000	46%
2007	$2,000,000	$1,000,000	45%
2008	$2,000,000	$1,000,000	45%
2009	$3,500,000	$1,000,000	45%
2010	Estate tax repealed	$1,000,000	35% (gifts only)
2011	$1,000,000	$1,000,000	55%

Although the estate tax exemption and the gift tax exemption now differ in amount, these exemptions are still cumulative and work together to determine an individual's federal estate tax liability. That is, in 2005, an individual does not have a $1,000,000 gift tax exemption and a separate $1,500,000 estate tax exemption. Rather, during life an individual can transfer up to $1,000,000 without incurring federal gift tax, and at death, the individual can transfer an additional $500,000 without incurring federal estate tax if the individual has already used his or her $1,000,000 gift tax exemption. Thus, the aggregate amount that can be transferred during life and at death without incurring federal estate tax will be $1,500,000 in 2005.

2.   Reduction in Estate, Gift and GST Tax Rates & Repeal of Estate and GST Tax

Under the Act, the maximum estate, gift and GST tax rates are scheduled to decline (see chart above) until the repeal of the estate tax and GST tax in 2010. During the scheduled one-year repeal of the estate tax and the GST tax in 2010, the gift tax is to remain in effect at the top income tax rate of 35%.

3.   Additions to GST Tax Rules

The Act contains additional GST tax relief retroactive to December 31, 2000. These rules are highly technical and add another layer of complexity to the transfer tax rules.

4.   Carryover Basis

Under the Act, beginning in 2010, the current "step-up in basis rule" for determining the basis of inherited property is replaced with a set of complicated "carryover basis" rules that apply even after repeal of the estate tax and GST tax.

E. Conclusion

More than ever, clients are looking to a myriad of professional practitioners, including attorneys specializing in estate planning, general practice attorneys, financial planners, accountants, banking professionals, life insurance agents, and other advisors, to guide them through these complex transfer tax rules and to provide them with financial, tax, and estate planning advice. Because minimizing taxes is an important goal of these clients, it is imperative that advisors have a detailed understanding of the transfer tax rules. A thorough comprehension of the rules and the effect of the Act on these rules will help practitioners recognize potential issues, identify potential solutions, and provide sound planning advice.

The following three chapters of this book discuss in detail the rules governing the federal estate tax (Chapter 2), the federal gift tax (Chapter 3), and the federal GST tax (Chapter 4). In general, these chapters cover the transfers subject to the tax; the deductions, exclusions and credits available to offset the tax; the computation of the tax; special rules applicable to the tax; and changes made by the Act. The next two chapters discuss the valuation of assets for transfer tax purposes (Chapter 5) and the federal income taxation of trusts and estates (Chapter 6). These initial chapters are intended to give the reader an understandable, yet thorough, discussion of the principal rules governing the transfer tax system and the income taxation of trusts and estates. The balance of the first volume is devoted to a comprehensive discussion of the numerous planning techniques (Chapters 7 though 17) available to address the otherwise potentially confiscatory gift, estate and GST taxes, the ethical considerations for practitioners (Chapter 18), the duties and liabilities of practitioners and fiduciaries (Chapters 19 and 20), and comprehensive wealth management (Chapter 21).

II. FEDERAL ESTATE TAX

A. Introduction

The federal estate tax is an excise tax imposed on a decedent's privilege of being able to transfer his or her entire taxable estate at death. Internal Revenue Code ("IRC") § 2001(a). The federal estate tax is an indirect tax on the transfer of property rather than a direct tax on the property itself. Because of various exclusions, credits and deductions, only significant transfers of property are subject to the federal estate tax.

Minimizing taxes at death is an important goal for many clients seeking financial and estate planning advice. Although the tax rules applicable to transfers at death are complex, a basic understanding of these rules will help practitioners recognize potential issues and provide sound tax planning advice to such clients.

This chapter discusses the following topics relating to the federal estate tax and applicable changes made by the Economic Growth and Tax Relief Reconciliation Act of 2001 (the "Act"):

- Types of property and property interests subject to federal estate tax.
- Valuation for federal estate tax purposes.
- Federal estate tax deductions.
- Federal estate tax credits.
- Calculation of federal estate tax.
- Payment of federal estate tax.

B. Types of Property and Property Interests Subject to Federal Estate Tax

Generally, a decedent's "gross estate" includes the value of all property owned by the decedent at death and the value of all property in which the decedent had an interest at death. IRC §§ 2031(a) and 2033. This definition is very broad, and includes all kinds of property and property interests, both real and personal and tangible and intangible, wherever situated, to the extent of the interest beneficially owned by the decedent. Examples of such property and property interests include, but are not limited to, the following:

- Tangible personal property (*e.g.*, jewelry, furniture, furnishings, clothing, furs, collections of tangibles, automobiles, artwork, hobby equipment, video and audio equipment, cameras and camera equipment, computer equipment, sporting equipment, together with any assignable insurance policies on any such items).
- Cash on hand or on deposit (*e.g.*, checking accounts, savings accounts and certificates of deposit).
- Stocks, bonds and notes (*e.g.*, shares in a corporation, U.S. savings bonds, promissory notes of which the decedent was the lender).

- Business interests (*e.g.*, interest in a partnership or unincorporated business).
- Real property and interests in real property (*e.g.*, interest in principal residence, vacation home, business real property).
- Annuities and retirement accounts (*e.g.*, IRAs, 401(k) accounts).
- Life insurance (*e.g.*, proceeds payable to the decedent's estate).
- Certain payments received after death (*e.g.*, compensation received after death, post-death employee benefits, tax refunds due to decedent) but <u>not</u> wrongful death proceeds. Rev. Rul. 55-87, 1955-1 C.B. 112.

The Internal Revenue Code also addresses the inclusion of <u>specific</u> types of property and property interests in a decedent's gross estate. These provisions are discussed below.

C. Property Owned by Decedent

1. Jointly-Owned Property

The general provisions of IRC §§ 2031(a) and 2033 govern the estate tax treatment of property owned by the decedent and another person as tenants in common. IRC § 2040 specifies the estate tax treatment of: (1) property owned by the decedent and another person as joint tenants with rights of survivorship, and (2) property owned by the decedent and his or her spouse as tenants by the entirety.

a. <u>Property Owned as Tenants in Common</u>. Generally, the value of property owned by the decedent and another person as tenants in common is included in the decedent's estate to the extent of the decedent's fractional interest in the property. IRC §§ 2031(a) and 2033.

> **EXAMPLE:** A and her sister B own a home as tenants in common. B dies first when the home is worth $150,000. At B's death, one-half of the value of the home ($75,000) will be included in B's estate.

b. <u>Property Owned as Joint Tenants With Rights of Survivorship or as Tenants by the Entirety</u>. Generally, the value of property owned by the decedent and another person in joint tenancy with rights of survivorship is included in the decedent's estate except to the extent that it can be shown that the other joint tenant contributed to the cost of the property. IRC § 2040(a).

➔ **<u>Planning Point</u>:** Practitioners should advise clients to keep track of contributions to such jointly-owned property for estate tax purposes and also for income tax purposes with respect to the step-up in basis at death.

> **EXAMPLE:** A and her sister B own a home as joint tenants with rights of survivorship. A contributed the entire purchase price of the

home ($100,000). B contributed nothing. B dies first. At B's death, the full value of the home will be included in B's estate unless B's estate can show that B did not contribute to any of the cost of acquiring the home.

> **EXAMPLE:** A and her sister B own a home as joint tenants with rights of survivorship. A contributed $75,000 to the purchase price of the home. B contributed $25,000. A dies first. At A's death, the home is worth $200,000, and A's share of the home, $150,000 (3/4 of $200,000), is included in A's estate.

(1) **Property Acquired by Gift, Bequest, Devise or Inheritance.** Where the decedent and the other joint tenant(s) acquired the property by gift, bequest, devise or inheritance, the decedent's fractional interest in the property is included in the decedent's gross estate. IRC § 2040(a).

> **EXAMPLE:** X makes a gift of real property to his four children A, B, C and D. A dies first. At A's death, one-fourth of the property will be included in A's gross estate, and the property will pass by operation of law to B, C and D. If B dies next, one-third of the property will be included in B's gross estate, and the property will pass by operation of law to C and D, and so on.

(2) **Qualified Joint Interests.** A special rule applies to married joint tenants. If the joint tenants are married, then only one-half of the value of a qualified joint interest is included in the estate of the first spouse to die. This is true regardless of the amount each spouse contributed towards the property. A "qualified joint interest" is any interest in property held by the decedent and the decedent's spouse as tenants by the entirety or as joint tenants with rights of survivorship but only if they are the only joint tenants.

> **EXAMPLE:** H and W own real estate as joint tenants with rights of survivorship. W paid the entire purchase price of $200,000. H dies first. At H's death, the property is worth $300,000, and $150,000 (one-half of the value of the property on the date of death) is included in H's estate even though W paid the entire purchase price of the property. If H and W had owned the real estate with a third party, then the general rule would apply because the property would not be a qualified joint interest.

2. Life Insurance

IRC § 2042 governs the estate tax treatment of life insurance proceeds.

---

a. <u>Proceeds Payable to Insured's Estate</u>. Life insurance proceeds payable to the insured's estate or the executor of the insured's estate will be included in the insured's gross estate, regardless of who owned the policy. IRC § 2042(1).

> **<u>EXAMPLE</u>:** A owned a $100,000 policy of insurance on B's life. The insurance policy named B's estate as beneficiary of the proceeds. At B's death, $100,000 is included in B's gross estate even though A owned the policy.

b. <u>Proceeds Payable to Beneficiary Other Than Insured's Estate</u>. Life insurance proceeds will be included in the insured's estate if the proceeds are payable to another beneficiary or beneficiaries, but the insured possessed any incident of ownership in the policy, exercisable alone or in conjunction with another person. IRC § 2042(2). An "incident of ownership" is the ability to control any of the economic benefits of the property. It includes the power to change the beneficiary, to surrender or cancel the policy, to assign the policy, to revoke an assignment, to pledge the policy for a loan or to obtain from the insurer a loan against the surrender value of the policy. Treas. Reg. § 20.2042-1(c)(2).

> **<u>EXAMPLE</u>:** A owned a $100,000 policy of insurance on A's own life. The insurance policy named B as beneficiary. A assigned ownership of the policy to B in 1997 but retained the right to revoke the assignment. At A's death in 2005, $100,000 will still be included in A's estate under IRC § 2042 because A's right to revoke the assignment was an incident of ownership in the policy.

> **<u>EXAMPLE</u>:** A owned a $100,000 policy of insurance on B's life. The insurance policy named A as beneficiary. At B's death, none of the proceeds will be included in B's estate because B did not have any incident of ownership in the policy and because the policy did not name B's estate as beneficiary.

c. <u>Transfer of Ownership Within 3 Years of Death</u>. If an insured transfers ownership of a policy within three years of the insured's death, the proceeds will be brought back into the insured's gross estate. IRC § 2035(a).

> **<u>EXAMPLE</u>:** A owned a $100,000 policy of insurance on A's own life. The insurance policy named B as beneficiary. In 2002, A transferred ownership of the policy to B. A died in 2004. Because A died within three years of transferring the policy to B, the $100,000 policy proceeds will be included in A's estate.

3. Certain Property for Which Marital Deduction Was Previously Allowed

IRC § 2044 provides that a decedent's gross estate includes the value of any property in which the decedent had a qualifying income interest for life if:

- An estate tax marital deduction (IRC § 2056) or gift tax marital deduction (IRC § 2523) was previously allowed with respect to the transfer of the property to the decedent; and
- The decedent did not make a taxable gift of the decedent's income interest in the property under IRC § 2519.

Property includible in a decedent's estate under IRC § 2044 is treated as property owned by and passing from the decedent rather than the decedent's predeceased spouse.

> **EXAMPLE:** At H's death, a trust was created for W's sole benefit. The trust qualified for the estate tax marital deduction in H's estate. W did not otherwise dispose of her income interest in the trust. The value of the trust at W's date of death will be included in W's estate, and the trust will be treated as owned by and passing from W.

4. Certain Property Transferred by Decedent During Decedent's Lifetime

a. Transfers Within Three Years of Death. Prior to 1982, all non-annual exclusion gifts made within three years of death were brought back into a decedent's estate as gifts made in contemplation of death. After 1982, only certain gifts made by a decedent within three years of death are brought back into the decedent's estate under IRC § 2035.

(1) General Rule. Outright gifts made by a decedent within three years of death are not includible in a decedent's estate. IRC § 2035(e) treats a gift by a decedent's revocable trust (a trust of which the decedent is treated as the owner under IRC § 676) as a gift by the decedent.

➔ **Planning Point:** One of the estate tax benefits of making lifetime gifts is the removal from the donor's gross estate of the value of the gifted property and any future appreciation in value of and income generated by the gifted property. Any gift tax paid on the gifted property also will be removed from the donor's estate (unless paid within three years of death under IRC § 2035(b)).

EXAMPLE: On October 18, 2002, D gave real property worth $700,000 to A. At D's death on July 3, 2005, the property was worth $1,000,000. Even though D made the gift within 3 years of D's death, the gifted property will not be included in D's estate because it was an outright gift. In addition, the appreciation on the property between the date of gift and D's date of death ($300,000) is removed from D's estate.

(2) **Transfers (or Releases of a Power) Under IRC §§ 2036, 2037, 2038 or 2042.** IRC § 2035(a) brings back into a decedent's gross estate certain interests transferred (or powers released) by the decedent within three years of the decedent's death that would have been included in the decedent's estate under one of the "string provisions" (IRC §§ 2036, 2037, 2038 and 2042) had they not been transferred (or released).

EXAMPLE: D contributed real property worth $100,000 to a revocable trust for the benefit of A. D retained the right to revoke the trust. D releases his right to revoke the trust on August 1, 2001 and then dies on January 31, 2004. The gifted trust property will be brought back into D's estate because it would have been includible in D's estate under IRC § 2038 had D not released the right to revoke.

(3) **Gift Taxes Paid Within Three Years of Death.** IRC § 2035(b) brings back into a decedent's estate gift taxes paid within three years of death.

➔ **Planning Point:** Note that even if the gift taxes are brought back into the decedent's estate, the decedent's estate still benefits from the removal of the gifted property and the future appreciation in value of and income generated by the gifted property.

EXAMPLE: D paid gift taxes on a gift to A of real property worth $500,000. D dies within three years of the gift when the property is worth $700,000. D's gift is not includible in D's estate under IRC § 2035(a) because it would not have been includible in D's estate under IRC §§ 2036, 2037, 2038 or 2042 had D not transferred the property. The gift taxes on D's gift, however, will be brought back into D's estate under IRC § 2035(b). D's estate still benefits from the removal of the appreciation in value of and income generated by the gifted property between the date of gift and D's date of death ($200,000).

b. **Transfers With Retained Life Estate.**

        (1)   **General Rule**.   Generally, IRC § 2036 brings back into a decedent's gross estate the entire value of property gifted by the decedent if the decedent retained for life or for a period that does not in fact end before the decedent's death:

- the possession or enjoyment of the property;
- the right to the income from the property; <u>or</u>
- the right, either alone or in conjunction with another person, to determine who would possess or enjoy the property or the property's income.

> **EXAMPLE:** D transferred $100,000 to a new trust for A but retained the right to the income of the trust for 5 years. If D dies 4 years after the trust was created, the value of the trust property will be included in D's estate because D's right to the income did not in fact end before D's death. If D had died 6 years after the trust was created, none of the trust property would be includible in D's estate because D no longer retained the right to the income.

> **EXAMPLE:** D transferred $100,000 to a new trust for A but retained the right to change the beneficiaries of the trust to A's children. The entire trust property will be included in D's estate because D's right to change the beneficiary is a right to determine who will enjoy the trust property.

A decedent has a retained right under IRC § 2036 if the decedent's use, possession, right to the income or other enjoyment is applied towards the discharge of a legal obligation of the decedent (such as a legal obligation to support a dependent during the decedent's lifetime). Treas. Reg. § 20.2036-1(b)(2).

> **EXAMPLE:** D transferred $100,000 to a new trust for A but retained the right to income to support D's minor child, B. Under state law, D is legally obligated to support B. Accordingly, the trust property will be included in D's estate.

        (2)   **External Standard Exception**. Any part of the gifted property subject to a power to distribute principal in favor of a beneficiary that is limited by an external standard will not be included in the decedent's gross estate under IRC § 2036. *Budlong, Milton Est.*, 7 T.C. 756 (1946), *acq.* 1947-1 C.B. 1, *aff'd & rev'd sub nom. Industrial Trust Co.*, 36 A.F.T.R. 502, 165 F.2d 142 (1947, CA1), 48-1 U.S.T.C. ¶10593; *Frew, Walter Est.*, 8 T.C. 1240 (1947), *acq. Jennings v. Smith*, 161 F.2d 74 (2d Cir. 1947).

The following are examples of external standards that sufficiently limit a grantor-trustee's power of distribution to prevent inclusion of the trust property in the grantor-trustee's gross estate under IRC § 2036:

- For the beneficiary's support, maintenance and education.
- If the beneficiary's other sources of income are insufficient to provide for the proper care, support and medical attention of such beneficiary during any period of incapacity or illness.
- In the event of sickness, accident, misfortune or other emergency.

> **EXAMPLE:** D transferred $100,000 to a new trust for A but retained the right to the income of the trust for D's health and support. The value of the trust property will not be included in D's estate because D's right to the income was limited by an ascertainable external standard.

c. Transfers Taking Effect at Death. IRC § 2037 brings back into a decedent's gross estate the entire value of property gifted by the decedent if all three of the following requirements are met:

- Possession or enjoyment of the property can be obtained only by surviving the decedent;
- The decedent retained a "reversionary interest" (a possibility that the gifted property may return to the decedent or the decedent's estate or may be subject to a power of disposition by the decedent); and
- The value of the reversionary interest immediately before death exceeds 5% of the value of the gifted property.

> **EXAMPLE:** D contributed $100,000 to a trust that provided that the principal of the trust will be distributed to A in 5 years if D is not living at that time. Otherwise, the principal of the trust would revert to D. D dies 4 years later. The value of D's reversionary interest exceeds 5% of the value of the trust. The trust property will be included in D's gross estate because A can enjoy the property only if A survives D, and D retained a possibility that the trust property would revert to D if D had survived 5 years. If the trust had instead provided that the principal would be paid to A in 5 years if A had finished college, A's enjoyment of the trust property would not depend on surviving D, and the property would not be included in D's estate under IRC § 2037.

d. Transfers With Retained Right to Revoke.

(1) **General Rule**. IRC § 2038 brings back into a decedent's gross estate the entire value of property gifted where the decedent, either alone or in conjunction with someone else, retained a right or power to alter, amend, revoke or terminate the transfer.

> **EXAMPLE:** D transferred $500,000 to a trust for A's benefit but retained the right, in conjunction with A, to revoke the trust. At D's death, the entire value of the trust property is included in D's estate.

(2) **External Standard Exception**. The property will not be included in the decedent's gross estate under IRC § 2038 if the decedent's right or power is subject to an external standard. *Jennings v. Smith*, 161 F.2d 74 (2d Cir. 1947).

The following are examples of powers limited by an external standard that prevent inclusion of trust property in the gross estate:

- Reserved power to amend only to clarify, but not to change substance.
- Reserved power to increase trust principal.
- Reserved power as grantor-trustee to distribute principal to or for a beneficiary if the beneficiary is suffering a prolonged illness.

> **EXAMPLE:** D transferred $500,000 to a trust for the benefit of A and B but retained the power to amend the trust to clarify the trust terms only. None of the trust property will be includible in D's estate under IRC § 2038. Although D retained the power to amend the trust terms, D's power was limited by an external standard (to clarify the trust terms).

(3) **Power to Remove Trustee.**

(a) **Power to Appoint Self as Trustee**. IRC § 2038 applies if the decedent-grantor had the unrestricted power to remove or discharge a trustee and appoint himself as trustee. In that case, the decedent would be considered as having the discretionary powers of distribution of the trustee. Treas. Reg. § 20.2038-1(a)(3). If the trustee's powers are sufficiently limited by an external standard, however, the power of the decedent-grantor to appoint himself as trustee will not cause inclusion in the decedent-grantor's estate.

> **EXAMPLE:** D transferred $500,000 to a trust for the benefit of A and B but retained the power, as trustee, to remove the trustee and appoint himself as successor trustee. The entire value of the trust property is included in D's estate.

(b) <u>**Power to Appoint Unrelated and Nonsubordinate Trustee**</u>. IRC § 2038 does not apply, however, if the decedent-grantor had the unrestricted power to remove or discharge a trustee and appoint an individual or corporate successor trustee that is not related or subordinate to the decedent (within the meaning of IRC § 672(c)). Such a power is not considered a reservation by the decedent of the trustee's discretionary powers of distribution over the property transferred by the decedent-grantor to the trust. Rev. Rul. 95-58, 1995-2 C.B. 191.

> **EXAMPLE:** D transferred $500,000 to a trust for the benefit of A and B but retained the power, as trustee, to remove the trustee and appoint an individual or corporate successor trustee that is not related or subordinate to D. The trust property is not includible in D's estate under IRC § 2038.

5.   Property Controlled By Decedent — Powers of Appointment

a. <u>What is a Power of Appointment?</u> A "power of appointment" simply is the power to decide who will take the trust property next, and the time, terms, shares and conditions under which they will receive it. A power of appointment can be exercisable during the powerholder's lifetime (a "lifetime" power of appointment) or exercisable upon the powerholder's death by will (a "testamentary" power of appointment). Powers of appointment often are used in trusts to give the powerholder a degree of control over the disposition of trust property or to achieve certain tax planning goals.

> **EXAMPLE:** H creates a trust for W's benefit. The trust gives W a power to appoint the trust property at death by W's will in favor of any one or more of the descendants of H and W. The trust also provides that if W does not exercise this power, at W's death, the trust property will be divided equally between their children, A (who is financially independent) and B (who is less stable financially). If W wishes, W may exercise her power of appointment in W's will to leave a greater share of the trust property to B after W's death.

The term "power of appointment" includes any power that is in substance and effect a power of appointment.

EXAMPLE: A decedent's power to remove or discharge a trustee and appoint himself as trustee may be a power of appointment. For example, if the trustee or his successor has the power to appoint the principal of the trust for the benefit of individuals including himself, and the decedent has the unrestricted power to remove or discharge the trustee at any time, the decedent is considered as having a power of appointment. However, the decedent is not considered to have a power of appointment if he only had the power to appoint a successor, including himself, under limited conditions which did not exist at the time of his death, without an accompanying unrestricted power of removal. Treas. Reg. § 20.2041-1(b)(1).

b. __Estate Tax Treatment of Powers of Appointment__. IRC § 2041 addresses the estate tax treatment of certain powers of appointment.

(1) __General Rule__. Only the value of property over which a decedent held a general power of appointment is included in the decedent's estate. IRC § 2041(a). A "general power of appointment" is a power of appointment exercisable in favor of the holder, the holder's estate, the holder's creditors or the creditors of the holder's estate. IRC § 2041(b)(1).

EXAMPLE: A trust provides that beneficiary A has a power to withdraw any or all principal for his own benefit. At A's death, the value of the trust property is included in A's gross estate for estate tax purposes because A's unlimited power to withdraw principal for his own benefit is a general power of appointment. The result is the same regardless of whether A actually withdrew the principal or not.

(2) __Exceptions__. There are several exceptions to the general rule that general powers of appointment are taxable for estate tax purposes.

(a) __Ascertainable Standard Exception__. First, the ascertainable standard exception provides that a holder's power to appoint the property to himself that is limited by an ascertainable standard relating to the holder's health, education, support or maintenance is not a general power of appointment. Certain other standards (such as "welfare" or "happiness") are not considered an ascertainable standard.

EXAMPLE: A trust provides that the trustee has a power to withdraw any or all of the principal for his own health. None of the trust property is included in the trustee's estate because his power to withdraw principal for himself was limited to an ascertainable standard (health). If the trustee had the power to withdraw principal for his health and welfare, all of the trust property would be included in the trustee's estate because "welfare" is not an ascertainable standard.

(b) <u>**Pre-October 22, 1942 General Powers of Appointment**</u>. Property subject to a general power of appointment created before October 22, 1942 is not includible in the holder's gross estate unless the holder exercised the power either (1) by will, or (2) by a disposition which is of such nature that if it were a transfer of property owned by the decedent, the property would be includible in the decedent's estate under IRC § 2035 (relating to transfers in contemplation of death), IRC § 2036 (relating to transfers with retained life estate), IRC § 2037 (relating to transfers taking effect at death) or IRC § 2038 (relating to revocable transfers).

> **EXAMPLE:** Beneficiary B has a general power of appointment over property in a trust created in 1939. B never exercised that power. At B's death, B's general power of appointment is not included in B's estate because B never exercised the power.

(c) <u>**Power Exercisable Only With Consent or Joinder**</u>. A power exercisable only with the consent or joinder of the creator of the power or a person having substantial adverse interest is not a general power of appointment. IRC § 2041(b)(1)(C).

(3) <u>**Special Powers of Appointment**</u>. A special power of appointment is a power of appointment that is *not* a general power of appointment (not exercisable in favor of the holder, the holder's estate, the holder's creditors or the creditors of the holder's estate). Special powers of appointment are not includible in the holder's gross estate. A special power of appointment often is used when the donor wants to give the holder the flexibility to control the disposition of trust property but still limit the group benefiting from the holder's exercise of the power.

> **EXAMPLE:** A trust gives beneficiary A power to appoint trust principal in favor of anyone other than A, A's estate or the creditors of either. None of the trust property will be included in A's estate because A's power is a special power of appointment.

> **EXAMPLE:** A trust gives beneficiary A a power to appoint trust principal in favor of A's descendants. A's power of appointment is a special limited power of appointment limited to the class of A's descendants. None of the trust property will be included in A's estate.

D. Valuation for Federal Estate Tax Purposes

1. General Rule

Generally, unless the executor elects the alternative valuation method (discussed below), property included in a decedent's gross estate is subject to estate tax based on its fair market value on the decedent's date of death. "Fair market value" is the price at which the property would change hands between a willing buyer and a willing seller, neither being under any

---

compulsion to buy or to sell and both having reasonable knowledge of relevant facts. Treas. Reg. § 20.2031-1(b). The Regulations provide guidelines on the valuation of specific types of property for federal estate tax purposes:

- Treas. Reg. § 20.2031-2 (stocks and bonds).
- Treas. Reg. § 20.2031-3 (business interests).
- Treas. Reg. § 20.2031-4 (notes).
- Treas. Reg. § 20.2031-5 (cash on hand or on deposit).
- Treas. Reg. § 20.2031-6 (household and personal effects).
- Treas. Reg. § 20.2031-7 (annuities, interests for life or term of years, and remainder or reversionary interests).
- Treas. Reg. § 20.2031-8 (certain life insurance and annuity contracts).
- Treas. Reg. § 20.2031-9 (other property).

➔ **Planning Point:** Some documentation helpful in determining what assets the decedent owned at death and their value include the decedent's bank statements, brokerage account statements, and prior income tax returns.

The following discussion briefly summarizes the <u>general</u> rules as to the valuation of the above types of property. Exceptions to these general rules are discussed in detail in a separate chapter on valuation.

a. **Stocks and Bonds**. The fair market value of a decedent's stocks and bonds is based on the mean between the highest and lowest selling prices on the date of death. If the date of death falls on a weekend or holiday, the value is determined by taking a weighted average of the means between the highest and lowest sales on the nearest date before and the nearest date after the date of death.

> **EXAMPLE:** D died owning 100 shares of common stock of Company X, a publicly traded company. D died on a Friday, which was a holiday. The nearest trading date before D's date of death ("DOD") was Thursday (1 day before) when the mean sales price per share was $10. The nearest trading date after D's date of death was the following Monday (3 days later) when the mean sales price per share was $15. The value of D's 100 shares is $1,375. The value per share of $13.75 on D's date of death is calculated as follows:
>
> $$\text{Value} = \frac{(1 \text{ day before x } \$10) + (3 \text{ days after x } \$15)}{4 \text{ days total}} = \$13.75/\text{share}$$

b. **Business Interests.** Generally, the fair market value of any interest of a decedent in a business is the net amount which a willing purchaser, whether an individual or corporation, would pay for the interest to a willing seller. The net value is determined on the basis of all relevant factors, including a fair appraisal of the business's assets and the business's demonstrated earning capacity.

      c. Notes. Generally, the fair market value of a decedent's note, secured or unsecured, is the amount of unpaid principal, plus interest accrued to the date of death unless the executor establishes the value is lower or that the note is worthless.

      d. Cash on Hand or on Deposit. Generally, the amount of cash belonging to the decedent at the date of his death, whether in his possession or in the possession of another, or deposited with a bank, is included in the decedent's estate.

      e. Household and Personal Effects. Generally, the fair market value of a decedent's household and personal effects is the price which a willing buyer would pay to a willing seller. An appraisal is required for items of artistic or intrinsic value (*e.g.*, jewelry, furs, silverware, paintings, etchings, engravings, antiques, books, statuary, vases, oriental rugs, coin or stamp collections) having a total value in excess of $3,000.

      f. Annuities, Interests for Life or Term of Years, and Remainder or Reversionary Interests. Generally, the fair market value of a decedent's annuities, life estates, terms of years, and remainder and reversionary interests is the present value of such interests. The Regulations provide tables with standard actuarial factors used to compute the present value of these interests.

      g. Certain Life Insurance and Annuity Contracts. Generally, the fair market value of a decedent's life insurance and annuity contracts is established through the sale by the issuing company of comparable contracts.

      h. Other Property. The valuation of any property not specifically described above is made in accordance with the general principles in the Regulations.

    2.   **Alternate Valuation Date**

      As discussed above, property generally is valued as of the decedent's date of death for federal estate tax purposes. Subject to certain requirements, however, IRC § 2032 allows a decedent's personal representative to elect to value the gross estate as of the date that is six months after the decedent's date of death (the "alternate valuation date").

      a. Purpose of Alternate Valuation. The main purpose of alternate valuation is to reduce the amount of estate tax that would otherwise be payable if the gross estate decreases in value during the six-month administration period following the decedent's date of death.

EXAMPLE: D died on July 6, 2001. D's gross estate, consisting mostly of technology stock, was worth $2,000,000 on D's date of death. On January 6, 2002, the value of D's gross estate dropped to $1,500,000, which was caused by a drop in technology stock prices. D's executor can elect to value the estate as of January 6, 2002 on D's federal estate tax return.

b. Requirements of Alternate Valuation.

(1)   Reduce Gross Estate and Estate Taxes Due. The alternate valuation election may be used only if the election will reduce the value of the gross estate and reduce the total estate tax due. IRC § 2032(c). This is to discourage estates, especially nontaxable estates, from using alternate valuation to obtain a higher step-up in basis for income tax purposes in order to reduce taxable gain. The step-up in basis rule is discussed later in this chapter.

(2)   Valuation Date Used. If alternate valuation is used, all property still in the estate six months after the decedent's date of death is valued as of the alternate valuation date. Any property sold or otherwise disposed of prior to that date is valued as of its date of disposition. IRC § 2032(a).

(3)   Election. The decedent's personal representative must make the election on the decedent's federal estate tax return. An estate cannot make the election on an estate tax return that is filed more than one year after the due date (including extensions) for filing the return. Once made, the election is irrevocable. IRC § 2032(d). No partial election is allowed; the election must be made for the decedent's entire estate.

Proposed regulations issued on December 23, 2003 provide that estates that fail to make the alternate valuation election on the last estate tax return filed before the due date or the first return filed after the due date could request an extension of time to make the election under Treas. Reg. §§ 301.9100-1 and 301.9100-3, which apply to all requests for an extension of time to make any election. However, no request for an extension of time would be granted if it were submitted to the IRS more than one year after the due date of the return (including filing extensions actually granted).

The proposed regulations also would provide guidance on making a protective election under IRC § 2032 in cases where, based on the return as filed, alternate valuation does not result in a decrease in transfer tax but it is later determined that such a decrease would occur. While a protective election generally would be irrevocable, it could be revoked on a subsequent return filed by the due date (including filing extensions actually granted). Absent a revocation, if the decrease occurred, alternate valuation would apply and could not later be changed. REG-139845-02; Prop. Reg. § 20.2032-1(b).

E. Federal Estate Tax Deductions

1.   Estate Tax Marital Deduction

IRC § 2056 allows an unlimited estate tax marital deduction for qualified interests that pass to a decedent's surviving spouse.

a. Requirements. An interest transferred to a surviving spouse must meet all of the following requirements in order to qualify for the estate tax marital deduction.

(1)   Interest Must be Includible in Decedent's Gross Estate. It would not make sense to apply a deduction if the property against which the deduction is to apply were not included in the gross estate.

(2)   Decedent is Survived by a Surviving Spouse Who is a U.S. Citizen. If the surviving spouse is not a U.S. citizen, the marital deduction is available only for transfers to a qualified domestic trust under IRC §§ 2056(d) and 2056A. See discussion below.

(3)   Interest Must "Pass" to the Surviving Spouse. Under IRC § 2056(c), an interest in property "passes" to the surviving spouse if it passes to the surviving spouse by bequest or devise, inheritance, dower or curtesy, *inter vivos* transfer, joint tenancy with right of survivorship, the exercise or nonexercise of a power of appointment or life insurance.

(4)   Interest Must be Deductible (Not a Nondeductible Terminable Interest). See discussion below on terminable interests.

b. Nondeductible Terminable Interests: The Terminable Interest Rule. The terminable interest rule provides that the marital deduction is not available for interests that terminate or fail upon a lapse of time or the occurrence or nonoccurrence of an event if a person other than the surviving spouse receives the property after the termination of the surviving spouse's interest. IRC § 2056(b)(1).

> **EXAMPLE:** H's will provides that $300,000 will pass to a trust for W's benefit for 10 years after H's death, at which time the trust will terminate and be distributed to H's children. H's estate is not entitled to a marital deduction for the $300,000 transferred to the trust for W because W's interest in the trust will terminate upon a lapse of time (10 years) and persons other than W (H's children) will receive the property from H.

> **EXAMPLE:** H's will provides that $300,000 will pass to a trust for W. If W remarries or cohabits with another person, however, the trust will terminate and be distributed to H's children. H's estate is not entitled to a marital deduction for the $300,000 transferred to the trust

for W because W's interest in the trust will terminate upon the occurrence of an event (W's remarriage or cohabitation with another person) and persons other than W (H's children) will receive the property from H.

c. Deductible Terminable Interests: Exceptions to The Terminable Interest Rule. Despite the terminable interest rule, certain terminable interests still qualify for the marital deduction. Some of these interests include the following:

(1) **Limited Survivorship Exception**. IRC § 2056(b)(3) provides that the marital deduction is available for transfers to a surviving spouse with a limited survivorship requirement. Specifically, a terminable interest is deductible if: (1) the only condition under which the interest will terminate is the death of the surviving spouse within 6 months after the decedent's death, or the surviving spouse's death as a result of a common disaster that also resulted in the decedent's death, and (2) the condition does not in fact occur. Treas. Reg. § 20.2056(b)-3(a).

> **EXAMPLE:** H's will provides that $500,000 will pass to a trust for W. If W dies within 6 months of H's death or dies in a common disaster with H, however, the trust will terminate and be distributed to H's children. W survives H for at least 6 months. Therefore, H's estate would be entitled to a marital deduction for the $500,000 transferred to the trust for W. If W and H had died together in a plane crash, however, H's estate would not be entitled to the deduction.

(2) **General Power of Appointment Trust Exception**. Under IRC § 2056(b)(5), a marital deduction is allowed for an interest that passes to a surviving spouse in trust if all of the following requirements are met:

- The surviving spouse is entitled for life to all of the income from the entire interest or a specific portion of the entire interest, or to a specific portion of all the income from the entire interest.
- The income payable to the surviving spouse must be payable at least annually.
- The surviving spouse must have the power to appoint the entire interest or the specific portion to either himself or herself or to his or her estate.
- The power must be exercisable by the surviving spouse alone and (whether by will or during life) must be exercisable in all events.
- The entire interest or specific portion must not be subject to a power in any other person to appoint any part to any person other than the surviving spouse.

> **EXAMPLE:** H died, leaving $500,000 to a trust for W. All of the income of the trust was payable to W annually. W had a power to

appoint the trust property at death by W's will in favor of W's estate. The trust qualifies for the estate tax marital deduction as a general power of appointment trust under IRC § 2056(b)(5). If the trust had also provided that W's child, C, had a power to appoint the trust property in favor of C's children, the trust would not have qualified for the estate tax marital deduction.

(3) Qualified Terminable Interest Property ("QTIP") Trust Exception. Under IRC § 2056(b)(7), a marital deduction is allowed for an interest that passes to a surviving spouse in trust if all of the following requirements are met:

- The surviving spouse is entitled for life to all of the income from the entire interest or a specific portion of the entire interest, or to a specific portion of all the income from the entire interest.
- The income payable to the surviving spouse must be payable at least annually.
- The entire interest or specific portion must not be subject to a power in any other person to appoint any part to any person other than the surviving spouse.
- A QTIP election must be made on the decedent's federal estate tax return with respect to a specific portion or all of the trust.

→ **Planning Point:** The QTIP trust exception is similar to the general power of appointment trust exception except that the surviving spouse need not have a power of appointment over a QTIP trust in order to qualify for the estate tax marital deduction.

> **EXAMPLE:** H died, leaving $500,000 to a trust for W. All of the income of the trust was payable to W annually. If H's executor makes a QTIP election on H's estate tax return, the trust will qualify for the estate tax marital deduction. If the trust had also provided that W's child, C, had a power to appoint the trust property in favor of C's children, the trust would not have qualified for the estate tax marital deduction under IRC § 2056(b)(7).

d. Estate Tax Marital Deduction for Non-U.S. Citizen Surviving Spouse. Generally, the estate tax marital deduction is not allowed for transfers to a non-U.S. citizen surviving spouse. IRC § 2056(d)(1). The rationale is to make sure that the property for which the marital deduction is allowed will later be subject to federal estate tax in the surviving spouse's estate. There are two exceptions to this rule:

(1) Resident Spouse Becomes Citizen Prior to Due Date of Estate Tax Return. The estate tax marital deduction is allowed if the non-U.S. citizen surviving spouse was a U.S. resident at all times after the decedent's date of death and before becoming a U.S.

citizen, and if the surviving spouse becomes a U.S. citizen before the federal estate tax return is due (including extensions). IRC § 2056(d)(4).

> **EXAMPLE:** H, a U.S. citizen, died leaving $500,000 to a trust for W, a Canadian citizen. H and W lived in the U.S. prior to and at H's death, and W continued to live in the U.S. If W becomes a U.S. citizen before the due date of H's federal estate tax return, H's estate will be entitled to a marital deduction under IRC § 2056(d)(4) even though W was not a U.S. citizen at H's date of death.

(2)   Qualified Domestic Trust ("QDOT"). The estate tax marital deduction is allowed for property transferred to a QDOT for the non-U.S. citizen surviving spouse's benefit. IRC § 2056(d)(2).

(a)   QDOT Requirements. IRC § 2056A(a) provides that a trust is a QDOT that qualifies for the estate tax marital deduction if all of the following requirements are met:

- At least one trustee is a U.S. citizen or a domestic corporation.
- No distribution (other than income) may be made from the trust unless the trustee who is a U.S. citizen or domestic corporation has the right to withhold from the distribution the tax imposed by IRC § 2056A on such distributions.
- The decedent's executor makes an irrevocable election to treat the trust as a QDOT on the decedent's federal estate tax return.
- The trust separately meets the requirements of IRC § 2056(b) (*e.g.*, a general power of appointment trust, QTIP trust).

(b)   Tax on Distributions From QDOT. Under IRC § 2056A(b), certain distributions from a QDOT (other than income or hardship distributions) before the surviving spouse's date of death and any property remaining in the QDOT at the surviving spouse's death may be subject to estate tax at the rate described in IRC § 2056A(b)(2).

e.   Use of Marital Deduction to Defer Estate Tax. The estate tax marital deduction essentially defers estate taxes until the death of the surviving spouse. All of the assets of the deceased spouse that are left outright or in a marital trust for the surviving spouse are potentially available for the needs of the surviving spouse and are not reduced by estate tax at the first death. Deferring the estate tax is advantageous because of the increasing estate tax exemption amount available to the surviving spouse, and because the surviving spouse, with careful planning, can reduce the size of his or her taxable estate.

> **EXAMPLE:** H died in 2000 leaving $500,000 to a QTIP trust for W, all of which qualifies for the estate tax marital deduction in H's estate. No estate tax was due at H's death. W dies in 2005 when the estate

tax exemption amount is $1,500,000, and the QTIP trust is worth $550,000. Estate tax will be payable by W's estate only if W's other assets exceed $950,000.

2. Estate Tax Charitable Deduction

IRC § 2055(a) allows an estate tax charitable deduction for transfers to the following types of recipients:

- IRC § 501(c)(3) corporations operated exclusively for religious, charitable, scientific, literary or education purposes, which do not attempt to influence elections and are not substantially engaged in carrying on propaganda or influencing legislation.
- Federal government, state government or subdivisions thereof for exclusively public purposes.
- IRC § 501(c)(3) fraternal or veterans' organizations.
- Certain employee stock ownership plans if the transfer is an IRC § 664(g) qualified gratuitous transfer of qualified employer securities.

a. **Property Must Be Included in Estate**. None of the percentage and other limitations on the income tax charitable deduction under IRC § 170 apply to the estate tax charitable deduction. In this sense, the estate tax charitable deduction is "unlimited." Charitable deduction property, however, must be property that was included in the decedent's gross estate. Accordingly, the only ceiling on the estate tax charitable deduction is the value of the gross estate. IRC § 2055(d).

b. **Certain Conditional Gifts and Certain Gifts Subject to a Power Do Not Qualify For Charitable Deduction**. A transfer to a qualified charity that is conditional at the time of decedent's death will not qualify for the charitable deduction unless the likelihood that the charity will not receive the bequest is so remote as to be considered negligible. Further, if a legatee, devisee, donee or trustee has a power to divert a portion or all of the gifted property or interest, the charitable deduction will be limited to that portion which is exempt from an exercise of that power. Treas. Reg. § 20.2055-2(b).

> **EXAMPLE:** D dies leaving an empty lot to a city government for as long as the lot is used by the city for a public park. If the city accepts the lot and if, on the date of D's death, the possibility that D will not use the land for a public park is so remote as to be negligible, a charitable deduction will be allowed.

c. **Split Interests**. A split interest is simply a gift in which a charitable beneficiary and a noncharitable beneficiary share interests. Split interest gifts, such as charitable remainder trusts, charitable lead trusts, pooled income funds, and other charitable techniques are discussed in detail in the chapter on charitable planning.

(1) **Charitable Interest is Deductible**. The estate tax charitable deduction is limited to the charitable interest in a split interest. IRC § 2055(e)(2). The value of the charitable interest must be currently ascertainable (subject to a reasonably precise valuation). In addition, the split interest must be one of the deductible types specified in the Internal Revenue Code. Otherwise, no charitable deduction is allowed for any portion of a split interest gift.

(2) **Deductible Interests**. A charitable deduction is allowed for: (a) the remainder interest in a charitable remainder annuity trust ("CRAT"), a charitable remainder unitrust ("CRUT") or a pooled income fund; (b) the income interest in a charitable lead annuity trust ("CLAT"), a charitable lead unitrust ("CLUT"); and (c) the nontrust remainder interest in a personal residence or a farm.

d. **Death Taxes Payable Out of Charitable Bequest**. The charitable deduction is reduced by the amount of any estate, succession, legacy or inheritance tax payable out of the charitable bequest. IRC § 2055(c).

> **EXAMPLE:** D's will leaves $100,000 to a qualified charity. The $100,000 is subject to a state inheritance tax of $5,000 (payable out of the bequest per D's will). The estate tax charitable deduction is limited to $95,000.

➔ **Planning Point:** In addition to express directions in the decedent's estate planning documents, state law can determine the source of payment of such death taxes. In determining the correct charitable deduction amount, practitioners should be aware of applicable state law on the source of payment of death taxes.

e. **Charitable Deduction for Qualified Conservation Transfer**. IRC § 2055(f) allows an estate tax charitable deduction for any transfer of a "qualified real property interest" under Section 170(h) to a qualified charity for conservation purposes. A "qualified real property interest" includes the entire interest of the donor other than a qualified mineral interest, a remainder interest or a restriction (granted in perpetuity) on the use which may be made of the real property. IRC § 170(h)(2).

f. **Estate Tax Exclusion for Conservation Easements.** Subject to exclusion limitations, IRC § 2031(c) excludes from a decedent's gross estate a portion of land subject to a conservation easement if the land meets certain requirements. For estates of decedents dying after December 31, 2000, the Act has expanded the availability of a qualified conservation easement by easing some of the technical requirements. For example, prior to the Act, there were certain limitations on the location of the land. Now, the land can be located anywhere in the U.S. or any U.S. possession and still qualify. IRC § 2031(c)(8)(A)(i).

3. Deduction for Expenses, Claims, Debts, Taxes and Losses

a. Classes of Deductions. IRC § 2053(a) allows an estate tax deduction for the following classes of expenses, indebtedness, taxes and losses:

(1) Funeral Expenses. In order to be deductible, funeral expenses must be actually expended and must be payable out of the decedent's estate under the laws of the local jurisdiction. Treas. Reg. § 20.2053-2. Funeral expenses include the casket, burial vault, funeral director's fee, flowers purchased by the estate, food for mourners, the cost of transporting the person bringing the body to the place of burial, tombstone, monument, mausoleum, burial lot, and the expense of landscaping the lot.

(2) Administration Expenses. An administration expense must be actually and necessarily incurred in the administration of the estate in order to be deductible. The administration expenses of an estate include the collection of assets, the payment of debts and the distribution of property to persons entitled to it. Administration expenses include executor's commissions, attorneys' fees and miscellaneous expenses. Expenditures that are not essential to the administration of the estate, but incurred for the individual benefit of an heir, legatee or devisee are not deductible. Treas. Reg. § 20.2053-3(a). For estates of decedents dying on or after December 3, 1999, certain administration expenses may or may not affect the marital deduction.

(a) Estate Transmission Expenses. Estate transmission expenses are expenses that would not have been incurred except for the decedent's death, such as the collection of the decedent's assets, the payment of the decedent's debts and death taxes, and the distribution of the decedent's property. Examples include executors' commissions, attorneys' fees, probate fees, appraisal fees, and expenses incurred in construction proceedings and defending against will contests. Executors' commissions and attorneys' fees that are related to the investment, preservation or maintenance of estate assets, however, would not be considered estate transmission expenses. Estate transmission expenses reduce the marital deduction on a dollar-for-dollar basis if they are paid from the income or principal of marital deduction property. Treas. Reg. § 20.2056(b)-4(d)(2).

(b) Estate Management Expenses. Estate management expenses are those expenses incurred with respect to the investment of estate assets and with their preservation and maintenance during a reasonable period of administration. Examples of estate management expenses include investment advisory fees, stock brokerage commissions, custodial fees and interest. Generally, the marital deduction is not reduced by these expenses if they are paid from the income or principal of marital deduction property. Treas. Reg. § 20.2056(b)-4(d)(3). There are 2 exceptions to this rule: (1) if estate management expenses are deducted on the federal estate tax return as an IRC § 2053 deduction; or (2) if estate management expenses are incurred for non-marital deduction property. Treas. Reg. §§ 20.2056(b)-4(d)(3) and 20.2056(b)-4(d)(4).

> → **Planning Point:** In drafting estate planning documents, practitioners should take advantage of these regulations by providing flexible language to charge administration expenses to either principal or income of the estate or trust.

       (3)   **Claims Against the Estate.** An estate can deduct claims which were personal obligations of the decedent that existed and were enforceable against the decedent at the time of the decedent's death, whether or not then matured, and interest thereon which had accrued at the time of death. Deductible claims include certain taxes (such as income taxes, gift taxes and property taxes) owed by the decedent before his death. Treas. Reg. § 20.2053-6. If a claim is founded on a promise or agreement, it is deductible if the claim is bona fide and contracted for full and adequate consideration in money or money's worth. Treas. Reg. § 20.2053-4.

> **EXAMPLE:** During D's lifetime, D promised to pay A $10,000 after D's death if A promised to release B from an obligation to pay A $10,000. D's estate would be entitled to a deduction for A's $10,000 claim against D's estate because the claim was created in good faith and for adequate and full consideration.

       (4)   **Unpaid Mortgages or Other Indebtedness.** An estate may deduct the full amount of any unpaid mortgage on or other debt relating to property included in the decedent's gross estate. The liability must have been contracted in good faith for full and adequate consideration. Treas. Reg. § 20.2053-7.

       (5)   **Losses.** IRC § 2054 allows an estate tax deduction for losses incurred during the settlement of the estate arising from fires, storms, shipwrecks or other casualties, or from theft, when such losses are not compensated for by insurance or otherwise. The loss must have occurred during the settlement of the estate before the asset is distributed. Partial deductions are allowed for that portion not compensated for by insurance or otherwise.

> **EXAMPLE:** D's attorney embezzled funds from D's estate. The estate was partially reimbursed by a client security trust fund. The estate's theft loss deduction would be reduced by the amount of payment received by the fund.

       b. Disallowance of Double Deduction. Amounts allowable as a deduction pursuant to IRC § 2053 or 2054 are not allowed as an income tax deduction unless the right to take such deduction for federal estate tax purposes is waived. IRC § 642(g).

4. Deduction for State Death Taxes

For estates of decedents dying after 2004, the state death tax credit under IRC § 2011 is repealed. Instead of the credit, there will be a deduction for state death taxes actually paid with respect to property included in the decedent's gross estate. IRC § 2058. Under current law, IRC § 2058 itself is repealed after 2010.

Under IRC § 2058, a deduction for state death taxes will be allowed after 2004 only for taxes actually paid and claimed as a deduction during the time period that ends before the later of: (1) four years after the filing of the estate tax return; (2) if a timely petition for redetermination of a deficiency has been filed with the Tax Court, 60 days after the Tax Court decision becomes final; (3) if an extension of time has been granted under IRC § 6161 or IRC § 6166 for payment of the tax, the expiration date of the extension period; or (4) if a timely claim for refund or credit of an overpayment of tax has been filed, the latest of:

- 60 days after the IRS mails to the taxpayer by certified or registered mail a notice of disallowance of any part of the claim,
- 60 days after a decision by a court of competent jurisdiction becomes final as to a timely suit started upon the claim, or
- two years after a notice of the waiver of disallowance is filed under IRC § 6532(a)(3).

Despite IRC § 6511 (time limits on filing refund claims) and IRC § 6512 (limitations on Tax Court petitions), a refund based on the state death tax deduction may be made if the refund claim is filed within the time period discussed above. Any refund will be made without interest.

F. Unified Credit

1. Allowance of Unified Credit

IRC § 2010(a) allows a tax credit of the applicable credit amount against a decedent's federal estate tax. The applicable credit amount often is also referred to as the "unified credit." The applicable credit amount is the amount of estate tax that would be generated on a transfer of property in the amount of the "applicable exclusion amount." The applicable exclusion amount often is referred to as a decedent's estate tax exemption. The following is a table of applicable credit amounts and applicable exclusion amounts under the Act.

YEAR OF DEATH	APPLICABLE CREDIT AMOUNT ("UNIFIED CREDIT")	APPLICABLE EXCLUSION AMOUNT ("ESTATE TAX EXEMPTION")
2005	$555,800	$1.5 million
2006-2008	$780,800	$2 million
2009	$1,455,800	$3.5 million
2010	Estate Tax Repealed	Estate Tax Repealed
2011	$345,800	$1 million

EXAMPLE: D dies in 2005 with a $2,000,000 estate. Assuming D has not previously used any of his unified credit, $1,500,000 of D's $2,000,000 estate would be exempt from estate tax.

2. Effect of the Act

As the table above indicates, prior to the repeal of the estate tax in 2010, the Act increases the estate tax exemption. Beginning in 2011, when the estate tax is scheduled to reappear, the estate tax exemption amount reverts to the amount under the law prior to enactment of the Act.

➔ **Planning Point:** In light of the increasing estate tax exemption amount, practitioners should review clients' estate plans to make sure that: (1) the estate plan is taking advantage of the scheduled increase in the estate tax exemption amount, (2) the allocation between the marital and nonmarital share of the estate plan is appropriate, and (3) spouses are appropriately dividing assets between them so that each spouse can take advantage of the estate tax exemption amount, regardless of who dies first.

3. Adjustment to Credit for Certain Pre-1977 Gifts

The allowable applicable credit amount is reduced by an amount equal to 20% of the aggregate amount allowed as a specific exemption under IRC § 2521 with respect to gifts made by a decedent after September 8, 1976.

4. Limitations

There are certain limitations on the amount and use of the applicable credit amount.

a. Amount. The amount of the unified credit cannot exceed a decedent's federal estate tax liability. In other words, the decedent's federal estate tax exemption cannot exceed a decedent's taxable estate. IRC § 2010(d).

b. Nature. The applicable credit amount is a lifetime amount and has mandatory application. It is cumulative and does not renew annually. Therefore, it cannot be skipped during lifetime and saved for transfers at death.

> **EXAMPLE:** D made a gift in 1998 of $500,000. No gift tax is paid because $500,000 of D's applicable exclusion amount covers the gift. D dies in 2005 with an estate of $1,500,000. Even though the applicable exclusion amount is $1,500,000 in 2005, D has used up $500,000 of his applicable exclusion amount. Therefore, $500,000 of D's estate is still subject to the estate tax.

G. Calculation of Federal Estate Tax

1. Computation of Federal Estate Tax

IRC § 2001(b) describes the computation of a decedent's federal estate tax liability.

 a. <u>Gross Estate</u>. The first step is to determine what property of the decedent is subject to the estate tax. This property is called the decedent's "gross estate." IRC §§ 2031(a) and 2033 through 2044 describe the various types of property includible in a decedent's gross estate for federal estate tax purposes.

 b. <u>Estate Tax Deductions</u>. The second step is to determine the total allowable estate tax deductions under IRC §§ 2053-2058.

 c. <u>Taxable Estate</u>. Next, the decedent's "taxable estate" is determined by subtracting from the decedent's gross estate the total allowable deductions. IRC § 2051.

 d. <u>Tax Base</u>. A decedent's tax base is the sum of the decedent's taxable estate and adjusted taxable gifts. A decedent's "adjusted taxable gifts" is the total amount of post-1976 taxable gifts made by the decedent that are not otherwise includible in the decedent's gross estate. IRC § 2001(b). Because the estate tax and the gift tax are part of a unified transfer tax system, the decedent's prior gifts are included in the decedent's estate tax computation.

 e. <u>Tentative Tax</u>. A "tentative tax" is determined by applying the applicable tax rate from the tax rate table in IRC § 2001(c) to the decedent's tax base. IRC § 2001(b)(1).

 f. <u>Reduction for Certain Gift Taxes</u>. In order to avoid double taxation, the tentative tax is then reduced by gift taxes paid by the decedent on prior post-1976 gifts. IRC § 2001(b)(2).

 g. <u>Estate Tax Credits</u>. The tentative tax is further reduced by applicable estate tax credits. IRC §§ 2010-2016 cover these credits, which include the unified credit against estate tax, the credit for gift taxes paid on pre-1977 gifts, the credit for tax on prior transfers, and the credit for foreign death taxes.

> **EXAMPLE:** D, a widow, died on January 1, 2004 owning the following property: a bank account worth $100,000, real estate worth $700,000, tangible personal property worth $50,000 and a $500,000

life insurance policy on D's own life. D was the beneficiary of a QTIP marital trust created at the death of D's predeceased spouse worth $500,000. At death, D had debts of $50,000, funeral expenses of $10,000 and administration expenses of $100,000. D's will left $10,000 to a qualified charity. D's estate actually paid $50,000 in state inheritance taxes. D's estate tax liability is calculated by taking her gross estate of $1,850,000 and subtracting her total allowable deductions of $220,000 to arrive at a taxable estate of $1,630,000. D's tentative tax of $614,300 is determined by applying the tax rate table to D's tax base of $1,630,000.

D's tentative tax is reduced by D's unified credit amount of $555,800 for 2005 (which is equivalent to an applicable exclusion amount of $1,500,000). Accordingly, D's federal estate tax liability is $58,500 ($614,300 - $555,800).

2.   Effect of the Act on Computation of Federal Estate Tax

a.   Increased Exemptions & Declining Maximum Rates. Under the Act, the federal estate tax gradually reduces through increased exemptions and declining maximum federal estate tax rates. The federal estate tax is then repealed for estates of decedents dying in 2010. Under the sunset provisions of the Act, however, the federal estate tax will return in 2011 unless repealed again by a future Congress and President.

YEAR OF DEATH	MAXIMUM ESTATE & GIFT TAX RATE	APPLICABLE EXCLUSION AMOUNT ("ESTATE TAX EXEMPTION")
2005	47%	$1.5 million
2006	46%	$2 million
2007	45%	$2 million
2008	45%	$2 million
2009	45%	$3.5 million
2010	35% (gifts only)	Estate Tax Repealed
2011	55%	$1 million

b.   Repeal of 5% Surtax. The 5% surtax applied to estates and total taxable gifts exceeding $10 million was repealed in 2002.

H. Payment of Federal Estate Tax

1.   General Rule

Generally, the federal estate tax and estate tax return are due nine months after the decedent's date of death. IRC §§ 6075(a) and 6151(a). Extensions of time to pay the estate tax are allowed under certain circumstances. IRC §§ 6161, 6163, 6165 and 6166 cover those circumstances.

2. Installment Payments of Federal Estate Tax Allowed for Certain Estates

One of the most important provisions relating to extending the time for payment of federal estate tax is IRC § 6166(a), which allows certain estates to pay some or all of their federal estate tax liability in installments.

a. Requirements. The estate must meet the following requirements to qualify for installment payments under IRC § 6166(a).

(1) U.S. Citizen or Resident Decedent. The decedent must have been a U.S. citizen or resident.

(2) Interest in a Closely Held Business Exceeds 35% of Estate. The decedent's gross estate must have included an interest in a closely held business which exceeded 35% of the decedent's adjusted gross estate. For estates of decedents dying after December 31, 2001, the Act increased the number of partners of a partnership or shareholders in a corporation eligible for installments from 15 to 45.

(a) Interest in Closely Held Business. IRC § 6166(b)(1) defines "interest in closely held business" as:

- an interest in a proprietorship in a trade or business carried on as a proprietorship;

- an interest as a partner in a partnership carrying on a trade or business, if (1) 20% or more of the total capital interest in such partnership is included in determining the gross estate of the decedent, or (2) such partnership had 45 or fewer partners; or

- stock in a corporation carrying on a trade or business if (1) 20% or more in value of the voting stock of such corporation is included in determining the gross estate of the decedent, or (2) such corporation had 45 or fewer shareholders.

(b) Adjusted Gross Estate. IRC § 6166(b)(6) defines "adjusted gross estate" as the value of the gross estate reduced by the sum of the amounts allowable as a deduction under IRC § 2053 or IRC § 2054. Such sum will be determined on the basis of the facts and circumstances in existence on the date (including extensions) for filing the federal estate tax return (or, if earlier, the date the return is filed).

(3) Up to 10 Installments. The executor may elect to pay part or all of the federal estate tax in two or more (but not exceeding 10) equal annual installments.

(4) **Amount Limitation**. The maximum amount of federal estate tax that can be paid in installments is an amount that bears the same ratio to the total estate tax as the ratio of the closely held business interest to the adjusted gross estate.

(5) **Election**. The executor must make an IRC § 6166 election on the decedent's federal estate tax return. IRC § 6166(d).

b. **Rationale.** The rationale for IRC § 6166 is to relieve the estate from the hardship of having to sell a portion or all of the decedent's closely held business interest in order to pay federal estate taxes, which might otherwise interrupt or cease business operations.

c. **Deferral.** If the estate elects to pay federal estate taxes in installments, the executor can defer the first installment for up to 5 years after the original due date. Each succeeding installment payment must be made one year after the date of the first payment. IRC § 6166(a)(3).

> **EXAMPLE:** D died on April 4, 2004. D's estate tax liability was $3,500,000. D's estate included a closely held business which comprised 75% of his adjusted gross estate. If D's estate makes an IRC § 6166 election on D's federal estate tax return, D's estate may pay up to $2,625,000 (75% of the federal estate tax liability) in up to 10 annual installments. D's estate may defer the first installment until January 4, 2010 (five years after the due date on January 4, 2005).

d. **2% Interest Rate.** Generally, if the estate elects to pay federal estate taxes in installments, then a 2% interest rate applies to a portion of the tax. IRC §§ 6601(j) and 6166.

e. **Acceleration of Payments.** Under certain circumstances, the IRS will accelerate the estate's installment payments. IRC § 6166(g). For example, the disposition of the business interest can trigger the acceleration because the rationale for the installment payments is no longer applicable. IRC § 6166(g)(1). Certain late payments or the nonpayment of principal or interest also can trigger acceleration. IRC § 6166(g)(3).

I. Income Tax Consequences of Inherited Property

1. Step-Up in Basis Under Current Law

Basis is the amount used to calculate income tax gain or loss on the sale of property. It usually is the cost of acquiring the asset. Under current law, the basis of property inherited from a decedent usually is the federal estate tax value of the property in the decedent's gross estate. IRC § 1014. If the value at the date of death is lower than the basis of the property, the basis takes a step down to the value on the decedent's date of death. Because property generally appreciates over time, however, there usually is a step-up in basis at death.

EXAMPLE: D's gross estate included 100 shares of ABC company stock, which D's will left to B. The price per share on D's date of death was $100. Therefore, the value of the stock on D's date of death was $10,000. D originally purchased the 100 shares for $50 per share ($5,000). B's basis in the shares becomes $10,000 ($100/share), eliminating the $5,000 of gain that would have been taxed if D had sold the stock immediately before his death.

2. Modified Carryover Basis Rule Under the Act

Under the Act, in 2010, a modified carryover basis rule replaces the step-up in basis rule. IRC § 1014 (repealed); IRC §§ 1040, 6018, and 6019 (amended); IRC §§ 1022 and 6716 (new). Recipients of inherited property will receive a carryover basis equal to the lesser of the decedent's adjusted basis and the fair market value of the property on the decedent's date of death. The decedent's personal representative can allocate up to $1.3 million in basis increase among the decedent's assets. In addition, the personal representative can allocate an additional $3,000,000 of basis increase among the decedent's assets that pass to a surviving spouse outright or in a QTIP trust. These amounts may be indexed annually for inflation beginning in 2011. There are a number of assets that are not eligible for the step-up in basis, including property acquired by gift within 3 years of death from a person other than the decedent's surviving spouse and property that would constitute a right to receive income in respect of a decedent.

→ **Planning Point:** Although these new rules do not apply until 2010, practitioners should start advising their clients now to keep careful records so their personal representatives can determine when the asset was acquired and what the decedent's basis was in the asset. In addition, spouses may wish to consider establishing credit shelter and QTIP trusts to make maximum use of both spouses' basis increases.

Chapter II
Bibliography

2001 Tax Legislation: Law, Explanation and Analysis, CCH Incorporated (2001).

Regis W. Campfield et al., *Taxation of Estates, Gifts and Trusts* (21st ed. 1999).

The Economic Growth and Tax Relief Reconciliation Act of 2001: An Analysis, Matthew Bender & Co., Inc. (2001).

Estate Planning and Taxation Coordinator, Research Institute of America (2001).

Roy D. Madoff et al., *Practical Guide to Estate Planning* (2nd ed. 2001).

Charles F. (Monty) Newlin, "Sophisticated Estate Planning For Uncertain Times: Covering All the Bases For Today and Tomorrow," Illinois Institute for Continuing Legal Education Master Teacher Program (June 21, 2001).

Thomas G. Opferman, "The Marital Deduction in Depth: Formula Provisions (Pecuniary, Fractional, Hybrid); Hubert's Impact on Administration Expenses; Impacting of Family Business Deduction; Impact of Generation-Skipping Transfer Tax; Funding Problems and Forms," Illinois Institute for Continuing Legal Education (April 18 and May 4, 2000).

John R. Price, *Price on Contemporary Estate Planning* (2nd ed. 2001).

III. FEDERAL GIFT TAX

A. Introduction

Clients seek to make lifetime gifts for a variety of reasons. The reasons can be personal, tax-motivated or both. Certain transfers can inadvertently result in unintended gifts with transfer tax consequences. A basic understanding of the gift tax system will help practitioners recognize when a transfer constitutes a gift for gift tax purposes, and to recognize the significant transfer tax advantages that can be achieved through the utilization of lifetime gifts.

This chapter discusses the following issues relating to the federal gift tax and applicable changes made by the Economic Growth and Tax Relief Reconciliation Act of 2001 (the "Act"):

- Transfers subject to the federal gift tax.
- Valuation for federal gift tax purposes.
- Federal gift tax exclusions and deductions.
- Gift-splitting.
- Calculation of federal gift taxes.
- Gift tax returns and payment of gift taxes.
- Practical effects of lifetime giving.

B. Transfers Subject to the Federal Gift Tax

1. "Gift" for Federal Gift Tax Purposes

The definition of a "gift" for gift tax purposes is very broad. The regulations state that "any transaction in which an interest in property is gratuitously passed or conferred upon another, regardless of the means or device employed, constitutes a gift subject to gift tax." Treas. Reg. § 25.2511-1(c). The elements of a "gift" for gift tax purposes coincide with many (but not all) of the elements of a "gift" for property law purposes:

      a. Competent Donor. The individual making the gift is the "donor." The donor must be competent at the time the gift was made.

      b. Identity of Donee Not Necessary. The individual receiving the gift is the "donee." The fact that the identity of the donee is not known or ascertainable does not matter for gift tax purposes. Treas. Reg. § 25.2511-2(a).

      c. Donative Intent Not An Essential Element. The definition of a "gift" for property law purposes requires the donor to have donative intent. For gift tax purposes, however, donative intent is not an essential element of a transfer subject to gift tax. Treas. Reg. § 25.2511-1(g)(1).

EXAMPLE: B furnishes the entire purchase price of a $100,000 vacation home. B adds C to the title so that B and C own the vacation home as tenants in common. Although B did not intend to make a gift to C, B has made a gift to C for gift tax purposes of one-half of the purchase price of the vacation home, $50,000.

d. Complete and Irrevocable Gift. A gift must be complete and irrevocable for gift tax purposes. A gift is complete and irrevocable when "the donor has so parted with dominion and control as to leave in him no power to change its disposition, whether for his own benefit or for the benefit of another...." Treas. Reg. § 25.2511-2(b).

(1) Gifts By Attorney-in-Fact / Agent. A gift made by an attorney-in-fact (or agent) on behalf of a principal will be complete only if the attorney-in-fact has authority to make such gifts under state law. If state law allows the donor's power of attorney to authorize gifts, and if the donor's power of attorney explicitly authorizes the attorney-in-fact to make gifts, the gift will be treated as complete.

➔ **Planning Point:** Practitioners should check applicable state law concerning an attorney-in-fact's authority to make gifts under a durable power of attorney. If state law requires an explicit grant of authority to the attorney-in-fact to make gifts on behalf of the principal, the benefits and drawbacks of explicitly granting this power to a trusted attorney-in-fact should be considered.

(2) Gifts By Check. Generally, a gift by check is complete on the earlier to occur of: (1) the date the donor no longer has any control over the check, or (2) the date the donee deposits or cashes the check, but only if:

- The check is honored by the donor's bank when presented.
- The donor is alive when the bank pays the check.
- The check is delivered unconditionally to the donee.
- The check is cashed or deposited within a reasonable time of receipt.

EXAMPLE: On Monday, A gives a $50,000 check to A's child, B. A dies on Wednesday in an auto accident before B has deposited the check. A's gift is not complete, because A could have cancelled the check and, thus, A retained control over the check at the time of death.

There is an exception to the general rule that "deathbed gifts" by check will not relate back to the date of delivery. A gift by check to a charitable donee will be treated as complete on the date of delivery even if the donor dies before the check is cashed or deposited. *Rosano Est. v. Comm'r.*, 245 F.3d 212 (2d Cir., Apr. 6, 2001), *aff'g* 67 F.Supp. 113 (E.D.N.Y., 1999).

➔ **Planning Point:** Practitioners should alert clients, especially terminally ill clients, that their gifts by check to a noncharitable donee will not be complete upon delivery of the check. Practitioners should advise clients to instead consider making such "deathbed gifts" by wire transfers, money orders or certified checks.

    (3)   **Gifts of Stock**. A gift of stock is complete on the date the donor delivers the properly endorsed stock certificate to the donee or the donee's agent. If the donor delivers the certificate to the donor's bank or broker or to the issuing corporation for transfer into the name of the donee, however, the gift is not complete until the date on which the stock is transferred on the corporation's books. Treas. Reg. § 25.2511-2(h).

    (4)   **Joint Interests**. The creation or termination of a joint interest can result in a completed gift under certain circumstances. The form of ownership and the consideration furnished by each joint tenant are the critical factors.

    (a)   **Forms of Joint Ownership**. Most states allow the co-ownership of property as tenants in common, as joint tenants with rights of survivorship and as tenants by the entirety. Each form of ownership has different effects at the death of a co-owner. When a tenant in common dies, his or her interest in the property may be disposed of by will. When a joint tenant with rights of survivorship dies, his or her interest in the property passes to the surviving joint tenant(s) by operation of law. A tenancy by the entirety is a special form of joint ownership for married couples, and works the same way at death as joint tenancy with rights of survivorship.

    EXAMPLE: A and B own a home. A dies first. If they own the home as tenants in common, A's interest will pass by A's will (or to his heirs under state law if A has no will). If they own the home as joint tenants with rights of survivorship, or if A and B are married and own the home as tenants by the entirety, A's interest will pass to B by operation of law.

    (b)   **Gift Tax Consequences.** If a co-owner provides more or all of the consideration for a purchase and takes title with another person as joint tenants or tenants in common, and either owner can unilaterally sever the joint ownership and receive a pro rata interest in the property, the individual providing the consideration has made a gift.

    EXAMPLE: A buys a house for $250,000 and takes title with A's sister, B, as tenants in common. A provided all of the consideration for the house. Under state law, either A or B can unilaterally sever the tenancy in common. A has made a completed gift to B of one-half of the interest ($125,000).

(c)   **Joint Bank Accounts.** If the accountholders of a joint bank account can unilaterally withdraw funds from the account, a completed gift does not occur when one of the accountholders deposits money into the joint account, because the depositor can simply withdraw the deposited funds. Thus, the depositor has not given up dominion and control over the funds. A completed gift will occur, however, when the accountholder (*i.e.*, the accountholder who did not make the deposit) withdraws the deposited funds from the account.

> **EXAMPLE:** P has a bank account with $100,000. On Date 1, P added C's name to the account. Under state law, either P or C can withdraw funds from the account. On Date 2, C deposits $10,000 to the account. On Date 3, C withdraws $20,000 from the account. On Date 1, P did not make a gift by adding C's name to the account. Similarly, C did not make a completed gift on Date 2 when C added funds to the account. P did, however, make a completed gift of $10,000 on Date 3 when C withdrew $20,000 from the account, because C withdrew $10,000 more than C contributed to the account.

(5)   **Joint and Mutual Wills**. Some states allow joint and mutual wills. Joint and mutual wills are identical wills created by two or more persons (usually spouses). In some states, joint and mutual wills become irrevocable and binding at the death of the first testator to die, resulting in a completed gift.

> **EXAMPLE:** H and W create identical wills that state that they are joint and mutual. The wills provide that the surviving spouse will receive a life estate in the deceased spouse's estate, and both estates will go outright to their children at the death of the surviving spouse. Under state law, the wills become binding and irrevocable at the first death. At W's death, there is a completed gift by H of a remainder interest in H's property to the children.

(6)   **Gifts in Trust.** In determining whether a donor's transfer in trust is a completed gift, the terms and the scope of the donor's powers must be examined. Treas. Reg. § 25.2511-2(b). Some of these powers include the following:

(a)   **Donor's Power to Revoke Trust or Revest Trust Property in Self**. A transfer to a trust is an incomplete gift if the donor has the power to revoke the trust or otherwise revest the trust property in himself. Treas. Reg. § 25.2511-2(c).

> **EXAMPLE:** D transfers $100,000 to D's revocable trust. D's transfer is not a completed gift because D retained the power to revoke the trust.

(b)   **Donor's Power to Name New Beneficiaries or Change Interests**. A transfer to a trust is an incomplete gift if the donor has the power to name new beneficiaries or to change the interests of the beneficiaries *unless* the power is a fiduciary power limited by an ascertainable standard relating to the health, education, maintenance and support of the beneficiary. Treas. Reg. §§ 25.2511-2(c); -2(g).

> **EXAMPLE:** D transfers $100,000 to a trust for the benefit of A and B. D, as trustee, retains the power to allocate income and principal to or for the benefit of A or B for their health. D's transfer is a completed gift because D's fiduciary power to reallocate property between the beneficiaries is limited by an ascertainable standard.

(c) **Donor's Power to Change Manner and Timing of Enjoyment**. A transfer to a trust is a complete gift if the donor only has the power to determine the manner or timing of the enjoyment of a gift. Treas. Reg. § 25.2511-2(d).

> **EXAMPLE:** D transfers $100,000 to a trust for the benefit of A. All income will be distributed to A annually for 10 years, and the trust property will be distributed to A at the end of 10 years. D retains the power to require that income be accumulated and added to principal until the end of the 10 years. D's transfer is a completed gift because D only has a power to determine the timing of A's enjoyment of D's gift.

2. Less Than Full and Adequate Consideration

a. General Rule. A transfer qualifies as a gift for gift tax purposes if the value transferred exceeds the consideration given. That is, a transaction such as a sale or exchange that is made for less than adequate and full consideration in money or money's worth will result in a gift. Internal Revenue Code ("IRC") § 2512(b); Treas. Reg. § 25.2512-8. The corollary of this rule is that a transfer for full and adequate consideration in money or money's worth is not a gift for gift tax purposes.

b. Ordinary Course of Business Exception. A sale, exchange or other transfer of property made in the ordinary course of business (*i.e.*, a transaction which is bona fide, at arm's length and free from donative intent) is not a gift, even if it is not for full and adequate consideration. Treas. Reg. §§ 25.2511-1(g)(2); 25.2512-8.

> **EXAMPLE:** B purchased a used car from a dealership for $15,000 even though the blue book price of the car was $17,000. Even though B did not pay the exact blue book price, there was no gift because the transaction was an arm's length business transaction.

3. Indirect Gifts

An indirect gifts is a transaction that does not look like a typical outright gift but confers an economic benefit on another person. Treas. Reg. § 25.2511-1(c).

a. **Interest-Free and Below-Market Interest Rate Loans**. Certain interest-free and below-market interest rate loans can result in a gift from the lender to the borrower.

(1) *Dickman* **Principle**. In Dickman v. Comm'r, 465 U.S. 330 (1984), the Supreme Court concluded that an interest-free loan of funds is a transfer of property by gift for gift tax purposes. The rationale was that the transaction conferred an economic benefit on the borrower.

(2) **Statutory Response**. In response to *Dickman*, IRC § 7872 was enacted. Section 7872 codifies the gift tax treatment of interest-free and low-interest rate loans.

(a) **Applicability**. IRC § 7872 applies to interest-free loans and loans with an interest rate below the applicable federal rate (AFR).

(b) **Amount of Gift**. Generally, the amount of the gift is the amount of the forgone interest, the difference between the amount of interest that would have been payable at the AFR and the interest actually paid. IRC § 7872(e)(2).

> **EXAMPLE:** P lends P's child, C, $100,000 at a 2% interest rate. The AFR is 8%. The amount of the gift in a given calendar year is the difference between the interest actually paid in that year and the interest that would have been paid at the 8% AFR.

(c) **Exceptions**. IRC § 7872 excepts certain loans between family members where tax avoidance is not the primary purpose. For example, a general de minimis exception allows certain gift loans between individuals of up to $10,000. IRC § 7872(c)(2)(A).

b. **Gift of Services.** An individual's personal services can sometimes result in a taxable gift. This issue often comes up when a personal representative foregoes a fee so that the beneficiaries will receive more from the estate. Such a fee would normally be included in the personal representative's gross income. In order for a personal representative to waive the fee without triggering income to himself and a deemed gift to the beneficiaries, the timing, purposes and effect of the personal representative's waiver of the fee must constitute evidence of an intent to render gratuitous services. An intention to serve gratuitously can be evidenced by an executor's waiver within six months of appointment or the executor's failure to claim fees or commissions as deductions. Rev. Rul. 66-167.

c. **Powers of Appointment.** A "power of appointment" is simply the power to decide who will take the trust property next, and the time, terms, shares and conditions under which they will receive it.

(1) **General Powers of Appointment**. IRC § 2514 provides that the exercise, release or lapse of certain general powers of appointment will result in a taxable transfer. IRC § 2514(c). Subject to certain exceptions, a "general power of appointment" is a

power of appointment exercisable in favor of the holder of the power, the holder's estate, the holder's creditors or the creditors of the holder's estate. Treas. Reg. § 25.2514-1(c).

(a) **Ascertainable Standard Exception**. The ascertainable standard exception provides that a holder's power to appoint the property to himself that is limited by an ascertainable standard (relating to the holder's health, education, support or maintenance) is *not* a general power of appointment. Certain other standards (such as "welfare" or "happiness") are *not* considered an ascertainable standard.

> **EXAMPLE:** A trust provides that beneficiary B has a power to invade principal for B's health. B's power is not a general power of appointment because B's power to invade principal for himself was limited by an ascertainable standard (health). If B had the power to invade principal for his health and welfare, B's power would be a general power of appointment because "welfare" is not an ascertainable standard.

(b) **General Powers of Appointment Created After October 21, 1942**. The exercise or release of a general power of appointment created after October 21, 1942 is a taxable transfer for gift tax purposes. IRC § 2514(b). A lapse of such a power is also treated as a release and, thus, as a taxable transfer, but only to the extent that the value of the property subject to the lapse exceeds the greater of $5,000 or 5% of the aggregate value of trust property out of which the power could have been satisfied. IRC § 2514(e).

➔   **Planning Point:** In trusts, a power given to take advantage of this rule is the "5 and 5 power." The 5 and 5 power gives the powerholder the right to withdraw the greater of $5,000 or 5% of the trust property each year. The power lapses at the end of the year if not exercised. The annual lapse of the 5 and 5 power is excluded from gift tax under IRC § 2514(e).

> **EXAMPLE:** P has a general power to appoint $100,000 out of a trust with a total value of $200,000. The trust was created in 1997. P permits the power to lapse. P is treated as having made a transfer of $90,000 (the excess of $100,000 over 5% of the trust).

(c) **General Powers of Appointment Created Before October 22, 1942**. Only the exercise of a general power of appointment created before October 22, 1942 is a taxable transfer for gift tax purposes. IRC § 2514(a).

(2) **Special Powers of Appointment**. Basically, a special power of appointment is a power of appointment that is *not* a general power of appointment (*i.e.*, not exercisable in favor of the holder, the holder's estate, the holder's creditors or the creditors of the holder's estate). The exercise or release of a special power of appointment is not a taxable transfer for gift tax purposes. A special power of appointment is often used when the donor

wants to give the holder the flexibility to control the disposition of trust property but still limit the group benefiting from the holder's exercise of the power.

> **EXAMPLE:** A trust gives beneficiary A a power to appoint trust principal in favor of anyone other than A, A's estate or the creditors of either. A exercises the power in favor of A's children. A's exercise is not a taxable transfer.

    d. Disclaimers. A disclaimer occurs when a donee refuses to accept property or a property interest transferred to the donee. The donee disclaiming the interest is called the "disclaimant." Certain disclaimers of property can result in a gift by the disclaimant to the person who receives the interest instead.

    (1) Qualified Disclaimers. IRC § 2518 provides that a "qualified disclaimer" is not a taxable transfer subject to gift tax. A disclaimer is "qualified" if it meets all of the following requirements. IRC § 2518(b).

➔   **Planning Point:** Qualified disclaimers are useful for post mortem planning purposes. They can be used to correct planning mistakes or omissions.

> **EXAMPLE:** H leaves his entire estate to H's child, C. C can disclaim a portion of his interest in favor of W to take advantage of the unlimited marital deduction.

    (a) Irrevocable and Unconditional. The disclaimant must irrevocably and unconditionally refuse to accept an interest in property.

    In Writing. The disclaimer must be in writing.

    (b) Timing. The disclaimer must be received by the transferor (or legal title holder) of the interest within 9 months of the date on which the transfer creating the interest in the disclaimant is made. For a disclaimant under age 21, the period is extended until 9 months after the disclaimant reaches age 21.

> **EXAMPLE:** D died on March 1, 2005 and left his entire estate to D's children, B (who is 25 years old) and C (who will turn 21 on April 4, 2005). Assuming B and C meet the other requirements of a qualified disclaimer, B can disclaim his interest in D's estate up until December 1, 2005 (9 months after D's date of death), and C can disclaim his interest in D's estate up until January 4, 2006 (9 months after C turns age 21).

    (c) No Acceptance or Benefit. The disclaimant must not have accepted any interest or benefit with respect to the disclaimed property.

➜ **Planning Point:** Immediately after a client's death, practitioners should consider whether a qualified disclaimer needs to be made *before* a beneficiary benefits from or accepts property.

(d) **Pass Without Direction or Control by Disclaimant.** The interest must in fact pass to another person without any direction or control by the disclaimant.

(2) **Non-Qualified Disclaimers.** A disclaimer of property that is not qualified will be treated as a taxable gift by the disclaimant.

4. Net Gifts

A "net gift" occurs when a donor makes a gift on the condition that the donee pays the gift tax.

a. Gift Tax Consequences. Because the donee's enjoyment of the gift is reduced by the amount of gift taxes paid, the "net gift" that is taxable is the difference between the amount of the gift and the gift taxes paid. Rev. Rul. 75-72 describes the interrelated calculation necessary to determine the amount of the gift and the amount of the gift tax due.

> **EXAMPLE:** P requires C to pay the gift tax liability of $200,000 on a $1,000,000 gift. The net gift principle says that P has made a net gift of $800,000.

b. Income Tax Consequences. An income tax issue arises with a net gift if the amount of gift tax discharged by the donee exceeds the donor's basis in the property transferred. In *Diedrich v. Comm'r*, 457 U.S. 191 (1982), the Supreme Court treated such a transaction as a sale for income tax purposes, and the excess was treated as the amount realized by the donor.

➜ **Planning Point:** In order to avoid income tax gain, the basis of gifted property in a net gift transaction should be equal to at least the amount of gift tax.

C. Valuation for Federal Gift Tax Purposes

1. General Rule

Generally, a gift is subject to gift tax based on its fair market value on the date of transfer (the date the gift becomes complete). IRC § 2512(a). "Fair market value" is the price at which the property would change hands between a willing buyer and a willing seller, neither being under any compulsion to buy or to sell and both having reasonable knowledge of the relevant facts. Treas. Reg. § 25.2512-1. Valuation issues are discussed in detail in a separate chapter.

2. Valuation of Specific Types of Property for Gift Tax Purposes

The regulations provide guidelines on the valuation of different types of property for gift tax purposes:

- Treas. Reg. § 25.2512-1 (property in general).
- Treas. Reg. § 25.2512-2 (stocks and bonds).
- Treas. Reg. § 25.2512-3 (business interests).
- Treas. Reg. § 25.2512-4 (notes).
- Treas. Reg. § 25.2512-5 (annuities, unitrust interests, interests for life or term of years, and remainder or reversionary interests).
- Treas. Reg. § 25.2512-6 (certain life insurance and annuity contracts and share in an open-end investment company).
- Treas. Reg. § 25.2512-7 (items subject to excise tax).
- Treas. Reg. § 25.2512-8 (transfers for insufficient consideration).

3. Discounts & Restrictions Affecting Valuation

Certain valuation discounts can be applied to *reduce* the value of a gift. For example, common discounts include (i) discounts for lack of marketability, (ii) discounts for minority interests and (iii) discounts for fractional interests. The rules in IRC §§ 2701-2704 (gifts of certain property subject to restrictions on the use of the property) can effectively establish a *higher* valuation than the fair market value standard. These discounts and rules are discussed in detail in a separate chapter.

D. Federal Gift Tax Exclusions

1. Gift Tax Annual Exclusion

The gift tax annual exclusion under IRC § 2503(b) permits an individual to give an amount equal to the annual exclusion ($11,000 in 2005) per donee without incurring gift tax liability, provided that the gift is of a present interest. A married donor can annually give up to $22,000 per donee if the donor's spouse agrees to apply his or her annual exclusion amount by gift-splitting. IRC § 2513.

> **EXAMPLE:** In 2005, A gave $15,000 in cash to B. The first $11,000 is not subject to gift tax because of the annual exclusion. If A and A's spouse had elected to split their gifts, the entire $15,000 gift would be covered by the annual exclusions of A and A's spouse.

a. Donee. Generally, the donee of an annual exclusion gift can be anyone. The donee need not be a relative in order to qualify for the annual exclusion. The number of potential donees is unlimited.

> **EXAMPLE:** A makes cash gifts totaling $220,000 in 2005 ($11,000 to each of A's 5 children, 10 grandchildren, 4 friends and 1 doorman). None of the gifts is subject to gift tax by reason of the annual exclusion.

b. Annual Exclusion Amount. The annual exclusion amount referred to in the Code is $10,000. However, that amount was indexed for inflation after 1998, and, as a result, the current gift tax annual exclusion amount is $11,000 for 2005. IRC § 2503(b)(2).

c. Annual Exclusion Gifts Not Subject to GST Tax. Annual exclusion gifts are not subject to the generation-skipping transfer (GST) tax for transfers to grandchildren or more remote descendants if the transfer is a "direct skip." IRC § 2642(c). Transfers directly (*i.e.*, not in trust) to grandchildren or more remote descendants always constitute "direct skips." This concept will be covered further in Chapter IV "Federal Generation-Skipping Transfer Tax."

> **EXAMPLE:** On January 1, 2005, B gave $11,000 to B's grandchild, G. Because the annual exclusion covers B's gift to G, and because the transfer is a "direct skip," B's gift to G is not subject to gift tax or GST tax.

d. Annual Exclusion Gifts Do Not Use Donor's Unified Credit. Annual exclusion gifts do not use any portion of the donor's unified credit against gift and estate tax. Accordingly, such gifts essentially escape transfer tax altogether. A donor's annual exclusion is applied to a gift before the donor's unified credit.

> **EXAMPLE:** During D's lifetime, D made only annual exclusion gifts of $10,000 to B. At D's death, D's entire unified credit amount remains intact.

> **EXAMPLE:** D makes a gift of $50,000 to B in 2005. No gift tax is due because the first $11,000 of D's gift is covered by the annual exclusion, and the remaining $39,000 utilizes a portion of D's unified credit.

e. No Carry Over to Subsequent Years. Unlike the unified credit, the gift tax annual exclusion does not carry over to the next calendar year.

> **EXAMPLE:** P gives $1,000 to A in 2004 and $20,000 to A in 2005. P's 2004 annual exclusion covers $11,000 of the $20,000 gift. P cannot, however, use the unused $9,000 of exclusion from 2004 to

cover the remaining taxable portion of his 2005 gift to A. As a result, P has made a taxable gift in 2005 of $9,000.

f. "Present Interest" Requirement. A gift of a "future interest" does not qualify for the annual exclusion. A gift must be of a "present interest" in order to qualify for the annual exclusion.

(1)   "Future Interest". A "future interest" is an interest in property, such as a reversion or remainder interest, that is limited in possession, use or enjoyment to a future date or time. Treas. Reg. § 25.2503-3(a).

(2)   "Present Interest". A "present interest" is an unrestricted right to the immediate use, possession, or enjoyment of property or the income from property (such as a life estate or term certain). Treas. Reg. § 25.2503-3(b).

(a)   Outright Gifts. Most outright gifts are present interest gifts that qualify for the annual exclusion because the donee has immediate use, possession or enjoyment of the gift. A substantial restriction, however, could prevent an outright gift from qualifying as a present interest gift.

➔   **Planning Point:** Practitioners advising clients who wish to make outright annual exclusion gifts of business interests should be sure that the operating agreement of the business does not prevent the donees from obtaining immediate use, possession or enjoyment of the transferred business interests. A member's (or partner's) inability, under the operating agreement, to; (1) unilaterally withdraw his or her capital account, (2) independently effectuate a dissolution of the business and (3) sell his or her business interest without the business manager's consent in the manager's sole discretion has been deemed to prevent transferred business interests from qualifying for the gift tax annual exclusion. *Hackl v. Comm'r*, 335 F.3d 664 (7th Cir. 2003).

This result might be avoided by giving a donee the unilateral right to sell his or her entire interest to third parties, subject to a right of first refusal by the entity and/or other interest holders to purchase the interest at the same price and terms as contained in a bona fide offer from a third party. In addition, perhaps the business manager's discretion to retain funds should be limited to amounts commensurate with the needs of the business with the balance of the funds being distributable to the interest holders. Alternatively, the business agreement could include a provision giving each donee the right to withdraw assets from the entity whenever gifts of entity interests are made. The right can be limited to the fair market value for the gifted interests and only be available for a limited period of time. Such a provision should foreclose any argument that the donee does not have the right to the immediate use, possession and enjoyment of the property in the economic sense.

(b) **Gifts in Trust**. Not all gifts in trust are gifts of present interests. A gift in trust must be a gift of a present interest to qualify for the annual exclusion. Certain gifts in trusts for the benefit of a minor qualify for the annual exclusion. These trusts ("*Crummey* trust" and "IRC § 2503(c) trust") are covered in a separate chapter.

> **EXAMPLE:** P transfers $11,000 to a trust for A in 2005. The trust provides that the trustee may make discretionary distributions of income and principal to A until P dies, at which time the entire trust property will be distributed to A. P's gift is not a gift of a present interest and does not qualify for the annual exclusion because A must wait for P to die before A gets the right to possess the trust property.

2. Unlimited Exclusion for Tuition Expenses and Medical Expenses

IRC § 2503(e)(1) excludes from gift tax certain "qualified transfers." "Qualified transfers" include amounts paid by a donor directly to a qualifying education institution or a medical provider on behalf of an individual for tuition expenses or medical care. IRC § 2503(e)(2).

a. Unlimited Exclusion Amount. The amount of the exclusion for such tuition and medical care expenses is unlimited. The exclusion is in addition to the gift tax annual exclusion. Treas. Reg. § 25.2503-6(a).

> **EXAMPLE:** In 2005, P gave $5,000 to C, paid $20,000 directly to State University for C's tuition expenses and paid $2,000 directly to State Hospital for C's medical expenses. None of these gifts are subject to gift tax. The annual exclusion covers P's $5,000 gift, and the exclusions for tuition expenses and medical expenses cover P's $20,000 and $2,000 gifts.

b. Exclusion Amount Not Subject to GST Tax. Gifts that qualify for the exclusion for tuition or medical expenses are not subject to GST tax. IRC § 2642(c).

➔ **Planning Point:** This exclusion is especially valuable for grandparents because their payments of a grandchild's tuition and medical expenses are: (1) unlimited in amount, (2) free of gift tax, (3) free of GST tax, and (4) remove significant amounts from their estates. In addition, the grandparents control the use of the gifts by making payments directly to the educational institution or medical provider.

c. Payments Must Be Direct. Payments of tuition expenses must be made *directly* to the educational institution to qualify for the exclusion. Similarly, payments of medical expenses must be made *directly* to the medical care provider to qualify for the exclusion. Section 2503(e)(2).

> **EXAMPLE:** P gives $20,000 to P's child, A, to pay for tuition at Private University. P's gift does not qualify for the exclusion because P paid A instead of paying Private University directly.

d. Permitted Donee. Generally, the donee of a such a gift can be anyone. The donee need not be a relative in order to qualify for the exclusion for tuition and medical expenses. The number of potential donees is unlimited.

e. Qualifying Education Institution. A "qualifying educational institution" is one that normally maintains a regular faculty and curriculum and normally has a regularly enrolled body of pupils or students in attendance at the place where the educational activities are regularly carried on. Treas. Reg. § 25.2503-6(b)(2).

f. Qualifying Education Expenses. Only tuition expenses qualify for the exclusion for educational expenses. Expenses for books, supplies, dormitory fees, board, or other similar expenses do not qualify for the exclusion. Treas. Reg. § 25.2503-6(b)(2).

g. Qualifying Medical Expenses. "Qualifying medical expenses" include expenses incurred for the diagnosis, cure, mitigation, treatment or prevention of disease, or for the purpose of affecting any structure or function of the body or for transportation primarily for and essential to medical care. In addition, amounts paid for medical insurance qualify. The exclusion does not apply, however, with respect to any amounts reimbursed by medical insurance. Treas. Reg. § 25.2503-6(b)(3).

E. Federal Gift Tax Deductions

1. Unlimited Gift Tax Marital Deduction

IRC § 2523 allows an unlimited gift tax marital deduction for qualified interests that a donor gives to the donor's spouse.

➜ **Planning Point:** The gift tax marital deduction is useful for spouses who wish to equalize their estates to give the "poorer" spouse more property. This is important for estate tax planning purposes so that both spouses' unified credits can be used, regardless of who dies first.

a. Requirements. An interest transferred to a donee-spouse must meet all of the following requirements in order to qualify for the gift tax marital deduction.

(1) Donee-Spouse is a U.S. Citizen. The donee-spouse must be a U.S. citizen on the date of the gift. The gift tax marital deduction is not available for gifts to donee-spouses who are not U.S. citizens at the time of gift.

(2)   Deductible Interest (Not a Nondeductible Terminable Interest).
The interest must not be a nondeductible terminable interest.   See discussion below on
terminable interests.

b.   The Terminable Interest Rule: Nondeductible Terminable Interests.
The terminable interest rule provides that the marital deduction is not available for interests that
terminate or fail upon a lapse of time or the occurrence or nonoccurrence of an event if a person
other than the donee-spouse receives the property after the termination of the donee-spouse's
interest.   IRC § 2523(b).

> **EXAMPLE:** H gives $300,000 to an irrevocable trust for W's benefit
> for 10 years, at which time the trust will terminate and be distributed to
> H's children. H is not entitled to a marital deduction for the $300,000
> transferred to the trust for W because W's interest in the trust will
> terminate upon a lapse of time (10 years) and persons other than W
> (H's children) will receive the property from H.

**c.   Exceptions to the Terminable Interest Rule: Deductible Terminable
Interests**. Despite the terminable interest rule, certain terminable interests still qualify for
the gift tax marital deduction. Some of these interests include the following:

(1)   General Power of Appointment Trust Exception. Under IRC §
2523(e), a marital deduction is allowed for an interest that passes to a spouse if all of the
following requirements are met:

- The donee-spouse is entitled for life to all of the income from the entire
  interest or a specific portion of the entire interest, or to a specific portion
  of all the income from the entire interest.
- The income payable to the donee-spouse must be payable at least
  annually.
- The donee-spouse must have the power to appoint the entire interest or the
  specific portion to either himself or herself or to his or her estate.
- The power must be exercisable by the donee-spouse alone (whether by
  will or during life) and must be exercisable in all events.
- The entire interest or specific portion must not be subject to a power in
  any other person to appoint any portion or all of the interest in favor of
  any person other than the donee-spouse.

> **EXAMPLE:** H gives $500,000 to an irrevocable trust for W. All of
> the income of the trust is payable to W annually and W has the power
> to appoint property to anyone, including herself and her estate. The
> trust qualifies for the gift tax marital deduction as a general power of
> appointment trust under IRC § 2523(e). If the trust had also provided
> that W's child, C, had a power to appoint the trust property in favor of

C's children, the trust would not have qualified for the gift tax marital deduction.

(2) **QTIP Trust Exception.** Under IRC § 2523(f), a marital deduction is allowed for an interest that passes to a spouse in a lifetime qualified terminable interest property (QTIP) trust if all of the following requirements are met:

- The spouse is entitled for life to all of the income from the entire interest or a specific portion of the entire interest, or to a specific portion of all the income from the entire interest.
- The income payable to the spouse must be payable at least annually.
- The entire interest or specific portion must not be subject to a power in any other person to appoint any part to any person other than the spouse.
- A QTIP election must be made on the donor's gift tax return with respect to a specific portion or all of the trust.

➔ **Planning Point:** The QTIP trust is similar to the general power of appointment trust except that the spouse need not have a general power of appointment over a QTIP trust in order to qualify for the gift tax marital deduction.

> **EXAMPLE:** H gives $500,000 to an irrevocable trust for W. All of the income of the trust is payable to W annually. W has a power to appoint the trust property in favor of W's descendants. If H makes a QTIP election on H's gift tax return, the trust will qualify for the gift tax marital deduction. If the trust had also provided that W's child, C, had a power to appoint the trust property in favor of C's children, the trust would not have qualified for the gift tax marital deduction.

2. Unlimited Gift Tax Charitable Deduction

IRC § 2522(a) allows an unlimited gift tax marital deduction for transfers to the following types of recipients:

- Federal government, State government or subdivisions thereof for exclusively public purposes.
- IRC § 501(c)(3) corporations, trusts, community chests, funds or foundations, operated exclusively for religious, charitable, scientific, literary or education purposes, which do not attempt to influence elections and are not substantially engaged in carrying on propaganda or influencing legislation.
- IRC § 501(c)(3) fraternal or veterans organizations.

a. Unlimited. None of the percentage and other limitations on the income tax charitable deduction under IRC § 170 apply to the gift tax charitable deduction. In this sense, the gift tax charitable deduction is "unlimited."

b. Nonresident Alien Donors. If the donor is not a U.S. resident or citizen at the time of gift, corporate donees must be domestic corporations, and gifts to trusts, community chests, funds or foundations, or fraternal organizations must be for use within the U.S. in order to be deductible for gift tax purposes. IRC § 2522(b).

c. Split Interests. A split interest is simply a gift in which a charitable beneficiary and a noncharitable beneficiary share interests. Split interest gifts, such as charitable remainder trusts, charitable lead trusts, pooled income funds, and other charitable techniques are discussed in detail in the chapter on charitable planning.

d. Charitable Deduction for Qualified Conservation Transfer. IRC § 2522(d) allows a gift tax charitable deduction for any transfer of a "qualified real property interest" under IRC § 170(h) to a qualified charity. A "qualified real property interest" includes the entire interest of the donor other than a qualified mineral interest, a remainder interest or a restriction (granted in perpetuity) on the use which may be made of the real property. IRC § 170(h)(2).

F. Gift Splitting

1. General Rule

Generally, IRC § 2513 allows one spouse to treat his or her gifts to any person other than his or her spouse as made one-half by each spouse.

> **EXAMPLE:** H makes a gift to A of $22,000. If H and W elect to split H's gift, one-half ($11,000) will be treated as made by H, and one-half ($11,000) will be treated as made by W.

2. Requirements

In order to "split gifts" under IRC § 2513, all of the following requirements must be met:

a. U.S. Citizen or Resident Spouses. Both spouses must be U.S. citizens or residents at the time of the gift. IRC § 2513(a)(1).

b. Married and No Subsequent Remarriage in Same Calendar Year. The donor must have been married at the date of gift. Further, the donor cannot remarry during the remainder of the calendar year in which the gift occurred. IRC § 2513(a)(1).

> **EXAMPLE:** H and W1 divorced on January 31, 2005. Prior to their divorce, H made a gift to A of $22,000. H subsequently marries W2

on December 4, 2005. H cannot split his gift to A with W1. Although H and W1 were married at the date of gift, H subsequently remarried during the same year. H cannot split his gift with W2 either because H was not married to W2 when H made the gift.

c. **Consent of Both Spouses on Gift Tax Return**. Both spouses must elect to split their gifts on their gift tax returns. IRC §§ 2513(a)(2) and 2513(b).

➔ **Planning Point:** Gift splitting is often used to take advantage of both spouse's gift tax and GST tax annual exclusions.

EXAMPLE: H gives $22,000 to H's grandchild, G. If H and W split H's gift, one-half ($11,000) will be treated as made by H, and one-half ($11,000) will be treated as made by W. Each spouse's gift tax and GST tax annual exclusion will cover his or her one-half of the gift.

3. **Joint and Several Liability**

The non-transferring spouse who consents to split gifts is jointly and severally liable for the entire gift tax liability. IRC § 2513(d).

G. Nature, Scope and Calculation of Federal Gift Tax

1. **Nature**

Like the federal estate tax, the federal gift tax is an excise tax on the <u>transfer</u> of property. The federal gift tax is a tax on a donor's <u>privilege</u> of being able to transfer property by gift during a calendar year. IRC § 2501(a)(1); Treas. Reg. § 25.2511-2(a).

2. **Scope**

The gift tax applies to all gifts made by U.S. citizens or residents and to gifts made by nonresident aliens of property situated in the U.S. Subject to certain exceptions, it does not apply to gifts made by nonresident aliens of intangible property. Shares of stock issued by a domestic corporation and debt obligations of any U.S. citizen or any federal or state government, however, are deemed to be property situated in the U.S. IRC §§ 2501(a)(2), 2511(a), and 2511(b); Treas. Reg. § 25.2511-3.

EXAMPLE: C, a Canadian citizen and resident, gives 500 shares of IBM stock to D. C's gift is subject to federal gift tax even though C is a nonresident alien, because the gifted shares are deemed to have a U.S. situs.

3. Calculation

IRC § 2502(a) and Treas. Reg. § 25.2502-1 describe the computation of a donor's gift tax liability.

a. Calculated Annually. A donor's gift tax liability for gifts made in the previous calendar year is calculated on an annual basis. IRC §§ 2501(a)(1) and 2502(a).

b. Computation. In general, a donor's gift tax liability is the amount equal to the excess of: (1) the tentative gift tax on the aggregate sum of the donor's taxable gifts for the current year and the donor's taxable gifts for all prior years, over (2) the tentative gift tax on the aggregate sum of the donor's taxable gifts for all prior years.

(1) Total Gifts. The first step is to determine the donor's total gifts during the calendar year in question.

(2) Allowable Exclusions and Deductions. The second step is to determine the donor's total allowable exclusions and deductions.

(3) Total Taxable Gifts. The donor's "total taxable gifts" is determined by adding the donor's taxable gifts for the calendar year in question to all of the donor's taxable gifts for prior calendar years.

(a) Taxable Gifts for Calendar Year in Question. The donor's taxable gifts for the current year is determined by subtracting from the value of the donor's total gifts the donor's total allowable exclusions and deductions. IRC § 2503.

(b) Taxable Gifts for All Prior Years. The donor's taxable gifts for a prior year is based on the donor's total gifts and exclusions, deductions and exemptions as were allowed under the gift tax laws applicable to that year. IRC § 2504.

(4) Tentative Tax. The donor's total tentative tax is determined by subtracting the tentative tax on taxable gifts for prior years from the donor's tentative tax on his total taxable gifts. IRC § 2502(a).

(a) Tentative Tax on Total Taxable Gifts. A tentative tax on the donor's total taxable gifts is determined by applying the applicable tax rate from the tax rate table in IRC § 2001(c) to the decedent's total taxable gifts. IRC § 2502(a)(1).

(b) Tentative Tax on Prior Taxable Gifts. A tentative tax on the donor's taxable gifts from all prior years (excluding the current year) is determined by applying the applicable tax rate from the tax rate table in IRC § 2001(c) to the decedent's taxable gifts from all such years. IRC § 2502(a)(2).

(5) **Reduction by Unified Credit**. The donor's total tentative tax is then reduced by the unused portion of the donor's unified credit. IRC § 2505.

> **EXAMPLE:** D made a taxable gift in 1997 of $100,000 and a taxable gift in 1998 of $200,000. In 2005, D gave B $100,000 in cash and paid for B's $20,000 tuition expense. D's 2005 gift tax liability is calculated as follows. D's taxable gifts for 2005 are $89,000 ($120,000 total gifts, less $11,000 annual exclusion, less $20,000 exclusion for tuition expenses). D's total taxable gifts are $389,000 ($100,000 in 1997 plus $200,000 in 1998 plus $89,000 in 2005). Applying the tax rate table in IRC § 2001(c), the tentative tax on D's total taxable gifts of $389,000 is $118,060, and the tentative tax on D's prior gifts of $300,000 is $87,300. D's tentative gift tax liability for 2005 is $30,760. This amount is reduced by the unused portion of D's unified credit. No gift tax is due in 2005.

c. Effect of the Act on Computation of Estate Tax.

(1) **Gift Tax Retained**. Unlike the estate tax and GST tax, the gift tax will not be repealed, and will remain in place after 2009. The gift tax was retained to deter income tax avoidance schemes.

(2) **Gift Tax Exemption**. Unlike the estate tax exemption, which increases in stages until 2010, the gift tax exemption remains at $1,000,000. Since 2004, the estate tax exemption has been larger than the gift tax exemption.

(3) **Declining Maximum Rate**. Under the Act, the maximum gift tax rate is scheduled to decline. Under the sunset provisions of the Act, however, the maximum gift tax rate will revert to 55%.

CALENDAR YEAR	MAXIMUM ESTATE & GIFT TAX RATE	GIFT TAX EXEMPTION	ESTATE TAX EXEMPTION
2005	47%	$1 million	$1.5 million
2006	46%	$1 million	$2 million
2007	45%	$1 million	$2 million
2008	45%	$1 million	$2 million
2009	45%	$1 million	$3.5 million
2010	35%	$1 million	Tax Repealed
2011	55%	$1 million	$1 million

H. Payment of Gift Tax, Gift Tax Returns & Statute of Limitations

1. Liability

The donor is primarily liable for payment of gift taxes. IRC § 2502(c); Treas. Reg. § 25.2502-2. The donee is secondarily liable if the donor does not pay. IRC §§ 6324(b) and 6901(a)(1)(A)(iii).

2. Gift Tax Return

a. Who Must File. Generally, any individual donor who in any calendar year makes a gift must file a gift tax return (IRS Form 709). No return is required, however, if all of the donor's gifts fall into one or more of the following categories of gifts: (1) annual exclusion gifts (without gift-splitting) under IRC § 2503(b), (2) gifts to an educational institution or health care provider under IRC § 2503(e), (3) gifts that qualify for the marital deduction under IRC § 2523, (4) certain outright gifts that qualify for the charitable deduction under IRC § 2522(d). IRC § 6019.

> **EXAMPLE:** D's only gifts in 2001 are cash gifts of $10,000 to each of D's children. D is not required to file a gift tax return because D's gifts qualify for the annual exclusion.

b. Due Date. The donor must file his or her federal gift tax return on or before April 15 of the year following the calendar year in which the gifts were made. IRC § 6075(b)(1). An extension to file the donor's individual income tax return is deemed an automatic extension of time to file the donor's gift tax return. IRC § 6075(b)(2). A donor can also request an extension of time to file. IRC § 6081. With respect to a donor who dies, the gift tax return must be filed no later than the time for filing the donor's estate tax return. IRC § 6075(b)(3).

> **EXAMPLE:** On January 3, 2004, D makes a gift of $50,000 to A. D dies on October 5, 2004. D's gift tax return reporting the gift is due at the same time as D's estate tax return on July 5, 2005.

c. Statute of Limitations and Adequate Disclosure.

(1) General Statute of Limitations Period. Generally, the IRS has three years to assess additional gift tax. The statute of limitations period begins to run on the filing date or the due date of the gift tax return, whichever is later. If the return is filed before April 15, the statute of limitations period begins on April 15. If the return is filed after April 15, the statute of limitations period begins on the actual filing date. IRC § 6501(a), (b).

> **EXAMPLE:** B files his 2004 gift tax return on March 30, 2005. The statute of limitations period begins on April 15, 2005.

EXAMPLE: B files his 2004 gift tax return on July 30, 2005. The statute of limitations period begins on July 30, 2005.

(2) **Exceptions**. There are several exceptions to the general limitations period:

(a) **Six Years**. If the gift tax return omits more than 25% of the total amount of gifts, the statute of limitations period becomes six years. IRC § 6501(e)(2).

(b) **Extension by Agreement**. The statute of limitations period can be extended by agreement with the IRS. IRC § 6501(c)(4). The IRS, however, is usually the party that initiates such an extension.

(c) **Assessment At Any Time**. If no gift tax return is filed, if the gift tax return is false or fraudulent with intent to evade tax, or if there is a willful attempt to evade tax or defeat tax, the IRS may assess gift tax at any time. In addition, for transfers made on or after January 1, 1997, the IRS may assess gift tax at any time for transfers that are not "adequately disclosed" on the gift tax return. IRC § 6501(c); Treas. Reg. § 301.6501(c)-1(f)(1).

(3) **Adequate Disclosure**. Generally, a disclosure on a gift tax return is "adequate" if all five of the following requirements are met. Treas. Reg. § 301.6501(c)-1(f)(2).

(a) **Description of Gift**. The gift tax return should describe the transferred property and any consideration received by the transferor.

(b) **Transferor and Transferee**. The gift tax return should disclose the identity and relationship of the transferor and each transferee.

(c) **Gifts in Trust**. For gifts in trust, the return should disclose the trust's tax ID number and a brief description of the trust terms (or a copy of the trust instrument).

(d) **Valuation Method**. The gift tax return must provide a detailed description of the method used to determine fair market value of the transferred property or provide a qualified appraisal. The regulations provide guidelines on what constitutes a detailed description and a qualified appraisal.

(e) **Contrary Position**. The return should disclose and describe any position taken by the taxpayer contrary to any proposed, temporary or final regulation or revenue ruling published at the time of the transfer.

➔ **Planning Point:** The IRS cannot challenge valuation or legal issues with respect to an adequately disclosed gift once the statute of limitations has run. Examples of legal issues that the IRS cannot challenge once the statute of limitations period has run include: (1) the availability of the annual exclusion, (2) a transfer in trust with an IRC §§ 2036 though 2038 string mistakenly treated as a completed transfer, and (3) a legal conclusion on the gift tax return that an incomplete transfer was complete.

I. Practical Effects of Lifetime Gifts

1. Transferred Property (Including Appreciation and Income) Removed From Estate

Property that a donor transfers by gift during lifetime is not included in the donor's estate. The donor's transfer tax liability for such a gift is calculated at the date of gift. Therefore, any post-gift income or appreciation generated by the transferred property will not be subject to gift tax or estate tax.

➔ **Planning Point:** Making lifetime gifts of property likely to appreciate or generate a significant amount of income can effectively reduce the donor's transfer tax liability at death.

> **EXAMPLE:** D gave a vacation home worth $100,000 to D's son, B. At D's death 20 years later, the vacation home had appreciated in value to $2,000,000. The vacation home was not included in D's estate. If D had retained the vacation home until death, the home would have been included in D's estate at a value of $2,000,000, and D's estate tax liability (assuming a 50% estate tax rate) would have increased by approximately $1,000,000.

2. Gift Tax Out of Donor's Estate if Donor Survives at Least Three Years

Assuming the donor survives at least three years after the date of gift, any gift tax paid on the gift is also removed from the donor's estate, even if the gift itself is included in the donor's estate. IRC § 2035(b).

> **EXAMPLE:** D paid gift taxes of $1,000,000 on a $2,000,000 gift to B in 2001. D dies in 2005. The gift taxes D paid on the gift are not included in D's estate because D survived at least three years after the gift.

3. Tax Exclusive Gift Tax v. Tax Inclusive Estate Tax

The gift tax is "tax exclusive" while the estate tax is "tax inclusive." That is, the tax used to pay gift tax is not itself subject to gift tax. The tax used to pay estate tax is itself, however, subject to estate tax. The tax exclusive nature of the gift tax makes the gift tax rate effectively lower than the estate tax rate. This is true even though the same tax rate schedule applies to both the gift tax and the estate tax.

EXAMPLE: D makes a $2 million gift to A and pays approximately $1 million in gift taxes. It cost D $3 million to give A a $2 million gift. If D had not made the gift and instead bequeathed the amount to A, D's estate would be increased by $3 million. D's estate tax would be approximately $1.5 million, and A would only receive $1.5 million. As this example illustrates, D can pass more to A by making a lifetime gift to A.

4. Taking Advantage of Gift Tax Exclusions Can Significantly Reduce Taxes

As discussed earlier in this chapter, an individual can give $11,000 each year to an unlimited number of donees, and may pay medical expenses and tuition expenses for another person free of gift tax and GST tax. All such property given away is also removed from the donor's estate. Therefore, such gifts are not subject to any transfer tax.

→ **Planning Point:** A planned giving program that takes advantage of these exclusions can significantly reduce an individual's total transfer tax liability.

EXAMPLE: D gave $10,000 a year in cash to each of D's 4 children, 8 grandchildren and 8 friends for each of the five years before D's death. D also paid tuition expenses for 2 of D's grandchildren totaling $100,000. None of these gifts were subject to gift tax or GST tax, and D effectively removed $1.1 million from D's estate. All future income and appreciation from the transferred funds was also removed from D's estate.

5. Income on Transferred Property Generally Taxed At a Lower Rate

Income on property transferred by gift is generally taxed to the donee. If the donee is in a lower income tax bracket than the donor, then less income tax will be paid on the same property. The "kiddie tax," however, subjects children under age 14 to the same marginal income tax rate as their parents, limiting this benefit. IRC § 1(g).

6. Basis Not Increased Except Portion of Gift Tax Paid On Appreciated Gift

Under current law, property transferred by gift retains the donor's basis, but property transferred at death gets a step up in basis to the property's fair market value at death. IRC §§ 1014 and 1015. If the donor pays gift tax on appreciated property, however, the donee's basis increases by the portion of the gift tax attributable to the appreciation in the property. Treas. Reg. § 1.1015-1(a)(2). To calculate the increase, the gift tax paid is multiplied by a fraction, of which the numerator is the appreciation, and the denominator is the fair market value of the gift.

EXAMPLE: D gives B a home worth $1,000,000 with a $300,000 basis. D pays gift tax of $500,000. The increase in basis of $350,000 is calculated by multiplying $500,000 (gift tax paid) by $700,000/$1,000,000 (appreciation over FMV). Therefore, B's basis is $650,000 (D's basis of $300,000 plus basis increase of $350,000).

➔ **Planning Point:** For property transferred by gift, all of the appreciation in excess of the donor's basis (plus any adjustment for gift taxes paid on appreciated property) will be subject to income tax on the sale of the property. For property transferred at death, only the appreciation after the decedent's death will be subject to income tax on the sale of the property. In determining whether to make lifetime gifts of appreciated property versus retaining such property until death, practitioners should consider the amount of appreciation in the property, the likelihood of a sale in the near future and the likelihood the client will survive until 2010 when the basis step-up becomes limited.

Chapter III
Bibliography

Regis W. Campfield et al., *Taxation of Estates, Gifts and Trusts* (21st ed. 1999).

The Economic Growth and Tax Relief Reconciliation Act of 2001: An Analysis, Matthew Bender & Co., Inc. (2001).

Roy D. Madoff et al., *Practical Guide to Estate Planning* (2nd ed. 2001).

Charles F. (Monty) Newlin, "Sophisticated Estate Planning For Uncertain Times: Covering All the Bases For Today and Tomorrow," Illinois Institute for Continuing Legal Education Master Teacher Program (June 21, 2001).

John R. Price, *Price on Contemporary Estate Planning* (2nd ed. 2001).

IV. FEDERAL GENERATION-SKIPPING TRANSFER TAX

A. Introduction

The generation-skipping transfer ("GST") tax is imposed on transfers to an individual who is two or more generations below the transferor (*e.g.*, a grandchild or more remote descendant) and certain trusts. The GST tax is one of the three federal transfer taxes, and was enacted to close a loophole in the transfer tax system. Prior to the enactment of the GST tax, after paying one transfer tax, an individual could pass property in trust through several generations free of any transfer tax. This loophole resulted from the fact that the estate tax does not apply to life estates created by others, and both the estate tax and the gift tax generally do not apply to trust distributions. By approximating the transfer taxes that would have been due if the trust property had been transferred at each generation level, the GST tax essentially closes the loophole.

The GST tax is imposed in addition to the estate tax and the gift tax. Unlike the progressive estate and gift tax rates, the GST tax rate is a flat rate (currently 47%), making it an extremely expensive tax. Nevertheless, a practitioner can effectively reduce or even eliminate a client's GST tax liability through the effective use of exemptions and exclusions that are available to a client.

This chapter discusses the following issues related to the GST tax and applicable changes made by the Economic Growth and Tax Relief Reconciliation Act of 2001 (the "Act"):

- Determining generation assignment.
- Types of generation-skipping transfers.
- GST exemption and exclusions.
- Valuation for GST tax purposes.
- Calculation of GST tax.
- Rules for allocating GST exemption.
- Severance of trusts with inclusion ratios greater than zero.
- Related transfer tax provisions.
- Benefits of GST tax planning.

B. Some GST Terminology

1. Transferor and Transferee

Generally, the GST tax is imposed on transfers by a "transferor" to a "skip person." For transfers subject to estate tax, the "transferor," for GST tax purposes, is the decedent. For transfers subject to gift tax, the "transferor," for the GST tax purposes, is the donor. Internal Revenue Code ("IRC") § 2652(a). The "transferee," on the other hand, is the recipient of a transfer of property by the transferor.

2.   Skip Person and Non-Skip Person

Every individual or trust can be categorized as a skip person or a non-skip person. A "skip person" is (a) an individual assigned to a generation two or more generations below the transferor, or (b) a trust in which all interests are held by skip persons or a trust in which no person holds an interest and from which no distribution may be made to a non-skip person. A "non-skip person" is any individual (or trust) who is <u>not</u> a skip person. IRC § 2613.

> **EXAMPLE:** T gives $50,000 to each of T's daughter, D, and T's grandson, G. For GST tax purposes, T is the transferor. With respect to T, D is a non-skip person because D is only 1 generation below T. G, however, is a skip person because G is 2 generations below T. Accordingly, T's transfer to G is a GST subject to the GST tax.

C. Determining Generation Assignment

All generation assignments are determined with respect to the transferor's generation. The rules for determining generation assignment are set forth in IRC § 2651, and depend upon the relationship between the transferor and the transferee.

1.   Generation Assignment for Relatives

a. "Relatives". Generally, the rules regarding generation assignment for a transferor's relatives apply to transfers to: (1) the transferor's spouse or former spouse, (2) the lineal descendants (and their spouses and former spouses) of the transferor's grandparents, and (3) the lineal descendants (and their spouses and former spouses) of the transferor's spouse's grandparents. Accordingly, relatives as remotely related as first cousins and their descendants.

b. Spouse or Former Spouse. A present or former spouse of the transferor is assigned the same generation as the transferor. IRC § 2651(c)(1). This rule applies even if there is a substantial age difference between the spouses.

> **EXAMPLE:** T, age 85, gives $50,000 to T's wife, W who is age 25. Because T and W are deemed to be in the same generation, W is a non-skip person. T's gift is not subject to GST tax.

c. Descendant of Transferor's Grandparent. Generation assignment for relatives is based on family lines. A transferee who is a lineal descendant of a grandparent of the transferor is assigned to a generation by comparing: (1) the number of generations between the recipient and the grandparent with (2) the number of generations between the transferor and the grandparent. IRC § 2651(b)(1). Accordingly, a transferor is at the same generation level as his or her siblings; one generation above his or her children, nieces and nephews; and two generations above his or her grandchildren, grandnephews and grandnieces.

EXAMPLE: T gives $50,000 to each of T's sister, daughter, niece, granddaughter and grandniece. Only T's transfers to T's granddaughter and grandniece are transfers subject to GST tax because those individuals are skip persons (*i.e.*, two generations below T).

d. Spouse (or Former Spouse) of Descendant of Transferor's Grandparent. A spouse (or former spouse) of a descendant of a grandparent of the transferor is assigned the same generation as that descendant (again, regardless of substantial age differences between the decedent and his or her spouse). IRC § 2651(c)(2).

> **EXAMPLE:** At T's death, T's will leaves $50,000 to his great-grandchild, G who is age 25, and $50,000 to G's husband, H who is age 85. G is three generations removed from T. H is deemed to be at the same generation level as G (three generations removed from T). Accordingly, T's bequests to G and H are both GSTs.

e. Descendant of Grandparent of Transferor's Spouse. The same general rule for descendants of the transferor applies to descendants of the transferor's spouse. IRC § 2651(b)(2). This rule is intended to apply to step-relatives. Therefore, a transferor is at the same generation level as the transferor's spouse; one generation above the spouse's children, nieces and nephews (the transferor's stepchildren, stepnieces and stepnephews); and two generations above the spouse's grandchildren, grandnephews and grandnieces (the transferor's stepgrandchildren, stepgrandnephews and stepgrandnieces).

> **EXAMPLE:** T, age 85, and W, age 25, are married. B is W's child from a prior marriage. B has one child, C. T gives $25,000 to each of B and C. For GST tax purposes, B is T's stepchild and is 1 generation below T. C is T's stepgrandchild and is 2 generations below T. Accordingly, only T's gift to C is a GST.

f. Spouse (or Former Spouse) of Descendant of Grandparent of Transferor's Spouse. A spouse or former spouse of a descendant of a grandparent of the transferor's spouse is assigned the same generation as that descendant. IRC § 2651(c)(2).

> **EXAMPLE:** T, age 90, gives $50,000 to his stepchild, S, age 30, and $30,000 to S's wife, W, age 20. S is 1 generation removed from T. W is deemed to be at the same generation level as S (1 generation below T). S and W are both non-skip persons. Accordingly, no GST has occurred.

g. Adoption/Half-Blood. A relationship by legal adoption or by half-blood is treated the same as a whole-blood relationship. IRC § 2651(b)(3).

EXAMPLE: T has a half-brother, B, who adopted C. For GST tax purposes, T and B are deemed to be whole-blooded brothers, and are deemed to be at the same generation level. For GST tax purposes, C is deemed to be T's nephew, and is deemed to be 1 generation below T.

h. Special Rule for Individuals Assigned to More Than One Generation. An individual that can be assigned to more than one generation under the above rules is assigned to the younger generation. IRC § 2651(f)(1);

EXAMPLE: T was previously married to W1 but is now married to W2. C is the child of T and W1. D is W2's child from a prior marriage. E is D's child. C and E marry. In this situation, E could be assigned to two different generations: E could be assigned to 2 generations below T because E is T's stepgrandchild, and E could be assigned to 1 generation below T because E is married to T's child, C. IRC § 2651(f)(1) resolves the conflict so that E is deemed to be 2 generations below T.

➔ **Planning Point:** Adoption of an individual who is a descendant of a parent, spouse or former spouse of the transferor will move the individual to a generation that is one generation below that of the adoptive parent as long as the individual is under 18 years of age at the time of adoption. Prop. Reg. § 26.2651-2.

EXAMPLE: T adopts T's minor grandchild, G. In the absence of the adoption, G would be assigned to 2 generations below T because G is T's grandchild. However, because of the adoption, G will be deemed to be 1 generation below T.

i. Predeceased Ancestor Exception. The predeceased ancestor exception acts to move up a transferee's generation assignment. IRC § 2651(e).

(1) General Rule. Specifically, under the predeceased ancestor exception, the transferee is treated as if he or she were a member of the generation which is one generation below the lower of: (a) the transferor's generation, or (b) the generation assignment of the youngest living ancestor of the transferee who is also a descendant of a parent of the transferor.

EXAMPLE: T gives $20,000 to T's grandchild, G. At the time of the gift, C (T's son and G's father) is deceased. G is moved up 1 generation so that G is treated as being 1 generation below T instead of 2. Accordingly, T's gift to G is not a GST subject to GST tax.

(2) **Requirements**. The predeceased ancestor exception applies only if the following requirements are met:

- With the exception below for certain collateral heirs, the transferee must be a descendant of a parent of the transferor, the transferor's spouse or the transferor's former spouse.
- The transferee's parent who is a descendant of the parent of the transferor must be deceased at the time the transfer is or was subject to gift tax or estate tax upon the transferor.
- The trust must not have made a reverse QTIP election under IRC section 2652. The predeceased ancestor rule is not needed in this situation because the transferor's GST exemption is usually allocated to the trust. Prop. Reg. § 26.2651-1(a)(3). Reverse QTIP elections are discussed in Chapter VIII, "Planning for the Marital Deduction."

This exception also affects other generation assignments. When an individual's generation assignment is adjusted under this exception, a corresponding adjustment is made to the generation assignment of that individual's spouse, former spouse, descendants and the descendants' spouses or former spouses. IRC § 2651(e)(1); Prop. Reg. § 26.2651-1(a)(2)(i).

(3) **Exception For Certain Collateral Heirs**. The predeceased ancestor exception applies to an individual who is not a lineal descendant of the transferor, the transferor's spouse or the transferor's former spouse only if the transferor has no living descendants at the time of the transfer. IRC § 2651(e)(2); Prop. Reg. § 26.2651-1(b).

> **EXAMPLE:** T's nephew, N, is deceased. T gives $50,000 to N's son, G (T's grandnephew). At the date of the gift, T has one living descendant, a granddaughter. The predeceased ancestor exception does not apply to this transfer because T has one living descendant. Accordingly, G is a skip person with respect to T, and T's gift to G is treated as a GST. If T had no living descendants at the date of the gift, the predeceased ancestor exception would apply, G would be treated as 1 generation below T, and T's gift would not be subject to GST taxes.

(4) **Exception for QTIP Trusts**. The proposed regulations provide an exception for remainder interests in trusts for which an election has been made under IRC § 2056, the qualified terminable interest property ("QTIP") election. Under the proposed regulations, the remainder beneficiary's interest is deemed established upon the death of the transferor's spouse (the income beneficiary), rather than upon the transferor's earlier death. Without this exception, a remainder beneficiary of a QTIP trust would not benefit from the predeceased ancestor exception in the event the remainder beneficiary's parent were alive when the QTIP was established but deceased when the income beneficiary's interest terminated. Prop.

Reg. § 26.2651-1(a)(3). QTIP trusts are discussed in Chapter VIII, "Planning for the Marital Deduction."

(5)   Drafting For Predeceased Ancestor Exception. The proposed regulations provide that a living descendant who dies no later than 90 days after the transfer is treated as having predeceased the transferor to the extent that either the governing instrument or applicable local law provides that such individual will be treated as predeceasing the transferor. Prop. Reg. § 26.2651-1(a)(2)(iii).

➔   **Planning Point:** Wills and trusts should include a provision that takes advantage of this rule.

2.   Generation Assignment for Nonrelatives

a. "Nonrelatives". Generally, the rules regarding generation assignment for nonrelatives apply to transfers to: (1) individuals outside of the transferor's family lines, and (2) individuals more remotely related to the transferor than first cousins and their descendants.

b. Age Comparison. Generation assignment for nonrelatives is determined based on the difference in age compared to the transferor. IRC § 2651(d).

(1)   12½ Years Younger or Less. An individual who is 12½ years younger or less than the transferor is treated as being in the same generation as the transferor.

> **EXAMPLE:** T gives $50,000 to T's doorman, D, who is 5 years younger than T. D is treated as being in the same generation as T, and T's gift to D is not subject to GST taxes.

(2)   More Than 12½ Years Younger But Not More Than 37½ Years Younger. An individual who is more than 12½ years younger but not more than 37½ years younger than the transferor is treated as being one generation below the transferor.

> **EXAMPLE:** T's will leaves $50,000 to T's friend, F, who is 20 years younger than T. F is treated as being 1 generation below T, and T's bequest to F is not subject to GST taxes.

(3)   More Than 37½ Years Younger. An individual who is more than 37½ years younger than the transferor is treated as being more than one generation below the transferor and is, thus, a skip person for purposes of applying the GST tax rules.

> **EXAMPLE:** T's will leaves $50,000 to T's second cousin, C, who is 40 years younger than T. C is treated as being 2 generations below T, and T's bequest to F is subject to GST taxes.

3. Generation Assignment for Trusts

a. Look-Through Rule. An individual with a beneficial interest in a trust is assigned to a generation under the foregoing rules regarding generation assignment. IRC § 2651(f).

> **EXAMPLE:** T creates a trust for the lifetime benefit of T's grandchild, G. G is deemed to be 2 generations below T.

b. Trust as a Skip Person. A trust may be a skip person under two circumstances:

(1) All Interests Held By Skip Persons. A trust may be a skip person if all interests in the trust are held by skip persons. IRC § 2613(a)(2)(A). A person generally has an "interest" in a trust if he or she: (a) has a present right to receive trust principal or income, or (b) is a permissible current recipient of trust principal or income.

> **EXAMPLE:** T creates a trust for the lifetime benefit of T's grandson, G. At G's death, the trust remainder will be distributed to G's children. The trust qualifies as a skip person because all current interests in the trust are held by skip persons.

(2) No Person Holds Interest and No Distribution to Non-Skip Person. A trust may also be a skip person if: (a) no person holds an interest in the trust; and (b) at no time after the transfer may a distribution be made to a non-skip person. IRC § 2613(a)(2)(B).

> **EXAMPLE:** T creates a trust for the benefit of T's grandson, G. Income of the trust will accumulate until distributed to G at age 21 (or to G's estate if G dies prior to age 21). The trust is a skip person because no person has an interest in the trust, and no distribution can be made to a non-skip person under the trust terms.

D. Types of Generation-Skipping Transfers

1. Generally

There are three types of generation-skipping transfers subject to GST tax: (1) a direct skip, (2) a taxable termination, and (3) a taxable distribution. Categorizing a generation-skipping transfer is important because the type of transfer will determine the amount subject to GST tax and who is responsible for paying the GST tax.

TYPE OF TRANSFER	TAXABLE AMOUNT	LIABILITY FOR PAYMENT OF TAX	TAX EXCLUSIVE v. INCLUSIVE
Direct Skip (not from trust)	Value of property received by transferee	Transferor	Tax Exclusive
Direct Skip (from trust)	Value of property received by transferee	Trustee	Tax Inclusive
Taxable Termination	Value of entire trust property, less any deduction for certain expenses, indebtedness and taxes	Trustee	Tax Inclusive
Taxable Distribution	Value of the trust property distributed to the skip person, less any deduction for certain expenses incurred by the transferee related to the determination, collection or refund of the GST tax	Transferee	Tax Inclusive

2. Direct Skip

A "direct skip" is a transfer to a skip person that is subject to estate tax or gift tax. IRC § 2612(c).

> **EXAMPLE:** T gives $100,000 to each of T's son, T's grandson and an irrevocable gift trust for the lifetime benefit of T's granddaughter (remainder to the children of T's granddaughter). The transfer to T's son is not a direct skip because T's son is not a skip person. The transfers to T's grandson and the trust for T's granddaughter are direct skips.

a. **Taxable Amount**. The taxable amount of a direct skip is the value of the property received by the transferee. IRC § 2623.

> **EXAMPLE:** In the above example, the taxable amount of T's gift to T's grandson for GST tax purposes is $100,000.

b. **Liability for GST Tax**. The transferor is responsible for paying the GST tax on a direct skip (other than a direct skip from a trust). The trustee, however, is responsible for paying the GST tax on a direct skip from a trust. IRC § 2603(a).

c. **Tax Exclusive v. Tax Inclusive**. A direct skip (other than a direct skip from a trust) is tax exclusive. That is, the GST tax paid on such a direct skip is paid only on the transferred property and not the dollars used to pay the GST taxes. A direct skip from a trust, however, is tax inclusive because the GST tax is imposed on the dollars used to pay the tax.

3. Taxable Termination

A "taxable termination" is a termination (by death, lapse of time, release of power, or otherwise) of an interest held in trust, <u>unless</u>: (1) immediately after the termination, a non-skip person has an interest in the trust property or (2) at or after the termination, no distribution may be made to a skip person. IRC § 2612(a).

> **EXAMPLE:** T creates a trust for the lifetime benefit of T's nephew, N. At N's death, the remainder of the trust is to be distributed to N's children. N's death is deemed to be a taxable termination of the trust. If the remainder of the trust were to be distributed to T's niece instead of N's children, N's death would not be a taxable termination because T's niece, a non-skip person, would receive an interest in the trust property.

a. Taxable Amount. The taxable amount of a taxable termination is the value of the entire trust property, less any deduction for certain expenses, indebtedness and taxes. IRC § 2622.

b. Liability for GST Tax. The trustee is responsible for paying the GST tax on a taxable termination. IRC § 2603(a)(2).

c. Tax Inclusive. A taxable termination is tax inclusive. That is, the GST tax paid on a taxable termination is paid on the transferred property and on the money used to pay the GST taxes.

4. Taxable Distribution

A "taxable distribution" is a distribution of income or principal from a trust to a skip person that is <u>not</u> a direct skip or a taxable termination. IRC § 2612(b). Distributions that are qualified transfers for medical expenses or tuition expenses under IRC § 2503(e) are <u>not</u> taxable transfers for GST purposes.

> **EXAMPLE:** T gives $100,000 to an irrevocable trust for the benefit of T's niece, N, and N's children. The trust is a non-skip person since N is a non-skip person and has an interest in the trust. T's transfer to the trust is not a direct skip. When distributions are made from the trust for the benefit of N's children, however, the distributions will be taxable distributions.

a. Taxable Amount. The taxable amount of a taxable distribution is the value of the trust property distributed to the skip person, less any deduction for certain expenses incurred by the transferee related to the determination, collection or refund of the GST tax. IRC § 2621(a). If the trustee pays any of the tax out of trust assets, the payment will be treated as an additional taxable distribution subject to GST tax. IRC § 2621(b).

        b. **Liability for GST Tax**. The transferee is responsible for paying the GST tax on a taxable distribution. IRC § 2603(a)(1).

        c. **Tax Inclusive**. A taxable distribution is tax inclusive. Because the transferee is liable for the GST tax, the transferee essentially is paying the GST tax out of the distributed property.

E. GST Exemption and Exclusions

1. GST Exemption

Every individual is entitled to a GST exemption which the individual (or the individual's executor) can allocate to any generation-skipping transfer with respect to which the individual is the transferor. IRC § 2631(a). The GST exemption amount is a lifetime amount. It is cumulative and does not renew annually (except to the extent the GST exemption amount increases by law).

> **EXAMPLE:** In 2003, T gives $1,120,000 to T's grandson, G. T allocates his entire GST exemption to the transfer so no GST tax is due. In 2005, T gives $380,000 to G. T can allocate T's remaining $380,000 GST exemption ($1,500,000 less $1,120,000 used exemption) to T's gift in 2005.

For 2005, the Act provides that the GST exemption is the same as the estate tax applicable exclusion amount. The GST tax is scheduled to be repealed in 2010. The sunset provisions of the Act, however, bring back the GST tax in 2011, and the GST exemption amount is scheduled to be $1,000,000, as adjusted for cost-of-living. The following is a chart of scheduled GST exemption increases:

CALENDAR YEAR	GST EXEMPTION
2005	$1.5 million
2006-2008	$2 million
2009	$3.5 million
2010	GST Tax Repealed
2011	$1.38 million*

* Estimate. Actual amount will depend on cost-of-living adjustment.

2. GST Tax Exclusion for Annual Exclusion Gifts

      a. Generally. The gift tax annual exclusion under IRC § 2503(b) permits an individual to give an amount equal to the annual exclusion ($11,000 in 2005) per donee without incurring any gift tax liability, provided that the gift is of a present interest. A "present interest" is an unrestricted right to the immediate use, possession, or enjoyment of property or the income from property (such as a life estate or term certain). A direct skip that qualifies for the gift tax annual exclusion under IRC § 2503(b) is excluded from GST tax under IRC § 2642. If the transfer is in trust, however, additional requirements must be met to qualify for the GST tax exclusion.

      b. Outright Gifts. An outright gift to a skip person qualifies for the annual exclusion for both gift tax and GST tax purposes because it is a direct skip (a transfer to a skip person subject to gift tax) and because it qualifies as a present interest under IRC § 2503(b).

➜   **Planning Point:** A planned giving program that takes advantage of these exclusions can significantly reduce an individual's total transfer tax liability without using up any portion of the individual's GST exemption or applicable credit amount.

EXAMPLE: T gives $10,000 a year in cash to each of T's 8 grandchildren for each of the 15 years before T's death. None of these gifts were subject to gift tax or GST tax because of the annual exclusion, T did not use up any of T's applicable credit amount or GST exemption by these gifts, and T effectively removed $1.2 million from T's estate. Any income from or appreciation on the transferred assets is also removed from T's estate.

c. Gifts in Trust. In order for a transfer in trust to qualify for the annual exclusion for GST tax purposes, (1) the transfer must be a direct skip, (2) the trust must meet the requirements of the gift tax annual exclusion under IRC § 2503(b), and (3) the trust must meet the additional requirements imposed by IRC § 2642(c).

(1) Direct Skip. A transfer in trust must be a direct skip (*i.e.*, a transfer to a skip person subject to gift tax) to qualify for the annual exclusion for GST tax purposes.

(a) Trust as Skip Person. As discussed earlier, a trust is a skip person if: (a) all interests in the trust are held by skip persons, or (b) if no person holds an interest in the trust and at no time after the transfer may a distribution be made to a non-skip person.

(b) Crummey Powers. Granting a Crummey power of withdrawal to a skip person does not by itself make the transfer in trust a direct skip. A Crummey power of withdrawal is often given to a trust beneficiary to qualify a transfer to a trust for the gift tax annual exclusion. The trust beneficiary essentially is given the power to withdraw property contributed to the trust not exceeding the annual exclusion amount for a finite period of time (*e.g.*, 30 days). A transfer to a trust subject to a beneficiary's right of withdrawal is treated as a transfer to the trust, not to the beneficiary.

(2) Annual Exclusion Requirement. The transfer in trust must be a transfer of a present interest in property in order to qualify for the annual exclusion for both gift and GST tax purposes. A transfer in trust generally does not qualify as a present interest. There are ways, however, to qualify a transfer in trust for the present interest requirement:

(a) IRC § 2503(c) Minor's Trust. IRC § 2503(c) provides a statutory exception to the present interest requirement for certain trusts created for the benefit of a minor. Transfers to such a trust will qualify for the annual exclusion for gift and GST tax purposes. These trusts are discussed in detail in a separate chapter.

(b) Crummey Trust. A trust beneficiary can be given a Crummey right to withdraw an amount up to the annual exclusion amount. Such a right will qualify the transfer for the annual exclusion for gift tax and GST tax purposes. The Crummey trust is discussed in a separate chapter.

(3)   IRC § 2642(c) Requirements. A transfer in trust will qualify for the annual exclusion for GST tax purposes if: (a) no part of the trust income or principal may be distributed to or for any person other than the skip person-beneficiary, and (b) the trust assets must be included in the skip person-beneficiary's gross estate if the skip person-beneficiary dies before the trust terminates. IRC § 2642(c).

➔   **Planning Point:** In order for the trust assets to be included in the skip person-beneficiary's estate, a general power of appointment usually is given to the beneficiary. To qualify for the annual exclusion for GST purposes, the trust must be created for the benefit of one beneficiary (or segregated into separate trusts if there are multiple beneficiaries).

3.   GST Tax Exclusion for Education Expenses and Medical Expenses

IRC § 2503(e)(1) excludes from gift tax certain "qualified transfers." "Qualified transfers" include amounts paid by a donor to a qualifying educational institution or a medical provider on behalf of an individual for tuition expenses or medical care. A transfer that qualifies for this exclusion for gift tax purposes is excluded from GST tax under IRC § 2642.

➔   **Planning Point:** This exclusion is especially valuable for grandparents because their payments of a grandchild's tuition and medical expenses are: (1) unlimited in amount, (2) free of gift tax, (3) free of GST tax, and (4) remove significant amounts from their estates. In addition, the grandparents control the use of the gifts by making payments directly to the educational institution or medical provider.

a.   **Unlimited Exclusion Amount.** The amount of the exclusion for such tuition and medical care expenses is unlimited. The exclusion is in addition to the gift tax annual exclusion.

b.   **Payments Must Be Direct**. Payments of tuition expenses must be made *directly* to the educational institution to qualify for the exclusion. Similarly, payments of medical expenses must be made *directly* to the medical care provider to qualify for the exclusion.

> **EXAMPLE:** T gives $20,000 to T's child, C, to pay for tuition at Private University. T's gift does not qualify for the exclusion for gift tax purposes or GST tax purposes because T paid C instead of paying Private University directly.

c.   **Qualifying Educational Institution and Qualifying Education Expenses**. A "qualifying educational institution" is one that normally maintains a regular faculty and curriculum and normally has a regularly enrolled body of pupils or students in attendance at the place where the educational activities are regularly carried on. Only tuition expenses qualify for the exclusion for education expenses. Expenses for books, supplies, dormitory fees, board, or other similar expenses do not qualify for the exclusion.

> **d. Qualifying Medical Expenses**. "Qualifying medical expenses" include expenses incurred for the diagnosis, cure, mitigation, treatment or prevention of disease, or for the purpose of affecting any structure or function of the body or for transportation primarily for and essential to medical care. In addition, amounts paid for medical insurance qualify. The exclusion does not apply, however, with respect to any amounts reimbursed by medical insurance.

F. Valuation for GST Tax Purposes

1. General Rule

Generally, a transfer is subject to GST tax based on its fair market value on the date of generation-skipping transfer. IRC § 2624(a). Valuation issues are discussed in detail in a separate chapter.

2. Value of Direct Skip Property Included in Transferor's Gross Estate

The value of direct skip property included in a transferor's gross estate reflects the alternate valuation or special use valuation under IRC §§ 2032 and 2032A. IRC § 2624(b).

3. Taxable Terminations Occurring At Death

If a taxable termination occurs because of the death of an individual, an alternate valuation election can be made to value the taxable termination on the alternate valuation date. IRC § 2624(c).

4. Reduction For Consideration Provided by Transferee

The value of property transferred is reduced by the amount of any consideration provided by the transferee. IRC § 2624(d).

G. Calculation of GST Tax

1. Nature

Like the estate tax and the gift tax, the GST tax is an excise tax on the _transfer_ of property. The GST tax is a tax on a transferor's _privilege_ of being able to transfer property to a skip person.

2. Calculation

IRC § 2602 describes the computation of GST tax liability.

a. Computation. In general, GST tax liability is determined by multiplying the taxable amount by the applicable rate.

GST Tax Liability = Taxable Amount x Applicable Rate

      (1)   Applicable Fraction. In general, the "applicable fraction" is determined by dividing the amount of GST exemption allocated by the value of the property transferred, less any federal or state estate taxes paid from the trust property and any charitable deduction allowed. The applicable fraction is rounded to the nearest thousandth. The applicable fraction for a trust is determined when the trust is funded, and continues for the duration of the trust. Additions to a trust, however, may change the applicable fraction.

$$\text{Applicable Fraction} = \frac{\text{Amount of GST exemption Allocated}}{\substack{\text{Value of Property Transferred - Any} \\ \text{Federal or State Estate Taxes Paid} \\ \text{From the Trust Property and Any} \\ \text{Charitable Deductions Allowed}}}$$

      (2)   Inclusion Ratio. The "inclusion ratio" is determined by subtracting the applicable fraction (rounded to the nearest thousandth) from 1. The inclusion ratio for a trust is determined when the trust is funded, and continues for the duration of the trust. Additions to a trust, however, may change the inclusion ratio.

Inclusion Ratio = 1 - Applicable Fraction

      (3)   GST Tax Rate. The GST tax rate is a flat rate equal to the maximum estate tax rate in effect. The GST tax rate is currently 47% for 2005.

GST Tax Rate = Maximum Estate Tax Rate

      (4)   Applicable Rate. The "applicable rate" is determined by multiplying the GST tax rate by the inclusion ratio.

Applicable Rate = GST Tax Rate x Inclusion Ratio

      (5)   Taxable Amount. As discussed earlier, the "taxable amount" of a GST transfer depends on the type of transfer.

      b. Examples. The following are some examples of how the GST tax is computed:

EXAMPLE: On January 5, 2005, T gives $2 million to T's grandchild, G. T has not previously used any of T's GST exemption. T's gift is a direct skip because it is a transfer to a skip person (G) subject to gift tax. The taxable amount of a direct skip is the value of property received by the transferee, $2 million. T, as transferor, is responsible for paying the GST tax on the direct skip. T's GST tax liability is calculated as follows.

Applicable Fraction = $1,500,000/$2,000,000 = .75
Inclusion Ratio = 1 - .75 = .25
Applicable Rate = 47% x .25 = .118
Tax = $2,000,000 x .118 = $236,000

➔ **Planning Point:** Since the applicable fraction and the inclusion ratio of a trust are determined at the time the trust is funded, if the transferor allocates GST exemption to the trust, the transferred property <u>and</u> any appreciation of the property in trust will be sheltered from GST tax.

EXAMPLE: T transfers $700,000 to a trust for the lifetime benefit of T's child, C. At C's death, the remainder is to be distributed to T's grandchild, G. T allocated GST exemption ($700,000) to T's transfer to the trust. C dies in 2003 when the trust property is worth $2 million. At C's death, a taxable termination occurs. The taxable amount of the taxable termination is $2 million (the value of the trust property, assuming no deduction for expenses). The trust is responsible for paying the GST tax on the direct skip. The trust's GST tax liability is calculated as follows.

Applicable Fraction = $700,000/$700,000= 1
Inclusion Ratio = 1 - 1 = 0
Applicable Rate = 47% x 0 = 0
Tax = $2 million x 0 = $0

c. **Effect of the Act on Computation of GST Tax.**

(1) **Declining GST Tax Rate and Eventual Repeal of GST Tax.** Because the GST tax rate equals the maximum estate tax rate, under the Act, the GST tax rate gradually reduces until both taxes are repealed in 2010. Under the sunset provisions of the Act, however, the estate tax and the GST tax will come back in 2011 unless repealed again by a future Congress and President.

➔ **Planning Point:** At least one commentator has noted the following. "Because the GST tax is scheduled to be repealed in 2010, any reasonable way to postpone a generation-skipping event until then (such as the introduction of new non-skip beneficiaries by the exercise of a special power of appointment or a trustee's discretion) should be considered."

(2) **Increasing GST Exemption**. For 2005, the Act provides that the GST exemption is the same as the estate tax applicable exclusion amount. In 2011, the GST tax is scheduled to return, and the GST exemption amount is scheduled to be $1,000,000, as adjusted for cost of living. The following is a schedule of changing GST tax rates and GST exemptions:

CALENDAR YEAR	RATE	GST EXEMPTION
2005	47%	$1.5 million
2006	46%	$2 million
2007	45%	$2 million
2008	45%	$2 million
2009	45%	$3.5 million
2010	35%	GST Tax Repealed
2011	55%	$1.38 million*

* Estimate. Actual amount will depend on cost-of-living adjustment.

➔ **Planning Point**: In light of the increasing GST exemption amount and the future repeal of the GST tax, practitioners may wish to review formula clauses that refer to the GST exemption. Unintended funding may result, depending on how the formula is drafted. For example, assume the formula provides that the maximum allowable GST exemption should be allocated to exempt trusts for grandchildren, and the balance should be allocated to non-exempt trusts for children. With the increasing exemptions, significantly more property may be left for the grandchildren than the decedent originally intended.

(3) **Additional Rules for Allocating GST exemption**. The Act contains provisions relating to the allocation of GST exemption that are retroactive to December 31, 2000. These provisions are complex and are discussed later in this chapter.

(4) **GST Tax Relief During Phase-Out Period**. The Act contains provisions for GST tax relief that are retroactive to December 31, 2000. These provisions are discussed later in this chapter.

H. Rules For Allocating GST exemption

1. General Rule

Generally, every individual (or the individual's executor) can allocate the individual's GST exemption to any GST with respect to which the individual is a transferor. IRC § 2631(a).

EXAMPLE: On January 5, 2005, T gives $500,000 to a trust for the sole benefit of T's grandchild, G. T has previously used $200,000 of T's GST exemption. T can allocate $500,000 of T's $1,300,000 unused GST exemption ($1,500,000 million, less $200,000) to the transfer so that no GST tax is due.

    a. **Time and Manner of Allocation**. GST exemption can be allocated at any time from the transfer date through the date for filing the individual's estate tax return (including extensions). GST exemption can be allocated on a Federal Gift (and Generation-Skipping Transfer) Tax Return (Form 709) or on a Federal Estate (and Generation-Skipping Transfer) Tax Return (Form 706).

    b. **Timely Allocation v. Late Allocation**. Whether an allocation is timely or late will determine the effective date of allocation and the amount of GST exemption allocated.

    (1) **Timely Allocation**. If the allocation is made on a timely filed return (including applicable extensions), the amount of GST exemption allocated relates back to the value of the transferred property as of the date of gift. An allocation made on a timely filed return can be modified up to the due date of the return. Treas. Reg. § 26.2632-1(b)(2). The IRS has been generous in allowing late allocations of GST exemption to be considered as having been made timely under Treas. Reg. § 301.9100.

    (2) **Late Allocation**. If the allocation is made on a late filed return, however, the amount of GST exemption allocated is based on the value of the transferred property as of the date of allocation (the date the return was filed) unless the transferor elects the special valuation rule for such late lifetime allocations.

> **EXAMPLE:** On January 5, 2004, T gives $500,000 to a trust for the sole benefit of T's grandchild, G. If T timely files a gift tax return on or before April 15, 2005 (assuming no extensions) when the trust property is worth $600,000, T need only allocate $500,000 of GST exemption to the transfer. If T files a late return on October 10, 2005 when the trust property is worth $700,000, T must allocate $700,000 of GST exemption to make the inclusion ratio zero.

    (a) **Special Valuation Rule for Late Lifetime Allocations**. Under the special valuation rule, if a transferor makes a late allocation, the transferor can, solely for purposes of determining the value of the trust assets, elect to treat the allocation as having been made on the first day of the month during which the late allocation is made (the "valuation date"). The election is not available, however, for a life insurance policy or a trust holding a life insurance policy. The transferor may make the election on Form 709 on which the allocation is made, and must state that the election is being made, the applicable valuation date and the fair market value of the trust assets on the valuation date. The election is effective when it is actually filed with the IRS. Treas. Reg. § 26.2642-2(a)(2).

(b) **Late Allocation Irrevocable**. A late allocation, once made, is irrevocable. Treas. Reg. § 26.2632-1(b)(2).

2. Deemed (Automatic) Allocation Rules

The deemed allocation rules are automatic rules that apply if an individual does not affirmatively allocate GST exemption to a transfer.

a. Deemed Allocation to Certain Lifetime Direct Skips. If an individual makes a direct skip during his or her lifetime, any unused portion of the individual's GST exemption is automatically allocated to the property transferred to the extent necessary to make the inclusion ratio zero (nontaxable for GST tax purposes) unless: (1) the individual elects out of this automatic allocation on a timely filed Form 709, or (2) the direct skip is to a trust with one skip person-beneficiary. IRC § 2632(b).

> **EXAMPLE:** On January 5, 2005, T gives $500,000 to T's grandchild, G. T has previously used $200,000 of T's GST exemption. If T does not allocate GST exemption to this transfer, $500,000 of T's $1,300,000 unused GST exemption ($1,500,000 - $200,000) will be automatically allocated to the transfer unless T opts out of the allocation on a timely filed Form 709.

(1) **Election Out of Automatic Allocation**. An individual can elect out of this automatic allocation on a timely filed Form 709. Form 709 is timely filed if it is filed on or before April 15 of the year following the calendar year in which the transfer was made (including any extensions actually granted). If no such election is made by the filing due date, the automatic allocation under IRC § 2632(b) becomes irrevocable. Treas. Reg. § 26.2632-1(b)(1)(ii).

(2) **Direct Skip to Trust With One Skip Person-Beneficiary**. As discussed earlier, under IRC § 2642(c)(2), the inclusion ratio is zero for a direct skip to a trust with only one skip person-beneficiary, if the trust property will be included in the beneficiary's estate. Since the inclusion ratio of such a trust is already zero, no automatic allocation of GST exemption is made to such a direct skip.

b. Deemed Allocation to Certain Lifetime Transfers to GST Trusts. The Act added IRC § 2632(c), effective for transfers made after December 31, 2000, which provides that if an individual makes an "indirect skip" during his or her lifetime, any unused portion of the individual's GST exemption is automatically allocated to the property transferred to the extent necessary to make the inclusion ratio zero (nontaxable for GST tax purposes) unless the individual elects out of this automatic allocation on a timely filed Form 709. Section 2632(c)(1)&(5).

> **(1)** **Indirect Skip**. An "indirect skip" is a transfer of property (other than a direct skip) subject to gift tax to a GST trust.

> **(2)** **GST Trust**. A "GST trust" is a trust that could have a generation-skipping transfer except a trust where one of the following is true. Each of the following non-GST trusts involve situations where a non-skip person is likely to receive the trust property.

- 25% of the trust principal must be distributed to or may be withdrawn by one or more non-skip person(s): (a) before the non-skip person turns 46, (b) on or before one or more dates specified in the trust instrument that will occur before the non-skip person turns 46, <u>or</u> (c) on the occurrence of an event that may reasonably be expected to occur before the non-skip person turns 46.

  > **EXAMPLE:** T creates a trust for T's child, C. C can withdraw one-half of the trust property at age 40, and the balance at age 50. This trust is not a GST because C, a non-skip person, can withdraw more than 25% of the trust property before age 46 (one-half at age 40). Accordingly, no automatic allocation of GST exemption will be made.

- More than 25% of the trust principal must be distributed to or may be withdrawn by one or more non-skip person(s) who are living on the death of a person identified in the trust instrument who is more than 10 years older than the non-skip person.

  > **EXAMPLE:** T creates a trust for T's child, C. At T's death, one-half of the trust property will be distributed to C. This trust is not a GST because more than 25% of the trust property (one-half) will be distributed to C, a non-skip person, on T's death (T, as C's parent, is more 10 years older than C). Accordingly, no automatic allocation of GST exemption will be made.

- If one or more non-skip person(s) die on or before a date described in the two paragraphs above, more than 25% of the trust principal must be distributed to the estate(s) of such non-skip person(s) or is subject to a general power of appointment exercisable by one or more of such non-skip person(s).

- The trust is includible in the gross estate of the non-skip person (other than the transferor) if such person died immediately after the transfer.

> **EXAMPLE:** T creates a trust for T's child, C. C has a testamentary general power of appointment over the trust property. The trust is not a GST trust because C's general power of appointment causes the trust to be included in the estate of C, a non-skip person. Accordingly, no automatic allocation of GST exemption will be made.

- The trust is a charitable lead annuity trust, charitable remainder annuity trust or charitable remainder unitrust.
- The trust is a charitable lead unitrust required to pay principal to a non-skip person if the non-skip person is alive at the end of the term.

For purposes of determining whether a trust is a "GST trust," the value of transferred property is <u>not</u> considered to be includible in the gross estate of a non-skip person or subject to a right of withdrawal by reason of such person holding a right to withdraw an amount that does not exceed the IRC § 2503(b) annual exclusion amount ($11,000 for 2005).

> **EXAMPLE:** T creates an irrevocable life insurance trust where T's children, A and B, each have a noncumulative annual right to withdraw an amount not to exceed the gift tax annual exclusion amount. This is a GST trust. GST exemption will be automatically allocated to the trust. The withdrawal right is not sufficient to make it a non-GST trust under one of the above exceptions.

➔ **Planning Point:** Under the Act, there is a possibility that if a client does nothing, a portion of the client's GST exemption might be allocated to a trust even though the trust is not intended to be generation-skipping, resulting in wasted GST exemption. In order to avoid this result, practitioners should advise clients to opt out of the automatic allocation rules by attaching a statement to a timely filed federal gift tax return (Form 709), regardless of whether the client otherwise needs to file a gift tax return.

➔ **Planning Point:** Determining whether a trust is a GST trust or non-GST trust under the new rules is difficult. Accordingly, for new trusts, practitioners may wish to indicate whether the trust is a GST trust either in separate memorandum or in the document itself.

(3) **Elections**. An individual can elect out of this automatic allocation for (a) an indirect skip or (b) any or all transfers made by such transferor to a particular trust.

The election can be made for all subsequent years in addition to the particular year in question. An individual can also elect to treat any trust as a GST trust for purposes of automatic allocation under IRC § 2632(c). The elections can be made on a timely filed Form 709. Form 709 is timely filed if it is filed on or before April 15 of the year following the calendar year in which the transfer was made (including any extensions actually granted). IRC § 2632(c)(5).

       c. Deemed Allocation to Transfers at Death. Generally, any unused portion of a deceased individual's GST exemption is automatically allocated first to direct skips at death and then to trusts with respect to which a taxable termination may occur or from which a taxable distribution may be made. Treas. Reg. § 26.2632-1(d)(2).

> **EXAMPLE:** At T's death in 2005, $250,000 is to be distributed to T's grandchild, G, and $450,000 is to be distributed to a trust for the benefit of T's child, C, and G. T previously used $800,000 of T's GST exemption, leaving $700,000 unused GST exemption ($1,500,000 - $800,000). $250,000 of T's unused GST exemption will first be automatically allocated to the direct skip to G. T's unused GST exemption, $450,000, will then be automatically allocated to the transfer to the trust.

3.   Retroactive Allocation

The Act also added IRC § 2632(d), which provides as follows:

       a. Generally. For the death of a non-skip person that occurs after December 31, 2000, a transferor may retroactively allocate his or her unused GST exemption to any previous transfer or transfers to a trust on a chronological basis if:

- A non-skip person has an interest or a future interest in a trust to which any transfer has been made;
- Such non-skip person (a) is a lineal descendant of a grandparent of the transferor or of a grandparent of the transferor's spouse or former spouse; and (b) is assigned to a generation below the transferor, <u>and</u>
- Such non-skip person predeceased the transferor.

       b. Retroactive Allocation Made in Calendar Year in Which Non-Skip Person's Death Occurs. If the transferor's retroactive allocation is made on a timely filed gift tax return (if the gift occurred in the same calendar year as the non-skip person's death), then:

- The value of such transfer(s) for purposes of IRC § 2642(a) is determined as if the allocation had been made on a timely filed gift tax return for each calendar year within which each transfer was made;

- The allocation will be effective immediately before the non-skip person's death, <u>and</u>
- The amount of the transferor's unused GST exemption that is available for allocation is determined immediately before the non-skip person's death.

4. Estate Tax Inclusion Period (ETIP) Rules

The GST exemption cannot be allocated to a lifetime gift during the period (estate tax inclusion period or "ETIP") the gift would be included in the transferor's or transferor's spouse's estate (other than by reason of IRC § 2035) if the transferor died. IRC § 2642(f).

> **EXAMPLE:** T transfers $1,000,000 to a trust. Income of the trust is payable to T for 10 years, at which time the remainder is to be distributed to T's grandchild, G. A taxable termination would occur at the end of the 10-year period. T cannot, however, allocate GST exemption to the trust until after the 10-year ETIP because the trust property would be includible in T's estate under IRC § 2036 if T died during that period.

a. **<u>Exceptions.</u>** There are exceptions to this general rule:

(1) **<u>Less Than 5% Probability of Being Included in Gross Estate.</u>** The value of transferred property is not considered as being subject to inclusion in the gross estate of the transferor or the transferor's spouse if the possibility that the property will be included is so remote as to be negligible. A possibility is so remote as to be negligible if it can be ascertained by actuarial standards that there is less than a 5% probability that the property will be included in the gross estate.

(2) **<u>Crummey Exception.</u>** The value of transferred property is not considered as being subject to inclusion in the gross estate of the transferor or the transferor's spouse if the spouse possesses with respect to any transfer to the trust a right to withdraw no more than the greater of 5% or $5,000 of the trust corpus, and the withdrawal right terminates no later than 60 days after the transfer to the trust.

b. **<u>ETIP.</u>** The ETIP terminates on the <u>first</u> to occur of the following:

- The transferor's death;
- The time at which no portion of the property is includible in the transferor's gross estate (other than by reason of IRC § 2035) or, in the case of an individual who is a transferor solely by reason of the gift-splitting election of IRC § 2513, the time at which no portion would be includible in the gross estate of the individual's spouse (other than by reason of IRC § 2035);

- The time of a GST; or
- For an ETIP arising by reason of an interest or power held by the transferor's spouse, at the first to occur of the spouse's death or the time at which no portion of the property would be includible in the spouse's gross estate (other than by reason of IRC § 2035).

     c. **Effective Date of Allocation.** An allocation of GST exemption to property subject to an ETIP that is made <u>prior</u> to termination of the ETIP cannot be revoked, but becomes effective on the termination date of the ETIP. An allocation of GST exemption on a gift tax return filed by the due date (if the ETIP termination were a taxable gift) is effective as of the ETIP termination date. An allocation of GST exemption <u>after</u> the due date of the gift tax return is effective as of the earlier of the date the gift tax return is filed or the date of the transferor's death.

> **EXAMPLE:** T transfers $1,000,000 to a trust on January 1, 1995. Income of the trust is payable to T for 10 years, at which time the remainder is to be distributed to T's grandchild, G. The ETIP is the 10-year period after the transfer, and terminates on January 1, 2005. If T allocates GST exemption prior to January 1, 2005, the allocation is irrevocable and does not become effective until January 1, 2005. If T allocates GST exemption on a gift tax return filed on or before April 15, 2006 (assuming no extensions), the allocation is effective as of January 1, 2005. If T allocates GST exemption on a late gift tax return filed on November 1, 2006, the allocation is effective as of November 1, 2006 (assuming T is still alive).

     d. **Valuation.** Whether the property is includible in the transferor's gross estate will determine the value of the ETIP property and the amount of GST exemption that must be allocated. IRC § 2642(f)(2).

     (1) **ETIP Property Includible in Transferor's Estate.** The value of ETIP property that is includible in the transferor's estate is its value for federal estate tax purposes.

     (2) **ETIP Property Not Includible in Transferor's Estate.** The value of ETIP property that is <u>not</u> includible in the transferor's estate is its value at the termination date of the ETIP if the allocation is timely made (or its value on the date of allocation if the allocation is late).

     5. **Relief For Late Elections and Substantial Compliance**

     Because the new rules for allocating GST exemption are so complex, the Act provides some relief provisions under certain circumstances:

a. Relief for Late Elections. IRC § 2642(g)(1) grants an extension of time under certain circumstances to (1) make an allocation of GST exemption under IRC § 2642(b)(1); or (2) to elect out of automatic allocation rules for direct skips under IRC § 2632(b)(3) or indirect skips under IRC § 2632(c)(5). The relief for late elections applies for requests pending on or filed after December 31, 2000. The Regulations, yet to be promulgated, will describe the circumstances and procedure to obtain such relief.

➔ **Planning Point:** Treas. Reg. § 301.9100 relief is currently available for extensions of time to allocate GST exemption and elect out of automatic allocation of GST exemption. Notice 2001-50, 2001-34 I.R.B. 189. Until the IRS issues Regulations under IRC § 2642(g)(1), practitioners may wish to apply to the IRS for an extension of time under the procedures described in Treas. Reg. § 301.9100, and indicate that the extension request is being made under both IRC §§ 2642(g) and Treas. Reg. § 301.9100.

b. Substantial Compliance. An allocation of GST exemption under IRC § 2632 that shows an intent to have the lowest possible inclusion ratio with respect to a transfer to a trust will be deemed an allocation of so much of the transferor's unused GST exemption as produces the lowest possible inclusion ratio. The relief for substantial compliance applies to transfers subject to estate tax or gift tax made after December 31, 2000. IRC § 2642(g)(2).

➔ **Planning Point:** Evidence of intent to have the lowest possible inclusion ratio might include contemporaneous letters to or from advisors and transferors and indications on relevant federal gift tax returns or federal estate tax returns.

I. Severance of Trust With Inclusion Ratio Greater Than Zero

1. Background

A single trust with an inclusion ratio of between zero and one is not as desirable for tax purposes as two separate trusts with inclusion ratios of zero and one, respectively. A single trust with an inclusion ratio of between zero and one wastes GST exemption. A distribution from such a trust to a non-skip person would generate GST tax that would not otherwise be due if non-exempt assets were distributed to the non-skip person. In addition, a distribution to a skip person would still generate some GST tax that would not otherwise be due if the inclusion ratio were zero. Instead, a trust with an inclusion ratio of zero and a separate trust with an inclusion ratio of one would optimize the tax benefit of the GST exemption. The trust with an inclusion ratio of zero could be used to provide for skip person/beneficiaries, and the trust with an inclusion ratio of one could be used to provide for non-skip person/beneficiaries.

EXAMPLE: At T's death in 2005, after taxes, T's estate has $3 million. Through lifetime taxable gifts, T has lowered his unified credit to $1 million. T still has his full $1.5 million GST exemption. T creates at death a credit shelter trust for the benefit of T's spouse, W, and T's descendants ($1 million), and a marital trust for the lifetime benefit of W ($2 million). Both trusts will be held for the benefit of T's descendants after W's death. $1 million of T's GST exemption is allocated to the credit shelter trust, and the balance, $500,000, is allocated to the marital trust. Accordingly, the credit shelter trust is wholly exempt from GST tax because its applicable fraction is 1 ($1 million allocated exemption divided by $1 million trust property), and its inclusion ratio is zero. The marital trust is only partially exempt from GST tax because its applicable fraction is .25 ($500,000 allocated exemption divided by $2 million trust property), and its inclusion ratio is .75. If W, a non-skip person, receives a trust distribution from the marital trust, some GST tax would be due, which wastes GST exemption. A better way to fund the trusts to maximize GST exemption would have been to split the marital trust into a non-exempt marital trust ($1.5 million) and an exempt marital trust ($500,000) and to allocate the balance of T's GST exemption ($500,000) to the exempt marital trust. Then, the exempt marital trust would be wholly exempt from GST tax because its applicable fraction would be 1 ($500,000 allocated exemption divided by $500,000 trust property), and its inclusion ratio would be zero. The non-exempt marital trust would be non-exempt from GST tax because its applicable fraction would be zero ($0 allocated exemption divided by $1.5 million trust property), and its inclusion ratio would be 1. Now, W, a non-skip person, could receive distributions out of the exempt trust without generating GST tax.

2. Severance of Trusts for GST Purposes

After GST exemption has been allocated to an existing trust, the trust generally cannot be severed to create two separate trusts with inclusion ratios of zero and one, <u>unless</u> one of the exceptions below applies. IRC § 2654(b). Accordingly, separate trusts generally should be established for GST tax purposes <u>before</u> GST exemption is allocated.

➔   **Planning Point:** Practitioners should be careful that boilerplate language in the governing trust instrument does not inadvertently provide that a trust with an inclusion ratio of zero be combined with or added to a trust with an inclusion ratio of one.

a. Separate Share Exception. Substantially separate and independent shares of different beneficiaries in a trust will be treated as separate trusts for GST purposes. The shares must exist at all times from and after the creation of the trust. IRC § 2654(b)(2); Treas. Reg. § 26.2654-1(a).

b. Multiple Transferor Exception. Portions of a trust attributable to transfers from different transferors will be treated as separate trusts for GST purposes. The regulations provide rules on the treatment of additions to and distributions from such trusts. IRC § 2654(b)(1); Treas. Reg. § 26.2654-1(a)(2).

> **EXAMPLE:** T gives $1,000,000 to a trust for T's descendants and allocates GST exemption to the trust so that the inclusion ratio is zero. When the trust property is worth $1,500,000, A transfers $3,000,000 to the trust but allocates no GST exemption to the transfer. The trust will be treated as two separate trusts for GST tax purposes: one-third will be attributable to T and have an inclusion ratio of zero, and the other two-thirds will be attributable to A and have an inclusion ratio of one.

c. Exception for Qualified Severance Allowed Under The Act. The Act added IRC § 2642(a)(3), which allows a "qualified severance" for a severance that occurs after December 31, 2000. If a trust is severed in a qualified severance, the two resulting trusts will be treated as separate for GST tax purposes.

(1) "Qualified Severance". A severance of a single trust is qualified if: (a) it is divided on a fractional basis, <u>and</u> (b) the terms of the new trusts, in the aggregate, provide for the same succession of interests of beneficiaries as the original trust.

(2) Trusts With Inclusion Ratio Between Zero and One. A severance of a trust with an inclusion ratio of between zero and one is qualified only if it is divided into two trusts, one of which receives a fractional share of the total value of all trust assets equal to the applicable fraction of the original trust. The trust receiving the fractional share will have an inclusion ratio of zero and the other trust will have an inclusion ratio of one. Proposed regulations issued in 2004 clarify that the new trusts simply must receive assets with a value equal to a fraction or percentage of the total value of the trust assets, rather than a pro rata portion of each individual asset held by the trust. Thus, the trustee does not need to divide each asset held by the trust on a fractional basis to make a qualified severance. Prop. Reg. § 26.2642-6.

> **EXAMPLE:** T gives $2,000,000 to a trust for T's descendants and allocates $500,000 of GST exemption to the trust so that the applicable fraction is 1/4 and the inclusion ratio is 3/4. A severance of the trust when the property is worth $4 million will be qualified if the trustee severs the trust so that one trust receives a 1/4 fractional share of the

trust property with an inclusion ratio of zero, and the other trust receives the balance of the property with an inclusion ratio of one.

Prop. Reg. § 26.2642-6 also provides that the beneficiaries of each trust resulting from the severance do not need to be identical to those of the original trust, for trusts that grant the trustee discretionary power to make non-pro rata distributions to beneficiaries, if all of these three conditions are met: (1) the separate trusts will have the same succession of interests of beneficiaries if terms are the same as the original, (2) the severance does not shift a beneficial interest in the trust to any beneficiary in a lower generation than the persons who held the beneficial interest in the original trust and (3) the severance does not extend the time for vesting of any beneficial interest in the trust beyond the period provided for in the original trust. This rule is intended to allow severance of trusts along family lines, which can be accomplished through a series of severances. For example, if two families are beneficiaries of one trust, the original trust may be severed first based on the inclusion ratio. Then, each resulting trust may be divided along family lines.

The proposed regulations also add that a qualified severance will not trigger gain or loss for income tax purposes under IRC § 1001 if the trustee is authorized under a state statute or the governing instrument to sever the trust and fund new trusts on a non-pro rata basis (that is, without transferring a pro rata portion of each asset to each trust). Prop. Reg. § 1.1001-1(h)(1)(i)-(ii). If IRC § 1001 does not apply, then, under IRC § 1015, the basis of the trust assets will be the same after the severance as before. Under IRC § 1223, the holding periods of the assets distributed to the new trusts will include the holding period of the assets in the original trust.

(3)   **Timing and Manner of Severance.** A qualified severance can be made at any time. Proposed regulations require that a qualified severance be reported by filing a Form 706-GS(T), "Generation-Skipping Transfer Tax Return for Terminations," with the words "Qualified Severance" written in red at the top of the form, and a Notice of Qualified Severance attached. Prop. Reg. § 26.2642-6.

J. Related Transfer Tax Provisions

1.   Payment of GST Tax on Direct Skip Treated as Gift

With respect to a taxable gift that is a direct skip, the amount of the gift is increased by the amount of any GST tax on the transfer paid by the transferor. IRC § 2515.

> **EXAMPLE:** On January 5, 2005, T gives $2 million to T's grandchild, G. T has not previously used any of T's GST exemption. T's gift is a direct skip because it is a transfer to a skip person, G, subject to gift tax. T's GST tax liability is $236,000. The gift tax is imposed on $2 million plus the $236,000 GST tax paid for a total taxable gift of $2,236,000. Assuming a gift tax rate of 47%, the gift

tax is $1,050,920. Total taxes for the transfer of $2 million are $1,286,920.

2. Related Income Tax Provisions

There are several income tax provisions related to the GST tax:

a. Income Tax Deduction For GST Taxes Paid on Income Distributions. IRC § 164(a)(4) grants an income tax deduction for GST taxes paid on income distributions. The deductible amount is the GST tax plus any state GST tax described in IRC § 2604. IRC § 164(b)(4)(A). If the GST tax is paid on or before the due date, it is treated as being paid on the last day of the taxable year in which the transfer was made. IRC § 164(b)(4)(B).

b. Income in Respect of a Decedent. With respect to a taxable termination or a direct skip as a result of the death of the transferor, IRC § 691(c)(3) allows an income tax deduction for that portion of the GST taxes attributable to items of gross income of the trust which were not properly includible in the gross income of the trust for periods before the due date of such termination.

c. Basis Adjustment for GST Tax Purposes.

(1) Basis Adjustment Generally. The basis of property transferred in a generation-skipping transfer is increased (but not above fair market value) by the GST tax that is attributable to the excess of the fair market value of the property over its adjusted basis immediately before transfer. The basis adjustment for GST tax is made after the basis adjustment under IRC § 1015. IRC § 2654(a)(1).

(2) Taxable Terminations At Death. The basis of property transferred in a taxable termination which occurs at the same time as and as a result of the death of an individual is adjusted in a manner similar to the adjustment in IRC § 1014(a) (*i.e.*, the basis is the federal estate tax value of the property), except that if the inclusion ratio is less than 1, any increase or decrease in basis will be limited by multiplying the increase or decrease by the inclusion ratio. IRC § 2654(a)(2).

> **EXAMPLE:** At T's death, T gave $2,000,000 to a trust for the lifetime benefit of T's child, C. At C's death, the trust will be held for the benefit of T's children. T's executor allocated $1,000,000 of T's GST exemption to the trust. Therefore, the trust's inclusion ratio is 50% (1 - $1,000,000/$2,000,000). At C's death, the basis of the trust property was $2,000,000, and the fair market value of the trust property was $4 million. The basis increase is $2,000,000 ($4,000,000 - $2,000,000), but this increase is limited by multiplying the increase ($2,000,000) by the inclusion ratio (.5), resulting in a basis increase of $1,000,000.

K. Benefits of GST Tax Planning

1.   Leveraging GST Tax Exclusions During Life

As discussed earlier, a planned giving program that takes advantage of the gift tax and GST tax exclusions can significantly reduce an individual's total transfer tax liability. Such transfers do not generate any gift tax or GST tax, do not use up the transferor's GST exemption or applicable credit amount, or remove the transferred property (and any post-transfer income from and appreciation) from the transferor's estate. The exclusions for tuition expenses and medical expenses are especially valuable since there is no limitation on the amounts that can be excluded for gift and GST tax purposes.

2.   Leveraging GST exemption During Life

The GST exemption, especially as it increases over the next few years, allows an individual to transfer a significant amount of property without incurring any GST tax. A transferor's lifetime use of his or her GST exemption removes the transferred property (and any post-transfer income from and appreciation) from the transferor's estate.

> ➔   **Planning Point:** Clients who wish to make lifetime gifts using his or her GST exemption should consider giving property likely to appreciate or generate significant income.
>
> > **EXAMPLE:** On January 1, 2005, T gives $1,100,000 to T's grandchild, G. No GST tax is due because $1,100,000 of T's GST exemption is allocated to the gift. Assuming the $1,100,000 grows to $4,000,000 at T's death four years later, not only has T removed the initial gift of $1,100,000 from his estate, T has also removed the appreciation ($2,900,000) from his estate. In addition, by T's lifetime gift, G has received more than G would have received if T had left $1,100,000 to G at T's death.

3.   Dynasty Trusts

An even more effective use of an individual's GST exemption is to allocate GST exemption to a dynasty trust for the benefit of multiple generations. A dynasty trust is designed to perpetuate for the maximum period of time permitted under applicable law. States differ with respect to the maximum allowable period. In some states, the common law rule against perpetuities allows the trust to exist for a period of time measured by lives in being at the creation of the trust, plus 21 years. Other states have abolished the rule against perpetuities or allowed a trust to opt out of the application of the rule against perpetuities, allowing a trust to exist perpetually.

Even if the estate tax and the GST tax are repealed, dynasty trusts will still be useful. A dynasty trust can be used to benefit multiple generations without gift tax.

EXAMPLE: After T's death, T wants to pass down $5 million to T's son, then to T's grandson, and then to T's great-grandson. If the property is left outright at each generation, the $5 million would be subject to estate tax at <u>each</u> generation before reaching T's great-grandson, reducing the amount left to T's great-grandson to only $625,000.

EVENT	TRANSFER TAX PAID (ASSUME 50% RATE)	PROPERTY LEFT FOR NEXT GENERATION
T's death	$2.5 million	$2.5 million
T's son's death	$1.25 million	$1.25 million
T's grandson's death	$625,000	$625,000

If T had instead established a dynasty trust for the lifetime benefit of T's son and grandson with the remainder passing to T's great-grandson, only <u>one</u> transfer tax would be paid when T created the trust, and T's great-grandson would receive $2.5 million (plus any appreciation of or income thereon and less any amounts distributed for T's son and grandson).

EVENT	TRANSFER TAX PAID (ASSUME 50% RATE)	PROPERTY LEFT FOR NEXT GENERATION
T's death	$2.5 million	$2.5 million
T's son's death	$0	$2.5 million
T's grandson's death	$0	$2.5 million

Chapter IV
Bibliography

2001 Tax Legislation: Law, Explanation and Analysis, CCH Incorporated (2001).

Ronald D. Aucutt, "An A-to-Z "To Do" List Following EGTRRA," *Est. Plan.* (December 2001).

The Economic Growth and Tax Relief Reconciliation Act of 2001: An Analysis, Matthew Bender & Co., Inc. (2001).

Carol A. Harrington and Frederick G. Acker, 850 T.M., *Generation-Skipping Transfer Tax.*

John B. Huffaker, "Generation-Skipping Transfer Tax Planning After The 2001 Act: Mostly Good News," *J. Tax'n* (September 2001).

Roy D. Madoff et al., *Practical Guide to Estate Planning* (2nd ed. 2001).

Charles F. (Monty) Newlin, "Sophisticated Estate Planning For Uncertain Times: Covering All the Bases For Today and Tomorrow," Illinois Institute for Continuing Legal Education Master Teacher Program (June 21, 2001).

John R. Price, *Price on Contemporary Estate Planning* (2nd ed. 2001).

V. VALUATION OF ASSETS FOR ESTATE, GIFT AND GENERATION-SKIPPING TRANSFER TAX PURPOSES

A. Introduction

This chapter discusses the rules for the valuation of assets for estate, gift, and generation-skipping transfer tax purposes. The valuation rules are important because they play an integral role in determining the amount of estate, gift, and generation-skipping transfer tax due on the lifetime and testamentary transfer of assets. The Treasury Regulations (the "regulations") provide a general definition of fair market value and specific valuation rules for certain assets.

The valuation of assets can also play an important role in planning for the disposition of assets during life and upon death. Certain techniques can be implemented to decrease the value of an asset prior to its disposition in order to reduce any gift or estate tax liability. Such techniques use fractional interest discounts, minority interest discounts, lack of marketability discounts and discounts on capital gains as a device to decrease the value of an asset. The topics that will be covered in this chapter include:

- Fair Market Value
- Valuation Date and Alternate Valuation Date
- Specific Valuation Rules for Certain Assets
- Valuation of Real Estate
- Business Interests Discounts
- Lapsing Rights
- Minimizing Valuation Risks for Lifetime Transfers

B. Fair Market Value

1. General Definition

The primary purpose of the regulations dealing with valuation is to provide guidance in determining the fair market value of property at the valuation date. As a general definition, the Regulations set forth fair market value as the price at which the property would change hands between a willing buyer and a willing seller, neither being under any compulsion to buy or to sell and both having reasonable knowledge of relevant facts. Treas. Reg. §§ 20.2031-1(b); 25.2512-1. This definition allows for positive and negative factors to be considered in the valuation of an asset much like a willing buyer and willing seller would do. For example, accrued interest will increase the value of an asset while an accrued tax liability, such as unrealized capital gain, will decrease the value of an asset.

All relevant factors that may affect value are to be considered. A relevant factor includes the fact that the decedent died. For example, a life insurance policy payable on the decedent's death is included in the decedent's estate at the full death benefit value because the value of the death benefit is not affected by the decedent's death. However, if the decedent was a "key-person" of a closely-held business and the business suffered a loss due to the death of the decedent, the value of the business may be discounted to allow for the effect of the decedent's death on the business.

→ **Planning Point:** The effect of the decedent's death should be taken into account in the valuation of assets that relied heavily on the talents and skills of the decedent. The decedent's death can affect the value of the property positively or negatively depending on the type of asset. Such assets include closely-held businesses, works of art created by the decedent, and intellectual property composed by the decedent. Intellectual property and works of art can increase in value because no other creations will be produced by the decedent. Whereas, a closely-held business can decrease in value if the decedent played a major role in the operations and success of the business.

2. Actual and Comparable Sales

a. Actual Sales.

(1) **General Rule.** Since fair market value is defined as the price that would be paid by a willing buyer to a willing seller, an actual bona fide sale of the property generally will be the best evidence of fair market value. For an actual sale to be a factor in the determination of fair market value, it must be a bona fide sale within a reasonable period of time of the valuation date. Additionally, there should not be any circumstances between the sale and the valuation date that would affect the property's value.

> **EXAMPLE:** If the property was severely damaged after the valuation date and then sold at a reduced price, the actual sale would not be a significant factor in the determination of fair market value.

(2) **Reasonable Time.** The definition of "reasonable time" varies widely and depends primarily on the facts and circumstances of each case. If the market fluctuates considerably between the valuation date and the actual sale date, the actual sale may be disregarded. As a general rule, the passing of a few years, even in a stable market, will be regarded as an unreasonable amount of time. *Estate of Krischer v. Comm'r.*, T.C. Memo 1973-172 (Tax Court held that seven years was too much time to find an actual sale useful). The passage of less than two years in a stable market tends to be regarded as a reasonable time. *Estate of Helen M. Noble v. Comm'r*, T.C. Memo. 2005-2 (sale by estate of closely-held stock approximately 14 months after the decedent's death occurred within a reasonable time when there were no intervening events that drastically changed the value of the property); *Gettysburg Nat'l Bank v. U.S.*, 806 F.Supp. 511 (M.D. Pa. 1992); *Estate of Kaplin v. Comm'r.*, T.C. Memo 1986-167.

→   **Planning Point:** Careful consideration should be given before actually selling any asset of an estate to ensure that the ultimate valuation of the property for tax reporting purposes as a result of the actual sale does not cause an adverse tax consequence.

      (3)   **Forced Sales.** The Regulations state that value is not to be determined by a forced sale. Treas. Reg. § 20.2031-1(b). Therefore, an auction generally is not determinative of value. However, if an auction has a reserve (a minimum price for which the item can be sold) or if there is a minimum opening bid, the auction price may be used as evidence of value. Rev. Proc. 65-19, 1965-2 C.B. 1002.

      b. **Comparable Sales.** The sale of comparable property is highly probative as to the value of the subject property. To be comparable, the property sold must be similar to the subject property. There must be a commonality between the two properties that would justify comparing the sales information. Some types of property are more readily comparable than others. It may be easier to find a comparable car than to locate comparable real properties. The job of the appraiser is to take into account the differences between the comparable properties and the subject property and make adjustments to account for the differences. If there are too many differences between the comparable properties and the subject property, the comparisons may not substantiate the value of the subject property.

      Additionally, the comparable sale must occur close in time to the valuation date in order to be meaningful or there must be a method for adjusting the value to account for the passage of time. There is not a recognized cut off point when a comparable sale is no longer meaningful. However, as a general proposition, the closer the sale date is to the valuation date, the more meaningful the comparable sale will be in determining the subject property's value.

      EXAMPLE: A died on January 1 of year 1, owning a personal residence in State X and owning another personal residence in State Y. There are six comparable sales for the residence in State X. All of the comparable sales are within two blocks of the State X personal residence and all the sales were made within the last two years of the valuation date. There is only one comparable sale for the personal residence in State Y. The comparable sale was made in a county different from that in which the State Y residence is located and occurred 5 years prior to the valuation date. The comparable sales in State X are highly probative in determining the value of the State X residence. However, the one comparable sale in State Y is marginally useful, if at all, in determining the value of the State Y residence. A different approach should be used to value the State Y residence.

C. Valuation Date and Alternate Valuation Date

1. Valuation Date

Generally, the valuation date for estate tax purposes is the date of the decedent's death. Internal Revenue Code ("IRC") § 2031(a). The alternate valuation date also can be used to value assets for estate tax purposes (see Subparagraph 2 below). For gift tax purposes, the valuation date is the date the gift is completed. IRC § 2512(a). There is no alternate valuation date for gift tax transfers.

The valuation date for generation-skipping transfers is the date the transfer is made; although, if the transfer is a direct skip made at death, then the alternate value used for estate tax purposes can be used to value the generation-skipping transfer.

2. Alternate Valuation Date

An alternate valuation date can be used to value the assets of an estate six months after the date of death. IRC § 2032. In order to elect the alternate valuation date, the value of the gross estate on the alternate valuation date must be less than the gross estate at the decedent's death and there must be a reduction in the amount of estate tax due. If an asset depreciates due to the mere passage of time, the alternate valuation date cannot be used. IRC § 2032(a)(3). If the alternate valuation date is elected, all of the assets must be valued as of that date. In other words, the estate cannot choose to value some assets on the alternate valuation date and other assets on the date of death. However, if an asset is sold or otherwise disposed of between the date of death and the alternate valuation date, the actual sale price will be the value of the asset for alternate valuation purposes.

> **EXAMPLE:** A patent and a life estate are examples of assets that decrease in value merely by the passage of time. A patent expires after a term of years. The passage of six months makes the interest less valuable because the term is shortened. Likewise, a life estate is less valuable as the life tenant ages, so the passage of six months will reduce the value of the life estate. The alternate valuation date cannot be utilized if the decrease in the value of the estate is attributed only to those assets that decrease in value merely by the passage of time.

➔ **Planning Point:** The alternate valuation date can be used to reduce the overall estate tax liability on an estate while increasing the value of other assets in the estate, such as a personal residence, thereby increasing the step-up in basis received. As long as the overall value of the gross estate and the estate tax liability decrease between the date of death and the alternate valuation date, individual assets can increase to achieve income tax benefits.

For a comprehensive discussion of the alternate valuation date, see Chapter 1, Federal Estate Tax.

D. Specific Valuation Rules for Certain Assets

1. Stocks and Bonds

a. General Rule. As a general rule, stocks and bonds are valued at their price per share on the valuation date. Treas. Reg. §§ 20.2031-2(a); 25.2512-2(a). If the stock or bond is publicly traded, the per share price is the mean between the high and low trading price on the valuation date. If there were no shares traded on the valuation date (*e.g.*, the valuation date is a holiday or weekend), the per share price equals the weighted average of the mean price on the nearest trading day preceding the valuation date and the mean price on the nearest trading day following the valuation date. The average of these two mean prices is weighted by the number of days they are from the valuation date.

> **EXAMPLE:** If A dies on a Saturday and has publicly-traded stock in his gross estate, the price per share will be the weighted average between the mean of the high and low trading prices on the Friday preceding A's death and on the Monday following A's death. Thus, if the mean share price on Friday (which is only one day from the valuation date) is $27 per share and the mean share price on Monday (which is two days after the valuation date) is $36 per share, the weighted average of these two prices will be $33, calculated as follows: $(($27 \times 1) + ($36 \times 2)) \div 3 = 33

If stocks or bonds are listed on more than one exchange, the exchange that primarily deals in the security should be used. If the securities are not listed on a public exchange, special care should be taken to determine the reliability of the information. The regulations suggest attaching a broker's letter or other credible confirming documentation to the tax return to establish the valuation of unlisted securities. Treas. Reg. §§ 20.2031-2(b); 20.2512-2(b). For a discussion of the valuation of closely-held business interests, see Paragraph 2 below.

b. Exceptions for Bonds. Since bonds ordinarily are not traded on a daily basis, the above-cited regulations provide an exception to the general rule stated above. If the only listed price for the bond is the closing selling price, then the value is the mean of the closing selling prices on the valuation date and the trading day before the valuation date. If there were no sales on the trading day before the valuation date, but there are sales on a day within a reasonable period of time before the valuation date, the value is determined by using a weighted average of the closing selling price on the valuation date and the closing selling price on the nearest day before the valuation date. If there was no trading of the bonds within a reasonable period of time prior to the valuation date, the value would be the closing selling price on the valuation date.

If none of the above methods of valuing a bond is available, the value can be determined by the mean of the bona fide bid and ask prices on the valuation date. Alternatively, the mean of the bona fide bid and ask prices on the day before and after the valuation date can be used if there are no bid and ask prices on the valuation date.

2. Business Interests

a. General Rule. The valuation of a closely-held business interest can be difficult to ascertain because there is no readily available market for the sale of the business interest. While the IRS is willing to accept the trading public's assessment of a company's value in publicly-traded shares, the valuation of a non-traded business interest is scrutinized more closely.

The regulations prescribe the same general rule for the valuation of a closely-held business interest as for any other asset; the price paid in an arm's-length transaction between a willing buyer and a willing seller. Fair market value is determined based upon all of the facts and circumstances, which include (i) a fair appraisal of all assets of the business including intangibles such as goodwill, (ii) the past, present and future earnings of the business, and (iii) the same rules used for the valuation of corporate stock in Treas. Reg. § 20.2031-2, discussed above.

In addition to the regulations, the IRS in Rev. Rul. 59-60, 1959-1 C.B. 237, has set forth its seminal pronouncement for the valuation of a closely-held business interest. The Ruling, as modified and amplified over the years,[1] states that the following factors should be considered:

(1) The Nature of the Business. The appraiser must consider the nature and history of the business. What the business does and how the business makes money are key considerations in the valuation of the business interest. Future performance also has a major impact on a business's value. Sometimes, a business's past financial performance can be used to predict the business's future performance. An analysis of the gross and net income and dividends over a long period of time can be particularly useful to assess the stability of the business and its probable future financial performance. Events that take place closer to the valuation date are given greater consideration than events that happened further from the valuation date. Nonrecurring events are given significantly less consideration because they have little or no effect on future performance and, therefore, should have little or no effect on value.

(2) The Economic Outlook in General and the Outlook of the Specific Industry. The general economic outlook of both the national economy and the economy of the specific industry in which the business operates will impact the valuation of the business interest. This factor includes the success of the business in relation to its competitors in the marketplace. The loss of a "key-person" may have a detrimental effect on the viability of the business and, therefore, also must be considered. If the business has purchased a life insurance policy on the "key-man," the value of the policy must be added to the value of the business interest. See, e.g., *Estate of Mitchell v. Comm'r*, 74 T.C.M. 872 (1997), *rev'd on other grounds*, 250 F.3d 696 (2001).

(3) **The Book Value of the Stock and Financial Condition of the Business.** A business' historical and current financial condition is of great importance in the determination of value. The IRS typically reviews two or more years' of the business's prior financial statements starting with the year immediately preceding the valuation date. The appraiser should determine from the business's financial statements the (i) liquidity of the business, (ii) gross and net book value of principal classes of fixed assets, (iii) working capital, (iv) long-term indebtedness, (v) capital structure, and (vi) net worth. The financial statements will determine what the business is worth based solely on its net asset value and will assist the appraiser in assessing the future performance of the business.

(4) **The Earning Capacity of the Business.** The profit-and-loss statements should be reviewed to determine the future earning capacity of the business. The profit-and-loss statements will separate the recurring from the nonrecurring earnings and expenses, and the investment income from the operating income. The profit-and-loss statements also would identify whether any portion of the business is operating at a loss. In attempting to assess how the risk of future profits would affect the business's value, an appraiser should consider the use of raw materials and supplies in the case of manufacturers, processors, and fabricators; the cost of purchased materials for merchandisers; utility services; insurance; taxes; depletion or depreciation; and interest.

After a proper earnings history is compiled, a capitalization rate or factor is applied to each of the years to determine the proper weight to be accorded each year's earnings or losses. There is no generally accepted method for determining the property capitalization rate, however, important factors to consider include the nature of the business, the risk involved and the stability or irregularity of earnings. One approach is to focus on particular earnings trends over the past few years. Clear trends can indicate cyclical business patterns. See, e.g., *Estate of Giselman v. Comm'r*, 57 T.C.M. 391 (1988).

(5) **The Dividend-Paying Capacity.** The business' ability to pay dividends is a relevant consideration in the valuation of a business interest. The major focus should be on the business' ability to pay, rather than the actual amount of dividends paid in prior years because the actual payment of the dividends is within the absolute discretion of the controlling shareholders.

Typically, courts will apply a capitalization factor to the dividend-paying capacity to generate a fair market value for the stock. The capitalization factor often comes from a review of comparable companies. See, e.g., *Central Trust Co. v. U.S.*, 305 F.2d 393 (Ct. Cl. 1962).

(6) **Goodwill and Other Intangible Value.** The value of a business's goodwill or other intangible assets can sometimes be illusive because of the difficulty in quantifying something that physically does not exist. Rev. Rul. 59-60 describes goodwill as the

21st Century Estate Planning:
Practical Applications
2005 Edition

©2005 Sonnenschein Nath & Rosenthal LLP
and Cannon Financial Institute, Inc.

100

excess of the net earnings over and above the fair return on the net tangible assets. However, goodwill also can be the value of the business' reputation and name. Another view is that goodwill need not be separately valued as it is included in the value of the entity as a whole, the amount in excess of the net book value of the assets. While there are a number of different methods that may be used to value goodwill or other intangible assets, the appraiser should recognize the existence of the intangible asset and give it due consideration in the appraisal.

In many cases, goodwill may not be present, or if present, may not be transferable. For example, if a corporation's goodwill depends primarily on one individual, the goodwill may be lost at the death of that person. Note that in various other valuation methods, the value of goodwill and other intangibles is already taken into account.

(7)   Sales of Stock and the Size of the Block of Stock to be Valued. Actual sales of stock may be determinative of value, provided the sale is an arm's-length transaction. As discussed below, with publicly-traded stock, a discount may be appropriate for the sale of a large block of stock. In contrast, large blocks of stock in a closely-held business, especially where they represent a controlling interest, more commonly increase the value of the stock because of the control premium.

(8)   The Market Price of Stock of Comparable Publicly-Traded Businesses. The market price of publicly-traded stock of comparable businesses also must be considered, pursuant to IRC § 2031(b). The stock must be traded on an active and public market as of the valuation date. Stocks listed on active and public market exchanges are given priority over stocks listed on less active, over-the-counter exchanges. Although the Internal Revenue Code only requires the businesses to be comparable, other relevant factors also must be considered. For example, a business with a shrinking market share and declining profits is not directly comparable, without adjustment, to a business with an expanding market share and growing profits. Comparability can be verified by reviewing the eight factors set forth in Rev. Rul. 59-60 to determine the extent to which each of the corporations is similar with respect to each factor.

Each of the relevant factors should be given a different weight depending on the particular facts and circumstances of each comparable business. For some operations, such as service-oriented businesses, earnings will be the most important factor in the determination of value. For other operations, such as financial institutions, a valuation of the business' capital assets will be the controlling factor.

b.   Valuation Methods. Rev. Rul. 59-60 also provides that an appraiser may elect to use one or more valuation methods to determine the value of a business in addition to the factors listed above. Four of the most common methods are discussed below:

(1)   Earnings Method. This method determines the fair market value of a business by assuming that an investor would pay for the present value of the business' future

21st Century Estate Planning:
Practical Applications
2005 Edition

©2005 Sonnenschein Nath & Rosenthal LLP
and Cannon Financial Institute, Inc.

101

earnings potential. The future earnings an investor would expect to receive are calculated over a term of years and then each year's projected earnings are discounted to present value.

A variation of the earnings method is the capitalization of earnings approach. See, e.g., *Estate of Deputy v. Comm'r*, T.C. Memo. 2003-176. This approach analyzes the price-to-earnings ratio of other comparable businesses. Such ratio is then applied to the subject business's earnings and a per share price is determined. Unfortunately, in order for this method to be accurate, it requires a comparison of only truly comparable businesses. Even where two businesses are similar, without certain adjustments to account for their differences, they may not be truly comparable. Thus, this approach can create a flawed valuation if not applied correctly.

> **EXAMPLE:** Company A has a price-to-earnings (PE) ratio of 2.5, Company B has a PE ratio of 3.0, and Company C has a PE ratio of 3.5. The average PE ratio between these three companies is 3.0. The earnings per share of Company D is $50. Applying the average PE ratio of 3.0 to Company D's earnings per share results in a share price of $150 ($50 x 3). However, if Companies A, B, and C are not truly comparable, some modifications to the average PE ratio would be necessary to achieve an accurate result in the valuation of Company D.

(2) **Asset Value Method.** This is one of the easiest methods appraisers use to value a business interest, but it can also be one of the least accurate methods. The value of the business is determined by taking the book value of the assets and subtracting liabilities, amortization and depreciation. This method does not attribute any value to the intangible assets of the business and frequently uses the historical or book value of a business' assets instead of the assets' fair market value. While a business's assets may be a factor in its overall value, this method alone rarely captures the whole value of the business.

A variation from this pure asset value method can be used to produce a more accurate appraisal. For example, the ratio of a comparable business' book value to its sales price can be applied to the subject business' book value to arrive at the fair market value. Although this is essentially a comparable sale approach, it uses a variation of the asset value method to determine a value. This method is only valid if there are comparable businesses with provable ratios. Another method assumes that the value of the corporation is based on the fair market value of its underlying assets, rather than their book value.

The Tax Court has agreed with the statement in Rev. Rul. 59-60 that "[t]he value of the stock of a closely held investment or real estate holding company, whether or not family owned, is closely related to the value of the assets underlying the stock." See, e.g., *Estate of Renier v. Comm'r*, T.C. Memo. 2000-298. However, most courts are reluctant to use book value alone without any modification, such as those discussed above. See, e.g., *Hagen v. Comm'r*, 57 T.C.M. 1489 (1989), *aff'd in part and rev'd in part*, 951 F.2d 1259 (10th Cir. 1991).

21ˢᵗ Century Estate Planning:
Practical Applications
2005 Edition

©2005 Sonnenschein Nath & Rosenthal LLP
and Cannon Financial Institute, Inc.

102

(3) **Dividend Method.** This method analyzes the history of a business' dividend-paying capacity to predict future dividends to value the business interest. The rationale of this method is that an investor would pay for the present value of a business' future dividend payments. The concern with this approach is that the actual dividends paid in prior years are often irrelevant because the decision to pay dividends in any given year is entirely within the absolute discretion of the controlling shareholders. In light of such discretion, the appraiser must perform a more subjective determination of the business' capacity to pay dividends, which is a function of earnings, current capital needs, and future capital needs.

As with the capitalization of earnings approach, dividend-paying capacity can be capitalized by using comparable figures from similar businesses. The appraiser's ability to select truly comparable businesses is critical to prevent inaccurate results.

(4) **Market Method.** This method compares the overall value of similar businesses, rather than comparing only the components of similar businesses. See, e.g., *Estate of Leichter v. Comm'r*, T.C. Memo. 2003-66. As with other comparable methods, finding a truly comparable business is crucial. Differences in geographic location, market share, management and structure, industries, positions within a given industry, product lines and competition can cause wide variations in value. Therefore, certain modifications may be required in the valuation of comparable businesses in order to achieve an accurate result.

> ➔ **Planning Point:** Courts have determined that an in-depth look at all the relevant facts and circumstances should be made before an appropriate value can be determined. See, e.g., *Provitola v. Comm'r*, 60 T.C.M. 939 (1990), *aff'd*, 963 F.2d 385 (11th Cir. 1992); *Estate of Gwinn v. Comm'r*, 25 T.C. 31 (1955). Also, the valuation method chosen may also be significant in determining whether particular types of discounts are available. Consequently, it is extremely important that a skilled and experienced appraiser value the business.

3. Valuation of Notes

The value of a promissory note is presumed to equal the unpaid principal balance plus interest accrued as of the valuation date. Treas. Reg. §§ 20.2031-4 and 25.2512-4. If a lower valuation is desired, the taxpayer must prove that the note is not collectable or that the note is worth less than the unpaid principal balance due. If the promissory note is secured, the burden of proof is on the taxpayer to prove that the pledged collateral to secure the note is insufficient to satisfy the obligation.

4. Valuation of Cash on Hand or on Deposit

Cash on hand or on deposit is one of the easiest assets to value. The value is equal to the amount included in the decedent's gross estate. Treas. Reg. § 20.2031-5. If there are

21ˢᵗ Century Estate Planning:
Practical Applications
2005 Edition

©2005 Sonnenschein Nath & Rosenthal LLP
and Cannon Financial Institute, Inc.

103

outstanding checks on the valuation date that were written for bona fide obligations and they are subsequently honored by the bank, the amount of cash included in the estate may be decreased by the amount of the outstanding checks. Obviously, the reduction is not allowed if the obligation is allowed as a separate deduction from the gross estate.

5. Household and Personal Effects

a. General Rule. Household and personal effects are valued based on the general rule of a willing buyer and a willing seller. Treas. Reg. § 20.2031-6. The price the grantor paid to purchase an item that was subject to excise tax can be used to prove its value where the purchase was made within a reasonable time before the valuation date. Treas. Reg. § 25.2512-7. In the valuation of personal property, the built-in obligation of any excise, luxury, or other taxes may be taken into account if it would affect the price a willing buyer would pay for that item.

b. Highly Valuable Personal Property. For personal property items that are highly valuable or have a unique market, an appraisal of such items often is recommended. If the value of a personal property item exceeds $3,000, an appraisal must be attached to the tax return. Treas. Reg. § 20.2031-6(b). As with the valuation of other property, the appropriate market must be used to determine value. The retail market is usually the relevant market for the valuation of personal property because that is where most people purchase personal property; thus, a car should be valued at its retail price, not its wholesale price. Price guides can be used to prove value, but an appraisal is better evidence of value.

c. Filing Requirements. The Regulations suggest preparing and filing with the tax return a room-by-room itemized list of personal effects. Items that do not individually exceed $100 in value can be grouped together on the itemized list. In lieu of the itemized list, the executor can attach to the tax return a written statement containing a declaration made under penalty of perjury setting forth the values determined by a competent appraiser or dealer.

→ **Planning Point:** Unless there is a significant amount of valuable personal property or unique objects, such as rare musical instruments or works of art, a written statement by the executor setting forth the value of personal property will suffice.

6. Annuities, Life Estates, Remainders and Other Actuarial Values

a. General Rule. Life interests and interests that vest in the future must be valued as of the valuation date. Since the interest is only for a life or does not become possessory until a future date, the value of that interest must be discounted to its present value. In applying the discount, the IRC § 7520 rate is used to determine the interest's present value for gift and estate tax purposes.

21st Century Estate Planning:
Practical Applications
2005 Edition

©2005 *Sonnenschein Nath & Rosenthal LLP*
and Cannon Financial Institute, Inc.

104

(1)   Calculation of Actuarial Interest. Generally, the valuation of an annuity, life estate, remainder interest or any other interest based upon the life expectancy of a person is determined by the present value, as of the valuation date, of such interest. The first step in the valuation of an actuarial interest is to determine the applicable IRC § 7520 discount rate. The IRC § 7520 rate is updated monthly and applies to most actuarial interests regardless of the taxpayer's gender. The IRC § 7520 rate is used for valuations made after April 30, 1989.

(2)   Factors and Tables. The IRC § 7520 rate is used in conjunction with the term of years or measuring life governing the actuarial interest to get the annuity, life estate, or remainder factor from tables published by the IRS. The appropriate factor is then multiplied by the value of the property on the valuation date to determine the present value of the actuarial interest. The tables for determining the present value of actuarial interests are contained in different sections of the Regulations. The present value of an actuarial interest that is valued between April 30, 1989 and May 1, 1999 is determined under Treas. Reg. § 20.2031-7A(d). For actuarial interests valued after April 30, 1999 the table contained in Treas. Reg. § 20.2031-7(d) is used.

(3)   100% Rule. The value of all the interests in a single property, both lifetime interests and remainder interests, must be equal to 100% of the value of the subject property on the valuation date. Thus, if the lifetime interest is equal to 75% of the property value, the remainder interest must be equal to the remaining 25%.

(4)   Exceptions to Use of IRC § 7520 Rate. The IRC § 7520 rate is not applicable for the valuation of life insurance, endowment, and annuity contracts subject to IRC § 72; deferred compensation under IRC §§ 83, 451, 457, 3121(v), and 3306(r); valuation statements evidencing compliance with qualified plan requirements under § 6058; interest-free and below-market loans under IRC § 7872; or the valuation of nonqualified retained interest under § 2702(a)(2)(A). See Treas. Reg. §§ 1.7520-3(a), 20.7520-3(a), and 25.7520-3(a).

(5)   Terminal Illness. Additionally, if the measuring life is a person who is terminally ill, the IRC § 7520 rate will not apply. The individual's actual life expectancy must be used for the valuation of the actuarial interest. To be terminally ill, the person must have an incurable illness or deteriorating physical condition with at least a 50% probability that the person will die within one year. If the individual lives for 18 months or longer, however, the IRS assumes that the individual was not terminally ill at the valuation date unless proven otherwise by clear and convincing evidence. Treas. Reg. § 1.7520-3(b)(3).

b. Remainder and Reversionary Interests.

(1)   Calculation of Remainder Interests. The present value of a remainder or reversionary interest is calculated by multiplying the value of the property by the remainder interest actuarial factor found in Table B (for interests taking effect after a term of years) or Table S (for interests taking effect after one measuring life). See Treas. Reg. § 20.2031-7(d)(6) and (d)(7).

21ˢᵗ Century Estate Planning:
Practical Applications
2005 Edition

©2005 Sonnenschein Nath & Rosenthal LLP
and Cannon Financial Institute, Inc.

105

The first step is to determine the applicable IRC § 7520 rate. The next step is to obtain the remainder factor from the appropriate table by using the IRC § 7520 rate and the term of years or the age of the measuring life. Note that the correct age of a person is the age as of that person's nearest birthday. Finally, the remainder factor is then multiplied by the value of the property on the valuation date and the product of that calculation is the present value of the remainder or reversionary interest.

(2)   **Ascertainable Remainder Requirement.** The IRC § 7520 rate will not be used to value a remainder interest if it is subject to excessive contingencies. An unimpeded right to invade trust corpus would render the remainder interest valueless. However, a principal invasion power will not render the remainder interest valueless if it is subject to an ascertainable standard. The Regulations state that the willing buyer/willing seller test must be applied to determine if the remainder interest has any value in light of the corpus invasion power. Treas. Reg. § 20.2031-9.

➔   **Planning Point:** If a grantor gifts a remainder interest in trust, but gives the lifetime beneficiary the right to invade corpus without an ascertainable standard, the remainder interest will not be valued using the IRC § 7520 rate and the value of the life estate will be 100% for gift and estate tax purposes. In order to avoid this potential adverse tax consequence, an ascertainable standard should be used to restrict the invasion power of the lifetime beneficiary so that the remainder interest can be valued using the IRC § 7520 rate and the associated tables.

c. **Term of Years and Life Interests.**

(1)   **Calculation of Interest.** The same steps described above are used to determine the present value of a life estate or a term of years interest. The life estate factor or term of years factor, as the case may be, is multiplied by the value of the property in order to determine the present value of the life estate or term of years. The life estate and term of years factors can be found in IRS Pub. 1457 by using the appropriate IRC § 7520 rate and the measuring life or term of years. The life estate or term of years factor also can be calculated by subtracting the remainder factor (discussed above) from 1.0. See Treas. Reg. § 20.2031-7(d)(2)(iii).

An easier way to determine the present value of a life estate or term of years is to subtract the present value of the remainder interest from the value of the property. Since the combination of the life estate and the remainder interest must equal 100% of the value of the property on the valuation date, the calculation of one of the two interests will result in the value of the other.

> **EXAMPLE:** X has given B a life estate and A a vested remainder interest in real property. The entire interest in the real property is worth $1,000,000 on the valuation date. A's interest will take effect on the death of the life tenant, B. On the valuation date, B is 46 years

21ˢᵗ Century Estate Planning:
Practical Applications
2005 Edition

©2005 Sonnenschein Nath & Rosenthal LLP
and Cannon Financial Institute, Inc.

106

old and the IRC § 7520 rate is 6.0%. Under Table S in Treas. Reg. § 20.2031-7(d)(7), the applicable remainder factor is .19725. The present value of the remainder interest is $197,250 ($1,000,000 x .19725). Therefore, the value of the life estate given to B is $802,750 ((1.0 - .19725) x $1,000,000). The life estate also can be valued by simply subtracting $197,250 from the $1,000,000 value of the property since the combination of the life estate and the remainder interest must equal 100% of the value.

(2) **Sale of Interests.** If the life tenant and the remainder beneficiary sell the interest and split the proceeds equally, the life tenant will be deemed to have made a gift to the remainder beneficiary to the extent the life tenant's proceeds from the sale are less than his or her fractional share of the interest, as determined by the Regulations discussed above. Rev. Rul. 79-225.

(3) **Terminal Illness.** The IRC § 7520 rate will not be used to value life estates if the life tenant is suffering from a terminal illness. The actual life expectancy of the person with the terminal illness would be used instead.

(4) **Unequivocal Right to Income Requirement.** The IRC § 7520 rate will apply only if the income beneficiary of a trust has an unequivocal right to the income. If the beneficiary's income interest can be altered or diverted to the benefit of another without the income beneficiary's consent, the use of the IRC § 7520 rate is precluded.

d. Annuities.

(1) **Calculation of Annuity.** Annuities are valued by multiplying the aggregate annual payments of the annuity by the annuity factor. The IRS sets forth the annuity factors in Publication 1457. The annuity interest also can be determined mathematically by subtracting the applicable remainder factor (contained in Table B or Table S of Treas. Reg. § 20.2031-7(d)(6) and (d)(7)) from 1.0 and then dividing the result by the IRC § 7520 rate.

(2) **Adjustment Factor.** If the annuity is payable at the end of semiannual, quarterly, monthly, or weekly periods, an adjustment must be made to the calculation. The adjustment is made by multiplying the adjustment factor found in Table K of Treas. Reg. § 20.2031-7(d)(6) by the present value of the annuity.

> **EXAMPLE:** A is 67 years old and has the right to receive an annuity of $50,000 per year for life, paid quarterly. The IRC § 7520 rate on the valuation date is 6%. Under Table S in Treas. Reg. § 20.2031-7(d)(6), the applicable remainder factor is .44556. Thus, the annuity factor is 9.2407 ((1.0 - .44556) / .06). Since the annuity payments are paid quarterly, an adjustment factor of 1.0222 from Table K of Treas.

21st Century Estate Planning:
Practical Applications
2005 Edition

©2005 Sonnenschein Nath & Rosenthal LLP
and Cannon Financial Institute, Inc.

107

Reg. § 20.2031-7(d)(6) must be used. The present value of the annuity is $472,292.18 (($50,000 x 9.2407) x 1.0222).

If the annuity payments are made at the beginning of semiannual, quarterly, monthly, or weekly periods, the adjustment factor is determined using Table J of Treas. Reg. § 20.2031-7(d)(6).

(3) **Terminal Illness.** As with life estate and remainder interests, the annuity tables are not used if the annuitant is terminally ill and death is imminent. In such a case, the actual life expectancy of the annuitant with the terminal illness is used to value the annuity interest.

E. Valuation of Real Estate

1. General Rule

Real property is valued using the general willing buyer/willing seller rule. In addition, vacant land is valued based on its "highest and best use." This means that if the decedent owned a vacant lot in the middle of a housing tract, the land would not be valued merely as barren land. The vacant lot would be valued as property that could be developed, subject to certain zoning restrictions.

Valuation of real property for transfer tax purposes always should be done by a competent appraiser.

2. Commercial Real Estate

a. **Income Method.** Commercial real estate often is valued based on the stream of income it derives. The valuation of apartments, office buildings and other commercial facilities often depends on a capitalization of income approach. Of course, the capitalized income must be adjusted to take into account costs associated with the real property. For example, a property that requires updating or extensive repairs would be less valuable than a new property or a newly remodeled property.

b. **Comparable Sales Method.** A comparable sales approach also can be used to value commercial real estate. This approach requires finding sales of similar properties and then adjusting the value of the subject property for any differences.

c. **Factors Affecting Value.** Whether an appraiser uses a capitalization of income approach, a comparable sales approach, or some other approach, there are a number of different factors that will affect value. These factors include:

- location of the property,
- zoning and local regulations,
- the proximity to transportation,

21ˢᵗ Century Estate Planning:
Practical Applications
2005 Edition

©2005 Sonnenschein Nath & Rosenthal LLP
and Cannon Financial Institute, Inc.

108

- availability of parking, and
- any negative factors associated with a nearby nuisance (such as loud noises close to a hotel).

As with most real property, location is usually the paramount factor for valuation purposes. Commercial property will be valued based on its proximity to a desired location for a particular type of use. For office buildings, it may be proximity to transportation and business centers. For retail shopping centers, the proximity to major thoroughfares will weigh heavily on value. For apartment buildings, locations away from commercial centers tend to be more valuable.

➔ **Planning Point:** By carefully scrutinizing the various factors that may affect the property's value, an appraisal can be increased or decreased, based upon a variety of relevant factors. Because the appraisal of real estate can be somewhat subjective, working closely with an appraiser may result in achieving the desired planning goal.

The aggregation of multiple buildings may also increase the value of the real property. For example, shopping centers are usually more valuable when considered as one property instead of a group of individual stores.

d. **Large Hotels and Commercial Complexes.** Large hotels and commercial complexes often are valued as businesses rather than as real estate. The value of these types of properties usually is more than the value of the underlying land and building. Large hotels and commercial complexes carry on various activities that are closely associated with a business, such as operating spas and providing convention or office services. Therefore, the valuation of this type of property is more closely akin to a business valuation rather than a valuation of only the land and building. A valuation of the entire endeavor requires, among other things, the inclusion of the income from all the various sources within the property and the deduction of the corresponding operating expenses.

3. **Residential Real Estate**

a. **Comparable Sales Method.** Residential real estate primarily is valued by using a comparable sales approach. Residential property usually does not produce income, except for multi-unit dwellings. It is important that an appraiser analyze a number of comparable sales so that the subject property can be properly valued. Once the comparable sales have been compiled, certain adjustments can be made to account for differences between the comparable sales and the subject property. Since no two pieces of real property are ever identical, failure to adjust for differences between properties may result in an inaccurate appraisal. Unfortunately, the types and amounts of each adjustment often are subjective.

b. **Time and Terms of Comparable Sales.** Comparable sales near the valuation date are probative of value. If there is a passage of time between the comparable sale

21st Century Estate Planning:
Practical Applications
2005 Edition

©2005 Sonnenschein Nath & Rosenthal LLP
and Cannon Financial Institute, Inc.

109

and the valuation date, adjustments must be made to the valuation to account for the effect of the passage of time. Additionally, if the comparable sale had unique circumstances surrounding the sale (*e.g.*, the comparable sale was a forced sale, the terms of the sale were more favorable than normal, or if the comparable sale was a part-gift, part-sale transaction), then adjustments would be required to account for the unique circumstances in order for the sale to be considered a comparable sale.

   c. <u>**Geographic Proximity of Comparable Sales.**</u> Comparable sales need to be in the same general geographic area as the subject property. If the comparable sale is located in a less desirable neighborhood, the value must be adjusted to account for the difference. A difference in the physical location of the comparable sale to the subject property also can affect value. For example, a property that is close to a busy street would be less valuable than a property on a cul-de-sac. Also, a property with a panoramic view is more valuable than a property with no view. Finally, the lot sizes and land use restrictions will affect the value. All of these various factors must be taken into account and properly adjusted to arrive at the fair market value of the subject property.

> ➔   <u>**Planning Point:**</u> Working closely with a competent appraiser can be the difference in achieving your planning objectives. Focusing on the differences between the comparable sales and the subject property can help justify an increase or decrease in value, depending on the desired result. Carefully analyzing the comparable sales with the appraiser can lead to a beneficial result.

  4. **Vacant Land**

   a. <u>**Highest and Best Use.**</u> Vacant land is to be valued at its "highest and best" use. This would be the use that will produce the highest value for the property. The use also must be one that is reasonable within the geographic area. Vacant land that is surrounded by farmland should not be valued as a possible residential development property. However, if there is a residential development in the surrounding area, it may be reasonable to value the vacant land as such.

   b. <u>**Factors Affecting Value.**</u> Comparable sales are primarily used to value vacant land, much like the valuation of residential real estate. In order for a comparable sale to be meaningful, it must be similar enough to the subject property and close enough in time to the valuation date. The IRS, in Rev. Proc. 79-24, sets forth the following factors for comparing similar pieces of vacant land:

• location	• easements
• configuration of property	• soil condition

21ˢᵗ Century Estate Planning:
Practical Applications
2005 Edition

©2005 Sonnenschein Nath & Rosenthal LLP
and Cannon Financial Institute, Inc.

110

- zoning
- accessibility
- water rights

- vegetation cover
- mineral rights
- riparian rights

5. Leases and Options

a. Leases.

(1) **Lessor's Interest.** An interest in a lease can be either an asset or a liability. The effect of the lease on the value of the property depends on an analysis of comparable leases. If a lease on the property has more favorable terms for the lessor than comparable leases, the property can be worth more. Conversely, if a lease has less favorable terms for the lessor, the property can be worth less.

(2) **Lessee's Interest.** A lessee's interest in a lease also can be considered an asset or a liability. If the lease is a long-term lease with terms favorable to the lessee, the lessee has a valuable interest. A lease also can be valuable if the lessee has a below-market lease with the right to sublease the property for a profit. In this case, the value of the lease would be the present value of the future net income from the sublease. On the other hand, if the lease is a long-term lease with less favorable terms for the lessee, the lessee has a potential liability if the interest were to be sold.

b. Options.
The IRS has stated in Rev. Rul. 80-186 that the value of an option to purchase real property depends on various factors including (i) the fair market value of the land on the date the option was given, (ii) the option price, (iii) any potential for appreciation or depreciation during the period, and (iv) the time period during which the option may be exercised.

The likelihood that the option will be exercised also affects its value. If the option price is unreasonably high, the likelihood of the option holder exercising the option decreases and so does the value of the option. Conversely, if the option price is low, the likelihood of the option holder exercising the option increases and so does the value of the option. All of these factors must be considered in determining what a willing buyer would pay to a willing seller for the option.

6. Fractional Interest Discounts

a. General Description.
The value of a fractional interest in any property is usually not equal to a proportionate share of the value of the entire property because the ownership of a partial interest is less desirable than ownership of the entire interest. The owner of a partial interest of property cannot freely or unilaterally make decisions on issues concerning the property. Co-owners of property are forced to (i) deal with each other, (ii) consider the rights

21st Century Estate Planning:
Practical Applications
2005 Edition

©2005 Sonnenschein Nath & Rosenthal LLP
and Cannon Financial Institute, Inc.

111

of the other co-owners, and (iii) make joint decisions on issues regarding the property. If a dispute arises between co-owners, the value of their fractional interests in the property could be compromised.

With respect to the ownership of real property, fractional interests are less desirable because co-tenants of real property have the right to occupy the entire property, provided it does not conflict with the use by the other co-tenants. Also, if an irreconcilable dispute arises between co-tenants, the property must be physically partitioned or sold.

> **EXAMPLE:** X owns a 10% interest in real property. The property is valued at $1,000,000. X's proportionate share of that value is $100,000. If X sold his 10% interest in the property, he would probably receive less than $100,000 because the sale of a fraction of the interest is less desirable to buyers than a sale of the whole interest.

b. The IRS's Position on Fractional Interest Discounts. Even though the IRC and Regulations do not provide any guidance on the validity or the amount of a fractional interest discount, the IRS has a strong bias against the use of fractional interest discounts. The IRS will generally disallow the fractional interest discount altogether or limit its value to the cost of partition.

The IRS's position that a fractional interest discount should be limited to the cost of partitioning the property is based partly on *Estate of Whitehead v. Comm'r*, T.C. Memo 1974-53. In *Whitehead*, the Tax Court allowed a fractional interest discount where the taxpayer was able to substantiate the value of the discount by providing evidence of the legal fees and surveying costs for partitioning the property. The taxpayer also proved that the fractional interest depressed the value of the entire property in the relevant marketplace.

The Court's rationale in *Whitehead* lead the IRS to hold in TAM 9336002 that a fractional interest discount is limited to partition costs. The IRS, in TAM 199943003, provides a method to determine the size of the fractional interest discount. Using this method, the IRS determines the proportionate value of the fractional interest and then subtracts the cost of partition allocable to the fractional interest.

TAM 9336002 was subsequently attacked by the Tax Court in *Shepherd v. Comm'r*, 115 T.C. 376 (2000). In *Shepherd*, the court held that the valuation of a fractional interest discount limited to only the partition costs failed to account for other factors that affect value, such as lack of control.

c. Case Law Development of Fractional Interest Discounts. The origin of fractional interest discounts is in case law. The courts tend to focus on the facts and circumstances surrounding the real property to determine if a fractional interest discount is appropriate.

21ˢᵗ Century Estate Planning:
Practical Applications
2005 Edition

©2005 *Sonnenschein Nath & Rosenthal LLP*
and Cannon Financial Institute, Inc.

112

(1) **<u>Cases Upholding Fractional Interest Discounts.</u>** The first case to hold in favor of a fractional interest discount was *In re Gilberts Estate*, 163 N.Y.S. 974 (1917). In *Gilberts*, the court allowed a 15% discount for a one-third fractional interest in property. Other courts following *Gilberts* have allowed fractional interest discounts:

- The court in *Propstra v. U.S.*, 680 F.2d 1248 (9th Cir. 1982), held that a fractional interest discount is appropriate for a one-half interest in real estate held as community property. In *Propstra*, the court reasoned that each spouse's interest should be valued separately because the family attribution rules do not apply in this context and that a fractional interest discount would apply to each of the spouse's interest.

- In *Estate of Bonner v. U.S.*, 84 F.3d 196 (5th Cir. 1996), the court held that a fractional interest discount was appropriate on the death of the surviving spouse where a QTIP trust owned an undivided one-half interest in property and the surviving spouse owned the other one-half interest. The court reasoned that even though the entire interest in the property is included in the surviving spouse's estate for estate tax reporting purposes, the surviving spouse has no control over the distribution of the property in the QTIP trust. Therefore, the two interests should be valued separately. <u>See</u>, <u>also</u>, *Estate of Mellinger v. Comm'r*, 112 T.C. 26 (1999), *acq.* AOD 99-006, 1999-35 I.R.B. 314; *Estate of Nowell v. Comm'r*, T.C. Memo. 1999-15; *Estate of Lopes v. Comm'r*, T.C. Memo. 1999-225.

(2) **<u>Cases Disallowing the Fractional Interest Discount.</u>** Courts have also disallowed the use of fractional interest discounts where there was limited evidence to support its use. The following cases illustrate a few of the circumstances where the discount was not allowed:

- In *Claflin v. Comm'r*, 2 B.T.A. 126 (1925), the decedent owned a nine-fourteenths interest in a Massachusetts trust and the trust owned three buildings. The estate's expert argued that the decedent's fractional share should be discounted by 25% because it was worth less than his proportionate share of the whole. The Court rejected the discount, holding that there were no "special conditions" that would reduce the value of the fractional share.

- In *Estate of Barclay v. Comm'r*, 2 B.T.A. 696 (1925), an estate attempted to get a 10% fractional interest discount based on the testimony of an expert who claimed that fractional interests were routinely discounted in the local real estate market. The court disallowed the discount because the IRS had evidence that actual sales of the fractional interest were routinely sold for more than their proportionate share of the entire value of the property.

21ˢᵗ Century Estate Planning:
Practical Applications
2005 Edition

©2005 Sonnenschein Nath & Rosenthal LLP
and Cannon Financial Institute, Inc.

113

- In *Estate of Young v. Comm'r*, 110 T.C. 297 (1998), the decedent owned property with his wife in joint tenancy with right of survivorship. The court held that a fractional interest discount was not appropriate because IRC § 2040(a) requires that joint tenancy property be included in the decedent's estate at 100% of its fair market value, less any contribution made by the surviving spouse. The fractional interest discount was not allowed because 100% of the value of the joint tenancy property was included in the decedent's estate. Furthermore, the joint tenancy property became the sole interest of the spouse after the decedent's death so there was no reason to discount the property.

➔ **Planning Point:** The IRS has aggressively sought to eliminate the use of fractional interest discounts. The courts, on the other hand, have allowed fractional interest discounts where there is evidence to support that a willing buyer would actually discount the price he would pay for the property because of the fractional interest. Anytime a taxpayer owns a fractional interest in real property, the use of a fractional interest discount should be considered.

7.   **Special Use Valuation**

    a. **General Rule.**

        (1)   **Highest and Best Use Exception.** IRC § 2032A allows an executor to value certain special use real property for estate tax purposes at a lower amount than the real property's fair market value. If certain requirements are satisfied, the executor may elect to value the real property using the special rules. The special use valuation rules allow the real property to be valued based on its given use instead of the "highest and best use" on the valuation date. Unfortunately, the special use valuation is not available for gifts. For GST tax purposes, the special use valuation is available only for direct skips at death (since the value of the generation-skipping transfer is the same as its estate tax value). IRC § 2624(b).

        (2)   **Special Use Valuation Limit.** The election can be made only to value real property used for farming or for a closely-held business. Since the property can be valued based on its given use instead of its "highest and best" use, a significant estate tax savings can be achieved. IRC § 2032A, however, can only be used to reduce the fair market value by $870,000 (for decedents dying in 2005).

➔ **Planning Point:** The special use valuation rule applies to the value of the entire real property. In community property states, the $870,000 reduction is against the entire community property interest instead of the decedent's one-half community property interest, except to the extent the surviving spouse contributed to the purchase of the property from his or her separate property.

21st Century Estate Planning:
Practical Applications
2005 Edition

©2005 Sonnenschein Nath & Rosenthal LLP
and Cannon Financial Institute, Inc.

114

b. Requirements for Election of Special Use Valuation.

(1) **Qualified Real Property.** Only "qualified real property" can obtain a special use valuation. IRC § 2032A defines "qualified real property" as property located in the U.S. that was acquired from or passed from the decedent to a qualified heir and was used for a qualified use by the decedent or his family on the decedent's date of death. Additionally, the decedent or a member of his family must have materially participated in the operation of the business for a total of five years out of the eight years preceding the decedent's death and the value of the property in the decedent's estate must meet certain percentage requirements. The date of the decedent's retirement from the business can be used for the eight-year look-back period rather than the date of death. IRC § 2032A(b)(4).

(2) **Qualified Use.** A "qualified use" is using the property as a farm for farming purposes or using the property in a trade or business other than the trade or business of farming. IRC § 2032A(b)(2).

(3) **Qualified Heir.** A "qualified heir" is a member of the decedent's family who acquires the property from the decedent. A qualified heir can subsequently dispose of the property to a member of his or her own family and the family member who receives the interest will be deemed the qualified heir with respect to the property transferred. A member of the decedent's family is defined to include (i) an ancestor of the decedent, (ii) the spouse of the decedent, (iii) a lineal descendent of the decedent, the decedent's spouse, or the decedent's parents, or (iv) the spouse of any lineal descendent described above. IRC § 2032A(c)(7)(C).

(4) **Percentage Tests.** There are two percentage tests that must be met in order to elect the special use valuation, a 50% test and a 25% test. Under IRC § 2032A(b)(1)(A), the adjusted value of all property, both real and personal, acquired from the decedent by a qualified heir and put to a qualified use must equal at least 50% of the decedent's gross estate. Under IRC § 2032A(b)(1)(B), the adjusted value of the real property acquired from the decedent by a qualified heir and put to a qualified use must equal at least 25% of the adjusted gross estate.

➔ **Planning Point:** It is essential that the qualified heirs receive sufficient assets to meet the rigid percentage requirements. If a portion of the property is distributed to an heir who is not qualified (*i.e.*, a non-family member), the special use valuation may not be available. This does not mean that there must be only one qualified heir. The number of heirs is not important as long as 50% or more of the qualified property is transferred to qualified heirs. The property can pass to more than one qualified heir and still meet the special use valuation requirements.

c. **Determining Value.** Farm property can be valued by the capitalization of rents method contained in IRC § 2032A(e)(7) or under a multifactor method in IRC

21ˢᵗ Century Estate Planning:
Practical Applications
2005 Edition

©2005 Sonnenschein Nath & Rosenthal LLP
and Cannon Financial Institute, Inc.

115

§ 2032A(e)(8). Closely-held business interests can be valued only by using the multifactor method.

(1) <u>**Capitalization of Rents Method.**</u> Under the capitalization of rents method, fair market value is determined by calculating the present value of the future cash flow. Such method analyzes the rental income of the property for the five years preceding the decedent's death. The average annual gross cash rental income of comparable farmland located in the same geographic area as the subject farmland is determined and then state and local real estate taxes are subtracted. The net income amount is then divided by the average annual effective interest rate for all new Federal Land Bank loans. IRC § 2032A(e)(7)(A). The term "gross cash rental" refers to the total amount of rents received during the year in question for the use of actual comparable farmland. Treas. Reg. § 20.2032A-4(b). The Regulations provide that comparable farmland is farmland in the same locality that meets generally accepted valuation rules for real property. Thus, as with the comparable sales approach, similar properties must be evaluated and the valuation must be adjusted to account for differences between the subject farmland and the comparable farmland, if necessary.

The factors that should be considered in the valuation of comparable farm properties include: (i) similarity of soil determined by objective means, (ii) the type of crops grown and their effect on the soil, (iii) soil conservation techniques, (iv) flooding, (v) slope of the land, (vi) capacity for livestock operations, (vii) similarity of timber for timberlands, (viii) whether property is segmented or unified, (ix) number and types of buildings, and (x) proximity of transportation facilities.

(2) <u>**Multifactor Method.**</u> Closely-held business interests can be valued only by using the multifactor method. Farmland also can be valued by this method. In using the multifactor method, five factors should be considered:

- capitalization of income that the property can be expected to yield for business or farm use over a reasonable period of time under prudent management;
- capitalization of the fair rental value of the land for farm or business purposes;
- Assessed land values in a state that provides a differential or use value assessment law for farmland or businesses;
- Comparable sales of other farms or business land in the same geographic area far enough removed from the metropolitan or resort area so that nonagricultural use is not a significant factor in the sales price; and
- Any other factor that fairly values the farm or business land value.

An appraiser must use all of the factors listed above that are relevant to the appraisal of the subject property. The appraiser is prohibited from selecting only those factors that are favorable to the planning goal. The appraiser, however, has the discretion to use different weightings for each factor in the appraisal. While the factors closely resemble normal appraisal

21ˢᵗ Century Estate Planning:
Practical Applications
2005 Edition

©2005 Sonnenschein Nath & Rosenthal LLP
and Cannon Financial Institute, Inc.

116

methods, there is no requirement that the property be valued at its "highest and best" use. Thus, even though the criteria are subjective, the real property can be valued at a lower amount than it would otherwise be valued if the "highest and best" use test were used.

               d. **Appraisal Requirement.** A written appraisal of the subject property must be obtained and attached to the estate tax return. Failure to do so would prevent the property from being valued at its special use. Treas. Reg. § 20.2032A-8(a)(3). If the executor makes a timely election and substantially complies with the Regulations, but files an incomplete appraisal, the executor would be allowed to provide the IRS with the omitted information within a reasonable period of time. IRC § 2032A(d)(3).

F. Business Interests Discounts

Business interests may be discounted if there are restrictions on ownership. Essentially, discounts are used because the value of a closely-held business as a whole is not equal to the sum of its parts. Thus, a ten percent ownership interest in a business is not necessarily worth ten percent of the entire value of the business. The minority interest may be worth less than ten percent because there is no control over the management of the business or because there is no readily available market to liquidate the interest.

In arriving at the appropriate discounts applicable to the interest being appraised, most appraisers compare the subject interest to other comparable publicly traded interests such as closed end equity mutual funds and studies of the sale of restricted securities. One example is the Institutional Investor Study conducted by the Securities Exchange Commission regarding sales of stock subject to Rule 144. Appraisers will also look at the governing instrument and the governing state law. The nature of the entity's assets are also important. A partnership owning real property will have a higher range of discounts than a partnership owning marketable securities. Return expectations and the level of risk at the entity level, as well as withdrawal and distribution rights are also important considerations.

The appropriateness of a discount or premium will always depend on whether the discount has already been accounted for in arriving at the base value of the business. For example, a minority discount would be inappropriate when the per share price for a minority position in a closely held company is determined based on comparable publicly traded stocks. Similarly, a discount for the loss of a key employee might be appropriate where the underlying valuation has not already accounted for such loss by utilizing reduced future earnings projections.

The most common discounts for business interests are: minority interest discount, lack of marketability discount, and discount for built-in capital gains.

21ˢᵗ Century Estate Planning:
Practical Applications
2005 Edition

©*2005 Sonnenschein Nath & Rosenthal LLP*
and Cannon Financial Institute, Inc.

117

1. Minority Interest Discounts

a. <u>Justification for Minority Discounts</u>. An investor who has a minority interest in a business, whether as a minority shareholder in a corporation or a limited partner in a limited partnership, lacks the ability to control the business. Since the investor cannot unilaterally make management decisions or control the distribution of dividends, the investor would discount the value of the minority interest.

> **EXAMPLE:** A owns 100% of a closely-held corporation. A gives 25% interests in the corporation to each of A's four children. Each gift will be valued separately and a minority interest discount can be taken for each child's 25% interest. The ownership interest of each child will not be attributed to the others based on their familial relationship. Note that the opportunity to obtain a minority interest discount is lost if the entire 100% interest is included in A's estate at his death.

Even though a particular minority business interest lacks control, both the IRS and the Tax Court have stated that no minority discount is available if the purpose of the transaction creating the minority interest is solely to avoid tax. In *Estate of Murphy v. Comm'r*, T.C. Memo. 1990-472, the Tax Court denied minority interest discounts for both gift and estate tax purposes where, 18 days before the decedent's death, the taxpayer made gifts designed to reduce her interest in a corporation from 51.41% to 49.65%, on the grounds that the transfers were made purely for tax avoidance. <u>But see</u> *Estate of Frank v. Comm'r*, 69 T.C.M. 2255 (1995).

b. <u>Swing Vote Premium</u>. In Rev. Rul. 93-12, 1993-1 C.B. 202, the IRS stated that each individual's interest in a business is valued separately and there is no attribution of ownership between family members. However, the IRS has argued that a premium should be added to a minority interest if it can be combined with another interest to gain control of the business. If each of two people has a 45% interest in a business and the interest being valued is the remaining 10%, the IRS can argue that the 10% interest has an additional value as a "swing vote" because it can be combined with one of the other two interests to gain control of the business. <u>See, e.g.</u>, TAM 9436005.

However, the Tax Court in *Estate of Magnin v. Comm'r*, T.C. Memo 2001-31, held that the swing vote approach works only where there is a definite ability by anyone owning the minority interest to gain control of the business. It must be likely that a hypothetical willing buyer can gain control of the business by combining with another shareholder. The hypothetical buyer must be considered without reference to the actual position of the minority interest holder. Therefore, if the minority interest holder is in a unique position to combine his interest and take control of the business, that position must be ignored for valuation purposes.

> **EXAMPLE:** Father owns a 35% interest in X Co. Father's Son owns a 16% interest in X Co. The remaining 49% of X Co. is owned by one hundred different individual investors with no one investor owning

21ˢᵗ Century Estate Planning:
Practical Applications
2005 Edition

©*2005 Sonnenschein Nath & Rosenthal LLP*
and Cannon Financial Institute, Inc.

118

more than 1%. Even though Son could combine his shares with Father to gain control of the business, a hypothetical buyer, one not in the same position as Son, could not be assumed to have the same ability to gain control of the business. Therefore, a swing vote premium is not appropriate. The hypothetical buyer rule is an objective standard that does not take into account the special relationship of Son and Father. A hypothetical willing buyer probably would not have the same relationship and, therefore, would not pay a premium for the minority interest.

     c. **Aggregation of Separate Interests Held by the Same Person**. The IRS has attempted to aggregate blocks of a particular business interest owned by the same person, but in different capacities, such as stock held in a trust for the taxpayer's benefit and stock held outright. Rev. Rul. 79-7, 1979-1 C.B. 294. The courts, however, have been less prone to aggregate such interests. Both the Fifth Circuit and the Tax Court have ruled that a beneficiary's interest in real estate held in a QTIP trust cannot be aggregated with other directly-held real estate interests in the same property for purposes of determining whether a controlling interest exists. *Estate of Bonnor v. U.S.*, 84 F.3d 196 (5th Cir. 1996); *Estate of Lopes*, T.C. Memo. 1999-225; see also *Estate of Bailey v. Comm'r*, T.C. Memo. 2002-152 (involving stock interests); *Estate of Nowell v. Comm'r*, T.C. Memo. 1999-15 (involving limited partnership interests). The IRS has acquiesced in the Tax Court's position. AOD 1999-0006 (Aug. 30, 1999). However, the Tax Court has aggregated stock held by the decedent outright and stock over which the decedent held a power of appointment. *Estate of Fontana v. Comm'r*, 188 T.C. 318 (2002).

     d. **Size of Minority Interest Discounts.** The amount of the minority interest discount varies. The IRS and the courts typically allow up to a 30% minority interest discount. Other special circumstances may justify a discount that is higher than 30%.

    ➔   **Planning Point:** A minority interest discount should be taken whenever a block of stock lacks control over a closely-held business. However, the amount of the minority interest discount should be carefully considered. While an aggressive discount may be appropriate, an overly aggressive discount may cost the client more than the benefit derived from the discount itself. A balance should be reached between the benefit derived from the discount and the cost associated with defending the discount.

     e. **The IRS' Use of Minority Interest Discounts.** Minority interest discounts can be used by the IRS to the taxpayer's disadvantage. For example, the value of a gift of a minority interest in a business to charity should be reduced to reflect the minority interest discount. If the use of the minority interest discount against the taxpayer is overlooked, it can result in significant adverse tax consequences.

21st Century Estate Planning:
Practical Applications
2005 Edition

©2005 Sonnenschein Nath & Rosenthal LLP
and Cannon Financial Institute, Inc.

119

2. Lack of Marketability Discounts

a. <u>Justification for Lack of Marketability Discounts</u>. The lack of marketability discount is a separate and distinct concept from a minority interest discount. While the two discounts may be somewhat related and often are used to discount the same interest, lack of marketability focuses on the ability of the investor to liquidate the interest. Therefore, it can apply to both a minority and a majority interest in a closely-held business, provided there is no readily available public market for the business interest. *Winkler v. Comm'r*, T.C. Memo. 1989-231. Of course, a controlling interest is more desirable and, therefore, may be easier to liquidate. But that consideration is merely a factor in determining the size of the discount, not the availability of the discount.

b. <u>Size of Lack of Marketability Discounts</u>. The size of the lack of marketability discount depends on the facts and circumstances of the business. Even though some appraisers have taken lack of marketability discounts of up to 70%, the courts tend to limit the lack of marketability discount to approximately 30%. See, e.g., *Mandelbaum v. Comm'r*, 69 T.C.M. 2852 (1995). Assuming both discounts are applicable, one discount percentage should be determined to reflect both a minority interest discount and a lack of marketability discount.

c. <u>Factors Affecting Size of Discount</u>. The lack of a public market is not the only factor that makes an interest unmarketable. Restrictions on the sale of the interest, such as options or buy-sell agreements, may justify a lack of marketability discount. However, not every option contract will reduce the value of the business interest. Treas. Reg. § 20.2031-2(h) states that an option contract held by a decedent that would allow him to dispose of the underlying securities at any price he chooses during his life will be given little weight. Even if the decedent is restricted from selling the securities during his lifetime, the option will be disregarded unless it is a bona fide arrangement and not a device to transfer the securities to the natural object of the decedent's bounty for less than full and adequate consideration. Moreover, buy-sell agreements and other arrangements may increase the lack of marketability discount, as long as they do not run afoul of Section 2703, discussed below.

Other restrictions on selling the interest can also give rise to a lack of marketability discount. Closely-held stock that cannot be sold for a certain period of time, because of agreements among the owners or because of securities laws, can result in substantial discounts. See, e.g., *Okerlund v. U.S.*, 53 Fed. Cl. 341 (2002), *aff'd*, 2004 WL 757972 (Fed. Cir. 2004). The cost of potential litigation may also be relevant in determining this discount. *Estate of Newhouse v. Comm'r*, 94 T.C. 193 (1990).

3. Discount for Built-In Capital Gains

A discount may be appropriate where an entity, such as a corporation or a partnership, holds an asset with a built-in capital gain. The IRS has suggested that the discount can be taken as a decrease in the entity's income stream or as a liability of the entity. IRS Guide for Income, Estate and Gift Taxes (May 1997).

21ˢᵗ Century Estate Planning:
Practical Applications
2005 Edition

©2005 Sonnenschein Nath & Rosenthal LLP
and Cannon Financial Institute, Inc.

120

Courts also have been willing to allow for these built-in capital gain discounts. See, e.g., *Eisenberg v. Comm'r*, 155 F.3d 50 (2d Cir. 1998). Still, however, the application and size of this discount will depend on the facts and circumstances. The size of the discount is largely determined by the likelihood of the recognition of the capital gain. The appraiser must discern the weight a willing buyer would place on purchasing the business interest with such a tax liability. For example, in situations where it is unlikely that a corporation would be liquidated and no disposition of the business' assets is expected to occur in the near future, the present value of the potential tax liability at a far off future date may be nominal. See, e.g., *Estate of Gray v. Comm'r*, T.C. Memo. 1997-67. If liquidation is likely, however, a discount for the tax liability flowing from such liquidation should be taken into account. See, e.g., *Estate of Davis v. Comm'r*, 110 T.C. 530 (1998).

The Fifth Circuit has stated that the weight to be given to such potential taxes should be the affect such potential taxes would have on a willing buyer. This same court added that when determining the asset-based value of a family-operated, closely-held corporation, there should be a dollar-for-dollar discount for the tax liability. However, the tax liability would not be considered in determining the earnings-based value of the business because this valuation assumes that there will be no sale of the assets. *Estate of Dunn v. Comm'r*, 301 F.3d 339 (5th Cir. 2002). The dollar-for-dollar discount was rejected in *Davis* because there was no planned liquidation or asset sale as of the valuation date.

4. Blockage Discount

Large blocks of publicly-traded stock are difficult to sell in the public marketplace without depressing the price of the stock. Since it is difficult to liquidate a large block of stock without lowering the per share price, the application of a valuation discount is appropriate. Treas. Reg. § 20.2031-2(e). The discount for the sale of large blocks of stock mainly is used for publicly-traded stock. The burden of proof is on the taxpayer to demonstrate that the sale of a large block of stock would depress the price per share in the open marketplace. A large block of stock generally is considered to be an amount of stock that exceeds the volume of shares traded in an average trading day.

The amount of the discount will depend on the effect the sale of the entire block would have on the market price of the stock. A block of stock that substantially exceeds the average daily trading volume of the stock will receive a higher discount than a block of stock that is about equal to the average daily volume. The objective is to arrive at a value that would represent the sales price for the shares had the entire block been liquidated on the valuation date.

Courts have expanded the concept of blockage discounts to such items as real estate and works of art. See, e.g., *Rimmer v. Comm'r*, T.C. Memo. 1995-215; *Estate of Auker v. Comm'r*, T.C. Memo. 1998-185.

21st Century Estate Planning:
Practical Applications
2005 Edition

©2005 Sonnenschein Nath & Rosenthal LLP
and Cannon Financial Institute, Inc.

121

5.   Valuation Discounts for Closely-Held Businesses After *Hackl*

Hackl v. Comm'r, 335 F.3d 664 (7th Cir., July 11, 2003), illustrates how structuring an operating or partnership agreement to restrict severely the rights of the holders of the business interests so as to obtain higher discounts such as the discounts discussed above may cause the donor of such interests to forfeit the ability to make annual exclusion gifts of such interests. The Seventh Circuit in *Hackl* upheld the Tax Court's decision that transfers of LLC interests did not qualify for the annual gift tax exclusion under Section 2503(b)(1). In reaching this conclusion, the court pointed to the LLC's operating agreement, which foreclosed an interest holder's ability to realize any substantial present economic benefit. As a result of this decision, practitioners advising clients who wish to make annual exclusion gifts of business interests should be sure that the operating agreement of the business does not prevent the donees from obtaining immediate use, possession or enjoyment of the gifted business interests. An interest holder's inability, under the entity agreement, to: (1) unilaterally withdraw his or her capital account, (2) independently effectuate a dissolution of the business and (3) sell his or her business interest without the business manager's consent in the manager's sole discretion could prevent the gifted business interests from qualifying for the gift tax annual exclusion.

This result might be avoided by giving a donee the unilateral right to sell his or her entire interest to third parties, subject to a right of first refusal by the entity and/or other interest holders to purchase the interest at the same price and terms as contained in a bona fide offer from a third party. In addition, perhaps the business manager's discretion to retain funds should be limited to amounts commensurate with the needs of the business with the balance of the funds being distributable to the interest holders. Alternatively, the business agreement could include a provision giving each donee the right to withdraw assets from the entity whenever gifts of entity interest are made, similar to a *Crummey* withdrawal right. The right can be limited to the fair market value of the gifted interests and only be available for a limited period of time. Such a provision should bar any argument that the donee does not have the right to the immediate use, possession and enjoyment of the property in the economic sense.

G. Chapter 14 Valuation Rules Regarding Certain Rights and Restrictions

1.   Buy-Sell Agreements and Other Sale Restrictions: Section 2703

IRC § 2703 limits the use of restrictions placed on a business interest contained in a buy-sell agreement or similar arrangement in the valuation of the business interest. Section 2703 was enacted to stop the perceived abuse in the use of such restrictions, especially in the closely-held business setting. The objective of Section 2703 is to nullify the effect on valuation of restrictions placed on a business interest in any agreement unless the agreement is truly a bona fide, arm's-length agreement. Under IRC § 2703(a), such restrictions are disregarded for estate, gift and GST tax purposes if the agreement is entered into after October 8, 1990 and obligates the owner to sell the business interest for less than fair market value. These limitations apply to any restrictions on a business interest contained in any corporate, partnership or LLC agreement, corporate bylaw, articles of incorporation and capital structure of any entity. Treas. Reg.

21ˢᵗ Century Estate Planning:
Practical Applications
2005 Edition

©2005 Sonnenschein Nath & Rosenthal LLP
and Cannon Financial Institute, Inc.

122

§ 25.2703-1(a)(3). Section 2703 does not affect the contractual rights of the parties to buy or sell the business interest under the buy-sell agreement.

IRC § 2703(b) provides an exception to the general rule in IRC § 2703(a), by setting forth the following factors when a restriction on a business interest will be upheld:

- the agreement must be a bona fide business agreement,
- the agreement must not be a device to transfer the business interest to members of the decedent's family without full and adequate consideration, and
- the terms of the agreement must be comparable to similar arrangements entered into by persons in arm's-length transactions.

A right or restriction is considered to meet each of the above requirements "if more than 50% by value of the property subject to the right or restriction is owned directly or indirectly by individuals who are not members of the transferor's family." Treas. Reg. § 25.2703-1(b)(3).

a. **Modification of Restrictions.** Any restriction on a business interest created prior to October 8, 1990, that is substantially modified after October 8, 1990, also will be subject to the requirements of IRC § 2703. The term "substantial modification" does *not* include:

- a modification that is required by the terms of a right or restriction,
- a discretionary modification that does not change the right or restriction,
- a modification of a capitalization rate provided it bears a fixed relationship to a specified market rate, and
- a modification that results in an option price that is closer to fair market value.

➔ **Planning Point:** Whenever the value of a business interest is being restricted pursuant to an agreement, or in any other manner, and the restricted value is being relied upon for transfer tax purposes, careful consideration of IRC § 2703 is required. By complying with the three requirements contained in IRC § 2703(b), the value of a business interest can be relied on for transfer tax purposes.

2. **Treatment of Certain Restrictions and Lapsing Rights: Section 2704**

Section 2704(a) applies to lapsing liquidation and voting rights and provides that a lapse is a transfer subject to estate, gift or GST tax by the individual holding the lapsing right. The amount of the transfer is the excess of the value of the transferred interest before the lapse over the value of the interest after the lapse. Section 2704(a) only applies if the interest holder and the members of his family control the entity immediately before and after the lapse.

> **EXAMPLE:** A general partner dies and the general partnership interest is converted to a limited partnership by reason of the death of the general partner and passes to the general partner's son. Section

21ˢᵗ Century Estate Planning:
Practical Applications
2005 Edition

©2005 Sonnenschein Nath & Rosenthal LLP
and Cannon Financial Institute, Inc.

123

2704(a) treats as a transfer the difference in the value of the decedent's general partnership interest and the value of the estate's limited partnership interest.

> **EXAMPLE:** D owns 84% of the single outstanding class of stock of corporation Y. The bylaws require at least 70% of the vote to liquidate Y. D gives one-half of D's stock in equal shares to D's three children. Section 2704(a) does not apply to the loss of D's ability to liquidate Y, because the voting rights with respect to the corporation are not restricted or eliminated by reason of the transfer. Treas. Reg. § 25.2704-1(f), Ex. 4.

Under Section 2704(b), if the governing instrument imposes an "applicable restriction," a restriction that is more severe than the default rules under state law, such restriction is ignored in valuing the interest for estate or gift tax purposes. The transfer at issue must be to a member of the donor's family and the family must control the entity immediately before the transfer.

> **EXAMPLE:** A provision in a partnership agreement might restrict a partner from dissolving the partnership, when this right is otherwise given to a partner under state law. Section 2704(b), if applicable, would treat the partnership interest as having the dissolution right otherwise provided under state law when determining the value of this interest for estate or gift tax purposes, thereby making it worth more than would be the case had the restriction on dissolution been taken into consideration.

➔ **Planning Point:** Because state law plays such a vital role in the application of Section 2704, practitioners should use the laws of those states that impose restrictions on the right of a limited partner or member to (1) withdraw from the entity, (2) liquidate or dissolve the entity and (3) transfer interests in the entity.

3. Valuation Freezes

The planning objective in any valuation freeze is to make a gift of property during the grantor's lifetime and allow the transferred property to appreciate outside the grantor's estate. The property can be given to an irrevocable trust or to individuals outright. By giving the property during the grantor's lifetime, the value of the property can be frozen for transfer tax purposes and any appreciation that occurs after the gift is made is not included in the grantor's estate.

Valuation freezes can be accomplished by making lifetime gifts through a number of different planning vehicles, such as the vehicles discussed below.

21st Century Estate Planning:
Practical Applications
2005 Edition

©2005 Sonnenschein Nath & Rosenthal LLP
and Cannon Financial Institute, Inc.

124

a. <u>Grantor Retained Annuity Trusts</u>. The Grantor Retained Annuity Trust ("GRAT"), the Grantor Retained Income Trust ("GRIT"), and the Grantor Retained Unitrust ("GRUT") involve an immediate gift of a remainder interest in property, thereby freezing the value of the remainder interest for transfer tax purposes. For all three trusts, the grantor retains an interest in the trust for a term of years. The remainder interest is transferred to the beneficiaries of the trust after the grantor's retained interest expires. By making a gift of the remainder interest in trust during the grantor's lifetime, the grantor can freeze the value of the remainder interest at the date the trust is established. The remainder interest appreciates outside the grantor's estate and is transferred to the remainder beneficiaries without any further gift or estate tax, provided the grantor dies after the expiration of the retained interest.

The grantor retains the right to an annuity amount with the GRAT, the right to an income interest with the GRIT, and a right to a fixed percentage of trust assets with the GRUT. Detailed rules governing the formation of GRATs, GRITs, and GRUTs are covered in Chapter XVII, Leveraging the Lifetime Transfer of Assets.

b. <u>Qualified Personal Residence Trust</u>. A Qualified Personal Residence Trust ("QPRT") freezes the value of a personal residence or a second/vacation home. The grantor transfers the residence to an irrevocable trust and retains the right to occupy the residence rent-free for a term of years. The remainder interest is given to the beneficiary of the trust, usually the grantor's children. The amount of the gift is the present value of the remainder interest using the applicable remainder factor in Table B. By making a gift of the remainder interest during the grantor's lifetime, the value of the gift is frozen for gift tax purposes. The property can appreciate for the benefit of the children outside of the grantor's estate and be transferred to the children without any further gift or estate tax, provided the grantor dies after the expiration of the term.

➔ **<u>Planning Point</u>:** A non-partition agreement can be used with a QPRT to significantly reduce the value of a jointly-owned residence and thereby reduce the amount of the remainder gift to the beneficiaries.

A detailed discussion of QPRTs and other types of personal residence trusts is presented in Chapter XVII, Leveraging the Lifetime Transfer of Assets.

c. <u>Family Limited Partnerships and Limited Liability Companies</u>. Family Limited Partnerships ("FLPs") and Limited Liability Companies ("LLCs") are planning vehicles used to freeze the value of assets. A variety of different types of properties can be transferred to an FLP or LLC. Due to the restrictions embodied in the FLP or LLC agreement, substantial valuation discounts often are taken on gifts of FLP or LLC interests. The value of the FLP or LLC interest transferred is determined on the date the gift is made and any appreciation that accrues thereafter on the gifted property is outside of the grantor's estate.

An in-depth discussion of FLPs and LLCs is presented in Chapter XV, The Use of Family Limited Partnerships and Family Limited Liability Companies in Estate Planning.

21st Century Estate Planning:
Practical Applications
2005 Edition

©2005 Sonnenschein Nath & Rosenthal LLP
and Cannon Financial Institute, Inc.

125

d. Sale to an Intentionally Defective Grantor Trust. In a sale to an intentionally defective grantor trust ("IDGT"), the grantor sells property at its fair market value to the IDGT in return for an installment note. At the end of the note term, any income and appreciation on the trust assets that exceed the payments required to satisfy the promissory note pass to the beneficiaries of the trust free of estate, gift and GST taxes.

A promissory note bearing interest at the applicable federal rate ("AFR") under Section 1274(d) is deemed to have a fair market value equal to its face amount. Therefore, the sale of assets to the IDGT in return for a promissory note will not be a gift as long as the promissory note equals the value of the property transferred and bears interest at the AFR. An accurate appraisal is essential to support the fair market value claimed in the transaction.

Gift tax concerns may arise if the property that is the subject of the sale is a hard-to-value asset, such as closely held stock. A taxable gift will occur if the value of the property transferred is later determined to be greater than the sale price. Section H. below discusses the most common methods used to minimize the risk that the IRS will increase the value of the property transferred.

A detailed discussion of sales to an intentionally defective grantor trust is presented in Chapter XVII, Leveraging the Lifetime Transfer of Assets.

4. Negotiated Securities Accounts[2]

A Negotiated Securities Account ("NSA") limits the control an owner has over a securities account and shifts the management and investment responsibilities to an account manager. The owner agrees not to withdraw any funds from the account for a term of years and the account manager is given wide discretion to invest and reinvest the funds in the account. Due to the restrictions imposed on the NSA structure, discounts can be taken for valuation purposes. The NSA is intended to compete with and sometimes replace the FLP or LLC structure. The obvious advantage of the NSA is that it is much easier to set up and less costly to maintain than an FLP or LLC.

a. Structure of NSAs. An NSA is created by depositing funds in a managed account with a bank or trust company (not a registered investment advisor). An agreement is then entered into by and between the owner and the account manager. Under the terms of the agreement, the owner is not allowed to withdraw the funds for a specified term of years (*e.g.,* 5 to 10 years) and the account manager has the discretion to invest and reinvest the assets in the account pursuant to a long-term investment strategy that has been previously agreed to by the owner. The owner of the account can give the account or a portion of the account to his or her spouse, children and grandchildren, but the account, or the portion transferred, would remain subject to the restrictions placed on the owner's account.

(1) NSA Agreement Term. The term of the NSA agreement is a critical point in the negotiations between the owner and the account manager. Obviously, the

21st Century Estate Planning:
Practical Applications
2005 Edition

©*2005 Sonnenschein Nath & Rosenthal LLP*
and Cannon Financial Institute, Inc.

126

longer the term, the more leverage the owner would have to negotiate a lower management fee. Additionally, a longer term will result in a larger valuation discount over the assets in the NSA for transfer tax purposes.

➔ **Planning Point:** The owner can extend the term of the agreement annually after the expiration of the first year so that the restrictions on the account are in place for the desired term of years. For example, if the initial term of the agreement is for six years, after year one, the owner can extend the agreement by one year so the six-year term of restriction on the account is maintained. The reason the owner would consider extending the restricted term in this manner is to ensure that the restriction period on the account is in place for a minimum number of years in order to maximize the amount of the discount to which the owner would be entitled if he or she were to die. The account also could have an automatic renewal provision. After the first year, the restricted term can automatically renew for another year to preserve the six-year term of restriction over the account. This would ease any administrative inconvenience on the owner to maintain the account. The owner also could consider an automatic renewal that would occur only after the end of the restriction period, but this alternative would limit the size of the discount if the owner dies near the end of the restriction period.

(2) **NSA Formation Considerations.** It is important for the owner to be comfortable with the restrictions on the NSA. The owner must select a term of years that, on balance, will provide the desired discount and not unduly burden or restrict his or her ability to obtain unfettered control over the account in the future. The owner also must determine who will be the permitted transferees of the NSA. Should the permitted transferees be limited to family members or also include unrelated parties? Finally, it is essential that the owner select an account manager that he or she is comfortable working with. When selecting an account manager, the owner should keep in mind that the NSA cannot be transferred to another account manager or terminated without the mutual consent of the owner and account manager. The account manager also should not be a related person as defined in IRC § 267(b) or a subordinated person as defined in IRC § 674(c).

(3) **NSA Income Distributions.** The owner of an NSA could require a distribution of all or a specified portion of the income earned in the account; however, such a requirement likely would decrease the amount of the discount because the owner would have the use and enjoyment of such property. By allowing the NSA to retain all of its income, the restrictions on the use and enjoyment of the property will be maximized and thereby the available discounts also will be maximized.

(4) **NSA Business Purpose.** The business purpose for entering into an NSA agreement is to allow the account manager to pursue a long-term investment strategy that should increase the overall performance of the investment. In exchange, the owner should

21st Century Estate Planning:
Practical Applications
2005 Edition

©2005 Sonnenschein Nath & Rosenthal LLP
and Cannon Financial Institute, Inc.

127

receive a reduced management fee for the management of the NSA since the account manager would control the account until the expiration of the term of the NSA agreement.

→ **Planning Point:** An NSA agreement is an agreement between the owner and an account manager. Since the owner does not have the power to unilaterally change the terms of the agreement, all of the issues that are of concern to the owner, (*e.g.*, permitted transferees, account manager duties, management fees, investment strategy, investment goals, and diversification of assets) should be thoroughly discussed and agreed upon before the NSA agreement is signed.

b. **Discounting the Value of the NSA.** The NSA utilizes two discounting principles: lack of marketability and lack of control. Both discounts can be utilized to reduce the value of the NSA for gift and estate tax purposes.

(1) **NSA Discounts.** The agreement entered into between the owner and account manager usually restricts the transfer of the NSA to anyone other than the owner's spouse, children, and grandchildren. Even after the owner transfers the account or a portion of the account to a spouse, child, or grandchild, the same restrictions on the NSA would remain in place. Therefore, the NSA lacks marketability. The owner also does not have control over the management and investment decisions of the account and cannot unilaterally terminate the agreement or transfer the account without the consent of the account manager. Therefore, the owner lacks control over the account.

(2) **Discount Comparison.** There is no authority that directly addresses valuation discounts for NSAs. However, discounts on NSAs can be analogized with valuation discounts taken on restricted stock and FLPs.

- Rule 144 of the Securities Act restricts the sale of stock for a period of one year. This restriction has resulted in a discount of approximately 25% on such restricted stock. See, e.g., *Trust Services of America, Inc. v. Comm'r*, 88-1 USTC ¶13,767, *rev'd in part*, 885 F.2d 561 (9th Cir. 1989). Since the period of restriction on an NSA usually will be greater than one year, a greater than 25% discount should be available.
- Since FLPs and LLCs use the same two discounting principles much in the same manner as an NSA, an NSA should also be able to receive discounts in the same range as the discounts taken on FLPs and LLCs. FLP and LLC discounts normally range from 20% to 60%.

(3) **Delay of Gift.** A transfer of the NSA by gift should be delayed for a reasonable period of time after the account is created so that the IRS cannot assert a position that, pursuant to IRC § 2703, the NSA was merely a device to transfer property to the next generation for less than full and adequate consideration.

21st Century Estate Planning:
Practical Applications
2005 Edition

©2005 Sonnenschein Nath & Rosenthal LLP
and Cannon Financial Institute, Inc.

128

EXAMPLE: X owns $3 million worth of securities in a managed account at a bank or trust company that is not a registered investment advisor. X and the account manager enter into an NSA agreement for a six-year term. The account manager has the exclusive right to manage and invest the account for the six-year term. X cannot withdraw the funds from the account, has no authority over the management and investment of the account assets, and can transfer the account, or an interest therein, only to his spouse, children and grandchildren. The account manager agrees to reduce the management fee normally charged by 10% over the term of the agreement. The account can be terminated only by the consent of X and the account manager.

One year after establishing the NSA, X decides to transfer $1,000,000 of assets in the NSA to his son. The $1,000,000 worth of securities is distributed from the NSA to a separate account for the benefit of X's son. The application of the lack of control and lack of marketability discounts reduces the value of the gift by 35%. Therefore, the value of the gift would be reduced by $350,000 ($1,000,000 x 35%) resulting in a gift valued at $650,000 instead of $1,000,000. These discounts would result in a potential gift tax savings of up to $175,000 (assuming X has no credit amount remaining and is subject to a gift tax rate of 50%).

Two years after establishing the NSA, X dies. X's NSA is then transferred to X's son. The remaining assets in X's NSA have a face value of $2 million at X's death. When the remaining assets in the NSA are appraised, they will still be eligible for the combined 35% discount because the NSA is still subject to the original restrictions. The value of the NSA in X's estate would be reduced by $700,000 ($2,000,000 x 35%), resulting in a transfer of $1.3 million ($2,000,000 - $700,000) for estate tax purposes. These discounts would result in an estate tax savings of up to $350,000 (assuming X has no credit amount remaining and his estate is subject to an estate tax rate of 50%).

By using an NSA, X will be able to transfer securities worth $3 million to X's son and pay transfer taxes only on $1,950,000 ($650,000 + $1,300,000), thereby saving X the transfer tax on $1,050,000. While X's son will still be bound by the restrictions imposed on the NSA, these restrictions will expire in four years.

21st Century Estate Planning:
Practical Applications
2005 Edition

©2005 Sonnenschein Nath & Rosenthal LLP
and Cannon Financial Institute, Inc.

129

c. **Statutory Restriction on NSAs.**

        (1)   **General Rule.** IRC § 2703 allows the IRS to disregard the valuation of a business interest in a buy-sell agreement or other agreement that attempts to restrict the value of the business interest. An NSA also is subject to general rules set forth in IRC § 2703.

        (2)   **Exception to the General Rule.** There is an exception to the general rule contained in IRC § 2703(b), which provides that a buy-sell or other restrictive agreement can be used to determine the value of the business interest if the agreement is (i) a bona fide business arrangement, (ii) not a device to transfer property to family members for less than full and adequate consideration, and (iii) comparable to similar arrangements entered into by persons in arm's-length transactions.

        (3)   **Bona Fide and Comparable Arrangement.** The NSA agreement should satisfy parts (i) and (iii) of IRC § 2703(b) because the agreement is a bona fide business arrangement and is entered into by two unrelated and independent parties in an arm's-length transaction. Both the owner of the account and the account manager have an interest in negotiating suitable terms for the agreement. The owner wants to have a lower management fee and an increased rate of return on his investment by using a long-term investment strategy. The account manager wants to have a long-term client and the freedom to buy and sell securities to accomplish the long-term strategy. Thus, the NSA arrangement easily should meet parts (i) and (iii) of IRC § 2703(b).

        (4)   **Not A "Device".** The NSA agreement also should satisfy part (ii) of IRC § 2703(b) because the NSA is not a device to transfer property to family members for less than full value. The IRS has held that the term "device" includes any restrictions that artificially reduce the value of the transferred interest for transfer tax purposes without ultimately reducing the value of the interest in the hands of the transferee. TAM 9842003 (October 6, 1998) and PLR 9730004 (April 3, 1997). In making this pronouncement, the IRS focused on FLPs wherein the grantor's general partnership interest is transferred to the grantor's children. The IRS held that since the children were general partners and could change or eliminate the restrictions placed on the FLP at any time, the restrictions on the FLP at the grantor's death were artificial, the transaction was merely a "device" under § 2703(b), and any reduction in value of the assets in the FLP should be ignored. In other words, the restrictions on the FLP interests that gave rise to the discounts were artificial and the FLP was just a sham used to reduce the value of the business interest for gift and estate tax purposes.

        In contrast, the restrictions placed on an NSA will remain in place even after the account is transferred by gift or on death to the owner's children. Therefore, the restrictions that give rise to the discounts remain in place and restrict the transferee's interest in the account. The restrictions in an NSA are real and not just a sham used to reduce the value of the assets for gift and estate tax purposes.

21st Century Estate Planning:
Practical Applications
2005 Edition

©2005 Sonnenschein Nath & Rosenthal LLP
and Cannon Financial Institute, Inc.

130

The IRS also has held that a "device" is a restriction imposed for the sole and primary reason of avoiding federal taxes. PLR 9736004 (June 5, 1997). Valuation discounts for the transfer of FLP interests created shortly before the transferor's death have been challenged by the IRS based on the argument that the creation and existence of the FLP is merely to avoid tax. Since the NSA has significant and credible non-tax benefits, the NSA should withstand an IRS attack based on the argument that its creation and existence is merely to avoid tax.

d. NSA Less Susceptible to IRS Attack. The IRS has taken the position that it will closely scrutinize FLP and LLC arrangements because they are agreements between family members. See *Kincaid v. U.S.*, 682 F.2d 1220 (5th Cir. 1982). An NSA is not susceptible to the same IRS attacks because the NSA arrangement is not an agreement between family members. To the contrary, the NSA arrangement is a negotiated transaction between two unrelated persons who have differing financial interests in the arrangement. Thus, even though the NSA uses the same discounting principles as the FLP, there are significant differences in the two planning vehicles that make the NSA far less susceptible to an IRS attack. Additionally, an NSA is not a corporation and, with only one owner, cannot be considered a partnership; therefore, IRC §§ 2701 and 2704 are not applicable to NSAs.

(1) Lack of Formalities. Certain formalities must be followed for an FLP to be recognized as a separate legal entity. The centerpiece of any FLP is a comprehensive partnership agreement. In most states, a limited partnership also is required to file a certificate of partnership. Federal and state partnership income tax returns also are required to be filed each year the partnership exists. By contrast, an NSA can be created with fewer formalities. An NSA would require a management agreement. The management agreement, however, would be between only the owner and an account manager and would be far less comprehensive and complex than an FLP partnership agreement. The owner would not be required to file a separate income tax return for the NSA or file any documents with the state.

➔   **Planning Point:** Even though an NSA would cost far less to set up and maintain over the years, it is essential that the management agreement is drafted in a manner that is consistent with the owner's overall estate planning goals.

(2) Restrictions on FLP Interests are More Suspect. Restrictions based on intra-family arrangements are more suspect than arrangements between independent third parties. An FLP is an agreement by and between family members. The discount in value for the transfer of an FLP interest is directly attributed to the restrictions created by the family members and placed upon themselves. The IRS regularly attacks the discounts taken in the FLP arrangement because the restrictions in the partnership agreement are controlled by the family members.

By contrast, an NSA is not an intra-family arrangement. It is an agreement between two independent third parties who have differing interests. The agreement is negotiated to benefit each party and is truly an arm's-length transaction. The restrictions imposed on the NSA by the

21ˢᵗ Century Estate Planning:
Practical Applications
2005 Edition

©2005 Sonnenschein Nath & Rosenthal LLP
and Cannon Financial Institute, Inc.

131

agreement can be changed only by mutual consent of both parties. Any proposed change by the owner will be closely scrutinized by the account manager, especially if the change would affect the account manager's compensation or ability to maintain the account for the long term.

(3) **Business Purpose.** There must be a valid non-tax business purpose. The validity of the business purpose depends on the facts and circumstances of each situation. In many FLPs it may be difficult to justify why family members should be involved in a common business enterprise at all, especially if certain family members do not possess the requisite skills or education needed to be involved in the enterprise.

The non-tax business purpose of an NSA is to obtain a better return on investment with a long-term management strategy and lower management fees. There is no need to justify a valid non-tax business purpose because one truly exists.

(4) **Contributions to FLP May Trigger Capital Gain.** A partner's contribution of non-identical assets to an FLP may result in recognition of capital gain unless each partner contributes a "diversified portfolio" of securities as defined in Treas. Reg. § 1.351-1(c)(6)(i). By contrast, since an NSA has only one owner, the owner may contribute any type of securities to the NSA and not trigger the recognition of any capital gain.

(5) **Gift on Formation of FLP.** Under the gift tax regulations and *Comm'r v. Wemyss*, 324 U.S. 303 (1945), an unequal exchange of assets constitutes a taxable gift unless the transfer can be characterized as a transfer in the ordinary course of business. The IRS has attacked an FLP arrangement as an "unequal exchange" where the grantor contributed property to the FLP in exchange for only a limited partnership interest. TAM 9842003. Since the grantor's children received a general partnership interest in the FLP by contributing an unequal amount of property or property with a *de minimis* value, the IRS attacked the FLP as an unequal exchange that resulted in a gift by the parent to the children.

By contrast, the NSA arrangement cannot create a gift on its formation because the owner has not transferred any interest in the NSA to anyone. In fact, all of the assets in the NSA are includable in the owner's estate. Additionally, the NSA arrangement cannot be considered an "unequal exchange" because it is a negotiated business agreement.

e. **Conclusion.** The restrictions placed on an NSA will support a discount to reduce the federal transfer tax value below the aggregate fair market value of the NSA. The NSA is simpler to create, less expensive to maintain, and should be less vulnerable to an IRS attack than an FLP. Therefore, when dealing with securities, the NSA is a superior estate planning device. When dealing with real property, however, the FLP remains a very important estate planning tool.

21st Century Estate Planning:
Practical Applications
2005 Edition

©2005 Sonnenschein Nath & Rosenthal LLP
and Cannon Financial Institute, Inc.

132

H. Minimizing Valuation Risks in Lifetime Transfers

Anytime a donor makes a lifetime gift of property, there is a risk that the IRS will attempt to increase the value of the property reported on the gift tax return. If the IRS is successful, an unexpected gift tax liability may arise along with the associated interest and penalties.

Different methods are used to minimize the risk that the IRS will increase the value of the property reported on the gift tax return. This section will discuss the methods most commonly used to minimize that risk.

1. *Procter* and Valuation Formulas

a. General Rule. The seminal case in the area of revaluation is *Comm'r v. Procter*, 142 F.2d 824 (4th Cir. 1944). *Procter* involved a transfer by gift to a trust. The trust provided that if a federal court of last resort held that any part of the transfer was a taxable gift, that portion of the property subject to gift tax would be excluded from the transfer. The court held that this was a condition subsequent and it violated public policy. The court stated that there were three reasons for declaring the condition subsequent void:

- It would deter the IRS from auditing returns because there would be no possibility to collect tax,
- The donees would not be parties to the tax litigation and might later try to enforce the gift and
- This type of provision would obstruct the administration of justice because as soon as a court rules that the value of the gift should be increased, the trust instrument revokes the gift and makes the court's ruling moot.

b. Valuation Formulas. The IRS and the courts have continued to confirm *Procter*. See, e.g., *Estate of McClendon v. Comm'r*, T.C. Memo. 1993-459, *rev'd on other grounds*, 77 F.3d 477 (5th Cir. 1995); *Ward v. Comm'r*, 87 T.C. 78 (1986); Rev. Rul. 86-41, 1986-1 C.B. 300. Practitioners have responded by creating valuation formulas (also called "valuation definition clauses" or "defined value gifts") that attempt to avoid the risk of revaluation. One valuation formula specifies the dollar amount of the gift and then calculates what portion of the property would be needed to satisfy the amount of the gift. This valuation formula arguably avoids the creation of a condition subsequent and the transferring of property back to the grantor. In other words, the donee never has a right to the portion of property that exceeds the specified dollar amount. While the IRS appeared at first to favor these valuation formulas (see, e.g., TAM 8611004, in which the IRS granted the ruling requests of a taxpayer who transferred "such interest in X partnership as has a fair market value of $13,000," although neither one of the issues at stake concerned the validity of this formula), the IRS has recently ruled that these clauses are invalid. In TAM 200337012, the taxpayer transferred "that fraction of Assignor's Limited Partnership Interest . . . which has a fair market value . . . of $a." The taxpayer reported the transfer on a federal gift tax return as a gift of a specific percentage

21st Century Estate Planning:
Practical Applications
2005 Edition

©2005 Sonnenschein Nath & Rosenthal LLP
and Cannon Financial Institute, Inc.

133

partnership interest with a value of $5,000 less than the figure mentioned in the deed of gift. Relying on the above-cited cases and ruling, the IRS stated that the formula gift clause was ineffective for gift tax purposes because it violated public policy. The IRS saw no difference between a valuation clause such as the one at issue in this TAM and the revaluation clauses in *Procter* and its progeny.

Other valuation formulas have not been any more successful. In TAM 200245053, the taxpayer, as trustee of a revocable trust, sold a fractional share of a 98.9% limited partnership interest to his irrevocable trust. The fraction used to determine the share of the limited partnership interest had a numerator equal to the stated purchase price and a denominator equal to the fair market value of a 98.9% interest in the limited partnership interest. The sale agreement stated that the fair market value of the limited partnership interest "shall be such value as finally determined for federal gift tax purposes." The sale agreement stated that the parties reached a tentative agreement that the percentage interest transferred was the revocable trust's entire interest. The sale agreement also stated that the agreement may be modified if the IRS determines that the sale actually conveyed a different percentage than 98.9%. Upon such a determination by the IRS, the ownership interests and prior distributions would be adjusted. The IRS stated that this clause was against public policy, relying on *Ward* and Rev. Rul. 86-41. The IRS stated that the formula was an "attempt to ameliorate any adverse consequences if the Service challenged the transaction and thereby to discourage any such challenge," and that the clause "does not serve a legitimate purpose."

While the IRS may disfavor valuation formulas, the Tax Court may have given some hope for the validity of these formulas. In *McCord v. Comm'r*, 120 T.C. 358 (2003), the taxpayers formed a limited partnership to hold various investment assets, including stocks, bonds, real estate and other limited partnership interests. The taxpayers then gave partnership interests to their children and certain charities under a formula clause that purported to give (a) $6,910,933 worth of partnership interest to the taxpayers' children and trusts for their benefit; (b) $134,000 worth of partnership interests to the Shreveport Symphony (but not more than the difference between the value of the total gift and the amount allocated to the children and their trusts) and (c) the balance to a second charity (later determined to be $324,345). The donees were required to determine the value of the partnership interests and to allocate the gift among themselves using gift tax valuation methods. The IRS valued the total gift at $12,426,086, and declined to recognize the validity of the formula clause, upholding its position in FSA 200122011, which dealt with a similar formula.

The Tax Court determined the value of the total gift to be $9,883,832. The court then stated that the specific formula clause might be valid to limit the amount given to the children and their trusts, but that it did not create a charitable deduction for the entire additional amount passing to the charity because it relied on the valuation fixed by the donees, rather than one fixed by the courts. The court stated that it did not, therefore, have to reach the question of whether such a formula clause would be enforced if it was tied directly to the gift tax values set by the court. The court stated, however, that it might have allowed the larger charitable deduction had the agreement given each donee the "enforceable right to a fraction of the gifted interest

21ˢᵗ Century Estate Planning:
Practical Applications
2005 Edition

©2005 Sonnenschein Nath & Rosenthal LLP
and Cannon Financial Institute, Inc.

134

determined with reference to the fair market value of the gifted interest as finally determined for Federal gift tax purposes." The taxpayers could, therefore, deduct as the gift to the second charity for gift tax purposes only the amount actually allocated to the second charity by the donees' agreement, rather than the difference between the court's valuation of the gift and the amount allocated to the children and the Shreveport Symphony, thus creating a $2,514,554 net additional taxable gift. ($9,883,832 - $7,044,933 - $324,345). Thus, *McCord* may be the beginning of a general acceptance of valuation formulas that rely on a value as finally determined for gift tax purposes. The remainder may be transferred to either a charity or a spouse, which avoids additional gift taxes. As of early 2005, *McCord* is on appeal to the Fifth Circuit.

2. Other Techniques to Minimize Valuation Risks

The Marital Formula and Charitable Formula are variations on the general valuation formula described above and also are used to avoid the risk of revaluation.

a. **Marital Formula.**
The marital formula provides that any part of a transfer that is determined to be a taxable gift is redirected to the spouse or a trust for the spouse's benefit. If the IRS increases the value of the property reported on the gift tax return, the marital formula would direct the taxable portion of the gift to the spouse or to a Qualified Terminable Interest Property ("QTIP") trust for the benefit of the spouse and thereby use the marital deduction to eliminate any gift tax liability.

The primary concern in using the marital formula is that it redirects the excess gift away from the trust beneficiaries and gives the property to the spouse or to a trust for the benefit of the spouse. Since the redirection of the excess gift would occur only after an audit, the marital formula also may appear to be more of a condition subsequent and therefore invalid.

➔ **Planning Point:** As a practical matter, marital formulas are not frequently used because of the risk of divorce. If the parties divorce, the excess gift cannot be diverted from the former spouse because an irrevocable gift already has been made. The former spouse would have full control over the gifted property and could transfer the property to whomever he or she wished.

b. **Charitable Formula.**
The charitable formula is similar to the marital formula except that the excess gift is transferred to a charity rather than the spouse or a QTIP trust. See *McCord*, supra. The charity can be a public charity or the grantor's private foundation.

The use of the charitable formula is subject to the same concerns as the marital formula described above. The IRS could argue that the charitable formula is a condition subsequent and therefore invalid. The charitable formula also will prevent the grantor's family from ever

21st Century Estate Planning:
Practical Applications
2005 Edition

©2005 Sonnenschein Nath & Rosenthal LLP
and Cannon Financial Institute, Inc.

135

succeeding to the property. If the amount of the excess gift is substantial, a larger than expected gift away from the grantor's family may occur.

3. Protective Limited Power of Appointment[3]

The Protective Limited Power of Appointment ("Protective LPA") is similar to the valuation formulas in that it protects against the revaluation of assets and imposition of additional gift tax. However, the Protective LPA does not change the beneficiary or change the characterization of the gift.

a. Structure of the Protective LPA. The Protective LPA may be used in an irrevocable trust. The trust provides that upon receipt of property from the grantor for less than adequate consideration (a gift), the property is divided into a "Protective LPA share" and a "non-Protective LPA share." The Protective LPA share receives that portion of the gift that exceeds the specified dollar amount of the gift (*i.e.*, the difference between the grantor's specified dollar amount of the gift reported on the gift tax return and the increased value of the gift determined by the IRS). The non-Protective LPA share receives the balance of the property gifted. The grantor is given an *inter vivos* and testamentary limited power of appointment over the Protective LPA share. Therefore, the grantor can appoint the Protective LPA share to anyone other than the grantor, his or her creditors, his or her estate, or the creditors of his or her estate.

Since the grantor reserves the power over the Protective LPA share to name a new beneficiary or change the interests of the existing beneficiaries, the gift of the Protective LPA share to the trust is not a completed gift pursuant to Treas. Reg. § 25.2511-2(c).

b. Revaluation Risk of the Protective LPA. The Protective LPA reduces the risk of revaluation (i) without changing the identity of the donee or the amount of the gift, and (ii) without eliminating the IRS' incentive to audit. The grantor would transfer the property to the trust and the property would be held in trust, subject to the terms of the trust agreement. The grantor would retain a power to alter the beneficiaries or to change the interests of the existing beneficiaries. If the IRS were to increase the value of the gift, an allocation of the excess gifted value would be made to the Protective LPA share. The grantor of the Protective LPA share would retain a limited power of appointment over that property. Since the Protective LPA share is defined at the outset of the transfer to the irrevocable trust, there is no condition subsequent.

The Protective LPA would not deter the IRS from auditing the gift tax returns. Since the Protective LPA share is included in the grantor's estate as a retained interest, the IRS has an incentive to audit the gift tax return to ensure that the value of the property allocated to the non-Protective LPA share is proper. If the IRS is able to increase the value of the gift, the excess could be added to the Protective LPA share, thereby increasing the size of the grantor's estate.

The IRS has recognized the use of a similar general power of appointment based on a formula in PLR 9110054. The general power of appointment-based formula operated over that portion of the trust that was not exempt from the generation-skipping transfer tax.

21st Century Estate Planning:
Practical Applications
2005 Edition

©2005 Sonnenschein Nath & Rosenthal LLP
and Cannon Financial Institute, Inc.

136

→ **Planning Point:** The Protective LPA and the valuation formulas can be used on the same gift. The grantor would then have a safety net against the risk of revaluation if one method fails. The grantor also should consider exercising the Protective LPA in favor of a marital trust to defer any estate taxes.

21ˢᵗ Century Estate Planning:
Practical Applications
2005 Edition

©2005 Sonnenschein Nath & Rosenthal LLP
and Cannon Financial Institute, Inc.

137

Chapter V
Bibliography

Michael F. Beausand, Jr. et al., 830 T.M., *Valuation: General and Real Estate.*

Jonathan G. Blattmachr and Richard S. Kinyan, *Valuation Techniques in Estate Planning* (1995).

Regis W. Campfield et al., *Taxation of Estates, Gifts and Trusts* (21st ed. 1999).

David A. Handler and Deborah V. Dunn, "The LPA Lid: A New Way to 'Contain' Gift Revaluations," 27 *Est. Plan.* 206.

Richard L. Lavoie et al., 831-2nd T.M., *Valuation of Corporate Stock.*

Ray D. Madoff et al., *Practical Guide to Estate Planning* (2001).

Carlyn S. McCaffrey, *Estate Freezes & Valuation Under Chapter 14: Implementing the New Regulations* (1991).

Carlyn S. McCaffrey and Mildred Kalik, "Using Valuation Clauses to Avoid Gift Taxes," 125 *Tr. & Est.* 47.

Louis A. Mezzullo, *Valuation Rules Under Chapter 14: The Impact on Gift and Estate Taxation* (1995).

John R. Price, *Price on Contemporary Estate Planning* (2nd ed. 2001).

Adena W. Testa et al., 835 T.M., *Chapter 14.*

Steven E. Zumback et al., 833 T.M., *Special Use Valuation.*

Online Research and Web Sites

Banister Financial, Inc.

http://www.businessvalue.com/valarticles.htm (provides many articles on the valuation of business interests).

Kelley Blue Book

http://www.businessvalue.com/valarticles.htm (provides information on vehicle valuations).

Timevalue Software Applicable Federal Rates

http://www.timevalue.com/afrindex.htm (provides monthly AFR information, including IRC § 7520 rates, from 1996 to the present).

21st Century Estate Planning:
Practical Applications
2005 Edition

©2005 Sonnenschein Nath & Rosenthal LLP
and Cannon Financial Institute, Inc.

138

Valuation Resources.com

http://valuationresources.com/(provides valuation resources for business appraisers).

---

[1] *Modified by* Rev. Rul. 65-193, 1965-2 C.B. 370 (deleting portions of Section 4.02(f) regarding intangibles valuation); *amplified by* Rev. Rul. 77-287, 1977-2 C.B. 319 (valuation of stock subject to SEC restrictions); *amplified by* Rev. Rul. 80-214, 1980-2 C.B. 101 (valuation of stock "stapled" or "paired" with another corporation); and *amplified by* Rev. Rul. 83-120, 1983-2 C.B. 170 (valuation of preferred stock). Additionally, the valuation methodology of Rev. Rul. 59-60 was extended to income tax and other tax situations and to the valuation of non-corporate business entities by Rev. Rul. 68-609, 1968-2 C.B. 327.

[2] This concept was developed by Roy M. Adams and his former colleagues while he was a member of Kirkland & Ellis LLP. For an excellent discussion of this concept, see Roy M. Adams, "Ethics at the Edge: Sophisticated Estate Planning and Professional Responsibility," *35th Annual Philip E. Heckerling Inst. on Est. Plan.*, Ch. 17 (2001); and Roy M. Adams, "Proprietary Estate Planning - For Your Eyes Only!," *Notre Dame Tax & Est. Plan. Inst.*, Ch. 21 (2000).

[3] This concept was developed by Roy M. Adams and his former colleagues while he was a member of Kirkland & Ellis LLP. For an excellent discussion of this concept, see Roy M. Adams, "Ethics at the Edge: Sophisticated Estate Planning and Professional Responsibility," *35th Annual Philip E. Heckerling Inst. on Est. Plan.*, Ch. 17 (2001); and Roy M. Adams, "Proprietary Estate Planning - For Your Eyes Only!," *Notre Dame Tax & Est. Plan. Inst.*, Ch. 21 (2000). See also David A. Handler and Deborah V. Dunn, "The LPA Lid: A New Way to 'Contain' Gift Revaluations," 27 *Est. Plan.* 206 (June 2000)

21st Century Estate Planning:
Practical Applications
2005 Edition

©2005 Sonnenschein Nath & Rosenthal LLP
and Cannon Financial Institute, Inc.

139

VI. FEDERAL INCOME TAXATION OF TRUSTS AND ESTATES

A. Introduction

In many ways, the federal income taxation of trusts and estates is similar to the federal income taxation of individuals. Concepts such as gross income, taxable income and deductions are common to both sets of income tax rules. Certain characteristics of trusts and estates, however, contribute to the complexity of the income tax rules for trusts and estates. For example, ownership of trusts and estates is split into a legal interest owned by the fiduciary and an equitable interest owned by the beneficiaries. This split ownership causes difficulty in identifying the appropriate taxpayer.

This chapter discusses the following topics related to the federal income taxation of trusts and estates:

- Working Definitions
- Computation of the Tax
- Taxation of Simple Trusts, Complex Trusts and Estates
- Throwback Tax
- Grantor Trusts
- Duties and Forms to File
- Income in Respect of a Decedent

B. Working Definitions

For trusts and estates, a preliminary issue is identifying who is subject to income taxation. For estates, it could be the estate or the beneficiaries. For trusts, it could be the trust, the grantor or the beneficiaries. The Internal Revenue Code sets forth tax rules devised specifically to deal with the varied: (1) interests of income and remainder beneficiaries, (2) distribution provisions in a given document and (3) discretionary decisions that alter the balance from account-to-account and year-to-year.

To sort out this complex taxation issue, it is important to first understand some key terms in the taxation of trusts and estates. This section provides the reader with some working definitions. Generally, there are three ways of looking at income: (1) "taxable income," (2) "fiduciary accounting income," and (3) "distributable net income." In addition, for federal income tax purposes, every trust can be classified as a "grantor trust" or "non-grantor trust," and every non-grantor trust can be further classified annually as either a "simple trust" or "complex trust," depending on what distributions or accumulations the trust makes during the year. These terms are defined below:

21st Century Estate Planning:
Practical Applications
2005 Edition

©2005 Sonnenschein Nath & Rosenthal LLP
and Cannon Financial Institute, Inc.

140

1.   Taxable Income

Generally, the computation and the definition of the "taxable income" of a trust or estate is the same as the computation and the definition of the taxable income of an individual, except as otherwise provided in Internal Revenue Code ("IRC") §§ 641 through 685. IRC § 641(b). IRC § 61 defines "gross income" for individual income tax purposes as income from whatever source derived, including (but not limited to) specifically enumerated items of income. Some of these listed items of income that also apply to trusts and estates include gross income derived from business, gains derived from dealings in property, interest, dividends, rents, royalties, income from life insurance and endowment contracts, the distributive share of partnership gross income, income in respect of a decedent and income from an interest in an estate or trust.

2.   Fiduciary Accounting Income

a. Definition. The term "fiduciary accounting income" ("FAI") is defined as the amount of income of the trust or estate for the taxable year, as determined under the terms of the governing instrument and applicable local law. Extraordinary dividends or taxable stock dividends which the fiduciary deems to be allocable to the trust principal under the trust instrument and local law, however, are <u>not</u> considered FAI. IRC § 643(b).

FAI refers to the <u>non-tax</u> concept of classifying receipts and expenditures as income versus principal in order to determine the amount of income distributable to the income beneficiaries from the trust or the estate each year. FAI does not determine the amount of taxable income allocated between the trust or estate and the beneficiaries. Taxable income allocated to the beneficiaries is determined by a separate concept of income.

(1)   Income. For FAI purposes, income is a net amount (*i.e.*, receipts minus expenditures), and is determined annually. Interest from bonds or certificates of deposit, cash dividends from stocks or mutual funds, rental income from investment real estate and other items of ordinary income are typically allocated to FAI. Fiduciary fees and administrative expenses are typically divided between income and principal but may be allocated entirely to income or to principal in accordance with the governing instrument or state law. When the controlling document is silent, allocation to accounting income and principal is determined under the Uniform Principal and Income Act or similar state law governing the trust or estate. Expenses that are typically allocated to income include income taxes, property taxes, maintenance costs and one-half of fiduciary fees.

(2)   Principal. For FAI purposes, principal includes capital gains, stock dividends, stock splits and proceeds from the sale of principal property. For estates, principal includes all estate assets at the decedent's date of death. Fiduciary fees and administrative expenses are typically divided between income and principal, unless specifically related to a principal transaction. Expenses typically allocated to principal include commissions on the sale of an asset, the cost of capital improvements and one-half of fiduciary fees.

21ˢᵗ Century Estate Planning:
Practical Applications
2005 Edition

©*2005 Sonnenschein Nath & Rosenthal LLP*
and Cannon Financial Institute, Inc.

141

b. __Governing Law.__ No generally accepted accounting principles or specific body of law govern FAI. Accordingly, income and principal for FAI purposes is generally determined with reference to the following sources in the order listed below:

- The governing instrument, whether a trust instrument or a will.
- Local law (generally a version of the Uniform Principal and Income Act).
- Uniform Principal and Income Act or court guidance.

If trust provisions fundamentally depart from the local law in determining what constitutes FAI income, the regulations provide that the trust will not be recognized for federal income tax purposes.

> __EXAMPLE:__ The trust instrument directs that all income be paid to B but defines ordinary dividends and interest as principal (even though these items are usually items of income). The trust will not be considered a trust which requires the distribution of all of its income currently for federal income tax purposes under IRC § 642(b) (personal exemptions) and IRC § 651 ("simple trusts"). Treas. Reg. § 1.643(b)-1.

c. __Definition of Income Under Final IRC § 643(b) Regulations.__ Final regulations regarding the definition of income were released on December 30, 2003. T.D. 9102. The final regulations are similar to the proposed regulations issued on February 15, 2001 (REG-106513-00) with some changes made to reflect comments. The regulations are a response to changing market conditions and state statutes governing prudent investing. Many trusts are investing primarily for capital appreciation, which has raised issues regarding whether an income beneficiary can receive more from a trust than what is traditionally labeled "income." This in turn has raised new issues regarding the tax treatment of characterizing certain receipts as income or principal.

Under the final regulations, "income" is defined as the amount of income of an estate or trust for the taxable year determined under the terms of the governing instrument and applicable local law. This definition is unchanged. The trust agreement and local law must follow traditional concepts of income and principal. Trust income, consistent with state law, may be defined as a unitrust amount or be determined in the trustee's discretion by making reasonable adjustments to trust income and principal to reflect total trust earnings, including ordinary and tax-exempt income, capital gains and appreciation. Treas. Reg. § 1.643(b)-1. Allocations to principal of traditional income items such as dividends or interest will be respected only in limited circumstances authorized by state law, including decisions by the state's highest court.

(1) __Adjustments to Income and Principal__. A state statute that "permits the trustee to make adjustments between income and principal to fulfill the trustee's

21ˢᵗ Century Estate Planning:
Practical Applications
2005 Edition

©2005 Sonnenschein Nath & Rosenthal LLP
and Cannon Financial Institute, Inc.

142

duty of impartiality between the income and remainder beneficiaries" is generally considered a reasonable apportionment of total return. Id. The trustee's adjustments do not have to be consistent from year to year, as long as they comply with state law. This allocation will be respected regardless of the number of income beneficiaries and regardless of whether the income must be paid or may be accumulated by the trust.

(2) **Unitrust Percentages**. A unitrust interest in the range of 3% to 5% (inclusive) and in accordance with state law, is considered a fair apportionment to income of the trust's total return. The periodic redetermination of the fair market value of the trust may occur on a particular date each year or be calculated as an average over several years.

(3) **Switching Methods**. The final regulations also describe the rules for switching between methods of distributing income. If the trust complies with state law in both the manner of switching and the types of methods available, then the switch will not be a taxable sale or disposition under IRC § 1001 and will not be treated as a gift.

➔   **Planning Point:** Note, however, that if the methods of distributing income are not specifically authorized by state statute, but are valid under state law (such as a switch in accordance with a judicial decision or a binding non-judicial settlement), the switch may constitute a recognition event for purposes of IRC § 1001 and may result in a taxable gift. Treas. Reg. § 1.643(b)-1.

(4) **Effective Dates**. The final regulations apply to trusts and estates for taxable years ending after January 2, 2004. Taxpayers may apply the final regulations to any year in which a trust or estate is governed by a state law described in the regulations that permits a trustee to adjust income and principal or that authorizes a unitrust payment to satisfy the income beneficiaries' interest.

3.   **Distributable Net Income**

a. **Definition of DNI.** Under IRC § 643(a), the term "distributable net income" ("DNI") is defined as, with respect to any taxable year, the taxable income of the trust or estate, computed with certain modifications. Some of these modifications include the following:

- No distribution deduction included in DNI under IRC §§ 651 and 661.
- No personal exemption included in DNI under IRC § 642(b).
- For simple trusts (defined later in this chapter), extraordinary dividends and taxable stock dividends that the fiduciary does not pay or credit to any beneficiary by reason of his determination that such dividends are allocable to principal under the trust terms and applicable local law are excluded from DNI.

21st Century Estate Planning:
Practical Applications
2005 Edition

©2005 Sonnenschein Nath & Rosenthal LLP
and Cannon Financial Institute, Inc.

143

- "Net tax-exempt interest" (interest excluded from income under IRC § 103, reduced by the expenses allocated to tax-exempt interest that would be deductible but for IRC § 265) is included in DNI.

The term DNI only applies in the realm of income taxation of trusts and estates and their beneficiaries. DNI is the tax concept used to allocate taxable income between the trust or estate and the beneficiaries. As discussed later in this chapter, DNI is the maximum <u>deduction</u> allowable to trusts and estates for amounts paid, credited, or required to be distributed to beneficiaries, and is used to determine the maximum amount paid, credited, or required to be <u>distributed</u> to a beneficiary that will be includible in his gross income. DNI also determines the character of distributions to the beneficiaries. Treas. Reg. § 1.643(a)-0.

b. **<u>Inclusion of Capital Gains in DNI Under Final IRC § 643(b) Regulations.</u>** Section 643(a)(3) provides that gains from the sale or exchange of capital assets generally are excluded from DNI to the extent that these gains are allocated to principal. However, an exception exists for capital gains that are either paid, credited or required to be distributed to a beneficiary during the year or paid, permanently set aside or to be used for charitable purposes. In these cases, capital gains are included in DNI, even though they are allocated to principal.

With regard to situations such as when the trustee is making adjustments between principal and income or when the trustee is distributing a unitrust amount following a statutory conversation, the final regulations under IRC § 643(b) state that "gains from the sale or exchange of capital assets are ordinarily excluded from [DNI] and are not ordinarily considered as paid, credited, or required to be distributed to any beneficiary." Treas. Reg. § 1.643(a)-3(a).

An exception to this rule states that capital gains will be included in the computation of DNI if: "pursuant to the terms of the governing instrument and applicable local law or pursuant to a reasonable and impartial exercise of discretion by the fiduciary (in accordance with a power granted to the fiduciary by applicable local law or by the governing instrument if not prohibited by local law)," such capital gains are:

- Allocated to income, but if income under the state statute is defined as, or consists of, a unitrust amount, a discretionary power to allocate gains to income must also be exercised consistently and the amount so allocated may not be greater than the excess of the unitrust amount over the amount of DNI determined without regard to this exception.
- Allocated to principal but treated consistently by the fiduciary on the books, records and tax returns as part of a distribution to a beneficiary.
- Allocated to principal but actually distributed to the beneficiary or used by the fiduciary in determining the amount that is distributed, or required to be distributed, to a beneficiary. Treas. Reg. § 1.643(a)-3(b).

21st Century Estate Planning:
Practical Applications
2005 Edition

©2005 Sonnenschein Nath & Rosenthal LLP
and Cannon Financial Institute, Inc.

144

The trustee may exercise discretion regarding capital gains differently for different trusts and different sales of assets.

→ **Planning Point:** Trustees who exercise discretion in deciding whether to allocate capital gains to income either as part of their power to adjust between income and principal under a state statute or following a conversion to a unitrust must do so "consistently," and must provide evidence of this consistent treatment. However, the examples in the regulations show only federal income tax reporting as evidence of the trustee's intent. A trustee may wish to go farther and make a specific statement at the outset of the trust's administration of the manner in which the trustee intends to treat capital gains.

c. **Calculation of DNI.** The following is an example of the calculation of DNI:

EXAMPLE: Under the terms of the trust instrument, the income of a trust is required to be currently distributed to W during her life. Capital gains are allocable to principal and are not distributed or used in determining the amount to be distributed or required to be distributed to the beneficiary, and all expenses are charged against principal. During the taxable year the trust has the following items of income and expenses:

Dividends for domestic corporations:	$30,000
Extraordinary dividends allocated to principal by the trustee in good faith:	$20,000
Taxable interest:	$10,000
Tax-exempt interest:	$10,000
Long-term capital gains:	$10,000
Trustee's commission and misc. expenses allocable to principal:	$ 5,000

"Income" under IRC § 643(b) is $50,000, calculated as follows:

Dividends for domestic corporations:	$30,000
Taxable interest:	$10,000
Tax-exempt interest:	$10,000
Total Income :	$50,000

"DNI" under IRC § 643(a) is $45,000, calculated as follows:

Dividends for domestic corporations	$30,000
Taxable interest :	$10,000

21st Century Estate Planning:
Practical Applications
2005 Edition

©2005 *Sonnenschein Nath & Rosenthal LLP*
and Cannon Financial Institute, Inc.

145

Tax-exempt interest:	$10,000
Expenses allocable to tax-exempt interest:	($1,000)
Expenses ($5,000 less $1,000 allocated to tax-exempt interest):	($4,000)
Total DNI:	$45,000

d. Tier System.

(1) Tier 1. Income required to be distributed to beneficiaries in the current year is tier 1 income and carries out DNI first. For a simple trust (defined below), this amount is the net accounting income. For a complex trust (defined below), this amount is generally a portion of FAI required to be distributed under the trust instrument. For most estates, no income is required to be distributed in the current year unless a support allowance of income is made by will or under state law. Income is included for this purpose if the trustee is legally required to distribute it even if the income has not been distributed when the return is filed. Treas. Reg. § 1.651(a)-2 and § 1.661(a)-2.

(2) Tier 2. Other amounts actually paid to beneficiaries (including discretionary distributions) are tier 2 distributions and carry out excess DNI on a pro-rata basis to beneficiaries receiving tier 2 distributions.

e. Apportioning DNI Among Beneficiaries.
If the estate or trust made distributions to beneficiaries during the tax year, DNI passes the tax effects of those distributions through to the estate or trust beneficiaries. The apportionment of DNI among the beneficiaries depends on the amount and type of distribution made to each. The actual source of payment for each distribution (whether income or principal) is irrelevant. Tracing payments back to their source is not permitted. A trustee cannot designate which beneficiaries receive taxable income and which receive non-taxable distributions of principal. If DNI is less than the income required to be distributed currently, DNI is distributed proportionately among the beneficiaries receiving tier 1 distributions.

4. Grantor Trusts v. Non-Grantor Trusts

A grantor trust is a trust in which the grantor or another individual is treated as the owner of a portion or all of the trust because of certain powers retained by the grantor or the individual. Income of a grantor trust is essentially passed down to and payable by the owner. Grantor trusts are discussed later in this chapter. A non-grantor trust is a trust where the trust entity itself is taxed for income tax purposes.

5. Simple Trusts

Under IRC § 651(a), a non-grantor trust is a "simple trust" if <u>all</u> of following requirements are met during the year in question:

21st Century Estate Planning:
Practical Applications
2005 Edition

©2005 Sonnenschein Nath & Rosenthal LLP
and Cannon Financial Institute, Inc.

146

- The trust terms require all of the income to be distributed currently.
- The trust terms do not provide that any amounts be paid, permanently set aside, or used for the charitable purposes described in IRC § 642(c).
- The trust must not actually distribute any amounts (other than the income required to be distributed currently).

Whether trust income is required to be distributed currently is determined under the trust terms and applicable local law. The Regulations provide guidelines for making this determination. Treas. Reg. § 1.651(a)-2. In addition, the Regulations state that the fact that the trust does not in fact distribute all income currently during the year does not disqualify the trust as a simple trust. Treas. Reg. § 1.651(a)-1.

> **EXAMPLE:** A trust instrument directs that all income be paid to B annually. The trustee does not distribute the 2004 income to B until January 1, 2005. The trust will still qualify as a simple trust for 2004 even though the income was not actually distributed in 2004.

6. Complex Trusts

A "complex trust" is a non-grantor trust that does not meet the requirements of a simple trust. Accordingly, a non-grantor trust is a complex trust if any <u>one</u> of the following is true during the year in question:

- The trust terms require that any portion of the income be accumulated.
- The trust terms give the trustee discretion to accumulate or distribute income, even if all current income is actually distributed.
- The trust distributes principal.
- The trust makes a charitable contribution.

> **EXAMPLE:** A trust instrument directs that all income be paid to B annually, and one-half of the trust principal be distributed to B at age 25. B turns 25 on December 31, 2004. The trustee distributes one-half of the principal to B on January 1, 2005. The trust will be considered a complex trust for 2005 when an actual distribution of principal is made.

➔ **Planning Point:** Whether a trust is a simple trust or a complex trust will affect its taxation. A trust may be simple one year and complex the next. A trust that is permitted but not required to distribute principal is a complex trust in years when principal is actually distributed, but may be a simple trust in a year when no distributions are made. A trust that can either distribute or accumulate income is always a complex trust even in years when all income is distributed. All non-grantor trusts are complex

21st Century Estate Planning:
Practical Applications
2005 Edition

©2005 Sonnenschein Nath & Rosenthal LLP
and Cannon Financial Institute, Inc.

147

in their final year because all principal must be distributed when the trust terminates.

7. Estates

An "estate" for federal income tax purposes is a decedent's estate, which is comprised of assets subject to probate administration under applicable local law. Property not subject to probate is not included in the definition of "estate" for federal income tax purposes. Accordingly, property that passes by contract (*e.g.*, retirement benefits or life insurance proceeds payable to a beneficiary other than the estate) or by operation of law (*e.g.*, property held in joint tenancy with rights of survivorship) is not included in a decedent's estate for income tax purposes.

→ **Planning Point:** Property includible in a decedent's "gross estate" for federal estate tax purposes may not necessarily coincide with property includible in the decedent's "estate" for federal income tax purposes. For example, life insurance proceeds payable to the decedent's spouse are included in the decedent's gross estate for federal estate tax purposes but are not included in the decedent's estate for income tax purposes. Life insurance proceeds payable to the decedent's estate, however, are included in the decedent's estate for both estate tax and income tax purposes.

Not surprisingly, the existence of the decedent's estate for income tax purposes commences with the decedent's date of death (regardless of when the probate estate is opened).

C. Computation of the Tax

1. General

The income tax liability of a non-grantor trust or estate is computed in much the same way as an individual's income tax liability is computed, with the exception of the distribution deduction, which is unique to trusts and estates:

- Gross Income (the total of all taxable income from all sources).
- Less: Deductions (much the same as for individuals with a few differences discussed later).
- Less: Distribution deduction (a device used to shift income tax liability to beneficiaries and thus avoid the trust or estate from always paying all the tax, as well as to avoid double taxation of the income).
- Less: Exemption (much the same as an individual's personal exemption, $600 for estates, $300 for trusts requiring all income to be distributed currently, and $100 for all others).
- Equals: Income taxable to the estate or trust.

21st Century Estate Planning:
Practical Applications
2005 Edition

©2005 Sonnenschein Nath & Rosenthal LLP
and Cannon Financial Institute, Inc.

148

2. Taxable Income

As discussed earlier, the taxable income of estates and non-grantor trusts generally is gross income less allowable deductions. If deductions exceed the gross income, the excess flows through to the beneficiaries only if the trust or estate has terminated during that year. IRC § 641(h).

3. Gross Income and Exclusions From Gross Income

The general definition of "gross income" in IRC § 61 applies for the most part to non-grantor trusts and estates. Not all items of income, however, will be taxed to the trust. For example, to the extent a portion or all of the trust is treated as a grantor trust, the income will not be taxed to the trust but to the individual treated as owner of the trust. Two examples of items of gross income received by a trust or estate include:

a. Income in Respect of a Decedent. If the estate receives an item of income in respect of a decedent ("IRD"), IRD will be includible in the estate's gross income. In general, IRD refers to those amounts to which a decedent was entitled as gross income but which were not properly includible in computing his taxable income for the taxable year ending with the date of his death. It is all income that the decedent would have received had death not occurred. IRC § 691(a). Examples of IRD include deferred compensation received after death and installment sales obligations payable after death. When an estate or trust receives an item of IRD, the estate may be allowed a deduction for the estate tax attributable to such IRD. IRC § 691(c).

b. Capital Gains. A trust or estate will have gross income from the sale, exchange or other disposition of assets to the extent of the amount realized in excess of basis in the property.

4. Deductions

Non-grantor trusts and estates are entitled to many of the same deductions as individuals, subject to certain exceptions and additions.

> "To determine if a deduction is allowed to an estate or trust, one considers the statutory provision granting the deduction, other statutory provisions limiting the deduction, and the exceptions applicable to estates and trusts."

There are several deductions that differ between individuals and estates or trusts. The three most significant are: (a) the charitable deduction, (b) the deduction for costs of administration, and (c) the distribution deduction. Also discussed here is the option to take certain deductions on the estate or income tax return, the non-deductibility of expenses allocated to tax-exempt income, and excess deductions.

a. Charitable Deduction. An estate or complex trust can fully deduct charitable contributions paid from the current year's gross income if the will, trust instrument, or

21st Century Estate Planning:
Practical Applications
2005 Edition

©2005 Sonnenschein Nath & Rosenthal LLP
and Cannon Financial Institute, Inc.

149

local law specifically requires the payment. Charitable contributions from principal are not deductible unless made from amounts included in the current year's gross income. Charitable contributions must be reduced by the proportion of tax-exempt income included in gross fiduciary accounting income. Unless the will, trust agreement, or state law requires payment from taxable income, charitable contributions are deemed to be paid from all types of income. Treas. Reg. § 1.642(c)-3(b)(2). This is a full deduction for charitable bequests as opposed to the limitations imposed on individuals to only a certain percentage of adjusted gross income that may be deducted for the year with any excess being carried forward for up to five years.

➜   **Planning Point:** All amounts which will be deductible under IRC § 642(c) should be paid or permanently set-aside in a year prior to the final year of the estate. Otherwise, they will be wasted.

Estates are also allowed a current deduction for amounts included in gross income permanently set-aside for qualifying charities. Only pooled income funds and trusts created before October 10, 1969 or by will executed before October 10, 1969 are allowed a set-aside deduction.

b.   Deduction for Costs of Administration. Estates and trusts are subject to the 2% AGI limitation on miscellaneous itemized deductions. Miscellaneous itemized deductions for an estate or trust are generally the same kinds of expenses as those incurred by individuals (*e.g.,* final Form 1040 tax preparation fees, investment expenses, etc.). However, under IRC § 67(e), expenses connected with the administration of an estate or trust which would not have been incurred if the property were not held in such trust or estate are allowed as a deduction in arriving at adjusted gross income and are not subject to the 2% AGI limitation. See *Scott v. United States*, 328 F.3d 132 (4th Cir. May 1, 2003), and *Mellon Bank N.A. v. United States*, 265 F.3d 1275 (Fed. Cir. 2001). Cf *O'Neill v. Comm'r*, 994 F.2d 302 (6th Cir. 1993). Nor are other miscellaneous itemized deductions such as the personal exemption of $600, $300 or $100, and the distribution deduction discussed next.

c.   Distribution Deduction. Taxable income earned by a trust or estate is taxable either to the trust or estate or to its beneficiaries but not to both. The trust or estate is allowed an income distribution deduction for income taxed to the beneficiaries. Beneficiaries receive Schedule K-1 informing them of the amount and types of income to include on their individual tax returns. Income passed through to the beneficiaries retains its original character (interest, dividends, capital gains, etc.).

Generally, the distribution deduction is the lesser of:

- Distributions less tax-exempt income included in distribution, or
- DNI less tax-exempt interest.

The effect of this deduction is to shift certain income treated as distributed currently, to the recipients of that income, rather than being taxed to the estate or trust. This deduction is granted

21st Century Estate Planning:
Practical Applications
2005 Edition

©2005 Sonnenschein Nath & Rosenthal LLP
and Cannon Financial Institute, Inc.

150

under IRC §§ 651 and 661 and limited to DNI under IRC § 663. The distribution deduction is discussed in context later in this chapter.

d. Deductibility of Expenses. In general, most estate or trust administrative expenses are deductible on Form 706 or Form 1041 but not on both. IRC § 642(g). Typical administrative expenses include the following:

- Trustee and personal representative estate or trust fees.
- Attorney and accountant fees for estate or trust administration.
- Form 1041, the decedent's final Form 1040, and other estate or trust tax return preparation costs.
- Court fees, court-required appraisal fees and other required expenses of the estate or trust.
- Investment expenses and advice, including expenses for managing, conserving, and maintaining estate or trust property.

➔ **Planning Point:** Since the lowest estate tax rate generally is higher than the highest income tax rate, when an estate owes estate taxes, the expenses should be taken on the Form 706, estate tax return. When there is no estate tax due to the size of the estate or use of the marital deduction or charitable deduction, expenses should be claimed on the Form 1041, fiduciary income tax return. Keep in mind that these expenses can also be apportioned between the two returns.

e. Non-Deductibility of Expenses Allocated to Tax-Exempt Income. Certain deductions that are otherwise allowable to an estate or trust are disallowed to the extent they are attributable or apportioned to tax-exempt income. IRC § 265. Tax-exempt interest includes interest on state and local bonds as well as tax-exempt interest dividends received from a mutual fund or other regulated investment company.

- Interest paid on debt used to purchase or carry tax-exempt obligations is not deductible.
- Administrative expenses under IRC § 212 directly attributable to tax-exempt interest are not deductible. Administrative expenses directly attributable to taxable income are fully deductible.
- A portion of indirect administrative expenses deductible under IRC § 212 must be allocated to tax-exempt interest, and that portion is not deductible. IRC § 265.

Indirect expenses are those not directly related to either taxable income or tax-exempt income.

EXAMPLE: Treas. Reg. § 1.652(c)-4 contains the following example:

21st Century Estate Planning:
Practical Applications
2005 Edition

©2005 Sonnenschein Nath & Rosenthal LLP
and Cannon Financial Institute, Inc.

151

Rents $25,000

Dividends 50,000

Tax-exempt interest 25,000

Total $100,000

Deductions:

Expenses directly attributable to rental income $5,000

Trustee's commission 3,900

Based on this information, the expenses allocable to tax-exempt interest are equal to a fraction, with a numerator of $25,000 and a denominator of $100,000, multiplied by the trustee's fee of $3,900. This calculation ignores the direct expenses of $5,000 attributable to the rental income. Thus $975 of the expenses (trustee's commission) is allocable to tax-exempt income, and as such, cannot be deducted against taxable income.

      f. **Excess Deductions.** In its final year, an estate or trust will generally have no tax liability since all income is distributed and capital gains that would ordinarily be taxed to the entity are allocated to the beneficiaries. If an estate or trust has deductions in excess of gross income in its final year, the excess deductions are allowed as deductions on the beneficiary's tax return. Treas. Reg. § 1.642(h)-2. Charitable deductions and the personal exemption are not allowed as excess deductions. This pass-through of deductions is allowed only in the taxable year the estate or trust terminates. The beneficiary cannot carry the deduction over to the following year. A capital loss may also be distributed to the beneficiaries in the final year. A loss received from a trust or estate can be carried over by the taxpayer if not fully used in the termination year.

D. Taxation of Simple Trusts, Complex Trusts and Estates

1. Simple Trusts and Their Beneficiaries

Because of the deduction available to simple trusts, a simple trust is generally taxed on two sources of income: (a) items allocated to principal for FAI purposes but subject to income tax (*e.g.*, capital gains and extraordinary dividends or taxable stock dividends allocated to principal in good faith), and (b) items that are taxable income but not FAI (*e.g.*, partnership income allocated but not distributed to the trust). Beneficiaries of a simple trust are generally taxed on the trust's items of ordinary income, less deductions.

21st Century Estate Planning:
Practical Applications
2005 Edition

©2005 Sonnenschein Nath & Rosenthal LLP
and Cannon Financial Institute, Inc.

152

a. Simple Trusts. Subject to certain limitations discussed below, a simple trust is generally entitled to a distribution deduction for the amount of FAI required under the trust instrument to be currently distributed to the beneficiaries. Treas. Reg. § 1.651(b)-1. Again, whether FAI is required to be distributed currently is determined under the trust terms and applicable local law. The Regulations provide guidelines for making this determination. Treas. Reg. § 1.651(a)-2. The distribution deduction cannot exceed the DNI. In addition, no deduction is allowed for net tax-exempt income (*i.e.*, tax-exempt income, less expenses). Treas. Reg. § 1.651(b)-1.

➔ **Planning Point:** The maximum distribution deduction available to a simple trust is the lesser of the trust's FAI or DNI, then reduced by net tax-exempt interest. Accordingly, in order to determine the applicable distribution deduction for a simple trust, practitioners should first calculate both FAI and DNI.

b. Beneficiaries of Simple Trusts. A simple trust has only one tier of beneficiaries, the beneficiaries entitled to receive current distributions of the trust's FAI. IRC § 652 provides that the income beneficiary must include in income the lesser of FAI or DNI (reduced by net tax-exempt income), regardless of whether or not the FAI is actually distributed. For multiple beneficiaries, the included income is prorated in proportion to the FAI each is required to receive under the trust instrument. The included income retains the same character (*e.g.*, earned income, dividends, exempt income) in the hands of the beneficiaries as in the hands of the trust. The income is included in the tax year that ends with or includes the end of the trust's year for that income.

> **EXAMPLE:** A trust instrument directs that one-third of income be paid to B annually, and two-thirds of income be paid to C annually. The income required to be distributed in 2005 is $60,000. B's income is $20,000 and C's income is $40,000. If the trust's DNI is only $30,000, however, B's income will be limited to $10,000, and C's income will be limited to $20,000.

2. Taxation of Complex Trusts and Estates and Their Beneficiaries

a. Taxation of Complex Trusts and Estates. IRC §§ 661 and 662 cover the taxation of complex trusts and estates and their beneficiaries.

(1) Distribution Deduction. A complex trust or estate is generally entitled to a distribution deduction equal to all of its distributions for the year to the extent of its DNI and subject to special rules for distributions in kind. IRC § 661(a). Specifically, the deduction is equal to the sum of: (a) the first-tier distributions, and (b) the second-tier distributions.

21ˢᵗ Century Estate Planning:
Practical Applications
2005 Edition

©2005 Sonnenschein Nath & Rosenthal LLP
and Cannon Financial Institute, Inc.

153

(a) **First-Tier Distributions**. First-tier distributions are "any amount of income for such taxable year required to be distributed currently (including any amount required to be distributed which may be paid out of income or corpus to the extent such amount is paid out of income for such taxable year)." IRC § 661(a)(1). Accordingly, first-tier distributions include distributions of income required to be distributed currently and annuity payments required to paid from income or principal.

(b) **Second-Tier Distributions.** Second-tier distributions are "any other amounts properly paid or credited or required to be distributed for such taxable year." IRC § 661(a)(2). Accordingly, second-tier distributions include discretionary distributions of income or principal, mandatory distributions of principal, and distributions out of principal for support of a person to whom the grantor or certain other persons are legally obligated to support or maintain.

b. Taxation of Beneficiaries of Complex Trusts and Estates. In a complex trust or estate, DNI may exceed the income required to be distributed currently. In that case, DNI is first apportioned dollar for dollar to the tier 1 beneficiaries. Excess DNI is divided proportionately among beneficiaries receiving tier 2 distributions.

> **EXAMPLE:** A simple trust has $100,000 of dividend income and $5,000 of trustee's fees. The fees are charged one-half against income and one-half against corpus. The trust's distribution deduction is equal to $95,000 computed as follows:
>
> (1) Fiduciary accounting income (FAI)
>
> | | |
> |---|---|
> | Dividends | $100,000 |
> | Less: 1/2 of trustee's fee | (2,500) |
> | = Fiduciary accounting income | $97,500 |
>
> (2) DNI =
>
> | | |
> |---|---|
> | Dividends | $100,000 |
> | Less: trustee's fee | (5,000) |
> | = Distributable Net Income | $95,000 |
>
> Distribution Deduction = $95,000
>
> Because DNI ($95,000) is less than FAI ($97,500), the distribution deduction is limited to $95,000.

21st Century Estate Planning:
Practical Applications
2005 Edition

©2005 Sonnenschein Nath & Rosenthal LLP
and Cannon Financial Institute, Inc.

154

EXAMPLE: Trust (T) has net accounting income of $60,000 for the current year. The trustee has the required income distribution language stated in each example below, and additional discretion to distribute income or principal to S and D. The trustee exercises its discretion and, in addition to the required amount of income, distributes $15,000 to S and $15,000 to D. T has no tax-exempt interest income.

(1) If T is required to distribute all income ($60,000) currently to S and D (one-third to S and two-thirds to D) and has $60,000 of DNI, S will have $20,000 of gross income (1/3 of DNI) and D, $40,000 (2/3 of DNI) for the first-tier distribution and no gross income from the second-tier distributions.

(2) If trust has $50,000 of DNI, and provides S is to have 25% of net accounting income and D is to have 50% of net accounting income, then S has $15,000 from his first-tier distribution and D $30,000 from her first-tier distribution. The remaining $5,000 of DNI ($50,000-45,000) will be allocated $2,500 to S and $2,500 to D. Thus, S will have $17,500 of income and D will have $32,500 of income.

E. Throwback Tax

Under the throwback rules, certain income that represents undistributed portions of DNI from earlier years may be subject to additional tax in later years when actually distributed. Trusts that did not distribute all of the current year's income used to have to deal with throwback rules. Since August 1, 1997, most domestic trusts are no longer subject to these rules. Trusts that are subject to these rules include foreign trusts, some domestic trusts that were foreign trusts, and certain trusts that were created before March 1, 1984 if they are treated as multiple trusts under IRC § 643(f).

As discussed earlier, each year, the DNI for a trust is calculated as the maximum amount of income for the year that may be treated as passed through to the beneficiaries through distributions in that year. Any undistributed amount of DNI is taxed to the trust. This undistributed net income however may be subject to additional tax if in a future year: (i) an amount in excess of DNI for the current year is distributed, and (ii) the income would have been taxed at a higher rate had it been distributed in the year originally earned. The calculation is complex, labor intensive, and due to the current compressed brackets for trusts, no longer generates the level of income it once did, and thus was eliminated for most domestic trusts.

21ˢᵗ Century Estate Planning:
Practical Applications
2005 Edition

©2005 Sonnenschein Nath & Rosenthal LLP
and Cannon Financial Institute, Inc.

155

F. Grantor Trusts

1. Definition of "Grantor"

The "grantor" is the person who creates a trust. For income tax purposes, however, the grantor may also be a substantial powerholder other than the person who created the trust. IRC § 678. When a person retains or is given substantial control of a trust, that person is considered the grantor for income tax purposes and is taxed on the trust's income, and the trust entity is disregarded for income tax purposes. IRC §§ 674(a); 675; 676; 678. If the grantor retains control of only part of a trust, the grantor is treated as the owner of only the portion of the trust controlled. Income from the other portion is taxed to the trust or its beneficiaries.

2. Adverse Party

Even if the grantor retains a power or right listed in the first four points below, he is not considered the owner of the trust for income tax purposes if an adverse party must consent to the grantor's exercise of control. An adverse party is a person who has a substantial beneficial interest in the trust and who would be adversely affected by the exercise or non-exercise of the grantor's power. IRC § 672(a). Trust beneficiaries generally are adverse parties. A beneficiary who has a right to only a portion of a trust's income or principal is only an adverse party as to that portion. A remainder beneficiary is generally not an adverse party with respect to a power over income. Income beneficiaries are generally adverse to distributions of principal only during the term of their interests. A grantor is also treated as owner of the trust if one of the powers listed in the first four points below is given to a non-adverse party. A grantor is considered to have retained any power or interest given to his spouse for transfers in trust after March 1, 1986. IRC § 672(e).

3. Independent Trustee

IRC § 674(a) sets forth a general rule that the grantor shall be treated as the owner of any portion of a trust where the beneficial enjoyment of income or principal is controlled by the grantor or a non-adverse party, or both, without the consent or approval of an adverse party. IRC § 674(c) provides that, if half or more of the trustees are "independent" (and neither the grantor nor his or her spouse is a trustee) within the meaning of IRC § 674, the general rule of IRC § 674(a) does not apply and the grantor will not be taxed on the trust's income. Who is "independent?" IRC § 674(c) defines this term in the negative:

> EXCEPTION FOR CERTAIN POWERS OF INDEPENDENT TRUSTEES.--
> Subsection (a) shall not apply to a power solely exercisable (without the approval or consent of any other person) by a trustee or trustees, none of whom is the grantor, and no more than half of whom are related or subordinate parties who are subservient to the wishes of the grantor . . . .

21st Century Estate Planning:
Practical Applications
2005 Edition

©2005 Sonnenschein Nath & Rosenthal LLP
and Cannon Financial Institute, Inc.

156

→ **Planning Point:** If the grantor of an irrevocable trust desires not to limit income and principal distributions by "a reasonably definite...standard which is set forth in the trust instrument" (see IRC §§ 674(b)(5) and 674(d)), and assuming grantor trust treatment is not desired, a grantor should choose at least half "independent" trustees within the above definition.

Treas. Reg. §§ 1.674(c)-1 confirms that an independent trustee may hold the power to sprinkle income or principal to any beneficiary without causing grantor trust status.

4. Related or Subordinate Party

A trustee is deemed "related or subordinate" if the trustee is not an adverse party (as defined above) and is the grantor's spouse (if living with the grantor), parent, issue, brother or sister, an employee of the grantor, a corporation or any employee of a corporation in which the stockholdings of the grantor and the trust are significant with respect to voting control, or in which the grantor is an executive. IRC § 672(c).

> **EXAMPLE:** Mother establishes a trust for the benefit of Son and Daughter and appoints her Brother as trustee. No distributions may be made that would discharge Mother's obligation of support. (see IRC § 677(b)). No one has the power to add beneficiaries to the trust (see IRC § 674(b) and (c)). Brother has no beneficial interest in the trust, and has the power to sprinkle income and principal between the beneficiaries. If Brother can exercise this discretionary distribution power without the consent of either beneficiary, Mother will be taxed on all trust income. The sprinkling power is held by a related or subordinate party, and no consent of an adverse party is required. If Brother has the discretionary distribution power but distributions to Son or Daughter must be approved by the other child, Mother will not be taxed on the trust income. The other child is an adverse party because any distributions to Son reduce the amount available to Daughter and vice versa.
>
> What if Mother appoints Bank instead of Brother as the third trustee? In that case, the trust falls within the exception in IRC § 674(c) for powers held by independent trustees, so the trust will not be a grantor trust.

5. Grantor Trust Rules

The grantor trust rules generally apply when the grantor:

- Derives benefits from the income (IRC § 677),

21st Century Estate Planning:
Practical Applications
2005 Edition

©2005 Sonnenschein Nath & Rosenthal LLP
and Cannon Financial Institute, Inc.

157

- Retains the power to revoke the trust or withdraw trust property (IRC §§ 676 and 678),
- Retains power to control beneficial enjoyment (IRC § 674),
- Retains power to exercise certain administrative powers over the trust's operation (IRC § 675) or
- Retains a reversionary interest in either principal or income (IRC § 673).

a. **Benefits From Income.** A grantor is treated as owner of a portion of a trust of which income can be distributed to the grantor or the grantor's spouse, held or accumulated for future distribution to the grantor or the grantor's spouse or used to pay premiums on policies insuring the life of the grantor or the grantor's spouse. If trust income is applied to discharge the grantor's or the grantor's spouse's legal obligation of support, income will be taxed to the grantor to that extent. IRC § 677.

b. **Power To Revoke.** A power of revocation gives the grantor the power to end all or part of a trust and take back the trust property. The grantor is treated as owner of the trust to the extent of that power. IRC § 676.

c. **Control of Beneficial Enjoyment.** A grantor is treated as the owner of a portion of a trust over which the grantor and/or a non-adverse person has the power to control who receives income or principal from a trust without an adverse party's consent. IRC § 674. IRC § 674(b) enumerates eight exceptions for powers that can be held by anyone and not result in grantor trust status. The regulations discuss these eight powers in detail. Treas. Reg. § 1.674(b)-1(b). An example of such a power is a power to distribute principal to trust beneficiaries limited by a reasonably definite standard set forth in the trust instrument that is held by the grantor or another person. IRC § 674(b)(5). A reasonably definite standard is one that is clearly measurable and allows the holder to be held legally accountable. Treas. Reg. § 1.674(b)-1(b)(5).

> **EXAMPLE:** A power to distribute principal for the education, support, maintenance or health of the beneficiary; for his reasonable support and comfort; or to enable him to maintain his accustomed standard of living; or to meet an emergency, would be limited by a reasonably definite standard. However, a power to distribute principal for the pleasure, desire or happiness of a beneficiary is not limited by a reasonably definite standard. Treas. Reg. § 1.674(b)-1(b)(5).

(1) **Power Over Income.** An additional exception to the general rule of IRC § 674 is IRC § 674(d). IRC § 674(d) provides that a power to distribute, apportion, or accumulate income limited by a reasonably definite standard can be given to any trustee other than the grantor or spouse. The power must be exercisable without consent of any other person. Treas. Reg. § 1.674(d)-1.

21st Century Estate Planning:
Practical Applications
2005 Edition

©2005 Sonnenschein Nath & Rosenthal LLP
and Cannon Financial Institute, Inc.

158

(2)   **Power to Remove and Replace Trustee.** If the grantor holds an unrestricted power to remove, substitute or add trustees and to designate any person including the grantor as successor trustee, the trustee's powers are deemed to be exercisable by the grantor for purposes of determining grantor trust status and the trust will not qualify as a non-grantor trust under IRC §§ 674(c) and 674(d). Treas. Reg. § 1.674(d)-2.

d. **Administrative Powers.** Generally, if the grantor or a non-adverse party has the power to deal with trust property for less than adequate consideration, to substitute assets for other assets of equivalent value (acting in a non-fiduciary capacity), to borrow funds without adequate interest or security, or to control certain other trust administrative functions in a non-fiduciary capacity, the grantor is considered the owner of the trust for income tax purposes. IRC § 675.

e. **Reversionary Interest.** For transfers in trust after March 1, 1986, a grantor generally is treated as the owner of that portion of a trust in which he has a reversionary interest, if the value of the reversionary interest at the time of the transfer exceeds 5% of the total property, based on IRS valuation tables. IRC § 673.

6.   **Person Other Than Grantor Treated As Owner**

A person other than the person who created and funded a trust may be considered the owner of all or part of the trust if he/she: (i) has an exclusive power to vest principal or income in himself/herself or (ii) previously released such a power and retained one of the rights that would cause the trust to be taxed to a grantor. IRC § 678(a). This rule does not apply to a power over income if the grantor is treated as the owner under IRC §§ 673-677. IRC § 678(b); Treas. Reg. § 1.678(b)-1. As an owner of the trust property for income tax purposes, the individual must include the trust income, deductions and credits on his or her personal income tax return instead of the trust's income tax return. IRC § 678 commonly applies in the case of beneficiaries who hold *Crummey* withdrawal rights. But see also, IRC § 677. See Chapter VII, Section D, regarding the income tax consequences of *Crummey* powerholders.

➔   **Planning Point:** IRC § 678 does not contain an explicit exception for a trustee whose powers are limited by an ascertainable standard. The same is true for beneficiaries who hold withdrawal rights. However, many practitioners believe such a trustee or beneficiary should not be taxed on trust income under IRC § 678. See *U.S. v. De Bonchamps* 278 F.2d 127 (9th Cir. 1960); cf. Treas. Reg. 1.678(c)-1(b), (c) (regarding the applicability of IRC § 678 to support trusts). But in PLR 8211057, the IRS applied IRC § 678 to a trustee who held withdrawal rights despite the existence of an ascertainable standard. A solution to this possible income tax problem is to designate a co-trustee to serve with the trustee who is also a beneficiary.

21st Century Estate Planning:
Practical Applications
2005 Edition

©2005 Sonnenschein Nath & Rosenthal LLP
and Cannon Financial Institute, Inc.

159

Note that IRC § 678 is the only provision of the Internal Revenue Code under which grantor trust status can apply, by the explicit terms of the statute, after the "real" grantor of the trust has died. Thus, any trust coming into existence under a post-death revocable trust or under a will cannot be a grantor trust for income tax purposes unless under IRC § 678.

7. Grantor Trust at Death

A grantor trust generally stops being a grantor trust when the grantor dies (unless there are multiple grantors). Income earned through the date of death is reported following the reporting requirements for grantor trusts. After-death income generally must be reported by the trust on Form 1041 as a simple or complex trust, even if the trust was not previously required to file a separate return because the grantor was taxed on all the income. A decedent's revocable trust may be treated as part of the estate for federal income tax purposes. The election must be made by the trustee and the personal representative of the estate by the due date for the estate's first year return. If no estate tax return is required, the election is effective for two years after the date of decedent's death. The election applies to trusts treated as grantor trusts because of a power held by the decedent. Trusts treated as grantor trusts because of a power held by a non-adverse party do not qualify. IRC § 645.

G. Duties and Forms To File

1. Identification Number

All taxable entities must have an employer identification number (EIN). An individual generally uses his social security number. Estates and irrevocable trusts must have an employer identification number assigned. Even revocable trusts will need an employer identification number, unless the grantor is at least a co-trustee. Form SS-4 (Application for Employer Identification Number) can be used for this purpose. At some point, a revocable trust will become irrevocable and need its own employer identification number, so most corporate trustees have one assigned right away. Individuals acting as their own trustee usually prefer to maintain the use of their social security number until resignation, incapacity, or death.

➔ **Planning Point:** Often it takes about 4 weeks to get an EIN from the IRS. It is possible to apply by phone and obtain the number immediately, but Form SS-4 will still need to be filed. A deceased individual's identifying number must not be used to file any returns after the decedent's final tax return, nor to make estimated tax payments for a tax year after the year of death.

2. Notice of Fiduciary Relationship

When an individual or entity is appointed to act in any fiduciary capacity for another, the individual or entity must file a written notice with the IRS stating this. Form 56 (Notice Concerning Fiduciary Relationship) can be used for this purpose.

21ˢᵗ Century Estate Planning:
Practical Applications
2005 Edition

©2005 Sonnenschein Nath & Rosenthal LLP
and Cannon Financial Institute, Inc.

160

3. Final Income Tax Return

A final individual income tax return (Form 1040) must be filed for a decedent for the year of death and for any prior years in which returns were not filed. The final income tax return covers income earned by the decedent from January 1 of the year of death until the date of death.

> **EXAMPLE:** Decedent dies on March 19, 2004 having earned $35,000 since January 1. Her securities portfolio and rental property continue to earn another $60,000 through December 31. The amount reported on her final income tax return is $35,000. The return is due by her regular due date of April 15, 2005. Also, since she died before the due date of her prior year tax return, a return will need to be filed for the prior year as well. The $60,000 of income earned after death will be reported on one or more of her estate's fiduciary income tax return(s).

If the decedent was married at the time of death, the personal representative and spouse may file a joint return as long as the surviving spouse does not remarry before the end of the year of the decedent's death.

> **EXAMPLE:** Decedent dies on October 19, 2004, having earned $60,000 since January 1. His surviving spouse earns $120,000 for the year. Their combined income of $180,000 is reported jointly on an income tax return due by the regular due date of April 15, 2005.

4. Fiduciary Income Tax Return

Most estates and irrevocable trusts must file a Form 1041 annually as well as a separate Schedule K-1, or acceptable substitute, for each beneficiary. Schedule K-1 must be furnished to the beneficiary by the date on which the Form 1041 is filed.

➔ **Planning Point:** Since the due date of the Schedule K-1 is the day the tax return is filed, it often comes too late for a beneficiary to file her own tax return on time. Advance discussion of this issue will increase awareness and decrease frustration on the part of the beneficiary.

The due date of the return is three months and fifteen days after the end of the tax year. Estates and wholly charitable trusts can elect a fiscal year for tax reporting purposes, while all other trusts must report on a calendar year basis.

a. Estate as Taxpayer. Estates come into existence as a taxpayer for federal income tax purposes at the death of the decedent and terminate at the final distribution of assets, as long as this is done in a reasonable time. An estate may elect a fiscal year that is a twelve-month reporting period other than the calendar year. IRC §§ 441 and 7701(a)(1), (14). This election is made simply by the Personal Representative's filing the first tax return for the estate.

21ˢᵗ Century Estate Planning:
Practical Applications
2005 Edition

©*2005 Sonnenschein Nath & Rosenthal LLP*
and Cannon Financial Institute, Inc.

161

The reporting period may be the end of any month not more than 12 months after the date of death.

> **EXAMPLE:** Decedent dies on March 3, 2005. His estate may elect a fiscal year ending on March 31, 2005 or any month-end until February 29, 2006. The executor elects a fiscal year ending June 30, 2005. The fiduciary income tax return is due three months and fifteen days after the end of the fiscal year; thus its due date is October 15.

Since estates may elect a fiscal year other than the calendar year and individuals report on a calendar year basis, there is an opportunity for the delay of taxation of distributions. Regardless of the year in which a distribution is received, the income is not recognized until the end of the estate's year when the amount and character of the distribution is determined and reported to the beneficiary. If this reporting takes place in a calendar year later than the distribution takes place, the beneficiary reports the income as of the later year rather than for the previous year in which the income was actually received.

> **EXAMPLE:** Decedent passes away on May 20, 2004. His estate elects a fiscal year ending on October 31, 2004. The fiduciary income tax return is due three months and fifteen days after the end of the fiscal year; thus its due date is February 15, 2005. A distribution is made to a beneficiary on November 12, 2004. It is not reported as income on the beneficiary's 2004 income tax return. The estate's fiduciary income tax return and related Schedule K-1 are filed on February 15, 2005. The income related to such distribution will be reported on the beneficiary's 2005 income tax return filed by April 15, 2006.

Every domestic estate with gross income $600 or more, or any beneficiary who is a nonresident alien must file a return. Estimated payments are only required for tax years ending two or more years after the decedent's death.

> **b. Trust as Taxpayer.** Trusts come into existence as a taxpayer for federal income tax purposes at the initial funding of the trust and terminate at the final distribution of assets. A trust "does not automatically terminate upon the happening of the event by which the duration of the trust is measured." Rather, it terminates after "the property held in trust has been distributed to the persons entitled to succeed to the property upon termination of the trust." The trustee is given a reasonable time to "perform the duties necessary to complete the administration of the trust." Treas. Reg. § 1.641(b)-3(b).

A trust must report income on a calendar year basis unless it is wholly a grantor trust or a trust exempt from taxation as a wholly charitable trust. IRC § 644; Rev. Rul. 90-55, 1990-2 C.B. 161. Trusts, therefore, do not have the ability to delay taxation on distributions in the way estates do. Every trust with any taxable income, gross income $600 or more, or any beneficiary

21ˢᵗ Century Estate Planning:
Practical Applications
2005 Edition

©2005 Sonnenschein Nath & Rosenthal LLP
and Cannon Financial Institute, Inc.

162

who is a nonresident alien must file a return. Estimated payments are required if tax is $1,000 or more. Safe harbor rules similar to those for individuals apply to estates and trusts. A trust or estate in its final year may allocate estimated tax payments to beneficiaries under IRC § 643(g).

           c. <u>Qualified Revocable Trusts</u>. Effective for individuals dying after August 5, 1997, an election may be made to treat a "qualified revocable trust" as part of the decedent's estate. IRC § 645. Both the executor and the trustee must agree to the election, and, the election, once made, is irrevocable. The election is effective for all taxable years ending within two years of the decedent's date of death where no estate tax return is filed and within six months of the final determination of estate tax liability where an estate tax return is filed. This provision allows the trust to be taxed as part of the estate and not as a separate taxpayer.

H. Income in Respect of a Decedent (IRD)

1. Definition

In general, the term "income in respect of a decedent" ("IRD") refers to those amounts to which a decedent was entitled as gross income but which were not properly includible in computing his taxable income for the taxable year ending with the date of his death. It is all income that the decedent would have received had death not occurred. IRC § 691(a). When an estate or trust receives an item of IRD, the estate may be allowed a deduction for the estate tax attributable to such IRD. IRC § 691(c).

2. Taxation of IRD

IRD must be included in the income of one of the following:

- The decedent's estate, if the estate receives it.
- The beneficiary, if the right to income is passed directly to the beneficiary and the beneficiary receives it.
- Any person to whom the estate properly distributes the right to receive it.

> **EXAMPLE:** The decedent was entitled at the date of his death to a large salary payment to be made in equal annual installments over five years. Her estate, after collecting two installments, distributed the right to the remaining installment payments to the residuary legatee of the estate. The estate must include in its gross income the two installments received by it, and the legatee must include in his gross income each of the three installments received by him.

21st Century Estate Planning:
Practical Applications
2005 Edition

©*2005 Sonnenschein Nath & Rosenthal LLP*
and Cannon Financial Institute, Inc.

163

EXAMPLE: A widow acquired, by bequest from her husband, the right to receive renewal commissions on life insurance sold by him in his lifetime, which commissions were payable over a period of years. The widow died before having received all of such commissions, and her son inherited the right to receive the rest of the commissions. The commissions received by the widow were includible in her gross income. The commissions received by the son must be included in the gross income of the son.

3. Income Tax Deduction For Estate Tax Paid Attributable To IRD

A person who is required to include in gross income for any taxable year an amount of IRD may deduct for the same taxable year that portion of the estate tax imposed upon the decedent's estate that is attributable to the inclusion in the decedent's estate of the right to receive such amount. IRC § 691(c).

21st Century Estate Planning:
Practical Applications
2005 Edition

©2005 Sonnenschein Nath & Rosenthal LLP
and Cannon Financial Institute, Inc.

164

Chapter VI
Bibliography

Mark L. Ascher, *Federal Income Taxation of Trusts & Estates: Cases, Problems, and Materials,* Carolina Academic Press (2nd ed. August 1996).

Bernard Barnett, "A Potpourri Of Perverse Puzzles And Problems Pervading Fiduciary Income Taxation Plus Positive Planning Possibilities To Pursue," *26th Annual Philip E. Heckerling Inst. on Est. Plan.* (1992).

Jonathan G. Blattmachr and Arthur M. Michaelson, *Income Taxation of Estates and Trusts,* Practicing Law Inst. (14th ed. June 1995).

Ira Mark Bloom, Ladson F. Boyle, John T. Gaubatz and Lewis D. Solomon, *Federal Taxation of Estates, Trusts and Gifts: Cases, Problems and Materials*, Matthew Bender (2nd ed. 1998).

John C. Bost, *Estate Planning and Taxation,* Kendall/Hunt Publishing Company.

Code and Regulations: Including Related Income Tax Provisions, Federal Estate and Gift Taxes, CCH Incorporated (May 2000).

Virginia F. Coleman, "Grantor Trust: Yesterday's Disaster, Today's Delight, Tomorrow's," *30th Annual Philip E. Heckerling Inst. on Est. Plan.* (1996).

M. Carr Ferguson, James J. Freeland and Mark L. Ascher, *Federal Income Taxation of Estates, Trusts, and Beneficiaries,* Aspen Publishers, Inc. (3rd ed. June 1998).

Fiduciary Income Taxation, BNA Treatise.

Fiduciary Tax Return Guide, Research Institute of America.

Norman H. Lane, *Federal Income Taxation Of Estates And Trusts,* Warren, Gorham & Lamont.

Michael L. Moore, *Income Taxation Of Estates, Trusts, And Beneficiaries,* Institute for Business Planning.

Jeffrey N. Pennell, *Cases and Materials on the Income Taxation of Trusts, Estates, Grantors and Beneficiaries* (American Casebook Series), West Publishing Company, College & School Division (January 2000).

Jeffrey N. Pennell, "Income Taxation of Trusts, Estates, Grantors & Beneficiaries," *33rd Annual Philip E. Heckerling Inst. on Est. Plan.* (1999).

Preparing Fiduciary Income Tax Returns, Massachusetts Continuing Legal Education (ed. 1997).

21st Century Estate Planning:
Practical Applications
2005 Edition

©2005 Sonnenschein Nath & Rosenthal LLP
and Cannon Financial Institute, Inc.

165

Jacob Rabkin, Mark Johnson with contributor Mary Howley, *Federal Income, Gift and Estate Taxation*, Matthew Bender.

Randall W. Roth, "The Intentional Use Of Tax-Defective Trusts," *26th Annual Philip E. Heckerling Inst. on Est. Plan.* (1992).

Stowell Rounds and Joseph J. O'Connell, How to Save Time and Taxes Preparing Fiduciary Income Tax Returns, Matthew Bender.

"Survivors, Executors, and Administrators," *IRS Publication 559,* Department of the Treasury.

Howard M. Zaritsky and Norman H. Lane, *Federal Income Taxation of Estates and Trusts*, Warren, Gorham & Lamont (2nd ed. 1993).

21st Century Estate Planning:
Practical Applications
2005 Edition

©2005 Sonnenschein Nath & Rosenthal LLP
and Cannon Financial Institute, Inc.

166

VII. ANNUAL EXCLUSION GIFT PLANNING

A. Introduction

Generally, the gift tax and GST tax annual exclusions permit an individual to give an amount equal to the annual exclusion ($11,000 in 2005) per donee without incurring any gift tax or GST tax liability, provided that the gift is of a present interest. A married donor can annually give up to double that amount ($22,000 for 2005) per donee if the donor's spouse agrees to apply his or her annual exclusion amount by gift-splitting. The requirements of annual exclusion gifts are discussed in detail in the federal gift tax chapter.

Although the annual exclusion amount may seem insignificant, a lifetime giving program that takes advantage of the gift tax and GST tax annual exclusions over a period of years can significantly reduce the donor's transfer tax liability.

This chapter discusses the following topics related to annual exclusion gift planning:

- Benefits of annual exclusion gifts.
- Annual exclusion gifts to custodial accounts.
- Annual exclusion gifts in trust (*i.e.*, IRC § 2503(c) minor's trusts and *Crummey* trusts).

B. Benefits of Annual Exclusion Gifts

1. Federal Transfer Tax Savings

The use of annual exclusion gifts can result in considerable federal transfer tax savings.

a. Generally. Generally, annual exclusion gifts are not subject to gift tax or GST tax. In addition, because the donor's annual exclusion is applied to a gift before the donor's applicable exclusion amount, annual exclusion gifts do not use up any portion of the donor's applicable exclusion amount. Accordingly, over a period of time, a planned giving program using annual exclusion gifts can remove a significant amount of property from the donor's gross estate without incurring any transfer tax or using up any portion of the donor's applicable exclusion amount. In addition, any future appreciation and income generated by the transferred property is also removed from the donor's gross estate, further reducing the donor's estate tax liability.

21st Century Estate Planning:
Practical Applications
2005 Edition

©2005 Sonnenschein Nath & Rosenthal LLP
and Cannon Financial Institute, Inc.

167

EXAMPLE: D gives $11,000 a year in cash to each of D's 3 children, 5 grandchildren, 10 great-grandchildren and 2 friends over the five-year period before D's death. Because of the annual exclusion, none of these gifts are subject to gift tax or GST tax. In addition, D did not use any portion of D's applicable exclusion amount or GST exemption, while effectively removing $1,100,000 from D's estate. Assuming a maximum estate tax rate of 50% at D's death, these annual exclusion gifts saved D's estate $550,000 in federal estate tax. In addition, any income and appreciation generated by the transferred property between the date of gift and D's date of death was also removed from D's estate.

    b. Leveraging the Annual Exclusion With Discounts. Structuring a gift so that valuation discounts will apply to the transfer enables the donor to "leverage" the amount of property that can be transferred via annual exclusion gifts. The valuation chapter discusses the types of applicable discounts that can reduce the value of a gift. For example, a discount for lack of marketability can be used to reduce the value of a business interest.

EXAMPLE: The concept of "leverage" can be illustrated as follows: P makes a gift of limited partnership interests to C. An appraiser determines that a 50% discount is applicable to the limited partnership interests being transferred. Accordingly, each gift of $1 of limited partnership interests represents $2 of underlying value.

    c. Avoidance of Gross-Up Rule. Another transfer tax benefit of annual exclusion gifts is the avoidance of the IRC § 2035(b) gross-up rule. Under the IRC § 2035(b) gross-up rule, gift taxes paid by the decedent on transfers within three years of death are included in the decedent's estate. Because annual exclusion gifts are not subject to federal gift tax, the gross-up rule is avoided. The advantage of avoiding the gross-up rule is the reduction in estate taxes that would be payable on gift taxes actually paid.

    d. Basis Considerations. In planning to make any gift, practitioners should weigh the benefit of the transfer tax savings against potential capital gain tax cost that results from the loss of the step-up in basis that would have occurred had the property been subject to estate tax in the donor's estate. Under current law, property transferred by gift retains the donor's basis, but property transferred at death gets a step-up in basis to the property's fair market value at death. IRC §s 1014 and 1015. If the donor pays gift tax on appreciated property, however, the donee's basis increases by the portion of the gift tax attributable to the appreciation in the property. Treas. Reg. § 1.1015-1(a)(2). Accordingly, annual exclusion gifts retain the donor's basis.

    →   **Planning Point:** For property transferred by gift, all of the appreciation in excess of the donor's basis (plus any adjustment for gift taxes paid on appreciated property) will be subject to income tax on the sale of the

21ˢᵗ Century Estate Planning:
Practical Applications
2005 Edition

©2005 Sonnenschein Nath & Rosenthal LLP
and Cannon Financial Institute, Inc.

168

property. For property transferred at death, only the appreciation after the decedent's death will be subject to income tax on the sale of the property. In determining whether to make lifetime gifts of appreciated property versus retaining such property until death, practitioners should consider the amount of appreciation in the property, the likelihood of a sale in the near future and the likelihood the client will survive until 2010 when the basis step-up becomes limited. For example, if the donee is not likely to sell the property after the donor's death, the capital gain issue may not be relevant.

2. State Transfer Tax Savings

Annual exclusion gifts can also reduce a donor's overall state transfer tax liability. This is true because most states impose some kind of death tax (*e.g.*, estate, inheritance, legacy or succession tax) after the donor's death. Not all states, however, impose a gift tax, and those states that impose a gift tax do so at lower tax rates than the death tax rates. Accordingly, making annual exclusion gifts over a period of time can result in considerable state transfer tax savings.

3. Income Shifting

Annual exclusion gifts can help reduce a family's overall income tax liability. This is accomplished in two ways. First, the donor can give income-producing assets to family members in lower income tax brackets. Second, the donor can transfer appreciated assets that will eventually be sold at a gain to a family member who is subject to a lower capital gains tax rate or who can offset the gain with losses.

➔ **Planning Point:** Practitioners should note that the income tax benefit of shifting income-producing assets to children may be reduced by the Kiddie tax. IRC §§ 1(g) and 63(c)(5).

4. Non-Tax Benefits

As the estate tax exemption increases in the future, the transfer tax benefits of annual exclusion gifts discussed above may not be as compelling for families of more modest wealth. These families, however, may still be compelled to make annual exclusion gifts for non-tax reasons. Some of these reasons include the following:

a. **Support Children or Other Beneficiaries.** One of the most common non-tax reasons for making annual exclusion gifts is to provide for the support of family members. Donors will still wish to support their children, regardless of the tax consequences.

b. **Provide Financial Experience to Beneficiaries.** Probably the most important non-tax reason for making annual exclusion gifts is to provide some financial experience to less wealthy and/or less financially sophisticated family members or other

21st Century Estate Planning:
Practical Applications
2005 Edition

©2005 Sonnenschein Nath & Rosenthal LLP
and Cannon Financial Institute, Inc.

169

individuals. This is especially true if the donor's wealth is considerable, and the beneficiary will eventually receive a significant amount of property. The donor could make annual exclusion gifts to a beneficiary in order to prepare the beneficiary for subsequent transfers of more significant amounts of property. Out of inexperience, some beneficiaries (especially minor beneficiaries) may make bad financial decisions or impulse purchases. These beneficiaries may benefit from learning from their mistakes made in investing or spending these relatively smaller amounts of property. If a beneficiary does not appear to have learned from these mistakes, the donor can adjust his or her gifting program or estate disposition accordingly.

      c. Transfer Control of Closely-Held Family Business. Another non-tax reason for making annual exclusion gifts is the gradual transfer of control in a closely-held family business to the younger family generation. By making annual exclusion gifts of business interests, the donor can control which beneficiaries will have ownership interests in the business. This also allows the donor to see how these beneficiaries handle their ownership interests.

➔   **Planning Point:** Practitioners advising clients who wish to make annual exclusion gifts of business interests should be sure that the operating agreement of the business does not prevent the donees from obtaining immediate use, possession or enjoyment of the gifted business interests. A member's (or partner's) inability, under the operating agreement, to: (1) unilaterally withdraw his or her capital account, (2) independently effectuate a dissolution of the business and (3) sell his or her business interest without the business manager's consent in the manager's sole discretion has been deemed to prevent gifted business interests from qualifying for the gift tax annual exclusion. *Hackl v. Comm'r*, 335 F.3d 664 (7th Cir. 2003).

This result might be avoided by giving a donee the unilateral right to sell his or her entire interest to third parties, subject to a right of first refusal by the entity and/or other interest holders to purchase the interest at the same price and terms as a bona fide offer from a third party. Also, the business manager's discretion to retain funds can be limited to the needs of the business with the balance of the funds being distributed to the interest holders. Alternatively, the business agreement could give each donee the right to withdraw assets from the entity. The right can be limited to the fair market value for the gifted interest and only be available for a limited period of time. Although such a provision might reduce the valuation discount, it should foreclose any argument that the donee does not have the right to the immediate use, possession and enjoyment of the property in the economic sense.

      d. Make Donor's Estate More Liquid. Another non-tax reason for making annual exclusion gifts is to shift illiquid assets in order to make the donor's estate more liquid. If the donor's gross estate is significant and is comprised mainly of illiquid assets (*e.g.*, stock in a

21ˢᵗ Century Estate Planning:
Practical Applications
2005 Edition

©2005 Sonnenschein Nath & Rosenthal LLP
and Cannon Financial Institute, Inc.

170

closely-held business), the estate may have to suffer the hardships of selling these illiquid assets or borrowing funds in order to pay the federal estate tax liability attributable to these illiquid assets. To avoid this problem, the donor could make annual exclusion gifts of the donor's illiquid assets and retain the liquid assets.

C. Annual Exclusion Gifts to Custodial Accounts

1. Background

Most states have adopted either the Uniform Gifts to Minors Act ("UGMA") or the Uniform Transfers to Minors Act ("UTMA"). These Uniform Acts basically authorize gifts of property to a minor without the appointment of a guardian. Generally, the UGMA allows securities, life insurance policies, annuity contracts or money to be transferred to a custodian for the minor's benefit, and the UTMA allows any type of property to be transferred to a custodian for the minor's benefit. The specific types of allowable property transfers vary from state to state.

➔   **Planning Point:** Before advising clients to transfer property to a custodial account for a minor, practitioners should verify what types of property can be transferred under applicable state law.

    a. Effecting Transfer. Typically, a donor gives property to a minor under the Uniform Acts by depositing funds or registering assets in the name of an adult individual or a trust company, "as custodian for [MINOR'S NAME] under [NAME OF APPLICABLE UNIFORM ACT]."

> **EXAMPLE:** T transfers $10,000 to a bank account for the benefit of T's minor nephew, N. N's father, B, created the account in Illinois and is the custodian. Title to the account might read as follows: "B, as custodian for N under the Illinois Uniform Transfers to Minors Act."

    b. Typical Provisions. The custodian is the fiduciary, and the prudent person standard of investment typically applies to the investment and reinvestment of custodial property. The custodian is typically authorized to distribute any portion or all of the property "for the minor's support, maintenance and education" or "as the custodian deems advisable for the use and benefit of the minor." Custodial property must typically be distributed to the donee when he or she reaches majority age (usually 18 or 21). If the donee dies prior to attaining that age, the custodial property must be paid to the donee's estate.

2. Tax Consequences

The tax consequences of a custodial account are as follows:

    a. Estate Tax Consequences. If the donor is _not_ acting as custodian, the custodial property will be included in the donee's estate at the donee's death. If, however, the

21st Century Estate Planning:
Practical Applications
2005 Edition

©2005 Sonnenschein Nath & Rosenthal LLP
and Cannon Financial Institute, Inc.

171

donor is acting as custodian at the donor's date of death and predeceases the donee, the custodial property will be included in the donor's estate under IRC §§ 2036, 2038 and/or 2041. Rev. Rul. 59-357, 1959-2 C.B. 212. When donors make related gifts to custodial accounts and appoint each other as custodian to avoid estate tax inclusion, the reciprocal transaction doctrine applies to unwind the transaction. *Exchange Bank & Trust Company v. U.S.*, 694 F.2d 1261 (Fed. Cir. 1982).

> **EXAMPLE:** H and W are married and have one minor child, C. In order to avoid inclusion in each other's estates, H gives 25 shares of stock to W, as custodian for C. W gives 10 shares of stock to H, as custodian for C. H dies. The 25 shares of stock will be included in H's estate even though W is custodian because under the reciprocal transaction doctrine, H effectively retained the same control over the stock as if H had named himself custodian.

    b. Gift Tax Consequences. A gift to a custodial account for a minor is a completed gift that qualifies for the annual gift tax exclusion to the extent of the annual exclusion amount. Rev. Rul. 59-357, 1959-2 C.B. 212. A donor may split gifts to a custodial account with the donor's spouse. IRC § 2513.

    c. GST Tax Consequences. A gift to a custodial account for a minor skip person is a completed gift and is a "direct skip" and, thus, qualifies for the annual exclusion for GST tax purposes to the extent of the annual exclusion amount. IRC § 2642(c). Accordingly, a grandparent can make gifts to a custodial account for a grandchild or more remote descendant (or other skip person) without incurring any GST tax liability.

    d. Income Tax Consequences. The income from custodial property is taxed to the minor, <u>regardless</u> of whether it is actually expended for the minor's benefit. The income is taxed to another individual, however, to the extent the income is used to discharge that individual's legal support obligation. Similarly, the income is taxed to the donor to the extent the income is used to satisfy the donor's obligations. Rev. Rul. 56-484, 1956-2 C.B. 23 *approved in* Rev. Rul. 59-357, 1959-2 C.B. 212; IRC § 677.

➔   **Planning Point:** Practitioners should check applicable state law regarding a parent's legal obligation to support a minor when determining who is responsible for paying the tax on income from a custodial account.

3. Advantages and Disadvantages

The advantages and disadvantages of gifts to a custodial account are as follows:

    a. Advantages. One advantage of gifts to a custodial account for a minor is the ease of transferring property. Proper reference to the applicable Uniform Act incorporates all

21ˢᵗ Century Estate Planning:
Practical Applications
2005 Edition

©2005 Sonnenschein Nath & Rosenthal LLP
and Cannon Financial Institute, Inc.

172

of its provisions. No separate document (such as a trust instrument) is necessary. Another advantage is that, unlike a guardian, a custodian can typically act without court supervision.

b. Disadvantages. As discussed above, custodial accounts are problematic for federal estate tax purposes if the donor is serving as custodian. Most donors are not aware of this estate tax consequence. Another disadvantage is that some states restrict the types of property that can be contributed to a custodial account. Finally, the most significant disadvantage of custodial accounts is the requirement that the property be distributed at a certain age (usually 18 or 21). Over a period of time, annual exclusion gifts to a custodial account can result in a significant amount of property passing to the beneficiary. Most clients would not desire a significant amount of property to be distributed outright to a beneficiary at such a young age.

D. Annual Exclusion Gifts In Trust

1. Generally

As discussed in the federal gift tax chapter, a gift must be a "present interest" (an unrestricted right to the immediate use, possession, or enjoyment of property or the income from property) in order to qualify for the gift tax and the GST tax annual exclusions under IRC §§ 2503(b) and 2642(c). Outright gifts typically qualify for the annual exclusion because the donee has the immediate use, possession and enjoyment of the gifted property. Generally, gifts in trust are gifts of a future interest that do <u>not</u> qualify for the annual exclusion, because the donee does not have the immediate use, possession and enjoyment of the trust property. Gifts to an IRC § 2503(c) minor's trust or a Crummey trust, however, are gifts of present interests and, therefore, <u>do</u> qualify for the annual exclusion. These two types of trusts are discussed below.

2. Gifts to IRC § 2503(c) Minor's Trusts

IRC § 2503(c) allows certain gifts in trust for a minor (an individual under age 21) to qualify for the annual exclusion. IRC § 2503(c) is a statutory exception to the general rule that a gift in trust is a gift of a future interest.

a. Requirements. A gift to an IRC § 2503(c) trust for the benefit of a donee under age 21 is a present interest qualifying for the annual exclusion if <u>all</u> of the following requirements are met:

(1) <u>Distributions Prior to Age 21</u>. The property and its income must be expendable by or for the benefit of the beneficiary <u>before</u> the beneficiary reaches age 21.

(a) <u>Either Principal Interest or Income Interest Can Qualify</u>. IRC § 2503(c) literally requires both the property <u>and</u> its income to be expendable by or for the benefit of the beneficiary prior to age 21. The Regulations, however, allow an annual exclusion to the extent the income interest <u>or</u> the principal interest meets this requirement. Treas. Reg. § 25.2503-4(b)(c).

21st Century Estate Planning:
Practical Applications
2005 Edition

©2005 Sonnenschein Nath & Rosenthal LLP
and Cannon Financial Institute, Inc.

173

EXAMPLE: T creates a trust for the benefit of T's minor child, C. All income is to be distributed annually to C, and the entire trust property is to be distributed to C at age 25. Such a transfer is a gift of a present interest qualifying for the annual exclusion with respect to C's right to income but is a gift of a future interest with respect to C's right to corpus.

(b) **No Substantial Restriction.** The terms of the trust must <u>not</u> substantially restrict the exercise of the trustee's discretion to determine the amounts, if any, of the income or property to be expended for the minor beneficiary's benefit and the purpose for which the expenditure is to be made. Treas. Reg. § 25.2503-4(b)(1). A distribution standard with no objective limitation (*e.g.*, welfare, happiness, or convenience) is <u>not</u> a substantial restriction. Rev. Rul. 67-270, 1967-2 C.B. 349. A more limited distribution standard (*e.g.*, education expenses only, if beneficiary is disabled, or if the beneficiary is not otherwise adequately provided for) would substantially restrict the trustee's discretion and disqualify the trust for the annual exclusion. Rev. Rul. 69-345, 369-1 C.B. 226; *Illinois National Bank of Springfield v. U.S.*, 91-1 U.S.T.C. ¶60,063 (C.D. Ill. 1991).

EXAMPLE: T creates a trust for the benefit of T's minor child, C. The trust provides that the income is distributable to C for his welfare, and the principal is distributable to C for his education only. Such a transfer is a gift of a present interest qualifying for the annual exclusion with respect to C's right to income but is a gift of a future interest with respect to C's right to corpus.

(2) **Passes at Age 21.** Any portion of the property and the income not expended by or for the donee must "pass" to the donee at age 21.

(a) **Extension of Trust After Age 21**. The trust need not terminate when the donee reaches age 21 in order to "pass" to the donee at age 21. Treas. Reg. § 25.2503-4(b)(2). The donee's right to withdraw the entire trust property at age 21 will satisfy the requirement that the entire property pass to the donee at age 21. This is true even if the donee's right of withdrawal lasts for a finite period of time after reaching age 21. Rev. Rul. 74-43, 1974-1 C.B. 285.

(b) **Passed to Beneficiary Prior to Age 21.** IRC § 2503(c) literally requires any portion of the property and the income not expended by or for the donee to pass to the donee <u>at</u> age 21. The IRS, however, has allowed an annual exclusion to the extent such property passes to the donee <u>prior to</u> age 21. The IRS reasoned that IRC § 2503(c) only sets the maximum age requirement at age 21. Rev. Rul. 73-287, 1973-2 C.B. 321.

(3) **Distribution at Death Prior to Age 21.** If the beneficiary dies before reaching age 21, the property and the income must be payable: (a) to the beneficiary's estate, <u>or</u> (b) as the beneficiary may appoint under a general power of appointment.

21ˢᵗ Century Estate Planning:
Practical Applications
2005 Edition

©2005 Sonnenschein Nath & Rosenthal LLP
and Cannon Financial Institute, Inc.

174

(a) **Lifetime or Testamentary General Power of Appointment Sufficient**. A lifetime general power of appointment or a testamentary general power of appointment qualifies. Treas. Reg. § 25.2503-4(b).

(b) **No Substantial Restriction on Exercise of Power.** If the beneficiary has a general power of appointment, the terms of the trust must _not_ substantially restrict the beneficiary's exercise of that power. Treas. Reg. § 25.2503-4(b).

> **EXAMPLE:** T creates a trust for the benefit of T's minor child, C. The trust terms are as follows: (1) income and principal are distributable to C for his welfare prior to age 21; (2) at age 21, C may withdraw the entire trust property; (3) at age 20, C will have a testamentary general power of appointment over the trust property. State law allows individuals 18 years of age to execute wills. Accordingly, the trust will not qualify for the exclusion under IRC § 2503(c) because the trust substantially restricts C's right under state law to exercise C's general power of appointment in C's will.

(c) **Inability to Exercise Power Due to Disability.** The fact that under local law a minor is under a disability and, thus, is unable to exercise a lifetime general power of appointment or to execute a will does _not_ disqualify the trust under IRC § 2503(c). Treas. Reg. § 25.2503-4(b). The possession of general power of appointment is sufficient.

> **EXAMPLE:** T creates a trust for the benefit of T's minor child, C. The trust terms are as follows: (1) income and principal are distributable to C for his welfare prior to age 21; (2) at age 21, C may withdraw the entire trust property; (3) C has a testamentary general power of appointment over the trust property. State law allows individuals 18 years of age to execute wills. Even though C is under age 18 and cannot execute a will, the trust still qualifies as a IRC § 2503(c) trust, transfers to which qualify for the gift tax annual exclusion to the extent of the annual exclusion amount.

b. **Tax Consequences.** The tax consequences of a IRC § 2503(c) trust are as follows:

(1) **Estate Tax Consequences.** IRC § 2503(c) trust property is included in the donee-beneficiary's gross estate because the trust provides that the trust property is payable to the beneficiary's estate or if the beneficiary has a general power of appointment over the trust property. If the donor serves as trustee, however, IRC § 2503(c) trust property will be included in the donor's estate under IRC §§ 2036 or 2038.

➔ **Planning Point:** The discretionary power the trustee must have to qualify for the exclusion under IRC § 2503(c) would cause the trust to be included

21ˢᵗ Century Estate Planning:
Practical Applications
2005 Edition

©2005 Sonnenschein Nath & Rosenthal LLP
and Cannon Financial Institute, Inc.

175

in the grantor's estate if the grantor were the trustee. Accordingly, the grantor of a IRC § 2503(c) trust should <u>not</u> serve as the trustee.

(2) **Gift Tax Consequences.** Obviously, transfers to a properly drafted IRC § 2503(c) will qualify for the gift tax annual exclusion.

(3) **GST Tax Consequences.** The grantor's transfer of property to an IRC § 2503(c) trust for a skip person (*e.g.*, a grandchild or more remote descendant) can qualify for the annual exclusion for GST tax purposes. As discussed in the federal generation-skipping transfer tax chapter, a transfer in trust qualifies for the annual exclusion for GST tax purposes if: (a) the transfer is a direct skip; (b) the trust meets the requirements for the gift tax annual exclusion under IRC § 2503(b); (c) no part of the income or principal may be distributed to or for any person other than the skip person-beneficiary; and (d) the trust assets must be included in the skip person-beneficiary's estate if the skip person-beneficiary dies before the trust terminates. IRC § 2642(c). An IRC § 2503(c) trust can be tailored to meet these requirements:

(a) **Direct Skip.** To qualify for the GST tax annual exclusion, the transfer to the IRC § 2503(c) trust must be a direct skip (*i.e.*, a transfer to a skip person subject to gift tax). A trust is a skip person if: (1) all interests in the trust are held by skip persons, <u>or</u> (2) if no person holds an interest in the trust and at no time after the transfer may a distribution be made to a non-skip person. An IRC § 2503(c) trust with a skip person (*e.g.*, a grandchild or more remote descendant) as sole beneficiary would meet this requirement.

(b) **Annual Exclusion Requirement Must Be Met.** To qualify for the GST tax annual exclusion, the trust must meet the requirements for the gift tax annual exclusion under IRC § 2503(b). An IRC § 2503(c) trust, by its nature, meets the present interest requirement of the gift tax annual exclusion under IRC § 2503(b).

(c) **No Distributee Other Than Skip Person-Beneficiary.** To qualify for the GST tax annual exclusion, no part of the income or principal of the IRC § 2503(c) trust may be distributed to or for any person other than the skip person-beneficiary. This requirement is met if the terms of the IRC § 2503(c) trust provide that income and principal are distributable only to or for the skip person-beneficiary.

(d) **Included in Beneficiary's Gross Estate.** To qualify for the GST tax annual exclusion, the IRC § 2503(c) trust assets must be included in the skip person-beneficiary's estate if the skip person-beneficiary dies before the trust terminates, regardless of when the skip person-beneficiary dies. This requirement is met if the IRC § 2503(c) trust provides that at the skip person-beneficiary's death, the trust property is payable to the beneficiary's estate or as the beneficiary may appoint under a general power of appointment.

> **EXAMPLE:** T creates a trust for the benefit of T's minor grandchild, G. The trust terms are as follows: (1) income and principal are distributable to G for his welfare prior to age 21; (2) at age 21, G may

21st Century Estate Planning:
Practical Applications
2005 Edition

©2005 Sonnenschein Nath & Rosenthal LLP
and Cannon Financial Institute, Inc.

176

withdraw the entire trust property; (3) if G dies prior to age 21, the trust property will be payable to G's estate, and (4) on or after age 21, G will have a lifetime general power of appointment over the trust property. The trust will be included in G's estate if G dies before the trust terminates, regardless of when G dies. Accordingly, the trust meets this requirement.

c. Income Tax Consequences. The income from an IRC § 2503(c) trust is taxed to the minor if it is distributed to or for the minor. Accordingly, the "kiddie tax" (*see* IRC § 1(g)) is applicable to an IRC § 2503(c) trust to the extent the income is distributed to or for a minor beneficiary under age 14. The income is taxed to another individual, however, to the extent the income is used to discharge that individual's legal support obligation. Similarly, the income is taxed to the donor to the extent the income is used to satisfy the donor's obligations. Otherwise, the income is taxed to the trust.

d. Advantages and Disadvantages. The advantages and disadvantages of a IRC § 2503(c) trust are as follows:

(1) Advantages. The main advantage of a IRC § 2503(c) trust is the potential transfer tax savings. Transfers to a IRC § 2503(c) trust will qualify for the gift tax annual exclusion to the extent of the annual exclusion amount ($11,000 in 2005 or $22,000 if gifts are split). If structured properly, transfers to a IRC § 2503(c) trust will also qualify for the annual exclusion for GST tax purposes to the extent of the annual exclusion amount. The transferred funds (and appreciation in value of or income generated by the transferred funds) will be removed from the donor's gross estate.

(2) Disadvantages. From a client's perspective, the main disadvantage of an IRC § 2503(c) trust is that the trust property must either be payable to the beneficiary at age 21 or subject to a right of withdrawal at age 21. The concern is that the beneficiary may be too young and financially irresponsible to handle the funds outside a trust. Clients who prefer the funds continue in trust for the beneficiary might instead consider a *Crummey* trust, discussed below.

3. Gifts to *Crummey* Trusts

A variation of the IRC § 2503(c) trust is the "*Crummey*" trust, named after the decision in *Crummey v. Comm'r.*, 397 F.2d 82 (9th Cir. 1968). A *Crummey* trust allows certain gifts in trust for a minor to qualify for the annual exclusion <u>without</u> requiring that the trust property be payable to or subject to a right of withdrawal by the beneficiary at age 21.

a. Background. Generally, transfers to a discretionary trust (a trust that gives the trustee discretion to distribute income and principal) do <u>not</u> qualify for the annual exclusion because the beneficiary is receiving a future interest. The annual exclusion is available,

21st Century Estate Planning:
Practical Applications
2005 Edition

©2005 Sonnenschein Nath & Rosenthal LLP
and Cannon Financial Institute, Inc.

177

however, for transfers to such a trust if the beneficiary is given a sufficient right of withdrawal (also called a "demand right") over the transferred property.

(1)   **Pre-*Crummey*.** Prior to the *Crummey* case, transfers to a trust subject to such a right of withdrawal by an <u>adult</u> beneficiary qualified for the gift tax annual exclusion. The beneficiary in these cases had a right of withdrawal over the <u>entire</u> trust property at <u>all</u> times.

(2)   **Crummey.** The *Crummey* case involved a <u>minor</u> beneficiary with a right of withdrawal and a substantially <u>narrower</u> right of withdrawal than in previous cases allowing the annual exclusion. The right of withdrawal in *Crummey* extended only to the amount of the annual transfer to the trust (not the entire trust property), and the right of withdrawal <u>expired</u> at the end of the calendar year in which the transfer was made. If the right of withdrawal was not exercised by the end of the calendar year, the right <u>lapsed</u>, and the annual transfer was retained in trust. The *Crummey* case allowed the annual exclusion for a minor beneficiary with such a right of withdrawal to the extent of the entire value of the transfer subject to the right of withdrawal. The court reasoned that the issue was whether the beneficiary had a right to enjoy the transferred property, <u>not</u> whether the beneficiary actually enjoyed the transferred property. Subsequent cases and rulings confirm the allowance of the annual exclusion for transferred property subject to such a right of withdrawal, regardless of the age or mental competency of the powerholder. *Fish v. U.S.*, 432 F.2d 1278 (9th Cir. 1970); Rev. Rul. 73-405, 1973-2 C.B. 321.

b.   **Amount Subject to Right of Withdrawal.** The typical *Crummey* clause gives the beneficiary a noncumulative right to withdraw some or all of a contribution to the trust for a limited time period. Because it is usually undesirable for the entire trust property to be subject to a right of withdrawal, the *Crummey* clause often limits the amount subject to withdrawal.

(1)   **Annual Exclusion Amount.** The trust could limit the amount subject to withdrawal to the amount that would qualify for the gift tax annual exclusion (with or without gift splitting). This limitation is appropriate if the donor does not wish for the beneficiary to withdraw any more trust property than necessary to qualify for the maximum gift tax annual exclusion.

> **EXAMPLE:** T creates a trust for the benefit of B. The trust terms are as follows: (1) income and principal are distributable to B for his support needs; (2) at age 30, B may withdraw the entire trust property; (3) B has a noncumulative right to withdraw that portion of each trust contribution not to exceed the gift tax annual exclusion amount. T transfers $5,000 to the trust in 2004 and $11,000 to the trust in 2005. If B does not exercise his rights of withdrawal, both of T's gifts will qualify for the gift tax annual exclusion.

21st Century Estate Planning:
Practical Applications
2005 Edition

©2005 Sonnenschein Nath & Rosenthal LLP
and Cannon Financial Institute, Inc.

178

(2) <u>**Greater of $5,000 or 5% of Trust Property**</u>. The annual lapse of a *Crummey* beneficiary's right of withdrawal in excess of the greater of $5,000 or 5% of the trust property (the "5 or 5 amount") is deemed to be a taxable gift by the powerholder. IRC § 2514(e). In order to prevent the lapse of the right of withdrawal from having any negative estate or gift tax consequences for the beneficiary, the amount subject to withdrawal could be limited to the greater of $5,000 or 5% of the trust property each year (a "5 or 5 power"). This is because the failure to exercise a 5 or 5 power is not a taxable gift, and the lapse of such a power will not cause any of the trust property to be included in the beneficiary's gross estate. IRC §§ 2514(e) and 2041(b)(2). The only drawback to a 5 or 5 power is that the annual exclusion allowed is limited to that amount.

> **EXAMPLE:** T creates a trust for the benefit of B. The trust terms are as follows: (1) income and principal are distributable to B for his support needs; (2) at age 30, B may withdraw the entire trust property; (3) B has a noncumulative right to withdraw the greater of $5,000 or 5% of the trust property. T transfers $11,000 to the trust in 2005 when the entire trust property is worth $80,000. B has a right to withdraw only $5,000 of the $11,000. Accordingly, only $5,000 qualifies for the gift tax annual exclusion.

(3) <u>**Unlimited Amount**</u>. The trust could provide that the <u>entire</u> transfer is subject to a right of withdrawal by the beneficiary. This would preserve the full benefit of the available annual exclusion amount. The lapse of such a right of withdrawal in excess of the 5 or 5 amount, however, may have adverse estate tax and gift tax consequences to the beneficiary unless the beneficiary has a general power of appointment (which prevents the beneficiary from inadvertently making a completed gift upon the lapse of his withdrawal right).

(4) <u>**Hanging Power**</u>. A "hanging power" can be used to obtain the protection of the 5 or 5 power <u>and</u> the full benefit of the annual exclusion. The hanging power is drafted as a cumulative power of withdrawal that lapses each year to the extent of the greater of $5,000 or 5% of the trust property. The drawback of a hanging power is that the amount subject to a hanging power at the powerholder's death is includible in his or her estate.

> **EXAMPLE:** T creates a trust for the benefit of B. B has a cumulative annual right of withdrawal over any property transferred to the trust during the year. The withdrawal right lapses to the extent of the greater of $5,000 or 5% of the trust property. T transfers $50,000 to the trust on October 12, 2005 (and B then has a right to withdraw the property). The trust property is worth $80,000 on December 31, 2005. B did not exercise B's right of withdrawal. Accordingly, $5,000 (because $5,000 is greater than 5% of $80,000) lapsed at the end of 2005 with no gift or estate tax consequences to B. B has a continuing power to withdraw $45,000.

21ˢᵗ Century Estate Planning:
Practical Applications
2005 Edition

©2005 Sonnenschein Nath & Rosenthal LLP
and Cannon Financial Institute, Inc.

179

c. Multiple _Crummey_ Powerholders. A trust may have multiple beneficiaries with identical withdrawal rights. Increasing the number of beneficiaries who have _Crummey_ withdrawal rights may maximize the number of annual exclusions that may be claimed. Accordingly, an incentive exists to use more _Crummey_ powerholders if the value of assets to be transferred to the trust in a given calendar year will be greater than the amount of a single annual exclusion.

To qualify for the annual exclusion, each beneficiary with a withdrawal right must have a legal right to exercise the withdrawal power. Transfers subject to a right of withdrawal, even such a right held by contingent beneficiary, qualify for the annual exclusion. _Cristofani Est. v. Comm'r_, 97 T.C. 74 (1991), _acq. in result only_, 1992-1 C.B. 1; see also _Kohlsaat Est._, T.C. Memo. 1997-212.

> **EXAMPLE:** T creates a trust for the lifetime benefit of T's child, C. The trust terms are as follows: (1) income and principal are distributable to C for his support needs; (2) at age 40, C may withdraw the entire trust property; (3) C and C's child, G, each have a noncumulative right to withdraw an amount equal to one-half of the value of any contribution to the trust (but not to exceed, in any calendar year, the amount of the federal gift tax annual exclusion for such year). T transfers $22,000 to the trust in 2005. The entire $22,000 subject to withdrawal, one-half by C and one-half by G, qualifies for the gift tax annual exclusion.

d. Notice and Reasonable Time to Exercise Right of Withdrawal. The beneficiary must have notice of his or her right of withdrawal and have a reasonable amount of time to exercise his or her right of withdrawal before it lapses. Rev. Rul. 81-7, 1981-1 C.B. 474. What is a "reasonable" amount of time varies. IRS rulings have approved withdrawal periods ranging from 30 to 90 days. PLR 8134135; PLR 8015133; PLR 8015133. The _Crummey_ case involved a two-week withdrawal period. At least one case held that knowledge of a contribution to a trust and right of withdrawal satisfies the adequate notice requirement. _Holland Est._, 73 T.C.M. (CCH) 3236 (1997).

➔   **Planning Point:** Although the beneficiary's knowledge of additions to and right of withdrawal from a trust may be adequate, the trustee of a _Crummey_ trust should still give beneficiaries immediate written notice of additions to the trust to secure the gift tax annual exclusion.

e. Tax Consequences. The tax consequences of a _Crummey_ trust are as follows:

(1) Estate Tax Consequences. The estate tax consequences of a _Crummey_ trust are essentially the same as the estate tax consequences of an IRC § 2503(c) trust. As discussed earlier, the amount subject to withdrawal in excess of the 5 or 5 amount is

21ˢᵗ Century Estate Planning:
Practical Applications
2005 Edition

©2005 Sonnenschein Nath & Rosenthal LLP
and Cannon Financial Institute, Inc.

180

includible in the beneficiary's estate if the right of withdrawal lapses. IRC § 2041. *Crummey* trust property should not be included in the donor's estate <u>unless</u> the trust income or principal is used to discharge the donor's legal obligations, or the donor is serving as trustee at the donor's date of death (and all discretionary distributions are not limited to ascertainable standards).

(2)   Gift Tax Consequences. Transfers to a properly drafted *Crummey* trust should qualify for the gift tax annual exclusion to the extent of the lesser of the annual exclusion amount or the amount subject to withdrawal.

➔   **Planning Point:** If a donor intends for a gift of a business interest to qualify for the gift tax annual exclusion, the practitioner must be sure that the transfer is in accordance with the *Hackl* decision, which is discussed earlier in this Chapter.

(3)   GST Tax Consequences. The donor's transfer of property to a *Crummey* trust for a skip person (*e.g.*, a grandchild or more remote descendant) can be structured to qualify for the annual exclusion for GST tax purposes.

(a)   Direct Skip. To qualify for the GST tax annual exclusion, the transfer to the *Crummey* trust must be a direct skip (*i.e.*, a transfer to a skip person subject to gift tax). A *Crummey* trust with a skip person (*e.g.*, a grandchild or more remote descendant) as beneficiary would meet this requirement.

(b)   Annual Exclusion Requirement Must Be Met. To qualify for the GST tax annual exclusion, the trust must meet the requirements for the gift tax annual exclusion under IRC § 2503(b). Transfers to a properly drafted *Crummey* trust, by its nature, would meet the present interest requirement of the gift tax annual exclusion under IRC § 2503(b).

(c)   No Distributee Other Than Skip Person-Beneficiary. To qualify for the GST tax annual exclusion, no part of the income or principal of the *Crummey* trust may be distributed to or for any person other than the skip person-beneficiary. This requirement is met if the terms of the *Crummey* trust provide that income and principal are distributable only to or for the skip person-beneficiary.

➔   **Planning Point:** Transfers to a single trust with <u>multiple</u> *Crummey* powerholders will not qualify for the annual exclusion for GST tax purposes. To qualify for the annual exclusion for GST purposes, the trust must be created for the benefit of one beneficiary (or segregated into separate trusts if there are multiple beneficiaries).

(d)   Included in Beneficiary's Gross Estate. To qualify for the GST tax annual exclusion, the *Crummey* trust assets must be included in the skip person-beneficiary's estate if the skip person-beneficiary dies before the trust terminates, regardless of

21st Century Estate Planning:
Practical Applications
2005 Edition

©2005 Sonnenschein Nath & Rosenthal LLP
and Cannon Financial Institute, Inc.

181

when the skip person-beneficiary dies. This requirement is met if the *Crummey* trust provides that at the skip person-beneficiary's death, the trust property is payable to the beneficiary's estate or as the beneficiary may appoint under a general power of appointment.

(4) Income Tax Consequences.

(a) Powerholder as Trust Owner. Since the beneficiary of the *Crummey* trust, through the utilization of the *Crummey* provision, has a power of withdrawal, the beneficiary will be treated as the owner of that portion of the trust subject to his or her power under IRC § 678(a). Rev. Rul. 81-6, 1981-1 C.B. 385. IRC § 678 is usually triggered by the mere existence of the power of withdrawal, rather than its exercise or the legal ability to exercise it. Accordingly, the beneficiary must include as taxable income the income to which he or she has a right during the appropriate calendar year (along with a corresponding portion of the trust's deductions and credits). IRC § 671. A specific method is provided for calculating the interest that a beneficiary would have in such a trust as well as the tax consequences of both the income and the corpus rights of withdrawal. See Treas. Reg. § 1.671-3(a)(3); (b)(3).

> **EXAMPLE:** B, a beneficiary of a *Crummey* trust, holds a power of withdrawal over annual transfers to the trust. Both B and the trust are calendar-year taxpayers. On January 1, the trust receives a $5,000 transfer subject to a power of withdrawal that continues until the end of the year. The corpus of the trust, as augmented by the $5,000 transfer, is $100,000. Under Treas. Reg. § 1.671-3(a)(3), the beneficiary would include for income tax purposes 5% ($5,000/$100,000) of the trust income, deductions and credits for the year. The 5% figure is the ratio of the property subject to the power of withdrawal over the total value of the trust property.

➔ **Planning Point:** If the trust has no income, deductions or credits (*e.g.*, a *Crummey* trust that holds only insurance on the life of the donor), IRC § 678 will not have any practical application. Furthermore, a *Crummey* power of withdrawal usually is restricted both in scope and in time. The donee can only withdraw the annual contribution to the trust and only for a limited period of time. As a result, if IRC § 678 is applicable, it should have partial application only. *See Oppenheimer v. Comm'r*, 16 T.C. 515 (1951); *Krause v. Comm'r.*, 56 T.C. 1242 (1971). The IRS has addressed this issue only indirectly by stating that the pro rata share of a trust to which IRC § 678 applies "should take into account the length of time during which [the beneficiary] has the power to vest in himself the additions of corpus to the trust." PLR 8142061. In any event, the income tax consequences to the beneficiaries should have little significance in a typical *Crummey* trust that holds only insurance.

21ˢᵗ Century Estate Planning:
Practical Applications
2005 Edition

©2005 Sonnenschein Nath & Rosenthal LLP
and Cannon Financial Institute, Inc.

182

Another aspect of the income tax consequences to a *Crummey* powerholder involves powerholders who allow a power of withdrawal to lapse but retain an interest in or a power over the trust that, were the beneficiary the trust's grantor, would trigger the grantor trust rules of IRC §§ 671 through 677. See IRC § 678(a)(2). This would arise in situations in which the powerholder is also, for example, a discretionary or mandatory income beneficiary, a remainder beneficiary or one who holds administrative powers. The IRS appears to have taken the position that the lapse of the *Crummey* power equates to a "contribution" to the trust by the powerholder, making him or her a grantor of that portion of the trust for purposes of current and future income taxes. PLRs 8521060, 8517052 and 200022035. The powerholder is treated in this manner because, when the powerholder allows a power of withdrawal to lapse, the economic result is the same as if the powerholder removed property from the trust and then immediately transferred that same property back to the trust. In the latter situation, the powerholder would clearly be deemed the owner of that portion of the trust that was withdrawn and then recontributed. When the powerholder in this situation is considered the grantor of a portion of the trust, the income taxation of the powerholder will then be determined like any other grantor of the trust - under IRC §§ 673-677 - not under IRC § 678. See Charles E. Early, Income Taxation of Lapsed Powers of Withdrawal: Analyzing Their Current Status, 62 J. of Taxation 198 (1985); David Westfall, Lapsed Powers of Withdrawal and the Income Tax, 39 Tax Law Review 63 (1983). In many *Crummey* trusts, lapses occur annually, and the application of this "recontribution rule" to the powerholder may be increasing each year. Because there is no regulation or ruling of general application that addresses this situation, the outcome of this issue remains unresolved.

(b) **Grantor vs. the Beneficiary as Trust Owner.** IRC § 677(a)(3) treats a grantor as the owner of any portion of a trust whose income can be used to pay premiums on insurance policies on the grantor's life. If Section 678 also treats the beneficiary as the owner of the same portion of the trust because of a power of withdrawal, one must question who really owns the trust for income tax purposes. This conflict is resolved in favor of the grantor's ownership because IRC § 678(b) states that, if the grantor is otherwise treated as the owner under IRC §§ 673-677 and the beneficiary holds an IRC § 678 power over the same income, the beneficiary's power is disregarded, and the grantor is taxed as the owner of the trust income. For a discussion of the grantor's income tax consequences, see Chapter VI, Federal Income Taxation of Trusts and Estates. IRC § 678, however, does not defer to the grantor when ownership of the trust principal is in question, leaving this issue open. On the differences between ownership of income and ownership of principal, see N. Lane & H. Zaritsky, *Federal Income Taxation of Estates and Trusts* ¶ 7.04[4] (WG&L 1989).

➔ **Planning Point:** Thus, to avoid income tax consequences to *Crummey* powerholders (along with the uncertainties and complexities of IRC § 678(a)), the governing instrument of a *Crummey* trust could be intentionally drafted to create a trust as to which the grantor is treated as the owner of all trust income and principal. After the grantor dies, however, the *Crummey* beneficiaries may find themselves the owners of a significant portion of the trust as a result of prior lapses that occurred while the grantor was alive.

21st Century Estate Planning:
Practical Applications
2005 Edition

©2005 Sonnenschein Nath & Rosenthal LLP
and Cannon Financial Institute, Inc.

183

f. **Advantages and Disadvantages.** The advantages and disadvantages of a *Crummey* trust are as follows:

(1) **Advantages.** The main advantage of a *Crummey* trust is the potential transfer tax savings <u>without</u> requiring the termination of the trust at a certain age. Transfers to a *Crummey* trust will qualify for the gift tax annual exclusion to the extent of the annual exclusion amount ($11,000 in 2005 or $22,000 if gifts are split). If structured correctly, transfers to a *Crummey* trust will also qualify for the annual exclusion for GST tax purposes to the extent of the annual exclusion amount. The transferred funds (and appreciation in value of or income generated by the transferred funds) will be removed from the donor's gross estate.

(2) **Disadvantages.** The main disadvantage of a *Crummey* trust is the amount of administration involved (*e.g.*, sending notices to *Crummey* powerholders each year).

21st Century Estate Planning:
Practical Applications
2005 Edition

©2005 Sonnenschein Nath & Rosenthal LLP
and Cannon Financial Institute, Inc.

184

Chapter VII
Bibliography

2001 Tax Legislation: Law, Explanation and Analysis, CCH Incorporated (2001).

The Economic Growth and Tax Relief Reconciliation Act of 2001: An Analysis, Matthew Bender & Co. (2001).

Edward F. Koren, *Estate and Personal Financial Planning* (2003).

Henry J. Lischer, Jr., 846 T.M., *Gifts to Minors*.

Charles F. (Monty) Newlin, "Sophisticated Estate Planning For Uncertain Times: Covering All the Bases For Today and Tomorrow," Illinois Institute for Continuing Legal Education Master Teacher Program (June 21, 2001).

John R. Price, *Price on Contemporary Estate Planning* (2nd ed. 2001).

George M. Turner, *Irrevocable Trusts* (3d ed. 2003).

Howard M. Zaritsky & Stephan R. Leimberg, *Tax Planning With Life Insurance: Analysis with Forms* (2003).

21st Century Estate Planning:
Practical Applications
2005 Edition

©2005 Sonnenschein Nath & Rosenthal LLP
and Cannon Financial Institute, Inc.

185

VIII. PLANNING FOR THE MARITAL DEDUCTION

A. Introduction and History

1. Introduction

The federal estate tax marital deduction defers federal estate taxation until the death of the last to die of an individual and his or her spouse. Internal Revenue Code ("IRC") § 2056 allows for an unlimited federal estate tax marital deduction for qualified interests that pass to a decedent's surviving spouse. Therefore, the estate tax marital deduction may eliminate any estate tax on transfers between spouses at the death of the first spouse. IRC § 2523 allows for an unlimited federal gift tax marital deduction for transfers between spouses during their lifetime, and such gift tax marital deduction will be discussed at the end of this chapter.

Upon a client's death, a client may leave property directly to his or her spouse and obtain a marital deduction for such property. Outright transfers of property to the surviving spouse result in the decedent's loss of control over the use of the property during the lifetime of the surviving spouse and the ultimate disposition of the property at the surviving spouse's death. Such transfers allow the surviving spouse to use and distribute the property as the surviving spouse chooses as opposed to how the decedent desired. By giving property to a marital trust, a client may obtain the marital deduction and also retain control over the ultimate use and disposition of the property after the client's death. The client's estate planning documents may contain a marital deduction formula that gives the marital trust the optimal amount of property to defer and minimize federal estate tax upon the death of the client or his or her spouse, whichever comes first; this is referred to as the "optimal marital deduction."

This chapter will discuss the following issues relating to the marital deduction, the use of trusts and formulae for funding such trusts:

- The Estate Tax Marital Deduction – Outright Distribution and Transfers to Trusts.
- Qualifying for the Marital Deduction.
- The Terminable Interest Rule and Its Exceptions.
- Power of Appointment Marital Trusts.
- Estate Trusts.
- Qualified Terminable Interest Property Trusts.
- Qualified Domestic Trusts.
- Selecting Marital Deduction Trusts.
- Common Marital Deduction Formula Provisions.
- Guidelines for Selecting a Marital Deduction Formula.
- Creating and Funding Generation-Skipping Trusts with the Use of Martial Deduction Trusts.
- Selected Funding and Drafting Issues.

21st Century Estate Planning:
Practical Applications
2005 Edition

©2005 Sonnenschein Nath & Rosenthal LLP
and Cannon Financial Institute, Inc.

186

- The Use of Disclaimers.
- Deferring Tax and the Step-up in Basis.
- The Gift Tax Marital Deduction.

2.   History of the Marital Deduction

At the inception of the federal estate tax in 1916, estates of decedents owning community property and estates owning non-community property were not treated equally. The inequitable treatment occurred in both the transfer tax (gift and estate) and the income tax arenas. In 1948, Congress sought to equalize the treatment of decedents in community and non-community property states. Decedents in non-community property states were allowed to deduct up to 50% of the non-community property which was transferred to a surviving spouse as long as the surviving spouse's interest in the property was sufficient to cause such property to be included in the surviving spouse's gross estate. Congress also provided for gift-splitting between spouses and the filing of joint tax returns for income tax purposes.

In 1976, Congress allowed for a deduction in the amount of $250,000 or 50% of the adjusted gross estate, whichever was larger. This deduction eliminated estate taxes in modest estates. In 1981, Congress removed the dollar limit and allowed a deduction for the full amount of property passing to the surviving spouse, whether during lifetime or at death. The deduction was allowable only if the property passing to the surviving spouse was includible in the surviving spouse's gross estate unless such property was consumed during the surviving spouse's lifetime. The 1981 act also introduced the qualified terminable interest property (QTIP) trust and the elective basis for the QTIP. There is more flexibility in post-mortem planning when a QTIP trust is involved.

The most recent tax law changes have not directly affected the marital deduction, but have modified other areas which impact the use of the marital deduction as more thoroughly discussed in the remainder of this chapter. Marital deduction planning remains one of the most complex areas of estate planning, and, at minimum, a basic understanding of the area is required when advising clients with regard to their estate planning.

3.   Definitions

The following terms will be used throughout this chapter and an understanding of them is recommended before moving forward:

- "Funding" is the selection of assets, whether cash, property or sales proceeds, to satisfy a gift or bequest under a will or trust.
- A "formula" gift or bequest is one whose size, composition or value is determined with reference to some external criteria.

   EXAMPLE: "I bequeath my son an amount equal to the value of 100 shares of IBM stock."

21ˢᵗ Century Estate Planning:
Practical Applications
2005 Edition

©2005 Sonnenschein Nath & Rosenthal LLP
and Cannon Financial Institute, Inc.

187

> **EXAMPLE:** "I give my son an amount equal to the value of all the gifts I made to my daughter during my lifetime."

- A "lead" gift or bequest is a formula bequest that is calculated first, that is, before the residuary gift or bequest.
- A "residuary" gift or bequest is a disposition of the balance of the assets of the estate after all the lead gifts or bequests, taxes, debts and expenses have been paid.
- A "marital deduction formula" is a formula gift or bequest that is determined with reference to the maximum available marital deduction under the Internal Revenue Code, (usually) after taking into account other available estate tax deductions and credits.
- An "applicable exclusion formula" is a formula gift or bequest determined with reference to the largest amount that may be transferred free of federal estate tax by reason of the applicable exclusion amount – also called the unified credit. IRC § 2010(c).

4. Pecuniary, Fractional Share, Residuary and Hybrid Gifts and Bequests

The characterization of a bequest or gift is critical to a determination of the nature and extent of a beneficiary's entitlement. It is necessary to determine whether a gift or bequest is pecuniary, fractional or residuary in nature to determine whether the gift or bequest: (i) shares in income during administration; (ii) can be satisfied in kind without the recognition of capital gain or the revaluation of assets; (iii) will participate in gains and losses during administration; or (iv) will share in the burden of taxes, debts, claims and expenses during administration. The following discussion of different types of gifts and bequests does not involve marital deduction formula clauses but explains how to characterize a gift or bequest. Marital deduction formula clauses, discussed further below, follow the same rules, although they can be more difficult to analyze, are generally more complex and are invariably more intimidating.

a. Pecuniary Gifts and Bequests.

A gift or bequest is referred to as pecuniary if it is of a sum certain, that is, equal to a specified dollar value that can readily be determined as of the date of death of a decedent. A few examples of pecuniary gifts will assist in understanding the characteristics and concepts of such gifts:

> **EXAMPLE:** "I give my wife the sum of $100,000." "I give to the Trustees of the Family Trust the sum of $1,000,000."

The primary characteristics of a gift or bequest of a pecuniary amount are:

- All post-death appreciation (and depreciation) in the estate benefits the residuary beneficiaries.

21ˢᵗ Century Estate Planning:
Practical Applications
2005 Edition

©2005 Sonnenschein Nath & Rosenthal LLP
and Cannon Financial Institute, Inc.

188

- Pecuniary amounts may or may not share in income earned during the period of administration. This depends on the specific provisions of state law and the trust instrument.
- Capital gains will be incurred if appreciated assets are sold to raise the cash needed to satisfy the gift or bequest. The same result is obtained if the gift or bequest is <u>satisfied</u> by the distribution of specific assets in kind that have appreciated in value between the date of death and the date of funding.
- The distribution of assets in kind to satisfy a pecuniary bequest requires the revaluation of the assets at the time of distribution.
- Any taxes incurred during the "funding" process are generally paid out of the residuary share, along with expenses of administration, taxes, debts and claims.
- In general, the executor or trustee has broad latitude to select the assets to sell or distribute in order to pay the gift or bequest.

b. <u>Fractional Share</u>. A gift or bequest is referred to as fractional if it is expressed either as a percentage or as a fractional portion of the assets available for distribution.

<u>EXAMPLE</u>: "I give my son one-half of my estate."

The primary characteristics of a gift or bequest of a fractional share are:

- The satisfaction of fractional share gifts and bequests generally does not give rise to capital gains, unless assets are actually sold. As discussed further below, no capital gains are realized if assets are distributed pursuant to the formula in kind, as long as the assets are divided proportionately.
- In general, costs, expenses, debts, claims, taxes, appreciation, depreciation, and trust accounting income are shared ratably among fractional shares.
- Any non-pro rata distribution of available assets must comply with fiduciary standards of impartiality and fair dealing. Unless non-pro rata distributions are authorized either by (i) the governing instrument or (ii) state law, the IRS will treat a non-pro rata distributions made in satisfaction of a fractional share bequest as a taxable event for income tax purposes.
- Assets that are divided proportionately and distributed in kind to fund fractional shares do not require revaluation at the time of distribution.

21ˢᵗ Century Estate Planning:
Practical Applications
2005 Edition

©2005 Sonnenschein Nath & Rosenthal LLP
and Cannon Financial Institute, Inc.

189

c.   Residuary. A residuary gift or bequest is a gift or bequest of property not otherwise disposed of under the terms of a will or trust.

> **EXAMPLE:** "I give my daughter the sum of $100,000, and I give the balance of my estate to my spouse." The "balance of my estate" is a residuary bequest.

The primary characteristics of a residuary gift or bequest are:

- Any appreciation or depreciation during the administration of the estate benefits the residuary beneficiaries.
- No capital gains are realized if assets are distributed in kind to satisfy the residuary gift or bequest.
- Revaluation of the assets is not necessary when satisfying a residuary gift or bequest.
- Taxes, debts, claims and expenses of administration are satisfied with property from the residuary share.

d.   Hybrid. Sometimes it is difficult to determine whether a formula is pecuniary or fractional because characteristics of both appear to be present. These are referred to as hybrid formulae. When first examining the following gifts, some appear the same, but upon a closer examination the differences can be distinguished.

- "I give my son the sum of $100,000, not to exceed, however, 10% of my estate." The "sum of $100,000" is a pecuniary gift. The limitation of 10% does not change the classification of the gift, although it may change the size of the gift.
- "I give my son the sum of $100,000; provided, however, that if the value of my estate is less than $1,000,000, I give my son 10% of my estate." The provision that if the estate is less than the stated amount the son will receive "10% of my estate" *changes* the bequest from a pecuniary amount to a fractional share *if* the condition is met.
- "I give my son an amount equal to the lesser of (a) the sum of $100,000 and (b) 10% of the value of my estate." The language "an amount equal to" generally creates a pecuniary bequest, even when the amount is measured with reference to a percentage, because a percentage "of the value of my estate" is still an amount, and therefore, considered to be pecuniary.
- "I give my son 10% of my estate, not to exceed, however, the sum of $100,000." The language "10% of my estate" creates a fractional share of the estate, subject to a limitation.
- "I give my son 10% of my estate; provided, however, that if the value of my estate is more than $1,000,000, I give my son the sum of $100,000."

21ˢᵗ Century Estate Planning:
Practical Applications
2005 Edition

©2005 Sonnenschein Nath & Rosenthal LLP
and Cannon Financial Institute, Inc.

190

This example illustrates a fractional share that *changes* to a pecuniary gift *if* a specified condition is met.

- "I give my son a share of my estate equal to the lesser of (a) 10% of my estate and (b) $100,000." The language "a share of my estate" generally creates a fractional share. In the absence of language denoting an amount, the limitation probably does not change the character of the gift.

B. Basic Marital Deduction Planning

1. Outright Disposition

An outright transfer or distribution of an interest in property by a decedent to a surviving spouse will qualify for the marital deduction. An outright transfer not only includes property devised to the surviving spouse but also includes property jointly owned with a surviving spouse with rights of survivorship and spousal beneficiary designations. The policy reason behind allowing direct transfers to the spouse to qualify for the marital deduction is that the interest in property will be included in the surviving spouse's gross estate for federal estate tax purposes unless such property is consumed during the lifetime of the surviving spouse.

2. Disposition to Trust

Property interests transferred to trusts where the surviving spouse has an interest in such trust may qualify for the marital deduction if certain requirements are met. IRC § 2056(b) allows for a power of appointment trust, a QTIP trust, or an estate trust. Each of these trusts will be examined in detail later in this chapter.

3. Deferring Tax

The estate tax marital deduction essentially defers estate tax until the death of the surviving spouse. This is advantageous because of the increasing applicable exclusion amount available to the surviving spouse, and because the surviving spouse, with careful planning, may reduce the size of his or her taxable estate after the death of his or her spouse.

At a minimum, when federal estate taxes are applicable, the utilization by each spouse of their applicable exclusion amount and the deferral of tax by use of the marital deduction should be considered.

Deferring taxes has several benefits in addition to the obvious benefit of not paying taxes upon the death of the first spouse. Assets will not need to be liquidated in order to pay estate taxes, thereby avoiding the payment of taxes on capital gains for such liquidation and allowing more assets to be available to support the surviving spouse during his or her lifetime. By splitting interests between a marital share and an applicable exclusion amount share, fractional interests in property may be created allowing a discount to be taken when valuing the property in the surviving spouse's estate.

21st Century Estate Planning:
Practical Applications
2005 Edition

©2005 Sonnenschein Nath & Rosenthal LLP
and Cannon Financial Institute, Inc.

191

Deferring taxes, however, may have some disadvantages. Assets retained by the spouse or a marital trust may appreciate during the surviving spouse's lifetime thereby increasing the federal estate tax at the death of the surviving spouse. Depending upon the age and health of both spouses, it may be more advantageous to pay some tax at the death of the first spouse at lower estate tax rates than to have property taxed in the surviving spouse's estate at higher estate tax rates, although this becomes less significant as the estate tax brackets become more compressed.

4. Step-Up in Basis

a. Current Law. When property is sold, gain or loss on the sale of such property is calculated by determining the difference between the amount realized and the adjusted basis of the property. The basis of property is usually the cost of acquiring the property. Under current law, the basis of property acquired from a decedent is the property's fair market value on decedent's date of death or on the alternate valuation date, whichever is used on the federal estate tax return filed by decedent's executor. IRC § 1014. This is sometimes called the "step-up in basis" rule and is to be contrasted with the "carryover basis" rule applicable to property acquired by gift. See the discussion regarding gifts, Chapter III, Federal Gift Tax. Property is considered "acquired" from the decedent when the property is acquired by bequest, gift or inheritance, when the property is transferred from a revocable trust created by decedent during the decedent's lifetime, and when the property is transferred as a result of the exercise of a general power of appointment. IRC § 1014(b). Some property, however, is not afforded a step-up in basis. This includes the following:

- Property received from the decedent during decedent's lifetime, but disposed of before decedent's death. IRC § 1014(a).
- A right to receive an item of income in respect of a decedent ("IRD") from decedent. IRC § 1014(c). For further discussion of IRD, see Section H.1 below.
- Property passing to a beneficiary if the decedent acquired the property by gift from such beneficiary within one year of decedent's death. IRC § 1014(e).
- Property purchased by an executor with funds obtained by selling property acquired from the decedent. Treas. Reg. § 1.1014-3(c).

b. Basis Rules Under the New Act. Under the Economic Growth and Tax Relief Reconciliation Act of 2001, in 2010, a modified carryover basis rule replaces the step-up in basis rule. Recipients of inherited property will receive a carryover basis equal to the lesser of the decedent's adjusted basis and the fair market value of the property on the decedent's date of death. The decedent's executor can allocate up to $1.3 million in basis increase among the decedent's assets. In addition, the executor can allocate an additional $3 million of basis increase among the decedent's assets that pass to a surviving spouse outright or in a QTIP trust. These amounts may be indexed annually for inflation beginning in 2011. There are a number of assets that are not eligible for the step-up in basis, including property acquired by gift within 3

21ˢᵗ Century Estate Planning:
Practical Applications
2005 Edition

©2005 Sonnenschein Nath & Rosenthal LLP
and Cannon Financial Institute, Inc.

192

years of death from a person other than the decedent's surviving spouse and property that would constitute a right to receive income in respect of a decedent.

C. Qualifying for the Marital Deduction

In general, a marital deduction is allowed for the value of any property interest which *passes* from the decedent to his or her surviving spouse if the interest is a *deductible interest*. The executor has the burden to establish that the decedent was survived by a spouse, the interest passed to the spouse, the interest is deductible and the value of the interest in property. Treas. Reg. § 20.2056(a)-1(b)(i).

1. Interest Must be Includible in Decedent's Gross Estate

In order for an interest in property to qualify for the marital deduction, the asset must be includible in the decedent's gross estate for federal estate tax purposes.

2. Decedent is Survived by a Surviving Spouse Who is a U.S. Citizen

If the surviving spouse is not a U.S. citizen, the marital deduction is only available for transfers to a qualified domestic trust (QDOT) under IRC § 2056A, or if the non-U.S. citizen surviving spouse, who was a resident of the U.S. at decedent's date of death, becomes a U.S. citizen before the date the federal estate tax return for the decedent is timely filed.

3. Interest Must "Pass" to the Surviving Spouse

Under IRC § 2056(c), an interest in property "passes" to the surviving spouse if it passes to the surviving spouse by bequest or devise, inheritance, dower or curtesy, inter vivos transfer, joint tenancy with right of survivorship, the exercise or nonexercise of a power of appointment, or beneficiary designation of a life insurance policy. Treas. Reg. § 20.2056(c)-1.

4. Interest Must be Deductible

The regulations describe a "deductible interest" as an interest that is not a "nondeductible interest." A nondeductible interest is defined as a property interest that: (i) is not included in the decedent's gross estate; (ii) generates deductions under IRC § 2053 or 2054; or (iii) in general, is a terminable interest. Reg. § 20.2056(a)-2(b). A terminable interest, as will be described more thoroughly below, is a nondeductible interest unless it meets the requirements of IRC § 2056(b).

5. Value of Property Interest

Once the requirements listed above are met, the value of the property interest must be determined. The property interest is valued as of the decedent's date of death, unless the executor elects the alternate valuation date under IRC § 2032. This election is not permitted unless both the value of the gross estate and the amount of federal estate tax and generation-skipping transfer tax imposed by reason of the decedent's death are thereby reduced. IRC §

21st Century Estate Planning:
Practical Applications
2005 Edition

©2005 Sonnenschein Nath & Rosenthal LLP
and Cannon Financial Institute, Inc.

193

2032(c). The marital deduction is allowed only to the extent of the net value of any deductible interest. If a decedent passes a property interest to his or her surviving spouse and such interest is subject to an encumbrance or obligation, the value of the interest, for purposes of determining the amount of the marital deduction allowable with respect to such interest, must be reduced by the amount of the encumbrance or obligation. Treas. Reg. § 20.2056(b)-4(b). If the executor is required to discharge the encumbrance or obligation, however, the discharge is considered an interest passing to the surviving spouse and is therefore deductible.

> **EXAMPLE:** Decedent devised property valued at $100,000 to her surviving spouse, and such property was subject to a $50,000 debt. If all other requirements for a marital deduction were met, the marital deduction would be $100,000 if the executor was required to discharge such debt, and $50,000 if the executor was *not* required to discharge the debt.

D. Terminable Interest Rule and Its Exceptions

The terminable interest rule provides that the marital deduction is not permitted for interests that terminate or fail upon a lapse of time or the occurrence or nonoccurrence of an event if a person other than the surviving spouse receives the property after the termination of the surviving spouse's interest, unless one of the exceptions to such rule are met. Treas. Reg. § 20.2056(b)-1(b). Examples of terminable interests include life estates, terms for years, annuities, patents, and copyrights. The following are exceptions to the terminable interest rule.

1. Limited Survivorship Exception

IRC § 2056(b)(3) provides that the marital deduction is available for transfers to a surviving spouse with a limited survivorship requirement. Specifically, a terminable interest is deductible if: (1) the only condition under which the interest will terminate is the death of the surviving spouse within six months after the decedent's death, or if the surviving spouse's death is a result of a common disaster that also resulted in decedent's death; and (2) the condition does not in fact occur. Treas. Reg. §20.2056(b)-3(a).

> **EXAMPLE:** Decedent bequeathed his estate to his spouse on the condition that she survive him by 6 months. If she did not survive the decedent by 6 months, such property was to be distributed to the decedent's child. If the spouse died within the 6 month period such interest would be a nondeductible interest as it passed to a person other than the surviving spouse. If the spouse survived the decedent by 6 months, the conditions of IRC § 2056(b)(3) have been met, and such interest is deductible.

> **EXAMPLE:** A decedent bequeathed her estate to her husband if he was living on the date of distribution. Even if the distribution occurred

21st Century Estate Planning:
Practical Applications
2005 Edition

©2005 Sonnenschein Nath & Rosenthal LLP
and Cannon Financial Institute, Inc.

within six months of the decedent's death, the interest would still be a nondeductible interest as the distribution *could have* occurred after the 6 month period. Therefore, the marital deduction is not allowed.

2.   General Power of Appointment Trust

Use of general power of appointment marital trusts, also referred to as a life estate with power of appointment, has declined since the Economic Recovery Tax Act of 1981, in part because of the larger degree of control that a property owner may exert through the use of one or more QTIP trusts. Under IRC § 2056(b)(5) and the regulations thereunder, a marital deduction is allowed for an interest that passes to a surviving spouse in trust if all the following conditions are met:

- The surviving spouse is entitled for life to all the income from the entire interest, or a specific portion of the entire interest, or to a specific portion of all the income from the entire interest;
- The income payable to the surviving spouse must be payable at least annually;
- The surviving spouse must have the power to appoint the entire interest or a specific portion of the entire interest to himself or herself or to his or her estate;
- The power must be exercisable by the surviving spouse alone and in all events;
- The entire interest or specific portion must not be subject to a power in any other person to appoint any part to any person other than the surviving spouse; and
- The surviving spouse must have the right to require the trustee to make unproductive property productive or to convert such unproductive property within a reasonable amount of time. Alternatively, applicable rules for administration of the trust must require the trustee to use the degree of judgment and care in the exercise of a power to retain unproductive property which a prudent man would use if he were the owner of the trust assets. Treas. Reg. § 20.2056(b)-5(f)(4).

If the right to income or the power of appointment is limited to a specific portion of the property interest, the marital deduction is allowed only to the extent that the rights in the surviving spouse meet the requirements listed above. Treas. Reg. § 20.2056(b)-5(b). The right to income and the power of appointment do not need to be in the same proportion; however, the marital deduction is limited to the smaller amount.

> **EXAMPLE:** The surviving spouse is entitled to receive all the income from the property, but the surviving spouse's power of appointment only extends to one-half of the property. The marital deduction is limited to one-half of the value of such property.

21ˢᵗ Century Estate Planning:
Practical Applications
2005 Edition

©2005 Sonnenschein Nath & Rosenthal LLP
and Cannon Financial Institute, Inc.

195

A surviving spouse who is a beneficiary of a general power of appointment marital trust can possess a number of rights and powers which would be inconsistent with the concept of, or would be impermissible in, a QTIP trust:

- An unlimited right to withdraw any or all of the principal of the marital trust during the life of the surviving spouse;
- The right, as sole trustee or co-trustee, to participate in discretionary principal distribution decisions under a non-ascertainable standard; and
- A lifetime power of appointment exercisable in favor of third parties.

3.   Life Insurance or Annuity Payments with General Power of Appointment

It is possible for an interest that consists of proceeds from an annuity, endowment or life insurance policy that are to be paid in installments or held by the insurer under an agreement to pay interest, to qualify for the marital deduction. Under IRC § 2056(b)(6), a marital deduction is allowed for such interests passing to a surviving spouse if the following conditions are met:

- The proceeds, or a specific portion of the proceeds, must be held by the insurer under an agreement to pay the entire proceeds or a specific portion of the proceeds in installments or to pay interest. Such payments must be payable only to the surviving spouse during the surviving spouse's lifetime;
- The installment or interest payments must be payable to the surviving spouse at least annually, and such payments must begin no later than 13 months after the decedent's death;
- The surviving spouse must have the power to appoint the entire interest or a specific portion of the entire interest to either the surviving spouse or the surviving spouse's estate;
- The power must be exercisable by the surviving spouse alone and in all events; and
- The entire interest or specific portion must not be subject to a power in any other person to appoint any part to any person other than the surviving spouse.

4.   Estate Trust

An estate marital trust allows the trustee broad discretion to distribute any, all or none of the income to the surviving spouse. Undistributed income is added to principal. Principal may be distributed to the surviving spouse pursuant to whatever standard the deceased spouse wishes to provide in the governing instrument. At the death of the surviving spouse, the entire trust, including accrued and accumulated income, must be distributed to the surviving spouse's estate.

➔   **Planning Point:** This lack of control over the ultimate disposition of the
         trust at the death of the surviving spouse is one of the disadvantages of the

21ˢᵗ Century Estate Planning:
Practical Applications
2005 Edition

©2005 Sonnenschein Nath & Rosenthal LLP
and Cannon Financial Institute, Inc.

196

estate trust for many individuals. In addition, the distribution to the surviving spouse's estate creates a probate estate that can be avoided by use of a QTIP trust or a general power of appointment marital trust.

→ **Planning Point:** If an estate consists of a business interest which is not income producing and which the decedent does not want to be sold, the decedent may want to use an estate trust because an estate trust is not subject to the productivity standards of Treas. Reg. § 20.2056(b)-5(f)(4).

The ability of the trustee to accumulate income of an estate trust during the life of the surviving spouse and the ability to hold unproductive property are among the advantages of an estate trust. See Rev. Rul. 68-554, 1968-2 C.B. 412; PLR 9634020 (May 24, 1996).

5.   Qualified Terminable Interest Property Trust

Under IRC § 2056(b)(7), a marital deduction is allowed for an interest that passes to a surviving spouse even if the interest is a terminable interest. The Qualified Terminable Interest Property ("QTIP") Trust is a vehicle which allows a decedent to provide for a surviving spouse yet retain control of the ultimate disposition of the decedent's property. If the QTIP requirements are met, the subject property is treated as property passing to the surviving spouse and as not passing to any person other than the surviving spouse. Treas. Reg. § 20.2056(b)-7(a).

a.   **Requirements.** A marital deduction is allowed for a terminable interest that passes to the surviving spouse if all of the following requirements are met:

- The surviving spouse is entitled to all the income from the property for life;
- No person, including the surviving spouse, may possess a power to appoint any part of such property to, or for the benefit of, any person other than the surviving spouse;
- The property passes from the decedent;
- The income payable to the surviving spouse must be payable at least annually; and
- An election must be made on the decedent's estate tax return with respect to a portion or all of the trust.

b.   **Dispositive Provisions of a QTIP Trust.**

(1)   **Income.** The spouse must receive all the income from the QTIP trust for his or her lifetime. IRC § 2056(b)(7)(B)(ii)(I). Some clients may wish the surviving spouse to receive the greater of the income from the QTIP trust or a unitrust amount, defined as a fixed percent of the trust determined annually.

21st Century Estate Planning:
Practical Applications
2005 Edition

©2005 Sonnenschein Nath & Rosenthal LLP
and Cannon Financial Institute, Inc.

197

(2) **Principal.** Principal may be distributed to the spouse pursuant to an ascertainable standard relating to health, education, support and maintenance or pursuant to a broad standard such as best interests. If a non-ascertainable distribution standard is used and the spouse is a trustee, the spouse will have a general power of appointment over all of the QTIP trust, which will cause inclusion in the gross estate of the spouse under IRC § 2041(a)(2) in addition to IRC § 2044. The inevitability of such inclusion would make effectively impossible a partial QTIP election when the marital trust is created.

A broad principal distribution standard may be used if a third party serves as sole trustee of a QTIP trust. In addition, a broad principal distribution can be used when the spouse is serving as a co-trustee of the QTIP trust if the governing instrument precludes the spouse as co-trustee from participating in discretionary principal distribution decisions or if the governing instrument limits the spouse's right to participate in discretionary distribution decisions to the narrower ascertainable standard and allows the third party trustee to make principal distributions pursuant to a broader standard.

Principal of a QTIP trust may not be distributable to anyone other than the surviving spouse without disqualifying the trust for the marital deduction. IRC § 2056(b)(7)(B)(ii)(II); Treas. Reg. § 20.2056(b)-7(d)(1).

(3) **Withdrawal Right.** A QTIP trust may contain a lifetime withdrawal right exercisable by the spouse, but such withdrawal right should be limited both in terms of the amount withdrawable as well as the time when it can be exercised. Such a withdrawal right is often limited to the greater of $5,000 or 5% of the value of the trust assets ("5 or 5" standard). See IRC §§ 2514(e) and 2041(b)(2). If a spouse is given an unlimited right, as opposed to a "5 or 5" standard, to withdraw the principal of the QTIP trust, the unlimited right assures inclusion of the trust in the gross estate of the surviving spouse. If an unlimited right of withdrawal given to the spouse makes the trust not a QTIP trust, then the trust would be ineligible for the special election available to a QTIP trust for purposes of the generation-skipping transfer tax under IRC § 2652(a)(3).

Annual withdrawal rights should be limited to the "5 or 5" standard to avoid estate tax and gift tax problems for the spouse under IRC §§ 2041(b)(2) and 2514(e). If only part of a QTIP trust is elected to qualify for the marital deduction, powers which allow withdrawals in excess of the "5 or 5" standard and which lapse during the surviving spouse's lifetime may eliminate the post-mortem estate tax planning available at the death of the settlor or testator. Even if all of a QTIP trust has been elected to qualify for the marital deduction, a lifetime lapse that exceeds the "5 or 5" safe harbor may result in the spouse's making a taxable gift of the remainder interest in the excess property.

Additionally, there is a potential grantor trust income tax problem under IRC § 678(a)(1) with lapsing rights of withdrawal over a QTIP trust. For a detailed discussion of the grantor trust rules, see Chapter VI, Income Taxation of Trust and Estates.

21st Century Estate Planning:
Practical Applications
2005 Edition

©2005 Sonnenschein Nath & Rosenthal LLP
and Cannon Financial Institute, Inc.

198

(4) **QTIP Election.** The QTIP election is made by the executor. IRC §§ 2056(b)(7)(B)(v) and 2203. If the decedent has a revocable trust agreement and pour-over will, the QTIP election is made by the legal representative of the estate, or, if none, by the trustee of the revocable trust. Treas. Reg. § 20.2056(b)-7(b)(3). The governing instrument may direct the fiduciary to elect to qualify all of the QTIP trust for the marital deduction. While such direction limits the flexibility to make a partial QTIP election (discussed below), it may be desirable when the interests of the surviving spouse and the remainder beneficiaries are different (*e.g.*, second spouse and children of first marriage).

(5) **Limited Testamentary Power of Appointment.** A limited testamentary power of appointment can be given to the spouse over the QTIP trust to allow the spouse to appoint the marital trust among a class of beneficiaries defined and limited by the testator or settlor, such as his or her descendants, their spouses and charities. This permits the spouse to take a second look at the family's estate plan after the death of the testator or settlor of the trust and adjust for events and circumstances that have occurred subsequent to his or her death.

- A limited testamentary power of appointment may be given to the spouse without jeopardizing the marital deduction.
- No one, including the surviving spouse, can be given a lifetime power of appointment without disqualifying the QTIP trust for the marital deduction. IRC § 2056(b)(7)(B)(ii)(II); Treas. Reg. § 20.2056(b)-7(d)(1).

(6) **Income Accrued or Undistributed at Death.** Income accrued or undistributed at the death of the surviving spouse can be paid to the spouse's probate estate or can be added to the principal of the QTIP trust or paid to the next income beneficiary of the trust.

- Treas. Reg. § 20.2056(b)-7(d)(4) permits such income to be paid to someone other than the spouse or the spouse's estate without jeopardizing the qualification of the QTIP trust for the marital deduction.
- If the accrued or undistributed income is not distributed to the estate of the spouse, it nevertheless must be included in the gross estate of the surviving spouse. Treas. Reg. § 20.2044-1(d)(2).
- In *Estate of Rose Howard v. Comm'r*, 91 T.C. 923 (1988), the Tax Court ignored the predecessor proposed regulation and disallowed the marital deduction for a QTIP trust that did not pay the accrued or undistributed income to the spouse's estate or make it subject to a general power of appointment by the spouse. The *Howard* case was reversed on appeal, *Estate of Howard v. Comm'r*, 910 F.2d 633 (9th Cir. 1990), but some estate planners still exercise caution and comply with the Tax Court's *Howard* decision even though the Treasury Regulations have subsequently been amended to reflect the decision of the Ninth Circuit Court of Appeals.

21ˢᵗ Century Estate Planning:
Practical Applications
2005 Edition

©2005 Sonnenschein Nath & Rosenthal LLP
and Cannon Financial Institute, Inc.

199

- In *Estate of Lucille Shelfer*, 103 T.C. 10 (1994), the Tax Court followed its decision in *Howard*. It held that a marital trust that did not pay the accrued and undistributed income to the spouse was not a QTIP trust and thus was not included in the gross estate of the surviving spouse at her death under IRC § 2044, even though a marital deduction had previously been claimed (and allowed) for the trust in her husband's estate. A dissenting opinion noted that the taxpayers had "whipsawed" the IRS. The Court of Appeals for the Eleventh Circuit agreed with the dissent and reversed the Tax Court. *Estate of Lucille Shelfer v. Comm'r*, 96-2 USTC ¶ 60,238 (11th Cir. 1996).

(7)   Definition of Income Under the IRC § 643(b) Final Regulations. The final regulations regarding the definition of income were issued on December 30, 2003. For further discussion of these regulations, see Chapter VI, "Federal Income Taxation of Trusts and Estates" and Chapter XVIII, "Charitable Giving." The final regulations amend the regulations governing marital deduction treatment for transfers to trust in both the gift and estate tax contexts. A trust will qualify for the gift and estate tax marital deduction if the trust operates under a state law that allows a reasonable allocation of the trust's total return between the income and remainder beneficiaries. A spouse will be treated as entitled to receive all net income from a trust, as required for the trust to qualify as QTIP for purposes of the gift and estate tax marital deductions, if the trust is administered under applicable state law that provides for a reasonable apportionment between the income and remainder beneficiaries of the total return of the trust and that meets the requirements of Treas. Reg. § 1.643(b)-1. Furthermore, the QTIP election requirements under Treas. Reg. § 20.2056(b)-7 state that a power under applicable local law permitting the trustee to adjust between income and principal that fulfills the trustee's duty of impartiality and that meets the requirements of Treas. Reg. § 1.643(b)-1 will not be considered a power to appoint trust property to a person other than the surviving spouse.

It is not sufficient that the trust agreement alone authorize the unitrust payment; state law must allow payment of a unitrust amount as income. The deduction will not be jeopardized if in some years trust income as traditionally defined will exceed the unitrust amount.

c.   Partial Election.

(1)   Single Fund Marital Trust. If a partial QTIP election is made, the QTIP trust may be held as a single fund marital trust with an elected share (which qualifies for the marital deduction) and a non-elected share (which does not so qualify). The governing instrument may provide that principal payments to the spouse are charged against the elected share first, thereby reducing the portion that will later be included in the spouse's gross estate for federal estate tax purposes. Treas. Reg. §§ 20.2044-1(d)(3) and (e), Ex. 4.

- The current fair market values of the elected share and the non-elected share are calculated immediately prior to the principal distribution. The principal distribution is then made solely from the elected portion of the single fund

21st Century Estate Planning:
Practical Applications
2005 Edition

©*2005 Sonnenschein Nath & Rosenthal LLP*
and Cannon Financial Institute, Inc.

200

marital trust. The amount of the principal distribution is then reflected by an adjustment based on current value to both the elected portion and the non-elected portion of the marital trust, thereby reducing the fraction or percentage of the marital trust consisting of property that will be subject to estate tax at the death of the surviving spouse.

- A single fund marital trust with a rolling fraction can present some administrative difficulties and so must be used with care.
- A single fund marital trust for which a partial QTIP election is to be made can also be used in lieu of a marital trust/family trust estate plan without wasting the applicable exclusion amount of the first to die.

(2) **Elected and Non-Elected Marital Trusts.** With a partial QTIP election, the governing instrument can provide that the QTIP trust may be severed into two separate trusts, elected and non-elected, that are held under the same dispositive terms and that principal payments shall be made to the spouse from the elected marital trust first. See Treas. Reg. § 20.2056(b)-(7)(b)(2)(ii). This avoids the need to revalue the QTIP trust each time principal is distributed to the spouse and reduces the assets that will be included in the gross estate of the spouse when principal distributions are made from the elected portion.

- The non-elected portion clearly will qualify for the credit for tax on prior transfers should the surviving spouse die within 10 years of the deceased spouse whose governing instrument created the QTIP trust for which the partial QTIP election is made. See IRC § 2013(a).
- The division of a marital trust to reflect a partial QTIP election must be done on a fractional or percentage basis. However, the funding of the separate trusts so created need not be done by transferring a pro rata share of each of the assets in the marital trust prior to division into elected and non-elected trusts. Treas. Reg. §§ 20.2056(b)-7(b)(2)(ii)(B), 20.2056(b)-7(h), Ex. 14.

➔ **Planning Point:** If the governing instrument is silent on a trustee's right to divide a QTIP trust into two separate trusts, state law may allow the fiduciary to sever the marital trust.

(3) **Non-Elected Portion Added to Family Trust.** Alternatively, the governing instrument can provide that, when a partial QTIP election is made by the executor, the non-elected portion of the marital trust is severed from the marital trust and added to the applicable exclusion disposition. Treas. Reg. § 20.2056(b)-7(d)(3)(i). Where the governing instrument provides for an applicable exclusion disposition consisting of a family trust in which income or principal can be distributed to the surviving spouse and the descendants of the decedent for their best interests in the discretion of an independent trustee, additional flexibility is gained by using a QTIP trust for which a partial election can be made in appropriate circumstances.

21st Century Estate Planning:
Practical Applications
2005 Edition

©2005 Sonnenschein Nath & Rosenthal LLP
and Cannon Financial Institute, Inc.

201

(4)   Partial Election and Post-Mortem Planning.   Providing for a partial QTIP election in the governing instrument can facilitate post-mortem estate tax planning. A partial QTIP election can allow the executor at the first death to try to equalize the taxable estates of the decedent and the surviving spouse or to use the decedent's lower graduated estate tax brackets to achieve a taxable estate of $2,500,000 at the first death.

- Utilizing a QTIP trust for which a partial election can be made provides more flexibility than use of alternative marital formulae (*e.g.,* "50% of adjusted gross estate" formula, equalizer formula based on *Estate of Smith v. Comm'r,* 565 F.2d 455 (7th Cir. 1977), and Rev. Rul. 82-23, 1982-1 C.B. 139).

➜   **Planning Point:** The governing instrument needs to address the burden of federal and state estate taxes generated by the partial QTIP election.

(5)   Portion of Family Trust to Qualify for Marital Deduction.   In limited circumstances, the executor may wish to qualify a portion of the family trust for the marital deduction, including planning for a decedent who did not revise his or her estate planning documents after the Economic Recovery Tax Act of 1981 ("ERTA").

- If the decedent dies with a pre-1981 document that uses a "maximum marital deduction" formula, funding of the marital trust may be limited to 50% of the adjusted gross estate under the unlimited marital deduction transitional rule of the ERTA. P.L. 97-34, § 403(a)(1)(A).
- The executor may elect to have part of the family trust qualify for the marital deduction as qualified terminable interest property. Disclaimers and related post-mortem planning may be necessary to enable the family trust to meet the requirements of a QTIP trust discussed above.
- A partial QTIP election must be a fractional or percentage share of the QTIP trust and may be defined by means of a formula. Treas. Reg. § 20.2056(b)-7(b)(2)(i). A formula election is advisable, since it automatically adjusts in case the values of estate assets or the amount of deductions are changed on audit by the IRS.

  EXAMPLE: Decedent dies with a pre-1981 document subject to the ERTA transitional rule. The executor may elect to qualify a fractional share of the family trust for the marital deduction as QTIP, of which (i) the numerator is the smallest marital deduction amount which will result in no federal estate tax payable by reason of testator's death, and (ii) the denominator is the federal estate tax value of the assets included in testator's gross estate which became (or the proceeds, investments or reinvestments of which became) a part of the family trust after payment of all taxes and expenses.

21ˢᵗ Century Estate Planning:
Practical Applications
2005 Edition

©2005 Sonnenschein Nath & Rosenthal LLP
and Cannon Financial Institute, Inc.

202

d. Generation-Skipping Transfer Tax Planning. The generation-skipping transfer ("GST") tax is imposed on any transfer of property from an individual to persons who are more than one generation younger than the transferor (*e.g.*, transfers to grandchildren, great-grandchildren, grand nieces and nephews), and to non-relatives who are more than 37-1/2 years younger than the transferor. The tax applies whether the transfer is an outright gift or bequest, a distribution of current income or principal from a trust, or a distribution on termination of a trust. The tax is imposed at a flat rate, which is equal to the highest estate tax rate on the largest of estates. It is assessed *in addition to* any gift or estate tax that may be incurred by reason of the transfer.

In 2005, an individual can transfer up to $1,500,000 or the amount of his or her unused GST exemption (whichever is lower) free of the GST tax. After 2005, the GST exemption is scheduled to increase as follows:

Calendar Year(s)	GST Exemption
2006-2008	$2,000,000
2009	$3,500,000
2010	Tax Repealed

An individual (or his or her executor) may allocate the GST exemption to transfers made during life or at death. The GST exemption is cumulative during life and at death. In addition to the GST exemption, the following transfers are excluded from application of the GST tax: (a) outright gifts qualifying for the gift tax annual exclusion; (b) gifts in trust that qualify for the gift tax annual exclusion if certain requirements are met (*e.g.,* generally, annual exclusion gifts made to an irrevocable life insurance trust are not exempt from GST tax); (c) medical and tuition payments that are exempt from gift tax; (d) pre-September 26, 1985 irrevocable trusts, which are "grandfathered" from GST tax if there are no additions or substantial changes in the trust provisions; and (e) gifts or bequests to a grandchild if the grandchild's parent was a child of the transferor and is deceased at the time of the gift or bequest.

(1) **QTIP Trust.** A QTIP trust enables some married individuals to use their GST exemption fully to the extent it is not otherwise used during life or at death. IRC §§ 2631(a), (c).

- An individual could create a lifetime generation-skipping trust and fully fund it with $1,500,000 of assets, incurring a gift tax of $205,270, assuming no prior lifetime taxable gifts. If his or her spouse consented to split gift

21ˢᵗ Century Estate Planning:
Practical Applications
2005 Edition

©2005 Sonnenschein Nath & Rosenthal LLP
and Cannon Financial Institute, Inc.

203

treatment, $3,000,000 of assets could be set aside in a generation-skipping trust during life, incurring a gift tax of $410,540.

- Alternatively, the individual could establish a $1,500,000 generation-skipping trust at his or her death. No estate tax will be incurred if the decedent still has his or her $1,500,000 applicable exclusion at his or her death.
- Many married individuals are unwilling to incur gift or estate tax any earlier than absolutely necessary and therefore do not want to create a trust to utilize their GST exemption until the death of both spouses.

(2) **GST Exempt and Non-Exempt Trusts.** Accordingly, many married individuals who want to use their full $1,500,000 GST exemption and defer all gift and estate taxes until the death of the surviving spouse will create one or two trusts at the first death:

- A family trust that uses the applicable exclusion amount (also called the credit shelter amount) and GST exemption, which are both $1,500,000 for 2005.
- The balance will pass either outright to the surviving spouse or in a marital trust.

If the taxpayer has eroded his or her GST exemption but has kept his or her entire applicable exclusion amount intact, the taxpayer's estate plan can create an exempt family trust that will be funded with the remaining GST exemption and a non-exempt family trust that will be funded with the taxpayer's applicable exclusion amount minus the remaining GST exemption. The balance will pass either outright to the surviving spouse or in a non-exempt marital trust.

Conversely, if the taxpayer has eroded his or her applicable exclusion amount but has kept the entire GST exemption intact, the taxpayer's estate plan can create a family trust that will be funded with the remaining applicable exclusion amount and an exempt QTIP marital trust that will be funded with the amount of the GST exemption minus the remaining applicable exclusion amount. The balance will pass either outright to the surviving spouse or in a non-exempt marital trust. As to the exempt marital trust, the executor will make a "reverse QTIP election" for generation-skipping transfer tax purposes under IRC § 2652(a)(3) so that the decedent remains the transferor for GST tax purposes of this trust after the death of the surviving spouse even though the trust is includible in the surviving spouse's gross estate.

> **EXAMPLE:** Decedent died in 2005 with an estate of $1,800,000. Decedent's GST exemption was unused at Decedent's death, but his applicable exclusion amount had been reduced to $1,000,000. To fully utilize Decedent's GST exemption, Decedent's estate plan created a family trust funded with $1,000,000, an exempt QTIP trust funded with $500,000 and a separate non-exempt QTIP trust funded with the remaining $300,000. Decedent's executor allocated $1,000,000 of Decedent's GST exemption to the family trust and $500,000 to the exempt QTIP trust for which the executor also made a reverse QTIP

21st Century Estate Planning:
Practical Applications
2005 Edition

©2005 Sonnenschein Nath & Rosenthal LLP
and Cannon Financial Institute, Inc.

204

election. This estate plan fully allocates Decedent's GST exemption and defers estate taxes until the death of the surviving spouse.

→ **Planning Point:** A partial reverse QTIP election is not allowed. Therefore, the election must be made for the entire value of the trust to which the reverse QTIP election applies.

(3) **Drafting Non-GST Exempt Marital Trusts.** The non-GST exempt marital trust can be either a QTIP trust or a general power of appointment trust. This non-GST exempt trust often will provide that, at the death of the surviving spouse, the federal and state estate taxes payable by reason of the inclusion of the GST exempt QTIP trust and the non-exempt marital trust in the gross estate of the surviving spouse will be paid from the non-exempt marital trust so that the exempt QTIP trust will not be reduced by estate taxes.

→ **Planning Point:** The non-exempt marital trust also can provide for the use of the surviving spouse's GST exemption. To do so, an amount or fraction of the non-exempt marital trust equal to the unused GST exemption of the surviving spouse would be added to the family trust and the exempt QTIP trust, to pass directly to or in trust ultimately for the benefit of one or more skip persons.

(4) **Other Options.** If a client's estate plan does not contain distributions to or in trust for skip persons, the estate plan can incorporate other, less complex provisions regarding the GST exemption, including the following:

- In order to provide for an unusual order of deaths or other unplanned distributions to skip persons, the governing instrument can (i) provide for a QTIP trust and (ii) give the trustee the power to divide a trust into exempt and non-exempt trusts for GST tax purposes or
- The trustee can use the above administrative power to divide a QTIP trust into two separate trusts, a GST exempt QTIP trust and a non-GST exempt QTIP trust. At the death of the surviving spouse, the administrative power could authorize the trustee to (i) pay death taxes solely from the non-exempt QTIP trust and (ii) allocate to the exempt QTIP trust distributions that are more likely to be to skip persons or generation-skipping trusts.

→ **Planning Point:** The election to allocate the unused portion of a decedent's GST exemption must be made within the time allowed to file the federal estate tax return, including extensions. Such allocation is irrevocable. If a timely election was not made, the executor may request an extension of time within which to make the election. Treas. Reg. § 301.9100-1.

21ˢᵗ Century Estate Planning:
Practical Applications
2005 Edition

©2005 Sonnenschein Nath & Rosenthal LLP
and Cannon Financial Institute, Inc.

205

6. Non-U.S. Citizen Surviving Spouse

Generally, the estate tax marital deduction is not allowed for transfers to a surviving spouse who is a non-U.S. citizen whether it is an outright distribution or a transfer to trust. IRC § 2056(d). The rationale for such rule is to make sure the property for which the marital deduction is allowed will later be subject to federal estate tax in the surviving spouse's estate. When the IRS is certain the assets will be subjected to federal estate tax in the surviving spouse's estate, the IRS permits an exception to the above rule.

a. <u>Resident Spouse Becomes a Citizen Prior to Due Date of Estate Tax Return.</u>

The estate tax marital deduction is allowed if the non-U.S. citizen surviving spouse was a U.S. resident at all times after the decedent's death and before becoming a U.S. citizen, and if the surviving spouse becomes a U.S. citizen before the estate tax return is filed.

➔ **Planning Point:** Practitioners should include a question on their estate planning questionnaires regarding citizenship. Although the IRS allows the marital deduction if a surviving spouse becomes a U.S. citizen before the estate tax return is due, as a practical matter, it is extremely difficult to complete the citizenship requirements within that time frame. Therefore, citizenship issues should be dealt with before the death of the first spouse.

b. <u>Qualified Domestic Trust.</u>

A qualified domestic trust ("QDOT") is not a separate type of marital deduction trust. Rather, a QDOT is a marital deduction trust which has additional requirements imposed upon it because the surviving spouse is not a U.S. citizen. IRC § 2056A provides that a trust is a qualified domestic trust and qualifies for the estate tax marital deduction if the following requirements are met:

- At least one trustee of the trust must be a U.S. citizen or a domestic corporation;
- No distribution (other than income) may be made from the trust unless the trustee who is a U.S. citizen or domestic corporation has the right to withhold from the distribution the tax imposed by IRC § 2056A on such distributions;
- The trust must satisfy requirements detailed in the regulations to ensure the collection of estate tax from the trust, including use of a U.S. bank, bond or letter of credit if the fair market value of the assets passing to the QDOT exceeds $2,000,000 at the decedent's date of death or the alternate valuation date. Treas. Reg. § 20.2056A-2(d)(1)(i)(A), (B), or (C);
- The decedent's executor makes an irrevocable election on the decedent's estate tax return to treat the trust as a QDOT; and
- The trust meets the requirements of IRC § 2056(b) (*e.g.*, a general power of appointment trust or QTIP trust).

21st Century Estate Planning:
Practical Applications
2005 Edition

©*2005 Sonnenschein Nath & Rosenthal LLP*
and Cannon Financial Institute, Inc.

206

(1)   Tax on Distributions from QDOT. Certain distributions from a QDOT (other than income or hardship distributions) before the surviving spouse's death, and certain distributions of any remaining property in the QDOT at the surviving spouse's death, are subjected to estate tax at the rate described in IRC § 2056A(b)(2).

(2)   QDOT May Be Created by the Decedent or Surviving Spouse. If a surviving spouse who is not a U.S. citizen receives a bequest or trust distribution by reason of the death of his or her spouse, the surviving spouse may transfer that property to a QDOT before the filing date for the federal estate tax return, and the transfer will be treated as a transfer from the decedent to a QDOT that qualifies for the federal estate tax marital deduction. IRC § 2056(d)(2)(B).

➜   **Planning Point:** The ability of the surviving spouse to add assets to a QDOT is helpful where the spouse receives property from the decedent outright, either through the client's probate estate or outside of probate (*e.g.*, joint tenancy property, life insurance proceeds, individual retirement accounts).

(3)   Individual Retirement Accounts. One of the decedent's largest investment assets may be an individual retirement account (IRA). If the surviving spouse is not a U.S. citizen, the question arises as to how the decedent's interest in the IRA can qualify for the marital deduction.

- If the beneficiary of the IRA is a QTIP marital trust, the solution is straightforward. The QTIP trust simply is drafted to satisfy the QDOT requirements.
- If the beneficiary of the IRA is the surviving spouse outright, the spouse probably will withdraw the property in the IRA and roll it over to his or her own IRA account, titled in the name of the surviving spouse. The surviving spouse's IRA account should have a domestic corporation as trustee. It will satisfy the requirements of a general power of appointment marital trust (IRC § 2056(b)(5)) because the spouse may withdraw any part or all of the income and principal of the IRA trust at any time. The spouse and the IRA trustee can amend the IRA trust to satisfy all of the QDOT requirements. Thus, the spouse's IRA trust serves as the qualified domestic trust.

➜   **Planning Point:** An appropriate IRA trustee is needed. With the spousal rollover approach, the financial institution that serves as IRA trustee must be knowledgeable about estate tax and trusts. Many financial institutions (*e.g.*, mutual funds, brokerage firms, savings and loan associations) may not completely understand the rules applicable to a QDOT. Also, the qualified domestic trust amendments to the financial institution's IRA trust form should be handled in such a manner that they do not jeopardize the favorable IRS determination letter issued to the prototype IRA trust.

21ˢᵗ Century Estate Planning:
Practical Applications
2005 Edition

©2005 Sonnenschein Nath & Rosenthal LLP
and Cannon Financial Institute, Inc.

207

(4) <u>**QDOT and the Repeal of the Estate Tax.**</u> Special rules will apply to a QDOT that is established before the repeal of the estate tax in 2010. Even though the estate tax will be repealed, distributions from a QDOT and assets remaining in the QDOT at the surviving spouse's death will continue to be subjected to estate tax for a limited period of time. For decedents dying before January 1, 2010, distributions from a QDOT to a surviving spouse, prior to the surviving spouse's death, will continue to be subjected to estate tax until January 1, 2021. IRC § 2210(b)(1). Additionally, the value of property remaining in a QDOT on the surviving spouse's death will be subjected to estate tax if the surviving spouse dies before January 1, 2010.

E. Selecting Marital Deduction Trusts – QTIP v. GPOA

1. Advantages of a QTIP Trust over a GPOA Trust

As discussed earlier, the QTIP trust was created by the Economic Recovery Tax Act of 1981, and it has since become the predominant marital deduction trust. The QTIP marital trust has significant advantages over the traditional general power of appointment (GPOA) marital trust.

a. <u>**Control**</u>. The testator or settlor can determine how much or little control to give the surviving spouse over the QTIP trust. In order to qualify for the gift and estate tax marital deduction, the spouse is required to have only an income interest for life. On the other hand, many individuals wish to give the spouse broad control over and benefits from a QTIP trust (*e.g.*, generous principal distribution provisions, "5 or 5" annual withdrawal rights, limited testamentary power of appointment, and spouse as sole trustee or as co-trustee). With a GPOA trust, the spouse must have a power to appoint the entire trust, and the deceased spouse has no control over such power.

b. <u>**Protection Against Remarriage of Surviving Spouse.**</u> A QTIP trust can be drafted to preclude a spouse who remarries from appointing the marital trust at death to his or her second spouse or children of the spouse's second marriage. However, with a GPOA trust, the power to appoint must be unlimited.

c. <u>**Post-Mortem Planning.**</u> Use of a QTIP trust facilitates post-mortem marital deduction planning, including a partial QTIP election and division of the marital trust into elected and non-elected portions or adding the non-elected portion to the family trust. The GPOA trust is not as flexible as the QTIP trust.

d. <u>**Minimizing Generation-Skipping Transfer Tax.**</u> A QTIP trust can facilitate planning for minimizing the generation-skipping transfer tax by allowing the testator or settlor to create a marital trust for which the reverse QTIP election is made under IRC § 2652(a)(3). The GPOA trust does not allow for the ability to minimize generation-skipping transfer tax.

21ˢᵗ Century Estate Planning:
Practical Applications
2005 Edition

©2005 Sonnenschein Nath & Rosenthal LLP
and Cannon Financial Institute, Inc.

208

e. **Valuation Discounts.** Use of a QTIP trust can facilitate obtaining valuation discounts at the death of the surviving spouse. Following the Fifth Circuit decision in *Bonner v. United States*, 84 F.3d 196 (5th Cir. 1996), the Tax Court has held in three separate cases that the assets of a QTIP marital trust includible in the gross estate of the surviving spouse under IRC § 2044 are not aggregated with other assets includible in the surviving spouse's gross estate under IRC § 2033 (outright ownership) or IRC §§ 2036 and 2038 (the surviving spouse's revocable trust) for purposes of valuing the assets of the QTIP trust. *Estate of Mellinger v. Comm'r*, 112 T.C. 26 (1999), *acq.* AOD 99-006, 1999-35 I.R.B. 314; *Estate of Nowell v. Comm'r*, T.C. Memo. 1999-15; *Estate of Lopes v. Comm'r*, T.C. Memo. 1999-225. Because such interests are not aggregated, a valuation discount may be obtained for each of the separate interests in the gross estate of the surviving spouse, thereby reducing the federal estate tax obligation of the surviving spouse.

2. Advantages of a GPOA Trust over a QTIP Trust

Even though the QTIP trust is used more frequently, there are some advantages to the general power of appointment trust.

a. **Spouse as Trustee.** A surviving spouse may serve as the sole trustee of a GPOA trust, and the trust may have broad discretionary principal distribution provisions. Adverse tax consequences are possible if a QTIP trust has such provisions.

b. **Unlimited Right to Withdraw.** The surviving spouse has an unlimited right to withdraw any or all of the principal of a GPOA trust during the surviving spouse's lifetime. Such right may allow the surviving spouse the ability to make inter vivos gifts to third parties from the trust property. A decedent may grant this power to the surviving spouse to allow more flexibility to the surviving spouse to reduce the amount subject to taxation in the estate of the surviving spouse and to shift income during the surviving spouse's lifetime.

c. **Elective Share.** With a QTIP trust, a surviving spouse may be more likely to exercise the spouse's elective share rights as the surviving spouse does not have control over the use or ultimate distribution of the trust's assets. Whereas with a GPOA trust, the surviving spouse controls the ultimate distribution of the trust assets, and may have a lifetime general power of appointment.

d. **Assignment of Income.** For a surviving spouse who may be in the higher income tax brackets, the use of a GPOA trust may allow the spouse to assign income to a beneficiary who is in a lower tax bracket. The surviving spouse is permitted to have a lifetime general power of appointment under the GPOA trust, and the spouse may use that power to distribute income to the beneficiary in the lower tax bracket.

21st Century Estate Planning:
Practical Applications
2005 Edition

©2005 Sonnenschein Nath & Rosenthal LLP
and Cannon Financial Institute, Inc.

209

F. Common Marital Deduction Formula Provisions

1. Unlimited Marital Deduction Formula Clauses

The marital deduction formula determines how much property will be distributed to the surviving spouse or to a marital trust for the benefit of the surviving spouse and how that distribution is to be funded. An optimal marital deduction formula automatically adjusts the amount of the marital disposition so that generally no federal or state estate tax is payable at the death of the first spouse and all estate tax is deferred until the death of the surviving spouse.

The most common marital deduction formulae that are discussed in this chapter are:

- True pecuniary marital formula
- Fractional share marital formula – pro rata and pick and choose
- Fairly representative pecuniary marital formula
- Reverse pecuniary formula
- Minimum worth pecuniary marital formula

2. True Pecuniary Marital Deduction Formula

A true pecuniary marital deduction formula is one in which the marital distribution is a *dollar amount* determined and satisfied in cash or in kind. When satisfied in kind, assets are *valued on the date of distribution*. This type of marital funding provision is also sometimes called a *true worth funding* because the marital distribution consists of cash or other assets that on the date of funding have a value exactly equal to the pecuniary amount of the marital distribution.

> **EXAMPLE:** An example of a true pecuniary marital deduction formula is as follows:
>
> "If my spouse survives me, the trustee shall set aside, to be administered as provided in the Marital Trust, the minimum amount that, if allowed as a marital deduction in determining the federal estate tax on my estate, will cause my estate to incur no, or the least, such tax.
>
> In computing such amount, the asset values, deductions and credits as finally determined in the federal estate tax proceedings in my estate shall control, and, among available credits, only the unified credit shall be used.
>
> In funding such amount, only assets for which a marital deduction is allowable shall be used, and all assets used shall be set aside at then current fair market values. I recognize that the amount described in

21st Century Estate Planning:
Practical Applications
2005 Edition

©2005 Sonnenschein Nath & Rosenthal LLP
and Cannon Financial Institute, Inc.

210

this Article may be affected by the exercise of, or failure to exercise, certain tax elections. I also acknowledge the possibility that no property will be set aside under this Article.

Despite any other provision in this instrument, the amount described in this Article shall be computed after considering payments made or to be made to pay for my debts, the administration expenses of my estate, my funeral expenses, the expenses of my last illness and death taxes that are deducted for estate tax purposes. The property set aside or to be set aside under this Article shall not be reduced, however, by the amount of any such payments.

If my spouse survives me, the balance of the Residuary Trust (and any other property that, but for the making of a qualified disclaimer by my spouse, would be set aside under the preceding provisions of this Article) shall be administered as provided in the Family Trust."

a. **Advantages of a True Pecuniary Marital Deduction Formula.** The advantages of a true pecuniary marital deduction formula include the following:

- The executor or trustee can pick and choose the assets with which to fund the marital deduction.

➜ **Planning Point:** Assets having the greatest potential for appreciation can be used to fund the family trust, and assets that are expected to appreciate more slowly or decline in value can be used to fund the marital distribution or trust. Similarly, in a rising market, the marital deduction distribution can be funded later and with less property since date of distribution values are used, which increases the amount of property in the family trust and decreases the estate tax at the death of the surviving spouse.

- A true pecuniary marital funding provision is generally considered to be the simplest to compute and to fund.

➜ **Planning Point:** Commentators suggest that a true pecuniary marital deduction formula should be used if the estate contains real property subject to special use valuation under IRC § 2032A.

21ˢᵗ Century Estate Planning:
Practical Applications
2005 Edition

©2005 Sonnenschein Nath & Rosenthal LLP
and Cannon Financial Institute, Inc.

211

b. Disadvantages of a True Pecuniary Marital Deduction Formula. There are a number of disadvantages of a true pecuniary marital deduction formula that may or may not offset its flexibility and simplicity, including the following:

- Capital gains will be generated if the marital distribution is funded with assets that have appreciated between the date of death (or alternate valuation date) and date of distribution because a fixed dollar obligation is being satisfied and the funding is treated as a sale or exchange. Treas. Reg. § 1.1014-4(a)(3); *Suisman v. Comm'r*, 15 F. Supp. 113 (D.C. Conn. 1935), *aff'd*, 83 F.2d 1019 (2d Cir. 1936); *Kenan v. Comm'r*, 114 F.2d 217 (2d Cir. 1940); see Treas. Reg. § 1.661(a)-2(f).

➔ **Planning Point:** Capital gains are realized by the estate or trust that funds the pecuniary marital distribution. See Rev. Rul. 60-87, 1960-1 C.B. 286. The tax in effect is borne by the non-pecuniary family trust since distributions to pay income taxes will reduce the amount of the residue.

- Capital losses would be realized where an executor funds a true pecuniary marital distribution with assets that had depreciated between the date of death (or alternate valuation date) and the date of distribution.

➔ **Planning Point:** In general, only $3,000 of capital losses may be taken in any year. IRC § 1211(b).

➔ **Planning Point:** Capital losses incurred by a trustee of a revocable trust in funding a marital trust pursuant to a pecuniary formula cannot be recognized. IRC §§ 267(a)(1), (b)(5). This problem can be avoided by the trustee selling the depreciated assets to recognize the loss before funding and then distributing cash in satisfaction of the distribution to the marital trust.

TRA '97 amended IRC § 267 by adding a new paragraph that generally disallows the recognition of loss on a sale or exchange of property between an executor of an estate and a beneficiary of such estate "[e]xcept in the case of a sale or exchange in satisfaction of a pecuniary bequest...." IRC § 267(a)(1), (b)(13) as amended by TRA '97 § 1308(a), effective for tax years beginning after August 5, 1997.

Hence, it appears that a loss that is realized in funding a true pecuniary marital distribution under a will still can be recognized subject to the $3,000 per year limitation.

- Another disadvantage of a true pecuniary funding formula, whether for the marital or family trust, is that funding such a distribution with the right to

21st Century Estate Planning:
Practical Applications
2005 Edition

©2005 Sonnenschein Nath & Rosenthal LLP
and Cannon Financial Institute, Inc.

212

receive income in respect of a decedent ("IRD"), *e.g.*, individual retirement accounts, a professional entitled to receive substantial contractual death benefits, or a real estate developer with installment sales contracts, is a transfer that accelerates the taxability of the IRD. IRC § 691(a)(2); Treas. Reg. § 1.691(a)-4; *Noel v. Comm'r*, 50 T.C. 702 (1968).

➔ **Planning Point:** This can be a significant issue in the case of a decedent whose estate consists mostly of IRD. This problem can be minimized by making the pecuniary trust the smaller of the two trusts. The problem can also be minimized by making a specific bequest of the item of IRD of a decedent either to the residuary trust or to the marital trust (as circumstances require), or by using a fractional share marital formula.

- A true pecuniary marital distribution requires the executor or trustee to revalue the assets being distributed on the date or dates of distribution.

➔ **Planning Point:** With interests in real estate, closely-held businesses or valuable artwork, a true pecuniary marital deduction provision creates a substantial added expense. However, a non-pro rata fractional share marital formula (discussed below) would also require a revaluation of the assets.

- In a falling market, the executor or trustee will be under pressure to fund the pecuniary amount trust early because any decline in the overall value of the assets will reduce the residuary family trust. If the marital disposition is funded early, the estate loses the advantage (admittedly nominal with compressed income tax brackets) of being a separate taxpayer with respect to the assets distributed in satisfaction of the marital gift. Early funding may also result in decisions being made before all of the variables, such as the amount of the marital deduction, death taxes and cash requirements, are known.

21ˢᵗ Century Estate Planning:
Practical Applications
2005 Edition

©2005 Sonnenschein Nath & Rosenthal LLP
and Cannon Financial Institute, Inc.

213

EXAMPLE: Decedent's estate is valued at $5,000,000 on the date of death. Pursuant to Decedent's estate plan utilizing a true pecuniary marital deduction formula, the marital disposition is to receive $3,500,000, and the nonmarital disposition is funded with the residue ($1,500,000 based on date of death values). During administration, the estate declines 20% in value to $4,000,000. At funding, the marital trust receives $3,500,000 (the pecuniary amount), and the nonmarital disposition receives 500,000 (the residue). Unhappy beneficiaries of the nonmarital disposition may sue the fiduciary. To protect itself, the executor or trustee may fund the marital disposition shortly after death to ensure the nonmarital disposition is not eliminated if the value of the estate declines between the date of death and the date of funding. If the marital disposition is funded shortly after death with $3,500,000 and all assets passing under the estate plan then decline in value by 20%, the nonmarital disposition would eventually receive $1,200,000, while the marital disposition would eventually decline in value to $2,800,000.

Similarly, if the estate appreciates substantially in value after death, the spouse may sue the fiduciary, arguing that it should have funded the marital disposition shortly after death with assets that later increased in value. See, e.g., *Smail v. Smail*, 617 S.W.2d 889 (Tenn. 1981); *In re Estate of Marks*, 211 Ill. App. 3d 53 (2nd Dist. 1991).

- The holding period for long-term capital gains purposes begins on the date of satisfaction of the pecuniary distribution rather than on the earlier date of death.
- All excess deductions on termination of the estate will be allocated to the residuary nonmarital disposition, which may not have sufficient income to utilize the deductions. See IRC § 642(h).
- In the second marriage situation, where the children of the first marriage are the beneficiaries of the residuary nonmarital disposition, there may be conflicts of interest if the surviving spouse is the executor with the authority to allocate the most desirable assets to the pecuniary marital distribution.

➔ **Planning Point:** A true pecuniary marital formula may not be appropriate where beneficiaries of the marital trust and the family trust are contentious (*e.g.*, second spouse and children by first marriage), regardless of whether the surviving spouse is named as the fiduciary.

- Funding a pecuniary formula distribution will carry out distributable net income from the estate or trust even though the distribution is in satisfaction of a pecuniary amount. Treas. Reg. § 1.663(a)-1(b)(1).

21st Century Estate Planning:
Practical Applications
2005 Edition

©2005 Sonnenschein Nath & Rosenthal LLP
and Cannon Financial Institute, Inc.

214

3. Fractional Share Marital Formula

The marital disposition may be computed as a fractional share of the residue of the estate or trust.

> **EXAMPLE:** An example of a fractional share marital formula is as follows:
>
> "If my spouse survives me, the trustee shall set aside, to be administered as provided in the Marital Trust, a fraction of the Residuary Trust. The numerator of such fraction shall equal the minimum amount that, if allowed as a marital deduction in determining the federal estate tax on my estate, will cause my estate to incur no, or the least, such tax. The denominator of such fraction shall equal the value of the Residuary Trust.
>
> In computing such fraction, the asset values, deductions and credits as finally determined in the federal estate tax proceedings in my estate shall control, and, among available credits, only the unified credit shall be used.
>
> In funding such fraction, only assets for which a marital deduction is allowable shall be used. I recognize that the numerator of the fraction described in this Article may be affected by the exercise of, or failure to exercise, certain tax elections. I also acknowledge the possibility that no property will be set aside under this Article. Despite any other provision in this instrument, the numerator of the fraction described in this Article shall be computed after considering payments made or to be made to pay for my debts, the administration expenses of my estate, my funeral expenses, the expenses of my last illness and death taxes that are deducted for estate tax purposes. The property set aside or to be set aside under this Article shall not be reduced, however, by the amount of any such payments.
>
> If my spouse survives me, the balance of the Residuary Trust (and any other property that, but for the making of a qualified disclaimer by my spouse, would be set aside under the preceding provisions of this Article) shall be administered as provided in the Family Trust."

a. The Minimum Amount Marital Distribution. The marital formula set forth above involves a *minimum amount* marital distribution. This marital formula gives the marital trust a share measured by "the minimum amount that … will cause my estate to incur no, or the least, such tax." In most cases, the "… no, or the least, such tax." will be zero. This formula is a *reduce estate tax to zero* formula. It gives the marital trust a share measured by the

21ˢᵗ Century Estate Planning:
Practical Applications
2005 Edition

©*2005 Sonnenschein Nath & Rosenthal LLP*
and Cannon Financial Institute, Inc.

215

optimal marital deduction amount allowed by the unlimited marital deduction used in conjunction with the applicable exclusion amount.

- The concept is not to fund the marital trust with any more assets than required to reduce the federal estate tax to zero. The *minimum amount* requirement keeps the marital trust as small as possible.
- The *minimum amount* formula will automatically adjust the amount of the marital trust to obtain the optimal marital deduction. The formula automatically considers expenses and other legacies which affect the optimal marital amount, so that the governing instrument need not expressly mention those items. The formula also automatically adjusts for yearly increases in the applicable exclusion amount.

> **EXAMPLE:** The *minimum amount* formula is illustrated in the following simplified example. Assume the testator died in 2005 and has a gross estate of $2,000,000.
>
> | | |
> |---|---|
> | $2,000,000 | Gross estate |
> | (70,000) | Administration expenses deducted on Form 1041 |
> | (30,000) | Cash legacies to children |
> | $1,900,000 | Balance |
>
> The marital trust will be funded with $500,000, which is the smallest marital deduction amount that will result in no federal estate tax being payable. The remaining $1,500,000 is allocated to the family trust. Note that part of the client's $1,500,000 applicable exclusion amount is used up by payments ($70,000) and bequests ($30,000) that are not deductible for federal estate tax purposes.
>
> If the $70,000 of administration expenses were deducted on the federal estate tax return (Form 706), the marital trust would be funded with only $430,000, because that amount would be the smallest marital deduction that would result in no federal estate tax being payable. The family trust would be funded with $1,570,000, and $100,000 of that amount would then be used to pay the expenses and legacies.

The marital formula set forth above provides that "the numerator of the fraction… shall be computed after considering payments made or to be made to pay for my debts, the administration expenses of my estate, my funeral expenses, the expenses of my last illness and death taxes that are deducted for estate tax purposes." This ensures that the marital deduction distribution is not inadvertently diminished. The will and revocable trust agreement (if any) should also contain coordinated tax and expense clauses that specify which assets or portion of the estate and trust bear the burden of death taxes and expenses.

21st Century Estate Planning:
Practical Applications
2005 Edition

©2005 Sonnenschein Nath & Rosenthal LLP
and Cannon Financial Institute, Inc.

216

→ **Planning Point:** The practitioner should always obtain copies of any estate planning documents that the client has executed. The tax clauses must be reviewed, and it must be determined who should bear the burden of paying the taxes on the assets which will be includible in the client's gross estate for federal estate tax purposes.

The phrase "only assets for which a marital deduction is allowable shall be used" is included in the marital deduction formula because this funding provision may be used with a QTIP marital trust.

- Not all of the QTIP trust may be qualified for the marital deduction. The executor may make only a partial QTIP election. Regardless of the election actually made, however, the marital trust should be funded with sufficient assets so that, if all of the trust did qualify for the marital deduction, the optimal marital deduction would be obtained taking into account the applicable exclusion amount.
- In calculating the distribution to the marital trust, it is assumed that all of the assets passing to the trust will qualify for the marital deduction, regardless of any partial QTIP election or disclaimer.

b. **Advantages of a Fractional Share Marital Formula.** Advantages of a fractional share marital funding formula include the following:

- As discussed further below, generally, no capital gain taxes are incurred in funding either the marital or nonmarital disposition.
- Both the marital and nonmarital shares bear a proportionate amount of any increase or decrease in value of the estate on an equal basis between date of death and date of funding.
- There is no acceleration of income in respect of a decedent ("IRD") in funding the marital and non-marital shares, and no need to make a specific gift of items of income in respect of a decedent. See Treas. Reg. § 1.691(a)-4(b).
- There is no need to revalue the assets on date of distribution unless non-pro rata distributions are made.
- Excess deductions on termination of an estate are allocated proportionately to the marital and non-marital distributions.
- There is no pressure to fund early because the date of funding does not alter the share of appreciation or depreciation borne by the marital and non-marital shares. The estate can be used longer as a separate income tax entity.
- In a second marriage situation or in others where absolute fairness is more important than saving taxes at the death of the surviving spouse, a fractional share marital formula is often used to avoid family conflicts and other difficulties.

21ˢᵗ Century Estate Planning:
Practical Applications
2005 Edition

©2005 Sonnenschein Nath & Rosenthal LLP
and Cannon Financial Institute, Inc.

217

c. __Disadvantages of the Fractional Share Marital Formula.__ The disadvantages of a fractional share marital formula include the following:

- If the assets of the estate or trust increase in value from the date of death to the date of funding, more assets are used to fund the marital share than would be used with a true pecuniary marital deduction formula using date of distribution funding language. If a true pecuniary marital deduction formula were used, all the appreciation would be allocated to the family trust.

- If an allocation between the marital and nonmarital shares is made on a non-pro rata basis and there is no specific authority in the governing instrument or under state law for making such distributions, the transaction will be treated as a sale or exchange between the marital and nonmarital trusts causing recognition of gain on any appreciation in the allocated assets from the date of death or alternate valuation date until the date of funding. See Rev. Rul. 69-486, 1969-2 C.B. 159; Treas. Reg. §§ 1.661(a)-2(f); 1.1014-4(a)(3). If the governing instrument gives the executor or trustee the authority to make a non-pro rata allocation between the marital and nonmarital shares such that the executor or trustee can choose the assets in funding the two trusts, many - probably most - commentators believe that no capital gain will be recognized in these circumstances. See _In re Fiedler's Estate_, 151 A.2d 201 (N.J. Super. 1959); Rev. Rul. 69-486, 1969-2 C.B. 159. However, marital and nonmarital dispositions funded on a non-pro rata basis would have to be revalued and issues of fairness and impartiality might arise.

- A fractional share marital formula is generally considered to be more inflexible and difficult to administer than a true pecuniary marital deduction formula.

- A fractional formula is generally believed to require the executor or trustee to fractionalize each asset in funding the marital and non-marital shares, except for de minimis amounts.

➡ __Planning Point:__ Fractionalizing some assets (_e.g._, round lots of listed securities, investment real estate and closely-held business interests) may reduce the value of the assets, or may be simply impossible.

- The fraction must be recomputed if there is a partial distribution that is non-pro rata, or if the federal estate tax values are changed on audit, or if administration expenses are different than the amount estimated when the fraction is computed.

21st Century Estate Planning:
Practical Applications
2005 Edition

©2005 Sonnenschein Nath & Rosenthal LLP
and Cannon Financial Institute, Inc.

218

d. Pro Rata Fractional Share Funding. Pro rata funding of a fractional share marital formula involves the executor dividing each and every asset according to the fraction determined using the formula. For example, if the formula created a fraction of 1,000,000/3,000,000, each asset would be allocated 33.33% to the marital trust and 66.67% to the family trust.

The advantages of the pro rata fractional share funding include no gain or loss on funding of the marital trust and family trust shares, the depreciation and appreciation are ratably apportioned between the two trusts avoiding any problems with Rev. Proc. 64-19 (discussed below), and revaluation of the assets is not required when funding. However, the pro rata fractional share funding does have several significant disadvantages:

- Because the appreciation and depreciation are ratably apportioned, the marital trust may be overfunded or underfunded depending on the date of distribution values;
- The trustee has no discretion when selecting which assets to use to fund the trusts;
- As explained further above, if non-pro rata distributions are made, capital gains are incurred; and
- A pro rata fractional share funding formula is difficult to administer.

e. Pick and Choose Fractional Share Funding. A pick and choose fractional share funding formula utilizes the same fractional formula; however, it allows the trustee to pick and choose, as the name applies, which assets should be distributed in kind when funding the marital bequest. The advantages are maximum flexibility, no Rev. Proc. 64-19 issues (discussed below), and favorable income tax treatment. Disadvantages include the fact that a revaluation of the assets must be performed upon each distribution in satisfaction of the fractional bequest, and uncertainty exists as the pick and choose method is not well established.

4. Fairly Representative Pecuniary Marital Formula

A fairly representative pecuniary marital formula (also referred to as a Rev. Proc. 64-19 marital formula) provides that the amount of the marital distribution is determined as a ***dollar amount*** that is satisfied in cash or in kind, with assets which are distributed in kind ***valued at their federal estate tax values*** (or income tax basis if acquired after death) rather than using date of distribution values in determining the amount of the marital distribution. This clause is based on the requirements of Rev. Proc. 64-19, 1964-1 C.B. 682. This is a pecuniary formula that seeks to avoid the capital gain on funding issue that is present with the true pecuniary marital deduction formula using date of distribution values, as discussed above.

> **EXAMPLE:** An example of a fairly representative pecuniary marital formula provision is as follows:

21ˢᵗ Century Estate Planning:
Practical Applications
2005 Edition

©2005 Sonnenschein Nath & Rosenthal LLP
and Cannon Financial Institute, Inc.

219

"If my spouse survives me, the trustee shall set aside, to be administered as provided in the Marital Trust, the minimum amount that, if allowed as a marital deduction in determining the federal estate tax on my estate, will cause my estate to incur no, or the least, such tax.

In computing such amount, the asset values, deductions and credits as finally determined in the federal estate tax proceedings in my estate shall control, and, among available credits, only the unified credit shall be used.

In funding such amount, only assets for which a marital deduction is allowable shall be used, and all assets used shall be set aside at the value as finally determined for federal estate tax purposes, except any property purchased after my death shall be valued at its cost. *The assets, including cash, so distributed shall be fairly representative of the appreciation or depreciation in the value to the date or dates of distribution of all property available for distribution in satisfaction of such devise.* I recognize that the amount described in this Article may be affected by the exercise of, or failure to exercise, certain tax elections. I also acknowledge the possibility that no property will be set aside under this Article.

Despite any other provision in this instrument, the amount described in this Article shall be computed after considering payments made or to be made to pay for my debts, the administration expenses of my estate, my funeral expenses, the expenses of my last illness and death taxes that are deducted for estate tax purposes. The property set aside or to be set aside under this Article shall not be reduced, however, by the amount of any such payments.

If my spouse survives me, the balance of the Residuary Trust (and any other property that, but for the making of a qualified disclaimer by my spouse, would be set aside under the preceding provisions of this Article) shall be administered as provided in the Family Trust."

a. **Advantages of a Fairly Representative Pecuniary Marital Formula Funding Provision.** The advantages of a fairly representative pecuniary marital formula funding provision are as follows:

- A fairly representative pecuniary marital funding formula avoids capital gain on funding of the marital trust by using federal estate tax values (or cost for property purchased after death) in determining the amount distributed to the marital disposition;

21st Century Estate Planning:
Practical Applications
2005 Edition

©2005 Sonnenschein Nath & Rosenthal LLP
and Cannon Financial Institute, Inc.

220

- Unlike the fractional share marital formula, the executor or trustee can pick and choose the assets for distribution to the marital trust and need not fractionalize each asset, although when a marital trust is funded at federal estate tax values instead of date of distribution values, Rev. Proc. 64-19 requires that funding be implemented with assets (including cash) that are fairly representative of the post-death appreciation or depreciation in value of all assets that are available to fund the marital trust. Hence, the name "fairly representative."

→ **Planning Point:** Rev. Proc. 64-19 does not prevent the executor or trustee from distributing to the nonmarital disposition those assets that such fiduciary believes have the greatest potential for future appreciation and distributing the other assets to the marital trust so long as appreciation or depreciation to the date of distribution is fairly allocated to the marital trust.

- Both the marital disposition and the nonmarital disposition are treated fairly in that both share in appreciation and depreciation to the date of funding on an equal basis.
- There is less pressure to fund early as compared with a true pecuniary marital formula, and the estate can be used as a separate income tax entity for a longer period.

b. **Disadvantages of a Fairly Representative Pecuniary Marital Formula Funding Provision.** The disadvantages of a fairly representative pecuniary marital formula funding provision are as follows:

- The assets must be revalued at date of distribution to demonstrate that the marital share has received a fairly representative amount of appreciation and depreciation during administration of the estate;
- If the assets of the estate or trust appreciate during the period of administration, the marital share is greater than it would be if a true pecuniary marital provision were used;
- A fairly representative pecuniary marital funding formula probably would be treated as a pecuniary formula with respect to both the acceleration of IRD issue and the allocation of excess expenses on termination issues discussed above as disadvantages of true pecuniary deduction formulas; and
- Proving that the marital share has received a fairly representative amount of appreciation and depreciation during estate administration is administratively difficult unless either the assets are revalued and careful records are kept on funding or the assets are fractionalized.

21st Century Estate Planning:
Practical Applications
2005 Edition

©2005 Sonnenschein Nath & Rosenthal LLP
and Cannon Financial Institute, Inc.

221

5. Reverse Pecuniary Marital Deduction Formula

When it is clear that the marital disposition will exceed the applicable exclusion amount, the amount of the applicable exclusion is sometimes stated as a pecuniary amount using date of distribution values. The marital disposition is the residue of the estate or trust. This type of funding is also sometimes referred to as a "credit shelter lead formula" and was created in response to the unlimited marital deduction brought about by the Economic Recovery Tax Act of 1981. See Richard B. Covey, *Marital Deduction and Credit Shelter Dispositions and the Use of Formula Provisions* (U.S. Trust Company, 1997), page 25.

> **EXAMPLE:** An example of a reverse pecuniary formula is as follows:
>
> "If my spouse survives me, the trustee shall set aside, to be administered as provided in the Family Trust, the maximum amount that, if not allowed as a marital deduction in determining the federal estate tax on my estate, will cause my estate to incur no such tax.
>
> In computing such amount, the asset values, deductions and credits as finally determined in the federal estate tax proceedings in my estate shall control. Despite the preceding sentence, all property passing under the following Article with respect to which my spouse has made a qualified disclaimer, or of which treatment as qualified terminable interest property is not effectively elected, shall be considered property for which a marital deduction is allowed. In computing such amount, among available credits, only the unified credit shall be used.
>
> In funding such amount, assets for which a marital deduction is allowable shall be used only to the extent other assets are not available, and all assets used shall be set aside at then current fair market values. I recognize that the amount described in this Paragraph may be affected by the exercise of, or failure to exercise, certain tax elections. I also acknowledge the possibility that no property will be set aside under this Article.
>
> Despite any other provision in this instrument, the amount described in this Paragraph shall be computed after considering payments made or to be made to pay for my debts, the administration expenses of my estate, my funeral expenses, the expenses of my last illness and death taxes that are not deducted for estate tax purposes. The property set aside or to be set aside under this Article shall not be reduced, however, by the amount of any such payments.

21ˢᵗ Century Estate Planning:
Practical Applications
2005 Edition

©*2005 Sonnenschein Nath & Rosenthal LLP*
and Cannon Financial Institute, Inc.

222

If my spouse survives me, the balance of the Residuary Trust shall be administered as provided in the Marital Trust. Despite the preceding sentence, any property directed in this Article to be administered as provided in the Marital Trust with respect to which my spouse has made a qualified disclaimer and any assets for which a marital deduction is not allowable shall be administered as provided in the Family Trust."

a. **Advantages of a Reverse Pecuniary Marital Deduction Formula.** The advantages of a reverse pecuniary marital deduction formula are as follows.

- As with the true pecuniary marital deduction formula, this type of funding provision is generally considered to be the simplest to compute and to fund.
- The executor or trustee may pick and choose the assets with which to fund the distribution. Assets having the greatest potential for appreciation can be used to fund the nonmarital disposition, and assets that are expected to appreciate more slowly or decline in value can be used to fund the marital disposition.
- Because the residuary marital disposition bears all risk of depreciation in value during administration of the estate, the nonmarital disposition will not be reduced by depreciation during the period of administration. This risk of depreciation does not jeopardize the marital deduction. In Rev. Rul. 90-3, 1990-1 C.B. 174, the IRS held that, if a pecuniary bequest of the then applicable exclusion amount of $600,000 is required to be paid with assets valued at the date of distribution, the possibility of post-death fluctuations in the value of the residuary bequest to the surviving spouse does not cause the residuary bequest to be a nondeductible terminable interest for purposes of IRC § 2056(b).
- Since the pecuniary gift to the nonmarital disposition is the smaller amount in a larger estate situation, using a reverse pecuniary marital deduction formula will minimize potential capital gain on funding as compared with a true pecuniary marital deduction formula.

b. **Disadvantages of a Reverse Pecuniary Marital Deduction Formula.** The reverse pecuniary marital deduction formula in general has the same disadvantages as the true pecuniary marital deduction formula. In addition, if there is appreciation during the administration period, it all accrues to the residuary marital disposition, which will have the effect of increasing estate taxes at the surviving spouse's death.

6. **Minimum Worth Marital Deduction Formula**

Another variation of the pecuniary marital funding language is the minimum worth marital deduction formula, which directs funding of the marital disposition at the *lower of* (a) federal estate tax values or (b) date of distribution values. There are two variations of the

21ˢᵗ Century Estate Planning:
Practical Applications
2005 Edition

©2005 Sonnenschein Nath & Rosenthal LLP
and Cannon Financial Institute, Inc.

223

minimum worth marital deduction formula: the individual asset variation and the aggregate asset variation.

EXAMPLE: An example of the *aggregate asset variation*, which is specifically mentioned in Rev. Proc. 64-19 as an acceptable form of a marital deduction formula, is as follows:

"If my spouse survives me, the trustee shall set aside, to be administered as provided in the Marital Trust, the minimum amount that, if allowed as a marital deduction in determining the federal estate tax on my estate, will cause my estate to incur no, or the least, such tax.

In computing such amount, the asset values, deductions and credits as finally determined in the federal estate tax proceedings in my estate shall control, and, among available credits, only the unified credit shall be used.

In funding such amount, only assets for which a marital deduction is allowable shall be used, and all assets used shall be set aside at the value as finally determined for federal estate tax purposes, except any property purchased after my death shall be valued at its cost. The assets, including cash, so distributed shall have an aggregate fair market value on the date or dates of distribution amounting to no less than the amount of this bequest. I recognize that the amount described in this Article may be affected by the exercise of, or failure to exercise, certain tax elections. I also acknowledge the possibility that no property will be set aside under this Article.

Despite any other provision in this instrument, the amount described in this Article shall be computed after considering payments made or to be made to pay for my debts, the administration expenses of my estate, my funeral expenses, the expenses of my last illness and death taxes that are deducted for estate tax purposes. The property set aside or to be set aside under this Article shall not be reduced, however, by the amount of any such payments.

If my spouse survives me, the balance of the Residuary Trust (and any other property that, but for the making of a qualified disclaimer by my spouse, would be set aside under the preceding provisions of this Article) shall be administered as provided in the Family Trust."

EXAMPLE: An example of the *individual asset variation* would be to change the bolded language in the above example as follows:

21ˢᵗ Century Estate Planning:
Practical Applications
2005 Edition

©*2005 Sonnenschein Nath & Rosenthal LLP*
and Cannon Financial Institute, Inc.

224

"In funding such amount, only assets for which a marital deduction is allowable shall be used, and the value of each asset shall be the lower of (a) the value finally determined for federal estate tax purposes (or cost, if it was purchased after my death) or (b) the value on the date of distribution."

The individual asset variation is generally assumed to qualify for the marital deduction although not specifically mentioned in Rev. Proc. 64-19 since, if federal estate tax values are lower, all funding is at federal estate tax values, and, if date of distribution values are lower, the marital trust will have to receive more assets in order for it to be fully funded.

a. **Advantages of the Minimum Worth Marital Deduction Formula.** The advantages of the minimum worth marital deduction formula are as follows:

- Capital gain on funding is avoided because appreciation in the value of assets is not "used" by the executor to meet the obligation to fund the pecuniary amount; and
- The minimum worth marital deduction formula grants the fiduciary substantial flexibility in selecting assets for the marital disposition.

b. **Disadvantages of the Minimum Worth Marital Deduction Formula.** The disadvantages of the minimum worth marital deduction formula are as follows:

- If values increase during post-death administration, the marital disposition will be overfunded (i.e., it will receive more value than that for which a marital deduction was claimed);
- In the case of a decline in values from the date of death or alternate valuation date to the date of funding, the minimum worth marital deduction formula reduces the value of the nonmarital disposition;
- A minimum worth marital deduction formula may not be appropriate in a second marriage situation or other circumstances where the beneficiaries of marital and nonmarital trusts are different; and
- Some commentators have suggested that use of a minimum marital deduction worth formula is inappropriate where a charitable deduction is being made from the residuary estate on the theory that the charitable deduction may fail because the amount is unascertainable at the date of death or alternate valuation date. See, e.g., Steve R. Akers, "An Overview of Post-Mortem Tax Planning Strategies," 34th Annual Philip E. Heckerling Ins. on Est. Plan. (2000).

7. **Double Pecuniary Drafting**

In the last several years, the option of utilizing a double pecuniary formula has been receiving more attention. The purpose is to limit the exposure of a residuary family trust to

21st Century Estate Planning:
Practical Applications
2005 Edition

©2005 Sonnenschein Nath & Rosenthal LLP
and Cannon Financial Institute, Inc.

225

reduction by reason of a decline in the value of the assets in an estate or funded revocable trust between the date of death and the date of funding. Several articles have been published regarding the double pecuniary drafting. Two of such articles include: D. Keith Bilter, "Marital Deduction and Generation-Skipping Formula Clauses: How to Get More Bang For Your Buck," *35th Annual Philip E. Heckerling Inst. on Est. Plan.* (2001); and Max Gutierrez, Jr., ACTEC 1999 Summer Meeting.

Mr. Gutierrez suggested that estate planners consider using a traditional pecuniary marital lead formula together with two other family trusts. The first family trust would be funded with a pecuniary amount equal to a large percentage of the remaining applicable exclusion amount (*e.g.*, 80% of $1,500,000), and the second family trust would be funded with the residue of the estate or revocable trust.

- If there is an increase in value during the period between death and funding, the residuary family trust would get the benefit, just as with a more traditional two trust pecuniary marital lead formula.
- In the event of a decline in value between death and funding, the double pecuniary formula suggested by Mr. Gutierrez would result first in reduction of the residuary family trust and then in pro rata abatement of both the pecuniary family trust and the pecuniary marital gift (provided that state law or the governing instrument provided for pro rata abatement).

Mr. Bilter suggests the use of true pecuniary formulas for the marital and family trust followed by a gift of the residue. Under this arrangement, the entire residue would be disposed of through the use of pecuniary gifts and the residue would be extinguished after payment of the decedent's debts, expenses and taxes. The use of the two "lead" pecuniary gifts would maximize the use of the applicable exclusion amount (and the GST exemption) if the estate appreciates in value and the applicable exclusion is protected if the estate depreciates in value. Under this approach, appreciation or depreciation from date of death until date of funding is dealt with as follows:

- If the estate appreciates in value, the appreciation passes under the residuary clause; and
- If the estate depreciates in value, the marital and family trusts are reduced pro rata under the abatement provisions.

G. General Guidelines for Selecting a Marital Deduction Formula

1. Pecuniary Marital Formula

It is recommended to use a pecuniary amount formula if possible. The pecuniary amount formula allows for selection of assets to fund the disposition, is inherently flexible and understandable, and is easiest to administer.

21ˢᵗ Century Estate Planning:
Practical Applications
2005 Edition

©*2005 Sonnenschein Nath & Rosenthal LLP*
and Cannon Financial Institute, Inc.

226

➔ **Planning Point:** If the nonmarital disposition will be larger than the marital disposition, the true pecuniary marital deduction formula may be preferred. If the marital disposition will be the larger, use of a reverse pecuniary marital deduction formula with a residuary marital disposition may be better if there is concern about declining values.

2. Fractional Share Marital Formula

The fractional share marital formula is the best single, "all purpose" formula. It operates satisfactorily in both small and large estates. The fractional share marital formula also is the best formula for certain specific situations (*e.g.*, no recognition of IRD or capital gains on funding, treats contentious beneficiaries equitably, avoids need to revalue assets). It can, however, be difficult to understand and implement.

3. Optimal Marital Deduction with the Applicable Exclusion Amount

Using the optimal marital deduction in conjunction with the applicable exclusion amount may not be appropriate for some clients. For example, the client may desire to have his or her children receive a significant amount of property at the client's death. This often is especially important in second marriage situations. In other situations, it may be advantageous to equalize the value of the estates of husband and wife, which would cause tax to be incurred at the death of the first spouse to die but reduce aggregate estate tax over the two deaths.

4. Planning Points When Not Using the Optimal Marital Deduction

The practitioner may decide not to use optimal marital deduction estate planning in certain situations as discussed in the previous paragraph. The following estate planning techniques should be considered in such circumstances:

- The use of a QTIP marital trust in first marriage situations will facilitate post-mortem tax planning and allow the fiduciary to evaluate all the facts after the death of the testator or settlor;
- A simple percentage marital formula may provide for a marital disposition equal to a percentage of the client's adjusted gross estate. Alternatively, the governing instrument could provide that the marital disposition and nonmarital disposition are to be funded with specified fractions or percentages of the client's net residuary estate;
- The will or revocable trust instrument can provide fixed pecuniary gifts to children, either outright or in trust (*e.g.*, $300,000 to each child);
- The client might provide a fixed pecuniary gift to a marital trust and leave the residue to a nonmarital trust (*e.g.*, $500,000 to marital trust; residue to nonmarital trust); and
- The governing instrument could contain a specific bequest of assets that are expected to appreciate substantially in value (*e.g.*, closely held stock)

21ˢᵗ Century Estate Planning:
Practical Applications
2005 Edition

©2005 Sonnenschein Nath & Rosenthal LLP
and Cannon Financial Institute, Inc.

227

to the nonmarital trust or a separate QTIP trust for which a partial or no election might be made.

→ **Planning Point:** In all of the situations discussed above, it is critical that the governing instrument clearly specify which distributions bear the burden of the estate tax. The source of payment of the estate tax may drastically affect the dispositive provisions in an estate plan.

H. Selected Funding and Drafting Issues

1. Income in Respect of a Decedent

Some clients may have substantial amounts of income in respect of a decedent ("IRD"). Some kinds of IRD may involve payments over an extended period of time (*e.g.*, individual retirement accounts, qualified employee benefit plans, deferred compensation, installment sale contracts, royalties, insurance renewal commissions). This long-term IRD may cause funding problems for the estate.

An estate generally includes IRD in its gross income only when it receives the IRD. IRC § 691(a)(1)(A). If the estate transfers the right to receive IRD, however, the IRD is prematurely realized and is taxed at that time. IRC § 691(a)(2). A transfer includes a sale, exchange or other disposition of the IRD, but it does not include a transfer to a person by bequest from a decedent.

If an estate satisfies a pecuniary amount legacy with IRD, the transfer will cause immediate realization (and taxation) of the IRD. The legatee is entitled to a pecuniary amount of property, and the estate's transfer of the IRD in satisfaction of the pecuniary amount is treated as a sale. IRC § 691(a)(2); Treas. Reg. § 1.691(a)-4; *Noel v. Comm'r*, 50 T.C. 702 (1968).

→ **Planning Point:** IRD is not prematurely realized when the estate transfers it to a specific or residuary legatee, including allocation of the IRD among residuary trusts. <u>See</u> Treas. Reg. § 1.691(a)-4(b)(2).

→ **Planning Point:** To avoid premature realization of IRD, the client's estate should be planned so that IRD is <u>not</u> used to fund a pecuniary amount legacy, including a pecuniary marital deduction formula or a reverse pecuniary formula.

> **EXAMPLE:** If a client has a multi-million dollar estate comprised mainly of IRD, a pecuniary funding formula would not be appropriate. Note that the IRD is realized even if assets distributed in kind to satisfy the pecuniary amount marital trust are valued at their federal estate tax values.

A fractional share marital formula avoids the IRD problem entirely because it does not involve a pecuniary amount. It also has flexibility, since a fiduciary who is authorized to make

21st Century Estate Planning:
Practical Applications
2005 Edition

©2005 Sonnenschein Nath & Rosenthal LLP
and Cannon Financial Institute, Inc.

228

non-pro rata distributions may allocate the IRD to the marital trust, the family trust or partly to each, depending on which allocation produces the most favorable overall income and estate tax result.

➔ **Planning Point:** In large estates, a residuary marital disposition of IRD is generally a good solution, since the IRD would be allocated to the spouse or the residuary marital trust along with most of the estate.

To minimize federal estate tax at the death of the client's surviving spouse, many estate planners recommend that IRD be distributed to the spouse or to a marital trust. IRD is a shrinking asset, since the income tax which it generates is paid to the Internal Revenue Service and thus reduces the surviving spouse's gross estate. For purposes of the marital deduction funding, however, IRD is not discounted because of its built-in income tax liability. See Rev. Rul. 66-348, 1966-2 C.B. 433. If IRD is distributed to the marital share, this enables the fiduciary to allocate to the family disposition other assets that do not have built-in income tax liability.

2. Section 691(c) Deduction

If IRD was included in a decedent's gross estate for federal estate tax purposes, the recipient includes the IRD in gross income and is allowed an income tax deduction for the incremental amount of federal estate tax attributable to the IRD. IRC § 691(c).

Prior to the enactment of the Economic Recovery Tax Act of 1981 allowing an unlimited marital deduction beginning in 1982, practitioners carefully drafted wills to preserve all of the IRC § 691(c) deduction that was created by paying estate tax on the death of the first spouse to die. Because Treas. Reg. § 1.691(c)-1(a)(2) reduced the amount of the IRC § 691(c) deduction if the IRD had been allowed as a marital deduction, wills often directed that all IRD be allocated to the non-marital family trust. See also Rev. Rul. 67-242, 1967-2 C.B. 227.

With the unlimited marital deduction, drafting for the IRC § 691(c) deduction is simplified. At the first death, no federal estate tax is payable because of the unlimited marital deduction, so no IRC § 691(c) deduction is created.

In some estates, federal estate tax will be incurred on the death of the first spouse to die. In most cases the client's governing instruments utilize the unlimited marital deduction, so estate tax is incurred at the first death either because (a) a partial election is made in a QTIP marital trust or (b) the surviving spouse disclaims part or all of the marital distribution. In some situations, a married couple may intentionally incur federal estate tax at the first death (*e.g.*, client bequeaths $3,000,000 to children even if spouse survives).

➔ **Planning Point:** If a married client does incur federal estate tax, the fiduciary might allocate IRD away from the marital distribution in order to preserve fully the IRC § 691(c) deduction.

21ˢᵗ Century Estate Planning:
Practical Applications
2005 Edition

©2005 *Sonnenschein Nath & Rosenthal LLP*
and Cannon Financial Institute, Inc.

229

In *Estate of Kincaid v. Comm'r*, 85 T.C. 25 (1985), however, the Tax Court stated that when an estate's marital deduction is determined by a formula, the allocation of IRD to the marital or non-marital share is irrelevant in determining the IRC § 691(c) deduction.

If the fiduciary relies on *Kincaid*, it can allocate IRD to the marital trust, receive a full IRC § 691(c) deduction, and obtain the estate tax benefit of having the marital trust funded with a shrinking asset due to the built-in income tax liability of the IRD. <u>See</u> <u>also</u> TAM 9219006 (January 31, 1992).

3.   Income Earned During Administration

Trust accounting income earned during the period of estate administration is generally allocated among testamentary trusts in proportion to their respective interests from time to time unpaid or undistributed in the principal of the estate. <u>See, e.g.</u>, IRC § 6(b)(2) of the Illinois Principal and Income Act, 760 ILCS 15/6(b)(2). The executor determines the relative sizes of the marital trust and the family trust and allocates the income of the estate between them proportionately. Each trust receives its portion or fraction of the accounting income of the estate. This fraction can change during the administration of the estate.

Disproportionate partial funding of testamentary trusts can change the fraction of the accounting income of the estate to which each trust is entitled.

> **EXAMPLE:** In a $2,500,000 estate, the executor may fund half of the marital trust, so its interest in the estate is reduced from $1,000,000 to $500,000:
>
> Before partial funding:
>
> | | |
> |---|---|
> | Marital Trust | $1,000,000 |
> | Family Trust | $1,500,000 |
>
> After partial funding:
>
> | | |
> |---|---|
> | Marital Trust | $ 500,000 |
> | Family Trust | $1,500,000 |
>
> The marital trust is entitled to 40% of the income of the estate earned before the partial funding, but it is entitled to only 25% of the income of the estate earned after the funding.

The fraction of income of the estate to which each trust is entitled can change when taxes or expenses are paid out of the family trust.

21ˢᵗ Century Estate Planning:
Practical Applications
2005 Edition

©2005 Sonnenschein Nath & Rosenthal LLP
and Cannon Financial Institute, Inc.

230

EXAMPLE: Assume that the executor of a $2,000,000 estate elects to qualify none of the true pecuniary QTIP marital trust for the marital deduction because the surviving spouse has cancer and may die soon. The will provides that the federal estate tax of $435,000 is paid from the residue of the estate, *i.e.*, the Family Trust.

Before payment of estate tax:

Marital Trust	$500,000
Family Trust	$1,500,000

After payment of estate tax:

Marital Trust	$500,000
Family Trust	$1,065,000

The family trust receives 3/4 of the income of the estate earned before the payment of estate tax, even though it is entitled to only 68.1% (1,065,000/1,565,000) of the income earned after the tax payment.

➜ **Planning Point:** The adjustment to the fraction is especially significant when the marital trust and family trust have different income beneficiaries and the adjustment (or lack thereof) affects a substantial amount of income of the estate.

4. *Estate of Hubert*

a. **Introduction and Summary of Decision.** The U. S. Supreme Court decision in *Comm'r v. Estate of Hubert*, 520 U.S. 93 (1997), has created new opportunities in funding marital trusts and family trusts, as well as increased complexity and uncertainty. The *Hubert* case deals in part with the question of which charges against marital deduction property will cause the marital deduction to be reduced for federal estate tax purposes.

Before the *Hubert* case and the subsequently issued amendments to the marital deduction regulations, if an administration expense was paid out of principal of marital deduction property, this payment would reduce the amount of the marital deduction for federal estate tax purposes. In addition, administration expenses might be charged against the income of a marital trust. Any material limitation upon the spouse's right to income from the marital trust would cause a reduction in the marital deduction. See Treas. Reg. §§ 20.2056(b)-4(a), (b).

In the *Hubert* case, the executors charged $1,500,000 of administration expenses against the income of the residuary estate, which passed approximately one-half to a marital trust and one-half to charities. The expenses were deducted on the estate's income tax return. The IRS argued that the estate tax marital and charitable deductions should be reduced by $1,500,000

21ˢᵗ Century Estate Planning:
Practical Applications
2005 Edition

©2005 Sonnenschein Nath & Rosenthal LLP
and Cannon Financial Institute, Inc.

231

(*i.e.*, on a *dollar-for-dollar* basis). The Supreme Court rejected the position of the IRS and found for the executors. Justice O'Connor also invited the IRS to amend the marital deduction regulations to define a "material limitation" on the spouse's right to income from the marital trust.

    b. Proposed and Final Regulations. In December 1998, the IRS issued proposed regulations in response to the *Hubert* case. Final regulations were issued in December of 1999. The regulations dispensed with the concept of a material limitation on the spouse's right to income, which was considered too complex and difficult to administer. Treas. Reg. § 20.2056(b)-4(d). The material limitation test was replaced with two categories of expenses:

- Estate transmission expenses; and
- Estate management expenses.

    (1) Estate Management Expenses. Estate management expenses are defined as expenses incurred in connection with the investment of estate assets and with their preservation and maintenance during a reasonable period of administration – similar to expenses charged to income. The regulations specifically include the following examples: investment advisory fees, custodial fees, stock brokerage commissions, and interest. Treas. Reg. § 20.2056(b)-4(d)(1)(i). The preamble to the final regulations provides that estate management expenses are those expenses that would be incurred with respect to the property even if the decedent had not died.

    (2) Estate Transmission Expenses. All other estate administration expenses are considered to be estate transmission expenses. Estate transmission expenses are expenses that would not have been incurred except for the decedent's death, and they include expenses incurred in the collection of the decedent's assets, the payment of the decedent's debts and death taxes, and the distribution of the decedent's property – similar to expenses charged to principal. Examples of transmission expenses include executor's commissions and attorneys fees (except to the extent specifically related to investment, preservation and maintenance of the estate assets), probate fees, will construction and contest expenses, and appraisal fees. Treas. Reg. § 20.2056(b)-4(d)(1)(ii).

    (3) Effect on Marital Deduction. If estate *transmission* expenses are paid from the income or principal of the marital share, the marital deduction is reduced by the amount of the payment (on a *dollar-for-dollar* basis). Treas. Reg. § 20.2056(b)-4(d)(2). If estate *management* expenses are paid from the income or principal of the marital share, the marital deduction is generally not reduced by these payments. Treas. Reg. § 20.2056(b)-4(d)(3).

    The final regulations contain two exceptions to the general rule that payment of estate *management* expenses does not reduce the federal estate tax marital deduction.

- The marital deduction is reduced on a dollar-for-dollar basis if estate management fees are paid from the income or principal of the marital

21ˢᵗ Century Estate Planning:
Practical Applications
2005 Edition

©2005 Sonnenschein Nath & Rosenthal LLP
and Cannon Financial Institute, Inc.

232

share and such fees are deducted on the federal estate tax return (Form 706) under IRC § 2053. Treas. Reg. § 20.2056(b)-4(d)(3); *see* IRC § 2056(b)(9).

- The marital deduction is reduced if estate management fees charged to the marital share are incurred for the non-marital share where the spouse is not entitled to the income from that non-marital share. Treas. Reg. § 20.2056(b)-4(d)(3).

➔ **Planning Point:** A corporate fiduciary's fee, attorney fees, accounting fees, etc. may be partly an estate management expense and partly an estate transmission expense. In general, record keeping for the various types of administration expenses may be difficult, but it is advisable to distinguish between the services rendered to provide for more flexibility during the administration of the estate.

c. **Effect of *Hubert* Regulations on Marital Formula and Trust Funding.** When estate *transmission* expenses are paid, each of the marital deduction formulae discussed in this chapter generally operates the same way as before the issuance of the regulations in response to the *Hubert* case with respect to (i) computation of the amount of the marital deduction for federal estate tax purposes and (ii) funding of the marital and family trusts.

EXAMPLE: A $30,000 estate administration expense is deducted on the estate's income tax return (Form 1041). If the $30,000 is an estate *transmission* expense, the marital deduction funding formula creates a $1,470,000 family trust, assuming no change in values between date of death (or alternate valuation date) and date of trust funding.

When estate *management* expenses are paid, the formula operates differently than before *Hubert* regarding both the amount of the federal estate tax marital deduction and the funding of the marital and family trusts, depending on whether the management expenses are taken as a deduction on Form 1041 or Form 706.

- Form 1041 income tax deduction. In the above example, assume that the $30,000 is an estate *management* expense. The formula creates a $1,500,000 family trust, regardless of whether the management expenses are charged to income or principal.
- Form 706 federal estate tax deduction. Assume that the $30,000 estate *management* expense is taken as a federal estate tax deduction on Form 706. Applying the regulations, the marital deduction formula will create a family trust of $1,500,000 and the marital deduction will be reduced by $30,000.

EXAMPLE: Decedent had a gross estate of $2,000,000, and administrative expenses of $30,000. Applying an optimal marital

21st Century Estate Planning:
Practical Applications
2005 Edition

©2005 Sonnenschein Nath & Rosenthal LLP
and Cannon Financial Institute, Inc.

233

formula, the family trust would be $1,500,000 and the marital deduction would be $470,000. The estate would still have a federal estate tax deduction in the amount of $500,000 (marital deduction of $470,000 plus an administrative expense deduction of $30,000) resulting in a taxable estate of $1,500,000 and an estate tax of zero by applying the applicable exclusion amount.

      d. Drafting under the *Hubert* Regulations. In drafting wills and revocable trusts to take advantage of the *Hubert* regulations, practitioners should continue to maintain maximum flexibility regarding charging administrative expenses – whether estate transmission expenses or estate management expenses – to either principal or income of the estate or trust. The formula for computing the funding of the marital and family trusts does not need to be revised as a result of the issuance of the final regulations, so long as the formula is self-adjusting and operates to obtain the optimal marital deduction, as do the various funding formulae discussed in this chapter.

➔   **Planning Point:** If the funding formula refers to specific deductions or provisions of the Internal Revenue Code that are to be taken into account in calculating the marital deduction disposition, the governing instrument may need to be revised in light of the *Hubert* regulations.

5.   Creating and Funding GST (The Reverse QTIP Election)

      The advantages of lifetime use of the GST exemption or the creation of a generation-skipping trust at death without the use of the so-called reverse QTIP election were discussed above at Section D.5.(d). Lifetime use of the GST exemption without the use of the marital deduction is the most tax efficient method of planning for the GST tax as all future appreciation escapes the estate of the client and the client's spouse. Full use of the GST exemption at the first death for a married client without creating an exempt marital trust for which the reverse QTIP election is made under IRC § 2652(a)(3) is more tax efficient than using the marital deduction to shelter the portion of the GST exemption that exceeds the applicable exclusion amount. The two or three trust approach discussed above at Section D.5.(d) does have the advantage of generally deferring all federal and state estate taxes until the death of the survivor.

      In order to properly allocate GST exemption to a trust – regardless of whether it is an exempt marital trust for which a reverse QTIP election is made – and to be sure that trusts are created that have an inclusion ratio of zero or one for GST purposes, it is essential that each trust be treated as a separate trust for Chapter 13 (the GST tax) purposes.

➔   **Planning Point:** In drafting and funding trusts at death that will be treated as separate trusts for purposes of Chapter 13, it is necessary to pay close attention to the valuation and division of trust rules contained in the generation-skipping tax regulations. In general, these rules are similar to some of the marital trust funding rules discussed above.

21st Century Estate Planning:
Practical Applications
2005 Edition

©2005 Sonnenschein Nath & Rosenthal LLP
and Cannon Financial Institute, Inc.

234

If a trust created under a will or a revocable trust is divided into two or more trusts pursuant to a *mandatory direction* under the governing instrument, the separate trusts thereby created will be recognized for Chapter 13 purposes without needing to meet the funding and appropriate interest requirements discussed below.

If a trust created under a will or a revocable trust is divided into two or more trusts pursuant to *discretionary authority* granted to the fiduciary, certain additional requirements must be met in order for the trusts thereby created for state law purposes to be recognized for Chapter 13 purposes. Treas. Reg. § 26.2654-1(b)(1)(ii). Among the requirements contained in the regulations are the following:

- The severance must occur prior to the date prescribed for filing the federal estate tax return (including extensions actually granted).

➔ **Planning Point:** Trusts will be treated as meeting this requirement if the federal estate tax return indicates that separate trusts will be created or funded and clearly sets forth the manner in which the trusts are to be divided and funded. Treas. Reg. § 26-2654-1(b)(2).

➔ **Planning Point:** Meeting this disclosure requirement on Form 706 is essential when the trusts will not be funded prior to filing the estate tax return, as is often the case.

- If the new trusts are severed on a fractional basis, the separate trusts need not be funded pro rata based on the assets held in the original trust. The trusts may be funded on a non-pro rata basis provided the funding is based on either: (1) the fair market value of the assets on the date of funding; or (2) in a manner that fairly reflects the net appreciation or depreciation in the value of the assets from the date of death (or alternate valuation date) to the date of funding.
- If the severance is required by the terms of the governing instrument to be made on the basis of a pecuniary amount, the trustee must pay appropriate interest and, if the funding is made in kind, the funding must be based either: (1) on the fair market value of the assets on the date of funding; or (2) in a manner that fairly reflects the net appreciation or depreciation in the value of the assets from the date of death (or alternate valuation date) to the date of funding. Treas. Reg. §§ 26.2654-1(b)(1)(ii)(C)(2), (a)(1)(ii).

The appropriate interest requirement may be met in several different ways contained in the regulations.

- Interest must be paid from the date of death until the date of funding at a rate at least equal to the statutory rate of interest applicable to pecuniary bequests under the applicable state law.

21st Century Estate Planning:
Practical Applications
2005 Edition

©2005 Sonnenschein Nath & Rosenthal LLP
and Cannon Financial Institute, Inc.

235

- If no statutory rate is provided by state law, interest must be paid at a rate equal to at least 80 % of the IRC § 7520 rate in effect at the death of the decedent.
- The appropriate interest requirement is deemed to be met if the funding of the pecuniary trust is irrevocably done within 15 months of the decedent's death.
- The appropriate interest requirement is also deemed to be met if the governing instrument or applicable state law requires the funding of the pecuniary trust to receive a pro rata share of the income earned by the fund from which the payment is being made from the date of death until the date of funding. Treas. Reg. § 26.2642-2(b)(4).

6. Savings Clauses

Marital deduction savings clauses have proven useful for expressing the grantor's intent and therefore securing a deduction that otherwise might be lost. An example of a savings clause is as follows:

> I intend that all property passing under this Article qualify for the marital deduction. Accordingly, all powers and discretions conferred on the Trustee by law or other provisions of this instrument shall be exercisable and exercised only in such manner as to give my spouse substantially that degree of beneficial enjoyment of the trust property during my spouse's life that the principles of trust law accord to a person who is unqualifiedly designated as the sole life beneficiary of a trust. All such powers and discretions shall be subject to the imposing of reasonable limits on their exercise by a court. Any power to retain or invest in assets that consist substantially of unproductive property shall also be subject to the requirement that the Trustee use the degree of judgment and care in the exercise of that power that a prudent person would use as the owner of the trust property. This provision supersedes all other provisions in this instrument to the extent of any inconsistency.

a. Rulings and Cases. A number of rulings and cases have approved savings clauses. For example, in *Ellingson v. Comm'r*, 964 F.2d 959 (9th Cir. 1992), a trust instrument provided that all income be distributed to the surviving spouse, but the trustee could accumulate income that was not required for the support of the surviving spouse. The trust instrument also contained a savings clause. The Ninth Circuit allowed the marital deduction, stating that the trust instrument evidenced an intent that the marital bequest qualify for the marital deduction. Thus, the trustee's power to accumulate income, which was inconsistent with an intent to qualify for the marital deduction, could not be given effect. In Rev. Rul. 75-440, 1975-2 C.B. 372, the trust instrument authorized the trustee to invest in life insurance, which is an unproductive asset. The IRS considered the savings clause included in the trust instrument and found that this language applied only to the nonmarital trust. In TAM 199932001, a QTIP marital trust with a savings clause and support trust limitations arguably limited another provision requiring income distribution. The IRS construed the support trust limitations to apply only with respect to

21ˢᵗ Century Estate Planning:
Practical Applications
2005 Edition

©2005 Sonnenschein Nath & Rosenthal LLP
and Cannon Financial Institute, Inc.

236

principal distributions. The IRS found that this language did not restrict the surviving spouse's right to all the trust income because a different interpretation would disqualify the trust for the marital deduction, which would be contrary to the indicated intent. In PLR 8440037, the trust contained a provision that expressly authorized the trustee of the marital trust to invest in or retain unproductive properties. However, because the will contained a savings clause, the trust was not disqualified for marital deduction purposes.

The IRS reached a different conclusion, however, in PLR 8437093, which involved a will that made fractional share marital formula gifts to a marital deduction power of appointment trust. The trust instrument also authorized the trustee, both during and after the surviving spouse's life, to make principal distributions to a child and descendants. Distinguishing Rev. Rul. 75-440, the IRS found that the savings clause was not merely an aid in interpretation but was an attempt to revoke the power to make principal distributions to a person other than the surviving spouse, which would disqualify the marital deduction. The IRS, therefore, refused to give effect to the savings clause. However, the IRS concluded that another provision authorizing the surviving spouse to make unlimited withdrawals of principal was inconsistent with the provision authorizing principal distributions to a child and descendants during the surviving spouse's life. Because the will expressed an intent to primarily benefit the surviving spouse and qualify for the marital deduction, the IRS concluded that the relevant state court would interpret the will to prevent principal distributions to the child or descendants during the surviving spouse's life. Consequently, the IRS allowed the marital deduction despite the invalidity of the savings clause.

In TAM 9325002, a revocable inter vivos trust granted a power after the grantor's death to either the trustee or any beneficiary to petition a court to amend the trust if the purposes of the trust may be defeated because of a changes in circumstances or a change in the law. Although the grantor clearly expressed an intent that the trust qualify for the marital deduction and that the trustee cannot exercise any powers contrary to that intent, the IRS held that power to amend disqualified the trust from receiving a marital deduction. The IRS stated that this provision essentially authorized a court to restrict or even remove the surviving spouse's income interest if the spouse no longer needed that income or could not manage the money or some other change in circumstances occurred.

➔   **Planning Point:** As the above rulings show, savings clauses should not be relied upon to provide any protection against disqualifying provisions that clearly apply to the gift intended to support the marital deduction. See, e.g., TAM 200234017 (savings clause did not save marital deduction for disposition to trust that gave the surviving spouse a power of appointment in violation of IRC § 2056(b)(7)).

21st Century Estate Planning:
Practical Applications
2005 Edition

©2005 Sonnenschein Nath & Rosenthal LLP
and Cannon Financial Institute, Inc.

237

I. Funding Examples

Assume that an estate has a federal estate tax value of $3,000,000, the applicable exclusion amount is $1,500,000, and the optimal marital deduction is $1,500,000.

1. 20% Increase in Value of the Estate Before Funding

Federal Estate Tax Value: $3,000,000
Date of Distribution Value: $3,600,000

	True Pecuniary	Fractional	Reverse Pecuniary
Marital Trust	$1,500,000	1/2 x $3,600,000 = $1,800,000	$2,100,000
Family Trust	$2,100,000	1/2 x $3,600,000 = $1,800,000	$1,500,000
Capital Gain	$1,500,000 $\underline{(1,250,000)}$[1] $250,000	None	$1,500,000 $\underline{(1,250,000)}$[2] $250,000
Tax on Capital Gain	$250,000 $\underline{\text{x } 15\%}$ $37,500	None	$250,000 $\underline{\text{x } 15\%}$ $37,500

The basis amount was calculated as follows:

The amount of the marital trust divided by the total value of the trust on date of distribution (1,500,000/3,600,000) yields the percent of assets received by the marital trust (41.6666%). The percent of assets received is then multiplied by the total basis of the trust which is equivalent to the federal estate tax value (41.6666% x 3,000,000).

The same method of calculating the basis in 1 above was used ((1,500,000/3,600,000) x 3,000,000).

2. 20% Decrease in Value of the Estate Before Funding

Federal Estate Tax Value: $3,000,000
Date of Distribution Value: $2,400,000

21ˢᵗ Century Estate Planning:
Practical Applications
2005 Edition

©2005 Sonnenschein Nath & Rosenthal LLP
and Cannon Financial Institute, Inc.

238

	True Pecuniary	Fractional	Reverse Pecuniary
Marital Trust	$1,500,000	1/2 x $2,400,000 = $1,200,000	$900,000
Family Trust	$900,000	1/2 x $2,400,000 = $1,200,000	$1,500,000
Capital Loss	$1,500,000 ($1,875,000)[3] ($ 375,000)	None	$1,500,000 ($1,875,000)[4] ($ 375,000)

The same method of calculating the basis in 1 above was used ((1,500,000/2,400,000) x 3,000,000).

The same method of calculating the basis in 1 above was used ((1,500,000/2,400,000) x 3,000,000).

21st Century Estate Planning:
Practical Applications
2005 Edition

©2005 Sonnenschein Nath & Rosenthal LLP
and Cannon Financial Institute, Inc.

239

J. Comparison of Characteristics of Funding Formulae

Characteristic	True Pecuniary	Fractional Share	Reverse Pecuniary	Fairly Representative
Which trust enjoys appreciation or suffers depreciation?	Family Trust (residuary)	Both	Marital Trust (residuary)	Both
Is capital gain recognized on funding?	Yes	No	Yes	No
Do assets have to be revalued on funding?	Yes	No	Yes	Yes
Which trust bears the burden of taxes and expenses?	Family Trust (residuary)	Both	Marital Trust (residuary)	Family Trust (residuary)
Is income in respect of a decedent realized on funding?	Yes	No	Yes	Yes
Is funding formula impartial between Marital and Family Trust beneficiaries?	No	Yes	No	Yes
Can formula produce a larger than desirable Marital Trust?	No	Yes	Yes	Yes
Can formula produce a larger than desirable Family Trust?	Yes	Yes	No	Yes
Is formula time-sensitive (*i.e.* may require early funding)?	Yes	No	Yes	No

21ˢᵗ Century Estate Planning:
Practical Applications
2005 Edition

©2005 Sonnenschein Nath & Rosenthal LLP
and Cannon Financial Institute, Inc.

240

K. Post-Mortem Planning

Post-mortem planning provides the practitioner flexibility, and also allows the practitioner the ability to provide some planning for the clients who did not complete their estate plans during their lifetime.

1. Partial QTIP Election

Several options are available utilizing the QTIP trust election. A partial QTIP election, discussed at Section D.5.c, may allow the practitioner to equalize the estates of the decedent and the surviving spouse. It may be advisable to create a taxable estate in order to take advantage of the climb in tax brackets for each spouse, although this becomes less relevant as we approach 2007 and achieve a flat tax rate of 45% for amounts in excess of the applicable exclusion amount. Some commentators believe that the time-value of money will offset the tax saved in the bracket climb. But see Jeffrey N. Pennell, 843 T.M., *Estate Tax Marital Deduction*, p. 15.

➔ **Planning Point:** If it is determined that paying estate taxes at the death of the first spouse is desirable, sufficient assets must be available to liquidate to pay the tax.

If a partial QTIP election is made, separate trusts for the elected and non-elected portions should be created if permitted in the governing instrument or under applicable state law. Any payments made to the surviving spouse should be made out of the elected portion, thereby reducing the amount that will be included in the surviving spouse's gross estate at death.

➔ **Planning Point:** If a general power of appointment trust was utilized under IRC § 2056(b)(5), the surviving spouse may make a qualified disclaimer of the general power of appointment. Such a disclaimer will change the GPOA trust into a QTIP trust and a partial QTIP election may be made.

➔ **Planning Point:** If a decedent created a trust that does not meet the qualifications for a QTIP trust because the decedent's children also have an interest in the trust, it may be possible for the children to disclaim their interest in order to meet the requirements of a QTIP trust.

2. Disclaimer Provisions

Instead of using a formula marital deduction provision, a disclaimer provision may be utilized whereby all of the decedent's property is left to the surviving spouse. The surviving spouse may elect to disclaim all or any portion of the property, and such disclaimed property will pass to a family trust. Typically, the disclaimed amount will be equal to the decedent's remaining applicable exclusion amount. The family trust may provide the surviving spouse with

21ˢᵗ Century Estate Planning:
Practical Applications
2005 Edition

©*2005 Sonnenschein Nath & Rosenthal LLP*
and Cannon Financial Institute, Inc.

241

the income for life and discretionary principal to or for the benefit of the surviving spouse and the decedent's descendants.

> **EXAMPLE:** An example of a disclaimer provision is as follows:
>
> "If my spouse survives me, the Residuary Trust shall be distributed to my spouse. Despite the preceding sentence, any property directed in this Paragraph to be distributed to my spouse with respect to which my spouse has made a marital disposition qualified disclaimer shall be administered as provided in the Family Trust."
>
> .   .   .
>
> "The term "marital disposition qualified disclaimer" means a qualified disclaimer with respect to property passing under Remaining Trust Property Section for which, but for the making of such qualified disclaimer, a marital deduction would be allowed (or, on the making of an election under IRC § 2056(b)(7) of the Code, would be allowable) in determining the federal estate tax on my estate."

A qualified disclaimer under IRC § 2518 must be made within nine months after the decedent's death, must be in writing, the surviving spouse must not have accepted any benefits from the disclaimed property, and the disclaimed interest must pass without any direction from the surviving spouse.

Including a disclaimer provision is not mandatory, but it provides direction as to the ultimate disposition of the disclaimed property. A disadvantage of using a disclaimer provision is the surviving spouse may decide that he or she wants absolute control of the property and refuse to disclaim any interest in the property. There is a possibility that a surviving spouse may not possess the necessary capacity to exercise a disclaimer at the death of the first spouse.

➔　　**Planning Point:** As mentioned above, the surviving spouse cannot receive any benefits from the disclaimed property. Therefore, a disclaimer should be discussed immediately following the death of the decedent to avoid the possibility of the surviving spouse inadvertently accepting any benefits from property that might later be disclaimed.

L. The Gift Tax Marital Deduction

IRC § 2523 provides an unlimited gift tax deduction for property passing to a donee spouse. The purpose of the gift tax marital deduction, like the estate tax marital deduction, was to equalize the treatment in community and non-community states, hence the gift tax marital deduction has very similar rules to the estate tax marital deduction. Such rules will be summarized below and the differences between the gift tax and estate tax marital deductions will be outlined.

21st Century Estate Planning:
Practical Applications
2005 Edition

©2005 Sonnenschein Nath & Rosenthal LLP
and Cannon Financial Institute, Inc.

242

One of the main reasons to use a gift tax marital deduction, especially the QTIP trust as discussed below, is to equalize the size of the spouses' estates, and to allow the donee spouse to fully utilize the applicable exclusion amount. *See, e.g.,* PLR 200406004.

> **EXAMPLE:** Donor has an estate of $3,000,000 and Spouse's estate is $500,000. If Spouse dies in 2005 before Donor, Spouse will only utilize one-third of the applicable exclusion amount. If Donor gifts property valued at $1,000,000 to Spouse and Spouse dies immediately thereafter, Spouse will have enough assets to fully utilize Spouse's applicable exclusion amount, and an overall estate tax savings of as much as $470,800 as a result of reducing the size of Donor's taxable estate.

Additionally, all future appreciation from the transferred property escapes taxation in the donor spouse's estate which may save taxes as the property may have been taxed at higher estate tax rates in the donor's estate than in the donee spouse's estate.

1.　Requirements

A gift tax deduction is not allowed for a "nondeductible interest." A nondeductible interest is defined as a "terminable interest," or an interest that is not required to be included in a gift tax return for the year of the gift. Treas. Reg. § 25.2523(a)-1(b)(3). A terminable interest is a property interest that will terminate or fail upon the occurrence or non-occurrence of some event or contingency. The marital deduction is not allowed if the donor spouse transfers a terminable interest in property to the donee spouse and (i) the donor spouse retains an interest in the property, (ii) the donor spouse transfers an interest in the property to a person other than the donee spouse, or (iii) the donor retains a power of appointment under IRC § 2523(b)(2). Additionally, if a donor spouse retains a power to appoint an interest in the transferred property, and the donor spouse may exercise such power in a manner that the appointee may possess or enjoy any part of the property after such termination or failure of the interest transferred to the donee spouse, such transfer will be a nondeductible interest.

2.　Exceptions to the Terminable Interest Rule

a.　Power of Appointment. Under IRC § 2523(e), a marital deduction is allowed for an interest transferred to a donee spouse if it meets the following requirements:

- Donee spouse is entitled to all of the income from the entire interest, or from a specific portion, and such income must be paid at least annually;
- The donee spouse has a general power of appointment over the entire interest, or a specific portion of the interest, and such power is exercisable by the donee spouse alone and in all events; and
- No other person possesses the power to appoint such interest to any person other than the donee spouse.

21ˢᵗ Century Estate Planning:
Practical Applications
2005 Edition

©2005 Sonnenschein Nath & Rosenthal LLP
and Cannon Financial Institute, Inc.

243

EXAMPLE: Donor transferred $500,000 to an irrevocable trust. The trust provided that Spouse was to receive all trust income during her lifetime. Spouse also has a testamentary general power of appointment over the entire trust principal. A gift tax marital deduction is allowed for such transfer.

EXAMPLE: The facts are the same as the above example except Spouse's testamentary power of appointment is only over one-half of the trust principal. Even though spouse was entitled to all of the trust income, the gift tax marital deduction is only allowed for one-half of the value of the property transferred to the trust.

b. Qualified Terminable Interest Property. Similar to the estate tax QTIP trust, a donor spouse may transfer an interest to the donee spouse and retain control of the ultimate disposition of the property upon the donee spouse's death with the use of an irrevocable QTIP trust. IRC § 2523(f). The requirements of IRC § 2523(f) are as follows:

- The property is transferred by the donor spouse;
- The donee spouse has a qualifying income interest for life;
- The donor spouse elects to treat such transfer as qualified terminable interest property;
- The donee spouse must have the right to require the trustee to make the trust property productive or convert it within a reasonable time; and
- No person, including the donee spouse, is permitted to possess a power to appoint the property to any person other than the donee spouse during the spouse's lifetime.

The donor spouse may retain a right to receive income from the QTIP trust if the donor survives the donee spouse without such property being included in the donor's gross estate under IRC §§ 2036 or 2038. IRC § 2523(f)(5); Treas. Reg. § 25.2523(d). This allows the donor spouse to continue to receive income from the property if the donor survives the donee spouse. An exception to this rule is where the donee spouse disposes of a qualifying income interest during the donee spouse's life or the property is includible in the donee spouse's gross estate under IRC § 2044. Treas. Reg. § 25.2523(f)-1(d)(2).

EXAMPLE: Decedent transfers a property interest to an irrevocable trust. The income from the trust is payable to Spouse during Spouse's lifetime. Upon Spouse's death, the income is payable to Decedent for life, and upon Decedent's death, the entire trust is to be distributed to Decedent's children. Decedent elects to treat the property as QTIP. Decedent dies survived by Spouse. No part of the trust is included in Decedent's gross estate because Decedent elected QTIP treatment. However, the entire trust will be included in Spouse's gross estate under IRC § 2044.

21ˢᵗ Century Estate Planning:
Practical Applications
2005 Edition

©2005 Sonnenschein Nath & Rosenthal LLP
and Cannon Financial Institute, Inc.

244

EXAMPLE: The facts are the same as the above example, except Spouse predeceases Decedent. The entire trust is included in Spouse's gross estate under IRC § 2044, and Spouse is treated as the transferor of such property pursuant to IRC § 2044(c). At Decedent's death, the exception does not apply because the property was included in Spouse's estate under IRC § 2044. However, the property is still not included in Decedent's gross estate as Spouse is treated as the transferor of the property. The property may be included in Decedent's gross estate if Spouse's executor elected to treat the property as QTIP property under IRC § 2056(b)(7).

➔ **Planning Point:** If the donee spouse disposes of any interest in the qualified terminable interest property, whether a subsequent gift or sale of any portion of the interest, careful attention must be given to IRC § 2519 and the gift tax consequences of such a transfer.

    c. **Joint Interests**. IRC § 2523(d) also creates an exception to the terminable interest rules for joint interests that meet the following requirements:

- Donor spouse and donee spouse are the sole joint tenants or tenants by the entirety; and
- Donor's interest in the property exists solely by reason of the possibility of the donor spouse surviving the donee spouse, or a severance of the tenancy may occur.

If the above requirements are satisfied, the donor spouse is not treated as retaining an interest in the transferred property. The transfer is considered a deductible interest for which a marital deduction is allowed for one-half of the value of the transferred property.

3. Non-Citizen Spouse

The gift tax marital deduction is not allowed for a transfer to a donee spouse who is not a U.S. citizen. However, the annual exclusion amount under IRC § 2503(b) is increased to $100,000 for transfers to a non-U.S. citizen spouse, adjusted annually for inflation ($117,000 for 2005). IRC § 2523(i).

21ˢᵗ Century Estate Planning:
Practical Applications
2005 Edition

©2005 Sonnenschein Nath & Rosenthal LLP
and Cannon Financial Institute, Inc.

245

Chapter VIII
Bibliography

Roy M. Adams, "The Great Repeal Hoax: The More Things Change, The More They Remain the Same!," *Tr. & Est.* (August 2001).

Roy M. Adams, "The New Tax Laws and Increased Risk of Liability (Or the Omnipresent Rule - Don't Do Something if You Don't Know What You're Doing)," *Tr. & Est.* (October 2001).

Roy M. Adams, "The Sacred A/B Plan Under Assault By The 2001 Tax Act; The Need for Adaptation and Change, But Not Abandon," *Tr. & Est.* (November 2001).

Roy M. Adams, "Sunset Or Not On 1/1/2011 - Our World Has Changed," *Tr. & Est.* (September 2001).

Roy M. Adams, "Surviving Spouse's Tax Liability In A Partial QTIP Election," *Tr. & Est.* (July 2001).

Steve R. Akes, "An Overview of Post-Modern Tax Planning Strategies," *34th Annual Philip E. Heckerling Inst. on Est. Plan.* (2000).

D. Keith Bilter, "Marital Deduction And Generation-Skipping Formula Clauses: How To Get More Bang For Your Buck," *35th Annual Philip E. Heckerling Inst. on Est. Plan.* (2001).

Stuart Kessler, 844 T.M., *Estate Tax Credits and Computations*.

Henry J. Lischer, Jr., 845 T.M., *Gifts*.

Thomas G. Opferman, "The Marital Deduction In Depth: Formula Provisions (Pecuniary, Fractional, Hybrid); Hubert's Impact on Administration Expenses; Impact of Family Business Deduction; Impact of Generation-Skipping Transfer Tax; Funding Problems and Forms," Illinois Institute for Continuing Legal Education (April 18 and May 4, 2000).

Jeffrey N. Pennell, 843 T.M., *Estate Tax Marital Deduction*.

Jeffrey N. Pennell, "Funding Marital Deduction (and other) Bequests," *35th Annual Philip E. Heckerling Inst. on Est. Plan.* (2001).

John R. Price, *Price on Contemporary Estate Planning* (2nd ed. 2001).

Richard B. Stephens, Guy B. Maxfield, Stephen A. Lind and Dennis A. Calfee, *Federal Estate and Gift Taxation* (7th ed. 2001).

21st Century Estate Planning:
Practical Applications
2005 Edition

©2005 Sonnenschein Nath & Rosenthal LLP
and Cannon Financial Institute, Inc.

246

IX. PLANNING WITH THE APPLICABLE EXCLUSION AMOUNT

A. Introduction

When clients seek estate planning advice from practitioners, often one of the client's main goals is to transfer property to the next generation while incurring no, or the least amount of, tax. The purpose of the federal transfer tax system, which includes estate taxes, gift taxes and generation-skipping transfer taxes, is to tax property when an interest in such property is transferred to another person. Congress has created some exceptions to the transfer tax system. One of these exceptions is utilization of the applicable exclusion amount (also referred to as the unified credit, or the estate or gift tax exemption). In order to achieve the goals of clients, practitioners should have a basic understanding of the rules regarding the applicable exclusion amount.

This chapter discusses the following issues relating to the applicable exclusion amount and will assist the practitioner in meeting his or her client's goals of minimizing or eliminating federal estate and gift taxes:

- History of the Unified Tax System.
- Unified Credit Against Estate Tax.
- Use of the Applicable Exclusion at Death.
- Unified Credit Against Gift Tax.
- Lifetime Use of the Applicable Exclusion Amount.
- The Applicable Exclusion and the Marital Deduction.
- The Family Trust.
- Selection of Trustees.

B. History of the Unified Tax System

Before 1977, separate rate schedules and exemption amounts were in effect for the federal estate and gift taxes. The estate tax rate ranged from 3% to 77%, and a specific exemption of $60,000 was allowed. The gift tax rate ranged from 2¼% to 57¾%, and a specific exemption of $30,000 and an annual exclusion of $3,000 were allowed.

In 1976, Congress replaced the separate rate schedules and exemptions with a unified estate and gift tax system. With the 1976 Act, Congress sought to eliminate the disparity between transfers during lifetime and at death, and to eliminate the preference for lifetime transfers which was created by the tax laws before 1976. See, generally, HR Rep. No. 1380, 94th Cong., 2nd Sess. 10-17 (1976), Estate and Gift Tax Reform Act of 1976.

The specific exemption was also changed to a unified credit. The specific exemption created a deduction that reduced the tax at the highest tax rate which benefited the wealthy taxpayer who paid tax at the higher rates. The unified credit is a dollar-for-dollar reduction in the tax due which provides more tax savings for small to medium size estates.

21ˢᵗ Century Estate Planning:
Practical Applications
2005 Edition

©2005 Sonnenschein Nath & Rosenthal LLP
and Cannon Financial Institute, Inc.

247

In 2001, Congress again significantly revised the transfer tax system. *See* Economic Growth and Tax Relief Reconciliation Act of 2001 (the "Act"). In 2005, each U.S. citizen has a gift tax applicable exclusion amount of $1,000,000, and an estate tax applicable exclusion amount of $1,500,000. The estate tax applicable exclusion amount is scheduled to gradually increase over the next few years until it reaches $3,500,000 in 2009. The gift tax applicable exclusion amount will remain $1,000,000 and is not indexed for inflation. The rate schedules for the estate and gift tax will gradually decrease over the next few years until the estate tax is repealed in 2010. The gift tax will not be repealed, but the rate will be reduced to 35% for gifts made after 2009. The following chart summarizes the adjustments in the estate tax applicable exclusion amount and rate schedule.

Calendar Year	Estate Tax Applicable Exclusion Amount	Rate
2005	$1,500,000	47%
2006	$2,000,000	46%
2007	$2,000,000	45%
2008	$2,000,000	45%
2009	$3,500,000	45%
2010	Repealed	Repealed
2011	$1,000,000	55%

Although the Act repeals the federal estate tax (and GST tax) in 2010, the Act contains a "sunset" provision, which provides that the Act does not apply for tax years beginning after December 31, 2010. In other words, the estate tax and the GST tax will reappear in 2011, under the law as it existed prior to the Act, unless repealed again by a future Congress and President. Accordingly, many expect that over the next several years additional changes will be made to the federal transfer tax system as it exists today.

C. Unified Credit Against Estate Tax

1. Definitions

The use of the estate tax applicable exclusion amount may reduce or even eliminate estate taxes. Internal Revenue Code ("IRC") § 2010 grants each estate of a decedent a credit equal to the applicable credit amount against the estate tax.

21ˢᵗ Century Estate Planning:
Practical Applications
2005 Edition

©2005 Sonnenschein Nath & Rosenthal LLP
and Cannon Financial Institute, Inc.

248

a. **Applicable Credit Amount**: The applicable credit amount is defined as the amount of tentative tax determined under the estate tax rate computed on the applicable exclusion amount. IRC § 2010(c).

b. **Applicable Exclusion Amount**: The applicable exclusion amount for a given year is stated in IRC § 2010(c) and is listed in the chart in the previous section.

c. **Tentative Tax**: In order to determine the applicable credit amount, the tentative tax is determined by applying the estate tax rate schedule in IRC § 2001(c) to the applicable exclusion amount. IRC § 2010(c).

> **EXAMPLE:** In 2005, the applicable exclusion amount is $1,500,000. Using the tax rates under IRC § 2001, an estate of $1,500,000 would create a tentative tax in the amount of $555,800. Therefore, the applicable credit amount for 2005 is $555,800.

2. Use of Applicable Exclusion at Death

In 2005, each U.S. citizen has an estate tax applicable exclusion in the amount of $1,500,000, which allows a person to transfer such amount at death to anyone without incurring federal estate tax, provided the decedent has not made any lifetime taxable gifts that may be included in calculating the decedent's gross estate. If a person utilized his or her gift tax applicable credit during lifetime, the amount of post-1976 adjustable taxable gifts is added to the decedent's taxable estate when determining the amount of the decedent's gross estate. The tentative tax is then determined on the total amount of the adjustable taxable gifts and taxable estate. If any gift tax was paid during life, the gift tax paid reduces the amount of tentative tax. The applicable credit amount is then deducted from the tentative tax to determine the net federal estate tax due.

> **EXAMPLE:** Decedent made post-1976 gifts in the amount of $500,000. At Decedent's death in 2004, her taxable estate was $1,500,000. The net federal estate tax is determined as follows:
>
> | | |
> |---|---|
> | Taxable Estate | $1,500,000 |
> | Adjustable Taxable Gifts | $500,000 |
> | Total | $2,000,000 |
> | | |
> | Tentative Tax | $780,800 |
> | Gift Tax Paid | $0 |
> | Total Federal Estate Tax | $780,800 |
> | | |
> | Available Applicable Credit | ($555,800) |
> | Net Federal Estate Tax | $225,000 |

21st Century Estate Planning:
Practical Applications
2005 Edition

©2005 Sonnenschein Nath & Rosenthal LLP
and Cannon Financial Institute, Inc.

249

➔ **Planning Point:** If gifts were made between September 8, 1976 and January 1, 1977, the applicable credit will be reduced by a portion of the specific exemption that was allowed.

If the value of an estate is less than the applicable exclusion amount, a refund is not available, and the credit is nontransferable. An executor is required to file an estate tax return only if the decedent's gross estate exceeds the applicable exclusion amount. IRC § 6018. If prior taxable gifts were made by the decedent, the applicable exclusion amount is reduced by the amount of the prior gifts to determine whether an estate tax return is necessary.

> **EXAMPLE:** Decedent's gross estate was $1,300,000, and Decedent made taxable gifts in the amount of $500,000 during Decedent's life. Based on the value of the gross estate only, an estate tax return is not required. However, the taxable gifts reduce the amount of the applicable exclusion in determining whether a return is required. Therefore, the applicable exclusion amount is $1,000,000 and the gross estate exceeds the applicable exclusion, thereby requiring the filing of an estate tax return.

➔ **Planning Point:** Even if a return is not required to be filed, some practitioners file a return in order to start the statute of limitations period on assessments. However, the time and cost associated with filing an estate tax return probably is too burdensome in an estate where valuation issues are not present.

D. Unified Credit Against Gift Tax

Every individual has a $1,000,000 gift tax applicable exclusion that shelters transfers during life aggregating such amount. Any taxable gifts in excess of such amount will be subject to gift tax. The gift tax rate is the same as the estate tax rate, and it is scheduled to decline along with the estate tax rate through 2009. Beginning in 2010, the gift tax will be imposed on transfers in excess of the $1,000,000 gift tax applicable exclusion at the rate of 35%. The Act did not repeal the gift tax, and the gift tax applicable credit is not indexed for inflation.

1. The Applicable Exclusion and the Determination of Gift Tax

IRC § 2505 is similar to language in IRC § 2010 regarding the estate tax applicable exclusion. Each person is allowed a credit equal to the applicable credit under the estate tax scheme determined as if the applicable exclusion amount was $1,000,000. As the gift tax applicable exclusion will remain constant at $1,000,000, the gift tax applicable credit is $345,800.

> **EXAMPLE:** In 2005, Donor transferred publicly traded stock to Donee. Such stock was valued at $511,000 on the date of transfer.

21ˢᵗ Century Estate Planning:
Practical Applications
2005 Edition

©2005 Sonnenschein Nath & Rosenthal LLP
and Cannon Financial Institute, Inc.

250

Donor had made no previous gifts and did not make any additional gifts in 2005. Donor filed a gift tax return for the 2005 tax year reporting the $511,000 gift. Because the gift was of a present interest, $11,000 of the gift qualified for the gift tax annual exclusion. Therefore, Donor made a taxable gift of $500,000. The tentative tax on such amount is $155,800. Because Donor's available applicable credit is $345,800, no gift tax is due and donor utilized $155,800 of Donor's applicable credit amount (or $500,000 of Donor's applicable exclusion amount).

In general, when determining the gift tax for a given year, that year's current taxable gifts are added to the taxable gifts from previous years, and the tentative gift tax is determined on the aggregated sum utilizing the applicable tax rate from IRC § 2001(c). The tentative gift tax is then reduced by the applicable credit.

> **EXAMPLE:** In 2005, Donor made a taxable gift of $1,000,000 to Son. Donor previously made a $500,000 post-1976 gift which utilized $155,800 of Donor's gift tax applicable credit. The gift tax for 2005 is determined as follows:

Taxable Gift	$1,000,000
Previous Taxable Gifts	$ 500,000
Total Taxable Gifts	$1,500,000
Tentative Tax on Total Taxable Gifts	$555,800
Tentative Tax on Previous Taxable Gifts	$155,800
Gross Gift Tax on 2005 Gift	$400,000
Applicable Credit	$345,800
Applicable Credit used on Prior Gifts	$155,800
Available Applicable Credit	$190,000
Net Gift Tax on 2005 Gift	$210,000

For a more detailed discussion on the computation of federal gift taxes, see Chapter III, Federal Gift Tax.

2.   Benefits of Lifetime Use of the Applicable Exclusion Amount

The use of the gift tax applicable exclusion amount has several advantages over not making gifts and utilizing only the estate tax applicable exclusion amount.

- Any future appreciation of, or income from, the gifted property is removed from the donor's estate for federal estate tax purposes.

21st Century Estate Planning:
Practical Applications
2005 Edition

©*2005 Sonnenschein Nath & Rosenthal LLP*
and Cannon Financial Institute, Inc.

251

- Any gift tax actually paid by the donor is removed from the donor's estate if the donor survives at least three years after the gift.
- The tax used to pay the gift tax is not itself subject to tax ("tax exclusive"), whereas the tax used to pay the estate tax is subject to tax ("tax inclusive").

For a more detailed discussion on the benefits of lifetime gifts, <u>see</u> Chapter III, Federal Gift Tax.

E. The Applicable Exclusion and the Marital Deduction

If married clients only use their gift tax and estate tax marital deduction (as discussed in Chapter VIII, Planning for the Marital Deduction), the clients will have eliminated federal estate tax at the first death, but will have effectively "wasted" the applicable exclusion amount of the first spouse to die. Depending on the size of the surviving spouse's estate at death, the surviving spouse's estate may incur up to $555,800 in additional federal estate taxes (based on 2005 applicable credits and rates) caused by the lack of use of the first spouse's applicable exclusion. Most practitioners will recommend to married clients that they fully utilize both the marital deduction *and* applicable exclusion amount to eliminate or minimize the federal and state estate taxes at the death of both spouses.

In general, formula clauses, as discussed in Chapter VIII, Planning for the Marital Deduction, provide for the marital trust to be funded so that no federal and state estate taxes, or the minimum amount of such taxes, would result. This type of planning is referred to as an "optimal marital deduction plan." Depending on the type of formula selected, the plan would create a marital trust share and a family trust share. In general terms, the family trust would hold assets with a value equal to the available applicable exclusion amount, and the amount in excess of the applicable exclusion amount would be held in the marital trust share. The marital trust share must be distributed outright to the spouse or held in a trust that qualifies for the marital deduction. The family trust share can be held in several different ways, as will be discussed in the following section.

> **EXAMPLE:** Decedent and Spouse have a total estate worth approximately $4,000,000. During Decedent's lifetime, they used the gift tax marital deduction to equalize their estates. Neither spouse made any other lifetime taxable gifts. Decedent died in 2004. At Decedent's death, Decedent and Spouse each owned property in their individual names in the amount of $2,000,000. Decedent did not use any of her gift tax applicable exclusion amount during her lifetime. Decedent's estate plan provided for the "optimal marital deduction." Therefore, under Decedent's plan, the Family Trust received $1,500,000 and the Marital Trust $500,000. The applicable exclusion amount exempts the Family Trust from estate tax, and, because Decedent's executor elected QTIP treatment for the Marital Trust, the

21ˢᵗ Century Estate Planning:
Practical Applications
2005 Edition

©2005 Sonnenschein Nath & Rosenthal LLP
and Cannon Financial Institute, Inc.

252

value of the Marital Trust qualified for the marital deduction. Therefore, at the death of the first spouse, no tax is due as a result of using both the marital deduction and the applicable exclusion amount.

EXAMPLE: Spouse died the following year, 2005, with an estate of $2,000,000. Because a QTIP election was made for Marital Trust, the value of the Marital Trust at Spouse's date of death is also included in Spouse's gross estate. Therefore, Spouse has a gross estate of $2,500,000. Applying the credits and rates in effect for 2005, a gross estate of $2,500,000 will generate federal estate tax of $460,000. If Decedent used only the marital deduction at her death and not her applicable credit amount, Spouse's estate would have been $4,000,000 at her death creating federal estate tax in the amount of $1,165,000 – an increase of $705,000.

Properly drafted marital deduction and applicable exclusion formulae must take into account property passing outside the will or trust agreement to the surviving spouse or others so that neither the marital trust nor the family trust will be funded with more assets than intended in order to minimize or eliminate federal and state estate taxes.

➔ **Planning Point:** As an alternative to using marital gifts to equalize the estates of two spouses, as used in the example above, the IRS in PLR 200403094 approved a technique in which the wealthier of spouses confers a general power of appointment on the poorer spouse to transfer property to the estate of the poorer spouse if the poorer spouse dies first. This technique enables equalization of the spouses' estates if the poorer spouse dies first without having the wealthier spouse make an irrevocable transfer during his or her lifetime to the other spouse, thereby losing control of the distribution of the transferred assets.

F. The Family Trust

As discussed above, the family trust is usually satisfied with an amount equaling the available estate tax applicable exclusion amount. There are unlimited ways which the family trust can be administered, and several of them will be discussed below.

1. During Spouse's Life

a. **Mandatory Income to Spouse.** The trust assets may be held in one trust during the lifetime of the surviving spouse. The trustee may be required to distribute the income to or for the benefit of the surviving spouse during the surviving spouse's life. The trustee may also have discretion to distribute the principal to or for the benefit of the surviving spouse alone or to or for the benefit of the spouse and others, such as decedent's descendants (and possibly descendants' spouses). The trustee's discretion may be limited to ascertainable standards such as

21st Century Estate Planning:
Practical Applications
2005 Edition

©2005 Sonnenschein Nath & Rosenthal LLP
and Cannon Financial Institute, Inc.

253

health, education, maintenance and support or may be as broad as best interests. If distributions are permitted to be made to anyone other than the spouse, the drafter should consider whether the trustee should be required to give preference to the needs of the spouse. Also the trust may provide for equal or unequal distributions to the beneficiaries.

➔ **Planning Point:** Many clients prefer this type of arrangement to assure that the surviving spouse has a guaranteed income stream for the remainder of the surviving spouse's life. The age of decedent's children will also impact the distribution provisions of the trust.

➔ **Planning Point:** The scope of the trustee's discretion also will impact the selection of trustee – whether the spouse may serve alone or with a co-trustee. The following section discusses the selection of trustees in more detail.

      b. Discretionary Payments of Income and Principal. In the alternative, the trust may provide for discretionary distributions of both income and principal to the spouse alone or to the spouse and decedent's descendants. The trustee's discretion may be limited to ascertainable standards or be as broad as best interests. As in the above arrangement, this trust share may be established for the primary benefit of the spouse.

      c. Other Provisions for the Spouse. The trust may provide the surviving spouse with other rights such as the following:

- A right to withdraw principal not to exceed the greater of $5,000 or 5% of the trust principal each year. Note that the annual withdrawal right should be limited to the "5 or 5" standard to avoid estate tax and gift tax problems for the spouse under IRC §§ 2041(b)(2) and 2514(e). See further discussion of "5 or 5" withdrawal rights in Chapter III, Federal Gift Tax, and Chapter VII, Annual Exclusion Gift Planning.

➔ **Planning Point:** A properly limited "5 or 5" withdrawal right will result in inclusion in the surviving spouse's gross estate of the amount of property subject to this right at the time of the surviving spouse's death, even if the right is never exercised by the surviving spouse.

- A lifetime or testamentary limited power of appointment in which property may be appointed to one or more persons *other than* the surviving spouse, surviving spouse's estate or creditors of the surviving spouse or the surviving spouse's estate. In the alternative, the decedent may grant the surviving spouse the power to appoint such property to a certain class of beneficiaries such as the descendants of the decedent. Caution should be exercised to avoid giving the spouse a general testamentary power of appointment, as this will result in the trust assets

21ˢᵗ Century Estate Planning:
Practical Applications
2005 Edition

©2005 Sonnenschein Nath & Rosenthal LLP
and Cannon Financial Institute, Inc.

254

which are subject to such power being includible in the surviving spouse's gross estate.

2. At the Surviving Spouse's Death

a. <u>Outright Distribution to Descendants</u>. At the death of the surviving spouse, the remaining trust assets may be distributed outright to individuals designated by the decedent, such as to the descendants of the decedent, *per stirpes*. If such descendants are minors, the assets should be held in trust at least until the beneficiaries attain the age of majority to avoid the establishment of a guardianship and/or conservatorship.

b. <u>Assets Held in Trust</u>. If the assets are not distributed outright, the assets remaining in the trust may be held in a single trust for the benefit of individuals designated by the decedent, such as decedent's descendants. This type of trust is commonly referred to as a "pot" trust as the assets are held in a single "pot" instead of being distributed into separate shares for each of the beneficiaries. The assets are held in trust until a certain event as determined by the decedent. For example, many clients hold the assets in the "pot" trust until their youngest child reaches a certain age, such as 23, when most children will have completed college. Upon the occurrence of the determined event, the "pot" trust may be divided into separate shares for each of decedent's then living descendants, *per stirpes*, and continue to be held in separate trusts, or may be distributed outright to designated beneficiaries.

Instead of a "pot" trust, the client may decide to immediately divide the remaining trust assets into separate shares at the spouse's death. There are a number of possibilities regarding the administrative provisions of the separate trust shares, and a few of them are outlined below:

- The trustee may have discretion to distribute income to or for the benefit of the beneficiary, and such discretion may be limited by ascertainable standards or be broadened to include best interests.
- A mandatory distribution of income may be required when the beneficiary reaches a certain age, such as age 21.
- Principal distributions may also be discretionary until a certain event when mandatory distributions are required. Examples of events include: the beneficiary reaching a certain age; the beneficiary completing his or her education; or the passage of a specified number of years after the death of the decedent and the decedent's spouse.

➔ **Planning Point:** Many clients choose to stagger the mandatory distribution of principal.

> **EXAMPLE:** An example of a provision allowing for staggered distributions is as follows:

21st Century Estate Planning:
Practical Applications
2005 Edition

©2005 Sonnenschein Nath & Rosenthal LLP
and Cannon Financial Institute, Inc.

255

"When such individual reaches age 25, or if such individual has already reached such age but not age 30 when the trust for such individual is established, the trustee shall distribute one-third of the remaining trust property to such individual. When such individual reaches age 30, the trustee shall distribute one-half, or if such individual has already reached such age when the trust for such individual is established, two-thirds, of the remaining trust property to such individual. When such individual reaches age 35, or if such individual has already reached such age when the trust for such individual is established, the trustee shall distribute all remaining trust property to such individual."

- The trustee may be specifically required to consider other assets available to the beneficiary before making any discretionary distribution of income or principal, or may be specifically permitted to ignore such other resources.

- Special discretionary distributions of principal may be permitted for certain purposes such as the following:

  - To enable the beneficiary to make gifts to or in trust for any one or more of the descendants of such beneficiary.
  - To pay tuition directly to an educational organization for the education or training of any one or more of the descendants of such beneficiary.
  - To make payments directly to a provider of medical care for the medical care of any one or more of the descendants of such beneficiary.
  - To purchase real property, including buildings, permanent improvements and fixtures located within such real property, to be used as such beneficiary's primary residence.
  - To establish an office for the practice of a profession or trade by such beneficiary which, in the judgment of the trustee, has a reasonable likelihood of success.
  - To invest in a business in which such individual intends to participate actively and which, in the judgment of the trustee, has a reasonable likelihood of success.

- Certain beneficiaries may be granted a right to withdraw principal not to exceed the greater of $5,000 or 5% of the trust principal each year. See the discussion in Section G.2.a.(2) ("5 or 5 Power") below regarding limitation of withdrawal rights.

- A lifetime or testamentary power of appointment, which may be limited or general, may be granted to certain beneficiaries. Note that the granting of

21st Century Estate Planning:
Practical Applications
2005 Edition

©2005 Sonnenschein Nath & Rosenthal LLP
and Cannon Financial Institute, Inc.

256

a general power of appointment will result in assets subject to such power being includible in the gross estate of the powerholder.

- Rather than mandatory distribution of principal, the trust may allow the beneficiary the right to withdraw trust property at designated ages. This may avoid the need for a beneficiary who is satisfied with the management of the trust assets by the trustee to create his or her own revocable trust to manage the assets.

There are countless ways in which to distribute the trust assets to the intended beneficiaries. Practitioners should gain an understanding of the family dynamics in order to facilitate a discussion with the clients regarding the various possibilities.

G. Selection of Trustees

Trustees are required to administer trusts actively for years or even decades. In addition, they must be able to handle the increasingly complex tax laws and a volatile investment climate. Thus, in selecting a trustee, the client, with the guidance of his or her advisors, must carefully consider who is the proper individual or entity to serve as trustee. The selection of an appropriate trustee is of prime importance to insure that the grantor's[1] wishes are fulfilled and the trust's beneficiaries receive all of the benefits to which they are entitled.

As discussed below, many factors must be considered when selecting a trustee, and most clients find this process difficult. It is the role of the client's advisors to assist the client by laying out the duties of a trustee and providing guidance to enable the client to evaluate the attributes of each individual or entity the client is considering as a trustee.

1.   Non-Tax Considerations

A balance of the factors discussed below and the facts and circumstances of each family situation will play a significant role in the final determination of a trustee. It is advisable for practitioners to consult with their clients every few years, for among many reasons, to review the selections of their trustees (and other fiduciaries) to assure that the individuals or entities selected remain the right choice after factoring in any changes in circumstances.

a.   <u>Most Common and Important Duties of the Trustee</u>. The grantor and any person being considered as a trustee must understand the amount of time and skill required to serve as a trustee. Some clients appoint a trustee because they feel it is an "honorary" position. However, as anyone who has served as a trustee knows, the position can absorb a large amount of time and requires a great deal of expertise.

(1)   <u>Investments</u>. A trustee has a duty to make trust property productive. The trustee must prudently invest trust property to assure both sufficient current income for the current income beneficiaries and appropriate capital appreciation for the remainder beneficiaries. The grantor may instruct the trustee in the trust instrument[2] that, in

21st Century Estate Planning:
Practical Applications
2005 Edition

©2005 Sonnenschein Nath & Rosenthal LLP
and Cannon Financial Institute, Inc.

257

making investment decisions, the trustee should emphasize either current income or long-term appreciation. If the principal is invested so that the principal does not appreciate, the impact of inflation could significantly erode the value of the remainder interest. If the trust's governing instrument or applicable state law is up-to-date, the trustee may be permitted, or even encouraged, to implement a style of investing promoting total return.

(2) **Exercise Appropriate Discretion While Making Distributions**. One of the trustee's most important duties is to make distributions to beneficiaries in accordance with the grantor's wishes as expressed in the trust instrument. This will often require the prudent exercise of discretion to sprinkle income and, possibly, principal to one or more beneficiaries, in accordance with the trust instrument. The trustee must be loyal and fair to all beneficiaries, both current and remainder. For the trustee to know how the grantor of the trust wants the trustee to exercise his or her discretion, or to ascertain the standard of living the grantor and beneficiaries are maintaining, it may be useful for the grantor and the trustee to discuss this subject (and for the results of the discussion to be reduced to writing for future reference) while the grantor is living and available to participate in such discussion. Although not legally binding, having had such a discussion can prove invaluable in assisting the trustee when the time comes for the trustee to exercise dispositive discretion. In addition, the trustee may have to take into account (but not necessarily be controlled by) the federal income tax situation of each beneficiary to assure that the overall income tax liabilities for the trust and the various beneficiaries will be minimized to the extent consistent with the grantor's objectives.

(3) **Maintenance of Property**. The trustee must secure possession of trust assets, conduct careful recordkeeping and maintenance of trust property, refrain from commingling property and perform other appropriate custodial and bookkeeping functions.

(4) **Other Duties**. The following are some other common and important duties of the trustee:

- Manage assets that are not typical investment assets (*e.g.*, farming operations or oil and gas investments).
- Be aware of and exercise, when necessary, other powers granted in trust instrument.
- Prepare (or arrange for the preparation of) and file tax returns and pay any taxes due.
- Defend the trust against attack.
- Terminate the trust and wind up its affairs.
- Seek and act upon professional advice when necessary.

b. **Characteristics of the Trust That Should be Considered When Selecting a Trustee.** A trustee's duties must be considered in light of the characteristics of the particular trust at issue. These characteristics include:

- The purposes of the trust.

21ˢᵗ Century Estate Planning:
Practical Applications
2005 Edition

©2005 Sonnenschein Nath & Rosenthal LLP
and Cannon Financial Institute, Inc.

258

- The prospective size of the trust. For a small trust, the appointment of a corporate trustee may be uneconomical.
- The types of assets the trust will hold.
- The probable duration of the trust.
- The relationships between the trustee and beneficiaries and among the beneficiaries as well as the individual personalities of the beneficiaries and of the trustee.
- Geographical differences in location of the assets, location of the trustee and location of the beneficiaries and whether or not the trust can be properly administered if any one of these is not in geographic proximity to the other two.
- The need for guardians for minor children to be able to have a co-operative working relationship with the trustees.
- Compensation of the trustee.

No single factor is determinative of who is best to serve as trustee; the client must balance the advantages and disadvantages of the various possible candidates.

c. Individual Trustee vs. Corporate Trustee. A large portion of the time spent selecting a trustee will be concerned with deciding whether the trustee should be an individual or an entity (or whether there should be two or more individuals or whether there should be one or more individuals along with an entity). The advantages and disadvantages of individual and corporate trustees are provided below to assist the practitioner in advising clients when facing this difficult decision.

(1) Advantages of an Individual Trustee

- An individual trustee who is a family member or friend of the family may have a better understanding of the family dynamics and be more familiar with the family members.
- If a family business is to be held and managed in the trust, an individual trustee may be more knowledgeable regarding such business operations.
- The costs associated with an individual trustee are sometimes less than those associated with a corporate trustee.
- The trust assets remain in "control" of a family member.

(2) Disadvantages of an Individual Trustee

- Typically, an individual trustee lacks sophisticated financial knowledge and detailed knowledge about trust administration. Even though usually authorized to retain agents and investment counsel to assist him or her in these matters, an individual acting as

21st Century Estate Planning:
Practical Applications
2005 Edition

©2005 Sonnenschein Nath & Rosenthal LLP
and Cannon Financial Institute, Inc.

259

sole trustee might find that the burdens of investment and administration are too complex and stressful.

- The time commitment necessary to be a responsible trustee may be greater than a given individual has available; most individuals have another "full-time" job, but, with a corporate trustee, trust administration is its "full-time" job.

- An individual trustee may be unduly influenced by the trust beneficiaries.

- An individual may have a real or perceived conflict of interest between his or her duties as trustee and his or her personal interest as a beneficiary or otherwise. For example, if a grantor names his son from his first marriage as trustee of a trust for his second wife, the son and the second wife may end up in conflict. The wife may request distributions for travel and luxuries, and the son may resist because he secretly hopes to preserve the trust assets until the wife's death, when they will be distributable to him. Conflicts of interest can also arise if the trustee, personally, has an interest in any asset in which the trust also will have an interest, such as stock in a closely held business.

- An individual may die, become disabled or become unsuitable to act while serving as trustee or may resign as trustee at any time.

(3) **Advantages of a Corporate Trustee**

- Where the trust is likely to be of substantial size or hold complex assets - such as closely held business interests or real estate - administration of the trust may require special competence and expertise beyond the ability of any individual, whether a relative, friend or business colleague. A corporate trustee provides professional handling of investment, tax, accounting and other aspects of trust administration, as opposed to individual trustees, who may not have the time or expertise to perform an adequate job. Although an individual named as trustee might be willing to serve without compensation, the resulting savings is often offset by the need to retain and compensate attorneys, accountants, investment advisors and other agents.

- A corporate trustee is intuitively knowledgeable concerning the laws and regulations that impose and relate to the duties of a trustee. Moreover, because they are considered experts in trust administration, corporate trustees are generally held to a higher standard of care than individual trustees.

- A corporate trustee is also appropriate in situations in which a trustee situated in a particular state is needed so that the trust and

21st Century Estate Planning:
Practical Applications
2005 Edition

©2005 Sonnenschein Nath & Rosenthal LLP
and Cannon Financial Institute, Inc.

260

its beneficiaries can benefit from flexible trust laws, low or no state income tax, a high degree of protection from creditors and/or lack of a rule against perpetuities.

- A corporate trustee's business is audited internally and by state and federal authorities.

- A corporate trustee, unlike an individual trustee, does not die or become legally incompetent.

- Appointing a corporate trustee usually eliminates most adverse tax consequences associated with a spouse or a child serving as trustee because a corporate trustee is independent and is never a beneficiary of the trust.

- A corporate trustee is a neutral party. The corporate trustee's neutrality helps minimize or eliminate potential conflicts among beneficiaries, especially those who are family members. Should family disharmony appear, the corporate trustee can serve as a liaison between the quarreling family members. Moreover, the corporate trustee is unlikely to show favoritism to one or more beneficiaries while making decisions regarding distributions or investments.

(4)   Disadvantages of a Corporate Trustee

- A corporate trustee is sometimes viewed as an insensitive, distant entity that is too rigid and inflexible. Some have the perception that a beneficiary will have to "beg for money" if a corporate trustee is involved. Beneficiaries of smaller trusts sometimes believe that corporate trustees pay less attention to them so they can favor their larger clients.

- The fees charged by corporate trustees can be higher than compensation to be paid to an individual trustee. Furthermore, the fees charged by a corporate trustee for administering a trust may increase at a rate that is irreconcilable with the increase (if any) in value of the trust portfolio. While a corporate trustee can usually do a better job of handling administrative details, investment decisions and accounting matters than an individual trustee, an individual trustee may usually retain accountants, investment advisors, attorneys and others who can provide the trust with essentially the same services that are available from a corporate trustee.

- A corporate trustee usually charges additional fees for managing a closely-held business. A corporate trustee's management of a family business may be less effective than management of that business by a knowledgeable family member.

21st Century Estate Planning:
Practical Applications
2005 Edition

©2005 Sonnenschein Nath & Rosenthal LLP
and Cannon Financial Institute, Inc.

261

- A corporate trustee may be quite unfamiliar with a given family's dynamics.
- Clients may perceive a loss of control when designating a corporate trustee as opposed to an individual trustee.
- A corporate trustee is more likely than an individual trustee to reject the administration of a trust if there are provisions in the trust instrument that it finds unacceptable. These provisions may deal with the amount of the discretion given to the trustee to make distributions, the extent of liability to which a trustee may be subject for the actions of a predecessor trustee, for a loss of value or for otherwise mishandling trust property or restrictions on the types of actions for which the corporate trustee can charge a fee. Rather than rejecting the administration altogether, the corporate trustee may demand that the trust instrument be amended to remove the provisions that are unacceptable, which of course may be to the disadvantage to the beneficiaries.
- To serve as trustee, the corporate trustee may need to be a resident or otherwise be qualified to do business within a given state or be able to act in other states where trust assets would be located. Unless adequate provisions are made in the trust instrument for removal and replacement of trustees, there may be an element of inflexibility in the selection of the trustee. The corporate trustee may become unable to act with respect to assets in another state, or one or more beneficiaries may take up residence in another state. Furthermore, a corporate trustee in one state may have to pay state and fiduciary income taxes that would not have to be paid if the trust were administered in another state.

        d.   **Additional Aspects of Choosing a Corporate Trustee**.   If the grantor chooses a corporate trustee, there are additional considerations beyond a corporate trustee's advantages over an individual trustee. The grantor can take steps to ensure that the disadvantages of a corporate trustee listed above do not turn into pitfalls for the grantor and the beneficiaries.

        As mentioned above, the beneficiaries may view a corporate trustee as inflexible and unsympathetic to their financial needs. To avoid having these perceptions turn into a reality, a grantor should do his or her homework by investigating and interviewing several banks to learn about their policies, responsiveness, ability to serve adequately as a "parental substitute," level of professionalism, concern for beneficiaries' needs and fee structure.

        Of course, the grantor should also review the corporate trustee's investment performance and investment philosophy. Corporate trustees will typically wish to have authority to invest the assets of all but the largest trusts in their own mutual funds, of which they typically offer a variety designed to serve varying investment objectives. Thus, a corporate trustee typically

21st Century Estate Planning:
Practical Applications
2005 Edition

©2005 Sonnenschein Nath & Rosenthal LLP
and Cannon Financial Institute, Inc.

262

offers funds designed to maximize income, to generate a balance of income and growth or to produce maximum growth.

The quality of services provided by a corporate trustee varies according to the ability and interest of the personnel assigned to a particular trust. If a client wishes, a trust instrument may express the grantor's desire that a designated trust officer work on, or supervise, the account and provide that the trust should follow the trust officer if he or she later moves to a different corporate trustee. Of course, such a provision introduces a degree of instability and could result in the imposition of higher trustees' fees if the designated trust officer changes employment.

Once a corporate trustee has been selected, the trust instrument may have to be customized to take into consideration the particularities of the corporate trustee selected. Many corporate trustees have specific language they require to be used in estate planning documents before they will agree to serve as trustee. It is advisable to consult with them before their designation, especially if they are to serve immediately or are one of the first successor trustees.

The trust document, of course, can and should provide for the removal of a corporate trustee. As discussed below, because of the usually disadvantageous tax consequences, a beneficiary generally should not be empowered to remove the trustee and appoint himself or herself as successor trustee. *See, e.g.*, Rev. Rul. 95-58, 1995-2 C.B. 191. The beneficiary can sometimes determine that a trust administration problem is not with the corporate trustee as an institution but rather with the account administrator, in which case the beneficiary can request another account administrator.

Often the grantor may name one or more individuals and a corporate trustee as co-trustees. The right to exercise discretion with respect to distributions might be vested with a "special trustee" who is familiar with the family situation and who is appointed solely for this purpose. This special trustee might understand the needs of the various family members better than a corporate trustee. The details of investments, recordkeeping and other administrative matters would normally be handled by the corporate trustee. Alternatively, a family member might be designated as the trustee, with the right to delegate other responsibilities (*e.g.*, investment management and custodial activities) to professionals. In this situation as well, the individual trustee would make the determinations concerning the discretionary distributions of income and principal.

If a special trustee is used, the trust document should give each co-trustee exclusive authority over specific activities of the trust. Doing so may avoid ambiguities in trust administration and adverse tax consequences that would follow if certain powers were shared with the other trustee. See, e.g., IRC § 2041.

However, the use of multiple trustees can present problems. Unless a statute or the trust instrument provides otherwise, each trustee may be liable for any loss arising from actions taken by a majority of the trustees. Usually these problems can be anticipated by appropriate provisions in the trust instrument to the effect that a majority vote of the trustees is to control and that a trustee is not to be liable if he or she specifically dissents from the decision of the majority. Moreover, a trustee may be authorized to delegate the trustee's powers, but, in the absence of specific governing instrument language, the trustee may not be relieved of liability for actions taken by the person to whom delegation was made.

e.　**Trustee Who is Also a Beneficiary**.　An individual beneficiary can serve as trustee.　However, the grantor should consider possible conflicts of interest that may exist or arise between the person he or she considers naming as trustee and the interests of such person as a beneficiary.　For example, where the trustee is the income beneficiary, he or she may be tempted to administer the trust in such a way as to increase the income even at the risk of diminishing the principal.　Where the trustee has also a discretionary power to invade the principal if the income is insufficient for his or her support, there is a greater danger that the trustee will unduly favor him or herself.　A conflict of interest situation also arises where the surviving spouse is named to act as trustee for him or herself and the children from the grantor's prior marriage are named as the remainder beneficiaries.　Worse yet, a child and surviving spouse may be named co-trustees, with the child having the discretion to make distributions to the surviving spouse that would reduce the child's remainder interest.　In several states, by statute, a current beneficiary may not usually act as sole trustee if he or she has the discretionary power to distribute trust income or principal to him or herself. *See, e.g.,* N.Y. EPTL 10-10.1; N. Car. G.S. § 32-34; Wis. S.A. 701.19(10).

These conflicts can usually be solved by appointing an additional or substitute trustee.　If the grantor did not originally appoint the beneficiary as sole trustee, but because of the disclaimer, death or resignation of a prior trustee or co-trustee the beneficiary becomes the sole trustee, the courts will ordinarily appoint a new co-trustee or will refuse to permit the trustee to exercise discretionary powers without first obtaining the approval of the court. *See, e.g.,* W.Va. Code §§ 44-5-13.　However, many courts have decided that, in situations in which the grantor appointed the beneficiary as sole trustee in spite of the fact that he or she was also a beneficiary, the trustee may administer the trust notwithstanding the danger that the trustee may favor him or herself. *See, e.g., Lovett v. Peavy*, 316 S.E.2d 754 (Ga. 1984).

2.　**Tax Considerations**

In examining the tax considerations of selecting a trustee, the main question to consider is: what limits, if any, are imposed by the trust instrument or state law regarding to whom and for what purposes the trustee may make discretionary distributions.　This question will be addressed below with regard to a spouse's serving as a trustee, and a few supplementary remarks will be made regarding a child's serving as a trustee.

a. **Definitions**.　A basic understanding of a few terms is necessary before proceeding to the following discussion.

(1)　**Powers of Withdrawal.**　If a trust's grantor has conferred on another person an unrestricted power of withdrawal over trust property, and if such person dies

21ˢᵗ Century Estate Planning:
Practical Applications
2005 Edition

©2005 Sonnenschein Nath & Rosenthal LLP
and Cannon Financial Institute, Inc.

264

holding such power, the value of the property subject to the power of withdrawal is included in such person's gross estate for federal estate tax purposes. IRC § 2041(a)(2); Treas. Reg. § 20.2041-1(b). Even if the person exercises or releases the power, the value of the property still will be included in such person's gross estate if the person exercised or released the power in a manner that, if the release or exercise were a transfer of property owned by such person, such transfer would be included in his or her estate under IRC §§ 2035 to 2038. Also, for estate tax purposes, a lapse of a power is considered a release of such power. IRC § 2041(b)(2).

Under IRC § 2514(b), the exercise or release of a general power of appointment is a transfer for gift tax purposes. Also, for gift tax purposes, a lapse of a power is considered a release of such power except to the extent the lapse relates to the greater of $5,000 or 5% of the trust property. IRC § 2514(e). Additionally, if a trustee has a beneficial interest in trust property and has an unrestricted power to distribute trust property to another beneficiary, the exercise of such power constitutes the making of a gift. However, if such power is limited by a reasonably fixed or ascertainable standard, the exercise of such power will not be subject to gift tax. Treas. Reg. § 25.2511-1(g)(2).

> **EXAMPLE:** Decedent was the trustee of a trust established by her father, and the trust instrument allowed Decedent to make distributions, not limited by any standard, for the benefit of herself and her brother. During Decedent's life, Decedent distributed $100,000 of principal to her brother. Because Decedent had an unrestricted power to distribute the trust principal to herself and her brother and she distributed $100,000 of principal to her brother, Decedent is considered to have made a gift of $100,000 to her brother. Further, upon Decedent's death, any remaining assets in the trust will be includible in her gross estate for federal estate tax purposes.

    (2)   <u>**Ascertainable Standards**</u>. If a trust grantor gives another person an unrestricted power to distribute trust assets, such power is considered a general power of appointment if the person has the power to distribute the assets to or for the benefit of him or herself. IRC § 2041(b)(1). The value of the trust assets will be included in the estate of a person who holds such power. IRC § 2041. If, however, such a power is limited by an "ascertainable standard relating to health, education, support or maintenance," the power is not considered a general power of appointment, and property subject to such power is not included in the estate of the powerholder. IRC § 2041(b)(1)(A).

➜   <u>**Planning Point:**</u> When ascertainable standards are used and general power treatment is sought to be avoided, the use of additional, broader words and phrases like "happiness" or "pleasure" or "absolute control" should not be used as such use may convert an otherwise non-general power of appointment to a general power of appointment.

21ˢᵗ Century Estate Planning:
Practical Applications
2005 Edition

©2005 Sonnenschein Nath & Rosenthal LLP
and Cannon Financial Institute, Inc.

265

(3)   **Joint Powers**. A power to distribute trust property to oneself not limited by an ascertainable standard is not a general power of appointment if the holder of the power cannot exercise the power except in conjunction with a person having a substantial interest in the property, subject to the power, which is adverse to an exercise of the power in favor of the holder. IRC § 2041(b)(1)(C)(ii).

> **EXAMPLE**: Mother created a testamentary trust for Son and Daughter, naming Son and Daughter as co-trustees. Son and Daughter were entitled to receive income and principal distributions, without being constrained by any standard, in the sole and absolute discretion of the trustees. Son predeceases Daughter. Son's dispositive power as co-trustee is not a general power of appointment because, to exercise his power, he would have had to be joined by Daughter, who would have had a substantial economic incentive not to allow Son to invade trust property frivolously or recklessly. If Daughter were to die immediately after Son's death, however, she would have a general power of appointment, and the full value of the trust property would be includable in her taxable estate.

(4)   **5 or 5 Power**. Another exception regarding the rules of general powers of appointment is that a power of withdrawal limited to the greater of $5,000 or 5% of the value of the trust property ("5 or 5 power") is not a general power of appointment and does not cause inclusion of the entire value of the trust property in the gross estate of the powerholder. IRC § 2041(b)(2). However, a 5 or 5 power will result in inclusion in the powerholder's gross estate of the amount of property subject to the power at the time of the powerholder's death, even if the power is never exercised.

(5)   **Income Tax Considerations: Grantor Trusts**

(a)   **Definition of "Grantor."** The "grantor" is the person who creates a trust. For income tax purposes, however, the grantor may also be a substantial powerholder other than the person who created the trust. IRC § 678. When a person retains or is given substantial control of a trust, that person is considered the grantor for income tax purposes and is taxed on the trust's income, and the trust entity is disregarded for income tax purposes. IRC §§ 674(a); 675; 676; 678. If the grantor retains control of only part of a trust, the grantor is treated as the owner of only the portion of the trust controlled. Income from the other portion is taxed to the trust or its beneficiaries.

(b)   **Adverse Party; Treatment of Spouse**. Even if the grantor retains a power or right listed in subparagraph (e) below, he is not considered the owner of the trust for income tax purposes if an adverse party must consent to the grantor's exercise of control. An adverse party is a person who has a substantial beneficial interest in the trust and who would be adversely affected by the exercise or non-exercise of the grantor's power. IRC § 672(a). Trust beneficiaries generally are adverse parties. A beneficiary who has a right to only a

21ˢᵗ Century Estate Planning:
Practical Applications
2005 Edition

©2005 Sonnenschein Nath & Rosenthal LLP
and Cannon Financial Institute, Inc.

266

portion of a trust's income or principal is only an adverse party as to that portion. A remainder beneficiary is generally not an adverse party with respect to a power over income. Income beneficiaries are generally adverse to distributions of principal only during the term of their interests. A grantor is also treated as owner of the trust if one of the powers listed in subparagraph (e) below is given to a non-adverse party. A grantor is considered to have retained any power or interest given to his spouse for transfers in trust after March 1, 1986. IRC § 672(e).

(c) **Independent Trustee**. IRC § 674(a) sets forth a general rule that the grantor shall be treated as the owner of any portion of a trust where the beneficial enjoyment of income or principal is controlled by the grantor or a non-adverse party, or both, without the consent or approval of an adverse party. IRC § 674(c) provides that, if half or more of the trustees are "independent" (and neither the grantor nor his or her spouse is a trustee) within the meaning of IRC § 674, the general rule of IRC § 674(a) does not apply and the grantor will not be taxed on the trust's income. Who is "independent?" IRC § 674(c) defines this term in the negative:

(6) **EXCEPTION FOR CERTAIN POWERS OF INDEPENDENT TRUSTEES.** Subsection (a) shall not apply to a power solely exercisable (without the approval or consent of any other person) by a trustee or trustees, none of whom is the grantor, and no more than half of whom are related or subordinate parties who are subservient to the wishes of the grantor . . . .

→ **Planning Point:** If the grantor of an irrevocable trust desires not to limit income and principal distributions by "a reasonably definite...standard which is set forth in the trust instrument" (see IRC § 674(b)(5) and IRC § 674(d)), and assuming grantor trust treatment is not desired, a grantor should choose at least half "independent" trustees within the above definition.

Treas. Reg. §§ 1.674(c)-1 confirms that an independent trustee may hold the power to sprinkle income or principal to any beneficiary without causing grantor trust status.

(7) **Related or Subordinate Party**. A trustee is deemed "related or subordinate" if the trustee is not an adverse party (as defined above) and is the grantor's spouse (if living with the grantor), parent, issue, brother or sister, an employee of the grantor, a corporation or any employee of a corporation in which the stockholdings of the grantor and the trust are significant with respect to voting control, or in which the grantor is an executive. IRC § 672(c).

EXAMPLE: Mother establishes a trust for the benefit of Son and Daughter and appoints her Brother as trustee. No distributions may be made that would discharge Mother's obligation of support. (see IRC § 677(b)). No one has the power to add beneficiaries to the trust (see IRC § 674(b) and (c)). Brother has no beneficial interest in the trust, and has the power to sprinkle income and

21st Century Estate Planning:
Practical Applications
2005 Edition

©2005 Sonnenschein Nath & Rosenthal LLP
and Cannon Financial Institute, Inc.

267

principal between the beneficiaries. If Brother can exercise this discretionary distribution power without the consent of either beneficiary, Mother will be taxed on all trust income. The sprinkling power is held by a related or subordinate party, and no consent of an adverse party is required. If Brother has the discretionary distribution power but distributions to Son or Daughter must be approved by the other child, Mother will not be taxed on the trust income. The other child is an adverse party because any distributions to Son reduce the amount available to Daughter and vice versa.

What if Mother appoints Bank instead of Brother as the third trustee? In that case, the trust falls within the exception in IRC § 674(c) for powers held by independent trustees, so the trust will not be a grantor trust.

(a) **Grantor Trust Rules**. The grantor trust rules generally apply when the grantor:

- Derives benefits from the income (IRC § 677),
- Retains the power to revoke the trust or withdraw trust property (IRC §§ 676 and 678),
- Retains power to control beneficial enjoyment (IRC § 674),
- Retains power to exercise certain administrative powers over the trust's operation (IRC § 675) or
- Retains a reversionary interest in either principal or income (IRC § 673).

1. **Benefits From Income.** A grantor is treated as owner of a portion of a trust of which income can be distributed to the grantor or the grantor's spouse, held or accumulated for future distribution to the grantor or the grantor's spouse or used to pay premiums on policies insuring the life of the grantor or the grantor's spouse. If trust income is applied to discharge the grantor's or the grantor's spouse's legal obligation of support, income will be taxed to the grantor to that extent. IRC § 677.

2. **Power To Revoke.** A power of revocation gives the grantor the power to end all or part of a trust and take back the trust property. The grantor is treated as owner of the trust to the extent of that power. IRC § 676.

3. **Control of Beneficial Enjoyment.** A grantor is treated as the owner of a portion of a trust over which the grantor and/or a non-adverse person has the power to control who receives income or principal from a trust without an adverse party's consent. IRC § 674. IRC § 674(b) enumerates eight exceptions for powers that can be held by anyone and <u>not</u> result in grantor trust status. The regulations discuss these eight powers in detail.

21st Century Estate Planning:
Practical Applications
2005 Edition

©2005 Sonnenschein Nath & Rosenthal LLP
and Cannon Financial Institute, Inc.

268

Treas. Reg. § 1.674(b)-1(b). An example of such a power is a power to distribute principal to trust beneficiaries limited by a reasonably definite standard set forth in the trust instrument that is held by the grantor or another person. IRC § 674(b)(5). A reasonably definite standard is one that is clearly measurable and allows the holder to be held legally accountable. Treas. Reg. § 1.674(b)-1(b)(5).

> **EXAMPLE:** A power to distribute principal for the education, support, maintenance or health of the beneficiary; for his reasonable support and comfort; or to enable him to maintain his accustomed standard of living; or to meet an emergency, would be limited by a reasonably definite standard. However, a power to distribute principal for the pleasure, desire or happiness of a beneficiary is not limited by a reasonably definite standard. Treas. Reg. § 1.674(b)-1(b)(5).

4.   **Power Over Income.** An additional exception to the general rule of IRC § 674 is IRC § 674(d). IRC § 674(d) provides that a power to distribute, apportion, or accumulate income limited by a reasonably definite standard can be given to any trustee other than the grantor or, if living with the grantor, the grantor's spouse. The power must be exercisable without consent of any other person. Treas. Reg. § 1.674(d)-1.

5.   **Power to Remove and Replace Trustee.** If the grantor holds an unrestricted power to remove, substitute or add trustees and to designate any person including the grantor as successor trustee, the trustee's powers are deemed to be exercisable by the grantor for purposes of determining grantor trust status and the trust will not qualify as a non-grantor trust under IRC §§ 674(c) and 674(d). Treas. Reg. § 1.674(d)-2.

6.   **Administrative Powers.** Generally, if the grantor or a non-adverse party has the power to deal with trust property for less than adequate consideration, to substitute assets for other assets of equivalent value (acting in a non-fiduciary capacity), to borrow funds without adequate interest or security, or to control certain other trust administrative functions in a non-fiduciary capacity, the grantor is considered the owner of the trust for income tax purposes. IRC § 675.

7.   **Reversionary Interest.** For transfers in trust after March 1, 1986, a grantor generally is treated as the owner of that portion of a trust in which he has a reversionary interest, if the value of the reversionary interest at the time of the transfer exceeds 5% of the total property, based on IRS valuation tables. IRC § 673.

(b)   **Person Other Than Grantor Treated As Owner.** A person other than the person who created and funded a trust may be considered the owner of all or part of the trust if he/she: (i) has an exclusive power to vest principal or income in himself/herself or (ii) previously released such a power and retained one of the rights that would cause the trust to be taxed to a grantor. IRC § 678(a). This rule does not apply to a power over income if the grantor is treated as the owner under IRC §§ 673-677. IRC § 678(b); Treas. Reg. § 1.678(b)-1.

21st Century Estate Planning:
Practical Applications
2005 Edition

©2005 Sonnenschein Nath & Rosenthal LLP
and Cannon Financial Institute, Inc.

269

As an owner of the trust property for income tax purposes, the individual must include the trust income, deductions and credits on his or her personal income tax return instead of the trust's income tax return. IRC § 678 commonly applies in the case of beneficiaries who hold Crummey withdrawal rights. But see also, IRC § 677. See Chapter VII, Section D, regarding the income tax consequences of Crummey powerholders.

→ **Planning Point:** IRC § 678 does not contain an explicit exception for a trustee whose powers are limited by an ascertainable standard. The same is true for beneficiaries who hold withdrawal rights. However, many practitioners believe such a trustee or beneficiary should not be taxed on trust income under IRC § 678. See *U.S. v. De Bonchamps* 278 F.2d 127 (9th Cir. 1960); cf. Treas. Reg. 1.678(c)-1(b), (c) (regarding the applicability of IRC § 678 to support trusts). But in PLR 8211057, the IRS applied IRC § 678 to a trustee who held withdrawal rights despite the existence of an ascertainable standard. A solution to this possible income tax problem is to designate a co-trustee to serve with the trustee who is also a beneficiary.

Note that IRC § 678 is the only provision of the Internal Revenue Code under which grantor trust status can apply, by the explicit terms of the statute, after the "real" grantor of the trust has died. Thus, any trust coming into existence under a post-death revocable trust or under a will cannot be a grantor trust for income tax purposes unless under IRC § 678.

b.   **Considerations When a Spouse is Trustee**

(1)   **Power of Appointment**. When a spouse is serving as trustee of a family trust (also known as a credit shelter trust or a non-marital trust), the trust instrument must be drafted carefully to avoid inclusion of the value of the trust assets in the spouse's estate. Otherwise, the purpose of establishing the family trust is defeated. If the spouse is serving as the sole trustee, any power to make discretionary principal distributions should be limited by ascertainable standards (health, education, maintenance and support), and the trustee should be expressly prohibited from using trust funds to satisfy his or her legal obligations, including any support obligations. In the absence of these restrictions, the spouse, as sole trustee would be considered as possessing a general power of appointment, thereby causing the trust assets to be includible in the spouse's estate. IRC § 2041. To avoid inclusion of the family trust in the spouse's estate if such restrictions are not used, there should be a co-trustee with the spouse (or a sole trustee who is not the spouse) who is vested with the sole discretion to make distributions.

Trust assets remaining in a general power of appointment marital trust at the spouse's death are includible in the spouse's gross estate, and, therefore, giving the spouse unrestricted dispositive rights as trustee does not create any adverse tax consequences. However, with a QTIP marital trust, if the spouse is given any powers that result in the spouse holding a general power of appointment, a partial QTIP election, as a practical matter, would not be available.

21ˢᵗ Century Estate Planning:
Practical Applications
2005 Edition

©*2005 Sonnenschein Nath & Rosenthal LLP*
and Cannon Financial Institute, Inc.

270

Therefore, it is important that the governing instrument of a QTIP trust be drafted to avoid the spouse having, or being deemed to have, a general power of appointment.

If a spouse trustee has a beneficial interest in trust property and has an unrestricted power to distribute trust property to another beneficiary, the exercise of such power is a gift. However, such will not be the result if such power is limited by a reasonably fixed or ascertainable standard that is set forth in the trust instrument. Treas. Reg. § 25.2511-1(g)(2).

(2) **Income Tax Consequences**. With regard to income tax consequences when a grantor's spouse is trustee or a co-trustee of an *inter vivos* irrevocable trust, it will be necessary to analyze the trust's administrative and dispositive provisions to determine grantor trust status. Most importantly, under IRC § 672(e), a grantor is generally treated as holding any power held by his or her spouse. Thus, if the spouse holds any power over a portion of a trust under IRC § 674(a) (which is not within the IRC § 674(b) exceptions), IRC § 675, IRC § 676 or IRC § 677, the trust will be a grantor trust with respect to such portion. To avoid the problem (assuming avoidance of grantor trust status is desired), the spouse's discretion over disposition of income should be limited (see IRC § 674(b)(6) and (b)(7)), and the spouse's power over disposition of principal should be restricted by a reasonably definite standard that is set forth in the trust instrument. (see IRC § 674(b)(5)). If grantor trust status is desired, that status should be triggered by including in the trust instrument one or more administrative powers set forth in IRC § 675, or a power to add beneficiaries other than after-born or adopted children, that would apply to any trustee and should not be dependent on the identity of the trustee because who is the trustee can change at any time.

(3) **Irrevocable Life Insurance Trusts**. The governing instrument of a typical irrevocable life insurance trust contains provisions that allow sprinkling of principal and income to family members during the life of the insured. After the insured's death, the trust may pay out immediately to the family members, or be retained in further trust, possibly even as a dynasty trust. Obviously, the insured should not be the trustee. If the insured has control over the insurance policy through the trust, he or she will have "incidents of ownership," which will cause the policy proceeds to be included in the insured's taxable estate under IRC § 2042. Inclusion of ascertainable standards is of no avail in avoiding inclusion under IRC § 2042. If the trust holds a second-to-die policy, neither insured should be a trustee.

What if the spouse of the insured acts as trustee and the trust holds a single-life policy on the life on the grantor? If the spouse can distribute property to herself, not subject to an ascertainable standard, he or she would be deemed to have a general power of appointment. This would cause all trust income to be taxed to the spouse under IRC § 678 and the trust property to be included in the spouse's taxable estate under IRC § 2041.

What if the distributions were subject to an ascertainable standard? Even assuming the spouse did not contribute any property to the trust, the trust would be a grantor trust as to the grantor since the exception of IRC § 674(d) would not be met because the trustee was the spouse of the grantor. For this purpose, a spouse's deemed gift to an irrevocable insurance

21st Century Estate Planning:
Practical Applications
2005 Edition

©2005 Sonnenschein Nath & Rosenthal LLP
and Cannon Financial Institute, Inc.

271

trust because of a gift-splitting election does not make her a donor for purposes of IRC §§ 673-677, 2036 or 2038. PLR 200130030.

Of course, income tax consequences regarding an irrevocable insurance trust are not ordinarily a serious concern because most if not all income in such a trust typically occurs inside one or more life insurance policies, and such income ordinarily does not lead to income taxes.

(4)   **Discharge of Support Obligations**. As alluded to above, an insidious problem arises if a beneficiary of the trust is a dependent of the trustee spouse. If the spouse has the ability to discharge the spouse's support obligations to the dependent with trust assets, the spouse is considered to have a general power of appointment over the trust assets, as the spouse can use the trust assets to benefit him or herself by discharging his or her support obligations. Treas. Reg. § 20.2041-1(c)(1). This is true even if the spouse's powers are limited by ascertainable standards. If a spouse trustee actually distributes trust income to discharge a support obligation, the distributions may result in trust income being taxable to the spouse to the extent of such distributions. IRC § 678.

(5)   **Removal of Trustee**. If the spouse is granted the right to remove a trustee and appoint another trustee who is "related or subordinate," the spouse is considered as having a general power of appointment if the appointed trustee would have the unrestricted right to distribute trust assets. If the removal and replacement power is limited to appointing someone who is not related or subordinate, such as a corporate trustee, then the spouse is not considered as having a general power of appointment. Rev. Rul. 95-58, 1995-2 C.B. 191. Also, if the spouse is required to have the consent of an adverse party in order to remove and replace a trustee, the issues regarding the power of appointment are eliminated.

c.   **Considerations When a Child is Trustee**. The tax rules that apply when a child of the property owner serves as trustee or a co-trustee are very similar to those applying when a spouse is serving as trustee or co-trustee. Indeed, in the estate and gift tax context, the rules are virtually identical. There is, however, an important exception worth noting in the context of what will trigger grantor trust treatment for income tax purposes when a child of the property owner serves as trustee or a co-trustee: the spousal unity rule of IRC § 672(e) has no application.

21ˢᵗ Century Estate Planning:
Practical Applications
2005 Edition

©2005 Sonnenschein Nath & Rosenthal LLP
and Cannon Financial Institute, Inc.

272

Chapter IX
Bibliography

Alan S. Acker, 820 T.M., *Administrative Powers*.

Alan S. Acker, 852 T.M., *Income Taxation of Trusts and Estates*.

Roy M. Adams, "The New Tax Laws and Increased Risk of Liability (Or the Omnipresent Rule - Don't Do Something If You Don't Know What You're Doing)," *Tr. & Est.* (October 2001).

Roy M. Adams, "The Sacred A/B Plan Under Assault By The 2001 Tax Act; The Need for Adaptation and Change, But Not Abandon," *Tr. & Est.* (November 2001).

Roy M. Adams, "Selection of Trustees in the Context of Rights of Withdrawal," *The Eleventh Annual Federal Estate Planning Symposium*, UMKC/CLE (May 15, 1992).

Christopher P. Cline, 825 T.M., *Powers of Appointment – Estate, Gift and Income Tax Considerations*.

Ralph M. Engel, "Reducing Risk in Successor Trusteeships," *ABA Trust & Investments*, Nov./Dec. 2002, at 29.

C. John Guenzel and David Ludtke, "Selecting a Fiduciary: Corporate or Individual," Nebraska Continuing Legal Education, Estate Planning and Probate.

Stuart Kessler, 844 T.M., *Estate Tax Credits and Computations*.

Henry J. Lischer, Jr., 845 T.M., *Gifts*.

Thomas G. Opferman, "The Marital Deduction In Depth: Formula Provisions (Pecuniary, Fractional, Hybrid); Hubert's Impact on Administration Expenses; Impact of Family Business Deduction; Impact of Generation-Skipping Transfer Tax; Funding Problems and Forms," Illinois Institute for Continuing Legal Education (April 18 and May 4, 2000).

Laura H. Peebles, *Tax Aspects of Choice of Trustee*, 31 *Estate Planning* 43 (Jan. 2004).

Jeffrey N. Pennell, 843 T.M., *Estate Tax Marital Deduction*.

Jeffrey N. Pennell, "Funding Marital Deduction (and other) Bequests," 35th *Annual Philip E. Heckerling Inst. on Est. Plan.* (2001).

John R. Price, *Price on Contemporary Estate Planning* (2nd ed. 2001).

Richard B. Stephens, Guy B. Maxfield, Stephen A. Lind and Dennis A. Calfee, *Federal Estate and Gift Taxation* (7th ed. 2001).

21st Century Estate Planning:
Practical Applications
2005 Edition

©2005 Sonnenschein Nath & Rosenthal LLP
and Cannon Financial Institute, Inc.

273

Kimbrough Street, "Practical Guidelines for Selecting an Individual Trustee," 20 *Estate Planning* 268 (Oct. 1993).

William P. Streng, 800 T.M., *Estate Planning*.

Howard M. Zaritsky, 858-2nd T.M., *Grantor Trusts: Sections 671-679*.

---

[1] The term "grantor" is used throughout this Section to refer to the creator of a trust. Such term may also include a testator in the context of a testamentary trust.

[2] Within the context of a testamentary trust, the term "trust instrument" refers to a will.

21ˢᵗ Century Estate Planning:
Practical Applications
2005 Edition

©2005 Sonnenschein Nath & Rosenthal LLP
and Cannon Financial Institute, Inc.

274

X. EDUCATION AND MEDICAL EXPENSES

A. Introduction

This chapter discusses various vehicles that may be utilized for payment of education and medical expenses and their tax benefits. Some payments of medical and education expenses are excluded for gift and generation-skipping transfer ("GST") tax purposes, while other medical and education expenses may be paid from various accounts that are allowed to grow tax-free. This chapter also discusses the relevant tax law changes that were made by the Economic Growth and Tax Relief Reconciliation Act of 2001 (the "Act").

Specifically, this chapter discusses the following topics related to the payment of education and medical expenses and relevant changes made by the Act:

- Unlimited Exclusion for Tuition Expenses and Medical Expenses Under Internal Revenue Code ("IRC") § 2503(e)
- Qualified Tuition Programs ("QTPs")
- Coverdell Education Savings Accounts ("Coverdell ESAs")
- Comparison of IRC § 2503(e) Exclusions, QTPs, and Coverdell ESAs

B. Brief Overview of GST Tax

A large part of this chapter discusses the transfer tax consequences (especially the GST tax consequences) of IRC § 2503(e) exclusions, QTPs and Coverdell ESAs. A brief summary of the GST tax follows. For a more detailed discussion, see Chapter 4 ("Federal Generation-Skipping Transfer Tax").

Generally, the GST tax is imposed on any transfer of property in excess of the GST exemption from a transferor to individuals who are more than one generation level younger than the donor, if the donor and the donee are related (e.g., transfers to grandchildren, great-grandchildren, grand-nieces and grand-nephews, and so forth), and if they are not related, if the donee is 37½ years or more younger than the donor. Such donees are called "skip persons." The GST tax applies whether the transfer to the skip person is an outright gift or bequest (a "direct skip"), a distribution to a skip person of income or principal from a trust (a "taxable distribution"), or a distribution to a skip person on the termination of a trust (a "taxable termination"). The GST tax is imposed on non-exempt transfers at a rate equal to the maximum estate tax rate, and is assessed in addition to any federal gift tax or estate tax that may be imposed on the transfer.

An outright gift to a skip person that qualifies for the federal gift tax annual exclusion will also be exempt from GST tax. A gift in trust for a skip person, however, will not be exempt from GST tax unless the skip person is the sole beneficiary of the trust and the trust will be included in the skip person's gross estate for federal estate tax purposes.

21st Century Estate Planning:
Practical Applications
2005 Edition

©2005 Sonnenschein Nath & Rosenthal LLP
and Cannon Financial Institute, Inc.

275

C. Unlimited Exclusion for Tuition Expenses and Medical Expenses Under IRC § 2503(e)

1. General

IRC § 2503(e)(1) excludes from gift tax certain "qualified transfers." "Qualified transfers" include amounts paid by a donor to a qualifying educational organization on behalf of an individual for tuition expenses or to a medical care provider for medical care expenses. IRC § 2503(e)(2). The amount of the exclusion for such tuition and medical expenses is unlimited, and the exclusion is *in addition to* the gift tax annual exclusion. Treas. Reg. § 25.2503-6(a). Gifts that qualify for the exclusion for tuition or medical expenses are considered nontaxable gifts and are not subject to GST tax. IRC §§ 2611(b)(1) and 2642(c)(3)(B).

Payments of tuition expenses must be made *directly* to the education institution to qualify for the exclusion. Similarly, payments of medical expenses must be made *directly* to the medical care provider to qualify for the exclusion. IRC § 2503(e)(2). As the donee need not be a relative in order to qualify for the exclusion for tuition and medical expenses, the number of potential donees is unlimited.

2. Definitions

a. Qualified Transfer. A "qualified transfer" is defined as payment on behalf of an individual for: (i) tuition expenses incurred at a qualifying educational organization described in IRC § 170(b)(1)(A), (ii) for the education or training of such individual, or (ii) medical care, as defined in IRC § 213(d), paid to the provider of medical services.

b. Qualifying Educational Organization. A "qualifying educational organization" is one that normally maintains a regular faculty and curriculum and normally has a regularly enrolled body of pupils or students in attendance at the place where the education activities are regularly carried on. Treas. Reg. § 25.2503-6(b)(2). The term includes primary, secondary, preparatory or high schools, and universities or colleges. Treas. Reg. § 1.170A-9(b). The tuition expenses may be paid on behalf of a part-time or full-time student. The payments must be made, however, directly to such qualifying educational organization. Only tuition expenses qualify for the exclusion for education expenses. Expenses for books, supplies, dormitory fees, board, or other similar expenses do *not* qualify for the exclusion. Treas. Reg. § 25.2503-6(b)(2).

➔ **Planning Point:** Qualifying educational organizations also may include day-care centers and pre-schools if they meet the above requirements. See Rev. Rul. 78-446; PLR 7942038 (July 19, 1979) (both focusing on the day-care or pre-school's primary function of the presentation of formal instruction).

21st Century Estate Planning:
Practical Applications
2005 Edition

©2005 Sonnenschein Nath & Rosenthal LLP
and Cannon Financial Institute, Inc.

276

The IRS has held that prepayment of tuition may qualify as a qualified transfer if certain requirements are satisfied. See PLR 199941013 (October 15, 1999). In the PLR, the IRS listed the following facts as determinative of the prepayments qualification:

- The prepayment must be made directly to the qualifying educational organization.
- The prepayment was made on behalf of a designated beneficiary for specified tuition costs.
- The prepayment was nonrefundable and subject to forfeiture if the designated beneficiary did not attend the school.

Payments to a qualified tuition program under IRC § 529, however, do not satisfy the requirements of IRC § 2503(e), and, to the extent such payments exceed the gift tax annual exclusion amount, such payments are taxable gifts.

      c. Qualifying Medical Expenses. "Qualifying medical expenses" include expenses incurred for the diagnosis, cure, mitigation, treatment or prevention of disease, or for the purpose of affecting any structure or function of the body or for transportation primarily for and essential to medical care. In addition, amounts paid for medical insurance, transportation for and essential to medical care, and qualified long-term care services qualify. The exclusion does not apply, however, with respect to any amounts reimbursed by medical insurance. Treas. Reg. § 25.2503-6(b)(3). A nonexclusive list of services that qualify as medical care is provided in Treas. Reg.§ 1.213-1(e)(1)(ii). The expenses must be incurred for more than a mere benefit to the general health of an individual. For example, a vacation that promotes healthy living is not an expenditure for medical care. See Treas. Reg. § 1.213-1(e)(ii). It also is possible for part or all of a capital expenditure to qualify as a medical expense if the expenditure has as its principal purpose medical care.

> **EXAMPLE:** A physician advised that Beneficiary needed a detachable air conditioner installed for medical reasons related to Beneficiary's lung condition. The full cost of the air conditioner, including related installation costs, would qualify as a medical expense. If a donor paid the air conditioner company directly, such payment would qualify under IRC § 2503(e) as an excludible medical expense.

3. GST Tax Advantages

Under IRC § 2611(b), transfers that are nontaxable gifts pursuant to IRC § 2503(e) are not subject to GST tax.

➔   **Planning Point:** The IRC § 2503(e) exclusion is especially valuable for grandparents because their payments of a grandchild's tuition and medical expenses: (1) are unlimited in amount, (2) are free of gift tax, (3) are free

21ˢᵗ Century Estate Planning:
Practical Applications
2005 Edition

©2005 Sonnenschein Nath & Rosenthal LLP
and Cannon Financial Institute, Inc.

277

of GST tax, and (4) remove significant amounts from their estates. In addition, the grandparents control the use of the gifts by making payments directly to the educational institution or medical provider.

4. Use of Trusts

Generally, a transfer of funds from a donor to a trust which provides for the distribution of income and/or principal to cover tuition costs incurred by the trust beneficiaries is not a direct transfer to a qualifying educational organization, and therefore does not qualify as a qualifying transfer under IRC § 2503(e), or for the exclusion from GST taxation under IRC § 2611(b).

> **EXAMPLE:** Donor transferred $50,000 to a trust which allows the trustee to make distributions of income and principal for tuition expenses incurred by Donor's grandchild. The transfers from the trust to the qualifying educational organization meet the requirements of IRC § 2503(e). The transfer to the trust by the Donor, however, does not qualify for IRC § 2503(e) treatment, and if the Donor's grandchild is the only beneficiary, the transfer is considered a direct skip for GST purposes and is subject to GST tax. See Treas. Reg. § 25.2503-6(c), Ex. 2.
>
> Contributions to such a trust which do not exceed the annual exclusion amount under IRC § 2503(b) and which are subject to "*Crummey*" withdrawal rights held by the skip person-beneficiary will be exempt from gift tax under IRC § 2503(b). See Chapter 7 ("Annual Exclusion Gift Planning") for a discussion of *Crummey* withdrawal rights. Additionally, such contributions will not be subject to GST tax because the trust will have a zero inclusion ratio under IRC § 2642(c) if the grandchild is the only beneficiary and any amounts remaining in the trust at the grandchild's death are includible in the grandchild's gross estate.

It is possible to structure a trust for more than one beneficiary so that it is exempt for gift and GST tax purposes. A donor can make a transfer to a trust that provides that the trustee may distribute funds only to cover tuition expense payments to qualified educational organizations or for medical care payments to a medical services provider as specified in IRC § 2503(e). The distribution from such a trust to a qualified educational organization or to a medical services provider will meet the requirements of IRC § 2503(e). In order for the initial transfer from the donor to the trust to qualify as nontaxable for gift tax purposes, however, the beneficiaries must have *Crummey* withdrawal rights that qualify the transfer for the IRC § 2503(b) gift tax annual exclusion.

For GST tax purposes, if a transfer is made to a trust where skip persons, such as grandchildren, are the only beneficiaries, such transfer is a direct skip subject to immediate GST

21st Century Estate Planning:
Practical Applications
2005 Edition

©2005 Sonnenschein Nath & Rosenthal LLP
and Cannon Financial Institute, Inc.

278

taxation. In order for the transfer to be nontaxable for GST tax purposes, the trust, as initially created, must include beneficiaries who are <u>not</u> skip persons. To accomplish this, a child of the donor could be a beneficiary of the trust, thereby giving a non-skip person an interest in such trust. Therefore, the transfer from the donor to the trust would not be a direct skip, and would not be subject to GST tax. Upon the death of the child, however, if the only beneficiaries are skip persons, the death of the child would be considered a taxable termination subject to GST tax.

If a charity is named as a beneficiary of the trust and the charity receives more than a nominal interest in such trust, the trust will not qualify as a skip person as the charity is assigned to the same generation level as the donor. The interest provided for the charity must be intended to truly benefit the charity to overcome the nominal limitation of IRC § 2652(c)(2). <u>See</u> Treas. Reg. § 26.2612-1(e)(2)(ii).

In addition to the above considerations, it is possible for such a trust to run afoul of the separate share rules. If a charity's interest can be separated from the non-charitable interest in the trust, the charitable and non-charitable interests are considered separate shares. The non-charitable share may be considered a skip person, thereby defeating the GST tax exempt nature of such trust. To avoid the separate share rules, the charity must be provided an interest that cannot be separated from the non-charitable interest, such as the right to receive all the income for several years and then a certain percentage of the income in future years.

EXAMPLE:

Facts: Donor creates a trust, the beneficiaries of which are Donor's grandchildren and Charity. The grandchildren are given *Crummey* withdrawal rights over contributions received by the trust. The charity is given an interest in the annual income from such trust which cannot be separated from the non-charitable interest as stated above. Distributions from the trust are permitted for the benefit of the grandchildren only to the extent such distributions qualify as tuition or medical expenses under IRC § 2503(e). If the assets of the trust are not fully utilized by the grandchildren and their descendants, such remaining assets will be distributed to Charity.

Results:

Transfers by Donor to Trust: Provided the transfers do not exceed the annual exclusion amount each year for any beneficiary, such transfers are excluded for gift tax purposes under IRC § 2503(b) as a result of the *Crummey* withdrawal powers of each beneficiary. Because a non-skip person (Charity) has an interest in the trust, the initial transfer is not a direct skip and is not subject to GST tax. Therefore, the initial transfers to the trust are not subject to gift tax or GST tax.

21st Century Estate Planning:
Practical Applications
2005 Edition

©2005 Sonnenschein Nath & Rosenthal LLP
and Cannon Financial Institute, Inc.

279

Transfers from the Trust: Under the trust, only transfers to the non-charitable beneficiaries that qualify under IRC § 2503(e) are permitted. Therefore, the distributions from the trust for tuition or medical expenses are not subject to GST tax under IRC § 2611(b)(1).

5. Advantages and Disadvantages of Exclusion for Tuition Expenses and Medical Expenses

There are several advantages of the exclusion under IRC § 2503(e). First, the donor can retain ultimate control and actual use of the assets until actual payments are made for such expenses. Also, a donor can withhold payment of expenses until expenses are actually incurred. Because payments for education and medical expenses are not considered taxable gifts, those payments do not utilize the donor's gift tax annual exclusion or gift tax exemption, and can be structured to be nontaxable gifts for GST tax purposes. A disadvantage of IRC § 2503(e) is that non-tuition expenses (such as room and board expenses) are not qualified education expenses excluded from gift tax.

D. Qualified Tuition Programs

1. Introduction

In 1996, Congress enacted IRC § 529, which exempts a "qualified tuition program" ("QTP") from federal income taxation, except for the tax on unrelated business income, and provides rules for the taxation of donors and beneficiaries. Amendments passed in 1997, 1998 and 2001 expanded the tax benefits available. IRC § 529 applies to QTPs established by a state or an agency or instrumentality of a state or by one or more "eligible educational institutions" as either a prepaid tuition program or an education savings account ("529 ESA") program. IRC § 529(b)(1). Today, every state has one or both types of these programs. Nearly every state's plan has been privatized and most states provide an incentive for taxpayers to participate in the state's own 529 plan, such as state income tax deductions.

Under a prepaid tuition program, an individual purchases tuition credits or certificates on behalf of a beneficiary to prepay tuition and fees while locking in current tuition rates. These plans are designed to hedge the increasing cost of higher education. The prepaid tuition programs may be established and maintained by state programs or by eligible private institutions that satisfy the requirements of IRC § 529.

Under a 529 ESA, an individual contributes to a state's savings account, established to pay for the designated beneficiary's "qualified higher education expenses" at an "eligible educational institution." These terms are defined below. These programs usually are managed by professional investment companies and have various investment options. The primary investment option is a managed allocation, age-based approach, whereby assets are shifted from equities to more conservative fixed-income investments as the child approaches college age. Neither the account owner nor the designated beneficiary may directly or indirectly participate in

21ˢᵗ Century Estate Planning:
Practical Applications
2005 Edition

©2005 Sonnenschein Nath & Rosenthal LLP
and Cannon Financial Institute, Inc.

280

investment decisions regarding a QTP, IRC § 529(b)(4), but the IRS does allow the account owners to change their investment options without changing beneficiaries once per calendar year. Notice 2001-55, 2001-2 C.B. 299 (Sept. 24, 2001). In addition, some states have added single-fund options to their portfolio choices, which allow account owners to exert more control over the investment of the 529 plan assets.

The following is a summary of the federal law regarding the requirements of both types of QTPs, and their federal tax treatment. Each state has its own program with its own rules and regulations, and the practitioner is encouraged to study each state's plan that he or she may be considering for the benefit of a client.

2. Definitions

a. **Qualified Higher Education Expenses**. "Qualified higher education expenses" include costs of tuition, fees, books, supplies, equipment required for enrollment or attendance at an eligible educational institution (including a graduate school at such institution), and expenses for "special needs services" of a "special needs beneficiary" incurred "in connection with such enrollment or attendance." IRC § 529(e)(3)(A)(ii). For students enrolled for at least one-half of a full-time load, qualified higher education expenses also include costs of "room and board while attending such institution" up to the greater of (1) the allowance for room and board in the institution's budget for federal financial aid or (2) "the actual invoice amount the student residing in housing owned or operated by the eligible educational institution is charged by such institution for room and board costs for such period." IRC § 529(e)(3).

b. **Eligible Educational Institution**. An "eligible educational institution" is an accredited, post-secondary education institution offering credit toward a bachelor's degree, an associate's degree, a graduate level or professional degree or other recognized post-secondary credential. IRC § 529(e)(5). According to the IRS, "virtually all accredited public, nonprofit, and proprietary postsecondary institutions" are eligible educational institutions. Notice 97-60, 1997-2 C.B. 310.

➔ **Planning Point:** Costs of attending high school, junior high school, elementary school and pre-school are *not* covered by QTPs.

c. **Account Owner**. The "account owner" is the individual entitled to select or change the designated beneficiary and to designate any person (including the account owner) other than the designated beneficiary to whom funds may be paid from the account. Prop. Reg. § 1.529-1(c). In contrast to a Uniform Gifts to Minors Act or a Uniform Transfers to Minors Act ("UTMA") account, the account owner always has complete control and ownership over the 529 plan. The designated beneficiary never has direct access to the account. Beneficiary changes can occur at any time and as often as desired. However, as discussed below, the change may be subject to taxes and penalties. Also, the account owner cannot use an account or an interest under the QTP as security for a loan.

21st Century Estate Planning:
Practical Applications
2005 Edition

©2005 Sonnenschein Nath & Rosenthal LLP
and Cannon Financial Institute, Inc.

281

The account owner may also retain the right to terminate the account and refund the account funds to him or herself. For example, if a designated beneficiary decides not to go to college, the account owner can defer use of the account, change beneficiaries or withdraw the assets (subject to income tax and a 10% penalty).

→ **Planning Point:** Some states permit persons other than the account owner to make contributions or permit a change in the identity of the account owner. Accordingly, the account owner is not always a donor; any entity, including a trust, can be an account owner. Any asset may be used to establish the trust, including real estate, appreciated stock or bonds. Depending on the nature of the asset contributed, a valuation discount for such asset may be obtained. Such a trust could have a purpose of making distributions of cash to the QTP for the benefit of the designated beneficiary, although it should have other purposes. Gift tax (and possibly GST tax) may apply to the initial transfer to such a trust, and the transfer to the Section 529 ESA.

After the account owner's death, the account will then be controlled by the account owner's designee, as stated in the plan form or in the account owner's will. To prevent the beneficiary from inheriting the account with full control, the owner could name a trust as the successor owner with restrictions on the trust as to how the funds in the 529 plan are to be expended.

d. **Designated Beneficiary**. A "designated beneficiary" is defined as: (i) the individual designated as the beneficiary when the account is established, (ii) the new beneficiary when a beneficiary change is made, or (iii) the individual who receives the benefits accumulated in the account as a scholarship in the case of a 529 ESA established by a state or local government or an IRC § 501(c)(3) charitable organization as part of a scholarship program operated by such government or organization. IRC § 529(e)(1). The designated beneficiary (if not the account owner) need not be related to the account owner. The program must keep a separate account for each designated beneficiary.

3. Contribution Rules

Only cash contributions are permitted. There are no age, time or income limitations applicable to investing in or owning a QTP. Contributions to a QTP are not deductible for federal income tax purposes, but most states allow a state income tax deduction for a limited amount of contributions. Contribution limits generally are between $100,000 and $235,000 and vary from state to state.

A QTP must provide adequate safeguards to prevent contributions in excess of those necessary to provide for the qualified higher education expenses of the designated beneficiary. The regulations provide a safe harbor for this requirement that states that the QTP must bar any additional contributions to an account once the account reaches a specified account balance limit.

21st Century Estate Planning:
Practical Applications
2005 Edition

©2005 Sonnenschein Nath & Rosenthal LLP
and Cannon Financial Institute, Inc.

282

To come within the safe harbor, total contributions may not exceed the amount determined by actuarial estimates that is necessary to pay tuition, required fees and room and board expenses of the designated beneficiary for five years of undergraduate enrollment at the highest cost institution allowed by the program. Prop. Reg. § 1.529-2(i).

→ **Planning Point:** Most states allow a transfer of existing Coverdell Education Savings Accounts ("Coverdell ESAs") and UTMA accounts to a 529 ESA. Because the beneficiary is considered the owner of those accounts, however, certain restrictions will apply to such a 529 ESA. For example, the 529 ESA can be used only for the benefit of the original designated beneficiary, and no distribution can be made to the initial donor of the Coverdell ESA or UTMA.

There is no limit on account growth; earnings on a QTP are not taxable to the account owner or the designated beneficiary for federal income tax purposes at least as long as they remain in the plan.

4. Distribution Rules

Distributions from a QTP or prepaid tuition program made for qualified higher education expenses are excluded from the designated beneficiary's gross income for federal income tax purposes. IRC § 529(c)(3). For purposes of the exclusion, qualified higher educational expenses are reduced by (1) scholarships excluded from gross income under IRC § 117, various federal educational assistance allowances and any excludable payment (other than a gift or inheritance) covering the educational expenses and (2) any portion of the expenses "taken into account in determining" the Hope Scholarship or Lifetime Learning Credit. Scholarship funds may be withdrawn income tax and penalty free.

→ **Planning Point:** If a Coverdell ESA is also utilized, the remaining expenses must be allocated among the QTP and the Coverdell ESA. IRC § 529(c)(3)(B)(iv).

The earnings portion (as determined under IRC § 72) of any distribution that is not used for qualified higher education expenses is subject to a 10% penalty, along with ordinary income tax treatment. The penalty and income tax is paid either by the account owner or the designated beneficiary, depending on who initiated the withdrawal. IRC § 529(c)(3)(A)&(c)(6). A state may also tax and penalize such distributions. The penalty is waived if the distribution is made after the designated beneficiary's death or becoming disabled or is made on account of the designated beneficiary's qualified expenses being covered by a scholarship, federal education assistance allowance or other payment excluded from gross income. Prop. Reg. § 1.529-2(e)(4)(ii)(B). To facilitate the inclusion of income, the program must file an annual information return with the IRS and make an annual report to the distributee. IRC § 529(d); Prop. Reg. § 1.529-4. No other amount is included in the gross income of the donor or designated beneficiary. IRC § 529(c)(1).

21ˢᵗ Century Estate Planning:
Practical Applications
2005 Edition

©2005 Sonnenschein Nath & Rosenthal LLP
and Cannon Financial Institute, Inc.

283

Each plan must have procedures for verifying the use of distributions. The proposed regulations provide a safe harbor for such procedures, which includes having payments made directly to an eligible educational institution or requiring the designated beneficiary to provide substantiation that payments are in reimbursement for qualified higher education expenses. Prop. Reg. § 1.529-2(e)(4)(ii).

> **EXAMPLE:** X contributes $10,000 to a 529 plan. In six years, that amount has grown to $15,000. Two withdrawals are made: $7,500 for qualified higher education expenses and $7,500 for a vacation. The $7,500 withdrawn for college expenses is tax-free. Regarding the vacation withdrawal, $2,500 is treated as a withdrawal of earnings (the proportionate amount of the total earnings). This amount is taxed as ordinary income. In addition, there is a 10% penalty attached to this amount. No other amount is taxed.

5. Federal Gift and GST Tax Treatment

A contribution to a QTP is treated as a completed gift and may be subject to gift tax. IRC § 529(c)(2). However, the donor can elect to contribute up to five times the gift tax annual exclusion limit in one calendar year without making a taxable gift ($55,000 in 2005 or $110,000 in 2005 if gift-splitting between spouses is elected). IRC § 529(c)(2)(B); Prop. Reg. § 1.529-5(b)(2). Upon the election, if the total contributions by a donor in a particular calendar year are in excess of the $11,000 gift tax annual exclusion amount, the total contributions for that year can be taken into account ratably over five years beginning with the calendar year of contribution. The election to do so must be made on the donor's United States Gift and Generation-Skipping Transfer Tax Return (Form 709). Unless state law provides otherwise, no distribution from a QTP is treated as a taxable gift.

➔ **Planning Point:** If the donor makes a contribution of five times the annual exclusion amount in Year 1, and makes the above election, the donor cannot make additional annual exclusion gifts to the same donee in Years 2, 3, 4 and 5, except to the extent the annual exclusion is adjusted for inflation in those years.

➔ **Planning Point:** Contributions to a QTP do not qualify as qualified transfers for education expenses under IRC § 2503(e).

6. Rollovers and Changes of Beneficiary

The account owner can make a tax-free rollover of the 529 plan if, within 60 days, the plan is rolled over to another QTP to the credit of the same beneficiary or is transferred to a QTP for another beneficiary who is a member of the family of the previous beneficiary and is in the same generation as (or in a higher generation than) the previous beneficiary. IRC §

21ˢᵗ Century Estate Planning:
Practical Applications
2005 Edition

©2005 Sonnenschein Nath & Rosenthal LLP
and Cannon Financial Institute, Inc.

284

529(c)(3)(C)(i)&(c)(5)(B) (as amended by P.L. 108-311, 118 Stat. 1166, Oct. 4, 2004). Only one rollover is allowed during a 12-month period. A rollover can be an effective way to handle a situation in which the original designated beneficiary cannot use the funds for education or when the account owner wants to exert more control over investments.

Under IRC § 529(e)(2), "member of the family" is defined as a person who has the following relationship to the previously designated beneficiary: (1) a child or other descendant; (2) a stepchild; (3) a sibling, half-sibling or step-sibling; (4) a parent or other ancestor; (5) a step-parent; (6) a nephew or niece; (7) an uncle or aunt; (8) a son-in-law, daughter-in-law, father-in-law, mother-in-law, brother-in-law or sister-in-law; (9) a spouse of any individual listed above or the spouse of the designated beneficiary; or (10) a first cousin.

The account owner can make a tax-free designation of a new beneficiary if the new beneficiary is a member of the family of the previous beneficiary and is assigned to the same generation as (or a higher generation than) the previous beneficiary. IRC § 529(c)(3)(C)(ii)&(c)(5)(B) (as amended by P.L. 108-311, 118 Stat. 1166, Oct. 4, 2004); Prop. Reg. § 1.529-5(b)(3).

If a rollover is made to a new beneficiary or a designation of a new beneficiary is made, and the new beneficiary is assigned to a lower generation level than the previous beneficiary, a taxable gift is made from the previous beneficiary to the new beneficiary even if the new beneficiary is a member of the family of the previous beneficiary. Such a gift is still eligible for the gift tax annual exclusion and the 5-year averaging rule. If the new beneficiary is more than one generation lower than the previous beneficiary, such a gift is subject to GST tax as well as gift tax. IRC § 529(c)(5)(B) (as amended by P.L. 108-311, 118 Stat. 1166, Oct. 4, 2004); Prop. Reg. § 1.529-5(b)(3)(ii). If the new beneficiary is not a member of the previous beneficiary's family, income and gift tax, in addition to a 10% penalty, will be due on the accumulated earnings portion of the transfer.

> **EXAMPLE:** In year one, P makes a contribution to each of two 529 ESAs for the benefit of P's children, A and B. P directs distributions from A's account to be made for A's qualified higher education expenses. Because B never attends an eligible educational institution, no distributions are made from B's account. P then rolls over the assets in B's account to an account for the benefit of A's child, D (B's nephew). Pursuant to the regulations, B is treated as making a taxable gift to D for the entire amount of the account, even though B had no control over the gift B is deemed to have made. Such a gift is eligible for the gift tax annual exclusion and the 5-year averaging rule.

7. **Federal Estate Tax Treatment**

Even if the account owner retains the right to change the designated beneficiary or the right to terminate and receive a refund of the account, the account assets are excluded from the

21st Century Estate Planning:
Practical Applications
2005 Edition

©2005 Sonnenschein Nath & Rosenthal LLP
and Cannon Financial Institute, Inc.

285

account owner's gross estate for federal estate tax purposes. IRC § 529(c)(4)(A); Prop. Reg. § 1.529-5(d)(1). If a donor elects to spread contributions over 5 years as discussed above, the portion of the excess contributions allocable to calendar years beginning after the donor's date of death will be included in the donor's gross estate for federal estate tax purposes. IRC § 529(c)(4)(C); Prop. Reg. § 1.529-5(d)(2).

> **EXAMPLE:** W gives $55,000 to a 529 plan. No gift tax results from this transfer. If W dies in the second year after the gift, $22,000 is excluded from his gross estate but $33,000 is included in his estate.

➔ **Planning Point:** Even though a portion of the contribution may be includible in the account owner's gross estate, only the unamortized gifts are included, and any appreciation in value of or earnings generated by the gifted funds are not includible.

The value of the account is, however, included in the gross estate of the designated beneficiary for federal estate tax purposes if amounts are distributable on the death of the designated beneficiary. IRC § 529(c)(4)(B); Prop. Reg. § 1-529-5(d)(3).

8.   Effect on Financial Aid

For federal financial aid purposes, a pre-paid tuition program is considered a "resource" of the student that reduces a student's financial need on a dollar-for-dollar basis. Therefore, a student's eligibility for subsidized loans, work-study or certain grants may be reduced. A 529 ESA generally is treated as an asset of the account owner (usually the parents) for financial aid purposes. Therefore, if the student is not the donor, the account does not count as an asset of the student. When calculating the parental contribution under the Free Application for Federal Student Aid, however, a certain percentage of the 529 ESA is included in such calculation (5.64% maximum for 2005). Additionally, when distributions are made in a given year, any taxable income from such distribution is included in the student's income for the following year's financial aid determination.

➔ **Planning Point:** Because of the Act, the inclusion of taxable distributions in a student's income should not be an issue in 2005-2010 with distributions for qualified higher education expenses. If Congress, however, does not amend the current law with regard to the sunset provision, it may be an issue again in 2011.

9.   Act Sunset

The tax exemption for qualified withdrawals expires on December 31, 2010, unless future legislation is passed by Congress and signed by the President. After this date, the previous IRC § 529 rules will return: earnings will be taxed to the beneficiary at his or her rate when withdrawn regardless of the purpose for withdrawal. Thus, now may be a good time to fund a

21ˢᵗ Century Estate Planning:
Practical Applications
2005 Edition

©2005 Sonnenschein Nath & Rosenthal LLP
and Cannon Financial Institute, Inc.

286

IRC § 529 account because any future legislation may "grandfather" accounts in place before such legislation takes effect.

10. Advantages and Disadvantages

a. **Advantages**. The advantages of QTPs include the following:

- Funds contributed grow tax-free.
- Anyone may participate in a QTP.
- A donor may contribute any amount to a QTP.
- Contributions to a QTP are gifts of a present interest which can qualify for the federal gift tax annual exclusion.
- Up to five years' annual exclusion gifts may be made to a QTP in a single funding.
- Even though the account owner can retain some control over the assets (even after the beneficiary reaches the age of majority), the value of the account assets are usually excluded from the account owner's gross estate for federal estate tax purposes.
- The account owner also may retain the right to terminate the account or to change the beneficiary.
- Earnings on a 529 QTP will not be taxed to the account owner or the designated beneficiary for income tax purposes as long as the withdrawals from the account are used for qualified higher education expenses, and the contributions grow tax-free.
- Some states offer state income tax deductions for contributions to a QTP.

b. **Disadvantages**. The disadvantages of QTPs include the following:

- Only after-tax cash contributions may be made to a QTP.
- The account owners and the designated beneficiaries lack complete control over investment decisions.
- Although the donor may select from a range of investment options similar to a 401(k) account, the donor does not have the same ability to change the investment options as the donor has with respect to the donor's own funds or a custodial account for a minor beneficiary.
- An interest in a QTP may not be pledged as security. Prop. Reg. § 1-529-2(h).
- The law surrounding QTPs has changed significantly over the last few years, and some of the rules and regulations are still being developed.
- As a result of the Act's sunset provision, a future change to Section 529 programs may be imminent.

21ˢᵗ Century Estate Planning:
Practical Applications
2005 Edition

©2005 Sonnenschein Nath & Rosenthal LLP
and Cannon Financial Institute, Inc.

287

c.   **Pre-Paid Tuition Programs vs. 529 ESAs**.   Under pre-paid tuition programs, individuals purchase tuition credits or certificates on behalf of a beneficiary to prepay tuition and fees while locking in current tuition rates.   A contribution to this type of plan purchases a specific amount of future tuition (*e.g.,* 12 credit hours).   The programs were established to be used at a public university.   Accordingly, if a student decides to attend a private or out-of-state college, most programs penalize the distributions for such purposes.   As discussed above, the funds held in the account are considered a resource to the student when determining the student's need for financial aid.

By using a 529 ESA, the amount of funds available to the beneficiary for education purposes is dependent on how the account was invested and how such investments performed.   It is possible that the funds will not be sufficient to cover the education costs of the beneficiary.   As stated above, the 529 ESA is treated as an account of the donor (typically the parents) for financial aid purposes.

E.   Coverdell Education Savings Accounts

1.   General

Another device for contributing to another individual's education is a Coverdell Education Savings Account ("Coverdell ESAs"), formerly called an Education IRA.   A Coverdell ESA is created to pay "qualified education expenses" of the designated beneficiary.

a.   **Qualified Education Expenses**.   "Qualified education expenses" include "qualified higher education expenses" and "qualified elementary and secondary education expenses."

b.   **Qualified Higher Education Expenses**.   "Qualified higher education expenses" include tuition, fees, books, supplies and equipment required for the enrollment or attendance of a beneficiary at a post-secondary educational institution.   They also include contributions to a QTP on behalf of the beneficiary.   Qualified higher education expenses include costs of room and board.

c.   **Qualified Elementary and Secondary Education Expenses**.   "Qualified elementary and secondary education expenses" include tuition, fees, academic tutoring, books, supplies, computer equipment and other equipment in connection with the enrollment of the beneficiary at a public, private or religious school.   They also include costs of room and board, uniforms, transportation, and the purchase of computer technology or equipment or Internet access if they are to be used while the beneficiary is in school.

➔   **Planning Point:** Expenses for special needs services for a special needs beneficiary are included in the definitions of qualified higher education expenses and qualified elementary and secondary education expenses if

21ˢᵗ Century Estate Planning:
Practical Applications
2005 Edition

©2005 Sonnenschein Nath & Rosenthal LLP
and Cannon Financial Institute, Inc.

288

such expenses are incurred in connection with enrollment and attendance at an eligible institution. IRC § 530(b)(2) and (4).

2.   Contribution Rules

The amount a donor can contribute to a Coverdell ESA is limited. Through 2010, a donor may make nondeductible cash contributions to a Coverdell ESA of up to $2,000 per year per beneficiary. The $2,000 limit applies in the aggregate to all Coverdell ESAs for the same beneficiary whether the contributions were made by one or more donors. IRC § 530(b)(1)(A).

> **EXAMPLE:** Grandparent created a Coverdell ESA for Grandchild and contributed $1,500. Parent also created a Coverdell ESA for Grandchild (Parent's child) in the amount of $1,000. The Coverdell ESA allowance for Grandchild is over-funded, and an excess contribution of $500 is created.

The donor's adjusted gross income may reduce the allowable contribution amount. Through 2010, the amount a single taxpayer can contribute to a Coverdell ESA is reduced beginning at $95,000 of adjusted gross income and completely phased out at $110,000, whereas the amount that a married couple filing jointly can contribute is reduced beginning at $190,000 and completely phased out at $220,000 of adjusted gross income. Under the Act, entities, such as an employer, are permitted to make contributions to a Coverdell ESA. Entities are not subject to the adjusted gross income limitations. IRC § 530(c)(1).

Contributions to a Coverdell ESA must be made in cash and cannot be made after the beneficiary reaches age 18. IRC § 530(b)(1)(A). The account may remain open, however, until the child turns 30, at which time any balance remaining in the account must be distributed. IRC § 530(b)(1)(E). Contributions for a special needs beneficiary may be made after such beneficiary reaches age 18, and mandatory distribution at age 30 is not required. IRC § 530(b)(1).

Contributions are permitted until the return due date for the tax year of the contribution, not including extensions. A tax is assessed on excess contributions. Under the Act, the time for making a corrective withdrawal of an excess contribution is extended to May 30 following the tax year of contribution. If the excess contribution is withdrawn by such date and the net income attributable to such distribution also is distributed, such distribution will not be subject to the 10% penalty. IRC § 530(d)(4)(C).

> **EXAMPLE:** In 2005, Donor contributed $2,500 to a Coverdell ESA for Beneficiary. Contributions are limited to $2,000 in 2005. Therefore, Donor made an excess contribution of $500. The earnings on the $500 excess distribution in 2005 amounted to $50. If Donor withdraws the $500 plus the $50 in earnings on or before May 30, 2006, the 10% penalty will not be assessed on such distribution. The

21ˢᵗ Century Estate Planning:
Practical Applications
2005 Edition

©2005 Sonnenschein Nath & Rosenthal LLP
and Cannon Financial Institute, Inc.

289

$50 earnings distribution will be includible in Donor's gross income for 2005.

3.   Distribution Rules

In contrast to the 529 ESA, the Coverdell ESA must be administered solely for the benefit of the designated beneficiary, and all distributions must be made to or for the benefit of the beneficiary. No distributions may be made to the account owner. Distributions are tax-free if such distributions are made for qualified higher education expenses. IRC § 530(d)(2)(A). If a distribution is in excess of qualified higher education expenses incurred for the designated beneficiary, the earnings portion of such excess distribution is subject to income tax as ordinary income and a penalty of 10%. IRC § 530(d)(2)(B).

→ **Planning Point:** If qualified higher education expenses are being paid with distributions from both a 529 ESA and a Coverdell ESA, such expenses must be allocated between both accounts. A double distribution is not permitted. IRC § 530(d)(2)(D).

→ **Planning Point:** If a client also is utilizing the Hope or Lifetime Learning Credit, such use will impact the amount of tax-free withdrawals from a Coverdell ESA. IRC § 530(d)(2)(C).

A change of a designated beneficiary to a member of the family of the previous beneficiary (as earlier defined) is not subject to income tax or a penalty if the new beneficiary is under the age of 30. IRC § 530(d)(6). Additionally, a distribution as a result of the death or permanent disability of a designated beneficiary or the receipt of a scholarship by the designated beneficiary is not subject to the 10% penalty, but the earnings portion of such distribution will be included in gross income. IRC § 530(d)(4)(B). The income tax consequence can be avoided if a new designated beneficiary is provided who is a family member of the previously designated beneficiary. IRC § 530(d)(7). An account may be rolled over into another Coverdell ESA once during each 12-month period without incurring any income tax or penalties. IRC § 530(d)(5).

→ **Planning Point:** The assets of a Coverdell ESA can be transferred to a QTP if such program is for the benefit of the same designated beneficiary and the account is established within the same taxable year.

4.   Federal Income Tax Treatment

Contributions to a Coverdell ESA are not income tax deductible. Earnings on contributions to a Coverdell ESA, however, are not taxed when earned. IRC § 530(a). If distributions equal the amount of qualified education expenses, then the distributions are not included in the beneficiary's gross income. IRC § 530(d)(2)(A). If the amount of distributions exceeds the qualified education expenses during the taxable year, then the earnings portion of the distribution will be included in the beneficiary's gross income. IRC § 530(d)(2)(B).

21ˢᵗ Century Estate Planning:
Practical Applications
2005 Edition

©2005 Sonnenschein Nath & Rosenthal LLP
and Cannon Financial Institute, Inc.

290

Additionally, with limited exceptions, there is a 10% penalty imposed to the extent that a distribution from a Coverdell ESA is includible in gross income. IRC § 530(d)(4)(A). When a beneficiary reaches age 30 and the account is distributed, the earnings portion of the distribution will be included in the beneficiary's gross income and subject to an additional 10% penalty because the distribution is not for education purposes.

A distribution from a Coverdell ESA that is rolled over into another Coverdell ESA for the benefit of the same beneficiary or a member of the beneficiary's family who has not reached age 30 is excluded from income. IRC § 530(d)(5). Additionally, a change in the beneficiary is not treated as a distribution and not subject to income tax if the new beneficiary is a member of the family of the old beneficiary and has not reached age 30. IRC § 530(d)(6).

5.   Federal Gift Tax and GST Tax Treatment

The IRS has not issued Regulations regarding the gift tax and GST tax consequences of a Coverdell ESA. The rules, however, should be similar to those for QTPs. A contribution to a Coverdell ESA is a completed gift and qualifies for the gift tax annual exclusion and exemption from GST tax. Generally, no distribution from a Coverdell ESA is treated as a taxable gift.

A rollover to an account for a new beneficiary or a designation of a new beneficiary will not be subject to gift tax or GST tax if the new beneficiary is in the same generation as the previous beneficiary. If the new beneficiary is not more than one generation level lower than the designated beneficiary, the rollover is subject to gift tax but not GST tax. However, if the new beneficiary is two or more generation levels lower than the designated beneficiary, the rollover is subject to both gift tax and GST tax.

6.   Federal Estate Tax Treatment

Generally, the value of the Coverdell ESA is not included in the gross estate of the donor. Amounts distributed on account of the death of the designated beneficiary are included in the beneficiary's gross estate.

7.   Effect on Financial Aid

A Coverdell ESA is considered an asset of the beneficiary for financial aid purposes. Any distributions which are included in taxable income will be included in the calculation of financial aid in the year following the distribution, thereby reducing the amount of financial aid received.

21ˢᵗ Century Estate Planning:
Practical Applications
2005 Edition

©2005 Sonnenschein Nath & Rosenthal LLP
and Cannon Financial Institute, Inc.

291

8. Advantages and Disadvantages

The advantages of Coverdell ESAs include the following:

- Funds contributed to a Coverdell ESA grow tax-free.
- Distributions from a Coverdell ESA are income tax-free if used entirely for education expenses.
- Distributions from a Coverdell ESA may be used for elementary and secondary education expenses along with higher education expenses.
- A donor has greater control over the investments of a Coverdell ESA than a QTP.

The disadvantages of Coverdell ESAs include the following:

- Contributions that are not used for qualified higher education expenses must be distributed to the beneficiary as opposed to the option of distributing such funds to the account owner under a QTP.
- Any assets remaining in the account when the beneficiary attains the age of 30 must be fully withdrawn or such assets will be subject to income tax and penalties.
- Coverdell ESAs could count against the beneficiary when applying for financial aid.
- Contributions currently are limited to $2,000 a year per child.
- There is an adjusted gross income limit for participants.

F. Comparison of Section 2503(e) Exclusions, Section 529 QTPs, and Coverdell ESAs

The following chart summarizes various characteristics of the above plans. The chart is intended as a generalization, and the practitioner is encouraged to review the appropriate sections of the Internal Revenue Code and not to rely solely on the following chart:

21st Century Estate Planning:
Practical Applications
2005 Edition

©2005 Sonnenschein Nath & Rosenthal LLP
and Cannon Financial Institute, Inc.

292

	Section 2503(e) Exclusions	Section 529 QTPs	Coverdell ESAs
Ownership/Control of Account	Donor.	Donor.	Donor controls on behalf of the beneficiary.
Guidelines for Use	Must be for tuition paid to a qualifying educational institution or payment to a provider for medical care under § 213(d).	Must use for qualified higher education expenses at participating accredited post-secondary schools anywhere in the U.S.	Must use for qualified elementary, secondary or higher education expenses by the time beneficiary turns 30.
Annual Contribution Limit	Unlimited exclusion and in addition to gift tax annual exclusion.	Unlimited contributions (except for specific program limitations) but amount over the annual exclusion subject to gift tax. Contribution greater than annual exclusion may be ratably taken over 5 years.	$2,000 per designated beneficiary under 18.
Adjusted Gross Income Limit	None.	None.	Single: $95-110K Joint: $190-220K
Taxation of Earnings	Not applicable.	Tax-free growth. Qualified distributions are federal income tax-free. State tax varies.	Tax-free growth. Qualified distributions are federal income tax-free. State tax varies.
Taxation/Penalty Upon Early Withdrawal	Not applicable.	Earnings portion of nonqualified withdrawals taxed as ordinary income and subject to federal 10% penalty.	Earnings portion of nonqualified withdrawals taxed as ordinary income and subject to federal 10% penalty.
Gift and GST Consequences	Not subject to gift tax or GST tax.	Subject to gift tax and GST tax; however, the use of the gift tax annual exclusion is permitted.	Subject to gift tax and GST tax; however, the use of the gift tax annual exclusion is permitted.
Estate Tax Consequences	Not included in estate of donor or beneficiary.	Included in beneficiary's estate, but not included in donor's estate.	Included in beneficiary's estate, but not included in donor's estate.
Change of Beneficiary	Not applicable.	Can transfer account penalty-free to benefit member of beneficiary's family.	Can transfer account penalty-free to benefit member of beneficiary's family.
Financial Aid	Not counted as a resource for student or parent.	Pre-paid tuition program - student resource. 529 ESA - included in calculating parental contribution, not a student resource.	Counted as a student resource.

21st Century Estate Planning:
Practical Applications
2005 Edition

©2005 Sonnenschein Nath & Rosenthal LLP
and Cannon Financial Institute, Inc.

293

Chapter X
Bibliography

Roy M. Adams, "Estate Planning 2000: Never A Greater Need to Adapt to Change," Bank of America (June 15, 2000).

Roy M. Adams, "A New Twist On Sec. 2503(e): Health and Education Exclusion Trust (HEET)," *Tr. & Est.* (July 2000).

Susan T. Bart, Timothy G. Carroll, Robert E. Hamilton, Louis S. Harrison and Donna E. Morgan, "Irrevocable Non-Charitable Lifetime Gift Trusts," Illinois Institute for Continuing Legal Education (January 2002).

Boris I. Bittker & Lawrence Lokken, "Qualified Tuition Programs," *Federal Taxation of Income, Estates and Gifts* ¶ 16.8A (2003).

L. Henry Gissel, Jr., "Planning Techniques for Large Estates," SG041 ALI-ABA 361 (November 2001).

Law, Explanation and Analysis: Economic Growth and Tax Relief Reconciliation Act of 2001, CCH Incorporated (2001).

Henry J. Lischer, Jr., 845 T.M., *Gifts.*

Henry J. Lischer, Jr., 846 T.M., *Gifts to Minors.*

James Edward Maule and Lisa Starczewski, 503-2nd T.M., *Deductions: Overview and Conceptual Aspects.*

David M. Pfefferkorn, "The Investment of Custodial Funds in Section 529 Qualified Tuition Programs: Tax Advantages and Fiduciary Concerns," 30 Est. Plan. 571 (Nov. 2003).

John R. Price, *Price on Contemporary Estate Planning* (2nd ed. 2001).

Michael Schlesinger, "Qualified State Tuition Programs: More Favorable After 2001 Tax Act," 28 *Est. Plan* 412 (September 2001).

Online Research

Savingforcollege.com, Joseph F. Harley, http:/www.savingforcollege.com

21st Century Estate Planning:
Practical Applications
2005 Edition

©2005 Sonnenschein Nath & Rosenthal LLP
and Cannon Financial Institute, Inc.

294

XI.   LIFE INSURANCE

Life insurance has long played a critical role in fulfilling many estate planning needs. Life insurance is used as an income replacement mechanism for surviving spouses, to provide liquidity to estates, to facilitate purchases under buy-sell agreements, to help "carry" small businesses through the transition phase after the loss of a "key person," and as a vehicle to transfer wealth to future generations. Through careful planning, all of these estate planning needs can be satisfied without causing the insurance proceeds to be included in the gross estate of the insured. Nevertheless, to avoid estate tax inclusion, practitioners must navigate through the unique tax rules that apply to life insurance policies. The planning process is further complicated by the fact that as many as four different parties may be involved in any insurance contract: the owner, the insured, the beneficiary and the individual or entity paying the premium. As a result of this complexity, there are many "traps" and "pitfalls" that practitioners must avoid to successfully match the life insurance death benefit proceeds with the estate planning "need" without triggering unnecessary transfer taxes.

This chapter provides an overview of planning with life insurance, including a discussion of the following topics:

- Estate Tax Inclusion Rules;
- Gifts of Life Insurance;
- Viatical and Senior Settlements;
- Split Dollar Life Insurance; and
- Use of Insurance in Buy-Sell Agreements

A. Estate Tax Inclusion Rules

In general, life insurance proceeds will be included in an insured's estate if (i) the life insurance proceeds are payable to the insured's estate, (ii) the insured possesses any incidents of ownership in the policy at the time of death, or (iii) the insured transferred his or her interest in an insurance policy within three years of his or her death.

1.   Insurance Proceeds Payable to the Insured's Estate

Life insurance proceeds from insurance policies on the decedent's life will be included in a decedent's estate under Internal Revenue Code ("IRC") § 2042(1) if the insurance proceeds are receivable by the executor of the decedent's estate. Moreover, Regulation § 2042-1(b)(1) provides "if under the terms of an insurance policy the proceeds are receivable by another beneficiary but are subject to an obligation, legally binding upon the other beneficiary, to pay taxes, debts, or other charges enforceable against the estate, then the amount of such proceeds required for the payment in full ... of such taxes, debts, or other charges is includible in the gross estate." Thus, insurance proceeds will be included in the decedent's estate under IRC § 2042(1) whenever insurance proceeds are payable to the decedent's estate or for the benefit of the decedent's estate.

21ˢᵗ Century Estate Planning:
Practical Applications
2005 Edition

©2005 Sonnenschein Nath & Rosenthal LLP
and Cannon Financial Institute, Inc.

295

→ **Planning Point:** If the decedent has created an Irrevocable Life Insurance Trust ("ILIT") and has named the ILIT as owner and beneficiary of the policy, the ILIT should never require the trust to pay obligations of the decedent's estate, because such a provision will cause inclusion in the decedent's estate under IRC § 2042. In a recent private letter ruling (See PLR 200147039 (August 21, 2001)), the Internal Revenue Service ("IRS") ruled that a provision in a trust giving the trustee *discretion* to use trust assets to pay taxes and expenses due on the death of the insured would not cause inclusion in the decedent's estate, because there was no legally binding obligation to do so. One should note, however, that the IRS did not rule on what the result would be had the trustee in fact exercised his discretion to pay such taxes or expenses. The regulations under IRC § 2042 do not preclude the IRS from taxing insurance proceeds under other Code sections that might apply. The ILIT, rather than distributing property to the estate to enable it to pay taxes and expenses, could use the insurance proceeds to purchase assets from the decedent's estate (at fair market value) as a means of providing liquidity to the decedent's estate without risking estate tax inclusion. Typically, the step-up in basis rules for assets included in the decedent's estate will prevent the estate from incurring a capital gain upon the sale of assets to the ILIT. Alternatively, the ILIT can be drafted so that the trustee is permitted to lend money to the estate for a commercially reasonable amount of interest.

→ **Planning Point:** Should you discover that an ILIT impermissibly requires the trustee to use the insurance proceeds to pay obligations of the decedent's estate, one means of rectifying the problem is to have the "defective" ILIT sell the policy to a new ILIT that does not contain the offending provision. As long as both trusts are grantor trusts with respect to the insured, there should not be a taxable event for income tax purposes. The new trust would acquire an income tax basis in the life insurance policy equal to the basis that the "defective" ILIT had in the policy. In addition, the carryover basis from the "defective" ILIT to the new ILIT should exempt the sale from the transfer-for-value rule under IRC § 101(a)(2).

2. Incidents of Ownership

Life insurance proceeds will also be includible in the decedent's estate under IRC § 2042(2) if the decedent possessed any "incidents of ownership" in the policy, either alone or in conjunction with any other person, at the time of the decedent's death. Regulation § 2042-1(c) provides that "the term 'incidents of ownership' is not limited in its meaning to ownership of the policy in the technical sense…. Thus, it includes the power to change the beneficiary, to surrender or cancel the policy, to assign the policy, to revoke an assignment, to pledge the policy for a loan, or to obtain from the insurer a loan against the surrender value of the policy, etc."

21ˢᵗ Century Estate Planning:
Practical Applications
2005 Edition

©2005 Sonnenschein Nath & Rosenthal LLP
and Cannon Financial Institute, Inc.

296

→ **Planning Point:** The Regulation quoted above clarifies that even if the insured does not own the policy and the insurance proceeds are paid to someone other than the insured's estate, the insurance proceeds will be includible in the decedent's estate if the decedent held any "incidents of ownership" at the time of his or her death. Practitioners should plan carefully to avoid the application of IRC § 2042 because any incident of ownership held directly by the insured will cause inclusion of the *entire* proceeds in the decedent's estate, even if the right can only affect a *portion* of the policy (See Regulation § 20.2042-1(a)(3)).

> **EXAMPLE:** Insured pledges a policy on his life to a bank to secure a loan. The insured is personally liable on the loan. Subsequently, the insured transfers ownership of the policy, subject to the loan, to an ILIT and the ILIT is named the beneficiary of the policy. The insured dies while the loan is outstanding. The insured has retained an incident of ownership, because he continued to benefit from the use of the policy as security for his loan. Accordingly, the *entire* proceeds of the life insurance would be includible in the insured's estate under IRC § 2042.

There is a split in authority regarding whether the retention by an insured of a right to elect a settlement option that affects the timing of payments to the beneficiary, but not the total amount that the beneficiary will receive, is an incident of ownership. See *Lumpkin v. Comm'r*, 474 F.2d 1092 (5th Cir. 1973), where the court held that a right affecting the timing of the payment was an incident of ownership. See also *Connelly v. U.S.*, 551 F.2d 545 (3d Cir. 1977), where the court held that an identical right did not constitute an incident of ownership. The IRS has indicated that it will follow *Lumpkin*, except in the Third Circuit in cases involving identical facts to *Connelly*. In addition, the following rights have been deemed to be "incidents of ownership:" (i) an option to repurchase a policy from an assignee (See TAM 9128008); and (ii) a right to veto any change in beneficiary designation, assignment or cancellation of the policy (See *Schwager v. Comm'r*, 64 T.C. 781 (1975)). Rights that have been deemed *not* to be "incidents of ownership" include the following: (i) the right to substitute a policy of equivalent value (See *Jordahl v. Comm'r*, 65 T.C. 92 (1975)); (ii) the payment of premiums and the receipt of policy dividends (because a dividend represents a refund of premium payments) (See *Jordahl, Bowers Est. v. Comm'r*, 23 T.C. 911 (1955), and *Old Point Nat'l Bank v. Comm'r*, 39 B.T.A. 343 (1939)); and (iii) the right to convert a group term life insurance policy to an individual policy if the insured ceases to be employed (See Rev. Rul. 84-130).

3. Incidents of Ownership in Corporate Owned Insurance

Regulation § 20.2042-1(c)(6) provides that if a corporation owns life insurance on the life of the insured and "the decedent is the sole or controlling stockholder, the corporation's incidents of ownership will not be attributed to the decedent through his stock ownership to the extent the proceeds of the policy are payable to the corporation." Conversely stated, where the decedent is

21ˢᵗ Century Estate Planning:
Practical Applications
2005 Edition

©*2005 Sonnenschein Nath & Rosenthal LLP*
and Cannon Financial Institute, Inc.

297

the controlling shareholder of a corporation and the corporation owns insurance on the decedent's life, the corporation's incidents of ownership in the policy at the time of the decedent's death will be attributed to the decedent to the extent the proceeds are payable to anyone other than the corporation.

> **EXAMPLE:** Decedent is a controlling stockholder in a corporation. The corporation owns an insurance policy on the decedent's life. The life insurance proceeds are payable 40% to the decedent's spouse and 60% to the corporation. Only 40% of the proceeds are includible in the decedent's estate under IRC § 2042. Note that this rule is an exception to the general rule that any *direct* incident of ownership held by the insured (*i.e.*, that is not attributed to him through the corporation), will cause inclusion of the *entire* proceeds in the insured's gross estate, even if it only affects a portion of the policy.

Thus, even if the insured is a controlling shareholder, if the entire proceeds are payable to the corporation or to a third party for a valid business purpose (*e.g.*, in satisfaction of a valid business debt), none of the proceeds will be included in the insured's gross estate. This is due to the fact that the insurance proceeds will be reflected in the value of the decedent's stock (*i.e.*, because the insurance proceeds will increase the value of the company).

The insured is deemed a "controlling" stockholder if, at the time of his or her death, the decedent owned stock possessing more than 50% of the total combined *voting power* of the corporation (See Regulation § 20.2042-1(c)(6)). Note that owning more than 50% of the value of the stock will not cause the insured to be a "controlling" shareholder, if the decedent does not own 50% of the voting power. Stock is considered owned by the decedent if legal title, at the time of the decedent's death, is owned by: (i) the decedent (or his agent or nominee); (ii) the decedent and another person jointly (but only to the extent of the pro rata number of shares that corresponds to the proportion of the total consideration considered to have been furnished by the decedent under IRC § 2040); or (iii) by a trustee of a voting trust (to the extent of the decedent's beneficial interest therein) or any other trust with respect to which the decedent was treated as an owner under IRC §§ 671-679 (*i.e.*, the grantor trust rules).

> **EXAMPLE:** Decedent owns 60% of the combined value of both the outstanding voting and non-voting stock, but only 20% of the voting power in a corporation. The corporation owns an insurance policy on the decedent's life. The life insurance proceeds are payable 40% to the decedent's spouse and 60% to the corporation. None of the proceeds are includible in the decedent's estate under IRC § 2042 because the decedent is not a "controlling" shareholder under Regulation § 20.2042-1(c)(6).

In a recent private letter ruling (200214028 (April 5, 2002)), the IRS addressed this issue in a partnership context. In that ruling, the decedent was a one-third partner in a general

21ˢᵗ Century Estate Planning:
Practical Applications
2005 Edition

©*2005 Sonnenschein Nath & Rosenthal LLP*
and Cannon Financial Institute, Inc.

298

partnership at the time of the partner's death. Under the terms of the partnership agreement, on the death of a partner, the partnership was required to purchase the deceased partner's interest in the partnership from his or her estate. The partnership was required to maintain life insurance policies on the partners to fund the purchase of the partnership interest. The insurance proceeds were paid to the partnership upon the decedent's death. The IRS sought to determine the estate tax treatment of these insurance policy proceeds under IRC § 2042.

In Rev. Rul. 83-147, 1983-2 C.B. 158, a partnership owned a life insurance policy on the life of a partner and paid the premiums. The beneficiary was the partner's son. The IRS ruled that because the proceeds were payable other than to or for the benefit of the partnership, the proceeds were includable in the partner's estate under IRC § 2042(2).

The IRS stated that incidents of ownership held by a partnership over a policy insuring the life of a general partner should be attributable to the insured unless the proceeds are paid to the partnership itself. Because in this case the insurance proceeds were necessary to purchase the interest of a deceased partner without liquidating the partnership assets, the IRS ruled that the proceeds of the life insurance policies held by the partnership on a deceased partner's life were payable for the benefit of the partnership. Consequently, the proceeds were not includable in the deceased partner's gross estate under IRC § 2042.

4. The Three-Year Rule - IRC § 2035(d)(2)

Transfers by an insured of incidents of ownership in a life insurance policy within three years of the insured's death are included in the insured's gross estate under IRC § 2035.

> **EXAMPLE:** Insured purchases a $1,000,000 term life insurance policy on his life, and names his wife as beneficiary of the policy. He transfers ownership of the policy to an ILIT and the ILIT is, in turn, named beneficiary of the policy. The insured dies two years after the transfer. The insurance proceeds are included in the insured's gross estate under IRC § 2035, because he transferred incidents of ownership in a life insurance policy within three years of his date of death.

→ **Planning Point:** The result in the above example could be avoided simply by having the trustee of the ILIT purchase the insurance policy directly, rather than having the insured acquire the insurance and then transfer it to the ILIT. The 3-year rule will not apply if the transaction is structured in this manner because the decedent will never hold any incidents of ownership in the policy. Accordingly, the life insurance proceeds will be excluded from the insured's gross estate, even if the insured makes annual exclusion gifts to the ILIT to cover the costs of the annual insurance premiums (See *Leder Est. v. Comm'r*, 893 F.3d 237 (10th Cir. 1989) and *Headrick Est. v. Comm'r*, 918 F.2d 1263 (6th Cir.

21st Century Estate Planning:
Practical Applications
2005 Edition

©2005 Sonnenschein Nath & Rosenthal LLP
and Cannon Financial Institute, Inc.

299

1990), *acq. recommended*, AOD 1991-012). Nevertheless, the ILIT should be drafted to provide that the trustee may use these future contributions, but is not required to do so, to pay premiums.

Just as incidents of ownership in a controlled corporation are attributed to the controlling shareholder, so too is the transfer of an insurance policy within three years of the insured's death. In Rev. Rul. 82-141, the insured was the "controlling" shareholder of X corporation, which possessed all the incidents of ownership in an insurance policy on the insured's life. The corporation assigned all of its incidents of ownership in the insurance policy to A and there was no valid business purpose for the assignment. The insured died within three years of the transfer and the insurance proceeds were paid to A. The IRS held that the insurance proceeds were includible in the decedent's gross estate, noting that the principle underlying the attribution rule or Regulation § 20.2042-1(c)(6) mandates that the incidents of ownership possessed by X corporation be attributed to the insured for purposes of IRC § 2035.

The three-year rule can also cause problems when an employee assigns his group term life insurance coverage in order to remove the proceeds from his gross estate, and the employer later changes group term carriers (thereby acquiring a new policy). In this situation, the employee will have to assign his coverage under the new policy, which will start the beginning of a new three-year period.

→ **Planning Point:** To avoid having to survive a new three-year period if an employer switches group-term life insurance carriers, the employee should, when assigning his rights in the initial policy, assign not only his rights in the existing policy, but also his rights in any replacement policy. In Rev. Rul. 80-289, the IRS approved such an anticipatory assignment, but limited it to situations "where the assignment was necessitated by the change of the employer's master insurance plan carrier and the new arrangement is identical in all relevant aspects to the previous arrangement with the first insurance carrier." Thus, if the replacement policy is significantly different from the original policy, the insured may have to survive an additional three years in order to avoid inclusion in his or her gross estate.

B. Gifts of Life Insurance

Persons with estates of less than $3,000,000 are often reluctant to transfer assets during their lifetime, because they may need the assets to maintain their own standard of living. Life insurance, however, is often viewed as an asset that is designed to replace earnings that are lost upon an individual's untimely death, rather than as an income-producing asset. As a result, whether a client's estate is large or small, most clients are usually very willing to transfer life insurance in order to remove the insurance proceeds from their estate for estate tax purposes.

21st Century Estate Planning:
Practical Applications
2005 Edition

©2005 Sonnenschein Nath & Rosenthal LLP
and Cannon Financial Institute, Inc.

300

➜ **Planning Point:** One should note that this section deals with gifts of life insurance and, thus, assumes the insured already owns the life insurance. Gifts of life insurance by the insured, however, are subject to the three-year rule under IRC § 2035. If a practitioner is in the planning stage (*i.e.*, insurance has not yet been purchased), the preferred approach is to have the would-be donee purchase the life insurance directly. The insured could then make annual exclusion gifts of cash to help fund the premium payments. This approach will avoid the application of IRC § 2035.

Additional reasons for making gifts of life insurance (*i.e.*, in addition to removing the life insurance from the insured's estate) include: (i) removing the policy and the eventual proceeds from the reach of the donor's creditors, (ii) the client can transfer the policy at its significantly lower lifetime value, thereby reducing transfer tax costs and (iii) creating a source of liquidity from which the donee can draw to help pay the insured's estate taxes.

1. Donees of Life Insurance: Individual vs. Trust

The key to removing life insurance from an individual's estate is to make sure that the individual does not possess any incidents of ownership. This is accomplished by giving the life insurance to a third party (and by the insured surviving the three-year rule). The question that arises is who is the appropriate donee of the life insurance (*e.g.*, an individual vs. a trust)?

a. Spouse as Donee vs. ILIT. If the insured intends for the life insurance proceeds to benefit his or her spouse, then an ILIT will almost always be preferable.

> **EXAMPLE:** Insured owns a $1,000,000 whole life policy on his life, with a cash value of $500,000 and his wife is named as beneficiary. The insured decides to transfer ownership of the policy to his wife. If the insured predeceases the spouse, the effect of this transfer is estate tax neutral, because there would be no estate tax due regardless of whether or not the transfer occurred. Assuming the insured survived the transfer by three years, the policy is removed from his estate; had the transfer not occurred, the proceeds would qualify for the estate tax marital deduction. In either case, the proceeds are still taxable in the surviving spouse's gross estate (unless dissipated by the surviving spouse). If, on the other hand, the insured transferred the policy to an appropriately designed ILIT, he could prevent the proceeds from being taxed in both his and his spouse's estate, while allowing his spouse to enjoy the benefits of the insurance proceeds as a trust beneficiary.

The outright transfer to the spouse in the above example, however, could be beneficial if (i) the spouse predeceased the insured and (ii) the spouse had only a small estate of her own. The benefit, under these circumstances, is that the cash value of the policy would be included in her gross estate, thereby enabling her to make greater use of her applicable credit.

21st Century Estate Planning:
Practical Applications
2005 Edition

©2005 *Sonnenschein Nath & Rosenthal LLP*
and Cannon Financial Institute, Inc.

301

b. Children as Donee vs. ILIT. If the spouse will not be a beneficiary of the insurance proceeds and the insured's children (or other beneficiaries) are adults, transferring the policy directly to the children may be simpler than using an ILIT. Assuming the insured survives the transfer by three years, no part of the insurance proceeds should be includible in the insured's gross estate. In addition, if the insured pays the policy premiums by making gifts to the children, the gifts should automatically qualify for the IRC § 2503(b) gift tax annual exclusion.

Nevertheless, transferring ownership of the policy to a trust and naming the trust as beneficiary is definitely preferable if the children are minors, because the insured's spouse (or another trusted relative or friend) could act as trustee of the trust and thereby exercise a tremendous amount of control over the transferred property. In addition, transferring the insurance policy to a trust for the benefit of children provides numerous other advantages that are associated with trusts in general (*e.g.*, creditor protection, protection from a divorcing spouse, the client can control timing of outright distributions to descendants, and can determine who will manage the trust property (*i.e.*, the client appoints the trustee) in the event the children lack the financial acumen to do so themselves, etc.).

→ **Planning Point:** If you decide to name children as beneficiaries of an insurance policy, the transaction should never be structured where the husband is the insured and the wife is the owner of the policy (or vice-versa), because, in this situation, upon the death of the husband (*i.e.*, the insured), the wife will be treated as having made a gift of the insurance proceeds to the children (See *Goodman v. Comm'r*, 156 F.2d 218 (2d Cir. 1946)). In fact, there is the potential for an inadvertent gift in any situation where three different parties are involved as owner, insured and beneficiary. To avoid this problem whenever the insured is not the policy owner, the policy owner should always be named as the policy beneficiary.

c. Irrevocable Life Insurance Trusts. As noted above, transferring the insured's insurance policy to an ILIT (and naming the trust as beneficiary) has a number of advantages over an outright transfer to an individual, including the following:

- If properly drafted, the ILIT will remove the life insurance from the insured's estate (assuming the insured survives the transfer by three years);
- The trust provides a flexible tool for the management and distribution of assets. For example, without causing inclusion in the surviving spouse's estate, the trust can provide that the surviving spouse and children are entitled to so much or all of the income and/or corpus as the trustee shall determine in the trustee's discretion (the spouse, however, should not be the trustee, unless distributions to the spouse are limited to an ascertainable standard);

21ˢᵗ Century Estate Planning:
Practical Applications
2005 Edition

©2005 Sonnenschein Nath & Rosenthal LLP
and Cannon Financial Institute, Inc.

302

- The ILIT can provide the insured's estate with liquidity to pay taxes and administration expenses, if the ILIT is drafted to provide the trustee with authority to purchase assets from the insured's estate or loan money to the insured's estate; and
- The insurance proceeds will be protected from the beneficiaries' creditors and from claims of spouses.

While use of an ILIT has a number of advantages, it also creates additional complexity. The main cause of the additional complexity is the need to structure the ILIT to avoid incurring gift tax on (i) the transfer of the life insurance policy to the trust and (ii) the transfer of cash to pay the annual policy premiums. In order to qualify these transfers for the gift tax annual exclusion, it is necessary to grant the beneficiaries Crummey powers (*i.e.*, a right to withdraw the beneficiary's pro rata share of the property contributed to the trust). For an overview of the issues that arise in connection with the use of Crummey powers <u>see</u> Chapter VII regarding Annual Exclusion Gift Planning.

2.   Valuation of Life Insurance for Gift Tax Purposes

As will occur with the transfer of any other type of asset, the transfer of a life insurance policy for less than full and adequate consideration will result in a taxable gift. (<u>See</u> IRC § 2512(b)). Similarly, the payment by the insured of premiums on a life insurance policy owned by another person (*e.g.*, the insured's children or an ILIT) will be considered a gift by the insured to such other person (<u>See</u> Treas. Reg. § 25.2511-1(h)(8)).

The value of the life insurance policy for gift tax purposes will differ depending on the type of policy being transferred. The following material discusses how to value various types of policies for gift tax purposes.

      a. <u>Single Premium or Paid-Up Policy</u>. A gift of a single premium or paid-up policy is essentially the replacement cost that the same company would charge, as of the date of the gift, for a contract of the same specified amount on the life of a person of the same age as the insured (See Treas. Reg. § 25.2512-6(a), Example (3)). Thus, if the insured's health is much worse on the replacement cost date (thereby increasing the cost of a replacement contract), the value of the gift will be greater than if the insured had been in excellent health.

      b. <u>Cash Value Policies</u>. A gift of a cash value policy on which further premiums will be due (*i.e.*, a cash value policy that is not a single premium or paid-up policy) will equal the sum of the interpolated terminal reserve (the terminal reserve is the reserve that an insurance company must set aside each year to meet its contractual obligation to the policy owner and is approximately equal to the cash surrender value of the policy) at the date of the gift, plus any unexpired premium, less any policy loans and plus any accumulated dividends (See Treas. Reg. § 25.2512-6(a)).

21ˢᵗ Century Estate Planning:
Practical Applications
2005 Edition

©2005 Sonnenschein Nath & Rosenthal LLP
and Cannon Financial Institute, Inc.

303

EXAMPLE: P has owned a whole life insurance policy for nine years and 4 months. P transfers the policy to C by gift four months after the last premium due date. The policy has a gross annual premium of $2,811. The gift is calculated as follows:

Terminal reserve at end of 10th year	$14,601.00
Terminal reserve at end of 9th year	12,965.00
Increase in terminal reserve	$ 1,636.00
Interpolation of the terminal reserves, equals 1/3 (4 months divided by 12 months) multiplied by the $1,636 increase in the terminal reserve	$ 545.33
Terminal reserve at end of 9th year	12,965.00
Interpolated terminal reserve at date of gift	$13,510.33
Unexpired portion of gross premium (2/3 multiplied by $2,811)	1,874.00
Value of the gift	$15,384.33

     c. Term Insurance. The value of term insurance is equal to the unexpired premium as of the date of transfer, because term insurance has no interpolated terminal reserve. Thus, the value of a term insurance policy decreases by 1/365 for each day of the policy year.

> **EXAMPLE:** H purchased a term life insurance policy on January 1, 2005. The policy has an annual premium of $2,000. If H transfers the policy on June 30, 2005, the amount of the gift is $991.78 (181/365 x $2,000). Had H transferred the policy on December 31, 2005 (*i.e.*, the day before the next premium payment is due), no taxable gift would occur.

     d. Group Term Insurance. The value of an employee's assignment of his or her interest in group term insurance is, like regular term insurance, dependent on the date of the gift. If the transfer occurs on the premium due date, the policy will have no ascertainable value and, thus, there will be no gift (See Rev. Rul. 76-490, 1976 C.B. 300). If the gift occurs on any other day, however, the value of the gift will equal the unexpired premium.

     ➔   **Planning Point:** Group term life insurance coverage expires at the end of each month and a new premium is paid for the following month. Accordingly, to avoid a gift, group term insurance should generally be transferred on the premium due date (or close enough thereto to exclude the gift by reason of the insured's annual exclusion).

     Following the assignment of the employee's group term insurance, each of the employer's future premium payments is an indirect gift from the employee to the assignee (See Rev. Rul. 76-490). In terms of valuing these indirect gifts, Rev. Rul. 84-147, 1984-2 C.B. 201,

21st Century Estate Planning:
Practical Applications
2005 Edition

©2005 *Sonnenschein Nath & Rosenthal LLP*
and Cannon Financial Institute, Inc.

304

provides that if the group term plan is not discriminatory, or if the plan is discriminatory but the insured is not a key employee (See IRC § 416(i), for definition), the value of the gift is the lower of (i) the amount taxable as income under the Table I of IRC § 79, or (ii) the actual cost of the group term coverage. If, on the other hand, the insured is a key employee and the group term plan is discriminatory, the actual cost of the coverage must be used to measure the value of the indirect gift.

e. Valuation Where Insured has Limited Life Expectancy. Treas. Reg. § 25.2512-1 indicates that "[a]ll relevant facts and elements of value as of the time of the gift shall be considered" when valuing property. Accordingly, where an insured is terminally ill, the gift is not to be calculated using normal valuation principles (*e.g.*, with a cash value policy, the value of the gift would not merely be the interpolated terminal reserve plus unearned premium). This principle is illustrated in *Pritchard Est. v. Comm'r*, 4 T.C. 204 (1944), where a terminally ill insured sold insurance policies on his life with an aggregate face amount of $50,000 to his wife for $10,482.55 (approximately the cash surrender value of the policies). The Tax Court held that the wife did not pay adequate and full consideration for the policies, noting that "the value [of the policy] rises in inverse ratio to the length of life expectancy."

C. Viatical and Senior Settlements[1]

With the rapid improvements in the healthcare industry, life expectancies for the average individual have been increasing. A corollary of longer life expectancies is that older individuals will need more money to sustain their accustomed standard of living and may need to access the value contained in life insurance policies to satisfy this need. Accordingly, it will be increasingly important to ensure that insureds can access the value of life insurance that they own either directly or indirectly. In response to this need, viatical and senior settlements have become important vehicles that enable insureds to reach the value embedded in life insurance contracts.

A viatical settlement involves the purchase by a third party of a life insurance policy from an insured who is terminally or chronically ill. The sale price will be more than the cash value of the policy but less than the policy's face value, and will depend on such factors as the insured's life expectancy, the annual premiums, interest rates and the amount of any outstanding loans. The use of viatical settlements has exploded since the enactment of the Health Insurance Portability and Accountability Act of 1996 (HIPAA), which expressly excludes the proceeds from a viatical settlement from the gross income of an insured who is terminally ill and from the gross income of some insureds who are chronically ill.

The growth in popularity of viatical settlements has, in turn, prompted a new breed of settlement providers to enter the industry. These companies have begun to offer "age-based settlements" to people who are not terminally or chronically ill. These settlements have become known as "senior settlements." To be eligible to participate in a senior settlement, a senior must typically be age 65 or older, and must have experienced some decline in health since the policy was issued.

21st Century Estate Planning:
Practical Applications
2005 Edition

©2005 Sonnenschein Nath & Rosenthal LLP
and Cannon Financial Institute, Inc.

305

1. Income Tax Treatment Where Insured is Terminally or Chronically Ill

Under IRC § 101(g)(2), if any portion of the death benefit under a life insurance contract on the life of an insured who is terminally or chronically ill is sold or assigned to a viatical settlement provider, the amount paid for the sale or assignment of such portion is treated as an amount paid by reason of the death of the insured. Because a viatical payment is treated as paid by reason of the death of the insured, the amount received in the settlement is excluded from the insured's gross income in whole or in part under IRC § 101(a). The classification of an insured as either terminally ill or chronically ill will impact the amount that the insured will receive income tax free.

    a. Terminally Ill Individual. An individual is terminally ill if he or she has been certified by a physician as having an illness or physical condition that can reasonably be expected to result in death in 24 months or less after the date of the certification (See IRC § 101(g)(4)(A)). If an insured is classified as terminally ill, the entire amount paid to the insured in the viatical settlement will be excluded from gross income.

    b. Chronically Ill Individual. An individual is chronically ill if he or she has been certified by a licensed health care practitioner as (i) being unable to perform (without substantial assistance) at least two activities of daily living for a period of at least 90 days due to a loss of functional capacity, (ii) having a similar level of disability as determined under regulations or (iii) requiring substantial supervision to protect the individual from threats to health and safety due to severe cognitive impairment (See IRC § 101(g)(4)(A) and IRC § 7702B(c)(2)). If an insured is classified as chronically ill, the maximum amount of the viatical settlement that may be excluded from gross income is generally $63,875 annually (adjusted annually for inflation). Other conditions also apply. (See IRC § 101(g)(3)).

2. Income Tax Treatment if Insured is not Terminally or Chronically Ill

If an insured is not terminally or chronically ill, the income tax treatment of life settlement proceeds is governed by IRC § 1001. Under that section the amount realized on the sale of property is the fair market value of the consideration received, while the gain that must be recognized on the sale is the difference between the amount realized and the seller's adjusted basis in the contract. It is not clear, however, whether the seller's basis in the insurance policy should be determined under IRC § 72(e)(6) or under IRC § 1001(a).

21st Century Estate Planning:
Practical Applications
2005 Edition

©2005 Sonnenschein Nath & Rosenthal LLP
and Cannon Financial Institute, Inc.

306

a. The Insured's Basis in the Contract Under IRC § 72(e)(6). IRC § 72(e)(6) determines the insured's basis in a contract where the policyholder surrenders or redeems the policy. Under that section, the insured's basis is equal to the aggregate amount of premiums paid, less the aggregate amount received under the contract that was not included in the recipient's gross income (*e.g.*, nontaxable dividends, which are essentially the return of excess policy premiums).

b. The Insured's Basis in the Contract Under IRC § 1001(a). In PLR 9443020 the IRS stated that the basis in a life insurance policy that is sold (as opposed to being surrendered or redeemed under IRC § 72(e)(6)) should be reduced by the cost of insurance protection provided through the date of the sale. There is no similar ruling or other precedent, however, suggesting that a policy holder's basis as determined under IRC § 72(e)(6) should be reduced by the "cost of insurance" as an amount received under the contract. Thus, an issue has arisen regarding which method is the correct method of calculating an insured's basis in an insurance policy for purposes of a sale of the policy.

The issue is confused further by a footnote in PLR 9443020 that cites IRC § 1016(a)(1) (which provides for basis adjustments for "expenditures, receipts, losses, or other items, properly chargeable to capital account") and then directs the reader to "see also" IRC § 72(e). The reference to IRC § 72(e) indicates that the IRS believes that IRC § 72(e)(6) applies, at least to some extent, in the sale context. Nevertheless, by citing IRC § 1016(a)(1) the IRS also implies that the basis as determined under IRC § 72(e) must be adjusted for "expenditures, receipts, losses, or other items, property chargeable to capital account" under IRC § 1016.

Whether an insured's basis in an insurance contract should be reduced by the "cost of insurance" for purposes of determining his or her gain on the sale of the policy is an important issue, as it will obviously have a significant impact on the amount of gain that must be recognized. Nevertheless, there is no case law squarely addressing the proper calculation of basis in determining *gain* on the sale of an insurance contract (in PLR 9443020 the IRS relied on cases that are distinguishable on their facts). As a result, the proper treatment of the amount received by an insured in a senior settlement (*i.e.*, where the insured is not terminally or chronically ill) may not be finally resolved until this issue is squarely addressed by the IRS or a court.

3.   The Mechanics of a Viatical or Senior Settlement

The life settlement process is similar to applying for an insurance policy. Generally, a broker or agent representing the insured will contact various life settlement companies, provide them with appropriate medical information about the insured and will assist the insured in collecting, comparing and eventually choosing among various settlement offers. After accepting an offer, the owner will be required to execute several instruments to transfer the policy and to change beneficiary designation. After the policy is transferred and the beneficiary designation is changed, the proceeds from the settlement are paid to the seller.

21st Century Estate Planning:
Practical Applications
2005 Edition

©2005 Sonnenschein Nath & Rosenthal LLP
and Cannon Financial Institute, Inc.

307

a. Who is Eligible? As discussed above, settlement providers will purchase policies from persons who are either terminally or chronically ill (*i.e.*, viatical settlements). Additionally, at least three commercial life settlement providers are currently purchasing policies from seniors whose health has declined but who are not classified as either terminally ill or chronically ill (*i.e.*, senior settlements). The definition of "seniors" varies depending on the company; some companies will only enter into settlements with seniors who are over age 65, while others require the senior to be at least age 70.

b. What Types of Policies May Be Subject to Viatical or Senior Settlements? Virtually any type of policy may be sold, including whole life, universal, split-dollar, and even term life policies, notwithstanding the fact that term life policies have no cash value. The only potential roadblocks to the sale of a policy are (i) if the contestability period (typically two years) has not yet expired or (ii) if the terms of the policy prohibit it from being assigned. Fractional interests in a policy (*e.g.*, one-third of the policy) may also be sold.

c. Overview of the Application, Due Diligence and Offer Process. In order to enter into a viatical or senior settlement, the seller must fill out an application that provides basic demographic data and complete consent forms that give the settlement company authority to obtain the insured's medical records and to verify that the insurance policy is currently in force. If the seller is not the same person as the insured (*e.g.*, the seller is the trustee of a trust), the seller will have to request that the insured provide the settlement company with the necessary information and consent forms. The life settlement provider's own medical experts use this information to independently determine the insured's life expectancy.

The settlement offer depends largely upon the results of the settlement provider's independent determination of the insured's life expectancy, the estimate of the future premiums it will have to pay to keep the policy in force, and the policy's cash value, if any. A reasonable estimate of amounts paid in settlement of a contract is 50% to 80% of the face value of the policy for viatical settlements and 10% to 40% of the face value of the policy for senior settlements.

21st Century Estate Planning:
Practical Applications
2005 Edition

©2005 Sonnenschein Nath & Rosenthal LLP
and Cannon Financial Institute, Inc.

308

d. Assignment, Payment and Rescission. Once the seller accepts an offer, he will be required to sign an instrument assigning his rights in the policy to the life settlement provider. After the policy has been assigned and the beneficiary designation has been changed, the settlement company will pay the agreed amount. Generally, the process from application to payout takes two to eight weeks, although it could take longer depending on how long it takes the insured's physicians to provide the settlement company with the necessary information. A seller is allowed a set period of time to rescind a life settlement after he or she receives the settlement proceeds.

e. Settlement Options. Some settlement providers offers a number of payment options, including the following: (1) a lump sum payment; (2) installments payments; (3) treating the proceeds as a tax-free loan; and (4) use of the proceeds to purchase an annuity.

→ **Planning Point:** If an insured is classified as chronically ill, the maximum amount of the viatical settlement that may be excluded from gross income is generally $63,875 *annually* (adjusted annually for inflation). Thus, when selecting a settlement option for a chronically ill insured, it will usually be better for the individual to receive the settlement proceeds in installments, so as to ensure that most (if not all) of the proceeds will be excludable from the seller's gross income under IRC § 101(g).

f. Post Settlement Issues. The seller may use settlement proceeds for any purpose, including paying for medical or day-to-day living expenses or engaging in estate planning. IRC § 6050Q requires viatical settlement providers to report the aggregate benefits they pay and certain other information on Form 1099-LTC, Long-Term Care and Accelerated Death Benefits or an acceptable substitute. The seller should provide a copy of this form to his or her tax return preparer.

4.   **Rethinking Common Estate Planning Techniques in Light of Lifetime Settlement Options**

In light of the increasing popularity of viatical and senior settlements, estate planners should reconsider the manner in which they structure some common estate planning techniques. With an eye towards the fact that clients may at some point desire to enter into lifetime settlements with respect to their life insurance policies, estate planners should concentrate on building flexibility into any planning that is done with life insurance.

a. Irrevocable Life Insurance Trusts. One of the primary tools estate planners have used to remove insurance proceeds from a client's estate is the irrevocable life insurance trust. To avoid causing inclusion in the insured's estate, however, the ILIT must limit the insured's power over both the policy and the trust property. As a result, under most ILITs, the insured will not be able to access the policy if a lifetime settlement becomes desirable. To prevent this result, estate planners should seek to build flexible terms into ILITs. One obvious

21ˢᵗ Century Estate Planning:
Practical Applications
2005 Edition

©2005 *Sonnenschein Nath & Rosenthal LLP*
and Cannon Financial Institute, Inc.

309

way to increase flexibility is to name the insured's spouse as beneficiary of the trust during the insured's life. By using this approach, if lifetime settlement becomes desirable, the trustee can distribute either the policy or the settlement proceeds to the beneficiary spouse, who can then transfer the policy or proceeds to the insured spouse pursuant to the unlimited gift tax marital deduction (or use the proceeds for the benefit of the insured spouse).

In addition, the terms of the trust should give the trustee an express power to sell any policy held by the trust, and to move the trust's situs to another jurisdiction. This will enable the trustee to engage in a settlement transaction that would otherwise be prohibited under the then applicable state law or to seek a jurisdiction that favorably regulates viatical and/or senior settlements.

b. Family Limited Partnerships. Practitioners should consider using family limited partnerships as an alternative to irrevocable life insurance trusts, because partnership agreements are freely amendable and thus provide greater flexibility (in comparison to an irrevocable trust). Moreover, an insured can retain substantially greater control as a general partner than he or she could under an irrevocable insurance trust. Partnerships, however, only shelter the value of the discount from estate or gift tax, whereas a life insurance trust (if properly drafted and administered) will completely shelter the full value of the policy.

> **EXAMPLE:** H has a portfolio of securities worth $2 million that he wishes to transfer to a family limited partnership. He plans to retain the limited partner units and wants to structure the partnership so that his limited partnership interest will be discounted at the death of the survivor of him and his wife, W. H and W form a corporation to act as the general partner of the partnership, and each receives one-half of the stock. Accordingly, neither H nor W has independent control of the corporation. Corporation contributes $20,000 of cash to the partnership in return for a 1% general partnership interest, and H contributes $1,800,000 of stock in return for a 99% limited partnership interest. The partnership uses the $20,000 cash to purchase insurance on H's life. Because H does not have a controlling interest in the corporation that is acting as general partner, none of the incidents of ownership of the life insurance policy owned by the partnership are attributable to H. Each year, H and Corporation make additional capital contributions to the partnership to enable it to fund the insurance premiums, and each takes back his or its respective limited or general partnership interests (*e.g.*, H contributes $19,800 and receives a pro rata amount of limited partnership units in return, while Corporation contributes $200 and receives a pro rata amount of general partnership units in return). After several years of paying premiums, H decides that he wants to sell the policy and use the proceeds. Partnership sells the insurance and distributes 99% of the proceeds to H. The remaining one percent is distributed to

21st Century Estate Planning:
Practical Applications
2005 Edition

©2005 Sonnenschein Nath & Rosenthal LLP
and Cannon Financial Institute, Inc.

310

Corporation. The limited partnership interests retained by H will be subject to estate tax at his death, but should be subject to valuation discounts.

If the practitioner opts to use a family limited partnership in lieu of an ILIT, the practitioner should verify that, under applicable state law, the partnership has an insurable interest in the insured. If not, then use of a family limited partnership may not be feasible. A drawback to the use of a partnership, in the life settlement context, is that the life settlement proceeds paid to the partnership will, in all likelihood, be taxable, because life settlement proceeds payable to a taxpayer, other than the insured, will not be eligible for exclusion under IRC § 101(g) if the payee has an insurable interest with respect to the life of the insured by reason of a business or financial relationship with the insured (See IRC § 101(g)(5)).

      c.   Asset Protection Trusts. Another alternative to the traditional irrevocable insurance trust is the Alaska or Delaware asset protection trust or an offshore asset protection trust. Under this approach the insured would transfer the insurance policy to a trust created in Alaska or Delaware (or an offshore jurisdiction) and retain a beneficial interest in the trust as a discretionary trust beneficiary.

Under the laws of most U.S. and other common law jurisdictions, if an individual creates a trust, even one that is irrevocable, and retains a beneficial interest in the trust, his or her creditors can reach the trust property. As a result, the transfer to the trust is deemed to be revocable and, therefore, at the settlor's death, is included in his or her estate for estate tax purposes under IRC § 2038.

Delaware and Alaska, in an attempt to attract trust business to their states, have modified their asset protection laws to allow U.S. citizens to achieve some of the benefits, from an asset protection standpoint, that could previously be obtained only via the laws of certain offshore jurisdictions. Under the new Delaware and Alaska statutes, the settlor may be a discretionary trust beneficiary of an irrevocable trust without causing the transfer to the trust to be an incomplete gift or risking inclusion under IRC §§ 2036 or 2038. Thus, if the settlor/insured wishes to obtain cash, the trustee could enter into a lifetime settlement of the insurance policy that was transferred to the trust, and the settlement proceeds could be paid out to the insured as a discretionary trust beneficiary.

The Delaware and Alaska trusts, however, are new and thus are not "time tested." As a result, despite a recent favorable IRS private ruling (See PLR 9837007 (June 10, 1998)), practitioners have legitimate reasons for being cautious about using this technique. Nevertheless, if these trusts withstand IRS scrutiny, they will allow clients to accomplish substantial transfer tax savings, while retaining access to the trust assets – and would be excellent vehicles for life insurance.

      d.   Use of Viatical and Senior Settlements to Fund Gift Tax. Even in this current climate of potential estate tax repeal, making a taxable gift may be beneficial for a

21st Century Estate Planning:
Practical Applications
2005 Edition

©2005 Sonnenschein Nath & Rosenthal LLP
and Cannon Financial Institute, Inc.

311

chronically ill client, because a client can pass significantly more wealth to his descendants by making gifts during life and paying gift tax (assuming he survives the transfer by three years so the gift tax is not included in his estate tax base) than leaving property to them at death subject to estate tax. Most clients, however, are unwilling to pay gift tax, and those who are willing may not have sufficient liquidity to pay gift tax. A life settlement may enable a client to make a large taxable gift and pay gift tax when he otherwise might not be able or willing to do so, thereby transferring greater wealth to his or her descendants.

> **EXAMPLE:** H, who is chronically ill, owns a $2 million life insurance contract on his life in which he has a basis of $500,000, which amount is greater than the policy's cash value. The beneficiaries of the policy are his children. H's wealth is largely tied up in a closely-held business. H wants to make a taxable gift of non-voting stock in his business, which qualifies for a 40% valuation discount, to his children; however, he is concerned that he may not have significant liquidity to pay the gift tax. H should consider a viatical settlement.

> Assume that H receives $1,000,000 (50% of the face value) from selling the policy. He will then have $900,000 ($1,000,000 – (20% x ($1,000,000 - $500,000))) of the settlement proceeds available after income taxes with which to pay gift tax. Therefore, assuming a 50% gift tax, H can use the $900,000 to pay the gift tax on an $1,800,000 gift ($1,800,000 x 50% = $900,000). Thus, client will be able to transfer closely-held stock having an undiscounted value of $3.0 million ($1,800,000 ÷ 60 % = $3.0 million).

    e. **Life Settlements Coupled with a Gift-Giving Program**. Life settlements coupled with an annual exclusion gift-giving program should be considered as another alternative means for removing a policy from a policyholder's estate. Using a life settlement avoids the complication of using an insurance trust or the other techniques for policy removal discussed above.

> **EXAMPLE:** H, who is terminally ill, owns a $2 million life insurance contract on his life. If H retains ownership of the policy, the entire death benefit will be included in his estate and his family will receive only $1,000,000 (assuming a 50% estate tax rate). H could remove the policy from his estate by transferring it to another individual or to an irrevocable trust; however, by doing so he risks having the policy brought back into his estate under IRC §§ 2035 and 2042 if he dies within three years of the transfer.

> If, instead, H chooses to sell his policy and use the proceeds to fund an annual exclusion gift-giving program, he may benefit his children and

21ˢᵗ Century Estate Planning:
Practical Applications
2005 Edition

©2005 Sonnenschein Nath & Rosenthal LLP
and Cannon Financial Institute, Inc.

312

grandchildren immediately and, depending upon the size of the settlement, he may ultimately transfer more wealth to his family.

For example, if H has six married children and twelve grandchildren, and he receives $1,200,000 as the viatical settlement in November of this year, H will not owe any tax on the settlement proceeds because he is terminally ill. If, via gift-splitting with his spouse, H makes $22,000 annual exclusion gifts to each child, each child's spouse and each grandchild, and then makes a second round of gifts early in the following calendar year, he could transfer $1,056,000 to his descendants free of gift tax. If he dies prior to the next calendar year, then $72,000 of the remaining $144,000 of the settlement proceeds will pass to his children (net of estate tax) upon his death. In total, H's beneficiaries receive $1,128,000 if he uses the settlement proceeds to fund annual exclusion gifts, whereas they would receive only $1,000,000 (net of estate tax) if he dies owning the policy.

5. New Estate Planning Techniques in Response to Lifetime Settlement Options

In response to the growing lifetime settlement industry, estate planners should not only rethink traditional techniques, but should also consider the following innovative estate planning uses for life settlements. The following examples, however, do not take into account subjective economic factors, such as disappointing investment performance, which may provide additional incentives for one to consider life settlements.

a. Private Viatical and Senior Settlements. Alaska and Delaware trusts offer a vehicle for clients to give away property, yet retain an interest in the trust as a discretionary beneficiary of the trust. As we have seen, however, many practitioners are reluctant to use these techniques due to the uncertainty as to whether they will withstand IRS scrutiny. Many clients, on the other hand, are reluctant to create irrevocable trusts for family members, even if the potential transfer tax savings are significant, unless the trust can be structured so that they can be named as a beneficiary of the trust. Clients with this concern might employ a "private viatication" strategy as an alternative way to access the assets in an irrevocable trust.

Under this strategy, the insured would sell an insurance policy on his life to an irrevocable trust for his family. The trust would pay exactly what a commercial life settlement provider would pay for the policy. Thus, the transfer should not constitute a taxable gift. The client will receive assets out of the trust, but, more importantly, the insurance proceeds will continue to benefit the client's family.

> **EXAMPLE:** H created a Dynastic Trust for his family in 1991, fully utilizing both his and W's applicable exclusion amounts. The Dynastic Trust now has roughly $3 million that H wants to access. H

21st Century Estate Planning:
Practical Applications
2005 Edition

©2005 Sonnenschein Nath & Rosenthal LLP
and Cannon Financial Institute, Inc.

313

owns a fully paid-up $2 million life insurance policy on his life (in which he has a basis of $200,000, an amount in excess of the policy's cash surrender value). H's health has declined, and he now intends to sell the policy. Assuming that a commercial life settlement provider would pay 15% of the face value of the policy, the Trust purchases the policy for $300,000. H will have $285,000 net of income tax ($300,000 – (15% capital gain tax rate x ($300,000 - $200,000))), and the Trust will acquire the $2 million policy and name itself as the beneficiary. If H dies two years after the sale, and if over that period the trust property continued to grow at eight percent, then upon H's death, the Dynastic Trust would hold approximately $5.15 million. By comparison, if H had retained the policy, at the end of two years his children would have received policy proceeds of $1,000,000 (net of estate tax), and the Dynastic Trust would hold approximately $3.5 million, for a total of $4.5 million for the benefit of H's descendants. By entering into a "private senior settlement" with respect to the policy, H will have transferred approximately $650,000 more for the benefit of his descendants, and he will have transferred value from the policy to the GST-exempt Dynastic Trust. In effect, the client has used a private senior settlement to shift almost all of the life insurance proceeds down one generation without any transfer tax cost. In addition, the client is able to use the $280,000 of net settlement proceeds for other purposes.

b. **Realizing Discounts Through the Use of Viatical and Senior Settlements**. Life settlements may be used to create discounts in an insured's estate, even if the insured has previously transferred the policy to an ILIT. As the following example illustrates, life settlement proceeds held by a client's insurance trust can be used to purchase controlling interests in an entity previously controlled by the client, thereby creating minority interest discounts that can save significant estate taxes.

> **EXAMPLE:** H is terminally ill and is the sole shareholder in a closely-held business valued at $4 million. H is also the settlor of an irrevocable life insurance trust, which owns a $2.4 million face value policy on H's life. The trustee of the insurance trust sells the policy for 50% of the face value and receives $1.2 million income tax free under IRC § 101(g). The trustee can use the proceeds to buy a substantial minority interest in H's business. The interest should be valued at a discount to reflect both its lack of control and lack of marketability. Assuming that the interest is entitled to a 40% discount, the trustee can purchase a 49% interest in the company for $1.176 million (($4 million x 49%) x (1-40%)). This transaction passes the amount of the discount attributable to the 49% interest (*i.e.*, $784,000)

21ˢᵗ Century Estate Planning:
Practical Applications
2005 Edition

©2005 Sonnenschein Nath & Rosenthal LLP
and Cannon Financial Institute, Inc.

314

to the children free of tax. The insurance trust now owns an asset with a non-discounted value of $1,960,000 for the benefit of H's children.

H then gives 2% of his remaining stock to his children, valued for gift tax purposes at $48,000 (*i.e.*, a non-discounted value of $80,000), and pays a gift tax of approximately $24,000, using the remaining settlement proceeds to pay the gift tax ($1.2 million of settlement proceeds = $1.176 million for stock purchase + $24,000 gift tax).

After the gift, H owns only 49% of the stock, a minority interest. At H's death, this interest should also be discounted by 40%. Taking the discount into account, H's interest is now worth only $1.176 million for estate tax purposes, rather than $1,960,000, thereby transferring an additional $784,000 (*i.e.*, $1.96 million less $1.176 million) to his children free of tax.

The gift of the 2% interest in the preceding example is an aggressive transaction and could be subject to attack under the Tax Court's holding in *Murphy v. Comm'r*, 60 T.C.M. 645 (1990). In *Murphy*, the decedent had a general power of appointment over 51.41% of closely-held stock. Eighteen days before her death, she exercised her power of appointment to transfer a 1.76% interest to her children, thereby reducing the amount subject to her power of appointment to 49.56% (and seemingly creating a minority interest discount). The Tax Court, however, denied the discount, stating that the "sole purpose" of the transaction was to obtain a minority interest discount. The *Murphy* decision, however, has been widely criticized in the estate planning community, because the language contained in the decision is so ambiguous that it is difficult to determine on what basis the court included the transferred assets in the decedent's estate. Many practitioners believe *Murphy* was repudiated by the Tax Court's decision in *Frank Est. v. Comm'r*, T.C. Memo 1995-132, whose facts are very difficult to distinguish from those of *Murphy* (*i.e.*, there was a transfer of stock days before the decedent's death, reducing the decedent's ownership interest in the corporation from over 50% to under 50%) and, yet, the Tax Court, without even mentioning *Murphy*, ignored any motive for the transfer and found the transfer to be valid, as all corporate formalities were followed. As a result, the current status of this issue is unclear and, thus, practitioners should proceed with caution when transferring a small percentage interest in an entity that results in a switch in the overall control of the entity.

21st Century Estate Planning:
Practical Applications
2005 Edition

©2005 Sonnenschein Nath & Rosenthal LLP
and Cannon Financial Institute, Inc.

315

c. **Using Viatical and Senior Settlements to Achieve Charitable Objectives**.

All things being equal, a client who intends to leave all or most of his estate to charity would typically prefer to donate highly appreciated assets to a charity during life so that he could enjoy the goodwill and recognition resulting from his philanthropy and to obtain a current fair market value income tax deduction. Nevertheless, many clients hesitate to do so for fear of losing the income stream and security associated with retaining the assets. A life settlement might facilitate the gift.

> **EXAMPLE:** H owns a $3 million insurance policy on his own life (with a basis of $400,000), as well as publicly traded securities worth $450,000, which has a basis of $275,000. H sells his policy and receives a $480,000 settlement. Assuming that the basis in the contract is greater than the policy's cash surrender value, the difference between the settlement proceeds and the basis will be taxed as capital gain at 15%, resulting in H receiving $468,000 of the settlement proceeds after tax ($480,000 – (15% x ($480,000 - $400,000))). Having $468,000 in cash, H feels free to donate his securities to a public charity. As a result of the donation, H receives a full fair market value income tax deduction on the appreciated securities. Assuming a 35% marginal income tax rate, the deduction saves him approximately $157,500 in income tax ($450,000 x 35%).

Of course, in the above example, if the client is terminally ill, he could expect to receive a higher amount in settlement proceeds, perhaps $1,500,000 free of income taxes. In that case, he could afford to make a greater charitable contribution, either of additional appreciated securities, or of a portion of the settlement proceeds.

D. Split Dollar Life Insurance

1. The History of the Taxation of Split Dollar Life Insurance Plans

Split dollar life insurance plans are not an insurance product, but rather a system for financing the purchase of an insurance policy. In its classic configuration, an employer and an employee purchase an insurance policy on the employee's life, and agree to a method for splitting the premiums on the policy, the cash value of the policy and the death benefit. Commonly, the employer would agree to pay the entire premium with the exception of that portion of the premium that represented the economic value of the death benefit provided to the employee. The employee would contribute toward the premium (or be deemed to have received as taxable income) an amount equal to the economic value of the death benefit payable to the employee. The split dollar agreement would provide that on the termination of the agreement or the payment of proceeds under the policy, the employer would be reimbursed for all funds advanced for premium payments, or the cash value of the policy. The balance of the policy proceeds (if any) would be paid to the employee. Often the split dollar agreement would be between the employer and an irrevocable life insurance trust established by the employee, so that

21st Century Estate Planning:
Practical Applications
2005 Edition

©2005 Sonnenschein Nath & Rosenthal LLP
and Cannon Financial Institute, Inc.

316

the insurance benefits paid at the employee's death would escape estate taxation in the employee's estate. In that case, the economic value of the death benefit payable to the trust is also the measure of the employee's annual gift to the trust.

Split dollar plans have been popular for many years, particularly after the IRS ruled that the employer's payment of premiums under a split dollar life insurance arrangement did not constitute loans to the employee. (See Rev. Rul. 64-328, 1964-2 C.B. 11, Rev. Rul. 66-10, 1966-1 C.B. 12, and Rev. Rul. 67-154, 1967-1 C.B. 11.) Many variations have developed, including equity split dollar (in which cash value build-up within the policy in excess of premiums paid by the employer is the property of the employee); private split dollar (in which the parties are not employer and employee); and reverse split dollar (in which the burdens of premium payments and economic benefits are reversed from the traditional plan).

In the 1960's, when these rulings were issued, they were consistent with prevailing law, under which interest-free loans were not treated as taxable events for income or gift tax purposes. However, once IRC § 7872 was enacted, imposing gift and income tax consequences on interest-free or below-market loans, the tax treatment of split dollar insurance arrangements under these old rulings made less sense.

The IRS has made several attempts to address what it considers abuses in the split dollar arena. The first issue with which the IRS has been concerned is the failure to characterize premium payments by the employer under a split dollar arrangement as a loan. A second perceived abuse developed from the recognition that the economic benefit being provided to the employee by virtue of the employer's premium payments could include not only death benefit protection, but also any equity build-up within the policy that exceeded the amount required to be repaid to the employer. The third perceived abuse related to the insurance rates used to quantify the economic benefit being provided to the employee for death benefit protection. In Rev. Rul. 55-747, 1955-2 C.B. 228, the IRS provided that so-called PS 58 tables could be used to measure the economic value of the death benefit protection. However, the PS 58 tables are based on mortality statistics that are very outdated. As a result, it is more common for participants in split dollar arrangements to use tables provided by the insurance company issuing the policy. The difficulty with this alternative, originally permitted by the IRS, is that insurance companies have developed rates for this purpose that the IRS perceives as being artificially low. Often an insurance company will use single life term rates for split dollar products that are not available for any other products sold to the general public.

2. Split-Dollar Regulations

On September 11, 2003, the Treasury released the final version of regulations governing the taxation of split-dollar life insurance arrangements (T.D. 9092).

a. Background. The final regulations are the culmination of a series of rulings, notices and regulations issued by the IRS over the previous 8 years that cumulatively have modified the tax treatment of split-dollar life insurance arrangements under Rev. Rul. 64-

21st Century Estate Planning:
Practical Applications
2005 Edition

©2005 Sonnenschein Nath & Rosenthal LLP
and Cannon Financial Institute, Inc.

317

328, 1964-2 C.B. 11, and Rev. Rul. 66-110, 1966-1 C.B. 12, discussed above. The following is a summary of the recent guidance concerning split-dollar arrangements.

(1) **TAM 9604001**. This TAM applied for the first time the concept that increases in the cash surrender value of an equity split-dollar arrangement, i.e., an arrangement in which an employer's interest in the cash surrender value of a life insurance contract is limited to the aggregate amount of its premium payments - are taxable annually under IRC § 83.

(2) **Notice 2001-10**. This notice provided "interim guidance" pursuant to which the taxpayer is offered a choice, "pending consideration of public comments and the publication of further guidance," of treating the equity split-dollar arrangement either as a loan, taxable under IRC § 7872, or as a transfer of property (cash value build-up) upon "rollout" under IRC § 83. Notice 2001-10 also promulgated Table 2001, based on the mortality experience reflected in Table (i) under IRC § 79, with extensions for ages below 25 and above 70, and the elimination of the five-year age brackets. The Table 2001 rates replace the P.S. 58 rates set forth in Rev. Rul. 55-747, 1955-2 C.B. 228, and are materially lower than the P.S. 58 rates at all ages.

(3) **Notice 2002-8**. The notice revoked Notice 2001-10, and announced the government's intention to publish regulations providing comprehensive guidance concerning split-dollar life insurance arrangements under which the taxation of the arrangement would depend on the parties' designation of the formal ownership of the insurance contract. This notice also provided interim guidance regarding the valuation of current life insurance protection and stated certain effective date and safe harbor rules with respect to existing arrangements.

(4) **2002 Proposed Regulations**. These regulations provided comprehensive proposed guidance, based generally on the principles announced in Notice 2002-8, for the income, gift and employment taxation of both equity and nonequity split-dollar life insurance arrangements.

(5) **2003 Proposed Regulations**. Published on May 9, 2003, the proposed rules provided for the valuation of the economic benefits provided under an endorsement equity split-dollar life insurance arrangement. The 2003 proposed regulations rejected the taxation of equity under IRC § 83 only on a rollout of the contract, and instead adopted a regime for current (annual) taxation of equity under IRC § 61.

21st Century Estate Planning:
Practical Applications
2005 Edition

©2005 Sonnenschein Nath & Rosenthal LLP
and Cannon Financial Institute, Inc.

318

b. Scope. The preface to the final regulations states specifically that they do not address the issues arising out of Section 402 of the Sarbanes Oxley Act, which falls within the jurisdiction of the SEC. The preface also states that the final regulations do not affect the estate taxation of split-dollar life insurance arrangements, which will continue to be governed by IRC § 2042. Future guidance may be issued on the estate tax implications of "co-owned" policies.

The Treasury and the IRS released with these regulations Rev. Rul. 2003-105, obsoleting Rev. Rul. 79-50, 1979-1 C.B. 138, Rev. Rul. 78-420, 1978-2 C.B. 67, Rev. Rul. 66-110 (except as provided in Section III, Paragraph 3 of Notice 2002-8, regarding the permitted use of the insurer's alternative term rates - as modified in some cases - for arrangements in existence before September 17, 2003, and Notice 2002-59, 2002-2 C.B. 481, to the same effect, except with regard to certain reverse split-dollar arrangements) and Rev. Rul. 64-328. TAM 9604001 is effectively obsolesced because the Revenue Rulings upon which it relied are obsolesced.

c. Split-Dollar Life Insurance Arrangement Defined. A split-dollar life insurance arrangement is defined as any arrangement (other than a group-term life insurance plan) between an "owner" and a "nonowner" of a life insurance contract, under which either party to the arrangement pays all or part of the premiums and one of the parties paying the premiums is entitled to recover all or any part of those premiums from the proceeds or cash surrender value of the contract. Employer/employee arrangements, corporation/shareholder arrangements and private (i.e., donor/donee) arrangements are all covered in the final regulations. In the context of employer/employee split-dollar and corporation/shareholder split-dollar, the arrangement is subject to the regulations even where the obligation of repayment is not secured by the policy or its proceeds, so long as the beneficiary of all or part of the death benefit is designated by the employee or shareholder or is someone whom the employee or shareholder would be reasonably expected to designate as a beneficiary. "Reverse" split-dollar arrangements are not discussed, because they have been dealt with in Notice 2002-59. The final regulations retain the special rules from the 2002 proposed regulations that treat certain arrangements entered into either in connection with the performance of services or between a corporation and another person in that person's capacity as a shareholder in the corporation as split-dollar life insurance arrangements regardless of whether the arrangements otherwise satisfy the general definition of a split-dollar life insurance arrangement.

The regulations exclude arrangements in which one party to the transaction pays the premiums for the benefit of another party without expectation of repayment. In that case, the payment is taxable to the recipient under the general rules of IRC § 61, or, in a non-compensatory context, as a gift. The preamble to the final regulations also makes clear that definition of "arrangement" does not cover the purchase of an insurance contract in which the only parties to the arrangement are the policy owner and the life insurance company acting only in its capacity as issuer of the contract. The final regulations also make clear that key person insurance, where the employer or corporation owns the policy and all of its benefits, is outside the scope of the regulations.

21ˢᵗ Century Estate Planning:
Practical Applications
2005 Edition

©*2005 Sonnenschein Nath & Rosenthal LLP*
and Cannon Financial Institute, Inc.

319

The regulations do, however, appear to cover loans used to pay premiums that are secured by the policy, including, presumably, third-party (e.g., bank) premium financing arrangements. However, the effect of including premium financing arrangements in the definition is not clear, unless the parties have an employment, shareholder or gift relationship and the interest rate is less than the AFR (or issues of original issue discount ("OID") are involved). The final regulations also are silent on the effect of a guarantee of a third-party loan by a related party (employer or donor) who may later step into the original lender's position with respect to the collateral.

        d. Owner and Nonowner Defined. As under the 2002 proposed regulations, the income and gift tax consequences of the split-dollar arrangement follow (with two exceptions) the formal ownership of the policy, thus making the definition of "owner" and "nonowner" key to the new rules. In general, payments made by an "owner" of the policy for the benefit of a nonowner in a split-dollar life insurance arrangement (typically an endorsement arrangement) are taxed to the parties through the use of an "economic benefit" analysis, while payments made by a "nonowner" of the policy for the benefit of the owner (typically a collateral assignment arrangement) are treated as loans subject to the rules of IRC § 7872 (and the OID provisions).

        (1)   General Rule. The "owner" of the policy is defined as the person who is named as the owner of the policy. A nonowner is anyone (other than the owner) who has a direct or indirect interest in the policy.

        (2)   Exceptions. Notwithstanding the formal designation of ownership, the employer in an employer/employee arrangement and the donor in a private split-dollar arrangement is treated as the owner of the contract where the arrangement is not of the "equity" variety. The purpose of these exceptions appears to be aimed, at least in part at allowing the use of the restricted collateral assignment method for estate planning purposes in a controlling (more than 50%) shareholder situation without requiring that the arrangement be reported as a loan.

        (3)   Attribution. The final regulations provide attribution rules (not present in the 2003 proposed regulations) for compensatory split-dollar life insurance arrangements. Under these rules, the employer is treated as the owner of a life insurance contract owned by (i) a member of the employer's "controlled group," (ii) an IRC § 403(b) secular trust, (iii) a grantor trust of which the employer is treated as the owner (such as a "rabbi" trust) or (iv) an IRC § 419(e)(1) welfare benefit fund.

        e. Economic Benefit Regime. Where the employer or donor is the owner of the contract, the following results, essentially the same as under the 2002 and 2003 proposed regulations, are prescribed:

        (1)   Nonequity Arrangements. The value of current life insurance protection paid for by an employer, corporation or donor (reduced by any amount contributed by

21st Century Estate Planning:
Practical Applications
2005 Edition

©2005 Sonnenschein Nath & Rosenthal LLP
and Cannon Financial Institute, Inc.

320

an employee, shareholder or donee) is taxable - as compensation, dividend or gift, as the case may be - on an annual basis. The value of current life insurance protection is measured by reference to a premium factor (currently Table 2001) that will change from time to time in accordance with published guidance. The final regulations do not allow the continued use of the insurer's alternative term rates for arrangements entered into after September 17, 2003.

The timing of the measurement of current life insurance protection value is changed under the final regulations. The 2002 proposed regulations provided that the "average death benefit" during the taxable year be used to compute the value of current life insurance protection, while the final regulations, subject to an anti-abuse rule, permit the value to be determined on the last day of the nonowner's taxable year, unless the parties agree to use the policy anniversary date. The valuation date may be changed with the consent of the Commissioner.

(2)   **Equity Arrangements**. Where the employer, corporation or donor is entitled to recover from the employee, shareholder or donee the lesser of its premium advances or the cash surrender value of the policy, the benefited party is required to take into income (or the donor is required to report as a gift) the value of the current life insurance protection, as described above respecting nonequity arrangements, and the amount of the annual increase in the value of his or her interest in the policy's equity to which the nonowner has "current access" (as described below). This increase must be taken into account on a current basis, and not just upon "rollout" of the policy. The nonowner also must take into account any other economic benefit provided by the owner. Thus, the final regulations ground the taxation of equity under the economic benefit regime in the constructive receipt analysis of IRC § 61, not IRC § 83.

(3)   **Safe Harbors for Pre-Final Regulations Arrangements**. A split-dollar term loan is any split-dollar loan, other than a split-dollar demand loan, and thus is the default classification (as is the case for all below-market interest rate loans under IRC § 7872). If a loan has a stated maturity date, that will be binding with respect to the taxation of the arrangement.

For pre-final regulations arrangements that have not yet accumulated equity, the parties can convert to the loan regime (discussed below) even after 2003 and possibly avoid a detrimental tax effect. The IRS stated in Notice 2002-8 that it will not challenge "reasonable efforts to comply with" the regulations' imputed interest rules after a pre-final regulations has converted. This technique can preserve the presumably lower economic benefit costs right up to the point in which equity arises.

(4)   **Measurement of Current Life Insurance Protection Under Pre-Final Regulations Arrangements**. The Table 2001 rates, published in Notice 2001-10, can be used for any arrangement entered into before September 18, 2003. For split-dollar arrangements entered into before January 28, 2002, where required by the terms of an agreement between employer and employee, actual P.S. 58 rates can continue to be used in these arrangements to determine the value of current life insurance protection provided to the employee. However, a

21st Century Estate Planning:
Practical Applications
2005 Edition

©2005 Sonnenschein Nath & Rosenthal LLP
and Cannon Financial Institute, Inc.

321

footnote in the preamble to the 2002 proposed regulations confirmed that P.S. 58 rates may not be used in reverse split-dollar or other non-compensatory arrangements.

For arrangements entered into before January 28, 2002, old carrier alternative term rates that comply with prior IRS requirements can continue to be used to measure current life insurance protection, if lower than the Table 2001 rates. For these arrangements, the ability to continue to use old carrier alternative term rates combined with the safe harbor protections previously discussed results in maximum future flexibility and preserves the most favorable options for these split-dollar arrangements. For arrangements entered into after January 28, 2002 and before September 18, 2003, old carrier alternative term rates can also continue to be used only if those rates meet tough new standards applicable to commonly sold term policies.

(5) **Modification**. This topic was reserved in the 2002 proposed regulations. The final regulations provide that a nonequity arrangement that becomes an equity arrangement will result (in the case of an existing endorsement arrangement) in the continued taxation of the arrangement under the economic benefit regime. Where the existing arrangement was a collateral assignment arrangement, the conversion to an equity arrangement will be treated as a transfer of the contract from the employer or donor to the employee or donee as of the date of the modification. At that point the loan regime becomes operative.

(6) **Loans, Withdrawals, Dividends, etc**. The nonowner (employee, shareholder or donee) will also be taxable on any amount received by him or her under a life insurance contract as a policy loan, a withdrawal or dividend, as if the amount had been just distributed directly to the owner (employer, corporation or donor) and then transferred to the nonowner. The constructive distribution to the owner is reportable under the rules of IRC § 72. The amount of the transfer is reduced by the amount previously paid or taken into taxable income by the nonowner as the equity portion (but not the term coverage portion) of the economic benefit.

(7) **Basis**. No nonowner of a policy will receive a basis in the contract for any portion of the premium paid by, or taxed to, him or her under the split-dollar arrangement, even though, as noted above, offsets against income recognition is, in part, permitted with respect to policy cash distributions.

(8) **Transfer of the Contract**. Where a contract (or an undivided interest in a contract) is transferred by an owner to a nonowner, the nonowner is taxable under IRC § 83 on the fair market value of the contract (defined, in general, as its cash surrender value) reduced by any consideration paid for the transfer or previously taken into account with respect to the equity portion of the contract. As with loans, withdrawals and dividends directly from the policy, no amount that was paid or previously taken into account for tax purposes by the transferee and was attributable to current life insurance protection may either (i) reduce the (former) nonowner's gain on the transfer or (ii) be added to the (former) nonowner's basis in the policy after the transfer. The employer, in a compensatory situation, may deduct the amount included in income by the employee as a result of the transfer of the contract to the employee.

21st Century Estate Planning:
Practical Applications
2005 Edition

©2005 Sonnenschein Nath & Rosenthal LLP
and Cannon Financial Institute, Inc.

322

(9)   Contributory Arrangements. The final regulations reaffirm that any payment for life insurance protection made by the nonowner of a contract is treated as income to the policy owner. This is the case even in a private split-dollar arrangement, where any contribution by the donee is taxable as income to the donor.

(10)   Death Benefits. The final regulations provide that any amount paid to a beneficiary (other than the owner) of a life insurance contract by reason of the death of the insured is excludable from gross income under IRC § 101 only to the extent attributable to amounts previously paid or taken into account for tax purposes by the nonowner for life insurance protection. While this rule would appear at first blush to present the potential for taxation of any untaxed equity component of the death benefit, under the final regulations, all transfers of economic benefit of either a nonequity or equity variety should be fully accounted for and taxed during the insured's lifetime. The split dollar import of this rule thus should in most cases be minimal.

The final regulations omit the statement in the 2002 proposed regulations that amounts received by a nonowner in his, her or its capacity as a lender (such as the employer or donor in an equity split-dollar arrangement that is treated as a loan under the principles described below) by reason of the death of the insured will not be treated as an amount received by reason of the death of the insured for purposes of IRC § 101. However, the repayment of a loan usually does not result in tax consequences to the lender, unless the repayment includes accrued interest not previously taxed.

f.   "Current Access" and Constructive Receipt.

(1)   Constructive Receipt, Economic Benefit and Cash Equivalence. The final regulations, like the 2003 proposed regulations, provide that, in the case of an endorsement equity split-dollar life insurance arrangement, the value of the economic benefits provided to the nonowner under the arrangement for a taxable year equals (i) the cost of any current life insurance protection provided to the nonowner, (ii) the amount of policy cash value to which the nonowner has current access (to the extent that such amount was not actually taken into account for a prior taxable year) and (iii) the value of any other economic benefits provided to the nonowner (to the extent not actually taken into account for a prior taxable year).

The concept of "current access" to policy cash value is based on the income tax doctrine of "constructive receipt," i.e., income (whether or not actually received) is taxed at the time that it is either credited to the taxpayer's account, set apart for him, or otherwise made available to the taxpayer so that he may draw upon it at any time.

As broadly construed in the regulations, a nonowner is deemed to have current access to "any portion of the policy cash value that is directly or indirectly accessible by the nonowner, inaccessible to the owner, or inaccessible to the owner's general creditors." The term "access" includes any direct or indirect right of the nonowner "to obtain, use or realize potential economic

---

21ˢᵗ Century Estate Planning:
Practical Applications
2005 Edition

©2005 Sonnenschein Nath & Rosenthal LLP
and Cannon Financial Institute, Inc.

323

value from the policy cash value." The right to withdraw from the policy, borrow from the policy or affect a total or partial surrender of the policy is considered "access."

→ **Planning Point:** A practitioner should be aware that merely limiting access by the nonowner will not suffice to avoid adverse tax consequences, if the owner is also denied access to those cash values.

→ **Planning Point:** Because of the rule that the cash value must not be inaccessible to the owner's general creditors to be considered inaccessible to the nonowner, care should be taken in those states in which life insurance cash value is not reachable by the creditors of the owner of a policy. For example, in Missouri the first $150,000 may not be accessible to creditors, 513.430 RSMo., and in Pennsylvania all cash of life insurance policies are completely exempt from creditors in certain circumstances. 42 P.a.C.S.A. § 8124.

(2) **Accessibility and Creditors' Rights.** Policy cash value is deemed to be accessible to a nonowner if he or she can "anticipate, assign (either at law or in equity), alienate, pledge, or encumber the policy cash value," or if the policy cash value is subject to attachment, levy or other legal or equitable process by the nonowner's creditors. Policy cash value is deemed to be inaccessible to the owner if the owner does not have the full rights to policy cash value normally held by an owner of a life insurance contract. Policy cash value is inaccessible to the owner's general creditors if, under the terms of the split-dollar life insurance arrangement or by operation of law of any contractual undertaking, the creditors cannot, for any reason, effectively reach the full policy cash value in the event of the owner's insolvency.

→ **Planning Point:** In non-equity agreements, which are often entered into between corporations and unrelated employees, the nonowner is considered to have current access to policy cash value only if, under the arrangement, the nonowner has a current or future right to policy cash value. In a true non-equity arrangement, the nonowner will have no such right and, therefore, will not be taxable with respect to the cash value.

(3) **Acceleration Rule/IRC § 457.** The final regulations add an acceleration rule for those cases that may require a nonowner to include an amount in income earlier than would otherwise be required under the general split-dollar rules. The regulations state that an equity endorsement split-dollar life insurance arrangement constitutes a deferred compensation arrangement. Therefore, so the Treasury states, an employee of a tax-exempt organization or of a state or local government subject to IRC § 457 may have to include an amount in gross income attributable to an equity split-dollar life insurance arrangement even if the employee does not have current access to the policy cash value under these regulations.

(4) **Measurement of Policy Cash Value.** In a change from the 2003 proposed regulations, the final regulations provide that, subject to an anti-abuse rule, policy cash

21st Century Estate Planning:
Practical Applications
2005 Edition

©2005 Sonnenschein Nath & Rosenthal LLP
and Cannon Financial Institute, Inc.

324

values are to be determined on the last day of the nonowner's taxable year, unless the parties agree to use the policy anniversary date. Policy cash values are still determined, however, without regard to surrender charges or other similar charges or reductions. If any "artifice or devise" is used to artificially understate the value of any economic benefit, the date on which such value is determined is the date on which the amount of policy cash value is greatest during that taxable year.

> **g. Loan Regime.** If the employee, shareholder or donee is formally designated as the owner of the contract and is obligated to repay the employer, corporation or donor, whether out of contract proceeds or otherwise, the premiums paid by the nonowner for the direct or indirect benefit of the owner is treated as a series of loans to the owner - i.e., each premium payment is a separate loan. Under this regime, such loans are subject to the principles, where applicable, of IRC §§ 1271-1275 (regarding the taxation of original issue discount or "OID") and IRC § 7872 (below-market interest rate loans). If only a portion of the premium payment made by the nonowner is repayable (or is reasonably expected to be repaid), the portion that is not repayable will not be considered to be a split-dollar loan and is taxed to the owner under the general principles of IRC § 61.

> → **Planning Point:** The loan regime should apply to all collateral assignment arrangements, except that a collateral assignment arrangement in which the employee or donee has no equity in the policy (i.e., a "non-equity" collateral assignment arrangement) may be treated as an endorsement arrangement and taxed under the economic benefit regime, regardless of who owns the policy. Presumably, this exception will allow for a non-equity corporate controlling stockholder or insured private split-dollar arrangement that will avoid incidents of ownership in the insured for estate tax purposes.

> **(1) De Minimis Rules Not Applicable.** The rules of IRC § 7872 are generally not applicable to "gift" loans, "compensation-related" loans or "corporate-shareholder" loans on any day on which the aggregate amount of indebtedness outstanding does not exceed $10,000. In the split-dollar context, however, the IRC § 7872 rules will apply whether or not the $10,000 threshold is exceeded.

> **(2) Indirect Loans.** The regulations recognize that many split-dollar arrangements involve third parties, such as life insurance trusts, and provide that such transactions will be viewed, for purposes of IRC § 7872, as a series of back-to-back loans for income and gift tax purposes. Thus, where an employer/lender advances premiums to a life insurance trust/borrower of which the employee (the "indirect participant") is the insured, any forgone interest is computed as if the employer made a compensatory below-market loan to the employee (likely generating income recognition), and the employee took the loan proceeds and made a second below-market gift loan to the life insurance trust (likely generating a taxable gift). The tax results of each deemed loan are determined in accordance with the relationship of the parties.

21st Century Estate Planning:
Practical Applications
2005 Edition

©*2005 Sonnenschein Nath & Rosenthal LLP*
and Cannon Financial Institute, Inc.

325

(3) **Nonrecourse Loans/Written Representation.** Where a split-dollar loan is nonrecourse to the borrower, the payment is treated as a "contingent" payment. To avoid contingent payment treatment (which generally will result in the imposition of unfavorable assumptions when testing the loan for adequate stated interest), the parties to the loan must represent in writing (and must attach to the parties' returns) no later than the due date for the return of the borrower or lender for the year in which the first split-dollar loan is made, that a "reasonable person" would expect that all payments under the loan will be made. The final regulations have eliminated a second requirement with respect to nonrecourse loans, - i.e., that the loan bear interest at a stated rate.

h. **Demand and Term Loans.** Loans subject to the foregone interest rules of IRC § 7872 are generally classified as demand loans or term loans.

(1) **Demand Loans.**

(a) **Definition.** A split-dollar demand loan is any split-dollar loan that is payable in full at any time on the demand of the lender - a circumstance that is characteristic of most split-dollar arrangements.

(b) **Taxation and Timing of Demand Loans.** In each year that a split-dollar demand loan is outstanding, the loan is tested for adequate stated interest under IRC § 7872. A split-dollar demand loan is deemed to have adequate stated interest if the interest rate, which may be a variable rate, is no lower than the "blended annual rate" for the year (an average of the January and July short-term rates) based on annual compounding.

(2) **Term Loans.**

(a) **Definition.** A split-dollar term loan is any split-dollar loan, other than a split-dollar demand loan, and thus is the default classification (as is the case for all below-market interest rate loans under IRC § 7872). If a loan has a stated maturity date, that will be binding with respect to the taxation of the arrangement.

(b) **Taxation and Timing of Term Loans.** A split-dollar term loan is tested on the day the loan is made to determine if it has adequate stated interest. Interest is adequate if the face amount of the loan is equal to or greater than the "imputed loan amount." The "imputed loan amount" is the present value of all payments due under the loan, determined as of the date the loan is made, using the discount rate equal to the applicable federal rate (AFR) on that date. The AFR/discount rate must be appropriate to the loan's term: short-term (not over 3 years); mid-term (over 3 years, but not over 9 years) or long-term (over 9 years). A loan's term is the period from the date the loan is made to its stated maturity date.

The difference between the split-dollar term loan's face amount and the imputed loan amount is taken into income as compensation or as a dividend by the borrower in the year that the loan is made. Special rules, described below, apply to gift loans and certain other types of

21ˢᵗ Century Estate Planning:
Practical Applications
2005 Edition

©2005 Sonnenschein Nath & Rosenthal LLP
and Cannon Financial Institute, Inc.

326

loans. The amount treated as income to the borrower is treated as OID to the lender, and is taken into income by the lender ratably over the term of the loan, together with any other amount of OID on the loan (determined without reference to IRC § 7872).

→ **Planning Point:** The required acceleration of income recognition, coupled with the higher interest rates that generally apply to term loans of any duration, will make their use unattractive in most situations. However, if adequate interest is charged, then IRC § 7872 generally does not apply. Accordingly, especially when interest rates are low, it has been suggested that the best course of action may be to arrange the transaction as a term loan that states adequate interest. Because adequate interest is stated, it can be paid annually, or even accrued until the end of the term, instead of treated as being transferred upon creation of the loan. However, if the employer directly or indirectly pays the interest to the employee, the stated interest will be disregarded, and the loan will be treated as a below-market loan under IRC § 7872.

(3) **Exception to Upfront Taxation of Imputed Interest on Term Loans.** Foregone interest on (1) split-dollar term loans payable on the death of an individual, (2) gift term loans (which would be the norm in a private split-dollar transaction) and (3) split-dollar term loans conditioned on the future performance of substantial services by an individual, is determined annually, in a manner similar to a demand loan, but using an AFR that is appropriate for the loan's term and that is determined when the loan is issued (not annually, as would be the case in a true demand loan). The final regulations clarify this last point.

(4) **Loan Terms.** With exceptions, the terms of life expectancy loans, gift loans and loans conditioned on the performance of future services are determined as follows:

(a) **Life Expectancy Loans.** The loan's term in the case of a split-dollar term loan payable on the death of an individual will be the individual's life expectancy determined under the appropriate table in the IRC § 72 regulations.

(b) **Gift Loan.** The loan's term in the case of a gift loan is the period from the date the loan is made to its stated maturity date.

(c) **Loans Conditioned on the Performance of Future Services.** The term of a split-dollar term loan that is conditioned on the future performance of future services is based on its stated maturity date.

(5) **Effect of OID Rules.** The OID rules of IRC §§ 1271-1275 are very complicated. However, these rules (which are income tax rules and not gift tax rules) will, in general, tax interest that is accrued, but unpaid, to the lender in a split-dollar transaction, even though the borrower is not entitled to a deduction for that interest. If unpaid interest is later forgiven, all or part of that interest, to the extent prescribed in the regulations (which in turn

21st Century Estate Planning:
Practical Applications
2005 Edition

©2005 Sonnenschein Nath & Rosenthal LLP
and Cannon Financial Institute, Inc.

327

depends on whether the loan is a term or demand loan and whether the loan bears adequate stated interest), is treated as transferred to the lender by the borrower on the date the interest is forgiven, and is treated as re-transferred by the lender to the borrower on that date. The amount deemed retransferred to the borrower is taken into income by the borrower in accordance with the relationship of the parties.

(6)   **Other**. The proposed regulations contain other provisions with respect to split-dollar loans, including provisions for variable interest rate loans, term loans containing unconditional options and contingent payment loans. In general, these rules respecting contingent payments assume that interest rates will apply and payments will be made in a manner that ascribes the lowest possible value to a contingent payment.

i.   **Material Modifications**. As stated above, the regulations are effective for arrangements entered into after September 17, 2003, and arrangements entered into before that date that are "materially modified" after that date. The final regulations provide a "non-exclusive" list of changes that are "non-material modifications," as follows:

- A change solely in the mode of premium payment (for example, a change from monthly to quarterly premiums),
- A change solely in the beneficiary of the life insurance contract, unless the beneficiary is a party to the arrangement,
- A change solely in the interest rate payable under the life insurance contract on a policy loan,
- A change solely necessary to preserve the status of the life insurance contract under IRC § 7702,
- A change solely to the ministerial provisions of the life insurance contract (for example, a change in the address to send payment),
- A change made solely under the terms of any agreement (other than the life insurance contract) that is a part of the split-dollar life insurance arrangement if the change is non-discretionary by the parties and is made pursuant to a binding commitment (whether set forth in the agreement or otherwise) in effect on or before September 17, 2003,
- A change solely in the owner of the life insurance contract as a result of a transaction to which IRC § 381(a) applies and in which substantially all of the former owner's assets are transferred to the new owner of the policy,
- A change to the policy solely if such change is required by a court or a state insurance commissioner as a result of the insolvency of the insurance company that issued the policy or
- A change solely in the insurance company that administers the policy as a result of an assumption reinsurance transaction between the issuing insurance company and the new insurance company to which the owner and the nonowner were not a party.

21st Century Estate Planning:
Practical Applications
2005 Edition

©2005 Sonnenschein Nath & Rosenthal LLP
and Cannon Financial Institute, Inc.

328

A conversion of an existing, pre-January 28, 2002, equity split-dollar life insurance arrangement to a loan pursuant to Section IV, Paragraph 4 of Notice 2002-8, also will not be considered a "material modification" for purposes of these final regulations. We note, however, that IRC § 1035 exchanges are not included among the "non-material modifications." The final regulations state that the Commissioner, in revenue rulings, notices and other published guidance, may provide additional guidance with respect to other modifications that are not material.

j. Planning for Post-Final Regulations Arrangements.

It appears that planning for post-final regulations split-dollar arrangements will have to begin by deciding whether it is in the client's interest to measure the ongoing benefit provided by the arrangement under the economic benefit regime (measuring the benefit by term cost) or under the loan regime (measuring the benefit by the foregone interest). Generally, for younger insureds and for survivorship policy arrangements, the economic benefit regime will be preferable (at least initially), while in the current, historically low interest rate environment, the loan regime will be preferable either for older insureds in single life policies or where providing an interest in policy cash values to the employee or donee without tax is important. When an economic benefit arrangement becomes uneconomic (for instance, at the first death in a survivorship arrangement), conversion to a split-dollar loan or replacement with a premium financing arrangement should be considered.

Once that decision has been made, for arrangements where economic benefit treatment is desired, the next decision will be whether the arrangement should be an equity or a non-equity arrangement. If the arrangement is a donor/donee or an employer/employee non-equity arrangement, it can be documented under the collateral assignment method and the economic benefit regime will be used to measure the benefit to the donee or the employee. But since it is a non-equity arrangement, a rollout using only policy values is not possible-a rollout will require funds of the owner not derived from the policy - meaning third party arrangements will require early and, hopefully, leveraged trust funding to allow for a rollout when economic benefits are not advantageous. That will increase the gift tax "cost" of third party split-dollar arrangements, compared to those done before the regulations.

On the other hand, if the arrangement is an equity arrangement, the employer, donor, or other premium provider will have to be the actual owner of the policy and the arrangement will need to be documented under the endorsement method. However, given the extremely broad definition of the phrase "access" in the final regulations for equity arrangements, it is not likely that many post-final regulations equity arrangements will be planned to be taxed under the economic benefit regime, especially those that are third party owned.

If, on the other hand, measuring the benefit from the arrangement is to be determined by interest rates, rather than term costs, or providing access to policy cash values to the employee or donee without tax is critical, then the arrangement will be treated initially under the loan regime - using a collateral assignment, equity arrangement. Even for arrangements initially treated under

21st Century Estate Planning:
Practical Applications
2005 Edition

©2005 Sonnenschein Nath & Rosenthal LLP
and Cannon Financial Institute, Inc.

329

the economic benefit regime, at some point, a switch to the loan regime may make sense (when economic benefits are not advantageous).

If the parties expect the borrower will use the borrower's own funds to actually pay interest, then in any arrangement in which the parties desire loan treatment, the best choice is likely to be to create a loan which provides for adequate interest (based on the applicable federal rate), either paid annually (or, less likely, accrued and paid with the principal at the insured's death).

E. Use of Insurance in Buy-Sell Agreements

Life insurance often is used as a means of funding the purchase of a shareholder's stock or a partner's partnership interest pursuant to the terms of a buy-sell agreement. If the transaction is properly structured, the life insurance can be excluded from the insured's estate. In a typical buy-sell arrangement, each shareholder owns and is the beneficiary of life insurance on the life or lives of the other shareholders.

> **EXAMPLE:** A and B form a corporation and enter into a buy-sell agreement, which, in part, provides that upon the death of one of the other shareholders, the surviving shareholder may purchase the deceased shareholder's stock at fair value, which is to be determined by an appraiser. In order to ensure that each shareholder will have sufficient liquidity to purchase the other shareholder's interest in the corporation, A takes out an insurance policy on B's life, while B takes out an insurance policy on A's life.

In the preceding example, because neither A nor B has an ownership interest in the policy on their own life, the proceeds will not be includible in either of their estates, even though the policies were purchased pursuant to a reciprocal agreement (See Rev. Rul. 56-397, 1956 C.B. 599).

➔ **Planning Point:** Should you come across a situation where the insured, rather than the other shareholder, was named as owner of the insurance policy, you may be able to prevent the insurance proceeds from being included in the insured's gross estate if you can establish that the insured's retention of incidents of ownership was due to a mistake by the agent who sold the policy (See *National Metropolitan Bank v. U.S.*, 87 F. Supp. 773 (Ct. Cl. 1950), and *Watson v. Comm'r*, 36 T.C. Memo 1084 (1977)). Alternatively, if the proceeds are included in the insured's estate, the value of the decedent's interest in the entity should be reduced by the amount of the insurance proceeds (See *Mitchell Est. v. Comm'r*, 37 B.T.A. 1 (1938) and *Tompkins Est. v. Comm'r*, 13 T.C. 1054 (1949), *acq.* 1950 C.B. 5).

21st Century Estate Planning:
Practical Applications
2005 Edition

©2005 Sonnenschein Nath & Rosenthal LLP
and Cannon Financial Institute, Inc.

330

Buy-sell agreements also may be structured so that the corporation, rather than the shareholders, will own insurance on the lives of the shareholders. Upon a shareholder's death, the proceeds will be payable to the corporation to fund the redemption of the deceased shareholder's stock. In this situation, even if the deceased shareholder is a "controlling" shareholder, the corporation's incidents of ownership will not be attributed to the insured, because the proceeds are payable to the corporation (although the insurance will be reflected in the value of the decedent's stock interest when it is valued for estate tax purposes). The same result should obtain in the partnership context (*see Knipp Est. v. Comm'r*, 25 T.C. 153 (1955), *acq. in result* 1959-1 C.B. 4).

21ˢᵗ Century Estate Planning:
Practical Applications
2005 Edition

©2005 Sonnenschein Nath & Rosenthal LLP
and Cannon Financial Institute, Inc.

331

Chapter XI
Bibliography

Roy M. Adams, Glenn Kurlander and Kimberly L. Marlar, "Unlocking New Value From Old Policies: Life Insurance Planning And Life Settlements," *Tr. & Est.* (May 2000).

Jeffrey A. Baskies and Brian J. Samuels, "Aggressive Viatical Settlement Transactions: Gambling on Human Lives," *Est. Plan.* (February 2001).

Lawrence Brody and Lucinda A. Althauser, "Typical Life Insurance Planning Mistakes and Some Suggested Solutions," *Est. Plan.* (February 2001).

Thomas F. Commito, "FLPs and LLCs Vs. Trusts In Life Insurance Planning," *Tr. & Est.* (March 1999).

Richard B. Covey, "Irrevocable Life Insurance Trusts," Loews New York Hotel, New York, NY (June 28, 1994).

Bernard Eizen and Victor S. Levy, "New and Expanded Uses of Viatical Settlements in Insurance Planning," *Est. Plan.* (December 1999).

Mitchell Gans and Jonathan G. Blattmachr, "Life Insurance and Some Common 2035/2036 Problems: A Suggested Remedy," *Tr. & Est.* (May 2000).

Sidney Kess and Lee Slavutin, "Planning Techniques and Tips," *Estate Planning Review* (July 21, 1999).

Stephan R. Leimberg, "'Policies' For Valuation Of Life Insurance," *Tr. & Est.* (March 2000).

Kevin D. Millard, Lawrence Brody and Norman H. Lane, *The Insurance Counselor, Federal Gift, Estate, and Generation-Skipping Transfer Taxation of Life Insurance* (2nd ed.).

Howard J. Saks, "Viatical Settlements: New Opportunities for Wealthy Individuals and Business Owners," *Est. Plan.* (January 1999).

Lee Slavutin, "Life Insurance Tax Traps," *Tr. & Est.* (August 1999).

Michael H. Zuckerman and John G. Grall, "Corporate Buy-Sell Agreements as Estate and Business Planning Tools," *Est. Plan.* (December 2001).

---

[1] The material in this section was derived principally from Roy M. Adams, Glenn Kurlander and Kimberly L. Marlar, "Unlocking New Value From Old Policies: Life Insurance Planning and Life Settlements." *Tr. & Est.* (May 2001).

21st Century Estate Planning:
Practical Applications
2005 Edition

©2005 Sonnenschein Nath & Rosenthal LLP
and Cannon Financial Institute, Inc.

332

XII. PLANNING FOR IRAS, QUALIFIED PLANS AND OTHER RETIREMENT BENEFITS

A. Introduction

The amount of wealth amassed in workplace retirement plans and IRAs is staggering. An understanding of the types of retirement plans, their distinguishing characteristics, their tax treatment and the available distribution options during life and at death is essential for all estate planners. This chapter will review a number of important concepts relating to employee benefit plans, and how to integrate them into your client's estate plan. Included will be discussion of the following topics:

- An overview of the common types of tax qualified and non-qualified employee benefit plans.
- A discussion of the different types of individual retirement plans, including Roth IRAs.
- An explanation of the importance of tax deferred savings.
- A review of the income tax rules that apply to both qualified and non-qualified employee benefit and individual retirement plans, including how contributions to and withdrawals from these plans are treated for federal income tax purposes.
- A description of the penalties that can apply when a taxpayer contributes too much, withdraws too soon, or fails to withdraw on time, from a qualified plan or IRA.
- A detailed explanation of the rules for calculating minimum required distributions from qualified plans and IRAs.
- An overview of the estate and gift taxation of qualified plans and IRAs, including an explanation of the income tax deduction for federal estate taxes paid on such plans under Code § 691(c).
- Basic estate planning strategies and considerations for qualified plans and IRAs.
- Marital deduction issues that arise in connection with the post-death distribution of qualified plans and IRAs.
- Charitable giving strategies for qualified plans and IRAs.

This chapter will primarily address benefits received from "qualified" retirement plans under Internal Revenue Code ("IRC") § 401(a), which include pension, profit sharing, 401(k) and self-employed (Keogh) plans; not-for-profit corporation, school and church sponsored plans under IRC § 403(b); individual retirement plans (IRAs) under IRC § 408(a); and simplified employee plans (SEPs) under IRC § 408(k).

21st Century Estate Planning:
Practical Applications
2005 Edition

©2005 Sonnenschein Nath & Rosenthal LLP
and Cannon Financial Institute, Inc.

333

B. Types of Retirement Plans

1. Qualified Plans and Non-Qualified Plans

Most employees are covered under employer sponsored retirement plans that are "qualified" retirement plans under IRC § 401(a). A qualified plan is one that provides favorable income tax benefits for the employer (income tax deduction for contributions to the plan), as well as for the employee (both contributions to the plan and earnings in the plan are not subject to income tax until they are withdrawn). However, in order to receive these tax benefits the plans must by design, funding and administration meet a complex set of federal statutory and regulatory requirements.

In contrast, a non-qualified plan is any other retirement plan or deferred compensation plan. Non-qualified plans are subject to much simpler federal regulation, along with less favorable income tax treatment. Non-qualified plans are created primarily for executives, highly compensated and select employees as a form of deferred compensation or supplemental retirement benefit.

2. Defined Benefit Plans and Defined Contribution Plans

An employer may establish and maintain one or more of several different types of plans as qualified employee benefit plans. Such plans are classified as either *defined benefit* plans or as *defined contribution* plans.

a. Defined Benefit Plans. A *defined benefit plan* is a plan designed primarily to provide income at retirement. Benefits are generally not available until the participant reaches a specified age, referred to as normal retirement age, and are usually paid in the form of an annuity. Some plans also provide an optional benefit at an earlier age (early retirement age). Treas. Reg. § 1.401-1(b)(1)(i). The employee's entitlement under the plan is calculated with reference to the benefit formula contained in the plan, and not with reference to the amount of contributions made, or earnings in, the plan. As a result, a defined benefit plan can accumulate assets in excess of those actually required to pay benefits under the plan (an "over-funded" plan), or may not have enough assets in the plan to pay all benefits (an "under-funded" plan).

A pension plan benefit formula must be designed so that an employee's retirement benefit is definitely determinable. The potential types of benefit formulas in a defined benefit plan are unlimited, but generally fall into four categories: fixed benefit, flat benefit, unit credit and cash balance.

- A *fixed benefit plan* provides a benefit that is a stated amount, such as $150 per month. The same benefit is paid to all participants, regardless of compensation.
- A *flat benefit plan* calculates a participant's normal retirement benefit as a percentage of the participant's compensation. A retirement benefit

21st Century Estate Planning:
Practical Applications
2005 Edition

©2005 Sonnenschein Nath & Rosenthal LLP
and Cannon Financial Institute, Inc.

- 334 -

equal to 50% of the employee's average compensation would be a flat benefit.

- A *unit credit plan* usually provides a benefit that is a combination of length of service and the participant's annual average compensation. This is accomplished by multiplying the participant's compensation (as defined in the plan) times years of service.

  > **EXAMPLE**: A *unit credit plan* contains a benefit formula that provides that the annual retirement benefit of each participant will equal 2% of compensation (average of all years) times years of service. If the employee's average compensation was $50,000 and the employee worked for 30 years, the annual retirement benefit would be $50,000 x 2% = $1,000, times 30 years of service = $30,000 annual benefit. The monthly benefit would be $30,000/12 months = $2,500 monthly benefit.

- A *cash balance plan* is a defined benefit plan that is made to look like a defined contribution plan. In a cash balance plan, the participant is given a hypothetical account that increases or decreases annually as a result of two types of credits: a compensation credit, based on the participant's compensation, and an interest credit, equal to a guaranteed rate that is stated in the plan.

Since the purpose of any defined benefit plan is to provide retirement security, the employer is subject to minimum funding rules that require the employer to make regular contributions to the plan. IRC § 412. Failure to make these contributions will subject the employer to a penalty. IRC § 4973.

b. Defined Contribution Plans. Plans that provide for individual participant account balances are classified as defined contribution plans. ERISA § 3(2)(A), 29 US § 1002 (2)(A). With a defined contribution plan, the participant's benefit under the plan is based solely on the amount of contributions made for or by the participant, increased by reallocated forfeitures (if applicable), and increased or decreased by gains, losses, and expenses. It is not possible for a defined contribution plan to be over-funded or under-funded.

Since each participant's benefit is ultimately based on contributions, a defined contribution plan must maintain individual bookkeeping accounts for each participant. However, this separate individual account requirement is merely a bookkeeping requirement. It does not require a plan to actually physically segregate each participant's account. IRC § 414(i).

c. Pension, profit sharing and stock bonus plans. Another way to distinguish among qualified plans is with reference to whether they are pension, profit sharing or stock bonus plans. Almost all defined benefit plans are pension plans. However, not all pension plans are defined benefit plans. A "money purchase pension plan," for example, is actually a

21st Century Estate Planning:
Practical Applications
2005 Edition

©2005 Sonnenschein Nath & Rosenthal LLP
and Cannon Financial Institute, Inc.

- 335 -

defined contribution plan to which the employer contributes a defined or fixed percentage of the participating employee's compensation each year. It is called a money purchase pension plan because the employer must fund the plan each year, under the minimum funding rules of IRC § 412 (similar to defined benefit plans), and the amount in the participant's account at retirement is usually not distributed in a lump sum, but rather is used to purchase an annuity.

Most defined contribution plans are profit sharing plans. Profit sharing plans acquired their name from the regulations prior to 1986 when an employer could contribute to a profit sharing plan only if the employer had current or accumulated profits. Treas. Reg. § 1.401-1(b)(1)(ii). This requirement was eliminated by the Tax Reform Act of 1986 ("TRA 1986"), P.L. 99-514. An employer may now make contributions to a profit sharing plan without regard to profits (IRC § 401(a)(27)(A)), and the plan does not have to require that a contribution be made each year, as long as contributions are "reoccurring and substantial." Treas. Reg. § 1.401-1(b)(2).

3. Characteristics and Features of Qualified Plans

a. Defined Benefit Plans. Employer contributions to a defined benefit plan are actuarially determined each year. The employer receives an income tax deduction for all contributions made to the plan when contributed. IRC § 404(a) and § 403(a). The contributions and all earnings in the plan are not subject to income tax when received by the plan, and accumulate in the plan without current income tax. IRC § 501(a).

The maximum benefit that can be provided to a participant under a defined benefit plan is measured two ways: the percentage limitation and the dollar amount limitation. Under the percentage limitation, the retirement benefit may not exceed 100% of average compensation for the highest three consecutive years of employment. (For a self-employed person, compensation is limited to "net" self-employment income, *i.e.*, gross income less the contribution and one half of the deduction for the self-employment tax.) The dollar amount limitation is indexed at $170,000 per year (for 2005) for a retirement age of 65. For early retirement age, the amount is actuarially reduced.

The normal form of benefit from a defined benefit plan must be a Qualified Joint and Survivor Annuity. Other forms of distribution are available with spousal consent. Distributions are generally taxed as ordinary income under IRC § 72. However, those participants born before 1936 may be able to elect favorable income tax treatment in the form of 10-year forward averaging or capital gains treatment. Distributions also may be rolled over to an IRA or another workplace retirement plan at retirement (if the plan allows lump sum distributions). IRC § 402 and § 403.

b. Defined Contribution Plans. In a defined contribution money purchase pension plan, the employer contributes a fixed percentage of the employee's compensation each year (under the minimum funding rules in IRC § 412). In a defined contribution profit sharing plan, the employer determines the amount the employer wishes to contribute to the plan in a

21st Century Estate Planning:
Practical Applications
2005 Edition

©2005 Sonnenschein Nath & Rosenthal LLP
and Cannon Financial Institute, Inc.

- 336 -

gross dollar amount, usually on an annual basis (but possibly more frequently). Contributions are then allocated to each participant's account based on each participant's compensation in relation to that of all compensation of participants in the plan. In each case, the employer receives an income tax deduction in an amount equal to the contribution. IRC § 404(a). Contributions are not currently taxed to the employee (IRC § 402(a) and 403 (a)), and both contributions and earnings accumulate in the plan without current income tax. IRC § 501(a).

The maximum annual contribution is 25% of covered payroll, not to exceed 100% of the individual participant's compensation up to $42,000 (Section 616 of the Economic Growth and Tax Relief Reconciliation Act of 2001 ("EGTRRA 2001"), P.L. 107-16) for 2005. The maximum compensation recognized in 2005 is $210,000, and for those who are self-employed, compensation is limited to "net" self-employment income (gross income less the contribution and one half of the deduction allowed for self-employment tax).

Distributions are not allowed from money purchase plans while the participant is employed ("in-service withdrawals")(IRS Memorandum of the District Director of the Los Angeles Key District dated August 10, 1995). In service withdrawals maybe allowed from profit sharing plans, however. A profit sharing plan may allow distributions after a fixed number of years, the attainment of a stated age, or upon the occurrence of stated events such as layoffs, illness or disability. Treas. Reg. § 1.401-1(6)(1)(ii).

When distributions are made they are generally taxed as ordinary income under IRC § 72. However, participants born before 1936 may be able to elect favorable income tax treatment in the form of 10-year forward averaging or capital gains treatment. Distributions also may be rolled over to another workplace retirement plan or IRA. IRC § 402 and § 403.

c. **Stock Bonus Plans**. The requirements of a stock bonus plan are identical to those of a profit sharing plan with two major exceptions. First, benefits under a stock bonus plan may be distributed in cash or stock of the employer maintaining the plan. Second, the plan may, but is not required to, invest primarily in the employer's stock.

d. **Employer Stock Ownership Plans (ESOPs)**. An ESOP is first and foremost a qualified stock bonus plan. But there are some important basic differences. The primary difference is that an ESOP must be primarily invested in stock of the employer company. Income tax treatment (to the employer and to the employee) of contributions to and earnings in an ESOP is the same as any other profit sharing plan.

An ESOP has a number of unique characteristics. An ESOP is exempt from many of the prohibited transaction rules applicable to most qualified plans, such as the normal prohibition against borrowing funds to purchase securities from a shareholder or the plan sponsor. The plan sponsor in turn may guaranty the loan. For these transactions to be deemed exempt from the penalties normally imposed on prohibited transactions, they must be entered into for the primary benefit of the participants and their beneficiaries. Treas. Reg. § 54.4975-7(b)(3).

21st Century Estate Planning:
Practical Applications
2005 Edition

©2005 Sonnenschein Nath & Rosenthal LLP
and Cannon Financial Institute, Inc.

- 337 -

Unlike any other qualified plans, an ESOP may serve as a financing tool for the employer. The intricacies of the leveraged ESOP are beyond the scope of this chapter. But the concept is straightforward. Under a leveraged ESOP, the plan borrows money from a commercial lender to purchase the stock owned by a shareholder of the plan sponsor. The loan is secured by the stock and is guaranteed by the sponsor. Contributions to the ESOP are in amounts sufficient to amortize the loan. The ESOP uses the contributions to the plan to repay the loan and, as the loan is repaid, shares of stock are released from the loan collateral and allocated to participant accounts. IRC § 404(a)(9).

An individual who sells a substantial amount of stock to an ESOP may be able to defer recognition of the gain on the sale by investing the proceeds in qualified replacement securities. IRC § 1042.

      e. <u>**401(k) Plans**</u>. In 1978, IRC § 401(k) was added to the Code, creating what is known as a "cash or deferred arrangement," or, more commonly, 401(k) plans. A 401(k) plan is a qualified profit sharing plan that includes an option for participants to direct the employer to put money in the plan in lieu of paying the employee taxable cash compensation. A 401(k) plan can be an independent plan, or it can be part of a profit sharing or stock bonus plan. A 401(k) plan can accept both employee and employer contributions, or it can be funded entirely through salary deferrals.

Since a 401(k) plan allows employees to choose deferrals or cash, a disproportionate benefit could be provided under the plan for highly compensated employees, who have more income to save. Consequently, the law requires that the plan comply with certain contribution limitations for highly compensated employees, as compared to all other employees covered by the plan. These limitations are commonly referred to as the ADP test, or average deferred percentage test, and the ACP test, or actual contribution percentage test. IRC § 401(k)(3), § 401(a), § 401(m)(2), and § 410(b).

In a 401(k) plan, the employee elects to defer a portion of salary or bonus. Amounts deferred are subject to FICA and FUTA taxes, but are not subject to current income tax. The employer may provide a voluntary matching contribution, which is tax deductible to the employer. IRC § 404(a). Contributions and earnings accumulate in the plan without current income tax, either to the employee or to the plan. IRC §§ 510(a), § 402(a) and § 403(a). Employers may make additional profit sharing contributions from year to year, as long as they are non-discriminatory.

New employee contribution limits under IRC § 402(g) were enacted under EGTRRA 2001. The employee deferral limit is 100% of compensation up to a maximum of $14,000 in 2005. The limit is increased to $15,000 in 2006. After 2006, the contribution limit is indexed to the cost of living annually, rounded down to the nearest $500. A new provision for "catch-up" contributions for individuals 50 years of age or older was added to IRC § 414(v), effective for years after 2001. An individual 50 years old or older will be able to elect additional deferrals of

21st Century Estate Planning:
Practical Applications
2005 Edition

©2005 *Sonnenschein Nath & Rosenthal LLP*
and Cannon Financial Institute, Inc.

- 338 -

$4,000 in 2005 and $5,000 in 2006. After 2006, the amount of catch-up deferrals is indexed to the cost of living annually, rounded down to the nearest $500.

f. Other Types of Qualified Plans or Hybrid Plans. Each of the following hybrid plans is a variation on a deferred contribution plan that has a unique allocation formula for the contributions that are made to the plan.

(1) Target Benefit Plans. This is a hybrid money purchase pension plan under which an employer establishes a targeted retirement benefit for each participant. However, the projected benefit is merely a target the plan uses to determine current contributions; it is not a guarantee.

(2) Age Weighted Profit Sharing Plans. Age weighted plans are no different from other types of profit sharing plans except that the contribution is allocated among the participants based not only on each participant's compensation, but also on each participant's age.

(3) New Comparability Plans. New comparability plans are profit sharing plans structured to provide a more uniform allocation of contributions among members of a group (such as among all highly compensated employees or among all non-highly compensated employees). Thus, unlike an age-weighted plan, the plan's allocation of contributions will not be age based.

4. Plan Qualification Requirements: An Overview

A complete discussion of qualified plan requirements is beyond the scope of this text. The following is intended to review and summarize some of the most significant requirements for employee benefit plan qualification. Keep in mind that these are general rules only, to which many complex exceptions and limitations apply.

a. Eligibility and Coverage. A qualified employer plan may contain an eligibility requirement, which sets forth who may participate in the plan and when they may join. However, as a general rule, the law prohibits basing eligibility on a minimum age higher than 21 and minimum service of more than one year. Moreover, in operation, a qualified plan must benefit a certain proportion of non-highly-compensated employees in relation to highly compensated employees.

b. Nondiscrimination in Benefits and Contributions. Much of the law pertaining to qualified plans was written to ensure that the plan does not unduly or unfairly benefit a company's officers, directors or key executives at the expense of rank and file employees. Consequently, a plan must be designed so that it does not discriminate, either in benefits provided or in contributions made, in favor of highly compensated employees.

c. Funding. Qualified plans must be funded in advance of employee retirement. Normally this is accomplished through contributions to an irrevocable trust fund or

21st Century Estate Planning:
Practical Applications
2005 Edition

©*2005 Sonnenschein Nath & Rosenthal LLP*
and Cannon Financial Institute, Inc.

- 339 -

under an insurance contract. The law also requires that a fiduciary -- a person or entity empowered to hold funds of another -- must control the fund for the sole benefit of the participants and their beneficiaries. This limits the control the employer has over the plan's funds, as was the intent.

d. Vesting. Vesting refers to the point at which an employee has a non-forfeitable and undeniable right to the benefit provided for the employee under the plan. Under current vesting rules, an employee must be fully vested at the normal retirement date specified in the plan and, in the event of termination prior to retirement, after a specified period of service. The purpose of the vesting rules is to make it difficult for an employer to deny benefits to employees by selective turnover, termination or other arbitrary acts.

The law has established two alternative vesting schedules. Five-year "cliff" vesting provides for no vesting during the first four years of service, and 100% vesting at five years. Three-year to seven-year vesting provides for a gradual vesting of the benefit, beginning the third year of service with 20%, and increasing each year by 20%, with 100% vesting in the seventh year.

e. Limitations on Contributions and Benefits. The Code limits the amount of benefit that can be received (under a defined benefit plan) or the amount of contribution that can be made (to a defined contribution plan). These limitations are stated above in the discussion of defined benefit plans and defined contribution plans.

f. Reporting and Disclosure. All qualified plans must meet certain reporting and disclosure requirements -- some simple, many complex. Generally, these requirements consist of four reports that must be provided to plan participants and/or filed with the government.

- A *Summary Plan Description* describes the plan, identifies the plan sponsor, indicates the funding mechanism, explains the plan's eligibility requirements and identifies procedures for making benefit claims. This report is furnished to plan participants and the Department of Labor.
- An *Annual Report* includes detailed financial information about the plan, including actuarial valuations if the plan is subject to minimum funding requirements, and identifies participants with vested benefits who have separated from the plan. This report is filed with the IRS.
- A *Summary of Annual Report* summarizes the annual report, and is provided to plan participants.
- A *Report on Termination, Merger or Other Changes* reports on any plan that is to be terminated, merged, split-up, etc.

g. Top-Heavy Plans. Special qualification rules were added to address plans that are "top heavy," *i.e.*, plans in which the accrued benefits or account balances of key employees (as defined in the Code) exceed the value of all accrued benefits or all account

21st Century Estate Planning:
Practical Applications
2005 Edition

©2005 Sonnenschein Nath & Rosenthal LLP
and Cannon Financial Institute, Inc.

- 340 -

balances by a specified percentage. Essentially, these special top-heavy rules were imposed to restrict the use of qualified plans as tax shelters for business owners and highly compensated employees, and to provide a way to measure potential discrimination in benefits. A plan must provide that if it ever meets the definition of a top-heavy plan on a given determination date, all of the top-heavy restrictions will automatically become part of the plan.

Many small plans -- those that cover 10 or fewer participants, for example -- are by their nature top-heavy, and these plans are actually designed according to top-heavy requirements and restrictions. Generally, these requirements (which are in addition to, not in lieu of, the qualification requirements all plans must meet) subject top-heavy plans to accelerated vesting, minimum contribution or benefit requirements for non-key employees, and lowered benefit or contribution levels for key-employees.

> **h. <u>Distributions</u>.** To ensure that qualified plans are primarily used for the purpose of providing retirement or deferred compensation benefits, there are a number of restrictions and rules that apply to distributions. These are discussed in more detail below. The rules are complex and to some extent vary according to the type of plan. Pension plans, for example, do not allow withdrawal of funds prior to termination of employment, whereas profit sharing plans may.

> **5. Not-for-Profit Corporations, School and Church Sponsored Plans**

Section 403(b) plans (also known as tax-sheltered annuities or TDAs) are available to public school systems and tax-exempt organizations described in IRC § 503(c)(3) of the Code, which include those operating exclusively for religious, charitable, scientific, literary or educational purposes. This definition encompasses a wide range of non-profit institutions such as churches, private and public schools and colleges, hospitals and charitable organizations.

EGTRAA 2001 § 632 amended IRC § 403(b) so that the benefits available under 403(b) plans are similar to those available under qualified profit sharing plans -- more specifically, Section 401(k) plans. The most common type of 403(b) plan is a salary reduction plan. It allows the participant to elect to contribute part of his or her salary to the plan (as opposed to receiving it as taxable income). The typical arrangement involves the use of a deferred annuity, fixed or variable, as the funding instrument. Premiums paid into the contract (within limits) are excluded from the employee's gross income. Mutual funds are another accepted funding vehicle.

> **a. <u>Contribution Limits</u>.** Since the beginning of 2002, employees who participate in 403(b) plans are not taxed currently on either salary reductions or employee contributions as long as the total does not exceed the lesser of $40,000 or 100% of the employee's compensation. Salary reductions also are subject to an aggregate annual limit. The employee must add together each year all of his or her salary reductions for TDA plans, Section 401(k) plans, salary reduction SEPs and Simple IRAs. The total must not exceed the elective deferral limit, which is $14,000 in 2005 and $15,000 in 2006. After 2006, the elective deferral limit is scheduled to be adjusted for cost-of-living increases annually, in increments of $500.

21st Century Estate Planning:
Practical Applications
2005 Edition

©2005 Sonnenschein Nath & Rosenthal LLP
and Cannon Financial Institute, Inc.

- 341 -

b. Unique Salary Reduction Catch-up for 403(b) Plans. If the employee has completed 15 years of service for the employer, and the employer is an education organization, a hospital, a home health care agency, a health and welfare service agency, or a church, synagogue or related organization, the elective deferral limit (above) is increased by an additional sum equal to the lower of:

- $3,000;
- $15,000, reduced by any amounts excluded from gross income for prior taxable years by reason of the catch-up provision; or
- $5,000 times the employee's years of service with the employer, less all prior salary reductions with that employer.

The elective deferral limit, plus the salary reduction catch-up provision described in the preceding paragraph, is generally the absolute limit on the amount of annual salary reductions for any employee. However, § 403(b) plan participants who are age 50 and over are eligible for additional elective deferrals. The additional elective deferral amount is $4,000 in 2005 and $5,000 in 2006.

21st Century Estate Planning:
Practical Applications
2005 Edition

©2005 Sonnenschein Nath & Rosenthal LLP
and Cannon Financial Institute, Inc.

- 342 -

c. **Unique Distribution rule for § 403(b) Plans**. Section 403(b) plans generally are subject to the qualified retirement plan distribution rules at retirement or later. However those plans that allow for in-service withdrawals are faced with a complex and unclear set of regulations based on the investment vehicles agreed upon by the plan.

Allowable Distributions From 403(b) Plans				
Insurance Contract Plans			**403(b)(7)(Mutual Fund) Plans**	
Events	**Employer Contributions**	**Salary Reductions**	**Employer Contributions**	**Salary Reductions**
At or after age 59 ½ , death, severance from employment, disability	All amounts	All amounts	All amounts	All amounts
Hardship	All amounts	All amounts attributable to pre-1989 assets; for post-1988 assets, principal only (no income)	Amounts attributable to pre-1989 assets only	All amounts attributable to pre-1989 assets; for post-1988 assets, principal only (no income)
Other	All amounts	Amounts attributable to pre-1989 assets only	No distributions permitted	No distributions permitted

d. **Plan Requirements for § 403(b) Plans**. The requirements previously discussed for qualified plans relating to eligibility, coverage, nondiscrimination, funding, vesting and disclosure also apply to Section 403(b) plans.

21st Century Estate Planning:
Practical Applications
2005 Edition

©2005 Sonnenschein Nath & Rosenthal LLP
and Cannon Financial Institute, Inc.

- 343 -

6. Workplace Individual Retirement Plans

a. <u>SEP IRAs</u>. Introduced in 1978, SEPs were created as an alternative to the more burdensome and expensive defined benefit and defined contribution plans, to encourage more employers to adopt retirement plans for themselves and their employees. SEPs are particularly attractive to small business and professional firms. Under a SEP Plan, individual retirement accounts are established for each participating employee. The employer makes tax-deductible contributions to these accounts. These contributions and the earnings they generate are not taxed as income to the employee when made, and accumulate without current income tax until they are distributed to the employee. The employee is always fully vested in the amounts contributed to the employee's SEP account on his or her behalf; with SEPs, there is a 100% vesting requirement. Once contributions are made to an employee's SEP account, the funds belong to the employee and cannot be forfeited.

Although SEP plans are not subject to the same set of rules as conventional defined benefit and defined contribution plans, they must meet certain requirements with regard to coverage. Basically, for every year an employer makes a contribution to a SEP plan, the plan must cover each employee who is age 21 or older, who worked for the employer during at least three of the previous five years, and who earned at least a certain level of compensation ($500 in 2003) for that year.

A SEP plan is an employer plan, but it effectively operates as an expanded IRA. In other words, once an employer makes a contribution to an employee's SEP account, the control of those funds resides with employee. The employee can direct how those funds are invested and when they are distributed. The distribution rules for SEPs are similar to those that apply to traditional IRAs, and are discussed in that section.

A SEP plan is entirely employer funded. Currently, the maximum amount that an employer can contribute on behalf of any one participant in any one year is limited to $40,000, or 25% of the participant's compensation. Job Creation and Worker Assistance Act of 2002, § 411(1)(3). Only the first $200,000 of compensation can be taken into account for this purpose.

21st Century Estate Planning:
Practical Applications
2005 Edition

©2005 Sonnenschein Nath & Rosenthal LLP
and Cannon Financial Institute, Inc.

- 344 -

These contributions are not included in the participant's income, and the employer may deduct the amount contributed. SEP Plans must be treated as defined contribution plans for purposes of the overall limits on employer contributions to qualified plans.

The employee can treat his or her SEP account as an individual retirement account – which, in fact, it is – and make deductible or nondeductible contributions to it under the rules applicable to traditional IRAs, discussed below.

b. Simple IRAs. The Small Business Job Protection Act of 1996 (HR 3448) created a savings incentive match plan for employees known as a Simple Plan. These plans are available to employers that do not have qualified plans in place and that employ 100 or fewer individuals. A Simple plan can be set up like an IRA or a 401(k) plan. Both provide for elective employee contributions, employer contributions (under a formula that either matches employee contributions or under a non-elective formula) and the immediate 100% vesting of plan funds.

Employees who received at least $5,000 in compensation from the employer during any two preceding years and who are expected to receive at least that amount during the current year must be allowed to participate, if they choose, by making contributions to the plan. All contributions to a Simple plan, whether made by the employee or the employer, vest fully and immediately in the employee, and cannot be forfeited. These contributions are not currently taxable to the employee and they remain tax deferred until distributed.

Under a Simple plan, contributions are made to an IRA established for each employee. Employees who earn at least $5,000 in the current year can contribute (through salary reductions) up to $8,000 annually. The contribution limits increased to a maximum amount of $10,000 in 2005.

Since the beginning of 2002, participants who have reached the age of 50 during the plan year may be permitted to make "catch-up" contributions, in addition to the limits listed above. The limit for catch-up contributions is $2,000 in 2005 and $2,500 in 2006.

The employer is required to make a contribution equal to either:

- A dollar for dollar matching contribution of up to 3% of the employee's compensation (the employer can elect a lower percentage, not less than 1%, in no more than two out of the five years ending with the current year), or
- 2% of compensation for all eligible employees earning at least $5,000 (whether or not they elect salary reductions).

Distributions to employees are generally treated the same as distributions from a traditional IRA, discussed below. However, the 10% penalty tax on early distributions is increased to 25% during the first two years of participation. Furthermore, while a rollover may be made at any time from one SIMPLE IRA to another SIMPLE IRA, a rollover from a SIMPLE

21st Century Estate Planning:
Practical Applications
2005 Edition

©2005 *Sonnenschein Nath & Rosenthal LLP*
and Cannon Financial Institute, Inc.

- 345 -

IRA to a traditional IRA during the first two years of participation is permitted only in the case of distributions to which the 25% early distribution penalty does not apply.

7. Individual Retirement Accounts

IRAs were first introduced in 1974 as a way for those who were not covered by an employer plan to save on a tax-deferred basis for their retirement. Since their introduction IRAs have been subject to many changes – some expansive, other restrictive. The most recent changes were the introduction of the Roth IRA and the so-called Education IRA, which has sparked a flood of new interest in these plans.

a. **Traditional IRAs**. A traditional IRA can be established by anyone who is under age 70½ and has earned income. Earned income includes wages, salaries, fees, tips and commissions; it does not include investment earnings, interest or dividends, rental income, retirement benefits or disability benefits. Since the beginning of 2002, up to $3,000 or 100% of earned income, whichever is less, may be contributed to an IRA on an annual basis. The earnings on IRA funds are not currently taxable to the IRA owner, and thus the account grows on a tax-deferred basis. Working spouses who file joint returns may each establish an IRA and contribute up to $3,000 each, or $6,000 combined.

The maximum allowable annual IRA contribution is scheduled to increase in 2005 to $4,000, and in 2008 to $5,000. Beginning in 2009, the maximum allowable annual contribution amount will be adjusted for inflation. Since the beginning of 2002, individuals who are 50 years of age or older can contribute additional "catch-up" contributions to an IRA of $500 per year. This amount is scheduled to increase in 2006 to $1,000.

(1) **Spousal IRAs**. A spousal IRA allows for additional contributions of up to $3,000 a year for a spouse who does not have any earned income, or whose earned income is less than $3,000. The typical arrangement is to establish two separate IRA accounts – one for the working spouse and the other for the non-working spouse. A maximum of $6,000 can be contributed for both accounts each year, though no more than $3,000 can be directed to either one account. Annual contribution limits for spousal IRAs will increase in the same manner as contribution limits for Traditional IRAs.

(2) **Traditional IRA Funding**. There are two basic approaches to funding an IRA: through an individual retirement account or an individual retirement annuity. An individual retirement account is a plan established by a written trust or custodial agreement through a bank, brokerage house, mutual fund or other approved sponsor. In this way, IRA funds can be invested in certificates of deposit, stocks, bonds, mutual funds or commodities. They cannot be invested in collectibles (works of art, gem stones, antiques), though certain silver, gold and platinum coins are acceptable. A bank or institution that serves as trustee or custodian may prepare its own prototype IRA agreement for IRS approval, or use IRS prototypes. By contrast, an individual retirement annuity is a contract issued by a life insurance

21st Century Estate Planning:
Practical Applications
2005 Edition

©2005 Sonnenschein Nath & Rosenthal LLP
and Cannon Financial Institute, Inc.

- 346 -

company that meets requirements similar to those described above. The premium on the contract is the contributions made. The product used is a flexible premium annuity, variable or fixed.

(3)   Traditional   IRA   Contributions: Deductible   and Nondeductible. When IRAs were first created, only those who were not actively participating in an employer-sponsored retirement program were eligible to establish an IRA and claim a deduction for any contribution. This law was changed in 1981, opening IRA eligibility to anyone who had earned income, and allowing full deductions for any IRA contribution within the prescribed limits. In 1986, the law changed again and returned to the earlier rule, limiting deductible IRA contributions only to those employees who were not active participants in another qualified retirement plan.

Today, anyone who is earning income (and is under age 70½) can establish and contribute to a traditional IRA. The IRA participant's ability to deduct those contributions depends in part on whether the IRA participant also is an active participant in an employer-sponsored plan. An individual who is not an active participant in another qualified plan can deduct the full amount of a traditional IRA contribution. An individual who is an active participant in another qualified plan can deduct IRA contributions fully, partially or not at all, depending on the level of his or her adjusted gross income ("AGI"). If your spouse is an active participant in a qualified plan, your spouse's participation will be attributed to you, limiting your ability to deduct IRA contributions, after another, higher level of AGI. All of these AGI limitations on the deductibility of IRA contributions are adjusted for inflation, and change periodically.

Individuals who cannot deduct any part of an IRA contribution can still make nondeductible IRA contributions. Conversely, IRA owners can elect to treat contributions that would otherwise be deductible as nondeductible.

Deductible or nondeductible, contributions to an IRA cannot exceed the allowable annual amount. Under the provisions of IRC § 4973, if a contribution greater than the allowable amount is made, the excess is subject to a six percent penalty tax each year until it is withdrawn.

b.   Roth IRAs. In 1997, the Taxpayer Relief Act (P.L. 105-34) introduced a new kind of IRA: the Roth IRA. Roth IRAs are unique in that they provide for "back-end" tax benefits. No deduction can be taken for contributions made to a Roth IRA, but the earnings on those contributions are entirely tax-free, both while in the Roth IRA and when they are withdrawn.

Up to $3,000 a year can be contributed to a Roth IRA for any one eligible individual; up to $3,000 can be contributed on behalf of a non-working spouse. Active participant status is not relevant – an individual can contribute to a Roth IRA regardless of whether he or she is covered by another employer plan or maintains and contributes to other IRA accounts. However, it should be noted that the $3,000 annual limit on contributions applies collectively to both traditional and Roth IRAs. No more than this amount can be contributed in any year for any account or combination of accounts. (An employer contribution to a SEP IRA or a SIMPLE IRA does not affect the contribution limit for an individual IRA account, traditional or Roth.) The annual contribution limit for Roth IRAs will increase in the same manner as the contribution limits for traditional IRAs.

Unlike traditional IRAs, which are limited to those under 70½, Roth IRAs impose no age limit. Any individual with earned income can establish a Roth IRA at any age and make contributions. ("Earned income" for this purpose is defined exactly the same as it is for traditional IRAs.) On the other hand, Roth IRAs are subject to income limits that traditional IRAs are not. High-income earners may not be able to contribute to a Roth IRA. The maximum annual contribution that can be made to a Roth IRA ($4,000 in 2005) begins to phase out for individuals whose modified adjusted gross incomes reach certain levels. Once AGI exceeds those levels, Roth contributions are no longer allowed.

The AGI phase-out for Roth IRA contributions is:

- For unmarried individuals: $95,000-$110,000.
- For married individuals filing joint returns: $150,000 - $160,000.
- For married individuals filing separate returns: $0-$10,000.

➔ **Planning Point**: There is a debate over whether it is better to make deductible IRA contributions or nondeductible Roth IRA contributions. But there is no debate between nondeductible IRA contributions and Roth IRA contributions. If you are not eligible to deduct IRA contributions, you are always better off making Roth IRA contributions, if you are eligible to do so.

    c. Education IRAs. Education IRAs are not really IRAs at all, and are more properly called Coverdell Education Savings Accounts. They are governed by IRC §530. Many (but not all) of the rules that apply to Education Savings Accounts are similar to the rules that apply to IRAs, and contributions are limited both by the amount that can be added to such accounts each year and the AGI of the person contributing to the account. However, Education Savings Accounts (as the name implies) are a vehicle for saving for educational expenses, not retirement, and are discussed in another chapter.

    d. Limits on the Deductibility of IRA Contributions. The available IRA options and contribution limits have become increasingly complex. The following chart from IRS Publication 590 summarizes the AGI limitations for the deductibility of IRA contributions for tax year 2005.

21st Century Estate Planning:
Practical Applications
2005 Edition

©2005 Sonnenschein Nath & Rosenthal LLP
and Cannon Financial Institute, Inc.

- 348 -

If you are covered by a retirement plan at work, use this table to determine if your modified AGI affects the amount of your deduction.

IF your filing status is …	AND your modified adjusted gross income (modified AGI) is …	THEN you can take…
Single or Head of Household	$45,000 or less	A full deduction
	More than $45,000 but less than $55,000	A partial deduction
	$55,000 or more	No deduction
Married Filing Jointly or Qualifying Widow(er)	$65,000 or less	A full deduction
	More than $65,000 but less than $75,000	A partial deduction
	$75,000 or more	No deduction
Married Filing Separately	Less than $10,000	A partial deduction
	$10,000 or more	No deduction

C. The Economic Advantages of Tax Deferred Savings

The primary advantage of saving for retirement within any type of tax deferred investment program is the impact of compounding earnings on a tax deferred basis. It is impossible to exactly compare a taxable investment program with a tax deferred investment program because of the numerous variables that come into play, such as the income tax rates that apply to different types of investments (ordinary income versus capital gains rates), state and local taxes, the timing of the payment of taxes (either when earned or on the sale of a security), and varying rates of investment return (*e.g.*, the interest rate on tax-free municipal bonds versus the after-tax rate on taxable bonds). However, a hypothetical example that has clear assumptions may be useful to illustrate the economic advantages of tax deferred savings over time. Consider the following:

Assumptions:

Annual Contribution: $2,000

Annual Return: 10%

Combined state and federal marginal income tax bracket: 30%

Contributions are made at the end of each year.

Taxes are due when the funds are distributed from the IRA.

21st Century Estate Planning:
Practical Applications
2005 Edition

©2005 Sonnenschein Nath & Rosenthal LLP
and Cannon Financial Institute, Inc.

- 349 -

	Tax Deferred		Currently Taxable	
Years Until Withdrawal of Funds	IRA Balance Assuming a $2,000 Annual Deductible Contribution	After-tax Amount if Withdrawn from the IRA at a 30% Income Tax Rate	$1400 Annual Contribution Invested at an Equivalent After-Tax Rate of 7.0%	Benefit Due to Tax-Deferral
5	$12,210	$8,547	$8,051	$496
10	$31,875	$22,312	$19,343	$2,969
15	$63,545	$44,481	$35,181	$9,301
20	$114,550	$80,185	$57,394	$22,791
25	$196,694	$137,686	$88,549	$49,137
30	$328,988	$230,292	$132,245	$98,047
35	$542,049	$379,434	$193,532	$185,902
40	$885,185	$619,630	$279,489	$340,140

This is fundamentally a time use of money analysis. For the period of tax deferral, you are using the government's money (the deferred income taxes) to earn money for you. The longer the period of tax deferral, the larger the overall economic benefit. This analysis holds true even if the applicable income tax rates on a currently taxable investment program are lower than ordinary rates, or are partially deferred (*i.e.* capital gains). It may take a longer period of deferral to show an economic advantage under those circumstances, but over time compounded tax deferred earnings is almost always economically superior.

D. The Income Tax Treatment of Distributions from Qualified Plans and IRAs

1. Types of Distributions

There are generally four types of distributions that might be made from a qualified plan: a lump sum distribution, a loan, an annuity and discretionary distributions.

21st Century Estate Planning:
Practical Applications
2005 Edition

©2005 Sonnenschein Nath & Rosenthal LLP
and Cannon Financial Institute, Inc.

- 350 -

a. **Lump-Sum Distributions. A lump-sum distribution by IRS definition is one that:**

- Is taken from a qualified pension, profit-sharing or stock bonus plan;
- Is made in one taxable year of the participant;
- Consists of the entire balance in the participant's plan (for this purpose, all pension plans must be treated as one plan, all profit-sharing plans must be treated as one plan and all employer stock bonus plans must be treated as one plan); and
- Is payable on account of the participant's death, disability, attainment of age 59½ or separation from the employer's service. (The disability requirement applies only to self-employed individuals; the separation from service requirement applies only to common-law employees and not to the self-employed.)

Only qualified *employer* plans can make lump sum distributions. Lump sum distributions are normally associated with account-based plans, such as 401(k) and profit-sharing plans, but may be available under certain defined benefit plans as well. Lump sum distributions are, by definition, eligible for certain types of favorable income tax treatment, including forward averaging, discussed below. Since it is not possible to take a lump sum distribution from an IRA, SEP or 403(b) plan, none of these plans are eligible for forward averaging or other forms of favorable income tax treatment.

Many lump sum distributions are rolled over. A *rollover* allows a participant to take a tax-free distribution from one qualified plan and deposit it into another plan (or plans), continuing tax deferral.

b. **Loans**. It may be a stretch to call a *loan* a distribution, but given that our definition of distribution is "any outflow from a retirement plan," a loan would qualify. The law allows certain plans to include provisions for loans to participants. Such provisions are not required, however, and a participant cannot borrow from his or her plan unless the plan specifically allows it. Loan provisions are common to profit-sharing plans, 401(k) plans and 403(b) plans. However, IRAs and SEPs are not allowed to make loans.

Plan loans taken in accordance with the conditions prescribed by the plan and by law are without tax consequences at the time the loan is made, and when it is repaid. Loans are not treated as taxable distributions or penalized distributions. In this way, loans do have an advantage over regular distributions.

c. **Annuity Distributions**. *Annuity distributions* are specifically defined as life contingent immediate annuities or life contingent annuitizations. Withdrawals from deferred annuity plans are not annuity distributions for these purposes; they would be considered discretionary distributions. Taking distributions in the form of an annuity as defined here is not a

21st Century Estate Planning:
Practical Applications
2005 Edition

©*2005 Sonnenschein Nath & Rosenthal LLP*
and Cannon Financial Institute, Inc.

- 351 -

very popular form of plan distribution. Interestingly enough, some plans -- notably defined benefit pension plans -- offer no alternative.

Annuity payouts are taken in a variety of forms: joint and 100% survivor annuities, joint and 50% survivor annuities, single life annuities, or life annuities (single or joint) with a guaranteed minimum term. Most qualified plans offer at least some of these alternatives. Many plans, in fact, require that married participants receive their retirement benefit in the form of a joint and survivor annuity, unless both participant and spouse waive this form of benefit.

The common thread among all the annuity options is the life contingency. The advantage of the life contingency is that the participant and his or her beneficiary cannot outlive the payment stream. The disadvantage is a complete lack of flexibility and inflation protection. The annuitization of pension benefits is commonly fixed, which locks the participant and his or her beneficiary into an irrevocable income stream -- at today's dollars -- for the rest of their lives. This, of course, would become quite unattractive in an inflationary environment. Annuitized pension benefits typically cease upon the death of the participant or the participant's beneficiary. There is usually no benefit paid to any other beneficiary, other than the guaranteed minimum payment, if there is one.

d. Discretionary Distributions. The best way to define a *discretionary distribution* is by elimination. Discretionary distributions are any distributions that are not lump sum distributions, loans or annuity payouts. Discretionary distributions are just as the name implies: they are taken at the participant's discretion. They do not have to be structured. They can be taken, at will, and changed up or down, at will. They can be stopped and reinstated later. Alternatively, discretionary distributions *can* be structured, if the participant desires, so that withdrawals are taken on a systematic basis. The flexibility inherent in this method of distribution makes it quite popular.

It should be noted that not all plans allow for discretionary distributions. Typically, pension plans and most profit-sharing plans do not provide for discretionary distributions; their benefit structures are normally designed for annuitized or lump sum payments. However, payments from IRAs and SEPs are almost always discretionary distributions. A qualified plan participant who wants distribution flexibility should consider the advantages of rolling over his or her qualified plan funds to an IRA.

e. Distributions by Age. Another way to differentiate the applicability of distribution rules is by the age of the participant: pre-59½; between 59½ and 70½; and post-70½.

(1) Pre-59 ½. Generally, the law does not allow distributions from a qualified or individual retirement plan prior to the participant or owner's age 59½. Any distributions taken before this age are considered to be "early" or "premature" distributions. Typically, early distributions are subject to a ten percent penalty (in addition to any applicable income taxes) unless the circumstances under which the distribution is made qualify as an exception to the penalty.

21st Century Estate Planning:
Practical Applications
2005 Edition

©*2005 Sonnenschein Nath & Rosenthal LLP*
and Cannon Financial Institute, Inc.

- 352 -

(2) __Between 59½ and 70½.__ There are no special rules regarding distributions between the ages of 59½ and 70½. During this period, according to tax law, distributions may be taken, but they are not required to be taken. Consequently, plan participants need only comply with the rules of their employer's plan. IRA and SEP owners need not comply with any rules.

From the standpoint of the IRS, the time period between ages 59½ and 70½ is considered to be "normal" or "regular" retirement age. Recent studies have shown, however, that there are more retirees pre-59½ and post-70½ (combined) than there are between 59½ and 70½. That which is normal or typical in real life does not always correspond to that which is deemed "normal" under the tax laws.

(3) __Post-70½.__ Just as the law mandates an age before which distributions are not allowed (at least not without penalty), it also stipulates a point at which distributions must begin. The point at which distributions must begin is generally regarded to be age 70½. See the discussion of the required beginning date ("RBD") below. Distributions from employer plans may be delayed until the individual retires if that is later than age 70½ (unless the participant is a 5% owner), but as a general rule the recognized required distribution point is age 70½.

Distributions at and after this point are subject to the *required minimum distribution* rules or *RMD* regulations, and are also discussed below. Failure to take a required minimum distribution results in a severe penalty: a 50% excise tax on the amount that should have been, but was not, withdrawn. This is one of the highest penalties the tax law imposes.

2. General Rule of Taxation as an Annuity Under IRC § 72

The income tax treatment of retirement plan distributions is fairly straightforward and follows a basic rule: that which was not taxed prior to distribution is taxed upon distribution. This means that any contributions and any interest earnings that were not taxed on "the front end" will be subject to tax when distributed from the plan; conversely, any contribution that was taxed to the participant or owner before it was deposited in the plan is recovered income tax-free. Thus, a distribution from a plan that consists entirely of deductible contributions is fully taxable as ordinary income.

Distributions from retirement plans that contain both deductible and nondeductible contributions will be partly taxable and partly tax-free. Nondeductible contributions represent the participant's *cost basis*, or *investment in the contract*, and they are not taxed when they are distributed. Only the portion of a distribution that represents deductible contributions and interest earnings is taxed. While the income taxation of annuities is complex, in general, each distribution received from a qualified plan or IRA to which nondeductible contributions have been made will be treated in part as a tax-free return of investment (*i.e.*, the tax-free return of nondeductible contributions) and in part as taxable income (the distribution of deductible

21st Century Estate Planning:
Practical Applications
2005 Edition

©2005 Sonnenschein Nath & Rosenthal LLP
and Cannon Financial Institute, Inc.

- 353 -

contributions and earnings on contributions), until all nondeductible contributions have been distributed. IRC § 72.

3. Lump Sum Distributions from Qualified Plans

The rules for the taxation of lump sum distributions from qualified plans are slightly more complex.

a. <u>Ten Year Forward Averaging and Capital Gains Treatment</u>. Certain lump-sum distributions may be eligible for 10-year forward averaging tax treatment. Forward averaging operates to tax the distribution as if it were received over 10 years instead of in a single year, thus reducing the tax liability. The tax is still paid all at once, for the year of the distribution. But the amount of tax is less than it would be if forward averaging were not used. (Basically, you compute the tax on one-tenth of the total taxable amount, then multiply that by ten.) Tax rate tables as in effect in 1986 are used to calculate the 10-year forward averaging tax.

To take advantage of 10-year forward-averaging, certain conditions must apply:

- The distribution must qualify for lump-sum treatment, as explained above (and since only qualified employer plans can distribute lump sums, IRA, SEP and 403(b) distributions cannot be forward-averaged);
- the participant must be over the age of 59½ when the distribution is received;
- the participant must elect averaging treatment on all lump sum distributions received during the same year. (For example, if a participant received lump sum distributions from a pension plan and a profit sharing plan and rolled one of them over to an IRA, the other plan would not be eligible for forward averaging.)
- The participant must have reached age 50 by January 1, 1986;
- The participant must have been a participant in the plan for at least five years before the year of the distribution; and
- The participant must not have elected forward averaging on any prior lump sum distribution.

Participants who attained age 50 prior to January 1, 1986, also (or alternatively) can elect capital gains treatment at a 20% long-term capital gains rate for any portion of the distribution attributable to plan participation prior to 1974.

As is the case with other types of distributions, any portion of a lump-sum distribution attributable to after-tax (nondeductible) contributions is returned tax-free to the participant.

b. <u>Net Unrealized Appreciation in Employer Securities</u>. On a distribution of employer securities from a qualified plan, certain appreciation will not be taxed. If the distribution is part of a lump sum distribution, the entire net unrealized appreciation with respect

21st Century Estate Planning:
Practical Applications
2005 Edition

©2005 Sonnenschein Nath & Rosenthal LLP
and Cannon Financial Institute, Inc.

- 354 -

to employer securities will escape taxation at the time of distribution. IRC § 402(e)(4)(A) and (B). The net unrealized appreciation is the excess of the market value of the securities at the time of distribution over the cost or other basis of the securities to or in the qualified plan.

On a subsequent sale of employer securities received in a lump sum distribution from a qualified plan, all of the (previously untaxed) appreciation in the securities will be taxed at the lowest capital gains tax rate. This can be a very attractive distribution option for a qualified plan balance that consists primarily of low basis employer stock that the participant wants to hold for some period of time.

> **EXAMPLE:** An employee has a vested account balance in a qualified retirement plan of $1,000,000, consisting of: (1) $600,000 in stocks, bonds and mutual funds (2) and $400,000 in employer securities. The employer securities have a cost basis to the plan of $100,000.
>
> The employee has two tax-favored distribution options. The employee can direct that the entire account balance be directly rolled over to an IRA. This has no current tax consequences to the employee. All distributions are taxed as ordinary income when made. Alternatively, the employee can direct that the $600,000 in stocks, bonds and mutual funds be rolled over to an IRA. This has no current tax consequences to the employee. When withdrawn, distributions from the IRA will be subject to ordinary income tax. The $400,000 of employer securities can be distributed (in kind) to the employee and placed in a personal investment management account. This results in ordinary income tax on the $100,000 of cost basis in the employer securities. The $300,000 of net unrealized appreciation is taxed as long term capital gain (at 15% rates) only when and as the securities are sold. The effect of this is to reduce the income tax on the distribution by as much as $60,000 (the difference between maximum ordinary income tax rates and maximum capital gains rates on $300,000 of net unrealized appreciation.).
>
> In determining which alternative is better, the timing of the payment of the capital gains tax becomes important. If the employee wants to diversify his or her holding in the employer securities, the rollover might be preferred, as the deferral of the income tax on the $100,000 cost basis in the securities and the $15,000 capital gains tax may be worth more economically than the $90,000 tax saved. If the employee plans to hold the stock, or if the employee needs cash for other reasons, this is an excellent strategy for minimizing income taxes.

21st Century Estate Planning:
Practical Applications
2005 Edition

©2005 Sonnenschein Nath & Rosenthal LLP
and Cannon Financial Institute, Inc.

- 355 -

4.   Distributions from IRAs

The rules regarding IRAs have been subject to a myriad of changes. However, very little has changed with regard to the taxation of IRA distributions until the introduction of the Roth IRA. The rules regarding the taxation of IRA distributions now vary, depending on whether the instrument is a traditional IRA or a Roth IRA. (SEP IRA and SIMPLE IRA plans are set up using traditional IRAs, so the distribution rules that pertain to traditional IRAs also apply to these plans.)

a.   Traditional IRAs.

The general rules regarding distributions from traditional IRAs are similar to those that pertain to qualified employer plans: they are not allowed prior to age 59½ (at least, not without the imposition of a ten percent penalty unless qualified under an exception to the penalty); they *may* be taken after age 59½; and they *must* be taken, in at least minimum amounts, once the owner reaches age 70½. Upon withdrawal or distribution, traditional IRA earnings are subject to ordinary income tax under Section 72, as are any contributions that were deducted when they were initially contributed to the account. If the account consists of contributions that were fully deducted by the owner, the entire amount of each distribution is subject to tax. On the other hand, it is not uncommon to find traditional IRA accounts that contain both deductible and nondeductible contributions. The way in which one would determine the taxable and nontaxable portion of a distribution in this circumstance is determined under IRC § 72, with nondeductible contributions representing the participant's cost basis, or investment in the contract, that are distributed to the participant without income tax.

Distributions from traditional IRAs are, by their nature, "discretionary." The timing and amount of each distribution is at the discretion of the account owner. However, it is important that IRA owners review the provisions of their account documents prior to the required distribution date, since a certain methodology of calculating required distributions may apply under the plan documents, unless changed by the owner.

b.   Roth IRAs.

The general rules regarding the distribution and taxation of funds from a Roth IRA are more straightforward than those imposed on traditional IRAs. The reason is that a traditional IRA is a *tax-deferred* vehicle and a Roth IRA is a *tax-exempt* or *tax-free* vehicle. With a tax-deferred product, taxes are still due and owing; every traditional IRA contribution that is deducted and every dollar that is earned while in a traditional IRA account carries an obligation to pay future taxes. These taxes are typically applied when a distribution is made. With a tax-exempt or tax-free Roth IRA, taxes have been paid "up front" -- as long as the rules are followed, there are no future taxes due. Consequently, with Roth IRAs the IRS really has a minimal ongoing interest because, theoretically, there are no other taxes to collect. That is, as long as the distribution rules are followed.

(1)   Qualified and Nonqualified Distributions from Roth IRAs.

Distributions from a Roth IRA are either *qualified* or *nonqualified*. A *qualified distribution* is one that provides for the full tax advantage the Roth IRA offers: tax-free distribution of earnings. To be a qualified distribution, two requirements must be met:

21st Century Estate Planning:
Practical Applications
2005 Edition

©2005 Sonnenschein Nath & Rosenthal LLP
and Cannon Financial Institute, Inc.

- 356 -

- the funds must have been held in the account for a minimum of five years, *and*
- the distribution occurs for one of the following reasons:

  ➢ the owner has reached age 59½; *or*
  ➢ the owner dies; *or*
  ➢ the owner becomes disabled; *or*
  ➢ the distribution is used to purchase a first home.

If these requirements are met, no portion of the distribution is subject to tax.

To be considered a "qualified" distribution from a Roth IRA and therefore completely tax free, one of the requirements is that the amount attributed to the distribution must have been held in the account for at least five years. The five-year holding period begins the first year for which a contribution was made. Individuals may even delay an initial contribution until April 15 of the next year, designate it as a contribution for the previous year and initiate the five-year holding period as of the previous year.

A *nonqualified distribution* is one that does not meet the above criteria. The result is that distributed Roth *earnings* are subject to tax. This would occur when the distribution is taken without meeting the above requirements *and* the amount of the distribution exceeds the total amount that was contributed to the Roth IRA. Remember, Roth contributions are made with after-tax dollars; they are not subject to taxation again upon distribution. Therefore, the only portion of a nonqualified Roth distribution that is subject to taxation is earnings, and only when those earnings are withdrawn from the account without having met the above requirements. Amounts taken from a Roth IRA are treated on a FIFO (first-in/first-out) basis: they will be considered first as withdrawals of nontaxable contributions until all contributions have been distributed. After that, nonqualified distributions will be treated as distributions of taxable earnings. As with the taxation of other distributions from qualified plans and IRAs, the distribution of basis (after-tax or nondeductible contributions) is not subject to tax or penalty. In the case of distributions from a Roth IRA, all distributions are deemed to be a return of basis until all basis is fully recovered. Only then might earnings be distributed, and subject to tax and a possible penalty.

If the owner of a Roth IRA is younger than 59½ when a distribution is taken, the distribution will be considered "early," or "premature," and, if the distribution does not qualify under an exception to the early distribution rules, the earnings portion will be assessed a ten percent penalty in addition to the applicable ordinary income tax.

21st Century Estate Planning:
Practical Applications
2005 Edition

©2005 Sonnenschein Nath & Rosenthal LLP
and Cannon Financial Institute, Inc.

- 357 -

Type of Distribution	Roth IRA Held Less Than 5 Years		Roth IRA Held 5 Years or More	
	Earnings Taxed	10% PenaltyTaxed	Earnings Taxed	10% Penalty Taxed
Pre-59½	Yes	Yes	Yes	Yes
Pre-59½, but distribution due to death, disability, or for a first home purchase	Yes	No	No	No
Post-59½	Yes	No	No	No

(2) **Minimum Required Distributions and Roth IRAs**. Unlike traditional IRAs, Roth IRAs do not require mandatory distributions during the lifetime of the participant. There is no minimum distribution requirement for the account owner; the funds can remain in the account as long as the owner desires. In fact, the account can be left intact and passed on to heirs or beneficiaries. However, upon the owner's death, any funds that do remain in a Roth IRA must be distributed to the beneficiary in accordance with the same minimum distribution requirements that apply to other qualified plans and IRAs, as discussed below.

(3) **Roth IRA Conversions**. Only an individual with an AGI of less than $100,000 for the year in which the conversion takes place can convert traditional IRA funds to a Roth IRA. Married couples filing separately are not eligible to make a Roth IRA conversion at all. For purposes of applying the five-year holding period to converted amounts, no separate period applies to amounts converted separately at different times; there is only one-five-year holding period. Taxable IRA distributions and minimum required distributions from other qualified plans do not have to be included in AGI in determining eligibility to make a Roth IRA conversion.

21st Century Estate Planning:
Practical Applications
2005 Edition

©2005 Sonnenschein Nath & Rosenthal LLP
and Cannon Financial Institute, Inc.

- 358 -

c. Comparing Distribution Rules: Traditional and Roth IRAs.

	Traditional IRA	Roth IRA
Allowable Distributions	After owner's age 59 ½	After holding period of 5 years *and:* - age 59 ½ *or* - death *or* - disability *or* - first-time home purchase
Tax Treatment	Subject to ordinary income tax, to extent distribution represents deductible contributions and earnings	No tax
Premature Distributions	Prior to owner's age 59 ½	Prior to owner's age 59 ½
Tax Treatment	Income tax plus a 10% penalty on amount included in income, unless distribution qualifies as an exception to the premature distribution penalty	10% penalty on distributed earnings, unless distribution qualifies as an exception to the premature distribution penalty; earnings subject to income tax unless distribution is taken due to death, disability or for first-time home purchase
Required Distributions	After owner's age 70 ½	None while owner is alive
Tax Treatment	Subject to ordinary income tax, except for the return of non-deductible contributions	None on qualified distributions

5. Rollovers and Transfers of IRAs and Qualified Retirement Plan Assets

The Economic Growth and Tax Relief Reconciliation Act of 2001 ("EGTRRA 2001," P.L. 107-16) dramatically changed and expanded the ability of individuals to transfer assets between IRAs and qualified retirement plans (EGTRRA § 641 - § 643). Under the old law there were many outdated rules restricting a participant's ability to move money from one type of retirement plan to another. EGTRRA significantly broadens those rules, allowing almost complete portability for eligible rollover distributions from qualified retirement plans, Section 403(b) annuities, and governmental Section 457 plans. Effective for years beginning on or after January 1, 2002, any of these plans now may be rolled over to any other qualified retirement plan or individual retirement arrangement. IRA distributions also may be rolled over to other workplace retirement plans (if the accepting plan allows it) and individual retirement arrangements. IRC § 408(d)(3). Spousal rollovers may now be made to a qualified plan, Section 403(b) annuity, or governmental Section 457 plan in which the surviving spouse participates, as

21st Century Estate Planning:
Practical Applications
2005 Edition

©2005 Sonnenschein Nath & Rosenthal LLP
and Cannon Financial Institute, Inc.

- 359 -

well as to an individual retirement plan. However, the penalty and withholding requirements, which are covered later, still apply.

Any distribution from a qualified retirement plan or IRA that is rolled over to another qualified plan or IRA in a qualifying rollover contribution is income tax free in the year of the rollover. For distributions in 2002 and after, tax-free rollovers of distributions to and from qualified plans, Section 403(b) tax deferred annuity plans, traditional IRAs, SEPs and eligible Section 457 governmental plans are specifically authorized by the Internal Revenue Code. IRC § 402(c)(8)(B) and IRC § 408(d)(3), as amended by EGTRRA 2001. Rollovers between different types of plans are permitted. For example, a participant could rollover an eligible rollover distribution from a qualified retirement plan under Section 401(a) to a Section 403(b) tax deferred annuity, and then back to a qualified retirement plan.

Any distribution from an "eligible retirement plan" is eligible for rollover to another eligible retirement plan, except:

- A required minimum distribution (generally beginning at age 70 ½);
- A distribution that is one of a series of substantially equal periodic payments payable (a) for a period of ten years or more, or (b) for the life or life expectancy of the employee or the employee and a designated beneficiary;
- A "hardship" distribution;
- In most cases, after-tax contributions or other amounts not included in gross income.

An "eligible retirement plan" is a qualified plan under IRC § 401(a), a Section 403(b) tax deferred annuity plan or an IRA. There may be some restrictions on particular assets that cannot be rolled over. For example, a life insurance contract held under a qualified plan cannot be rolled over to an IRA, for which life insurance is not a permitted investment. Loans also cannot always be rolled over.

Eligible rollover distributions received from an eligible retirement plan must either be transferred to another eligible retirement plan by means of a "direct rollover" at the employee's election, or transferred by the participant to the other plan not later than the 60th day after distribution from the plan.

A "direct rollover" is defined as an eligible rollover distribution that is paid directly to another eligible retirement plan for the benefit of the employee. It can be accomplished by any reasonable means of direct payment, including the use of a wire transfer or a check that is negotiable only by the trustee of the new plan or rollover IRA. If the "direct rollover" method is not chosen in the case of a distribution from a qualified retirement plan, a Section 403(b) plan, or an eligible Section 457 governmental plan, the distribution is subject to mandatory withholding at 20%. Distributions from an IRA (other than direct IRA trustee to IRA trustee transfers) are subject to 10% withholding, which may be waived by the IRA participant.

21st Century Estate Planning:
Practical Applications
2005 Edition

©2005 *Sonnenschein Nath & Rosenthal LLP*
and Cannon Financial Institute, Inc.

- 360 -

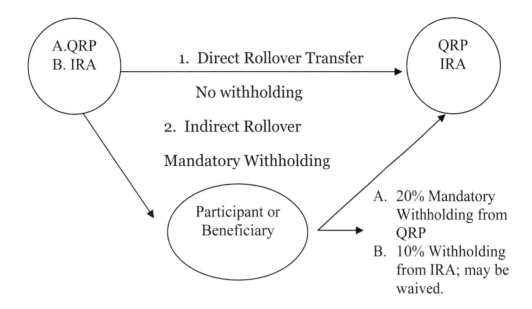

A. QRP
B. IRA

1. Direct Rollover Transfer

No withholding

2. Indirect Rollover

Mandatory Withholding

QRP
IRA

Participant or Beneficiary

A. 20% Mandatory Withholding from QRP
B. 10% Withholding from IRA; may be waived.

IRA rollovers may only be made once a year, but a direct trustee to trustee transfer is not considered a rollover for purposes of this rule. Partial rollovers are allowed. However the amount not rolled over is subject to the 10% early withdrawal penalty (if applicable) and must be reported as ordinary income.

➔ **Planning Point:** If the distribution is first paid to the employee before being rolled over (within 60 days), the qualified retirement plan will withhold 20% of the distribution. In order to rollover the entire distribution and avoid current income taxation (and a possible 10% penalty tax) on the 20% of the distribution that is withheld, the employee will have to make up the 20% withholding from some other source.

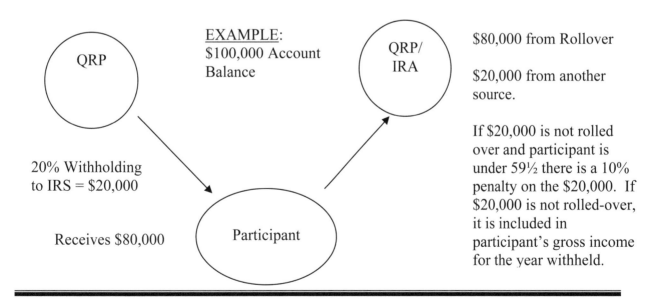

QRP

EXAMPLE:
$100,000 Account Balance

QRP/ IRA

$80,000 from Rollover

$20,000 from another source.

20% Withholding to IRS = $20,000

Receives $80,000

Participant

If $20,000 is not rolled over and participant is under 59½ there is a 10% penalty on the $20,000. If $20,000 is not rolled-over, it is included in participant's gross income for the year withheld.

21st Century Estate Planning:
Practical Applications
2005 Edition

©2005 Sonnenschein Nath & Rosenthal LLP
and Cannon Financial Institute, Inc.

- 361 -

In order to preserve capital gains and special averaging treatment for a lump sum distribution from a qualified retirement plan, a "conduit IRA" must be used to hold qualified plan funds for transfer from one qualified plan to another when an employee changes employers. The initial transfer from the qualified plan to the IRA is income tax-free if the amount is transferred within 60 days. (The distribution will be subject to 20% mandatory withholding unless transferred by means of a "direct rollover.") If the IRA contains no assets other than those attributable to the distribution from the qualified plan, then the amount in the IRA may subsequently be transferred, tax-free, to another qualified plan, if that plan allows such transfers. The special income tax treatment is preserved. Special income tax treatment will not be preserved if the qualified plan distribution is commingled with traditional IRA funds. An existing IRA should not be used for conduit rollovers; a new IRA always should be established for that purpose.

E. Penalties Applicable to Qualified Plans and Individual Retirement Accounts

1. Penalty for Excess Contribution to IRA

An excess contribution is a contribution in excess of the maximum permissible contribution to Traditional IRAs, Roth IRAs, Education Saving Accounts, Simple IRAs, SEP IRAs and qualified retirement plans. IRC § 4973. The IRA or qualified retirement plan is not disqualified as a result of excess contributions, but various excise taxes and penalties are imposed.

Generally, there is a 6% excise tax on the amount of the excess contribution to any IRA account or qualified retirement plan. This excise tax must be paid each year until the contribution is withdrawn. IRC § 4973(b)(2). This tax is imposed on the IRA owner, rather than the IRA or trustee. Prop. Reg. § 54.4973(b)(1).

If the IRA participant removes the excess contribution (and all earnings on the excess contributions) prior to filing his or her individual income tax return for that year, there is no 6% (or 10%) tax on the excess contribution or on the earnings on the excess contribution. The participant must include the earnings on the excess contribution in gross income. These earnings are taxable in the year the excess contribution is made (not in the year withdrawn). No deduction is allowed for the excess contribution. An excess contribution left in the IRA after the tax return filing date is subject both to the annual 6% excise tax and the 10% premature distribution tax on withdrawal, if the IRA participant is under age 59½ and no exception to the penalty applies. The distribution also will be subject to ordinary income tax in the year withdrawn.

➔ **Planning Point:** One way to eliminate excess contributions is to not make allowable contributions in future years. The excess contribution is treated as (or applied against) the contribution that would have been allowed, but is not made. You still can claim an income tax deduction (if otherwise allowable) for the amount allowable as a contribution but that is not made is order to offset an excess contribution.

21st Century Estate Planning:
Practical Applications
2005 Edition

©2005 Sonnenschein Nath & Rosenthal LLP
and Cannon Financial Institute, Inc.

- 362 -

2. Penalty for Early (Premature) Distribution from Qualified Plan or IRA

We noted earlier that one element that differentiates types of distributions from qualified plans and IRAs is the age of the participant. Distributions taken between age 59½ and 70½ are "normal" or "regular" (or more precisely, they are what the IRS considers normal or regular). Thus, by extension, a distribution taken before age 59½ is "early" or "premature."

a. Early Distribution Defined. According to IRC § 72(t), an early distribution is one that takes place prior to age 59½. The participant's age 59½ is the designated point: any distribution received before that is early, or "premature"; any distribution received on or after that date is regular, or "normal."

b. The Taxation of Early Distributions. The premature distribution rules under IRC § 72(t) impose a 10% penalty on distributions taken before the age of 59½. More precisely, this penalty is applied to the portion of the distribution that is includable in income -- in other words, it is imposed on the same amount that is subject to income tax. The purpose of the early distribution penalty is to discourage the use of qualified plans and individual retirement accounts as short-term tax shelters.

In the case of SIMPLE IRA plans, the impact can be even more significant. Because these employer plans are so accessible by the participant, Congress added an extra level of impediment to discourage premature distributions. This impediment is an additional 15% penalty for early withdrawals, in addition to the normal 10% penalty, during the first two years of plan participation. After the two-year period has passed, the penalty reverts to 10% (assuming the participant is still under age 59½). Other than this, SIMPLE IRAs operate identically to traditional IRAs with regard to premature distributions.

c. Exceptions to the Ten Percent Penalty on Early Distributions. Not all early distributions are subject to the 10% penalty. For certain reasons and under certain circumstances, distributions can be taken before the age of 59½ without imposition of the 10% penalty. The following list cites these exceptions; however, it is important to know that not all of the exceptions on the list apply to every type of plan:

- Death
- Disability
- separation from service after age 55
- certain (qualifying) medical expenses
- health insurance premiums while unemployed
- higher education expenses
- first-time home purchase
- qualified domestic relations orders
- ESOP dividends
- to reduce excess contributions or deferrals

21st Century Estate Planning:
Practical Applications
2005 Edition

©2005 Sonnenschein Nath & Rosenthal LLP
and Cannon Financial Institute, Inc.

- 363 -

- as substantially equal periodic payments over life

Despite what many people think, most of these exceptions have very limited applicability.

Ten Percent Early Distribution Penalty Exceptions by Plan Type			
	Qualified Pension, Profit Sharing and 403(b) Plans	401(k) and SIMPLE 401(k) Plans	Traditional IRA, SEP IRA, SIMPLE IRA* and Roth IRA
Death	X	X	X
Disability	X	X	X
Separation from service after age 55	X	X	
Certain medical expenses	X	X	X
QDROs	X	X	
To reduce excess contributions and/or deferrals	X	X	X
As substantially equal payments over life	X	X	X
First-time home purchase			X
Higher education expenses			X
Health insurance premiums while unemployed			X
ESOP dividends	X**		

**Except 403(b) Plans

* For SIMPLE IRAs, the premature distribution penalty is 25% if the distribution is taken during the first two years of participation.

21st Century Estate Planning:
Practical Applications
2005 Edition

©2005 Sonnenschein Nath & Rosenthal LLP
and Cannon Financial Institute, Inc.

- 364 -

Reason for Distribution	Roth IRA Held Less than 5 Years		Roth IRA Held 5 Years or More		Traditional IRA	
	Earnings Taxed	10% Penalty	Earnings Taxed	10% Penalty	Distributions Taxed	10% Penalty
Pre-59 ½	Yes	Yes	Yes	Yes	Yes	Yes
Death	Yes	No	No	No	Yes	No
Disability	Yes	No	No	No	Yes	No
First-time home purchase	Yes	No	No	No	Yes	No
Substantially equal payments	Yes	No	Yes	No	Yes	No
Medical payments	Yes	No	Yes	No	Yes	No
Health insurance while unemployed	Yes	No	Yes	No	Yes	No
Higher education expenses	Yes	No	Yes	No	Yes	No
Post-59 ½	Yes	No	No	No	Yes	No

3. Penalty for Failing to Make a Required Distribution from a Qualified Plan or IRA

Minimum distributions from qualified retirement plans, Section 403(b) tax deferred annuity plans, IRAs, SEPs, SIMPLE IRAs and Section 457 governmental deferred compensation plans must begin not later than April 1 of the year following the later of: (1) The year in which the employee attains age 70 1/2; or (2) the year an employee (who is not a 5% owner) retires. IRC § 4974. The second (retirement year) alternative is not available for a participant who owns more than 5% of the business sponsoring the qualified plan, or for an IRA participant.

If the annual distribution is less than the minimum amount required, there is a penalty equal to 50% of the amount that was not distributed, but should have been.

➔ **Planning Point:** If the taxpayer has more than one IRA, the required minimum distribution amount must be calculated separately for each IRA. However the IRA participant can receive the total minimum distribution amount in whole or in part from any one or more of the IRAs, as long as the aggregate amount distributed from all of the IRAs equals the aggregate minimum required distribution from all of the IRAs. Treas. Reg. § 408-8, A-9.

21st Century Estate Planning:
Practical Applications
2005 Edition

©2005 Sonnenschein Nath & Rosenthal LLP
and Cannon Financial Institute, Inc.

- 365 -

This "aggregate dollar approach" may not be used for qualified retirement plans. Each qualified retirement plan must make its own required minimum distribution.

A qualified retirement plan can be disqualified, and no longer entitled to the tax benefits of qualified status, if the plan consistently fails to make required distributions.

4. Prohibited Transactions

IRAs and qualified retirement plans may not engage in prohibited transactions. There are many different types of prohibited transactions, primarily centered around investments and "self-dealing" transactions. Any type of sale or exchange, lending of money, extension of credit, furnishing of goods or services, or other act of dealing with plan assets for personal benefit that is engaged in by a disqualified person and the plan is prohibited, unless subject to exemption, either under the statute or by special exemption. IRC § 4975. A disqualified person is any person who is a fiduciary under the plan, a sponsoring employer, an employee organization whose members are covered by the plan, a 50% owner of a sponsoring employer, a member of the family of any of the above, any corporation, partnership, trust or estate that is 50% owned by any of the above, and officers, directors, 10% shareholders and highly compensated employees of a sponsoring employer, employee organization, controlling shareholder or related entity. IRC § 4975(e). Estate planners will most frequently encounter the penalties imposed on IRAs when the participant or beneficiary engages in a prohibited transaction.

There are three possible penalties if an IRA is involved in a prohibited transaction:

a. Disqualification of the IRA. The most common IRA penalty for a prohibited transaction is disqualification of the IRA. The penalty applies whenever the IRA participant engages in a prohibited transaction. IRC § 408(e)(2)(a). The tax consequences of disqualification are disastrous. The IRA loses its tax-exempt status (IRC § 408(e)(2)(a)) and the IRA participant is deemed to have received a distribution of the entire account balance on the first day of the tax year in which the prohibited transaction occurs. The IRA participant is subject to ordinary income tax on the previously tax deductible contributions and all earnings. If the participant is under 59½, the 10% excise tax is also charged on the taxable portion of the deemed distribution (unless an exception to the penalty applies).

b. Excise Taxes. The second type of penalty for prohibited transactions is the 15% excise tax under IRC § 4975. This penalty applies if someone other than the participant engages in a prohibited transaction. The excise tax is imposed on the persons participating in the prohibited transaction and only on the amount involved in the transaction. The IRA does not lose its tax-exempt status, and the fair market value of the amount involved in the prohibited transaction is not taxable to the participant in the year of the transaction.

c. Taxation of Prohibited Investments. The third type of penalty for a prohibited transaction is imposed when a prohibited investment is made in an IRA. The fair

21st Century Estate Planning:
Practical Applications
2005 Edition

©2005 Sonnenschein Nath & Rosenthal LLP
and Cannon Financial Institute, Inc.

- 366 -

market value of the improper investment is treated as a taxable distribution to the IRA participant, and is subject to ordinary income tax and (if applicable) the 10% penalty for early distributions. The IRA is not disqualified and there are no excise taxes under IRC § 4975. IRA investments in collectibles, the assignment of the IRA, pledging the IRA as security for a loan, and purchasing life, health or accident insurance in the IRA are prohibited transactions subject to this type of penalty.

F. The Income Taxation of Non-Qualified Plans

Non-qualified employee benefit plans are not eligible for the special income tax treatment afforded qualified plans. The employee must include in income the value of any property transferred to him or her in connection with the performance of services as soon as it is no longer subject to "a substantial risk of forfeiture." IRC § 83(a). This rule also applies if the property is transferred to a trust for the benefit of the employee. IRC § 402(b). If the property is subject to risk of forfeiture, which includes a condition that the employee remain employed in order to become entitled to receive the property, it is not taxable to the employee, but the employer does not get a current income tax deduction either. IRC § 83(h). Note that stock options are subject to special rules, and are treated in another chapter of this book.

There is a certain tension between employers and employees in the design of non-qualified employee benefit plans. From the employer's perspective, the employer does not want to lose control of (or give up) property for which it gets no current income tax deduction. This can be addressed by creating an unfunded plan - that is, a plan that is based only on the employer's contractual obligation to pay the promised benefit, and that is not secured by a trust or other assets. There is no deduction to the employer, but the employer also has not given up anything of current economic value. From the employee's point of view, the employee does not want to pay income tax currently on property the employee has not yet received. At the same time, the employee is less sure of receiving a benefit based solely on the employer's unsecured promise to pay the benefit some time in the future.

Most non-qualified employee benefit plans are unfunded. If the employer does transfer assets to a trust to secure the plan, the trust is not tax-exempt. Income earned in the trust either is subject to income tax under the traditional rules governing the income taxation of trusts, or the trust may be characterized as a grantor trust to the employer. The trust assets will be taxed to the employee as ordinary income when they are no longer subject to a substantial risk of forfeiture under IRC § 83. When distributions are made to the employee from the trust after the employee has been subject to income tax on part or all of the trust assets, the distribution is taxed as an annuity under IRC § 72, with the amount previously subject to income tax constituting the employee's cost, or investment, which is distributed to the employee without further income tax. A trust that is part of a funded non-qualified employee benefit plan does not become a grantor trust to the employee by virtue of the fact that some or all of its assets have been taxed to the employee as income. Special rules apply to these trusts with respect to highly compensated employees. IRC § 402(b).

21st Century Estate Planning:
Practical Applications
2005 Edition

©*2005 Sonnenschein Nath & Rosenthal LLP*
and Cannon Financial Institute, Inc.

- 367 -

An employee may elect to accelerate the recognition of income on property transferred as part of a non-qualified employee benefit plan. This has a benefit to the employee if the property transferred under the plan is likely to appreciate. The value of the property at the time of the election is subject to ordinary income tax; post-election increases in value will be taxed as capital gains on disposition of the property. There is a risk as well. If this election is made but the right to receive the property is subsequently forfeit (*e.g.*, because the employee terminates employment), the employee will get no deduction, and will have paid income tax on assets never received.

The advantage of non-qualified employee benefit plans is that they are not subject to the funding, vesting, contribution and benefits limitations applicable to qualified plans. They can (and often do) discriminate in favor of executives, officers and highly paid employees.

G. Minimum Required Distributions from Qualified Plans and IRAs

1. Introduction

Income tax deferral on qualified plans and IRAs is an extremely important consideration for most retired clients. Beneficiary designations that accomplish estate-planning goals at the expense of income tax deferral are not always in the client's best interests. Understanding the IRS rules regarding the minimum amounts that must be withdrawn from qualified plans and IRAs after retirement will permit you to advise clients, not only on the proper disposition of the plan benefits as part of the client's overall estate plan, but how to structure distributions to maximize the potential for income tax deferral.

Income tax deferral does not have to end at death. In fact, it is as important a consideration for the survivors as it is for the plan participant, and for the same reasons. This is particularly true when there is a surviving spouse. In that case, the estate tax is deferred, but the income tax is a current obligation, the payment or deferral of which could significantly affect the spouse's standard of living.

Congress and the IRS have promulgated complex "minimum distribution" rules, set forth IRC § 401(a)(9) and in Treas. Reg. § 1.401(a)(9), that are intended to limit the deferral of income attributable to qualified plan and IRA benefits by requiring that certain minimum distributions be made annually after a participant has reached age 70½. The rules governing the calculation of minimum required distributions (or "MRDs") originally were set out in proposed treasury regulations issued in 1987. These 1987 proposed regulations were superseded by a new set of proposed regulations issued on January 17, 2001. The 2001 proposed regulations introduced significant simplification into the process of calculating minimum required distributions from most qualified plans and IRAs, particularly for distributions made during the participant's lifetime, but remained problematic in a number of respects. Final regulations were issued on April 17, 2002 that addressed some, but not all, of these concerns.

21st Century Estate Planning:
Practical Applications
2005 Edition

©2005 Sonnenschein Nath & Rosenthal LLP
and Cannon Financial Institute, Inc.

- 368 -

Special distribution rules are contained in the regulations for annuities. These rules are of primary interest to plan administrators, not estate planners. The most important estate planning issues and opportunities arise with respect to retired individuals who are receiving discretionary distributions from defined contribution plans and IRAs. The minimum distribution rules for these types of accounts are described in detail below.

2. Distributions During Life

Under the old proposed regulations, during a participant's lifetime the minimum required distribution for any year was calculated by dividing the account balance as of the last day of the previous year by the life expectancy of the participant and his "Designated Beneficiary." Under the new final regulations, the minimum required distribution for any year during the participant's life is the amount obtained by dividing the account balance as of the last valuation date of the previous year by the factor set forth in the "Uniform Table" (below) for the participant's age on the participant's birthday during the distribution year. Treas. Reg. § 1.401(a)(9)-5, A-3 and A-4. The concept of Designated Beneficiary is no longer relevant for purposes of calculating <u>lifetime</u> minimum required distributions from a qualified plan or IRA.

> **EXAMPLE:** Your client's birthday is October 1, 1920. The balance in his IRA on December 31, 2001 was $100,000. The client's minimum required distribution for the distribution year 2002 is calculated by dividing the December 31, 2001 balance by the factor on the Uniform Table for age 82, or 17.1. The MRD for 2002 is $5,848 ($100,000/17.1=$5,848).

a. <u>Required Beginning Date</u>. Distributions must begin from a qualified plan or IRA no later than the participant's "Required Beginning Date." A participant's Required Beginning Date generally is April 1 of the year following the year in which the participant reaches age 70½. This general rule applies to all IRA participants. A participant of a qualified plan who is not a 5% owner may, however, defer his Required Beginning Date until April 1 of the year following the year in which the participant retires. A 5% owner who participates in a qualified plan is treated for this purpose the same as an IRA participant. The Required Beginning Date for a 5% owner is April 1 of the year following the year in which the owner reaches age 70½, whether or not he or she is retired. Treas. Reg. § 1.401(a)(9)-2, A-2. IRC § 416 defines a 5% owner as a person who owns 5% of the outstanding stock of a corporation or stock with more than 5% of the total combined voting power. If the employer is not a corporation, a 5% owner is a person who owns more than 5% of the capital or profits interest.

21st Century Estate Planning:
Practical Applications
2005 Edition

©2005 Sonnenschein Nath & Rosenthal LLP
and Cannon Financial Institute, Inc.

- 369 -

> **EXAMPLE:** Your client's birthday is November 15, 1930. The client will reach age 70 on November 15, 2000. The client will reach age 70½ on May 15, 2001. The client retires on June 30, 2002. If the client is a qualified plan participant who is not a 5% owner, the client's Required Beginning Date is April 1, 2003 (April 1 of the year after the year the participant retires). In all other cases, including all IRA participants, the client's Required Beginning Date is April 1, 2002 (the year after the year the participant reaches age 70½).

b. **First Distribution Year.** The distribution required to be made on a participant's Required Beginning Date is actually the distribution for the participant's "first distribution year." The first distribution year generally is the year in which the participant reaches age 70½. (The first distribution year for a qualified plan participant who is not a 5% owner is the later of the year in which the participant reaches age 70½ and the year in which the participant retires.) The year in which the Required Beginning Date occurs is the second distribution year. The required distribution for the second distribution year must be made before December 31 of that year. Treas. Reg. § 1.401(a)(9)-5.

> **EXAMPLE:** Your client's birthday is November 15, 1930, and her Required Beginning Date is April 1, 2002. Assume that the client's IRA balance is $100,000 on December 31, 2000, and $110,000 on December 31, 2001. The minimum required distribution to be paid on April 1, 2002 is calculated for the first distribution year, or 2001. This calculation is made by dividing the year end account balance for the preceding year (the December 31, 2000 balance of $100,000) by the Uniform Table factor for the participant's age on her birthday during 2001, the first distribution year (the factor for age 71 is 26.5). The MRD required to be paid on April 1, 2002 is $3,774.

c. **Other Distributions.** While a qualified plan or IRA participant must begin to take mandatory distributions on the participant's Required Beginning Date in the defined minimum amounts, there is no IRS prohibition against taking larger amounts. After age 59½, there is no penalty for taking out more than the minimum required distribution. Ideally, a participant will want to qualify for the longest permitted distribution period, which produces the smallest *mandatory*, or minimum, payments, both during lifetime and after death. This allows for the most income tax deferral, and is the most flexible.

➔ **Planning Point:** Although after age 59½ there is no prohibition against withdrawing more than the MRD in any year, excess distributions taken in one year cannot be used to reduce minimum required distributions to be made in another year. Treas. Reg. § 1.401(a)(9)-5, A-2. There is one exception to this general rule. A MRD paid during the first distribution year can be treated as the MRD required to be paid by April 1 of the following year.

21st Century Estate Planning:
Practical Applications
2005 Edition

©2005 Sonnenschein Nath & Rosenthal LLP
and Cannon Financial Institute, Inc.

- 370 -

EXAMPLE: Your client's birthday is November 15, 1930, and her Required Beginning Date is April 1, 2002. Assume that the client's IRA balance is $100,000 on December 31, 2000, and $110,000 on December 31, 2001. The minimum required distribution to be paid on April 1, 2002 is $3,774. This distribution can be made at any time during 2001, or in 2002 before April 1.

d. After the First Distribution Year. After the first distribution year, the MRD for any year is calculated by dividing the year-end account balance for the preceding year by the factor from the Uniform Table for the participant's age on his or her birthday during the distribution year. Generally, no adjustments are made to account for prior distributions in excess of the MRD, or for any distributions required, but not made, in a prior year. (This is a change from earlier proposed regulations.)

EXAMPLE: Your client's birthday is November 15, 1930, and her Required Beginning Date is April 1, 2002. Assume that the client's IRA balance is $100,000 on December 31, 2000, and $110,000 on December 31, 2001. The minimum required distribution for the first distribution year, to be paid on or before April 1, 2002, is $3,774. If the distribution is deferred to 2002, the 2001 year end account balance includes the deferred payment. Nevertheless, to calculate the 2002 MRD, you still divide the December 31, 2001 year-end account balance, of $110,000, by the factor from the Uniform Table for your client's age on her birthday during 2002 (72), or 25.6. $110,000 ÷ 25.6 = $4,297. This is the MRD for the second distribution year, which has to be paid on or before December 31, 2002. Note that if the MRD for the first distribution year is paid *during* the first distribution year, the MRD for the second distribution year is reduced to $4,149 ($110,000 - $3,774 = 106,226 ÷ 25.6 = $4,149).

e. The Uniform Table. The Uniform Table sets forth factors representing the joint, recalculated life expectancy of an individual and another person ten years younger. The Uniform Table is used to calculate MRDs for all distributions during the lifetime of a participant, with a single exception. If the participant's spouse is more than 10 years younger than the participant, and the participant's spouse is the sole beneficiary of the account or plan for the entire year, then the participant may use the actual recalculated joint life expectancy of the participant and the spouse instead of the factor set forth in the Uniform Table. Life expectancy factors are determined by reference to the tables promulgated by the Internal Revenue Service in the regulations under IRC § 401(a)(9), which are reproduced as Appendix B and Appendix C to this chapter.

21st Century Estate Planning:
Practical Applications
2005 Edition

©2005 Sonnenschein Nath & Rosenthal LLP
and Cannon Financial Institute, Inc.

- 371 -

Uniform Table for Calculating
Minimum Required Distributions
For IRAs and Qualified Plans

Age of Employee	Factor	Age of Employee	Factor	Age of Employee	Factor
70	27.4	85	14.8	100	6.3
71	26.5	86	14.1	101	5.9
72	25.6	87	13.4	102	5.5
73	24.7	88	12.7	103	5.2
74	23.8	89	12.0	104	4.9
75	22.9	90	11.4	105	4.5
76	22.0	91	10.8	106	4.2
77	21.2	92	10.2	107	3.9
78	20.3	93	9.6	108	3.7
79	19.5	94	9.1	109	3.4
80	18.7	95	8.6	110	3.1
81	17.9	96	8.1	111	2.9
82	17.1	97	7.6	112	2.6
83	16.3	98	7.1	113	2.4
84	15.5	99	6.7	114	2.1
				115 and older	1.9

➔ **Planning Point:** Another way to calculate minimum required distributions is to *multiply* the year-end account balance by the percentage obtained by dividing 100 by the factor for any stated age. These percentages, for all ages, are shown in the table contained in Appendix A. This method provides a clearer understanding of whether MRDs are exceeding investment returns in the account. For example, at age 80, the MRD represents 5.3476% of the account balance. As long as the investment return exceeds 5.4%, the account balance will continue to grow, notwithstanding the payments of MRDs.

➔ **Planning Point:** Ordinarily, the MRD has to be calculated separately for each qualified plan and IRA, and paid separately from the account with respect to which it is calculated. There is one exception to this general rule. If your client has multiple IRAs, the aggregate MRDs for any one or more of them may be paid out of any one or more of them in any proportions, as long as total IRA distributions from all IRAs each distribution year at least equal the total MRDs for all IRAs for that distribution year. The MRD for each IRA still has to be calculated separately, for each separate account.

21st Century Estate Planning:
Practical Applications
2005 Edition

©2005 Sonnenschein Nath & Rosenthal LLP
and Cannon Financial Institute, Inc.

- 372 -

3. The "Designated Beneficiary"

It is important to name a "Designated Beneficiary" to receive post-death distributions from a qualified plan or IRA in order to maximize income tax deferral after death. If a Designated Beneficiary is not named, post-death distributions either must be made within 5 years after death (if the participant died before his or her "Required Beginning Date") or over the participant's remaining single life expectancy (if the participant died after his or her "Required Beginning Date"). If a Designated Beneficiary is named, however, the life expectancy of the Designated Beneficiary can be used to measure post-death distributions from the account. Unless the beneficiary is very elderly, the account will be eligible to be distributed over a longer period of time if a Designated Beneficiary is named, and income tax deferral will be maximized. So it is important to understand who is eligible to be a "Designed Beneficiary."

➔ **Planning Point:** Under the final regulations, only post-death distributions are affected if the named beneficiary is not a Designated Beneficiary. Consequently, whether or not there is a Designated Beneficiary is unimportant if post-death income tax deferral is not required. For example, if the participant wants his or her remaining account balance to pass to a qualified charity at death, the post-death deferral of income tax is not a concern, because the charitable beneficiary is income tax exempt. The fact that a qualified charity is not a Designated Beneficiary is not relevant for calculating distributions during the participant's lifetime, and does not matter after the participant's death.

The same situation can arise if the qualified plan or IRA assets are the only source of liquid assets in the participant's estate, and will be required to pay debts, taxes and administration expenses. While one might prefer to avoid this situation, that is not always possible. If the qualified plan or IRA has to be liquidated shortly after death to meet estate cash requirements, the fact that the estate does not qualify for an extended distribution period because the estate is not a Designated Beneficiary is not a concern.

➔ **Planning Point:** If a qualified plan or IRA is the only source of liquid assets available in a participant's estate to pay debts, taxes and administration expenses, overall taxes may be reduced if the account is liquidated immediately prior to death. This potential opportunity should be included on your pre-mortem planning checklist, for consideration in appropriate cases.

a. Eligible Designated Beneficiaries. A Designated Beneficiary is either an individual or a qualified trust. Treas. Reg. § 1.401(a)(9)-4. A charity, a corporation, a partnership, an estate or a nonqualified trust cannot be a Designated Beneficiary. If the qualified plan or IRA can be used to pay estate obligations, such as debts, taxes or administration

21st Century Estate Planning:
Practical Applications
2005 Edition

©2005 Sonnenschein Nath & Rosenthal LLP
and Cannon Financial Institute, Inc.

- 373 -

expenses, the estate is considered the (non-designated) beneficiary. The beneficiaries of an estate, whether the participant died testate or not, cannot be treated as the designated beneficiaries of a qualified plan or IRA of which the estate is the named beneficiary (whether expressly or by default).

If a participant names a *qualified* trust as the beneficiary of a qualified plan or IRA, then the trust beneficiaries will be treated as the beneficiaries of the account for purposes of determining whether there is a Designated Beneficiary and who it is. Treas. Reg. § 1.401(a)(9)-4, A-5. A qualified trust is a trust that satisfies the following four requirements on or before October 31 of the year following the year of the participant's death):

- The trust must be valid under local law. In making this determination the existence or requirement of trust corpus is disregarded.
- The trust must have identifiable beneficiaries. A class, such as descendants, may identify the beneficiaries; they do not need to be identified by name.
- The trust must be, or by its terms become, irrevocable on or before the participant's death.
- One of two documentation requirements must be satisfied. Either a copy of the trust instrument (and all subsequent amendments) must be provided to the plan administrator or trustee, or the plan administrator or trustee must be provided with a list of all the trust beneficiaries, including contingent and remainder beneficiaries, and a statement as to the circumstances under which they will take, determined as of September 30 of the year following the year of the participant's death. The participant must certify that this list is correct and complete and that the three above requirements are satisfied. The participant also must agree to provide a copy of the trust instrument to the plan administrator or trustee on demand.

By far the easier of these two documentation requirements is to provide a copy of the trust instrument to the plan administrator or IRA trustee or custodian. Under the proposed regulations, the date for providing trust documentation (under either option) is October 31 of the year following the year of the participant's death. It is no longer necessary to satisfy the trust documentation requirement during the participant's lifetime, unless the participant's spouse is the sole beneficiary of the trust and wants to be treated as the sole Designated Beneficiary of the account for purposes of the lifetime minimum distribution rules. This relieves some of the privacy concerns about providing a copy of the entire trust instrument. Note that a testamentary trust can be a qualified trust. Treas. Reg. § 1.401(a)(9)-5, A-7(c)(3), Ex. 2.

b. Multiple Beneficiaries. Special rules apply in determining who the Designated Beneficiary is when there is more than one beneficiary of an account. These rules provide that if *any* beneficiary is not a Designated Beneficiary, then there is *no* Designated Beneficiary. These rules also provide that if all of the beneficiaries are eligible Designated

21st Century Estate Planning:
Practical Applications
2005 Edition

©2005 Sonnenschein Nath & Rosenthal LLP
and Cannon Financial Institute, Inc.

- 374 -

Beneficiaries, then *the* Designated Beneficiary is that beneficiary with the shortest life expectancy (that is, the oldest). Because trusts usually have more than one beneficiary, the rules for determining the Designated Beneficiary when multiple beneficiaries are named ordinarily apply to trusts. Treas. Reg. § 1.401(a)(9)-5, A-7.

> **EXAMPLE:** An IRA participant names his three children as beneficiaries of the IRA. All of the children are individuals, so there is *a* Designated Beneficiary. The oldest child, who has the shortest life expectancy, is *the* Designated Beneficiary.

There is a "separate share" rule that in certain cases permits benefits payable under a plan to be treated as payable from separate accounts for purposes of applying this and the other minimum distribution rules, including those relating to the determination of the Designated Beneficiary. Treas. Reg. § 1.401(a)(9)-8, A-2. Two requirements must be met. First, the beneficiaries' interests must generally be fractional or percentage interests in the benefit as of the date of the participant's death (rather than fixed-dollar amount shares). Second, the separate shares must be established by December 31 of the year following the year of the participant's death. If these two requirements are satisfied, the life of the designated beneficiary of the separate share with respect to whom such separate share was established may be used as the measuring life for post-death distributions from that share. Treas. Reg. § 1.401(a)(9)-8; PLR 200208029; but see PLRs 200317041 and 200317043-44 (IRA distributable to trust that divided IRA into separate shares and distributed them to separate trusts held not to qualify for separate share treatment). The separate share rule will be effective for MRDs made during the year that the separate shares are established. Treas. Reg. §§ 1.401(a)(9)-6; -8 A-2(a) (69 FR 33288, June 15, 2004). Note that these separate share rules are not applicable when a qualified trust is designated as the account beneficiary. Treas. Reg. § 1.401(a)(9)-4, A-5(c). The related issue of contingent and successor beneficiaries is discussed below.

> **EXAMPLE:** An IRA participant names her three children as beneficiaries of the IRA. The participant dies on January 27, 2003, and all three children survive her. In November of 2003, before any IRA distributions are made, the IRA Trustee divides the IRA into three equal separate accounts, one for each of the three surviving children. The separate share rule applies, and the minimum distribution rules are applied separately to each share. As a result, each child is considered the sole Designated Beneficiary of his or her separate share of the account.

> ➔ **Planning Point:** To avoid a very technical ambiguity in the regulations related to the calculation of post-death MRDs under the separate share rules, it is advisable to establish separate shares by September 30 of the year following the year of the participant's death (the "Applicable Date" for determining the identity of the Designated Beneficiary), rather than December 31 of that year.

21st Century Estate Planning:
Practical Applications
2005 Edition

©2005 Sonnenschein Nath & Rosenthal LLP
and Cannon Financial Institute, Inc.

- 375 -

c. <u>Contingent Beneficiaries</u>. Contingent beneficiaries are included in determining whether there is a Designated Beneficiary, and who it is, unless the contingency relates to surviving either the participant or another beneficiary (which is the most common, but not the only, kind of contingency). Treas. Reg. § 1.401(a)(9)-5, A-7(b) and (c). The new regulations clarify that remainder beneficiaries after a life estate are counted in determining who the beneficiaries of a trust are, if any part of the qualified plan benefit or IRA could be accumulated in the trust for later distribution to the remainder beneficiaries. Treas. Reg. § 1.401(a)(9)-5, A-7(c)(3), Example 2. As a result, the ability to characterize one of the beneficiaries of a dynasty trust as the Designated Beneficiary is still an issue.

> **EXAMPLE:** An IRA participant names her daughter as the beneficiary of the IRA. If the daughter dies before the participant, or before the complete distribution of benefits from the account, the participant names a qualified charity as the beneficiary of the IRA. The daughter survives the participant. In determining whether there is a Designated Beneficiary after the participant's death, the qualified charity does not have to be considered. The charity's interest takes effect only if the daughter predeceases the participant, or the complete payment of benefits. This is a death contingency under Treas. Reg. § 1.401(a)(9)-5, A-7(b) and (c). The charity can be disregarded. The only remaining beneficiary (the daughter) is an eligible Designated Beneficiary.

> **EXAMPLE:** An IRA participant names his revocable living trust as the beneficiary of the IRA. The trust is a qualified trust under Treas. Reg. § 1.401(a)(9)-1. The trust provides that if the spouse survives the participant, the spouse will receive all of the income of the trust for life, plus principal in the discretion of the trustee for the spouse's health and support. At the spouse's death, or if the spouse predeceases the participant, any remaining trust property will be distributed to a qualified charity. The spouse survives the participant. In determining whether there is a Designated Beneficiary after the participant's death, the charity has to be included as one of the trust beneficiaries if any part of the benefits payable to the trust from the IRA can be accumulated in the trust. The charity's interest in the IRA is not contingent on surviving the spouse. It is contingent on the existence of any IRA assets remaining in the trust property at the spouse's death. This is not a death contingency under Treas. Reg. § 1.401(a)(9)-5, A-7(b) and (c). If the charity is included as one of the trust beneficiaries, there is no Designated Beneficiary, because a charity is not eligible to be a Designated Beneficiary.

21st Century Estate Planning:
Practical Applications
2005 Edition

©2005 Sonnenschein Nath & Rosenthal LLP
and Cannon Financial Institute, Inc.

- 376 -

d. **The Ability to Change Beneficiaries**. Under the original 1987 proposed regulations, if anyone other than the surviving spouse had the power to change the participant's beneficiaries, then there was no Designated Beneficiary for purposes of these rules. In general, this concept was carried forward in the 2001 proposed regulations. (Prop. Reg. § 1.401(a)(9)-5, A-7(d).) However, the 2001 proposed regulations also made it clear that a vested beneficiary could designate a successor beneficiary to receive unpaid benefits in the event of the beneficiary's death before all payments had been received. Although this entire section was eliminated from the final regulations, it is widely believed that the same rule continues to apply under the final regulations, by reason of the way in which the identity of the Designated Beneficiary is established for post-death distributions under the final regulations.

> **EXAMPLE:** An IRA participant names his son as his primary beneficiary, and provides that if his son dies before him, the IRA will be paid to the son's surviving children. The IRA custodial account agreement provides that if a beneficiary dies before the complete payment of benefits, the beneficiary can designate who will receive any remaining benefits. The son survives his father, and names a qualified charity to receive any remaining IRA benefits that are not distributed to the son during his lifetime. The son is the Designated Beneficiary. The children are not considered under the "death contingency" rules. Nothing in the final regulations limits the son's ability to name a successor beneficiary.

e. **The "Applicable Date" for Determining the Designated Beneficiary**. Under the regulations, the Designated Beneficiary is determined on September 30 of the year following the year of the participant's death (the "Applicable Date"). Treas. Reg. § 1.401(a)(9)-4, A-4. The actual death of a Designated Beneficiary after the participant's death and before the Applicable Date is disregarded, and in that case, the deceased Designated Beneficiary would continue to be considered a Designated Beneficiary for purpose of applying the post-death distribution rules.

The reason the proposed regulations deferred the date for determining the Designated Beneficiary until at least nine months after the participant's death is to avoid some of the hardships that had occurred under the old rules, which required that the designated beneficiary be determined as of December 31 of the year following the year of the participant's death. For example, when a trust is named as a beneficiary and one or more of the trust beneficiaries is not a Designated Beneficiary, the existence of *any* non-Designated Beneficiary requires the distribution of the account within five years after the participant's death. The application of this rule could be harsh, particularly if the interest of the non-designated beneficiary in the trust was relatively small, or could be satisfied in full out of other assets.

> **EXAMPLE:** An IRA participant named her revocable living trust as the beneficiary of the IRA. The trust was a qualified trust under Treas. Reg. § 1.401(a)(9)-4, A-5. The trust provides that after paying a

21st Century Estate Planning:
Practical Applications
2005 Edition

©2005 Sonnenschein Nath & Rosenthal LLP
and Cannon Financial Institute, Inc.

- 377 -

bequest to charity of $10,000, a gift to the participant's brother of $20,000, and paying all debts, taxes and expenses, the remaining trust property is to be distributed in equal shares to the participant's three adult children. All of the trust beneficiaries have to be included in determining whether there is a Designated Beneficiary, and who it is.

If the Designated Beneficiary were determined as of the date of the participant's death, the charity, the participant's brother, the participant's estate (because trust assets could be used to discharge estate obligations) and the participant's children all arguably would be trust beneficiaries. Because some of these beneficiaries are not eligible to be a Designated Beneficiary, there would be no Designated Beneficiary, and the entire account would have to be distributed within five years of the participant's death, if the participant died before her Required Beginning Date, or over the participant's remaining life expectancy, if she died thereafter.

However, assume that the Designated Beneficiary is determined on the Applicable Date, and that the charity, the brother and all estate debts, taxes and administration expenses are paid before the Applicable Date. Then the only beneficiaries of the trust on the Applicable Date are the participant's three children. Because each child is an eligible Designated Beneficiary, the account could be distributed over the life expectancy of the oldest child.

➜ **Planning Point:** In administering a trust that is named as the beneficiary of a qualified plan or IRA, you may be able to avoid the unnecessarily rapid distribution of the account, or qualify for a long-term distribution of the account, by completing estate administration duties within nine months after death.

Disclaimers also may be used after death to eliminate non-designated beneficiaries, or Designated Beneficiaries with short life expectancies.

4. Distributions After Death

With that background, the specific rules for calculating MRDs after death follow.

21st Century Estate Planning:
Practical Applications
2005 Edition

©2005 Sonnenschein Nath & Rosenthal LLP
and Cannon Financial Institute, Inc.

- 378 -

a. **Death Before Required Beginning Date**. In general, all qualified plans and IRA benefits must be distributed within five years after death, if the participant dies before reaching the participant's Required Beginning Date. IRC § 401(a)(9)(B)(ii). The rule that mandates distribution within five years after death can be avoided by naming a Designated Beneficiary during lifetime.

        (1)   **The "five-year rule"**. If the "five-year rule" applies, the decedent's entire interest in the qualified plan or IRA must be distributed on or before December 31 of the year that contains the fifth anniversary of the date of the decedent's death. Treas. Reg. § 1.401(a)(9)-3, A-2. However, if a Designated Beneficiary is named, distributions after the participant's death may be made over the beneficiary's life expectancy. In that case, distributions must commence by December 31 of the year following the year of the participant's death. IRC § 401(a)(9)(B)(iii); Treas. Reg. 1.401(a)(9)-3, A-2.

> **EXAMPLE:** A qualified plan participant dies on May 5, 2002. The general rule is that the participant's entire interest in the plan must be completely distributed on or before December 31, 2007. It does not matter how distributions are made during that time. The account may be distributed in a lump sum or in installments. In fact, the entire account can be distributed on December 31, 2007, with no intervening distributions. However, if the participant has named a Designated Beneficiary, distributions may be made over a period measured by the beneficiary's life expectancy, but only if distributions begin on or before December 31, 2003.

     Special rules may apply if the participant's spouse is the Designated Beneficiary. These are discussed at length below.

        (2)   **Calculating MRDs After Death Under the Exception to the 5-year Rule**. The procedure for calculating minimum required distributions if there is a Designated Beneficiary for the account and the participant dies before his or her Required Beginning Date is somewhat similar to the calculation of lifetime MRDs. First, determine the Designated Beneficiary's life expectancy for his or her age on his or her birthday in the year following the year of death, using the life expectancy tables contained in the regulations under Treas. Reg. § 401(a)(9)-9, A-1. That becomes the distribution factor for the first distribution year (the year following the year of death). Second, divide the account balance at the end of the preceding year (which would be the year of death) by the distribution factor. That calculation yields the MRD for the first distribution year. In each subsequent year, repeat the calculation, using the same method, after reducing the life expectancy factor for the prior year by one. Treas. Reg. § 1.401(a)(9)-5, A-5(c). You do not recalculate life expectancies on an annual basis unless the beneficiary is the surviving spouse. Special rules that apply to surviving spouses are discussed below.

21st Century Estate Planning:
Practical Applications
2005 Edition

©2005 Sonnenschein Nath & Rosenthal LLP
and Cannon Financial Institute, Inc.

- 379 -

EXAMPLE: An IRA participant dies on May 1, 2003, at age 65, before his Required Beginning Date. The participant named his adult child as the beneficiary of the IRA. The child survived the participant, and was living on December 31, 2004. The child's birthdate was September 15, 1968. The child's age on the child's birthday in 2004 is 36. The life expectancy factor for a person age 36 is 47.5 years, under Treas. Reg. § 401(a)(9)-(9) Single Life Table (<u>see</u> Appendix B). To calculate the MRD for 2004, divide the December 31, 2003 year-end account balance by 47.5. To calculate the MRD for 2005, divide the December 31, 2004 year-end account balance by 46.5 (47.5 minus 1). To calculate the MRD for 2006, divide the December 31, 2005 year-end account balance by 45.5 (46.5 minus 1).

b. Death After Required Beginning Date. If a participant dies after the participant's Required Beginning Date, qualified retirement plan and IRA benefits must be distributed "at least as rapidly" as they were being distributed to the participant during the participant's lifetime. IRC § 401(a)(9)(B)(i). The regulations interpret this rule differently, depending on whether or not the participant has named a Designated Beneficiary.

(1) If There is No Designated Beneficiary. If the participant dies after the participant's Required Beginning Date and has no Designated Beneficiary, post-death distributions are to be made over the participant's remaining single life expectancy, without further recalculation.

In this case, a MRD must be made for the year of death. The MRD for the year of death is calculated as if the participant were still alive. (If the year of death MRD was paid to the participant prior to death, the MRD requirement for that year is satisfied, and does not have to be paid again after the participant's death.) To calculate the MRD for the year following the year of death, you determine the participant's life expectancy as of the participant's age on his or her birthday in the year of death, and reduce that number by one. This becomes the distribution factor for calculating the MRD in the year after the year of death. This factor is then reduced by one for each succeeding year. Treas. Reg. § 1.401(a)(9)-5, A-5(c)(3).

EXAMPLE: An IRA participant dies at age 75 in 2002. She names her estate as her beneficiary. The account balance on December 31, 2001 is $250,000. In 2002, the MRD is calculated under the Uniform Table. The December 31, 2001 account balance is divided by the factor on the Uniform Table for age 75 (22.9). The MRD is $10,917 ($250,000/22.9=$10,917).

The MRD for 2003 is calculated by determining the participant's single life expectancy for age 75 (13.4) and reducing that number by 1 (12.4). Then, the December 31, 2002 account balance is divided by this factor to determine the MRD. If the account balance on December

21st Century Estate Planning:
Practical Applications
2005 Edition

©2005 Sonnenschein Nath & Rosenthal LLP
and Cannon Financial Institute, Inc.

- 380 -

31, 2002 is $275,000, the MRD for 2003 is $22,177 ($250,000/12.4=$22,177).

(2) **If There is a Designated Beneficiary**. If the participant has a Designated Beneficiary, post-death payments may be made from a qualified plan or IRA over the *longer of*: (i) the participant's remaining single life expectancy and (ii) the *beneficiary's* remaining single life expectancy, in either case without recalculation (unless the Designated Beneficiary is the surviving spouse, discussed further below). As is the case when the participant dies after his or her Required Beginning Date without a Designated Beneficiary, a minimum required distribution must be made for the year of death. This is calculated as if the participant were still alive, and is satisfied to the extent of distributions made to the participant prior to death. The distribution period for the year after the year of death is calculated with reference to the beneficiary's life expectancy as of his or her age on his or her birthday in that year (the year following the year of death). That age is reduced by one for each succeeding year. Treas. Reg. § 1.401(a)(9)-5, A-5(c)(1). Life expectancies are not recalculated or re-determined after the participant's death, unless the participant's Designated Beneficiary is the surviving spouse. If the Designated Beneficiary is the surviving spouse, special rules may apply, as described more fully below. Treas. Reg. § 1.401(a)(9)-5, A-5.

c. **Special Rules for the Surviving Spouse**. There are a number of special rules that apply if the participant of a qualified plan or IRA names his or her spouse as the beneficiary of the account.

(1) **Distributions During Participant's Life**. If the participant's spouse is more than 10 years younger than the participant, and the participant's spouse is the sole beneficiary of the account or plan for the entire year, then the participant may use the actual recalculated joint life expectancy of the participant and the spouse (instead of the factor set forth in the Uniform Table) as the distribution factor for calculating the MRD for that year. Treas. Reg. § 1.401(a)(9)-5, A-4(b). Life expectancy factors are determined by reference to the tables promulgated by the Internal Revenue Service in the regulations under IRC § 401(a)(9)-(9), reproduced as Appendix C. Although, generally, this younger spouse has to be the sole beneficiary of the entire account for the whole year, a change in marital status (by reason of death or divorce) during the year will not affect the calculation of the MRD until the following year.

> **EXAMPLE:** An IRA participant was born on March 15, 1930. Her first distribution year is 2000, and her Required Beginning Date is April 1, 2001. The participant has named her spouse as the sole beneficiary of the account. If the spouse was born before December 31, 1940, the MRD distribution factor for the participant's first distribution year (2000) is 27.4, based on the Uniform Table, because the participant was age 70 on her birthday that year. Suppose the participant's spouse was born on October 10, 1955. In that case, the MRD distribution factor for the first distribution year can be the actual

21st Century Estate Planning:
Practical Applications
2005 Edition

©2005 Sonnenschein Nath & Rosenthal LLP
and Cannon Financial Institute, Inc.

- 381 -

joint life expectancy of the participant and her spouse that year, based on Treas. Reg. § 1.401(a)(9)-9, Joint and Last Survivor Table (Appendix C). The participant's age on her birthday in her first distribution year is still age 70. Her spouse's age on his birthday in the participant's first distribution year is 45. The joint life expectancy of two persons aged 70 and 45 is 39.4. The participant's MRD for her first distribution year is calculated by dividing the 1999 year-end account balance by 39.4.

(2) __Death Before Required Beginning Date__. If the participant names his or her spouse as the Designated Beneficiary and dies before his or her Required Beginning Date, then the spouse may defer post-death payments until the participant's (hypothetical) age 70½. That is, distributions to the spouse do not have to begin until December 31 of the year in which the participant would have reached age 70½, had the participant survived. When payments are required to begin to the spouse in that year, the spouse's single recalculated life expectancy is used to calculate minimum required distributions. The factor for calculating the MRD for the first distribution year (the year in which the participant would have reached age 70½, had the participant survived) is the spouse's life expectancy factor based on the spouse's age on the spouse's birthday during that year. The factor for calculating the MRD for the next year is the spouse's recalculated life expectancy factor based on the spouse's age on the spouse's birthday during that next year. Treas. Reg. § 1.401 (a)(9)-5, A-5(c)(2).

If the spouse dies before distributions to the spouse commence, distributions are required to be made from the account under the same rules that would have applied if the spouse were the participant and had died before his or her Required Beginning Date. Treas. Reg. § 1.401(a)(9)-3, A-5. In other words, the general rule is that the entire remaining balance in the account must be distributed on or before December 31 of the year that contains the fifth anniversary of the date of the spouse's death. However, if a Designated Beneficiary is named, post-death distributions may be made over the beneficiary's life expectancy. In such a case, the first distribution must be made by December 31 of the year following the year of the spouse's death. The distribution factor for that first distribution year is the beneficiary's life expectancy based on his or her age on his or her birthday in that first distribution year. For each succeeding year, this factor is reduced by one.

If the spouse dies after distributions have begun to the spouse, minimum required distributions after the spouse's death are calculated using the spouse's remaining single life expectancy without further recalculation, in the same manner as if the spouse were the participant and had died, without naming a Designated Beneficiary, after his or her Required Beginning Date. The MRD for the year of the spouse's death is calculated as if the spouse were living. The factor for the first distribution year after the year of death is the factor corresponding with the spouse's age on the spouse's birthday in the year of the spouse's death, reduced by one. Treas. Reg. § 1.401(a)(9)-5, A-5(c). This factor is reduced by one in each succeeding year.

21st Century Estate Planning:
Practical Applications
2005 Edition

©2005 Sonnenschein Nath & Rosenthal LLP
and Cannon Financial Institute, Inc.

- 382 -

EXAMPLE: An IRA participant died in 2002 at age 67. He was born on October 10, 1935. His spouse was born on October 10, 1930. The participant named his spouse as the sole beneficiary of his IRA. The spouse is not required to begin distributions from the IRA until December 31, 2006, because the deceased participant would have reached age 70½ that year. If the spouse dies in 2005 with no Designated Beneficiary, the IRA must be completely distributed by December 31, 2010 (the year in which the fifth anniversary of the spouse's death occurs).

The spouse's MRD for 2006 is calculated by dividing the 2005 year-end account balance by the spouse's life expectancy in 2006. In that year, the spouse is age 76, and the life expectancy of a person aged 76 is 12.7. If the spouse dies in 2007 with no Designated Beneficiary, the IRA may be distributed over the spouse's remaining single life expectancy, without recalculation. In the year of death, the MRD distribution factor is based on the life expectancy of a person aged 77 (12.1) (as if the spouse were still alive). In the year following the year of death, the MRD distribution factor is the spouse's life expectancy based on her age on her birthday in the year of the spouse's death, reduced by 1, or 11.1. The *following* year, that factor is again reduced by 1, to 10.1.

(3) **Death After Required Beginning Date**. If a qualified plan or IRA participant dies after the participant's Required Beginning Date and names his or her surviving spouse as beneficiary, distributions after the participant's death must continue to be made at least as rapidly as they were being made during the participant's lifetime. As with other Designated Beneficiaries, post-death distributions may be made over the spouse's remaining single life expectancy. However, unlike other Designated Beneficiaries, the surviving spouse is entitled to recalculate the spouse's life expectancy each year. As in all cases when the participant dies after the participant's required distribution date, a MRD is required for the year of death, and is calculated as if the participant had not died. The distribution factor for the year following the year of death, and for all subsequent years during the spouse's lifetime, is the spouse's life expectancy, based on the spouse's age on the spouse's birthday in that distribution year.

After the spouse's death, distributions may continue to be made over the spouse's remaining single expectancy, but without recalculation. In the year of death, the MRD is calculated as if the spouse were still alive. In the year following the year of death, the distribution factor is the spouse's life expectancy, based on his or her age on his or her birthday in the year of the spouse's death, reduced by one. The distribution factor continues to be reduced by one in each succeeding year.

21st Century Estate Planning:
Practical Applications
2005 Edition

©2005 Sonnenschein Nath & Rosenthal LLP
and Cannon Financial Institute, Inc.

- 383 -

EXAMPLE: An IRA participant died in 2002 at age 77. He was born on October 10, 1925. His spouse was born on October 10, 1930. The participant named his spouse as the sole beneficiary of his IRA. The spouse is not required to begin distributions from the IRA until December 31, 2003. The spouse's MRD for 2003 is calculated by dividing the 2002 year-end account balance by the spouse's life expectancy in 2003. In that year, the spouse is age 73, and the life expectancy of a person aged 73 is 14.8. If the spouse dies in 2007, the IRA may be distributed over the spouse's remaining single life expectancy, without recalculation. In the year of death, the MRD distribution factor is based on the life expectancy of a person aged 77 (12.1) (as if the spouse were still alive). In the year following the year of death, the MRD distribution factor is the spouse's life expectancy based on her age on her birthday in the year of the spouse's death, reduced by 1, or 11.1. The *following* year, that factor is again reduced by 1, to 10.1.

      (4)   **Spousal Rollovers**. A very important special rule available exclusively to participants' spouses is the spouse's ability to rollover an eligible distribution from a qualified plan or IRA to another IRA. IRC § 402(c)(9) and § 408(d)(3)(C). Treas. Reg. 1.408-2(b)(7)(ii) also permits the surviving spouse, if named as the beneficiary of an IRA, to elect to treat the spouse's entire interest in the IRA as the spouse's own IRA. The use of these options is very important for income tax deferral planning. A surviving spouse who rolls over an IRA inherited from a participant has all of the income tax deferral opportunities available to the participant during the participant's lifetime, including the right to defer distributions until the spouse's Required Beginning Date, to measure lifetime MRDs to the spouse using the factors from the Uniform Table, and to designate new beneficiaries whose life expectancies may be used to measure distributions from the IRA after the spouse's death.

      If the spouse is under age 59½ a rollover of the entire inherited IRA may not be an appropriate option, if the spouse needs any of the IRA funds for the spouse's support prior to reaching that age. If the spouse rolls over an inherited IRA, the spouse is subject to the same penalties as any IRA participant for early distributions. Unless a pre-59½ distribution qualifies for one of the exceptions noted in IRC §72(t), funds paid out of the spouse's IRA prior to the spouse's age 59½ will be subject to the 10% early distribution penalty.

➔   **Planning Point:** One of the exceptions to the 10% penalty for early distributions is payment to a beneficiary by reason of a participant's death. One strategy for taking advantage of rollover opportunities for the younger surviving spouse is to keep in the participant's IRA only that amount of property needed to provide for the surviving spouse's support to age 59½, and to distribute that portion of the participant's IRA to the spouse in a manner that satisfies the applicable post-death minimum required

21st Century Estate Planning:
Practical Applications
2005 Edition

©*2005 Sonnenschein Nath & Rosenthal LLP*
and Cannon Financial Institute, Inc.

- 384 -

distribution rules and meets the spouse's support needs. The spouse can rollover the balance of the account.

Another exception to the 10% tax on early distributions is payment of the account to the participant in equally or substantially equal installments over life, or over the joint life expectancy of the participant and his or her designated beneficiary. IRC §72(t)(2)(a)(iv). Another way for a surviving spouse to take advantage of rollover options prior to age 59½ without incurring the 10% penalty is to rollover the entire account, and immediately begin distributions over life or joint lives, as provided in this section.

(5) **Conduit Trusts**. With one exception, the special rules available to spouses for calculating post-death MRDs are not available if a trust is named as the beneficiary of a qualified plan or IRA, even if the trust is a qualified trust and the spouse is treated as the Designated Beneficiary. The exception relates to "Conduit Trusts." A Conduit Trust is a trust that distributes to the current beneficiary all amounts paid to the trust from a qualified plan or IRA, and that cannot accumulate distributions from a qualified plan or IRA in the trust for later distribution to anyone else. Treas. Reg. § 1.401(a)(9)-5, A-7(c)(3), Exs. 1 and 2. If a Conduit Trust for the benefit of the spouse is named as the beneficiary of an IRA or qualified plan, most of the special rules available when the spouse is named as the direct beneficiary can apply to distributions to the Conduit Trust. PLR 200105058. The Conduit Trust exception does not apply to spousal rollovers, however, or to a spouse's election to treat an "inherited" IRA as the spouse's own IRA.

There also has developed a set of rules for determining when a spouse, who is the beneficiary of a trust, can rollover a qualified plan or IRA benefit payable to the trust, and not to the spouse directly. If the qualified plan or IRA benefits are allocated entirely to the spouse, or to a trust for the benefit of the spouse which the spouse is entitled to withdraw without restriction, either by the terms of the governing instrument or by the exercise of fiduciary discretion *that is controlled by the spouse*, the spouse can rollover the benefit. PLR 9533042; PLR 9524020; PLR 9515041; PLR 9515042; PLR 9545010; PLR 9623056. For an example of a situation where a rollover was not permitted because the non-spouse trustee had discretion to determine the allocation and distribution of trust assets, including the IRA, see PLR 9445029.

➔ **Planning Point:** Do not give up entirely on rollover options if a trust has been designated as the beneficiary of a qualified plan or IRA. Review the terms of the governing instruments with care, to see if the spouse might qualify for a rollover under this exception.

Because the Designated Beneficiary is not determined until the Applicable Date, consider if disclaimers might be used so that the qualified plan or IRA benefits are payable to the spouse, or to a trust for the spouse that qualifies for this exception.

21st Century Estate Planning:
Practical Applications
2005 Edition

©2005 Sonnenschein Nath & Rosenthal LLP
and Cannon Financial Institute, Inc.

- 385 -

d. <u>Some Improvements Made to the 1987 Regulations</u>. The final regulations eliminate a number of problems that existed under the original proposed regulations. Two in particular have ongoing importance.

(1)   <u>Recalculation Election</u>. Under the original proposed regulations, a qualified plan or IRA participant was required to elect whether or not to recalculate life expectancies no later than the participant's Required Beginning Date. This election, once made, was irrevocable. The new rules eliminate the concept of the lifetime recalculation election in its entirety. They contemplate that during the lifetimes of the participant and spouse, life expectancies will always be recalculated annually. Any prior election or failure to elect to recalculate life expectancies is no longer relevant, and can be disregarded entirely.

(2)   <u>Changes of Beneficiary</u>. Under the old proposed regulations, if a participant changed his or her beneficiary after the Required Beginning Date, it could have an adverse effect on the distribution period during the participant's lifetime. This made it difficult to correct a beneficiary designation that did not maximize income tax deferral, or to change a beneficiary designation to accommodate changing estate planning needs, after a participant's Required Beginning Date. This rule no longer applies. As a result, plan participants can change their beneficiaries without restriction, before or after their Required Beginning Date, without any impact on the calculation of lifetime minimum required distributions.

e. <u>Reporting</u>. One of the reasons the IRS has adopted these new more liberal regulations is because it was not only difficult for plan participants, administrators and trustees to calculate minimum required distributions accurately, it was equally impossible for the IRS to enforce minimum distribution requirements. One of the features of the new proposed regulations is that qualified plan trustees and IRA sponsors are going to be required to report to the IRS identifying information for all accounts from which minimum required distributions must be made. The IRS can use this information to "match" reported qualified plan and IRA distributions on the participant's federal income tax return. Qualified plan trustees and plan sponsors also will have to advise participants when MRDs are required, and how to calculate them.

f. <u>Effective Dates</u>. The minimum distribution rules contained in the 2002 final regulations are effective for all plan years beginning in 2003, and may not be used for plan years prior to 2002. In 2001, MRDs can be calculated under either the 2001 proposed regulations or the 1987 proposed regulations. In 2002, MRDs can be calculated either under the 2001 proposed regulations, the 1987 proposed regulations, or the 2002 final regulations. Note that a minimum required distribution for 2001 that is properly deferred to April 1, 2002 is still a year 2001 distribution, and is not eligible to be calculated under the final regulations. For IRAs, the underlying plan documents do not have to be amended in order for participants to rely on the new rules. Qualified plans must be amended to incorporate the new rules before the plan administrator may use them to calculate participant MRDs. IRS Announcement 2001-18, 2001-10 I.R.B. 791. However, if a qualified plan is not amended, and as a result a participant receives a distribution calculated under the old proposed regulations that is larger than the distribution

21st Century Estate Planning:
Practical Applications
2005 Edition

©2005 Sonnenschein Nath & Rosenthal LLP
and Cannon Financial Institute, Inc.

- 386 -

that would have been made under the new regulations, it appears that the participant is entitled to rollover the excess. IRS Announcement 2001-23, 2001-10 I.R.B. 791.

➔ **Planning Point.** Distributions made before 2003 that fail to comply either with the 1987 or the 2001 proposed regulations under IRC § 401(a)(9) should not be automatically subject to penalty. Many non-complying distributions might be defended as based on a "reasonable interpretation" of the statutory requirements, particularly now that the IRS has developed three such "reasonable interpretations" itself.

There are two other effective date rules to keep in mind. If an employee filed an election under "TEFRA 242(b)" (The Tax Equity and Fiscal Responsibility Act of 1982, P.L. 97-248) on or before January 1, 1984, and has not since revoked the election, the employee is entitled to receive distributions under the plan provisions as in effect in 1983. Some long-standing distribution schemes that do not comply with any of the proposed regulations under IRC § 401(a)(9) may be grandfathered by this election, and, if so, are entitled to continue to use their elected method of distribution without penalty. See, IRS Notice 83-23, 1983 - 2 C.B. 418.

The 1987 proposed regulations under IRC § 401(a)(9) were issued in 1987, but related to tax law changes effective in 1985. These old proposed regulations contain a number of transitional rules for distributions made in 1985, 1986 and 1987. Do not assume that distributions for those years that do not appear to comply with the proposed regulations are incorrect, without first reviewing the transitional rules contained in the 1987 proposed regulations.

H. Estate and Gift Taxation of Qualified Plans and IRAs

1. General Rule - Estate Taxation

As a general rule, the value of qualified plans and individual retirement accounts are included in the gross estate under IRC § 2039, dealing with the estate taxation of annuities. IRC § 2039 annuities are not limited to annuity contracts. For purposes of IRC § 2039, an annuity includes *any* payment receivable by *any* beneficiary under *any* form of contract or agreement under which a payment was to be made to the decedent during his lifetime. If the decedent contributed the entire purchase price for the annuity, then the entire value of the annuity is included in the decedent's gross estate. Contributions made by a decedent's employer (or former employer) to the purchase price of an annuity (within the meaning of IRC § 2039) are considered to be contributions by the decedent. The value of the annuity or other payment itself is determined under IRC § 2031 and Treas. Reg. §§ 20.2031-7; 20.2031-8; 20.2031-9.

Although there are certain cases in which it has been successfully argued that payments made to a beneficiary after the decedent's death in connection with the decedent's employment were not taxable as part of the decedent's gross estate, for the most part IRC § 2039 will capture

21st Century Estate Planning:
Practical Applications
2005 Edition

©2005 Sonnenschein Nath & Rosenthal LLP
and Cannon Financial Institute, Inc.

- 387 -

in the gross estate the value of all employment related compensation, including pension and profit sharing plans, whether qualified or non-qualified, and individual retirement accounts.

→ **Planning Point.** The regulations under IRC § 2031 relating to the valuation of annuities emphasize the valuation of traditional annuity contracts. Because many qualified plan accounts and IRAs are invested by, and can be withdrawn by, the participant at any time, most planners have valued such accounts with reference to the value of the underlying securities or investments in the account. An argument could be made, however, that qualified plans and IRAs should be valued only after taking into account plan restrictions (such as non-alienability) or other features of the qualified plan or IRA that define it, such as the tax burden inherent in the account if it is distributed, and the income tax deferral benefit that can be obtained if distributions from the account are restricted. However, the IRS has consistently resisted such an approach.

2.   Grandfather Provisions For Estate Tax Exclusion under IRC § 2039

Before 1983, the proceeds of many qualified plans and IRAs were exempt from federal estate tax if certain requirements were met. The exclusion applied to employer contributions to a qualified plan, tax deductible contributions to an IRA and rollover IRAs. The proceeds had to be payable to a beneficiary other than the participant's estate. There developed from this requirement a rule that if qualified plan or IRA proceeds could be used to discharge an estate obligation, they would be included in the gross estate under § 2039. (For this reason, it was important to exclude the proceeds of a qualified plan or IRA from the funds out of which tax payments and other obligations could be satisfied.) For qualified plans, the estate tax exclusion did not apply if the recipient of the proceeds elected favorable income tax treatment (that is, ten-year forward averaging or capital gains treatment for pre-1974 participation) for a lump sum distribution of the plan proceeds. An IRA, which was not eligible for favorable income tax treatment, had to be paid in equal installments over a minimum of thirty-six months to be eligible for estate tax exclusion under IRC § 2039, as in effect before 1983.

The estate tax exclusion for qualified plans and IRAs was cut back to a maximum of $100,000 for estates of decedents dying after December 31, 1982. The exclusion was eliminated entirely in 1984 for estates of decedents dying after December 31, 1984.

The Tax Reform Act of 1984 (P.L. 98-369) included special "grandfather" provisions that applied retroactively to retain part or all of the estate tax exclusion under IRC § 2039 for certain qualified plans and IRAs. In its original form, the grandfather provision was largely irrelevant. However, in the Tax Reform Act of 1986 (P.L. 99-514) the 100% federal estate tax exclusion for a qualified plan or IRA was reinstated if the following conditions were met:

- the participant separated from service before 1983.

21st Century Estate Planning:
Practical Applications
2005 Edition

©2005 Sonnenschein Nath & Rosenthal LLP
and Cannon Financial Institute, Inc.

- 388 -

- the participant elected the form of benefit to be paid under the plan before 1983.
- the participant did not change the form of benefit paid under the plan prior to the participant's death.
- the participant was in "pay status" (that is, received at least one payment pursuant to the benefit option elected) before 1983.
- the distribution otherwise qualified for estate tax exclusion under IRC § 2039, as it existed prior to repeal.

The 1986 Tax Act also reinstated the $100,000 federal estate tax exclusion for qualified plans or IRAs under similar circumstances, with reference to an effective date of July 18, 1984 (P.L. 99-514).

EXAMPLE: Your client retired in 1980, and elected to receive distributions from her qualified plan in installments payable over 30 years. This was a permissible form of distribution in 1980. Payments began to your client in 1981. The client provided that at her death any unpaid installments would be paid, in installments as originally elected, to her revocable trust. The revocable trust precluded the use of qualified plan assets to pay estate obligations and taxes. It further provided that any property that was not eligible for the federal estate tax marital deduction would be allocated to the Family Trust. The client died in 2000, and her spouse survived her.

The undistributed plan benefits should be eligible for estate tax exclusion under the IRC § 2039 provisions. First, the payments would have been exempt from estate tax under IRC § 2039 prior to repeal, because they were not payable to or for the benefit of the estate, and they were not payable in a lump sum distribution for which favorable income tax treatment was elected. Second, the participant had retired prior to 1983, and had elected a form of benefit (30-year installments) prior to 1983 that began before 1983 and had not been changed.

Property that is not included in the gross estate is not eligible for the federal estate tax marital deduction. As a result, under the terms of the trust, the remaining qualified plan installments should be allocated to the Family Trust.

➔ **Planning Point:** If qualified plan assets are excluded from the gross estate under IRC § 2039, they also are exempt from Generation Skipping Transfer Tax under IRC § 2612 (dealing with the taxation of direct skips). The preservation of this estate tax exclusion when it is otherwise available can be enormously valuable. You may think that it is not possible to preserve the exclusion if the form of payment elected prior to 1983 does

21st Century Estate Planning:
Practical Applications
2005 Edition

©2005 Sonnenschein Nath & Rosenthal LLP
and Cannon Financial Institute, Inc.

- 389 -

not conform to current minimum distribution requirements. This is not necessarily the case. Many forms of benefit elections not permitted under current law remain valid if they were elected prior to 1983, under the so-called "TEFRA 242(b)" election (see, P.L. 97-248).

The IRS has acknowledged that these grandfather provisions apply to eligible qualified plan benefits (PLR 9211041 (Dec. 17, 1991)). However, the IRS also has taken the position that these grandfather provisions do *not* apply to IRAs under any circumstances. Rev. Rul. 92-22, I.R.B. 1992-13 (March 20, 1992). There are no known decided cases challenging the IRS position on this point, even though it appears to be inconsistent with the original intent of the grandfather provisions and is not supported by the statute.

With the passage of time, the potential benefit of estate tax exclusion under the IRC § 2039 grandfather provisions becomes more and more remote. Eligible individuals would have had to separate from service before 1985, which for the most part would make them well into their 80's today, if they retired at normal retirement age. What is more, in order for the exclusion to apply, the form of benefit elected prior to the grandfather date cannot be changed prior to the participant's death. Given all of the changes made in the rules governing the calculation of minimum required distributions from qualified plans and IRAs since 1983, an unchanged form of benefit is uncommon. Most forms of benefit have, in fact, been changed, either to comply with revised minimum distribution requirements or in order to avoid a more rapid lifetime distribution than would otherwise be required. Nevertheless, these situations continue to surface from time to time.

➔ **Planning Point:** If your client retired before 1985, be sure to evaluate the status of the client's qualified plans or IRAs under the IRC § 2039 estate tax exclusion grandfather provisions before making any changes in the client's beneficiary designation or distribution election. Consider if you can maximize the benefit of the exclusion, such as by allocating a grandfathered plan to a GST exempt trust or share, without disqualifying the plan for the exclusion. Can you qualify the plan for the estate tax marital deduction on a contingent basis, if the exclusion is disallowed? Can you use a formula gift if you are unsure about qualifying for the exclusion (*i.e.*, "allocate to the Family Trust that part of the plan excluded from my gross estate …").

3.   **Income Tax Deduction for Estate Taxes Paid Under IRC § 691(c)**

The basis for the former estate tax exclusion for qualified plans and IRAs was the two-fold concern of (i) imposing income tax and estate tax on the same asset, and (ii) imposing estate tax at a time when the plan benefits themselves might not be available to the beneficiary. With the introduction of the unlimited federal estate tax marital deduction and an easing of the constructive receipt rules (which gave to plan participants and their beneficiaries more flexibility in deciding how to withdraw plan benefits), both of these concerns are alleviated, at least if there

21st Century Estate Planning:
Practical Applications
2005 Edition

©*2005 Sonnenschein Nath & Rosenthal LLP*
and Cannon Financial Institute, Inc.

- 390 -

is a surviving spouse. However, if there is no spouse, or if the spouse is not the beneficiary of the plan, or if the spouse's benefits under the plan fail to qualify for the marital deduction, the double taxation issue remains severe.

Under IRC § 691, any item that would have been income if payable to a decedent during the decedent's lifetime is taxed as income to the recipient of that item after the decedent's death. This applies to many items, including most employee benefits payable after death, whether qualified or non-qualified. Rev. Rul. 92-47, 1992-1 C.B. 198; Rev. Rul. 69-297, 1969-1 C.B. 131; Rev. Rul. 75-125, 1975-1 C.B. 254. Items of "Section 691" income (or "income in respect of a decedent") do not receive any basis step up at death. IRC § 1014(c).

> **EXAMPLE:** An unmarried employee dies in 2005 with a deferred compensation account valued at $350,000, plus $1,500,000 in other assets. The employee did not make any lifetime gifts. The deferred compensation account is included in the employee's gross estate under IRC § 2039. This generates an estate tax of approximately $157,500. When the deferred compensation account is distributed to the employee's beneficiaries, all amounts distributed are included in the gross income of the beneficiaries. Without reference to the special deduction allowed under IRC § 691(c), and assuming the employee's beneficiaries have an average rate of income tax of 25%, the total income tax on the date of death plan balance will be approximately $87,500. The total effective rate of tax (both income and estate) on the deferred compensation plan is about 70%.

To relieve the burden of this estate taxation and income taxation of the same asset, there is an income tax deduction, allowed under IRC § 691(c), for the federal estate tax attributable to Section 691 income. This deduction is calculated with respect to the net value of all Section 691 items included in the decedent's estate, and then prorated among them. The tax attributable to Section 691 income is calculated at marginal rates. It is measured as the difference between the federal estate tax, calculated on the estate *including* all items of Section 691 income, and the federal estate tax, calculated on the estate *excluding* all items of Section 691 income.

21st Century Estate Planning:
Practical Applications
2005 Edition

©2005 Sonnenschein Nath & Rosenthal LLP
and Cannon Financial Institute, Inc.

- 391 -

EXAMPLE: An unmarried employee dies in 2005 with a deferred compensation account valued at $350,000, plus $1,500,000 in other assets. The employee's estate tax is approximately $166,300. The employee's state of residence imposes a "decoupled" state estate tax which represents $16,000 of the total estate tax. The federal estate tax represents the remaining $150,300. The entire estate tax is attributable to the deferred compensation account because, if that account were not included in the employee's gross estate, there would be no estate tax. (The entire estate tax would have been absorbed by the available applicable credit amount.) When the deferred compensation account is distributed to the employee's beneficiaries, all amounts distributed are included in the gross income of the beneficiaries. Taking into account the special deduction allowed under IRC § 691(c), and assuming the employee's beneficiaries have an average rate of income tax of 25%, the total income tax on the date of death plan balance will be $49,925. This is calculated as follows:

691 income:	$350,000
691(c) deduction:	(150,300)
Taxable amount:	$199,700
25% tax:	$49,925

Note that the IRC § 691(c) deduction is only available for the federal estate tax, not the state estate tax. The total effective rate of tax (both income and estate) on the deferred compensation plan (after the IRC § 691(c) deduction) is about 60%.

There are a number of important things to remember about the IRC § 691(c) deduction. First, it is complicated to calculate. The actual facts in an estate administration are rarely as simple as those assumed above. Section 691 income includes many items, such as accrued interest and dividends after the record date, and a number of offsets and deductions as well. Further, Section 691 income can be, and often is, received over a period of several years. Second, the deduction is often forgotten, or overlooked. Third, the deduction does not fully compensate for the double taxation of Section 691 income (including qualified plans and IRAs) at death. Finally, the IRC § 691(c) deduction is not available if the Section 691 income is not subject to estate tax. Consequently, the distribution of qualified plan or IRA assets at death to the surviving spouse or a qualified charity will not enjoy the benefit of the IRC § 691(c) deduction.

➜   **Planning Point:** In any administration of a taxable estate, be sure to calculate the § 691(c) deduction. If the right to receive items of Section

21st Century Estate Planning:
Practical Applications
2005 Edition

©2005 Sonnenschein Nath & Rosenthal LLP
and Cannon Financial Institute, Inc.

- 392 -

691 income are allocated to beneficiaries as part of their distributive share of the estate, be sure to advise them, *and their accountants*, of the amount of the IRC § 691(c) deduction they are entitled to claim against their share of Section 691 income as received.

→ **Planning Point:** Because the IRC § 691(c) deduction is not the same as (or as good as) eliminating the unpaid income tax from the decedent's taxable estate, there are two strategies that might be considered in planning prior to death, if your client will have a taxable estate at death. One is a Roth IRA conversion. This preserves tax-free growth for the future, but does not preserve deferral of the income tax on the current plan balance. Not all clients (particularly those that have taxable estates) will be eligible for a Roth IRA conversion, because of the applicable income limitations.

Another strategy is to withdraw the qualified plan or IRA balance prior to death. While this sacrifices *all* income tax deferral, it can still be a useful strategy in some cases, particularly if a large portion or all of the qualified plan or IRA will have to be liquidated shortly after death to meet estate cash requirements, or if a distribution of the qualified plan or IRA balance over a number years is unavailable for other reasons.

Neither strategy is right in every case. But each is worth considering and merits an analysis of the relative advantages and disadvantages.

4.   General Rule for Gift Taxation of Qualified Plans and IRAs

As a general rule, qualified plans and individual retirement accounts do not attract gift tax, because beneficiary designations and other elections are generally revocable by the participant during life. Further, in order to be treated as a qualified plan or IRA under the applicable sections of the Internal Revenue Code, the participant's interest in the plan or IRA must be non-alienable and non-forfeitable. IRC § 401(a)(13)(A). The inability of a participant to transfer his or her interest in the plan during life in general precludes the gift taxation of plan benefits.

Prior to 1986, Internal Revenue IRC § 2517 expressly provided that the exercise of elections under qualified plans did not constitute a gift, even if the election were irrevocable. The one common situation in which gift treatment might arise with respect to a qualified plan under current law relates to an irrevocable election by a qualified plan participant to receive a joint and survivor annuity at retirement, either with the participant's spouse or another beneficiary.

The characteristics of qualified plans and IRAs that limit the occasions when a gift tax issue might arise do not apply to most non-qualified plans. Irrevocable beneficiary designations

21st Century Estate Planning:
Practical Applications
2005 Edition

©2005 *Sonnenschein Nath & Rosenthal LLP*
and Cannon Financial Institute, Inc.

- 393 -

or other elections under non-qualified plans may attract gift tax, under the traditional rules governing when a gift is made and completed for federal gift tax purposes. IRC § 2511.

5. Automatic QTIP Treatment for Annuities

In order to prevent the election of a joint and survivor spousal annuity from constituting a taxable gift for federal gift tax purposes, IRC § 2523(f)(6) was added to the Internal Revenue IRC in 1988 as part of the Technical and Miscellaneous Revenue Act of 1988 ("TAMRA," P.L. 100-647). This provision specifies that when only a husband and wife have the right to receive payments under an annuity (as defined for purposes of IRC § 2039) during the lifetimes of husband and wife, an irrevocable election to receive a joint and survivor annuity will be treated as a qualifying income interest for life in the donee spouse, eligible for the federal gift tax marital deduction under IRC § 2523. What is more, the election normally required to qualify such an income interest for the gift tax marital deduction under IRC § 2523(f)(2)(C) and IRC § 2523(f)(4) is considered to have been made automatically, unless the donor or spouse affirmatively elects otherwise on a timely filed gift tax return. The interest of a donee spouse who predeceases the participant is not included in the gross estate of the donee spouse under IRC § 2044.

These rules apply retroactively to all irrevocable elections made after December 31, 1981. However, these provisions will not apply if they are inconsistent with the treatment given to such a transfer on a prior estate or gift tax return. Every participant had two years after date of enactment (November 10, 1988) either to elect QTIP treatment for an irrevocable joint and survivor annuity that was inconsistently reported on a prior return, or to elect out of automatic marital deduction treatment for a joint survivor annuity. (See, TAMRA § 6152(c)(2) and (3), P.L. 100-647.)

6. Waiver of Rights Under Retirement Equity Act of 1984 ("REA")

The Retirement Equity Act of 1984 ("REA") requires that defined benefit plans, money purchase plans, profit sharing plans (including HR-10 or KEOGH plans but *not* IRAs) and stock bonus plans all provide survivor benefits (both pre- and post-retirement) for the surviving spouse of any vested plan participant. Generally, participants may waive the survivor annuity requirements, but, for such a waiver to be effective, the participant's spouse must consent to the waiver in writing before either the plan administrator or a notary public. In certain profit sharing plans, the spouse also must consent to the designation of a beneficiary other than the spouse. If a spouse consents to the waiver of the spouse's survivor benefits during the participant's lifetime, this is not considered a gift by the spouse. IRC § 2503(f). There are no provisions describing the gift tax treatment that may apply to waivers after the participant's death of rights or consents under REA, however.

21st Century Estate Planning:
Practical Applications
2005 Edition

©2005 Sonnenschein Nath & Rosenthal LLP
and Cannon Financial Institute, Inc.

- 394 -

I. Planning for Distributions of Qualified Plans and IRAs at Death

1.   Maximizing Deferral

The economic principles that make deferring distributions from a qualified plan or IRA advantageous during the participant's lifetime, apply equally well after the participant's death. In planning for the distribution of qualified plans and IRAs after death, structuring the beneficiary designation and distribution options to maximize income tax deferral should be a primary objective. The difficulty is how to achieve estate tax minimization and deferral at the same time.

        a. Spouse as Beneficiary.   Maximum income tax deferral ordinarily is obtained by naming the surviving spouse as the primary beneficiary of a qualified plan or IRA. The spouse has a number of distribution options that are not available to other beneficiaries. The spouse can defer distribution from a qualified plan or IRA to the participant's age 70½, if the participant dies before that age. Alternatively, if the spouse has the right to rollover the qualified plan or IRA to another IRA, or to treat the IRA as the spouse's own IRA, distributions can be deferred until the spouse's age 70½. If the participant's spouse is the sole beneficiary of an IRA or qualified plan account for the entire year, the minimum required distribution for that year can be based upon the actual joint life expectancy of the participant and the participant's spouse, rather than the Uniform Table. If the participant's spouse is more than 10 years younger than the participant, this can produce a longer distribution period both during the participant's lifetime and after the participant's death. If the participant's surviving spouse rolls over a qualified plan or IRA to another IRA, the spouse can name new beneficiaries and recommence the uniform lifetime distribution period, further extending account distributions. If the participant's spouse is the Designated Beneficiary, the spouse can recalculate the spouse's life expectancy in calculating required distributions after the participant's death.

➔   **Planning Point:** There is a significant difference between the distribution period available to the spouse if the spouse rolls over an IRA or qualified plan benefit and the distribution period available to the spouse if the spouse is treated as a Designated Beneficiary after the participant's death without the ability to rollover (as would be the case if the surviving spouse failed to rollover within the 60-day rollover period). Compare the distribution period, MRDs and the value of the IRA under the Uniform Table for a person aged 70 - 75, with the recalculated life expectancy of a person aged 70 - 75.

21st Century Estate Planning:
Practical Applications
2005 Edition

©*2005 Sonnenschein Nath & Rosenthal LLP*
and Cannon Financial Institute, Inc.

- 395 -

	Uniform Table Calculation				Life Expectancy Calculation		
Age	Account Value	Distribution Factor	MRD	Age	Account Value	Distribution Factor	MRD
70	100,000	27.4	3,650	70	100,000	17	6,250
71	96,350	26.5	3,636	71	94,118	16.3	5,882
72	92,714	25.6	3,622	72	88,344	15.5	5,774
73	89,092	24.7	3,606	73	82,644	14.8	5,700
74	85,486	23.8	3,592	74	77,060	14.1	5,465
75	81,894	22.9	3,576	75	71,595	13.4	5,343
Total Distributions			21,682				33,748
Balance in Account	78,318				66,252		
Percent Change					(15.4%)		56%

The results are far more dramatic when account earnings are taken into account.

There are a number of other advantages, both tax and non-tax, in naming the spouse as the primary beneficiary of a qualified plan or IRA. Perhaps most important of these is the fact that the unrestricted payment of qualified plan and IRA benefits to the surviving spouse should qualify for the unlimited federal estate tax marital deduction in the participant's estate, thus deferring any federal estate tax that might otherwise be imposed with respect to the plan benefits. On the non-tax side, designating the spouse as the sole primary beneficiary of a qualified plan or IRA avoids any community property issues that might arise with respect to an IRA and assures compliance with the Retirement Equity Act of 1984 for a qualified plan. Both of these issues are discussed at greater length below.

  b. "Stretch" Distributions and IRAs. A "Stretch" Distribution or a Stretch IRA is simply a qualified plan or IRA that is eligible to be distributed over a long period of time after death, usually when payable to a beneficiary other than the spouse. For income tax deferral

21st Century Estate Planning:
Practical Applications
2005 Edition

©*2005 Sonnenschein Nath & Rosenthal LLP*
and Cannon Financial Institute, Inc.

- 396 -

purposes, you want post-death distributions from a qualified plan or IRA to qualify for a Stretch Distribution or as a Stretch IRA. This is accomplished by making sure that the plan or account is payable at the participant's death to a Designated Beneficiary.

→ **Planning Point:** There are two strategies that will assist you in implementing a Stretch IRA. One is to make sure that there are sufficient other liquid assets available for the payment of debts, claims and other obligations in the decedent's estate. Qualifying for a stretch distribution is of little use if the account has to be liquidated to pay taxes. Second, consider advising your client to rollover from a qualified plan into an IRA prior to death. IRAs generally are more flexible in their distribution options, and can qualify for stretch distribution more easily. In making this recommendation, review with your client the advantages of qualified plan participation that will be given up in an IRA rollover. These may include investment management costs, when they are absorbed or subsidized in the qualified plan, eligibility for certain favorable income tax treatment, or eligibility for the application of certain grandfather provisions, such as estate tax exclusion under the IRC § 2039 grandfather provisions, or exemption from the current minimum distribution rules, under the "TEFRA 242(b)" (See, P.L. 97-248) grandfather provisions. The existence of loans against the plan, or life insurance in the plan, also may be issues, as neither can be rolled over to an IRA.

One or more individual beneficiaries can qualify as the "Designated Beneficiary" for purposes of implementing a Stretch Distribution or creating a Stretch IRA. But when naming individual beneficiaries of a qualified plan or IRA for stretch distribution purposes, there are a number of issues that should be considered:

- Is the possibility of minor beneficiaries adequately provided for, either under the beneficiary designation or the underlying plan documentation?
- Will the beneficiary designation be appropriate if there is an unusual order of deaths (*i.e.*, child predeceases parent)?
- Is adequate provision made for the distribution of the account in the event of the death of the individual beneficiary before the complete distribution of his or her share of the account?
- Is the taxation of the account on the death of an individual beneficiary before the complete distribution of his or her share clear? The account will be subject to estate tax in the beneficiary's estate if the beneficiary has the right to withdraw the account at will, or to designate a successor beneficiary without restriction (either of which constitute a general power of appointment under IRC § 2041), or if the beneficiary's estate will receive any undistributed assets at the beneficiary's death.

21st Century Estate Planning:
Practical Applications
2005 Edition

©2005 Sonnenschein Nath & Rosenthal LLP
and Cannon Financial Institute, Inc.

- 397 -

- Do you want to use the qualified plan or IRA as a form of generation-skipping transfer? If so, are you certain that the beneficiary does not have any rights or powers (either under the participant's beneficiary designation or distribution election or under the plan documentation itself) that will cause the value of the account to be included in the beneficiary's estate?
- Is the distribution of the qualified plan or IRA to individual beneficiaries consistent with other (non-tax) provisions of the participant's estate plan, including the allocation or apportionment of estate taxes?
- Are there adequate provisions governing investment management in the account after the participant's death?

➜ **Planning Point:** The plan and trust documents for a qualified plan, and the trust or custodial account agreement for an IRA, contain all of the provisions governing the participant's interest under the plan. Although these documents have to comply with IRS requirements, they do not have to include all available options allowed by the IRS, and may specify their own rules regarding investments, distributions and defaults, to the extent not inconsistent with the Internal Revenue Code and ERISA. It is important to keep this in mind when planning for distributions from qualified plans and IRAs, as your planning options may be restricted by the terms of these documents. You may not have the ability to address the issues outlined above in a manner other than as provided in the plan documents.

c. **Dynasty Trusts or Other Trusts for Children**. To avoid many of the issues noted above, estate planners commonly recommend that payments from a qualified plan or IRA be made after death to a trust for the benefit of individual family members. Naming a trust as a beneficiary of a qualified plan or IRA, while appealing for this reason, must be approached with care if income tax deferral is a primary objective. As discussed above, in addition to complying with the documentation requirements described in the regulations, you also must make sure that all of the trust beneficiaries (including any contingent beneficiaries) are eligible Designated Beneficiaries.

The final regulations permit a trust beneficiary to be considered the sole Designated Beneficiary of the account only if the trust is a "Conduit Trust" - that is, a trust that immediately distributes all qualified plan benefits payable to the trust to the beneficiary. This is not a traditional way to draft a trust, and in many cases such an approach would defeat the purposes for using a trust in the first instance. However, if the trust is *not* a Conduit Trust, then all beneficiaries for whom plan benefits could be accumulated for future distribution have to be taken into account in determining who the Designated Beneficiary is.

This is a particularly trying issue when naming a dynasty trust (or multi-generation-skipping transfer tax exempt trust) as the beneficiary of a qualified plan or IRA, and trying to

21st Century Estate Planning:
Practical Applications
2005 Edition

©2005 Sonnenschein Nath & Rosenthal LLP
and Cannon Financial Institute, Inc.

- 398 -

qualify for a stretch distribution. These trusts typically will not be conduit trusts. The final regulations do not indicate how many levels of contingent beneficiaries need to be considered in this context. How far out do you have to go? If your trust is not subject to the rule against perpetuities, perhaps forever. Nor do the final regulations indicate how to treat potential appointees under a power of appointment. Do broad powers of appointment create a class of beneficiaries that is not "identifiable"? Can a trust be designed that never under any circumstances distributes to anyone other than identifiable individual beneficiaries? Maybe, but it would require unusual provisions to do so.

If a trust were intended to be distributed when the beneficiary attained a stated age or ages that is within the beneficiary's actuarial life expectancy, it could be argued in that case that only the first level of default beneficiaries need be taken into account - that is, the members of the default beneficiary class presently living. If this class were descendants, the trust distribution could arguably be made over the life expectancy of the oldest living child (as all other descendants would be younger). While this seems a logical result, the final regulations do not give any specific guidance, and the IRS has been less than clear in its private rulings on the subject.

In PLR 200228025, a trust for the benefit of children was named as the beneficiary of an IRA. Under the trust terms, separate trusts were established for each child. Each trust continued until the child reached a stated age. If the child died before attaining that age, the trust distributed to the child's descendants, or if none, to the child's siblings (or the descendants of a deceased brother or sister), or if none, to the child's uncle. At the time of the participant's death, the children had not reached the stated distribution age. The IRS ruled that the uncle was a beneficiary of the trust who had to be taken into account in determining the designated beneficiary of the IRA. Taken to its logical conclusion, this analysis is extremely problematic. Whether expressed in the trust or not, every trust has some default taker, which may not be an eligible designated beneficiary, or who may be an older family member.

Other rulings are more encouraging. In PLRs 200235038-41, the decedent named his revocable trust as the beneficiary of his IRA and died after his RBD. The trust provided that a non-relative was to receive outright 25% of the trust property upon the decedent's death. This distribution was satisfied by distributing 25% of the IRA to a separate IRA for the benefit of that non-relative. The remaining 75% of the trust was divided into equal trusts for the benefit of the decedent's surviving children. Daughter A was the oldest.

Each child's trust provided that the child had a mandatory income interest and could receive discretionary principal distributions. Each child also had a broad special testamentary power of appointment. In addition, the child was prohibited from exercising that power in favor of a "Disqualified Appointee," which was defined as any person older than Daughter A, any person other than a trust or an individual or any trust that has or may have a beneficiary who is older than Daughter A. The IRS ruled that the MRDs to each child's trust could be taken from the IRA based on the life expectancy of Daughter A, the oldest child of the decedent. Thus, the IRS in these rulings gave its apparent approval of the above savings clause. Also, the

21st Century Estate Planning:
Practical Applications
2005 Edition

©2005 Sonnenschein Nath & Rosenthal LLP
and Cannon Financial Institute, Inc.

- 399 -

disqualified appointee provisions were added after the decedent's death by way of a court reformation. Practitioners therefore can not only use these provisions in drafting the trust agreement but also use them effectively in post-mortem planning.

When drafting a savings clause such as the one in the above ruling, there are three (at least) rules to be attentive to: (a) that all of the beneficiaries of the trust with respect to the IRA (including contingent and successor beneficiaries) be eligible designated beneficiaries; (b) that all of the beneficiaries of the trust with respect to the IRA (including contingent and successor beneficiaries) be identifiable; and (c) that all of the non-primary beneficiaries of the trust with respect to the IRA be younger than the primary trust beneficiary.

Some planners are concerned that such a comprehensive savings clause might introduce significant dispositive distortions or ambiguities into the estate plan or create an administrative nightmare. Thus, in some cases, a preferable approach when a trust is required may be to use a conduit trust.

There also is a practical problem in naming a trust as the beneficiary of a qualified plan or IRA. In the normal course of trust administration, trust assets are allocated among or distributed to the trust beneficiaries, who may be individuals or continuing trusts for the benefit of those individuals. There is no tax or trust law reason why the right to receive benefits under a qualified plan or IRA could not be allocated or distributed in the same way. PLR 200008044; PLR 199947036; PLR 9751037; Rev. Rul. 78-406, 1978-2 C.B. 157. However, in some cases the plan administrator or IRA sponsor will interpret a beneficiary designation literally, and insist on paying the plan benefits to the named trust, even though there is no other reason for the named trust's continued existence. This interferes with Marital and Family Trust splits, allocation among separate trusts for different beneficiaries, and the distribution of trust assets at stated ages, among other things. Even in the best case, it precludes the efficient administration of the trust. Some plan administrators have argued that this approach is required, as no one is permitted to transfer an interest in a qualified plan or IRA. It is not always possible to persuade them that this form of devolution is not a transfer, but simply the passage of entitlement by operation of the terms of the beneficiary trust.

2. Marital Deduction Qualification Issues

One common situation in which a spouse should not be designated as a direct, unrestricted beneficiary of a qualified plan or IRA is when the participant wants to insure that some portion of the account will pass at the spouse's death to the participant's selected beneficiaries. In other words, the participant does not want the spouse to have unrestricted access to or control over the disposition of the qualified plan or IRA. There are two ways this concern might be addressed. One would be by naming the spouse as the direct beneficiary of the account, but restricting in some way the spouse's rights over the account. Another way would be by naming a trust for the benefit of the spouse as the beneficiary of the account. Either approach raises marital deduction issues.

21st Century Estate Planning:
Practical Applications
2005 Edition

©2005 Sonnenschein Nath & Rosenthal LLP
and Cannon Financial Institute, Inc.

- 400 -

a. Restrictions on the Spouse. In naming the spouse as the primary beneficiary of the qualified plan or IRA assets, it is important that the distribution to the spouse qualify for the federal estate tax marital deduction, or be eligible to elect to qualify for the federal estate tax marital deduction. Problems can arise with the marital deduction whenever restrictions are imposed on the distribution of the account. For example, if instead of allowing the spouse the unrestricted right to rollover the account balance or to make withdrawals at the spouse's election, a participant might decide to direct that a qualified plan or IRA be paid to the spouse in annual installments equal to the minimum required distribution, and that any unpaid installments at the spouse's death will be paid to a beneficiary other than the spouse's estate. On what basis would such an interest qualify for the federal estate tax marital deduction?

Under IRC § 2056(b), there are three exceptions to the general rule that a terminable interest will not qualify for the federal estate tax marital deduction. Two of them, a general testamentary power of appointment marital trust under IRC § 2056(b)(5) and a qualified terminable interest property trust (QTIP) under IRC § 2056(b)(7), each require that the spouse receive all of the income for life. The payment of minimum required distributions by no means guarantees that the spouse will receive all of the income of the underlying account each year.

> **EXAMPLE:** An IRA participant has an IRA that is invested in a certificate of deposit earning 4.5%. The participant provides that in the event of death, MRDs are to be paid to the participant's spouse for life. Any undistributed balance in the account at the spouse's death will be paid to the participant's surviving children in equal shares. The participant dies at age 67 in 2002. The value of the IRA at that time is $100,000. The spouse was age 62 in 2002.
>
> The accounting income in the IRA and the MRDs for the first five years after death is as follows:

Year	Account Income	MRD
2003	$4,500	-0-
2004	$4,703	-0-
2005	$4,914	-0-
2006	$5,135	$5,649
2007	$5,112	$5,856
Total	*$24,364*	*$11,505*

21st Century Estate Planning:
Practical Applications
2005 Edition

©2005 Sonnenschein Nath & Rosenthal LLP
and Cannon Financial Institute, Inc.

- 401 -

In this example, no MRDs are required until the participant would have reached age 70½. As a result, during the first three years after the participant's death, no income at all was required to be distributed to the surviving spouse, and the MRDs paid to the spouse during the first five years after death are less than one-half of the accounting income earned in the IRA.

Results of the type postulated in the above example do not occur only when the participant dies before the participant's Required Beginning Date. This type of result could occur as well if the participant died after reaching his or her Required Beginning Date, depending on the earnings in the account and the age of the spouse. Because for marital deduction purposes the spouse must receive all of the income in all events, this form of distribution would not qualify for the marital deduction under IRC § 2056(b)(5) or § 2056(b)(7).

In Treas. Reg. § 20.2056(b)-7(h), Ex. 10, it is provided that, if the amount to be paid to the spouse is the *greater of* the trust accounting income and the minimum required distribution, the installment form of payout will qualify for the federal estate tax marital deduction as qualified terminable interest property. In Rev. Rul. 2000-2, 2000-3 I.R.B. 305, the IRS further held that the spouse's continuing right to compel the distribution of the income of the underlying account is sufficient for marital deduction qualification, even if the distributions actually made are limited to the minimum required distribution. This is consistent with Treas. Reg. § 20.2056(b)-(7)(d)(2) and Treas. Reg. § 20.2056(b)-5(f)(8). In either case, however, it is clear that the spouse must have either the right to receive, or the unfettered right to demand the distribution of, all of the accounting income of the underlying qualified plan account or IRA, and that minimum distributions alone will not satisfy the estate tax marital deduction requirements.

b. **Annuities**. IRC § 2056(b)(7)(C) provides that in the case of an annuity that is included in the gross estate of the decedent under IRC § 2039 where only the surviving spouse has the right to receive payments during the spouse's lifetime, the interest of the spouse will automatically be treated as a qualifying income interest for life, eligible for the federal estate tax marital deduction, unless the executor elects otherwise on the decedent's federal estate tax return. It is possible to argue that minimum required distributions that are made directly to the surviving spouse should qualify as an "annuity" under IRC § 2039, and as qualified terminable interest property under IRC § 2056(b)(7)(C). It is not likely, however, that this provision could be used to claim a federal estate tax marital deduction for minimum required distributions to a trust that otherwise did not provide for the distribution to the spouse, at least annually, of all of the accounting income earned in the underlying qualified plan or IRA.

c. **QTIP and General Power of Appointment Marital Trusts**. Participants often name a trust for the benefit of the spouse as the beneficiary of a qualified plan or IRA so as to gain more control over the ultimate disposition of the principal while still obtaining the marital deduction for the IRA or qualified plan benefits. The disadvantage of this approach is a loss of

21st Century Estate Planning:
Practical Applications
2005 Edition

©2005 Sonnenschein Nath & Rosenthal LLP
and Cannon Financial Institute, Inc.

- 402 -

income tax deferral. As explained above, the spouse can substantially delay the beginning of MRDs and reduce the amount of such MRDs. A trust, on the other hand, does not have these advantages. The trustee would be required to distribute to the surviving spouse at least annually all of the current income of the trust, including any and all internally generated income inside the qualified plan or IRA.

Qualifying an IRA or interest in a qualified plan for the marital deduction when proceeds are payable to a trust is complex. The IRS views the employee benefit account itself as a vehicle that must qualify for the marital deduction. Treas. Reg. §§ 20.2056(b)-5(f)(8) and 20.2056(b)-7(d)(2). Thus, it is not simply enough to give the trustee of the trust the ability to withdraw distributions from the qualified plan or IRA in excess of the minimum required distribution. Either the trustee has to be mandated to exercise that power so that all of the trust accounting income of the underlying plan is distributed to the trust at least annually, or the spouse has to be given the right to do so, or to compel the trustee to do so. In addition, there must be a mechanism, either under the trust instrument itself, under state law rules, or both, to guarantee that all of the trust accounting income that is distributed to the trust from the underlying qualified plan or IRA (or that the spouse can compel to be distributed) will be allocated to the income account and distributed to the spouse as income. If distributions to the trust from the qualified plan or IRA of income earned in the qualified plan or IRA are allocated to principal, marital deduction qualification is jeopardized. Finally, the surviving spouse must be able to compel the trustee to make the qualified plan or IRA assets income producing.

> **EXAMPLE:** An IRA participant has an IRA that is invested in a certificate of deposit earning 4.5%. The participant provides that in the event of death, MRDs are to be paid to the participant's revocable trust. The revocable trust provides that during the spouse's lifetime, the spouse will receive all the income of the trust. Any undistributed balance in the trust at the spouse's death will be paid to the participant's surviving children in equal shares. The participant dies at age 67 in 2002. The value of the IRA at that time is $100,000. The spouse is age 62 in 2002.
>
> Assume that the trustee does not have the ability to withdraw funds from the IRA in excess of the MRD. Assume further that the trust requires that receipts be allocated between income and principal in accordance with state law, and that state law allocates all retirement plan payments to principal.
>
> The following chart shows the accounting income in the IRA, the MRDs, and the income distributions to the spouse for the first five years after death.

21st Century Estate Planning:
Practical Applications
2005 Edition

©2005 Sonnenschein Nath & Rosenthal LLP
and Cannon Financial Institute, Inc.

- 403 -

Year	Account Income	MRD	Income to Spouse
2003	$4,500	-0-	-0-
2004	$4,703	-0-	-0-
2005	$4,914	-0-	-0-
2005	$5,135	$5,649	-0-
2007	$5,112	$5,856	$254
Total	*$24,364*	*$11,505*	*$254*

In this example, the MRDs paid to the trust during the first five years after death are allocated to principal. The spouse's right to income under the trust does not include either the income earned in the IRA or the MRDs, but just the earnings on MRDs paid to the trust and allocated to principal, *after income tax*.

→ **Planning Point:** State law rules vary significantly in how they allocate qualified plan and IRA payments payable to a trust between income and principal. When naming a trust as the beneficiary of a qualified plan or IRA, make sure that the trustee or the spouse can withdraw accounting income earned in the plan or IRA in excess of the MRD, and that accounting income distributed from the qualified plan or IRA is allocated to income in the trust for income and principal accounting purposes, if you want the qualified plan or IRA to qualify for the federal estate tax marital deduction.

Instead of giving the trustee or the surviving spouse the discretion to compel distributions from the underlying plan or account, the beneficiary designation and distribution election could require that annual distributions be made in an amount equal to the *greater of* the trust accounting income and the minimum required distribution. This less flexible approach may be required if the underlying plan documents do not permit the beneficiary to make withdrawals in excess of MRDs or otherwise will not accommodate the type of distribution provisions required for marital deduction qualification purposes.

   d. "Estate-Type" Marital Deduction Trust. A time-honored (although not often used) form of distribution to a spouse that qualifies for the federal estate tax marital deduction is a form of trust that pays income (and, perhaps, principal) to the spouse in the discretion of the trustee, coupled with a provision that transfers any trust property remaining at the spouse's death to the spouse's estate. This "estate type" marital deduction trust qualifies for

21st Century Estate Planning:
Practical Applications
2005 Edition

©2005 Sonnenschein Nath & Rosenthal LLP
and Cannon Financial Institute, Inc.

- 404 -

the federal estate tax marital deduction because it is not a terminable interest. Any form of distribution of a qualified plan or IRA to a qualifying "Estate-Type" marital deduction trust should qualify for the federal estate tax marital deduction.

e. **"Conduit Trusts"**. A Conduit Trust is not really a type of Marital Deduction Trust. In a Conduit Trust, all qualified plan or IRA distributions paid to the trust (whether MRDs or discretionary distributions made at the direction of the trustee) are immediately distributed to the beneficiary, and not accumulated for future distribution to the successor beneficiaries. Because none of the minimum required distributions made during the spouse's lifetime can ever be accumulated for the ultimate benefit of anyone but the spouse, the spouse is treated as the sole beneficiary of the IRA or qualified plan. Treas. Reg. § 1.401(a)(9)-5 A-7, Ex. 2. To the extent that a client wants both maximum income tax deferral and to use a trust instead of outright distribution to the spouse, you should consider structuring your Marital Deduction Trust as a Conduit Trust. This means that *in addition* to satisfying the requirements for the type of marital trust you are using, you *also* must provide for the complete distribution of all qualified plan benefits and IRA payments made to the trust to the spouse.

Conduit Trusts used as a marital deduction qualification vehicle are a mixed blessing. They avoid trapping income associated with qualified plan and IRA payments in the trust, where they will be taxed at the higher trust income tax rates. But if the spouse lives a long time, most or all of the IRA or qualified plan proceeds will be distributed to the spouse, free of the trust. This may defeat, at least in part, the client's objectives in using the trust in the first instance.

3. Marital Deduction and GST Formulas

Another situation in which a client may not want to name the spouse as the direct, unrestricted beneficiary of a qualified plan or IRA is when the plan assets are anticipated to be needed to minimize estate taxes over two estates, usually by means of Marital Trust and Family Trust "zero-tax" estate planning. However, this type of estate planning is generally accomplished by means of a formula gift or bequest, which raises a special problem in the context of Section 691 income.

A formula gift or bequest is one in which the amount of the gift is determined with reference to some external measurement. The most common formula gift is one that measures the value of the gift either with reference to the "applicable exclusion" (or "unified credit equivalent"), or with reference to the unlimited marital deduction. It would be typical, in Marital Trust and Family Trust "zero-tax" estate planning, for example, to allocate to the Marital Trust the smallest amount necessary to eliminate the estate tax, or to allocate to the Family Trust the largest amount possible without generating any estate tax. These are typically called "Marital Deduction Formulas." "GST Formulas" operate in the same way, except that they are calculated with reference to the GST exemption. A typical GST formula would allocate an amount equal to the remaining unused GST exemption to a GST exempt trust.

21st Century Estate Planning:
Practical Applications
2005 Edition

©2005 Sonnenschein Nath & Rosenthal LLP
and Cannon Financial Institute, Inc.

- 405 -

There are many ways to draft formula gift or bequest clauses, and the choice of language can have an effect both on the amount of property allocated to the disposition under the formula, and on the income tax consequences of allocating assets in kind in satisfaction of the formula gift. While there are many different kinds of formulas, two of the most common are "pecuniary" formulas and "fractional share" formulas. A fractional share formula allocates to the trust (or other beneficiary) that *percentage* of the trust assets required to fund the gift. A pecuniary formula allocates to the trust (or other beneficiary) that *amount or value* of trust assets required to fund the gift. (For example, the formulas described in the preceding paragraph are pecuniary formulas.) One of the primary characteristics of any gift of a pecuniary amount, including a pecuniary formula gift, is that, when assets (rather than money) are used to satisfy the gift, the transaction is treated as a sale of the assets. *Kenan v. Comm.,* 40 B.T.A. 824 (1939), *aff'd* 114 F. 2d 217 (Cir. 2, 1940); *Suisman v. Comm.,* 15 Fed. Supp. 113, *aff'd,* 83 F. 2d 1019, *cert. den.* 299 U.S. 573; Rev. Rul. 56-270, 1956-1 C.B. 325; Rev. Rul. 66-207, 1966-2 C.B. 243; PLR 9507008; PLR 9315016. In the context of estate administration, the "sale" is often between related parties under IRC § 267, so that gain (but not loss) is recognized.

> **EXAMPLE:** A decedent makes a gift under his revocable trust to his daughter of $250,000. Included in the trust assets is 100 shares of XYZ Company stock, with a cost basis for measuring gain or loss of $100,000, and a fair market value of $250,000. The trustee distributes the stock to the decedent's daughter in satisfaction of her gift.
>
> The gift to the daughter of $250,000 is a pecuniary gift. The transfer of XYZ Company stock to the daughter is the transfer of assets (instead of cash) in satisfaction of a pecuniary gift. The transfer of stock to the daughter under these circumstances is considered a sale, and the trust will recognize $150,000 of capital gains income in the year of the transfer. The daughter's cost basis in the stock for measuring gain or loss on a subsequent sale is $250,000. See, *Ewing v. Comm.,* 40 B.T.A. 912 (1939); GCM 36783 (July 8, 1976).

This concept has special significance in the context of Section 691 income. IRC § 691(a)(2) provides that, if an item of Section 691 income is transferred, either by the estate or anyone else, the fair market value of the right to receive that item of income (at the time of transfer) will be included in the recipient's gross income. For this purpose, the term "transfer" includes any sale or exchange. It does not include a transfer after the decedent's death to the person entitled to receive it by reason of the decedent's death. PLR 9324024.

If the satisfaction of a pecuniary gift with assets (or "in kind") is treated as a sale for federal income tax purposes, then logically the transfer of an item of Section 691 income in satisfaction of a pecuniary formula gift is a transfer, which results in the immediate income taxation of the Section 691 income. Most planners believe this is, in fact, what happens.

21st Century Estate Planning:
Practical Applications
2005 Edition

©2005 Sonnenschein Nath & Rosenthal LLP
and Cannon Financial Institute, Inc.

- 406 -

EXAMPLE: Your client's revocable trust provides that, at her death, an amount equal to the largest amount that can be transferred free of federal estate tax will be allocated to the Family Trust, and the balance of the trust property will be allocated to the Marital Trust. Your client's estate consists of a $2,500,000 IRA, payable to the revocable trust. The client's available applicable exclusion amount is $1,500,000. After the client's death, the trustee allocates $1,500,000 of the IRA to the Family Trust and $1,000,000 of the IRA to the Marital Trust. The revocable trust will have $1,500,000 of ordinary income in the applicable taxable year as a result of using part of the IRA to fund the pecuniary amount to which the Family Trust is entitled. The transfer of the IRA in satisfaction of a pecuniary formula gift is a "sale," and a sale is a "transfer" under IRC § 691(a)(2), resulting in the immediate recognition of income.

EXAMPLE: Your client's revocable trust provides that at her death, a fractional share of the trust property will be allocated to a Family Trust, and the balance of the trust property will be allocated to the Marital Trust. The numerator of the faction to be allocated to the Family Trust is equal to the largest amount that can be transferred free of federal estate tax. The denominator of the fraction is the value of the trust property. Your client's estate consists of a $2,500,000 IRA, payable to the revocable trust. The client's available applicable exclusion amount is $1,500,000. This produces a fraction (in this case) of 60% ($1,500,000/$2,500,000). After the client's death, the trustee allocates 60% of the IRA, or $1,500,000, to the Family Trust and 40% of the IRA, or $1,000,000, to the Marital Trust. The revocable trust will not recognize any income in the applicable taxable year as a result of using part of the IRA to fund the fractional amount to which the Family Trust is entitled. The transfer of the IRA is *not* in satisfaction of a pecuniary formula gift, so it is *not* a "sale." Because it is not a sale, it is not a "transfer" under IRC § 691(a)(2). Instead, it is a non-taxable transfer to the person entitled to receive the IRA by reason of the decedent's death.

This problem is easily avoided. It often is possible to fund the pecuniary formula gift with other assets, and not Section 691 income. Further, planners may wish to avoid the use of a pecuniary formula when the estate consists in large part of Section 691 income and instead use a fractional share formula. Another method of dealing with this problem is specifically to allocate items of Section 691 income to a particular beneficiary or trust, perhaps employing cut-back or limiting language (in the case of a trust) or consider the use of disclaimers (in the case of individuals) to deal with the possibility that the Section 691 income will be more than the trust or beneficiary is intended to receive. Rev. Rul. 55-117, 1955-1 C.B. 233; PLR 9537011. But in all

21st Century Estate Planning:
Practical Applications
2005 Edition

©2005 Sonnenschein Nath & Rosenthal LLP
and Cannon Financial Institute, Inc.

- 407 -

events, be aware of the issue, whenever a client's estate includes large items of Section 691 income.

This problem is not limited to qualified plans and IRAs. It could arise with any items of Section 691 income, including installment sales contracts, non-qualified employee benefits, annuities and so on. Nor is this issue limited to pecuniary formula gifts. Any kind of pecuniary gift (*i.e.*, "I give my friend Jack $1,000,000) could attract this problem.

→ **Planning Point:** If you are required by circumstances to fund a pecuniary gift with qualified plan or IRA assets, consider withdrawing assets from the plan, reserving the income tax on the withdrawn funds, and funding the gift with the net proceeds. The allocation of the right to receive an IRA or qualified plan in satisfaction of a pecuniary gift will have the same income tax result. But if the assets remain in the plan when the right to receive the plan benefits is allocated to the beneficiary, will subsequent distributions from the plan be taxed to the beneficiary for federal income tax purposes *again*?

It is important to keep in mind that in most cases the use of a trust as the beneficiary of a qualified plan or IRA will not provide for the greatest amount of income tax deferral. Consequently, there often is a trade off to be made at the death of the first spouse to die. Either the client minimizes estate taxes by fully funding the credit shelter amount with plan benefits (which, as income in respect of a decedent, may not fully fund the credit shelter amount in any case), or the client minimizes income taxes by paying the plan benefits to the spouse. It is important that the client understand this trade off.

A common approach is to pay the benefits to the spouse, and provide that, if the spouse predeceases the participant, the benefits will then pass to the trust. This permits the spouse to decide about this trade off based on the circumstances that exist at the time of the participant's death, and to use disclaimers to achieve the desired result at that time. This approach is not perfect, of course, as the spouse also must disclaim any powers of appointment over the disclaimed benefits, limiting the flexibility of the credit shelter trust. Also, the time period within which a disclaimer may be made (nine months from the participant's death) could elapse. Still further, the spouse may inadvertently accept the benefits before disclaiming, thus destroying his or her ability to disclaim them. Furthermore, the spouse may choose not to disclaim, even if good tax planning would clearly indicate the desirability of disclaiming, particularly if the trust to which the disclaimed benefits will pass restricts the spouse's access to funds. However, when a nonmarital trust is needed primarily for estate tax minimization at the second death, this approach has merit, especially in the current estate tax environment of constant change. Other solutions might include making the credit shelter trust a Conduit Trust, or using a Charitable Remainder Unitrust as the credit shelter vehicle (discussed below).

→ **Planning Point:** An often recommended beneficiary designation for qualified plans and IRAs is to name the spouse as the primary beneficiary

21st Century Estate Planning:
Practical Applications
2005 Edition

©*2005 Sonnenschein Nath & Rosenthal LLP*
and Cannon Financial Institute, Inc.

- 408 -

(if the spouse survives the participant), and the Family Trust (or other nonmarital disposition) as the contingent beneficiary (if the spouse predeceases the participant). The thought behind this plan is that, by naming the spouse first, the spouse has every opportunity to maximize wealth by deferring income taxes. If there are not enough assets to fully fund the Family Trust from other sources, the spouse has the option to disclaim part of the qualified plan interest or IRA. In most jurisdictions, disclaimed property passes as if the disclaiming beneficiary (in this case, the spouse) had predeceased the decedent. As a result, the disclaimed portion will pass to the Family Trust, and supplement its funding. Such a disclaimer would not result in the surviving spouse's making a taxable gift of the IRA to the Family Trust. By specifically naming the Family Trust as the contingent beneficiary, the IRC § 691(a)(2) issue discussed above is avoided. The qualified plan or IRA proceeds also end up in the right place if the spouse actually predeceases the participant.

A variation on this theme is to name the participant's revocable trust as the contingent beneficiary, and to include in the revocable trust language that specifically allocates Section 691 income to the appropriate beneficiary.

4.   Tax Apportionment Issues

There are no Internal Revenue Code provisions providing for tax reimbursements for qualified plans or individual retirement accounts taxable under IRC § 2039, other than general transferee liability. If a qualified plan or IRA passes to beneficiaries outside the provisions of a decedent's will and revocable trust, the issue of how estate taxes on those qualified plans and IRA benefits are to be paid must be addressed.

A non-apportionment tax clause in your estate planning documents, which allocates the burden of tax payments to the residue of the estate (whether passing by will or revocable living trust) might bankrupt an estate, or create a significant disproportion in the distribution of assets. Conversely, the apportionment of the tax burden to the qualified plan or IRA beneficiaries might force the beneficiaries to withdraw funds from the plan or account prematurely in order to meet their estate tax obligations, minimizing the potential for income tax deferral. The distribution of funds from a qualified plan or IRA to pay estate taxes will accelerate the income taxation of the distribution. It also will further increase the tax burden imposed on the beneficiary, by creating an income tax liability to the beneficiary with respect to income the beneficiary does not have, or cannot keep.

There also is the concern that if a qualified plan or IRA is required to contribute to the payment of estate taxes, the estate is functionally a beneficiary of the qualified plan or IRA. The estate is not a Designated Beneficiary for purposes of the minimum distribution rules, so that if the estate is functionally a beneficiary of the account or plan, distribution of the plan benefits after the participant's death over the lifetime of the beneficiary may not be available. Finally,

21st Century Estate Planning:
Practical Applications
2005 Edition

©2005 Sonnenschein Nath & Rosenthal LLP
and Cannon Financial Institute, Inc.

- 409 -

there always is the question of how to calculate a tax that is to be apportioned, and whether that calculation should be made at marginal estate tax rates or at average estate tax rates. Without statutory guidance, the method of making the calculation, including who is to get the benefit of deductions or credits associated with the distribution, needs to be addressed.

A number of states, either by statute or case law, have developed a scheme for the apportionment of estate taxes to non-probate property that may provide for tax apportionment to employee benefit plans. The Uniform Estate Tax Apportionment Act and the Uniform Probate Code each contain such provisions. Some planners also have argued that tax apportionment under IRC § 2036 may apply to employee benefit plans, though there is no published IRS authority or case law to support the argument.

The issue of who is responsible for the payment of estate taxes on qualified plan benefits and IRAs should be carefully provided for in the estate planning documents whenever the surviving spouse, a qualifying marital deduction trust, a qualified charity or the participant's estate (or other vehicle that provides for the payment of taxes) are not named as the only beneficiaries of the plan proceeds at the participant's death.

5.   Charitable Gifts with Qualified Plans and IRAs

The use of employee benefits such as qualified plans and IRAs for charitable giving after-death is extremely tax efficient. A qualified charity is both income and estate tax exempt, and the payment of such benefits to charity is income tax free. PLR 9253038 (January 1, 1993); PLR 9237020 (September 11, 1992).

> **EXAMPLE**: Assume a client with a taxable estate wants to make a gift at his death of $100,000 to charity, and $100,000 to his niece. The client has a $100,000 IRA. Here is how the net after-tax gifts look if the IRA is given to charity, or the niece. Assume the client's estate tax bracket is 45%, and that the niece is in a 25% income tax bracket. Paying the IRA to the niece produces a 45% estate tax on the client's gift to the niece, and a 15% income tax on the IRA payable to the niece, after the applicable income tax deduction under IRC § 691(c).

IRA to Charity			IRA to Niece		
Charity	*Niece*	*IRS*	*Charity*	*Niece*	*IRS*
$100,000	$100,000	$45,000	$100,000	$85,000	$60,000

While this approach fails to take into account any benefit the niece might derive from the income tax deferral she could enjoy if she were named as the beneficiary of the IRA, in many cases the benefits of using Section 691 income to fund charitable gifts outweigh even these

21st Century Estate Planning:
Practical Applications
2005 Edition

©2005 Sonnenschein Nath & Rosenthal LLP
and Cannon Financial Institute, Inc.

- 410 -

additional benefits. The advantage applies equally to all items of Section 691 income, including non-qualified employee benefit plans, stock options and other assets burdened by income tax.

This planning strategy was difficult to implement for qualified plans and IRAs when lifetime MRDs were tied to the identity of the participant's Designated Beneficiary. This is no longer the case. Lifetime income tax deferral is not affected by naming a charitable beneficiary to receive a qualified plan or IRA at the participant's death.

This planning strategy also can be implemented by naming a Charitable Remainder Trust ("CRT") as the beneficiary of a qualified plan or IRA. A CRT is a trust that pays to a non-charitable beneficiary a fixed annuity or a percentage of the trust assets valued annually (a "unitrust" interest), for life or for a period of years. At the end of the non-charitable interest, the remaining trust assets pass to charity. The CRT is not a qualified trust, for purposes of identifying the Designated Beneficiary of a qualified plan or IRA, but this is unimportant, as the plan proceeds can be paid to the CRT, an income tax exempt entity, in a lump sum distribution, without income tax. PLR 9634019 (August 23, 1996); PLR 9237020 (September 11, 1992). The value of the annuity or unitrust interest payable to the non-charitable beneficiary of the CRT will not be exempt from estate tax. But there will be an estate tax charitable deduction for the present value of the charitable interest. If the spouse is the only non-charitable beneficiary of the CRT, the spouse's interest will qualify for the federal estate tax marital deduction. IRC § 2056(b)(8). If there are other family beneficiaries of the CRT, the CRT still might be used for the estate tax free portion of the estate.

The proceeds of the qualified plan or IRA in the CRT will remain and grow on an income tax exempt basis, the same as if they had remained in the qualified plan or IRA. Distributions to the non-charitable beneficiary will be subject to ordinary income tax, for the most part, again, the same as if they were paid from a qualified plan or IRA. But the minimum distribution rules will not apply, and the non-charitable beneficiary's interest will be as it is defined in the CRT - no more, and no less.

Some plan participants would like to make lifetime charitable gifts of qualified plan assets or IRAs. Because these plans are not transferable, however, lifetime gifts cannot be made to a charitable beneficiary with qualified plan or IRA assets without first taking the value of the assets into the participant's income. Even though the participant can claim an income tax charitable deduction to offset this income, the charitable deduction is limited to a percentage of the participant's adjusted gross income, so that it is not often possible for the income received on the distribution from the qualified plan or IRA to be entirely offset by the charitable deduction. Legislation has been introduced in Congress on several occasions to change this situation, and to permit participants to make charitable gifts out of qualified plans and IRAs without income tax effect. While this legislation has yet to pass, expect to see it reintroduced.

21st Century Estate Planning:
Practical Applications
2005 Edition

©2005 Sonnenschein Nath & Rosenthal LLP
and Cannon Financial Institute, Inc.

- 411 -

6. Non-Tax Issues In Estate Planning For Qualified Plans and IRAs

a. Retirement Equity Act of 1984. The Retirement Equity Act of 1984 ("REA") requires that defined benefit plans, money purchase plans, profit sharing plans (including HR-10 or KEOGH plans but *not* IRAs) and stock bonus plans all provide survivor benefits (both pre- and post-retirement) in the form of a survivor annuity or qualified (50%) survivor annuity for the surviving spouse of any vested plan participant. There is an exception to this requirement for profit sharing and stock bonus plans that applies if the participant does not elect distribution in the form of a life annuity and the plan provides that 100% of the account balance will be paid to the participant's surviving spouse at death (the "profit sharing plan exception"). Defined contribution plans otherwise satisfy the pre-retirement survivor annuity requirement if 50% of the participant's vested account balance is applied to the purchase of an annuity for the spouse.

Generally, participants may waive the survivor annuity requirements, but the participant's spouse must consent to the waiver in writing before either the plan administrator or a notary public. The spouse's consent must acknowledge the effect of the waiver. The spouse also must consent to the designation of a beneficiary other than the spouse (if the profit sharing exception applies), and to any cashout of annuity benefits payable at death or on retirement. If a spouse consents to the waiver of the spouse's survivor benefits during the participant's lifetime, this is not a gift by the spouse IRC § 2503(f). There are no provisions, however, describing the gift tax treatment that may apply to post-death waivers or consents. Nor is it entirely clear that REA rights can be disclaimed after death in a qualified disclaimer under IRC § 2518.

b. ERISA Preemption. The Supreme Court has recently held that ERISA preempts state law rules that are not consistent with qualified plan requirements. In *Boggs v. Boggs*, 118 S. Ct. 9 (U.S. 1997), the Supreme Court specifically held that ERISA preempts the community property law rights of the non-participant spouse with respect to qualified plan assets. In a more recent case, the Supreme Court ruled that state laws revoking beneficiary designations after divorce do not apply to ERISA plans. *Egelhoff v. Egelhoff ex rel Breiner*, 121 S. Ct. 1322 (S. Ct., 2001).

Although, like *Boggs*, the *Egelhoff* case only applies to ERISA plans, and not IRAs or other nonprobate assets, its implications may be dramatic. The dissent, written by Justice Breyer, describes the usefulness of relying on state property and inheritance laws to resolve ambiguities in the administration of ERISA plans. "Why would Congress want the courts to create an ERISA-related federal property law to deal with such problems?" asks Justice Breyer (*at p. 1332*). Nonetheless, after *Egelhoff*, it will be difficult to predict whether state laws will be preempted by ERISA in such matters as disclaimers, missing persons, presumption of fact or order of deaths, competency at the time of execution, so-called "slayer" statutes, the construction of ambiguous or contradictory language and many other issues.

21st Century Estate Planning:
Practical Applications
2005 Edition

©*2005 Sonnenschein Nath & Rosenthal LLP*
and Cannon Financial Institute, Inc.

- 412 -

c. Community Property Issues. As a result of the Supreme Court decision in *Boggs v. Boggs*, supra, it is clear that ERISA and REA preempt the application of community property laws in community property jurisdictions, at least with respect to qualified plans. However, ERISA preemption and REA do not apply to individual retirement accounts or to nonqualified plans. As a result, community property law issues must be considered both with respect to the participant and the non-participant spouse in a nonqualified plan or IRA, to the extent that the participant was married and resided in a community property state during his or her employment.

Community property laws vary considerably from state to state, and do not always address clearly how they apply to IRAs and other employee benefit plans not governed by ERISA. The community property rules of a jurisdiction may apply differently in the event of a divorce, than they do on death (as is the case under ERISA, which recognizes the ability of the state court to divide a qualified plan on divorce by means of a qualified domestic relations order, or QDRO, but does not permit a similar division on death). The community property rights of the parties may or may not be addressed in the IRA trust or other governing instruments for the plan, and even if they are addressed still may be superceded by state law. Few, if any, courts have attempted to reconcile state community property laws with IRC § 408(g), which expressly provides that IRC § 408 (which governs the qualification requirements and taxation of IRAs and distributions from IRAs) "shall be applied without regard to any community property laws."

Given this state of the law, be forewarned, and seek the advice of a knowledgeable state law community property expert whenever this issue arises outside of your own jurisdiction.

21st Century Estate Planning:
Practical Applications
2005 Edition

©2005 Sonnenschein Nath & Rosenthal LLP
and Cannon Financial Institute, Inc.

- 413 -

APPENDIX A

Uniform Table for Calculating
Minimum Required Distributions
For IRAs and Qualified Plans

Age of Employee	Factor	% of Account	Age of Employee	Factor	% of Account
50	46.5	2.1505	83	16.3	6.1350
51	45.5	2.1978	84	15.5	6.4516
52	44.6	2.2422	85	14.8	6.7568
53	43.6	2.2936	86	14.1	7.0922
54	42.6	2.3474	87	13.4	7.4627
55	41.6	2.4039	88	12.7	7.8740
56	40.7	2.4570	89	12.0	8.3333
57	39.7	2.5189	90	11.4	8.7719
58	38.7	2.5840	91	10.8	9.2593
59	37.8	2.6455	92	10.2	9.8039
60	36.8	2.7174	93	9.6	10.4167
61	35.8	2.7933	94	9.1	10.9890
62	34.9	2.8653	95	8.6	11.6279
63	33.9	2.9499	96	8.1	12.3457
64	33.0	3.0303	97	7.6	13.1579
65	32.0	3.1250	98	7.1	14.0845
66	31.1	3.2154	99	6.7	14.9254
67	30.2	3.3313	100	6.3	15.8730
68	29.2	3.4247	101	5.9	16.9492
69	28.3	3.5336	102	5.5	18.1818
70	27.4	3.6496	103	5.2	19.2308
71	26.5	3.7736	104	4.9	20.4082
72	25.6	3.9063	105	4.5	22.2222
73	24.7	4.0486	106	4.2	23.8095
74	23.8	4.2017	107	3.9	25.6410
75	22.9	4.3668	108	3.7	27.0270
76	22.0	4.5455	109	3.4	29.4118
77	21.2	4.7170	110	3.1	32.2581
78	20.3	4.9261	111	2.9	34.4828
79	19.5	5.1282	112	2.6	38.4615
80	18.7	5.3476	113	2.4	41.6667
81	17.9	5.5866	114	2.1	47.6191
82	17.1	5.8480	115 and older	1.9	52.6316

21st Century Estate Planning:
Practical Applications
2005 Edition

©2005 Sonnenschein Nath & Rosenthal LLP
and Cannon Financial Institute, Inc.

APPENDIX B
Life Expectancy Tables - Single Life

AGE	DIVISOR	AGE	DIVISOR	AGE	DIVISOR
0	82.4	40	43.6	80	10.2
1	81.6	41	42.7	81	9.7
2	80.6	42	41.7	82	9.1
3	79.7	43	40.7	83	8.6
4	78.7	44	39.8	84	8.1
5	77.7	45	38.8	85	7.6
6	76.7	46	37.9	86	7.1
7	75.8	47	37.0	87	6.7
8	74.8	48	36.0	88	6.3
9	73.8	49	35.1	89	5.9
10	72.8	50	34.2	90	5.5
11	71.8	51	33.3	91	5.2
12	70.8	52	32.3	92	4.9
13	69.9	53	31.4	93	4.6
14	68.9	54	30.5	94	4.3
15	67.9	55	29.6	95	4.1
16	66.9	56	28.7	96	3.8
17	66.0	57	27.9	97	3.6
18	65.0	58	27.0	98	3.4
19	64.0	59	26.1	99	3.1
20	63.0	60	25.2	100	2.9
21	62.1	61	24.4	101	2.7
22	61.1	62	23.5	102	2.5
23	60.1	63	22.7	103	2.3
24	59.1	64	21.8	104	2.1
25	58.2	65	21.0	105	1.9
26	57.2	66	20.2	106	1.7
27	56.2	67	19.4	107	1.5
28	55.3	68	18.6	108	1.4
29	54.3	69	17.8	109	1.2
30	53.3	70	17.0	110	1.1
31	52.4	71	16.3	111+	1.0
32	51.4	72	15.5		
33	50.4	73	14.8		
34	49.4	74	14.1		
35	48.5	75	13.4		
36	47.5	76	12.7		
37	46.5	77	12.1		
38	45.6	78	11.4		
39	44.6	79	10.8		

21st Century Estate Planning:
Practical Applications
2005 Edition

©2005 Sonnenschein Nath & Rosenthal LLP
and Cannon Financial Institute, Inc.

- 415 -

APPENDIX C
Life Expectancy Tables - Joint and Last Survivor

Ages	0	1	2	3	4	5	6	7	8	9
1	90.0	89.5	89.0	88.6	88.2	87.8	87.4	87.1	86.8	86.5
2	89.5	89.0	88.5	88.1	87.6	87.2	86.8	86.5	86.1	85.8
3	89.0	88.5	88.0	87.5	87.1	86.6	86.2	85.8	85.5	85.1
4	88.6	88.1	87.5	87.0	86.5	86.1	85.6	85.2	84.8	84.5
5	88.2	87.6	87.1	86.5	86.0	85.5	85.1	84.6	84.2	83.8
6	87.8	87.2	86.6	86.1	85.5	85.0	84.5	84.1	83.6	83.2
7	87.4	86.8	86.2	85.6	85.1	84.5	84.0	83.5	83.1	82.6
8	87.1	86.5	85.8	85.2	84.6	84.1	83.5	83.0	82.5	82.1
9	86.8	86.1	85.5	84.8	84.2	83.6	83.1	82.5	82.0	81.6
10	86.5	85.8	85.1	84.5	83.8	83.2	82.6	82.1	81.6	81.0
11	86.2	85.5	84.8	84.1	83.5	82.8	82.2	81.6	81.1	80.6
12	85.9	85.2	84.5	83.8	83.1	82.5	81.8	81.2	80.7	80.1
13	85.7	84.9	84.2	83.5	82.8	82.1	81.5	80.8	80.2	79.7
14	85.4	84.7	84.0	83.2	82.5	81.8	81.1	80.5	79.9	79.2
15	85.2	84.5	83.7	83.0	82.2	81.5	80.8	80.1	79.5	78.9
16	85.0	84.3	83.5	82.7	82.0	81.2	80.5	79.8	79.1	78.5
17	84.9	84.1	83.3	82.5	81.7	81.0	80.2	79.5	78.8	78.1
18	84.7	83.9	83.1	82.3	81.5	80.7	80.0	79.2	78.5	77.8
19	84.5	83.7	82.9	82.1	81.3	80.5	79.7	79.0	78.2	77.5
20	84.4	83.6	82.7	81.9	81.1	80.3	79.5	78.7	78.0	77.3
21	84.3	83.4	82.6	81.8	80.9	80.1	79.3	78.5	77.7	77.0
22	84.1	83.3	82.4	81.6	80.8	79.9	79.1	78.3	77.5	76.8
23	84.0	83.2	82.3	81.5	80.6	79.8	78.9	78.1	77.3	76.5
24	83.9	83.1	82.2	81.3	80.5	79.6	78.8	77.9	77.1	76.3
25	83.8	83.0	82.1	81.2	80.3	79.5	78.6	77.8	76.9	76.1
26	83.7	82.9	82.0	81.1	80.2	79.3	78.5	77.6	76.8	75.9
27	83.6	82.8	81.9	81.0	80.1	79.2	78.3	77.5	76.6	75.8
28	83.6	82.7	81.8	80.9	80.0	79.1	78.2	77.4	76.5	75.6
29	83.5	82.6	81.7	80.8	79.9	79.0	78.1	77.2	76.4	75.5
30	83.4	82.6	81.6	80.7	79.8	78.9	78.0	77.1	76.2	75.4
31	83.4	82.5	81.6	80.7	79.7	78.8	77.9	77.0	76.1	75.2
32	83.3	82.4	81.5	80.6	79.7	78.8	77.8	76.9	76.0	75.1
33	83.3	82.4	81.5	80.5	79.6	78.7	77.8	76.8	75.9	75.0
34	83.2	82.3	81.4	80.5	79.5	78.6	77.7	76.8	75.9	74.9
35	83.2	82.3	81.3	80.4	79.5	78.5	77.6	76.7	75.8	74.9
36	83.1	82.2	81.3	80.4	79.4	78.5	77.6	76.6	75.7	74.8
37	83.1	82.2	81.3	80.3	79.4	78.4	77.5	76.6	75.6	74.7
38	83.0	82.2	81.2	80.3	79.3	78.4	77.4	76.5	75.6	74.6
39	83.0	82.1	81.2	80.2	79.3	78.3	77.4	76.4	75.5	74.6
40	83.0	82.1	81.1	80.2	79.2	78.3	77.3	76.4	75.5	74.5
41	82.9	82.1	81.1	80.2	79.2	78.3	77.3	76.4	75.4	74.5
42	82.9	82.0	81.1	80.1	79.2	78.2	77.3	76.3	75.4	74.4
43	82.9	82.0	81.1	80.1	79.1	78.2	77.2	76.3	75.3	74.4
44	82.9	82.0	81.0	80.1	79.1	78.2	77.2	76.2	75.3	74.3
45	82.8	81.9	81.0	80.0	79.1	78.1	77.2	76.2	75.2	74.3

21st Century Estate Planning:
Practical Applications
2005 Edition

©2005 Sonnenschein Nath & Rosenthal LLP
and Cannon Financial Institute, Inc.

- 416 -

Ages	0	1	2	3	4	5	6	7	8	9
46	82.8	81.9	81.0	80.0	79.1	78.1	77.1	76.2	75.2	74.3
47	82.8	81.9	81.0	80.0	79.0	78.1	77.1	76.1	75.2	74.2
48	82.8	81.9	80.9	80.0	79.0	78.0	77.1	76.1	75.2	74.2
49	82.8	81.9	80.9	80.0	79.0	78.0	77.1	76.1	75.1	74.2
50	82.7	81.8	80.9	79.9	79.0	78.0	77.0	76.1	75.1	74.1
51	82.7	81.8	80.9	79.9	79.0	78.0	77.0	76.0	75.1	74.1
52	82.7	81.8	80.9	79.9	78.9	78.0	77.0	76.0	75.1	74.1
53	82.7	81.8	80.9	79.9	78.9	78.0	77.0	76.0	75.0	74.1
54	82.7	81.8	80.8	79.9	78.9	77.9	77.0	76.0	75.0	74.0
55	82.7	81.8	80.8	79.9	78.9	77.9	76.9	76.0	75.0	74.0
56	82.6	81.8	80.8	79.8	78.9	77.9	76.9	76.0	75.0	74.0
57	82.6	81.7	80.8	79.8	78.9	77.9	76.9	75.9	75.0	74.0
58	82.6	81.7	80.8	79.8	78.9	77.9	76.9	75.9	75.0	74.0
59	82.6	81.7	80.8	79.8	78.8	77.9	76.9	75.9	74.9	74.0
60	82.6	81.7	80.8	79.8	78.8	77.9	76.9	75.9	74.9	74.0
61	82.6	81.7	80.8	79.8	78.8	77.8	76.9	75.9	74.9	73.9
62	82.6	81.7	80.8	79.8	78.8	77.8	76.9	75.9	74.9	73.9
63	82.6	81.7	80.7	79.8	78.8	77.8	76.9	75.9	74.9	73.9
64	82.6	81.7	80.7	79.8	78.8	77.8	76.8	75.9	74.9	73.9
65	82.5	81.7	80.7	79.8	78.8	77.8	76.8	75.9	74.9	73.9
66	82.5	81.7	80.7	79.8	78.8	77.8	76.8	75.8	74.9	73.9
67	82.5	81.7	80.7	79.7	78.8	77.8	76.8	75.8	74.9	73.9
68	82.5	81.7	80.7	79.7	78.8	77.8	76.8	75.8	74.9	73.9
69	82.5	81.6	80.7	79.7	78.8	77.8	76.8	75.8	74.8	73.9
70	82.5	81.6	80.7	79.7	78.8	77.8	76.8	75.8	74.8	73.9
71	82.5	81.6	80.7	79.7	78.8	77.8	76.8	75.8	74.8	73.9
72	82.5	81.6	80.7	79.7	78.7	77.8	76.8	75.8	74.8	73.8
73	82.5	81.6	80.7	79.7	78.7	77.8	76.8	75.8	74.8	73.8
74	82.5	81.6	80.7	79.7	78.7	77.8	76.8	75.8	74.8	73.8
75	82.5	81.6	80.7	79.7	78.7	77.8	76.8	75.8	74.8	73.8
76	82.5	81.6	80.7	79.7	78.7	77.8	76.8	75.8	74.8	73.8
77	82.5	81.6	80.7	79.7	78.7	77.8	76.8	75.8	74.8	73.8
78	82.5	81.6	80.7	79.7	78.7	77.7	76.8	75.8	74.8	73.8
79	82.5	81.6	80.7	79.7	78.7	77.7	76.8	75.8	74.8	73.8
80	82.5	81.6	80.7	79.7	78.7	77.7	76.8	75.8	74.8	73.8
81	82.5	81.6	80.7	79.7	78.7	77.7	76.8	75.8	74.8	73.8
82	82.4	81.6	80.7	79.7	78.7	77.7	76.8	75.8	74.8	73.8
83	82.4	81.6	80.7	79.7	78.7	77.7	76.8	75.8	74.8	73.8
84	82.4	81.6	80.7	79.7	78.7	77.7	76.8	75.8	74.8	73.8
85	82.4	81.6	80.7	79.7	78.7	77.7	76.8	75.8	74.8	73.8
86	82.4	81.6	80.6	79.7	78.7	77.7	76.8	75.8	74.8	73.8
87	82.4	81.6	80.6	79.7	78.7	77.7	76.7	75.8	74.8	73.8
88	82.4	81.6	80.6	79.7	78.7	77.7	76.7	75.8	74.8	73.8

21st Century Estate Planning:
Practical Applications
2005 Edition

©2005 Sonnenschein Nath & Rosenthal LLP
and Cannon Financial Institute, Inc.

- 417 -

Ages	0	1	2	3	4	5	6	7	8	9
89........................	82.4	81.6	80.6	79.7	78.7	77.7	76.7	75.8	74.8	73.8
90........................	82.4	81.6	80.6	79.7	78.7	77.7	76.7	75.8	74.8	73.8
91........................	82.4	81.6	80.6	79.7	78.7	77.7	76.7	75.8	74.8	73.8
92........................	82.4	81.6	80.6	79.7	78.7	77.7	76.7	75.8	74.8	73.8
93........................	82.4	81.6	80.6	79.7	78.7	77.7	76.7	75.8	74.8	73.8
94........................	82.4	81.6	80.6	79.7	78.7	77.7	76.7	75.8	74.8	73.8
95........................	82.4	81.6	80.6	79.7	78.7	77.7	76.7	75.8	74.8	73.8
96........................	82.4	81.6	80.6	79.7	78.7	77.7	76.7	75.8	74.8	73.8
97........................	82.4	81.6	80.6	79.7	78.7	77.7	76.7	75.8	74.8	73.8
98........................	82.4	81.6	80.6	79.7	78.7	77.7	76.7	75.8	74.8	73.8
99........................	82.4	81.6	80.6	79.7	78.7	77.7	76.7	75.8	74.8	73.8
100.......................	82.4	81.6	80.6	79.7	78.7	77.7	76.7	75.8	74.8	73.8
101.......................	82.4	81.6	80.6	79.7	78.7	77.7	76.7	75.8	74.8	73.8
102.......................	82.4	81.6	80.6	79.7	78.7	77.7	76.7	75.8	74.8	73.8
103.......................	82.4	81.6	80.6	79.7	78.7	77.7	76.7	75.8	74.8	73.8
104.......................	82.4	81.6	80.6	79.7	78.7	77.7	76.7	75.8	74.8	73.8
105.......................	82.4	81.6	80.6	79.7	78.7	77.7	76.7	75.8	74.8	73.8
106.......................	82.4	81.6	80.6	79.7	78.7	77.7	76.7	75.8	74.8	73.8
107.......................	82.4	81.6	80.6	79.7	78.7	77.7	76.7	75.8	74.8	73.8
108.......................	82.4	81.6	80.6	79.7	78.7	77.7	76.7	75.8	74.8	73.8
109.......................	82.4	81.6	80.6	79.7	78.7	77.7	76.7	75.8	74.8	73.8
110.......................	82.4	81.6	80.6	79.7	78.7	77.7	76.7	75.8	74.8	73.8
111.......................	82.4	81.6	80.6	79.7	78.7	77.7	76.7	75.8	74.8	73.8
112.......................	82.4	81.6	80.6	79.7	78.7	77.7	76.7	75.8	74.8	73.8
113.......................	82.4	81.6	80.6	79.7	78.7	77.7	76.7	75.8	74.8	73.8
114.......................	82.4	81.6	80.6	79.7	78.7	77.7	76.7	75.8	74.8	73.8
115.......................	82.4	81.6	80.6	79.7	78.7	77.7	76.7	75.8	74.8	73.8
116+.....................	82.4	81.6	80.6	79.7	78.7	77.7	76.7	75.8	74.8	73.8

Ages	10	11	12	13	14	15	16	17	18	19
10........................	80.0	79.6	79.1	78.7	78.2	77.9	77.5	77.2	76.8	76.5
11........................	79.6	79.0	78.6	78.1	77.7	77.3	76.9	76.5	76.2	75.8
12........................	79.1	78.6	78.1	77.6	77.1	76.7	76.3	75.9	75.5	75.2
13........................	78.7	78.1	77.6	77.1	76.6	76.1	75.7	75.3	74.9	74.5
14........................	78.2	77.7	77.1	76.6	76.1	75.6	75.1	74.7	74.3	73.9
15........................	77.9	77.3	76.7	76.1	75.6	75.1	74.6	74.1	73.7	73.3
16........................	77.5	76.9	76.3	75.7	75.1	74.6	74.1	73.6	73.1	72.7
17........................	77.2	76.5	75.9	75.3	74.7	74.1	73.6	73.1	72.6	72.1
18........................	76.8	76.2	75.5	74.9	74.3	73.7	73.1	72.6	72.1	71.6
19........................	76.5	75.8	75.2	74.5	73.9	73.3	72.7	72.1	71.6	71.1
20........................	76.3	75.5	74.8	74.2	73.5	72.9	72.3	71.7	71.1	70.6
21........................	76.0	75.3	74.5	73.8	73.2	72.5	71.9	71.3	70.7	70.1
22........................	75.8	75.0	74.3	73.5	72.9	72.2	71.5	70.9	70.3	69.7
23........................	75.5	74.8	74.0	73.3	72.6	71.9	71.2	70.5	69.9	69.3

21st Century Estate Planning:
Practical Applications
2005 Edition

©2005 Sonnenschein Nath & Rosenthal LLP
and Cannon Financial Institute, Inc.

- 418 -

Ages	10	11	12	13	14	15	16	17	18	19
24	75.3	74.5	73.8	73.0	72.3	71.6	70.9	70.2	69.5	68.9
25	75.1	74.3	73.5	72.8	72.0	71.3	70.6	69.9	69.2	68.5
26	75.0	74.1	73.3	72.5	71.8	71.0	70.3	69.6	68.9	68.2
27	74.8	74.0	73.1	72.3	71.6	70.8	70.0	69.3	68.6	67.9
28	74.6	73.8	73.0	72.2	71.3	70.6	69.8	69.0	68.3	67.6
29	74.5	73.6	72.8	72.0	71.2	70.4	69.6	68.8	68.0	67.3
30	74.4	73.5	72.7	71.8	71.0	70.2	69.4	68.6	67.8	67.1
31	74.3	73.4	72.5	71.7	70.8	70.0	69.2	68.4	67.6	66.8
32	74.1	73.3	72.4	71.5	70.7	69.8	69.0	68.2	67.4	66.6
33	74.0	73.2	72.3	71.4	70.5	69.7	68.8	68.0	67.2	66.4
34	73.9	73.0	72.2	71.3	70.4	69.5	68.7	67.8	67.0	66.2
35	73.9	73.0	72.1	71.2	70.3	69.4	68.5	67.7	66.8	66.0
36	73.8	72.9	72.0	71.1	70.2	69.3	68.4	67.6	66.7	65.9
37	73.7	72.8	71.9	71.0	70.1	69.2	68.3	67.4	66.6	65.7
38	73.6	72.7	71.8	70.9	70.0	69.1	68.2	67.3	66.4	65.6
39	73.6	72.7	71.7	70.8	69.9	69.0	68.1	67.2	66.3	65.4
40	73.5	72.6	71.7	70.7	69.8	68.9	68.0	67.1	66.2	65.3
41	73.5	72.5	71.6	70.7	69.7	68.8	67.9	67.0	66.1	65.2
42	73.4	72.5	71.5	70.6	69.7	68.8	67.8	66.9	66.0	65.1
43	73.4	72.4	71.5	70.6	69.6	68.7	67.8	66.8	65.9	65.0
44	73.3	72.4	71.4	70.5	69.6	68.6	67.7	66.8	65.9	64.9
45	73.3	72.3	71.4	70.5	69.5	68.6	67.6	66.7	65.8	64.9
46	73.3	72.3	71.4	70.4	69.5	68.5	67.6	66.6	65.7	64.8
47	73.2	72.3	71.3	70.4	69.4	68.5	67.5	66.6	65.7	64.7
48	73.2	72.2	71.3	70.3	69.4	68.4	67.5	66.5	65.6	64.7
49	73.2	72.2	71.2	70.3	69.3	68.4	67.4	66.5	65.6	64.6
50	73.1	72.2	71.2	70.3	69.3	68.4	67.4	66.5	65.5	64.6
51	73.1	72.2	71.2	70.2	69.3	68.3	67.4	66.4	65.5	64.5
52	73.1	72.1	71.2	70.2	69.2	68.3	67.3	66.4	65.4	64.5
53	73.1	72.1	71.1	70.2	69.2	68.3	67.3	66.3	65.4	64.4
54	73.1	72.1	71.1	70.2	69.2	68.2	67.3	66.3	65.4	64.4
55	73.0	72.1	71.1	70.1	69.2	68.2	67.2	66.3	65.3	64.4
56	73.0	72.1	71.1	70.1	69.1	68.2	67.2	66.3	65.3	64.3
57	73.0	72.0	71.1	70.1	69.1	68.2	67.2	66.2	65.3	64.3
58	73.0	72.0	71.0	70.1	69.1	68.1	67.2	66.2	65.2	64.3
59	73.0	72.0	71.0	70.1	69.1	68.1	67.2	66.2	65.2	64.3
60	73.0	72.0	71.0	70.0	69.1	68.1	67.1	66.2	65.2	64.2
61	73.0	72.0	71.0	70.0	69.1	68.1	67.1	66.2	65.2	64.2
62	72.9	72.0	71.0	70.0	69.0	68.1	67.1	66.1	65.2	64.2
63	72.9	72.0	71.0	70.0	69.0	68.1	67.1	66.1	65.2	64.2
64	72.9	71.9	71.0	70.0	69.0	68.0	67.1	66.1	65.1	64.2

21st Century Estate Planning:
Practical Applications
2005 Edition

©*2005 Sonnenschein Nath & Rosenthal LLP*
and Cannon Financial Institute, Inc.

- 419 -

Ages	10	11	12	13	14	15	16	17	18	19
65	72.9	71.9	71.0	70.0	69.0	68.0	67.1	66.1	65.1	64.2
66	72.9	71.9	70.9	70.0	69.0	68.0	67.1	66.1	65.1	64.1
67	72.9	71.9	70.9	70.0	69.0	68.0	67.0	66.1	65.1	64.1
68	72.9	71.9	70.9	70.0	69.0	68.0	67.0	66.1	65.1	64.1
69	72.9	71.9	70.9	69.9	69.0	68.0	67.0	66.1	65.1	64.1
70	72.9	71.9	70.9	69.9	69.0	68.0	67.0	66.0	65.1	64.1
71	72.9	71.9	70.9	69.9	69.0	68.0	67.0	66.0	65.1	64.1
72	72.9	71.9	70.9	69.9	69.0	68.0	67.0	66.0	65.1	64.1
73	72.9	71.9	70.9	69.9	68.9	68.0	67.0	66.0	65.0	64.1
74	72.9	71.9	70.9	69.9	68.9	68.0	67.0	66.0	65.0	64.1
75	72.8	71.9	70.9	69.9	68.9	68.0	67.0	66.0	65.0	64.1
76	72.8	71.9	70.9	69.9	68.9	68.0	67.0	66.0	65.0	64.1
77	72.8	71.9	70.9	69.9	68.9	68.0	67.0	66.0	65.0	64.1
78	72.8	71.9	70.9	69.9	68.9	67.9	67.0	66.0	65.0	64.0
79	72.8	71.9	70.9	69.9	68.9	67.9	67.0	66.0	65.0	64.0
80	72.8	71.9	70.9	69.9	68.9	67.9	67.0	66.0	65.0	64.0
81	72.8	71.8	70.9	69.9	68.9	67.9	67.0	66.0	65.0	64.0
82	72.8	71.8	70.9	69.9	68.9	67.9	67.0	66.0	65.0	64.0
83	72.8	71.8	70.9	69.9	68.9	67.9	67.0	66.0	65.0	64.0
84	72.8	71.8	70.9	69.9	68.9	67.9	67.0	66.0	65.0	64.0
85	72.8	71.8	70.9	69.9	68.9	67.9	66.9	66.0	65.0	64.0
86	72.8	71.8	70.9	69.9	68.9	67.9	66.9	66.0	65.0	64.0
87	72.8	71.8	70.9	69.9	68.9	67.9	66.9	66.0	65.0	64.0
88	72.8	71.8	70.9	69.9	68.9	67.9	66.9	66.0	65.0	64.0
89	72.8	71.8	70.9	69.9	68.9	67.9	66.9	66.0	65.0	64.0
90	72.8	71.8	70.9	69.9	68.9	67.9	66.9	66.0	65.0	64.0
91	72.8	71.8	70.9	69.9	68.9	67.9	66.9	66.0	65.0	64.0
92	72.8	71.8	70.9	69.9	68.9	67.9	66.9	66.0	65.0	64.0
93	72.8	71.8	70.9	69.9	68.9	67.9	66.9	66.0	65.0	64.0
94	72.8	71.8	70.8	69.9	68.9	67.9	66.9	66.0	65.0	64.0
95	72.8	71.8	70.8	69.9	68.9	67.9	66.9	66.0	65.0	64.0
96	72.8	71.8	70.8	69.9	68.9	67.9	66.9	66.0	65.0	64.0
97	72.8	71.8	70.8	69.9	68.9	67.9	66.9	66.0	65.0	64.0
98	72.8	71.8	70.8	69.9	68.9	67.9	66.9	66.0	65.0	64.0
99	72.8	71.8	70.8	69.9	68.9	67.9	66.9	66.0	65.0	64.0
100	72.8	71.8	70.8	69.9	68.9	67.9	66.9	66.0	65.0	64.0
101	72.8	71.8	70.8	69.9	68.9	67.9	66.9	66.0	65.0	64.0
102	72.8	71.8	70.8	69.9	68.9	67.9	66.9	66.0	65.0	64.0
103	72.8	71.8	70.8	69.9	68.9	67.9	66.9	66.0	65.0	64.0
104	72.8	71.8	70.8	69.9	68.9	67.9	66.9	66.0	65.0	64.0
105	72.8	71.8	70.8	69.9	68.9	67.9	66.9	66.0	65.0	64.0

21st Century Estate Planning:
Practical Applications
2005 Edition

©2005 Sonnenschein Nath & Rosenthal LLP
and Cannon Financial Institute, Inc.

- 420 -

Ages	10	11	12	13	14	15	16	17	18	19
106	72.8	71.8	70.8	69.9	68.9	67.9	66.9	66.0	65.0	64.0
107	72.8	71.8	70.8	69.9	68.9	67.9	66.9	66.0	65.0	64.0
108	72.8	71.8	70.8	69.9	68.9	67.9	66.9	66.0	65.0	64.0
109	72.8	71.8	70.8	69.9	68.9	67.9	66.9	66.0	65.0	64.0
110	72.8	71.8	70.8	69.9	68.9	67.9	66.9	66.0	65.0	64.0
111	72.8	71.8	70.8	69.9	68.9	67.9	66.9	66.0	65.0	64.0
112	72.8	71.8	70.8	69.9	68.9	67.9	66.9	66.0	65.0	64.0
113	72.8	71.8	70.8	69.9	68.9	67.9	66.9	66.0	65.0	64.0
114	72.8	71.8	70.8	69.9	68.9	67.9	66.9	66.0	65.0	64.0
115+	72.8	71.8	70.8	69.9	68.9	67.9	66.9	66.0	65.0	64.0

Ages	20	21	22	23	24	25	26	27	28	29
20	70.1	69.6	69.1	68.7	68.3	67.9	67.5	67.2	66.9	66.6
21	69.6	69.1	68.6	68.2	67.7	67.3	66.9	66.6	66.2	65.9
22	69.1	68.6	68.1	67.6	67.2	66.7	66.3	65.9	65.6	65.2
23	68.7	68.2	67.9	67.1	66.6	66.2	65.7	65.3	64.9	64.6
24	68.3	67.7	67.2	66.6	66.1	65.6	65.2	64.7	64.3	63.9
25	67.9	67.3	66.7	66.2	65.6	65.1	64.6	64.2	63.7	63.3
26	67.5	66.9	66.3	65.7	65.2	64.6	64.1	63.6	63.2	62.8
27	67.2	66.6	65.9	65.3	64.7	64.2	63.6	63.1	62.7	62.2
28	66.9	66.2	65.6	64.9	64.3	63.7	63.2	62.7	62.1	61.7
29	66.6	65.9	65.2	64.6	63.9	63.3	62.8	62.2	61.7	61.2
30	66.3	65.6	64.9	64.2	63.6	62.9	62.3	61.8	61.2	60.7
31	66.1	65.3	64.6	63.9	63.2	62.6	62.0	61.4	60.8	60.2
32	65.8	65.1	64.3	63.6	62.9	62.2	61.6	61.0	60.4	59.8
33	65.6	64.8	64.1	63.3	62.6	61.9	61.3	60.6	60.0	59.4
34	65.4	64.6	63.8	63.1	62.3	61.6	60.9	60.3	59.6	59.0
35	65.2	64.4	63.6	62.8	62.1	61.4	60.6	59.9	59.3	58.6
36	65.0	64.2	63.4	62.6	61.9	61.1	60.4	59.6	59.0	58.3
37	64.9	64.0	63.2	62.4	61.6	60.9	60.1	59.4	58.7	58.0
38	64.7	63.9	63.0	62.2	61.4	60.6	59.9	59.1	58.4	57.7
39	64.6	63.7	62.9	62.1	61.2	60.4	59.6	58.9	58.1	57.4
40	64.4	63.6	62.7	61.9	61.1	60.2	59.4	58.7	57.9	57.1
41	64.3	63.5	62.6	61.7	60.9	60.1	59.3	58.5	57.7	56.9
42	64.2	63.3	62.5	61.6	60.8	59.9	59.1	58.3	57.5	56.7
43	64.1	63.2	62.4	61.5	60.6	59.8	58.9	58.1	57.3	56.5
44	64.0	63.1	62.2	61.4	60.5	59.6	58.8	57.9	57.1	56.3
45	64.0	63.0	62.2	61.3	60.4	59.5	58.6	57.8	56.9	56.1
46	63.9	63.0	62.1	61.2	60.3	59.4	58.5	57.7	56.8	56.0
47	63.8	62.9	62.0	61.1	60.2	59.3	58.4	57.5	56.7	55.8
48	63.7	62.8	61.9	61.0	60.1	59.2	58.3	57.4	56.5	55.7

21st Century Estate Planning:
Practical Applications
2005 Edition

©2005 Sonnenschein Nath & Rosenthal LLP
and Cannon Financial Institute, Inc.

- 421 -

Ages	20	21	22	23	24	25	26	27	28	29
49	63.7	62.8	61.8	60.9	60.0	59.1	58.2	57.3	56.4	55.6
50	63.6	62.7	61.8	60.8	59.9	59.0	58.1	57.2	56.3	55.4
51	63.6	62.6	61.7	60.8	59.9	58.9	58.0	57.1	56.2	55.3
52	63.5	62.6	61.7	60.7	59.8	58.9	58.0	57.1	56.1	55.2
53	63.5	62.5	61.6	60.7	59.7	58.8	57.9	57.0	56.1	55.2
54	63.5	62.5	61.6	60.6	59.7	58.8	57.8	56.9	56.0	55.1
55	63.4	62.5	61.5	60.6	59.6	58.7	57.8	56.8	55.9	55.0
56	63.4	62.4	61.5	60.5	59.6	58.7	57.7	56.8	55.9	54.9
57	63.4	62.4	61.5	60.5	59.6	58.6	57.7	56.7	55.8	54.9
58	63.3	62.4	61.4	60.5	59.5	58.6	57.6	56.7	55.8	54.8
59	63.3	62.3	61.4	60.4	59.5	58.5	57.6	56.7	55.7	54.8
60	63.3	62.3	61.4	60.4	59.5	58.5	57.6	56.6	55.7	54.7
61	63.3	62.3	61.3	60.4	59.4	58.5	57.5	56.6	55.6	54.7
62	63.2	62.3	61.3	60.4	59.4	58.4	57.5	56.5	55.6	54.7
63	63.2	62.3	61.3	60.3	59.4	59.4	58.4	56.5	56.5	54.6
64	63.2	62.2	61.3	60.3	59.4	58.4	57.4	56.5	55.5	54.6
65	63.2	62.2	61.3	60.3	59.3	58.4	57.4	56.5	55.5	54.6
66	63.2	62.2	61.2	60.3	59.3	58.4	57.4	56.4	55.5	54.5
67	63.2	62.2	61.2	60.3	59.3	58.3	57.4	56.4	55.5	54.5
68	63.1	62.2	61.2	60.2	59.3	58.3	57.4	56.4	55.4	54.5
69	63.1	62.2	61.2	60.2	59.3	58.3	57.3	56.4	55.4	54.5
70	63.1	62.2	61.2	60.2	59.3	58.3	57.3	56.4	55.4	54.4
71	63.1	62.1	61.2	60.2	59.2	58.3	57.3	56.4	55.4	54.4
72	63.1	62.1	61.2	60.2	59.2	58.3	57.3	56.3	55.4	54.4
73	63.1	62.1	61.2	60.2	59.2	58.3	57.3	56.3	55.4	54.4
74	63.1	62.1	61.2	60.2	59.2	58.2	57.3	56.3	55.4	54.4
75	63.1	62.1	61.1	60.2	59.2	58.2	57.3	56.3	55.3	54.4
76	63.1	62.1	61.1	60.2	59.2	58.2	57.3	56.3	55.3	54.4
77	63.1	62.1	61.1	60.2	59.2	58.2	57.3	56.3	55.3	54.4
78	63.1	62.1	61.1	60.2	59.2	58.2	57.3	56.3	55.3	54.4
79	63.1	62.1	61.1	60.2	59.2	58.2	57.2	56.3	55.3	54.3
80	63.1	62.1	61.1	60.1	59.2	58.2	57.2	56.3	55.3	54.3
81	63.1	62.1	61.1	60.1	59.2	58.2	57.2	56.3	55.3	54.3
82	63.1	62.1	61.1	60.1	59.2	58.2	57.2	56.3	55.3	54.3
83	63.1	62.1	61.1	60.1	59.2	58.2	57.2	56.3	55.3	54.3
84	63.0	62.1	61.1	60.1	59.2	58.2	57.2	56.3	55.3	54.3
85	63.0	62.1	61.1	60.1	59.2	58.2	57.2	56.3	55.3	54.3
86	63.0	62.1	61.1	60.1	59.2	58.2	57.2	56.2	55.3	54.3
87	63.0	62.1	61.1	60.1	59.2	58.2	57.2	56.2	55.3	54.3
88	63.0	62.1	61.1	60.1	59.2	58.2	57.2	56.2	55.3	54.3
89	63.0	62.1	61.1	60.1	59.1	58.2	57.2	56.2	55.3	54.3

21st Century Estate Planning:
Practical Applications
2005 Edition

©2005 Sonnenschein Nath & Rosenthal LLP
and Cannon Financial Institute, Inc.

- 422 -

Ages	20	21	22	23	24	25	26	27	28	29
90	63.0	62.1	61.1	60.1	59.1	58.2	57.2	56.2	55.3	54.3
91	63.0	62.1	61.1	60.1	59.1	58.2	57.2	56.2	55.3	54.3
92	63.0	62.1	61.1	60.1	59.1	58.2	57.2	56.2	55.3	54.3
93	63.0	62.1	61.1	60.1	59.1	58.2	57.2	56.2	55.3	54.3
94	63.0	62.1	61.1	60.1	59.1	58.2	57.2	56.2	55.3	54.3
95	63.0	62.1	61.1	60.1	59.1	58.2	57.2	56.2	55.3	54.3
96	63.0	62.1	61.1	60.1	59.1	58.2	57.2	56.2	55.3	54.3
97	63.0	62.1	61.1	60.1	59.1	58.2	57.2	56.2	55.3	54.3
98	63.0	62.1	61.1	60.1	59.1	58.2	57.2	56.2	55.3	54.3
99	63.0	62.1	61.1	60.1	59.1	58.2	57.2	56.2	55.3	54.3
100	63.0	62.1	61.1	60.1	59.1	58.2	57.2	56.2	55.3	54.3
101	63.0	62.1	61.1	60.1	59.1	58.2	57.2	56.2	55.3	54.3
102	63.0	62.1	61.1	60.1	59.1	58.2	57.2	56.2	55.3	54.3
103	63.0	62.1	61.1	60.1	59.1	58.2	57.2	56.2	55.3	54.3
104	63.0	62.1	61.1	60.1	59.1	58.2	57.2	56.2	55.3	54.3
105	63.0	62.1	61.1	60.1	59.1	58.2	57.2	56.2	55.3	54.3
106	63.0	62.1	61.1	60.1	59.1	58.2	57.2	56.2	55.3	54.3
107	63.0	62.1	61.1	60.1	59.1	58.2	57.2	56.2	55.3	54.3
108	63.0	62.1	61.1	60.1	59.1	58.2	57.2	56.2	55.3	54.3
109	63.0	62.1	61.1	60.1	59.1	58.2	57.2	56.2	55.3	54.3
110	63.0	62.1	61.1	60.1	59.1	58.2	57.2	56.2	55.3	54.3
111	63.0	62.1	61.1	60.1	59.1	58.2	57.2	56.2	55.3	54.3
112	63.0	62.1	61.1	60.1	59.1	58.2	57.2	56.2	55.3	54.3
113	63.0	62.1	61.1	60.1	59.1	58.2	57.2	56.2	55.3	54.3
114	63.0	62.1	61.1	60.1	59.1	58.2	57.2	56.2	55.3	54.3
115+	63.0	62.1	61.1	60.1	59.1	58.2	57.2	56.2	55.3	54.3

Ages	30	31	32	33	34	35	36	37	38	39
30	60.2	59.7	59.2	58.8	58.4	58.0	57.6	57.3	57.0	56.7
31	59.7	59.2	58.7	58.2	57.8	57.4	57.0	56.6	56.3	56.0
32	59.2	58.7	58.2	57.7	57.2	56.8	56.4	56.0	55.6	55.3
33	58.8	58.2	57.7	57.2	56.7	56.2	55.8	55.4	55.0	54.7
34	58.4	57.8	57.2	56.7	56.2	55.7	55.3	54.8	54.4	54.0
35	58.0	57.4	56.8	56.2	55.7	55.2	54.7	54.3	53.8	53.4
36	57.6	57.0	56.4	55.8	55.3	54.7	54.2	53.7	53.3	52.8
37	57.3	56.6	56.0	55.4	54.8	54.3	53.7	53.2	52.7	52.3
38	57.0	56.3	55.6	55.0	54.4	53.8	53.3	52.7	52.2	51.7
39	56.7	56.0	55.3	54.7	54.0	53.4	52.8	52.3	51.7	51.2
40	56.4	55.7	55.0	54.3	53.7	53.0	52.4	51.8	51.3	50.8
41	56.1	55.4	54.7	54.0	53.3	52.7	52.0	51.4	50.9	50.3
42	55.9	55.2	54.4	53.7	53.0	52.3	51.7	51.1	50.4	49.9

21st Century Estate Planning:
Practical Applications
2005 Edition

©2005 Sonnenschein Nath & Rosenthal LLP
and Cannon Financial Institute, Inc.

- 423 -

Ages	30	31	32	33	34	35	36	37	38	39
43	55.7	54.9	54.2	53.4	52.7	52.0	51.3	50.7	50.1	49.5
44	55.5	54.7	53.9	53.2	52.4	51.7	51.0	50.4	49.7	49.1
45	55.3	54.5	53.7	52.9	52.2	51.5	50.7	50.0	49.4	48.7
46	55.1	54.3	53.5	52.7	52.0	51.2	50.5	49.8	49.1	48.4
47	55.0	54.1	53.3	52.5	51.7	51.0	50.2	49.5	48.8	48.1
48	54.8	54.0	53.2	52.3	51.5	50.8	50.0	49.2	48.5	47.8
49	54.7	53.8	53.0	52.2	51.4	50.6	49.8	49.0	48.2	47.5
50	54.6	53.7	52.9	52.0	51.2	50.4	49.6	48.8	48.0	47.3
51	54.5	53.6	52.7	51.9	51.0	50.2	49.4	48.6	47.8	47.0
52	54.4	53.5	52.6	51.7	50.9	50.0	49.2	48.4	47.6	46.8
53	54.3	53.4	52.5	51.6	50.8	49.9	49.1	48.2	47.4	46.6
54	54.2	53.3	52.4	51.5	50.6	49.8	48.9	48.1	47.2	46.4
55	54.1	53.2	52.3	51.4	50.5	49.7	48.8	47.9	47.1	46.3
56	54.0	53.1	52.2	51.3	50.4	49.5	48.7	47.8	47.0	46.1
57	54.0	53.0	52.1	51.2	50.3	49.4	48.6	47.7	46.8	46.0
58	53.9	53.0	52.1	51.2	50.3	49.4	48.5	47.6	46.7	45.8
59	53.8	52.9	52.0	51.1	50.2	49.3	48.4	47.5	46.6	45.7
60	53.8	52.9	51.9	51.0	50.1	49.2	48.3	47.4	46.5	45.6
61	53.8	52.8	51.9	51.0	50.0	49.1	48.2	47.3	46.4	45.5
62	53.7	52.8	51.8	50.9	50.0	49.1	48.1	47.2	46.3	45.4
63	53.7	52.7	51.8	50.9	49.9	49.0	48.1	47.2	46.3	45.3
64	53.6	52.7	51.8	50.8	49.9	48.9	48.0	47.1	46.2	45.3
65	53.6	52.7	51.7	50.8	49.8	48.9	48.0	47.0	46.1	45.2
66	53.6	52.6	51.7	50.7	49.8	48.9	47.9	47.0	46.1	45.1
67	53.6	52.6	51.7	50.7	49.8	48.8	47.9	46.9	46.0	45.1
68	53.5	52.6	51.6	50.7	49.7	48.8	47.8	46.9	46.0	45.0
69	53.5	52.6	51.6	50.6	49.7	48.7	47.8	46.9	45.9	45.0
70	53.5	52.5	51.6	50.6	49.7	48.7	47.8	46.8	45.9	44.9
71	53.5	52.5	51.6	50.6	49.6	48.7	47.7	46.8	45.9	44.9
72	53.5	52.5	51.5	50.6	49.6	48.7	47.7	46.8	45.8	44.9
73	53.4	52.5	51.5	50.6	49.6	48.6	47.7	46.7	45.8	44.8
74	53.4	52.5	51.5	50.5	49.6	48.6	47.7	46.7	45.8	44.8
75	53.4	52.5	51.5	50.5	49.6	48.6	47.7	46.7	45.7	44.8
76	53.4	52.4	51.5	50.5	49.6	48.6	47.6	46.7	45.7	44.8
77	53.4	52.4	51.5	50.5	49.5	48.6	47.6	46.7	45.7	44.8
78	53.4	52.4	51.5	50.5	49.5	48.6	47.6	46.6	45.7	44.7
79	53.4	52.4	51.5	50.5	49.5	48.6	47.6	46.6	45.7	44.7
80	53.4	52.4	51.4	50.5	49.5	48.5	47.6	46.6	45.7	44.7
81	53.4	52.4	51.4	50.5	49.5	48.5	47.6	46.6	45.7	44.7
82	53.4	52.4	51.4	50.5	49.5	48.5	47.6	46.6	45.6	44.7
83	53.4	52.4	51.4	50.5	49.5	48.5	47.6	46.6	45.6	44.7

21st Century Estate Planning:
Practical Applications
2005 Edition

©2005 Sonnenschein Nath & Rosenthal LLP
and Cannon Financial Institute, Inc.

- 424 -

Ages	30	31	32	33	34	35	36	37	38	39
84	53.4	52.4	51.4	50.5	49.5	48.5	47.6	46.6	45.6	44.7
85	53.3	52.4	51.4	50.4	49.5	48.5	47.5	46.6	45.6	44.7
86	53.3	52.4	51.4	50.4	49.5	48.5	47.5	46.6	45.6	44.6
87	53.3	52.4	51.4	50.4	49.5	48.5	47.5	46.6	45.6	44.6
88	53.3	52.4	51.4	50.4	49.5	48.5	47.5	46.6	45.6	44.6
89	53.3	52.4	51.4	50.4	49.5	48.5	47.5	46.6	45.6	44.6
90	53.3	52.4	51.4	50.4	49.5	48.5	47.5	46.6	45.6	44.6
91	53.3	52.4	51.4	50.4	49.5	48.5	47.5	46.6	45.6	44.6
92	53.3	52.4	51.4	50.4	49.5	48.5	47.5	46.6	45.6	44.6
93	53.3	52.4	51.4	50.4	49.5	48.5	47.5	46.6	45.6	44.6
94	53.3	52.4	51.4	50.4	49.5	48.5	47.5	46.6	45.6	44.6
95	53.3	52.4	51.4	50.4	49.5	48.5	47.5	46.5	45.6	44.6
96	53.3	52.4	51.4	50.4	49.5	48.5	47.5	46.5	45.6	44.6
97	53.3	52.4	51.4	50.4	49.5	48.5	47.5	46.5	45.6	44.6
98	53.3	52.4	51.4	50.4	49.5	48.5	47.5	46.5	45.6	44.6
99	53.3	52.4	51.4	50.4	49.5	48.5	47.5	46.5	45.6	44.6
100	53.3	52.4	51.4	50.4	49.5	48.5	47.5	46.5	45.6	44.6
101+	53.3	52.4	51.4	50.4	49.5	48.5	47.5	46.5	45.6	44.6

Ages	40	41	42	43	44	45	46	47	48	49
40	50.2	49.8	49.3	48.9	48.5	48.1	47.7	47.4	47.1	46.8
41	49.8	49.3	48.8	48.3	47.9	47.5	47.1	46.7	46.4	46.1
42	49.3	48.8	48.3	47.8	47.3	46.9	46.5	46.1	45.8	45.4
43	48.9	48.3	47.8	47.3	46.8	46.3	45.9	45.5	45.1	44.8
44	48.5	47.9	47.3	46.8	46.3	45.8	45.4	44.9	44.5	44.2
45	48.1	47.5	46.9	46.3	45.8	45.3	44.8	44.4	44.0	43.6
46	47.7	47.1	46.5	45.9	45.4	44.8	44.3	43.9	43.4	43.0
47	47.4	46.7	46.1	45.5	44.9	44.4	43.9	43.4	42.9	42.4
48	47.1	46.4	45.8	45.1	44.5	44.0	43.4	42.9	42.4	41.9
49	46.8	46.1	45.4	44.8	44.2	43.6	43.0	42.4	41.9	41.4
50	46.5	45.8	45.1	44.4	43.8	43.2	42.6	42.0	41.5	40.9
51	46.3	45.5	44.8	44.1	43.5	42.8	42.2	41.6	41.0	40.5
52	46.0	45.3	44.6	43.8	43.2	42.5	41.8	41.2	40.6	40.1
53	45.8	45.1	44.3	43.6	42.9	42.2	41.5	40.9	40.3	39.7
54	45.6	44.8	44.1	43.3	42.6	41.9	41.2	40.5	39.9	39.3
55	45.5	44.7	43.9	43.1	42.4	41.6	40.9	40.2	39.6	38.9
56	45.3	44.5	43.7	42.9	42.1	41.4	40.7	40.0	39.3	38.6
57	45.1	44.3	43.5	42.7	41.9	41.2	40.4	39.7	39.0	38.3
58	45.0	44.2	43.3	42.5	41.7	40.9	40.2	39.4	38.7	38.0
59	44.9	44.0	43.2	42.4	41.5	40.7	40.0	39.2	38.5	37.8
60	44.7	43.9	43.0	42.2	41.4	40.6	39.8	39.0	38.2	37.5
61	44.6	43.8	42.9	42.1	41.2	40.4	39.6	38.8	38.0	37.3

21st Century Estate Planning:
Practical Applications
2005 Edition

©2005 Sonnenschein Nath & Rosenthal LLP
and Cannon Financial Institute, Inc.

- 425 -

Ages	40	41	42	43	44	45	46	47	48	49
62	44.5	43.7	42.8	41.9	41.1	40.3	39.4	38.6	37.8	37.1
63	44.5	43.6	42.7	41.8	41.0	40.1	39.3	38.5	37.7	36.9
64	44.4	43.5	42.6	41.7	40.8	40.0	39.2	38.3	37.5	36.7
65	44.3	43.4	42.5	41.6	40.7	39.9	39.0	38.2	37.4	36.6
66	44.2	43.3	42.4	41.5	40.6	39.8	38.9	38.1	37.2	36.4
67	44.2	43.3	42.3	41.4	40.6	39.7	38.8	38.0	37.1	36.3
68	44.1	43.2	42.3	41.4	40.5	39.6	38.7	37.9	37.0	36.2
69	44.1	43.1	42.2	41.3	40.4	39.5	38.6	37.8	36.9	36.0
70	44.0	43.1	42.2	41.3	40.3	39.4	38.6	37.7	36.8	35.9
71	44.0	43.0	42.1	41.2	40.3	39.4	38.5	37.6	36.7	35.9
72	43.9	43.0	42.1	41.1	40.2	39.3	38.4	37.5	36.6	35.8
73	43.9	43.0	42.0	41.1	40.2	39.3	38.4	37.5	36.6	35.7
74	43.9	42.9	42.0	41.1	40.1	39.2	38.3	37.4	36.5	35.6
75	43.8	42.9	42.0	41.0	40.1	39.2	38.3	37.4	36.5	35.6
76	43.8	42.9	41.9	41.0	40.1	39.1	38.2	37.3	36.4	35.5
77	43.8	42.9	41.9	41.0	40.0	39.1	38.2	37.3	36.4	35.5
78	43.8	42.8	41.9	40.9	40.0	39.1	38.2	37.2	36.3	35.4
79	43.8	42.8	41.9	40.9	40.0	39.1	38.1	37.2	36.3	35.4
80	43.7	42.8	41.8	40.9	40.0	39.0	38.1	37.2	36.3	35.4
81	43.7	42.8	41.8	40.9	39.9	39.0	38.1	37.2	36.2	35.3
82	43.7	42.8	41.8	40.9	39.9	39.0	38.1	37.1	36.2	35.3
83	43.7	42.8	41.8	40.9	39.9	39.0	38.0	37.1	36.2	35.3
84	43.7	42.7	41.8	40.8	39.9	39.0	38.0	37.1	36.2	35.3
85	43.7	42.7	41.8	40.8	39.9	38.9	38.0	37.1	36.2	35.2
86	43.7	42.7	41.8	40.8	39.9	38.9	38.0	37.1	36.1	35.2
87	43.7	42.7	41.8	40.8	39.9	38.9	38.0	37.0	36.1	35.2
88	43.7	42.7	41.8	40.8	39.9	38.9	38.0	37.0	36.1	35.2
89	43.7	42.7	41.7	40.8	39.8	38.9	38.0	37.0	36.1	35.2
90	43.7	42.7	41.7	40.8	39.8	38.9	38.0	37.0	36.1	35.2
91	43.7	42.7	41.7	40.8	39.8	38.9	37.9	37.0	36.1	35.2
92	43.7	42.7	41.7	40.8	39.8	38.9	37.9	37.0	36.1	35.1
93	43.7	42.7	41.7	40.8	39.8	38.9	37.9	37.0	36.1	35.1
94	43.7	42.7	41.7	40.8	39.8	38.9	37.9	37.0	36.1	35.1
95	43.6	42.7	41.7	40.8	39.8	38.9	37.9	37.0	36.1	35.1
96	43.6	42.7	41.7	40.8	39.8	38.9	37.9	37.0	36.1	35.1
97	43.6	42.7	41.7	40.8	39.8	38.9	37.9	37.0	36.1	35.1
98	43.6	42.7	41.7	40.8	39.8	38.9	37.9	37.0	36.0	35.1
99	43.6	42.7	41.7	40.8	39.8	38.9	37.9	37.0	36.0	35.1
100	43.6	42.7	41.7	40.8	39.8	38.9	37.9	37.0	36.0	35.1
101	43.6	42.7	41.7	40.8	39.8	38.9	37.9	37.0	36.0	35.1
102	43.6	42.7	41.7	40.8	39.8	38.9	37.9	37.0	36.0	35.1
103	43.6	42.7	41.7	40.8	39.8	38.9	37.9	37.0	36.0	35.1

21st Century Estate Planning:
Practical Applications
2005 Edition

©2005 Sonnenschein Nath & Rosenthal LLP
and Cannon Financial Institute, Inc.

- 426 -

Ages	40	41	42	43	44	45	46	47	48	49
104	43.6	42.7	41.7	40.8	39.8	38.8	37.9	37.0	36.0	35.1
105	43.6	42.7	41.7	40.8	39.8	38.8	37.9	37.0	36.0	35.1
106	43.6	42.7	41.7	40.8	39.8	38.8	37.9	37.0	36.0	35.1
107	43.6	42.7	41.7	40.8	39.8	38.8	37.9	37.0	36.0	35.1
108	43.6	42.7	41.7	40.8	39.8	38.8	37.9	37.0	36.0	35.1
109	43.6	42.7	41.7	40.7	39.8	38.8	37.9	37.0	36.0	35.1
110	43.6	42.7	41.7	40.7	39.8	38.8	37.9	37.0	36.0	35.1
111	43.6	42.7	41.7	40.7	39.8	38.8	37.9	37.0	36.0	35.1
112	43.6	42.7	41.7	40.7	39.8	38.8	37.9	37.0	36.0	35.1
113	43.6	42.7	41.7	40.7	39.8	38.8	37.9	37.0	36.0	35.1
114	43.6	42.7	41.7	40.7	39.8	38.8	37.9	37.0	36.0	35.1
115+	43.6	42.7	41.7	40.7	39.8	38.8	37.9	37.0	36.0	35.1

Ages	50	51	52	53	54	55	56	57	58	59
50	40.4	40.0	39.5	39.1	38.7	38.3	38.0	37.6	37.3	37.1
51	40.0	39.5	39.0	38.5	38.1	37.7	37.4	37.0	36.7	36.4
52	39.5	39.0	38.5	38.0	37.6	37.2	36.8	36.4	36.0	35.7
53	39.1	38.5	38.0	37.5	37.1	36.6	36.2	35.8	35.4	35.1
54	38.7	38.1	37.6	37.1	36.6	36.1	35.7	35.2	34.8	34.5
55	38.3	37.7	37.2	36.6	36.1	35.6	35.1	34.7	34.3	33.9
56	38.0	37.4	36.8	36.2	35.7	35.1	34.7	34.2	33.7	33.3
57	37.6	37.0	36.4	35.8	35.2	34.7	34.2	33.7	33.2	32.8
58	37.3	36.7	36.0	35.4	34.8	34.3	33.7	33.2	32.8	32.3
59	37.1	36.4	35.7	35.1	34.5	33.9	33.3	32.8	32.3	31.8
60	36.8	36.1	35.4	34.8	34.1	33.5	32.9	32.4	31.9	31.3
61	36.6	35.8	35.1	34.5	33.8	33.2	32.6	32.0	31.4	30.9
62	36.3	35.6	34.9	34.2	33.5	32.9	32.2	31.6	31.1	30.5
63	36.1	35.4	34.6	33.9	33.2	32.6	31.9	31.3	30.7	30.1
64	35.9	35.2	34.4	33.7	33.0	32.3	31.6	31.0	30.4	29.8
65	35.8	35.0	34.2	33.5	32.7	32.0	31.4	30.7	30.0	29.4
66	35.6	34.8	34.0	33.3	32.5	31.8	31.1	30.4	29.8	29.1
67	35.5	34.7	33.9	33.1	32.3	31.6	30.9	30.2	29.5	28.8
68	35.3	34.5	33.7	32.9	32.1	31.4	30.7	29.9	29.2	28.6
69	35.2	34.4	33.6	32.8	32.0	31.2	30.5	29.7	29.0	28.3
70	35.1	34.3	33.4	32.6	31.8	31.1	30.3	29.5	28.8	28.1
71	35.0	34.2	33.3	32.5	31.7	30.9	30.1	29.4	28.6	27.9
72	34.9	34.1	33.2	32.4	31.6	30.8	30.0	29.2	28.4	27.7
73	34.8	34.0	33.1	32.3	31.5	30.6	29.8	29.1	28.3	27.5
74	34.8	33.9	33.0	32.2	31.4	30.5	29.7	28.9	28.1	27.4
75	34.7	33.8	33.0	32.1	31.3	30.4	29.6	28.8	28.0	27.2
76	34.6	33.8	32.9	32.0	31.2	30.3	29.5	28.7	27.9	27.1
77	34.6	33.7	32.8	32.0	31.1	30.3	29.4	28.6	27.8	27.0

21st Century Estate Planning:
Practical Applications
2005 Edition

©2005 Sonnenschein Nath & Rosenthal LLP
and Cannon Financial Institute, Inc.

- 427 -

Ages	50	51	52	53	54	55	56	57	58	59
78	34.5	33.6	32.8	31.9	31.0	30.2	29.3	28.5	27.7	26.9
79	34.5	33.6	32.7	31.8	31.0	30.1	29.3	28.4	27.6	26.8
80	34.5	33.6	32.7	31.8	30.9	30.1	29.2	28.4	27.5	26.7
81	34.4	33.5	32.6	31.8	30.9	30.0	29.2	28.3	27.5	26.6
82	34.4	33.5	32.6	31.7	30.8	30.0	29.1	28.3	27.4	26.6
83	34.4	33.5	32.6	31.7	30.8	29.9	29.1	28.2	27.4	26.5
84	34.3	33.4	32.5	31.7	30.8	29.9	29.0	28.2	27.3	26.5
85	34.3	33.4	32.5	31.6	30.7	29.9	29.0	28.1	27.3	26.4
86	34.3	33.4	32.5	31.6	30.7	29.8	29.0	28.1	27.2	26.4
87	34.3	33.4	32.5	31.6	30.7	29.8	28.9	28.1	27.2	26.4
88	34.3	33.4	32.5	31.6	30.7	29.8	28.9	28.0	27.2	26.3
89	34.3	33.3	32.4	31.5	30.7	29.8	28.9	28.0	27.2	26.3
90	34.2	33.3	32.4	31.5	30.6	29.8	28.9	28.0	27.1	26.3
91	34.2	33.3	32.4	31.5	30.6	29.7	28.9	28.0	27.1	26.3
92	34.2	33.3	32.4	31.5	30.6	29.7	28.8	28.0	27.1	26.2
93	34.2	33.3	32.4	31.5	30.6	29.7	28.8	28.0	27.1	26.2
94	34.2	33.3	32.4	31.5	30.6	29.7	28.8	27.9	27.1	26.2
95	34.2	33.3	32.4	31.5	30.6	29.7	28.8	27.9	27.1	26.2
96	34.2	33.3	32.4	31.5	30.6	29.7	28.8	27.9	27.0	26.2
97	34.2	33.3	32.4	31.5	30.6	29.7	28.8	27.9	27.0	26.2
98	34.2	33.3	32.4	31.5	30.6	29.7	28.8	27.9	27.0	26.2
99	34.2	33.3	32.4	31.5	30.6	29.7	28.8	27.9	27.0	26.2
100	34.2	33.3	32.4	31.5	30.6	29.7	28.8	27.9	27.0	26.1
101	34.2	33.3	32.4	31.5	30.6	29.7	28.8	27.9	27.0	26.1
102	34.2	33.3	32.4	31.4	30.5	29.7	28.8	27.9	27.0	26.1
103	34.2	33.3	32.4	31.4	30.5	29.7	28.8	27.9	27.0	26.1
104	34.2	33.3	32.4	31.4	30.5	29.6	28.8	27.9	27.0	26.1
105	34.2	33.3	32.3	31.4	30.5	29.6	28.8	27.9	27.0	26.1
106	34.2	33.3	32.3	31.4	30.5	29.6	28.8	27.9	27.0	26.1
107	34.2	33.3	32.3	31.4	30.5	29.6	28.8	27.9	27.0	26.1
108	34.2	33.3	32.3	31.4	30.5	29.6	28.8	27.9	27.0	26.1
109	34.2	33.3	32.3	31.4	30.5	29.6	28.7	27.9	27.0	26.1
110	34.2	33.3	32.3	31.4	30.5	29.6	28.7	27.9	27.0	26.1
111	34.2	33.3	32.3	31.4	30.5	29.6	28.7	27.9	27.0	26.1
112	34.2	33.3	32.3	31.4	30.5	29.6	28.7	27.9	27.0	26.1
113	34.2	33.3	32.3	31.4	30.5	29.6	28.7	27.9	27.0	26.1
114	34.2	33.3	32.3	31.4	30.5	29.6	28.7	27.9	27.0	26.1
115+	34.2	33.3	32.3	31.4	30.5	29.6	28.7	27.9	27.0	26.1

Ages	60	61	62	63	64	65	66	67	68	69
60	30.9	30.4	30.0	29.6	29.2	28.8	28.5	28.2	27.9	27.6
61	30.4	29.9	29.5	29.0	28.6	28.3	27.9	27.6	27.3	27.0

21st Century Estate Planning:
Practical Applications
2005 Edition

©2005 Sonnenschein Nath & Rosenthal LLP
and Cannon Financial Institute, Inc.

- 428 -

Ages	60	61	62	63	64	65	66	67	68	69
62	30.0	29.5	29.0	28.5	28.1	27.7	27.3	27.0	26.7	26.4
63	29.6	29.0	28.5	28.1	27.6	27.2	26.8	26.4	26.1	25.7
64	29.2	28.6	28.1	27.6	27.1	26.7	26.3	25.9	25.5	25.2
65	28.8	28.3	27.7	27.2	26.7	26.2	25.8	25.4	25.0	24.6
66	28.5	27.9	27.3	26.8	26.3	25.8	25.3	24.9	24.5	24.1
67	28.2	27.6	27.0	26.4	25.9	25.4	24.9	24.4	24.0	23.6
68	27.9	27.3	26.7	26.1	25.5	25.0	24.5	24.0	23.5	23.1
69	27.6	27.0	26.4	25.7	25.2	24.6	24.1	23.6	23.1	22.6
70	27.4	26.7	26.1	25.4	24.8	24.3	23.7	23.2	22.7	22.2
71	27.2	26.5	25.8	25.2	24.5	23.9	23.4	22.8	22.3	21.8
72	27.0	26.3	25.6	24.9	24.3	23.7	23.1	22.5	22.0	21.4
73	26.8	26.1	25.4	24.7	24.0	23.4	22.8	22.2	21.6	21.1
74	26.6	25.9	25.2	24.5	23.8	23.1	22.5	21.9	21.3	20.8
75	26.5	25.7	25.0	24.3	23.6	22.9	22.3	21.6	21.0	20.5
76	26.3	25.6	24.8	24.1	23.4	22.7	22.0	21.4	20.8	20.2
77	26.2	25.4	24.7	23.9	23.2	22.5	21.8	21.2	20.6	19.9
78	26.1	25.3	24.6	23.8	23.1	22.4	21.7	21.0	20.3	19.7
79	26.0	25.2	24.4	23.7	22.9	22.2	21.5	20.8	20.1	19.5
80	25.9	25.1	24.3	23.6	22.8	22.1	21.3	20.6	20.0	19.3
81	25.8	25.0	24.2	23.4	22.7	21.9	21.2	20.5	19.8	19.1
82	25.8	24.9	24.1	23.4	22.6	21.8	21.1	20.4	19.7	19.0
83	25.7	24.9	24.1	23.3	22.5	21.7	21.0	20.2	19.5	18.8
84	25.6	24.8	24.0	23.2	22.4	21.6	20.9	20.1	19.4	18.7
85	25.6	24.8	23.9	23.1	22.3	21.6	20.8	20.1	19.3	18.6
86	25.5	24.7	23.9	23.1	22.3	21.5	20.7	20.0	19.2	18.5
87	25.5	24.7	23.8	23.0	22.2	21.4	20.7	19.9	19.2	18.4
88	25.5	24.6	23.8	23.0	22.2	21.4	20.6	19.8	19.1	18.3
89	25.4	24.6	23.8	22.9	22.1	21.3	20.5	19.8	19.0	18.3
90	25.4	24.6	23.7	22.9	22.1	21.3	20.5	19.7	19.0	18.2
91	25.4	24.5	23.7	22.9	22.1	21.3	20.5	19.7	18.9	18.2
92	25.4	24.5	23.7	22.9	22.0	21.2	20.4	19.6	18.9	18.1
93	25.4	24.5	23.7	22.8	22.0	21.2	20.4	19.6	18.8	18.1
94	25.3	24.5	23.6	22.8	22.0	21.2	20.4	19.6	18.8	18.0
95	25.3	24.5	23.6	22.8	22.0	21.1	20.3	19.6	18.8	18.0
96	25.3	24.5	23.6	22.8	21.9	21.1	20.3	19.5	18.8	18.0
97	25.3	24.5	23.6	22.8	21.9	21.1	20.3	19.5	18.7	18.0
98	25.3	24.4	23.6	22.8	21.9	21.1	20.3	19.5	18.7	17.9
99	25.3	24.4	23.6	22.7	21.9	21.1	20.3	19.5	18.7	17.9
100	25.3	24.4	23.6	22.7	21.9	21.1	20.3	19.5	18.7	17.9
101	25.3	24.4	23.6	22.7	21.9	21.1	20.2	19.4	18.7	17.9
102	25.3	24.4	23.6	22.7	21.9	21.1	20.2	19.4	18.6	17.9
103	25.3	24.4	23.6	22.7	21.9	21.0	20.2	19.4	18.6	17.9

21st Century Estate Planning:
Practical Applications
2005 Edition

©2005 Sonnenschein Nath & Rosenthal LLP
and Cannon Financial Institute, Inc.

- 429 -

Ages	60	61	62	63	64	65	66	67	68	69
104...........	25.3	24.4	23.5	22.7	21.9	21.0	20.2	19.4	18.6	17.8
105...........	25.3	24.4	23.5	22.7	21.9	21.0	20.2	19.4	18.6	17.8
106...........	25.3	24.4	23.5	22.7	21.9	21.0	20.2	19.4	18.6	17.8
107...........	25.2	24.4	23.5	22.7	21.8	21.0	20.2	19.4	18.6	17.8
108...........	25.2	24.4	23.5	22.7	21.8	21.0	20.2	19.4	18.6	17.8
109...........	25.2	24.4	23.5	22.7	21.8	21.0	20.2	19.4	18.6	17.8
110...........	25.2	24.4	23.5	22.7	21.8	21.0	20.2	19.4	18.6	17.8
111...........	25.2	24.4	23.5	22.7	21.8	21.0	20.2	19.4	18.6	17.8
112...........	25.2	24.4	23.5	22.7	21.8	21.0	20.2	19.4	18.6	17.8
113...........	25.2	24.4	23.5	22.7	21.8	21.0	20.2	19.4	18.6	17.8
114...........	25.2	24.4	23.5	22.7	21.8	21.0	20.2	19.4	18.6	17.8
115+...........	25.2	24.4	23.5	22.7	21.8	21.0	20.2	19.4	18.6	17.8

Ages	70	71	72	73	74	75	76	77	78	79
70...........	21.8	21.3	20.9	20.6	20.2	19.9	19.6	19.4	19.1	18.9
71...........	21.3	20.9	20.5	20.1	19.7	19.4	19.1	18.8	18.5	18.3
72...........	20.9	20.5	20.0	19.6	19.3	18.9	18.6	18.3	18.0	17.7
73...........	20.6	20.1	19.6	19.2	18.8	18.4	18.1	17.8	17.5	17.2
74...........	20.2	19.7	19.3	18.8	18.4	18.0	17.6	17.3	17.0	16.7
75...........	19.9	19.4	18.9	18.4	18.0	17.6	17.2	16.8	16.5	16.2
76...........	19.6	19.1	18.6	18.1	17.6	17.2	16.8	16.4	16.0	15.7
77...........	19.4	18.8	18.3	17.8	17.3	16.8	16.4	16.0	15.6	15.3
78...........	19.1	18.5	18.0	17.5	17.0	16.5	16.0	15.6	15.2	14.9
79...........	18.9	18.3	17.7	17.2	16.7	16.2	15.7	15.3	14.9	14.5
80...........	18.7	18.1	17.5	16.9	16.4	15.9	15.4	15.0	14.5	14.1
81...........	18.5	17.9	17.3	16.7	16.2	15.6	15.1	14.7	14.2	13.8
82...........	18.3	17.7	17.1	16.5	15.9	15.4	14.9	14.4	13.9	13.5
83...........	18.2	17.5	16.9	16.3	15.7	15.2	14.7	14.2	13.7	13.2
84...........	18.0	17.4	16.7	16.1	15.5	15.0	14.4	13.9	13.4	13.0
85...........	17.9	17.3	16.6	16.0	15.4	14.8	14.3	13.7	13.2	12.8
86...........	17.8	17.1	16.5	15.8	15.2	14.6	14.1	13.5	13.0	12.5
87...........	17.7	17.0	16.4	15.7	15.1	14.5	13.9	13.4	12.9	12.4
88...........	17.6	16.9	16.3	15.6	15.0	14.4	13.8	13.2	12.7	12.2
89...........	17.6	16.9	16.2	15.5	14.9	14.3	13.7	13.1	12.6	12.0
90...........	17.5	16.8	16.1	15.4	14.8	14.2	13.6	13.0	12.4	11.9
91...........	17.4	16.7	16.0	15.4	14.7	14.1	13.5	12.9	12.3	11.8
92...........	17.4	16.7	16.0	15.3	14.6	14.0	13.4	12.8	12.2	11.7
93...........	17.3	16.6	15.9	15.2	14.6	13.9	13.3	12.7	12.1	11.6
94...........	17.3	16.6	15.9	15.2	14.5	13.9	13.2	12.6	12.0	11.5
95...........	17.3	16.5	15.8	15.1	14.5	13.8	13.2	12.6	12.0	11.4
96...........	17.2	16.5	15.8	15.1	14.4	13.8	13.1	12.5	11.9	11.3
97...........	17.2	16.5	15.8	15.1	14.4	13.7	13.1	12.5	11.9	11.3

21st Century Estate Planning:
Practical Applications
2005 Edition

©2005 Sonnenschein Nath & Rosenthal LLP
and Cannon Financial Institute, Inc.

- 430 -

Ages	70	71	72	73	74	75	76	77	78	79
98	17.2	16.4	15.7	15.0	14.3	13.7	13.0	12.4	11.8	11.2
99	17.2	16.4	15.7	15.0	14.3	13.6	13.0	12.4	11.8	11.2
100	17.1	16.4	15.7	15.0	14.3	13.6	12.9	12.3	11.7	11.1
101	17.1	16.4	15.6	14.9	14.2	13.6	12.9	12.3	11.7	11.1
102	17.1	16.4	15.6	14.9	14.2	13.5	12.9	12.2	11.6	11.0
103	17.1	16.3	15.6	14.9	14.2	13.5	12.9	12.2	11.6	11.0
104	17.1	16.3	15.6	14.9	14.2	13.5	12.8	12.2	11.6	11.0
105	17.1	16.3	15.6	14.9	14.2	13.5	12.8	12.2	11.5	10.9
106	17.1	16.3	15.6	14.8	14.1	13.5	12.8	12.2	11.5	10.9
107	17.0	16.3	15.6	14.8	14.1	13.4	12.8	12.1	11.5	10.9
108	17.0	16.3	15.5	14.8	14.1	13.4	12.8	12.1	11.5	10.9
109	17.0	16.3	15.5	14.8	14.1	13.4	12.8	12.1	11.5	10.8
110	17.0	16.3	15.5	14.8	14.1	13.4	12.7	12.1	11.5	10.8
111	17.0	16.3	15.5	14.8	14.1	13.4	12.7	12.1	11.5	10.8
112	17.0	16.3	15.5	14.8	14.1	13.4	12.7	12.1	11.5	10.8
113	17.0	16.3	15.5	14.8	14.1	13.4	12.7	12.1	11.4	10.8
114	17.0	16.3	15.5	14.8	14.1	13.4	12.7	12.1	11.4	10.8
115+	17.0	16.3	15.5	14.8	14.1	13.4	12.7	12.1	11.4	10.8

Ages	80	81	82	83	84	85	86	87	88	89
80	13.8	13.4	13.1	12.8	12.6	12.3	12.1	11.9	11.7	11.5
81	13.4	13.1	12.7	12.4	12.2	11.9	11.7	11.4	11.3	11.1
82	13.1	12.7	12.4	12.1	11.8	11.5	11.3	11.0	10.8	10.6
83	12.8	12.4	12.1	11.7	11.4	11.1	10.9	10.6	10.4	10.2
84	12.6	12.2	11.8	11.4	11.1	10.8	10.5	10.3	10.1	9.9
85	12.3	11.9	11.5	11.1	10.8	10.5	10.2	9.9	9.7	9.5
86	12.1	11.7	11.3	10.9	10.5	10.2	9.9	9.6	9.4	9.2
87	11.9	11.4	11.0	10.6	10.3	9.9	9.6	9.4	9.1	8.9
88	11.7	11.3	10.8	10.4	10.1	9.7	9.4	9.1	8.8	8.6
89	11.5	11.1	10.6	10.2	9.9	9.5	9.2	8.9	8.6	8.3
90	11.4	10.9	10.5	10.1	9.7	9.3	9.0	8.6	8.3	8.1
91	11.3	10.8	10.3	9.9	9.5	9.1	8.8	8.4	8.1	7.9
92	11.2	10.7	10.2	9.8	9.3	9.0	8.6	8.3	8.0	7.7
93	11.1	10.6	10.1	9.6	9.2	8.8	8.5	8.1	7.8	7.5
94	11.0	10.5	10.0	9.5	9.1	8.7	8.3	8.0	7.6	7.3
95	10.9	10.4	9.9	9.4	9.0	8.6	8.2	7.8	7.5	7.2
96	10.8	10.3	9.8	9.3	8.9	8.5	8.1	7.7	7.4	7.1
97	10.7	10.2	9.7	9.2	8.8	8.4	8.0	7.6	7.3	6.9
98	10.7	10.1	9.6	9.2	8.7	8.3	7.9	7.5	7.1	6.8
99	10.6	10.1	9.6	9.1	8.6	8.2	7.8	7.4	7.0	6.7
100	10.6	10.0	9.5	9.0	8.5	8.1	7.7	7.3	6.9	6.6
101	10.5	10.0	9.4	9.0	8.5	8.0	7.6	7.2	6.9	6.5

21st Century Estate Planning:
Practical Applications
2005 Edition

©2005 Sonnenschein Nath & Rosenthal LLP
and Cannon Financial Institute, Inc.

- 431 -

Ages	80	81	82	83	84	85	86	87	88	89
102	10.5	9.9	9.4	8.9	8.4	8.0	7.5	7.1	6.8	6.4
103	10.4	9.9	9.4	8.8	8.4	7.9	7.5	7.1	6.7	6.3
104	10.4	9.8	9.3	8.8	8.3	7.9	7.4	7.0	6.6	6.3
105	10.4	9.8	9.3	8.8	8.3	7.8	7.4	7.0	6.6	6.2
106	10.3	9.8	9.2	8.7	8.2	7.8	7.3	6.9	6.5	6.2
107	10.3	9.8	9.2	8.7	8.2	7.7	7.3	6.9	6.5	6.1
108	10.3	9.7	9.2	8.7	8.2	7.7	7.3	6.8	6.4	6.1
109	10.3	9.7	9.2	8.7	8.2	7.7	7.2	6.8	6.4	6.0
110	10.3	9.7	9.2	8.6	8.1	7.7	7.2	6.8	6.4	6.0
111	10.3	9.7	9.1	8.6	8.1	7.6	7.2	6.8	6.3	6.0
112	10.2	9.7	9.1	8.6	8.1	7.6	7.2	6.7	6.3	5.9
113	10.2	9.7	9.1	8.6	8.1	7.6	7.2	6.7	6.3	5.9
114	10.2	9.7	9.1	8.6	8.1	7.6	7.1	6.7	6.3	5.9
115+	10.2	9.7	9.1	8.6	8.1	7.6	7.1	6.7	6.3	5.9

Ages	90	91	92	93	94	95	96	97	98	99
90	7.8	7.6	7.4	7.2	7.1	6.9	6.8	6.6	6.5	6.4
91	7.6	7.4	7.2	7.0	6.8	6.7	6.5	6.4	6.3	6.1
92	7.4	7.2	7.0	6.8	6.6	6.4	6.3	6.1	6.0	5.9
93	7.2	7.0	6.8	6.6	6.4	6.2	6.1	5.9	5.8	5.6
94	7.1	6.8	6.6	6.4	6.2	6.0	5.9	5.7	5.6	5.4
95	6.9	6.7	6.4	6.2	6.0	5.8	5.7	5.5	5.4	5.2
96	6.8	6.5	6.3	6.1	5.9	5.7	5.5	5.3	5.2	5.0
97	6.6	6.4	6.1	5.9	5.7	5.5	5.3	5.2	5.0	4.9
98	6.5	6.3	6.0	5.8	5.6	5.4	5.2	5.0	4.8	4.7
99	6.4	6.1	5.9	5.6	5.4	5.2	5.0	4.9	4.7	4.5
100	6.3	6.0	5.8	5.5	5.3	5.1	4.9	4.7	4.5	4.4
101	6.2	5.9	5.6	5.4	5.2	5.0	4.8	4.6	4.4	4.2
102	6.1	5.8	5.5	5.3	5.1	4.8	4.6	4.4	4.3	4.1
103	6.0	5.7	5.4	5.2	5.0	4.7	4.5	4.3	4.1	4.0
104	5.9	5.6	5.4	5.1	4.9	4.6	4.4	4.2	4.0	3.8
105	5.9	5.6	5.3	5.0	4.8	4.5	4.3	4.1	3.9	3.7
106	5.8	5.5	5.2	4.9	4.7	4.5	4.2	4.0	3.8	3.6
107	5.8	5.4	5.1	4.9	4.6	4.4	4.2	3.9	3.7	3.5
108	5.7	5.4	5.1	4.8	4.6	4.3	4.1	3.9	3.7	3.5
109	5.7	5.3	5.0	4.8	4.5	4.3	4.0	3.8	3.6	3.4
110	5.6	5.3	5.0	4.7	4.5	4.2	4.0	3.8	3.5	3.3
111	5.6	5.3	5.0	4.7	4.4	4.2	3.9	3.7	3.5	3.3
112	5.6	5.3	4.9	4.7	4.4	4.1	3.9	3.7	3.5	3.2
113	5.6	5.2	4.9	4.6	4.4	4.1	3.9	3.6	3.4	3.2
114	5.6	5.2	4.9	4.6	4.3	4.1	3.9	3.6	3.4	3.2
115 +	5.5	5.2	4.9	4.6	4.3	4.1	3.8	3.6	3.4	3.1

Ages	100	101	102	103	104	105	106	107	108	109
100	4.2	4.1	3.9	3.8	3.7	3.5	3.4	3.3	3.3	3.2
101	4.1	3.9	3.7	3.6	3.5	3.4	3.2	3.1	3.1	3.0

21st Century Estate Planning:
Practical Applications
2005 Edition

©*2005 Sonnenschein Nath & Rosenthal LLP*
and Cannon Financial Institute, Inc.

- 432 -

Ages	100	101	102	103	104	105	106	107	108	109
102	3.9	3.7	3.6	3.4	3.3	3.2	3.1	3.0	2.9	2.8
103	3.8	3.6	3.4	3.3	3.2	3.0	2.9	2.8	2.7	2.6
104	3.7	3.5	3.3	3.2	3.0	2.9	2.7	2.6	2.5	2.4
105	3.5	3.4	3.2	3.0	2.9	2.7	2.6	2.5	2.4	2.3
106	3.4	3.2	3.1	2.9	2.7	2.6	2.4	2.3	2.2	2.1
107	3.3	3.1	3.0	2.8	2.6	2.5	2.3	2.2	2.1	2.0
108	3.3	3.1	2.9	2.7	2.5	2.4	2.2	2.1	1.9	1.8
109	3.2	3.0	2.8	2.6	2.4	2.3	2.1	2.0	1.8	1.7
110	3.1	2.9	2.7	2.5	2.3	2.2	2.0	1.9	1.7	1.6
111	3.1	2.9	2.7	2.5	2.3	2.1	1.9	1.8	1.6	1.5
112	3.0	2.8	2.6	2.4	2.2	2.0	1.9	1.7	1.5	1.4
113	3.0	2.8	2.6	2.4	2.2	2.0	1.8	1.6	1.5	1.3
114	3.0	2.7	2.5	2.3	2.1	1.9	1.8	1.6	1.4	1.3
115 + ...	2.9	2.7	2.5	2.3	2.1	1.9	1.7	1.5	1.4	1.2

Ages	110	111	112	113	114	115+
110	1.5	1.4	1.3	1.2	1.1	1.1
111	1.4	1.2	1.1	1.1	1.0	1.0
112	1.3	1.1	1.0	1.0	1.0	1.0
113	1.2	1.1	1.0	1.0	1.0	1.0
114	1.1	1.0	1.0	1.0	1.0	1.0
115 + ...	1.1	1.0	1.0	1.0	1.0	1.0

21st Century Estate Planning:
Practical Applications
2005 Edition

©2005 Sonnenschein Nath & Rosenthal LLP
and Cannon Financial Institute, Inc.

- 433 -

Chapter XII
Bibliography

Burton T. Beam, Jr. and John J. McFadden, *Employee Benefits* (5th ed.).

Frederick J. Benjamin, Jr. and Nicholas P. Damico, 370 T.M., *Qualified Plans - Taxation of Distributions*.

Edward V. Brennan and Steven E. Trytten, "A Second Look at Spousal Rights in an IRA," *State Bar of California Estate Planning, Trust & Probate News,* p. 1 (Fall 1994).

Michael J. Canan and David Rhett Baker, *Qualified Retirement Plans*.

David J. Cantano, *Individual Retirement Account Answer Book* (2001 ed.).

Natalie B. Choate, *Life and Death Planning for Retirement Benefits* (4th ed. 2002).

Richard S. Franklin, "Should Retirement Distributions be Accelerated or Deferred," *Est. Plan.,* p. 257 (July 1997).

Edward B. Horahan, III and Ellen A. Hennessy, 365 T.M., *ERISA - Fiduciary Responsibility and Prohibited Transactions*.

Christopher R. Hoyt, "Solution for Estates Overloaded with Retirement Plan Accounts: The Credit Shelter CRUT," *Tr. & Est.* (May, 2002).

Stephen J. Krass, *The Pension Answer Book* (2002 ed.).

Ronald D. Larson, 821 T.M., *Tax Issues of Employee Plans and Commercial Annuities*.

Gary S. Lesser and Susan D. Diehl, *Simple, SEP and SARSEP Answer Book* (5th ed.).

Pamela D. Perdue, *Qualified Pension and Profit Sharing Plans* (2nd ed.).

Alan N. Polasky, "Marital Deduction Formula Clauses in Estate Planning - Estate and Income Tax Considerations," 63 Mich. L. Rev. 809 (March 1965).

Edward N. Polisher and Charles Bender, "Appointing a CRUT as a Retirement Plan Beneficiary," *Tr. & Est.,* p. 16 (July 1996).

Denny S. Rosenbloom, *The Handbook of Employee Benefits* (4th ed.).

Irving S. Schloss and Deborah V. Abildsoe, "Off the Map: More on TIAA - CREF and Paradoxes of Retirement Planning," *Tax Mgmt. Est. Gifts & Tr. J.,* p. 107 (May/June 1998).

21st Century Estate Planning:
Practical Applications
2005 Edition

©2005 *Sonnenschein Nath & Rosenthal LLP*
and Cannon Financial Institute, Inc.

- 434 -

Susan B. Slater-Jansen and Ronald M. Finkelstein, "The Case for an Estate Tax Valuation Discount for IRAs," *The New York Law Journal*, p. 9 (April 2002).

Mervin M. Wilf, "Informed Consent by Spouse Necessary to Waive Plan Benefits," *Est. Plan.*, p. 251 (July 1997).

Online Research and Websites

American College of Trust and Estate Counsel

http://www.actec.org

Natalie B. Choate, Bingham Dana LLP

http://www.ataxplan.com

Noel C. Ice, Cantey & Hanger, L.L.P.

http://www.trustsandestates.net

Gift Planner's Digest

http://www.pgdc.ne0074

21st Century Estate Planning:
Practical Applications
2005 Edition

©2005 Sonnenschein Nath & Rosenthal LLP
and Cannon Financial Institute, Inc.

- 435 -

XIII. PLANNING FOR STOCK OPTIONS AND EMPLOYER STOCK OWNERSHIP PLANS

A. Introduction

Stock options and employer stock ownership plans ("ESOPs") are commonly used forms of employee compensation. Stock options allow an employee to participate in the potential future appreciation of the stock of the employer. The basic types of stock options are (i) incentive stock options and (ii) nonqualified incentive stock options. Both types of stock options allow the employee to defer the recognition of tax on any appreciation of the stock from the exercise date to the date the stock is sold.

An ESOP is a qualified plan that allows employers to make contributions of the employer's stock to an account for the benefit of an employee. Like other types of qualified plans, contributions of the employer's stock to the ESOP are not taxed to the employee and the stock can appreciate within the ESOP tax-free until distributed.

This chapter analyzes the unique estate planning issues that must be considered when using stock options and employer stock ownership plans. The topics covered in this chapter include:

- Incentive stock options;
- Nonqualified incentive stock options;
- Stock Appreciation Rights; and
- Employee Stock Ownership Plans.

B. Incentive Stock Options

1. General Description

An incentive stock option ("ISO") gives an employee of a corporation the right to purchase stock of the employer at a set price (the "exercise price"). The employee then is allowed to "wait and see" whether the stock of the employer will appreciate over the exercise price. The question becomes when should the employee exercise the ISO? If the employee waits until the fair market value of the stock significantly exceeds the exercise price, the difference between the fair market value of the stock on the date of exercise and the exercise price may trigger an alternative minimum tax, even though the exercise of the ISO does not trigger regular income tax. If the employee exercises the ISO when the fair market value is close to the exercise price, no alternative minimum tax would be triggered, but the employee could suffer an unnecessary economic loss if the fair market value of the stock declines or the corporation goes out of business. On the other hand, if the fair market value of the stock significantly increases, the employee could enjoy long-term capital gain treatment on the disposition of the stock, provided the employee satisfies certain holding-period requirements.

21st Century Estate Planning:
Practical Applications
2005 Edition

©2005 Sonnenschein Nath & Rosenthal LLP
and Cannon Financial Institute, Inc.

- 436 -

2. ISO Requirements

a. IRC § 422(b). In order to obtain the advantageous tax treatment and deferral benefits of an ISO, the ISO must satisfy the following requirements set forth in Internal Revenue Code ("IRC") § 422(b):

- The option must be granted pursuant to a plan adopted by the corporation and the plan must be approved by the stockholders within 12 months before or after the date the plan is adopted;
- The option must be granted within 10 years from the date such plan is adopted by the corporation or approved by the stockholders, whichever is earlier;
- The option by its terms must not be exercisable after the expiration of 10 years from the date the option is granted;
- The option price must not be less than the fair market value of the stock at the time the option is granted;
- The option cannot be transferred, other than by will or the intestacy laws, and is only exercisable by the employee (the employee's personal representative can exercise the ISO after the employee's death); and
- At the time the option is granted, the employee cannot own stock equal to more than 10% of the total combined voting power of all classes of stock of the employer corporation or of its parent or subsidiary corporation.

b. Employment Requirement. ISOs can be held only by employees of the issuing corporation or a related corporation. The employee must exercise the ISO during employment or within three months after termination of employment. IRC § 422(a).

c. Exercise Price. The exercise price of an ISO must equal the fair market value of the stock on the date the ISO is *granted*. If the exercise price is lower than the fair market value of the stock on the date the ISO is granted, the ISO will not satisfy the requirements of IRC § 422(b) and therefore becomes a nonqualified incentive stock option. When the employee exercises an ISO, if the fair market value on the date of exercise is greater than the exercise price, the difference will not be included into the employee's regular income, but it may trigger alternative minimum tax.

d. Limitation on Amount of Exercise. IRC § 422(d) limits the amount of ISOs an employee can exercise in each calendar year to $100,000 of the aggregate fair market value of the stock.

> **EXAMPLE:** C was granted an option to purchase 50,000 shares of his employer's stock pursuant to an ISO agreement. The exercise price under the ISO agreement is $2 per share. In year 5, all of the shares of stock under the ISO agreement become vested and exercisable. In year 5, the fair market value of the stock is $10 per

21st Century Estate Planning:
Practical Applications
2005 Edition

©2005 Sonnenschein Nath & Rosenthal LLP
and Cannon Financial Institute, Inc.

- 437 -

share. If C exercises all 50,000 shares of stock pursuant to the ISO, only 10,000 ($100,000 ÷ $10) shares of stock would qualify for tax-favored ISO treatment pursuant to the $100,000 limitation, and the remaining 40,000 shares would receive nonqualified stock option treatment. To preserve the tax-favored ISO treatment on the remaining 40,000 shares, C could exercise the number of shares up to the $100,000 limitation in each of the four succeeding years.

e. Holding-Period. In order for the employee to enjoy long-term capital gain treatment on the disposition of the stock of the employer obtained through an ISO, the employee must satisfy the holding-period requirements set forth in IRC § 422(a)(1). Pursuant to IRC § 422(a)(1), the employee must hold the stock of the employer for 2 years from the date the ISO is *granted* and for 1 year from the date the stock of the employer is received (*i.e.*, the date the ISO is *exercised*). The employee's tax basis in the stock is equal to the exercise price paid.

> **EXAMPLE:** C was granted an ISO on January 30, 1995. The exercise price of the stock of the employer was $5 per share. On January 30, 2002, C exercised his ISO. On the exercise date, the stock of the employer was worth $10 per share. C's basis in the stock is $5 per share. On February 22, 2003, C sold the stock for $25 per share. Since C satisfied the holding-period requirements of IRC § 422(a)(1), C would recognize a long-term capital gain of $20 per share ($25 - $5).

3. Alternative Minimum Tax

a. General Description. The alternative minimum tax ("AMT") is a tax based on the recalculation of a taxpayer's taxable income. Adjustments called "preference items" are generally added to the taxpayer's taxable income to arrive at the taxpayer's alternative minimum taxable income. The alternative minimum taxable income is then subject to tax at an alternative, and usually lower, tax rate. The economic benefit an employee obtains, when he or she exercises an ISO at a time when the fair market value of the stock significantly exceeds the exercise price, is not included in the employee's regular taxable income because of IRC § 421(a). The difference, however, is a preference item for alternative minimum tax purposes and could subject the employee to an alternative minimum tax liability.

b. Alternative Minimum Taxable Income. Alternative minimum taxable income is an employee's regular taxable income with various adjustments. Alternative minimum taxable income includes an amount equal to the difference between the exercise price and the fair market value of the stock of the employer on the date of exercise. This difference is a preference item that is added to the employee's regular taxable income for purposes of calculating alternative minimum taxable income.

c. AMT Calculation. AMT is calculated by multiplying the employee's alternative minimum taxable income by the tentative minimum tax rate of approximately 28%.

21st Century Estate Planning:
Practical Applications
2005 Edition

©2005 Sonnenschein Nath & Rosenthal LLP
and Cannon Financial Institute, Inc.

- 438 -

The product of this calculation is the employee's tentative minimum tax. The employee's tentative minimum tax is then compared to his or her regular income tax liability. If the tentative minimum tax exceeds the employee's regular income tax liability, the difference is the employee's additional AMT liability.

> **EXAMPLE:** W, a married man, has regular taxable income of $800,000 in tax year 2001. During 2001, W also exercises an ISO with an economic benefit (fair market value of the stock on the date of exercise over the exercise price) of $25,000. W's tax liability on his regular taxable income for year 2001 is $284,843. W's tax liability on his alternative minimum taxable income is approximately $231,000 (($800,000 + $25,000) x 28%); therefore, W has no AMT liability for tax year 2001 because his alternative minimum tax liability ($231,000) does not exceed his tax liability on his regular taxable income ($284,843). If, however, W exercises an ISO with an economic benefit of $500,000, W would have a tax liability on his alternative minimum taxable income of approximately $364,000 (($800,000 + $500,000) x 28%) and an AMT liability amount of $79,157 ($364,000 - $284,843).

➔ **Planning Point:** AMT can be avoided by limiting the number of shares that are purchased through an ISO to a number that would cause the taxpayer's tentative minimum tax to be equal to, or less than, his or her regular income tax liability. By staggering the number of shares purchased in an ISO over a number of different tax years, AMT liability can be significantly minimized or altogether avoided.

d. **AMT Credit**. The employee is entitled to claim a credit for the amount of AMT paid in prior years. In the tax years following the exercise of an ISO, the employee may no longer be subject to an AMT. In these subsequent years, the employee can claim a credit against his or her regular income tax liability for the AMT paid in the previous tax years. The credit, however, is sometimes limited and the employee may be unable to recover the entire amount of AMT paid.

➔ **Planning Point:** The use of the AMT credit can be maximized by timing the amount of regular taxable income in the subsequent tax years. If the employee has the ability to bunch income or expenses in any given year, the AMT credit could be used in the year when the employee's regular taxable income is being taxed in the highest marginal tax rates.

4. **Estate Planning for ISOs**

a. **Lifetime Planning**. Lifetime planning opportunities dealing with ISOs are limited because of the stringent requirements of IRC § 422. Lifetime transfers of unexercised ISOs by the employee are not permitted. Therefore, unexercised ISOs cannot be transferred to a

21st Century Estate Planning:
Practical Applications
2005 Edition

©2005 Sonnenschein Nath & Rosenthal LLP
and Cannon Financial Institute, Inc.

- 439 -

revocable trust or to any other planning vehicles. Additionally, in order to obtain long-term capital gain treatment, the stock received upon exercising an ISO should be transferred only after the employee has met the holding-period requirements. If the stock is transferred before the expiration of the holding-period requirements, the appreciation on the stock may be taxed as ordinary income rather than as a capital gain. Therefore, the lifetime planning opportunities to transfer ISOs and remove the corresponding appreciation out of the employee's estate are limited.

        b. Testamentary Planning. Many of the restrictions placed on an ISO for lifetime transfers do not apply after the employee dies. The requirement that the employee exercise the ISO during employment or within 3 months after termination of employment does not apply after the employee's death. Also, the holding-period requirements on the stock received under an ISO do not apply after the employee's death. The ISO can be exercised by the employee's personal representative at any time prior to the expiration of the 10-year period set forth in IRC § 422(b), provided the employee was employed by the company within 3 months of his or her death.

➔   **Planning Point:** The elimination of the requirement that the ISO be exercised within 3 months after the employee terminates employment allows the employee's personal representative to step into the shoes of the employee. The personal representative can exercise the ISO, at any time after the date of the employee's death, to the date that is 10 years from the date the ISO is granted. Therefore, the personal representative can take the requisite time needed to fully consider when and how the ISO should be exercised.

The employee's estate planning documents should provide the personal representative with the power to exercise the ISO, to borrow funds to pay the exercise price, to pledge the stock as collateral, and the authority to act on the ISOs without court supervision.

C. Nonqualified Incentive Stock Options

1. General Rule

Nonqualified incentive stock options ("NISOs") are options that do not meet the requirements of IRC § 422 and therefore are not afforded the corresponding tax benefits described above. There is, however, more planning flexibility in dealing with NISOs because NISOs are not subject to the restrictions of IRC § 422.

2. Income Tax Consequences on Grant and Exercise of NISOs

The grant of a NISO to an employee is generally not includable in the income of the employee. In some limited circumstances, the value of a grant of a NISO can be includable in the income of the employee if (i) the option is transferable, (ii) the option is exercisable immediately and in full, (iii) there are no restrictions imposed on the ownership or sale of the NISO that would affect its value, and (iv) the option's value is reasonably ascertainable using a

21st Century Estate Planning:
Practical Applications
2005 Edition

©2005 Sonnenschein Nath & Rosenthal LLP
and Cannon Financial Institute, Inc.

- 440 -

predictive formula. Treas. Reg. § 1.83-7(b). However, most NISO plans avoid this adverse tax consequence by requiring a vesting period in the NISO agreement.

Unlike an ISO, the *exercise* of a NISO will create ordinary income for the employee. The amount of ordinary income that must be recognized upon the exercise of a NISO is the difference between the fair market value of the stock on the date of exercise and the exercise price. Since the exercise of the NISO is included in the employee's regular taxable income, there is no AMT liability associated with the exercise of a NISO. The employee's tax basis in the shares of stock received from the exercise of the NISO would be the fair market value of the stock on the date of exercise.

3. Gift of NISO

a. Gift and Income Tax Consequence. A NISO can be gifted by the employee during his or her lifetime, provided the NISO plan permits the transfer of ownership. The employee will not incur any immediate income tax liability on the transfer of the NISO by gift. Upon the exercise of the NISO by the donee, the employee will include into income the difference between the exercise price and the fair market value of the stock on the date of exercise. The donee's basis in the stock received pursuant to the exercise of the NISO is equal to the exercise price paid by the donee plus the amount of taxable income recognized by the employee as a result of the exercise (*i.e.*, the fair market value of the stock on the exercise date). If the employee pays the exercise price, the employee will be deemed to have made an additional gift to the donee for the amount paid.

➔ **Planning Point:** The employee's payment of income taxes due to the exercise of the NISO by the donee is not an additional gift by the employee to the donee. This result would allow the employee to further deplete his or her estate for the benefit of the donee without incurring any additional transfer tax.

b. Incomplete Gift. The gift of a NISO is not completed until the option is fully vested and exercisable. Rev. Rul. 98-21. The value of the NISO that is not fully vested and exercisable is included in the donor's estate. If the donor has gifted the NISO and the NISO vests and becomes exercisable in subsequent years, then each time a portion of the NISO vests and becomes exercisable, the donor has made a completed gift over that portion of the NISO in that particular year.

4. Valuation of NISO for Gift Tax Purposes

A NISO has value because it gives the option holder the ability to wait and see if the stock appreciates beyond the exercise price before the stock is purchased. The value of a NISO for transfer tax purposes can be illusive because of the potential uncertainties that may surround the stock of a NISO.

21st Century Estate Planning:
Practical Applications
2005 Edition

©2005 Sonnenschein Nath & Rosenthal LLP
and Cannon Financial Institute, Inc.

- 441 -

a. Black Scholes Method of Valuation. The Black Scholes method of valuation is the most widely used method to value nonpublicly traded options. The Black Scholes method considers the following factors:

- The exercise price of the option;
- Expected life of the option;
- Current trading price of the underlying stock;
- The expected volatility of the underlying stock;
- Expected dividends on the underlying stock; and
- The risk-free interest rate over the remaining option term.

Once the value of the NISO is determined by using the Black Scholes method, a lack of marketability discount can also be applied to decrease the value of a nonpublicly traded NISO.

b. NISO Valuation Safe Harbor. The IRS in Rev. Proc. 98-34 has set forth a "safe harbor" for valuing nonpublicly traded stock options. The safe harbor applies only to nonpublicly traded NISOs where the underlying stock is publicly traded on an established securities exchange. The safe harbor uses the Black Scholes method to value the NISO, but precludes the application of a lack of marketability discount.

➔ **Planning Point:** The potential benefits and detriments of using the IRS safe harbor to value nonpublicly traded NISOs should be carefully weighed. The safe harbor may produce a value that is too high because the lack of marketability discount cannot be used. The alternative is to have the NISOs independently appraised with a lack of marketability discount, even though the appraisal may be more susceptible to an IRS attack.

5. Estate Planning for NISOs

Unlike ISOs, it is possible to transfer unexercised NISOs during the employee's lifetime. The transfer tax goal is to shift the appreciation of the underlying stock of the NISO out of the employee's estate by making lifetime gifts of the NISO. The gifts can be made outright to family members, to a trust for the benefit of family members, to a family limited partnership, or any combination thereof. Once the gift of the NISO is completed, the underlying stock is removed from the employee's estate and the donee would enjoy the benefits of the post-transfer appreciation free from transfer tax.

a. Transfer of NISOs to Grantor Retained Annuity Trust. The employee could transfer the NISO to a Grantor Retained Annuity Trust ("GRAT"). The GRAT would pay the employee an annuity amount over a term of years. The annuity amount could be paid with stock. At the end of the retained annuity term, the remaining assets would be distributed to the named beneficiaries, outright or in trust. The transfer of the NISO to the GRAT is a gift equal to the present value of the remainder interest. This technique allows the employee to retain a portion of the stock, transfer the remainder to his or her children, and shift the future appreciation

21st Century Estate Planning:
Practical Applications
2005 Edition

©2005 Sonnenschein Nath & Rosenthal LLP
and Cannon Financial Institute, Inc.

- 442 -

in the stock to his or her children. See Chapter XVII, Leveraging the Lifetime Transfer of Assets, for a full discussion of GRATs.

b. Transfer of NISOs to Family Limited Partnership. The employee could transfer the NISO to a family limited partnership ("FLP"). The employee would contribute the NISO to the FLP and receive a general and limited partnership interest in return. The employee would then transfer the limited partnership interest to his or her children. The gift of the limited partnership interest would be discounted in value because the partnership agreement would significantly restrict the marketability of the limited partnership interest and restrict the control that a limited partner may have over the FLP. This technique allows the employee to retain control over the FLP while making discounted gifts of the limited partnership interests to his or her children. See Chapter XV, The Use of Family Limited Partnerships and Family Limited Liability Companies in Estate Planning, for a full discussion of FLPs.

c. Transfer of NISOs to FLP/GRAT Combination. The employee could also transfer the NISO to an FLP, receive general and limited partnership interests in return, then transfer the discounted limited partnership interests into a GRAT for a term of years. This would allow the employee to pay gift tax only on the present value of the remainder interest. Additionally, the limited partnership interest would appreciate for the benefit of the children outside the employee's estate.

➜   **Planning Point:** A gift of a NISO to a charitable organization can result in an unexpected and undesirable consequence. Even though the NISO has been gifted to a charity, the employee, upon the exercise of the NISO by the charity, would still be required to include into his or her income the difference between the fair market value of the stock on the date of exercise and the exercise price. The employee should coordinate with the charity to find solutions to this outcome.

D. Stock Appreciation Rights

1. General Description

Stock Appreciation Rights ("SARs") can be viewed as "phantom stock options." The company agrees to pay the employee cash, stock, or both, based on the "applicable measuring factor." The applicable measuring factor is usually tied to the market price of the corporation's stock. The SAR can be granted to an employee in conjunction with stock options to provide the liquidity needed to exercise the stock options.

2. Taxation of SARs

The grant of a SAR to an employee does not generally trigger an income tax consequence to the employee. When the SAR is exercised, the employee must recognize ordinary income equal to the cash received plus the fair market value of any property received.

21st Century Estate Planning:
Practical Applications
2005 Edition

©2005 Sonnenschein Nath & Rosenthal LLP
and Cannon Financial Institute, Inc.

- 443 -

3. Estate Planning for the SARs

The same planning techniques used for NISOs can be used for SARs if the SAR plan allows for transfer of ownership. The employee would incur a gift tax liability on the value of the SAR transferred. As with NISOs, the employee will also recognize ordinary income when the donee exercises the SAR and the payment of income tax by the donor will not constitute an additional gift to the donee.

E. Employee Stock Ownership Plans

1. General Description

Employee stock ownership plans ("ESOP") are generally available to employees in public and privately held corporations. An ESOP is a defined contribution plan governed by IRC § 409 that invests primarily in the stock of the issuing corporation. The employer's contribution to the ESOP plan is usually made without any corresponding tax consequences to the employee. The stock in an ESOP can also appreciate in value over time without any corresponding tax consequence to the employee. An employee is usually given the right to receive distributions in either cash or employer securities. ESOP plans are sometimes included as part of a 401(k) plan, but the ESOP portion must still comply with the separate ESOP requirements.

2. Distribution Requirements

An employee's entire interest in an ESOP must be distributed to him or her outright or over his or her lifetime beginning on April 1 of the calendar year in which the employee retires from the company or reaches age 70½. IRC § 401(a)(9)(C)(i). If distributions to the employee begin and then the employee dies, the undistributed portion of the ESOP must be distributed to the employee's beneficiaries over a period that is equal to or shorter than the employee's original distribution schedule. If the employee dies before any distributions are made, the ESOP interest must be distributed within 5 years of the employee's death, unless the ESOP is transferred to a designated beneficiary. IRC § 401(a)(9)(B)(ii), (iii).

If the designated beneficiary is the employee's spouse, the distributions can be delayed until the later of 1 year after the date of the employee's death or the year in which the employee would have been 70½. The employee's spouse can also roll over the ESOP interest into an IRA and delay the distributions from the IRA until the spouse attains age 70½.

21st Century Estate Planning:
Practical Applications
2005 Edition

©*2005 Sonnenschein Nath & Rosenthal LLP*
and Cannon Financial Institute, Inc.

- 444 -

3. Planning Considerations

a. Lifetime Planning. During the term of employment, the employee cannot receive distributions from his or her ESOP account. However, once employment has been terminated, the employee can withdraw the vested portion of his or her ESOP account. The employee can receive the distribution in cash or in stock of the issuing corporation. The distributions received in cash can be rolled over into an IRA.

Once employment has been terminated, the employee can also request a distribution of stock from the issuing corporation in lieu of a cash distribution. The employee's tax basis in the stock is equal to the cost of the securities to the plan. If the employee elects to take a lump-sum distribution of stock, the employee will be required to include into his or her ordinary income an amount equal to the tax basis in the stock.

The "net unrealized appreciation" of the stock is not taxed until the securities are sold. "Net unrealized appreciation" is the difference between the fair market value of the stock on the date of distribution and the cost of the securities to the plan. Treas. Reg. § 1.402(a)-1(b)(2)(i). The cost of the securities to the plan is usually the employer's contributions to the plan. If the employee elects a lump-sum distribution, the recognition of the entire amount of the "net unrealized appreciation" is deferred until the employee sells the stock. If the employee elects a partial distribution, then only the portion of net unrealized appreciation that is attributable to the employee's nondeductible contributions, if any, is deferred. IRC § 402(e)(4)(A).

➔ **Planning Point:** If the cost of the securities to the plan is low, the employee should strongly consider electing a lump-sum distribution of stock because there will be little to no tax consequence resulting from the distribution. Any gain from the sale of the stock thereafter will result in long-term capital gain treatment.

b. Testamentary Planning. If the employee dies while still employed by the corporation, the beneficiary of the employee will receive the same tax-deferred benefits of an ESOP as the employee. The beneficiary can also choose to take a distribution of cash or of stock. If the beneficiary receives stock and elects a lump-sum distribution, he or she can defer tax on the "net unrealized appreciation" until the stock is sold. Unfortunately, the beneficiary would not, however, receive a step-up in basis on the stock at the death of the decedent because the "net unrealized appreciation" is treated as income in respect of a decedent. Any gain on the sale of the stock by the beneficiary will result in long-term capital gain treatment.

4. Succession Planning for Closely Held Businesses

a. Sale of Closely Held Stock. IRC § 1042 allows an owner of a closely held corporation to sell his or her shares of stock to an ESOP and recognize no gain on the sale. The owner must sell his or her shares of stock to an ESOP, and immediately after the sale the ESOP must own at least 30% of each class of outstanding employer stock or 30% of the total value of all outstanding stock. IRC § 1042(b)(2). The owner, in order to have no recognition of gain on

21st Century Estate Planning:
Practical Applications
2005 Edition

©2005 Sonnenschein Nath & Rosenthal LLP
and Cannon Financial Institute, Inc.

- 445 -

the sale, must purchase qualified replacement property within a 15-month period beginning 3 months prior to his or her sale of stock to the ESOP.

      b. <u>Qualified Replacement Property</u>. The term "qualified replacement property" is defined under IRC § 1042(c)(4) as securities issued by a domestic operating corporation other than the corporation that issued the stock involved in the ESOP sale transaction or any of its controlled group members. A domestic operating corporation is a corporation with more than 50% of its assets used in the active conduct of a trade or business during the replacement period. Additionally, the domestic operating corporation cannot have passive investment income exceeding 25% of the gross receipts for the preceding taxable year.

      c. <u>Disposition of Qualified Replacement Property</u>. If the owner of qualified replacement property sells or transfers the qualified replacement property, he or she will recognize gain. However, no gain is recognized if the owner transfers the property:

- In any reorganization under IRC § 368 that does not involve another corporation owned by the owner;
- By reason of the death of the person making such election;
- By gift; or
- In any transaction to which IRC § 1042(a) applies.

Qualified replacement property can be gifted without triggering the recognition of gain. The donee, however, would receive a carryover basis in the stock received.

➔   **<u>Planning Point</u>:** The business owner can diversify his interest in a closely held corporation into publicly traded securities without triggering a capital gain tax. On the other hand, the securities distributed do not get the basis step-up at death that other securities would receive. The "net unrealized appreciation," not included in the income of the employee at the time the stock was distributed, is treated as income in respect of a decedent to the beneficiary.

21st Century Estate Planning:
Practical Applications
2005 Edition

©2005 Sonnenschein Nath & Rosenthal LLP
and Cannon Financial Institute, Inc.

- 446 -

Chapter XIII
Bibliography

David Ackerman, "Innovative Uses of ESOPs in Estate Planning for Business Owners," *33rd Annual Philip E. Heckerling Inst. on Est. Plan.* (1999).

S. Stacy Eastland and Daniel H. Markstein, "Consider your Options: Income and Estate Planning Strategies for Non-qualified Stock Options," American College of Trust and Estate Counsel 2001 Annual Meeting.

S. Stacy Eastland, "Navigating the Employee Stock Option Maze," American College of Trust and Estate Counsel 2001 Annual Meeting.

Michael G. Goldstein et al., 808-2nd T.M., *Estate Planning for the Corporate Executive*.

Jared Kaplan et al., 354 T.M., *ESOPs*.

Ray D. Madoff et al., *Practical Guide to Estate Planning* (2001).

Daniel H. Markstein, III, and L. Wayne Pressgrove, Jr., "New Developments Create Opportunities via Gifts of Stock Options," 24 *Est. Plan.* 403.

Thomas Z. Reicher et al., 381-2nd T.M., *Statutory Stock Options*.

Max J. Scwhartz and Scott P. Spector, *Hot Issues in Executive Compensation* (2001).

Victoria M. Trumbower, "Optimizing Stock Option Strategies for Corporate Executives," 125 *Tax Mgmt. Est. Gifts & Tr. J.* 163.

John L. Utz, 383-3rd T.M., *Nonstatutory Stock Options*.

Online Research and Web Sites

Fairmark Press

http://www.fairmark.com (provides tax information for investors, including compensation in stock options).

Internal Revenue Service Digital Daily

http://www.irs.gov/ Keyword: Stock Options (provides information on stock options and employee stock ownership plans along with IRS forms and publications.).

The National Center for Employee Ownership

http://www.nceo.org/index.html (provides research information on employee stock ownership plans).

21st Century Estate Planning:
Practical Applications
2005 Edition

©2005 Sonnenschein Nath & Rosenthal LLP
and Cannon Financial Institute, Inc.

- 447 -

XIV. PLANNING FOR BUSINESS INTERESTS

Although estate planners commonly are asked to assist clients in striking an appropriate balance between tax and non-tax issues, this balancing is particularly difficult to achieve when dealing with closely held business interests. The reason for this is twofold: (1) the asset is unique in that it typically has substantial value, but often limited marketability, and (2) dealing with the asset frequently is emotionally charged, due to the fact that family relationships are often intertwined with the business interest. Thus, the role of the advisor is to balance these issues, while helping clients achieve an orderly succession of both management and ownership of their businesses.

This chapter will provide an overview of the following subjects, which often arise when advising clients regarding their business interests:

- Succession Planning for Business Interests;
- S Corporation Planning;
- Stock Redemptions -- Internal Revenue Code ("IRC") § 303; and
- Extension of Time for Payment of Estate Tax -- IRC § 6166.

A. Succession Planning for Business Interests

Owners of closely held businesses often are consumed by the demands of running the day-to-day operations of their businesses. This is, in part, reflected by the fact that less than one-third of family-owned businesses survive the succession from one generation to the next. The fact that so many businesses fail to survive the transfer to the next generation illustrates the challenges that planners face when advising clients regarding succession planning. As noted above, planning for the disposition of a client's closely held business interest is complicated by the fact that other family members often are intricately involved in the business. While these family relationships may provide a foundation on which a successful business can be built, these same relationships can splinter when family members confront the emotionally charged issue of succession planning. The estate planner can help reduce the potential for family discord by adequately addressing business and estate planning issues that must be confronted by their clients in order to adopt a successful succession plan.

1. Factors to Consider

In order to develop a successful succession plan, the advisor should, at a minimum, ensure that his client address the following issues:

21st Century Estate Planning:
Practical Applications
2005 Edition

©2005 Sonnenschein Nath & Rosenthal LLP
and Cannon Financial Institute, Inc.

- 448 -

a. Sell or Continue the Business. A threshold issue that must be addressed is whether the client intends to sell the business during his or her lifetime or intends for the business to continue after his or her death.

b. Ownership and Control of the Business. If the client intends for the business to continue, the client must determine who or whom should own the business. A related issue is who or whom the client wants to control the business, and whether some owners should hold voting stock, while others hold only non-voting stock. Similarly, the client must determine whether descendants who do not participate in the business should hold equity interests in the business (generally, this is not a good idea, as those who do not actively participate in the business typically want to siphon cash out of the business, while those who participate want to reinvest cash in order to grow the business).

c. Transition. The client must determine when transition should occur and how he or she intends to effectuate the transition.

d. Spouse. If there is a spouse who does not have a significant ownership interest in the business, the client must determine what the spouse's role will be if he or she survives the owner. If the client intends for the children to own the business, the client must determine whether the spouse is adequately provided for.

e. Provisions for Owner. If the client intends to transfer control of the business during his or her lifetime, the client must determine whether he or she wants to remain involved in the business in a diminished capacity (*e.g.*, the client could be retained as a consultant).

2. Alternatives for Transferring Ownership

There are essentially three ways to transfer ownership in business interests to the next generation. You can sell it to them, you can give it to them or you can effectuate a transfer of ownership via a combination of gifts and sales. The estate planner has no shortage of techniques that can be used to effectively transfer ownership in a business. The following is a brief overview of some of the more common techniques used by estate planners to transfer ownership of business interests:

21st Century Estate Planning:
Practical Applications
2005 Edition

©2005 Sonnenschein Nath & Rosenthal LLP
and Cannon Financial Institute, Inc.

- 449 -

a. Buy-Sell Agreements. A buy-sell agreement is an agreement among the owners of the business and the entity to purchase and sell interests in the business at a price set under the agreement upon the occurrence of a specified triggering event (*e.g.*, death, disability, an offer to purchase an owner's interest from an outside party, or termination of employment). One of the primary benefits of a well drafted buy-sell agreement is that it may alleviate disputes among the owners (a benefit that cannot be understated in the family context). Additionally, a well drafted buy-sell agreement may establish the value of a deceased owner's interest for estate tax purposes if the agreement satisfies the requirements of IRC § 2703. There are essentially three types of buy-sell agreements:

(1) Cross-Purchase Agreement. The typical cross-purchase agreement provides that upon the occurrence of a triggering event (*e.g.*, death, disability or termination of employment), the continuing shareholders will acquire the withdrawing shareholder's interest at a purchase price that is determined under the agreement.

(2) Corporate Redemption Agreement. Under a corporate redemption agreement, upon the occurrence of the triggering event, the corporation redeems the party's interest in the entity at a price specified in the agreement.

(3) Hybrid Agreement. An agreement can combine aspects of both the cross-purchase agreement and the corporate redemption agreement, by giving the corporation the primary right to acquire the selling shareholder's interest, and permitting or requiring the remaining shareholders to redeem the withdrawing shareholder to the extent that the primary right is not exercised (the order of priority obviously can be reversed, thereby giving the shareholders the primary right to purchase the interest).

b. The Use of an FLP or Family LLC to Transfer Business Interest. Generally, by transferring assets to either a family limited partnership or an LLC in return for interests in the entity, significant tax savings can be achieved. This results from the fact that the interests in the entity are cloaked with transfer restrictions that reduce the value of the interest for transfer tax purposes (*i.e.*, a willing buyer would not pay as much for an interest in the entity as he would for the entity's underlying assets). As a result, a transferor can transfer a significantly larger percentage interest in the entity via annual exclusion gifts (or, if a taxable gift occurs, at a significantly reduced tax cost). Similarly, the owner of the interest simply could sell an interest in the entity to a family member at a significantly reduced sale price. For a detailed discussion of FLPs and LLCs, see Chapter XV.

c. Grantor Retained Annuity Trusts. A Grantor Retained Annuity Trust ("GRAT") is an irrevocable trust that pays the creator an annuity, typically annually, for a fixed term of years. The annuity interest is described as a percentage of the initial value of the assets transferred to the GRAT. If the creator survives the trust term, any property remaining in the GRAT at the end of the term (which will be the case if the total return on the trust assets is greater than the actuarial discount rate in effect when the GRAT is created) will pass to the

21st Century Estate Planning:
Practical Applications
2005 Edition

©2005 Sonnenschein Nath & Rosenthal LLP
and Cannon Financial Institute, Inc.

- 450 -

remainder beneficiaries free of all transfer taxes. For a detailed discussion of GRATs, see Chapter XVII, Leveraging the Lifetime Transfer of Assets.

>   **d. Sale to a Grantor Trust**. A sale to a grantor trust involves the creation of an irrevocable trust that is a "grantor trust" for income tax purposes. A "grantor trust" is a trust that is structured so that all items of income, deduction and credit generated by the trust are taxed to the creator of the trust (*i.e.,* the "grantor") for income tax purposes. The result of grantor trust status is that the trust is ignored for income tax purposes and, as a result, the trust's income, deductions, and credits are passed through the trust to the grantor and reported on the grantor's individual income tax return rather than being reported by the trust as a separate entity. Although the trust is a "grantor trust" for income tax purposes, the trust is structured so that the trust assets are not includible in the grantor's gross estate for federal estate tax purposes. After creating the trust, the grantor sells assets to the trust at their fair market value in return for a promissory note that bears interest at the applicable federal rate sanctioned by the Code. At the end of the note term, any income from and appreciation on the trust assets that exceed the payments required to satisfy the promissory note passes to the beneficiaries of the trust (usually the grantor's children and/or grandchildren) free of estate, gift and, if appropriately structured, generation-skipping transfer taxes. For a detailed discussion of a sale to a grantor trust, see Chapter XVII, Leveraging the Lifetime Transfer of Assets.

B. S Corporation Planning

Many closely held businesses are formed as corporations. In order to avoid the negative income tax aspects of corporations (*i.e.,* corporate profits distributed to shareholders in the form of dividends generally are subject to income tax at both the corporate and shareholder levels), the shareholders typically elect for the corporation to be taxed under subchapter S of the Code. Corporations electing to be taxed under subchapter S have become known as "S corporations." S corporations receive favorable tax status under subchapter S, which allows the corporation to be treated as a conduit, much like a partnership, through which the corporation's income and losses flow to the shareholders on a current basis (thereby avoiding the corporate level tax that applies to regular corporations). Nevertheless, to achieve this tax benefit, there are a number of requirements that the corporation and its shareholders must satisfy.

The American Jobs Creation Act of 2004 ("AJCA"), P.L. 108-357 (Oct. 22, 2004), created a number of changes to subchapter S. Most of these changes broaden the availability of S status, while others minimize problems that can occur in electing and preserving the S election. The changes are effective for tax years beginning after 2004. Some of the more pertinent changes have been incorporated into the following discussion.

1. Eligibility for S Corporation Status

In general, to qualify for S corporation status, the corporation must not be an "ineligible corporation" as defined in IRC § 1361(b)(2) and must satisfy the following criteria provided in IRC § 1361(b)(1):

21st Century Estate Planning:
Practical Applications
2005 Edition

©2005 Sonnenschein Nath & Rosenthal LLP
and Cannon Financial Institute, Inc.

- 451 -

a. Domestic Corporation. First, the corporation must be a domestic corporation that is incorporated in the United States.

b. Limit on the Number of Shareholders. Second, the corporation may not have more than 100 shareholders. Section 1361(b)(1)(a). For purposes of the shareholder limit, a husband and wife (and their estates) are considered as one shareholder (see IRC § 1361(c)(1)), while individuals (other than a husband and wife) who hold stock as tenants in common or as joint tenants are each considered a separate shareholder for purposes of applying this rule (see Treas. Reg. § 1.1361-1(e)(2)).

For tax years beginning after 2004, Section 1361(c) is amended to allow a family to elect to be treated as one shareholder. Members of a family are defined as the common ancestor, lineal descendants of the common ancestor, and the spouses (or former spouses) of such lineal descendants or common ancestor. The amended provision also incorporates the expansive definition of a family member in Section 152(b)(2). A family member includes a legally adopted child, a child who is a member of an individual's household, if placed with such individual by an authorized placement agency for legal adoption, or a foster child. The provision does not limit the number of families that can each elect to be treated as one shareholder. Thus, it is possible for an S corporation to have far in excess of 100 shareholders.

An individual will not be considered a common ancestor if, as of the later of December 31, 2004 or the time that the S election is made, that individual is more than six generations removed from the youngest generation of shareholders who would, but for this restriction, be a member of the family. Spouses and former spouses are considered to be in the same generation as the individual to whom the spouse is or was married.

The election can be made by any member of the family. Once the election is made, it remains in effect until terminated, as will be provided in regulations to be issued. There is no requirement that any minimum number of family members consent this election.

In conjunction with this election, Section 1362(f) is amended to qualify family elections for relief for inadvertent or invalid elections or terminations. This Section gives specific authority to the Treasury to provide relief where a family election is invalid and results in an invalid S election, or a family election is inadvertently terminated, thereby terminating the S election.

The family election applies only for purposes of determining the number of shareholders - each family member must be otherwise eligible to be an S corporation shareholder.

c. Shareholder Restrictions. Third, all shareholders must be individuals and either U.S. citizens or resident aliens. There are, however, a number of important exceptions to the "individual" rule that allow the following entities to hold S corporation stock: (i) a deceased shareholder's estate, (ii) a bankrupt shareholder's estate, (iii) a qualified subchapter S trust ("QSST"), (iv) an electing small business trust ("ESBT"), (v) voting trusts and (vi) specified tax-

21st Century Estate Planning:
Practical Applications
2005 Edition

©2005 Sonnenschein Nath & Rosenthal LLP
and Cannon Financial Institute, Inc.

- 452 -

exempt organizations. The exceptions for estates, QSSTs and ESBTs are extremely important from an estate planning perspective and are, therefore, discussed in greater detail below.

For purposes of applying the "all individual rule," stock that is held by a nominee, guardian, custodian or agent is considered to be held by the beneficial owner of the stock (*see* Treas. Reg. § 1.1361-1(e)(1)).

> **EXAMPLE:** A partnership may be a nominee of S corporation stock for a person who qualifies as a shareholder of S corporation stock (because, as nominee, the partnership is not deemed an S corporation shareholder). However, if the partnership is the beneficial owner of the stock, then the partnership is the shareholder, and the corporation does not qualify as an S corporation.

d. One Class of Stock. Fourth, an S corporation may not have more than one class of stock outstanding. Nevertheless, for purposes of this rule, voting rights are disregarded. Thus, an S corporation may issue both voting and non-voting stock (*see* Treas. Reg. § 1.1361-1(l)(1)).

2. Estates and Trusts as S Corporation Shareholders

Although, generally, all shareholders of an S corporation must be individuals, there is an important exception for an estate and certain types of trusts.

a. A Decedent's Estate as an S Corporation Shareholder. Although a deceased shareholder's estate is a permitted shareholder (see IRC § 1361(b)(1)(B)), prolonging the administration of an estate may cause the estate to terminate and become a trust that may not be a permitted shareholder (*see Old Va. Brick Co. v. Comm'r*, 44 T.C. 724 (1965), *aff'd*, 367 F.2d 276 (4th Cir. 1966)). For purposes of applying the S corporation rules, the estate, rather than the beneficiaries of the estate, is considered to be the S corporation shareholder.

> **EXAMPLE:** X Corporation, an S corporation, has 100 shareholders, including P. P dies and, at P's death, P's stock is then held by P's estate. P's estate has five beneficiaries. Because the estate, rather than the beneficiaries, is deemed to be X Corporation's shareholder, X Corporation will not violate the 100 shareholder limit under the S corporation rules.

b. Trusts as S Corporation Shareholders. IRC § 1361(c)(2) authorizes the following types of trusts to be S corporation shareholders:

(1) Grantor Trusts. A trust, all of which is treated under IRC §§ 671 through 678 as owned by an individual (whether or not the grantor) who is a citizen or resident of the United States, is permitted to hold S corporation stock. In addition, after the death of the

21st Century Estate Planning:
Practical Applications
2005 Edition

©*2005 Sonnenschein Nath & Rosenthal LLP*
and Cannon Financial Institute, Inc.

- 453 -

deemed owner, the trust may continue as a permitted S corporation shareholder for up to two years after the date of the deemed owner's death.

> ➔ **Planning Point:** The grantor trust must be treated as owned by one individual to satisfy this rule and he or she must be treated as owning both the income and principal of the trust under the grantor trust rules (*see* Treas. Reg. § 1.1361-1(h)(1)(i)).

For purposes of applying the S corporation rules, (i) the individual who is the deemed owner for income tax purposes is considered to be the S corporation shareholder (rather than the trust), and, upon his or her death, if the trust continues to hold the S corporation stock, his or her estate will be considered the shareholder (for up to two years after the decedent's death).

> **EXAMPLE:** X Corporation, an S corporation, has 100 shareholders, including Trust. Trust is a grantor trust for income tax purposes and P is Trust's deemed owner. P is X Corporation's shareholder for purposes of applying the S corporation rules. At P's death, if Trust continues to hold X Corporation stock, P's estate will be X Corporation's shareholder for purposes of applying the S corporation rules. Nevertheless, two years and one day after P's death, Trust will no longer be a permitted shareholder, unless Trust is either a grantor trust, a QSST or an ESBT (in which case the Trust will have a new deemed shareholder for purposes of applying the S corporation rules).

(2) **Testamentary Trusts**. A trust that receives S corporation stock pursuant to the terms of a will may hold such stock for up to two years, beginning on the day of the deemed owner's death. For purposes of applying the S corporation rules, the estate of the testator is regarded as the shareholder. On the first day after the expiration of the two-year period, the general prohibition against trusts as shareholders of S corporation stock applies.

> **EXAMPLE:** X Corporation, an S corporation, has 100 shareholders, including P. P dies and pursuant to P's will, X Corporation stock is transferred to Trust. Trust has six beneficiaries. Because P's estate, rather than the beneficiaries of Trust, is deemed to be X Corporation's shareholder, X Corporation will not violate the 100 shareholder limit under the S corporation rules. Nevertheless, two years and one day after P's death, Trust will no longer be a permitted shareholder, unless Trust is either a grantor trust, a QSST or an ESBT (in which case the Trust will have a new deemed shareholder for purposes of applying the S corporation rules).

(3) **Voting Trusts**. A trust created to exercise the voting power of S corporation stock transferred to it will be permitted to hold S corporation stock if several conditions are satisfied. First, the beneficial owners of the stock must be regarded as the owners

21st Century Estate Planning:
Practical Applications
2005 Edition

©2005 Sonnenschein Nath & Rosenthal LLP
and Cannon Financial Institute, Inc.

- 454 -

of their respective portions of the trust under the grantor trust rules of IRC §§ 671 through 678. Second, the trust must have been created pursuant to a written trust agreement entered into by the shareholders that (1) delegates to one or more trustees the right to vote, (2) requires all distributions with respect to the stock of the corporation held by the trust to be paid to, or on behalf of, the beneficial owners of that stock, (3) requires title and possession of that stock to be delivered to those beneficial owners upon termination of the trust, and (4) terminates, under its terms or by state law, on or before a specific date or event.

When a voting trust satisfies the above conditions, each beneficiary of the voting trust is regarded as a shareholder. Accordingly, each member of the voting trust will count in identifying the number of shareholders of the S corporation, and each member must be a permitted S corporation shareholder (*e.g.*, a U.S. citizen or resident alien).

(4) **Electing Small Business Trusts**. A trust that qualifies as an ESBT may hold stock in an S corporation. In the case of an ESBT, each potential current beneficiary of the trust is regarded as a shareholder for purposes of applying the S corporation rules, unless for any period no potential current beneficiary exists, in which case the trust will be treated as the shareholder. Current beneficiaries include every person that may or will receive a distribution of principal or income from the trust (*see* IRC § 1361(e)(2)). Thus, each potential current beneficiary (i) will be counted toward the 100 shareholder limit and (ii) must be a permitted S corporation shareholder.

(5) **Qualified Subchapter S Trusts**. A QSST is regarded as a grantor trust for purposes of IRC § 1361(c)(2)(A)(i) and, thus, is an eligible S corporation shareholder, provided the beneficiary makes a proper election (*see* IRC § 1361(d)). Only the current income beneficiary is treated as an S corporation shareholder, which, in comparison to the ESBT, simplifies the determination as to whether the shareholder is a permitted S corporation shareholder and in determining if the corporation satisfies the 100 shareholder limit.

3.   Qualifying as an ESBT and the Income Tax Ramifications of ESBT Status

The ESBT provisions are designed to create a vehicle through which gifts of S corporation stock in trust may be made, while avoiding the "one beneficiary" rule applicable to grantor trusts and the "all income distribution" requirement of QSSTs.

a. ESBT Requirements. A trust will qualify as an ESBT if the following requirements are satisfied (*see* IRC § 1361(e)(1)(A) and (B)):

(1) **Limitation on Beneficiaries**. The only permitted beneficiaries of an ESBT are individuals, estates or certain charitable organizations. For purposes of applying this first requirement, the term "beneficiary" does not include a distributee trust (other than a trust described in paragraphs (2) or (3) of IRC § 170(c)), and, instead, looks through the distributee trust to include those persons who have a beneficial interest in the property held by

21st Century Estate Planning:
Practical Applications
2005 Edition

©2005 Sonnenschein Nath & Rosenthal LLP
and Cannon Financial Institute, Inc.

- 455 -

the distributee trust. Thus, a distributee trust is ignored as long as the beneficiaries of the distributee trust are permitted S corporation shareholders.

> **EXAMPLE:** Trust intends to make an ESBT election. The terms of the Trust provide that the trustee may make discretionary distributions of income or principal to C for life and, upon C's death, Trust is to divide into separate trusts for the benefit of C's children. For purposes of IRC § 1361(e)(1)(A)(i), the beneficiaries of the intended ESBT are C and C's children, and not the separate trusts for the benefit of C's children. Thus, all of the beneficiaries of the intended ESBT are individuals. Nevertheless, once C's children are entitled to receive distributions from the separate trusts (*i.e.*, upon C's death), the S corporation election will terminate unless (1) the distributee trusts are either grantor trusts, QSSTs or ESBTs and (2) C's children are permitted S corporation shareholders.

Section 1361(e)(2) provides that with respect to any period, any person to whom distributions of income or principal could be made under a power of appointment will be considered a potential income beneficiary and, therefore, treated as a shareholder. For tax years beginning after 2004, 1361(e)(2) is amended to provide that in determining the potential current income beneficiaries of an ESBT, any power of appointment will be disregarded if the power remains unexercised at the end of such period. Thus, the fact that a person has a power to make distributions to a large number of persons or to ineligible persons will not result in those persons being treated as potential income beneficiaries if the power remains unexercised.

This provision is further amended to provide that, for tax years beginning after 2004, the ESBT now has one year, instead of 60 days, to sell stock following the date a disqualified person becomes a potential income beneficiary.

(2) **No Interest Acquired by Purchase**. No interest in the ESBT may be acquired by purchase (*i.e.*, although the ESBT may acquire S corporation stock by purchase, the beneficiaries must acquire their interest as a result of a gratuitous transfer).

(3) **Election is Made**. An election must be made to be classified as an ESBT.

(4) **No QSST Election Made**. The trust must not have made a QSST election with respect to any stock held by the trust to qualify as an ESBT.

(5) **Not Tax-Exempt**. The trust may not be a tax-exempt trust, including a charitable remainder annuity trust or charitable remainder unitrust.

b. Mechanics of the ESBT Election. The ESBT election must be made within the sixteen-day-and-two-month period beginning on the day that the S corporation stock

21st Century Estate Planning:
Practical Applications
2005 Edition

©2005 Sonnenschein Nath & Rosenthal LLP
and Cannon Financial Institute, Inc.

- 456 -

is transferred to the trust. The *trustee* (as opposed to the beneficiaries) must make the election and file it with the IRS Service Center at which the S corporation files its income tax return. Once made, the election is irrevocable. *See* Treas. Reg. § 1.1361-1(m)(2).

> c. **ESBT Income Tax Ramifications**. The flexibility offered by ESBTs comes at a cost from an income tax perspective. Once the election is made, the portion of the trust that consists of S corporation stock is treated as a separate trust for federal income tax purposes (*see* IRC § 641(c)(1)). The income generated by this deemed separate trust is subject to tax at the highest individual income tax rate applicable to estates and trusts (currently 35% for 2005), except to the extent the capital gains rate applies (*see* IRC § 641(c)(2)(A)). Moreover, the trust's alternative minimum tax exemption amount under IRC § 55(d) is zero (*see* IRC § 641(c)(2)(B)). The taxable income generated by the separate trust is not included in distributable net income of the trust (*see* IRC § 641(c)(3)). Thus, there is no deduction available for distributions to beneficiaries, and no taxable income is passed through to beneficiaries (*see* IRC § 641(c)(2)(C)). Upon termination of all or any part of the separate portion of the ESBT, any loss carryovers or excess deductions under IRC § 642(h) are taken into account by the entire trust, subject to the usual rules (*see* IRC § 641(c)(4)).

If the trust has assets other than S corporation stock, that portion of the trust is treated as a separate trust and is subject to the normal income tax rules for trusts and estates.

> > **EXAMPLE:** Trust makes an ESBT election. During the year, Trust has $200 attributable to S corporation ordinary income and $150 of other distributable net income. Trust distributed $160 to beneficiaries during the year. Trust has taxable income of $200 that is taxed at the 35% rate. The trust also has a distribution deduction of $150. Thus, of the amount distributed to the beneficiaries, $150 will be taxed as part of the beneficiaries' income and $10 will be distributed to them free of further tax (as it was already taxed as part of the ESBT).

Thus, in summary, ESBTs offer increased flexibility in that the trust can accumulate income and spray distributions among multiple beneficiaries; nevertheless, all of the income attributable to the S corporation is taxed at the maximum income tax rate, and the impact of this high rate cannot be minimized by making distributions to beneficiaries.

> ➔ **Planning Point:** Although ESBTs are subject to a higher income tax rate, they are particularly beneficial in connection with generation-skipping trusts, where the ability to accumulate income and sprinkle income and principal among multiple beneficiaries is a particularly attractive attribute. If you have an existing QSST and determine that it would be beneficial to convert to an ESBT, Treas. Reg. § 1.1361-1(j)(12) specifies the method for converting a QSST to an ESBT or an ESBT to a QSST.

21st Century Estate Planning:
Practical Applications
2005 Edition

©2005 *Sonnenschein Nath & Rosenthal LLP*
and Cannon Financial Institute, Inc.

- 457 -

4. Qualifying as a QSST and the Income Tax Ramifications of QSST Status

Although QSSTs are not as flexible as ESBTs, a QSST generally will be preferable from an income tax perspective, because the beneficiaries typically will be taxed at a lower rate and the administration is less complicated (*i.e.*, the administration of an ESBT tends to be more complicated because the S portion of an ESBT is treated as a separate trust for purposes of computing the ESBT's tax liability during the year).

      a. QSST Requirements. In order to qualify as a QSST, the following requirements under IRC § 1361(d)(3) must be satisfied:

      (1)   **Terms of Trust**. The terms of the trust must require that:

- During the life of the current income beneficiary, there will be only one income beneficiary of the trust;
- Any trust corpus that is distributed during the life of the current income beneficiary may be distributed only to that beneficiary;
- The income interest of the current income beneficiary will terminate upon the first to occur of that beneficiary's death and the termination of the trust; and
- Upon termination of the trust during the life of the income beneficiary, the trust must distribute all of its assets to that beneficiary.

The terms of the trust must satisfy these requirements from the date the QSST election is made or from the effective date of the QSST election, whichever is earlier, throughout the entire period during which the current income beneficiary and any successor income beneficiary is the income beneficiary of the trust.

      (2)   **Income Required to be Distributed or Must Actually be Distributed**. All the trust income (as defined in IRC § 643(b)) must be required to be distributed or must actually be distributed currently to one individual who is a U.S. citizen or resident. The 65-day rule applies to QSSTs, so that a trustee may elect to treat any amount distributed to a trust beneficiary within the first 65 days after the end of the trust's taxable year as if that distribution had been made on the last day of that taxable year (*see* Treas. Reg. § 1.1361-1(j)(1)(i)).

➜   **Planning Point:** If (i) a husband and wife are income beneficiaries of the same trust, (ii) the husband and wife file a joint return and (iii) each is a U.S. citizen or resident, the husband and wife are treated as one beneficiary for purposes of applying the QSST rules (see Treas. Reg. § 1.1361-1(e)(2)).

➜   **Planning Point:** Because only one individual may receive distributions from a QSST, the income beneficiary cannot be given a lifetime limited

21st Century Estate Planning:
Practical Applications
2005 Edition

©2005 Sonnenschein Nath & Rosenthal LLP
and Cannon Financial Institute, Inc.

- 458 -

power of appointment over any part of the trust (*see* Treas. Reg. § 1.1361-1(j)(1)(i)). Similarly, for the same reason a trust that permits income or principal distributions among a class of beneficiaries cannot qualify as a QSST. Thus, the trust must be drafted to preclude the *possibility* that distributions will be made to someone other than the current income beneficiary.

> **EXAMPLE:** The terms of the trust are silent with respect to principal distributions, however, under state law principal may be distributed to a person other than the current income beneficiary during the current income beneficiary's life. Because the trust's terms do not preclude the possibility that principal may be distributed to a person other than the current income beneficiary, the trust does not qualify as a QSST.

b. Mechanics of the QSST Election. An election to treat the trust as a QSST and to treat the income beneficiary as the owner of the trust's S corporation stock must be made by the income beneficiary (not the trustee) within two months and 16 days after the trust's receipt of the S corporation stock (*see* IRC § 1361(d)(1) and (2) and Treas. Reg. § 1.1361-4(j)(6)(iii)(C)). Once made, the election is irrevocable. Treas. Reg. § 1.1361-1(j)(6)(ii) sets forth the procedure for making the QSST election.

c. QSST Income Tax Ramifications. The QSST's income beneficiary is treated as the S corporation shareholder for most income tax purposes (*see* IRC § 1361(d)(1)(B)). Accordingly, the trust's *share of the S corporation's income tax items* will be reported by the income beneficiary for tax purposes, even if he or she does not receive any distributions. The income beneficiary will not, however, report and pay the capital gains tax resulting from the sale of S corporation stock held by the QSST (*see* Treas. Reg. § 1.1361-1(j)(8)); instead the QSST will report and pay capital gains tax with respect to such sale. The QSST itself also will report any other income tax items (*i.e.*, non-S corporation income tax items). Thus, with respect to any non-S corporation income tax items, the QSST is taxed according to traditional trust taxation rules. Accordingly, because the QSST is required to distribute all of its income currently, the income beneficiary will be taxed on the fiduciary income of the trust up to the amount of the trust's distributable net income, while the QSST will be taxed on items of income that constitute principal for fiduciary accounting purposes.

5. Death of an S Corporation Shareholder

Upon the death of an S corporation shareholder, an advisor must be aware of the resulting tax ramifications, including the following:

a. Effect on S Corporation Status. In situations where a trust is permitted to hold S corporation stock, the death of a deemed S corporation shareholder could result in the inadvertent termination of the S corporation election. As we have seen, where a trust is permitted to hold S corporation stock under IRC § 1361(c)(2), IRC § 1361(c)(2)(B) deems

21st Century Estate Planning:
Practical Applications
2005 Edition

©2005 Sonnenschein Nath & Rosenthal LLP
and Cannon Financial Institute, Inc.

- 459 -

certain individuals or their estates as the S corporation shareholder (*e.g.*, where a trust is a grantor trust for income tax purposes, the deemed income tax owner (rather than the trust) is treated as the S corporation shareholder; similarly, where a trust receives S corporation stock pursuant to a decedent's will, the trust is a permitted shareholder under IRC § 1361(c)(2)(iii); however, the decedent's estate is treated as the S corporation shareholder). Accordingly, upon the death of a deemed shareholder, advisors must carefully monitor the disposition of the S corporation stock to determine whether or not the successors in interest qualify as permitted S corporation shareholders.

> **EXAMPLE:** P, a U.S. citizen, creates a revocable trust and transfers S corporation stock to the trust. The trust is a grantor trust for income tax purposes and, thus, may hold S corporation stock (*see* IRC §1361(c)(2)(A)(i)). P is the deemed shareholder during his life. Upon P's death, the stock of the S corporation remains in the trust. P's estate is an eligible S corporation shareholder for 2 years after P's death (*see* IRC § 1361(c)(2)(A)(ii) and (B)(ii)).

> **EXAMPLE:** Same facts as above, except one year after P's death, his revocable trust is terminated and the S corporation stock is distributed in equal shares to A, B and C. Neither P's estate nor his trust is thereafter deemed the S corporation shareholder. Instead, A, B, and C are treated as the new shareholders and the factual situation must be reanalyzed to determine if each of them is a permitted S corporation shareholder and to verify that the S corporation does not exceed the 100 shareholder limit.

> **EXAMPLE:** P created a trust for the benefit of C and C's children. The trust qualifies as an ESBT and makes the appropriate election. The terms of the trust provide that the trustee may make discretionary distributions of income or principal to C for life and upon C's death the trust is divided into separate trusts for the benefit of C's children. Upon C's death, the S corporation election will terminate unless (1) the distributee trusts are either grantor trusts, QSSTs or ESBTs and (2) C's children are permitted S corporation shareholders.

21st Century Estate Planning:
Practical Applications
2005 Edition

©2005 Sonnenschein Nath & Rosenthal LLP
and Cannon Financial Institute, Inc.

- 460 -

b. **Impact on Basis**. A disadvantage of an S corporation, when compared to an entity that is taxed as a partnership (including a limited liability company), is that an entity taxed as a partnership has the ability to step-up the inside basis (*i.e.*, the assets owned by the entity) of its assets to fair market value in the event of a sale or exchange of an interest or on the death of an owner (*see* IRC §§ 743(a) and 754). There is no similar election available to a corporation. Thus, although an S corporation shareholder's basis in his or her S corporation stock will be "stepped-up" to its fair market value on the date of the deceased shareholder's death, the underlying assets in the S corporation will not receive a similar step-up in basis.

C. Stock Redemptions -- IRC § 303

Under current law, IRC § 303 offers an unparalleled opportunity to receive tax-free corporate distributions of cash. IRC § 303 provides that a redemption of stock the value of which has been included in the gross estate of a decedent for federal estate tax purposes is, if certain requirements are met, treated as a sale of stock even though the redemption would, but for IRC § 303, be taxed as a dividend under IRC § 301. Because stock included in a decedent's estate ordinarily receives a basis step-up under IRC § 1014, a redemption that qualifies under IRC § 303 usually results in recognition of little or no gain or loss. The policy reason behind IRC § 303 is to provide a mechanism that facilitates the tax-free withdrawal of funds from a closely held business in order to provide a source of funds from which estate taxes and administration expenses incurred by the decedent's estate can be paid.

In order to qualify for the tax-favored treatment under IRC § 303, the stock redemption must satisfy, or fall within, the following requirements and restrictions:

1. The Stock is Included in Decedent's Estate

First, in order to qualify under IRC § 303, the redeemed stock must have been included in the decedent's gross estate (<u>see</u> IRC § 303(a)) for estate tax purposes, or the stock must take its basis from stock that was included in the decedent's gross estate and the "old stock" would have qualified for exchange treatment under IRC § 303(a).

2. 35% Requirement

Second, the value of the stock at issue must exceed 35% of the value of the decedent's gross estate, less the amount of deductions allowable under IRC §§ 2053 and 2054 (*i.e.*, debts, claims, administrative expenses and casualty losses).

> **EXAMPLE:** A's gross estate is $2,000,000, which included stock in X Corporation that was valued at $680,000 for estate tax purposes. $120,000 was allowable as estate tax deductions under IRC § 2053. A's estate satisfies the 35% requirement ($680,000 ÷ ($2,000,000 - $120,000) = 36.17%).

21st Century Estate Planning:
Practical Applications
2005 Edition

©2005 Sonnenschein Nath & Rosenthal LLP
and Cannon Financial Institute, Inc.

- 461 -

→ **Planning Point**: For purposes of the computation under IRC § 303(b)(2)(a)(ii), the amounts deductible under IRC §§ 2053 and 2054 are taken into account whether or not they are claimed as deductions for federal estate tax purposes. Also, one should note that the amount of charitable and marital deductions are not included as part of the computation.

→ **Planning Point**: A redemption which qualifies under IRC § 303 is almost always desirable for an estate, because it provides large amounts of cash on a tax-free or low-tax basis (by avoiding dividend treatment). Thus, in planning the administration of the estate, the estate's advisors must be cognizant of the fact that the valuation of the corporate stock and other assets will affect whether or not the 35% rule is satisfied.

→ **Planning Point**: Advisors should monitor a shareholder's lifetime gift-giving program to make sure that the shareholder does not, unintentionally, reduce his or her stake in the corporation, thereby causing the value of the closely-held stock in his or her estate to fall below 35% of the value of his or her gross estate. If a decedent inadvertently transfers shares that drop him or her below the 35% threshold, he or she could contribute additional property to the corporation in return for additional shares of stock in an amount sufficient to raise his or her interest in the corporation above 35%.

If a decedent's estate has an interest in two or more corporations, the interests may be aggregated for purposes of satisfying the 35% rule if certain requirements are met. Specifically, under IRC § 303(b)(2)(B), the stock of two or more corporations may be aggregated for purposes of the 35% rule if 20% or more in value of each corporation's total outstanding stock is included in the decedent's gross estate. For purposes of the 20% requirement, stock held by the decedent and the decedent's surviving spouse as community property, or held by the decedent and the decedent's surviving spouse as joint tenants, tenants-by-the-entirety or tenants-in-common shall be treated as if it were included in determining the value of the decedent's gross estate (see IRC § 303(b)(2)(B)).

> **EXAMPLE**: D died with a gross estate of $1,200,000. IRC §§ 2053 and 2054 expenses were $200,000. D owned, as his separate property, X Corporation stock valued at $250,000 (X Corporation's total value was $1,000,000). D also owned jointly with his wife stock in Y Corporation. D's one-half interest in Y Corporation was valued at $150,000 (Y Corporation's total value was $1,000,000). By including D's wife's interest ($150,000) in Y Corporation as if it were included as part of D's estate for purposes of the 20% requirement, both X Corporation and Y Corporation will satisfy the 20% requirement. In addition, the combined value of D's interests in X Corporation and Y

21st Century Estate Planning:
Practical Applications
2005 Edition

©2005 Sonnenschein Nath & Rosenthal LLP
and Cannon Financial Institute, Inc.

- 462 -

Corporation (*i.e.*, $400,000) will satisfy the 35% requirement ($400,000 ÷ ($1,200,000 - $200,000) = 40%).

A further complication to satisfying the 35% rule is that IRC § 2035(c)(1) includes in the decedent's estate, for purposes of the 35% requirement, all property transferred by the decedent within three years of death. Thus, stock transferred within three years of the decedent's death is included for purposes of determining whether the 35% rule is satisfied, even though the stock is not included in the decedent's estate and is not eligible for redemption.

> **EXAMPLE:** D transferred $500,000 of X Corporation stock to C in 2000. D died in 2001. His estate was valued at $2,000,000, which included $600,000 in X Corporation stock. Deductions allowable under IRC §§ 2053 and 2054 were $250,000. For purposes of determining whether the 35% rule is satisfied, D's estate includes the stock transferred to C in 2000. Thus, for purposes of the 35% rule, D's estate is valued at $2,500,000, including X Corporation stock of $1,100,000. Thus, D's estate satisfies the 35% rule ($1,100,000 ÷ ($2,500,000 - $250,000) = 48.89%). Nevertheless, only the X Corporation stock actually included in D's estate (*i.e.*, the stock valued at $600,000) may be redeemed under IRC § 303.

> **EXAMPLE:** D transferred $900,000 of real estate to C in 2000. D died in 2001. His estate was valued at $3,000,000, which included $1,200,000 in X Corporation stock. Deductions available under IRC §§ 2053 and 2054 were $300,000. Although D's estate would have satisfied the 35% rule if the transferred real estate was not taken into account ($1,200,000 ÷ ($3,000,000 - $300,000) = 44.44%), it will not satisfy the 35% rule once the $900,000 of real estate transferred in 2000 is taken into account ($1,200,000 ÷ ($3,900,000 - $300,000) = 33.33%).

3. Maximum Redemption Amount

Under IRC § 303(a), the maximum amount that can be received in redemption of the decedent's stock is the sum of (1) state and federal death taxes imposed because of the decedent's death, and (2) funeral and administration expenses allowed as an estate tax deduction under IRC § 2053. The redemption, however, will qualify only to the extent the interest of the shareholder is reduced directly (or through a binding obligation to contribute) by any payment of death taxes and funeral and administration expenses. Thus, stock that passes to a beneficiary will not be eligible for redemption treatment under IRC § 303 if the obligation to pay expenses and administration expenses is borne by another party (see IRC § 303(b)(3)).

21st Century Estate Planning:
Practical Applications
2005 Edition

©2005 Sonnenschein Nath & Rosenthal LLP
and Cannon Financial Institute, Inc.

- 463 -

4. Time Period During which Redemption Must Occur

An IRC § 303 redemption generally must occur within 90 days after the expiration of the statute of limitations for assessment of federal estate taxes, typically three years (see IRC § 303(b)(1)(A)). If a petition for redetermination of estate tax is filed in the Tax Court, the time period is extended to include the 60-day period after the Tax Court's decision becomes final. Also, if an IRC § 6166 election is made to defer estate tax, the period for redemption is extended to include the period during which installment payments will be made.

If a redemption is made more than four years after the decedent's death, the redemption will qualify under IRC § 303 only to the extent it does not exceed the lesser of (1) the amount of death taxes and funeral and administration expenses that remained unpaid immediately before the distribution and (2) the amount paid toward those expenses within one year following the date of the distribution (see IRC § 303(b)(4)).

➔ **Planning Point:** If an IRC § 6166 election has been made to defer estate taxes, any redemption made more than four years after the decedent's death must be carefully coordinated with payment of the estate tax under IRC § 6166 to ensure that the estate does not trigger the acceleration provisions contained in IRC § 6166(g).

D. Extension of Time for Payment of Estate Tax -- IRC § 6166

IRC § 6166 provides that the portion of the estate tax attributable to an interest in a closely held business may be deferred if the value of the closely held business interest exceeds 35% of the decedent's adjusted gross estate (and if the decedent is a U.S. citizen or a resident alien). The purpose behind the statute is to prevent the estate from having to sell the business in order to obtain the necessary liquidity to pay the estate tax. In general, IRC § 6166 permits the estate to elect to defer paying the tax attributable to a closely held business for five years, followed by installment payments over a period not to exceed ten years. Because year one of the installment period overlaps with year five of the deferral period, the maximum extension period is fourteen years.

1. The 35% Requirement

The 35% requirement under IRC § 6166 is calculated in the same manner as the 35% requirement under IRC § 303, and generally is subject to the same rules and restrictions. Accordingly, in calculating the decedent's "adjusted gross estate," the decedent's gross estate is reduced only by the deductions allowable under IRC §§ 2053 and 2054 (see IRC § 6166(b)(6)). In addition, if a decedent's estate has an interest in two or more corporations, the interests may be aggregated for purposes of satisfying the 35% rule if 20% or more in value of each business is included in the decedent's gross estate (see IRC § 6166(c)). For purposes of the 20% requirement, stock held by the decedent and the decedent's surviving spouse as community property, or as joint tenants, tenants-by-the-entirety or tenants-in-common is treated as if it were

21st Century Estate Planning:
Practical Applications
2005 Edition

©2005 Sonnenschein Nath & Rosenthal LLP
and Cannon Financial Institute, Inc.

- 464 -

included in determining the value of the decedent's gross estate (see IRC § 6166(c)). Although the 35% requirement for IRC § 6166 generally is calculated in the same manner as the 35% requirement under IRC § 303, there are two important distinctions: (1) under IRC § 2035(c)(2), the estate will satisfy the 35% requirement only if the estate meets such requirement both with and without the application of IRC § 2035(a), and (2) IRC § 6166(b)(9) specifically disregards the value of passive assets owned by a business in determining whether the 35% requirement is satisfied under IRC § 6166.

2. Interest in a Closely Held Business

For purposes of IRC § 6166 an "interest in a closely held business" includes: (i) a sole proprietorship; (ii) an interest in a partnership if 20% or more of the capital interest in the partnership is included in the decedent's gross estate or the partnership had 45 or fewer partners; or (iii) stock in a corporation engaged in a trade or business if 20% or more of the voting interest in the corporation is included in the decedent's gross estate or there are 45 or fewer shareholders (see IRC § 6166(b)(1)). The determination as to whether the decedent's interest constitutes an "interest in a closely held business" is made as of the time immediately before the decedent's death (see IRC § 6166(b)(2)(A)).

a. Interests Held by Husband and Wife. For purposes of determining whether the decedent's interest is an "interest in a closely held business," the stock or partnership interests held by a husband and wife as community property or as joint tenants, tenants-in-common or tenants-by-the-entirety is considered to be owned by one person (see IRC § 6166(b)(2)(B)).

b. Indirect Ownership. Similarly, in determining whether the decedent's interest is an "interest in a closely held business," property owned, directly or indirectly, by or for a corporation, partnership, estate or trust is considered to be owned proportionately by the persons who hold an interest in such entity; however, a person is treated as having an interest in a trust only if such person has a present interest in the trust.

> **EXAMPLE:** H and W own stock in X Corporation as joint tenants. There are 43 other shareholders. In addition, a trust, in which there are two beneficiaries with present interests, owns stock in X Corporation. Although H and W are considered one shareholder, each of the beneficiaries of the trust is considered a shareholder. Thus, X Corporation has 46 shareholders and, thus, is not an "interest in a closely held business."

21st Century Estate Planning:
Practical Applications
2005 Edition

©2005 Sonnenschein Nath & Rosenthal LLP
and Cannon Financial Institute, Inc.

- 465 -

c. Family Attribution. For purposes of determining the number of partners or shareholders (*i.e.*, in determining whether an interest is an "interest in a closely held business"), a decedent is treated as owning all of the partnership interests or stock held by the decedent's spouse, siblings, ancestors or descendants (see IRC § 6166(b)(2)(D)).

d. Trade or Business Requirement. Even though a business seemingly may fall within the definition of an "interest in a closely held business," the business also must constitute a "trade or business." Thus, only businesses that produce income from active involvement, rather than solely from property ownership, are eligible for estate tax deferral under IRC § 6166.

3. Nature of the IRC § 6166 Relief

Once it is determined that the decedent's interest is an "interest in a closely held business" that satisfies the 35% requirement, the estate may elect to pay all or a portion of the estate tax in two but not more than 10 installments and may take advantage of the reduced interests rates under IRC § 6601(j).

a. Limitation on the Amount That May be Paid in Installments. IRC § 6166(a)(2) places a cap on the amount of estate tax that can be paid in installments. The cap is equal to an amount which bears the same ratio to the estate tax as (a) the value of the closely-held business bears to (b) the value of the adjusted gross estate.

> **EXAMPLE:** H died with a gross estate of $2,200,000. His estate had allowable deductions under IRC §§ 2053 and 2054 of $200,000 (thus, H's adjusted gross estate for purposes of IRC § 6166 was $2,000,000 (*i.e.*, $2,200,000 - $200,000). His estate consisted of an 80% interest in a closely held business, which was valued at $900,000. H's estate incurred estate tax of $1,000,000. Accordingly, the maximum amount qualifying for IRC § 6166 treatment is calculated as follows: ($900,000 ÷ $2,000,000) x $1,000,000 = $450,000.

b. Number of and Due Dates for Installments. The tax may be paid in two to ten equal annual installments, the first of which is due not more than five years after the date on which the federal estate tax was due to be paid (see IRC § 6166(a)(3)). The date chosen for payment of the first installment of tax does not have to be the anniversary of the original due date of the return, but must be the same date within any month corresponding to the day of the month on which the return was due (see Treas. Reg. § 20.6166-1(e)(2)).

> **EXAMPLE:** If D died on April 2, 2004, the tax would be due on January 2, 2005 (*i.e.*, nine months later). If an IRC § 6166 election is made, the first installment of the deferred estate tax is due on the 2nd of any month through January 2010.

21st Century Estate Planning:
Practical Applications
2005 Edition

©2005 Sonnenschein Nath & Rosenthal LLP
and Cannon Financial Institute, Inc.

- 466 -

c. **Rate and Due Date for Interest**. If the executor elects to take advantage of the maximum deferral, only interest is paid for a maximum of four years following the date on which the estate tax was due (see IRC § 6166(f)). IRC § 6601(j) establishes a 2% rate for interest payable on the deferred tax attributable to the first $1,000,000 (for decedents dying after 1998, this amount is adjusted annually for inflation -- the amount for 2005 is $1,170,000) in taxable value of a closely held business (this amount is referred to as the "2% portion"). Interest on the deferred tax that exceeds the 2% portion is payable at a rate equal to 45% of the annual underpayment rate established under IRC § 6621 (see IRC § 6601(j)(1)(B)).

> **EXAMPLE:** D died in 2005 owning a closely held business, which is valued at $4,000,000 for estate tax purposes. The first $1,500,000 is not subject to tax by reason of the applicable exclusion amount. After application of the unified credit, D's estate has a business interest of $2,500,000 in taxable value. D's executor makes the IRC § 6166 election to pay the estate tax. Interest on the tax attributable to the inclusion of $1,170,000 of value in D's estate is payable at the 2% rate. The interest attributable to the remaining $1,330,000 is payable at 45% of the underpayment rate.

4. **Making the IRC § 6166 election**

The election must be made no later than the date on which the estate tax return is required to be filed, taking into account any extensions of time that are granted for filing the return (see IRC § 6166(d)). Treas. Reg. § 6166-1(a) provides that if the election is made when the estate tax return is filed, the election is applicable both to the tax originally determined to be due and to certain deficiencies. If, on the other hand, no election is made when the return is filed, up to the full amount of certain later deficiencies (but not the tax originally determined to be due) may be paid in installments.

An estate may make a protective election, even if the estate does not appear to satisfy the requirements of IRC § 6166. The protective election will defer payment of so much of the tax as remains unpaid when the estate tax values are finally determined (see Treas. Reg. § 20.6166-1(d)).

5. **Acceleration of Estate Tax Payment**

IRC § 6166(g) provides a number of circumstances which will trigger the acceleration of the due date for payment of estate tax, including the following:

a. **Withdrawal of Money or Disposition of Interest**. The estate tax is accelerated if withdrawals of money or other property from the business equal or exceed 50% of the value of the closely held business. A redemption that qualifies under IRC § 303, however, is not counted for purposes of the 50% withdrawal rule if an amount equal to the redemption

21st Century Estate Planning:
Practical Applications
2005 Edition

©2005 Sonnenschein Nath & Rosenthal LLP
and Cannon Financial Institute, Inc.

- 467 -

distribution is paid on the remaining balance of the estate tax no later than one year after the distribution is made (see IRC § 6166(g)(1)(B)).

    b.   **Undistributed Income of Estate**. If an electing estate has undistributed net income for a taxable year ending on or after the due date for the first installment, the estate must pay an amount equal to the undistributed income toward the unpaid estate tax on or before the date the income tax return must be filed for the year (see IRC § 6166(g)(2)).

    c.   **Failure to Pay Principal or Interest on Time**. If there is a failure to pay any principal or interest on time, the unpaid portion of the tax must be paid upon notice and demand from the IRS (see IRC § 6166(g)(3)(A)). Nevertheless, if the unpaid balance is paid within six months of the due date, acceleration does not occur and, instead, the preferential 2% interest rate will not apply to the payment and a penalty is imposed in an amount equal to the product of (a) 5% of the unpaid payment and (b) the number of months or fractions of months after the payment date and before payment is actually made (see IRC § 6166(g)(3)(B)).

21st Century Estate Planning:
Practical Applications
2005 Edition

©2005 Sonnenschein Nath & Rosenthal LLP
and Cannon Financial Institute, Inc.

- 468 -

Chapter XIV
Bibliography

Boris I. Bittker and James S. Eustice, "Federal Income Taxation of Corporations and Shareholders," *Stock Redemptions,* Warren Gorham & Lamont.

Boris I. Bittker and Lawrence Lokken, "Estate, Gift and Generation-Skipping Transfer Tax Procedure," *Federal Taxation of Income, Estates & Gifts*, Ch. 134, Warren Gorham & Lamont.

Charles D. Fox, IV, "Passing and Not Dropping the Baton: Non-Tax Considerations in the Succession of Closely Held Businesses," *36th Annual Philip E. Heckerling Inst. on Est. Plan.* (2002).

Jon J. Gallo and David A. Hjorth, "Handling the Nontax Issues in Business Succession Planning," *Est. Plan.* (January 1998).

C. Wells Hall, III, "The Electing Small Business Trust -- Where Are We Now?," *Business Entities* (September/October 1999).

Kathryn G. Henkel, "Estate Planning & Wealth Preservation: Strategies & Solutions," *S Corporations*, Ch. 18, Warren Gorham & Lamont.

Jerry A. Kasner, *Post Mortem Tax Planning*, Warren Gorham & Lamont (3rd ed.).

Louis A. Mezzullo, "Creating Order Out of Chaos - Planning for the Orderly Devolution of the Closely Held Business," *36th Annual Philip E. Heckerling Inst. on Est. Plan.* (2002).

Christopher Stoneman, 809 T.M., *Estate Planning for Owners of Closely Held Business Interests*.

John B. Truskowski, "AJCA Changes to Subchapter S Broaden the Availability of the S Election," *J. of Tax'n*, at 327 (Dec. 2004).

Howard M. Zaritsky and Norman H. Lane, "Special Trusts," *Federal Income Taxation of Estates and Trusts*, Ch. 17, Warren Gorham & Lamont.

21st Century Estate Planning:
Practical Applications
2005 Edition

©2005 Sonnenschein Nath & Rosenthal LLP
and Cannon Financial Institute, Inc.

- 469 -

XV. THE USE OF FAMILY LIMITED PARTNERSHIPS & FAMILY LIMITED LIABILITY COMPANIES IN ESTATE PLANNING

A. Introduction

The use of family limited partnerships ("FLPs") and family limited liability companies ("LLCs") in estate planning has exploded in recent years. The popularity of these vehicles as a means of transferring wealth from one generation to the next results from not only the fact that they can help achieve significant transfer tax savings, but also from the fact that they allow families to achieve significant non-tax benefits.

The estate, gift and generation-skipping taxes that can be saved through the utilization of these vehicles have been well documented. A predictable side effect of this publicity is intense scrutiny from the IRS, which, in turn, has resulted in a number of disputes that have recently worked their way through the nation's court systems. As the IRS has the ability to "pick and choose" cases for audit, the IRS naturally selects the cases with the worst facts from a taxpayer's perspective. Despite this adverse selection process, taxpayers were able to obtain some early victories that eliminated a number of weapons from the IRS's arsenal. However, courts have recently issued a string of decisions that make estate planning involving FLPs and LLCs a risky endeavor.

This chapter will review the use of these vehicles in estate planning, focusing particular attention on the following:

- Overview of FLPs and Family LLCs;
- Non-Tax Benefits of FLPs and Family LLCs;
- Tax Benefits of FLPs and Family LLCs;
- Inclusion of FLP/LLC Interests Under IRC § 2036
- Formation Issues;
- Avoiding Estate Tax Inclusion -- Operational Concerns;
- Overview of IRS Attacks Under the Business Purpose Doctrine, Internal Revenue Code ("IRC") § 2703 and IRC § 2704;
- Avoiding IRS Attacks on Annual Gift Tax Exclusion for Gifts of FLP or Family LLC Interests; and
- Federal Income Tax Considerations.

B. Brief Overview of FLPs and LLCs

An FLP is simply a partnership created by two or more family members in accordance with state law. The family members contribute property that they expect to appreciate in value and in return receive general partnership interests and/or limited partnership interests. The FLP is managed by the general partners, who have unlimited liability for the activities of the partnership. The limited partners, on the other hand, are essentially passive investors with few, if

21st Century Estate Planning:
Practical Applications
2005 Edition

©2005 Sonnenschein Nath & Rosenthal LLP
and Cannon Financial Institute, Inc.

- 470 -

any, management rights. A limited partner's liability for the activities of the partnership is limited to the amount of his or her investment in the partnership.

> **EXAMPLE:** H and W form an FLP. H contributes a diversified portfolio of securities valued at $250,000 and an interest in real estate worth $250,000 in return for a 1% general partnership interest and a 49% limited partnership interest. W similarly contributes a diversified portfolio of securities valued at $250,000 and an interest in real estate worth $250,000 in return for a 1% general partnership interest and a 49% limited partnership interest.

An LLC, on the other hand, is an entity formed by family members under state law that has characteristics of both a partnership and a corporation. The family members with ownership interests in the LLC are called "members." Like shareholders in a corporation, members are not personally liable for the activities of the LLC. In addition, like partners in a partnership, the legal specifications of one's ownership interest are governed by an operating agreement. An LLC can either be "member-managed," where each member has equal rights in the management and operation of the LLC, or "manager-managed," where a manager or managers specified in the LLC agreement are given the right to manage and operate the LLC. In addition, an LLC could have voting and non-voting membership interests, in which case it is managed by the voting members, or a managing member designated by them.

> **EXAMPLE:** H and W form an LLC. By creating voting and non-voting membership interests, H and W could structure the LLC in an identical manner to the FLP in the previous example. Assuming the same property is contributed, H could receive in return for his contribution a 1% Class A membership interest (with voting rights) and a 49% Class B membership interest (without voting rights). W would receive identical interests in return for her contribution.

The choice of whether to use an FLP or an LLC for estate planning purposes will depend upon which state law the practitioner intends to use. Either entity can be used to accomplish a client's estate planning objectives.

C. Non-Tax Reasons for Using FLPs and Family LLCs

In addition to the highly publicized valuation discounts that can be achieved through the use of FLPs and LLCs, there are a number of non-tax benefits (*e.g.*, the degree of control that one can retain over the assets in these entities vis-à-vis the control one can retain over the assets in a trust without causing estate tax inclusion) that can be achieved through owning assets in these vehicles. Although a number of recent cases have held that a valid business purpose is not necessary for the entity to be respected for transfer tax purposes (See e.g., *Knight v. Comm'r,* 115 T.C. 506 (Nov. 30, 2000); *Estate of Strangi v. Comm'r*, 115 T.C. 478 (2000), *aff'd and rev'd*

21st Century Estate Planning:
Practical Applications
2005 Edition

©2005 Sonnenschein Nath & Rosenthal LLP
and Cannon Financial Institute, Inc.

- 471 -

in part by Gulig v. Comm'r, 293 F.3d 279 (5th Cir. 2002)), there always have been and always will be valid non-tax reasons for establishing an FLP or LLC, including the following:

1. Provides a Vehicle to Transfer Assets while Retaining Control over Distributions to Family Members

In making gifts to descendants, probably the single biggest non-tax benefit derived from the use of an FLP or LLC, in contrast to the use of a trust, is that the donor can retain control over both the management of the underlying assets and the distributions to his or her descendants. A concern of many wealthy clients is that transferring substantial wealth to descendants will inhibit the initiative of the beneficiaries and may prevent them from becoming productive members of society (*i.e.*, fear that their generosity will spawn a "trust fund baby"). By creating an FLP or LLC and transferring limited partnership interests or non-voting membership interests, the donor can relieve some of that fear, as the donor is able to retain control over the underlying assets and can reinvest cash flow rather than making distributions. Moreover, because there are substantial transfer restrictions on these interests, they are largely non-marketable and cannot be readily converted by the beneficiary into cash. By contrast, retention of the same degree of control, as trustee of a trust for the benefit of one's descendants, would likely cause the trust assets to be included in the donor's estate (but see section E. below regarding the inclusion of the donor's FLP or LLC interest in his or her gross estate under IRC § 2036).

2. Protection from Creditors and Failed Marriages

An FLP or LLC provides protection from a partner or member's personal creditors (*i.e.*, "outside creditors"), by limiting their remedy to obtaining a "charging order" against the interest in the entity. Unless the partner or member made a fraudulent conveyance of the partner or member's assets to the FLP or LLC, his or her personal creditors cannot reach the entity's assets and, instead, will be limited to obtaining a charging order. A charging order gives the creditor the rights of an assignee of a membership/partnership interest. As such, the creditor is only entitled to receive distributions which otherwise would be made to the partner or member whose interest is charged. The rationale behind limiting the creditor to assignee status is to prevent a partner or member's individual creditors from seizing entity assets and thereby interrupting the business and adversely impacting innocent partners or members. Because the creditor is limited to a charging order and, thus, cannot force distributions from the entity, the creditor will likely be more willing to settle than if the assets were not held in an FLP or LLC. If the creditor chooses to litigate the matter and obtains a charging order, the creditor could be saddled with income taxes even though no distributions are made to the creditor (*i.e.*, the creditor, and the other partners or members, would be forced to report "phantom income"). See Rev. Rul. 77-137, 1977-1 C.B. 178; Osborne & Schurig, 2 Asset Protection: Domestic and International Law and Tactics § 16.06.

➜ **Planning Point:** Additional creditor protection can be obtained by drafting the partnership or operating agreement so that an involuntary

---

21st Century Estate Planning:
Practical Applications
2005 Edition

©2005 Sonnenschein Nath & Rosenthal LLP
and Cannon Financial Institute, Inc.

- 472 -

transfer of an interest to a creditor or any other third party triggers buy-sell provisions that allow the other partners or members or the entity itself to purchase the interest at its fair market value (*i.e.*, at the interest's discounted fair market value). An added degree of protection can also be obtained by prohibiting partners or members from pledging their interests for their individual debts.

In addition to providing protection from personal creditors, an FLP or LLC may provide some protection from a divorced spouse, as these vehicles provide a convenient means of ensuring that a child or grandchild does not commingle his or her separate property with that of his or her spouse.

➔ **Planning Point**: Again, additional protection can be obtained by drafting the partnership or operating agreement so that an involuntary transfer of an interest pursuant to a divorce decree will trigger buy-sell provisions that allow the divorced partner or member (in the event the former spouse held an interest in the entity), the other partners or members or the entity itself to purchase the interest at its fair market value. As the fair market value of the interests is less than the value of the underlying interest, even if a court awards the value of an entire interest to the former spouse, the former spouse will not be able to reach the total value of the underlying assets.

3. Consolidate Ownership

FLPs and LLCs can be used to consolidate a family's ownership interest in a "family" asset. For example, an FLP or LLC is an excellent vehicle for holding an interest in a family farm. If owned outside of one of these entities, fractional interests among family lines would result over time, which would make dealing with the asset as a whole extremely difficult (*e.g.*, if a parent transferred his interest in a farm to his three children in equal shares and, at the death of each of the children, they each transferred their one-third share to their three children (*i.e.*, the grandchildren of the original transferor), the farm would be owned in equal shares by nine different individuals). By owning the assets in an FLP or LLC, the general partner or managing member would be able to manage the property on behalf of the others, thereby significantly reducing administrative headaches that result from fractional ownership.

4. One Level of Federal Income Taxation

Unlike a corporation, in which the corporation pays federal income tax at the corporate level and the shareholders are again taxed at the individual level, the partners of an FLP and the members of an LLC are subject to federal income tax only at the individual level. FLPs and LLCs do not pay federal income tax. Instead, they "pass-through" all taxable items to their partners or members, as the case may be, who are then obligated to report such times on their

21st Century Estate Planning:
Practical Applications
2005 Edition

©*2005 Sonnenschein Nath & Rosenthal LLP*
and Cannon Financial Institute, Inc.

- 473 -

personal income tax return and to pay any federal income tax due. Some states, however, may impose a state income tax on the entity itself.

5. Facilitate Gifts

Creating an FLP or LLC simplifies the making of gifts to the next generation. The parents may make gifts of their limited partnership interests or membership interests rather than direct gifts of the underlying assets. The gifts can be made by simply signing a form and without the necessity of reregistering securities or accounts. A gift of partnership interests or membership interests should qualify for the gift tax annual exclusion and, if the gift is structured correctly, the exemption from the generation-skipping transfer tax. In addition to annual exclusion gifts, the donor can use a portion or all of the donor's remaining gift tax exemption to transfer more partnership interests or membership interests to family members during the donor's life. See section I. below regarding the qualification of these gifts for the annual exclusion.

6. Investment Advantages

An FLP or LLC can serve as an investment vehicle to consolidate assets and reduce the costs associated with the management of an investment portfolio for the family of the entity's creator. A larger pool of assets also may allow the FLP or LLC to gain access to investment opportunities that would not be available to single investors. The parents can also use the entity as a means of teaching their children to handle investment decisions in a responsible manner.

7. Flexibility

The partnership agreement (for an FLP) and the operating agreement (for an LLC) can provide that the agreement can be amended or the FLP or LLC terminated with the consent of the partners without adverse tax consequences. This attribute makes an FLP or LLC a ;more flexible estate planning tool than, for example, an irrevocable trust (but see section E, below regarding the inclusion of the donor's FLP or LLC interest in his or her gross estate under IRS § 2036).

D. Tax Reasons for Using FLPs and Family LLCs

Although there are non-tax reasons for creating FLPs and LLCs, the driving force behind these vehicles is their ability to achieve significant reductions in gift, estate and generation-skipping transfer tax. There are essentially two types of FLPs and LLCs used in estate planning: the "discount FLP/LLC" and the "frozen FLP/LLC." As the names indicate, the primary tax motive for a discount FLP/LLC is to obtain minority interest and lack of marketability discounts for gift and estate tax purposes, while a frozen FLP/LLC is designed to partially freeze the value of an individual's estate and shift future appreciation to the next generation.

21st Century Estate Planning:
Practical Applications
2005 Edition

©2005 Sonnenschein Nath & Rosenthal LLP
and Cannon Financial Institute, Inc.

- 474 -

1. Tax Reasons for Creating Discount FLPs/LLCs

A discount FLP/LLC is a technique that can be used both as a value-reduction technique or a value-shifting technique. For individuals with less than $3,000,000, the discount FLP/LLC will primarily be used as a value reduction technique, as people in this economic class typically want to save estate tax, but generally do not want to undertake an annual gift-giving program (*i.e.*, because they will likely need the cash flow, including the cash flow from future appreciation, that is generated from the assets for their own needs). Conversely, for larger estates, this technique may be used as both a value-reduction technique (*i.e.*, an appropriately designed discount FLP/LLC can achieve estate tax savings even if no lifetime gifts are made) and a value-shifting technique (through lifetime gift giving programs).

Regardless of whether the discount FLP/LLC is intended to be used as a value-shifting or value-reducing technique, the key to this type of transaction is achieving valuation discounts. The discounts are generated from the fact that interests in FLPs and LLCs are cloaked with restrictions, such as lack of control, prohibitions preventing interest holders from withdrawing from the entity, and severe limitations on transfers. As a result of these restrictions, the value of these interests may be discounted, thereby permitting the transferor to leverage the amount of wealth he or she is able to give away to family members.

> **EXAMPLE:** The concept of "leverage" can be illustrated as follows: Assume P intends to make a gift of limited partnership interests to C and, for purposes of simplicity, assume that a combined 50% discount is applicable to the FLP interests being transferred. Under these assumptions each gift of $1 of limited partnership interests represents $2 of underlying value.

The discounts that are typically available in the FLP/LLC context are discounts for lack of control and lack of marketability. Discounts for lack of control flow from the fact that the holder of a limited partnership interest (or a minority interest or non-voting interest in the case of an LLC) does not have the ability to manage the underlying assets or direct distributions from the entity. Lack of marketability discounts, on the other hand, flow from the restrictions in the partnership or operating agreement that limit one's ability to transfer his or her interest in the entity (*i.e.*, thereby preventing the development of a ready market for the purchase and sale of interests in the entity). In determining the amount of the discount, several factors must be considered, including the specific provisions partnership or operating agreement, the type of assets held by the entity, the prospect for distributions and the financial risk to the limited partner or member. The discounts can produce substantial transfer tax savings. For estate and gift tax purposes, discounts generally range from 25% to 40%, and may be even higher, depending on the circumstances.

If the primary reason, from a tax perspective, for forming the FLP/LLC is to produce valuation discounts for estate tax purposes, it may now be important for the taxpayer not to retain any power to participate in liquidating the entity. If a taxpayer, as a partner or member (or as

21st Century Estate Planning:
Practical Applications
2005 Edition

©2005 Sonnenschein Nath & Rosenthal LLP
and Cannon Financial Institute, Inc.

- 475 -

manager of an LLC), has a power to participate in liquidating the entity, all interests in the entity owned by such individual may be valued for estate tax purposes at the value of the entity's underlying assets attributable to the decedent's interest in the entity. The alleged statutory support for this position is IRC § 2036(a)(2).

A discount FLP/LLC can also be used as a value-shifting technique, if the initial partners or members (usually a husband and wife) make lifetime gifts of limited partnership interests or membership interests to their children and other beneficiaries. Using this approach, an individual will typically retain control over the entity (*e.g.*, by retaining the general partnership interests an FLP) and then making gifts of limited partnership interests to his or her children and/or grandchildren (but see section E. below regarding the inclusion of the individual's interest in his or her gross estate under IRC § 2036).

> **EXAMPLE:** H and W each own a 1% general partnership interest and a 49% limited partnership interests in an FLP, which owns $4,000,000 of marketable securities. H and W want to begin transferring assets to their three children, but want to retain the ability to not only manage the securities, but also control the amount and timing of distributions to their children. Accordingly, H and W decide to make annual exclusion gifts (currently $11,000) to each of their children of limited partnership interests. A qualified appraiser determines that a combined 30% discount for minority interest and lack of marketability should apply to their interests in the FLP. As a result, each transfer of $11,000 of limited partnership interests will represent $15,714 of value in the underlying securities ($11,000 ÷ 70%). See Section H. below regarding the qualification of these gifts for the annual exclusion.

2.   Tax Reasons for Creating Frozen FLPs/LLCs

Frozen FLPs and LLCs are used primarily as value-shifting devices. The value of the various interests in a frozen FLP/LLC is determined under the special valuation rules contained in IRC § 2701. Although a detailed discussion of the special valuation rules under IRC § 2701 is beyond the scope of this chapter, the following material provides a general overview of the mechanics of a frozen FLP/LLC and discusses some situations in which a practitioner may want to consider using a frozen FLP/LLC.

In a typical frozen FLP/LLC structure, three classes of interests will be created: (i) a common general partnership interest (typically representing 1% of the value of the FLP), (ii) a common or "unfrozen" limited partnership interest (which must represent not less than 10% of the value of the FLP) and (iii) a preferred limited partnership interest, which represents the balance of the interests (a similar capital structure would be used for an LLC). The holder of the general partnership interest has the ability to control and manage the entity.

21st Century Estate Planning:
Practical Applications
2005 Edition

©2005 Sonnenschein Nath & Rosenthal LLP
and Cannon Financial Institute, Inc.

- 476 -

The preferred interest pays the holder a fixed and certain rate of return with no participation in equity growth, while the holders of the common interests have rights to all income, growth and appreciation in excess of the preferred distributions. Thus, as the holders of the preferred limited partnership interests are assured a fixed and certain rate of return with no participation in equity growth, their interest is referred to as a "frozen" interest. Similarly, as all income, growth and appreciation above the preferred return inures to the holders of the common limited partnership interests, their interest is referred to as an "unfrozen" interest.

The individual creating a frozen FLP typically transfers the common or unfrozen interest to his or her children and/or grandchildren and retains the general partner interest and the preferred limited partner interests. This will partially freeze the value of the interest retained, as all earnings and growth over the preferred amount will pass to the children's common interest (except 1% of such amount inures to the holder of the general partnership interest, thereby causing a "leak" in the freeze).

Depending on the creator's specific circumstances and desires, he or she can either retain control over the entity's activities (by retaining the general partnership interests) and make annual exclusion gifts of the preferred limited partnership interests, or the creator can transfer his or her general partnership interest to his or her children and retain the preferred limited partnership interest (thereby retaining a guaranteed payment right during his or her lifetime).

➔ **Planning Point:** A frozen FLP/LLC will only make sense if the total rate of return generated by the underlying assets exceeds the preferred distribution rate. In fact, if the total rate of return on the underlying assets is less than the preferred distribution rate, the "unfrozen" limited partnership interest which was previously transferred by gift will be paid back to the donor in satisfaction of the preferred distribution (thereby resulting in a "phantom gift"; *i.e.*, a taxable gift that fails to transfer any value). This result would be even worse if the donor's children contributed their own assets in return for the "unfrozen" limited partnership interest, because the children's assets would be paid back to the donor in satisfaction of the preferred distribution amount.

As a result of this risk, practitioners should carefully analyze a situation before opting to use a frozen FLP/LLC. Despite this risk, a frozen FLP/LLC may be well tailored for the following situations:

- The business or other asset in the frozen FLP/LLC is likely to experience significant short-term growth and then likely will be sold. The frozen FLP/LLC is well suited for this type of situation, because the preferred distributions can be deferred for up to four years, thereby providing an additional source of funds to fuel the growth. Upon the sale of the underlying asset, the sale proceeds can be used to pay the distributions that are in arrears and the FLP/LLC can be liquidated with most of the growth inuring to the holders of the "unfrozen" interest.

21st Century Estate Planning:
Practical Applications
2005 Edition

©2005 Sonnenschein Nath & Rosenthal LLP
and Cannon Financial Institute, Inc.

- 477 -

- The asset in the frozen FLP/LLC consistently generates a predictable total return in excess of the preferred distribution rate.

- Your client wants to purchase a life insurance policy; however, because he or she fully utilized his or her annual exclusion elsewhere, an irrevocable life insurance trust is not an option. Instead, the policy could be owned by a frozen FLP/LLC. The children own the "unfrozen" limited partnership interests, your client owns the preferred limited partnership interests and an independent third party owns the general partnership interest. At the insured's death, the insurance proceeds effectively inure to the benefit of the children. Only the value of the preferred interest should be included in the parents' gross estate. Other assets would have to be owned by the FLP/LLC so that the entity could use these other assets to pay the insurance premiums. By having the FLP/LLC pay the insurance premiums, the necessity of annual gifts is avoided. Thus, unlike when an irrevocable life insurance trust is used, there is no need for Crummey notices or gift tax returns, and additional GST exemption is not used if skip persons are involved.

E. Inclusion of FLP/LLC Interests Under IRC § 2036: The *Estate of Strangi* Decision

Estate of Strangi v. Comm'r, T.C. Memo. 2003-145 (*Strangi III*), and the two previous decisions involving these parties ((*Estate of Strangi v. Comm'r*, 115 T.C. 478 (2000) (*Strangi I*), *aff'd and rev'd in part by Gulig v. Comm'r*, 293 F.3d 279 (5th Cir. 2002) (*Strangi II*)) have substantially impacted the approach that practitioners and clients must take towards estate planning with FLPs and LLCs. Below is a basic discussion of the case and, in subsequent sections of this chapter, an explanation of the case's impact (along with the impact of other recent cases) on the formation and operation of FLPs and LLCs.

In 1988, Albert Strangi, suffering from severe health problems, executed a broad power of attorney in favor of his son-in-law, Michael Gulig. In July 1994, after attending a seminar on the use of FLPs, Gulig formed SFLP (a Texas FLP) and its general partner, Stranco (a Texas corporation), on behalf of Strangi.

Following SFLP's formation, Gulig made a series of transfers pursuant to the power of attorney. Gulig transferred $9,876,929 (or approximately 98%) of Strangi's assets to SFLP in exchange for a 99% limited partnership interest. Approximately 75% of the value of the assets contributed to the partnership were cash and securities. Gulig also transferred Strangi's primary residence to SFLP.

Gulig also opened a bank account for Stranco and, as its incorporator, appointed Strangi and his four adult children as directors of the company. In August 1994, Gulig (acting as Strangi's attorney-in-fact) and Strangi's children authorized execution of a management agreement under which Gulig would be employed by Stranco to handle its day-to-day business, as well as that of SFLP.

21st Century Estate Planning:
Practical Applications
2005 Edition

©*2005 Sonnenschein Nath & Rosenthal LLP*
and Cannon Financial Institute, Inc.

- 478 -

Stranco was then funded with $49,350 of cash from Strangi (transferred by Gulig pursuant to the power of attorney), in exchange for 47% of the company's outstanding stock, and $55,650 of cash contributed by the Strangi children, in exchange for 53% of the company's outstanding stock. Stranco then contributed all of the cash to SFLP in exchange for a 1% general partnership interest therein. Thereafter, the Strangi children transferred 1% of the outstanding Stranco stock to a local public charity.

Strangi died in October 1994, just a few months following the creation and funding of SFLP and Stranco. In January 1996, the executor filed the federal estate tax return with the IRS, which, after applying substantial minority interest and lack of marketability discounts to Strangi's interests in SFLP and Stranco, reported the value of Strangi's gross estate as $6,823,582; substantially less than the $11,100,922 date-of-death value of SFLP's assets. The IRS issued a notice of deficiency in the amount of $2,545,826 of federal estate tax (and, alternatively, $1,629,947 of federal gift tax). In response, the estate filed suit in the Tax Court.

Before trial, the IRS moved to raise IRC § 2036(a) as grounds for including in Strangi's estate all the assets that Gulig, acting on Strangi's behalf, transferred to SFLP and Stranco. Finding the motion untimely, the court denied it and subsequently held, among other things, that (1) SFLP was validly formed under state law and, therefore, would be respected for federal estate tax purposes, (2) no taxable gift resulted from Strangi's transfers to SFLP and (3) Strangi's interest in SFLP should be valued by applying the discounts proposed by the IRS. The IRS timely appealed the denial of its IRC § 2036(a) motion to the U.S. Court of Appeals for the Fifth Circuit. While it affirmed the Tax Court's other rulings, the Fifth Circuit reversed the Tax Court's holding on the timeliness of the motion and remanded the case for consideration of the motion (or, alternatively, articulation of the Tax Court's basis for its denial).

On remand, the Tax Court considered application of IRC § 2036(a) to Strangi's estate. Focusing first on IRC § 2036(a)(1), the Tax Court concluded that Strangi had retained both the right to possess and enjoy the transferred assets and the right to the income generated therefrom. In reaching this conclusion, the court found that an implied agreement existed between Strangi and Gulig (and presumably the Strangi children) that the transferred assets, as well as the income generated by the assets, would be available to Strangi should he need them. In accordance with the provisions of Treas. Reg. § 20.2036-1(a), such agreement amounted to the retention of rights with respect to such property. Absent such an agreement, the court found it implausible that Strangi, a man in rapidly declining health, would dispose of 98% of his assets, including his primary residence, leaving him with a relatively insignificant amount of liquid assets with which to meet his personal expenses.

The court noted that the factor most probative of such an agreement was the fact that Strangi's relationship to his assets was largely unchanged by their transfers to SFLP and Stranco. He continued to occupy his primary residence after its transfer to SFLP and did so rent-free (although Strangi's estate eventually paid accrued rent to SFLP in 1997, the court dismissed the importance of that fact). In addition, Gulig managed the assets for Strangi's benefit both before and after their transfer to SFLP and Stranco. In fact, Gulig, by virtue of his ability to cause SFLP

21st Century Estate Planning:
Practical Applications
2005 Edition

©2005 Sonnenschein Nath & Rosenthal LLP
and Cannon Financial Institute, Inc.

- 479 -

to make distributions (pursuant to his employment under the management agreement), authorized several partnership distributions for Strangi's benefit. In the months preceding - as well as the months following - Strangi's death, Gulig authorized over $3,000,000 of distributions from SFLP for Strangi's personal expenses, Strangi's home health care costs, the surgery expenses of Strangi's nurse (necessitated by an injury she sustained while caring for him), Strangi's funeral and estate administration expenses, a specific bequest under Strangi's will and state inheritance and federal estate taxes. Although the estate vigorously argued that the distributions were made on a pro rata basis and, therefore, made to Stranco as well as Strangi, the court found the estate's argument unpersuasive because distributions were dictated largely by the expenses of Strangi and his estate and also because Strangi owned more than 99% of SFLP, rendering the distributions received by Stranco insignificant. Moreover, giving further support to the court's finding of an implicit agreement between Strangi and Gulig (and presumably the Strangi children), none of the Strangi children ever challenged or otherwise objected to any of SFLP's distributions.

The Tax Court could have based its conclusion solely on IRC § 2036(a)(1). Nevertheless, the court saw fit to focus on the application of IRC § 2036(a)(2) to Strangi's estate. The court concluded that Strangi had retained the right to designate the person who would possess or enjoy the transferred assets and the income therefrom, with the result that the transferred assets were also includible in the estate under IRC § 2036(a)(2). In doing so, the court rejected the estate's assertions that *U.S. v. Byrum*, 408 U.S. 125 (1972), was controlling. In *Byrum*, the Supreme Court held that IRC § 2036(a)(2) did not warrant the inclusion of closely-held stock that had been transferred to a family trust in the gross estate of the transferor, despite the fact that the transferor retained the right to vote the stock and, accordingly, to elect the directors who would authorize dividends. The Court reached this holding because the transferor did not maintain the ability to regulate the payment of dividends to the trust. This was largely due to the existence of fiduciary duties that he owed to the other corporate shareholders not to promote his personal interest at the expense of the corporation. The Court also relied on the fact that the transferor did not have the ability to decide which trust beneficiaries would enjoy the income of the trust because of the existence of an independent trustee for the trust.

The *Strangi* court found that, unlike the transferor in *Byrum*, Strangi had retained an absolute right to determine who would enjoy the income from the transferred assets because his attorney-in-fact was authorized under the management agreement to declare distributions for SFLP or could, with the other directors of Stranco, terminate SFLP and cause a distribution of the partnership assets to the partners (*i.e.*, Stranco and Strangi). In reaching this finding, the court, relying on Treas. Reg. § 20.2036-1(b)(3), noted that a retained power (such as Strangi's right as a shareholder of Stranco to terminate SFLP or his right as a director of Stranco to authorize dividends from Stranco) need not be exercisable alone, but could require the exercise of others to be effective under IRC § 2036(a)(2).

The court further distinguished *Byrum* by noting that the impediments that could have prevented the transferor in *Byrum* from exercising his right to vote to compel dividends (such as the corporate need for retained earnings, the relative operating health of the company and the

21st Century Estate Planning:
Practical Applications
2005 Edition

©2005 Sonnenschein Nath & Rosenthal LLP
and Cannon Financial Institute, Inc.

- 480 -

existence of fiduciary duties to the other shareholders) or from exercising his right to control which trust beneficiaries would possess or enjoy the income from the trust (such as the existence of an independent trustee to determine discretionary trust distributions) were absent in this case. The *Strangi* court found that (1) there was no need for retained earnings because neither SFLP nor Stranco were actively operating business entities, (2) the respective operating health of SFLP and Stranco were irrelevant for the same reason, (3) Strangi, whether as a partner of SFLP or a shareholder of Stranco, was not subject to fiduciary duties to act in the best interests of the other partners or shareholders because of the intra-family dynamics of the situation and (4) neither SFLP distributions nor Stranco dividends were subject to the approval of an independent party (similar to the independent trustee of the family trust in *Byrum*). The court further noted that Gulig, given his role as Strangi's attorney-in-fact, would be compelled to operate SFLP and Stranco in Strangi's best interests and that the local public charity which held a 1% interest in Stranco, given the size and gratuitous receipt of its interest, was unlikely to exercise any oversight with regard thereto, whether meaningful or otherwise.

Having found that Strangi retained the right to the income from the transferred assets, the right to possess and enjoy the transferred assets and the right to designate the persons who were to possess and enjoy the transferred assets and their income, the court next considered whether inclusion of the transferred assets in Strangi's estate would be precluded by the bona fide sale exception of IRC § 2036. The Tax Court found that no bona fide sale of property (whether to SFLP or to Stranco) had ever occurred because the transfers were not made at arms' length - a requisite element of a bona fide sale. Instead, the court concluded that Gulig unilaterally had made all decisions regarding the structure, formation and funding of SFLP and Stranco, evidencing a general absence of negotiation between the parties to the transaction.

Even if there had been a bona fide sale, the court noted that the transaction also lacked adequate and full consideration. Relying on a series of cases, the court held that changing the form of an interest in property without also changing the underlying property itself merely results in the "recycling" of value and does not amount to the receipt of adequate and full consideration. Finding no bona fide sale for adequate and full consideration, the court concluded that the transferred assets were includible in Strangi's estate under Section 2036(a)(1) and (a)(2).

→ **Planning Point:** The court's discussion regarding Section 2036(a)(2) is particularly troubling because it suggests that this Section may be triggered in the event that the decedent owns any interest in a corporate general partner, regardless of whether that interest is a minority interest or a controlling interest, since in such case the decedent would have the ability, alone or in conjunction with others, to control the distribution of the income. Thus, while the *Strangi* decision may certainly be characterized as a "bad fact" decision, it does appear that the Tax Court has once again raised the bar with respect to its scrutiny of FLPs.

21st Century Estate Planning:
Practical Applications
2005 Edition

©2005 Sonnenschein Nath & Rosenthal LLP
and Cannon Financial Institute, Inc.

- 481 -

F. Formation Issues

Generally, an FLP or LLC can be formed without the partners or members recognizing any income or gain on the unrealized appreciation of assets transferred to the entity. There are, however, exceptions to this general rule, including the following:

- The partners or members must recognize gain if the liabilities assumed by the entity exceed the basis of the assets transferred to the entity plus the partner or member's share of the debt under IRC § 752 (See IRC § 752(b)).

> **EXAMPLE:** P transfers an asset with a basis of $500 subject to a $1,000 liability that is assumed by the FLP and in return receives a 40% limited partnership interest. P's 40% share of the partnership's $1,000 liability is $400. Accordingly, P will recognize income of $100 ($1,000 - ($500 + $400)).

- If a partner or member transfers services in exchange for a capital interest in a partnership, the partner or member will recognize compensation income equal to the fair market value of the capital interest he or she receives (See Treas. Reg. § 1.721-1(b)(1)).
- Partners and members will recognize gain if the entity is treated as an investment company and any of the owners are diversifying their investments (See IRC §§ 351(e) and 721(b) and Treas. Reg. § 1.351-1(c)).

Fortunately, in the FLP and LLC context the first two exceptions to the general non-recognition rule are easily avoided. The third exception, however, is more troublesome. Nevertheless, through effective planning, the recognition of gain under the investment company rules can be avoided. Once the planner has devised a strategy to avoid the potential recognition of gain on formation of the entity, the planner will need to focus on structuring the partnership to avoid the IRS's gift on formation argument.

1. Avoiding the Investment Company Rules

The investment company rules require recognition of gain on the unrealized appreciation in property transferred to an FLP or LLC if (1) the entity is treated as an investment company after its formation and (2) the partners or members have diversified their investments as a result of the formation of the entity. The purpose behind this rule is to prevent a partner or member from contributing non-diversified assets and receiving back a mix of assets that effectively diversifies his or her holdings.

a. What Constitutes an Investment Company? An FLP or LLC, under Treas. Reg. § 1.351-1(c)(1) and IRC § 721(b), will be deemed an investment company if more than 80% of the value of the FLP's or LLC's assets are held for investment and are cash, stocks, or securities, whether or not readily marketable, certain other investments listed in IRC §

21st Century Estate Planning:
Practical Applications
2005 Edition

©2005 Sonnenschein Nath & Rosenthal LLP
and Cannon Financial Institute, Inc.

- 482 -

351(e)(1) or the regulations thereunder or interests in regulated investment companies ("RICs") or real estate investment trusts ("REITs") (See Treas. Reg. § 1.351-1(c)(1), as modified by Section 1002 of the Tax Reform Act of 1997, amending IRC § 351(e)).

> **EXAMPLE:** P and C form an LLC. P contributes $1,000,000 of securities and C contributes real property valued at $270,000. Because the securities represent less than 80% of the value of the LLC's assets, the LLC will not be deemed to be an investment company and, as a result, P and C will not recognize any gain upon formation of the entity.

➔ **Planning Point:** The easiest way to avoid the investment company rules is to structure the transaction so that the FLP or LLC is not deemed to be an investment company. As the above example illustrates, this can be accomplished by having the partners contribute sufficient "other" assets (*i.e.,* assets other than cash, stocks, or securities, whether or not readily marketable, certain other investments listed in IRC § 351(e)(1) or the regulations thereunder or interests in RICs or REITs).

b. Have the Partners or Members Diversified Their Investments? Even if an FLP or LLC is deemed an investment company, the partners or members will not recognize gain as a result of contributing appreciated property to the entity if they have not diversified their interests.

> **EXAMPLE:** P and C form an LLC. P contributes $1,000,000 of securities, which consists of 50% Microsoft stock and 50% AT&T stock. C contributes $300,000 consisting of 50% Microsoft stock and 50% AT&T stock. The LLC is an investment company, because more than 80% of its assets consist of marketable securities. Nevertheless, because neither P nor C diversified their interests, they will not recognize gain.

➔ **Planning Point:** As the above example illustrates, if the FLP or LLC is deemed to be an investment company, one means of avoiding the recognition of gain on the assets contributed to the entity is to have the partners contribute identical percentages of the same investments. The total dollar values of each security contributed do not need to be the same to avoid diversification -- the key is that each partner contributes the same percentage of each security.

Even if you are unable to structure the transaction so that the partners or members contribute identical percentages of each security, there are other means available to avoid the recognition of gain. Specifically, Regulation § 1.351-1(c) provides both a safe harbor and a de minimis exception that can be utilized to avoid gain recognition.

21st Century Estate Planning:
Practical Applications
2005 Edition

©2005 Sonnenschein Nath & Rosenthal LLP
and Cannon Financial Institute, Inc.

- 483 -

(1)　The Diversification Safe Harbor. The safe harbor provides that diversification can be avoided if each partner or member transfers an already diversified portfolio of stocks and securities to the FLP or LLC (see Treas. Reg. § 1.351-1(c)(6)(i)). A portfolio will be treated as diversified if (i) not more than 25% of its value is invested in stocks and securities of any one issuer; and (ii) not more than 50% of its value is invested in stocks and securities of five or fewer issuers (see IRC § 368(a)(2)(F)(ii)).

> **EXAMPLE:** P and C form an LLC and each transfers a $1,000,000 portfolio of stocks to the LLC. P's portfolio consists of $240,000 of General Motors and $63,333.33 of stock in twelve different corporations, while C contributes $90,909.09 of stock in eleven different corporations. The portfolios contributed by both P and C will be deemed already diversified because (i) no company's stock in either portfolio exceeds 25% of the total value of that portfolio and (ii) the value of the stock of any five companies within each portfolio does not exceed 50% of the value of that portfolio.

➔ **Planning Point:** This safe harbor is particularly effective where the FLP or LLC is being created solely for the purpose of investing in marketable securities. Many practitioners have concerns about creating these vehicles solely for the purpose of investing in marketable securities. This concern, however, ignores the many provisions in the Code and related regulations that specifically recognize investment partnerships (See IRC § 731(c) for an example). In addition, a recent Tax Court decision allowed a 40% aggregate discount for lack of marketability and minority interest with respect to a limited partnership interest in an FLP that held only marketable securities and cash (See *Dailey v. Comm'r*, T.C. Memo 2001-263).

(2)　Exception to the Diversification Rule. The exception to the diversification rule provides that if one or more partners or members transfers non-identical assets that, when taken in the aggregate, constitute an insignificant portion of the total value of the assets transferred, it will be disregarded in determining whether diversification has occurred (See Regulation § 1.351-1(c)(5)).

> **EXAMPLE:** A, B and C form an LLC. A and B each transfer $20,000 of IBM stock to the LLC, while C transfers $400 of McDonald's stock to the LLC. Because C's contribution is an insignificant portion of the assets transferred, C's participation in the transaction is disregarded. As a result, there is no diversification, and gain or loss is not recognized.

> **EXAMPLE:** A and 50 other members form an LLC. A transfers $20,000 of IBM stock to the LLC. Each of the other 50 transferors

21st Century Estate Planning:
Practical Applications
2005 Edition

©*2005 Sonnenschein Nath & Rosenthal LLP*
and Cannon Financial Institute, Inc.

- 484 -

transfers $400 of stock in various other corporations to the LLC. Although the transfers by the other 50 members may be insignificant on an individual basis, in the aggregate, they constitute a significant portion of the total assets transferred to the LLC. Accordingly, diversification is present and gain or loss will be recognized.

The above examples, which are consistent with the examples in the regulations, indicate that, if less than 1% of the assets are non-identical, the non-identical assets will be disregarded. The IRS, however, has indicated in a private letter ruling (See PLR 200006008) that transfers of non-identical assets which amount to less than 5% of the total value of the assets transferred to an LLC are disregarded in determining whether or not diversification occurred upon formation.

→ **Planning Point:** PLR 200006008 tells us that the IRS's current opinion is that a non-identical asset which amounts to less than 5% of the total value of the assets transferred to an FLP or LLC will be disregarded for purposes of determining whether or not diversification occurred. Nevertheless, prudent advisors should keep in mind that private letter rulings have no precedential value. Accordingly, if an advisor seeks certainty that a non-identical asset, representing between 0.99% (the amount approved by the examples in the regulations) and 5% (the amount approved in PLR 200006008) of the total value of the assets transferred to an FLP or LLC, will be disregarded, he or she should obtain their own private letter ruling.

2.   Avoiding the IRS's Gift on Formation Argument

The IRS has raised the argument that a gift occurs upon formation of an FLP or LLC equal to the difference between the fair market value of the assets contributed to the entity and the value of the interests received in return. In other words, the IRS argues that there is a gift equal to the amount of the valuation discount.

> **EXAMPLE:** Assume P and C create an FLP. P contributes $800,000 of assets in return for a 1% general partnership interest and a 79% limited partnership interest, while C contributes $200,000 of assets in return for a 20% limited partnership interest. An appraiser determines that a 35% discount is applicable to the interest in the partnership. Based on the discount, P's 80% interest in the FLP is worth $520,000 ($800,000 x (1-35%)). Accordingly, based on the IRS's argument, P has made a gift to C of $280,000 (*i.e.*, the difference between the assets he contributed ($800,000) and the value of the partnership assets he received in return ($520,000)).

The IRS first raised this theory in TAM 9842003. In this TAM the donor and two of the donor's children formed an FLP. The FLP's underlying property consisted of $1,740,144 of

21st Century Estate Planning:
Practical Applications
2005 Edition

©2005 Sonnenschein Nath & Rosenthal LLP
and Cannon Financial Institute, Inc.

- 485 -

securities, $253,000 in real estate and $268,463 in cash. The donor contributed approximately 99% of the property and in return received a 99% limited partnership interest. The donor's two children each contributed the balance of the property in return for 0.5% general partnership interests. Upon the donor's death, her estate valued her 99% limited partnership interest at $1,343,400, which reflected a 40% valuation discount. The IRS concluded that there was a gift upon formation equal to the amount by which the value of the property the donor transferred to the FLP exceeded the value of the limited partnership interests received in return.

The IRS's conclusion was based on IRC § 2512(b), which provides that if "property is transferred for less than an adequate and full consideration in money or money's worth, then the amount by which the value of the property exceeds the value of the consideration shall be deemed a gift...." The estate, on the other hand, argued that no gift occurred because the value of the other partners' interests in the FLP were not enhanced by the formation of the partnership (*i.e.*, each partner's net worth declined upon formation of the partnership and, as a result, there was no donee and no basis for asserting that a gift was made). The IRS, however, determined that the other partners' interests were enhanced by reason of the fact that they obtained control over the partnership assets (via the fact that they received general partnership interests), despite transferring only 1% of the underlying value of the partnership assets.

The IRS's gift on formation argument, however, ignores the fact that before IRC § 2512 can be applied to a transaction in order to impose gift tax there must first be a transfer of property. Where an FLP or LLC is established as a pro rata partnership (*i.e.*, where each partner or member receives back an interest in the entity that is proportional to the property they transferred), no transfer of property occurs on formation of the entity. Although each partner's net worth declines in value upon formation of the entity, no property is transferred to any other partner. This is evidenced by the fact that, if the partnership was liquidated immediately after creation, each partner would get back precisely what he or she transferred to the partnership. Moreover, this principle has been recognized in recent court decisions.

In *Estate of Church v. U.S.*, 85 A.F.T.R. 2d 2000-804, *aff'd by* 268 F.3d 1063 (5th Cir., 2001), the Fifth Circuit affirmed a district court decision which rejected (among other arguments) the IRS's gift on formation argument, noting that the entity was a pro rata partnership, with each partner's interest in proportion to his or her capital account. Accordingly, the court found that no one benefited from the decline in value that occurred on formation and, as a result, there was no donative transfer (despite the fact that the donor contributed the majority of the property and did not receive back a general partnership interest).

The Tax Court also rejected the IRS's gift on formation argument in *Estate of Strangi v. Comm'r*, 115 T.C. 478 (2000), *aff'd and rev'd in part by Gulig v. Comm'r*, 293 F.3d 279 (5th Cir. 2002), noting that, because the decedent retained a 99% limited partnership interest and 47% interest in the corporate general partner, "he did not transfer more than a minuscule proportion of the value that would be 'lost' on the conveyance of his assets to the partnership in exchange for a partnership interest." Although the convoluted language in the *Strangi* decision can be interpreted to mean that the Tax Court might recognize a gift on formation equal to the increase

21st Century Estate Planning:
Practical Applications
2005 Edition

©2005 Sonnenschein Nath & Rosenthal LLP
and Cannon Financial Institute, Inc.

- 486 -

in value realized by the donee (as opposed to the diminution in value of the donor's assets), the same judge who wrote the Tax Court opinion in *Strangi* also wrote the Tax Court opinion in *Estate of Jones v. Comm'r*, 116 T.C. 121 (Mar. 6, 2001). In *Jones*, the Tax Court, citing *Strangi* as precedent, noted that "[a]ll of the contributions of property were properly reflected in the capital accounts of decedent, and the value of the other partners' interests was not enhanced by the contributions of decedent," thereby rejecting the IRS's gift on formation argument (again, despite the fact that the decedent contributed the vast majority of the property and did not retain a general partnership interest).

→ **Planning Point:** Although the *Church, Strangi I* and *Jones* cases indicate that the donor can relinquish control upon formation of the entity without causing a gift, the more conservative approach is to structure the entity in a manner that does not shift control. Thus, if parent and child intend to form an FLP where the parent will contribute 99% of the property and the child 1% of the property, the parent should receive, in return, a controlling general partnership interest. To be conservative, any shift in control should be made in the future by means of a lifetime gift. To further guard against the gift on formation argument, the FLP or LLC could be structured so that the principal contributor has the ability to liquidate the entity (but see section E. above regarding the inclusion of the principal contributor's interests in his or her gross estate under IRC § 2036). Giving the principal contributor a liquidation right, however, should not be necessary to avoid the gift on formation argument and should be avoided if the FLP or LLC is intended to achieve estate tax discounts (as opposed to creating the FLP or LLC to achieve leverage in a lifetime annual exclusion gift giving program). In addition, if you give a principal contributor a liquidation right and intend to make a future transfer to eliminate the liquidation right, you could run afoul of IRC § 2704(a) (see discussion below).

EXAMPLE: P and C intend to create an FLP for various non-tax reasons and to facilitate a lifetime gift giving program of the underlying assets, which primarily consists of real estate. P contributes real estate that comprises 80% of the value of the FLP and in return receives a 0.80% general partner interest and a 79.20% limited partner interest. C contributes securities that represent 20% of the total value of the underlying assets and, in return, receives a 0.20% general partnership interest and 19.80% limited partnership interest. In addition, the partnership agreement provides that a 75% vote of the general partner interest is required to liquidate the FLP. Because the partnership is set up as a pro rata partnership and because P has retained control and has the ability to liquidate the FLP, this structure should be immune from a gift on formation argument.

21st Century Estate Planning:
Practical Applications
2005 Edition

©2005 Sonnenschein Nath & Rosenthal LLP
and Cannon Financial Institute, Inc.

- 487 -

3. Formation Issues Post-*Strangi*

The *Strangi* decision, discussed in the previous section, and other recent cases allow us to glean certain facts that the courts and the IRS deem relevant when scrutinizing FLPs and LLCs under IRC § 2036. The following is a nonexclusive list of the guidelines that practitioners and their clients should follow when forming one of these entities so as to avoid inclusion under IRC § 2036.

a. Organize and fund the entity and make gifts of interests in the entity before death is imminent. Deathbed transfers will be scrutinized closely by the IRS. Similarly, to the extent possible, avoid the use of durable powers of attorney and revocable trusts (when the grantor is incapacitated and he or she is not serving as the trustee of his or her revocable trust) to form and fund the entity (and related entities such as a corporate general partner).

b. Fund the entity with assets requiring ongoing management - such as income-producing real estate or interests in a closely held business - rather than just passive investment assets. If only passive investment assets are available, it is especially important to document the reasons for the existence of the entity, such as to provide creditor protection, to centralize investment authority or to take advantage of investment opportunities not available on a smaller scale. Once all assets are contributed to the entity, the parties should ensure that the assets owned by the entity will be able to meet the partnership's investment objectives. It may be prudent for the asset portfolio to be redesigned; there should not be a "recycling" of assets.

c. Do not transfer personal use assets to the entity. If personal assets are transferred, discontinue any personal use after the transfer of such assets to the entity.

d. Do not transfer substantially all of the donor's assets to the entity; instead, he or she should retain sufficient assets to provide support outside the entity. If the donor's support is dependent on distributions from the entity, the IRS may argue that the donor retained an income interest in the assets contributed. If children will be shareholders of the corporate general partner or member, they should contribute their own assets to the corporation. If a child cannot independently afford to contribute assets to the corporation, he or she should execute a promissory note payable to the corporation. Alternatively, the parent can gift the anticipated contribution to the child. However, such a gift should occur well in advance of the funding of the corporation and should not be for the exact amount of the anticipated contribution.

e. Have more than one donor make substantial contributions to the entity in exchange for an interest. A pooling of interests will help establish the entity as a true joint venture or enterprise and not merely a testamentary vehicle. However, pay careful attention to the investment company rules under Section 721, discussed above, to avoid gain upon formation of the entity. *Strangi* itself suggested that pooling is one method of avoiding inclusion under Section 2036(a)(2). Similarly, if possible, have more than one general partner or member corporation. If there is only one general partner or member corporation, the corporation should

21st Century Estate Planning:
Practical Applications
2005 Edition

©2005 *Sonnenschein Nath & Rosenthal LLP*
and Cannon Financial Institute, Inc.

- 488 -

be controlled by more than one individual. In fact, at least for new entities, the donor should not own any interest in the corporate general partner or member.

      f.   The donors should contribute assets to the entity with a value equal to their initial percentage ownership interests in the entity. The same should apply to shareholders contributing assets to a corporate general partner or member. With respect to the general partner or member's contribution, assets should first be contributed to the corporation, and then from the corporation to the entity.

      g.   Transfer and title all entity assets properly in the name of the entity. If real estate is contributed, the deed should be signed and recorded. Assign any leases to the entity and pay all rental income directly to the entity. If certificated securities are contributed, each certificate should be assigned, delivered to the transfer agent, and retitled in the name of the entity. If a closely held business or investment interest is contributed, comply with any applicable transfer restrictions (*e.g.*, transfer notice requirements).

      h.   If possible, more than an insignificant amount of limited partnership units should be transferred to unrelated parties.

      i.   When drafting the governing instrument, do not waive the fiduciary duties of the general partner or the member who manages the entity. In fact, ensure that there is a provision in the agreement regarding such person's affirmative fiduciary duty to the other interest holders.

      j.   The general partner or member who manages the entity should be paid a management fee based on a written management agreement between such individual and the entity. Make sure that any compensation paid is reasonable.

G. Operational Concerns

      Once you have safely navigated your client through the formation of the FLP or LLC, the hard work begins: namely, educating your client regarding the importance of operating the entity as a separate entity, which means preventing the commingling of entity assets with personal assets, the maintenance of books and records, making distributions only in accordance with entity interests, etc. Failure to respect the entity as a separate entity will risk causing inclusion of the entity in the donor's gross estate under IRC § 2036(a). This is, in many ways, a more challenging task than dealing with the technical tax aspects of creating and operating an FLP or LLC, because you lose control over the transaction when your client takes control of the operation of the entity. The following is just one example of a number of recent cases that illustrate how not to operate an FLP or LLC.

      In *Harper v. Comm'r*, T.C. Memo. 2002-121, Morton Harper set up a living trust to which he transferred substantially all of his investment assets, including brokerage accounts and a promissory note. He retained a life estate and named his two children as the remainder

21st Century Estate Planning:
Practical Applications
2005 Edition

©2005 Sonnenschein Nath & Rosenthal LLP
and Cannon Financial Institute, Inc.

- 489 -

beneficiaries of the trust. Harper and his children later formed a limited partnership. The purpose of establishing the partnership was to protect assets from creditors. Harper's children received a total of a 1% general partnership interest, and the trust received a 99% limited partnership interest for contributing the investment portfolio. Harper's son, the managing general partner, had complete management authority. The trust then transferred 60% of its limited partnership interest to the two children. Harper filed a gift tax return reporting this transfer. Upon Harper's death in 1995, the IRS determined deficiencies in the estate tax return, arguing that the full value of the limited partnership assets was includable in his gross estate.

At issue was the treatment of the partnership interests that Harper transferred to his children during his life and the interest included through the trust in his gross estate. The IRS argued that Section 2036(a) applied to include the value of the contributed property in the gross estate due to Harper's retention of the economic benefit of the assets. Furthermore, the IRS believed that even if the previous argument failed, the discounts applied to the value of the interest included in Harper's estate was excessive. The estate countered that Section 2036(a) was inapplicable because the trust unconditionally transferred the investment portfolio to the partnership, it received full consideration for the transfer, and there was no express or implied agreement that Harper would retain a right to control the property or the income generated by it. The estate further argued that the value of the partnership interest was appropriately established by their expert.

The court began by stating that the issue was whether there was an implicit agreement that decedent would retain the economic benefit of the assets he transferred. The Tax Court agreed with the IRS, concluding that the value of the property Harper contributed to the partnership was includable in his gross estate under Section 2036(a). The court pointed to the fact that because a partnership bank account was not set up initially, funds were deposited in Harper's personal account, resulting in a commingling of partnership funds with Harper's trust funds. The parties otherwise ignored the formal structure of the partnership. Harper also made disproportionate distributions to himself for personal purposes. The court also relied on the many testamentary characteristics of the partnership, stating that Harper's relationship with the assets he transferred to the partnership did not change until his death. The court essentially found that the partnership was created principally as an alternate testamentary vehicle to the trust and that the above mentioned implicit agreement existed.

The court also found that the partnership's formation fell short of meeting the bona fide sale exception to 2036(a). The court stated that for the exception to apply, two requirements must be met: (1) a bona fide, arm's-length transaction; and (2) adequate and full consideration. Because Harper did not receive any consideration from his children or the partnership and essentially stood on both sides of the transaction, this exception was not met.

See also *Estate of Abraham v. Comm'r*, T.C. Memo. 2004-39; *Estate of Strangi v. Comm'r,* T.C. Memo. 2003-145; *Kimbell v. U.S.*, 244 F.Supp.2d 700 (N.D. Tex. 2003); *Estate of Thompson v. Comm'r,* T.C. Memo. 2002-246; *Estate of Reichardt v. Comm'r*, 114 T.C. 144 (2000); *Estate of Schauerhamer v. Comm'r,* T.C. Memo 1997-242.

21st Century Estate Planning:
Practical Applications
2005 Edition

©2005 Sonnenschein Nath & Rosenthal LLP
and Cannon Financial Institute, Inc.

- 490 -

As discussed in the previous section, these cases allow us to glean certain facts that the courts and the IRS deem relevant when scrutinizing FLPs and LLCs. The following is a nonexclusive list of the guidelines that practitioners and their clients should follow when operating one of these entities so as to avoid inclusion under IRC § 2036.

a. Establish a separate bank or brokerage account for the entity and make all contributions to, and distributions from, the account. Ensure the separate accounts are continuously maintained in the name of the entity and that the assets in such accounts remain separate from non-entity accounts (such as personal or trust accounts).

b. An initial meeting of the interest holders should be held and minutes should be taken. Investment and distribution plans should be discussed. Similarly, require the general partner or the member operating the entity to (1) prepare and distribute annual financial statements, (2) calculate capital accounts annually and (3) adjust percentages of ownership for distributions and contributions. Annual meetings should be held to discuss entity business, including future investment plans.

c. Make distributions of income pro rata to all the interest holders, unless the governing instrument specifically provides for non-pro rata distributions. If additional assets are contributed to the entity, they should be made by the interest holders in accordance with their respective ownership percentages at the time of the additional contribution.

d. The governing instrument should preclude the major contributor from participating in any decisions with respect to distributions or any other major decisions that could affect the timing of distributions (*i.e.*, removing and replacing interest holders).

e. Gifts of cash to other individuals (*i.e.*, $11,000 annual exclusion gifts) should not be made immediately after distributions from the entity.

f. Signatures on all formation documents should be properly executed. Officers of the corporate partner or member should sign as such. When the president of the corporation executes a document on behalf of the partnership (acting on behalf of the corporation), the president should sign in such capacity. Trustees should also sign in their fiduciary capacity. Separate accounts should be established in the name of the partnership or LLC and the corporation.

g. Ensure that personal obligations and expenses incurred by interest holders are satisfied from such interest holder's personal, non-entity accounts.

h. If an interest holder uses any entity property for any purpose, such individual should pay fair market value rent for such use and a lease should be executed between the parties. Similarly, if the entity loans money to an interest holder, the note should be structured in an "arms-length" transaction.

21st Century Estate Planning:
Practical Applications
2005 Edition

©2005 Sonnenschein Nath & Rosenthal LLP
and Cannon Financial Institute, Inc.

- 491 -

H. IRS Attacks Under the "Business Purpose Doctrine," IRC §§ 2703 and 2704

Beginning in 1997 and continuing into 1998, the IRS in a series of technical advice memoranda began a full-scale attack on FLPs and LLCs (See TAM 9719006, 9723009, 9725002, 9730004 and 9842003). The factual scenarios in each of these TAMs involved situations where the taxpayer died shortly after creating the FLP. In attacking these transactions the IRS asserted four arguments:

- The IRS relied on the Tax Court's decision in *Estate of Murphy v. Comm'r*, T.C. Memo 1990-472, and income tax cases requiring a "business purpose" to conclude that the formation of the partnership and the subsequent transfer of partnership interests upon the death of a partner should be treated as a single testamentary transaction occurring upon the decedent's death;

- The IRS argued that (i) the property that was transferred for purposes of IRC § 2703 was the underlying partnership property that was contributed to the FLP and not the limited partnership interests that were transferred; and (ii) the safe harbor provision under IRC § 2703(b) was not met. Under this argument, if the property transferred was the underlying property, the partnership agreement itself would be an impermissible agreement under IRC § 2703(a);

- In the alternative (*i.e.*, if the property transferred was limited partnership interests), the IRS argued that (i) certain provisions in the FLP agreement constituted an impermissible restriction on the right to sell or use the partnership interests under IRC § 2703(a); and (ii) the safe harbor provision under IRC § 2703(b) was not met; and

- The IRS argued that a fixed term in the partnership agreement was an "applicable restriction" under IRC § 2704(b) that should be disregarded for valuation purposes. The agreements at issue prohibited a limited partner from withdrawing from the partnership or from demanding return of his or her capital account until the termination of the partnership. Under the IRS's argument, if the term restriction was disregarded, the partner's interests would be valued under the assumption that he or she could immediately withdraw or demand access to his or her partnership account.

The IRS has subsequently lost each of these arguments in various court cases arising between 1999 and 2001. Nevertheless, the IRS has not given up on its legal arguments and has appealed a number of the decisions in which they have lost. Accordingly, practitioners need to be aware of these arguments and should carefully plan their transaction to limit exposure to IRS attacks.

21st Century Estate Planning:
Practical Applications
2005 Edition

©2005 Sonnenschein Nath & Rosenthal LLP
and Cannon Financial Institute, Inc.

- 492 -

1. Business Purpose Doctrine

In each of the TAMs, the IRS, relying on *Murphy*, argued that the FLP should be ignored for federal tax purposes, because the formation of the entity was intended primarily for tax reduction purposes (*i.e.*, the creation of the FLP and the transfer of partnership interests was a single "testamentary transaction," causing the underlying assets to be included in the decedent's gross estate under IRC § 2033). In *Murphy* the decedent had a general power of appointment over a marital trust which held 51.45% of the stock of a corporation. Eighteen days before her death, the decedent exercised her power of appointment over the marital trust by appointing 1.76% of the stock to certain beneficiaries, thereby reducing the marital trust's interest in the corporation to 49.65% (and seemingly qualifying it for minority interest discounts). The Tax Court, however, denied the minority interest discount, noting that the "sole motive" for the transaction was tax reduction, and stating that, because nothing of substance changed as a result of the transaction, the transfer could be ignored for transfer tax purposes.

The *Murphy* case has been widely criticized by the estate planning community, because the language contained in the decision is so ambiguous that it is difficult to determine on what basis the court included the transferred assets in the decedent's estate. Regardless of the factors on which *Murphy* may have been based, one thing is clear: the *Murphy* case does not stand for the proposition that a validly created entity under state law can be disregarded. The entity in *Murphy* was not disregarded; instead, the decedent was treated as having retained control over the transferred stock (although the rationale for this conclusion is not clearly elucidated in the case). Moreover, many practitioners believe that *Murphy* was repudiated by the Tax Court's decision in *Frank Est. v. Comm'r*, T.C. Memo 1995-132, whose facts are very difficult to distinguish from those of *Murphy* (*i.e.*, there was a transfer of stock days before the decedent's death, reducing the decedent's ownership interest in the corporation from over 50% to under 50%) and, yet, the Tax Court, without even mentioning *Murphy*, ignored any motive for the transfer and found the transfer to be valid, as all corporate formalities were followed.

In addition, the IRS's argument that there must be a valid business purpose when creating an FLP or LLC in order for the entity to be respected has been rejected in recent court decisions. In *Estate of Strangi v. Comm'r*, 115 T.C. 478 (2000), *aff'd and rev'd in part by Gulig v. Comm'r*, 293 F.3d 279 (5th Cir. 2002), the decedent's son-in-law, acting under a power of attorney, formed an FLP and its corporate general partner on behalf of the decedent two months before the decedent's death. The decedent contributed the vast majority of the property to the FLP and in return received a 99% limited partnership interest and 47% of the corporate general partner, which owned the remaining 1% interest in the FLP. In response to the IRS's argument that the FLP should be disregarded due to lack of economic substance (*i.e.*, the IRS argued that the assets to be valued for estate tax purposes are the underlying assets rather than the decedent's interest in the FLP), the Tax Court stated that the FLP "was validly formed under state law. The formalities were followed and the proverbial 'i's were dotted' and 't's were crossed.' The partnership, as a legal matter, changed the relationships between decedent and his heirs and decedent and actual and potential creditors. Regardless of subjective intentions, the partnership had sufficient substance to be recognized for tax purposes. Its existence would not be disregarded by potential

21st Century Estate Planning:
Practical Applications
2005 Edition

©2005 Sonnenschein Nath & Rosenthal LLP
and Cannon Financial Institute, Inc.

- 493 -

purchasers of decedent's assets, and we do not disregard it in this case." The Tax Court in *Strangi* reached that decision despite referring to the non-tax reasons asserted for creating the FLP as "mere window dressing to conceal tax motives."

The Tax Court rejected a similar IRS argument in *Knight v. Comm'r*, 115 T.C. 506 (2000), stating that "[s]tate law determines the nature of property rights, and federal law determines the appropriate tax treatment of those rights…. The parties stipulated that the steps followed in the creation of the partnership satisfied all requirements under Texas law, and that the partnership has been a limited partnership under Texas law since it was created. Thus, the transferred interests are interests in a partnership under Texas law. Petitioners have burdened the partnership with restrictions that apparently are valid and enforceable under Texas law…. We apply the willing buyer, willing seller test to value the interests in the partnership that petitioners transferred under Texas law. We do not disregard the partnership because we have no reason to conclude from this record that a hypothetical buyer or seller would disregard it."

In addition, the court in *Estate of Church v. U.S.*, 85 A.F.T.R. 2d 2000-804, *aff'd by* 268 F.3d 1063 (5th Cir. 2001), respected the non-tax reasons set forth for creating the FLP (*i.e.*, centralized management of the ranch that was contributed to the partnership and creditor protection), despite the fact that the FLP was created two days before the decedent's death.

→ **Planning Point:** The *Strangi* and *Knight* cases illustrate that the courts will respect an entity validly created in accordance with state law, even if the court questions the non-tax reasons set forth for creating the entity. This is the correct decision in light of the Supreme Court's declaration in *Morgan v. Commissioner*, 309 U.S. 78 (1940), that "[s]tate law creates legal interests and rights. The federal revenue acts designate what interests or rights, so created, shall be taxed." Thus, applying this doctrine in the estate and gift tax context, once a court determines that an FLP or LLC was validly formed under state law, the court is bound by *Morgan* to apply the estate or gift tax to the asset transferred (*i.e.*, the limited partnership interest or membership interest, rather than the underlying assets of the entity). Any attack on a validly formed FLP or LLC should be based on general valuation principles, rather than attempting to disregard an entity that was validly created under state law. Nevertheless, prudent practitioners will continue to emphasize the non-tax reasons for creating these entities, thereby giving courts, like the court in *Church*, additional reasons to rule for the taxpayer.

2.   IRS Attacks Under IRC § 2703

Despite the fact that the legislative history of IRC § 2703 indicates that this Section should have limited applicability in the partnership context, the IRS used this Code section as its primary means of attack in the series of TAMs that were issued in 1997 and 1998.

21st Century Estate Planning:
Practical Applications
2005 Edition

©2005 Sonnenschein Nath & Rosenthal LLP
and Cannon Financial Institute, Inc.

- 494 -

IRC § 2703(a) provides that the value of any property shall be determined without regard to (1) any option, agreement or other right to acquire or use the property at a price less than the fair market value of the property (without regard to such option, agreement, or right) or (2) any restriction on the right to sell or use such property. IRC § 2703(b), on the other hand, provides that IRC § 2703(a) shall not apply to any option, agreement, right or restriction that meets each of the following requirements: (i) it is a bona fide business arrangement; (ii) it is not a device to transfer such property to members of the decedent's family for less than full and adequate consideration in money or money's worth; and (iii) its terms are comparable to similar arrangements entered into by persons in arm's length transactions.

In the TAMs referred to above, the IRS assessed estate or gift tax on the entity's underlying assets, stating that the property transferred for purposes of IRC § 2703 was the FLP's or LLC's underlying assets, rather than the limited partnership or member interests in the entity itself. Under the IRS's interpretation, if the property transferred was the underlying property, IRC § 2703(a) would require those assets to be valued without regard to the partnership or operating agreement (and thus the restrictions contained therein). The IRS also stated in the TAMs that, even if the property that was transferred was the interests in the entity (and not the underlying assets), certain provisions in partnership and operating agreements constitute an impermissible restriction on the right to sell or use the partnership interests under IRC § 2703(a).

The *Church* court and the *Strangi* court, however, rejected the IRS's first argument, noting that there is neither a statutory nor a regulatory basis for the IRS's interpretation that the property transferred was the partnership's underlying assets (rather than the partnership interests). The *Church* court also rejected the IRS's second argument, noting that the legislative history indicates that IRC § 2703 was intended to target the use of options and buy-sell agreements to artificially reduce the value of an asset. The court noted that while restrictions in option and buy-sell agreements are not inherent components of the property interest itself (and, thus, artificially reduced value), the restrictions in partnership and operating agreements, on the other hand, are "part and parcel" of the property interest created upon formation of the entity, and, as a result, are not the type of restrictions that IRC § 2703 was designed to target.

→ **Planning Point:** The *Church* and *Strangi* decisions likely spell the death knell for the IRS's IRC § 2703 arguments in the FLP and LLC context. The legislative history clearly indicates that IRC § 2703 was added to target specific abuses and these cases demonstrate that the courts will, as they should, narrowly construe the provisions of IRC § 2703.

3. IRS Attacks Under IRC § 2704

Congress enacted IRC § 2704 to address perceived valuation abuses resulting from the lapse of voting or liquidation rights. Specifically, IRC § 2704 was the legislative response to the Tax Court's decision in *Estate of Harrison v. Comm'r*, T.C. Memo 1987-8. In *Harrison*, the decedent, less than 6 months before his death, contributed property worth $59,476,523 to an FLP in return for a 1% general partnership interest and 77.8% limited partnership interest. The

21st Century Estate Planning:
Practical Applications
2005 Edition

©2005 Sonnenschein Nath & Rosenthal LLP
and Cannon Financial Institute, Inc.

- 495 -

decedent's two sons each contributed $7,981,351 to the partnership in exchange for the remaining 21.2% general partnership interests. After decedent's death, his sons exercised options to purchase the decedent's general partnership interest for $757,116 and agreed to continue the partnership. The IRS argued that the decedent's limited partnership interest should be valued at $59,555,020, which was 77.8% of the value of the entire partnership as of the decedent's date of death. The decedent's estate, on the other hand, argued that the value of the limited partnership interests was $33,000,000, the stipulated value of the limited partnership interest the moment it passed from the decedent to his estate. The difference, $26,555,020, was due entirely to the decedent's right, as general partner, immediately before death to dissolve and liquidate the partnership (a right both parties agreed did not pass to his estate), and thereby realize his proportionate value in the FLP. Because the liquidation right lapsed at death, the Tax Court ruled in favor of the estate.

To prevent the type of valuation abuse that occurred in *Harrison*, Congress enacted IRC § 2704(a) to prevent taxpayers from impermissibly structuring a transaction so that a voting or liquidation right exists immediately before death (thereby reducing the asset's value for estate and gift tax purposes) but then "vanishes" at the time of the transfer. Similarly, Congress enacted IRC § 2704(b) to allow the IRS, under certain circumstances, to disregard certain restrictions on a taxpayer's power to liquidate a corporation or partnership (including an LLC).

    a. IRC § 2704(a): Treatment of Lapsed Voting or Liquidation Rights. The IRS has not launched an attack against FLPs and LLCs under IRC § 2704(a). Nevertheless, a thorough understanding of this Section is necessary to thwart potential IRS arguments. Under IRC § 2704(a), whenever there is a lapse of a voting or a liquidation right in a corporation or partnership (including an LLC) and the individual holding such right, together with members of his or her family, has control both before and after the lapse, the lapse will be treated as a transfer for estate and gift tax purposes. The value of the transfer is the excess of the value of all interests in the entity held by the individual immediately before the lapse over the value of such interests after the lapse.

> **EXAMPLE:** If IRC § 2704(a) had been in effect at the time of the *Harrison* case, the deemed transfer under IRC § 2704(a) would have been $26,555,020, the difference between the value of the decedent's interest in the FLP immediately before and after the lapse of his liquidation right.

> **EXAMPLE:** D and his two children, A and B, are partners in FLP. Each has a 3 1/3% general partnership interest and a 30% limited partnership interest. The partnership is to last 65 years, unless a majority of the general partners agree to terminate the partnership sooner (this provision is the default provision under state law). The agreement also provides that if any general partner attempts to transfer his or her interest, that general partnership interest will be converted to a limited partnership interest. D dies leaving his limited partnership

21st Century Estate Planning:
Practical Applications
2005 Edition

©2005 Sonnenschein Nath & Rosenthal LLP
and Cannon Financial Institute, Inc.

- 496 -

interest to his spouse. IRC § 2704(a) should not apply to this transaction, because prior to D's death, D did not have the ability to unilaterally liquidate the partnership. Accordingly, there was no lapse of a liquidation right under IRC § 2704(a).

Thus, as the above example illustrates, IRC § 2704(a) will not apply where the transferor of an interest in an FLP or LLC does not have the unilateral right to liquidate the entity because no lapse can occur upon the transfer. Regulation § 2704-1(c)(1) provides a further limitation on the application of IRC § 2704(a), as it provides that IRC § 2704(a) does not apply if the voting or liquidation right with respect to the transferred interest is not restricted or eliminated as a result of the transfer.

> **EXAMPLE:** D owns 84% of the single outstanding class of stock of Corporation Y. The by-laws require at least 70% of the vote to liquidate Y. D gives one-half of his stock to his three children (*i.e.,* 14% to each). IRC § 2704(a) does not apply to the loss of D's ability to liquidate Y, because the voting rights with respect to the corporation are not restricted or eliminated by the transfer (See Example 4 of Regulation § 2704-1(f)).

The above example clearly illustrates that IRC § 2704(a) does not apply to a transfer of a voting or liquidation right which does not terminate the voting power of the transferred shares.

➔ **Planning Point:** As discussed above, a conservative approach to avoiding the IRS's gift on formation argument is to structure the transaction so that the principal contributor has the power to liquidate the FLP or LLC. If you intend to achieve discounts for estate tax purposes (as opposed to discounts for gift tax purposes), however, you will need to make a future transfer that eliminates this liquidation power. A stumbling block, however, is that, to avoid a lapse, the transferee must immediately become a general partner or managing member; however, under state law a transferee of a general or limited partnership interest typically becomes an assignee, and an assignee does not have the rights of a partner, thereby causing a lapse of the transferred interest. Thus, if the FLP/LLC is intended to achieve discounts for estate tax (rather than strictly for gift tax) purposes, no partner should have the unilateral right to liquidate the partnership or his or her partnership interest.

Treas. Reg. § 2704-1(c)(1) also provides that, if a transfer results in the elimination of the transferor's ability to compel the entity to acquire an interest that is subordinate to the transferred interest, the transfer is a lapse of a liquidation right with respect to the subordinate interest. Accordingly, if a limited partnership interest is treated as a subordinate interest to a general partnership interest, there could be a lapse when a person transfers a general partnership interest and retains a limited partnership interest (the lapse would occur with respect to the retained

21st Century Estate Planning:
Practical Applications
2005 Edition

©2005 Sonnenschein Nath & Rosenthal LLP
and Cannon Financial Institute, Inc.

- 497 -

subordinate interest), because the transfer of the general partnership interest could result in the elimination of the transferor's ability to compel the entity to acquire a limited partnership interest (*i.e.*, a subordinate interest). An interest is subordinate if there is a senior equity interest that carries a right to distribution of income or capital that is preferred to the rights of the subordinate interest.

➔ **Planning Point:** You can avoid having a limited partnership interest treated as a subordinate interest simply by providing in the partnership agreement that a general partnership interest does not have a preferred right to distributions. Accordingly, a partner's transfer of a general partnership interest while retaining a limited partnership interest (with no lapse of the general partner's powers in the hands of the transferee) should not be a lapse under IRC § 2704(a) in a typical pro rata limited partnership where the items of income, deduction, loss and credit are allocated among partners based on their capital accounts.

b. IRC § 2704(b): Certain Restrictions on Liquidation Disregarded. While the IRS has not launched an offensive against FLPs and LLCs under IRC § 2704(a), IRC § 2704(b), on the other hand, has proven to be fertile ground for IRS attacks. IRC § 2704(b) and the regulations thereunder provide that if

(a) there is a transfer of an interest in a corporation or partnership (including an LLC) to (or for the benefit of) a member of the transferor's family;

(b) the transferor and members of the transferor's family hold, immediately before the transfer, control of the entity; and

(c) after the transfer, either (i) the "applicable restriction" lapses, in whole or in part, or (ii) the transferor or any member of the transferor's family, either alone or collectively, has the right to remove, in whole or in part, the "applicable restriction,"

then any "applicable restriction" is to be disregarded in determining the value of the transferred interest. An "applicable restriction" is any restriction that (i) effectively limits the ability of the corporation or partnership to liquidate and (ii) is more restrictive than the limitations that would generally apply under state law in the absence of the restrictions in the governing instrument.

EXAMPLE: Family creates an FLP. The partnership agreement provides that there must be unanimous consent of all of the partners to liquidate the partnership, while state law, on the other hand, requires only partners owning at least 75% of the partnership interests to consent to the liquidation of the FLP. Because the agreement's restriction on liquidation is more restrictive than the default provision under state law, the liquidation restriction may be an "applicable restriction" under IRC § 2704(b).

21st Century Estate Planning:
Practical Applications
2005 Edition

©2005 Sonnenschein Nath & Rosenthal LLP
and Cannon Financial Institute, Inc.

- 498 -

In the series of TAMs referred to above, the IRS argued that the fixed term used in each of the partnership agreements constituted an "applicable restriction" under IRC § 2704(b) that should be disregarded for valuation purposes. The agreements in the TAMs prohibited a limited partner from withdrawing from the partnership or from demanding return of his or her capital account until the termination of the partnership, while, in each case, the state law default provisions stated that a limited partner could withdraw upon not less than six months' prior written notice. Under the IRS's argument, if the term restrictions were disregarded, the partner's interest would be valued as if he or she could immediately withdraw or demand access to his or her partnership account (thereby eliminating the valuation discounts).

The IRS, however, lost this argument in a series of recent Tax Court cases. The first Tax Court case to address the issue was *Kerr v. Comm'r*, 292 F.3d 490 (5th Cir. 2002). In 1993, Blaine and Mildred Kerr (the taxpayers) and their children formed two family limited partnerships under Texas law: the KIL partnership and the KFLP partnership. The taxpayers contributed all the capital and then transferred interests to their children. In KFLP, the taxpayers and their children were general partners and the taxpayers were limited partners. In KIL, KFLP was the general partner while taxpayers and their children were limited partners. The University of Texas later received a limited partnership interest in both partnerships. In 1994, the taxpayers each created a GRAT and transferred to it a 44.5% limited partnership interest in KFLP. The partnership agreements said that the partnerships would dissolve and liquidate in 2043 by agreement of all partners or on the occurrence of certain narrowly defined acts of dissolution, whichever occurred earlier. No limited partner could withdraw from the partnership before it dissolves and liquidates.

The taxpayers reported all their transfers on their 1994 and 1995 gift tax returns and valued the interests by applying marketability discounts reflecting the partnership agreements' restrictions on liquidation. The taxpayers considered the interests transferred to the GRATs to be assignee interests only. The taxpayers were seeking through this characterization to avoid the valuation rules of IRC § 2704(b). The IRS issued a deficiency notice, arguing that all the interests transferred were subject to IRC § 2704(b), and, thus, the discount should not have reduced their value.

The Tax Court ruled that the interests transferred to the GRATs were partnership interests and not assignee interests. The court found, however, that the partnership agreement restrictions were not applicable restrictions, as they were no more restrictive than the limitations imposed under Texas law. On appeal, the U.S. Court of Appeals for the Fifth Circuit affirmed the Tax Court but relied on a different provision of IRC § 2704(b). The Fifth Circuit based its decision on IRC § 2704(b)(2)(B), which states that an applicable restriction is a restriction that lapses or can be removed by the family after the transfer of the interest. Because lapsing of the interest was not a consideration, the court considered the "removability" of the restriction. The University of Texas, as a limited partner, could oppose the removal of the restrictions. The IRS argued that, because the University of Texas would have no reason to oppose the removal of the restrictions in the partnership agreement, the partnership restrictions should be treated as capable

21st Century Estate Planning:
Practical Applications
2005 Edition

©*2005 Sonnenschein Nath & Rosenthal LLP*
and Cannon Financial Institute, Inc.

- 499 -

of being removed by the Kerr family. In fact, the evidence indicated that the University of Texas would not oppose removal of the restrictions.

Noting that Treas. Reg. § 2704(b)(2)(B)(ii) requires that the transferor or family member must have the right to remove the restriction, the Fifth Circuit then stated that no exception to this regulation exists that would permit the court to disregard the nonfamily partners who would likely consent to removal of a restriction. Thus, the court concluded that the probable consent of the nonfamily partner did not fulfill the requirement that the family be able to remove the restriction on its own. The restrictions were thus not applicable restrictions, and the taxpayers could apply the discounts.

In *Estate of Harper v. Comm'r*, T.C. Memo 2000-202, the Tax Court, in response to the same argument (*i.e.*, that the prohibition against withdrawal was an applicable restriction within the meaning of IRC § 2704(b) -- except that it was made under California law), reached the same conclusion. The court in *Harper* noted that there was no substantial differences between the partnership agreements in *Kerr* and *Harper* or between California law and Texas law with respect to the liquidation of a limited partnership. Thus, the Tax Court, citing *Kerr* as precedent, found that the prohibition against withdrawal was not an applicable restriction under IRC § 2704(b), because it is a restriction on withdrawal, not liquidation.

The Tax Court, again citing *Kerr*, reached similar conclusions in response to the same argument in *Knight v. Comm'r*, 115 T.C. 506 (2000), and in *Estate of Jones v. Comm'r*, 116 T.C. No. 11 (2001).

➔ **Planning Point:** In response to IRS attacks on FLPs under IRC § 2704(b), a number of states have changed their limited partnership acts to provide that a limited partner may withdraw from a limited partnership only at the time or upon the occurrence of events specified in writing in the partnership agreement. These statutes thwart the IRC § 2704(b) arguments raised by the IRS in *Kerr, Harper, Knight* and *Jones*. Accordingly, practitioners, when forming an FLP or LLC, should select a state that has favorable state law default provisions concerning the partnership term and withdrawal rights in order to avoid the IRS's recent attacks under IRC § 2704(b).

I. Avoiding IRS Attacks on Annual Gift Tax Exclusion for Gifts of FLP or Family LLC Interests

The IRS has, in a number of rulings, stated that transfers of limited partnership interests qualify for the gift tax annual exclusion. In those rulings, the IRS has relied on the fiduciary duty that general partners owe to the limited partners and the ability of limited partners to dispose of their interests (see e.g., PLR 9415007). Nevertheless, having lost cases involving (i) their gift on formation argument, (ii) business purpose doctrine, (iii) arguments under IRC § 2703, (iv) arguments under IRC § 2704 and (v) many cases involving valuation discounts, the

21st Century Estate Planning:
Practical Applications
2005 Edition

©2005 Sonnenschein Nath & Rosenthal LLP
and Cannon Financial Institute, Inc.

- 500 -

IRS has "circled the wagons" and is now trying to disallow the gift tax annual exclusion in connection with the transfer of interests in FLPs and LLCs. In a recent case, *Hackl v. Comm'r*, 335 F.3d 664 (7th Cir. 2003), the U.S. Court of Appeals for the Seventh Circuit ruled in favor of the IRS and held that, under the facts at issue, a gift of units in an LLC was ineligible for the gift tax annual exclusion.

In 1995, A.J. and Christine Hackl formed Treeco, a limited liability company that A.J. formed to hold and operate tree-farming properties. The operating agreement of the LLC vested A.J. with management authority for life. When A.J. bought the properties, he sought to provide investment diversification in the form of long-term growth and future income. The land he bought had little or no salable timber. At the time of the purchase, A.J. correctly projected that Treeco and several successor entities would generate losses and make no distributions for many years.

The LLC operating agreement vested control of the business in the manager, and A.J. was named as the initial manager of the LLC. The operating agreement also provided that (i) before dissolution "no Member shall have the right to withdraw the Member's Capital Contribution, except as may be approved by the Manager," (ii) "No Member shall be entitled to transfer, assign, convey, sell, encumber or in any way alienate all or any part of the Member's interest except with the prior written consent of the Manger, which consent may be given or withheld, conditioned or delayed as the Manger may determine in the Manger's sole discretion" and (iii) after the tenure of A.J. as manager, voting members could dissolve the company by an 80% majority vote.

In 1995 and 1996, A.J. and his wife gave interests in Treeco to family members. The couple reported the gifts on their gift tax returns and elected to treat them as made one-half by each under Section 2513. They also treated the gifts as qualifying for the $10,000 gift tax annual exclusion under Section 2503(b). The IRS disallowed the exclusions for 1996.

At issue was whether the transfers of LLC interests amounted to gifts of a present or future interest. The Tax Court concluded that the donees did not possess a present interest and thus the gifts were not excluded under Section 2503(b).

The Seventh Circuit also concluded that the transfers of Treeco interests were gifts of future interests. In reaching this conclusion, the court pointed to Treeco's operating agreement, which clearly foreclosed the donee's ability to realize any substantial present economic benefit. Although the voting shares that the Hackls gave away had the same legal rights as those that they retained, Treeco's restrictions on the transferability of the shares meant that they were essentially without immediate value to the donees. While a shareholder might violate the agreement and sell his or her shares without the manager's approval to a transferee who would then not have any membership or voting rights, the court reasoned that this possibility could hardly be called a substantial economic benefit. Thus, the court concluded that the Hackl's gifts, while outright, were not gifts of present interests.

21st Century Estate Planning:
Practical Applications
2005 Edition

©2005 Sonnenschein Nath & Rosenthal LLP
and Cannon Financial Institute, Inc.

- 501 -

→ **Planning Point:** One way for clients to avoid the result in *Hackl* is to give the donee the unilateral right to sell his or her entire interest to third parties, subject to a right of first refusal by the entity and/or other interest holders to purchase the interest at the same price and terms as a bona fide offer from a third party. Also, the business manager's discretion to retain funds can be limited to the needs of the business with the balance of the funds being distributed to the interest holders. Alternatively, each donee could be given the right to withdraw assets from the entity (as opposed to interests in the entity) in the governing instrument, similar to a Crummey withdrawal right. The right can be limited to the fair market value of the gifted interest and be available only for a limited period of time. Although such a provision might reduce the valuation discount, it should foreclose any argument that the donee does not have the right to the immediate use, possession and enjoyment of the property in the economic sense.

J. Income Tax Provisions Entities Taxed as Partnerships

Although a detailed discussion of the income taxation of partnerships is beyond the scope of this chapter, the following material (in addition to the investment company rules under IRC § 721(b) discussed above) is intended to guide practitioners to some of the typical income tax provisions that their clients may encounter while operating an FLP or LLC.

1. Taxation of the Entity

Unlike a corporation, in which the corporation pays federal income tax at the corporate level and the shareholders are again taxed on the individual level, the partners of an FLP and the members of an LLC are subject to federal income tax only at the individual level. Partnerships do not pay federal income tax. Instead, they "pass-through" all taxable items to their partners, who are then obligated to report such times on their personal income tax return and to pay any federal income tax due. Income and loss are taxed to the partners or members (whether or not they actually receive a distribution) in proportion to their interest in the FLP or LLC. Some states, however, impose a state income tax on the partnership entity itself.

→ **Planning Point:** When selecting a state in which to form an FLP or LLC, practitioners should be sure to check whether or not the state imposes a state income tax on the partnership itself. All other things being equal, practitioners will typically want to select a state that does not impose a separate state income tax on the partnership entity.

2. Family Partnership Rules

Under the "family partnership rules" of IRC § 704(e), a person to whom a partnership interest is transferred by gift will not be recognized for income tax purposes (*i.e.*, income will instead be taxed to the donor) unless certain requirements are met. An FLP or LLC should be

21st Century Estate Planning:
Practical Applications
2005 Edition

©2005 Sonnenschein Nath & Rosenthal LLP
and Cannon Financial Institute, Inc.

- 502 -

able to satisfy these requirements provided there are at least some regular distributions, all formalities are observed, and any gifts of partnership interests are made either outright to adult donees or to a trust or Uniform Transfers to Minors Act account that is not controlled by the donor.

3. Allocation of Built-in Gain or Loss on Contribution

Income or loss attributable to appreciation or depreciation existing when property is contributed to the FLP or LLC is allocated to the contributing partner or member under IRC § 704(c).

4. Loss Limitations

Tax losses are typically allocated to limited partners only to the extent of their capital accounts, with the balance being allocated to the general partners. Subsequent income is allocated first to the general partners, to the extent of prior losses (See IRC § 465 "at risk limitations").

5. In-Kind Distributions

Distributions of assets (other than cash, and, in certain cases, marketable securities) upon liquidation or otherwise are generally tax-free to the extent the property distributed does not exceed the distributee partner's basis in his or her partnership interest. Gain will not be recognized by a partner upon the distribution of marketable securities by an "investment partnership," which generally means a partnership that has never engaged in a trade or business and substantially all of the assets of which have always consisted of money, stocks, bonds, derivatives and certain similar other investments (See IRC § 731(c)(3)(A)(iii) and (C)(i)). Also, gain generally will not be recognized upon distribution of marketable securities if a partner receives only his or her pro rata share of such securities held by the partnership.

6. Basis Adjustment

Under partnership tax rules (which also apply to LLCs that are taxed as partnerships), each partner has a basis in the partner's partnership interest ("outside basis") and a share of the partnership's basis in the property owned by the partnership ("inside basis"). If a partner dies, the partner's outside basis will be stepped-up to fair market value. The partner's inside basis, on the other hand, will only receive a step-up in basis if an election is made under IRC § 754. Generally, the election will be made if the basis of the deceased partner's interest in the partnership is higher than a pro rata portion of the partnership assets attributed thereto. The result of this election will be to increase the basis of the partnership assets. The tax items attributable to such increase will generally be allocated to the transferees of the deceased partner's partnership interest.

> **EXAMPLE:** H and W each own 50% of a piece of real estate that they contribute to an FLP. The tax basis of the real estate is

21st Century Estate Planning:
Practical Applications
2005 Edition

©2005 Sonnenschein Nath & Rosenthal LLP
and Cannon Financial Institute, Inc.

- 503 -

$1,000,000. Thus, each partner has an inside basis of $500,000 and an outside basis of $500,000. H dies and his partnership interest is valued at $1,200,000 for estate tax purposes. H's estate's outside basis is $1,200,000. If an IRC § 754 election is made, H's estate's inside basis also becomes $1,200,000.

7. Anti-Abuse Regulations Under IRC § 701

Under the "Anti-Abuse" Regulations, the IRS may attempt to re-characterize a partnership for income tax purposes under certain circumstances. These regulations apply only for income tax purposes (*i.e.,* not for estate and gift tax purposes). As long as an FLP or LLC is managed in accordance with all formalities, the entity should be able to avoid these rules.

8. Disguised Sale Rules

IRC § 707(a)(2)(B) is designed to prevent the sale of property between a partner and partnership from being structured as a nontaxable contribution and distribution under IRC § 721 and § 731. IRC § 707(a)(2)(B) should not be a problem if distributions are limited to "operating cash flow" under Treas. Reg. § 1.707-4(b) or if contributions and distributions are more than two years apart (See Treas. Reg. § 1.707-3(d)).

When first enacted, IRC § 704(c) did not apply to distributions of contributed property. As a result, a contributing partner could avoid an allocation of pre-contribution gain or loss if the partnership distributed the contributed property to another partner instead of selling the property. Neither the partnership nor the contributing partner normally would recognize gain or loss on the distribution, and built-in gain often was shifted to the distributee partner. To prevent this type of income shifting, IRC § 704(c)(1)(B) provides that, if property contributed by a partner is distributed to another partner within seven years of its contribution, the contributing partner must recognize gain or loss from the sale or exchange of the property in an amount equal to the gain or loss that would have been allocated to that partner under IRC § 704(c)(1)(A). Practitioners should be cognizant of this rule to make sure they do not inadvertently run afoul of the rule.

IRC § 737 was designed to thwart transactions where a partner contributes appreciated property to a partnership and later receives a distribution of other property, with the partnership retaining the contributed property. The concern was that, under the normal contribution and distribution rules, a contributing partner would be able to avoid recognition of gain on a swap of properties when a similar transaction outside the partnership would not have qualified for non-recognition. Under IRC § 737, a contributing partner will recognize gain if the partner contributes appreciated property to a partnership and within seven years of the contribution receives property other than money as a distribution from the partnership. The gain will be recognized to the extent the value of other property distributed to the partner by the FLP or LLC exceeds the partner's outside basis (*i.e.*, the partner's basis in his or her partnership interest).

21st Century Estate Planning:
Practical Applications
2005 Edition

©2005 Sonnenschein Nath & Rosenthal LLP
and Cannon Financial Institute, Inc.

- 504 -

➔ **Planning Point:** IRC § 737 will not apply (even if the contribution and distribution occur within the seven-year time period) if the distributed property was contributed by the partner to whom it is distributed.

21st Century Estate Planning:
Practical Applications
2005 Edition

©2005 Sonnenschein Nath & Rosenthal LLP
and Cannon Financial Institute, Inc.

- 505 -

Chapter XV
Bibliography

Ronald D. Aucutt, "Valuation Developments Highlight the Importance of Appraisals," *Est. Plan.* (July 2001).

Cannon Financial Institute, Inc. & Sonnenschein Nath & Rosenthal LLP, "Gifting of Significant Amounts Without Taxation," The 2003 Estate Planning Teleconference Series With Roy M. Adams (Dec. 2003).

Jerald David August and Adi Rappoport, "Recent Decisions Frustrate Service's Efforts to Challenge FLPs," *Est. Plan.* (November 2000).

John A. Bogdanski, "Closely Held Businesses and Valuation - Family Limited Partnerships: The Open Issues," *Est. Plan.* (June 2001).

Richard L. Dees, "Now That the Monster Is Dead, Can You Avoid the Hot Seat? The Cold Facts of Partnership Freezes Under Chapter 14," *Taxes* (December 1993).

John D. English, "Family Limited Partnerships vs. Limited Liability Companies: Which to Use for Estate Planning Purposes," *Illinois Institute for Continuing Legal Education 41*[st] *Annual Estate Planning Short Course* (1998).

Owen G. Fiore, "Coping with Continuing Uncertainty in FLP/LLC-Based Valuation Discount Strategies," *ACTEC Journal* (2001).

Lance S. Hall, "The Current State of FLP Valuation Discounts," *Tr. & Est.* (December 2001).

Alan S. Halperin, "Discount Shopping as Family Limited Partnerships Become Retail," *Tax Mgmt. Est. Gifts & Tr. J.* (May 10, 2001).

A. Kel Long, III, "Statutory Freeze Partnerships: A Useful Estate Planning Technique," *Est. Plan.* (February 2001).

Louis A. Mezzullo, 812 T.M., *Family Limited Partnerships and Limited Liability Companies*.

Michael D. Mulligan, "Dealing with the IRS's Arguments Against Family Limited Partnerships," *Est. Plan.* (June 1999).

David Pratt, "Bad Facts Are Making Bad Law: Putting Our Clients in a Defensive Posture in Order to Avoid a Successful IRS Attach Under Section 2036," Meeting of the Florida Fellows of the American College of Trust and Estate Counsel (Aug. 8, 2003).

John W. Porter, "Defending the Family Limited Partnership: Litigation Perspective; IRS Claims, Taxpayer Defenses, Use of Experts, Discovery and Privilege; How to Prepare at the Estate

21st Century Estate Planning:
Practical Applications
2005 Edition

©*2005 Sonnenschein Nath & Rosenthal LLP*
and Cannon Financial Institute, Inc.

- 506 -

Planning Level for Disputes with the IRS," *27ʰ Annual Notre Dame Tax & Est. Plan. Inst.* (September 20-21, 2001).

Igor Potym, "Technical Arguments of Internal Revenue Service and Arsenal of Attack: The Partnership Agreement," *Using Pro Rata Partnerships for Advanced Estate Planning Purposes: A Practitioner's Guide*, Illinois Institute of Continuing Legal Education (1999).

Arthur D. Sederbaum, Esq., "Family Limited Partnerships: The Latest Cases," *Tax Mgmt. Memo.* (May 2001).

Howard M. Zaritsky and Ronald D. Aucutt, *Structuring Estate Freezes*, Warren Gorham & Lamont (2ⁿᵈ ed.).

21st Century Estate Planning:
Practical Applications
2005 Edition

©2005 Sonnenschein Nath & Rosenthal LLP
and Cannon Financial Institute, Inc.

- 507 -

XVI. CHARITABLE GIVING

A. Introduction

The charitable deduction is allowed by three separate areas of the Internal Revenue Code: the income tax, Internal Revenue Code ("IRC") §§ 170 and 642(c); the estate tax, IRC § 2055; and the gift tax, IRC § 2522. Although these Sections cover the same basic areas, there are differences among them. Therefore, one must carefully review these Sections to determine whether contributions to an organization will qualify for the desired deductions. If the donee organization qualifies under the appropriate Sections, lifetime gifts that meet the requirements of both the income and gift tax provisions will be entitled to both an income tax and a gift tax charitable deduction, while gifts at death will be entitled to an estate tax deduction.

This chapter will address the basic rules for qualifying a transfer for an income, gift and estate tax charitable deduction, will illustrate how the charitable deduction is calculated and will review several charitable planning techniques ranging from outright gifts to the more complex charitable family limited partnership. Along the way, this chapter will discuss the following topics:

- The percentage and valuation limitations that affect the income tax charitable deduction and the income tax substantiation rules;
- Outright gifts to public charities, private foundations, donor advised funds, and charitable gift annuities; and
- Restrictions on split-interest trusts, which include charitable remainder trusts and charitable lead trusts, and the requirements for qualifying such trusts for the charitable deduction.

B. Income Tax Charitable Deduction

For federal income tax purposes, an individual who itemizes deductions is allowed a charitable deduction for gifts to charitable organizations if the requirements of IRC § 170 are met. IRC § 170 sets forth the types of organizations to which deductible contributions may be made, the types of property that will qualify for an income tax deduction, the percentage limitations on income tax deductions, and the valuation rules for determining the deductible amount. Generally, any gift of money, property (*e.g.*, stock, real estate, tangible personal property) or a right with value qualifies as a charitable gift. If a donor receives value in return (*e.g.*, dinner or a prize), the contribution may not be wholly deductible.

1. Organizations for Which an Income Tax Deduction is Permitted

Generally, contributions to an organization organized and operated exclusively for charitable, scientific, educational, literary or religious purposes are deductible for federal income tax purposes. IRC § 170(c)(2)(B). Specifically, under IRC § 170(c), an income tax deduction is allowed for transfers to the following types of recipients:

21st Century Estate Planning:
Practical Applications
2005 Edition

©2005 Sonnenschein Nath & Rosenthal LLP
and Cannon Financial Institute, Inc.

- 508 -

- IRC § 501(c)(3) corporations and trusts organized and operated exclusively for religious, charitable, scientific, literary or educational purposes, no part of the net earnings of which inures to the benefit of a private individual, and that do not attempt to influence elections and are not substantially engaged in influencing legislation;
- Federal government, state government or subdivisions thereof, if the contribution is made for exclusively public purposes;
- IRC § 501(c)(3) fraternal or veterans organizations; and
- Cemetery corporations.

The income tax deduction is limited to gifts to domestic organizations. However, gifts to a foreign organization for which an income tax deduction is desired may be made to a "Friends of" domestic organization.

Contributions to organizations that have certain discriminatory policies or engage in certain activities, such as gifts to organizations with racially discriminatory policies or to an organization a substantial portion of whose activities is participating in any political campaign, carrying on propaganda, or otherwise attempting to influence legislation, are not deductible. IRC § 170(c)(2)(D); Treas. Reg. § 1.170A-1(j).

2. Gifts of Partial Interests

As a general rule, gifts of partial interests in property are not deductible for federal income tax purposes. A partial interest is any interest in property that consists of less than the donor's entire interest in the property. IRC § 170(f)(3)(A); Treas. Reg. § 1.170A-7(a)(1). For example, the right to use the property is a gift of a partial interest. *Id.*

> **EXAMPLE:** Donor owns a building and allows a charity to use one floor of the building rent-free for administrative purposes. Donor's gift of the right to use the space is a gift of a partial interest that is not deductible.

a. **Partial Interest Gifts Not in Trust**. The general rule is subject to several exceptions, the application of which depends on whether the gift of the partial interest is outright or in trust. For example, an outright gift of a donor's entire interest in property (*e.g.*, a life estate or a remainder interest), even if it is a partial interest in the property, will be deductible. Treas. Reg. § 1.170A-7(a)(2)(i).

> **EXAMPLE:** Donor owns the remainder interest in stock while another party owns the right to the income from the stock for life. If Donor contributes her remainder interest to charity, she has made a deductible contribution.

21st Century Estate Planning:
Practical Applications
2005 Edition

©2005 Sonnenschein Nath & Rosenthal LLP
and Cannon Financial Institute, Inc.

- 509 -

Another exception exists for the contribution not in trust of a remainder interest in a personal residence or a farm if the remainder interest is not the donor's entire interest in the property. IRC § 170(f)(3)(B)(i). "Personal residence" includes any property used by the donor as a personal residence and is not limited to the donor's principal residence. Treas. Reg. § 1.170A-7(b)(3).

> **EXAMPLE:** Donor transfers to charity the remainder interest in his personal residence, retaining the right to use the residence during his life. Donor is entitled to a deduction for the gift of the remainder interest.

Other exceptions exist for a gift to charity of all interests a donor has in the property (Treas. Reg. § 1.170A-7(a)(2)(ii)), an undivided portion of the donor's entire interest (IRC § 170(f)(3)(B)(ii)), a qualified conservation contribution (IRC § 170(f)(3)(B)(iii); Treas. Reg. § 1.170A-7(b)(5)), and future interests in tangible personal property (IRC § 170(a)(3); Treas. Reg. § 1.170A-5(a)(1)). A qualified conservation contribution is a contribution of a qualified real property interest, to a qualified organization, exclusively for conservation purposes. IRC § 170(h). A qualified real property interest is the entire interest of the donor other than a qualified mineral interest, a remainder interest or a perpetual conservation restriction. IRC § 170(h)(2). A qualified organization is a governmental unit, a publicly supported charity or a supporting organization of a governmental unit or publicly supported charity. IRC § 170(h)(3). Conservation purposes mean preservation of a land for outdoor recreation by or education of the general public, protection of relatively natural habitat, or preservation of open space which will yield a significant public benefit. IRC § 170(h)(4).

b. Partial Interest Gifts in Trust (Split-Interests). A split-interest trust is a trust that has both charitable and noncharitable beneficiaries. The deductibility of gifts to split-interest trusts is subject to strict limitations. See Treas. Reg. § 1.170A-6. If a donor creates a trust and gives or retains a life or term interest for the taxpayer or another individual and gives the remainder interest to charity (a charitable remainder trust), no deduction is available for the charitable remainder interest unless the noncharitable beneficiary's interest takes a specific form. If a donor creates a trust and gives a life or term interest to charity and gives the remainder interest to the donor or another individual (a charitable lead trust), no deduction is available for the charity's lead interest unless the interest qualifies as an annuity or unitrust interest. The requirements for the deductibility of split-interest gifts will be discussed in greater detail below.

3. Limitations on Deductibility

The amount of the income tax charitable deduction allowed for a contribution to a charitable organization depends in part on the type of organization to which the gift is made and in part on the type of property being contributed.

a. Percentage Limitations. The amount deductible depends on whether the organization is a public charity or a private foundation. Contributions, whether to private

21st Century Estate Planning:
Practical Applications
2005 Edition

©2005 Sonnenschein Nath & Rosenthal LLP
and Cannon Financial Institute, Inc.

- 510 -

foundations or public charities, that exceed the percentage limitation in the year of the gift may be carried over for five succeeding taxable years. IRC § 170(b)(1)(B), (b)(1)(D)(ii). Any unused carryover is lost at the donor's death.

(1)   **Public Charities**. Public charities include churches, educational organizations (*e.g.*, high schools, colleges and universities that are publicly supported), hospitals, governmental units, and organizations that generally receive a substantial amount of their support from governmental units or from the general public. IRC § 170(b)(1)(A)(i)-(vi), (viii).

(a)   **Fifty Percent Limitation**. The income tax charitable deduction for gifts to public charities of cash and ordinary income property generally is limited to 50% of the donor's contribution base (generally, the donor's adjusted gross income ("AGI")). IRC § 170(b)(1)(A).

(b)   **Thirty Percent Limitation**. The income tax charitable deduction for a gift to a public charity of long-term capital gain property (*e.g.*, stock held for more than one year) is limited to 30% of the donor's AGI. Additionally, a contribution "for the use of" a public charity is deductible only to the extent of 30% of the donor's AGI (versus a 50% limitation on contributions "to" a public charity). IRC § 170(b)(1)(B); Treas. Reg. § 1.170A-8(a)(2). A contribution is made "for the use of" a public charity if property is transferred in trust and is held for the continuing benefit of the charity. Treas. Reg. § 1.170A-8(a)(2).

➔   **Planning Point:** A contribution of an income interest in property is made "for the use of" charity, whether or not the interest is transferred in trust. *Id.*

➔   **Planning Point:** A contribution of a remainder interest in property is made "to" the charity, whether or not such interest is transferred in trust, and, therefore, qualifies for the 50% limitation, provided that the remainder interest is to be distributed outright to the charity when the noncharitable term ends. If the trust property is to be held further in trust for the benefit of the remainder beneficiary, then the gift is "for the use of" the charity and is subject to the 30% limitation. *Id.*

In the case of contributions to a public charity of long-term capital gain property, a donor can avoid the 30% limitation by electing to limit the income tax charitable deduction to the donor's cost basis in the property (the deduction generally is equal to the fair market value of the property, as discussed below). If the election is made, then the contribution is subject to the 50% limitation rather than the 30% limitation. IRC § 170(b)(1)(C)(iii). The election must be made by attaching a statement to the donor's income tax return for the year to which the election applies.

Unrealized capital gains generally are not subject to income tax when a gift of appreciated assets is made to a public charity, even though they may be part of the income tax charitable deduction.

21st Century Estate Planning:
Practical Applications
2005 Edition

©2005 Sonnenschein Nath & Rosenthal LLP
and Cannon Financial Institute, Inc.

- 511 -

(2)   **Private Foundations**. A private foundation generally is a charitable organization that has been established by an individual donor or family.

(a)   **Thirty Percent Limitation**. The income tax charitable deduction for gifts of cash or ordinary income property to private foundations generally is limited to 30% of the donor's AGI in the year of the contribution. IRC § 170(b)(1)(B).

(b)   **Twenty Percent Limitation**. The income tax charitable deduction for a gift of long-term capital gain property to a private foundation generally is limited to 20% of a donor's AGI in the year of the contribution. IRC § 170(b)(1)(D)(i).

The maximum deduction allowable for contributions to a private foundation must be determined after the donor's contributions to public charities are considered. As noted above, the deduction for contributions to public charities is limited to 50% of donor's AGI. IRC § 170(b)(1)(A). Therefore, the maximum deduction allowable for a contribution of cash to a private foundation would be equal to the lesser of (i) 30% of donor's AGI or (ii) the amount of donor's 50% limitation remaining after donor's contributions to public charities are considered.

> **EXAMPLE:** If the donor contributes cash equal to 40% of donor's AGI to a public charity, then the donor is limited to a deduction equal to 10% of his or her AGI for contributions to which the 30% limitation applies, such as the donor's contribution to a private foundation.

b. **Valuation Limitations**. The value of the property that is deductible depends on the nature of the property and may depend on whether the gift is made to a public charity or a private foundation.

(1)   **Ordinary Income Property**. Contributions of ordinary income property, such as stock held for less than one year, are reduced by the amount of ordinary income that would have been realized had the contributed property been sold at its fair market value at the time of the contribution. IRC § 170(e)(1); Treas. Reg. § 1.170A-4(b)(1). This means that the income tax deduction is limited to the donor's cost basis in the property. This rule applies regardless of the identity of the charitable donee (*i.e.*, public charity or private foundation).

(2)   **Long-Term Capital Gain Property**. Generally, the amount of a charitable deduction for a contribution of long-term capital gain property is the property's fair market value. Treas. Reg. § 1.170A-1(c)(1). For example, securities that are held for more than one year are deductible for income tax purposes at their full fair market value. The deduction for contributions to a private foundation of appreciated long-term capital gain property, however, must be reduced by the amount of long-term capital gain that would have been realized had the property been sold at its fair market value at the time of the contribution, so the donor receives a deduction in an amount equal to the donor's basis in the property.

21st Century Estate Planning:
Practical Applications
2005 Edition

©2005 Sonnenschein Nath & Rosenthal LLP
and Cannon Financial Institute, Inc.

- 512 -

EXAMPLE: A donor contributes to a private foundation land held for investment for more than one year. The land has a fair market value at the time of the contribution of $90,000, and an adjusted basis of $30,000. The donor's charitable deduction is limited to $30,000 ($90,000 fair market value less $60,000 long-term capital gain).

There is an exception for contributions of "qualified appreciated stock" to a private foundation, which are not subject to the long-term capital gain reduction. Thus, the donor receives a deduction for the stock's full fair market value. Qualified appreciated stock is stock for which market quotations are readily available on an established securities market and that is long-term capital gain property. IRC § 170(e)(5).

(3)   **Tangible Personal Property**. The deduction for gifts of tangible personal property (*e.g.*, works of art, books, antiques) held long term is the full fair market value of the property if use of the property is related to the charity's exempt function. IRC § 170(e)(1)(B)(i); Treas. Reg. § 1.170A-4(b)(3). If the gift is not related to the charity's exempt function, the deduction must be reduced by the amount of gain that would have been long-term capital gain if the property were sold at its fair market value (*i.e.*, the deduction is limited to the donor's basis). IRC § 170(e)(1)(B). Gifts of tangible personal property held short term are deductible at their cost basis. IRC § 170(e)(1)(A).

4.   **Substantiation Rules**

The substantiation requirements for charitable contributions vary depending on the nature and value of the property contributed.

a. **Money or Property Less Than $250**. Contributions of money in an amount less than $250 must be substantiated by a cancelled check or a receipt from the donee showing the donee's name and the date and amount of the contribution. Treas. Reg. § 1.170A-13(a)(1). A receipt may consist of a letter from the donee acknowledging receipt of the contribution.

Contributions of property other than money in an amount less than $250 must be substantiated by a receipt from the donee showing the donee's name, the date and location of the contribution, and a description of the property. Treas. Reg. § 1.170A-13(b)(1). A receipt may consist of a letter from the donee acknowledging receipt of the contribution. The fair market value of the donated property need not be stated in the receipt. If a receipt is impractical to obtain, for example, if property is deposited in a charity's unattended drop box, the donor must maintain written records with respect to the property that contain the required information. *Id.*; Treas. Reg. § 1.170A-13(b)(2)(ii).

b. **Contributions of $250 or More**. No income tax deduction is allowed for any charitable contribution of money or property of $250 or more unless the donor has a contemporaneous written acknowledgment of the contribution from the charity. IRC §

21st Century Estate Planning:
Practical Applications
2005 Edition

©2005 Sonnenschein Nath & Rosenthal LLP
and Cannon Financial Institute, Inc.

- 513 -

170(f)(8)(A); Treas. Reg. § 1.170A-13(f)(1). In order to be "contemporaneous," the substantiation must be obtained by the time the donor files his or her income tax return for the year the contribution was made. Treas. Reg. § 1.170A-13(f)(3).

Separate contributions of less than $250 to one charitable donee are not subject to the substantiation requirements of IRC § 170(f)(8), and, therefore, do not require a contemporaneous written acknowledgment, regardless of whether the sum of the contributions during the taxable year equals $250 or more. Treas. Reg. § 1.170A-13(f)(1).

> **EXAMPLE:** Donor makes monthly contributions to her church of $200. Because each separate contribution is less than $250, a contemporaneous written acknowledgment is not required, even though the aggregate contributions exceed $250.

The written acknowledgment may take any form, such as a letter, receipt or postcard. It must include the amount of the cash contribution and must describe any property donated, but need not include the value of the property donated. If the charity has provided goods or services to the donor, the charity must provide a description and a good faith estimate of the value of the goods or services provided, which reduces the amount of the charitable contribution. Treas. Reg. § 1.170A-13(f)(2).

> **EXAMPLE:** A donor pays $100 for a ticket to charity's fundraising event. The ticket entitles the donor to dinner with a fair market value of $40. The donor's payment of $100 exceeds by $60 the value of the goods and services he will receive, so the donor has made a charitable gift of $60.

(1) **Split-Interest Trusts**. The IRC § 170(f)(8) substantiation rules do not apply to transfers to charitable remainder trusts or charitable lead trusts, which are split-interest trusts. Treas. Reg. § 1.170A-13(f)(13). The exemption of such trusts from the substantiation rules reflects the fact that such trusts do not have to identify the charitable beneficiary at the time the trust is created. Contributions to pooled income funds, another form of split-interest trust, however, are subject to the substantiation rules of IRC § 170(f)(8). *Id.* The donee organization maintaining the fund provides the contemporaneous written acknowledgment.

(2) **Charitable Gift Annuities**. A charitable gift annuity is a transaction in which a donor transfers money or other property to a charity in exchange for the charity's promise to pay an annuity to the donor or other person. The donor is entitled to a charitable deduction for the excess of the value of the property transferred to the charity over the value of the annuity. Treas. Reg. § 1.170A-1(d)(1). The substantiation rules apply if the deduction equals or exceeds $250. Treas. Reg. § 1.170A-13(f)(16). The donor's right to receive the annuity is not treated as goods or services furnished in consideration for the transfer. *Id.*

21st Century Estate Planning:
Practical Applications
2005 Edition

©2005 Sonnenschein Nath & Rosenthal LLP
and Cannon Financial Institute, Inc.

- 514 -

c. **Additional Requirements for Contributions of $500 or More**. Donors who make contributions of property with a claimed deduction of more than $500 and not more than $5,000, and donors of certain publicly traded securities with a claimed deduction of more than $5,000, must maintain reliable written records containing the information specified in Treas. Reg. § 1.170A-13(b)(2)(ii) (relating to the written records for contributions of property of $250 or less). Treas. Reg. § 1.170A-13(b)(3)(i). Additionally, the records must contain information on the manner and approximate date of acquisition of the property and the donor's adjusted basis in the property. *Id.* A donor must disclose on his or her income tax return most of the information required to be maintained in the written records.

In applying the valuation limitation, the amount claimed as a deduction is the aggregate amount claimed for all similar items of property contributed to the same donee in the same year. Treas. Reg. § 1.170A-13(c)(1). The term "similar items of property" means property in the same generic category or type, such as books, stamp or coin collections, jewelry, toys and clothing. Treas. Reg. § 1.170A-13(c)(7)(iii).

➔ **Planning Point:** A donor must file Form 8283, Noncash Charitable Contributions, if the amount of the deduction for all noncash gifts is more than $500 and attach it to the income tax return. A donor lists on Schedule A items for which the donor claims a deduction of $5,000 or less per item or group of similar items and certain publicly traded securities, even if the deduction is more than $5,000. For all such items, the donor must furnish the name and address of the donee organization and a description of the donated property. If the amount claimed as a deduction with respect to an item exceeds $500 but is less than $5,000, additional information must be supplied, including the date of the contribution, the date on which the donor acquired the property and the manner of acquisition, the donor's adjusted basis in the property, the fair market value of the property, and the method used to determine the fair market value.

(1) **Qualified Appraisal for Contributions of $5,000 or More**. A donor who claims a deduction in excess of $5,000 for property other than certain publicly traded securities must obtain a "qualified appraisal" prepared by a "qualified appraiser" and attach an appraisal summary to the return, in addition to maintaining written records. Treas. Reg. § 1.170A-13(c)(2)(i). The qualified appraisal must be made no earlier than 60 days prior to the date of the contribution, and it must be received before the due date, including extensions, of the income tax return on which the deduction is claimed. Treas. Reg. § 1.170A-13(c)(3)(i). One qualified appraisal is sufficient in the case of a group of similar items contributed in the same year. Treas. Reg. § 1.170A-13(c)(3)(iv)(A). The income tax regulations set forth the information that must be included in a qualified appraisal, such as a description of the property, the date of the contribution, the appraisal date, and the valuation method used. See Treas. Reg. § 1.170A-13(c)(3)(ii).

21st Century Estate Planning:
Practical Applications
2005 Edition

©2005 Sonnenschein Nath & Rosenthal LLP
and Cannon Financial Institute, Inc.

- 515 -

→ **Planning Point:** A donor lists on Schedule B of Form 8283 items for which the donor claims a deduction of more than $5,000 (omitting publicly traded securities reportable on Schedule A). Generally, items reported on Schedule B will require a "qualified appraisal" prepared by a "qualified appraiser."

A qualified appraiser is an individual who holds himself or herself out to the public as an appraiser or performs appraisals on a regular basis. Treas. Reg. § 1.170A-13(c)(5)(i). Certain persons cannot serve as a qualified appraiser, including the donor, the donee, or a party to the transaction in which the donor acquired the property (*e.g.*, the dealer who sold the property to the donor) unless the property is donated within two months of the date of acquisition and its appraised value does not exceed its acquisition price. Treas. Reg. § 1.170A-13(c)(5)(iv).

(2)   **Substantiation Rules for Certain Securities**. The extent of substantiation required for contributions of securities depends on the nature of the securities. The term "publicly traded securities" generally refers to securities for which market quotations are readily available on an established securities market (*e.g.*, the security is listed on the New York Stock Exchange or the American Stock Exchange or is traded in an over-the-counter market for which published quotations are available). Treas. Reg. § 1.170A-13(c)(7)(xi)(A). The additional substantiation rules in Treas. Reg. § 1.170A-13(c) do not apply to gifts of such securities, even if the claimed deduction exceeds $5,000. Treas. Reg. § 1.170A-13(c)(1)(i). If the value of the securities is $250 or more, however, the donor must obtain a contemporaneous written acknowledgment.

C. Estate and Gift Tax Charitable Deductions

IRC § 2055(a) allows an estate tax charitable deduction, and IRC § 2522(a) allows a gift tax charitable deduction, for transfers to the following types of recipients:

- IRC § 501(c)(3) corporations and trusts organized and operated exclusively for religious, charitable, scientific, literary or educational purposes that do not attempt to influence elections and are not substantially engaged in carrying on propaganda or influencing legislation;
- Federal government, state government or subdivisions thereof, if the contribution is made for exclusively public purposes;
- IRC § 501(c)(3) fraternal or veterans organizations; and
- For estate tax purposes only, certain employee stock ownership plans if the transfer is a gratuitous transfer of qualified employer securities from a charitable remainder trust.

→ **Planning Point:** The gift tax does not apply to transfers to political organizations (defined in IRC § 527), meaning that the transfer is never subject to the gift tax. IRC § 2501(a)(5). In the case of transfers to

21st Century Estate Planning:
Practical Applications
2005 Edition

©2005 Sonnenschein Nath & Rosenthal LLP
and Cannon Financial Institute, Inc.

- 516 -

charitable organizations, the transfer is subject to gift tax but is entitled to a deduction. Of course, the effect is the same. Gifts at death to political organizations are subject to estate tax.

The charitable deductions for income, estate and gift taxes cover the same basic areas, although they are not identical. For example, the estate and gift tax charitable deductions are not limited to gifts for use in the United States or to domestic corporations, as is the case with the income tax deduction. Treas. Reg. §§ 20.2055-1(a), 25.2522(a)-1(a). Therefore, it is important to consult the applicable Code sections to determine the exact parameters of the desired deduction.

1. Deduction is Unlimited

Unlike the rules governing the income tax charitable deduction, no distinction is made for estate and gift tax charitable deduction purposes among the types of qualified donees or between long-term and short-term capital gain property. Thus, none of the percentage and valuation limitations on the income tax charitable deduction under IRC § 170 apply to the estate tax or gift tax charitable deduction. In this sense, the gift tax and estate tax charitable deductions are "unlimited." For estate tax purposes, however, charitable deduction property must be property that was included in the decedent's gross estate, and the amount of the deduction cannot exceed the value of the transferred property required to be included in the gross estate. IRC § 2055(d). Generally, the value of the gift or estate tax deduction is the value of the property on the date of gift or on the date of death, as the case may be.

A charitable deduction may be denied if the charitable gift is indefinite or discretionary. A deduction will not be disallowed, however, if the testator designates a third party to select the charitable organizations and to allocate the bequest among them. See Rev. Rul. 81-20, 1981-1 C.B. 471.

2. Split-Interests

As discussed above, a split-interest trust is a gift in which a charitable beneficiary and a noncharitable beneficiary share interests in the same property. The estate tax or gift tax charitable deduction is limited to the charitable interest in a split-interest, and a charitable deduction will not be allowed for transfers to a trust that has both charitable and noncharitable beneficiaries unless the trust meets certain requirements for split-interest trusts. IRC §§ 2055(e)(2), 2522(c)(2).

Under IRC §§ 2055(e)(2) and 2522(c)(2), gift tax and estate tax charitable deductions are allowed for: (a) the remainder interest in a charitable remainder annuity trust, a charitable remainder unitrust, or a pooled income fund; (b) the income interest in a charitable lead annuity trust or a charitable lead unitrust; and (c) the nontrust remainder interest in a personal residence or a farm. Split-interest gifts will be discussed in detail below.

21st Century Estate Planning:
Practical Applications
2005 Edition

©2005 Sonnenschein Nath & Rosenthal LLP
and Cannon Financial Institute, Inc.

- 517 -

D. Outright Gifts to Charity

This section will discuss several charitable planning techniques that do not involve the use of a trust.

1. Public Charities

Outright gifts to public charities will qualify for the income tax and/or gift tax or estate tax charitable deductions. The types of organizations that qualify as public charities include churches, educational organizations, hospitals, governmental units, and organizations that generally receive a substantial amount of their support from governmental units or from the general public. IRC §§ 170(b)(1)(A)(i)-(vi), (viii). As discussed above, the income tax deduction is limited to 50% of the donor's AGI, or 30% if long-term capital gain property is donated or if the gift is "for the use of" the public charity. The estate and gift tax deductions are unlimited.

2. Private Foundations

A private foundation is a charitable organization that is not publicly funded. That is, it is funded primarily by a single donor or a small number of major donors. A private foundation uses its assets to carry out the charitable giving program of the people contributing to the foundation. The private foundation does so by making grants to the public charities that the contributors wish to support rather than engaging directly in a charitable activity. Contributors to the private foundation receive an immediate income tax deduction for the contribution, yet the funds may be held in the foundation for distribution over time.

➔ **Planning Point:** A private foundation is a way for the donor to fund a charitable gift-giving program without surrendering control of investment of assets. By using a private foundation, the donor and the donor's family members can centralize the management of the family's charitable giving and pool the family's resources to make a larger impact in that giving. A private foundation also allows the donor to establish an endowment that will appreciate, permitting funds to be accumulated and distributed in the future for charitable purposes. Potentially significant estate, gift and income tax deductions may be available for contributions to a private foundation.

a. <u>Taxation of Contributions to a Private Foundation.</u>

(1) <u>Estate and Gift Taxes</u>. Contributions to a private foundation will qualify for a charitable gift tax deduction if made during a donor's lifetime, or a federal estate tax deduction if made at a donor's death under the donor's will or revocable trust. The donor can make a contribution to a foundation already in existence or to a foundation to be created at the

21st Century Estate Planning:
Practical Applications
2005 Edition

©2005 Sonnenschein Nath & Rosenthal LLP
and Cannon Financial Institute, Inc.

- 518 -

donor's death under the terms of his or her will or revocable trust. As discussed above, the gift and estate tax charitable deductions are unlimited.

(2) **Income Taxes**. Unlike the estate and gift tax charitable deductions, the donor's income tax charitable deduction for gifts to a private foundation during his or her life is subject to percentage limitations, which are discussed above. Subject to the percentage limitations, a donor can deduct contributions of cash in full. A donor generally can deduct contributions of appreciated property only to the extent of his or her tax basis in the property, although an exception to this rule exists for "qualified appreciated stock" contributed to a private foundation, which can be deducted at its full fair market value at the time of the contribution. IRC § 170(e)(5).

b. **Private Foundation Restrictions**. Private foundations are subject to several operating rules and restrictions not applicable to public charities. Failure to follow these rules results in additional taxes and penalties. If the foundation fails to correct the activity, then the IRS may impose punitive second-tier taxes. These rules are summarized below.

(1) **Self-Dealing**. A private foundation cannot engage in "self-dealing" with any person or organization that might be classified as a "disqualified person" in relation to the private foundation. IRC § 4941. The law imposes an excise tax equal to 5% of the amount involved in the act of self-dealing, which is payable by any disqualified person who participates in the act of self-dealing. IRC § 4941(a)(1). A "disqualified person" includes substantial contributors (the creator of a foundation, for example), foundation managers (*e.g.*, officers, directors and trustees), family members, and entities subject to more than 20% control by any such persons and members of their families. IRC § 4946(a). The individual who creates a private foundation, the founder's spouse, the founder's children and their spouses would all be disqualified persons in relation to the founder's private foundation.

An additional initial tax of 2-1/2% of the amount involved may be assessed against the trustee or other foundation manager who has actual knowledge that an act constitutes self-dealing. IRC § 4941(a)(2). Ignorance is a defense to the foundation manager's initial tax. If the self-dealing is not corrected (which requires reversal of the transaction to the extent possible), then a "second-tier" tax of 200% of the amount involved is imposed on the disqualified person. IRC § 4941(b)(1). The second-tier tax on a trustee or other foundation manager who refuses to correct the act of self-dealing is 50% of the amount involved. IRC § 4941(b)(2).

In general, a disqualified person may not have any financial dealings with, and may receive no financial payments from, the private foundation. Acts of self-dealing include: (1) the sale, exchange, or leasing of property between a private foundation and a disqualified person; (2) the lending of money or other extension of credit between a private foundation and a disqualified person; (3) the furnishing of goods, services, or facilities between a private foundation and a disqualified person; (4) the payment of compensation by a private foundation to a disqualified person; (5) the transfer to, or for the benefit of, or use by, a disqualified person of the income or assets of a private foundation; and (6) the agreement by a private foundation to

21st Century Estate Planning:
Practical Applications
2005 Edition

©2005 Sonnenschein Nath & Rosenthal LLP
and Cannon Financial Institute, Inc.

- 519 -

make any payment of money or other property to a government official. IRC § 4941(d)(1); Treas. Reg. § 53.4941(d)-2.

→ **Planning Point:** Exceptions to the self-dealing rules exist for gifts the founder makes to the foundation, reimbursement of expenses incurred in conducting the private foundation's grant-making programs, and reasonable compensation for services as a trustee or director of the foundation.

(2) **Excise Tax on Investment Income**. An excise tax of 2% is imposed each year on the net investment income of a private foundation. IRC § 4940(a). This tax may be reduced to 1% if the foundation makes sufficiently large distributions to public charities.

(3) **Minimum Distribution Requirements**. A private foundation is required to make qualifying distributions for each taxable year equal to 5% of the net fair market value of the foundation's assets (other than those used in carrying out the foundation's charitable purposes). If such amount is not distributed, a tax will be imposed on the undistributed income of the foundation. IRC § 4942(a). This required distribution amount is reduced by any income and excise taxes for the year. In general, "qualifying distributions" include any amount paid to accomplish exempt purposes, other than payments to an organization controlled by the foundation or by disqualified persons or to a non-operating foundation, or any amount paid to acquire an asset used in carrying out charitable purposes. IRC § 4942(g). Charitable distributions in excess of the amount required to be distributed for a given year generally reduce the required distributions in subsequent years. The foundation must pay the required distribution amount before the beginning of the second year following the taxable year. Thus, the foundation must distribute the year one amount by the end of year two, the year two amount by the end of year three, and so forth.

(4) **Excess Business Holdings**. A foundation that owns more than 2% of the outstanding stock of any company may be subject to restrictions on excess business holdings. In general, combined holdings of the foundation and disqualified persons in any "business enterprise" are limited to 20%, or 35% if unrelated third parties have control of such business enterprise. IRC § 4943.

(5) **Jeopardizing Investments**. Generally, the law imposes a tax on high-risk investments, on the assumption that these investments jeopardize the carrying out of the exempt purposes of a foundation. IRC § 4944. The IRS has indicated that the following types of investments will be scrutinized closely: trading in securities on margin; trading in commodity futures; investments and working interests in oil and gas wells; purchase of puts, calls and straddles; purchase of warrants; and selling short. A standard portfolio of stocks and bonds should not violate the jeopardy investment restrictions. Treas. Reg. § 53.4944-1(a)(2).

21st Century Estate Planning:
Practical Applications
2005 Edition

©*2005 Sonnenschein Nath & Rosenthal LLP*
and Cannon Financial Institute, Inc.

- 520 -

(6) **Taxable Expenditures**. A foundation generally is subject to a 10% tax on the amount of a taxable expenditure. IRC § 4945(a). Taxable expenditures are payments by the foundation other than qualifying distributions and payments of taxes and expenses. Specifically, taxable expenditures include: lobbying expenditures; political campaign expenditures; most grants to individuals unless made pursuant to programs pre-approved by the IRS; grants to organizations other than public charities unless the foundation exercises "expenditure responsibility"; and expenditures for noncharitable purposes. IRC § 4945(d).

c. **Creating a Private Foundation.**

(1) **Corporation or Trust**. A private foundation may be created and organized as a wholly charitable trust or as a not-for-profit corporation under state law and receives its federal tax-exempt status under the Code. The not-for-profit corporation may be formed by founders known as "members" who elect directors of the corporation to choose officers and supervise management of the foundation. A not-for-profit corporation also may be formed with directors and officers but without members. If a corporate entity is used, various documents must be filed with the Secretary of State of the state in which the corporation is incorporated. A board of directors operates the foundation and decides on the charitable distributions to be made each year.

If an individual uses a trust, the individual creating the trust enters into a trust agreement with one or more designated trustees who are responsible for the management of the trust assets. The trustees or other persons selected in the trust agreement will operate the foundation and decide on the charitable distributions to be made each year.

(2) **Filing Requirements**. A private foundation must file federal Form 1023 with the IRS to obtain recognition of its tax-exempt status. A private foundation also must file federal Form 990-PF annually with the IRS. Form 990-PF reports income earned, includes details of the foundation's expenses of operation, lists charitable grants made, lists names and addresses of the foundation's directors and officers or its trustees and otherwise provides details on the foundation's activities.

Charitable organizations generally are subject to the supervision and control of the Attorney General of the state in which they are organized and operated. Many states require a private foundation to file with the Attorney General an initial registration statement and an annual return containing detailed financial information.

3. **Donor Advised Funds**

A donor advised fund is a separate fund, but not a separate entity, within a public charity. The donor's contributions are accounted for separately within the public charity's records, and often the donor is permitted to "name" a fund after the donor or the donor's family, thus providing the name recognition benefit of a private foundation.

21st Century Estate Planning:
Practical Applications
2005 Edition

©2005 Sonnenschein Nath & Rosenthal LLP
and Cannon Financial Institute, Inc.

- 521 -

The public charity must control the gift in all respects, including the right to control investments and to control the disposition of the donated funds for charitable purposes. The donor or his or her designees, however, generally exercises the privilege of making nonbinding recommendations to the governing body suggesting which public charities should receive grants from that particular fund. Treas. Reg. §§ 1.507-2(a)(8)(iv)(A)(2), (3) (listing factors indicating whether the donor retained control of the gift). Control is sacrificed because the donor's recommendations can be advisory only, and the right to advise generally is limited by life spans of the advisors. Although the public charity must retain control over investments, donors may be given the option of selecting types of investments within the overall investment portfolio of the public charity.

➔ **Planning Point:** Individuals reluctant to subject themselves to the private foundation rules and limitations frequently find that the creation of a donor advised fund permits them to achieve their charitable goal successfully. A donor advised fund program also is attractive to many donors who want advice and administrative services and are willing to sacrifice ultimate control over their funds. Others may prefer to exert more control over the disposition of the funds to other charities, as the public charities are not bound to follow the recommendations made by the donors of advised funds.

➔ **Planning Point:** Because the donor advised fund is a bookkeeping entry within the records of the public charity, the donor advised fund keeps all records and the donor is not required to keep records or prepare separate tax returns, as is the case with a typical private family foundation.

      a. **Income Tax Consequences**. The gift to a donor advised fund is a gift to a public charity. Therefore, the donor's income tax deduction is subject to the percentage limitations applicable to public charities.

A disadvantage of the donor advised fund is the lack of clear rules governing its operation. The most significant rules governing donor advised funds are found in the private foundation termination provisions. See Treas. Reg. § 1.507-2. If a donor advised fund contains any "material restriction" or condition, it may fail to be treated as a public charity and may instead be reclassified by the IRS as a private foundation or supporting organization and subject to a lower percentage limitation.

      b. **Where to Find Donor Advised Funds**. The community foundation is the traditional home of the donor advised fund. A community foundation is an organization established to receive gifts or bequests from the public and to administer them for charitable purposes, primarily in the community or area where it is located. The community foundation generally has a governing body comprised of representatives of the particular community or area it benefits. A donor can make a gift directly to open a donor advised fund account or indirectly

21st Century Estate Planning:
Practical Applications
2005 Edition

©2005 Sonnenschein Nath & Rosenthal LLP
and Cannon Financial Institute, Inc.

- 522 -

by creating a supporting organization to the community foundation donor advised fund account. All contributions are subject to the ultimate authority of the governing board.

➜ **Planning Point:** Some donor advised funds may be limited geographically to giving to a particular community or state. Others have policies against funding public charities unfamiliar to staff members. Almost all have policies against making grants to private foundations (except, in some cases, to private operating foundations because they already offer public-charity-sized deductibility) or to individuals.

Many public charities have, or will create upon request, donor advised funds dedicated to the furtherance of the public charity's exempt purposes. Some for-profit entities also have established donor advised funds (*e.g.*, the Fidelity Charitable Gift Fund).

4. Supporting Organizations

A supporting organization is organized and operated exclusively for the benefit of a church, educational organization, hospital, governmental unit or publicly supported charity (a "supported organization"), is operated, supervised or controlled by or in connection with the supported organization, and is not controlled directly or indirectly by disqualified persons. Section 509(01)(3).

EXAMPLE: A supporting organization may support a specific charity, such as a school, or may have a broader scope by supporting a community foundation.

For this purpose, a disqualified person is a person defined in Section 4946, or an employee of a disqualified person. A donor's non-employee advisors are generally not disqualified persons.

➜ **Planning Point:** A donor may be more comfortable with a supporting organization with a majority of the Board of Directors consisting of family members and advisors than with a donor advised fund. For example, a Board of Directors consisting of a donor, his spouse, his financial advisor and two representatives of the community foundation would qualify.

A supporting organization is treated as a public charity for all purposes. Thus, contributions to a supporting organization may include private company stock valued at full fair market value, and the higher percentage limitations apply. The supporting organization avoids the private foundation excise taxes.

5. Charitable Gift Annuities

A charitable gift annuity is a contract between a donor and a charity in which the donor transfers money or other property to a charity in exchange for the charity's promise to pay the beneficiary a fixed dollar amount each year for the beneficiary's lifetime. The annuity may be a

21st Century Estate Planning:
Practical Applications
2005 Edition

©2005 Sonnenschein Nath & Rosenthal LLP
and Cannon Financial Institute, Inc.

- 523 -

single life annuity, or a joint and survivor annuity, and payments may be made annually, semiannually, quarterly, monthly or more frequently. The annuity payments may be either immediate or deferred (*i.e.*, payments beginning now or payments beginning at a future date).

The Committee on Gift Annuities (a representative body of philanthropic organizations) recommends rates of return for gift annuities. The annuity rate depends on the age of the beneficiary. The annuity rates are conservative in order to ensure that the charity receives a significant benefit from the transaction and to minimize the possibility that the charity will be required to use its assets to make annuity payments.

      a. <u>Income Tax Consequences</u>. The transfer of appreciated property for a charitable gift annuity is deemed to be a bargain sale. Treas. Reg. §§ 1.170A-1(d)(3), 1.1011-2(a)(4)(i). A bargain sale is a transfer of property to a charity in exchange for consideration that is less than the fair market value of the property. For tax purposes, the transfer is treated in part as the purchase of an annuity and in part as a charitable gift.

      (1)   <u>Amount of the Charitable Deduction</u>. The donor can claim an immediate charitable income tax deduction for the portion of the transaction that represents the charitable gift element, which is the amount of money or fair market value of the property transferred to the charity less the present value of the annuity. Treas. Reg. § 1.170A-1(d)(1). The present value of the annuity is determined under IRC § 7520. The Section 7520 rate is published monthly. In determining the amount of the charitable deduction, the donor may elect to use either the rate for the month in which the valuation date falls, or either of the immediately preceding two months, whichever is the most favorable. In fact, because the Section 7520 rate is published on the 20th or 21st day of the preceding month, a donor may consider four months' rates. The charitable deduction for the gift portion is subject to the percentage limitations.

> **<u>EXAMPLE</u>:** Donor, age 60, purchased a charitable gift annuity from a museum, a public charity. Donor transferred to the museum stock qualifying as long-term capital gain property with a value of $1,000,000 and a basis of $200,000. The museum will pay Donor an annual annuity of $20,000, payable quarterly for Donor's life. Assuming a Section 7520 rate of 5.4%, the present value of the annuity is $233,305. The amount of Donor's charitable contribution is $766,695 ($1,000,000 - $233,305).

      (2)   <u>Recognition of Capital Gain</u>. In computing the amount of the capital gain, the basis of the transferred property is allocated between the gift portion and the actuarial value of the annuity. IRC § 1011(b). The amount of gain is the difference between the value of the annuity and the cost basis allocated to the value of the annuity. If certain requirements are met, the gain determined under the bargain sale rules need not be reported in full in the year the annuity is purchased, but may be reported ratably over the donor's life expectancy. Treas. Reg. § 1.1011-2(a)(4)(ii). This is accomplished by treating as gain the appropriate portion of each annuity payment that would otherwise be excluded from income.

21st Century Estate Planning:
Practical Applications
2005 Edition

©2005 Sonnenschein Nath & Rosenthal LLP
and Cannon Financial Institute, Inc.

- 524 -

Treas. Reg. §§ 1.1011-2(a)(4)(ii), 1.1011-2(c), Ex. 8. To qualify for this method of reporting gain, the annuity must be nonassignable or assignable only to the charity to which the property was transferred. Treas. Reg. § 1.1011-2(a)(4)(ii). In addition, the annuitants must be either the donor only or the donor and a designated survivor annuitant.

> **EXAMPLE:** Building on the example above, under the bargain sale rules, the portion of the basis of the stock allocable to the sale portion of the annuity transaction is $46,661 ($233,305/$1,000,000 x $200,000). Donor must recognize long-term capital gain of $186,644 ($233,305 - $46,661). The gain is reported ratably over Donor's life expectancy so long as the annuity is nonassignable or assignable only to the museum.

(3) **Taxation of Annuity Payments**. The income tax consequences of a charitable gift annuity are governed by the annuity rules in IRC § 72. The annuity rules treat the annuity payments as having three elements for income tax purposes: a tax-free recovery of basis; a capital gain portion (if gain can be deferred); and ordinary income (the annuity amount). Treas. Reg. § 1.72-1(a).

(a) **Tax-Free Portion**. A portion of each annuity payment will represent a tax-free recovery of basis until the donor has fully recovered his or her basis in the property. After the donor has fully recovered his or her basis, which occurs if the donor lives for his or her actuarial life expectancy, as determined under Table V of Treas. Reg. § 1.72-9, the balance of the payments received will be taxable as ordinary income. IRC § 72(b)(2). In the event that the donor dies before recovering his or her entire basis, the unrecovered amount can be taken as a deduction on his or her final income tax return. IRC § 72(b)(3).

The tax-free return of basis portion of each payment is determined by multiplying the exclusion ratio by each annuity payment received. The exclusion ratio is the ratio of the donor's investment in the contract (the present value of the annuity) to the expected return. The expected return is determined by multiplying the total annual annuity payment to be made by the donor's life expectancy, as determined under IRC § 72. Treas. Reg. § 1.72-9.

> **EXAMPLE:** Building on the examples above, Donor's life expectancy under the life annuity tables in Treas. Reg. § 1.72-9 Table V is 24.2. Therefore, his expected return is $484,000 ($20,000 x 24.2).
>
> The exclusion ratio is 48.2% ($233,305 value of the annuity divided by $484,000 expected return). Therefore, $9,640 ($20,000 x 48.2%) of each annuity payment Donor receives is treated as a tax-free return of investment.

21st Century Estate Planning:
Practical Applications
2005 Edition

©2005 Sonnenschein Nath & Rosenthal LLP
and Cannon Financial Institute, Inc.

- 525 -

(b) **Capital Gain Portion**. Because property was transferred to purchase the annuity, a portion of each excludable amount must be reported as long-term capital gain. This amount will be reported ratably over the donor's life expectancy. If the donor lives at least as long as his or her life expectancy at the time of the transfer, the donor eventually will pay a tax on his or her entire realized gain.

> **EXAMPLE:** Continuing the example above, the gain is reported over Donor's 24.2-year life expectancy, so that each year $7,713 is reported as capital gain ($186,644 divided by 24.2). Thus, of the $9,640 that is excludable, Donor must report $7,713 as long-term capital gain. The balance, $1,927, is excluded from income as a return of basis.

(c) **Ordinary Income Portion**. The ordinary income portion is the difference between the annuity payment and the return of basis portion.

> **EXAMPLE:** Continuing the preceding example, the balance of each annuity payment, $10,360 ($20,000 less $9,640), will be ordinary income.

b. **Gift Tax Consequences**. The donor is entitled to a gift tax charitable deduction for the value of the charitable gift element.

c. **Deferred Gift Annuities**. With a deferred payment gift annuity, a donor transfers money or property to a charitable organization in exchange for its promise to pay an annuity to the donor to begin at a future date. The donor is able to make a gift now and get an immediate income tax charitable deduction when he or she is in a high tax bracket, deferring distributions to the donor until those years when the donor may need the income more and may be in a lower income tax bracket. A portion of each annuity payment, when the payments begin, will be excludable from gross income over the donor's life expectancy. See Treas. Reg. § 1.72-1(a).

E. Use of Section 7520 Rate to Value Split-Interest Gifts

The charitable deduction for income, estate and gift tax purposes is equal to the present value of the charity's interest, determined using the IRS's mortality tables and 120% of the annual federal mid-term rate determined pursuant to IRC § 7520 (the "Section 7520 rate"). The Section 7520 rate is published monthly. In determining the amount of the charitable deduction, the donor is allowed to use either the rate for the month in which the gift occurs, or either of the immediately preceding two months, whichever is the most favorable. In fact, because the Section 7520 rate is published on the 20th or 21st day of the preceding month, a donor may consider four months' rates when planning the date on which to establish a charitable remainder trust or charitable lead trust.

21st Century Estate Planning:
Practical Applications
2005 Edition

©2005 Sonnenschein Nath & Rosenthal LLP
and Cannon Financial Institute, Inc.

- 526 -

F. Charitable Remainder Trusts

A charitable remainder trust ("CRT") allows an individual (the "donor") to donate assets to a charity while retaining an interest in the donated assets or providing another individual or entity with an interest in the donated assets for a specified period of time. The donor transfers property to an irrevocable trust that provides that the noncharitable beneficiary of the CRT will receive a stream of payments for a specified period of time, and at the expiration of this period, the remaining assets will be transferred to the charitable beneficiary. Thus, a CRT is a "split-interest" gift because both a charitable beneficiary and a noncharitable beneficiary receive interests in the same property. The donor will obtain an income tax charitable deduction and a gift tax charitable deduction or an estate tax charitable deduction based on the present value of the remainder interest ultimately passing to charity.

1.   Requirements for Charitable Estate, Gift and Income Tax Deductions

A charitable deduction is allowed only if the noncharitable beneficiary's interest is in the form of an annuity interest or a unitrust interest. Accordingly, a CRT may be established as a charitable remainder annuity trust (a "CRAT"), a charitable remainder unitrust (a "CRUT"), or a net income CRUT.

a. Annual Payments. The annual payment must be either an annuity or a unitrust amount, which must be fixed and may not change over time. No amount other than the annuity or unitrust payment may be distributed to any person except a charitable organization. IRC §§ 664(d)(1)(B), (2)(B).

(1)   Rules Common to CRATs and CRUTs. Certain rules apply to both CRATs and CRUTs, and they are discussed below.

(a)   Distributions for Emergencies. No distributions for emergency needs or other purposes may be made from a CRT. Treas. Reg. §§ 1.664-2(a)(4), 3(a)(4). See also Rev. Rul. 77-58, 1977-1 C.B. 175.

(b)   Proration in Short Years. The annuity or unitrust payment must be prorated in the case of a short taxable year other than the final year. Treas. Reg. §§ 1.664-2(a)(1)(iv)(a), 3(a)(1)(v)(a).

(c)   Incorrect Valuations. All CRUTs, and all CRATs basing the annuity amount on a percentage of the value of the CRAT assets, must include language directing the trustee to correct improper distributions made, or not made, due to the incorrect valuation of CRT assets. Treas. Reg. §§ 1.664-2(a)(1)(iii), 3(a)(1)(iii). Where there is an incorrect valuation, the trustee must pay to the beneficiary (in the case of an undervaluation) or receive from the beneficiary (in the case of an overvaluation) an amount equal to the difference between the amount paid to the beneficiary and the correct payment amount.

21st Century Estate Planning:
Practical Applications
2005 Edition

©2005 Sonnenschein Nath & Rosenthal LLP
and Cannon Financial Institute, Inc.

- 527 -

(d) Distributions to Charity. Interim distributions to charity may be permissible if within certain parameters. For example, income exceeding the annuity or unitrust amount could be paid to charity. Treas. Reg. §§ 1.664-2(a)(4), 3(a)(4). Alternatively, periodic distributions of principal or principal distributions at the death of one of the CRT beneficiaries is also permissible, provided that the adjusted basis of any distributions in kind is fairly representative of the adjusted basis of the property available for distribution. Treas. Reg. §§ 1.664-2(a)(4), 3(a)(4). This provision prohibits the trustee from distributing low basis assets to the charity, which is exempt from income tax, thereby benefiting the noncharitable beneficiary by retaining high basis assets. A donor is not entitled to an additional income tax deduction for any portion of an annuity or unitrust payment that is paid to charity. Treas. Reg. §§ 1.664-2(d), 3(d).

(e) Minimum and Maximum Payments. The amount paid must be equal to at least 5%, but not more than 50%, of the initial fair market value of the assets of the trust, in the case of a CRAT, and of the value of the trust revalued annually, in the case of a CRUT. IRC §§ 664(d)(1)(A), (d)(2)(A); Treas. Reg. §§ 1.664-2(a)(2)(i), 3(a)(2)(i). The present value of the remainder interest that passes to charity must be equal to at least 10% of the initial fair market value of the assets contributed to the trust. IRC §§ 664(d)(1)(D), (d)(2)(D).

➔ **Planning Point**: Note that the 10% minimum value for the charitable remainder trust may restrict the use of such trusts with younger generation beneficiaries, such as children of the grantor or for multiple beneficiaries. A CRT to be held for the life of a young beneficiary raises a significant risk of failing the 10% remainder test.

> **EXAMPLE:** Assuming a Section 7520 rate of 5.6%, a 6% annuity for the life of a 35-year-old fails the 10% remainder test. The value of the remainder is only 5.283%.

➔ **Planning Point**: The requirement that the remainder interest be at least 10% of the value of the property transferred to the trust could cause a problem in the case of a testamentary CRT because the value of the remainder cannot be determined until the death of the donor. A trust that does not meet the 10% test can be reformed to do so. IRC § 2055(e)(3)(J). Thus, a testamentary CRT should include a provision allowing the trustee to amend the trust by decreasing the payment or the term of the noncharitable interest in order to meet the 10% requirement.

(2) CRATs. A CRAT pays a defined annuity, either a fixed dollar amount or a fixed percentage of the initial fair market value of the trust assets, to the noncharitable beneficiary, at least annually, regardless of the value of the trust assets or the income generated by the trust. Treas. Reg. §§ 1.664-2(a)(1)(ii), (iii).

21st Century Estate Planning:
Practical Applications
2005 Edition

©2005 Sonnenschein Nath & Rosenthal LLP
and Cannon Financial Institute, Inc.

- 528 -

When the CRAT is created, there must be no more than a 5% chance that the required payments will exhaust the principal of the trust. Rev. Rul. 77-374, 1977-2 C.B. 329. If the chance exceeds 5%, no charitable deduction will be allowed. The basis for this position is language in the estate and gift tax regulations that prohibits a deduction where a charitable transfer is subject to a condition "unless the possibility that the charitable transfer will not become effective is so remote as to be negligible." Treas. Reg. §§ 20.2055-2(b)(1), 25.2522(c)-3(b)(1).

→ **Planning Point:** The 10% remainder test is in addition to the 5% probability of exhaustion test, and it is possible to pass one yet flunk the other.

> **EXAMPLE:** Assuming a Section 7520 rate of 5.6%, an annuity for the life of a 30-year-old paying a 5.64% annuity passes the probability of exhaustion test but fails the 10% remainder test. The probability of exhaustion is 3.81%, but the value of the remainder is only 8.29%.

> **EXAMPLE:** Still assuming a Section 7520 rate of 5.6%, an annuity for the life of a 60-year-old paying a 7% annuity fails the probability of exhaustion test but passes the 10% remainder test. The probability of exhaustion is 23.13%, and the value of the remainder is 19.77%.

The Section 7520 regulations contain a separate exhaustion rule for income, gift and estate tax purposes that applies to CRATs in which the annuity is measured by a life and the trust will be exhausted if the measuring life outlives his or her life expectancy. Treas. Reg. §§ 1.7520-3(b)(2), 20.7520-3(b)(2), 25.7520-3(b)(2). The rule is that if the trust will be exhausted if the measuring life lives until age 110, the annuity interest cannot be valued under Section 7520.

(3)   CRUTs. A CRUT pays a defined percentage of the net fair market value of the assets of the trust, valued as of a certain day each year, to the noncharitable beneficiary, at least annually. This amount is called the "unitrust amount." Treas. Reg. § 1.664-3(a)(1)(i). The valuation date can be any date during the year, provided that the same date is used each year. Alternatively, the valuation could be made on several different dates to produce an average valuation, as long as the same valuation dates and valuation methods are used each year. Treas. Reg. § 1.664-3(a)(1)(iv). The unitrust amount fluctuates as the net fair market value of the CRUT assets fluctuates, even though the defined percentage is fixed. Therefore, unlike the CRAT, a CRUT will not be exhausted by distributions to the noncharitable beneficiaries because the unitrust amount will decrease as the value of the assets of the trust decreases.

(a)   Net Income CRUT. A variation of the CRUT, called a net income CRUT, is a CRUT that pays the noncharitable beneficiary the lesser of the income of the trust or the unitrust amount. IRC § 664(d)(3); Treas. Reg. § 1.664-3(a)(1)(i)(b)(1). Income is trust accounting income as determined by the governing instrument and state law.

21st Century Estate Planning:
Practical Applications
2005 Edition

©2005 Sonnenschein Nath & Rosenthal LLP
and Cannon Financial Institute, Inc.

- 529 -

(b) **Net Income With Make-Up CRUT**. The Code allows a net income CRUT to include a "make-up" provision, specifying that any deficits between the required unitrust amount that would otherwise have been payable and the net income of the CRUT shall be made up in later years, to the extent that the CRUT income in those later years exceeds the required unitrust amount for such later years. Treas. Reg. § 1.664-3(a)(1)(i)(b)(2). A CRUT with a "make-up" provision is sometimes called a "NIMCRUT." The charitable deduction for the net income CRUT, whether or not it has a "make-up" feature, is determined by assuming that the unitrust amount will be paid each year.

→ **Planning Point:** The make-up feature means that a CRUT that holds low-yielding assets that are sold and converted into high-yielding assets may make the CRT beneficiary whole, to an extent. No allowance is made for the time value of money due to the "late" receipt of the required unitrust amounts.

> **EXAMPLE:** Donor transfers $1,000,000 to an irrevocable trust that pays the Donor for life the lesser of 5% of the value of the trust property each year or the net income of the trust. A deficiency in any year will be made up from excess income in later years. In year 1 the trust had income of $40,000. Therefore, only $40,000 would be distributed to Donor, rather than the required payment of $50,000. If in year 2 the trust income was $65,000 and the payment was $55,000 (the trust property having appreciated to $1,100,000), Donor would be entitled to all $65,000, $10,000 of which would be a deficiency distribution.

→ **Planning Point:** The 5% exhaustion rule discussed above does not apply to a NIMCRUT because the trust principal will not be invaded. It also should not apply to a standard CRUT because the unitrust payment increases and decreases as the value of the trust assets increases and decreases, so that the trust should never be exhausted.

(c) **Final Regulations Regarding the Definition of Income Under IRC § 643**. The final regulations regarding the definition of income were issued on December 30, 2003. For further discussion of these regulations, see Chapter VI, "Federal Income Taxation of Trusts and Estates." With regard to charitable trusts, the final regulations affect only CRUTs that make distributions partially by reference to "income," including net income CRUTs and NIMCRUTs. They do not affect CRATs or CRUTs that pay only a unitrust interest.

A charitable trust may follow its own definition of trust income or follow the definition under applicable state law. However, trust income may not be determined by reference to a fixed percentage of the annual fair market value of the trust property, notwithstanding any contrary provision in applicable state law. Treas. Reg. § 1.664-3(a)(1). As provided in IRC § 643(b),

21st Century Estate Planning:
Practical Applications
2005 Edition

©2005 Sonnenschein Nath & Rosenthal LLP
and Cannon Financial Institute, Inc.

- 530 -

capital gains from assets contributed to the trust by the donor or purchased by the trust may be allocated to income, pursuant to the terms of the governing instrument, if not prohibited by applicable local law. However, gains from the sale of assets contributed to the trust by the donor must be allocated to principal and not to trust income to the extent of the fair market value of those assets on the date of their contribution to the trust. In addition, capital gains may not be allocated to trust income to the extent of the trust's purchase price of those assets. Further, the trustee's discretionary power to make an allocation to income is acceptable only to the extent that a state statute permits the trustee to make adjustments between income and principal to treat beneficiaries impartially. Id.

→ **Planning Point:** It will be important to monitor enabling legislation in states where a practitioner practices with regard to how state law definitions of income will be taken into account in CRUTs. Affirmative steps may be required to protect the tax treatment of existing CRUTs, and revised income and principal allocation language may be needed for newly created CRTs.

(d) **FLIPCRUTs.** The position of the IRS previously was that a CRUT cannot use more than one of the types of payments during its term, that is, it cannot "flip" from a NIMCRUT to a standard CRUT, for example. This type of CRUT is known as a "FLIPCRUT." In the past, the IRS had indicated that a FLIPCRUT would not qualify under IRC § 664 as a CRUT.

EXAMPLE: A FLIPCRUT is beneficial if the trust is funded initially with illiquid assets that do not produce income. In that case, the CRUT can be an income-only CRUT until the property is sold because of the difficulty in paying the unitrust amount. After the asset has been sold, however, the donor can receive the unitrust payment rather than income only.

In regulations adopted in 1998, however, the IRS changed its position. Treas. Reg. § 1.664-3(a)(1)(i)(c). These regulations allow a trust that uses either the net income or net income with make-up provisions to pay out using such method for an initial period and then flip to a standard CRUT (i.e., the fixed unitrust amount) for the balance of the term. The "flip" must be triggered by a specific date or by a specific event, as long as the date or event is not within the discretion or control of the trustee or any other person. Id. The sale of unmarketable assets, or the death, birth of a child, marriage or divorce of any individual will not be considered to be within the discretion or control of the trustee or any person. Treas. Reg. § 1.664-3(a)(1)(i)(d). The flip will be effective at the beginning of the taxable year immediately following the year in which the triggering event or date falls. Treas. Reg. § 1.664-3(a)(1)(i)(c).

→ **Planning Point:** Any "make-up" amount is forfeited upon the conversion.

21st Century Estate Planning:
Practical Applications
2005 Edition

©2005 Sonnenschein Nath & Rosenthal LLP
and Cannon Financial Institute, Inc.

- 531 -

The term "unmarketable assets" includes assets that are not "cash, cash equivalents, or other assets that can be readily sold or exchanged for cash or cash equivalents." Treas. Reg. § 1.664-1(a)(7)(ii). Examples include real property, closely held stock, and unregistered securities for which there is no available exemption permitting public sale. *Id.*

      b. <u>**Timing of Payment**</u>. The annuity or unitrust payment may be made after the close of the taxable year if certain requirements are met. See Treas. Reg. §§ 1.664-2(a)(1)(i)(a), 3(a)(1)(i)(g).

A testamentary CRT is deemed created at death even if it is not funded until the end of the period of estate administration. The annuity or unitrust payment may be deferred until the end of the taxable year in which the CRT is funded. Treas. Reg. § 1.664-1(a)(5)(i). The governing instrument must set forth the method for retroactively determining the payments to which the noncharitable beneficiary was entitled from the date of death to the date the CRT was funded. Deferred payments must bear interest at the Section 7520 rate. Treas. Reg. §§ 1.664-1(a)(5)(i), (iv)(a).

      c. <u>**Reformation of Split-Interest Trusts**</u>. Reformation of split-interest trusts is allowed under IRC § 2055(e)(3) if certain requirements are met. The governing instrument must express the noncharitable beneficiary's interest in terms of an annuity or unitrust interest. IRC § 2055(e)(3)(C)(ii). Meeting this requirement demonstrates an intent to comply with the law. If this requirement is not met, reformation also may be accomplished if a judicial reformation proceeding is commenced within ninety days of the due date (including extensions) for the federal estate tax return on which the deduction is claimed. If no federal estate tax return is required, the judicial reformation proceeding must be commenced within ninety days after the last date (including extensions) for filing the first income tax return for the CRT. IRC § 2055(e)(3)(C)(iii).

The reformation may not change the actuarial value of the charitable interest by more than five percent. IRC § 2055(e)(3)(B)(i). Additionally, the durations of the charitable and noncharitable interests may not change. A noncharitable interest in a CRT of more than twenty years, however, may be reduced to twenty years. *Id.* In that case, the annual distribution to the noncharitable beneficiary must be increased so that the actuarial value of the charitable and noncharitable interests remains the same.

CRATs and CRUTs that do not meet the ten percent value of remainder interest test also can be reformed. IRC § 2055(e)(3)(J). Reformation may be necessary in the case of a testamentary CRT because, with such a trust, it is not possible to determine whether the trust satisfies the ten percent requirement until the grantor's death. This is because the Section 7520 rate is not fixed until the date of death, and if a noncharitable term has a measuring life, the length of that term will not be determinable until the donor's death.

      d. <u>**Beneficiaries of the CRT**</u>. The noncharitable beneficiaries of a CRT may include individuals, trusts, partnerships, corporations, or other legal entities that are not charities.

21st Century Estate Planning:
Practical Applications
2005 Edition

©2005 Sonnenschein Nath & Rosenthal LLP
and Cannon Financial Institute, Inc.

- 532 -

Treas. Reg. §§ 1.664-2(a)(3), 3(a)(3). If the noncharitable beneficiaries are individuals, all of them must be living when the trust is created.

The remainder must be distributed to or for the use of an organization described in IRC § 170(c) or held as a charitable trust. IRC § 664(d)(1)(C), (d)(2)(C). The CRT may provide that the interests of the charitable beneficiaries be enjoyed concurrently or successively. Treas. Reg. §§ 1.664-2(a)(6)(iii), 3(a)(6)(iii).

> **EXAMPLE:** Trust provides that, upon termination, the remainder will be held in trust, and the income will be payable 50% to each of two charities. The trust qualifies as a CRT.

> **EXAMPLE:** Trust provides that, upon termination, the remainder will be held in trust with all the income payable to Charity 1 for 10 years and thereafter the property is to be distributed outright to Charity 2. The trust qualifies as a CRT.

The trust instrument must set forth a method for selecting an alternate charitable remainder beneficiary in the event the designated charity does not qualify as an organization for which an income tax deduction is available. Treas. Reg. §§ 1.664-2(a)(6)(iv), 3(a)(6)(iv).

➜ **Planning Point:** Because IRC §§ 170(c), 2055(a) and 2522(a) differ in the type of organization contributions to which are deductible, the trust instrument should provide that both the designated and the alternate remainder beneficiaries qualify for a charitable deduction under whichever Code sections a deduction is sought.

The donor of an inter vivos CLT may retain the right to substitute the charitable remainder beneficiaries. Rev. Rul. 76-8, 1976-1 C.B. 179; PLR 200034019 (August 25, 2000); PLR 9331043 (August 6, 1993). Additionally, the income beneficiary or a trustee of a testamentary CRT may have the right to designate the remainder beneficiaries. Rev. Rul. 76-7, 1976-1 C.B. 179; PLR 8919016 (May 12, 1989).

    e. **Term of the CRT**. If the noncharitable beneficiary is an individual, then the term of the CRT may be for either the duration of the beneficiary's life or not more than twenty years. IRC § 664(d)(1)(A), (d)(2)(A); Treas. Reg. §§ 1.664-2(a)(5), 3(a)(5). If the noncharitable beneficiary is not an individual, then the term of the CRT must be for a term of years not to exceed twenty years. *Id.* An interest that could never exceed both the life interest of named beneficiaries who were living at the creation of the CRT or a term of twenty years would be permissible.

➜ **Planning Point:** The donor to the CRT must choose which measuring period -- a life interest or a term of years -- to use, and the CRT may not later deviate from that original choice. For example, a term of years

21st Century Estate Planning:
Practical Applications
2005 Edition

©2005 Sonnenschein Nath & Rosenthal LLP
and Cannon Financial Institute, Inc.

- 533 -

followed by a life interest, or vice versa, generally is not permissible, because of the possibility that the total duration of the CRT might exceed both the lives of named beneficiaries who were living at the creation of the CRT and a term of twenty years.

> **EXAMPLE:** An interest to A for A's life, followed by an interest to B (who was living at the creation of the CRT), for the shorter of twenty years or B's life, would qualify. In this example, the total term could not exceed A's and B's lives, so that the possibility of a term exceeding both the life interest of named beneficiaries and a term of twenty years is not possible.

In selecting the term of the CRT, the donor must bear in mind the requirements, discussed above, as to the probability of the exhaustion of trust assets and the amount that must be distributed to the charity at the end of the term. As illustrated in an example above, a CRAT for the life of a young beneficiary is unlikely to meet the 10% remainder test.

> **f. Valuation of Unmarketable Assets**. If the CRT will hold unmarketable assets, the trust will not qualify for an income, gift or estate tax deduction unless an independent trustee values the unmarketable assets, or, alternatively, the value is determined by a qualified appraisal from a qualified appraiser. Treas. Reg. § 1.664-1(a)(7)(i). For this purpose, a qualified appraisal is defined as it is for purposes of the income tax substantiation rules. An independent trustee is a person who is not the grantor of the CRT, a noncharitable beneficiary, or a person who is subordinate or related to the grantor, the grantor's spouse, or a noncharitable beneficiary. Treas. Reg. § 1.664-1(a)(7)(iii). Unmarketable assets are those that are not cash, cash equivalents, or other assets that can be readily converted into cash, such as real estate, closely held stock, and unregistered securities. Treas. Reg. § 1.664-1(a)(7)(ii).

➔ **Planning Point:** Because with a CRUT the assets must be valued each year, the appraisal requirement must be met each time the assets are revalued.

➔ **Planning Point:** If the transfer of assets to the CRT requires a qualified appraisal for the purpose of the substantiation rules, that same appraisal can be used to satisfy the requirements of Treas. Reg. § 1.664-1(a)(7).

21st Century Estate Planning:
Practical Applications
2005 Edition

©2005 Sonnenschein Nath & Rosenthal LLP
and Cannon Financial Institute, Inc.

- 534 -

g. IRS "Safe Harbor" Forms. The IRS has promulgated a number of "safe harbor" forms, stating that use of the language in the forms complies with all of the relevant rules and restrictions for CRTs. See Rev. Proc. 90-30, 1990-1 C.B. 534; Rev. Proc. 90-31, 1990-1 C.B. 539; Rev. Proc. 90-32, 1990-1 C.B. 546. The IRS forms are not complete trusts. Important sections, such as trustee powers, are completely missing, and the forms omit many popular CRT provisions. Consequently, although practitioners are well-advised to use the safe harbor forms, they may do so only by integrating general trust provisions into the safe harbor forms.

➔ **Planning Point:** Because of the safe harbor provisions, the IRS will not issue rulings on whether a particular trust qualifies as a CRT. Rev. Proc. 2002-3, 2002-1 I.R.B. 117. To the extent that a particular CRT document uses provisions not included in the safe harbor provisions, then the IRS may rule on whether or not such additional provisions will disqualify the trust as a CRT.

2. Income, Gift and Estate Tax Consequences

A charitable deduction will be available to the donor for the actuarial value of the charity's remainder interest in the CRT. If the CRT is established during the donor's lifetime, then the donor will be entitled to a charitable deduction for income tax purposes and for gift tax purposes. If the CRT is established upon the death of the donor (under the donor's will or revocable trust, for example), then the donor's estate will be entitled to a charitable deduction for estate tax purposes.

a. Income Tax Consequences.

(1) Charitable Deduction for Value of Charitable Remainder Interest. To qualify as a CRT, the charitable remainder beneficiary must be an organization described in IRC § 170(c). An income tax deduction is available for the actuarial value of the charity's remainder interest, determined under Section 7520. The deduction for a CRAT is calculated by subtracting the present value of the annuity from the fair market value of the property transferred to the CRAT. The deduction for a CRUT is the present value of the remainder interest.

➔ **Planning Point:** For CRATs, the higher the Section 7520 rate, the larger the charitable deduction. This is because the IRS is assuming that the higher the interest rate, the better the yield of the CRT assets, so that a larger amount is left for charity. The differences caused by rate changes for CRUTs are nominal, because the unitrust amount that is payable will be deemed to increase at the same rate as the CRUT assets are appreciating.

EXAMPLE: Assuming a Section 7520 rate of 5.6%, a $1,000,000 CRAT for the life of a 68-year-old donor that pays a 7% annuity

21st Century Estate Planning:
Practical Applications
2005 Edition

©2005 Sonnenschein Nath & Rosenthal LLP
and Cannon Financial Institute, Inc.

- 535 -

quarterly will result in a charitable deduction of $337,539 for the remainder interest. The present value of the annuity is $662,461. The value of the remainder interest is determined by subtracting the value of the annuity ($662,461) from the value of the property transferred to the CRAT ($1,000,000). If the Section 7520 rate is 7%, then the charitable deduction for the remainder interest is $399,018.

EXAMPLE: Assuming the same facts as in the previous example except that a CRUT is used, the charitable deduction for the remainder interest is $403,540 at a 5.6% Section 7520 rate, and $406,140 at a 7% Section 7520 rate. Comparing these results with the previous example illustrates how a change in the Section 7520 rate has little effect on the amount of the charitable deduction for a CRUT.

The amount of the deduction will be determined by the type of property contributed to the CRT (cash or capital gain property), the remainder charitable beneficiary (public charity or private foundation), and on whether the remainder interest will pass outright to the charitable beneficiary or be held in further trust for the benefit of the charitable beneficiary. If the property is retained in trust for the beneficiary, the gift is "for the use of" a public charity and is subject to the thirty percent limitation. The percentage limitations for purposes of the income tax charitable deduction are discussed in detail at the beginning of this chapter.

➔ **Planning Point:** If any person has the right to substitute the charitable remainder beneficiary, and the amount of the deduction depends upon the remainder beneficiary being a public charity, then the right to substitute the charitable remainder beneficiary should be limited to public charities. Rev. Rul. 79-308, 1979-2 C.B. 109.

(2) Character of Income Distributions (the Tier System). Charitable remainder trusts generally are exempt from income taxes. Distributions to the noncharitable beneficiaries of the CRT carry out the CRT's income to the beneficiaries, where it is taxed to the beneficiaries on a tier basis. The purpose of the tier system is to ensure that income taxed at the highest rate is distributed first to the beneficiaries before distributions taxed at a lower rate.

In any year in which the trust has any unrelated business taxable income ("UBTI"), the trust will forfeit its tax-exempt status, and all income realized by the trust for the year will be subject to income tax to the trust as a non-exempt complex trust. IRC § 664(c); Treas. Reg. § 1.664-1(c). See also *Leila G. Newhall Unitrust v. Comm'r*, 104 T.C. 236 (1995). UBTI usually results from income derived from a trade or business carried on by the trust that is unrelated to the charity's tax-exempt purposes.

➔ **Planning Point:** A CRT is often used in order to avoid tax on the sale of the contributed property. In this situation, it is critical to avoid UBTI, at

21st Century Estate Planning:
Practical Applications
2005 Edition

©2005 Sonnenschein Nath & Rosenthal LLP
and Cannon Financial Institute, Inc.

- 536 -

least in the year in which the contributed property is sold. Thus, contributions of property which create UBTI, such as trade or business partnerships and S corporations, should be avoided. Similarly reinvestment of proceeds of sale in investments which create UBTI, such as trade or business partnerships and S corporations, or margined securities, or investment partnerships with leveraged investments, should be avoided.

Every year, the CRT categorizes its income into one of three categories: ordinary income, capital gain income, and other income. IRC § 664(b).

(a) **First Tier: Ordinary Income**. All distributions are deemed to carry out first the ordinary income of the CRT for the current year, plus any undistributed ordinary income from previous years. IRC § 664(b)(1); Treas. Reg. § 1.664-1(d)(1)(i)(a). Ordinary income means the CRT's trust accounting income that is includible in its gross income. Ordinary losses reduce the current year's ordinary income first and then may reduce accumulated ordinary income from previous years. Ordinary losses that still remain may be carried forward indefinitely to offset ordinary income earned in later taxable years.

(b) **Second Tier: Capital Gain Income**. Once the payments to a beneficiary in a given year have carried out all of the current year's ordinary income and any previous years' undistributed ordinary income, then distributions, to the extent that they exceed this total accumulated amount, are deemed to consist, first, of capital gain income for the current year and then of undistributed capital gain income from previous years. IRC § 664(b)(2); Treas. Reg. § 1.664-1(d)(1)(i)(b).

(c) **Third Tier: Other Income**. Once the CRT's capital gain income for the current year and all undistributed capital gain income from previous years has been distributed, any additional distributions would be deemed to consist of other income (such as municipal bond income) from the current year and undistributed other income from prior years. IRC § 664(b)(3); Treas. Reg. § 1.664-1(d)(1)(i)(c).

(d) **Fourth Tier: Return of Capital**. If the third tier of income is exhausted, then any additional payments will be deemed to consist of trust corpus. IRC § 664(b)(4); Treas. Reg. § 1.664-1(d)(1)(i)(d).

If a CRT makes a distribution to a charity other than a distribution of a portion of the annuity or unitrust amount, the distribution is deemed made out of the same tiers as distributions to the noncharitable beneficiaries, but in the reverse order. Treas. Reg. § 1.664-1(e)(1). That is, distributions to the charitable beneficiary are attributed to corpus first, then other income, then capital gains, then ordinary income. If the charitable beneficiary receives a portion of the annuity or unitrust payment, however, the tier rules for noncharitable beneficiaries apply. Treas. Reg. § 1.664-1(d)(1)(i).

21st Century Estate Planning:
Practical Applications
2005 Edition

©2005 Sonnenschein Nath & Rosenthal LLP
and Cannon Financial Institute, Inc.

- 537 -

b. Gift Tax Consequences. To qualify as a CRT, the charitable remainder beneficiary must be an organization described in IRC § 170(c). Thus, the charitable remainder beneficiary must meet the requirements of both IRC §§ 2522 and 170(c) in order to qualify for the gift tax deduction. Because the category of permissible recipients is not the same in those sections, it is necessary to make sure that the charitable beneficiary qualifies under both sections.

If the CRT is established during the donor's life, the donor is entitled to a charitable gift tax deduction for the actuarial value of the charity's remainder interest. A transfer to a CRT in which the donor retains the annuity or unitrust interest does not have any gift tax consequences. In such a case, the only gift is the gift of the remainder interest, which qualifies for the gift tax charitable deduction.

If the donor gives the annuity or unitrust interest to another person, however, gift tax may be incurred. The value of the gift of the annuity interest is calculated by subtracting the present value of the remainder interest from the value of the property transferred, determined under Section 7520. The value of the gift of a unitrust interest is the present value of the unitrust interest. If the only noncharitable beneficiary other than the donor is the donor's spouse, the gift tax marital deduction will be available. IRC § 2523(g). If the noncharitable beneficiary is not the donor's spouse, then the actuarial value of the beneficiary's interest will be subject to gift tax, and as long as the value of the gift is less than the donor's unused gift tax applicable exclusion amount, the donor will not have to pay any gift tax on the transfer of the interest.

> **EXAMPLE:** Assuming a Section 7520 rate of 5.6%, a $1,000,000 CRAT for the life of a 68-year-old that pays a 7% annuity quarterly will result in a charitable deduction of $337,539 for the remainder interest. The present value of the annuity is $662,461. Thus, if the noncharitable beneficiary is someone other than the donor or the donor's spouse, the taxable gift is $662,461.

➔ **Planning Point:** If a donor wants to name a successor noncharitable beneficiary who is not a spouse, the donor should retain the right, exercisable by his or her will, to revoke the successor beneficiary's interest at the donor's death. Treas. Reg. §§ 1.664-2(a)(4), 3(a)(4). This renders the successor beneficiary's interest incomplete, so that no gift tax is assessed on the interest. The successor beneficiary's interest will, however, be subject to estate tax at the donor's death, unless that interest is revoked, in which case all of the CRT assets pass immediately to or for charity.

c. Estate Tax Consequences. The remainder beneficiary must be an organization described in IRC §§ 2055(a) and 170(c) in order to qualify for the estate tax charitable deduction. If the donor is a beneficiary of the CRT, then the CRT will be includible in the donor's gross estate for federal estate tax purposes. If the CRT is established at the donor's

21st Century Estate Planning:
Practical Applications
2005 Edition

©2005 Sonnenschein Nath & Rosenthal LLP
and Cannon Financial Institute, Inc.

- 538 -

death, however, an estate tax deduction will be available to the donor's estate for the remainder interest.

If the property is passing outright to charity at the donor's death, then the charitable deduction equals the net fair market value of the property at the time of the donor's death. If the property is remaining in trust for the benefit of another individual, then the estate tax charitable deduction is limited to the actuarial remainder value of the trust assets. The value of the noncharitable interests will be subject to estate tax. If the only noncharitable beneficiary other than the donor is the donor's spouse, then the estate tax marital deduction will be available. IRC § 2056(b)(8). If the noncharitable beneficiary is not the donor's spouse, then the actuarial value of the beneficiary's interest will be subject to estate tax, and the donor's unused estate tax applicable exclusion amount may be used to eliminate or reduce any estate tax.

3. Other Considerations

   a. Choice of Trustee. The donor may name any person, including the donor, or a corporate fiduciary to act as trustee. If the trustee will have the power to make distributions among a class of noncharitable beneficiaries or if any hard-to-value assets are transferred to the trust, the trust may be disqualified if the donor or a party controlled by the donor is acting as trustee. Under these circumstances, the trust should provide that all discretionary powers and valuations of hard-to-value assets will be done by an independent trustee.

➔ **Planning Point:** A charity that is a designated remainder beneficiary of the CRT may act as trustee if not prohibited by state law. Donors often name charities as trustee of their CRTs to minimize trustee fees, as charities customarily waive such fees. A charitable remainder beneficiary may not act, however, where the trust property includes hard-to-value assets, although it may choose to act and obtain an independent appraisal.

➔ **Planning Point:** Trustee fees that are paid may not be charged against the unitrust amount or the annuity amount. Doing so will result in disqualification of the CRT. See Rev. Rul. 74-19, 1974-1 C.B. 155.

➔ **Planning Point:** If the donor is acting as trustee, payment of trustee fees will not constitute self-dealing as long as the payments are reasonable. See PLR 8035078 (June 6, 1980).

If the donor is serving as trustee, he or she should not retain any powers that would cause the trust to be subject to the grantor trust rules. Treatment as a grantor trust prevents a trust from qualifying as a CRT. Treas. Reg. § 1.664-1(a)(4).

➔ **Planning Point:** If the donor wants the trustee to be able to "spray" the unitrust or annuity amount among a specified class of beneficiaries, then the donor's serving as trustee will cause the CRT to be treated as a grantor

21st Century Estate Planning:
Practical Applications
2005 Edition

©2005 Sonnenschein Nath & Rosenthal LLP
and Cannon Financial Institute, Inc.

- 539 -

trust for income tax purposes, thereby causing the CRT to be disqualified and its income to be taxable to the donor rather than taxable under the tier system. See Treas. Reg. §§ 1.664-2(a)(3)(ii), 3(a)(3)(ii).

➔ **Planning Point:** The retained power to designate the charitable remainder beneficiaries in the donor's will or other document will not cause the trust to be treated as a grantor trust. See IRC § 674(b)(4).

> **b. Choice of Assets to Contribute to a CRT.** Many CRTs are funded with appreciated property because no gain will be recognized on the transfer of property to the trust. Caution should be used if the donor wishes to contribute unproductive or low-yield assets, such as land or closely held stock.

➔ **Planning Point:** A net income CRUT, with or without the make-up provision, is a good candidate for such assets because it avoids mandatory unitrust payments in years in which the income yield on the trust assets is low. If the assets are sold and reinvested in more productive assets, then the trustee can begin to pay the full unitrust amount. A CRAT is a bad candidate for such assets because it requires the distribution of the specified amount regardless of whether the assets have generated income. Additionally, while additional property can be added to a CRUT to provide for the necessary payments, no additional property may be added to a CRAT.

As noted above, a CRT forfeits its tax-exempt status for any year in which UBTI is realized by the trust. Therefore, the donor must consider whether property contributed to a CRT will generate UBTI.

➔ **Planning Point:** In most situations, mortgaged property should not be contributed to a CRT, even if the CRT is not liable for the debt. Subject to certain exceptions, the mortgage is treated as acquisition indebtedness. This treatment means that the CRT could realize debt-financed income, which is treated as UBTI. IRC § 514(c)(2). Realizing UBTI would cause the CRT to forfeit its special income tax status for the year of receipt of the UBTI. If the donor is liable for the debt, the trust's payment of the debt would be self-dealing because it would have the effect of discharging a legal obligation of a disqualified person (*i.e.*, the donor).

➔ **Planning Point:** Even real estate not subject to a mortgage may generate UBTI, if real estate taxes are a lien on the property under state law and the real estate taxes are paid late. In that situation, late payment of the taxes would cause the lien on the property to be treated as a mortgage that would be characterized as acquisition indebtedness, thereby possibly generating debt-financed income.

21st Century Estate Planning:
Practical Applications
2005 Edition

©2005 Sonnenschein Nath & Rosenthal LLP
and Cannon Financial Institute, Inc.

- 540 -

➜ **Planning Point:** Limited partnership interests, including publicly traded limited partnership interests, often throw off UBTI.

    c. Using a CRAT or a CRUT. A CRAT may be preferred by individuals who are less tolerant to risk and are worried about deflation because the value of the annual annuity remains constant regardless of any increase or decrease in the value of the trust property. If the property contributed to the trust is difficult to value, a CRAT will be preferable because the asset must be valued only at the time of contribution rather than annually, as with a CRUT.

    A CRUT may be preferred by individuals who are more risk tolerant and are worried about the effect of inflation, on the assumption that the fair market value of the assets will increase with inflation. As the fair market value of the assets increases, the unitrust payment increases. If the donor wishes to make additional gifts to the trust, a CRUT should be selected because no additional gifts may be made to a CRAT.

    If a net income CRT is desired, then the donor can use only a CRUT. A CRUT offers more flexibility than a CRAT in designing an interest to meet cash flow needs or to deal with property contributed to the CRUT that is not producing income. This flexibility is not available with a CRAT.

➜ **Planning Point:** If older private beneficiaries are involved, a CRAT may be preferable, because of its greater certainty, and because the impact of inflation is not as large a factor if the expected duration of the CRT is shorter. This also means that the CRUT format usually is preferred for younger beneficiaries because of the anticipated longer duration of the CRT.

    d. Private Foundation Rules. CRTs are split-interest trusts within the meaning of IRC § 4947(a)(2). This means that the restrictions on operations of private foundations in IRC § 4941 (self-dealing), IRC § 4943 (excess business holdings), IRC § 4944 (jeopardy investments) and IRC § 4945 (taxable expenditures) may be applicable to CRTs, so the restrictions must be examined in detail to avoid excise taxes. These restrictions are discussed in greater detail above in the section on private foundations.

    (1) Self-Dealing. IRC § 4941 relating to self-dealing is applicable to CRTs, even during the term of the private beneficiary's noncharitable interest. The applicability of IRC § 4941 means that CRTs should not enter into any business or other arrangements with the donor of the CRT, members of his or her family, or any other persons who would be disqualified persons with respect to the CRT under the attribution rules of IRC § 4946.

    (2) Excess Business Holdings and Jeopardy Investments. A special exemption exists for the IRC § 4943 rule on excess business holdings and the IRC § 4944 rule on jeopardy investments if a charitable deduction was allowed for amounts payable to every remainder beneficiary, but not to any income beneficiary. IRC § 4947(b)(3)(B); Treas.

21st Century Estate Planning:
Practical Applications
2005 Edition

©2005 Sonnenschein Nath & Rosenthal LLP
and Cannon Financial Institute, Inc.

- 541 -

Reg. § 53.4947-2(b)(1)(ii). This is the case with most CRTs, which means that most CRTs are exempt from the rules on excess business holdings and jeopardy investments. If any portion of the income interest in a CRT is payable to a charity and a charitable deduction was allowed for the gift of such interest, IRC §§ 4943 and 4944 will apply.

➔ **Planning Point:** As discussed above, a CRT may pay a portion of the annuity amount or unitrust amount to charity, but no charitable deduction is allowed for such a payment. If no deduction is allowed, IRC §§ 4943 and 4944 will not apply. Some CRTs may, however, pay income other than the annuity or unitrust amount to charity for which a charitable deduction is permitted.

Although CRTs may be exempt from the jeopardy investment rules, the trust document must not prevent the trustee from being able to invest the assets in a way that realizes a reasonable amount of income or gain. Treas. Reg. § 1.664-1(a)(3).

➔ **Planning Point:** Consequently, directions in the trust document to retain certain assets, or restrictions on the sale or disposal of certain assets, may cause the CRT to be disqualified. See PLR 8041100 (July 21, 1980) (trustee directed to invest assets as investment counsel directed); PLR 7948108 (August 31, 1979) (beneficiary approval required to change CRT's investments); PLR 7802037 (October 14, 1977) (trustee required to invest only in tax-exempt securities).

The consequences of disqualification are that the donor loses the income, gift or estate tax charitable deductions that otherwise would have been available for the transfer of the assets into the CRT, and the CRT is subject to tax on its income just like any other complex trust would be.

G. Charitable Remainder Trusts as Retirement Plan Beneficiary

The income tax-exempt status of CRTs makes retirement assets, also known as income in respect of a decedent ("IRD") assets, particularly good assets for the CRT to receive at the donor's death. An IRD asset is inherited property that, had the decedent received it before death, would have been taxable income to the decedent. Although as a general rule inherited property is not subject to income tax, IRD is an exception to that rule. The individual who receives the IRD, or the decedent's estate if the IRD is distributed to the estate, must include the IRD on the income tax return for the year it was received. Additionally, IRD assets are included in a decedent's gross estate for federal estate tax purposes, and, therefore, are subject to estate tax. Although the recipient can claim an income tax deduction for the federal estate tax attributable to the IRD, the effect of the double taxation is to tax IRD assets at a very high rate.

➔ **Planning Point:** The most common sources of IRD are distributions from a decedent's IRA, 401(k) or profit sharing plan.

21st Century Estate Planning:
Practical Applications
2005 Edition

©2005 Sonnenschein Nath & Rosenthal LLP
and Cannon Financial Institute, Inc.

- 542 -

1. **Naming the CRT as Beneficiary**

If an individual wishes to make a charitable bequest, making a gift of IRD to a charity saves income taxes. The trustee of a CRT created under a person's will or revocable trust instrument is designated as primary or contingent beneficiary of such person's qualified retirement plan or IRA proceeds. The individual can give other assets that are not subject to income tax to heirs.

2. **Tax Consequences**

    a. **Income Tax**. The CRT does not realize taxable income upon receipt of the proceeds because the CRT is a tax-exempt entity. IRC § 664(c). The character of distributions out of the qualified retirement plan or IRA means nothing as far as the CRT is concerned (unless the CRT has UBTI). Because the IRD is distributed to the CRT, neither the donor's estate nor the donor's heirs will recognize taxable income when the IRD is distributed to the CRT.

    b. **Gift Tax**. There is no gift tax consequence to this transaction so long as the beneficiary designation remains revocable.

    c. **Estate Tax**. The decedent's estate will be entitled to an unlimited estate tax charitable deduction for the actuarial value of the remainder interest in the CRT. If the spouse of the participant or employee has an interest in the CRT and is the only noncharitable beneficiary, the marital deduction will shelter from estate tax the actuarially computed value of that interest, and the charitable deduction can be claimed for the balance of the value of the remaining trust property. IRC §§ 2056(b)(8), 2055(e)(2)(A).

If there are noncharitable beneficiaries other than the spouse of the participant or employee, the charitable deduction can be claimed only with respect to the actuarially computed value of the charitable remainder interest, and estate tax may be due on the actuarially computed value of all noncharitable interests. In this case, naming a CRT as the beneficiary will not eliminate estate taxes, but it will allow the children of the participant or employee to receive a benefit from the IRD assets, and the children will be taxed only on the distributions from the CRT rather than on all of the income from the IRD assets.

3. **Considerations**

    a. **Required Distributions from Qualified Plans and IRAs**. Qualified pension and profit sharing plans and IRAs are subject to special rules governing their distribution during life. Under the old proposed regulations, the distribution rules were not favorable for naming a charity as a beneficiary of a qualified plan or an IRA. The old proposed regulations tied the calculation of the minimum amount that must be distributed during the participant's or employee's life to the life expectancy of the participant or employee and a "designated beneficiary." Because a charity is not a "designated beneficiary," the use of a charitable beneficiary limited lifetime distributions from the IRA or qualified plan to a period measured by

21st Century Estate Planning:
Practical Applications
2005 Edition

©2005 Sonnenschein Nath & Rosenthal LLP
and Cannon Financial Institute, Inc.

- 543 -

the single life expectancy of the participant or employee, the effect of which was to increase the amount that must be distributed during life.

Under the new proposed regulations, however, this is no longer the case. The identity of the designated beneficiary is irrelevant in calculating the lifetime distributions from a qualified plan or IRA. Thus, even with a charitable beneficiary, lifetime distributions can be measured using a uniform table (which generally results in smaller required distributions during life), and the fact that a charity is not a "designated beneficiary" will not affect the amount of the lifetime distributions. For a more in-depth discussion of the changes to the distribution rules for qualified plans and IRAs, see Chapter 12 on planning for retirement benefits.

      b. <u>Naming a Spouse as the Primary Beneficiary</u>. If the participant or employee has a spouse, it adds flexibility to the estate plan if the spouse is designated as the primary beneficiary of the qualified retirement plan or IRA benefits, and the trustee of the CRT created under the will or revocable trust instrument of the participant or employee is designated as the contingent beneficiary. The spouse can either roll over such benefits and create his or her own CRT (or direct an outright charitable disposition) in his or her will or revocable trust instrument, or the spouse can make a qualified disclaimer to the participant's CRT.

      c. <u>Funding the CRT With Retirement Benefits</u>. The CRT could be funded directly in accordance with a qualified retirement plan or IRA beneficiary designation. Alternatively, the qualified retirement plan or IRA proceeds could pass by beneficiary designation to the trustee under the will or revocable trust instrument of the participant or employee, and such trustee would then use such proceeds, along with any other available assets, to fund the CRT in accordance with applicable provisions of the will or trust instrument. Such provisions should set out a specific asset allocation or a percentage or fractional share of property to be transferred to the trustee of the CRT rather than designating a pecuniary amount for the CRT. Funding the CRT with a pecuniary amount will result in the acceleration of IRD.

      d. <u>Advantages of Naming a CRT as a Retirement Plan Beneficiary</u>. The advantages of naming a CRT as a retirement plan beneficiary, as compared to designating someone other than a spouse (*e.g.*, a child of the participant or employee) as beneficiary of a qualified retirement plan or IRA include the following:

- Estate taxes are reduced because the actuarially computed value of the charitable remainder gives rise to a charitable deduction;
- The immediate recipient of the qualified retirement plan or IRA proceeds (the trustee of the CRT) realizes no taxable income upon receipt of such proceeds. Thus, there is a larger fund to invest from the outset;
- Because the CRT is an income tax-exempt entity, dividends, interest and capital gains are not diluted by income taxes. In sum, if the CRT lasts long enough after the death of the participant or employee, the economic

21st Century Estate Planning:
Practical Applications
2005 Edition

©2005 Sonnenschein Nath & Rosenthal LLP
and Cannon Financial Institute, Inc.

- 544 -

benefits of income tax-free investing and reinvesting within the CRT will outweigh the first disadvantage discussed below; and

- Using a CRT may involve a substantial gift to charity. If the participant or employee is otherwise charitably inclined, this technique may be a good vehicle through which to accomplish part or all of his or her desired charitable giving.

e. Disadvantages of Naming a CRT as a Retirement Plan Beneficiary. The primary disadvantage of naming a CRT as a retirement plan beneficiary, as compared to designating someone other than a spouse (*e.g.*, a child of the participant or employee) as beneficiary of a qualified retirement plan or IRA is that when a CRT terminates, regardless of how long after its creation, all remaining trust property passes to the charitable remainder beneficiary. This issue can be addressed by designating the children of the participant or employee as successor noncharitable beneficiaries. Doing so may have estate tax consequences as described above, but the actuarial joint life expectancy of the children often will be long enough so that the CRT may last long enough to provide a net benefit to the family.

H. Charitable Lead Trusts

A charitable lead trust ("CLT") is another type of split-interest gift because both a charitable beneficiary and a noncharitable beneficiary receive interests in the same property. A CLT allows the donor to donate a limited interest in specified assets to a charity. The donor transfers property to an irrevocable trust that pays the designated charity a stream of payments (the "lead" interest) for a specified period of time. At the expiration of this period of time, the grantor may reclaim his or her interest in the assets or provide for the assets to be transferred to noncharitable beneficiaries.

Depending upon the type of CLT the donor elects to establish, the donor may obtain an income tax charitable deduction and a gift tax charitable deduction or an estate tax charitable deduction.

➔ **Planning Point:** The grantor loses the income from the asset contributed to the CLT. Therefore, a CLT should be established only by a grantor possessing other assets.

1. Requirements for Estate, Gift and Income Tax Charitable Deductions

A charitable deduction is allowed only if the charitable interest is in the form of an annuity interest or a unitrust interest. Accordingly, a CLT may be established as a charitable lead annuity trust ("CLAT") or a charitable lead unitrust ("CLUT"). IRC §§ 170(f)(2)(B), 2055(e)(2)(B), 2522(c)(2)(B); Treas. Reg. §§ 1.170A-6(c)(2), 20.2055-2(e)(2)(vi) and (vii), 25.2522(c)-3(c)(2)(vi) and (vii). There is no minimum or maximum amount that must be paid to charity from a CLT.

21st Century Estate Planning:
Practical Applications
2005 Edition

©2005 Sonnenschein Nath & Rosenthal LLP
and Cannon Financial Institute, Inc.

- 545 -

a. **Annual Payments.**

(1) **Charitable Lead Annuity Trust**. A CLAT provides for the payment of a fixed dollar amount to one or more charitable beneficiaries for a specified period of time, at least yearly, regardless of the income generated by the trust. The amount paid to the charity may be a fixed percentage of the initial fair market value of the trust assets or a stated sum. The stated sum may be for a term of years or for the life of an individual living at the date of the transfer. The amount of the stated sum may be changed by a specified amount at the expiration of a term. Treas. Reg. §§ 1.170A-6(c)(2)(i)(A), 20.2055-2(e)(2)(vi)(a), 25.2522(c)-3(c)(2)(vi)(a).

> **EXAMPLE:** The CLT could provide that $50,000 be distributed to charity for 15 years and $100,000 for the remaining 10 years of a 25-year charitable term.

Income in excess of the annuity or unitrust payment may be distributed to the charitable beneficiary. The amount of the charitable deduction, however, is limited to the fair market value of the stated annuity or unitrust interest. Treas. Reg. §§ 1.170A-6(c)(2)(i)(C) and 6(c)(2)(ii)(C), 20.2055-2(e)(2)(vi)(d) and 2(e)(2)(vii)(d), 25.2522(c)-3(c)(2)(vi)(d) and 3(c)(2)(vii)(d).

(2) **Charitable Lead Unitrust**. A CLUT provides for the payment of a fixed percentage of the net fair market value of the assets of the trust, valued at least annually, to one or more charitable beneficiaries for a specified period of time, at least yearly. Because the trust assets are revalued annually, the unitrust payment fluctuates as the assets appreciate and depreciate.

b. **Term of the CLT**.
A CLT may be established for a term of years or for the life of one or more individuals who are living at the time the CLT is established. Treas. Reg. § 1.170A-6(c)(2)(i)(A). There is no limit on the number of years a CLT may operate, although the term of the CLT may be restricted by local law. Only the following individuals may be used as measuring lives: the donor, the donor's spouse, and an individual who, with respect to all noncharitable remainder beneficiaries, is either a lineal ancestor or the spouse of a lineal ancestor of those beneficiaries. Treas. Reg. §§ 20.2055-2(e)(2)(vi)(a) and (vii)(a), 25.2522(c)-3(c)(2)(vi)(a) and (vii)(a).

c. **Beneficiaries**.
A charitable lead trust may specify one or more charitable beneficiaries. Additionally, the governing instrument may allow the trustee to allocate the income interest between two or more charitable organizations. The noncharitable remainder beneficiary may be individuals, trusts, estates, partnerships or corporations.

2. Valuing the Charitable Interest

The charitable deduction for income, gift and estate tax purposes is equal to the actuarial value of the charity's annuity interest or unitrust interest, determined under Section 7520. As

21st Century Estate Planning:
Practical Applications
2005 Edition

©2005 Sonnenschein Nath & Rosenthal LLP
and Cannon Financial Institute, Inc.

- 546 -

noted above, a donor is allowed to use either the Section 7520 rate for the month in which the gift occurs, or either of the immediately preceding two months, whichever is the most favorable. In fact, because the Section 7520 rate is published on the 20th or 21st day of the preceding month, a donor may consider four months' rates when planning the date on which to establish a charitable remainder trust or charitable lead trust.

  a. **Value of an Annuity Interest**. The value of the annuity interest in a CLAT is determined by subtracting the value of the remainder interest from the value of the property transferred to the CLAT.

> **EXAMPLE:** Donor, age 55, transfers $1,000,000 to a CLAT when the Section 7520 rate is 5.4%. The CLAT will pay the charity an annuity of $100,000 for Donor's life. The present value of the annuity (and the amount of the charitable deduction) is $929,008, and the value of the remainder interest is $70,992 ($1,000,000 - $929,008). If the Section 7520 rate were 7%, the value of the annuity would equal $916,434.

  The Section 7520 regulations adopt the conclusion in Rev. Rul. 77-454, 1977-2 C.B. 351 that, in valuing an annuity payable for the life of an individual, the payment of which would exhaust the fund if the fund's total rate of return were limited to the Section 7520 rate used to value the annuity and if the measuring life outlived the exhaustion date, the value of the annuity must be calculated using a special method. Treas. Reg. §§ 1.7520-3(b)(2)(i), 20.7520-3(b)(2)(i), 25.2570-3(b)(2)(i). The value of such an annuity will be limited to the value of the right to receive it for the shorter of the measuring life or the period of time over which the trust could be expected to pay the annuity if its total return were limited to the Section 7520 rate used to value the annuity.

  b. **Value of a Unitrust Interest**. The value of a unitrust interest is determined by subtracting the present value of all interests in the transferred property other than the unitrust interest from the value of the property on the date of the transfer. Changes in the Section 7520 rate have little effect on the valuation of the charitable interest in a CLUT. The exhaustion rules should not apply to a CLUT because it should be impossible to exhaust such a trust.

> **EXAMPLE:** Donor, age 55, transfers $1,000,000 to a CLUT when the Section 7520 rate is 5.4%. The CLUT will pay the charity a unitrust amount equal to 8% of the value of the trust for Donor's life. The value of the remainder interest is $200,150, and the amount of the charitable deduction equals $799,850. If the Section 7520 rate were 7%, the amount of the charitable deduction would equal $797,440.

21st Century Estate Planning:
Practical Applications
2005 Edition

©2005 Sonnenschein Nath & Rosenthal LLP
and Cannon Financial Institute, Inc.

- 547 -

3. **Income, Gift, Estate and GST Tax Consequences**

A donor may be entitled to an income tax deduction and/or a gift or estate tax charitable deduction for the value of the charity's lead interest.

a. **Income Tax Consequences**. To obtain an income tax deduction, the grantor must be treated as the owner of the lead interest for purposes of the grantor trust rules. That is, the CLT must be a grantor trust. IRC § 170(f)(2)(B).

The recommended method of obtaining grantor trust status is for the grantor or the grantor's spouse to retain a reversionary interest equal to at least five percent of the value of the trust property on the date of transfer. IRC §§ 673(a), 672(e). The reversion is valued under Section 7520. Many of the other powers that are used to obtain grantor trust status should not be invoked because they could violate certain of the private foundation rules or other rules that would disqualify the charitable interest.

(1) **Grantor CLT**. A grantor CLT is established during the lifetime of the grantor, and it is a "grantor trust," which means that the grantor is treated as the owner of the income produced by the trust. Accordingly, all items of income, deduction and credit of the trust are reported by the grantor on his or her personal income tax return rather than by the trust as a separate entity. As a result, the grantor is taxed on the trust's income each year even though the income is being paid to the charitable beneficiary.

The grantor of a grantor CLT is entitled to a charitable income tax deduction upon the creation of the CLT but, as noted above, the grantor is taxed on the trust income each year. The initial charitable deduction is equal to the present value of the charity's annuity interest or unitrust interest upon the creation of the trust. See Treas. Reg. §§ 1.170A-6(c)(3), 20.2055-2(f)(2)(iv) and (v), 25.2522(c)-3(d)(2)(iv) and (v).

The grantor's charitable income tax deduction is subject to the percentage limitations on charitable gifts to public charities and private foundations. The income tax charitable deduction for a grantor lead trust is equal to the present value of the charity's income interest. For charitable lead trusts funded with cash or ordinary income property that benefit public charities, the charitable deduction for the value of the lead interest is limited to 30% of the donor's adjusted gross income (with a five-year carryover for any excess) because the gift is "for the use of" the charity rather than "to" the charity. IRC § 170(b)(1)(B); Treas. Reg. § 1.170A-8(a)(2). The same 30% limitation applies for cash gifts to CLTs that benefit private foundations. The limit on deductibility is 20% of adjusted gross income when a CLT that benefits a private foundation is funded with capital gain property. IRC § 170(b)(1)(D).

➔ **Planning Point:** A grantor CLT is advantageous for a donor who is in a high income tax bracket in the year the CLT is created, when the donor will be entitled to the income tax deduction, but who is expected to be in a

21st Century Estate Planning:
Practical Applications
2005 Edition

©2005 Sonnenschein Nath & Rosenthal LLP
and Cannon Financial Institute, Inc.

- 548 -

lower income tax bracket in subsequent years, when the donor will be taxed on the trust's income.

(2) **Nongrantor CLT**. A nongrantor CLT is not a grantor trust, so the income of a nongrantor CLT is not taxed to the grantor. Rather, a nongrantor CLT is taxed as a separate entity, with income taxable to the trust. It is not exempt from income tax. The trust will receive an income tax charitable deduction for the income distributed to charity each year pursuant to the terms of the trust instrument. IRC § 642(c). The trust instrument may specify its own tier system, and if it does not, payments made to the charitable beneficiary will be considered to consist of a pro rata share of all items of the trust's income. Treas. Reg. §§ 1.643(a)-5(b), 1.662(b)-2. Unlike CRTs, the character of payments made to charitable beneficiaries of CLTs for income tax purposes is not determined by a tier system.

➔ **Planning Point:** Without a specific allocation in the trust instrument, the trust may lose the benefit of the IRC § 642(c) deduction to the extent that capital gain or tax-exempt income is deemed distributed to the charitable beneficiary. Thus, the governing instrument should characterize distributions in the following order: ordinary income, capital gain, UBTI, tax-exempt income, and trust principal.

➔ **Planning Point:** Nongrantor lead trusts are advantageous for individuals who have reached their percentage limitations and, therefore, are not entitled to an income tax charitable deduction. By using a nongrantor trust, the grantor in effect receives an income tax deduction because the grantor is not subject to income tax on the income generated by the assets held by the trust.

➔ **Planning Point:** A charitable lead trust in which neither the donor nor the donor's spouse is taxable on the trust income and which names other family members as the remainder beneficiaries affords other benefits. The creation of the trust during life can result in assets passing to family members at reduced transfer tax costs. Future appreciation is not subject to estate or gift tax. The trust term and the yearly payment to charity often can be set up so that no or a small gift is deemed made to the family remainder beneficiaries even though family members may receive a substantial amount at the termination of the trust.

The tax on UBTI does not directly affect CLTs because CLTs are not tax-exempt trusts. A portion of a CLT's IRC § 642(c) charitable deduction may, however, be disallowed in any year in which the trust realizes UBTI. Treas. Reg. § 1.681(a)-2(b).

There are no percentage limitations on the amount of income that a CLT can deduct for payments made to charity. Thus, if all of the income is payable to a charitable beneficiary, the trust will be entitled to a charitable income tax deduction for the full amount paid. Because the

21st Century Estate Planning:
Practical Applications
2005 Edition

©2005 Sonnenschein Nath & Rosenthal LLP
and Cannon Financial Institute, Inc.

- 549 -

trust has an unlimited charitable deduction, the trust can be used to avoid the percentage limitations applicable to individuals.

b. <u>Gift and Estate Tax Consequences</u>. The charitable gift or estate tax deduction allows a donor to obtain a discount in the value of the gift to the remainder beneficiaries. In the case of a CLAT, if the rate of return on the CLAT assets exceeds the Section 7520 rate used to value the charitable gift, then the excess will be transferred to the noncharitable beneficiaries free of estate and gift tax. A CLAT offers a potentially gift tax-free method of shifting future appreciation to beneficiaries while enabling a charitably-inclined client to make a gift to charity. The CLUT does not offer the same transfer tax advantages as the CLAT does. Because the amount of the unitrust payment increases as the value of the CLUT assets increases, any additional value benefits the charity rather than the noncharitable remainder beneficiaries.

(1) <u>Gift Tax Consequences</u>. If the CLT is established during the grantor's life, the grantor is entitled to a charitable gift tax deduction for the value of the charity's interest upon the creation of the trust. If the remainder beneficiaries are individuals other than the grantor, then the value of the remainder interest is a gift that is subject to gift tax when the trust is created. The remainder interest passes to the beneficiaries free of additional gift tax or estate tax, however, at the expiration of the CLT term. If the trust is designed so that the grantor receives the trust assets back at the end of the term of the trust, however, then the grantor has not made a gift, and there is no gift tax.

> **<u>EXAMPLE</u>:** Donor transfers $1,000,000 to a CLAT on January 1, 2003 when the applicable federal rate is 5.0%. The term of the trust is 10 years, and the annual payment to the charity is $50,000. The present value of the annuity payments is $386,085, and the value of the remainder interest is $613,915. Therefore, Donor would receive a gift tax charitable deduction in the amount of $386,085. If Donor designated his children as the remainder beneficiaries, Donor would have a taxable gift in the amount of $613,915. If Donor has not fully utilized his gift tax applicable exclusion amount, however, the remaining exemption may be applied, thereby reducing or even eliminating any gift tax payable.

(2) <u>Zeroed-Out CLATs</u>. It is possible to create a CLAT with a charitable interest equal to the entire value of the property transferred to the trust. Thus, the value of the remainder interest, which is the interest gifted to the noncharitable beneficiaries, would equal zero (a "zeroed-out CLAT"). As a result, no gift will be made to the noncharitable remainder beneficiaries even though family members may receive a substantial amount at the termination of the trust. A zeroed-out CLAT can be created only for a term of years, however, because the exhaustion rule of the Treas. Reg. § 1.7520-3(b)(2)(i) and Rev. Rul. 77-454, 177 C.B. 351, prevent the creation of a zeroed-out CLAT, the term of which is measured by the life of an individual.

21st Century Estate Planning:
Practical Applications
2005 Edition

©2005 Sonnenschein Nath & Rosenthal LLP
and Cannon Financial Institute, Inc.

- 550 -

EXAMPLE: Donor transfers $2 million to a 20-year CLAT when the Section 7520 rate is 5.4%. The CLAT is zeroed-out, and the annual payment to the charitable lead beneficiary is $165,972. The present value of the annuity payments is $2,000,000, so the value of the remainder interest is $0. Therefore, Donor would receive a gift tax charitable deduction in the amount of $2,000,000 for the charity's lead interest, and Donor would not pay gift tax on the gift to the remainder beneficiaries. If the assets experience a total return of 8%, then at the end of 20 years, there will be $1,726,693 available for the remainder beneficiaries.

(3)   **Estate Tax Consequences**. If the CLT is established at the death of the donor, the donor's estate will be entitled to an estate tax charitable deduction in an amount equal to the present value of the charity's interest. If the trust is created during the donor's life and the trust is designed so that the donor receives the trust assets back at the end of the term of the trust, the assets of the trust will be included in the donor's gross estate for federal estate tax purposes.

c.   **GST Tax Consequences**.   The creation of a CLT is not subject to generation-skipping transfer ("GST") tax. If at the end of the term of the CLT the trust will terminate in favor of grandchildren or more remote descendants, such distributions will be subject to GST tax. Accordingly, to avoid the potential application of the GST tax, the trust assets should be distributed to the grantor's then living children when the CLT term ends.

(1)   **Allocating GST Exemption Generally**. The tax rate imposed on a generation-skipping transfer depends on the trust's inclusion ratio, which in turn depends on the trust's applicable fraction. The inclusion ratio is: 1 minus the applicable fraction. The applicable fraction generally is:

<u>the amount of GST exemption allocated to the property</u>
the value of the property.

The GST tax is determined by multiplying the inclusion ratio by the GST tax rate (the top estate tax rate, which currently is 49%). The goal is to achieve an applicable fraction of 1 so that the inclusion ratio is zero. In that case, the 49% tax rate multiplied by a zero inclusion ratio equals zero, so there is no GST tax.

(2)   **Allocating GST Exemption to CLATs**. Special rules apply for determining the applicable fraction of a CLAT. Treas. Reg. § 26.2642-3(a). The applicable fraction is:

<u>the "adjusted GST exemption"</u>
the value of the property immediately after the termination
of the charity's annuity interest.

21st Century Estate Planning:
Practical Applications
2005 Edition

©2005 Sonnenschein Nath & Rosenthal LLP
and Cannon Financial Institute, Inc.

- 551 -

The "adjusted GST exemption" is the amount of the donor's GST exemption allocated to the trust, increased by interest on that amount for each year of the charitable lead annuity term at the Section 7520 rate used to value the charitable gift or estate tax deduction. Treas. Reg. § 26.2642-3(b). Thus, if the Section 7520 rate is 5.4%, the adjusted GST exemption equals the GST exemption (currently $1.5 million) times 1.054^{years}.

> **EXAMPLE:** Donor funds a 20-year CLAT with $1,000,000 when the Section 7520 rate is 5.4%. At the end of the term of the charity's annuity interest, the assets are worth $4,500,000. Donor allocated all of her remaining GST exemption to the CLAT ($1,500,000). The applicable fraction is 95.43%, determined as follows:
>
> $$\frac{\$1,500,000 \times (1.054)^{20}}{\$4,500,000}$$
>
> The inclusion ratio is 1 - 95.43%, which equals 4.57%. This inclusion ratio is then multiplied by the GST tax rate (47%), which equals 2.15%. The GST tax due is $4,500,000 x 2.15% = $96,750.

Thus, the determination of the applicable fraction is not made until the end of the charitable term, using the value of the assets then in the trust. The donor does not know, when a CLAT is created that ultimately will pass to grandchildren or more remote descendants, whether or not there will be generation-skipping tax at the expiration of the charitable lead annuity interest. This special rule for CLATs discourages donors from using them with the remainder to grandchildren or more remote descendants because of the uncertainty of the ultimate result and the possibility of wasting GST exemption if the assets do not have a total return equal to the Section 7520 rate over the term of the trust.

(3) **Allocating GST Exemption to CLUTs**. Allocating GST exemption to a CLUT is easier than allocating it to a CLAT. Under IRC § 2642(a)(2), the applicable fraction for a CLUT is:

> the amount of GST exemption allocated to the trust
> the value of the property in the trust minus any
> estate tax or gift tax charitable deduction allowed.

> **EXAMPLE:** Donor creates a $100,000 CLUT to pay Charity a 10% unitrust amount for 18 years. At the end of the 18-year term, the trust property will be distributed to Donor's grandchildren. The value of the gift tax charitable deduction is $85,000. Thus, Donor allocates $15,000 of GST exemption to the trust. The applicable fraction is 1, determined as follows:

21st Century Estate Planning:
Practical Applications
2005 Edition

©2005 *Sonnenschein Nath & Rosenthal LLP*
and Cannon Financial Institute, Inc.

- 552 -

$$\frac{\$15,000}{\$100,000 - \$85,000}$$

The inclusion ratio is 1 - 1 = 0, which means that no GST tax will be due.

Thus, it is possible to effectively allocate GST exemption to a CLUT. The problem, however, is that if the value of the trust property increases, the amount payable to charity increases, the result of which is that some of the GST exemption allocated to the CLUT may be wasted.

4. Other Considerations

a. Designation of Trustee. The grantor may name any person or corporate fiduciary to act as trustee, and the grantor can act as trustee as long as the grantor's powers as trustee are limited. For example, if the trustee will have the power to select the charitable beneficiaries, the gift to the trust may be incomplete for gift tax purposes, resulting in the inclusion of the trust in the grantor's gross estate for federal estate tax purposes, if the grantor is acting as trustee. Under these circumstances, unless the grantor intends to have the CLT included in his or her gross estate, the trust should provide that the designation of charitable beneficiaries will be done by an independent trustee.

➜ **Planning Point:** In the case of a grantor CLT, this consideration may be less important because it is likely that the trust property will be included in the grantor's gross estate.

b. Private Foundation Rules. CLTs are split-interest trusts within the meaning of IRC § 4947(a)(2). This means that the restrictions on operations of private foundations in IRC § 4941 (self-dealing), IRC § 4943 (excess business holdings), IRC § 4944 (jeopardy investments) and IRC § 4945 (taxable expenditures) may be applicable to CLTs, so these restrictions must be examined in detail to avoid excise taxes. These restrictions are discussed in greater detail above in the section on private foundations.

(1) Self-Dealing. IRC § 4941 relating to self-dealing is applicable to CLTs. The applicability of IRC § 4941 means that CLTs should not enter into any business or other arrangements with the donor of the CLT, members of his or her family, or any other persons who would be disqualified persons with respect to the CLT under the attribution rules of IRC § 4946.

(2) Excess Business Holdings and Jeopardy Investments. The prohibition on excess business holdings could be a problem for CLTs that hold closely held stock or limited partnership interests. There is, however, an exception if certain requirements are met. First, the excess business holdings prohibition can be overcome if the actuarial value of the charitable lead interest does not exceed 60% of the value of all interests in the trust, valued at the inception of the trust. The effect of the lower charitable interest value necessary to qualify for

21st Century Estate Planning:
Practical Applications
2005 Edition

©2005 Sonnenschein Nath & Rosenthal LLP
and Cannon Financial Institute, Inc.

- 553 -

this exemption is to lower the charitable deduction. Second, the entire charitable interest and none of the remainder interest must be devoted to charitable purposes. Because the typical CLT provides that all income be distributed to the charitable beneficiaries, the trust should satisfy the second requirement. An identical exception exists for the jeopardy investment provisions.

I. Pooled Income Funds

A pooled income fund is another type of split-interest gift that is sanctioned by the Code. IRC § 642(c)(5). A donor transfers money or securities to a separately maintained fund created by a public charity, where it is invested with gifts of other donors. The donor retains an income interest for life but makes a gift of the remainder interest. The donor receives a pro rata share from the fund's earnings each year for life. Treas. Reg. § 1.642(c)-5(c)(1). At the donor's death, the donor's percentage of the fund is transferred to the charity. A donor also can name someone else as the income beneficiary of a gift to a pooled income fund.

➔ **Planning Point:** The donor cannot be the trustee and can have no management power over the resources in the trust fund.

1. Income Tax Consequences

The income the donor receives is taxed as ordinary income. The donor is entitled to an income tax charitable deduction for the value of the remainder interest.

The final regulations regarding the definition of income were issued on December 30, 2003. For further discussion of these regulations, see Chapter VI, "Federal Income Taxation of Trusts and Estates" and Section E. of this Chapter. With regard to pooled income funds, the charitable deduction for a contribution of long-term capital gain property is unavailable if the income beneficiary's right to income may be satisfied either as a unitrust amount or by adjusting between income and principal. Because the final regulations allow such a fund's income beneficiaries to receive a unitrust amount that may be paid in part from principal, not all capital gains can be conclusively presumed to be permanently set aside for charity.

The final regulations provide that a pooled income fund's governing instrument may be amended or reformed in a judicial proceeding to avoid the denial of the deduction. However, this reformation must have been completed by October 2, 2004.

2. Gift Tax Consequences

The charitable deduction for the remainder interest is determined by subtracting the present value of the life income interest from the fair market value of the property transferred. The discount rate is equal to the highest yearly rate of return of the pooled income fund for the three immediately preceding taxable years. Treas. Reg. § 1.642(c)-6(e)(3).

The value of the charitable remainder interest is not subject to gift tax. If the donor creates a pooled income fund with payments to another individual other than the donor's spouse,

21st Century Estate Planning:
Practical Applications
2005 Edition

©*2005 Sonnenschein Nath & Rosenthal LLP*
and Cannon Financial Institute, Inc.

- 554 -

however, the donor makes a gift equal to the present value of the income interest payable to the life beneficiary. The donor can avoid making a gift by retaining the right to revoke the successor life interest by the donor's will. The mere retention of the right to revoke the gift, whether or not exercised, avoids making a completed gift.

3. Estate Tax Consequences

If the donor retains the life interest in the pooled income fund, then the value of the donor's units in the fund at his or her death will be included in the donor's gross estate. The estate is, however, entitled to a charitable deduction, which offsets the amount included. If the successor beneficiary is the donor's spouse, an estate tax marital deduction will be allowed for the spouse's interest. If there is a successor beneficiary other than the donor's spouse, the value of such beneficiary's income interest is subject to estate tax, and the estate is entitled to a charitable deduction for the value of the charity's remainder interest.

J. Charitable Family Limited Partnerships

The charitable family limited partnership ("CFLP") is a charitable giving vehicle that provides a substantial gift to charity, produces income tax savings for the donor, transfers significant wealth to the donor's descendants, and allows a means for the donor's family to retain control over the transferred assets.

1. Basic CFLP Structure

Senior family members (*e.g.*, parents) contribute appreciated assets to a limited partnership in exchange for general partnership interests and limited partnership interests. The general partners manage the affairs of the partnership and generally receive a reasonable management fee for their services. The limited partners do not participate in management.

➔ **Planning Point:** As the general partners of the partnership, the parents retain control over the property transferred to the partnership. Thus, they determine the partnership's investment as well as if and when any distributions will be made.

Parents transfer a small portion of their limited partnership interests to their children and contribute their remaining limited partnership interests to charity, claiming a charitable income tax deduction for the fair market value of the limited partnership interests given to the charity.

The partnership sells the appreciated property, but because partnership income is allocated to partners in accordance with their pro rata shares and the charity owns nearly all of the limited partnership interests, nearly all of the gain is allocated to the charity, which is tax exempt. Therefore, most of the gain escapes taxation. This eliminates the need for the partnership to make tax distributions (assuming the other partners are otherwise able to pay their relatively small tax), thereby leaving more property in the partnership from which the children will benefit.

21st Century Estate Planning:
Practical Applications
2005 Edition

©2005 Sonnenschein Nath & Rosenthal LLP
and Cannon Financial Institute, Inc.

- 555 -

The proceeds are reinvested. Eventually the partnership liquidates, and the charity receives its share of the reinvested assets. Additionally, the partnership may make pro rata distributions to the partners, which would provide an immediate benefit to charity.

➔ **Planning Point:** The CFLP works like a CRT, except that it does not have to satisfy the requirements in the Code for a CRT. A CRT provides a guaranteed stream of payments to the donor and results in a gift of the remainder interest to charity. With a CFLP, the donor receives a stream of payments in the form of the management fee and any distributions that the partnership makes, and the assets eventually are distributed to charity when the partnership is liquidated or the partnership redeems the charity's limited partnership interests. Using a CFLP rather than a CRT allows the donor to transfer assets that may not be appropriate for a CRT, such as closely held stock or real estate, and may allow a more aggressive investment strategy. Further, it provides an opportunity to make current distributions to charity by means of partnership distributions rather than postponing the gift to charity until the noncharitable interest terminates.

Alternatively, the charity may be given a "put" right by which the partnership is required to buy the charity's interest after a certain period of time. The price may be discounted to reflect the lack of marketability of the limited partnership interest and the fact that the charity has no management control. A discount also may be appropriate because the charity will be liquidating its interest before the end of the partnership's term. The remaining assets then belong to the other partners, generally the donor's children. Because the amount the partnership pays in order to redeem the charity's LP interests is discounted, the amount of the discount is effectively transferred to the remaining partners. Thus, a significant amount of wealth is transferred to the children free of gift and estate tax.

➔ **Planning Point:** There should be no agreement between the charity and the partnership prior to the gift of partnership interests that the partnership will buy back the charity's partnership interest. Such an arrangement could lead to a finding that the gift was not complete.

➔ **Planning Point:** If the charity does not exercise its put right and instead retains its limited partnership interests until the dissolution of the partnership, the charity will realize the full, nondiscounted value of such interests. In such a case, the estate planning benefits of the CFLP (the transfer of the amount of the discount reflected in the purchase price for the charity's limited partnership interests) is lost.

> **EXAMPLE:** Parents own appreciated securities and would like to sell them in order to diversify their investments. Parents would like to transfer most of their wealth to Son, but also are interested in providing a benefit to charity. Parents create a limited partnership to

21st Century Estate Planning:
Practical Applications
2005 Edition

©2005 Sonnenschein Nath & Rosenthal LLP
and Cannon Financial Institute, Inc.

- 556 -

which they transfer $1,000,000 of securities. Parents take back a 2% general partnership (GP) interest and a 98% limited partnership (LP) interest.

Parents gift a 4% LP interest to Son and a 94% LP interest to Charity, retaining the 2% GP interest. Assuming the partnership interests are subject to a 30% valuation discount for gift and income tax purposes, the gift to the children's trust has a value of $28,000 ($1 million - 30% discount x 4%), resulting in gift tax of $14,000 (assuming a 50% gift tax rate). The gift to Charity has a value of $658,000 ($1 million - 30% discount x 94%), resulting in a charitable deduction equal to such amount. Assuming Parents have an adjusted gross income ("AGI") of $350,000, the charitable deduction could be used over 6 years (30% of AGI is the maximum deduction per year).

The partnership grants the limited partners (including Charity) a "put" right that allows them to sell their respective LP interests to the partnership in five years for their fair market value at that time, as adjusted for applicable marketability and minority interest discounts.

The partnership sells the $1 million of securities. The partnership is a "pass-through" entity, which means that all income and capital gains realized by the partnership are allocated to the partners in proportion to their respective interests. Thus, 94% of the capital gain triggered by the sale ($940,000) is allocated to Charity, which, as a tax-exempt entity, does not pay any capital gains tax. The remaining 6% of the capital gain ($60,000) is allocated between Parents and Son. Parents' aggregate income tax liability resulting from the sale is $3,000 ($20,000 x 15%), and Son's income tax liability is $6,000 ($40,000 x 15%).

Charity exercises its put right at the end of five years and sells its 94% LP interest to the partnership. Assuming the value of the partnership property increased at a rate of 10% per year and no distributions were made to the partners, the partnership property would be worth $1.6 million at the time of such sale. Accordingly, Charity receives $1.053 million for its 94% LP interest ($1.6 million - 30% discount x 94%), leaving $547,000 in the partnership. After Charity's interest is redeemed, Parents' 2% GP interest will represent one-third of the remaining outstanding partnership interests, and Son's 4% LP interest will represent two-thirds of such interests.

If Charity invests its $1.053 million proceeds at a 10% rate of return, it would have $4.4 million after 15 more years.

21st Century Estate Planning:
Practical Applications
2005 Edition

©2005 Sonnenschein Nath & Rosenthal LLP
and Cannon Financial Institute, Inc.

- 557 -

After 15 years, the Partnership is liquidated. Assuming the $547,000 of partnership property continues to grow at the same 10% rate, it would be worth approximately $2.3 million after 15 additional years. If the partnership is liquidated at that time, Son will receive $1.53 million ($2.3 million x 2/3), and Parents will receive $767,000 ($2.3 million x 1/3). Additionally, Parents' combined estates will be augmented by the income taxes Parents saved as a result of their charitable contribution deduction (and the growth thereon), less the income taxes Parents paid on the partnership income and gains allocated to them.

2. Charitable Income Tax Deduction

As noted above, the donor will receive an income tax charitable deduction for the value of the limited partnership interests transferred to charity in the year in which the gift is made. The gift will be subject to the income tax deduction percentage limitations. An income tax deduction is denied, however, for gifts of partial interests. IRC § 170(f)(3). Of concern is whether a gift of a limited partnership interest is a gift of a partial interest because the donor or his or her family retains control of the partnership as general partner and often retains a management fee. See Carolyn D. Duronio, "Let the Donor Beware of the Charitable Family Limited Partnership," 12 *J. Tax'n Exempt Org.* 272 (May/June 2001). Duronio states that this should not be an issue as long as all distributions are made pro rata and any management fee is reasonable. She notes that the argument that the gift is of a partial interest if the donor or the donor's family retains control as general partners is inconsistent with gifts of voting stock, which are deductible.

The income tax deduction is based on the value of the transferred limited partnership interests. Gifts of limited partnership interests generally are discounted to reflect the partnership interest's lack of marketability and that the partnership interest represents a minority interest and does not carry control of the partnership. The higher the discount, the greater the ability to transfer property at reduced transfer tax costs. In the case of a charitable income tax deduction, however, a lower discount will be desired in order to increase the amount of the charitable deduction.

> **EXAMPLE:** If in the example above the discount is 20% rather than 30%, the gift to charity has a value of $752,000 ($1 million - 20% discount x 94%), resulting in a charitable deduction of such amount.

➔ **Planning Point:** In order to achieve a lower discount, the partnership agreement should contain provisions that allow the charity to realize on its interest. For example, the agreement could mandate annual distributions, in which case the charity would be guaranteed a stream of income from the partnership. Additionally, the agreement could provide a "put" right for the charity at a certain price or the interest's fair market value. Giving

21st Century Estate Planning:
Practical Applications
2005 Edition

©2005 Sonnenschein Nath & Rosenthal LLP
and Cannon Financial Institute, Inc.

- 558 -

the charity a put right should increase the value of the charity's interest because it ensures the charity's ability to liquidate its interest.

→ **Planning Point:** The conflict between a lower discount for the charitable gift and a higher discount for the gift to family members could result in valuation issues. The donor could not, for example, claim a 20% discount on the gift to the charity but a 40% discount on the gift to a family member.

3. Other Considerations

a. **Substance Over Form Argument**. The IRS could attack the CFLP transaction using a substance over form argument, particularly if the charity has a put right, to find that the charity never had an interest in the partnership. In fact, the IRS used this argument in a recent Field Service Advisory, FSA 200122011 (February 20, 2001). In this FSA, the donors and their sons formed a limited partnership, and the donors took back limited partnership interests while the sons took back general and limited partnership interests. Donors transferred their entire limited partnership interests to their sons, trusts for the benefit of their sons, and two charities. The assignments were made by way of a formula that allocated the partnership interests to the sons, their trusts, and charity, with one charity to receive all remaining value. Approximately six months later, the sons redeemed the partnership interests of the charities.

On audit, the IRS determined that the value of the transferred partnership interests exceeded the amount stated in the formula. The donors, in turn, argued that, under the formula, any excess value would pass to the residuary charity, resulting in an increased charitable deduction and eliminating any gift tax.

The IRS applied the step transaction doctrine, concluding that the transaction was, in effect, a single transaction to transfer limited partnership interests to the sons. The IRS noted that at all times donors and their sons were in control of the transaction, and, after the transaction, the sons were in control of the partnership interests. There was no evidence of arm's-length negotiations with the charity. The IRS found that "the sole purpose of the presence of [the residuary charity] was to imbue the appraisals, which were an integral part of the donative plan, with the patina of third-party reliance." As such, any additional transfer to the residuary charity under the formula clause was illusory, and no additional charitable deduction was allowed. Therefore, the transaction was treated as the transfer of limited partnership interests to the sons. The IRS further ruled that the formula clause was void as against public policy and ineffective for transfer tax purposes because it would render any adjustment nontaxable.

→ **Planning Point:** FSA 200122011 shows that the IRS will attack what it views as an abusive CFLP, especially when the charity's participation appears to be incidental in light of the overall transaction.

21st Century Estate Planning:
Practical Applications
2005 Edition

©2005 Sonnenschein Nath & Rosenthal LLP
and Cannon Financial Institute, Inc.

- 559 -

b. <u>Self-Dealing</u>. The private foundation self-dealing rules prohibit transactions between a charity and any disqualified person (*e.g.*, the donor and the donor's family, or an officer or a director of the charity) with respect to the charity and impose an excise tax on self-dealing transactions. The partnership's purchase of the charity's partnership interest could result in a self-dealing excise tax. Thus, the charity should be a public charity as to which the donor is not a disqualified person and not the donor's private foundation.

c. <u>Unrelated Business Taxable Income</u>. Of concern for the charity is whether the partnership income will be subject to the UBTI rules. Although charities generally are exempt from income tax, a charity is subject to tax on UBTI, which is income derived from any trade or business carried on by the charity that is not related to the charity's exempt purposes. If a charity has an interest in a partnership that conducts an unrelated trade or business, the charity will be taxed on its share of such income.

There are exceptions to the UBTI rules, however, that should apply in the case of most CFLPs. Investment income, such as dividends, interest, royalties, capital gains and rent from real estate specifically are excluded. IRC § 512(b). These generally are the sources of income for most family limited partnerships, so the exceptions should apply.

d. <u>Excess Benefit Rule</u>. The excess benefit rule requires fair market value transactions between a charity and a disqualified person. The Code imposes excise taxes on certain disqualified persons if they engage in excess benefit transactions with a public charity and on the managers of the charity if they knowingly participate in the transactions. These issues should not be a concern if the charity does not control the flow of funds and if the charity is a public charity as to which the donor is not a disqualified person.

➔ **Planning Point:** In light of the income tax and excise tax concerns discussed above, the charity should review a CFLP transaction carefully with its tax advisor.

In addition, the IRS has successfully included the entire amount of a family limited partnership in a donor's estate in *Estate of Strangi*, T.C. Memo 2003-145, and *Kimbell v. U.S.*, 244 F.Supp. 2d 700 (N.D. Tex. 2003) on alternative and somewhat controversial theories. The parameters of acceptable planning remain uncertain. The ultimate resolution of the family limited partnership issues will undoubtedly affect or even control resolution of the charitable family limited partnership issues.

21st Century Estate Planning:
Practical Applications
2005 Edition

©2005 Sonnenschein Nath & Rosenthal LLP
and Cannon Financial Institute, Inc.

- 560 -

Chapter XVI
Bibliography

Roy M. Adams, "The Estate Planner's Bazaar: Making the Right Choices in a Confusing Market," *Notre Dame Tax & Est. Plan. Inst.*, Ch. 5 (1999).

Charitable Giving Techniques, ALI-ABA (June 3-4, 1999).

Edward J. Beckwith, 839 T.M., *Estate and Gift Tax Charitable Deductions*.

Larry Brickner, "Family Limited Partnerships and Charities: The Newest Planning Technique?," *Tr. & Est.*, p. 49 (October 2000).

Bonnie S. Brier and Nancy J. Knauer, 442-2nd T.M., *Charitable Income Trusts*.

Barbara L. Kirschten and Carla Neeley Freitag, 863 T.M., *Charitable Contributions: Income Tax Aspects*.

Robert J. Rosepink, 865 T.M., *Charitable Remainder Trusts and Pooled Income Funds*.

Conrad Teitell, *Charitable Contribution Tax Strategies*, ALI-ABA (June 15-20, 1997).

Conrad Teitell, *Deferred Giving: Explanation, Specimen Agreements, Forms* (2001).

21st Century Estate Planning:
Practical Applications
2005 Edition

©2005 Sonnenschein Nath & Rosenthal LLP
and Cannon Financial Institute, Inc.

- 561 -

XVII. LEVERAGING THE LIFETIME TRANSFER OF ASSETS

A. Introduction

Under the Internal Revenue Code (the "Code"), the Internal Revenue Service (the "IRS") prescribes certain interest rates to be used to value annuities, life estates, interests for a term of years, remainder interests, and reversionary interests for federal transfer tax purposes. The IRS also publishes base interest rates to be used for various sale and loan transactions. There are a number of estate planning techniques that take advantage of the spread between these growth rates assumed by the IRS and the actual rate of return that is realized on the asset transferred to transfer wealth to clients' descendants. The amount by which the rate of return on the asset transferred, whether by gift or sale, exceeds the applicable interest rate for the transaction is transferred to descendants free of transfer taxes. If the asset actually produces in income and appreciation a yield equal to the assumed interest rate, the asset will have been valued correctly. If the asset outperforms the assumed interest rate, however, the asset will have been undervalued. As a result, these techniques allow the client to "leverage" the difference between the assumed rate of return and the actual rate of return, meaning that the client can give away property with a value in excess of the value that the IRS places on the property.

Because the techniques that will be discussed in this chapter remove the transferred property and any appreciation thereon in excess of the IRS assumed growth rate from the gross estate with the payment of no, or minimal, gift tax, such techniques continue to be viable estate planning options in light of the changes made to the transfer taxes in the Economic Growth and Tax Relief Reconciliation Act of 2001 (the "Act"). Prior to the Act, practitioners would advise clients to make gifts to remove the transferred property and the appreciation thereon from their gross estates, even if they would have to pay gift tax, because paying gift tax is more tax effective than paying estate tax. In light of the Act, however, estate tax may never be paid, either because of the repeal of the estate tax or because of the increasing estate tax applicable exclusion amount. Additionally, because the Act establishes a $1 million gift tax applicable exclusion amount (which is not scheduled to increase), making large lifetime taxable gifts will quickly erode this amount. Therefore, counseling clients to make taxable gifts makes less sense than it did before the Act. Because the techniques discussed in this chapter result in the payment of no, or minimal, gift tax, however, practitioners should continue to consider them. Additionally, because the gift tax is not scheduled to be repealed, such techniques will continue to be effective even if the estate tax is repealed because clients will continue to make lifetime gifts for reasons other than estate tax savings.

The following techniques will be discussed in this chapter:

- Grantor retained annuity trusts and the recent change in the law that has made such trusts even more attractive;

21st Century Estate Planning:
Practical Applications
2005 Edition

©2005 Sonnenschein Nath & Rosenthal LLP
and Cannon Financial Institute, Inc.

- 562 -

- Sales and loans to grantor trusts, including how they compare to grantor retained annuity trusts;
- Private annuities and self-canceling installment notes, which are techniques that involve the sale of property and allow the seller to defer capital gain;
- Grantor retained income trusts and how they may be used in certain limited circumstances to make a discounted gift to the beneficiaries; and
- The sale of a remainder interest in a marital trust and how it avoids a taxable gift to the spouse yet escapes estate tax at the spouse's death.

B. General Principles

Following is an explanation of several principles and Code sections that apply to the techniques discussed in this chapter and to which several of the sections will refer.

1. Present Value

Suppose an individual would like to save $100,000 in ten years to send his or her children to school. He or she would like to know how much to set aside today to have $100,000 in ten years. This is the concept of present value. The fact that the asset will not be received for ten years makes the asset worth much less today.

The present value depends on the "discount rate," which is the interest rate assumed throughout the time period. The higher the discount rate, the lower the present value of a given future amount. That is, an individual would have to invest less today to reach a future sum if interest rates are high rather than low.

> **EXAMPLE:** If the discount rate is 8%, the present value of the right to receive $1 million 15 years from now is $315,242. If, however, the discount rate is 4%, the present value is $555,265.

The techniques discussed in this chapter are based on the concept of present value. That is, the value of the asset transferred, whether for purposes of determining the amount of the taxable gift or the sales price, will be the present value of the right of the beneficiaries to receive the asset at a future date or the present value of the right to receive a stream of payments over time.

> **EXAMPLE:** Grantor, age 55, transfers an asset valued at $1 million to an irrevocable trust for the benefit of his nieces and nephews. The applicable interest rate is 5.4%, and the trust will terminate in 10 years. The value of the remainder interest for gift tax purposes is $591,009, which is the present value of the right of the nieces and nephews to receive $1 million in 10 years at a discount rate of 5.4%.

21st Century Estate Planning:
Practical Applications
2005 Edition

©2005 Sonnenschein Nath & Rosenthal LLP
and Cannon Financial Institute, Inc.

- 563 -

2. Applicable Federal Rates

The success of the techniques discussed in this chapter depends upon whether the rate of return on the assets transferred, whether by gift or sale, exceeds the applicable interest rate for the transaction. The applicable interest rate for techniques discussed in this chapter generally will be determined by reference to either the applicable federal rate (the "AFR") under Internal Revenue Code ("IRC") § 1274(d) of the Code or the rate determined under Section 7520 of the Code (the "Section 7520 rate").

a. IRC §§ 1274 and 7872. Each month, the IRS publishes base interest rates known as the applicable federal rates. These interest rates are used for various purposes under the Code. IRC § 1274 provides rules for interest on debt instruments issued in consideration for the sale of property, and IRC § 7872 provides rules for the imputation of interest in the case of loans where the stated interest is less than the AFR (known as "below-market loans").

The AFR changes monthly and varies depending upon the term of the loan and how frequently interest compounds (*e.g.*, annually, semi-annually, quarterly or monthly). There are three AFRs that vary based on the term of the loan: 1) the short-term rate, which applies for instruments having a term of three years or less; 2) the mid-term rate, which applies to instruments having a term greater than three years and nine years or less; and 3) the long-term rate, which applies to instruments having a term greater than nine years.

b. Section 7520. Under Section 7520, the value of any annuity, life interest, term interest, remainder interest or reversionary interest is determined by use of certain tables and an interest rate that is equal to 120% of the federal mid-term rate in effect under IRC § 1274(d)(1) of the Code for the month in which the transfer occurs. The actuarial factors contained in the tables for interests that depend on life expectancy include a mortality component based on life expectancy and an interest rate component that is the growth rate assumed by the IRS for the purpose of valuing such interests, while the factors in the tables that are not dependent on life expectancy include only the interest rate component.

The Section 7520 rate cannot be used if the individual who is the measuring life is terminally ill. An individual who is known to have an incurable illness or other deteriorating physical condition is considered to be terminally ill if there is at least a 50% probability of death within one year of the transaction. If the individual survives for eighteen months or longer after the date of the transaction, however, he or she is presumed not to have been terminally ill at the time of the transaction, unless the contrary is established by clear and convincing evidence. Treas. Reg. § 25.7520-3(b)(3).

Additionally, the Section 7520 rate cannot be used if the trust instrument does not "provide the income beneficiary with that degree of beneficial enjoyment of the property during the term of the income interest that the principles of the law of trusts accord to a person who is unqualifiedly designated as the income beneficiary of a trust for a similar period of time." Treas. Reg. § 25.7520-3(b)(2)(ii). Thus, for example, if stock is transferred to a trust in which the grantor has retained an income interest and the stock historically pays dividends equal to one percent of fair market value, and the valuation tables assume an eight percent return, the income

21st Century Estate Planning:
Practical Applications
2005 Edition

©2005 Sonnenschein Nath & Rosenthal LLP
and Cannon Financial Institute, Inc.

- 564 -

interest should not be valued using the Section 7520 tables. Examples 1 and 2 in Treas. Reg. § 25.7520-3(b)(2)(v) make it clear that the income beneficiary should be given the power to direct the trustee to "make the trust corpus productive consistent with income yield standards for trusts under applicable state law," and specifically contemplate that the minimum rate of income that a productive trust may produce may be substantially below the Section 7520 interest rate on the valuation date. Moreover, Example 2 of these regulations shows that, so long as the beneficiary has the power to make the trust property productive of income, the fact that it actually does not produce income will not preclude use of the Section 7520 income factors.

3.   IRC § 2702

IRC § 2702 of the Code provides special valuation rules to determine the amount of a gift when an individual transfers property to a trust (or trust equivalent) to or for the benefit of a "member of the transferor's family," and immediately after the transfer the transferor or an "applicable family member" retains an interest in the trust (or trust equivalent). IRC § 2702(a)(1); Treas. Reg. § 25.2702-1(a). Under IRC § 2702, if such a transfer is made, the value of the interest retained by the transferor or applicable family member is valued at zero unless it is a "qualified interest" or the interest falls within an exception to IRC § 2702. IRC § 2702(a)(2) and (3). If the retained interest is valued at zero, the gift is a gift of the entire value of the property transferred. In contrast, if an exception to IRC § 2702 applies, or if the retained interest is a "qualified interest," the gift tax value of the transferred interest is determined by subtracting the value of the retained interest determined under Section 7520 from the value of the property that is the subject of the transfer.

> **EXAMPLE:** Grantor transfers $1 million to a trust and retains an annuity, which is a qualified interest. If the value of the retained annuity interest is $419,430, then the value of the gift is $1 million less the value of the retained annuity interest, or $580,570. If the grantor's retained interest were not a qualified interest, it would be valued at zero, and the value of the gift would be $1 million.

a. **Member of the Transferor's Family**. For IRC § 2702 to apply, the transfer in trust must be to or for the benefit of a "member of the transferor's family." A "member of the family" includes (i) the transferor's spouse, (ii) ancestors or descendants of the transferor or the transferor's spouse, (iii) siblings of the transferor, or (iv) the spouse of any of the foregoing. IRC §§ 2702(e); 2704(c)(2). A transfer to a relative that does not fall within this group (*e.g.*, a niece or nephew) is not subject to IRC § 2702's special valuation rules.

b. **Applicable Family Member**. For IRC § 2702 to apply, the transferor or an "applicable family member" must have retained an interest in the trust. An "applicable family member" includes (i) the transferor's spouse, (ii) ancestors of the transferor or the transferor's spouse, and (iii) spouses of any such ancestor. IRC §§ 2702(a)(1); 2701(e)(2).

➔   **Planning Point:** The transferor or the applicable family member must have retained an interest in the trust, which means that such individual has an interest in the trust both before and after the transfer. Thus, if an

21st Century Estate Planning:
Practical Applications
2005 Edition

©2005 Sonnenschein Nath & Rosenthal LLP
and Cannon Financial Institute, Inc.

- 565 -

individual transfers property in trust and retains the right to income for 5 years, after which time the property is payable to the individual's child, the individual has retained an interest in the trust. If, however, an individual creates a trust that provides that income is to be paid to the individual's spouse for life, after which time the property will be distributed to the individual's child, the individual has not retained an interest in the trust, nor has the individual's spouse retained an interest in the trust. Therefore, IRC § 2702 does not apply. See Treas. Reg. § 25.2702-2(d)(1), Ex. 3.

      c. Qualified Interest. If IRC § 2702 applies, and if an exception to IRC § 2702 does not apply, then in order for the transferor's retained interest to be valued under Section 7520 rather than being valued at zero, the transferor's retained interest must be in the form of a "qualified interest." Two types of qualified interests, a "qualified annuity interest" and a "qualified unitrust interest," will be discussed in this chapter.

> **EXAMPLE 1:** Grantor creates a trust, retaining the right to receive an annual annuity equal to 8% of the initial fair market value of the trust property for 5 years. When the 5-year term ends, the trust property will be distributed to the grantor's daughter. Grantor's retained annuity is a qualified annuity interest. The amount of the gift will equal the fair market value of the property transferred to the trust less the value of the retained qualified annuity interest determined under Section 7520.

> **EXAMPLE 2:** The facts are the same as in Example 1, except that the grantor receives the right to all of the income of the trust property, payable annually. Grantor's retained interest is not a qualified interest and is, therefore, valued at zero for purposes of determining the value of the gift of the remainder to the daughter. The amount of the gift equals the fair market value of the property transferred to the trust.

4.   Grantor Trust Status

    Under the grantor trust provisions of the federal income tax law (IRC §§ 671-679 of the Code), if the creator of a trust (known as the "grantor") retains certain powers over or benefits in a trust, the trust will be deemed to be owned by the grantor for federal income tax purposes. Such a trust is known as a "grantor trust." The grantor will be taxed individually on the grantor trust's income rather than the trust or its beneficiaries being taxed on the income. The grantor trust rules can be violated in certain ways so that the grantor retains sufficient controls over the trust property to be the owner of the trust for federal income tax purposes but not for gift, estate or generation-skipping transfer ("GST") tax purposes. The result of grantor trust status is that the trust is ignored for federal income tax purposes and, therefore, transactions between the grantor and the trust will be ignored for federal income tax purposes. See Rev. Rul. 85-13, 1985-1 C.B. 184. Thus, the following benefits result:

21st Century Estate Planning:
Practical Applications
2005 Edition

©2005 Sonnenschein Nath & Rosenthal LLP
and Cannon Financial Institute, Inc.

- 566 -

- The grantor will not recognize gain or loss on the sale of assets to a grantor trust.
- The grantor is not taxed on annuity payments or interest payments he or she receives from the trust.
- Because the grantor is treated for income tax purposes as if he or she still owns the trust assets, the grantor will report, for income tax purposes, all items of income, deduction and credit generated by the trust on his or her individual income tax return. Such items will not be taxable to the trust as a separate entity. Thus, if interest or dividends are received or capital gains are recognized by the trust, the grantor continues to be taxed on such items as though he or she had never sold the assets to the trust, regardless of whether the income actually is distributed to the grantor.

a. **Additional Gifts**. The grantor's payment of income tax on assets that eventually pass to the trust beneficiaries is effectively a tax-free gift to such beneficiaries (*i.e.*, it reduces the grantor's estate without any transfer tax consequences and leaves intact the trust assets, which eventually pass to the beneficiaries of the trust). In PLR 9444033 (August 5, 1994), the IRS took the position that the grantor's payment of income tax was an additional gift to the remaindermen. The language in that ruling was deleted, however, when the ruling was modified by PLR 9543049 (August 3, 1995). The consensus among practitioners is that the grantor's payment of income taxes with respect to income of a grantor trust should not be a gift because it is a payment to discharge a legal obligation imposed by the income tax laws.

b. **Reimbursement Rights**. If the grantor does not wish to pay the income taxes, the trust instrument can contain a provision allowing the trustee to reimburse the grantor for the income taxes. The planner should consider who has the right to reimburse the grantor for income taxes. If the trustee has the right and the grantor is the trustee, such a right could cause the gift to the trust to be incomplete or could cause the trust property to be included in his or her gross estate. Therefore, it may be advisable to give the right to an independent trustee.

C. Grantor Retained Annuity Trusts

A grantor retained annuity trust ("GRAT") provides the grantor with a "qualified annuity interest," which is the right to receive a fixed amount, payable at least annually. IRC § 2702(b)(1). Because the annuity is a "qualified interest," the value of the grantor's retained interest is valued under Section 7520, and the value of the gift will be the fair market value of the property transferred less the present value of the retained annuity interest determined under Section 7520.

1. Overview of Grantor Retained Annuity Trusts

A GRAT is an irrevocable trust that pays the grantor an annuity, at least annually, for a fixed term of years. The annuity interest generally is described as a percentage of the initial value of the assets transferred to the GRAT. If the grantor is living at the end of the term, any

21st Century Estate Planning:
Practical Applications
2005 Edition

©2005 Sonnenschein Nath & Rosenthal LLP
and Cannon Financial Institute, Inc.

- 567 -

property remaining in the GRAT after the last annuity payment is made will pass to the remainder beneficiaries (usually the grantor's children), either outright or in trust for their benefit. If the expected return on the GRAT assets is less than the applicable Section 7520 rate, all of the trust property will be distributed to the grantor as part of the annuity payments during the trust term and nothing will be left for distribution to the remainder beneficiaries. The grantor will be no worse off than if the grantor had not created the GRAT, except for the cost of creating the GRAT and any gift tax paid upon funding the GRAT. If the return exceeds the applicable Section 7520 rate, however, then the remaining trust property will be distributed tax free to the remainder beneficiaries. If the GRAT is appropriately designed and the assets appreciate significantly, substantial wealth can be transferred to the grantor's children free of both gift tax and estate tax.

EXAMPLE 1: Grantor, age 50, transfers $1,000,000 to a 5-year GRAT. The Section 7520 rate is 5.4%. The annual annuity payment to Grantor is $233,535.60. If the assets grow at the rate of 5%, all of the assets will be distributed to Grantor to satisfy the annuity, and no property will be left in the GRAT at the end of the term.

Year	Beginning Principal	5.00% Growth	Annual Payment	Remainder
1	$1,000,000.00	$50,000.00	$233,535.60	$816,464.40
2	$ 816,464.40	$40,823.22	$233,535.60	$623,752.02
3	$ 623,752.02	$31,187.60	$233,535.60	$421,404.02
4	$ 421,404.02	$21,070.20	$233,535.60	$208,938.62
5	$ 208,938.62	$10,446.93	$219,385.55	$ 0.00
	$1,000,000.00	$153,527.95	$1,153,527.95	$ 0.00

EXAMPLE 2: The facts are the same as in Example 1, except that the assets grow at the rate of 8%. Because the return on the assets exceeds the Section 7520 rate, there will be assets in the GRAT at the end of the term to be distributed to the beneficiaries. At an 8% return, $99,267.90 will be left for the beneficiaries.

Year	Beginning Principal	8.00% Growth	Annual Payment	Remainder
1	$1,000,000.00	$80,000.00	$233,535.60	$846,464.40
2	$ 846,464.40	$67,717.15	$233,535.60	$680,645.95
3	$ 680,645.95	$54,451.68	$233,535.60	$501,562.03
4	$ 501,562.03	$40,124.96	$233,535.60	$308,151.39
5	$ 308,151.39	$24,652.11	$233,535.60	$ 99,267.90
	$1,000,000.00	$266,945.90	$1,167,678.00	$ 99,267.90

21st Century Estate Planning:
Practical Applications
2005 Edition

©2005 Sonnenschein Nath & Rosenthal LLP
and Cannon Financial Institute, Inc.

- 568 -

Generally, any assets with appreciation potential or total return in excess of the Section 7520 rate are appropriate assets for a GRAT. Assets that can be valued at a discount, such as a minority interest in a closely held corporation, a limited partnership interest or a large block in a publicly traded company, can produce significant savings because the amount of the annuity will be based on the discounted value of the asset, rather than on the full value. This will be particularly beneficial if the asset has a high yield (because the effective yield will be made even higher by the discount) or if the asset can be valued at its full value (rather than its discounted value) when distributed as part of the annuity payment.

a. The Annuity. The annuity must be a fixed amount, that is, a stated dollar amount or a fixed fraction or percentage of the initial fair market value of the assets transferred to the GRAT. Treas. Reg. § 25.2702-3(b)(1)(ii).

> **EXAMPLE:** A payment of $50,000 each year would constitute a fixed amount, as would a payment of 10% of the initial fair market value of the property contributed to the trust.

→ **Planning Point:** It is generally more desirable to define the annuity amount as a percentage or fraction of the value of the initial trust assets in the event that the fair market value of the assets contributed to the GRAT is uncertain. If the value of the assets transferred to the GRAT is increased on audit, the taxable gift will increase. If the annuity amount is expressed as a percentage of the fair market value of the assets transferred to the GRAT, however, an increase in the value of the assets results in an increase in the annuity payable to the grantor, thus reducing or nearly eliminating the increase in the taxable gift.

The annuity amount may increase annually by up to 120% of the preceding year's annuity amount. *Id.*

→ **Planning Point:** For example, the annuity could be 10% in the first year, 12% in the second year, 14.4% in the third year, and so on. The advantage of an increasing annuity is that less property is distributed to the grantor in the beginning, and, therefore, property grows within the trust for a longer period of time. An increasing annuity is particularly useful for assets that are not expected to achieve a high return in the early years but that are expected to achieve an increasing return in the future.

The trust also may provide that income in excess of the annuity amount may be paid to the grantor. The right to receive the excess income is not, however, a qualified interest, and, therefore, it will not reduce the value of the transferor's retained interest. Treas. Reg. § 25.2702-3(b)(1)(iii). No distributions can be made to anyone other than the holder of the annuity interest during the term of the annuity interest. Treas. Reg. § 25.2702-3(d)(2).

21st Century Estate Planning:
Practical Applications
2005 Edition

©2005 Sonnenschein Nath & Rosenthal LLP
and Cannon Financial Institute, Inc.

- 569 -

b. <u>Payment of the Annuity</u>. The annuity can be paid from income, and, if income is insufficient, from principal.

        (1) <u>Payment in Kind</u>. If the income generated by the GRAT assets is insufficient to pay the annuity, the trustee can transfer trust principal in kind to the grantor to pay the annuity. This is a common practice when highly appreciating assets with low cash flow are contributed to a GRAT.

        (2) <u>Payment of the Annuity With a Note</u>. The trustee cannot make the annuity payment with a note from the trustee to the grantor. Treas. Reg. § 25.2702-3(b)(1)(i). In fact, the governing instrument must expressly prohibit the use of notes or similar financial arrangements to make the annuity payments. The trustee can, however, borrow from an unrelated third party, such as a bank, to satisfy the annuity payments. 65 Fed. Reg. 53587, 53588 (September 5, 2000).

c. <u>Timing of Payments</u>. The annuity payments can be made on a calendar year or anniversary year basis and can be made annually or more frequently. If the payment is for a short taxable year, the payment must be prorated. Treas. Reg. § 25.2702-3(b)(3).

d. <u>Term of the GRAT</u>. The term can be for any length. Generally, the longer the term (a) the smaller the amount of each annuity payment, and (b) the greater the possibility that the grantor will die during the term (in which case there will be no, or minimal, estate tax savings).

➔   <u>**Planning Point**</u>: It is accepted practice to create GRATs for a term as short as 2 years. The IRS approved a 2-year GRAT in PLR 9239015 (June 25, 1992).

➔   <u>**Planning Point**</u>: If the grantor desires to have most or all of the trust principal remain in the GRAT, the grantor can reduce the size of the required annuity payment by creating a GRAT with a longer term (*i.e.,* as the term of the GRAT is increased, the required annual annuity payment will decrease, thereby making it easier to satisfy the annual annuity from the cash flow generated by the GRAT assets).

2.   **Gift, Estate and Income Tax Consequences**

a. <u>Gift Tax</u>. The transfer of assets to a GRAT is a taxable gift. The amount of the gift will equal the excess of (a) the value of the property transferred to the GRAT over (b) the value of the interest retained by the grantor, determined under the actuarial tables in Section 7520.

        EXAMPLE: Grantor, age 50, transfers $5 million to a GRAT with a 5-year term. The GRAT assets increase in value at a rate of 15% per year during the GRAT term. The Section 7520 rate in effect at the creation of the GRAT is 6%.

21st Century Estate Planning:
Practical Applications
2005 Edition

©2005 Sonnenschein Nath & Rosenthal LLP
and Cannon Financial Institute, Inc.

- 570 -

The trust provides that Grantor will receive $1,186,972 from the GRAT each year during the 5-year term. The value of the annuity is $4,935,071. The amount of the taxable gift equals $64,929, which is $5 million less $4,935,071, the value of the retained annuity. The assets remaining in the GRAT at the end of the 5-year term will, based on the stated assumptions, equal $2,053,772 and are distributable to children free of gift or estate tax. Thus, Grantor has transferred over $2 million of assets to his children with a taxable gift of only $64,929.

➔ **Planning Point:** The gift made on the creation of a GRAT is a gift of a future interest. Therefore, it will not qualify for the gift tax annual exclusion. Gift tax will not be due, however, if the gift is sheltered by the grantor's applicable exclusion amount.

➔ **Planning Point:** The annuity rate and the length of the term can be adjusted so that the value of the initial gift is close to zero, so that no gift will result upon funding the GRAT. This type of GRAT is known as a "zeroed-out GRAT" and is accomplished by making the annuity large enough to have the value of the retained annuity interest equal the value of the property transferred, thereby reducing the value of the gift to zero. With a zeroed-out GRAT, the grantor will receive back all of the original assets transferred to the trust and some appreciation in the value of the trust assets, while shifting the appreciation in excess of the Section 7520 rate during the term of the GRAT to the beneficiaries. Zeroed-out GRATs will be discussed in detail below.

  b. Estate Tax. If the grantor is living at the end of the trust term, any property remaining in the GRAT (which will be the case if the total return on the trust assets is greater than the Section 7520 rate in effect when the GRAT is created) will pass to the named beneficiaries and avoid gift and estate tax. If the grantor dies during the trust term, however, some portion or all of the trust property will be included in the grantor's gross estate for federal estate tax purposes. In such a case, there will be no estate tax savings. Nevertheless, the grantor will be no worse off than if he or she had not created the GRAT, except for the cost of creating the GRAT and any gift tax paid upon funding the GRAT.

  (1) IRC § 2036. A portion of the trust property may be included in the grantor's gross estate under IRC § 2036. TAM 200210009; and FSA 200036012. See also Rev. Rul. 82-105, 1982-1 C.B. 133. IRC § 2036 provides that the value of a retained interest (e.g., a GRAT annuity) is included in the gross estate. In Rev. Rul. 82-105, the IRS determined the amount includable in the gross estate of the grantor of a charitable remainder annuity trust in which the grantor retained an annuity interest for his life. Based on that ruling, the value of the GRAT property that is includable in the grantor's gross estate is the amount necessary to yield the guaranteed annual payments using the Section 7520 rate applicable at the grantor's death.

  (2) IRC § 2039. The value of the entire trust property may be included in the grantor's gross estate under IRC § 2039. TAM 200210009; and FSA 200036012;

21st Century Estate Planning:
Practical Applications
2005 Edition

©2005 Sonnenschein Nath & Rosenthal LLP
and Cannon Financial Institute, Inc.

- 571 -

PLR 9451056; and PLR 9345035. IRC § 2039 provides that the value of an annuity or other payment receivable by any beneficiary by reason of surviving the decedent is included in the decedent's gross estate. If the GRAT provides that when the grantor's annuity interest terminates the remaining trust property is paid to the remaindermen, the survivorship requirement is met, and the value of the entire trust principal at the grantor's death is included in the grantor's gross estate under IRC § 2039.

It is the view of some commentators that if the annuity payments are not distributed at the grantor's death to the remaindermen but rather continue to be made to the grantor's estate for the balance of the term, the survivorship requirement will not be met. In that case, IRC § 2039 should not apply. See Jonathan G. Blattmachr and Georgiana J. Slade, 836 T.M., Partial Interests - GRATs, GRUTs, QPRTs (Section 2702), at A-34. In a recent technical advice memorandum, however, the IRS concluded that, in such a situation, IRC § 2039 applies to include the value of the entire GRAT in the grantor's gross estate. TAM 200210009.

In TAM 200210009, the decedent had created a ten-year GRAT that provided that, if he were to die before the end of the term, the annuity was to be paid to his estate for the balance of the term. At the end of the ten-year term, the GRAT would terminate and be distributed to his daughter, or, if she was not living, to his wife. The decedent died during the sixth year of the GRAT, and the annual annuity payments then were made to his estate.

The IRS first discussed inclusion of the GRAT under IRC § 2036 and concluded, based on Rev. Rul. 82-105, that a portion of the GRAT was includable in the decedent's gross estate. The IRS then addressed inclusion under IRC § 2039 and held that one 100% of the value of the GRAT property on the decedent's date of death was includable in the decedent's gross estate under IRC § 2039.

The decedent's estate argued that the survivorship requirement in IRC § 2039 was not met because the annuity was first payable to the estate for the balance of the term and then payable to the daughter, and, as such, the daughter must survive the term of the GRAT in order to receive the remainder interest rather than surviving the decedent. The IRS disagreed, stating that the annuity payments, "whether payable initially to the estate beneficiaries and then to the child, or initially to the child, commence by reason of the decedent's death and will be received by the ultimate beneficiaries because they survived the decedent." Therefore, all post-death payments from the GRAT were receivable by reason of surviving the decedent, and IRC § 2039 applied to include the entire value of the GRAT on the date of the decedent's death in the decedent's gross estate.

(3)   IRC § 2033. If the GRAT provides that, if the grantor dies during the term of the GRAT, the balance of the annuity payments are to be made to the grantor's estate, or, if the trust property reverts to the grantor's estate upon the grantor's death, the property will be includable under IRC § 2033. IRC § 2033 includes in the gross estate the value of all property of a decedent at the decedent's death.

21st Century Estate Planning:
Practical Applications
2005 Edition

©2005 Sonnenschein Nath & Rosenthal LLP
and Cannon Financial Institute, Inc.

- 572 -

c. Income Tax. The GRAT will be a grantor trust for income tax purposes. As a result of the grantor trust status, the following favorable income tax results are achieved:

- No gain or loss is recognized on the creation of the GRAT when the grantor transfers assets to fund the trust because the grantor is deemed to have transferred the assets to himself or herself for income tax purposes;
- The payment of the annual annuity by the GRAT to the grantor is ignored for income tax purposes, as the grantor is deemed to have paid it to himself or herself; and
- The income and capital gains generated by the GRAT assets are taxable to the grantor whether or not distributed to him or her.

➔ **Planning Point:** Thus, if the grantor funds the trust with appreciated property, the distribution of such property in satisfaction of the annuity will not cause the grantor to recognize gain.

3. Valuation of the Gift

The value of the retained annuity interest generally depends on the value of the property transferred to the GRAT, the annuity rate, the Section 7520 rate in effect for the month in which the GRAT is created, the age of the grantor at the creation of the GRAT and the length of the term for which the grantor is retaining the annuity.

a. Valuing the Reversion and Example 5. In addition to the annuity interest that the grantor retains, the grantor also can retain a contingent reversion in the property transferred to the GRAT. A reversion is the possibility that the trust property will revert to the grantor's estate if the grantor dies before the end of the term of the GRAT. Thus, if a GRAT provides that the trust property will be paid to the grantor's estate if the grantor dies before the end of the term, the grantor has retained a reversion in the trust property.

➔ **Planning Point:** Because a portion or all of the trust property will be includable in the grantor's gross estate for federal estate tax purposes if the grantor dies before the end of the annuity term, it is common for the trust to provide that, upon the grantor's death, assets will revert to the grantor's estate. In such a case, the GRAT property will be disposed of according to the grantor's will or revocable trust. If the grantor dies survived by a spouse and the grantor's estate plan contains a marital deduction formula, the reversion allows the grantor to obtain a marital deduction for the GRAT property. Additionally, because the GRAT assets are paid to the grantor's estate, they are available to pay estate tax. Because less than all of the trust assets may be included in the grantor's gross estate, depending upon which one of IRC §§ 2039, 2036 and 2033 applies, the trust instrument may provide that only the portion of the assets includable in the grantor's gross estate will be paid to the grantor's estate.

21st Century Estate Planning:
Practical Applications
2005 Edition

©*2005 Sonnenschein Nath & Rosenthal LLP*
and Cannon Financial Institute, Inc.

- 573 -

If the grantor retains a reversion in the GRAT property, three interests are created in the GRAT: (1) the grantor's right to the annuity interest for the shorter of the GRAT term or the grantor's life; (2) the remainder, which is paid to the remainder beneficiaries of the GRAT if the grantor survives the GRAT term; and (3) the reversion, which is paid to the grantor's estate if the grantor does not survive the GRAT term. The older the grantor, the less likely he or she is to survive the term of the GRAT, and, therefore, the more valuable the reversion.

A reversion is not a qualified interest, and, therefore, it is valued at zero for purposes of determining the taxable gift. See Treas. Reg. § 25.2702-3(e), Ex. 1. As such, a reversion does not reduce the value of the gift, and only the annuity interest is subtracted from the value of the property transferred to the GRAT in calculating the gift. If the GRAT is optimized to reduce the taxable gift to the smallest number possible, then in effect, the grantor makes a gift to the remainder beneficiaries equal to the value of the reversion, as illustrated below.

> **EXAMPLE 1:** Grantor, age 50, transfers $5 million to a 10-year GRAT. The GRAT pays Grantor an annuity of $660,162 for the shorter of 10 years or Grantor's life. If Grantor dies before the end of the term, the balance of the property will be distributed to his estate (*i.e.*, he retains a reversion). The Section 7520 rate is 5.4%.
>
> The value of the annuity interest is $4,856,082.
> The value of the reversion is $143,915.
> The value of the remainder interest is $3.
> The value of the taxable gift is $143,918 ($5,000,000 - $4,856,082 (annuity)) or ($143,915 (reversion) + $3 (remainder)).

If the grantor retains an annuity for a fixed term, however, so that the annuity payments are made regardless of whether the grantor is living, two interests are created in the GRAT: (1) the annuity interest for the fixed term, which is payable to the grantor if living, otherwise to the grantor's estate; and (2) the remainder, which is paid to the remainder beneficiaries at the end of the GRAT term. In this case, because there is no reversion, the value of the gift includes only the value of the remainder interest, which is zero or almost zero.

> **EXAMPLE 2:** The facts are the same as in Example 1, except that if Grantor dies before the end of the term, the remaining annuity payments will be made to his estate (*i.e.*, he does not retain a reversion).
>
> The value of the annuity interest is $4,999,997.
> The value of the remainder interest is $3.
> The value of the taxable gift is $3 ($5,000,000-$4,999,997).
>
> The difference in the value of the taxable gift in Examples 1 and 2 is the value of the reversion in Example 1.

21st Century Estate Planning:
Practical Applications
2005 Edition

©2005 Sonnenschein Nath & Rosenthal LLP
and Cannon Financial Institute, Inc.

- 574 -

Until recently, the position of the IRS, based on Example 5 of Treas. Reg. § 25.2702-3(e) ("Example 5"), however, was that, even if the grantor retains an annuity for a fixed term, an annuity for a fixed term must be valued as if the grantor's right to the annuity terminates at death, regardless of whether payments are made to the grantor's estate after death. Example 5 provided that an annuity for a term of years must be valued as if it were an annuity for the shorter of the term or the grantor's life because the possibility that the grantor may die during the term must be considered. Thus, under the prior version of Example 5, even if the grantor does not retain a reversion, the annuity must be valued as if the grantor had retained one.

Because the IRS considered the term of a fixed-term GRAT to be shorter than its term (because the possibility of the grantor's death during the term must be considered), the grantor was not expected to receive all of the annuity payments. Consequently, under Example 5, the present value of the annuity decreased and created a remainder subject to gift tax. However, the discussed further below, Example 5 has been invalidated by the *Walton* case, the IRS has acquiesced in *Walton* and revised its regulations in this regard.

b. Zeroed-Out GRATs and the *Walton* Case. A zeroed-out GRAT is a GRAT in which the value of the grantor's retained annuity interest equals the value of the property transferred to the GRAT, resulting in a remainder (and value of the taxable gift) of zero. Until recently, because of Example 5 discussed above, zeroing-out a GRAT was not possible because the possibility of the grantor's death during the term, which reduces the value of the retained interest, had to be considered.

The IRS's position that because of Example 5 zeroed-out GRATs were not possible was rejected by the Tax Court in *Walton v. Comm'r*, 115 T.C. 589 (2000); *acq.*, Notice 2003-72. In *Walton*, the grantor established two substantially identical GRATs, each for a two-year term, and transferred shares of stock in Wal-Mart to the GRATs. The grantor was to receive an annuity amount from each trust equal to 49.35% of the initial trust value for the first year of the trust, and 59.22% of the initial value for the second year of the trust. If the grantor died during the two-year term, the remaining GRAT payments would be made to her estate, with the balance of the GRAT property being paid to the remainder beneficiaries at the end of the two-year term.

The GRAT payments were designed to result in no gift on creation of the GRAT under the position that the grantor's mortality need not be considered in valuing the remainder (a position contrary to the IRS and Example 5). Therefore, the grantor reported the gift of the remainder interest on a gift tax return at a value of zero. The Wal-Mart stock did not perform as expected, and all of the property was distributed to the grantor to satisfy the annuity. As such, there was nothing left for the remainder beneficiaries. The IRS sought to impose gift taxes on the transfer.

The Tax Court held that Example 5 was an invalid interpretation of IRC § 2702 and that the grantor's retained annuity interest was to be valued as an annuity for a term of years rather than as an annuity for the shorter of a term of years or the grantor's life.

As a result of *Walton*, practitioners can create GRATs with an annuity that equals the value of the transferred property, which means that all of the property and income and

21st Century Estate Planning:
Practical Applications
2005 Edition

©2005 *Sonnenschein Nath & Rosenthal LLP*
and Cannon Financial Institute, Inc.

- 575 -

appreciation thereon at the assumed rate of return (that is, the Section 7520 rate) is returned to the grantor in the form of an annuity. The result is a gift (and a remainder interest) in the amount of zero. Any income and appreciation in excess of the Section 7520 rate will pass to the remainder beneficiaries of the GRAT free of any gift or estate tax.

> **EXAMPLE:** Grantor, age 50, transfers $10,000,000 to a zeroed-out GRAT with a 10-year term. The GRAT assets increase at a rate of 15% per year during the GRAT term. The GRAT instrument provides that, if the Grantor dies during the 10-year term, the remaining annuity payments will be paid to his estate for the balance of the term. The Section 7520 rate in effect at the creation of the GRAT is 6%.
>
> The trust instrument provides that Grantor will receive $1,358,677 from the GRAT each year during the 10-year term. Because the GRAT annuity payments received by Grantor have a present value equal to the value of the property transferred, there is no gift when the Grantor creates the GRAT. The assets remaining in the GRAT at the end of the 10-year term will, based on the stated assumptions, equal $12,869,382 and are distributable to Grantor's children free of gift and estate tax. Thus, by use of a zeroed-out GRAT, Grantor can transfer over $12.8 million of assets to his children free of any transfer tax consequences.

→ **Planning Point:** In light of *Walton*, practitioners should consider structuring GRATs for a fixed term with payments to be made to the grantor or, if the grantor dies during the fixed term, to the grantor's estate (hereinafter referred to as a "*Walton* GRAT"). If minimizing gift tax on creation of the GRAT is a primary goal, a GRAT should not be structured to terminate at the grantor's death and then to pay the remaining assets to the remainder beneficiaries or to the grantor's estate. Such a structure would result in the value of the annuity interest being valued as the lesser of the fixed term or the grantor's life, and, therefore, would not benefit from the holding in *Walton*. The value of the retained interest for the shorter of term or life will be less than the value of the retained interest for a term, resulting in a taxable gift.

→ **Planning Point:** A gift tax-free GRAT is an ideal technique in light of the changes made by the Act. If the estate tax is repealed, the grantor will be no worse off because he or she will have not paid gift tax needlessly. If the estate tax is not repealed and the grantor survives the term of the GRAT and the GRAT assets outperform the Section 7520 rate, the grantor will have succeeded in removing the excess return from his or her estate.

On February 25, 2005, the IRS finalized regulations that conform the regulations under Section 2702 to *Walton*. T.D. 9181. Example 5 now provides that the grantor's interest in that example will be a qualfied interest for the entire term of the interest, whether the grantor survives

21st Century Estate Planning:
Practical Applications
2005 Edition

©2005 Sonnenschein Nath & Rosenthal LLP
and Cannon Financial Institute, Inc.

- 576 -

the term or dies before the end of the term causing the remaining payments to be made to the grantor's estate. Thus, the example no longer treats the term of a fixed-term GRAT that continues making payments to the grantor's estate in the event of the grantor's death before the end of the fixed term as the shorter of the fixed term or the grantor's life. These regulations are effective as of July 26, 2004.

(1) **Estate Tax Inclusion**. If a GRAT is structured as a *Walton* GRAT, then the fact that the annuity payments will continue, rather than the remaining GRAT property being paid to the estate, must be considered in determining how estate taxes will be paid in the event that the grantor does not survive the term of the GRAT and some portion or all of the GRAT property is includable in the grantor's gross estate. Because the GRAT property will not be distributed to the estate, there may be insufficient assets with which to pay estate taxes. Therefore, it is important to consider the source of funds from which to pay estate taxes by reason of the inclusion of the GRAT in the grantor's gross estate for federal estate tax purposes.

➔ **Planning Point:** If the GRAT is a short-term GRAT, the annuity payment is very high, so payment of estate taxes may not be an issue because the annuity payments, which continue to be made to the grantor's estate, may be sufficient to cover the tax liability.

As discussed above, the IRS has taken the position that the entire GRAT is included in the grantor's gross estate under IRC § 2039 when payments continue to the grantor's estate. IRC § 2033 also should apply because annuity payments continue to be made to the grantor's estate, as will IRC § 2036. Under these Sections, however, only a portion of the GRAT would be includable in the grantor's gross estate. TAM 200210009 (discussed above).

(2) **Marital Deduction Planning**. When the grantor retains a reversionary interest in a GRAT, which is generally the case with a GRAT that is not structured as a *Walton* GRAT, and dies before the end of the GRAT term, the GRAT usually provides that some portion (that portion that is included in the grantor's gross estate) or all of the remaining GRAT property will be distributed to the grantor's estate. Such planning allows the GRAT property to be disposed of in accordance with the grantor's will or revocable trust and often will allow the GRAT property to qualify for the marital deduction. With a *Walton* GRAT, however, the remaining GRAT property is not paid to the grantor's estate, to be disposed of according to his or her will or revocable trust. Rather, the annuity payments continue to the grantor's estate. Therefore, if the grantor wants to ensure that the entire GRAT, including both the remainder interest and the grantor's right to continuing annuity payments for the balance of the term, qualifies for the marital deduction, some additional planning will be required. Two alternatives follow.[1]

(a) **Direction in Will that Payments Be Made to the Surviving Spouse**. The grantor's will can direct that the continuing annuity payments, once they are paid to the estate, will be distributed outright to the surviving spouse and that the remainder will be paid directly to the surviving spouse when the GRAT term ends. If, however, the planner believes that IRC § 2039 does not cause inclusion of all of the GRAT assets in the grantor's gross estate, but rather that IRC § 2036 applies to include only a portion of the GRAT property

21st Century Estate Planning:
Practical Applications
2005 Edition

©2005 Sonnenschein Nath & Rosenthal LLP
and Cannon Financial Institute, Inc.

- 577 -

in the grantor's gross estate, then the GRAT should be structured so that only that portion of the property that is included in the gross estate will be distributed to the surviving spouse.

    (b)   **Distribution to a Marital Trust**. The GRAT instrument can provide that, if the grantor dies during the fixed term and is survived by a spouse, the remaining annuity payments and the GRAT remainder will be distributed to a marital trust for the surviving spouse's benefit. To ensure that the surviving spouse receives all of the income earned by the GRAT (which is a requirement to qualify the trust for the marital deduction), the GRAT must distribute any income in excess of the annuity amount to the marital trust. The GRAT itself could establish the marital trust as a remainder trust, or a separate irrevocable marital trust could be established. The latter alternative may be preferable if more than one GRAT has been created, in which case all of the GRATs could be payable to the separate irrevocable marital trust.

    c.   **Revocable Spousal Annuity Interest**. One way that practitioners have sought to minimize the value of the gift on the creation of a GRAT was to provide that the grantor's spouse had an annuity interest that would take effect if the grantor died during the term of the GRAT and the spouse survived. In such a case, the remaining annuity amount would be paid to the surviving spouse for the balance of the term, unless the grantor revoked the spouse's interest. Because the grantor has the right to revoke the spouse's annuity interest, the grantor has not made a completed gift to the spouse. The possibility of either the grantor or the grantor's spouse surviving the GRAT term is greater than the possibility of only the grantor surviving, and, therefore, the value of the reversion (and, therefore, the gift) decreases.

> **EXAMPLE 1:** Grantor, age 50, transfers $5 million to a 10-year GRAT. The Section 7520 rate is 5.4%. The annual annuity is $660,162, which will be paid to Grantor until the end of the 10-year term or Grantor's prior death. The value of the reversion, and thus the gift, is $143,918.

> **EXAMPLE 2:** The facts are the same as in Example 1, except that, if Grantor dies before the end of the 10-year term, the remaining annuity payments will be made to his spouse, also age 50. Because of the two-life annuity and the possibility that either Grantor or his spouse will survive the GRAT term, the value of the reversion decreases to $6,340, with a corresponding decrease in the value of the taxable gift.

    Previously, the IRS's position was that the spouse's revocable annuity interest was a qualified interest so that, in determining the value of the gift, the value of both the grantor's annuity interest and the spouse's annuity interest could be deducted. The result was a significant reduction in the value of the gift, as evidenced by Examples 1 and 2 above. See PLR 9451056; and PLR 9449013.

    Later, the IRS reversed its position, however, concluding that a revocable annuity in the surviving spouse is not a qualified interest that reduces the value of the gift. See TAM 9848004; TAM 9717008; TAM 9741001; and TAM 9707001. The IRS's position was upheld by the Tax

21st Century Estate Planning:
Practical Applications
2005 Edition

©2005 Sonnenschein Nath & Rosenthal LLP
and Cannon Financial Institute, Inc.

- 578 -

Court and the Seventh Circuit in *Cook v. Comm'r*, 115 T.C. 15 (2000), *aff'd*, 269 F.3d 854 (7th Cir. 2001). In *Cook*, a husband and wife each created two separate GRATs in 1993 and in 1995. Both of the 1993 GRATs provided for annual payments to the grantor of 23.999% of the initial fair market value of the trust principal, for a period of five years. If the grantor survived the five-year term, the remainder would pass to a trust for the benefit of the grantor's son. If the grantor died before the expiration of the five-year term, a revocable spousal annuity was created for the spouse, whereby the spouse would receive the same annual payments for the remainder of the deceased grantor's five-year annuity term. The 1995 GRATs were structured in the same manner, except they had different terms and annuity payments.

In reporting the taxable value of their respective GRATs, both the husband and wife reported that the value of the dual-life annuities were exempt from gift tax liability. The IRS, on the other hand, claimed that the spousal interests created in each GRAT were not qualified interests, and, as a result, must be valued at zero for gift tax purposes (thereby creating a taxable gift). The Tax Court and the U.S. Court of Appeals for the Seventh Circuit agreed with the IRS, finding that the spousal interests were not qualified interests, and, therefore, they could not be considered in valuing the retained annuity interests. Accordingly, the IRS could value the retained interest as a one-life, not a two-life, annuity.

In *Schott v. Comm'r*, 319 F.3d 1203 (9th Cir. 2003), *rev'g* T.C. Memo. 2001-110, Patricia and Stephen Schott each created a GRAT with a two-life annuity. Both GRATs provided the grantor with an annuity for 15 years or until the grantor's death, whichever occurred first. If the grantor did not survive the 15-year term, the annuity payments would be made to the spouse if living unless the grantor revoked the spouse's annuity interest. If the grantor died before the end of the 15-year term, and if the spouse did not survive the grantor or if the grantor had revoked the spouse's interest, the annuity would end, and the property would be distributed to a trust for the benefit of the surviving spouse or for the grantor's descendants. If Stephen survived the term of his GRAT, the remaining assets would be held in trust for Patricia if living, or otherwise for Stephen's descendants. If Patricia survived the term of her GRAT, the assets would be held in trust for Patricia's descendants. The IRS found that the two-life annuities were not a qualified interest under Section 2702(b) and assessed a tax deficiency. The Tax Court, confirming its decision in *Cook*, upheld the IRS's assessment, finding that the two-life annuities were unqualified because the annuities could extend beyond the life of the term holder.

At issue on appeal was whether Treas. Reg § 25.2702-2(d)(1), Ex. 7, allows a contingent spousal annuity interest to be a qualified interest under Section § 2702(b). The example states that a two-life annuity in which both interests are qualified annuity or unitrust interests and in which the grantor has the power to revoke the spouse's annuity or unitrust interest will be a qualified interest under Section 2702(b). Treas. Reg. § 25.2702-2(a)(5) provided that the retention of a power to revoke a qualified interest of the transferor's spouse is the retention of a qualified interest.

The Ninth Circuit, reversing and remanding the Tax Court's decision, concluded that the Schotts' GRATs fell within Example 7. The Ninth Circuit noted that the amounts payable are a fixed percentage of the trust property under Section 2702(b) with a fixed termination after 15

21st Century Estate Planning:
Practical Applications
2005 Edition

©2005 Sonnenschein Nath & Rosenthal LLP
and Cannon Financial Institute, Inc.

- 579 -

years if the grantor and spouse live that long. Furthermore, the Ninth Circuit stated, the value of the two-life annuity is ascertainable under the annuity tables, and the value of each grantor's power to revoke is treated as the retention of a qualified interest under Treas. Reg. § 25.2702-2(a)(5).

The Ninth Circuit distinguished *Cook*, stating that, in that case, an additional contingency existed: the grantor and spouse had to be married at the time the spouse's annuity began. This interest was thus unascertainable by the annuity tables.

On February 25, 2005, the IRS finalized regulations regarding revocable spousal annuity interests. The final regulations clarify that a spouse's revocable successor annuity interest will be treated as a qualified interest only if the spouse's annuity or unitrust interest, standing alone, would meet the requirements for a qualified annuity or unitrust interest under Treas. Reg. § 25.2702-3(d)(3) but for the grantor's revocation power. Treas. Reg. § 2702-2(a)(6); -3(d)(2). Treas. Reg. § 25.2702-2(d)(1), Ex. 7, which was at issue in *Schott*, has been removed. These regulations are effective as of July 26, 2004.

4. Rolling GRATs

By creating a series of GRATs, often called rolling GRATs, rather than a single long-term GRAT, a grantor can take advantage of the benefits of short-term GRATs.

> **EXAMPLE:** Rolling GRATs work as follows: the grantor creates a GRAT for a short term, such as 2 years. The annuity payment in year 1 from the first GRAT is used to fund the second GRAT, also for a 2-year term. The annuity payments in year 2 of GRAT 1 and year 1 of GRAT 2 would be used to create the third GRAT. Annuity payments from GRAT 2 and GRAT 3 would be used to create the fourth GRAT.

a. Advantages of Short-Term GRATs. Short-term GRATs have the following advantages:

- The risk of death during the term of the GRAT is minimized. For example, if a grantor creates a six-year GRAT and dies in year five, the GRAT fails. If, however, the grantor creates three two-year GRATs, only the third GRAT will fail, and GRATs one and two (assuming the return on the property exceeds the Section 7520 rate) will have succeeded in transferring assets to the beneficiaries; and
- The risk that a year or two of poor performance during the term of the GRAT will adversely affect the overall benefit of the GRAT is minimized. The failure of one GRAT because of poor investment performance will not affect the success of the future GRATs in the series. Thus, a series of short-term GRATs may result in a larger gift to the remaindermen.

21st Century Estate Planning:
Practical Applications
2005 Edition

©*2005 Sonnenschein Nath & Rosenthal LLP*
and Cannon Financial Institute, Inc.

- 580 -

b. Disadvantages of Short-Term GRATs. Short-term GRATs have the following disadvantages:

- The risk of the Section 7520 rate increasing is an issue. With a long-term GRAT, the grantor can lock in the benefits of a low Section 7520 rate;
- A change in the tax law may prohibit later GRATs; and
- There will be additional transaction costs in doing a series of short-term GRATs, including fees to prepare trust instruments and, possibly, the revaluation of the trust property.

5. Allocation of GST Exemption to a GRAT

If the grantor survives the retained term and the trust property is distributed to grandchildren or trusts from which distributions can be made to grandchildren, GST tax may be imposed.[2] Under IRC § 2642(f)(1) of the Code, the grantor of a trust cannot allocate his or her GST exemption to property transferred during an estate tax inclusion period ("ETIP"). The ETIP is the period of time after the transfer during which the value of the trust property would be includable in the grantor's gross estate. Because some portion or all of the GRAT will be includable in the grantor's gross estate if he or she does not survive the term of the GRAT, GST exemption cannot be allocated to the GRAT until the end of the GRAT term. If the GRAT is successful (the total return on the trust property exceeds the Section 7520 rate, so that there is property left for the beneficiaries), allocating GST exemption at the end of the term, when the trust property has appreciated, does not leverage the GST exemption. As such, a GRAT generally is not considered to be an effective technique to transfer assets to grandchildren.

> **EXAMPLE:** Grantor, age 50, transfers $10 million to a 10-year GRAT when the Section 7520 rate is 5.4%. The GRAT will pay him an annuity of $1,320,323 each year for the shorter of Grantor's life or the 10-year term. The taxable gift is $287,836. Without the ETIP rules, Grantor could allocate $287,836 of his GST exemption to the transfer. As a result, the trust remainder, which would be almost $5 million at a 10% rate of return, could be distributed to a trust for grandchildren without any GST tax consequences. Because of the ETIP rules, however, Grantor must wait until the end of the GRAT term and allocate GST exemption to the higher amount, thus using all of his GST exemption, which would not shelter the entire remainder in this example.

➔ **Planning Point:** If GST exemption is not allocated to a GRAT, it is important to be sure that the GRAT terminates in favor of non-skip persons, *e.g.*, children. If a child is not then living, then his or her share should be distributed to the other then living children. Because the deceased child's descendants will not receive a share of the GRAT, it is necessary to consider whether adjustments must be made in the grantor's

21st Century Estate Planning:
Practical Applications
2005 Edition

©2005 *Sonnenschein Nath & Rosenthal LLP*
and Cannon Financial Institute, Inc.

- 581 -

other estate planning documents to compensate the family of a deceased child.

a. Sale of Remainder Interest in a GRAT. Having the grantor's children sell their remainder interests in the GRAT to a GST exempt trust for the benefit of the grantor's grandchildren may be a way to avoid the problem caused by the ETIP rules. The effect is to create a generation-skipping GRAT.

(1) Structure of the Transaction. When the GRAT is created, the remainder beneficiaries, generally the grantor's children, sell their remainder interests to an existing GST exempt trust previously created by the grantor for the benefit of the grantor's grandchildren. When the GRAT terminates, the remaining trust property will be distributed to the trust for the grantor's grandchildren from which distributions can be made to grandchildren and more remote descendants free of transfer taxes. As a result, the benefits of the GRAT are shifted to the GST trust. The purchase price is the fair market value of the remainder interest, which has little or no value when the GRAT is created. If a *Walton* GRAT is used, so that the gift has a value of zero, a nominal amount, such as $1, should be paid for the remainder.

> **EXAMPLE:** Grantor, age 55, transfers $5 million to a 10-year GRAT of which his children are the remaindermen. The Section 7520 rate is 5.4%. The GRAT will pay Grantor an annuity in the amount of $660,162 for the shorter of 10 years or Grantor's life. The resulting gift is approximately $223,732. Shortly after the creation of the GRAT, the children sell their remainder interest to an existing GST exempt trust for $223,732. At the end of the 10 years, assuming that the GRAT assets grow at a rate of 8%, $1,231,154 will be remaining in the GRAT, to be distributed to the GST exempt trust, free of any transfer taxes.

➔ **Planning Point:** The GRAT instrument can provide that, at the end of the term, the remainder is payable to a trust for the benefit of the grantor's children, in which case the trustee of such trust is the owner of the remainder interest, and the trustee can sell the remainder interest to the GST trust. Alternatively, the grantor's children themselves can be the beneficiaries, and they will sell their remainder interests. The GRAT should not, however, terminate in favor of the grantor's descendants, per stirpes, because of the likelihood of needing the consent of unborn beneficiaries to the transaction.

➔ **Planning Point:** The planner must be sure that the spendthrift clause in the GRAT does not prohibit the transfer of the remainder interest.

(2) Value of the Remainder. If the children sell the remainder interest for its value under Section 7520, the sale should be for full and adequate consideration, so there should be no gift tax consequences upon the sale or GST tax consequences when the GRAT remainder is distributed to the GST trust.[3]

21st Century Estate Planning:
Practical Applications
2005 Edition

©*2005 Sonnenschein Nath & Rosenthal LLP*
and Cannon Financial Institute, Inc.

- 582 -

Whether the payment of the actuarial value of the remainder interest in a trust as the purchase price for such interest constitutes adequate and full consideration has been the subject of a line of cases, the leading case on such issue being *Gradow v. U.S.*, 897 F.2d 516 (Fed. Cir. 1990). See also *U.S. v. Past*, 347 F.2d 7 (9th Cir. 1965); *Parker v. U.S.*, 894 F. Supp. 445 (N.D. Ga. 1995); and *Pittman v. U.S.*, 878 F. Supp. 833 (E.D.N.C. 1994). In *Gradow*, the IRS argued, and the court held, that the purchase of a remainder interest is deemed to be for full and adequate consideration for purposes of IRC § 2036's estate inclusion provisions only if the price paid for the remainder is equal to the full value of the property and not just the value of the remainder interest. The IRS could attempt to extend *Gradow*'s rationale by arguing that unless the children pay the grantor an amount equal to the full value of the GRAT property, as opposed to the actuarial value of the remainder interest, they will not have paid adequate and full consideration for the interest. Three Courts of Appeal have, however, held that consideration equal to the fair market value of the remainder interest is adequate for purposes of IRC § 2036 of the Code. See *Magnin v. Comm'r*, 184 F.3d 1074 (9th Cir. 1999); *Wheeler v. U.S.*, 116 F.3d 749 (5th Cir. 1997); and *D'Ambrosio v. Comm'r*, 101 F.3d 309 (3d Cir. 1996). More importantly, the IRS has conceded that this line of cases does not apply for purposes of the gift tax. *Wheeler v. U.S.*, 116 F.3d at 755 ("[b]oth parties [*i.e.*, the government and the taxpayer] agree that, for the purposes of the gift tax (section 2512 of the Code), consideration equal to the actuarial value of the remainder interest constitutes adequate consideration").

      b. **Severance of Trusts**. IRC § 2642(a)(3) of the Code, which was added by the Act, provides another alternative to allow a GRAT to take advantage of the GST exemption. Under IRC § 2642(a)(3), if certain requirements are met, an existing trust can be severed for GST tax purposes into two trusts, and GST exemption can be allocated to one of the trusts so that it is completely exempt from GST tax. The other trust would not be exempt from GST tax.

Under this Section, therefore, if a grantor wishes to allocate GST exemption to a GRAT but the value of the GRAT property at the end of the term exceeds the grantor's available GST exemption, the grantor can structure the GRAT so that the remainder is held in a continuing trust for the remaindermen, at least one of whom should be a child of the grantor (*i.e.*, a non-skip person). The remainder trust will then be severed to create a trust for the benefit of grandchildren and more remote descendants, and the trustee can allocate the grantor's remaining GST exemption to that portion of the remainder trust. The balance of the GRAT property will be held in a non-exempt trust from which distributions can be made to children.

    ➜   **Planning Point:** Although severing a trust as discussed above is a method for allocating a grantor's GST exemption to a GRAT, the basic problem with allocating GST exemption to a GRAT is that the GST exemption cannot be allocated until the end of the term of the GRAT. The fact that the GST exemption is not effectively leveraged must still be considered.

    6. **GRATs Without Mortality Risk[4]**

The primary disadvantage of a GRAT is that, if the grantor dies during the term of the annuity, a portion or all of the property is includable in his or her gross estate for federal estate tax purposes. As a result, the GRAT fails to achieve the goal of transferring property to the

21st Century Estate Planning:
Practical Applications
2005 Edition

©2005 Sonnenschein Nath & Rosenthal LLP
and Cannon Financial Institute, Inc.

- 583 -

beneficiaries at no, or a reduced, gift tax cost. Additionally, the grantor may have paid gift tax or used part of his or her applicable exclusion amount. One technique, called a "guaranteed GRAT,"[5] has been suggested to eliminate the mortality risk inherent in a GRAT.

a. Structure of the Transaction. A grantor creates a GRAT, retaining a contingent reversion in the GRAT property, so that such property will be paid to the grantor's estate if he does not survive the GRAT term. The grantor's children are the remainder beneficiaries and will receive the remaining property in the GRAT if the grantor survives the term.

Shortly after the creation of the GRAT, the grantor and his or her children enter into an agreement whereby the children purchase the equivalent of the grantor's contingent reversion for its fair market value. Pursuant to the agreement, the grantor agrees that his or her estate will pay the children the value of any amount it receives from the GRAT because of the contingent reversion, and the children pay the grantor an amount equal to the current actuarial value of the contingent reversion (hereinafter the "reversion equivalent") determined under Section 7520. Note that the agreement does not obligate the estate to pay the actual GRAT property that reverts to the grantor's estate to the children, but rather to pay the children an amount equal to the value of such property.

If the grantor dies during the GRAT term, the GRAT will terminate and distribute the remaining trust property to the grantor's estate. Pursuant to the terms of the agreement, the grantor's estate must pay the children an amount equal in value to the property distributed to the grantor's estate from the GRAT upon his or her death (*i.e.*, the contingent reversion interest). As explained in more detail below, the grantor's estate should be entitled to an estate tax deduction for the amount it pays to the children. Thus, although the GRAT property is included in the grantor's estate, the estate receives a deduction that offsets the value of the GRAT property included in the gross estate. Such a transaction eliminates the mortality risk because, as a result of the deduction, the GRAT property is effectively not included in the grantor's gross estate for federal estate tax purposes. Thus, the children receive the value of the GRAT property free of estate tax.

Additionally, there is a possible windfall to the children. If the grantor dies during the GRAT term before all of the annuity payments have been made to the grantor, more property will remain in the GRAT than there would have been if the grantor had survived the GRAT term and received all of the annuity payments. This additional amount remaining in the GRAT (which the children receive from the grantor's estate pursuant to the agreement) will represent a windfall to the children.

b. Why the Guaranteed GRAT Works. Although the GRAT property is includable in the grantor's gross estate for federal estate tax purposes, the estate should be entitled to a deduction under IRC § 2053(a) for the value of the GRAT property that is paid to the children. IRC § 2053(a) provides for an estate tax deduction for claims against the estate, to the extent the claims were contracted for an adequate and full consideration in money or money's worth. The purchase price of the reversion equivalent will be adequate and full consideration because the purchase price will equal the actuarial value of the reversion, as

21st Century Estate Planning:
Practical Applications
2005 Edition

©2005 Sonnenschein Nath & Rosenthal LLP
and Cannon Financial Institute, Inc.

- 584 -

determined under Section 7520. Thus, the requirements of IRC § 2053(a) should be satisfied. In contrast, a deduction would not be allowed under IRC § 2053(a) if the children received the reversionary interest by gift.

      c. <u>Funding the Purchase Price</u>. The children will need funds to purchase the reversion equivalent from the grantor. If the children have sufficient wealth to purchase the reversion equivalent from the grantor but do not have sufficient liquid assets, they could give the grantor a promissory note, although the children should have sufficient other assets to ensure they have the ability to make payments on the note. If not, their payment may be deemed illusory, and the IRS could recharacterize the transaction as a gift of the reversion equivalent. Interest payments made by the children to the grantor will be taxed as interest income to the grantor. If the reversion equivalent is purchased by a trust for the benefit of the children that is a grantor trust as to the grantor, however, any interest payments made by the trust will not be taxable interest income to the grantor. This is because with a grantor trust, as discussed above, transactions between the grantor and the trust are ignored for federal income tax purposes.

      If the children do not have sufficient funds to purchase the reversion equivalent or to make payments on a note, the grantor could make a gift to the children, which they may use to pay the purchase price. Unless such a gift qualifies for the gift tax annual exclusion or is sheltered by the applicable exclusion amount, a gift tax will be due. The timing of the gift and the purchase of the reversion equivalent should be irrelevant. The IRS has held, however, that the purchaser of a remainder interest must not have acquired the funds to buy such interest from the holder of the life estate. <u>See</u> TAM 9206006. It is reasonable to assume that the IRS would take a similar position with respect to the purchase of a reversion interest. Therefore, a lapse of time between the gift and the purchase (*e.g.*, six months) is preferable.

21st Century Estate Planning:
Practical Applications
2005 Edition

©2005 Sonnenschein Nath & Rosenthal LLP
and Cannon Financial Institute, Inc.

- 585 -

d. IRC § 2702 Does Not Apply. IRC § 2702, which applies to a "transfer of an interest in trust," should not apply to the reversion purchase. The grantor's sale of the reversion equivalent should not be deemed to be a transfer of an interest in trust. Under the purchase agreement, the children are entitled only to receive an amount equal in value to the property received by the grantor's estate by reason of his reversion, but they are not entitled to receive the specific property paid to the grantor's estate from the GRAT. Thus, there is no transfer with respect to the GRAT property. Accordingly, IRC § 2702 should not apply, and the reversion should be valued under Section 7520.

e. The *Gradow* Issue. As discussed above, the children must pay adequate and full consideration for the reversion equivalent for the estate's obligation to pay the children an amount equal to the reversion to be deductible under IRC § 2053(a). In *Gradow v. U.S.*, 897 F.2d 516 (Fed. Cir. 1990), the court held that the purchase of a remainder interest is deemed to be for full and adequate consideration for purposes of IRC § 2036's estate inclusion provisions only if the price paid for the remainder is equal to the full value of the property and not just the value of the remainder interest. The holding in *Gradow* specifically applies to the inclusion provisions of IRC § 2036, which may not apply to a guaranteed GRAT (because it may be included under IRC § 2033 or 2039).

The IRS could attempt to extend *Gradow*'s rationale by arguing that, unless the children pay the grantor an amount equal to the full value of the GRAT property, as opposed to the actuarial value of the reversion interest, they will not have paid full and adequate consideration for purposes of IRC § 2053. Consequently, the grantor's estate would not receive a deduction under IRC § 2053. As noted above in the discussion of the sale of a remainder interest in a GRAT, three Courts of Appeal have held that consideration equal to the fair market value of the remainder interest is adequate for purposes of IRC § 2036. See *Magnin v. Comm'r*, 184 F.3d 1074 (9th Cir. 1999); *Wheeler v. U.S.*, 116 F.3d 749 (5th Cir. 1997); *D'Ambrosio v. Comm'r*, 101 F.3d 309 (3d Cir. 1996). As recognized by the court in *Wheeler*, the sale of a remainder interest for its actuarial value does not result in the circumvention of the estate tax because the consideration received for the remainder interest, reinvested at the Section 7520 rate for the applicable life expectancy or term, will equal the value of the property in which the remainder interest is sold.

f. Cost of a Guaranteed GRAT. Even if the IRS were to succeed in arguing that an IRC § 2053 deduction is not allowed for the grantor's estate's obligation to pay the children under the purchase agreement, the children will be no worse off than if the guaranteed GRAT had been a traditional GRAT (in which the grantor retains the reversion) and the grantor died during the annuity term. This comes with two exceptions: first, the children will have incurred an additional "cost" associated with a guaranteed GRAT, discussed below; and, second, a shorter term might have been used with a traditional GRAT, and the grantor may have survived the shorter term.

The purchase price that the children pay for the reversion equivalent becomes part of the grantor's estate, and it, and any appreciation thereon, will be subject to estate tax at the grantor's death. Thus, the additional "cost" of a guaranteed GRAT compared to a traditional GRAT is the

21st Century Estate Planning:
Practical Applications
2005 Edition

©2005 Sonnenschein Nath & Rosenthal LLP
and Cannon Financial Institute, Inc.

- 586 -

estate tax on the amount the children pay the grantor for the contingent reversion (and on the appreciation thereof). The children place this amount into the grantor's estate, to be subject to estate tax before passing back to them.

If the GRAT assets grow at a rate that is less than the Section 7520 rate, or if the assets decline in value, the loss is greater with a guaranteed GRAT than with a traditional GRAT. In the case of a traditional GRAT, all that is lost is the grantor's use of the funds used to pay the gift tax. With the guaranteed GRAT, however, the purchase price paid by the children for their reversion equivalent will be subject to estate tax in the grantor's estate. Thus, in 2005, the children would lose 47% of the reversion equivalent purchase price (plus 47% of any appreciation thereon). This loss is in addition to the loss in the case of a traditional GRAT, *i.e.*, the use of the gift tax funds.

> **EXAMPLE 1**: 10-Year Guaranteed GRAT. When the Section 7520 rate is equal to 5.4%, the grantor, who is 50, transfers $10 million to a 10-year GRAT that will pay him or her an annuity of $1,320,323 per year. The grantor also retains a contingent reversion in the event he or she does not survive the GRAT term. His or her children are the remainder beneficiaries of the GRAT. The value of the gift (the contingent reversion) upon creation of the GRAT is $287,836. Assuming a 47% gift tax rate, the grantor will be required to pay $135,283 in gift tax. Shortly after the creation of the GRAT, the grantor and his or her children enter into an agreement whereby the children purchase the reversion equivalent from the grantor for $287,836. The grantor then dies just before the end of the GRAT term.
>
> If the GRAT's rate of return on its investments is 10%, the children will receive about $4,900,000 from the GRAT property. The children also will receive the $287,836 that the grantor received from the children as payment for the reversion, reduced by estate tax. However, the estate will be able to take a deduction for $287,836 under Section 2053. Assuming the grantor reinvested the purchase price at 10%, it will have grown to about $746,572. After estate taxes, the children will receive $395,683 + $4,900,000, which equals $5,295,683.
>
> **EXAMPLE 2**: Traditional 10-Year GRAT. If the grantor creates a traditional 10-year GRAT with identical terms and the grantor survives the 10-year term but dies immediately thereafter, the children will receive the same $4,900,000 from the GRAT at the end of 10 years. The children will have retained their $287,836 (not used to purchase the reversion equivalent), which will have grown to $746,572. The children will have $4,900,000 + $746,572, which equals $5,646,572. The difference between what they receive from the guaranteed GRAT and what they receive from the traditional GRAT, $350,889, results

21st Century Estate Planning:
Practical Applications
2005 Edition

©2005 *Sonnenschein Nath & Rosenthal LLP*
and Cannon Financial Institute, Inc.

- 587 -

because the children kept their $287,836, which grew to $746,572 over 10 years and was not subject to estate tax at the grantor's death. The "cost" of the guaranteed GRAT is the amount of estate tax saved on the $746,572.

If the grantor dies in year 5, however, the traditional GRAT would have failed to save any estate tax, while the guaranteed GRAT shifted all of the GRAT property at that time to the children free of estate tax.

g. **Factors Offsetting the Additional Cost**. The additional cost of a guaranteed GRAT is reduced or offset by three factors:

(1) **Economic Benefits of GRAT Increase With Longer Term**. The economic benefit produced by any type of GRAT (traditional or guaranteed) is that the amount by which the investments in the GRAT outperform the Section 7520 rate passes to the remainder beneficiaries free of gift or estate tax other than any gift tax paid when the GRAT is initially funded. Because the guaranteed GRAT does not have the mortality risk associated with a traditional GRAT, however, the GRAT term can be longer than one might otherwise use in a traditional GRAT. The economic benefit produced by the GRAT is increased because more property remains in GRAT for a longer period of time, thereby shifting to the children the spread between the actual rate of return and the Section 7520 rate on more property for a longer period.

As the GRAT term is increased, however, the value of the contingent reversion (and thus the amount of the gift tax triggered upon creation of the GRAT and the purchase price of the reversion equivalent) will also increase. This is because the longer the GRAT term, the greater the likelihood that the grantor will not survive the entire term, and, therefore, the more valuable the reversion equivalent (and the greater the purchase price of the reversion equivalent).

> **EXAMPLE 1:** Grantor, age 50, transfers $10 million to a 5-year GRAT and retains a contingent reversion. The Section 7520 rate is 5.4%. The GRAT will pay Grantor an annuity of $2,335,357 for the shorter of his life or the 5-year term. If the assets grow at 8%, at the end of the 5-year term, $992,673 will be available for the beneficiaries. The value of the grantor's reversion, and the value of the taxable gift, is $130,548.

> **EXAMPLE 2:** The facts are the same as in Example 1, except that the GRAT is for a 10-year term. In that case, the annuity payment is $1,320,323. At the end of 10 years, $2,462,308 will be available for the beneficiaries. The value of the grantor's reversion, and the value of the taxable gift, is $287,836.

➔ **Planning Point:** If a *Walton* GRAT is used, however, there is no reversion, and, therefore, no gift. Accordingly, a longer-term, traditional (non-guaranteed) GRAT can be used without the corresponding increase in the gift tax.

21st Century Estate Planning:
Practical Applications
2005 Edition

©2005 Sonnenschein Nath & Rosenthal LLP
and Cannon Financial Institute, Inc.

- 588 -

(2) <u>**Windfall Upon Premature Death**</u>. If the grantor dies during the term of a guaranteed GRAT, the children will receive a "windfall" because they will receive the property in the GRAT before all of the annuity payments are made to the grantor. (With a traditional (non-guaranteed) GRAT, such property returns to the grantor's estate and is subject to estate tax before passing to the children.) Thus, unlike a traditional (non-guaranteed) GRAT, a practitioner can consider a guaranteed GRAT for those clients who do not have a normal life expectancy but nevertheless are not terminally ill within the meaning of the regulations under IRC § 7520. (Recall that, if the grantor is terminally ill, the Section 7520 rate cannot be used to value the reversion. Treas. Reg. § 1.7520-3(b).) A guaranteed GRAT thus can function as a "bet to die" technique, providing a greater benefit when the grantor dies prematurely.

(3) <u>**Less Investment Risk**</u>. A longer GRAT term reduces the investment risk, *i.e.*, the risk that the GRAT's investment return will not exceed the Section 7520 rate over the GRAT term.

7. GRAT v. Direct Gift

The success of a GRAT must be compared with the alternative of making an outright gift. Whether a GRAT should be used depends on whether, at the end of the term of the GRAT, the remaindermen will receive more than they would have if the grantor had made an outright gift.

As discussed above, a GRAT serves to transfer property at a reduced gift tax cost to the remaindermen only if the GRAT assets achieve a rate of return in excess of the Section 7520 rate. If the grantor dies during the term of the GRAT, the remainder beneficiaries will not receive anything. Had the grantor made a direct gift to them, however, they would have received something. A GRAT may decrease the transfer tax cost of a gift, but a direct gift of an amount equal to the amount of the gift upon creation of the GRAT may result in more property being available for the beneficiaries because they receive the property immediately and are entitled to all of the income and appreciation on it.

> **EXAMPLE:** Grantor, age 55, transfers $5 million to a 5-year GRAT for Son. The Section 7520 rate is 5.4%, and the annuity payment is $1,167,679. Based on the value of the annuity for the shorter of 5 years or Grantor's life, the taxable gift is $102,406.
>
> If the GRAT property grows at 5.0% (less than the Section 7520 rate), nothing will be passed to Son. If, instead, Grantor had given Son $102,406 directly, which also grew at 5%, Son would have $130,699 after 5 years. Thus, the direct gift produces a better result than the GRAT.
>
> If the property in the GRAT grows at 8%, however, upon termination $496,337 will be distributed to Son. Had Grantor given Son $102,406 directly, which grew at 8%, Son would have $150,468, a less favorable result than with the GRAT.

21st Century Estate Planning:
Practical Applications
2005 Edition

©2005 Sonnenschein Nath & Rosenthal LLP
and Cannon Financial Institute, Inc.

- 589 -

Although it is said that a GRAT is successful if it outperforms the Section 7520 rate, it may not be as successful as an outright gift. At a 6% rate of return, the GRAT will result in $108,816 available for Son, while an outright gift of $102,406 will result in $137,042.

D. Grantor Retained Unitrusts

A grantor retained unitrust ("GRUT") is similar to a GRAT, except that it provides the grantor with a "qualified unitrust interest," which is another type of qualified interest under IRC § 2702. A "qualified unitrust interest" is the right to receive, at least annually, a fixed percentage of the fair market value of the property in the GRUT, determined annually. IRC § 2702(b)(2). Thus, a grantor transfers property to an irrevocable trust and, instead of paying an annuity as with a GRAT, the trust pays the grantor a fixed percentage of the fair market value of the property, determined annually. Trust distributions under a GRUT vary from year to year, depending on the value of the trust property. That is, because the payment is a percentage of the value of the trust property, as the value of the trust property increases (or decreases), so does the annual payment. This, of course, differs from a GRAT, where the distributions do not change from year to year.

A GRUT is more difficult to administer than a GRAT because the trust assets must be revalued each year in order to determine the annual payment. The revaluation is especially burdensome if the GRUT holds hard to value assets, such as closely held stock.

1.   Gift and Estate Tax Consequences

As with a GRAT, the transfer of property to a GRUT constitutes a taxable gift equal to the value of the property transferred to the GRUT less the value of the retained unitrust interest. Because the unitrust interest is a "qualified interest," it will be valued under Section 7520 of the Code. As with a GRAT, the GRUT property will be included in the grantor's gross estate if the grantor dies during the term of the GRUT.

2.   Why GRUTs Are Rarely Used

In general, practitioners do not use GRUTs because the unitrust payment returns more property to the grantor, which is contrary to the usual goal of removing property from the grantor's estate. That is, if the rate of return on the GRUT assets exceeds the Section 7520 rate, the unitrust payment will increase, so that the grantor shares in the excess, thereby eliminating any transfer tax savings from the high returns. In contrast, with a GRAT, the excess benefits the remaindermen exclusively.

The GRUT generally provides little benefit over a direct gift, regardless of whether the GRUT assets exceed or fall short of the Section 7520 rate, and a direct gift may be preferable because it eliminates the mortality risk associated with a GRUT.

21st Century Estate Planning:
Practical Applications
2005 Edition

©2005 Sonnenschein Nath & Rosenthal LLP
and Cannon Financial Institute, Inc.

- 590 -

EXAMPLE: Grantor, age 60, transfers $1,000,000 to a 5-year GRUT. The Section 7520 rate is 5.4%. The unitrust payment is 10% of the value of the trust. The taxable gift is $619,470.

If the assets grow at a rate of 10%, then, at the end of the GRUT term, the beneficiaries will receive $1,000,000. Had the grantor made a direct gift of $619,470, after 5 years at 10% growth, the beneficiaries would have $997,663, or $2,337 less than with a GRUT.

If the assets grow at a rate of 6%, the beneficiaries will receive $815,373 at the end of the term. Had the grantor made an outright gift of $619,470, the beneficiaries would have received $828,991, or $13,618 more than with the GRUT.

In either case, although the rate of return exceeds the Section 7520 rate, very little additional property, if any, is transferred to the remainder beneficiaries using a GRUT versus what they would receive from a direct gift.

E. Sale to an Intentionally Defective Grantor Trust

A sale to an intentionally defective grantor trust ("IDGT") is often proposed as an alternative to a GRAT, as it is a similar technique to transfer property to beneficiaries at no, or a reduced, transfer tax cost. As with a GRAT, the success of this technique depends upon the assets that are the subject of the transaction achieving a rate of return in excess of the IRS' assumed interest rate.

1. Structure of the Transaction

The grantor sells property at its fair market value to the IDGT in return for an installment note. There are two keys to the transaction: (1) the trust must be structured as a grantor trust so that it will be disregarded for income tax purposes; and (2) the transaction must be recognized as a bona-fide sale for adequate and full consideration to avoid the imposition of estate and gift taxes. At the end of the note's term, any income and appreciation on the trust assets that exceed the payments required to satisfy the promissory note pass to the beneficiaries of the trust (usually the grantor's children and/or grandchildren) free of estate, gift and, if appropriately structured, GST transfer taxes.

If the trust assets appreciate at a rate that is less than the interest rate used to determine the interest payments on the promissory note, or if the assets decline in value, the grantor will receive back (as promissory note payments) the value of the original property sold to the trust, and nothing will be left to distribute to the remainder beneficiaries. Thus, if the trust assets underperform, some of the grantor's assets could be subject to double taxation: assets that are gifted to the trust to fund the note payments will be subject to gift tax upon funding the trust and subject to estate tax at the grantor's death). Assets transferred to the grantor as payment on the note are eligible for a stepped-up basis at the grantor's death.

21st Century Estate Planning:
Practical Applications
2005 Edition

©*2005 Sonnenschein Nath & Rosenthal LLP*
and Cannon Financial Institute, Inc.

- 591 -

If the trust's total return exceeds the applicable interest rate but the income generated by the trust assets is insufficient to pay the interest on the note (*i.e.*, the assets have a high growth rate, but a low income yield), the trustee can transfer trust principal back to the grantor in order to make the annual interest payment. This method of payment is common where the assets sold to the trust are highly appreciating assets with low cash flow.

Generally, any assets with appreciation potential or yield in excess of the applicable interest rate are appropriate assets to sell to an IDGT. Assets that can be valued at a discount, such as a minority interest in a closely held corporation or limited partnership interests, can produce significant savings because the face amount of the note will be based on the discounted value of the assets sold, rather than on the full value.

a. The Grantor Trust.

A sale to an IDGT involves the creation of an irrevocable trust that is a grantor trust for income tax purposes. A grantor trust is ignored for federal income tax purposes and, as a result, the trust's income, deductions, and credits are passed through the trust to the grantor and reported on the grantor's individual income tax return rather than to the trust as a separate entity. Although the trust is a grantor trust for federal income tax purposes, the trust is structured so that the trust assets are not includable in the grantor's gross estate for federal estate tax purposes. The basis of the assets sold to the IDGT is equal to the grantor's basis in such assets (*i.e.*, a carryover basis). Because the value of the IDGT will not be included in the grantor's gross estate, the trust assets will not receive a stepped-up basis at the grantor's death. The loss of the step-up in basis for the assets sold to the IDGT must be considered in determining the tax consequences of the sale transaction.

→ **Planning Point:** One alternative to avoid the adverse income tax consequences of selling highly appreciated assets to an IDGT and losing the step-up in basis is to pay the note in kind before the grantor's death with appreciated assets. Because the trust is a grantor trust, no gain or loss would be recognized on the payment, and the appreciated property used to pay the note would be included in the grantor's gross estate and, therefore, would get a step-up in basis at the grantor's death.

Rather than creating a new trust to which the assets will be sold, the assets could be sold to an irrevocable grantor trust that already exists. Doing so will avoid the need to fund the trust with cash or other assets in order to support the assertion that the eventual sale is a bona-fide sale. The reasons for funding the trust with other assets will be discussed below.

b. Terms of the Sale.

After creating the trust, the grantor sells assets to the trust at their fair market value in return for a promissory note that bears interest at the interest rate sanctioned by the Code.

(1) The Interest Rate.

The interest rate on the note is determined by reference to IRC § 7872(f)(2)(A). This Section states that the AFR for a term loan is the AFR in effect under IRC § 1274(d) for the period represented by the loan, compounded semi-annually. The AFR changes monthly and varies depending upon the term of the note. The short term rate

21st Century Estate Planning:
Practical Applications
2005 Edition

©2005 Sonnenschein Nath & Rosenthal LLP
and Cannon Financial Institute, Inc.

- 592 -

applies for terms of three years or less, the mid-term rate applies to terms greater than three years and nine years or less, and the long-term rate applies to terms greater than nine years.

(2)   **The Note**. The promissory note will bear interest at the interest rate determined by reference to the applicable federal rate ("AFR") under IRC § 7872(f)(2)(A). Ideally, the note will be structured as a balloon note, where repayment of the principal is deferred until the end of the note term. Therefore, the trust will make only annual interest payments to the grantor. By using a balloon note, a larger percentage of the assets remains in the trust during the note term, thereby allowing the greatest compounding of appreciation inside the trust.

➜   **Planning Point:** The term of the promissory note can be for any length. Generally, the longer the term, the larger the required interest payment because the AFR will be higher. Because the death of the grantor during the note term only will result in the unpaid balance of the note being included in the grantor's estate (as opposed to the full value of the note), the grantor's survival of the term is not necessary to achieve transfer tax savings. In general, the length of the term will depend on interest rates at the time of the transaction (*e.g.*, if the AFR is low, the grantor may want to lock in this rate by using a longer term; alternatively, if the AFR is high, the grantor may want to use a shorter term and then enter into another sale transaction when rates are more favorable).

➜   **Planning Point:** The sale should be documented in the same way in which a sale to an unrelated party would be. Thus, there should be a sales contract, an assignment, a promissory note, an appraisal of the property, if necessary, and a security document, if applicable.

> **EXAMPLE:** Grantor, age 50, transfers $500,000 to an irrevocable grantor trust. The income and principal of the trust are to be paid, in the trustee's discretion, for his daughter's health, education, support and maintenance. At his daughter's death, the trust assets will be held in the trust for the benefit of his grandchildren. Grantor files a gift tax return to report the $500,000 gift to the trust (which is sheltered from tax by his applicable exclusion amount) and allocates GST exemption to the transfer. After funding the trust, Grantor sells $5,000,000 worth of assets to the trust in exchange for a 5-year, $5,000,000 promissory note. The promissory note is structured so that interest is paid annually at the mid-term AFR of 4.65%, and a balloon payment of principal is due at the end of the 5-year note.
>
> As discussed, the initial funding of the trust with $500,000 results in a taxable gift. Nevertheless, if Grantor's applicable exclusion amount is available, the initial transfer can be sheltered from gift tax. No gain or loss is recognized on the sale of $5,000,000 of assets to the trust, and the annual interest payments of $232,500 ($5,000,000 x 4.65%) will not be taxable as income to Grantor. Assuming a 15% annual growth

21st Century Estate Planning:
Practical Applications
2005 Edition

©*2005 Sonnenschein Nath & Rosenthal LLP*
and Cannon Financial Institute, Inc.

- 593 -

rate, at the end of the note term, the trust will pay Grantor a balloon payment of $5,000,000, which also will not be taxable income to Grantor. After the payment of the note, $3,489,183 will be left in the trust and will pass to the trust beneficiaries free of gift, estate and GST taxes.

If the assets were sold to an existing trust, however, Grantor would avoid the $500,000 gift.

2. Tax Consequences of a Sale to an Intentionally Defective Grantor Trust

a. Gift Tax. A promissory note bearing interest at the AFR is deemed to have a fair market value equal to its face amount. Therefore, the sale of assets to the IDGT in return for a promissory note will not be a gift as long as the promissory note equals the value of the property transferred and bears interest at the AFR. An accurate appraisal is essential to support the fair market value claimed in the transaction.

If the assets are not sold to an existing trust, the initial funding of the IDGT will be a taxable gift. The grantor can use, if available, a portion of his or her applicable exclusion amount to shelter the gift from tax.

(1) Avoiding the Undervaluation of Assets. Gift tax concerns may arise if the property that is the subject of the sale is a hard-to-value asset, such as closely held stock. A taxable gift will occur if the value of the property transferred is later determined to be greater than the sale price. This section discusses the most common methods used to minimize the risk that the IRS will increase the value of the property transferred.

(a) General Rule. The seminal case in this area is *Comm'r v. Procter*, 142 F.2d 824 (4th Cir. 1944). *Procter* involved a transfer by gift to a trust. The trust provided that if a federal court of last resort held that any part of the transfer was a taxable gift, that portion of the property subject to gift tax would be excluded from the transfer. The court held that this was a condition subsequent and it violated public policy. The court stated that there were three reasons for declaring the condition subsequent void:

- It would deter the IRS from auditing returns because there would be no possibility to collect tax,
- The donees would not be parties to the tax litigation and might later try to enforce the gift and
- This type of provision would obstruct the administration of justice because as soon as a court rules that the value of the gift should be increased, the trust instrument revokes the gift and makes the court's ruling moot.

(b) Valuation Formulas. The IRS and the courts have continued to confirm *Procter*. See, e.g., *Estate of McClendon v. Comm'r*, T.C. Memo. 1993-459, *rev'd on other grounds*, 77 F.3d 477 (5th Cir. 1995); *Ward v. Comm'r*, 87 T.C. 78 (1986); Rev. Rul. 86-

21st Century Estate Planning:
Practical Applications
2005 Edition

©2005 Sonnenschein Nath & Rosenthal LLP
and Cannon Financial Institute, Inc.

- 594 -

41, 1986-1 C.B. 300. Practitioners have responded by creating valuation formulas (also called "valuation definition clauses" or "defined value gifts") that attempt to avoid the risk of revaluation. One valuation formula specifies the dollar amount of the gift and then calculates what portion of the property would be needed to satisfy the amount of the gift. The valuation formula arguably avoids the creation of a condition subsequent and the transferring of property back to the grantor. In other words, the donee never has a right to the portion of property that exceeds the specified dollar amount. While the IRS appeared at first to favor these valuation formulas (see, e.g., TAM 8611004, in which the IRS granted the ruling requests of a taxpayer who transferred "such interest in X partnership as has a fair market value of $13,000," although neither one of the issues at stake concerned the validity of this formula), the IRS has recently ruled that these clauses are invalid. In TAM 200337012, the taxpayer transferred "that fraction of Assignor's Limited Partnership Interest . . . which has a fair market value . . . of $a." The taxpayer reported the transfer on a federal gift tax return as a gift of a specific percentage partnership interest with a value of $5,000 less than the figure mentioned in the deed of gift. Relying on the above-cited cases and ruling, the IRS stated that the formula gift clause was ineffective for gift tax purposes because it violated public policy. The IRS saw no difference between a valuation clause such as the one at issue in this TAM and the revaluation clauses in *Procter* and its progeny.

Other valuation formulas have not been any more successful. In TAM 200245053, the taxpayer, as trustee of a revocable trust, sold a fractional share of a 98.9% limited partnership interest to his irrevocable trust. The fraction used to determine the share of the limited partnership interest had a numerator equal to the stated purchase price and a denominator equal to the fair market value of a 98.9% interest in the limited partnership interest. The sale agreement stated that the fair market value of the limited partnership interest "shall be such value as finally determined for federal gift tax purposes." The sale agreement stated that the parties reached a tentative agreement that the percentage interest transferred was the revocable trust's entire interest. The sale agreement also stated that the agreement may be modified if the IRS determines that the sale actually conveyed a different percentage than 98.9%. Upon such a determination by the IRS, the ownership interests and prior distributions would be adjusted. The IRS stated that this clause was against public policy, relying on *Ward* and Rev. Rul. 86-41. The IRS stated that the formula was an "attempt to ameliorate any adverse consequences if the Service challenged the transaction and thereby to discourage any such challenge," and that the clause "does not serve a legitimate purpose."

While the IRS may disfavor valuation formulas, the Tax Court may have given some hope for the validity of these formulas. In *McCord v. Comm'r*, 120 T.C. 358 (May 14, 2003), the taxpayers formed a limited partnership to hold various investment assets, including stocks, bonds, real estate and other limited partnership interests. The taxpayers then gave partnership interests to their children and certain charities under a formula clause that purported to give (a) $6,910,933 worth of partnership interest to the taxpayers' children and trusts for their benefit; (b) $134,000 worth of partnership interests to the Shreveport Symphony (but not more than the difference between the value of the total gift and the amount allocated to the children and their trusts) and (c) the balance to a second charity (later determined to be $324,345). The donees were required to determine the value of the partnership interests and to allocate the gift among

21st Century Estate Planning:
Practical Applications
2005 Edition

©2005 Sonnenschein Nath & Rosenthal LLP
and Cannon Financial Institute, Inc.

- 595 -

themselves using gift tax valuation methods. The IRS valued the total gift at $12,426,086, and declined to recognize the validity of the formula clause, upholding its position in FSA 200122011, which dealt with a similar formula.

The Tax Court determined the value of the total gift to be $9,883,832. The court then stated that the specific formula clause might be valid to limit the amount given to the children and their trusts, but that it did not create a charitable deduction for the entire additional amount passing to the charity because it relied on the valuation fixed by the donees, rather than one fixed by the courts. The court stated that it did not, therefore, have to reach the question of whether such a formula clause would be enforced if it was tied directly to the gift tax values set by the court. The court stated, however, that it might have allowed the larger charitable deduction had the agreement given each donee the "enforceable right to a fraction of the gifted interest determined with reference to the fair market value of the gifted interest as finally determined for Federal gift tax purposes." The taxpayers could, therefore, deduct as the gift to the second charity for gift tax purposes only the amount actually allocated to the second charity by the donees' agreement, rather than the difference between the court's valuation of the gift and the amount allocated to the children and the Shreveport Symphony, thus creating a $2,514,554 net additional taxable gift. ($9,883,832 - $7,044,933 - $324,345). Thus, *McCord* may be the beginning of a general acceptance of valuation formulas that rely on a value as finally determined for gift tax purposes. The remainder may be transferred to either a charity or a spouse, which avoids additional gift taxes. As of early 2004, *McCord* is on appeal to the Fifth Circuit.

(2)   IRC § 2702 Should Not Apply. A gift could result if IRC § 2702 of the Code applies to the IDGT promissory note sale. Under IRC § 2702, the value of a retained interest in a trust that is not a "qualified interest" is valued at zero for purposes of determining the value of the gift. With a sale to an IDGT, only the interest payments on the note would constitute qualified interests. Thus, if IRC § 2702 were applicable, the balloon note payment at the end of the term would be deemed to be a gift.

Nevertheless, IRC § 2702 should not apply because the promissory note issued by the IDGT is not a retained interest of the grantor. A promissory note, unlike a retained beneficial interest in a trust, is governed by its own terms and is independent of the trust instrument. The note can be pledged or otherwise disposed of even if the trust from which it is issued contains a spendthrift provision. See PLR 9535026 (May 31, 1995) and PLR 9436006 (March 14, 1994) (concluding that IRC § 2702 does not apply to promissory notes issued to a trust to pay for assets sold to the trust).

b.   Estate Tax. If the grantor dies before the note is fully paid, then the balance due on the note will be included in the grantor's gross estate. Post-sale appreciation on the trust assets, however, will not be subject to estate tax.

(1)   Inclusion in the Gross Estate Generally. The trust must be designed so that the trust assets will be excluded from the grantor's gross estate for federal estate tax purposes. Accordingly, the grantor must not retain any interests in or powers over the

21st Century Estate Planning:
Practical Applications
2005 Edition

©2005 Sonnenschein Nath & Rosenthal LLP
and Cannon Financial Institute, Inc.

- 596 -

property transferred to the trust that would cause the trust property to be includable in his or her gross estate for federal estate tax purposes.

➔ **Planning Point:** To avoid inclusion of the IDGT property in the grantor's gross estate, the grantor should not be a beneficiary of the trust. Generally, state law allows a grantor's creditors to reach a grantor's retained beneficial interests in a trust. If state law allows a grantor's creditors to reach an irrevocable trust created by the grantor to satisfy claims against the grantor, the trust is included in the grantor's gross estate. See *Estate of Uhl*, 25 T.C. 22 (1955), *rev'd*, 241 F.2d 867 (7th Cir. 1957); Rev. Rul. 77-378, 1977-2 C.B. 347; Rev. Rul. 76-103, 1976-1 C.B. 293.

The grantor can be a trustee if his or her powers are appropriately limited. For example, if the grantor is acting as trustee, the grantor cannot have the power to distribute the trust property to discharge his or her legal obligations, including support obligations. If the grantor has such a power, the grantor's creditors can reach the trust property, and in that case, the trust property may be included in the grantor's gross estate. See *Estate of McTighe*, 36 T.C.M. 1655 (1977). In practice, the grantor generally is not the trustee of the grantor trust.

➔ **Planning Point:** The grantor's spouse can, however, be a beneficiary of the IDGT, which, in effect, allows the grantor to obtain benefits from the transferred property. If the spouse is a beneficiary, the spouse must not transfer property to the IDGT, as doing so could have adverse estate tax consequences for the spouse. Even if the spouse is a beneficiary, the spouse can split gifts with the grantor so that gifts by the grantor to the trust are treated as having been made one-half by each of them without causing inclusion of the trust property in the spouse's gross estate. Splitting gifts also is effective for GST tax purposes, so that both the grantor and the spouse will be deemed to be the transferor of one-half of the property that the grantor gifts to the IDGT. Depending on the terms of the trust, however, the spouse's ability to split gifts to such a trust could be limited. Treas. Reg. § 25.2513-1(b)(3), (4).

> **EXAMPLE:** Grantor contributes $1,000,000 to an IDGT of which spouse is a discretionary beneficiary. Grantor and spouse elect to split gifts. Each of Grantor and spouse is deemed to have transferred $500,000 to the trust, so that each uses $500,000 of his or her respective applicable exclusion amount. Each also is deemed to be the transferor for GST tax purposes with respect to $500,000, so that each uses $500,000 of his or her respective GST exemption.

(2) **Inclusion Under IRC § 2036(a)(1).** If the sale is structured correctly as a bona fide sale, then the grantor's sale of assets to the IDGT should not be

21st Century Estate Planning:
Practical Applications
2005 Edition

©2005 Sonnenschein Nath & Rosenthal LLP
and Cannon Financial Institute, Inc.

- 597 -

characterized as a transfer with a retained interest under IRC § 2036(a)(1). The argument for inclusion is that the right to annual interest payments on the note constitutes a right to receive the income from the transferred property. The concern is one of "coverage" or "thin capitalization," *i.e.*, if the only assets held by the trust are the assets the trust received in exchange for the note, then the grantor is relying on the income from the transferred property to make interest payments on the note. The result of thin capitalization would be that the trust assets would be included in the grantor's gross estate at their date of death value, including the appreciation and accumulated income.

> ➔ **Planning Point:** A number of commentators have stated that the obligation should not be secured by the property held in trust. Their concern is that using the trust property to secure the note might be deemed a retained interest, causing the assets to be included in the grantor's estate under IRC § 2036(a)(1). Others believe, however, that using the trust property to secure the assets in the trust will lend credence to the fact that the sale is a "bona fide sale" that is outside the purview of IRC § 2036.

The result in a number of cases illustrates how a sale to an IDGT should be structured to avoid inclusion of the property in the IDGT in the grantor's gross estate under IRC § 2036(a)(1). See, e.g., *Fidelity-Philadelphia Trust Co. v. Smith*, 356 U.S. 274 (1958); *Ray v. U.S.*, 762 F.2d 1361 (9th Cir. 1985); *Estate of Fabric v. Comm'r*, 83 T.C. 932 (1984); see also Rev. Rul. 77-193, 1977-1 C.B. 273. The cases set forth the following factors to determine whether inclusion under IRC § 2036 can be avoided.

(a) **No Tie Between Trust Income and Interest Payments**. The note should be structured so that the rate of interest is not tied to the income generated by the assets sold to the trust. This is accomplished by using the AFR.

(b) **Note is Obligation of Trustee**. The note should be the personal obligation of the trustee. It is unlikely, however, that the trustee would accept personal liability.

(c) **Note Not Charged to Trust Property**. The obligation on the note should not be charged to the transferred property. That is, the trust assets should not be the sole source of the debt repayment. This factor, as well as the previous factor ((b) above), should be satisfied if the IDGT is funded with assets other than those sold to the trust, which can be used to meet the trust's obligation under the note. One solution is to sell the assets to a preexisting, funded trust. If that is not possible, the following alternatives can be used to provide the necessary coverage.

1. Ten Percent Funding. The prevailing view is that the trust should be funded with assets equal to ten percent of the face amount of the note. This ten percent funding is often called "seed money" or a "downpayment." The contribution of seed money to the IDGT will be a gift and will generate a gift tax unless it is sheltered by the grantor's applicable exclusion amount. Funding the trust with assets other than those sold to the trust lends credence to the fact that the sale is a "bona fide sale." For the view that pre-sale

21st Century Estate Planning:
Practical Applications
2005 Edition

©2005 Sonnenschein Nath & Rosenthal LLP
and Cannon Financial Institute, Inc.

- 598 -

funding is unnecessary, see Elliott Manning and Jerome M. Hesch, "Deferred Payment Sales to Grantor Trusts, GRATs and Net Gifts: Income and Transfer Tax Elements," 24 *Tax Mgmt. Est., Gifts & Tr. J.* 3 (Jan. 1999) (hereinafter "Manning and Hesch").

2. <u>Beneficiary Guarantees</u>. As an alternative to a gift of seed money, coverage can be afforded by the personal guarantees of the beneficiaries. Guaranteeing payment of the note, however, might constitute a gift by the guarantors if it is possible that the guarantors might be required to make payments on the note.

The mere giving of a guarantee should not be a gift, especially if the remainder beneficiaries are the guarantors, who would be making a guarantee for their own benefit. Additionally, there should be no gift if the guarantee is a bona fide obligation of the beneficiary making the guarantee and the beneficiary has sufficient net worth to make payments in the event of default by the trust. <u>See</u> PLR 9515039; Milford B. Hatcher, Jr. and Edward M. Manigault, "Using Beneficiary Guarantees in Defective Grantor Trusts," 92 *J. Tax'n* 152 (Mar. 2000) (hereinafter "Hatcher and Manigault"). Hatcher and Manigault suggest that as long as the trust assets are expected to be sufficient to repay the note at the end of the term, and as long as there is no evidence that the parties do not expect or intend for the beneficiaries to honor their guarantees, the guarantee should be bona fide and should not cause the guarantors to have made taxable gifts.

Payment of a commercially reasonable guarantee fee by the IDGT to the guarantors should avoid the argument that such a guarantee is itself a gift by the guarantor to the trust or the grantor. If the trust does not pay a fee for the guarantee, or if the fee is inadequate, however, the guarantors could become contributors to the trust and thus grantors, with the result that the IDGT would not be wholly owned by the original grantor. In such a case, interest payments and any in-kind payments to the grantor would be taxable events to the grantor to the extent that the grantor is not treated as the owner of the trust.

The timing of the gift, if one is made, is uncertain. First, there could be an annual gift as long as the guarantee is outstanding. Second, there could be a one-time taxable gift when the guarantee is made. Finally, no gift might occur until the beneficiary actually makes a payment under the guarantee. For a discussion of the timing of the gift, see Michael D. Mulligan, "Sale to an Intentionally Defective Irrevocable Trust for a Balloon Note - An Estate Freeze Technique Avoiding the Heat of Chapter 14?," SG027 *ALI-ABA* 315 (Sept. 2001).

21st Century Estate Planning:
Practical Applications
2005 Edition

©2005 Sonnenschein Nath & Rosenthal LLP
and Cannon Financial Institute, Inc.

- 599 -

c. **Generation-Skipping Transfer Tax**. The IDGT can be designed so that the trust assets are exempt from GST tax. As discussed above in connection with GRATs, the grantor of a trust cannot allocate his or her GST exemption to property transferred during an estate tax inclusion period, which is the period of time after the transfer during which the value of the trust property would be includable in the grantor's gross estate. Because the IDGT will not be includable in the grantor's gross estate, the grantor can allocate a portion of his or her GST exemption to the assets used to fund the trust immediately upon the creation of the trust and thereby shelter the entire trust from the GST tax.

d. **Income Tax**. As discussed above, the trust is designed to be a grantor trust for income tax purposes. This means that transactions between the grantor and the trust have no income tax consequences (because the grantor is treated for income tax purposes as if he or she still owns the trust assets). The transaction has the following income tax ramifications:

- The grantor will not recognize gain or loss on the sale of assets to the trust in return for the promissory note. As the sale is ignored for income tax purposes, the income tax basis of the assets sold to the trust will not change as a result of the sale;

- The grantor is not taxed on interest payments he or she receives from the trust on the promissory note; and

- Because the grantor is treated for income tax purposes as if he or she still owns the trust assets, the grantor will report, for income tax purposes, all items of income, deduction and credit generated by the trust on his or her individual income tax return. Such items will not be taxable to the trust as a separate entity. Thus, if interest or dividends are received or capital gains are recognized in the trust, the grantor continues to be taxed on such items as though he or she had never sold the assets to the trust. The net effect of this income tax treatment is that the grantor is effectively able to make a tax-free gift to the beneficiaries of the trust, as the grantor's payment of income taxes reduces his or her estate without any transfer tax consequences while enhancing the assets that ultimately pass to the remainder beneficiaries by leaving the trust assets intact.

(1) **Achieving Grantor Trust Status**. Grantor trust status can be achieved by intentionally violating one of the grantor trust rules specified in IRC §§ 671-679 of the Code. Some of the typical provisions used to cause grantor trust status are as follows:

- Naming the grantor's spouse as a beneficiary of the IDGT. IRC § 677(a).

- Granting the grantor the power to borrow the income or principal of the IDGT without adequate interest or security. IRC § 675(2). There is concern, however, that the grantor's retention of the power to borrow income or principal without adequate interest may cause inclusion in the

21st Century Estate Planning:
Practical Applications
2005 Edition

©2005 Sonnenschein Nath & Rosenthal LLP
and Cannon Financial Institute, Inc.

- 600 -

grantor's estate as a retained right to the possession or enjoyment of, or the right to income from, the trust property under IRC § 2036(a)(1).

- Granting the grantor the power, in a nonfiduciary capacity, to reacquire the trust corpus by substituting property of equivalent value. IRC § 675(4). The IRS, in an apparent attempt to discourage the use of this provision as a means of achieving grantor trust status, has declined to rule on whether or not this provision will cause grantor trust status. Instead, the IRS has stated that the determination as to whether the grantor is acting in a nonfiduciary capacity is a factual issue that must await the filing of the fiduciary income tax return.

- Granting a person other than the grantor or an existing beneficiary the power to add beneficiaries. IRC § 674(c). See PLR 200030019 (April 28, 2000); and PLR 199936031 (June 10, 1999).

➔ **Planning Point:** The trust should provide for the ability to change from a grantor trust to a nongrantor trust if the law changes or other circumstances dictate such a change. For example, if the grantor's payment of income taxes is determined to be a gift, grantor trust status may result in unwanted gift, estate and GST tax consequences.

(2) **Basis of Property Sold to IDGT**. The basis of the assets sold to the IDGT is equal to the grantor's basis in such assets. That is, the assets have a carryover basis. Because the IDGT will not be included in the grantor's gross estate, the assets in the trust will not receive an increased basis, as is the case with assets held by the grantor at death (the basis is "stepped up" to equal the fair market value at death). If highly appreciated assets are sold to the IDGT and the assets do not continue to appreciate as expected, the grantor may have been better off had the sale not taken place, in which case the assets would be included in his or her gross estate, but they also would receive a stepped-up basis.

➔ **Planning Point:** One alternative to avoid the adverse income tax consequences of selling highly appreciated assets to an IDGT is to pay the note in kind prior to the grantor's death with appreciated assets. Because the trust is a grantor trust, no gain or loss would be recognized on the payment, and the appreciated property used to pay the note would be included in the grantor's gross estate and, therefore, would get a step-up in basis at the grantor's death.

(3) **Death of the Grantor During the Note Term**. If the grantor dies before the note is paid in full, the IDGT will lose its status as a grantor trust and become a separate entity for income tax purposes. When grantor trust status terminates, the grantor is treated as transferring assets to the IDGT for income tax purposes. Treas. Reg. § 1.1001-2(c), Ex. 5; *Madorin v. Comm'r*, 84 T.C. 667 (1985); Rev. Rul. 77-402, 1977-2 C.B. 222. Practitioners disagree, however, about whether the deemed transfer to the trust, usually presumed to be in exchange for the note, occurs before or after the grantor's death. The different views follow.[6]

21st Century Estate Planning:
Practical Applications
2005 Edition

©2005 Sonnenschein Nath & Rosenthal LLP
and Cannon Financial Institute, Inc.

- 601 -

(a) <u>**Sale at Death With Tax Consequences**</u>. Under Madorin, the loss of grantor trust status during the grantor's lifetime was treated as a transfer (sale) of property to a newly formed non-grantor trust causing the grantor to recognize income to the extent that the liability (*i.e.*, unpaid balance of note) exceeded the basis of the transferred property. The *Madorin* case, however, involved a situation where the grantor renounced certain powers, causing grantor trust status to terminate. In the IDGT situation, the grantor's death causes the loss of grantor trust status.

1. <u>A Sale Occurred Immediately Before Death</u>. Under the view that a sale occurred immediately before death, gain would be recognized by the grantor to the extent the balance due on the note exceeds the grantor's basis in the assets sold to the IDGT. The assets purchased would acquire a new income tax basis in the hands of the IDGT equal to the balance due on the note.

If the sale did not qualify for installment treatment under IRC § 453 because, for example, it involved marketable securities for which installment treatment is not available, the gain would be reportable on the grantor's final return. The additional income taxes generated by the gain would be deductible for estate tax purposes under IRC § 2053 as a claim against the estate.

If the sale qualifies for installment treatment, the gain would not be reported on the grantor's final return, but payments received by the grantor's estate after death would be income to the estate or a beneficiary of the estate.

2. <u>A Sale Occurred Immediately After Death</u>. Under the view that a sale occurred immediately after death, the property deemed sold would be considered owned by the grantor at death and, therefore, should acquire a new income tax basis under IRC § 1014 with no gain resulting. Manning and Hesch disagree with this conclusion, noting that the assets are owned by the trust, not the grantor, at death for transfer tax purposes. Therefore, the property cannot receive a step-up in basis at the grantor's death because it does not pass from the grantor at death. <u>See</u> Manning and Hesch, *supra*.

(b) <u>**Sale at Death With No Recognition of Income**</u>. Under the view that a sale occurs at death without any recognition of gain, the basis of the trust assets is the amount the IDGT paid for the assets, *i.e.*, the amount of the note. The note is included in the grantor's gross estate and receives a stepped-up basis to its fair market value at death. In this case, neither the grantor nor the grantor's estate will recognize gain. For a comprehensive discussion of this alternative, see Manning and Hesch, *supra*.

(c) <u>**Repaying the Note Prior to the Grantor's Death**</u>. Given the uncertainty as to which of the above views would prevail, every effort should be made to pay the note off with appreciated assets during the grantor's lifetime (thereby causing the appreciated assets to be included in the grantor's gross estate, where they will receive a stepped-up basis). Because the trust is a grantor trust, the grantor would not recognize gain or loss on the payment. Assuming the trust property has appreciated since the original transfer, the note could be satisfied with a return of only part of the original trust property, with sufficient assets remaining

21st Century Estate Planning:
Practical Applications
2005 Edition

©2005 Sonnenschein Nath & Rosenthal LLP
and Cannon Financial Institute, Inc.

- 602 -

in the trust for the benefit of the trust beneficiaries. The property remaining in the trust would retain the grantor's original basis. Satisfying the note in kind is preferable to the trust's selling property to satisfy the note because the trust would incur income tax upon the sale of the property, which could decrease the overall tax savings of the transaction.

Alternatively, it has been suggested that to avoid the loss of basis step-up for all of the trust property when the note is satisfied with part of the trust property, the grantor could reacquire the remaining property in the trust during the grantor's life by substituting it for a high-basis asset. Again, there would be no income tax consequences on the substitution, and the substitution would bring low-basis assets back into the grantor's estate to get a step-up in basis. This method could avoid both the problems of gain recognition and loss of step-up in basis for all of the assets. See Frederic A. Nicholson, "Sale to a Grantor Controlled Trust: Better Than a GRAT?," *Tax Mgmt. Memo* (February 22, 1996).

3. Sale to an IDGT vs. Grantor Retained Annuity Trust

A GRAT offers similar transfer tax saving opportunities as a sale to an intentionally defective grantor trust, in that they both result in tax savings when the trust assets outperform (from an investment return perspective) the applicable interest rate. Following is a discussion of how GRATs and sales to an IDGT compare on several important issues.

21st Century Estate Planning:
Practical Applications
2005 Edition

©*2005 Sonnenschein Nath & Rosenthal LLP*
and Cannon Financial Institute, Inc.

- 603 -

a. Inclusion in the Grantor's Gross Estate. If the sale to an IDGT is structured correctly, no portion of the IDGT will be included in the grantor's gross estate for federal estate tax purposes. If the grantor dies before the promissory note is fully paid, only the unpaid balance of the note is included in his or her gross estate. Any appreciation in the value of the assets in the grantor trust escapes taxation. In contrast, if the grantor of a GRAT dies during the GRAT term, most or all of the GRAT property, including any appreciation in the value of the GRAT property, will be included in the grantor's gross estate for federal estate tax purposes. Therefore, there is a mortality risk with a GRAT that is not an issue with a sale to an IDGT. The mortality risk of a GRAT, however, can be eliminated by use of the guaranteed GRAT approach discussed above.

b. Annual Payments. The Section 7520 rate, which is used to value the retained annuity interest in a GRAT, equals 120% of the federal mid-term rate under IRC § 1274. As such, the Section 7520 rate is almost always higher than the interest rate on the note (the short-, mid-, or long-term AFR). Thus, the annual annuity payments under a GRAT almost always will be greater than interest payments required under the promissory note used in a sale to an intentionally defective grantor trust. In addition, the GRAT annuity payments often result in a portion of the underlying trust assets being returned to the grantor at a time that is often earlier than would be the case where a sale to an IDGT is used. As a result, with a GRAT, more property will be returned to the grantor in the form of an annuity payment (to be subject to estate tax if not consumed by the grantor), and less property will pass to the beneficiaries. Thus, more property usually will pass to trust beneficiaries free of transfer taxes under the sale technique than under a GRAT.

c. GST Exemption. The sale technique, unlike a GRAT, permits the leveraging of the grantor's GST exemption. This is because the ETIP rules, which prohibit the allocation of GST exemption to a GRAT before its term of years expires, do not apply to an irrevocable trust of the type used in connection with the sale technique. Thus, a grantor of an IDGT can allocate GST exemption to an IDGT immediately, and any appreciation after the sale will avoid GST tax. To achieve a similar result for generation-skipping transfer tax purposes with a GRAT, the family needs to consider employing the remainder sale technique discussed above.

d. Backloading Payments. By structuring the transaction as a sale to an intentionally defective grantor trust, it is possible to use a balloon note in which the repayment of principal is deferred until the end of the term of the note. Thus, it is possible to delay payments to the grantor, which has the effect of causing more growth to occur inside the irrevocable trust. With a GRAT, however, the extent to which annuity payments may be postponed is limited because the annuity for a given year cannot exceed 120% of the preceding year's annuity amount. Treas. Reg. § 25.2702-3(b)(1)(ii). Thus, a sale to an IDGT allows the greatest compounding of appreciation inside the trust.

e. Amount of the Gift. The sale of assets to an IDGT, if structured correctly, will not be a taxable gift. The only gift will be the gift upon contributing the "seed" money to the IDGT. As discussed above, a gift can be avoided entirely if the sale is to an existing funded

21st Century Estate Planning:
Practical Applications
2005 Edition

©2005 Sonnenschein Nath & Rosenthal LLP
and Cannon Financial Institute, Inc.

- 604 -

grantor trust or if the beneficiaries guarantee payments on the note. In light of *Walton*, discussed in the section on GRATs above, a GRAT can be structured as a zeroed-out GRAT so that there is no gift upon creation. Before *Walton*, a sale to an IDGT was considered to have the advantage on this point because it could be structured to avoid any gift.

➔ **Planning Point:** If the sale is not to an existing funded trust, the creation of a new trust will require the transfer of "seed" money to the trust. Such a transfer may result in the payment of gift tax. Thus, a sale to a newly created IDGT may not be as attractive as a gift tax-free *Walton* GRAT in light of the possibility of estate tax repeal. That is, clients may be less likely to pay gift tax now to save estate taxes later if there is a possibility that estate taxes may never be paid. Therefore, techniques that do not involve the payment of gift tax, such as a *Walton* GRAT, may be preferable.

    f. **Post-Sale Adjustment of Sale Price**. As discussed above, if the value of the property sold to the IDGT is later increased on audit, the grantor will have made a taxable gift. Valuation concerns may be addressed by a price adjustment clause, but such provisions may be subject to attack by the IRS under the holding in *Procter*. With a GRAT, however, the regulations in effect sanction a post-transaction adjustment clause by permitting the annuity amount to be payable as a fraction or percentage of the fair market value of the GRAT assets. If the value of the assets increases, so will the amount of the annuity, which, in turn, results in no, or a minimal, increase in the taxable gift.

    EXAMPLE: Grantor transfers $10,000,000 to a 10-year, zeroed-out GRAT when the Section 7520 rate is 5.4%. The annuity is expressed as 13.20323% of the initial value of the property transferred to the GRAT. As such, the annual annuity amount is $1,320,323, and the taxable gift is $6.00. If the value of the GRAT property is increased to $13,000,000, then the amount of the annuity will increase to $1,716,420. The value of the taxable gift will, however, only increase to $7.00.

➔ **Planning Point:** Because of the possibility that the revaluation of the property sold to an IDGT could result in gift tax liability, and because the risk of revaluation of the property transferred to a GRAT is minimized if the annuity is expressed as a percentage of the value of the property, a sale to an IDGT may not be as attractive as a gift tax-free *Walton* GRAT in light of the possibility of estate tax repeal.

    Although the sale technique has a number of advantages over the GRAT, the GRAT has one significant advantage over the sale technique in that it is a creature of statute. There is a provision of the Code, along with associated regulations, that explicitly states what a GRAT is, what the rules are for creating and operating a GRAT, and what the transfer tax consequences will be upon creating a GRAT. In contrast, no such certainty exists with respect to the sale to an intentionally defective grantor trust. The sale technique has been created based on a number of

21st Century Estate Planning:
Practical Applications
2005 Edition

©2005 *Sonnenschein Nath & Rosenthal LLP*
and Cannon Financial Institute, Inc.

- 605 -

previously unconnected legal principles (*i.e.*, the technique was created based on logical connections and inferences that were drawn from court cases, published and private rulings by the IRS, Treasury Regulations and Code provisions). Thus, there is a risk that if the IRS, in litigation involving the viability of a sale to an intentionally defective grantor trust, is able to successfully dislodge any of the key premises upon which the sale technique is built, the technique could lose its advantage (*e.g.*, the entire value of the trust property could be brought into the gross estate of the grantor for federal estate tax purposes). Despite this risk, the sale technique is a viable planning tool for estate planners and their clients who understand the benefits and potential pitfalls involved.

F. Low-Interest Loans to Grantor Trusts

1. Overview of the Transaction

A low-interest loan, which is a loan at an interest rate equal to the AFR, to an IDGT is one of the simplest estate planning techniques available, and its ability to transfer wealth to descendants is similar to that of a GRAT or sale to an IDGT. Generally, the lender loans money to the IDGT in return for an installment note that bears interest at the AFR in effect for the period represented by the loan, compounded semiannually. See IRC § 7872(f)(2)(A). The borrower (the IDGT) uses the funds to purchase an asset. The amount by which the borrower's rate of return on the funds loaned to the trust (or on the asset purchased by the trust with the funds) exceeds the interest rate on the note is, in effect, a gift tax-free transfer to the borrower.

> → **Planning Point:** A sale to an IDGT is preferable to a loan where the client has an appreciating asset that he or she wants to remove from his or her estate by transferring it to an irrevocable trust. A loan to an IDGT, which has comparable results to a sale to an IDGT, is preferable where the client does not currently own the appreciating asset but is planning to acquire such an asset. In that case, the client lends the purchase price to the trustee of the IDGT, and the trust purchases the asset.

Ideally, the note will be structured as a balloon note, where repayment of the principal is deferred until the end of the note term. Therefore, the borrower will make only annual interest payments to the lender. By using a balloon note, a larger percentage of the assets remain in the trust during the note term, thereby allowing the greatest compounding of appreciation inside the trust.

> **EXAMPLE:** Father lends $2 million in cash to a grantor trust for the benefit of his children in exchange for a 5-year note with interest at the mid-term AFR of 4.65%. The annual interest payment will be $93,000. The trust uses the funds to purchase an appreciating asset. If the return on the investment of the asset is 10%, then at the end of 5 years, after the repayment of the $2 million loan, the trust will have $653,246, which will pass estate tax-free and gift tax-free to the trust beneficiaries.

21st Century Estate Planning:
Practical Applications
2005 Edition

©2005 Sonnenschein Nath & Rosenthal LLP
and Cannon Financial Institute, Inc.

- 606 -

2. Estate Tax Consequences

If the lender dies with the note outstanding, the note will be included in the lender's gross estate. Depending on the interest rates prevailing at the time of the grantor's death, the value of the note may be more or less than the outstanding principal balance. If the AFR is higher than the interest rate on the note, the note will be worth less than the outstanding principal balance; but if the AFR is lower than the note's interest rate, the note may be worth more than the outstanding principal balance, thus reducing the benefit of the strategy. The risk that the note will be worth more than its face if the note's interest rate is higher than the prevailing interest rate can be reduced by having the note prepayable at any time by the borrower.

Similar issues arise with a loan to an IDGT as with a sale to an IDGT with respect to the undercapitalization of the trust. That is, the IRS might argue that, in such a case, the note received by the grantor in exchange for the loan of cash or property to the trust should be recharacterized as a transfer with a retained life interest, with the result that the transferred property (*i.e.*, the property loaned to the trust) is includable in the grantor's gross estate under IRC § 2036.

As with a sale to an IDGT, these arguments should not succeed where the trust has other property, the income or principal of which can be used to service the debt, where the interest payments are not tied in to the income from the loaned property, and where the grantor has not retained any interests in the loaned property (such as, perhaps, a security interest). Thus, the loan should be made to an existing grantor trust, or the trust should be funded with cash or other property (*i.e.*, "seed" money) in an amount equal to ten percent of the value of the trust assets. For a more comprehensive discussion of the estate tax issues, see the section on sales to IDGTs above.

3. Gift Tax Consequences

The interest rate on the loan must be at least equal to the AFR in effect for the period represented by the loan, compounded semiannually, in order to avoid adverse income and gift tax consequences under IRC § 7872. See IRC § 7872(f)(2)(A). IRC § 7872 imputes interest in the case of below-market loans, which are loans where the stated interest is less than the AFR. Thus, if the stated interest on a loan to an IDGT is less than the appropriate AFR, the loan is subject to IRC § 7872.

IRC § 7872 recharacterizes a loan as a transaction in which the lender makes a loan to the borrower in exchange for a promissory note requiring interest to be paid at the AFR (rather than at the lower stated interest rate of the note). The deemed interest at the AFR in excess of the stated interest rate is called "imputed interest." Imputed interest generally is includable as taxable income to the lender. When loans are made to a grantor trust as to the lender, however, the imputed interest is not taxable interest to the lender.

The lender then is deemed to make a gift to the borrower (which the borrower is presumed to use to pay the imputed interest to the lender). The amount of the gift is equal to the amount loaned less the present value of the note determined using the AFR as the discount rate.

21st Century Estate Planning:
Practical Applications
2005 Edition

©2005 Sonnenschein Nath & Rosenthal LLP
and Cannon Financial Institute, Inc.

- 607 -

EXAMPLE: Father makes an interest-free $1,000,000 loan to a grantor trust for 10 years. The AFR is 8%, compounded semiannually. The present value of $1,000,000 payable in 10 years at 8% interest compounded semiannually is $456,387. The amount of the deemed gift is $543,613 ($1,000,000 - $456,387).

If the aggregate outstanding loans (both market and below-market) between the lender and borrower are $100,000 or less, the imputed interest is limited to the borrower's net investment income for the year. IRC § 7872(d)(1). Whether the aggregate outstanding loans between the lender and borrower are $100,000 or less, however, does not limit the amount of the gift to the borrower.

If accrued interest payable on the loan is waived, canceled, or forgiven by the lender, such interest is treated as if it were paid to the lender and then re-transferred by the lender to the borrower resulting in a taxable gift by the lender. Prop. Reg. § 1.7872-11(a).

4. Income Tax Consequences

Because the loan is made to a grantor trust as to the lender, the lender does not recognize interest income. That is, for income tax purposes, the loan is treated as between the lender and himself or herself.

The trust will cease to be a grantor trust upon the grantor's death. Pre-death accrued and unpaid interest should not be taxable income to the grantor or the grantor's estate for the following reasons.[7]

First, in the sale to an IDGT strategy, if the grantor dies with the note outstanding, a sale is deemed to have occurred. See Treas. Reg. § 1.1001-2(c), Ex. 5; *Madorin v. Comm'r.*, 84 T.C. 667 (1985); Rev. Rul. 77-402, 1977-2 C.B. 222. Practitioners disagree, however, about whether the deemed sale occurs before or after the grantor's death. If the sale occurs prior to the grantor's death, the capital gain will be reported on the grantor's final return or by the grantor's estate or a beneficiary of the estate, depending upon whether installment sale treatment applies.[8] If this theory is applied to the loan transaction, then if a loan is deemed to be made immediately prior to the grantor's death, no interest will have accrued during the grantor's lifetime that would be taxable. Post-death interest, however, will be taxable to the grantor's estate.

Second, the income would be taxable under the Code section and regulations that refer to "those amounts to which a decedent was entitled as gross income but which were not properly includible in computing his taxable income" for the taxable year ending with his or her death (or any prior year). See Treas. Reg. § 1.691(a)-1(b). The pre-death interest was not gross income because interest payable by a grantor trust to the grantor is not income to the grantor.

In order to avoid the taxable income issues when the lender dies, the trust should pay all accrued interest or pay off the outstanding indebtedness prior to the lender's death. The trust could pay the note in kind with appreciated assets. Because the trust is a grantor trust, no gain or loss would be recognized on the payment, and the appreciated property used to pay the note

21st Century Estate Planning:
Practical Applications
2005 Edition

©2005 *Sonnenschein Nath & Rosenthal LLP*
and Cannon Financial Institute, Inc.

would be included in the lender's gross estate and, therefore, would get a step-up in basis at the lender's death, thereby eliminating the capital gain.

5. Comparison to GRATs and Sales to IDGTs

As noted above, a loan to an IDGT is comparable to a GRAT and a sale to an IDGT, and, in fact, may have some advantages over these techniques.

a. GRAT. The most important difference between a loan to a grantor trust and a traditional GRAT is that the loan is not subject to the mortality risk that is inherent in a GRAT. If the lender dies before the note is retired, only the unpaid balance of the note will be included in his or her gross estate. In contrast, if the grantor of a GRAT dies during the term of a GRAT, the IRS can be expected to take the position that all the GRAT property would be subject to estate tax under IRC § 2039(a). See TAM 200210009. The difference between including the value of the note, on the one hand, and all the GRAT property, on the other, could be quite substantial.

There is greater flexibility in structuring the note than the annuity payment. The note may be fully amortizing or bear interest only; the note may be refinanced; and the interest rate may vary. The GRAT payment, on the other hand, may change only in accordance with the regulations. If the client's death appears imminent while the note is outstanding, the borrower may accelerate the entire indebtedness if it is advisable to retire the note to avoid the possible income tax consequences discussed above. On the other hand, the annuitant's interest in a GRAT may not be commuted (indeed, if the governing instrument does not prohibit commutation, the annuity will fail to be a qualified interest under IRC § 2702 and the grantor will be deemed to make a gift of the entire trust property).

b. Sale to IDGT. The loan is a simpler strategy and provides the same benefit as the sale to an IDGT: the spread between the interest rate on the note and the rate of return on the trust's investments is transferred to the trust and its beneficiaries free of gift and estate taxes.

If the grantor dies with the note from the sale to the grantor trust outstanding, the prevailing view is that either the grantor or his or her estate will be liable for capital gain tax on the amount of the unpaid principal. With the loan strategy, however, no gain should be recognized on death if the note is outstanding.

The loan does not require an appraisal or subject the grantor to the risk that the IRS disagrees with the value of the property sold, which could result in gift tax liability.

G. Private Annuities

A private annuity is a sale of property by one individual (the annuitant) to another individual or entity (the buyer) (usually by one family member to a younger generation family member) in exchange for the latter's unsecured promise to make fixed annual payments to the annuitant for the annuitant's lifetime. A private annuity affords the annuitant an opportunity to defer recognition of capital gain, retain a steady stream of income, and remove the transferred

21st Century Estate Planning:
Practical Applications
2005 Edition

©2005 Sonnenschein Nath & Rosenthal LLP
and Cannon Financial Institute, Inc.

- 609 -

property and the appreciation thereon from his or her gross estate without estate, gift or generation-skipping transfer tax.

→ **Planning Point:** A private annuity is a good estate planning technique if the annuitant wishes to keep ownership of certain property within his or her family, yet shift management of the property to his or her children and have the security of a fixed income for life.

→ **Planning Point:** The benefits of a private annuity will be maximized if the buyer has a lower marginal income tax rate than the annuitant. In such a case, the annuitant is able to shift the income tax burden on property to a family member with a lower tax rate.

The tax savings of a private annuity are greatest when the annuity is given in exchange for appreciating property, so that not only is the property removed from the annuitant's gross estate, but the appreciation also is removed from the annuitant's gross estate. This technique is particularly effective when the actual life of the annuitant is significantly less than his or her life expectancy under the IRS actuarial tables. Because at the death of the annuitant the annuity payments cease, premature death allows the buyer to actually purchase the property for less than its full sales price, and because the total number of annuity payments is reduced, less property goes back into the annuitant's gross estate, where it will be subject to estate tax if not consumed by the annuitant.

→ **Planning Point:** The property that is sold in exchange for the annuity should be expected to appreciate in value and should not be an asset that the buyer expects to sell in the short term. Additionally, the property should generate income, or the buyer must have another source of funds with which to make the annuity payments.

1. Gift Tax Consequences

A sale for a private annuity will not be subject to gift tax as long as the fair market value of the property transferred in exchange for the private annuity equals the present value of the annuity (that is, it is a sale for full and adequate consideration). The present value of the annuity payments must be computed using the Section 7520 actuarial tables for the month in which the sale occurs. The Section 7520 regulations prohibit the use of the actuarial tables if the transferor is terminally ill at the time of the transfer. If the individual survives for eighteen months or longer after the valuation date, however, he or she will be presumed not to have been terminally ill at the time of the transfer. Treas. Reg. § 25.7520-3(b)(3). Therefore, an individual whose health condition is likely to result in premature death, but not within eighteen months, can value the annuity payments under Section 7520, but will receive few of the annuity payments to increase his or her gross estate.

→ **Planning Point:** The required annuity payments that the buyer must make in order to avoid gift taxes decrease as interest rates decline. Thus,

21st Century Estate Planning:
Practical Applications
2005 Edition

©2005 Sonnenschein Nath & Rosenthal LLP
and Cannon Financial Institute, Inc.

- 610 -

lower annuity payments may make the transaction more feasible if the buyer is concerned about the ability to make payments.

There will be a taxable gift from the annuitant to the buyer to the extent that the present value of the annuity is less than the fair market value of the property sold. Thus, property that is difficult to value poses a risk of gift tax liability in the event of a later determination of a higher value for the property. Having a well documented appraisal significantly reduces (but does not completely eliminate) the gift tax exposure.

It may be possible to avoid the risk of gift tax liability with a valuation adjustment clause, which adjusts the payments to reflect the property value ultimately determined by court decision or by the IRS. The IRS does not, however, favor such clauses.[9] For example, PLR 9133001 (January 31, 1990) involved a private annuity transaction where the agreement provided that the annuity payments and the purchase price would be adjusted to reflect any changes in valuation resulting from a settlement with the IRS or a final decision by the Tax Court. The IRS disregarded the provision for estate and gift tax purposes.

2. Estate Tax Consequences

Because the buyer's obligation to make annuity payments ceases upon the annuitant's death, a private annuity does not have any value for estate tax purposes, and the assets subject to the sale should not be included in the seller's taxable estate. To the extent that the annuitant does not consume the annuity payments, however, they will be included in the annuitant's gross estate and subject to estate tax. Thus, a private annuity is ideal when the asset sold is one that generates most of the annuitant's income because, in such a case, the annuitant will consume most of the payments.

a. IRC § 2036. In structuring a private annuity transaction, the parties must ensure that the IRS cannot claim that the annuitant has a retained life estate in the transferred property so that the property would be includable in the annuitant's gross estate under IRC § 2036 of the Code. The IRS may make such an argument if the income from the transferred property equals the annual annuity payment. Therefore, annuity payments should never be tied to the income generated from the transferred property. Other ways to insulate the transaction from the application of IRC § 2036 are: (1) the buyer should not pay the annuity with a note; (2) the annuity agreement should impose personal liability on the buyer and make the buyer liable for annuity payments regardless of whether the property produces income; (3) the buyer should have sufficient other assets with which to make the annuity payments; (4) the buyer must make payments in a timely manner and the parties must respect the formalities of the transaction; (5) the annuitant should not take a security interest in the transferred property; and (6) the annuitant must not continue to possess or enjoy the transferred property.

b. Trust as Buyer. The buyer can be a trust, in which case it is particularly important to structure the transaction correctly, as the IRS has not favored private annuity arrangements where the trust is the purchaser. See *Ray, supra*; *Stern v. Comm'r*, 77 T.C. 614 (1981), *rev'd*, 747 F.2d 555 (9th Cir. 1984); *LaFargue v. Comm'r*, 73 T.C. 40 (1979), *aff'd in*

21st Century Estate Planning:
Practical Applications
2005 Edition

©2005 Sonnenschein Nath & Rosenthal LLP
and Cannon Financial Institute, Inc.

- 611 -

part and rev'd in part, 689 F.2d 845 (9th Cir. 1982); and *Lazarus v. Comm'r*, 58 T.C. 854 (1972), *aff'd*, 513 F.2d 824 (9th Cir. 1975).

(1) <u>**IRC § 2036**</u>. Whether the annuitant has retained the right to income from the transferred property in exchange for the private annuity is generally the issue where the trust is the buyer. Because clients may feel more comfortable selling property to a trust rather than outright to descendants, practitioners can minimize the risk of an IRS challenge under IRC § 2036 by ensuring that there is no "tie-in" between the trust income and the annual annuity payment. In the absence of such a tie-in, the annuitant should not be considered to have retained a life estate in the transferred property. See *LaFargue, supra* (no tie-in); *Ray, supra* (tie-in); *Stern, supra* (no tie-in); and *Lazarus, supra* (tie-in).

For example, in *LaFargue*, the taxpayer funded a trust for the benefit of her daughter and herself with $100. Two days later, the taxpayer transferred assets with a fair market value equal to $335,000 to the trust and executed a private annuity agreement with the trust. The Tax Court characterized the annual payments as distributions of trust income, taxable to the taxpayer under the grantor trust rules. The Ninth Circuit reversed and remanded to the Tax Court, holding that there was no tie-in between the trust income and the amount of the annuity and, therefore, the transaction was a bona fide sale.

In addition to a tie-in between income and the annuity payment, the courts also may consider other factors in determining the validity of a private annuity with a trust as the buyer. These include: (1) the degree of control the annuitant exercises over the transferred property; (2) the nature and extent of the annuitant's continuing interest in the transferred property; (3) the source of the annuity payment; and (4) the arm's-length nature of the transaction. *Weigl v. Comm'r*, 84 T.C. 1192, 1225 (1985) (citing *LaFargue, Stern, Lazarus* and *Fabric*). The courts also may consider whether the parties disregarded the substance of the transaction. See *Lazarus, supra*. Finally, if the distributions to make the annuity payments are subject to the approval of an adverse party, then IRC § 2036 should not apply. *Lazarus*, 58 T.C. at 864 n.8.

(2) <u>**IRC § 2702**</u>. In a properly structured transaction, the annuitant does not retain any interest in the transferred property. Therefore, IRC § 2702 does not apply. The IRS might, however, use IRC § 2702 to reach an annuity transaction in which a trust is the buyer. IRC § 2702 should not apply unless it can be shown that a fixed annuity is being paid from the trust. Thus, there should be no tie-in between the income produced by the annuity property and the annuity payment. Even if there is a tie-in, the interest retained would likely qualify as a "qualified annuity interest" under IRC § 2702 and the regulations thereunder. See PLR 9253031 (October 2, 1992).

3. Income Tax Consequences

The income tax consequences of a private annuity are governed by the annuity rules in IRC § 72. The annuity rules treat the annuity payments as having three elements for income tax purposes: a tax-free recovery of basis; a capital gain portion (to the extent the value of the transferred property exceeds the annuitant's basis in the property); and ordinary income (the annuity amount). If the private annuity is secured, however, the annuitant will recognize all

21st Century Estate Planning:
Practical Applications
2005 Edition

©2005 Sonnenschein Nath & Rosenthal LLP
and Cannon Financial Institute, Inc.

- 612 -

capital gain in full at the time of the transfer rather than deferring it over his or her life expectancy. *212 Corp. v. Comm'r.*, 70 T.C. 788 (1978); *Estate of Bell*, 60 T.C. 469 (1973).

If a trust is the buyer and the annuitant is the grantor of the trust, and if the trust has no assets other than the property acquired in exchange for the annuity, the annuitant will be treated as the owner of the trust under the grantor trust rules. Rev. Rul. 68-183, 1968-1 C.B. 308. In such a case, the annuitant will be taxed on the entire trust income each year, which means that instead of a portion of each annuity payment being taxed as capital gain and a portion being excluded from income, the entire payment would be ordinary income.

    a. The Annuitant. Rev. Rul. 69-74, 1969-1 C.B. 43 sets forth the following method for calculating the income tax components of a private annuity.

    (1) Tax-Free Portion. A portion of each annuity payment will represent a tax-free recovery of basis until the annuitant has fully recovered his or her basis in the property. After the annuitant has fully recovered his or her basis, which occurs if the annuitant lives for his or her actuarial life expectancy, as determined under Table V of Treas. Reg. § 1.72-9, the balance of the payments received will be taxable as ordinary income. IRC § 72(b)(2). In the event that the annuitant dies before recovering his or her entire basis, the unrecovered amount can be taken as a deduction on his or her final income tax return. IRC § 72(b)(3).

The tax-free return of basis portion of each payment is determined by multiplying the exclusion ratio by each annuity payment received. The exclusion ratio is the ratio of the annuitant's investment in the contract (the adjusted basis) to the expected return. The expected return is determined by multiplying each annuity payment to be made by the annuitant's life expectancy, as determined under IRC § 72. Treas. Reg. § 1.72-9.

> **EXAMPLE:** Father, age 70, transfers stock with a fair market value of $1,000,000 and a basis of $500,000 to Daughter in exchange for a private annuity. The Section 7520 rate for the month of the sale is 5.4%. The annual annuity that Daughter must make to ensure that Father does not make a taxable gift is $112,726.
>
> Father's life expectancy under the life annuity tables in Treas. Reg. § 1.72-9 Table V is 16 years. Therefore, his expected return is $1,803,616 ($112,726 x 16).
>
> The exclusion ratio is 27.72% ($500,000 basis divided by $1,803,616 expected return). Therefore, $31,248 ($112,726 x 27.72%) of each annuity payment Father receives is treated as a tax-free return of investment.

    (2) Capital Gain Portion. Because only a portion of each annuity payment is capital gain, a private annuity allows the annuitant to defer gain on the sale of the property by reporting it ratably over his or her life expectancy. If the annuitant lives at least as

21st Century Estate Planning:
Practical Applications
2005 Edition

©2005 Sonnenschein Nath & Rosenthal LLP
and Cannon Financial Institute, Inc.

- 613 -

long as his or her life expectancy at the time of the transfer, the annuitant will eventually pay a tax on his or her entire realized gain.

The total capital gain recognized on the sale is the difference between the annuitant's basis in the property and the present value of the annuity. The total capital gain is then divided by the annuitant's life expectancy, and the resulting number is the capital gain portion of each annuity payment.

> **EXAMPLE:** Continuing the example above, the capital gain is $500,000 ($1,000,000 present value of the annuity less $500,000 adjusted basis). The gain is reported over Father's 16-year life expectancy, so that each year $31,250 is reported as capital gain ($500,000 divided by 16).

(3) **Ordinary Income Portion**. The ordinary income portion is the difference between the annuity payment and the sum of the return of basis portion and capital gain portion.

> **EXAMPLE:** Continuing the preceding examples, the balance of each annuity payment, $49,778 ($112,726 less $31,248 less $31,250), will be ordinary income.

b. The Buyer. Although part of each annuity payment is a payment of interest, the buyer will not be entitled to an interest deduction for any part of the annuity payments.

If the buyer sells the asset after the annuitant's death, the buyer's basis in the property purchased from the annuitant is the sum of all the annuity payments actually made under the contract. Rev. Rul. 55-119, 1955-1 C.B. 352. As such, in the event of the annuitant's premature death, the buyer will have made few payments and, therefore, will have a low basis in the property.

If the buyer sells the asset before the annuitant dies, the buyer's basis depends upon whether the transaction results in a gain or a loss. For gain purposes, the buyer's basis equals the total annuity payments actually made at the date of sale plus the present value of the future annuity payments yet to be made. The present value is determined using the annuitant's life expectancy and the Section 7520 rate on the date the buyer sells the property. For loss purposes, the buyer's basis is the sum of all annuity payments actually made to the date of sale.

> **EXAMPLE:** Building on the previous example, Daughter sells the stock in 6 years for $1,500,000. The Section 7520 rate has increased to 7.4%. Daughter's basis for gain will be determined as follows:

21st Century Estate Planning:
Practical Applications
2005 Edition

©2005 Sonnenschein Nath & Rosenthal LLP
and Cannon Financial Institute, Inc.

- 614 -

$676,356 (total payments actually made), plus

$726,158 (present value of future payments based on Father's age at the sale (76) and a 7.4% Section 7520 rate)

$1,402,514 - Daughter's basis for gain

Daughter's capital gain will be $1,500,000 million less her adjusted basis of $1,402,514, for a capital gain of $97,486.

Daughter's basis for loss is $676,356. Therefore, had she sold the property for $675,000, she would realize a loss of $1,356.

→ **Planning Point:** Because of the possibility that a buyer may have a very low basis in the asset sold, the transferred property should be an asset that the buyer is not likely to sell, *e.g.*, an interest in the family business.

4. Advantages of a Private Annuity

Private annuities remove the transferred property from the annuitant's gross estate, and any appreciation on the transferred property subsequent to the sale avoids estate taxation in the annuitant's estate. Private annuities also serve to defer capital gain and to shift the taxation of income to individuals who are in a lower income tax bracket.

Private annuities have the greatest benefit for individuals who die prematurely because the value of the annuity will have been based on the assumption that the annuitant will receive all of the annuity payments. When the annuitant dies prematurely, the buyer will have paid less for the assets than what it is worth. Additionally, less annuity payments will be transferred to the annuitant to be included in his or her gross estate.

5. Disadvantages of a Private Annuity

Some of the disadvantages of a private annuity result from the uncertainty of death. The annuitant's children generally are in the awkward position of having an economic benefit if the annuitant does not survive his or her life expectancy under the IRS tables. Also, because the buyer's adjusted basis in the property is, in general, the total annuity payments made to the date of the annuitant's death, the annuitant's premature death may result in a lower basis than the buyer would have received if he or she had inherited the property and received a basis equal to the property's fair market value (a "stepped-up basis") at the annuitant's death. If the annuitant outlives his or her actuarial life expectancy, the annuity payments made may cause the estate tax to exceed what it would have been if the asset were still in the annuitant's estate (unless the annuitant consumes the annuity payments).

There are a number of risks inherent in the use of a private annuity. For example, there is the risk to the annuitant of nonpayment of the annuity by the buyer. This risk may be exacerbated if the buyer predeceases the annuitant. Additionally, the annuity payments may place a significant economic burden on the buyer, which is a risk he or she bears, regardless of increase or decrease in the value of the property transferred. The buyer must be prepared to

21st Century Estate Planning:
Practical Applications
2005 Edition

©2005 Sonnenschein Nath & Rosenthal LLP
and Cannon Financial Institute, Inc.

- 615 -

make continuous annuity payments to the annuitant even if the annuitant should outlive his or her life expectancy. In such a case, the annuity payments could exceed the original value of the property transferred by the annuitant to fund the private annuity.

H. Self-Canceling Installment Notes

A self-canceling installment note ("SCIN") is an installment note that is payable until the first to occur of the expiration of a stated term or the death of the seller. With a SCIN, property is sold in exchange for the buyer's promise to make periodic payments until a maximum sales price is received or the seller dies, whichever occurs first. A SCIN is generally viewed as an alternative to a private annuity. Like private annuities, SCINs provide estate tax savings, deferral of capital gain, and a stream of income to the seller.

For the SCIN to be a beneficial estate planning technique, the return on the asset that is sold must exceed the interest rate on the SCIN, or the seller must die before his or her life expectancy.

1. Estate Tax Consequences

SCINs remove the transferred property and any appreciation thereon in excess of the interest rate on the note from the seller's gross estate. The payments made on the note will, however, be included in the seller's gross estate to the extent that they are not consumed during the life of the seller, as is the case with the annuity payments in a private annuity. Because of the risk premium, discussed below, more money will be returned to the grantor's gross estate with a SCIN than with a private annuity.

➔ **Planning Point:** Because the term of a SCIN is less than the seller's life expectancy, the SCIN has an advantage over a private annuity in that the seller does not incur the risk of living beyond the installment term, thereby increasing his or her gross estate because of the continued annuity payments. The maximum term limits how much the buyer pays, but it also limits the seller's security because the seller may not receive payments for his or her life.

In addition to removing the transferred property from the seller's gross estate, the estate tax advantage of a SCIN is that because the buyer's obligation terminates at the seller's death, nothing is included in the seller's gross estate for federal estate tax purposes. *Estate of Moss v. Comm'r*, 74 T.C. 1239 (1980), *acq. in result* 1981-1 C.B. 2. The value of the remaining payments on the SCIN at death escapes estate tax.

21st Century Estate Planning:
Practical Applications
2005 Edition

©*2005 Sonnenschein Nath & Rosenthal LLP*
and Cannon Financial Institute, Inc.

- 616 -

2. Income Tax Consequences

A SCIN may be classified as either an installment sale or a private annuity for income tax purposes. Generally, it is structured so that it is treated as an installment sale, in which case the income tax consequences will be determined under the installment sale rules of IRC § 453.

→ **Planning Point:** The sale of marketable securities is not eligible for installment reporting.

Gain is reported over the period during which payments are received, and each payment is divided into a return of basis portion, a capital gain portion, and interest income. Any gain remaining at the seller's death will be recognized by the seller's estate. *Frane v. Comm'r*, 998 F.2d 567 (8th Cir. 1993); Rev. Rul. 86-72, 1986-1 C.B. 253. Commentators disagree with this result, however, arguing that the gain should be reported on the seller's final income tax return. See Jerome M. Hesch, "Installment Sale, SCIN and Private Annuity Sales to a Grantor Trust: Income Tax and Transfer Tax Elements," 23 *Tax Mgmt. Est., Gifts and Tr. J.* 114 (May 14, 1998).

Interest paid by the buyer on a SCIN is deductible by the buyer, although the extent to which it may be deducted depends on the type of property involved. GCM 39503 (May 7, 1986). In contrast, with a private annuity, the buyer cannot deduct interest paid.

If the SCIN is treated as an installment sale, it is generally believed that the buyer's basis in the property acquired in exchange for the installment note is the full face value of the note. Rev. Rul. 86-72, 1986-1 C.B. 253; GCM 39503 (May 7, 1986).

→ **Planning Point:** The seller may take a security interest in the property sold without jeopardizing installment sale treatment. This is in contrast to a private annuity, under which the entire gain is taxable at the time of the sale if the seller has a security interest in the property sold.

3. Gift Tax Consequences

The note will never be paid if the seller dies before all installments have been paid. Therefore, to avoid a gift upon the sale, a risk premium must be added to the note to compensate the seller for the risk of cancellation. The premium may be reflected in either a higher interest rate or a greater sales price. As such, if the seller lives the full term, the amount payable to the seller under the SCIN (and, therefore, the increase in the seller's gross estate if the payments are not consumed) is greater than if a standard promissory note were used.

→ **Planning Point:** A SCIN may be used in connection with a sale to an intentionally defective grantor trust. This strategy may be beneficial if the seller wants a stream of income greater than the amount required under a traditional promissory note (the AFR). Because of the risk premium, a higher interest rate may be paid on the SCIN, which results in more income to the seller.

21st Century Estate Planning:
Practical Applications
2005 Edition

©2005 *Sonnenschein Nath & Rosenthal LLP*
and Cannon Financial Institute, Inc.

- 617 -

I. Grantor Retained Income Trusts

A "grantor retained income trust" ("GRIT") is an irrevocable trust in which the grantor retains the right to receive all of the trust income for a specified number of years, after which time the remaining trust property is distributed to the remaindermen.

GRITs were practically eliminated when IRC § 2702 was enacted in 1990. As discussed in the section on general principles above, IRC § 2702 provides special valuation rules to determine the amount of a gift when an individual transfers property to a trust to or for the benefit of a "member of the transferor's family." A "member of the family" includes (i) the transferor's spouse, (ii) ancestors or descendants of the transferor or the transferor's spouse, (iii) siblings of the transferor, or (iv) the spouse of any of the foregoing. IRC §§ 2702(e); 2704(c)(2). A transfer to a relative that does not fall within this group (*e.g.*, a niece or nephew) is not subject to IRC § 2702's special valuation rules.

If such a transfer is made, the value of the interest retained by the transferor or applicable family member is valued at zero unless it is a "qualified interest" or the interest falls within an exception to IRC § 2702. The income interest in a GRIT is not a qualified interest under IRC § 2702. Therefore, in most cases, a transfer to a GRIT is treated for gift tax purposes the same as an outright gift to the remaindermen (because the retained income interest is valued at zero). There are three exceptions to IRC § 2702 that permit limited uses of GRITs: 1) a GRIT for an individual who is not a member of the grantor's family for purposes of IRC § 2702 (*e.g.*, nieces and nephews); 2) a GRIT that holds certain tangible property; and 3) a GRIT that holds a personal residence of the grantor.

→ **Planning Point:** GRITs can be used to transfer property to nieces and nephews and their descendants, to a partner in a non-marital relationship, or to an individual to whom one is engaged to be married. The fact that a premarital GRIT or other form of GRIT may eventually benefit a person who has become a member of the grantor's family but who was not a member of the grantor's family at the time the GRIT was created should not disqualify the GRIT. Thus, a GRIT for a future spouse could terminate in favor of the future spouse's children (who are the grantor's children), who would not have been members of the grantor's family when the GRIT was established.

21st Century Estate Planning:
Practical Applications
2005 Edition

©2005 *Sonnenschein Nath & Rosenthal LLP*
and Cannon Financial Institute, Inc.

- 618 -

1.   Gift, Estate and Income Tax Consequences

   a. Gift Tax. A GRIT for an individual who is not a member of the grantor's family will be valued under Section 7520. Thus, the amount of the taxable gift to the remaindermen upon the creation of a GRIT will equal the value of the property transferred to the GRIT less the value of the income interest retained by the grantor, determined under Section 7520 of the Code. The Section 7520 valuation tables assume that: (1) the GRIT's rate of return on its investments will equal the Section 7520 rate; and (2) all of the growth in value of the GRIT will be allocable to income, all of which must be paid to the grantor annually.

➔   **Planning Point:** A GRIT will transfer property to the remaindermen if either or both of the following occur: (1) the GRIT's rate of return actually exceeds the Section 7520 rate, in which case the excess will be distributed to the remaindermen free of gift tax; and (2) if the income realized and paid by the GRIT (as opposed to the capital appreciation) is less than the Section 7520 rate, more property will remain in the GRIT than was presumed under the valuation tables to value the income interest, and such excess will have been transferred to the remaindermen free of gift tax.

   A GRIT usually results in significant gift tax upon creation, although the gift can be sheltered from tax by the grantor's applicable exclusion amount. The taxable gift will equal the present value of the right to receive the property at the end of the term, valued under Section 7520.

   EXAMPLE: Grantor, age 50, transfers $1,000,000 to a 5-year GRIT. The Section 7520 rate is 5.4%. The taxable gift is $768,771, which is the present value of the right to receive $1,000,000 in 5 years at a 5.4% rate of return. As the term increases, the taxable gift decreases, so that if the GRIT lasts for 10 years, the taxable gift will be $591,009.

   b. Estate Tax. If the grantor of a GRIT dies before the end of the term of the GRIT, the GRIT property is included in his or her gross estate under IRC § 2036.

   c. Income Tax. The GRIT is a grantor trust for income tax purposes. Thus, all items of income, deduction and credit will be reported by the grantor on his or her personal income tax return rather than by the trust as a separate entity.

2.   Tangible Property GRITs

   IRC § 2702(c)(4) provides an exception to the IRC § 2702 gift tax valuation rules for the transfer of a term interest in tangible property where the nonexercise of rights with respect to the term interest would not have a substantial effect on the valuation of the remainder interest in such property. Where the special rule applies, the retained term interest will not be valued at zero. Rather, the value of the retained term interest will be the amount that the transferor

21st Century Estate Planning:
Practical Applications
2005 Edition

©2005 Sonnenschein Nath & Rosenthal LLP
and Cannon Financial Institute, Inc.

- 619 -

establishes that an unrelated third party would pay for the term interest. IRC § 2702(c)(4). Note that Section 7520 is not used to value the term interest.

> **EXAMPLE:** Collector transfers a painting to her daughter, retaining the use of the painting for 10 years. The value of Collector's retained right to use the painting is the value that a third party would pay for the use of the painting for 10 years.

a. **Definition of Tangible Property.** As a general rule, the tangible property provision only applies to tangible property that cannot be depreciated or depleted. Treas. Reg. § 25.2702-2(c)(2)(i)(A). Such property includes works of art and undeveloped land (the value of which primarily reflects future development potential). Treas. Reg. § 25.2702-2(d)(2), Ex. 8; 136 Cong. Rec. S15682 (Oct. 18, 1990).

b. **Conversion of Tangible Property.** If the tangible property is converted into property that does not qualify for the exception, the conversion is treated for gift tax purposes as a transfer of the value of the unexpired portion of the term interest. Treas. Reg. § 25.2702-2(c)(4)(i). A conversion occurs not only when the tangible property is sold and the proceeds are reinvested in property that does not qualify for the exception, but also may occur when an addition or improvement is made to the tangible property. Treas. Reg. § 25.2702-2(c)(5).

c. **Valuation.** If the transferor cannot reasonably establish the value of the term interest, the interest is valued at zero. Treas. Reg. § 25.2702-2(c)(1). To establish the value of the tangible property, the actual sales or rentals that are comparable both as to the nature and character of the property and the duration of the term interest are the best evidence of the value of the term interest. Treas. Reg. § 25.2702-2(c)(3). If the only evidence produced by the transferor is the amount paid by an organization for the use of a comparable painting for one year, such evidence does not indicate what the right to use the painting for ten years would be worth. Treas. Reg. § 25.2702(d)(2), Ex. 9. Appraisals are insufficient in the absence of comparable sales or rentals, and amounts determined under Section 7520 are not evidence of value. Treas. Reg. § 25.2702-2(c)(3). Given the difficulty in establishing the value of the term interest, tangible property GRITs are rarely feasible.

J. Personal Residence Trusts

IRC § 2702 does not apply to a transfer of an interest in a trust if the transferor or an applicable family member retains the right to use the trust property as a personal residence for a term. IRC § 2702(a)(3)(A)(ii). As such, the value of the remainder will be the value of the transferred property less the value of the term interest, valued under Section 7520. The value of the term interest will not be deemed to be zero. The regulations provide that only two types of trusts can qualify for this statutory exception: a personal residence trust and a qualified personal residence trust ("QPRT").

21st Century Estate Planning:
Practical Applications
2005 Edition

©2005 *Sonnenschein Nath & Rosenthal LLP*
and Cannon Financial Institute, Inc.

- 620 -

1. Overview of Personal Residence Trusts

In general, IRC § 2702 allows a grantor to transfer title to a personal residence to the trustee of an irrevocable trust, retaining the right to live in the residence rent-free for the term of years specified in the trust agreement. The grantor continues to pay all ordinary expenses relating to the residence, such as utilities, maintenance, taxes and repairs.

If the grantor is living at the end of the retained term, the residence passes to the remainder beneficiaries (typically the grantor's children or trusts for their benefit) designated in the trust agreement. Thereafter, the grantor may wish to lease the residence from its new owners (*e.g.*, his or her children or trusts for their benefit). If the grantor dies prior to the end of the term, the residence is included in his or her gross estate for federal estate tax purposes. This is, however, essentially the same result that would occur if the grantor had not established the trust.

The value of the gift of the residence for gift tax purposes is based on the present value of the right of the beneficiaries of the personal residence trust to receive the residence at the end of the term of years. Because the beneficiaries must wait until the end of the term to receive the residence, the value of the gift of the residence is essentially "discounted." In other words, the value of the gift is substantially lower than the actual value of the residence at the time of transfer.

2. Definition of Personal Residence

The residence must be: (1) the principal residence of the term holder within the meaning of IRC § 1034 (relating to the rollover of capital gain on the sale of a principal residence); (2) one other residence of the term holder within the meaning of IRC § 280A (generally referring to a residence used by the term holder for personal purposes for the greater of fourteen days each year or ten percent of the number of days during the year that it is rented to others); or (3) an undivided fractional interest in either of the foregoing. Treas. Reg. §§ 25.2702-5(b)(2)(i), (c)(2)(i). Thus, each individual may transfer no more than two residences, and, therefore, can establish no more than two personal residence trusts. For this purpose, multiple trusts holding fractional interests in the same residence are treated as one trust. Treas. Reg. § 25.2702-5(a)(1).

➜ **Planning Point:** Because an individual can transfer an undivided interest in a residence, a grantor can reduce the mortality risk associated with a QPRT by transferring undivided interests in a residence to two or more QPRTs of varying terms, such as 10 and 15 years. Thus, the grantor could increase the chance that he or she would survive the term of at least one of the QPRTs. The property transferred to the shorter term QPRTs will, however, produce a larger gift than if all of the property were transferred to a single QPRT for the longer term. For example, if a grantor, age 50, transfers a $1,000,000 residence to a 15-year QPRT when the Section 7520 rate is 5.4%, the taxable gift would be $391,140. If the grantor instead transferred $500,000 to a 10-year QPRT and $500,000 to a 15-year QPRT, the combined taxable gifts would be $469,215.

21st Century Estate Planning:
Practical Applications
2005 Edition

©2005 Sonnenschein Nath & Rosenthal LLP
and Cannon Financial Institute, Inc.

- 621 -

➜ **Planning Point:** While transferring a primary residence is permitted, vacation homes are often the preferred choice for several reasons. The primary reason is that when the personal residence trust term ends, the grantor must vacate the residence unless the instrument permits him or her to lease the residence from its new owners or they otherwise agree to do so.

Generally, the residence may not be used for any purpose other than the term holder's residence when occupied by the term holder. Treas. Reg. §§ 25.2702-5(b)(2)(iii), (c)(2)(iii). A residence will qualify as a personal residence, however, if a portion of it is used for a business use such that certain expenses are deductible business expenses for federal income tax purposes. Treas. Reg. §§ 25.2702-5(b)(2)(iii), (c)(2)(iii). A residence also may be rented during the portion of the year that it is not occupied by the term holder. Treas. Reg. § 25.2702-5(c)(2). See, e.g., PLR 200117021 (January 25, 2001) (where the taxpayer's stay at the vacation property exceeded the minimum required under IRC § 280A(d), and the taxpayer rented the property for two months a year and provided no services in connection with the rental of the property, the IRS determined that such property qualified as a personal residence eligible for a QPRT).

a. **Additional Property**. A personal residence also includes appurtenant structures used for residential purposes and adjacent land not in excess of that which is reasonably appropriate for residential purposes, considering the residence's size and location. Treas. Reg. §§ 25.2702-5(b)(2)(ii), (c)(2)(ii). There are numerous private letter rulings addressing the type of property and structures that will qualify as a personal residence, and the IRS has approved the treatment as a personal residence of:

- A parcel containing a residence, carport, pier, boat dock and guesthouse (PLR 199908032 (November 30, 1998));
- A parcel containing a residence, two outbuildings, a swimming pool and land subject to a conservation easement (PLR 200039031 (June 30, 2000)); and
- A parcel containing a vacation home, detached garage with an apartment used by a maintenance person, a cabin, tennis court, Jacuzzi and land subject to a conservation easement (PLR 200109017 (November 27, 2000)).

b. **Furnishings**. The term personal residence does not include personal property, such as furnishings. Treas. Reg. §§ 25.2702-5(b)(2)(ii), (c)(2)(ii).

c. **Mortgaged Property**. Mortgaged property will qualify as a personal residence. *Id.* For purposes of determining the value of the gift, however, the mortgage must be considered, in which case the gift is the value of the property net of the mortgage. The view of some practitioners is, however, that if the grantor enters into an indemnification agreement with the trustee pursuant to which the grantor remains liable on the mortgage and the trustee has the right to enforce the debt against the grantor, then the gift is the full value of the property, not its

21st Century Estate Planning:
Practical Applications
2005 Edition

©2005 Sonnenschein Nath & Rosenthal LLP
and Cannon Financial Institute, Inc.

- 622 -

net value. See Carlyn S. McCaffrey and Pam H. Schneider, "Planning for GRATs and QPRTs," 301 *PLI/Est* 395 (Feb./Mar. 2001).

> **EXAMPLE:** Grantor, age 50, transfers a residence worth $1,000,000 to a 15-year QPRT when the Section 7520 rate is 5.4%. The residence is subject to a $500,000 mortgage. If the transfer is not subject to the mortgage, the value for purposes of determining the gift is $1,000,000. Grantor's retained interest has a value of $608,860, and he makes a gift of $391,140. If Grantor transferred the house subject to the mortgage, however, its net value of $500,000 would be used in determining the amount of the gift. In that case, the value of Grantor's retained interest is $304,430, and he makes a gift of $195,570. As Grantor pays off the mortgage, he or she will be making an additional transfer to the trust in the amount of the principal portion of each mortgage payment, and a portion of the transfer will be treated as a taxable gift for which a gift tax return will need to be prepared and filed.

➔ **Planning Point:** If the residence is secured by a mortgage, the grantor should notify the bank of the transfer so the mortgage documents can be updated and to make sure the transfer does not accelerate the mortgage. The terms of the mortgage may prohibit a transfer to a QPRT or accelerate repayment if a transfer is made.

d. Joint Ownership by Spouses. Spouses who hold interests in the same residence may transfer their interests in the residence to the same trust, as long as the trust instrument prohibits any person other than one of the spouses from holding a term interest concurrent with the other spouse. Treas. Reg. §§ 25.2702-5(b)(2)(iv), (c)(2)(iv). Alternatively, each spouse may establish a personal residence trust and transfer his or her undivided interest to it.

➔ **Planning Point:** The transfer to separate trusts may result in fractional discounts, and it also may allow the spouses to take advantage of the longer life expectancy of one of the spouses by creating a trust with a longer term, thereby decreasing the taxable gift.

> **EXAMPLE 1:** Wife, age 55, transfers a $1,000,000 residence to a 10-year QPRT when the Section 7520 rate is 5.4%. The value of the gift will be $524,000. If Wife and Husband, both of whom are 55 years old, hold their residence in joint tenancy and each of them transfers his or her respective one-half interest to a QPRT, the value of the residence can be discounted. Assuming a discount of 15%, the value of each one-half interest would be $425,000. Assuming the same Section 7520 rate, the value of each gift would be $223,000, for a total gift of $446,000, which is $78,000 less than had Wife transferred the entire residence.

21st Century Estate Planning:
Practical Applications
2005 Edition

©2005 *Sonnenschein Nath & Rosenthal LLP*
and Cannon Financial Institute, Inc.

- 623 -

EXAMPLE 2: If, in Example 1 above, Wife transferred her undivided one-half interest to a 15-year QPRT because of her longer life expectancy, Wife would make a taxable gift of $154,000 rather than $223,000 (the amount of Husband's taxable gift). The total gift would be $377,000, which is $69,000 less than had Wife used a 10-year QPRT.

3. Personal Residence Trusts

A personal residence trust is a trust that must prohibit the trust from holding any asset other than one personal residence of the term holder and "qualified proceeds." Treas. Reg. § 25.2702-5(b)(1). "Qualified proceeds" are defined as proceeds payable as a result of damage, destruction or involuntary conversion of the personal residence if the proceeds are reinvested in a personal residence within two years of receipt of the proceeds. Treas. Reg. § 25.2702-5(b)(3). The trust instrument must prohibit the sale or transfer of the personal residence during the term of the trust. Treas. Reg. § 25.2702-5(b)(1).

The rules governing personal residence trusts are inflexible, and, therefore, such trusts are rarely used. Rather, QPRTs are used.

4. Qualified Personal Residence Trusts

In order for a trust to qualify as a QPRT, it must meet the requirements for a QPRT set forth in the regulations, and the governing instrument must contain several provisions, which are discussed below. For a sample governing instrument for a QPRT, along with annotations and optional provisions, see Rev. Proc. 2003-42, 2003-1 C.B. 993.

a. Permissible Distributions. All of the income must be distributed to the term holder at least annually, and no distributions of principal may be made to anyone other than the term holder prior to the end of the retained term. Treas. Reg. §§ 25.2702-5(c)(3), (c)(4).

b. Permissible Trust Property. The governing instrument trust must prohibit the trust from holding any asset other than one residence to be used as a personal residence by the term holder. Treas. Reg. § 25.2702-5(c)(5)(i). That said, the governing instrument also may permit the trust to hold the assets discussed below.

(1) Additions of Cash. Additions of cash or the holding of cash in a separate account are permitted for the following purposes:

- For the payment of trust expenses (including mortgage payments) already incurred or reasonably expected to be incurred within six months of the date on which the cash was contributed;
- For improvements to the residence to be paid for within six months of the date the cash was contributed; and
- For the purchase by the QPRT of the initial residence within three months of the date the trust is created, or for the purchase of a

21st Century Estate Planning:
Practical Applications
2005 Edition

©2005 Sonnenschein Nath & Rosenthal LLP
and Cannon Financial Institute, Inc.

- 624 -

replacement residence within three months of the cash addition; provided that, in either case, the trustee has entered into a contract to purchase the residence. Treas. Reg. § 25.2702-5(c)(5)(ii)(A)(1).

➔ **Planning Point:** Additions of cash to a QPRT may be additional gifts to the QPRT. Items that the grantor, as the life tenant, is required to pay under applicable law, such as mortgage interest payments, taxes and utilities, however, should not be treated as additional gifts to the trust.

(2) **Improvements**. The trust may permit improvements to the residence to be added to the trust as long as the residence continues to meet the definition of a personal residence. Treas. Reg. § 25.2702-5(c)(5)(ii)(B).

➔ **Planning Point:** This exception appears to be limited to improvements paid for directly by the term holder, whereas under the exception for cash additions to pay for improvements, the trustee would pay for the cost of the improvements.

(3) **Sale Proceeds**. The governing instrument may allow the QPRT to hold the proceeds from the sale of the personal residence, in a separate account, for a period not to exceed two years from the date of sale if the trustee plans to use the proceeds within that period to purchase another personal residence for the term holder. Treas. Reg. §§ 25.2702-5(c)(5)(ii)(C), (c)(7)(ii).

(4) **Insurance Proceeds**. The QPRT may hold insurance policies on the residence and the insurance proceeds payable to the trust as a result of damage to or destruction of the residence, if the proceeds are held in a separate account, for up to two years, for the repair, improvement or replacement of the residence. Treas. Reg. § 25.2702-5(c)(5)(ii)(D).

➔ **Planning Point:** After the transfer of the residence to the QPRT, the grantor should notify his or her insurance agent so the homeowner's policy can be updated to reflect the trust as the new owner of the residence.

c. **Commutation**. The governing instrument must prohibit commutation (the prepayment of the income interest at its actuarial value at the date of prepayment). Treas. Reg. § 25.2702-5(c)(6).

d. **Cessation of Use as a Personal Residence**. The governing instrument must provide that the trust ceases to be a QPRT if the residence held by the QPRT ceases to be the personal residence of the term holder. Treas. Reg. § 25.2702-5(c)(7). A trust may cease to be a QPRT if the personal residence is sold, damaged or destroyed. Treas. Reg. §§ 25.2702-5(c)(7)(ii), (c)(7)(iii).

21st Century Estate Planning:
Practical Applications
2005 Edition

©2005 Sonnenschein Nath & Rosenthal LLP
and Cannon Financial Institute, Inc.

- 625 -

(1) **Sale of Residence**. The sale of the personal residence is not a cessation of use if the sale proceeds are used to acquire a new residence within two years of the sale. Treas. Reg. § 25.2702-5(c)(7)(ii).

(2) **Destruction of Residence**. Damage to or destruction of the personal residence will not cause the trust to cease to be a QPRT if replacement of or repairs to the residence are completed, or the trust acquires a new residence, prior to the date that is two years after the date of such damage or destruction. Treas. Reg. § 25.2702-5(c)(7)(iii)(A).

Within thirty days of the trust's ceasing to be a QPRT, either (i) the assets must be distributed outright to the term holder, or (ii) the trust must be converted to a GRAT. Treas. Reg. § 25.2702-5(c)(8)(i). The regulations set forth the manner in which a QPRT may be converted to a GRAT. Treas. Reg. § 25.2702-5(c)(8)(ii).

→ **Planning Point:** The trustee may be given the discretion as to which of these results occurs. If the term holder is the trustee, however, such a provision may make the original transfer to the trust an incomplete gift. Requiring the trust to convert to a GRAT is the preferred option for this reason. Additionally, creating a GRAT allows at least a portion of the expected tax benefit of the QPRT to be preserved.

e. **Sale of Residence to Grantor**. The governing instrument must prohibit the trust from selling or transferring the residence to the grantor, the grantor's spouse, or a corporation or partnership controlled by the grantor or the grantor's spouse during the term of the trust or at any time after the retained term that the trust is a grantor trust. Treas. Reg. § 25.2702-5(c)(9). For this purpose, a sale or transfer to a grantor trust of the grantor or the grantor's spouse is a sale or transfer to the grantor or the grantor's spouse. If the grantor dies before the expiration of the retained term, however, the residence can be distributed to anyone, including the grantor's estate and the grantor's spouse, pursuant to the terms of the trust or the grantor's exercise of a power of appointment. Id.

5. **Gift, Estate and Income Tax Consequences**

a. **Gift Tax**. A QPRT allows the grantor potentially to transfer his or her personal residence to others (*e.g.*, his or her children) at a reduced gift tax cost. For federal gift tax purposes, the original transfer of the residence to the QPRT will be treated as a taxable gift of the remainder interest to the remainder beneficiaries determined by subtracting from the value of the property transferred to the QPRT an amount equal to the value of the retained interest, determined under Section 7520.

The value of the gift to the QPRT for gift tax purposes is based on the present value of the right of the QPRT beneficiaries to receive the residence at the end of the term of years. In determining the value of the residence, a number of factors are considered, such as the grantor's age, the initial term of the QPRT, and the Section 7520 rate in effect for the month of the transfer. Because the QPRT beneficiaries must wait until the end of the term to receive the residence, the value of the gift is substantially lower than the actual value of the residence at the

21st Century Estate Planning:
Practical Applications
2005 Edition

©2005 Sonnenschein Nath & Rosenthal LLP
and Cannon Financial Institute, Inc.

- 626 -

time of transfer. Therefore, the older the donor or the longer the term of years, the lower the value of the gift.

> **EXAMPLE:** Grantor, age 50, transfers a residence worth $300,000 to a QPRT when the Section 7520 rate is 6.2%. If the property grows at 4%, the following results will be achieved:

QPRT Term	Initial Value of Property	Value of Property at End of Term	Taxable Gift (Remainder Interest)	Estate Tax Savings @ 50% Estate Tax Rate
20 years	$300,000	$657,337	$69,588	$293,875
25 years	$300,000	$799,751	$43,638	$378,057
30 years	$300,000	$973,019	$25,161	$473,929

Not only is the initial transfer of the residence a gift to the QPRT, but also later contributions of cash to the trust and the direct payment by the grantor of certain expenses and improvements are gifts to the QPRT. When contributions of cash are made to the trust to pay for expenses or improvements, or payments are made by the grantor directly, the additional gift is valued using the factors (*i.e.*, term, age, Section 7520 rate) applicable to the date of contribution rather than those applicable on the date of the original transfer. Contributions of cash to pay for expenses that are allocable to income under applicable state law should not, however, be gifts to the trust because they are properly chargeable against the term holder. See PLR 9249014 (September 4, 1992). Thus, the grantor's payment of mortgage interest, taxes, maintenance charges, repairs and utilities will not result in a gift to the remaindermen. Similarly, the grantor's direct payment of such expenses will not constitute a gift. The payment of other expenses, such as principal on a mortgage loan, will be additional gifts.

b. Estate Tax. If the grantor survives the QPRT term, the full fair market value of the residence, including any appreciation in the value of the residence during the term of the trust, will not be included in the grantor's estate for federal estate tax purposes. Care must be taken to ensure that the grantor does not retain any interests in or powers over the trust after the retained term ends that would cause the trust property to be included in his or her gross estate. For example, although the grantor can act as trustee during the term of the retained use of the residence, he or she should cease to act at the end of the term to ensure that he or she does not retain any powers over the trust that would cause the trust property to be included in his or her gross estate.

(1) Gross Estate Inclusion. If the grantor dies during the term of the QPRT, the full value of the residence is included in his or her gross estate for federal estate tax purposes under IRC § 2036(a)(1). This Section includes in a grantor's gross estate the value of property transferred during life if the grantor retained for life the right to the income from or the right to possess or enjoy the transferred property. If the property is included in the grantor's gross estate, any of the grantor's applicable exclusion amount used to shelter the gift to the trust is restored. Consequently, the result for federal gift and estate tax purposes is the same as if the QPRT had never been established. The only "cost" if the grantor dies during the term of the

21st Century Estate Planning:
Practical Applications
2005 Edition

©2005 Sonnenschein Nath & Rosenthal LLP
and Cannon Financial Institute, Inc.

QPRT is the expense of creating and operating the QPRT and the loss of the use of the funds used to pay any gift tax upon creating the GRAT. If the grantor paid gift tax, the grantor's estate will be entitled to an adjustment for the gift tax paid.

→ **Planning Point:** Although the grantor's applicable exclusion will be restored, if the grantor's spouse consented to split the gift, the spouse's applicable exclusion will not be restored. Therefore, the grantor should not split gifts to a QPRT with his or her spouse because the spouse's applicable exclusion amount will be wasted if the grantor does not survive the term.

(2) Use of Residence After Retained Term. The QPRT instrument can include a "lease-back" provision. Pursuant to such a provision, if the grantor survives until the end of the term of the QPRT and the trust holds the residence at that time, the residence will continue to be held in trust for the benefit of the beneficiaries, subject to the grantor's right to lease the property for fair market value from the remainder beneficiaries. The grantor also could rent the residence from the children if the residence is distributed outright to them. If the trustee at any time decides to sell the residence, any sale would be subject to the grantor's continuing right to lease the property.

If the grantor or his or her spouse leases the residence from the remainder beneficiaries after the end of the QPRT term, the residence will not be subject to estate tax upon either spouse's death as long as the lease is at fair market value. See PLR 199931028 (May 10, 1999); and PLR 9723021 (March 7, 1997). Although the rental payments will be taxable income to the beneficiaries, the income tax rate is less than the estate tax rate. Paying rent also will save estate tax on the rental payments that would otherwise be included in the grantor's estate at death and will move assets from the grantor to the new owners free of estate or gift tax.

→ **Planning Point:** For a married individual, an alternative to renting the residence from the remainder beneficiaries is to provide that the residence will continue to be held in trust after the initial term with the grantor's spouse having the right to use and occupy the residence rent-free during the spouse's life. Thus, the grantor can continue to occupy the residence after the retained term without any adverse estate tax consequences.

In addition, the QPRT can provide that a continuing trust owns the residence after the expiration of the grantor's retained interest. If the continuing trust is structured as a grantor trust for income tax purposes and the grantor pays fair market rent for the use of the property, the rent payments will be out of the grantor's estate and will be not be income to the continuing trust or its beneficiaries.

c. Generation-Skipping Transfer Tax. As discussed above in connection with the discussion on GRATs, the ETIP rule prevents the allocation of a grantor's GST exemption to a trust that will be included in the grantor's gross estate until such time as the grantor's interest has terminated. Under the ETIP rule, because the QPRT will be included in the grantor's gross estate if he or she dies during the retained term, the grantor cannot allocate GST

21st Century Estate Planning:
Practical Applications
2005 Edition

©2005 Sonnenschein Nath & Rosenthal LLP
and Cannon Financial Institute, Inc.

- 628 -

exemption to a QPRT until the end of the retained term. Thus, it is preferable to designate the grantor's living children as the remaindermen of the QPRT.

> **d. Income Tax**. A QPRT allows the grantor to take advantage of certain income tax savings normally available to individual taxpayers.

A QPRT is designed to be a grantor trust, which, as discussed above, means that the trust will be ignored for federal income tax purposes. Therefore, the grantor can deduct all real property tax payments on the residence in the QPRT and mortgage interest payments on his or her personal income tax return as long as the QPRT owns the residence. Further, if the home is the grantor's principal residence and is sold during the QPRT term, the grantor can take advantage of the capital gain exclusion for the sale of a principal residence that is available to an individual under IRC § 121 ($250,000 for an individual, $500,000 for a married individual filing jointly).

If the property is sold after the term of the QPRT has expired, even though the grantor may be leasing the property, the capital gain will not be taxed to the grantor, but rather to the persons who received the property when the QPRT ended (*e.g.*, the grantor's children) unless the residence is held in a continuing trust that is treated as a grantor trust for federal income tax purposes.

It should be noted that a residence held in a QPRT that ends before the grantor dies does not get a step-up in basis at the grantor's death. Instead, the grantor's cost basis in the residence will carry over to the beneficiaries. Therefore, if the residence is eventually sold, the capital gains tax could be higher than if the grantor had owned the residence at his or her death. The beneficiary may still be able to use his or her own exclusion under IRC § 121, but only if the property is the beneficiary's principal residence for the required length of time.

K. Sale of Remainder Interest in a Marital Trust[10]

The sale of the remainder interest in a marital trust involves the grantor's transfer of property to an irrevocable trust for the benefit of the grantor's spouse, who receives an income interest or an annuity payment from the trust for life, and the grantor's simultaneous sale of the remainder interest in the trust to the remainder beneficiaries for its fair market value. The trust is designed to qualify for the gift tax marital deduction, but it will not be subject to estate tax at the spouse's death. As a result, the trust property passes to the grantor's children completely free of gift and estate taxes.

1. Gift Tax Marital Deduction

Generally, a lifetime transfer of property between a husband and a wife is not subject to gift tax because of the unlimited gift tax marital deduction provided in IRC § 2523.

> **a. Terminable Interest Rule**. When a husband or wife transfers a "terminable interest" in property to his or her spouse, however, the transfer will not qualify for the marital deduction, except in limited circumstances. An example of a "terminable interest" is where a

21st Century Estate Planning:
Practical Applications
2005 Edition

©2005 *Sonnenschein Nath & Rosenthal LLP*
and Cannon Financial Institute, Inc.

- 629 -

husband or wife transfers property in trust for the benefit of his or her spouse, and the spouse's right to receive payments from the trust will end at the spouse's death or at the end of a term of years, at which time the property passes to someone other than the spouse or the spouse's estate. Because the rights of the spouse or the spouse's estate terminate at some point, the spouse's interest is considered a terminable interest and may not qualify for the gift tax marital deduction.

> **b. Exceptions to the Terminable Interest Rule**. IRC § 2523 contains exceptions to the "terminable interest" rule pursuant to which certain terminable interests will qualify for the gift tax marital deduction.

>> **(1) Certain Trusts**. Under the exceptions, certain types of marital trusts that contain requisite statutory provisions (so-called qualified terminable interest property ("QTIP") trusts and general power of appointment marital trusts) will qualify for the gift tax marital deduction. Each of these types of trusts, either by statute or as a result of required provisions, however, will be included in the spouse's gross estate for federal estate tax purposes at the spouse's death under either IRC § 2041 (by reason of the general power of appointment) or IRC § 2044 (by reason of the QTIP election), thereby merely deferring, but not eliminating, estate taxes.

>> **(2) Transfer for Full and Adequate Consideration**. Another exception to the terminable interest rule applies if the person receiving the remainder of a terminable interest paid full and adequate consideration for that remainder interest. IRC § 2523(b). It is this exception upon which the marital trust remainder sale strategy is built. The marital trust should not be subject to the terminable interest rule (and thus should qualify for the marital deduction) because the grantor sells the remainder interest for full and adequate consideration at the same time that he or she transfers the lifetime interest to his or her spouse. Because the marital trust remainder sale strategy relies on this exception, the trust agreement need not contain any provisions that would cause the trust property to be included in the spouse-beneficiary's gross estate (the spouse will not have a general power of appointment, and a QTIP election will not have been made). As a result, transfer taxes should be eliminated, both on the initial transfer of property to the marital trust and on the transfer of the marital trust property to the remaindermen at the end of the marital trust term.

21st Century Estate Planning:
Practical Applications
2005 Edition

©2005 Sonnenschein Nath & Rosenthal LLP
and Cannon Financial Institute, Inc.

- 630 -

2. Marital Trust Remainder Sale Considerations

a. <u>Valuation of the Spouse's Interest</u>. In order to eliminate as many of the valuation issues as possible in determining the value of the remainder interest (and thus the purchase price to be paid by the remainder beneficiaries), the grantor's spouse should receive either only an income interest or an annuity in the trust; that is, an interest that requires that the spouse receive a fixed annuity or that all income be distributed to him or her. This structure makes the valuation of the spouse's interest a simple annuity or life estate calculation under Section 7520. The value of the remainder interest should be equal to the value of the property the grantor transfers less the value of the spouse's annuity interest or life estate, determined under Section 7520.

b. <u>Estate and Gift Tax Consequences</u>. As noted above, the spouse will not have a general power of appointment over the trust, and a QTIP election will not be made for the marital trust. Thus, the trust property should not be included in the spouse's gross estate at his or her death. Nonetheless, because the remainder beneficiaries pay the grantor adequate and full consideration for the remainder interest, the interest in the trust transferred to the grantor's spouse should qualify for the gift tax marital deduction. This is the case even though a person (*e.g.*, one or more of the grantor's children) will receive the trust property (*i.e.*, the remainder interest) after the termination of the spouse's interest.

The result of the transaction is that the property is removed from the grantor's estate, the grantor's spouse receives a benefit for life from the property in the trust, yet the trust property is not included in the spouse's gross estate for federal estate tax purposes. Thus, the property is not subject to estate tax or gift tax before reaching the children. Only the amount that the remainder beneficiaries pay to the grantor for the remainder interest and any appreciation thereon will be subject to estate tax in the grantor's gross estate.

The rationale for allowing the marital deduction in this case is that the remainder beneficiaries will have transferred to the grantor property having a value equal to the present value of what they will eventually receive from the marital trust. The property transferred to the grantor, as reinvested, will be subject to estate tax at his or her death, and thus, in theory, no circumvention of the estate tax will have occurred.

c. <u>Income Tax Consequences</u>. Income tax consequences also must be considered in determining the benefits of the transaction. If the asset being transferred to the trust has built-in appreciation, the grantor will recognize capital gain when he or she sells the remainder interest to the beneficiaries. The basis of the asset in the hands of the remainder beneficiaries will equal the purchase price, and the asset will not be entitled to a stepped-up basis at the grantor's death. Thus, when the remainder beneficiaries sell the asset, they will recognize more gain than if they had received the asset from the grantor by reason of the grantor's death.

3. Income Marital Trust

If the marital trust pays all of the trust income to the grantor's spouse for the shorter of a specified term or the spouse's life, and if the trust invests for growth rather than income, then, in

21st Century Estate Planning:
Practical Applications
2005 Edition

©2005 Sonnenschein Nath & Rosenthal LLP
and Cannon Financial Institute, Inc.

- 631 -

effect, all of the appreciation on the trust property should be transferred to the children free of gift and estate tax. State law may require that the trust pay at least some income to the spouse, and may give the spouse the right to recover the minimum amount of income out of capital gains if the trust does not in fact earn that income. Even if the trust generates income at the rate of 1% or 2% per year, which amount is paid to the spouse as the income beneficiary, all growth in excess of that amount will pass to the remainder beneficiaries.

EXAMPLE: Grantor transfers $2 million of cash and marketable securities to an income marital trust for Spouse's benefit, from which she will receive all of the income for 15 years or until her death if sooner. Grantor simultaneously sells the remainder interest in the trust (the right to receive the remaining trust property after the 15-year term) to a trust for the benefit of Grantor's children (the "Children's Trust").

Assume the transfer is made when Spouse is 55 and the Section 7520 rate is 7%. Given these facts, the value of the remainder interest is equal to $812,520. Thus, the Children's Trust pays Grantor $812,520 for such remainder. Because the Children's Trust purchases the remainder interest in the marital trust, the trust qualifies for the gift tax marital deduction. Thus, no gift tax is due as a result of the $2 million transfer to the marital trust.

If the trust property generates income of 1% per year and capital appreciation of 9% per year (10% total), at the end of 15 years, the trust assets would have a value of $7.28 million, as illustrated below, all of which would pass free of gift and estate taxes to the Children's Trust.

Year	Start of Year	Growth	Income Paid	End of Year
1	$ 2,000,000	$ 200,000	$ (20,000)	$ 2,180,000
2	$ 2,180,000	$ 218,000	$ (21,800)	$ 2,376,200
3	$ 2,376,200	$ 237,620	$ (23,762)	$ 2,590,058
4	$ 2,590,058	$ 259,006	$ (25,901)	$ 2,823,163
5	$ 2,823,163	$ 282,316	$ (28,232)	$ 3,077,248
6	$ 3,077,248	$ 307,725	$ (30,772)	$ 3,354,200
7	$ 3,354,200	$ 335,420	$ (33,542)	$ 3,656,078
8	$ 3,656,078	$ 365,608	$ (36,561)	$ 3,985,125
9	$ 3,985,125	$ 398,513	$ (39,851)	$ 4,343,787
10	$ 4,343,787	$ 434,379	$ (43,438)	$ 4,734,727
11	$ 4,734,727	$ 473,473	$ (47,347)	$ 5,160,853
12	$ 5,160,853	$ 516,085	$ (51,609)	$ 5,625,330
13	$ 5,625,330	$ 562,533	$ (56,253)	$ 6,131,609
14	$ 6,131,609	$ 613,161	$ (61,316)	$ 6,683,454
15	$ 6,683,454	$ 668,345	$ (66,835)	$ 7,284,965

21st Century Estate Planning:
Practical Applications
2005 Edition

©2005 *Sonnenschein Nath & Rosenthal LLP*
and Cannon Financial Institute, Inc.

- 632 -

If Spouse dies in year 8, however, the marital trust provides the Children's Trust with a "windfall" in that the property then held by the marital trust will pass to the Children's Trust several years earlier than anticipated. The marital trust would have $3.98 million after 8 years, which would grow to $7.75 million after an additional 7 years (*i.e.*, a total of 15 years).

The income Spouse receives from the marital trust and the $812,520 Grantor receives for the remainder interest can be reinvested and passed to their children after estate taxes (to the extent that they do not consume it). This provides their children with an additional $2.28 million (assuming a 10% rate of return and a 50% estate tax rate) after estate taxes.

If Grantor had retained the $2 million and the Children's Trust had kept its $812,520, in 15 years at a 10% rate of return, Grantor would have $8.35 million, only $4.175 million of which would pass to his children after estate tax, and the Children's Trust would have $3.39 million. Thus, the total amount received by the children would be $7.565 million.

Accordingly, the marital trust remainder sale, taking into account (1) the value of the marital trust at the end of the 15-year term ($7.28 million), and (2) the $2.28 million the children eventually inherit from Grantor's and Spouse's estates by reason of the payment for the remainder and the income Spouse received from the marital trust (a total of $9.56 million), increases the children's inheritance by almost $2 million.

    a. Advantages Over Other Techniques. This result clearly is better than a GRAT or a sale to an IDGT, both of which transfer to the remainder beneficiaries only the growth in excess of the Section 7520 rate (on the GRAT) or the IRC § 1274 interest rate (on the note). Those rates could be several times higher than the 1% or 2% minimum income rate that may apply to the marital trust. In effect, the children receive the amount of the estate tax that would have been imposed on the property transferred into the trust, and give up the amount of the estate tax on the property they transfer to the grantor to purchase the remainder interest.

    b. Use of Section 7520 Rate to Value the Income Interest. The Section 7520 rate cannot be used if the trust instrument does not "provide the income beneficiary with that degree of beneficial enjoyment of the property during the term of the income interest that the principles of the law of trusts accord to a person who is unqualifiedly designated as the income beneficiary of a trust for a similar period of time." Treas. Reg. § 25.7520-3(b)(2)(ii). Thus, for example, if stock is transferred to a trust in which the grantor has retained an income interest and the stock historically pays dividends equal to one percent of fair market value, and the valuation

21st Century Estate Planning:
Practical Applications
2005 Edition

©2005 Sonnenschein Nath & Rosenthal LLP
and Cannon Financial Institute, Inc.

- 633 -

tables assume an eight percent return, the income interest should not be valued using the Section 7520 rate.

A trust with a mandatory income interest in favor of the grantor's spouse should satisfy the foregoing requirements. Examples 1 and 2 in Treas. Reg. § 25.7520-3(b)(2)(v) make it clear that the spouse should be given the power to direct the trustee to "make the trust corpus productive consistent with income yield standards for trusts under applicable state law," and specifically contemplate that the minimum rate of income that a productive trust may produce may be substantially below the Section 7520 interest rate on the valuation date. Moreover, Example 2 of these regulations shows that, as long as the beneficiary has the power to make the trust property productive of income, the fact that it actually does not produce income will not preclude use of the Section 7520 rate factors. (In this example, the trust owned non-dividend-paying stock, and the beneficiary had the right to compel the trustee to make the trust property productive of income.)

4. Annuity Marital Trust

Alternatively, the marital trust could pay the grantor's spouse an annuity for a fixed term of years. The annuity will be valued using the Section 7520 tables. The annuity could be structured so that the remainder value is minimized, thereby significantly reducing the purchase price to be paid by the remainder beneficiaries. In this case, only the growth of the trust property in excess of the Section 7520 rate will pass to the remainder beneficiaries. As the example below illustrates, less property is available for the remainder beneficiaries if an annuity marital trust is used than if an income marital trust is used because of the higher payout rate to the spouse.

> **EXAMPLE:** Grantor transfers $2 million of cash and marketable securities to an annuity marital trust for Spouse's benefit, from which she (or her estate) will receive an annuity of approximately $203,000 for 15 years. Grantor simultaneously sells the remainder interest in the marital trust (the right to receive the remaining trust property after the 15-year term) to a trust for the benefit of Grantor's children (the "Children's Trust").
>
> Assuming a Section 7520 rate of 5.8%, the remainder is valued at $10,000. Thus, the Children's Trust pays Grantor $10,000 for the remainder. Because the Children's Trust purchases the remainder interest in the marital trust, the trust qualifies for the gift tax marital deduction. Thus, no gift tax is due as a result of the $2 million transfer to the trust.
>
> Assuming a 10% rate of return on the trust property, at the end of 15 years, the trust assets would have a value of $1.9 million, as illustrated below, all of which would pass free of gift and estate taxes to the Children's Trust.

21st Century Estate Planning:
Practical Applications
2005 Edition

©2005 Sonnenschein Nath & Rosenthal LLP
and Cannon Financial Institute, Inc.

- 634 -

Year	Start of Year	Growth	Annuity	End of Year
1	$ 2,000,000	$ 200,000	$ (202,687)	$ 1,997,313
2	$ 1,997,313	$ 199,731	$ (202,687)	$ 1,994,358
3	$ 1,994,358	$ 199,436	$ (202,687)	$ 1,991,106
4	$ 1,991,106	$ 199,111	$ (202,687)	$ 1,987,530
5	$ 1,987,530	$ 198,753	$ (202,687)	$ 1,983,596
6	$ 1,983,596	$ 198,360	$ (202,687)	$ 1,979,269
7	$ 1,979,269	$ 197,927	$ (202,687)	$ 1,974,509
8	$ 1,974,509	$ 197,451	$ (202,687)	$ 1,969,273
9	$ 1,969,273	$ 196,927	$ (202,687)	$ 1,963,514
10	$ 1,963,514	$ 196,351	$ (202,687)	$ 1,957,178
11	$ 1,957,178	$ 195,718	$ (202,687)	$ 1,950,209
12	$ 1,950,209	$ 195,021	$ (202,687)	$ 1,942,543
13	$ 1,942,543	$ 194,254	$ (202,687)	$ 1,934,111
14	$ 1,934,111	$ 193,411	$ (202,687)	$ 1,924,835
15	$ 1,924,835	$ 192,483	$ (202,687)	$ 1,914,631

The $10,000 Grantor receives for the remainder interest and the annuity payments Spouse receives from the marital trust can be reinvested and passed to their children after estate taxes (to the extent they do not consume it). This provides their children with an additional $2.7 million (assuming a 10% rate of return and a 50% estate tax rate) after estate taxes.

If Grantor had retained the $2 million and the Children's Trust had kept its $10,000, in 15 years at a 10% rate of return, Grantor would have $8.35 million, only $4.175 million of which would pass to his children after estate tax, and the Children's Trust would have $42,000. Thus, the total amount received by the children would be $4.217 million.

Accordingly, the marital trust remainder sale, taking into account (1) the value of the marital trust at the end of the 15-year term ($1.9 million), and (2) the $2.7 million the children eventually inherit from Grantor's and Spouse's estates by reason of the payment for the remainder and the income Spouse received from the marital trust (a total of $4.6 million), increases the children's inheritance by almost $400,000.

The marital trust remainder sale using an annuity marital trust has two advantages over a GRAT. First, there is no mortality risk. That is, if the grantor's spouse dies during the annuity term, only the present value of the remaining annuity payments is included in the spouse's taxable estate. The amount of the marital trust property is not subject to estate tax. Second, there is no taxable gift upon creation of the marital trust, assuming the Children's Trust has sufficient assets with which to purchase the remainder.

21st Century Estate Planning:
Practical Applications
2005 Edition

©2005 Sonnenschein Nath & Rosenthal LLP
and Cannon Financial Institute, Inc.

- 635 -

5. Valuation Issues

The success of the marital trust remainder sale depends on a finding that the remainder beneficiaries paid full and adequate consideration for the remainder interest so that the grantor does not make a taxable gift to his or her spouse. Thus, the following valuation issues should be considered.

a. <u>Consequences of Incorrect Valuation of Remainder Interest</u>. If the property contributed to the marital trust was undervalued or overvalued for any reason, then the amount paid for the remainder interest would either be too great or too little. If the property contributed was overvalued, then the remainder beneficiaries will not have paid adequate and full consideration for the remainder interest. It is unclear how such a determination would affect the availability of the marital deduction. Two different results are possible, which are discussed below.

(1)   <u>Spouse's Interest Does Not Qualify for the Marital Deduction</u>. It is possible that no portion of the spouse's interest in the marital trust would qualify for the gift tax marital deduction because the remainder beneficiaries did not pay adequate and full consideration, the result of which would be that the full value of the spouse's interest would be subject to gift tax. In that case, the value of the property transferred to the marital trust, less the amount paid by the remainder beneficiaries, would be subject to gift tax. Further, the grantor will have made a taxable gift to the remainder beneficiaries of the amount by which the value of the remainder interest exceeds the amount the remainder beneficiaries paid.

General Counsel Memorandum 38505 (September 19, 1980) supports this conclusion. In that memo, the taxpayer made a transfer to charity in a manner similar to the marital trust in a remainder sale only in that a third party paid for and would receive a future benefit. At issue was whether the gift to charity qualified for the gift tax charitable deduction under IRC § 2522. Like the marital deduction, IRC § 2522 permits a gift tax charitable deduction only for certain types of trusts that benefit both charity and individuals and that meet certain statutory requirements. If the individual paid full and adequate consideration for his or her interest, however, the trust has no formal requirements, and the charity's interest will qualify for the gift tax charitable deduction. This exception parallels, in concept and in language, the marital deduction exception upon which the marital trust remainder sale is based. In GCM 38505, the IRS determined that if the amount paid by the third party (remainder beneficiaries) was less than the value of his or her interest, the gift by the donor to charity failed to qualify for the gift tax charitable deduction in its entirety. Thus, no charitable deduction would be allowed -- not even an amount proportionate to the payment made by the remainder beneficiaries.

(2)   <u>A Fraction of Spouse's Interest Qualifies for the Marital Deduction</u>. The more appropriate result is that a fraction of the spouse's interest in the marital trust would qualify for the marital deduction. The numerator of the fraction is equal to the amount the remainder beneficiaries paid for the remainder interest, and the denominator is equal to the value of the remainder interest as determined by the IRS. The portion that does not qualify for the marital deduction is subject to gift tax. In addition, the remainder beneficiaries will have

21st Century Estate Planning:
Practical Applications
2005 Edition

©2005 Sonnenschein Nath & Rosenthal LLP
and Cannon Financial Institute, Inc.

- 636 -

received a taxable gift from the grantor of the amount by which the value of the remainder interest exceeds the amount the remainder beneficiaries paid.

Technical Advice Memorandum 7605283200D (May 28, 1976) supports this more favorable result. In this TAM, the IRS held that where the decedent's spouse received a terminable interest in an annuity from the decedent and only a portion of the interest passing to the remainder beneficiaries was paid for with full and adequate consideration, then the fraction that was so paid for will qualify for the marital deduction, and the balance will not. Thus, based on TAM 7605283200D, if the price paid by the remainder beneficiaries in a marital trust remainder sale is determined to be less than the fair market value of the remainder, only a fraction of the value of the spouse's interest in the marital trust will not qualify for the marital deduction.

Based on TAM 7605283200D and GCM 38505, it is unclear whether the IRS would disallow the entire marital deduction, or only a fraction of the deduction, if the remainder beneficiaries do not pay full and adequate consideration for the remainder. These two rulings have opposite results; neither is directly on point; and neither has precedential value. The TAM is more indicative of the IRS's anticipated position on the marital trust because the facts of TAM 7605283200D are more similar to a marital trust remainder sale than are the facts of GCM 38505, and the provision of IRC § 2523 that was at issue in TAM 7605283200D is the same provision on which the marital trust remainder sale technique is based.

Finally, the IRS might point to the "full and adequate consideration" language of IRC § 2523(b)(1) to deny the entire marital deduction if the remainder beneficiaries do not pay full and adequate consideration for the remainder interest. To bolster its argument, the IRS could argue that IRC § 2523 does not state that the deduction is allowed "to the extent" full and adequate consideration is received. On the other hand, the language of IRC § 2523 does not rule out that interpretation.

b. Price Adjustment Clause to Avoid Gift Taxes. To address the risk that the remainder beneficiaries will not have paid adequate and full consideration for the remainder interest, the marital trust could include a price adjustment clause if it is to be funded with property that is difficult to value (*e.g.*, limited partnership interests or closely held business stock). The purpose of a price adjustment clause is to adjust the price of the remainder interest if the value of the interest is increased on audit. If given effect, such an adjustment clause should eliminate the risk that an undervaluation would disqualify the trust entirely for the marital deduction. It is uncertain, however, whether any particular adjustment clause will be given effect. The subject of adjustment clauses is discussed above in greater detail in connection with the section on sales to intentionally defective grantor trusts.

6. IRC § 2702 and *Gradow*

As discussed above, it is necessary that the remainder beneficiaries pay full and adequate consideration for the remainder interest in order to avoid a gift. It also is important that full and adequate consideration for the remainder be equal to the actuarial value of such interest as

21st Century Estate Planning:
Practical Applications
2005 Edition

©2005 Sonnenschein Nath & Rosenthal LLP
and Cannon Financial Institute, Inc.

- 637 -

determined under IRC § 7520, and not to the value of the entire trust. Two potential areas of concern on this issue -- IRC § 2702 and the *Gradow* case -- should be irrelevant.

a. IRC § 2702. As discussed above, IRC § 2702(a)(1) provides that if property is transferred in trust for the benefit of a member of the transferor's family, and if the transferor retains (or certain family members retain) an interest in the trust, the value of any interest in the trust retained by the transferor (or by certain family members) will be valued at zero, resulting in a taxable gift of the entire amount to the remainder beneficiaries, unless the retained interest is a "qualified interest." In the case of a marital trust remainder sale, however, the transferor (*i.e.*, the creator of the trust) does not "retain" any interest in the trust; rather, he or she simultaneously transfers a life estate to his or her spouse and sells the remainder to his or her children. Treas. Reg. § 25.2702-2(a)(3) states that "[r]etained means held by the same individual both before and after the transfer in trust." Treas. Reg. § 25.2702-2(d)(1), Ex. 3 shows that if a grantor transfers property in trust that pays all of the income to his wife for life, remainder to children, IRC § 2702 does not apply because neither the grantor nor the spouse held an interest both before and after the transfer. With the marital trust remainder sale, the grantor will not hold an interest in the property both before and after the transfer, and thus IRC § 2702 would not apply.

b. *Gradow* and the Meaning of Adequate and Full Consideration. What constitutes full and adequate consideration for the sale of a remainder interest has been addressed in a series of cases arising under IRC § 2036. At issue in these cases was whether the transferor, who had a retained interest in the transferred property, had received adequate and full consideration for the sale of a remainder interest, thus avoiding estate tax inclusion under IRC § 2036. Some courts have held that, for purposes of the estate tax, full and adequate consideration for a remainder interest is not the actuarial value of the remainder interest but the full value of the property transferred. See, *e.g.*, *Gradow, supra*; *U.S. v. Past, supra*; *Parker v. U.S., supra*; and *Pittman v. U.S., supra*. If this authority applied to the marital trust remainder sale, the technique would not be viable.

This authority should not apply to the marital trust remainder sale. First, as noted above, the grantor of the marital trust does not retain any interest in the property. Rather, the grantor makes a gift of a lifetime income or annuity interest to his or her spouse and sells the remainder interest. Thus, there is no basis for including any of the trust property in the grantor's estate under IRC § 2036.

Second, the IRS has conceded that this line of cases does not apply for purposes of the gift tax. *Wheeler v. U.S.*, 116 F.3d 749, 755 (5th Cir. 1997) ("[b]oth parties [*i.e.*, the government and the taxpayer] agree that, for the purposes of the gift tax (section 2512 of the Code), consideration equal to the actuarial value of the remainder interest constitutes adequate consideration"). Thus, despite these cases, the remainder beneficiaries' payment of the actuarial value of the remainder interest should constitute adequate and full consideration.

Finally, even if *Gradow* and its progeny apply to a marital trust remainder sale, three Courts of Appeal have rejected its holding, recognizing that, in the context of the estate tax,

21st Century Estate Planning:
Practical Applications
2005 Edition

©2005 Sonnenschein Nath & Rosenthal LLP
and Cannon Financial Institute, Inc.

- 638 -

adequate and full consideration for the sale of a remainder interest is equal to the actuarial value of such interest. *Magnin, supra; Wheeler, supra;* and *D'Ambrosio, supra.*

7. **Funding The Purchase Price**

The Children's Trust will need funds in order to purchase the remainder from the grantor. If the trust has sufficient wealth to purchase the remainder interest but not sufficient liquid assets, it could give the grantor a promissory note, although the trust should have sufficient other assets to ensure that it has the ability to service the note. Otherwise, the payment may be deemed illusory and the IRS could recharacterize the transaction as a gift of the remainder. Interest payments made by the Children's Trust to the grantor will be taxed as interest income to the grantor, unless the Children's Trust is a grantor trust as to the grantor, in which case interest payments made by the trust will not constitute taxable interest income.

If the Children's Trust does not have sufficient assets with which to purchase the remainder or to service a note, the grantor could make a gift to the trust, which the trust could then use to pay the purchase price. Unless such a gift qualifies for the gift tax annual exclusion or is sheltered by the applicable exclusion amount, a gift tax will be due. Technically, the timing of the gift and the purchase of the remainder should be irrelevant. The IRS has held, however, that the purchaser of a remainder interest must not have acquired the funds to buy such interest from the holder of the life estate. See TAM 9206006 (January 7, 1992). Some lapse of time between the gift and the purchase (*e.g.*, six months) is thus advisable.

8. **Timing of Transaction**

The gift of the income or annuity interest to the grantor's spouse and the sale of the remainder interest to the remainder beneficiaries must be treated as occurring simultaneously. If the sale is deemed to occur after the gift, the gift will not qualify for the marital deduction because, at the time of the gift, the remainder beneficiaries will not have paid adequate and full consideration for their interest. If the sale is deemed to occur before the gift, the transaction would be treated as a transfer of property with an interest being retained by the grantor or an applicable family member, in which case IRC § 2702 would apply, causing the value of the remainder interest to be equal to the full value of the property for gift tax purposes.

➔ **Planning Point:** It should be possible to structure the gift and the sale as simultaneous transactions. For example, the remainder beneficiaries could sign the trust as purchasers of the remainder interest. If a parent transfers property to a child and the child then hands the parent a check for the fair market value of the property, the parent and child would not be deemed to have made successive gifts to one another. Rather, their actions would be viewed as a single transaction in which the parent sold property to the child.

21st Century Estate Planning:
Practical Applications
2005 Edition

©2005 Sonnenschein Nath & Rosenthal LLP
and Cannon Financial Institute, Inc.

- 639 -

9. Reporting the Marital Trust Remainder Sale

a. Gift Tax Return. The instructions to Form 709, the United States Gift (and Generation-Skipping Transfer) Tax Return, require a taxpayer to report all gifts of terminable interests the taxpayer made to his or her spouse during the year unless the terminable interest qualifies as a life estate with a power of appointment. Thus, the marital trust remainder sale must be reported on a gift tax return.

Line 16 of the gift tax return states that if a gift (i) is listed on Schedule A, (ii) is claimed on line 8 as qualifying for the marital deduction and (iii) otherwise qualifies as QTIP property, then a QTIP election is deemed to have been made with respect to that property. There is no way to elect out when these requirements are met. The marital trust in a marital trust remainder sale will not qualify for QTIP treatment, however, because it does not provide the spouse with an income interest for life.

b. Estate Tax Return. The consideration the grantor receives from the remainder beneficiaries will be a part of the grantor's gross estate. Further, the instructions to line 12a of Form 706, the United States Estate (and Generation-Skipping Transfer) Tax Return, require the grantor's executor to attach to the estate tax return a copy of all trusts created by the grantor during his or her life (which would include the marital trust) and to complete Form 706, Schedule G. The instructions to Schedule G, however, require the executor to list only gift tax paid on gifts made within three years of death and property transferred during the grantor's life included under IRC §§ 2035(a), 2036, 2037 or 2038. Thus, the marital trust need not be listed on Schedule G, as the grantor will not have retained any interest in nor have any power that would cause inclusion of the trust property in his or her estate under any of the enumerated sections. The required attachment of the marital trust agreement to the estate tax return, however, would at least disclose the existence of the trust.

On the spouse's death, the instructions to line 12b of Form 706 require his or her executor to attach to the return a copy of all trusts of which the spouse is a beneficiary at his or her death (which would include the marital trust if the spouse's interest had not terminated before his or her death) and to complete Schedule F. Schedule F lists miscellaneous property that is included in the gross estate, however, and the marital trust will not be so included. Thus, the marital trust would not have to be listed on Schedule F (although a copy would have to be attached to the return).

L. Sale of Remainder Interest in a Charitable Trust

For a charitably-inclined client, the sale of the remainder interest in a charitable trust provides a way for the client to transfer property to his or her children completely free of gift and estate taxes (the same result as with a sale of a remainder interest in a marital trust), while enabling the client to make charitable contributions that the client would otherwise make.

The sale of the remainder interest in a charitable trust is a transaction that is similar to the sale of a remainder interest in a marital trust, but it involves charitable, rather than spousal, interests. The grantor transfers property to an irrevocable trust for the benefit of a charity, which

21st Century Estate Planning:
Practical Applications
2005 Edition

©*2005 Sonnenschein Nath & Rosenthal LLP*
and Cannon Financial Institute, Inc.

- 640 -

receives an income interest from the trust for a period of time, and the grantor simultaneously sells the remainder interest in the trust to the remainder beneficiaries for its fair market value. The gift of the income interest to charity is designed to qualify for the gift tax charitable deduction. As a result, the trust property passes to the grantor's children completely free of gift and estate taxes.

> **EXAMPLE:** Grantor, age 62, transfers $5 million to a charitable trust that provides that all of the income will be distributed to charity for the shorter of 15 years or Grantor's life. Grantor simultaneously sells the remainder interest in the charitable trust (the right to receive the remaining trust property after Grantor's death or the 15-year term, whichever occurs first) to a trust for the benefit of Grantor's children (the "Children's Trust").
>
> Based on Grantor's life expectancy, the term of the trust, and the Section 7520 rate of 5.6%, the remainder is valued at $2,550,000. Thus, the Children's Trust pays Grantor $2,550,000 for the remainder. Because the Children's Trust purchases the remainder interest in the charitable trust, the charitable income interest qualifies for the gift tax charitable deduction. Thus, no gift tax is due as a result of the $5 million transfer to the trust.
>
> Assuming a 2% rate of return on income and capital appreciation of 8% each year (a total of 10%), at the end of 15 years, the trust assets will have a value of $15.86 million, all of which would pass free of gift and estate taxes to the Children's Trust.
>
> The charity will receive all of the income, which would be $100,000 in year 1, $136,000 by year 5, $200,000 by year 10, and $294,000 by year 15.
>
> If Grantor dies in year 8, however, the charitable trust provides the Children's Trust with a "windfall" in that the property then held by the charitable trust will pass to the Children's Trust several years earlier than anticipated. The charitable trust would have $9.25 million after 8 years, which would grow to $18 million after an additional 7 years (*i.e.*, a total of 15 years).
>
> Assuming a 2% rate of return on income and capital appreciation of 6% each year (a total of 8%), at the end of 15 years, the trust assets will have a value of $12 million, all of which would pass free of gift and estate taxes to the Children's Trust.
>
> Assuming a 2% rate of return on income and capital appreciation of 10% each year (a total of 12%), at the end of 15 years, the trust assets

21st Century Estate Planning:
Practical Applications
2005 Edition

©2005 *Sonnenschein Nath & Rosenthal LLP*
and Cannon Financial Institute, Inc.

- 641 -

will have a value of $20.9 million, all of which would pass free of gift and estate taxes to the Children's Trust.

Because the analysis of this technique is similar to that of the sale of a remainder interest in a marital trust, this section will highlight the differences in the techniques and aspects that apply only to the sale of a remainder interest in a charitable trust. The reader should refer to the previous section for a more in-depth discussion of the sale of a remainder interest and the issues that should be considered.

1. Gift Tax Charitable Deduction

IRC § 2522 provides an unlimited gift tax charitable deduction. If property is transferred to a trust that benefits both charitable and noncharitable beneficiaries, however, the charity's interest must be a specific type, and the trust must meet certain requirements. Like IRC § 2523 with respect to the marital deduction, however, if an individual pays full and adequate consideration for his or her interest, the trust has no formal requirements, and the charitable beneficiary's interest will qualify for the gift tax charitable deduction. IRC § 2522(c)(2). This exception parallels, in concept and in language, the marital deduction exception upon which the marital trust remainder sale is based.

2. Valuation Issues

One of the potential risks associated with the sale of a remainder interest in a charitable trust is that if the purchaser of the remainder interest does not pay full and adequate consideration for the remainder, the IRS could disallow the charitable deduction. This risk is discussed in detail with respect to the sale of a remainder interest in a marital trust immediately above, and a portion of that discussion bears repeating because it applies directly to the charitable trust. In GCM 38505 (September 19, 1980), the taxpayer made a transfer to charity, and a third party paid for and would receive a future benefit. At issue was whether the gift to charity qualified for the gift tax charitable deduction. The IRS determined that if the amount paid by the third party (remainder beneficiaries) was less than the value of his or her interest, the gift by the donor to charity failed to qualify for the gift tax charitable deduction in its entirety. Thus, no charitable deduction would be allowed -- not even an amount proportionate to the payment made by the remainder beneficiaries. In light of the holding in GCM 38505, therefore, the charitable trust should not be funded with any assets that are hard to value in order to avoid any possibility of undervaluation.

➔ **Planning Point:** It is important that the charitable trust be funded with income-producing assets so that the IRS will not challenge use of the Section 7520 valuation tables to value the remainder interest. See the discussion of this issue above in the section on the sale of a remainder interest in a marital trust.

3. Income Tax Charitable Deduction

The charitable trust can be structured as either a grantor trust or a nongrantor trust.

21st Century Estate Planning:
Practical Applications
2005 Edition

©2005 Sonnenschein Nath & Rosenthal LLP
and Cannon Financial Institute, Inc.

- 642 -

a. Nongrantor Trust. If the trust is structured as a nongrantor trust, the grantor will not be entitled to a charitable deduction for federal income tax purposes when property is transferred to the trust. The charitable trust, however, may deduct the income paid to charity each year. IRC § 642(c).

b. Grantor Trust. If the trust is structured as a grantor trust, all items of income, deduction and credit will be reported by the grantor on his or her income tax return rather than to the trust as a separate entity. The grantor will not receive a charitable deduction for federal income tax purposes in the year in which property is transferred to the trust. This is because in order for a transfer to a trust in which there are both charitable and noncharitable beneficiaries to qualify for an income tax deduction, the charity's interest must take a specific form. The grantor will be entitled to an income tax deduction, however, when the trust makes annual distributions of income to charity. Treas. Reg. § 1.671-2(c). If the charitable beneficiary is a public charity, the amount of the grantor's charitable income tax deduction will be limited to 50% of the grantor's adjusted gross income, or 30% if long-term capital gain property is used to fund the charitable trust. If the charitable beneficiary is a private foundation, the deduction is limited to 30% of adjusted gross income, or 20% if the property is long-term capital gain property. For an in-depth discussion of the percentage limitations, see Chapter XVI, Charitable Giving.

4. Reporting the Charitable Trust Remainder Sale

a. Gift Tax Return. The instructions to Form 709, the United States Gift (and Generation-Skipping Transfer) Tax Return, provide that if the taxpayer transfers a partial interest to charity, or transfers part of his or her interest to a person other than a charity, the taxpayer must file a gift tax return. Thus, the transfer of property to the charitable trust in a charitable trust remainder sale must be reported on a gift tax return.

b. Estate Tax Return. The consideration the grantor receives from the remainder beneficiaries will be a part of the grantor's gross estate. Further, the instructions to line 12a of Form 706, the United States Estate (and Generation-Skipping Transfer) Tax Return, require the grantor's executor to attach to the estate tax return a copy of all trusts created by the grantor during his or her life (which would include the charitable trust) and to complete Form 706, Schedule G. The instructions to Schedule G, however, require the executor to list only gift tax paid on gifts made within three years of death and property transferred during the grantor's life included under IRC §§ 2035(a), 2036, 2037 or 2038. Thus, the charitable trust need not be listed on Schedule G, as the grantor will not have retained any interest in nor have any power that would cause inclusion of the trust property in his or her estate under any of the enumerated sections. The required attachment of the charitable trust agreement to the estate tax return, however, would at least disclose the existence of the trust.

M. Charitable Lead Annuity Trusts

A charitable lead annuity trust ("CLAT") is a charitable vehicle that also serves to transfer assets to family members at a reduced transfer tax cost. Future appreciation in the value of the assets transferred to the CLAT is not subject to estate or gift tax. CLATs are discussed in

21st Century Estate Planning:
Practical Applications
2005 Edition

©2005 Sonnenschein Nath & Rosenthal LLP
and Cannon Financial Institute, Inc.

- 643 -

detail in the chapter on charitable planning, so the purpose of the following brief discussion is to illustrate how CLATs can be used to leverage the difference between the assumed rate of return and the actual rate of return on the assets used to fund the CLAT.

1.   Overview of Charitable Lead Annuity Trusts

A CLAT is a "split interest" gift, which means that both a charitable beneficiary and a noncharitable beneficiary receive interests in the same property. A CLAT allows an individual (the "donor") to donate a limited interest in specific assets to a charity. The donor transfers property to an irrevocable trust that pays the designated charity a fixed dollar amount (the "lead" interest) for a certain period of time, at least annually. At the expiration of this period of time, the grantor may reclaim his or her interest in the assets or provide for the assets to be transferred to noncharitable beneficiaries. Depending upon the type of CLAT the donor elects to establish, the donor may obtain an income tax charitable deduction, and/or a gift tax charitable deduction or an estate tax charitable deduction for the present value of the charity's lead interest.

The CLAT works in a manner similar to a GRAT. The GRAT offers a potentially gift tax-free method of shifting future appreciation to beneficiaries, and the CLAT offers the same kind of benefit to individuals who want to make a gift to charity. If the rate of return on the CLAT assets exceeds the Section 7520 rate used to value the charitable gift, then the excess will be transferred to the noncharitable beneficiaries free of estate and gift tax. This is the same result that a GRAT has. The CLAT has an advantage over a GRAT because there is no mortality risk with a CLAT.

2.   Estate and Gift Tax Consequences

The charitable deduction for income, estate and gift tax purposes is equal to the present value of the charity's interest determined under Section 7520. In determining the amount of the charitable deduction, the donor is allowed to use either the rate for the month in which the gift occurs, or either of the immediately preceding two months, whichever is the most favorable. In fact, because the Section 7520 rate is published on the 20th or 21st day of the preceding month, a donor may consider four months' rates when planning the date on which to establish a CRT.

➔   **Planning Point:** The lower the Section 7520 rate, the higher the charitable deduction will be for the charity's annuity interest in a CLAT. Thus, the donor will want to use the lowest of the four months' rates.

If the CLAT is established during the donor's life, the donor is entitled to a charitable gift tax deduction for the value of the charity's interest upon the creation of the trust. If the remainder beneficiaries are individuals other than the donor, then the value of the remainder interest is a gift that is subject to gift tax when the trust is created. The remainder interest passes to the beneficiaries free of additional gift tax or estate tax, however, at the expiration of the CLAT term. If the trust is designed so that the donor receives the trust assets back at the end of the term of the trust, however, then the donor has not made a gift, and there is no gift tax. In that event, the assets of the trust will be included in the donor's gross estate for federal estate tax purposes.[11]

21st Century Estate Planning:
Practical Applications
2005 Edition

©2005 Sonnenschein Nath & Rosenthal LLP
and Cannon Financial Institute, Inc.

- 644 -

It is possible to create a CLAT for a term of years with a charitable interest equal to the entire value of the property transferred to the trust. Thus, the value of the remainder interest, which is the interest gifted to the noncharitable beneficiaries, would equal zero (a "zeroed-out CLAT"). As a result, no gift will be made to the family remaindermen even though family members may receive a substantial amount at the termination of the trust.

> **EXAMPLE:** Donor transfers $2 million to a 20-year CLAT when the Section 7520 rate is 5.4%. The CLAT is zeroed-out, and the annual payment to the charity is $165,972. The present value of the annuity payments is $2,000,000, so the value of the remainder interest is $0. Therefore, Donor would receive a gift tax charitable deduction in the amount of $2,000,000 for the charity's lead interest, and if Donor designated his children as the remainder beneficiaries, Donor would not have made a taxable gift. If the assets had a total return of 8%, then at the end of 20 years, there will be $1,726,693 available for the remainder beneficiaries.

3. GST Tax Consequences

The creation of a CLAT is not subject to GST tax. If, at the end of the term of the CLAT, the trust will terminate in favor of grandchildren or more remote descendants, such distributions will be subject to GST tax. Special rules apply to the allocation of GST exemption to a CLAT, the effect of which is to discourage clients from using a CLAT for transfers to grandchildren. The rules regarding allocating GST exemption to a CLAT are discussed in detail in the chapter on charitable planning.

➔   **Planning Point:** Because of the special GST rules, CLATs are not a good vehicle to transfer assets to grandchildren. Accordingly, to avoid the potential application of the GST tax, the trust assets should be distributed to the donor's then living children when the CLAT term ends.

21st Century Estate Planning:
Practical Applications
2005 Edition

©2005 Sonnenschein Nath & Rosenthal LLP
and Cannon Financial Institute, Inc.

- 645 -

Chapter XVII
Bibliography

Roy M. Adams, "Cutting Edge Techniques: How to Use Them Effectively," *Notre Dame Tax & Est. Plan. Inst.*, Ch. 27 (1998).

Roy M. Adams, "The Estate Planner's Bazaar: Making the Right Choices in a Confusing Market," *Notre Dame Tax & Est. Plan. Inst.*, Ch. 5 (1999).

Roy M. Adams, "Ethics at the Edge: Sophisticated Estate Planning and Professional Responsibility," *35th Annual Philip E. Heckerling Inst. on Est. Plan.*, Ch. 17 (2001).

Roy M. Adams, "Proprietary Estate Planning - For Your Eyes Only!," *Notre Dame Tax & Est. Plan. Inst.*, Ch. 21 (2000).

Ronald D. Aucutt, "Installment Sales to Grantor Trusts," SG04 ALI-ABA 1005 (November 2001).

Thomas C. Baird, "A Potpourri of Leveraged Transfers Using Defective Grantor Trusts," SG020 ALI-ABA 661 (July 2001).

Jonathan G. Blattmachr and Georgiana J. Slade, 836 T.M., *Partial Interests - GRATs, GRUTs, QPRTs (Section 2702)*.

Deborah V. Dunn, "Coming to a Wal-Mart Near You: Tax-Free GRATs," *Tr. & Est.*, p. 10 (April 2001).

David A. Handler and Deborah V. Dunn, "'Guaranteed GRATs: GRATs Without Mortality Risk," *Tr. & Est.*, p. 30 (December 1999).

David A. Handler and Deborah V. Dunn, "Tax Consequences of Outstanding Trust Liabilities When Grantor Trust Status Terminates," 95 *J. Tax'n* 49 (July 2001).

David A. Handler and Steven J. Oshins, "GRAT Remainder Sale to a Dynasty Trust," *Tr. & Est.*, p. 20 (December 1999).

Milford B. Hatcher, Jr. and Edward M. Manigault, "Using Beneficiary Guarantees in Defective Grantor Trusts," 92 *J. Tax'n* 152 (March 2000).

Jerome M. Hesch, "Coordinating Income Tax Planning With Estate Planning: Uses of Installment Sales, Private Annuities and SCINs," *36th Annual Philip E. Heckerling Inst. on Est. Plan.*, Ch. 10 (2002).

Jerome M. Hesch, "Installment Sale, SCIN and Private Annuity Sales to a Grantor Trust: Income Tax and Transfer Tax Elements," 23 *Tax Mgmt. Est., Gifts & Tr. J.* 114 (May 1998).

21st Century Estate Planning:
Practical Applications
2005 Edition

©*2005 Sonnenschein Nath & Rosenthal LLP*
and Cannon Financial Institute, Inc.

- 646 -

Harry F. Lee and David L. Silvian, "The *Walton* GRAT and Marital Deduction Planning," *Taxes*, p. 35 (July 2001).

Scott H. Malin, "Self-Cancelling Installment Notes Maintain Estate Planning Usefulness," 65 *Prac. Tax Strategies* 141 (September 2000).

Elliott Manning and Jerome M. Hesch, "Deferred Payment Sales to Grantor Trusts, GRATs and Net Gifts: Income and Transfer Tax Elements," 24 *Tax Mgmt. Est., Gifts & Tr. J.* 3 (January 1999).

Carlyn S. McCaffrey, Lloyd Leva Paine and Pam H. Schneider, "The Aftermath of *Walton*: The Rehabilitation of the Fixed-Term, Zeroed-Out GRAT," *J. Tax'n*, p. 325 (December 2001).

Carlyn S. McCaffrey and Pam H. Schneider, "Planning for GRATs and QPRTs," 301 PLI/Est 395 (February/March 2001).

Michael D. Mulligan, "Sale to a Defective Grantor Trust: An Alternative to a GRAT," 23 *Est. Plan.* 3 (January 1996).

Michael D. Mulligan, "Sale to an Intentionally Defective Irrevocable Trust for a Balloon Note - An Estate Freeze Technique Avoiding the Heat of Chapter 14?," SG027 ALI-ABA 315 (September 2001).

Frederic A. Nicholson, "Sale to a Grantor Controlled Trust: Better Than a GRAT?," *Tax Mgmt. Memo.* (February 22, 1996).

Susan K. Smith and Alfred J. Olsen, "Post-Implementation Considerations in Sophisticated Estate Planning: The End is Only the Means to the Beginning," ACTEC 1998 Summer Meeting (July 1998).

Merrie Jeanne Webel, "Private Annuity Passes Wealth to Family Members - Other Than Uncle Sam," 27 *Tax'n for Law.* 68 (September/October 1998).

Edward P. Wojnaroski, Jr., 805-2nd T.M., *Private Annuities and Self-Canceling Installment Notes*.

Howard M. Zaritsky and Ronald D. Aucutt, *Structuring Estate Freezes*, Warren, Gorham & Lamont (2nd ed. 1999).

---

[1]   For a comprehensive discussion of marital deduction planning in light of the decision in *Walton v. Comm'r*, see Harry F. Lee and David L. Silvian, "The Walton GRAT and Marital Deduction Planning," *Taxes*, p. 35 (July 2001). <u>See</u> <u>also</u> Deborah V. Dunn, "Coming To A Wal-Mart Near You: Tax-Free GRATs," *Tr. & Est.*, p. 10 (April 2001).

21st Century Estate Planning:
Practical Applications
2005 Edition

©2005 Sonnenschein Nath & Rosenthal LLP
and Cannon Financial Institute, Inc.

- 647 -

[2]   For a discussion of the generation-skipping transfer tax and the generation-skipping transfer tax exemption, see Chapter 4, Federal Generation-Skipping Transfer Tax.

[3]   For a more in-depth discussion of the transfer tax consequences of the sale, see Roy M. Adams, "Cutting Edge Techniques: How to Use Them Effectively," *Notre Dame Tax & Est. Plan. Inst.,* Ch. 27 (1998). See also David A. Handler and Steven J. Oshins, "GRAT Remainder Sale to a Dynasty Trust," *Tr. & Est.,* p. 20 (December 1999).

[4]   This section is derived from Roy M. Adams, "Ethics at the Edge: Sophisticated Estate Planning and Professional Responsibility," *35th Annual Philip E. Heckerling Inst. on Est. Plan.,* Ch. 17 (2001).

[5]   This concept was developed by the author and his former colleagues while he was a member of Kirkland & Ellis. See David A. Handler and Deborah V. Dunn, "'Guaranteed GRATs': GRATs Without Mortality Risk," *Tr. & Est.,* p. 30 (December 1999).

[6]   For a discussion of the possible income tax consequences at the grantor's death, see Michael D. Mulligan, "Sale to an Intentionally Defective Irrevocable Trust for a Balloon Note - An Estate Freeze Technique Avoiding the Heat of Chapter 14?," SG027 *ALI-ABA* 315 (September 2001), and David A. Handler and Deborah V. Dunn, "Tax Consequences of Outstanding Trust Liabilities When Grantor Trust Status Terminates," 95 *J. Tax'n* 49 (July 2001).

[7]   For a discussion of the income tax consequences at the lender's death, see Roy M. Adams, "The Estate Planner's Bazaar: Making the Right Choices in a Confusing Market," *Notre Dame Tax & Est. Plan. Inst.,* Ch. 5 (1999).

[8]   See the discussion of this issue in the section on sales to intentionally defective grantor trusts, *supra.*

[9]   See the discussion of price adjustment clauses in the section on sales to intentionally defective grantor trusts, *supra.*

[10]   This section is derived from Roy M. Adams, "Ethics at the Edge: Sophisticated Estate Planning and Professional Responsibility," *35th Annual Philip E. Heckerling Inst. on Est. Plan.,* Ch. 17 (2001). This concept was developed by the author and his former colleagues while he was a member of Kirkland & Ellis. See also Roy M. Adams, "Proprietary Estate Planning – For Your Eyes Only!," *Notre Dame Tax & Est. Plan. Inst.,* Ch. 21 (2000); David A. Handler and Deborah V. Dunn, "RPM Trusts: Turning the Table on Chapter 14," *Tr. & Est.,* p. 31 (July 2000).

21st Century Estate Planning:
Practical Applications
2005 Edition

©2005 Sonnenschein Nath & Rosenthal LLP
and Cannon Financial Institute, Inc.

- 648 -

XVIII. ETHICAL CONSIDERATIONS FOR ESTATE PLANNING PROFESSIONALS

A. Introduction

Attorneys, financial planners, accountants, fiduciaries, and other individuals practicing in the area of estate planning are presented with a variety of ethical and legal issues in their daily practice. These issues arise with respect to the practitioner's obligations to the client, to third parties, and to the public as a whole. At times, the issues take the form of the attorney's ethical obligations. Other times, the actions raise issues of negligence and malpractice. The line between ethical violations and negligence or malpractice is often blurred and confused.

The purpose of this chapter and the following two chapters is to make the practitioner aware of some of the types of ethical and legal issues that may present themselves during the course of one's practice, some of which may be obvious and others that may seem counterintuitive. Many of the issues are similar to those encountered by practitioners in other disciplines of law and some that are unique to the estate planning practitioner.

This chapter is by no means intended to cover all areas of the practitioner's ethical obligations, and the practitioner is advised to review the specific ethical rules, opinions, and cases applicable to the jurisdiction in which he is practicing and to make inquiries when any action seems questionable. It is, however, intended that the material will raise an awareness of the types of issues that may arise and provide practical suggestions to address them. The following topics are discussed in this chapter:

- Resources For Ethical Guidance
- Clients Under a Disability
- Joint Representation and Confidentiality
- Permissibility of Attorney Signing Confidentiality Agreement
- Payment of Legal Fees by Third Parties
- Attorney-Draftsman as Fiduciary or Counsel for Fiduciary
- Obligations of Attorney When Maintaining Original Documents
- Multi-Disciplinary Practice
- Payment of Referral Fees to Attorneys
- Use of E-mail to Transmit Confidential Information

B. Resources for Ethical Guidance

The ethical challenges confronting estate planning practitioners has made the need for research guidance more important today than ever before. In addressing these issues, the practitioner has available a vast number of resources from which to seek guidance and direction regarding his ethical and legal obligations. The following are some of the primary sources of ethical guidance that should be utilized by the practitioner.

21st Century Estate Planning:
Practical Applications
2005 Edition

©2005 Sonnenschein Nath & Rosenthal LLP
and Cannon Financial Institute, Inc.

- 649 -

1. Model Rules of Professional Conduct (and Comments)

The Model Rules of Professional Conduct (the "Model Rules") adopted by the American Bar Association ("ABA") in 1983 sets forth the ethical rules governing attorneys. Almost every jurisdiction has adopted the Model Rules in one form or another. The Model Rules replaced the Ethical Considerations and Disciplinary Rules of the previous Model Code of Professional Conduct. The Model Rules consists of "Rules" and "Comments." The Rules define the standard of conduct for the attorney, including whether the attorney is afforded any discretion with respect to taking any action. The Comments provide guidance and examples for complying with the Rules.

2. Model Code of Professional Responsibility

The Model Code of Professional Conduct (the "Model Code"), the predecessor to the Model Rules, was adopted by the ABA House of Delegates in 1969. The Model Code is still applicable in some states that have not adopted the Model Rules. The Model Code is divided into three parts: Canons, Disciplinary Rules, and Ethical Considerations. The Canons are defined as "axiomatic norms." The Disciplinary Rules are rules that are intended to be enforced. Ethical Considerations are aspirational standards for the attorney. Neither the Model Rules nor the Model Code have the force of law unless the state or federal court officially adopts them.

3. American College of Trusts and Estates Counsel ("ACTEC") Commentaries to the Model Rules

The American College of Trusts and Estate Counsel issued their own commentaries to the Model Rules (the "Commentaries"). The Commentaries interpret and apply the Model Rules as they affect the trusts and estates practice and provide comments to the rules as well as references to case law, ethics opinions, and articles. The stated purpose of the Commentaries is to "fill th[e] gap" resulting from the absence of sufficiently explicit guidance regarding the professional responsibilities of attorneys engaged in a trusts and estates practice.

4. Report of Ethics 2000 Commission

The ABA set up a special committee to review the Model Rules and to propose changes they deemed necessary. One of the primary stated purposes of reviewing the Model Rules was to address the growing disparity in the rules being adopted among the various states. Although most states have adopted the Model Rules, minor differences between them have become more and more prevalent.

5. Published Formal and Informal Opinions

Most state and local bar associations issue advisory opinions addressing specific ethical issues raised by attorneys regarding their practice. The opinions are generally limited to interpreting the state's applicable ethical rules. The opinions can be either formal or informal. Formal opinions deal with broad general issues while informal opinions address specific facts. In most states, ethics opinions are advisory only and are not binding.

21st Century Estate Planning:
Practical Applications
2005 Edition

©2005 Sonnenschein Nath & Rosenthal LLP
and Cannon Financial Institute, Inc.

- 650 -

In addition, the ABA Standing Committee on Ethics and Professional Responsibility issues opinions that interpret the Model Rules and the Model Code and provide practical guidance to the practitioner. The opinions are not enforceable as a matter of law but are intended to provide useful guidelines for the attorney's conduct. As with state and local bar association opinions, these opinions are divided into formal and informal opinions.

6. State and Federal Cases

Often, the line between what are the attorney's ethical obligations and what may constitute the attorney's legal obligations, for which the attorney may be disciplined or held civilly liable, is litigated in state and federal court. The holdings in these cases have the force of law and can be used in litigation or disciplinary proceedings.

The practitioner is encouraged to familiarize himself with the sources cited above, as well as the myriad of other primary and secondary resources available, in order to better identify the important issues. As with all areas of the law, the first step is to understand and identify the issues; the next step is to resolve them. A sampling of resources, many of which are available on the Internet, are found at the end of this chapter.

7. Other Codes of Conduct

Finally, accountants, financial planners, insurance agents and other individuals practicing in the area of estate planning are subject to the standards of conduct pronounced by the various organizations governing their respective practices: AICPA Code of Professional Conduct, Code of Ethics of the Association of Life Underwriters, Code of the American Society of CLU and ChFC, Code of Professional Ethics of the International Association of Financial Planners and Model Standards of Practice for Charitable Gift Planners.

C. Clients Under a Disability

1. Relevant Issues

The estate planning practitioner is often asked to represent clients whose mental capacity is questionable. Often, though not exclusively, this occurs in the representation of the elderly and infirm. The following are a few of the questions that can arise:

- What are the attorney's ethical obligations to such a client?
- May the attorney discuss the client's condition with family members?
- May the attorney reveal confidences disclosed by the incompetent client? If so, to whom?
- Does the attorney have an obligation to see that a guardian is appointed?
- Under what circumstances is the attorney permitted to let the client sign a will or other dispositive document?

21st Century Estate Planning:
Practical Applications
2005 Edition

©2005 Sonnenschein Nath & Rosenthal LLP
and Cannon Financial Institute, Inc.

- 651 -

2. Model Rule 1.14

Model Rule 1.14(a) makes it clear that the attorney's duty to the client does not end simply because the client may be disabled. Specifically, the Rule provides that the attorney should "as far as reasonably possible, maintain a normal client-lawyer relationship with the client." This includes maintaining adequate communication with the client to determine the client's objectives and goals and the ways in which to achieve them.

If the attorney determines that a normal attorney-client relationship cannot be maintained, Model Rule 1.14(b) permits the attorney to take steps to protect the client's interests. This may, depending on the circumstances, include seeking guidance from medical diagnosticians or others to ascertain the client's mental state or petitioning the court for the appointment of a guardian.

3. Revealing Confidences of a Disabled Client

Most state ethics opinions have espoused relaxing the confidentiality requirements of the attorney if the attorney determines it to be in the client's best interests. Various jurisdictions, however, have expressed different opinions as to the point at which the attorney may reveal the confidence and to whom the confidence may be revealed. Illinois State Bar ASN, Op 00-02 (2000) (attorney may not reveal confidences to parent unless attorney is of the opinion that the adult client is disabled to the extent a guardian should be appointed; however, attorney may consult with physician); Alabama Op. 90-12 (1990) (attorney for an incompetent client may reveal confidences to an independent diagnostician without the consent of the client); Oregon Op. 1991-41 (1991) (attorney authorized to disclose confidential communications to family members in order to avoid more extreme protective actions); Pa. Bar Ass'n Comm. on Legal Ethics and Prof'l Responsibility, Informal Op. 90-89 (1990) (confidentiality should be protected at least until the lawyer determines that it is necessary to seek appointment of a guardian); Nassau County (NY) Bar Ass'n, Op. 90-17 (1990) (attorney's consultations with client, including the attorney's observations about the client's competency, may not be revealed to the client's family members).

The Ethics 2000 Commission recommended adding an additional paragraph to Rule 1.14 that provides as follows:

> Information relating to the representation of a client with diminished capacity is protected by Rule 1.6. When taking protective action pursuant to paragraph (b), the lawyer is impliedly authorized under Rule 1.6(a) to reveal information about the client, <u>but only to the extent reasonably necessary to protect the client's interests</u>. (emphasis added).

The comments to the Commission's report provide that the ability to disclose confidences is not open-ended and should generally be limited to situations where the client is at risk of substantial physical, financial or other harm unless action is taken and cannot adequately act in his own interest. "At the very least, the lawyer should determine whether it is likely that the person or entity consulted with will act adversely to the client's interests before discussing matters related

21st Century Estate Planning:
Practical Applications
2005 Edition

©2005 Sonnenschein Nath & Rosenthal LLP
and Cannon Financial Institute, Inc.

- 652 -

to the client." See also ABA Informal Opinion 89-1530 (1989) (Model Rule 1.6 impliedly authorizes an attorney to consult with a physician regarding client's disability).

> *Query*: What if the attorney concludes that the best interests of the client would be adverse to the express directions of the client made to the attorney prior to becoming disabled (*i.e.*, client previously advised attorney not to discuss mental capacity with family members)?

4. Recommending Appointment of Guardian

The appointment of a guardian for an individual is an extreme measure and should not be undertaken lightly.

a. Rule 1.14. Rule 1.14 gives the attorney discretion to seek the appointment of a guardian only when the lawyer reasonably believes that the client cannot adequately act in the client's own interest. Of importance is the discretionary wording of Rule 1.14. The intent is for the attorney to consider all of the options to determine what is in the client's best interests. See New York State Bar Association Committee on Professional Ethics, Opinion Number 746 (July 18, 2001) (attorney who serves as the client's attorney-in-fact may petition for the appointment of a guardian without the client's consent only if the lawyer determines that the client is incapacitated and that there is no practical alternative through the use of the power of attorney or otherwise, to protect the client's best interests). See also ABA Formal Opinion 96-404 (August 2, 1996).

b. Minority View. A minority view was held in California State Bar Standing Committee on Professional Responsibility and Conduct, Formal Opinion No. 1989-112 (1989) (it was held unethical for attorney to institute a conservatorship proceeding for a client he believed to be incompetent if against the client's express wishes and doing so would require the attorney to violate his client's confidences and represent potentially conflicting interests, notwithstanding attorney's view that it would be in client's best interests; attorney may withdraw under the circumstances). See also L.A. Opinion 450 (1988) (attorney may not institute a conservatorship proceeding without permission from the client).

c. Attorney's Role. Generally, if a guardian is appointed, the attorney should assist the guardian to benefit the ward. However, if the attorney representing the disabled client reasonably believes that the guardian is not acting in the ward's best interests, the attorney may be obligated to act contrary to the guardian to protect the client's interests. See *In re Makarewicz*, 516 N.W.2d 90 (Mich. App. 1984) (an attorney representing a guardian who becomes aware that the guardian is acting adverse to the ward has an obligation to prevent or rectify the guardian's misconduct). See also Alaska Ethics Op. 87-2 (1987).

5. Take Least Restrictive Measure

a. Protective Measures. The principal rule when representing disabled clients is to act in the client's best interests. This includes taking the least restrictive measures under the circumstances. See ABA Opinion 96-404. The ABA ethics committee ("Committee") addressed

21st Century Estate Planning:
Practical Applications
2005 Edition

©2005 Sonnenschein Nath & Rosenthal LLP
and Cannon Financial Institute, Inc.

- 653 -

various questions encountered by attorneys who serve disabled clients, including whether consultation with family or others might be appropriate or allowable, when should the attorney petition the court for the appointment of a guardian, and when should the attorney withdraw from representation? The Committee responded to each of the issues and, while giving the attorney broad discretion when representing a disabled client, instructed the attorney to use the least restrictive alternatives.

> "[T]he principle of respecting the client's autonomy dictates that the action taken by the lawyer…should be the action that it reasonably views as the least restrictive under the circumstances."

b. <u>Withdrawal</u>. The Committee advised that withdrawing from representation is disfavored, "even if ethically permissible under the circumstances."

6. Drafting Estate Planning Documents for an Incompetent Client

An attorney drafting estate planning documents for a client must ascertain that the client has the requisite mental capacity to execute the specific document in question. The attorney must keep in mind that the mental capacity required for executing various documents may not be identical. For example, the capacity needed for executing a will differs from the capacity for executing a contract. Additionally, the state of mind of the client at the time the document is executed must be ascertained. This is of critical importance for the client who may go in and out of various stages of dementia.

If the attorney believes a client is incapable of acting rationally, the attorney should not allow the client to sign the document. If the client is experiencing a lucid moment, however, the attorney is advised to document the occurrence and, if possible, to have witnesses to the execution. The Commentaries to Rule 1.14 provide:

> [B]ecause of the importance of testamentary freedom, the lawyer may properly assist clients whose testamentary capacity appears borderline. In such a case the lawyer should take steps to preserve evidence regarding the client's testamentary capacity.

In the case of a will, it is helpful for the attorney to read parts of the will out loud and to ask if the client understands what the attorney is reading. This should be balanced with the client's right to have the contents of the document kept confidential.

> *Query:* Is the attorney obligated to dissuade the client from appointing a fiduciary of her choice that is incapable of handling the client's affairs? Should it matter if the attorney has knowledge of the proposed fiduciary's inability? What if the client has the requisite capacity to execute the document but has limited mental ability? <u>See</u> *Persinger v. Holst*, 639 N.W.2d (Ct. App. Mich 2002) (attorney has no obligation to ensure that the client appoints an appropriate fiduciary).

21st Century Estate Planning:
Practical Applications
2005 Edition

©2005 Sonnenschein Nath & Rosenthal LLP
and Cannon Financial Institute, Inc.

- 654 -

→ **Planning Point:** An attorney who has doubts as to the mental capacity of a client should take the time to interview the client to see if the client has the requisite capacity. If the attorney cannot assess the client's capacity, it is permissible to seek guidance from appropriate diagnosticians. As a general rule, once the attorney is satisfied that a disability is present, the attorney should take whatever further steps he deems necessary to preserve the interests of the client. This may entail recommending that a guardian be appointed or disclosing, in limited circumstances, a client's confidences. Whatever action the attorney chooses to take, the attorney must first determine that it is in the client's best interests and should only act in a way that minimizes the adverse consequences to the client.

D. Joint Representation and Confidentiality

1. Duty to Disclose Confidences?

Perhaps the greatest and most ubiquitous ethical issue confronting practitioners in the trusts and estates area is the subject of joint representations and the obligations of the attorney to each of the parties. The most common joint representation is that of a husband and wife who come to an attorney to arrange for their estate plan, although it can also arise in multi-generational planning (*e.g.*, parents and children) or among different members of a corporation or partnership the attorney is representing.

Among the many problems that can arise is the issue of confidences that are revealed to the attorney by one party that are intended by that party to be kept confidential from the other party. An attorney put in this predicament is confronted with the following dilemma: Should the attorney (i) reveal the confidence, (ii) encourage the client to reveal the confidence, (iii) withdraw from the engagement for one or both parties, or (iv) not reveal the confidence and continue on with the representation?

Absent an express agreement among the parties to the contrary, the correct answer may very well depend on where the attorney is practicing.

2. Attorney Entitled to Disclose

This issue was presented in *A v. B v. Hill Wallack*, 726 A.2d 924 (New Jersey 1999).

In October 1997, the law firm of Hill Wallack was retained to jointly represent husband and wife in drafting their wills. Husband and wife each signed a "Waiver of Conflict of Interest" document and consented to and waived any conflict of interest that may arise. There was no express waiver, however, of the confidentiality of any information that may be told to the attorneys.

In January 1998, prior to the execution by the husband and wife of their wills, the mother of an illegitimate child of the husband (not wife) retained Hill Wallack to commence a paternity suit against the husband. At the time of the representation by the mother, the attorneys at Hill

21st Century Estate Planning:
Practical Applications
2005 Edition

©2005 Sonnenschein Nath & Rosenthal LLP
and Cannon Financial Institute, Inc.

- 655 -

Wallack who represented the husband and wife in connection with their estate planning were not aware of the conflict between the husband and the mother.

After the paternity suit was filed, the husband and wife signed their wills. Subsequently, Hill Wallack became aware of the conflict between the mother and husband and withdrew as attorneys for the mother. The firm then wrote to the husband and stated its view that it had an ethical obligation to inform the wife of the existence of the illegitimate child. The husband sued Hill Wallack to prevent it from disclosing any such information to the wife.

The court examined the New Jersey rules of professional conduct and concluded that the firm was entitled, but not required, to disclose the existence (but not identity) of the child. The court arrived at this conclusion because it held that the husband's deliberate omission of the existence of the child was a fraud on his wife. In addition, the court believed that the husband's child support requirements and other financial responsibilities towards the child could affect distributions to the wife or her estate.

The court rejected imposing an obligation on the firm to make any disclosure to the wife. It suggested that an attorney commencing the joint representation of co-clients should explicitly agree with the clients regarding the sharing of confidential information.

3. Attorney Not Entitled to Disclose

The court in *A v. B v. Hill Wallack* noted the contrary positions taken by New York and Florida whereby each <u>prohibited</u> the disclosure of confidential information obtained during the course of a joint representation. <u>See</u> New York State Bar Assn Comm. on Professional Ethics, Op. 555 (1984); Florida State Bar Assn Comm. on Professional Ethics, Op. No. 95-4 (1997).

a. <u>New York</u>. The New York opinion addressed the situation where A and B employed an attorney to represent them in connection with the formation and operation of a partnership. B then told the attorney in confidence that he was actively breaching the partnership agreement. The court held that the attorney may not disclose the confidential communication to A in the absence of B's consent.

b. <u>Florida</u>. The Florida opinion dealt with the case of an attorney who represented both husband and wife in a range of personal matters, including estate planning. Several months after the wills were executed, the husband informed the attorney that he had executed a codicil prepared by another law firm that made substantial provisions for a woman with whom he was having an extramarital relationship. The court held that, not only was the attorney not obligated to inform the wife of the new information, he did not have the discretion to do so. The attorney was then required to withdraw as attorney for both parties.

4. ACTEC Position – Attorney Entitled to Disclose

The Commentaries concur in giving the attorney discretion in determining how to respond. <u>See</u> Commentaries at 120. The attorney is first encouraged to advise the client to voluntarily reveal the confidence, and should make the client aware of the possible consequences

21st Century Estate Planning:
Practical Applications
2005 Edition

©2005 Sonnenschein Nath & Rosenthal LLP
and Cannon Financial Institute, Inc.

- 656 -

of not revealing the confidence. If the client refuses to reveal the confidence, the attorney should determine if he should reveal the confidence and whether he should withdraw from representing one or both clients.

5.   Attorney Obligated to Disclose

Some states have modified their rules to require an attorney to reveal confidences in certain joint representation situations. See Hawaii Rule of Professional Conduct 1.6(b), which provides, in pertinent part, that "[a]n attorney shall reveal information which clearly establishes a criminal or fraudulent act of the client in the furtherance of which the lawyer's services had been used, to the extent reasonably necessary to rectify the consequences of such act, where the act has resulted in substantial injury to the financial interests or property of another." The attorney will be put in the difficult position of determining what conduct falls under this standard. For example, what if the client who discloses to the attorney of an intent to change his will only changed his mind after the original will was signed? Does the subsequent change of mind imply that a fraud is being committed?

6.   Parent-Child Joint Representation

A similar conflict may arise in situations where an attorney represents both a parent and child. See *Chase v. Bowen*, 771 So.2d 1181 (Ct App. Florida 2000).

In *Chase*, an attorney from time-to-time represented a mother and daughter in connection with their respective estate planning and business needs. The attorney initially prepared a will for the mother naming her daughter as beneficiary. The attorney subsequently revised the mother's estate planning documents to omit the daughter as a beneficiary. After the mother died, the daughter sued the attorney for breaching his duty as "her lawyer." The court, holding that no such duty existed to the daughter, stated the following:

> If an attorney prepares the wills of various members of a family, he thereby assumes no obligation to oppose any testator or testatrix from changing such will. Nor is he precluded from assisting such testator or testatrix in the redrafting.... It is our view that an attorney who prepares a will owes no duty to any previous beneficiary, even a beneficiary he may be representing in another matter, to oppose the testator or testatrix in changing his or her will and, therefore, that assisting in that change is not a conflict of interest.

In this particular case, there was no evidence that the attorney was retained to jointly represent the mother and daughter.

21st Century Estate Planning:
Practical Applications
2005 Edition

©*2005 Sonnenschein Nath & Rosenthal LLP*
and Cannon Financial Institute, Inc.

- 657 -

7. Sign Engagement Letters

The attorney is strongly encouraged not to commence any representation of multiple clients without first disclosing the potential conflicts to each client and having the clients sign an engagement letter that carefully details the relationship and obligations of each of the parties.

a. Show and Tell Approach

The first approach is for each party to execute an engagement letter that states there will be joint representation and that specifies clearly that the attorney may reveal all confidences to either party and that no information may be withheld. This representation is referred to as a "show and tell approach." Appended to the end of this chapter is suggested language to include in the engagement letter that would cover this situation for joint representation of a married couple. A similar approach could be used for parent-child joint representation.

b. Priestly Approach

The alternative is for the attorney to represent the parties jointly (or separately) but be specifically prohibited from revealing any confidences. This approach has been referred to as the "priestly" approach. The priestly approach is fraught with potential conflicts and may result in the attorney having to withdraw as attorney for one or both clients if a conflict arises (*e.g.,* one spouse informs the attorney of his intention to withdraw all funds held as joint tenants).

➔ **Planning Point:** The relative uncertainty in this ethical conundrum strongly advocates that any attorney contemplating a joint representation arrange for each party to execute an engagement letter expressly stating whether the representation will be joint or several and also including instructions for the attorney in the event that confidences revealed by one of the parties conflict with the best interests of the other party.

E. Permissibility of Attorney Signing Confidentiality Agreement

1. General

An attorney has an ethical duty to provide competent and informed legal services to each of his clients. If the representation of one client restricts the attorney's ability to provide the same services to another client, a conflict of interest exists.

On occasion, attorneys are asked by clients to review "novel" or "innovative" tax packages presented to the client by accountants and financial advisors who then demand that the attorney sign a confidentiality agreement. The ramifications of signing such agreements impact both the client with respect to whom the confidentiality agreement is being signed <u>and</u> the attorney's other clients, both present and future.

Query: Does the fact that an attorney signs a confidentiality agreement required by an accounting firm that would prohibit the attorney from divulging a package of ideas developed by the accounting firm that may reduce one client's tax obligations create a conflict of interest to

21st Century Estate Planning:
Practical Applications
2005 Edition

©2005 Sonnenschein Nath & Rosenthal LLP
and Cannon Financial Institute, Inc.

- 658 -

the attorney's other clients (to whom the attorney would be contractually prohibited from revealing the information)?

2. Prohibition Against Signing Agreements

The ethical ability of the attorney to sign such agreements was addressed in Illinois State Bar Association, Opinion No. 00-01 (October 2000).

The Illinois State Bar Association ("Association") started with the assumption that the package of ideas included interpretations and applications of tax laws that would also be useful to the attorney in helping other clients. The tax information was distinguished from other types of information that an attorney may keep in confidence, such as a manufacturing process that may be disclosed to an attorney while he is conducting a due diligence investigation. The Association stated that in such cases:

> the industry related proprietary information might be beneficial to other clients whom the lawyer represents in the same industry. This information would not, however, be useful to the lawyer in performing legal services.

The Association concluded that if an attorney were to sign such an agreement, he would have a conflict of interest in representing other clients pursuant to Illinois Rule 1.7(b), which states as follows:

> A lawyer shall not represent a client if the representation of that client may be materially limited by the lawyer's responsibility to another client or to a third person, or by the lawyer's own interests, unless:
>
> (1) The lawyer reasonably believes that the representation will not be adversely affected; and
>
> (2) The client consents to the disclosure.

Since it was recognized that an attorney could not reasonably assume that withholding material tax strategies would not adversely affect other clients, a conflict was found. It also seemed unlikely any client would consent to an attorney withholding such information.

Accordingly, the Association concluded that it would not be permissible for an attorney to sign a confidentiality agreement whereby the attorney agrees not to divulge material tax strategies to other clients.

➔ **Planning Point:** If presented with a confidentiality agreement, the attorney should explain the ethical issues involved to the provider of the information and should resist signing it. If the provider of the information insists that the attorney sign the agreement, the attorney should at the very

21st Century Estate Planning:
Practical Applications
2005 Edition

©2005 Sonnenschein Nath & Rosenthal LLP
and Cannon Financial Institute, Inc.

- 659 -

least try to limit the scope of the non-disclosure in a way that is least restrictive to other clients.

F. Payment of Legal Fees by Third Parties

1. General Rule

It is not unusual for an attorney to be asked to represent a client and for a third party to pay the legal fees. This frequently occurs when the attorney is asked by a corporation to prepare estate planning documents for an officer or director or by a parent for a child. The general rule is that an attorney and client may enter into an arrangement whereby the legal fees incurred for the client's estate planning are paid by a third party.

2. Model Rule 1.8(f)

Model Rule 1.8(f) provides that an attorney may accept compensation from someone other than the client if: (1) the client consents after consultation, (2) there is no interference with the attorney's independence of professional judgment or the attorney-client relationship, and (3) the client's confidences are protected. See also Model Rule 5.4(c) (a person who pays the attorney may not direct or regulate the attorney's professional judgment).

Regardless of who pays the fees, the person for whom the services are being provided is the client, and the attorney owes that person a duty of loyalty and care.

> *Query:* What if the client, during the course of the representation, reveals a confidence that may be adverse to the party paying the fees? What if that third party is also a client of the attorney? Does the attorney owe any duties to the party paying the legal fees? (The potential conflicts of interest during multiple representations were discussed earlier in this chapter.)

The attorney should obtain an engagement letter that sets forth the attorney's obligations to each client and the scope of the representation.

3. Payment of Personal Legal Fees by Corporation

a. Proper Disclosure. In ABA Informal Opinion 86-1517 (February 9, 1986), the ABA re-addressed the issue of whether an attorney may bill a corporate client for personal non-corporate legal services furnished to an employee, officer, director, or shareholder of the corporation when the corporation requests that the bill should not identify the services as personal services and the charge for the services.

The Opinion superceded ABA Informal Opinion 1494. In Opinion 1494, the ABA opined that if an attorney is asked by a corporation to furnish them with the bill for non-corporate legal services performed for the corporation's sole shareholder without specifying the nature of the work, the attorney has a duty to inquire of the client the purpose of this request and,

21st Century Estate Planning:
Practical Applications
2005 Edition

©2005 Sonnenschein Nath & Rosenthal LLP
and Cannon Financial Institute, Inc.

- 660 -

if the attorney is not satisfied with the client's intended use for tax purposes, the attorney should not provide such a bill.

The Committee concluded that, regardless of any explanation provided by the client of the reason for the request, the attorney should not provide such a bill. In changing its position, the Committee stated:

> Submission to the corporation of a bill which includes personal services to the shareholder without identifying those services as personal services ... may, under the circumstances, constitute assistance to the client in conduct that the lawyer knows is criminal and fraudulent and is at least conduct involving deceit or misrepresentation by the lawyer.
>
> Thus, even though it might be argued that the lawyer does not actually "know" that the conduct of the client will be criminal or fraudulent, the facts would ordinarily present a sufficiently clear indication of criminal or fraudulent intent that the billing, without identification of the personal nature of the services and the charge applicable to them would violate [the rules].

b. Uncertainty as to Nature of Work. Very often, work performed by an attorney may qualify as either personal in nature or corporate-related. For example, an attorney restructuring a closely-held company and the ownership thereof may be performing personal estate planning work and legitimate corporate work. What if the attorney, as part of the restructuring plan, prepares a family limited partnership and different trusts to facilitate the new ownership structure? Should it matter if the restructuring itself is done solely for estate planning purposes? What portion is estate planning and what portion is corporate-related? These issues can arise whether the fees are being paid by the client or by a third party.

➔ **Planning Point:** The attorney should obtain the written consent of the client if the fees are to be paid by a third party. In addition, the engagement letter should clearly state who the client is and should address the treatment of confidences revealed by the client. The attorney should also protect himself by advising the client in advance that the attorney will clearly and separately identify in the bill the nature of the work done and the amount billed for such work. Finally, the attorney should discuss in advance with the client what work the attorney and client believe can properly be classified as business related work and what should be classified as personal.

21st Century Estate Planning:
Practical Applications
2005 Edition

©2005 Sonnenschein Nath & Rosenthal LLP
and Cannon Financial Institute, Inc.

- 661 -

G. Attorney-Draftsman as Fiduciary or Counsel for Fiduciary

1. General

A client is entitled to name the attorney preparing his will or other document as fiduciary, provided that the attorney discloses to the client: (a) the role and duties of the fiduciary, (b) that the client may appoint a non-attorney as fiduciary with legal and other assistance, (c) the comparative cost of appointing the attorney or another person or entity as fiduciary, and (d) the manner in which the attorney is to be compensated. It is not unethical for an attorney to accept the appointment. The attorney, however, should not suggest to the client that the attorney be appointed as fiduciary. To do so may constitute improper solicitation and the exercise of undue influence.

a. **Code of Professional Responsibility EC 5-6**. EC 5-6 provides that "[a] lawyer should not consciously influence a client to name the lawyer as executor, trustee, or lawyer in an instrument. In those cases where the client wishes to name the lawyer as such, care should be taken by the lawyer to avoid even the appearance of impropriety." There is no similar provision in the Model Rules.

b. **Commentaries to Model Rule 1.7**. The Commentaries provide that an attorney should be free to prepare documents that appoint the lawyer as fiduciary so long as the client is properly informed, the appointment does not violate any conflict of interest, and the appointment is not the result of any undue influence or improper solicitation by the attorney.

c. **ISBA Ethics Advisory Opinion No. 99-08 (1999)**. An attorney may prepare a trust agreement that, at the client's request, directs the trustee to retain that attorney to provide legal services for the trust. The attorney may follow the directions of the client only if the client consents after the attorney fully discloses the economic interest of the attorney in serving as counsel and indicates that such provision might not be enforceable.

➔ **Planning Point:** It should be noted that many traditional trusts and estates attorneys have an implied understanding with their clients that the client would be minimally charged for their estate planning work with the intention that the attorney would be substantially remunerated for such work when the client's estate is probated, either by acting as fiduciary or counsel to the fiduciary. It is recommended that the attorney document this understanding in a memorandum to the client in order to avoid any appearance of impropriety.

2. Attorney Acting as Executor and Attorney for Estate

An attorney named as fiduciary is not ethically prohibited from naming himself or his firm as attorney for the estate. The attorney, however, is advised to take steps to inform the beneficiaries of the attorney's dual role and should maintain meticulous records and timesheets documenting the work that is intended to be billed as legal fees. See Virginia Legal Ethics Opinion 1515 (1993) (an attorney-draftsman may be named as executor or as the attorney with

21st Century Estate Planning:
Practical Applications
2005 Edition

©2005 Sonnenschein Nath & Rosenthal LLP
and Cannon Financial Institute, Inc.

- 662 -

whom the fiduciary should consult, provided that the attorney fully discloses in writing to the client the potential fees that he will be entitled to prior to the execution of the will or trust agreement; attorney may not initiate suggestion that he be named fiduciary). It is equally important to inform the client in advance if the attorney intends to employ his law firm to represent the estate.

> *Query:* If the work done by the attorney-fiduciary can be properly classified as both legal and fiduciary work, is the attorney entitled to pay himself in that capacity (*e.g.,* transferring assets held by the estate to the beneficiaries)? Although the fiduciary may be within his right to pay an independent attorney to perform such services, it is advisable for the attorney-fiduciary not to pay himself under those circumstances without first receiving court approval or consent from the beneficiaries.

A number of states have passed legislation restricting the right of an attorney serving in a fiduciary capacity to recover compensation for providing legal services.

a. New York Rule. New York allows an attorney-draftsman to be paid as both an executor and an attorney for the estate if the attorney obtains a written acknowledgment from the client, either prior to or after signing the will, that the attorney can be paid a commission for acting as executor and a separate fee for acting as the attorney for the estate. New York Surrogate's Court Procedures Act Section 2307-a. In the absence of such an acknowledgment, the attorney can only receive one-half the statutory commission to which the attorney would otherwise be entitled.

b. California. California Probate Code Section §10804 ("Estate Attorney Acting as Personal Representative—Court Approval of Compensation") provides as follows:

> Notwithstanding any provision in the decedent's will, a personal representative who is an attorney may receive the personal representative's compensation, but shall not receive compensation for services as the attorney for the personal representative unless the court specifically approves the right to the compensation in advance and finds that the arrangement is to the advantage, benefit, and best interests of the decedent's estate.

➜ **Planning Point:** The attorney should advise the client that he is entitled to name anyone he chooses as fiduciary, including the attorney. The attorney should <u>not</u> suggest that he be appointed as fiduciary. If the client wishes for the attorney to act as fiduciary, the attorney should disclose to the client, preferably in writing, the responsibilities that the attorney will undertake as fiduciary, the fees payable to the attorney as fiduciary, that the attorney may act as counsel to the estate or trust, and that the attorney will be entitled to be paid for acting as such in addition to the fees payable as fiduciary.

21st Century Estate Planning:
Practical Applications
2005 Edition

©2005 Sonnenschein Nath & Rosenthal LLP
and Cannon Financial Institute, Inc.

- 663 -

H. Obligations of Attorney When Maintaining Original Documents

1.   General

It is commonplace for attorneys practicing in the trusts and estates field to maintain in a special vault the original wills and certain other estate planning documents of those clients for whom they have drafted the documents. Absent any express agreement to the contrary, does the attorney have any obligations when he learns that the client has died?

Generally, the obligations of an attorney who maintains original documents are determined by the agreement between the attorney and client. These obligations may arise if there are *express* or *implied* agreements or understandings between the client and the attorney in regard to the attorney's duties and responsibilities in relation to the will. The attorney and client may agree that the attorney will undertake the responsibility to learn of the client's death (*e.g.*, by reading death notices) or that the attorney, upon learning of the client's death, will file the will with the appropriate court.

2.   Implied Understanding

An implied understanding may exist if the attorney has in the past undertaken a greater role in the handling of the client's estate planning matters. This is more likely to occur where the attorney has regular contact with the client and performs ongoing services as is often the case with high net-worth clients.

3.   Obligation to Inform Beneficiaries/Executor

In New York Eth. Op. 724, N.Y. St. Bar Assn. Comm. Prof. Eth. (November 30, 1999), the Committee concluded that, in the absence of an agreement, if the attorney has maintained the client's original will, after the client's death, the attorney must assure that the executor and/or beneficiaries are aware of its existence, unless the attorney knows of a later valid will. The attorney, however, does <u>not</u> have an obligation to take steps to learn of the client's death or to file the original will with an appropriate court.

4.   Additional Obligations

At least one jurisdiction has imposed a greater obligation on the attorney who drafts a will and retains the original where the named executor refuses to file the will. <u>See</u> Pennsylvania Ethics Opinion 97-66 (1997).

The husband, the named executor, refused to probate the will. The husband, however, provided the attorney with some information for the inheritance tax return, and therefore entered into an attorney-client relationship with the attorney.

The Committee held that an "attorney who has drafted a will and is still in possession of it after death has an absolute obligation to take steps to see that the will is given effect." Such an

21st Century Estate Planning:
Practical Applications
2005 Edition

©2005 Sonnenschein Nath & Rosenthal LLP
and Cannon Financial Institute, Inc.

- 664 -

obligation was deemed to fall within the scope of Rule 8.4(d) which forbids an attorney from "[engaging] in conduct that is prejudicial to the administration of justice."

The attorney was directed to inform all the beneficiaries of the will of their interest thereunder. In addition, the attorney was encouraged to warn the husband of the attorney's actions and to ask him to seriously reconsider. If the husband demands that the attorney give him the will, the attorney must decline and either retain it or file the will with the court. Finally, unless the executor is completely cooperative, it was suggested that the attorney resign as the attorney settling the estate.

5. Other Estate Planning Documents

The extent that an obligation will be imposed on attorneys who retain other types of documents has not been addressed. For example, does an attorney who keeps an original insurance trust agreement in his files obligate himself to insure that the terms of the trust agreement are carried out upon the grantor's death? Should it matter if the trustees refuse to carry out their fiduciary responsibilities? Should it matter if the document is a health-care proxy or power of attorney?

➔ **Planning Point:** It is advisable for an attorney who drafts wills and other estate planning documents and who intends to maintain the originals of such documents for safekeeping to agree with his clients in advance what obligations the attorney is assuming, such as whether, after the client's death the attorney must assure that the executor and/or beneficiaries are aware of its existence and, for that matter, whether the attorney has a duty to inquire as to the health of the client.

I. Multi-Disciplinary Practice

1. General

One of the most contentious contemporary subjects confronting members of the legal profession is whether to allow attorneys to engage in business relationships with non-attorneys.

Query: Should an attorney be able to enter into a contractual relationship with an insurance agent whereby the attorney refers clients to the insurance agent and receives a fee for assisting in the sale of insurance? Should it matter if the attorney then separately charges the client for legal work done in connection with the client's estate planning needs?

This is especially important because of the proliferation of non-attorneys offering clients more and more services formerly the domain of the estate planning attorney (*i.e.*, almost every large accounting firm, trust company and investment bank today has an estate planning advisory and consulting group).

21st Century Estate Planning:
Practical Applications
2005 Edition

©2005 Sonnenschein Nath & Rosenthal LLP
and Cannon Financial Institute, Inc.

- 665 -

The basic ethical issues are whether or not such a relationship would compromise the obligations of the attorney to act with independent judgment and solely in the best interests of the client and would it raise insurmountable conflicts of interest and confidentiality issues.

Two schools of thought have developed in this area. One adheres to the historical view that the attorney's special relationship with the client should preclude the attorney from participating in any business relationship with a non-attorney that may raise the appearance of the attorney compromising his duty of loyalty to the client. The other believes that it is essential to the legal profession's economic viability and protection to allow attorneys to engage in contractual relationships with non-attorneys, provided that the interests of the client are protected.

2. New York Takes the Lead

New York has become the first state in the country to provide regulations allowing attorneys to participate in multi-disciplinary practices and to enter into contractual relationships and business alliances with non-attorneys.

The new rules create a regulatory framework that balances the attorney's ability to engage in financial relationships with non-attorneys while at the same time establishing the circumstances under which the attorney would remain subject to the ethical obligations governing the attorney's legal activities. It should be emphasized that the new rules permit, under various circumstances, attorney and non-attorney to enter into a relationship for the provision of <u>non-legal services</u>, but do not allow the attorney and non-attorney to enter into a relationship to provide <u>legal services</u> or for the non-attorney to share in legal fees.

The new rules have taken the form of two new Disciplinary Rules: DR 1-106 and DR 1-107.

DR 1-106 identifies the circumstances under which the attorney or law firm entering into the business of providing non-legal services remains subject to the Disciplinary Rules applicable to the provision of legal services. These circumstances include: (i) if the non-legal services provided by the attorney are not distinct from legal services, or (ii) if the client could "reasonably believe" that the non-legal services are the subject of an attorney-client relationship. The attorney can avoid application of the Disciplinary Rules in the latter situation by providing the client with a written statement that the services are non-legal and that they are not subject to the attorney-client privilege. DR 1-106 also prohibits a non-attorney from directing or regulating the attorney or law firm in the rendering of any legal services, or otherwise compromising the attorney's duties with respect to the client's confidences and secrets.

DR 1-107 first reinforces the attorney's traditional obligations to the client and provides that an attorney may "enter into and maintain a contractual relationship with a nonlegal professional or nonlegal professional service firm for the purpose of offering to the public, on a systematic and continuing basis, legal services performed by the lawyer or law firm, as well as other nonlegal professional services ...."; provided that certain requirements governing the type of person with whom the attorney may enter into a relationship are followed. The Rules require

21st Century Estate Planning:
Practical Applications
2005 Edition

©2005 Sonnenschein Nath & Rosenthal LLP
and Cannon Financial Institute, Inc.

- 666 -

that the profession of the non-attorney be on an approved list, that the non-attorneys have a certain level of education (including a bachelor's degree or equivalent), that the non-attorney be licensed by an agency of New York state or the federal government), that the non-attorney be subject to ethical requirements comparable to those of the legal profession, and that the non-attorney may not have any ownership interest in or right to control the legal aspects of the attorney's practice nor may the non-attorney share in legal fees.

a. **Relation to Other Ethical Rules**.

New York also modified the Rules relating to attorney advertising, the dissemination of professional notices and letterhead, and solicitation of clients to take into account the new Rules. Of particular note is the rule that the attorney is prohibited from giving any financial or other benefit for giving or receiving referrals to or from non-attorneys or from sharing legal fees.

b. **Consent Requirements**.

Finally, the Rules require the attorney, prior to the commencement of legal representation of a client referred by a non-legal service provider or prior to the referral of an existing client to a non-legal service provider, to provide the client with a statement of his rights and a disclosure of the attorney's relationship with the non-attorney. See DR Section 1205.4 ("Statement of Client's Rights in Cooperative Business Arrangements"). The new legislation provides a model statement setting forth the required disclosure that should be delivered to and signed by the client.

3. Other States

Several other states have issued reports favoring the adoption of some sort of regulations allowing attorneys to participate in multi-disciplinary activities. These states include Arizona, California, Colorado, District of Columbia, Georgia, Maine, Minnesota, North Carolina, South Carolina, Utah, and Wyoming. See Utah State Bar Multidisciplinary Task Force Report (11/1/00). In addition, the ABA ethics commission has encouraged states to revisit their rules regarding multi-disciplinary practices (subject to certain regulations designed to protect the attorney's independence).

4. Conclusion

While practitioners may welcome the opportunity to participate in financial contractual relationships with non-attorneys in ways that have been heretofore prohibited, it is incumbent for the attorney to take measures to protect the client's interests from any conflict with the attorney and with his non-attorney partners.

> *Query:* If the attorney representing a client with respect to both legal services and non-legal services discovers a problem with the client's activities in the non-legal capacity (*i.e.,* client has been doctoring the corporation's balance sheet), to whom does the attorney have an obligation to express his concerns? To the client and/or the corporation?

21st Century Estate Planning:
Practical Applications
2005 Edition

©2005 Sonnenschein Nath & Rosenthal LLP
and Cannon Financial Institute, Inc.

- 667 -

→   **Planning Point:** Consistent with the theme expounded throughout this chapter, attorneys are strongly encouraged to disclose in detail the relationship that the attorney has with the non-attorney and to set forth in detail the attorney's obligations (or lack thereof) to the client in an engagement letter. This is especially important in jurisdictions that allow multi-disciplinary practices with non-lawyers. In this post-Enron era, attorneys should take special steps to ensure that their legal and ethical obligations are not compromised.

J. Payment of Referral Fees to Attorneys

1. General

The close working and business relationships between trusts and estates attorneys, accountants, financial advisors, trust companies and other estate planning practitioners raise the ethical issue of whether the attorney may be paid a referral fee by these entities. (The issue of the attorney paying a referral fee to a non-lawyer (*e.g.,* accountant, fiduciary, financial planner) raises its own set of issues regarding unauthorized fee-splitting and will not be discussed here.)

The primary objection to allowing attorneys to accept referral fees is that it impinges on the basic duty of the attorney to exercise his professional judgment solely on behalf of the client without being impaired in any way by the attorney's obligations to or relationship with another client.

2. Model Rule 1.7(b)

Model Rule 1.7(b) governs the ability of attorneys to enter into such an arrangement. The Rule provides as follows:

> A lawyer shall not represent a client if the representation of that client may be materially limited by the lawyer's responsibilities to another client or to a third person, or by the lawyer's own interest, unless:
>
> > (1) the lawyer reasonably believes the representation will not be adversely affected; and
>
> > (2) the client consents after disclosure.

3. Potential Conflict

The potential conflict is especially problematic in instances where the entity paying the referral fee has an economic interest in the documents being prepared by the attorney. For example, an accountant or trust company that wishes to be named fiduciary, a charity that wishes to be included in the will, or a financial advisor or insurance company that intends to sell products to the client.

21st Century Estate Planning:
Practical Applications
2005 Edition

©*2005 Sonnenschein Nath & Rosenthal LLP*
and Cannon Financial Institute, Inc.

- 668 -

4. Referral Fee From Trust Company

In Illinois State Bar Association, Advisory Opinion on Professional Conduct, Opinion No. 99-06 (November 1999), the Committee addressed the ethics of an attorney receiving fees for referring clients to a trust company.

The trust company developed a program of entering into agreements with trusts and estates lawyers to furnish legal services as a "trust administrator" with respect to trusts of which the trust company had been named trustee.

Once accepted as a trust administrator, the attorney generally referred clients as potential customers for the trust company's services. The attorney continued to bill his clients for legal services in preparing trust instruments and other documents and was paid a fee by the trust company, based on a published fee schedule, from the fee paid to the trust company from the client's trust.

The attorney's relationship with the trust company, his compensation as trust administrator, and other relevant information were set out in an extensive written disclosure and consent form which the client was required to sign.

The Committee noted the attorney's incentive to recommend the trust company's services over those of a competing fiduciary. Accordingly, the relationship between the attorney and the trust company, and the compensation generated by that relationship, was a conflict of interest and involved the "responsibilities to a third person" and "the attorney's own interests" as described in Rule 1.7.

Notwithstanding the potential conflict, the Committee held that the relationship is not improper if the attorney reasonably believes that his representation of the client may not be adversely affected by his relationship with the trust company and discloses his relationship with the trust company, the fee arrangement and method of calculation (including the source of payment to him), and all other aspects of the relationship.

5. Other Referral Fee Situations

Other opinions have addressed the multitude of scenarios that arise with respect to attorneys accepting referral fees. The following are just a few of those opinions:

The Commentaries to Rule 1.5 provide that the attorney should not accept any referral fees from a non-lawyer or an attorney not acting in a legal capacity in connection with the representation of a client, even with full disclosure. The Committee determined that the risk of a conflict of interest is too great.

Supreme Court of Texas, Professional Ethics Committee, Opinion No. 536 (May 2001) (an attorney would violate his ethical obligations to the client if he accepts from an investment advisor referral fees while he continues to perform services for the client, notwithstanding disclosure to the client).

21st Century Estate Planning:
Practical Applications
2005 Edition

©2005 Sonnenschein Nath & Rosenthal LLP
and Cannon Financial Institute, Inc.

- 669 -

Philadelphia Bar Association, Professional Guidance Committee, Inquiry 2001-11 (December 2001) (an attorney may reimburse a bank for its out-of-pocket costs incurred in advertising the services of an attorney but may not make any "profit" payments to the bank; attorney is advised to disclose the relationship to the client).

Illinois State Bar Association, Advisory Opinion on Professional Conduct, Opinion No. 97-04 (January 23, 1998) (an attorney may not properly take a referral fee from an investment advisor for referring a client to the advisor unless the lawyer rebuts the presumption of undue influence that arises when an attorney enters into a business transaction with the client; the presumption may be rebutted by showing the transaction was fair, the client had the opportunity for independent advice of counsel, and the client consented to the transaction after full disclosure).

6. Multi-Disciplinary Jurisdictions

As discussed in the preceding section of this chapter, the issue regarding the ability of attorneys to pay and receive referral fees is directly affected by those jurisdictions allowing multi-disciplinary practices. <u>See</u> New York DR 2-103.

DR 2-103 provides that an attorney may not compensate or give anything of value to a person to recommend or obtain employment by a client, except that:

> A lawyer or law firm may refer a client to a nonlegal professional or nonlegal professional service firm pursuant to a contractual relationship with such nonlegal professional or nonlegal professional service firm to provide legal and other professional services on a systematic and continuing basis .... provided however that such referral shall not otherwise include any monetary or other tangible consideration or reward for such, or the sharing of legal fees.

To what extent other jurisdictions will amend their rules regarding referral fees is not known. The trend, however, seems to be in favor of allowing attorneys to enter into specific relationships with non-attorneys to provide legal and non-legal services. If these arrangements become permitted, it is likely that "referral fees" may become more prevalent but may take form other than outright money paid to or by the attorney.

7. Conclusion

The payment and acceptance of referral fees or other form of payment raises a number of ethical issues and implicates a number of the Model Rules. Often, the form of "payment" by and to the attorney is the back and forth referral of business between the attorney and the other service provider. In addition, further issues are raised if the attorney himself is wearing more than one hat (*i.e.*, attorney and accountant or insurance broker). Attorneys should not enter into such arrangements without first reviewing the applicable local rules and regulations governing accepting or paying referral fees and without first disclosing all material facts to the client.

21st Century Estate Planning:
Practical Applications
2005 Edition

©*2005 Sonnenschein Nath & Rosenthal LLP*
and Cannon Financial Institute, Inc.

- 670 -

→ **Planning Point:** Given the various ethical issues regarding attorneys being paid fees for referring clients and the multitude of approaches to these issues by different jurisdictions, it is suggested that, at the very least, the attorney should disclose to the client the nature and extent of any relationship the attorney may have with an accountant, financial advisor, or trust company with respect to whom the attorney may receive a fee. In addition, the attorney has an affirmative obligation to ascertain if the relationship with the client would in any way be adversely affected as a result of the financial benefit being conferred on him. If any adverse consequences may result, the attorney must decline to accept a fee even with the consent of the client.

K. Use of E-mail to Transmit Confidential Information

1. General

The increased use of electronic mail (e-mail) by attorneys and their clients as a means of communicating and transmitting information has raised the timely issue of whether e-mail may be used to communicate with clients regarding confidential client matters in view of an attorney's duty under the ethics rules to maintain the confidentiality of client information.

2. E-mail Permitted Means of Communication

Most state bar associations that have considered this issue have concluded, with few exceptions, that a reasonable expectation of privacy exists in the use of Internet e-mail and an attorney may use this form of communication to transmit confidential client information. See State of Hawaii, Office of Disciplinary Counsel, Formal Opinion No. 40 (April 26, 2001); Utah State Bar Ethics Advisory Opinion No. 00-01 (approved March 9, 2000); South Carolina Ethics Advisory Opinion 97-08 (June 1997); Massachusetts Ethics Op. No. 94-5 (1994).

In Illinois State Bar Association, Advisory Opinion on Professional Conduct, Opinion No. 96-10 (May 16, 1997), the Committee found that the major issue concerning the ability of an attorney to use e-mail to communicate with clients arises out of an attorney's duty to protect confidential client information under Rule 1.6(a) of the Illinois Rules of Professional Conduct.

The Rule provides that "a lawyer shall not, during or after termination of the professional relationship with the client, use or reveal a confidence or secret of the client known to the lawyer unless the client consents after disclosure." The duty to maintain the confidentiality of client information implies the duty to use methods of communication with clients that provide reasonable assurance that messages will be and remain confidential.

The Committee likened the use of e-mail with the use of a telephone and concluded that just as courts and ethics committees have uniformly held that persons using ordinary telephones for confidential communications have a reasonable expectation of privacy, messages transmitted by e-mail also have a reasonable expectation of privacy. The fact that Internet service provider administrators or hackers are capable of intercepting e-mail does not render the expectation of

21st Century Estate Planning:
Practical Applications
2005 Edition

©2005 Sonnenschein Nath & Rosenthal LLP
and Cannon Financial Institute, Inc.

- 671 -

privacy unreasonable, any more than the risk of the illegal eavesdropping on a telephone conversation removes the reasonable expectation of privacy in a land-line telephone call. In addition, the unauthorized interception of an Internet message is a violation of various federal and state laws.

Accordingly, the Committee concluded that because: (1) the expectation of privacy for e-mail is no less reasonable than the expectation of privacy for ordinary telephone calls, and (2) the unauthorized interception of an electronic message is illegal, a lawyer does not violate Rule 1.6 by communicating with a client using e-mail without encryption. Finally, it was found unnecessary to seek specific client consent to the use of unencrypted e-mail.

3.   ABA View

The ABA concurs that the use of Internet e-mail does not violate any rule of professional conduct. ABA Formal Opinion No. 99-413 (1999) provides that: "Lawyers have a reasonable expectation of privacy in communications made by all forms of e-mail, including unencrypted e-mail sent on the Internet, despite some risk of interception and disclosure. It therefore follows that its use is consistent with the duty under Rule 1.6 to use reasonable means to maintain the confidentiality of information relating to a client's representation."

4.   Special Considerations

Notwithstanding the general acceptance of the use of e-mail as a means of transmitting client information, the unrestricted use has been brought into question by certain jurisdictions when highly sensitive material is being transmitted. See Iowa Supreme Court Board of Professional Ethics and Conduct, Opinion No. 97-01 (9/18/97) (while the pure exchange of information or legal communications with clients may be transmitted with the client's consent, for sensitive material to be transmitted by e-mail counsel must have written acknowledgment by the client of the risk of violation of DR 4-101 which acknowledgment includes consent for communication thereof on the Internet or non-secure intranet or other forms of proprietary networks to be protected as agreed between counsel and client).

➔   **Planning Point:** Given the ever-changing modes of transmitting information, where highly sensitive material is transmitted over the Internet or the attorney has reason to believe that the risk of interception of the communication is higher, an attorney should seek the consent of the client to the use of e-mail (or other mode of communication) or the attorney should transmit the information by means of communication with greater security (*i.e.*, by using advanced e-mail encryption or by delivery of the information by messenger or courier). It may also be prudent for an attorney to advise a client at the time he is retained that the attorney intends to use unencrypted e-mail as a method of communicating with the client, including to transmit confidential material, and seek the client's consent to its use.

Appendix A – Joint Representation of Husband and Wife ("Show and Tell Approach")

21st Century Estate Planning:
Practical Applications
2005 Edition

©2005 Sonnenschein Nath & Rosenthal LLP
and Cannon Financial Institute, Inc.

- 672 -

Suggested language to add to engagement letter

<u>Joint Representation</u>.   You have indicated that the interests of the two of you, _____ and _____, presently coincide, and that you have agreed between yourselves that this firm should represent both of you. In the event that your interests continue to coincide, this joint representation should be more efficient and economical than would be the case if separate counsel were retained for each of you. Each of you, therefore, is our client. This means that, if one of you shares with us a matter in confidence, that matter is not protected by the attorney-client privilege from disclosure to the other of you. In fact, if one of you shares any information with us that might affect the other's estate planning needs, concerns and desires, we are ethically (and, therefore, legally) obligated to disclose such information to the other. By contrast, if we were to represent each of you separately, we would have to keep in confidence and conceal from the other of you any confidential information or instructions communicated to us by one of you even if such information or instructions had the effect of altering facts the other had relied on in formulating his or her own estate plan.

When we engage in estate planning for a married couple, we strongly encourage open discussions between the spouses of their objectives and interests, and we embark on the project with the assumption that the estate planning objectives of the two of you are, if not identical, at least harmonious. Nevertheless, sometimes spouses do not share the same or harmonious objectives, and, occasionally, whether or not the same or harmonious objectives are shared by the spouses, one spouse wishes to speak in confidence with his or her lawyer. We are willing to meet with either of you individually, but, since we will be representing the two of you jointly, we are not in a position to agree with either of you not to communicate freely with both of you.

It is possible that, during the course of our estate planning work, conflicts may arise between you with respect to, for example, the disposition of your assets or other matters. If a conflict of interest arises between you such that it is impossible in our judgment for this firm to fulfill its obligations to each of you in a professionally and ethically responsible manner, we will so advise you. At that point, we will withdraw from further joint representation of the two of you and recommend that each of you retain new and separate counsel to avoid the possibility that our advice to one of you will be influenced by our representation of the other. Moreover, you should be aware that if any such dispute among you ever results in litigation, you will be precluded from claiming, against one another, the attorney-client privilege of confidentiality with respect to the joint representation.

21st Century Estate Planning:
Practical Applications
2005 Edition

©2005 Sonnenschein Nath & Rosenthal LLP
and Cannon Financial Institute, Inc.

- 673 -

Chapter XVIII
Bibliography

ABA Report of Ethics 2000 Commission.

ABA/BNA Lawyer's Manual on Professional Conduct (looseleaf service).

ACTEC Commentaries on the Model Rules of Professional Conduct (3rd ed. 1999).

AICPA Code of Professional Conduct.

Annotated Code of Professional Responsibility, American Bar Foundation (1979).

Robert H. Aronson & Donald T. Weinstein, *Professional Responsibility in a Nutshell* (2nd ed. 1991).

Gary Blankenship, "Enron Case Boosts Bar's MDP Stance," *Florida Bar News* (February 15, 2002).

Ward Bower, "The Case for MDPs: Should Multidisciplinary Practices be Banned or Embraced?," *ABA Law Practice Management Magazine* (July/August 1998).

Peter W. Brown and Melinda M. Ward, "Ethical Issues for Estate Planners," SE14 ALI-ABA 185 (October 28, 1999).

John Caher, "Multidisciplinary Practice Rules Adopted by State, New York Takes Lead in Lawyer-Nonlawyer Partnerships," *New York Law Journal* (July 25, 2001).

Duke University School of Law Research Guides - Legal Ethics.

Barbara Glesner Fines, *Researching Professional Responsibility* (1997, updated 2000).

Robert B. Fleming and Rebecca C. Morgan, "Lawyers' Ethical Dilemmas, A "Normal" Relationship When Representing Demented Clients and their Families," 35 *Ga. Law Rev.* 735 (Winter 2001).

Georgetown Journal of Legal Ethics.

Charles Groppe, "Ethical Considerations," 110 PLI/NY 141 (November 26, 2001).

Mark E. Haranzo, "Use of Trusts in Estate Planning: Ethical Considerations," 97 PLI/NY 413 (April 18, 2001).

Geoffrey P. Hazard & W. William Hodes, *The Law of Lawyering: A Handbook on the Model Rules of Professional Conduct* (3rd edition).

Journal of the Institute for the Study of Legal Ethics (Hofstra University School of Law).

21st Century Estate Planning:
Practical Applications
2005 Edition

©2005 Sonnenschein Nath & Rosenthal LLP
and Cannon Financial Institute, Inc.

- 674 -

Journal of the Legal Profession (University of Alabama, School of Law).

Nancy Maurer and Patricia W. Johnson, "Representing Children and Disabled Clients," 114 PLI/NY 1143 (January 2002).

Louis A. Mezullo, "Ethics for Estate Planners," CA52 ALI-ABA 295 (October 1995).

Model Rules of Professional Conduct, Center for Professional Responsibility, American Bar Association, Annotated (3rd ed.).

"Ethics and Public Policy," *Notre Dame Journal of Law*.

Jeffrey N. Pennell, "Ethics, Professionalism, and Malpractice Issues in Estate Planning and Administration," SC75 ALI-ABA 67 (June 14, 1998).

Jan Ellen Rein, "Ethics and the Questionably Competent Client: What the Model Rules Say and Don't Say," 9 *Stan. Law & Pol'y Rev.* 241 (Spring 1998).

Restatement (Third) of the Law Governing Lawyers, American Law Institute (2000).

Randall W. Roth, "Current Ethical Problems in Estate Planning," SF68 ALI-ABA 275 (February 22, 2001).

Charles W. Wolfram, *Modern Legal Ethics* (1986) (Reserve).

Edith Ywu, "Why Say No to Multidisciplinary Practice," *Loyola Univ. of Chicago L. Rev.* (Spring 2001).

Online Research and Web Sites

AICPA - Professional Ethics Division of the AICPA

http://www.aicpa.org/members/div/ethics/index.htm (includes links to ethics resources and developments affecting accounts)

Duke University School of Law Research Guides – Legal Ethics

http://www.duke.edu/lib/libser/publicat/researchguides/ethics/ethics.html

Freivogal on Conflicts, Joint Multiple Representation (online guide)

http://www.freivogalonconflicts.com/new_page_8.htm

Westlaw and Lexis each provides links to case law, ethics codes and opinions, articles, treatises

Findlaw - Ethics and Professional Responsibility Law

21st Century Estate Planning:
Practical Applications
2005 Edition

©2005 Sonnenschein Nath & Rosenthal LLP
and Cannon Financial Institute, Inc.

- 675 -

http://findlaw.com/01topics/14ethics/index.html

LegalEthics.com

http://www.findlaw.com

Cornell Legal Information Institute – Ethics Section

http://www.law.cornell.edu/topics/professional_responsibility.html

ABA Center for Professional Responsibility

http://www.abanet.org/cpr/ethics.html

Edward Bennett Williams Law Library, Georgetown University Law Center, Research Guides, Legal Ethics

http.www.ll.georgetown.edu/lib/guides/legaleth.htm

21st Century Estate Planning:
Practical Applications
2005 Edition

©2005 Sonnenschein Nath & Rosenthal LLP
and Cannon Financial Institute, Inc.

- 676 -

XIX. PROFESSIONAL LIABILITY

A. Introduction

Attorneys practicing in the estate planning area are repeatedly being held legally accountable for their "mistakes" in drafting, judgment, and behavior. Unhappy clients are holding attorneys liable for mistakes made during the preparation of documents and during the administration of trusts and estates. Increasingly, liability is also being imposed on the attorney for damages caused to non-client third parties who are the purported beneficiaries of the services being provided. Attorneys have to be made aware that they will not only be held accountable for ethical lapses, but may subject themselves to civil liability and potential disbarment or suspension under the more extreme circumstances.

This chapter deals with professional liability of attorneys for the actions they take and for the actions they neglect to take. From the onset, it is important to point out that ethical violations are not necessarily the same as malpractice. Nevertheless, the basis of a claim for malpractice can originate from an ethical violation. Accordingly, each of the attorney's ethical obligations set forth in the previous chapter could, depending on the circumstances, give rise to a claim of malpractice. It is therefore advisable for the attorney to take the proper steps to ensure that he is acting within the ethically prescribed boundaries and thus be better able to protect himself from claims of malpractice and misconduct.

As with the previous chapter, this material is by no means intended to cover all areas of the attorney's potential professional liability. Rather, it is intended to raise an awareness of the types of issues that may arise and provide practical suggestions to address them. The following are the topics discussed in this chapter:

- Adequate Representation
- Liability for Actions of Non-Attorney Assistants
- Obligation of Attorney to Inform Client of Unsettled Nature of the Law
- Duty of Attorney and Others to Non-Client Third Parties
- Attorney for Fiduciary – Who is the Client?
- Continuing Obligations of Attorney Once Representation Ends
- Liability for Client's Failure to Execute Documents

B. Adequate Representation

1. General

One of the foremost duties of the attorney is to provide competent legal services to the client. The trusts and estates attorney, confronted with an ever-changing legal landscape, must be careful not to allow the representation to fall below acceptable standards. The constant evolution of the tax laws requires the attorney to stay current regarding changes in the law. In addition, the attorney must be knowledgeable about the specific estate and probate requirements of each jurisdiction and the rules of each court in which the attorney practices.

21st Century Estate Planning:
Practical Applications
2005 Edition

©2005 Sonnenschein Nath & Rosenthal LLP
and Cannon Financial Institute, Inc.

- 677 -

EXAMPLE: An attorney could be found negligent for not advising clients of the recent changes under New York law regarding the ability of a trustee to adjust between income and principal or to utilize the new unitrust regulations. Also, an attorney could be found negligent if he was not aware that a specific county required the execution of all self-proving affidavits to be officiated by an attorney.

Many attorneys not practicing exclusively in the trusts and estates field are of the belief that while they may not be trusts and estates "specialists," they are capable of handling basic matters. This type of thinking gives the attorney a false sense of security. The attorney preparing any estate planning document must have a strong working and current knowledge of a multitude of areas of law, including testate and intestate laws, elective share statutes, federal and state income, estate, and gift tax laws, rules governing IRA and 401(k) plans, elder law issues — each a sub-specialty in its own right. In addition, each of these areas may differ depending on the particular jurisdiction of the attorney and/or the client. For example, in New York, a non-resident alien may not be appointed as guardian of minor children even if such person is a close relative (*e.g.*, aunt or uncle) of the minor child.

The requirement to be competent extends beyond the necessity of having the requisite educational knowledge. The attorney is required to be thorough, careful, prepared, diligent and prompt.

The following are a few of the potential pitfalls for attorneys:

- Failure to properly draft documents (*e.g.*, improperly drafted estate tax allocation provisions).
- Failure to properly execute documents.
- Failure to properly advise clients of their legal options (*e.g.*, whether to hold real property as joint tenants or tenants in common).
- Failure to properly complete designated beneficiary forms.
- Failure to efficiently and promptly administrate the estate.

2. Model Rule 1.1 (Competence)

The text to Model Rule 1.1 provides as follows:

> A lawyer shall provide competent representation to a client. Competent representation requires the legal knowledge, skill, thoroughness and preparation reasonably necessary for the representation.

3. Model Code

DR 6-101(A)(1) of the Model Code is similar to Rule 1.1 and provides that an attorney should not handle matters "which he knows or should know that he is not competent to handle, without associating himself with a lawyer who is competent to handle it."

21st Century Estate Planning:
Practical Applications
2005 Edition

©2005 Sonnenschein Nath & Rosenthal LLP
and Cannon Financial Institute, Inc.

- 678 -

4. How to Protect Yourself

a. Education. The first thing an attorney must do is educate himself in each area of law he wishes to practice. This may include obtaining a working understanding of the basic principles of law and should include continuing legal education. The standard of care required by the attorney may depend on the type of work being performed and the manner in which the attorney holds himself out to the client. For example, an attorney who prints on his stationery or letterhead that he practices in the area of trusts and estates may be held to a higher standard than an attorney who merely identifies himself as a general practitioner.

b. Consult Specialists. The Commentaries provide that the needs of a client may also be met "by involving another lawyer or other professional who possesses the requisite degree of skill or care." If an attorney does not have sufficient learning and skill when undertaking legal services, the attorney may nonetheless perform the services competently by: (1) associating with or, where appropriate, consulting with another professional whom the attorney reasonably believes is competent, or (2) acquiring sufficient learning and skill before performance is required. An attorney can be held guilty of malpractice, not for lacking the requisite knowledge, but for failing to retain someone with the specialized knowledge. See *Lewis v. State Bar of California*, 170 Cal. Rptr. 634 (1981) (in a proceeding to review the recommendation of the disciplinary board of the state bar, it was held that an attorney who negligently and improperly conducts the administration of an estate without any previous probate experience and without associating or consulting with an experienced attorney warrants suspension for 30 days; in finding that there was no bad faith on the part of the attorney, the court stayed the suspension and placed the attorney on probation for one year).

5. Multi-Jurisdictional Issues

It is not uncommon for clients of an attorney to reside or have assets located in multiple jurisdictions (*e.g.*, New York and Florida). The attorney should make himself aware of the tax and estate administration nuances of each jurisdiction. This may entail having to retain local counsel to perform the work or to review the services of the attorney.

> **EXAMPLE:** The attorney must be aware of how a Connecticut client's assets located in California, a community property state, may affect the estate plan.

➔ **Planning Point:** The attorney undertaking any type of estate planning work should make sure that he has the requisite knowledge to perform the work. If the attorney lacks the knowledge, depending on the complexity of the assignment, the attorney should educate himself in the area of law or should consult with or retain experts. If the attorney intends to employ outside experts, the client should be informed of this in the engagement letter or follow-up correspondence. If the scope of knowledge is entirely outside of the attorney's ability, it may be appropriate to withdraw from the engagement.

21st Century Estate Planning:
Practical Applications
2005 Edition

©2005 Sonnenschein Nath & Rosenthal LLP
and Cannon Financial Institute, Inc.

- 679 -

C. Liability for Actions of Non-Attorney Assistants

1. General

A direct corollary to the requirement that the attorney be competent is the requirement that the attorney ensure the competence of his non-attorney assistants. The administrative functions of a trusts and estates practitioner, particularly in the areas of trust and estate administration, are ideal situations for the attorney to delegate responsibilities to paralegals, fiduciary accountants, and clerks. This usually provides a more economic and efficient way for the administration to proceed and should be disclosed to the client in the engagement letter. When delegating responsibility, the attorney is ethically obligated to properly instruct his assistants and must supervise and monitor all work performed. The attorney must also ensure that the assistant acts within the boundaries of the ethical rules. For example, the assistant may not reveal any confidences made known to him.

2. Model Rule 5.3

Model Rule 5.3 requires attorneys to ensure that non-attorney assistants conduct themselves appropriately and holds the attorney responsible for their work product. It provides, in pertinent part, as follows:

With respect to a non-lawyer employed or retained by or associated with a lawyer:

> (a) a partner in a law firm shall make reasonable efforts to ensure that the firm has in effect measures giving reasonable assurance that the person's conduct is compatible with the professional obligations of the lawyer;
>
> (b) a lawyer having direct supervisory authority over the non-lawyer shall make reasonable efforts to ensure that the person's conduct is compatible with the professional obligations of the lawyer; and
>
> (c) a lawyer shall be responsible for conduct of such a person that would be a violation of the Rules of Professional Conduct if engaged in by a lawyer if:
>
> > (1) the lawyer orders or, with the knowledge of the specific conduct, ratifies the conduct involved; or
> >
> > (2) the lawyer is a partner in the law firm in which the person is employed, or has direct supervisory authority over the person, and knows of the conduct at a time when its consequences can be avoided or mitigated but fails to take reasonable remedial action.

21st Century Estate Planning:
Practical Applications
2005 Edition

©2005 Sonnenschein Nath & Rosenthal LLP
and Cannon Financial Institute, Inc.

- 680 -

3. Liability for Action of Assistants

The attorney can be held liable for the incompetence of his employees. Attorneys have been held liable where the assistant to whom the attorney delegates the responsibility to administer an estate is delinquent in carrying out that responsibility. It is not sufficient for the attorney to merely delegate responsibility without continually supervising the assistant. See *Matter of Stenstrom*, 605 N.Y.S.2d 603 (App. Div. 1993) (attorney disbarred for neglect of matter and failure to supervise non-lawyers). See also *Matter of Carrigan*, 726 N.Y.S.2d 538 (App. Div. 2001) (attorney disbarred for, among other things, improperly delegating estate administration work to paralegal).

The attorney has also been held liable for the misconduct of his employees. See *Office of Disciplinary Counsel v. Ball*, 618 N.E.2d 159 (Ohio 1993) (failure to supervise secretary who misappropriates client funds resulted in suspension of attorney for violation of DR 6-101 which requires that an attorney not "[n]eglect a legal matter entrusted to him").

➔ **Planning Point:** The attorney should always inform the client that work may be performed by non-attorney assistants. The attorney should be careful when delegating responsibilities to supervise and instruct assistants in the carrying out of their duties. It is recommended that the attorney maintain a detailed checklist of obligations of the assistant (*e.g.*, estate administration checklist) and should periodically review the status of each matter with the assistant.

D. Obligation of Attorney to Inform Client of Unsettled Nature of the Law

1. Obligations of Attorney to Stay Current

The duty of the attorney to stay current in his knowledge of the law was discussed in an earlier section of this chapter. The duty of the attorney to be aware of legal trends is the subject of this section. Most attorneys are aware of their obligation to stay abreast of changes in the law and to advise clients when the law governing the advice being provided is known to be unsettled (*i.e.*, published disagreement as to the interpretations of statutes between the IRS and Tax Court or between different jurisdictions). To what extent are attorneys obligated to inform their clients of the uncertainty in the law and, if such an obligation exists, what is considered an uncertainty that would require such disclosure?

2. Model Rule 1.4(b)

Model Rule 1.4(b) provides that "[a] lawyer shall explain a matter to the extent reasonably necessary to permit the client to make informed decisions regarding the representation." Ethical Consideration 7-8 provides "[a] lawyer should exert his best efforts to insure that decisions of his client are made only after the client has been informed of relevant considerations…. Advice of an attorney need not be confined to purely legal considerations. An attorney should advise his client of the possible effects of each legal alternative."

21st Century Estate Planning:
Practical Applications
2005 Edition

©2005 Sonnenschein Nath & Rosenthal LLP
and Cannon Financial Institute, Inc.

- 681 -

3.   *Williams v. Ely*

The extent to which an attorney was held obligated to notify his client of uncertainty in the law was discussed in *Williams v. Ely*, 668 N.E.2d 799 (Mass. 1996).

In *Williams*, each plaintiff had a contingent remainder interest in two testamentary trusts, one created in 1926 and the other in 1948. In October 1975, one of the plaintiffs consulted his cousin, a partner in the law firm of Gaston Snow, and inquired whether he would be able to effectively disclaim his interest under the trusts and, if he did, whether there would be any gift tax consequences. The plaintiff was informed that he could effectively disclaim the property without gift tax consequences.

In December 1975, one of the plaintiffs executed a disclaimer for each trust. In December 1976, the other plaintiffs executed disclaimers of their contingent interests in the trusts. Gaston Snow did not advise the plaintiffs to file a gift tax return to begin the running of the statute of limitations nor did they advise the plaintiffs that the law was unsettled and that there was a risk of federal gift tax consequences if the disclaimers were made. At the time the advice was given, there was a difference of opinion between the United States Court of Appeals for the Eighth Circuit (*Keinath v. Comm'r.*, 58 T.C. 352 (1972), *overruled*, 480 F.2d 57 (8th Cir. 1973)) and the IRS (IRS AOD, 1973 WL 34941, Jul 12, 1973).

In February 1982, the United States Supreme Court ruled that a taxable gift results if a disclaimer of a pre-1977 property interest is not made within a reasonable time after creation, or knowledge is obtained by the disclaimant of the creation, of a contingent interest. *Jewett v. Comm'r.*, 455 U.S. 305 (1982). The plaintiffs had been aware of the contingent interest well before they disclaimed their interest in 1975.

In 1984, Gaston Snow advised the plaintiffs of the adverse tax consequences of their disclaimers. In 1986, a gift tax return was filed and plaintiffs paid their gift tax liability.

The plaintiffs sued Gaston Snow for failing to advise them of the risks of possible federal gift tax consequences for making the disclaimers.

The court held that the firm was negligent in failing to advise the plaintiffs of the unsettled state of the law.

> The problem is not that Gaston Snow gave reasonable advice that proved to be wrong. The problem is that the apparent uncertainty of the opinion, given when the issue was not conclusively resolved, denied the plaintiffs the opportunity to assess the risks and to elect to follow alternative estate planning options.... The absence of a guarantee does not, however, foreclose liability for the adverse consequences of a negligent failure to advise a client of the uncertainty of the advice given.

21st Century Estate Planning:
Practical Applications
2005 Edition

©*2005 Sonnenschein Nath & Rosenthal LLP*
and Cannon Financial Institute, Inc.

- 682 -

In addition, the court held that since the plaintiffs only became aware of the adverse tax consequences in 1984, the statute of limitations for actions against the firm did not begin to run until that time.

4. Conclusion

The holding in *Williams* should give all attorneys in the tax and estate planning fields pause to think of the nature of the advice we give and the obligation to warn clients of possible adverse positions taken by the IRS or among the various circuits. It is important to note that in *Williams*, Gaston Snow was found negligent notwithstanding that it provided a reasonable view of the law at the time it was given.

A survey of other cases illustrates the lack of consensus on this issue. See *Smith v. St. Paul Fire & Marine Ins. Co.*, 366 F.Supp. 1283 (M.D. La. 1973) ("If the attorney has reason to believe, or should have reason to believe that there could be some adverse consequences from taking the course advised, he is obligated to so advise his client. But if there is no reasonable ground for him to believe that his advice is questionable, he certainly has no obligation to advise clients of every remote possibility that might exist."); *Wood v. McGrath, North, Mullin & Kratz, P.C.*, 589 N.W.2d 103 (Neb. 1999) ("An allegation that an attorney did not properly inform a client of relevant unsettled legal issues does not provide the same need for immunity from suit as does an attorney's judgment or recommendation in an area of unsettled law"); *Conklin v. Hannoch Weisman*, 678 A.2d 1060 (N.J. 1996) ("we find no persuasive need to introduce into attorney malpractice the subjective standard of informed consent"); *First Nat'l Bank of Clovis v. Diane, Inc.*, 698 P.2d 5 (N.M. 1985) ("It is not the fact that defendant incorrectly interpreted the statutes that renders him liable; it is the failure to warn of potential liability to the client of adverse consequences which could result"); *Davis v. Damrell*, 119 Cal.App.3d 883 (1981) (stating that to impose a duty to inform a client of the unsettled nature of the law "would effectively undermine the attorney-client relationship and vitiate the salutary purpose of the error-in-judgment rule," which states that "if any attorney acting in good faith exercises an honest and informed discretion in providing professional advice, the failure to anticipate correctly the resolution of an unsettled legal principle does not constitute culpable conduct."); compare *Stake v. Harlan*, 529 So.2d 1183 (Fla.App. 1988) (attorney held to have breached duty to client where attorney did not inform the client of his awareness of a possible change in law that may occur through certification of question to the state Supreme Court that could have a materially adverse effect upon the client) with *Crosby v. Jones*, 705 So.2d 1356 (Fla. 1998) (good faith tactical decisions made by attorneys on fairly debatable point of law are generally not actionable).

> *Query*: What degree of uncertainty rises to the level of requiring a warning to clients? Also, will a court apply a different standard depending on whether the attorney has actual knowledge of an uncertainty in the law as compared to an attorney who perhaps should be, but is not, aware of the uncertainty?

Finally, as one commentator noted, the court seemed to place an additional obligation on the part of attorneys to inform clients of any changes in the law that may affect past advice

21st Century Estate Planning:
Practical Applications
2005 Edition

©2005 Sonnenschein Nath & Rosenthal LLP
and Cannon Financial Institute, Inc.

- 683 -

given, particularly if the law may have had any degree of uncertainty at the time the advice was given. The extent to which an attorney is obligated to advise clients of changes in settled areas of law that occur after the initial representation has ended will be discussed later in this material.

➔ **Planning Point:** The attorney's job is to advise clients as to the best approach to take with respect to the issue at hand. Notwithstanding that the attorney may deem one approach preferable to the other, the attorney should make the client aware (preferably in writing) of any potential uncertainty in the law regarding such advice and should further advise the client of the potential downside of any action taken if the applicable authority were to challenge the position.

E. Duty of Attorney and Others to Non-Client Third Parties

1. General

To what extent can an attorney or other practitioner (*e.g.*, accountant) be held liable to non-client third-party beneficiaries of the trusts and estates of the services they are providing? The answer depends on whether the jurisdiction in which the practitioner giving the advice adheres to the strict privity doctrine or whether such jurisdiction allows third parties to proceed against the practitioner under either a negligence theory, third-party beneficiary contract claim, or a combination of the two.

2. Strict Privity Doctrine

The one-time prevailing view was that of a strict privity doctrine. An attorney was held liable only to the client and not to the beneficiaries of the document being prepared. The jurisdictions adhering to this doctrine have refused to grant standing to non-client beneficiaries under either a negligence or third-party beneficiary contract theory. The primary reasons given for this doctrine have been:

- Absent strict privity, clients would lose control over attorney-client relationships, and the attorneys would be subject to almost unlimited liability.
- Allowing a broad cause of action against an attorney would create a conflict of interest between the client and third-party beneficiaries during the estate planning process, thereby limiting the attorney's ability to zealously represent his or her clients.
- Fears that suits by disappointed beneficiaries would cast doubt on the deceased testator's intentions.

States that adhere to strict privity rule include Nebraska, New York, Ohio, Virginia, Wisconsin (*Beauchamp v. Kemmeter*, 625 N.W.2d 297 (Wis.App. 2000) but see *Auric v. Continental Cas. Co.*, 331 N.W.2d 325 (Wis. 1983)), Alabama and Texas. See, *e.g.*, *Robinson v. Benton*, 842 So.2d 631 (Ala. 2002).

21st Century Estate Planning:
Practical Applications
2005 Edition

©2005 Sonnenschein Nath & Rosenthal LLP
and Cannon Financial Institute, Inc.

- 684 -

3. Changing Trend to Impose Liability

Recently, there has been a growing trend among many jurisdictions that is eroding the strict privity doctrine and is allowing non-client beneficiaries to bring claims under either a (1) "balancing factors method" under a negligence theory or (2) breach of contract theory as a third-party beneficiary. Over 25 states, including Florida, California, Pennsylvania and Illinois, allow non-client beneficiaries of estate planning services and/or trust and estate administration to bring a malpractice claim under either a negligence theory or a third-party beneficiary theory.

Blair v. Ing. One recent jurisdiction to adopt this approach is Hawaii in Blair v. Ing, 21 P.3d 452 (Hawaii 2001).

In 1988, Lloyd and Joan Hughes, the appellant's parents, retained attorney Lawrence Ing to prepare an estate plan, including a revocable living trust. After Mr. Hughes passed away in 1996, Mrs. Hughes, as executor, retained the services of accountant Thomas Thayer to prepare the necessary federal and state estate tax forms. Mrs. Hughes passed away in 1997.

Under the trust, the appellants were the sole named beneficiaries and successor trustees.

Upon review by another attorney of the trust drafted by Ing and the tax returns prepared by Thayer, the appellants were informed that there were costly errors and omissions. Subsequently, the appellants filed suit against Ing and Thayer. Ing was accused of not including a funding formula for the by-pass trust created under the trust and Thayer was accused of not recommending tax-saving techniques, such as disclaimers.

The lower court dismissed the claims against both Ing and Thayer because it concluded that the appellants lacked standing to sue. In addition, the lower court reasoned that because the trust did not on its face provide any intent to minimize taxes or to maximize the appellants' interests, Ing did not owe any duty to the appellants.

The court examined the history of the strict privity doctrine and the reasoning provided for its application and concluded that it was not applicable. It then proceeded to discuss the other applicable theories of liability.

(1) **Balancing Factors Approach Under a Negligence Theory.** The court in *Blair v. Ing* adopted the balancing approach cited in *Lucas v. Hamm*, 56 Cal. 2d 583, 15 Cal. Rptr. 821, 364 P.2d 685 (1961), *cert. denied*, 368 U.S. 987 (1962). *Lucas* stated that whether a particular defendant can be liable to a third person not in privity is a matter of public policy, requiring the balancing of six factors:

(a) The extent to which the transaction was intended affects the plaintiff;

(b) The foreseeability of harm to the plaintiff;

(c) The degree of certainty that the plaintiff suffered injury;

21st Century Estate Planning:
Practical Applications
2005 Edition

©2005 Sonnenschein Nath & Rosenthal LLP
and Cannon Financial Institute, Inc.

- 685 -

(d) The closeness of the connection between the defendant's conduct and the injury;

(e) The policy of preventing future harm; and

(f) Whether imposing liability places undue burden upon the legal profession.

(2) **Third-Party Beneficiary Under a Contract Theory**. The court in *Blair v. Ing* also examined the applicability of a third-party beneficiary theory to the case at hand. The focus on this theory is whether the primary purpose of the attorney-client relationship was to benefit the non-client beneficiary. The court then adopted the approach in *Guy v. Liederbach*, 501 Pa. 47, 459 A.2d 744 (1983). In *Guy*, the Pennsylvania Supreme Court provided a two-part test for determining whether a person is an intended beneficiary:

(1) The court should determine whether the recognition of the beneficiary's right is appropriate to effectuate the intention of the parties.

(2) The performance must satisfy an obligation of the promisee to pay money to the beneficiary or the circumstances indicate that the promisee intends to give the beneficiary the benefit of the promised performance.

The court held that a non-client beneficiary has standing to bring suit under *either* theory. In contrast, some jurisdictions have limited the beneficiaries to only one theory, either negligence or contract.

While holding that an attorney cannot be held liable for every mistake made in his or her practice, especially for errors as to a question of law on which reasonable doubt may be extended, the court held that the duty to a third party must be decided on a case-by-case basis.

The court first held that Ing owed a duty to the appellants, which duty was violated.

The court then found that the appellants did not have a strong case to sue the accountant, Thayer. The court reasoned that Thayer was retained only to prepare applicable tax returns and not to provide any estate planning advice. Accordingly, the postmortem services provided were not intended to benefit the non-client beneficiaries. Since the appellants were not intended beneficiaries of the retention of Thayer, the court refused to hold him liable under either a negligence or third-party beneficiary theory.

b. **Trustee's Liability for Providing Estate Planning Services**. In *Merrick v. Mercantile-Safe Deposit & Trust Co.*, 855 F.2d 1095 (4th Cir. 1988), the decedent through her will sought to exercise a power of appointment over trust assets given to her by her father. The power could be exercised only in favor of her descendants, but the decedent nevertheless attempted to exercise the power in favor of her daughter and her son-in-law, the plaintiff. The plaintiff later alleged that the resulting distortion of the decedent's estate plan was caused by the negligence of the defendant bank in failing to inform the decedent that the attempted

21st Century Estate Planning:
Practical Applications
2005 Edition

©2005 Sonnenschein Nath & Rosenthal LLP
and Cannon Financial Institute, Inc.

- 686 -

appointment would be ineffectual. The court held that, where the bank had undertaken to provide estate planning advice to the decedent in addition to managing her investments, an implied contractual relationship arose making the plaintiff a third party beneficiary to whom the bank also owed a duty to exercise due care. The bank's own files contained legal opinions to the effect that the plaintiff would not qualify as a descendant and, therefore, that the decedent's intent to leave one-half of the appointive property to the plaintiff could not be carried out. The fact that the decedent's attorney was also negligent did not immunize the bank from liability.

In *In re McCoy*, 419 N.W.2d 301 (Wis.App. 1987), the trust at issue benefited the grantor for her life, and the remaining trust property was to pass to her estate. The grantor later decided to give both the income and the principal to a charity but retain control over the principal until her death. She communicated this intent in a letter to the charity with a copy to the bank trustee. However, she never executed an amendment to the trust, so on her death her estate claimed the principal. The charity sued and settled with the estate for an equal division of the principal. The charity then sued the bank for negligence. The court found that the charity had a cause of action if the bank was negligent in fulfilling its duties to the grantor and its negligence was a substantial factor in causing loss to the intended beneficiary. The court held that "given the bank's expertise in trust matters," the bank had breached its duty by failing to warn the grantor of easily identifiable impediments of achieving her dispositive intent. Mere reminders at the time of the trust creation and at the meeting that she should consult a lawyer were insufficient.

These two cases illustrate the nature of a trustee's duties to his or her customers and third parties and are strongly suggestive of ethical standards to which a trustee may need to adhere.

4. Ramifications of Cases Imposing Liability

The ramifications of the trend to impose liability for damages caused to non-client third parties can be far-reaching. The list of potential "damaged" beneficiaries is unlimited:

- Beneficiaries of previous will disinherited by new will.
- Beneficiaries inadvertently omitted from will.
- Beneficiaries of will negligently prepared.
- Beneficiaries of will negligently executed.
- Intestate distributees of will executed by allegedly disabled client.
- Beneficiaries of mismanaged estate or trust.

5. States Not Imposing Liability

States that adhere to strict privity rule include Nebraska, New York, Ohio, Iowa, and Texas.

6. States Imposing Liability

States that permit third parties to proceed with either (or both) a balancing factors test of negligence theory or third-party beneficiary of contracts claim include: California, Delaware, Hawaii, Kansas, Missouri, Nevada, Pennsylvania, and Washington.

21st Century Estate Planning:
Practical Applications
2005 Edition

©2005 Sonnenschein Nath & Rosenthal LLP
and Cannon Financial Institute, Inc.

- 687 -

→ **Planning Point:** Whether or not any particular jurisdiction permits a claim by a third party against an attorney should have no bearing on the duties owed by the attorney to the client (*e.g.*, duty of loyalty and confidentiality). However, it is incumbent on each practitioner to be aware of the changing legal climate that is allowing potential liability claims by third parties against attorneys.

7. **Third-Party Claims Against Accountants**

An accountant, when performing accounting and tax/estate planning services for either the testator or the testator's estate, is subject to numerous potential liabilities in the course of his representation. The following are examples of such potential claims:

- Providing erroneous tax advice
- Failure to properly advise as to tax implications of client's actions or documents
- Failure to timely file tax returns
- Failure to detect inaccuracies in financial information
- Failure to correctly reflect information on tax returns
- Failure to properly interpret statutes

Similar to claims against an attorney, these claims may be alleged by the client based on either allegations of negligence by the accountant or breach of contract. See *Jerry Clark Equipment, Inc. v. Hibbits*, 612 N.E.2d 858 (Ill. Appl. 1993). In addition, the standard of care that an accountant will be held to is similar to that of an attorney described above.

To what extent is an accountant potentially liable to third-party beneficiaries of the services provided? As discussed above, this may depend on whether the jurisdiction in which the accountant is rendering its services adheres to the strict privity doctrine (*e.g.*, New York), whether it allows third parties to proceed against the practitioner under either a negligence theory or third-party beneficiary contract claim (*e.g.*, California, North Carolina), or whether it has enacted legislation governing the liability of accountants to clients and third-parties (*e.g.*, Kansas, New Jersey, Illinois, Utah). In addition, the potential liability may depend on the type of services being rendered (*e.g.*, estate planning and tax advice v. preparation of fiduciary tax returns) and whether the services are provided pre-mortem or post-mortem.

Jewish Hosp. v. Boatmen's Nat'l Bank. One of the seminal cases addressing this issue is *Jewish Hosp. v. Boatmen's Nat'l Bank*, 633 N.E.2d 1267 (Ill. Ct. App. 1994), *appeal denied*, *Jewish Hosp. v. Boatmen's Nat'l Bank*, 642 N.E.2d 1282 (1994).

In 1982, the attorney drafted a Will for the decedent and, together with the accountant, developed an estate plan for the decedent. It was shown that the attorney and the accountant both assured the decedent that no estate tax would be due under the Will.

21st Century Estate Planning:
Practical Applications
2005 Edition

©2005 *Sonnenschein Nath & Rosenthal LLP*
and Cannon Financial Institute, Inc.

- 688 -

In 1984, after the decedent's death, the attorney was retained to represent the estate and the accountant was retained to provide accounting services to the estate. The estate tax return was filed accordingly.

Finally, in 1986, the estate received notice that it owed in excess of $850,000 because the charitable deduction and a portion of the marital deduction claimed were disallowed. The problem was that the Will gave the trustees of the charitable trusts the right to invade the principal on behalf of the decedent's wife and sister. The defendant attorney's attempt to reform the Will was unsuccessful.

The plaintiffs, Jewish Hospital of St. Louis and Jewish Center for the Aged, were the remainder beneficiaries of the testamentary trusts established by the decedent. They claimed that the actions of the attorney and the accountant "unnecessarily" caused the estate to pay $878,709 in taxes. With respect to the accountants, the plaintiffs sought to recover the tax liability as money damages in the preparation of the decedent's Will and estate plan. In addition, plaintiffs allege the accountants failed to timely reform the Will or to notify them of the problem once it came to light.

The Circuit Court entered summary judgment against the plaintiffs. One of the issues presented to the Appellate Court was whether an accountant owes a duty in contract or tort to the remainder beneficiaries of a testamentary trust or for improperly preparing an estate tax return.

(1) **Accountant's Duties During Life of Testator.** With respect to the services rendered by the accountant during the life of the testator, the Court stated that the primary purpose and intent of the accountant-client relationship was to benefit the plaintiffs. The Court found the reason that the decedent hired the accountant was to obtain information about estate taxes and that since the decedent would not personally benefit from the avoidance of estate taxes, the only satisfaction was knowing that the remaindermen would benefit. Accordingly, it was held that the accountant owed a duty to the plaintiffs and that the plaintiffs could proceed with their claims for negligence and breach of contract against the accountant for services rendered to the decedent during his lifetime.

(2) **Accountant's Duties Administration of the Estate.** The next issue was whether the plaintiffs could proceed against the accountant with respect to services rendered to the estate. The Court noted that the accountant was only involved in assisting the attorney in preparing the estate tax return. The Court held that the "primary duty of an accountant hired by the executor or the attorney for the executor is not to benefit the beneficiaries, rather, his duty is to the executor so that the executor can fulfill his duties as required by law." *Id* at 1279. Accordingly, it was held that the plaintiffs could not proceed with their claims for negligence and breach of contract against the accountant for services rendered to during the administration of the estate.

A similar conclusion was reached in *Blair v. Ing, supra.* In *Blair*, as more fully discussed above, the accountant was retained to prepare the necessary federal and state estate tax forms. Upon review by another attorney of the tax returns, the appellants were informed that there were

21st Century Estate Planning:
Practical Applications
2005 Edition

©2005 *Sonnenschein Nath & Rosenthal LLP*
and Cannon Financial Institute, Inc.

- 689 -

costly errors and omissions. The appellants accused the accountant of not recommending tax-saving techniques, such as disclaimers. The Court found that the appellants did not have standing to sue the accountant because he was retained only to prepare applicable tax returns and not to provide any estate planning advice. Accordingly, the post-mortem services provided were not intended to benefit the non-client beneficiaries. Since the appellants were not intended beneficiaries of the retention of the accountant, the court refused to hold him liable under either a negligence or third-party beneficiary theory.

Both *Jewish Hosp.* and *Blair* stand for the proposition that it is the nature of the services being provided by the accountant and the reasonable expectations of the parties that the services are intended to benefit third-parties that gives a non-client standing to sue an accountant under either a negligence or contract claim. In both cases, the services rendered post-mortem were merely intended to assist the fiduciary in the administration of the decedent's estate. However, if an accountant were to expand his role in the post-mortem planning (*e.g.*, offer tax advice regarding disclaimers), he would subject himself to possible third-party claims in these jurisdictions.

The Court in *Blair* distinguished the facts from an allegation against an accountant for "negligent misrepresentation." See *Kohala Agriculture v. Deloitte & Touche*, 949 P.2d 141 (Hawaii App. 1997) (holding that an accountant can be held liable to a third party if it can shown that the accountant negligently misrepresented information that the third-party relied on).

➔　　**Planning Point:** Whether or not any particular jurisdiction permits a claim by a third party against an attorney or other practitioner should have no bearing on the duties owed by the practitioner to the client (*e.g.*, duty of loyalty and confidentiality). However, it is incumbent on each practitioner to be aware of the changing legal climate that is allowing potential liability claims by third parties.

F. Attorney for Fiduciary – Who is the Client?

1. General

An attorney who is engaged to represent an executor or a trustee is confronted with the issue of "who is the client?" To whom does the attorney owe a duty of loyalty and care? Is it to the fiduciary, the estate, the beneficiaries, or all of the above?

2. Majority Position

The majority of states hold that the fiduciary is the client and that the attorney's duties are to that person and not to the beneficiaries. See *Jewish Hosp. v. Boatmen's Nat'l Bank, supra,* (attorney owes professional obligations to estate and not the beneficiaries in handling probate administration due to the potentially adversarial relationship between the interests of the estate and the interests of the beneficiaries). See also *Goldberg v. Frye*, 266 Cal. Rptr. 483 (Cal. Ct. App. 1990) (the attorney represents administrator of the estate and not the beneficiaries); *Borissoff v. Taylor & Faust*, 96 Cal. Rptr.2d 138 (Cal. Ct. App. 2002) (approving *Goldberg*, held

21st Century Estate Planning:
Practical Applications
2005 Edition

©2005 Sonnenschein Nath & Rosenthal LLP
and Cannon Financial Institute, Inc.

- 690 -

attorney for administrator of estate represents administrator and not the estate); *Weingarten v. Warren*, 753 F. Supp. 491 (S.D.N.Y. 1990) (the federal court applying New York law held trustee's lawyer liable to beneficiaries for aiding conversion but declined to impose malpractice liability on the attorney because of strict privity doctrine); Virginia Legal Ethics Opinion 1452 (August 1992) ("[a]lthough the attorney, in providing [services to the estate], may benefit the beneficiaries of the estate, the Committee is of the further opinion that there is no contractual privity with the beneficiaries which can give rise to an attorney-client relationship with those beneficiaries").

> **Query**: What are the attorney's obligations to the beneficiaries if the attorney discovers misconduct by the fiduciary?

3. Minority Position

Several states have begun to impose obligations on the attorney to the beneficiaries: *Steinway v. Bolden*, 460 N.W.2d 306 (Mich. App. 1990) (the client is the estate and not the personal representative); *Estate of Larson*, 694 P.2d 1051 (Wash. 1995) (duty runs not only to fiduciary but also to heirs), but cf. *Trask v. Butler*, 872 P.2d 1080 (Wash. 1994) (the Supreme Court of Washington, applying a multi-balancing test, determined that the attorney did not owe a duty to the beneficiaries of the estate).

Many states are willing to impose liability on the attorney for damage caused to beneficiaries without directly imposing an attorney-client relationship between the attorney and the beneficiaries. This is being accomplished by applying the balancing factors method under a negligence theory or breach of contract theory and a third-party beneficiary theory discussed in the previous section of this chapter.

4. Agreement of the Parties

The particular obligations that the attorney is undertaking, either to the fiduciary, to the estate or to the beneficiaries, should be disclosed to the parties prior to commencing the representation and should be properly documented. The fact, however, that the parties are made aware that the attorney's duties are to the fiduciaries does not preclude a court from imposing liability on the attorney for his actions.

➔ **Planning Point:** The attorney should preempt problems that may arise representing fiduciaries by clarifying in writing to all interested parties at the commencement of the representation the identity of the client and fully disclosing the scope of the representation. The attorney should also advise the beneficiaries that it may be advisable to retain their own counsel to independently represent their interests.

21st Century Estate Planning:
Practical Applications
2005 Edition

©2005 Sonnenschein Nath & Rosenthal LLP
and Cannon Financial Institute, Inc.

- 691 -

G. Continuing Obligations of Attorney After Representation Ends

1. General

What is an attorney's continuing obligation to a client once the initial tasks of the representation are completed?

This obligation can take one of two forms. First, does the attorney have a duty to monitor the affairs of the client to ensure that the estate plan originally prepared and executed is not frustrated by subsequent actions of the client? Second, does the attorney have a continuing obligation to advise clients of changes in the law occurring after the initial representation has ended?

2. Duty to Monitor Affairs of the Client to Ensure that the Estate Plan is not Frustrated by Subsequent Actions

The first issue was addressed in *Stangland v. Brock*, 747 P.2d 464 (Wash. 1987).

In 1979, attorney Norman Brock prepared a will for Ralph Schalack that left all of his real property to Alvin Stangland and Bruce Kintschi (the respondents). At the time the will was signed, the decedent's farm was the substantial asset of his estate. The residue of the estate was bequeathed to different individuals.

In February 1982, attorney Kenneth Carpenter, a real estate lawyer practicing in the same law firm as Brock, prepared a sales contract for the decedent's farm. Brock was not aware that the property was being sold. Carpenter stated that he had no knowledge of the terms of Schalack's will.

Schalack died on May 7, 1982. Respondents brought an action against Brock, Carpenter and their law firm seeking damages for professional negligence. Specifically, the complaint alleged that Brock was negligent in not drafting the will to provide that the farm (or sales proceeds thereof) would ultimately pass to the respondents, as was the intent of the decedent. In addition, the attorneys were alleged to be negligent by not advising the decedent that entering into the sale of the property would frustrate the intent under his will.

The court first examined whether the respondents had standing to bring a suit. The court opted to follow the modern trend of relaxing the privity rule where there is found an implied duty to the intended beneficiaries under the will, and proceeded to review the facts under both the multi-factor balancing test and the third-party beneficiary theory.

The court found that, notwithstanding that Brock was a member of the same law firm as Carpenter, Brock had no duty to advise the decedent of the contract's possible effect on his estate plan. The court stated:

> If we held that Brock had such a duty, we would be expanding the obligation of a lawyer who drafts a will beyond reasonable limits.

21st Century Estate Planning:
Practical Applications
2005 Edition

©2005 Sonnenschein Nath & Rosenthal LLP
and Cannon Financial Institute, Inc.

- 692 -

While an individual retains an attorney to draft his will the attorney's obligation is to use the care, skill, diligence and knowledge that a reasonable, prudent lawyer would exercise in order to draft the will according to the testator's wishes. Once that duty is accomplished, the attorney has no continuing obligation to monitor the testator's management of his property to ensure that the scheme established in the will is maintained. The time and expense that would be required for the attorney to follow all of the testator's activities with respect to his property would prevent the attorney from being able to provide reliable and economical services to that client, and would constitute an overwhelming burden on the attorney's practice as a whole.

The court further found that Carpenter had no reason to know of the contents of the decedent's will and could not have foreseen that the sale of the property may harm the respondents.

3. Attorneys Beware

It should be noted that the court's holding should not be read to imply that an attorney does not have any obligation to monitor a testator's activities with respect to his assets where the attorney has actual knowledge of a subsequent transaction.

Further, courts may be more inclined to impose a greater level of implied knowledge in situations where the firm represents the client on an ongoing basis (*e.g.*, high net-worth clients who require legal representation on a regular basis).

In addition, courts in other jurisdictions could reach a result that is less favorable to estate planning attorneys.

4. Model Rule 1.4 and Dormant Representation

Model Rule 1.4 provides that an attorney must keep his clients reasonably informed about the status of a matter and promptly comply with reasonable requests for information and shall explain a matter to the extent reasonably necessary to permit the client to make informed decisions.

The Commentaries to Rule 1.4 introduces the concept of "dormant representation," which is applicable to both the first and second issues, and provides as follows:

> The execution of estate planning documents and the completion of related matters, such as changes in beneficiary designations and the transfer of assets to the trustee of a trust, normally ends the period during which the estate planning lawyer actively represents an estate planning client. At that time, unless the representation is terminated by the lawyer or client, the representation becomes dormant, awaiting activation by the client....

21st Century Estate Planning:
Practical Applications
2005 Edition

©*2005 Sonnenschein Nath & Rosenthal LLP*
and Cannon Financial Institute, Inc.

- 693 -

While the lawyer remains bound to the client by some obligation, including the duty of confidentiality, the lawyer's responsibilities are diminished by the completion of the active phase of the representation. As a service the lawyer may communicate periodically with the client regarding the desirability of reviewing his or her estate planning documents. Similarly, the lawyer may send the client an individual letter or a form letter, pamphlet, or brochure regarding changes in the law that might affect the client. <u>In the absence of an agreement to the contrary, the lawyer is not obligated to send a reminder to a client whose representation is dormant or to advise the client of the effect that changes in the law or the client's circumstances might have on the client's legal affairs</u>. (emphasis added).

The Commentaries provides the following examples:

> Example 1.4-1: Lawyer (L) prepared and completed an estate plan for Client (C) in 1992. At C's request L retained the original documents executed by C. L performed no other legal work for C in 1993 or 1994 but has no reason to believe that C has engaged other estate planning counsel. L's representation of C is dormant. L may, but is not obligated to, communicate with C regarding changes in the law. If L communicates with C about changes in the law, but is not asked by C to perform any legal services, L's representation remains dormant.

> Example 1.4-2: Assume the same facts as in Example 1.4-1 except that L's partner (P) in 1993 and 1994 renders legal services to C in matters completely unrelated to estate planning, such as a criminal representation. L's representation of C with respect to estate planning matters remains dormant, subject to activation by C.

5.   Newsletters

Attorneys should be careful when sending out newsletters to clients advising them of changes in the law not to make any implication that the attorney has assumed the obligation to continually update the client as to future changes in the law or that the attorney has assumed any obligation to review any client's particular estate plan without first being contacted by the client. If the client has a reasonable belief that the representation has not ended, the attorney may have a continuing duty to that client. For example, several commentators have suggested that the retention by the attorney of original documents may suggest to the client that the attorney is undertaking to inform the client of changes in the law may affect the carrying out of the will's intent.

> ***Query***:   Does this impose an obligation on all attorneys who retain original wills to inform their clients how recent changes in the federal estate tax affect their estate plan? If so, is it sufficient to send out a newsletter?

21st Century Estate Planning:
Practical Applications
2005 Edition

©2005 Sonnenschein Nath & Rosenthal LLP
and Cannon Financial Institute, Inc.

- 694 -

➔ **Planning Point:** An attorney should set out his responsibilities carefully and in great detail in an engagement letter with respect to the actions to be taken by the attorney and should also include what will not be required of the attorney (*e.g.*, the obligation to see that a trust is funded, assets properly transferred or designated beneficiary forms properly completed). The engagement letter should clarify whether the attorney has a continuing duty to advise the client or to take other actions regarding subsequent changes in the law or other circumstances that may affect the client's estate plan. In addition, the attorney might consider sending an "exit" letter to the client specifying that the engagement has been completed and that the attorney assumes no obligation to inform the client of any changes in the law or otherwise that might require a reconsideration of the estate plan completed.

H. Liability for Client's Failure to Execute Documents

1. Attorney's Obligation to Have Documents Executed — Issue

Once an attorney has undertaken the obligation of preparing a client's estate plan, what is the attorney's duty to see that the documents are executed, especially if the attorney has knowledge that the client is terminally ill?

2. Model Rules 1.3

Model Rule 1.3 provides that a "lawyer shall act with reasonable diligence and promptness in representing a client."

3. No Duty Imposed on Attorney

Surprisingly, notwithstanding that many jurisdictions have expressed a willingness to allow non-client beneficiaries to sue the drafting attorney where the will is negligently prepared, the major cases reported addressing this issue have found that an attorney who did not have the documents signed before the client died was not liable in tort to the disappointed beneficiaries. Such was the holding in *Radovich v. Locke-Paddon*, 41 Cal. Rptr. 2d 573 (Cal. Ct. App. 1995).

In *Radovich*, the client initially executed a will in 1985. In June 1991, the attorney met with the client to discuss drafting a new will. The attorney learned at that time that the client was suffering from breast cancer, for which she was receiving chemotherapy treatments. The attorney sent the client "a rough draft" of the new will in October 1991. The client subsequently died in December 1991 without signing the new will.

The proposed beneficiary of the "new" will brought a malpractice claim against the attorney for failing to obtain the decedent's execution of the new will. The theory of the claim was that the attorney owed a duty of care and reasonable diligence to the proposed beneficiary.

21st Century Estate Planning:
Practical Applications
2005 Edition

©2005 Sonnenschein Nath & Rosenthal LLP
and Cannon Financial Institute, Inc.

- 695 -

The court acknowledged the trend moving away from a strict privity rule to one holding attorneys potentially liable to third parties. However, the court refused to extend this trend to a situation where the decedent never signed the will. The court reasoned that to hold an attorney accountable for not having documents signed before a client's death may cause attorneys to rush clients into signing testamentary documents. This would clearly violate the attorney's duty to the client by putting the interests of the beneficiaries ahead of the client's interests.

The court cited the holdings of two other jurisdictions dealing with similar facts. *Krawczyk v. Stingle*, 543 A.2d 733 (Conn. 1988) and *Gregg v. Lindsay*, 649 A.2d 935 (Penn. Super. Ct. 1994).

> **a. Krawczyk v. Stingle**. In *Krawczyk*, the decedent instructed the attorney to prepare two trust agreements ten days before he died and after informing the attorney he was about to undergo open-heart surgery. The court held that "the imposition of liability to third parties for negligent delay in the execution of estate planning documents would not comport with a lawyer's duty of undivided loyalty to the client." The court felt that imposition of such a duty would create an incentive for the attorney to encourage clients to execute documents to avoid a potential suit by third parties.

> **b. *Gregg v. Lindsay***. In *Gregg*, the attorney visited with the client in the hospital and was directed to draft a new will. The attorney drafted a will and brought it to the hospital that night. When two witnesses could not be found, the attorney left and returned the next day with the will. However, the client had died by that time. The proposed beneficiary sued the attorney on a third-party beneficiary contract claim. The court held that "this is nothing more than a case in which the testator died before he had executed a new will" and refused to extend liability to the attorney. The court emphasized the potential for mischief by third parties who could theoretically call an attorney, dictate the terms of a will for a hospitalized client, and then sue the attorney as an intended beneficiary if the will is not signed.

The court in *Radovich* then determined that without an executed will it could not find an express intent to help the beneficiary ("the only person who can say what he or she intended – has died") and further that harm to the beneficiary was not sufficiently foreseeable.

The court implied that the testatrix may have wanted to discuss the documents with her sister prior to executing them and may have decided that the new documents would not effectuate her intent; or may simply have changed her mind.

> We acknowledge that in the circumstances it would have been professionally appropriate, at least, for [attorney] to have inquired of the decedent whether she had any question or wished further assistance in completing the change of testamentary disposition she had discussed with him. But on weighing the relevant policy considerations we conclude that [attorney] and the law firm owed no duty to [beneficiary].

21st Century Estate Planning:
Practical Applications
2005 Edition

©2005 Sonnenschein Nath & Rosenthal LLP
and Cannon Financial Institute, Inc.

- 696 -

4. Required Diligence by Attorney

The attorney should not interpret the cases cited as giving him license not to act diligently in getting documents prepared and executed. This is especially so if the client is in bad health and indicates a desire to sign the documents. The cases cited each went to great lengths to show why the attorney was not at fault for not having the documents signed, including laying partial blame for the failure on the client. <u>Cf.</u> *People v. James*, 502 P.2d 1105 (Colo. 1971) (attorney disbarred for failing to prepare a will for 8 months after being employed to do so); *Discipline of Helder*, 396 N.W.2d 559 (Minn. 1986) (attorney indefinitely suspended for, *inter alia*, failing to make requested changes to a client's will).

The ramifications of these cases may extend beyond the obligation of an attorney to see that a will or trust is properly executed. What is the obligation of an attorney to see that property is transferred to fund a trust, that assets are properly titled (*e.g.*, joint tenancy, tenancy-in-common)? This may depend on the agreement of the parties.

➔ **Planning Point:** The rising tide seems to be in favor of invoking greater obligations and liability on the attorney to third parties. The cases cited have each gone to great lengths to find a valid reason why the attorney did not complete the estate plan, including attributing some responsibility for the documents not being signed on the part of the testator. Accordingly, it would be imprudent for an attorney to rely on these cases when dealing with clients.

Attorneys should be careful to prepare documents promised with due diligence and to be vigilant in following up with their clients to complete the estate plan undertaken (*i.e.*, send follow-up letters and perhaps phone calls). Also, the attorney should be careful to document the steps taken to have the documents executed, especially if the client is in obvious poor health.

21st Century Estate Planning:
Practical Applications
2005 Edition

©2005 Sonnenschein Nath & Rosenthal LLP
and Cannon Financial Institute, Inc.

- 697 -

Chapter XIX
Bibliography

ACTEC Commentaries on the Model Rules of Professional Conduct (3rd ed. 1999).

"Duty of Care to Certain Nonclients," *Restatement (Third) of the Law*, Ch. 4, Topic 1, §51 (1998).

Bradley E.S. Fogel, "Attorney v. Client-Privity, Malpractice, and the Lack of Respect for the Primacy of the Attorney-Client Relationship in Estate Planning," 68 *Tenn. L. Rev.* 261 (Winter 2001).

Ronald Mallen and Jeffrey Smith, *Legal Malpractice* (5th ed. 2000).

William M. McGovern, Jr. and Sheldon F. Kurtz, *Wills, Trusts and Estates, Including Taxation and Future Interests* (2nd ed. 2001).

Louis A. Mezullo, "Ethics for Estate Planners," CA52 ALI-ABA 295 (October 1995).

Jeffrey N. Pennell, "Ethics, Professionalism, and Malpractice Issues in Estate Planning and Administration," SC75 ALI-ABA 67 (June 14, 1998).

"Supervision of Lawyers and Nonlawyers Within an Organization," *Restatement (Third) of the Law*, Ch. 1, Topic J, Title C (1998).

Paul Toner, "Attorney Liability in the Wake of William v. Ely," 3 *Suffolk Journal of Trial and Appellate Advocacy* 193 (1998).

Warren R. Trazenfeld, "Legal Malpractice: A Framework for Assessing Potential Claims," 70 *Fla. Bar Journal* 38 (January 1996).

"What Constitutes Negligence Sufficient to Render Attorney Liable to Person Other Than Immediate Client," 64 *A.L.R.* 4th 464 (1998).

Elizabeth Williams, "Cause of Action Against Accountant for Negligent Performance of Professional Services," 15 Causes of Actions 2d 395 (2000).

21st Century Estate Planning:
Practical Applications
2005 Edition

©*2005 Sonnenschein Nath & Rosenthal LLP*
and Cannon Financial Institute, Inc.

- 698 -

XX. FIDUCIARY LIABILITY

A. Introduction

The duties and obligations of the fiduciary extend to the trusts and estates being administered and to the beneficiaries of such trusts and estates. Often these obligations may result in conflicts between the fiduciary and the beneficiaries or between the various beneficiaries. The fiduciary's obligations are continuous and must be monitored with increasing vigilance. A fiduciary, whether an individual or entity, has a unique legally mandated fiduciary relationship with each interested party and can be held liable to each of them for breaches of his or its fiduciary duty.

The purpose of this chapter is to educate the fiduciary as to certain of his responsibilities in the day-to-day administration of a trust or estate and to make the fiduciary aware of the types of issues and consequential liability that he may encounter while carrying out those responsibilities. The following are the topics discussed in this chapter:

- Duty to Diversify
- Duty of Loyalty and Self-Dealing
- Duty to Deal Fairly With Multiple Beneficiaries
- Payment of Trust Funds to Beneficiary Whose Interest is Terminated or to Non-Beneficiary
- Use of Exculpatory Provisions
- Unauthorized Practice of Law

B. Duty to Diversify

1. General

A fiduciary is under a duty to exercise reasonable care under the prudent investor rule in decisions relating to investment of trust and estate property. The fiduciary must use diligence and care in creating and maintaining a proper trust portfolio. Each time that a fiduciary chooses to make an investment, he must be sure to act within the terms of the governing instrument and in accordance with the applicable law.

One of the generally accepted principles of modern portfolio management is the duty to diversify. The rationale is that, by diversifying, the fiduciary reduces the risk of loss by distributing the risk. A fiduciary who is found not to have diversified can be surcharged for losses to the trust. See Estate of Janes, 659 N.Y.S.2d 165 (1997) (co-executor surcharged for failing to diversify high concentration of a single security).

The duty to diversify is imposed on the fiduciary by statute and case law. See 24 A.L.R. 3d 730 (1969) ("Duty of Trustee to Diversify Investments, and Liability for Failure to Do So") and 14 Am. Jur. Proof of Facts 2d 253 (1977) ("Trustee's Failure to Diversify Investments") for an extensive discussion of the history and the case law of the duty to diversify.

21st Century Estate Planning:
Practical Applications
2005 Edition

©2005 Sonnenschein Nath & Rosenthal LLP
and Cannon Financial Institute, Inc.

- 699 -

a. Uniform Prudent Investor Act. A majority of states have adopted the Uniform Prudent Investor Act ("UPIA") in one form or another. Section 3 of the UPIA provides that "[a] trustee shall diversify the investments of the trust unless the trustee reasonably determines that, because of special circumstances, the purposes of the trust are better served without diversifying."

b. Restatement (Third) of the Law — Trusts. Section 227(b) ("General Standard of Prudent Investment") of the RESTATEMENT (THIRD) OF THE LAW — TRUSTS ("RESTATEMENT (THIRD)") provides that "[i]n making and implementing investment decisions, the trustee has a duty to diversify the investments of the trust unless, under the circumstances, it is prudent not to do so."

c. Majority View. The majority of jurisdictions follow the UPIA and the RESTATEMENT (THIRD) and have taken the view that a fiduciary has a duty to diversify. A large number of the reported cases involve the investment by the fiduciary of a large percentage of the trust assets in a single stock. See *First Alabama Bank of Huntsville, N.A. v. Spragins*, 515 So.2d 962 (Ala. 1987) (a trustee bank was found to have breached its fiduciary duty to its beneficiaries by investing 70-75% of the trust assets in its own bank stock); *Estate of Janes*, 659 N.Y.S.2d at 171 (71% of assets held in a single stock). In addition, the cases focus on a number of additional factors:

- Geographical concentration of investments.
- Sector concentration of investments.
- Size of the trust account.
- Duration of holding securities.
- Purpose of the trust (*i.e.*, was it established to retain family business?).

The fact that the trustee does not diversify is not *per se* negligence, and the circumstances will dictate if the fiduciary is acting prudently. The Comments to the UPIA provide examples of a trustee's reason for not diversifying:

> **EXAMPLE:** For example, if a tax-sensitive trust owns an undiversified block of low-basis securities, the tax cost of recognizing the gain may outweigh the advantages of diversifying the holding. The wish to retain a family business is another situation in which the purposes of the trust sometimes outweigh the conventional duty to diversify.

d. Minority View. A minority of jurisdictions do not impose a common law duty to diversify. See *In re Elkins' Estate*, 20 Pa. D. & C. 483 (1934), *aff'd* 325 Pa. 323 (1937) (the court held there was no duty to diversify in Pennsylvania). The court, however, may find the failure to diversify as evidence of imprudent investing. *Matter of Fleet Trust Co.*, 662 N.Y.S.2d 360 (Surr. Ct. New York Cty. 1997), *rev'd by In re Jakobson*, 683 N.Y.S.2d 860 (App. Div. 1998) ("there is no absolute duty to diversify in all circumstances, and although a failure to diversify will not automatically result in liability, neither is a fiduciary automatically insulated

21st Century Estate Planning:
Practical Applications
2005 Edition

©2005 Sonnenschein Nath & Rosenthal LLP
and Cannon Financial Institute, Inc.

- 700 -

from liability based on a "mere" failure to diversify where the lack of diversification itself presents an unreasonable risk to the assets of the estate or trust"). It is important to note that the common law rule of many of these jurisdictions has been superseded by statutes adopting the UPIA's duty to diversify. See Section 7204 ("Diversification") of the Pennsylvania Prudent Investor Rule; New York E.P.T.L. 11-2.3(b)(3)(C). Furthermore, notwithstanding the absence of a statutory or common law duty to diversify, a specific provision in the governing instrument requiring diversification will impose a fiduciary obligation to diversify.

2. Measuring the Loss

There is a division among jurisdictions as to how to measure damages caused by a failure to diversify. Some cases have held a fiduciary liable for the actual losses sustained by the trust. Other cases permit a surcharge for "opportunity cost" damages measured by the difference between the actual results achieved and the return that could have been achieved with a properly diversified portfolio. See *105 East Second Street Ass'n v. Bobrow*, 573 N.Y.S.2d 503 (App. Div. 1991), *appeal after remand*, 605 N.Y.S.2d 870 (App. Div. 1993) (the measure of damages for breach of fiduciary duty is the amount of loss sustained, including lost opportunities for profit on the properties by reason of the fiduciary's conduct).

3. Retaining Investment Advisor

A fiduciary can reduce his exposure by seeking investment advice when he deems it necessary and proper. Generally, most wills and trust agreements provide that a fiduciary, at least a non-corporate fiduciary, may retain investment advisors. In addition, the prudent investor rule of most states also allows for the fiduciary to retain investment advisors. See New York EPTL Section 11-2.3(b)(4)(C) (trustee is authorized to "delegate investment and management functions if consistent with the duty to exercise skill, including special investment skills"). Notwithstanding the appointment of an investment advisor, the fiduciary is still obligated to review the investment decisions made by the advisor to determine if they appear prudent under the circumstances. The level of scrutiny that will be required by the fiduciary will depend on the circumstances, including the level of skills of the fiduciary and the types of investments being made.

4. Statutory Exception to Duty to Diversify

Some states have legislated exceptions to the duty to diversify. Under Virginia law, the fiduciary has an absolute immunity from claims that it did not follow the "prudent investor" rule in managing trust assets, provided the fiduciary invests in the assets specified by statute. The Virginia law, § 26-45.1, specifies the securities and a list of stock of which the fiduciary may invest and such investment shall be conclusively presumed to have been prudent. See *Scott v. United States of America*, 186 F. Supp. 2d 664 (E.D. Va. 2002).

5. Direct Authorization to Retain Assets

An express provision in the governing instrument can relieve a trustee from the duty to diversify. SCOTT ON TRUSTS (4th ed.) Section 230.3. Some cases, however, have held that a

21st Century Estate Planning:
Practical Applications
2005 Edition

©2005 Sonnenschein Nath & Rosenthal LLP
and Cannon Financial Institute, Inc.

- 701 -

general authorization in an instrument to retain specific assets will not protect a trustee from liability for failure to diversify. See *Rutanen v. Ballard*, 678 N.E.2d 133 (Mass. 1997) (trustee not allowed to retain unproductive assets notwithstanding general authorization in trust agreement to retain assets); Comments to Section 229 of the RESTATEMENT (THIRD) ("The duty to diversify is not absolute. With or without a general authorization to retain inception assets, other considerations may properly affect the trustee's decision in these matters."). The same may apply if the instrument specifically provides that the trustee may retain a particular asset. See *In re Estate of Saxton*, 686 N.Y.S.2d 573, 577-578 (1998) (trustee of testamentary trust which consisted of high concentration of shares of stock in a single corporation breached its fiduciary duty by failing to diversify trust assets over 30-year life of trust notwithstanding written agreement allowing trustee not to diversify). See also Comments to Section 229 of the RESTATEMENT (THIRD), which provides:

> In most instances a trustee should not take a settlor's authorization to retain specific investments as special justification indefinitely if retention would otherwise be imprudent, especially if an apparent purpose of the authorization becomes outdated by changed circumstances or passage of time.

But cf. *Baldus v. Bank of California*, 530 P.2d 1350 (Wash. Ct. App. 1975) (holding that a trust instrument may relieve the trustee of duty to diversify trust assets in absence of showing that trustee abused its discretion in failing to diversify trust investments).

→ **Planning Point:** Modern investment theories are focusing on the total return of investments and may impact strategic investing by fiduciaries. The fiduciary is advised not to overly invest in any one stock or group of stocks without the express written authorization of the testator or grantor in the will or trust agreement. Notwithstanding a direct authorization, the fiduciary is further encouraged to seek professional investment advice to ensure that the particular investment objectives under the governing instrument are maintained and should continually monitor investments to ensure that they remain prudent under the circumstances as they may exist from time to time.

C. Duty of Loyalty and Self-Dealing

1.   General

One of the most fundamental obligations owed by the fiduciary to the beneficiaries is the duty of loyalty. See SCOTT ON TRUSTS (4th ed.), Section 170. It is this unique relationship that has led courts to place a higher and stricter standard for the fiduciary's conduct whenever there is a conflict between the fiduciary's interests and those of the beneficiaries. As a general rule, the fiduciary is not permitted to directly or indirectly have a personal interest in any transaction involving trust property, regardless of the fairness of the transaction. To do so may constitute prohibited self-dealing. The fiduciary is normally held to the standard of care of a reasonably

21st Century Estate Planning:
Practical Applications
2005 Edition

©2005 Sonnenschein Nath & Rosenthal LLP
and Cannon Financial Institute, Inc.

- 702 -

prudent person. However, if the fiduciary engages in self-dealing, the standard of care is raised to a higher level. Judge Benjamin Cardoza is often quoted as having written:

> Many forms of conduct permissible in a workaday world for those acting at arm's length, are forbidden to those bound by fiduciary ties. A trustee is held to something stricter than the morals of the marketplace. Not honesty alone, but the punctilio of an honor the most sensitive, is then the standard of behavior. Uncompromising rigidity has been the attitude of courts of equity when petitioned to undermine the rule of undivided loyalty by the 'disintegrating erosion' of particular exceptions … Only thus has the level of conduct for fiduciaries been kept at a level higher than that trodden by the crowd.

Meinhard v. Salmon, 249 N.Y. 458, 464 (1928).

The following are instances of potential self-dealing between the fiduciary and the estate or trust being administered:

- Sale of trust property to fiduciary individually.
- Sale of trust property to entity controlled by fiduciary.
- Purchase of trust property by fiduciary directly from trust or at auction.
- Sale by corporate trustee to one of its departments, officers, or directors.
- Loan by trustee to trust.
- Loan by trust to trustee.
- Investment of trust property in fiduciary's own securities or deposit of trust funds in fiduciary's account.
- Employment of fiduciary as accountant or investment advisor for trust or estate.
- Personal use of trust property.

2.   **RESTATEMENT (SECOND) OF THE LAW — TRUSTS**

Section 170 ("Duty of Loyalty") of the RESTATEMENT (SECOND) OF THE LAW — TRUSTS ("RESTATEMENT (SECOND)") sets forth the fiduciary's duty as follows:

- The trustee is under a duty to administer the trust solely for the benefit of the beneficiaries.
- The trustee, in dealing with a beneficiary on the trustee's own account, is under a duty to deal fairly and to communicate to the beneficiary all material facts the trustee knows or should know in connection with the transaction.

The comments to the RESTATEMENT (SECOND) provide that the trustee is acting in a fiduciary relationship with the beneficiary as to the matters within the scope of the relationship and is under a duty not to profit at the expense of the beneficiaries, unless doing so is in accordance

21st Century Estate Planning:
Practical Applications
2005 Edition

©2005 Sonnenschein Nath & Rosenthal LLP
and Cannon Financial Institute, Inc.

- 703 -

with the express terms of the documents or is with the beneficiaries' consent or with court approval. The duty of loyalty promulgated in the RESTATEMENT (SECOND) is not limited to trustees; it also extends to other fiduciary relationships (*e.g.*, guardians and executors).

3. Defenses to Self-Dealing

The prohibition against self-dealing is not absolute. The fiduciary has available a number of possible defenses to a claim of impropriety. See Section 802 (Duty of Loyalty) of the Uniform Trust Code (2000) for a list of possible defenses. It is important to note, however, that a fiduciary's assertion that he acted in good faith or that the transaction was fair will not be a sufficient defense.

a. Consent of Beneficiaries. A self-dealing transaction generally will be respected if the beneficiaries consent, unless the fiduciary does not properly disclose all material elements of the transaction or exercises undue influence. See *Ramsey v. Boatmen's First Nat. Bank*, 914 S.W.2d 384, 388 (Mo. Ct. App. 1996) (trustee's failure to communicate with the beneficiary to see if she understood the nature of the transaction or that a conflict of interest existed invalidated acquiescence by beneficiary); *Renz v. Beeman*, 589 F.2d 735, 744 (2d Cir. 1978), *cert. denied*, 444 U.S. 834 (1979); *Beyer v. First Nat'l Bank*, 843 P.2d 53 (Colo. Ct. App. 1992); *Ford City Bank v. Ford City Bank*, 441 N.E.2d 1192 (Ill. App. Ct. 1992).

b. Provision in Governing Instrument Allowing Self-Dealing. A specific provision in the will or trust agreement will exonerate the fiduciary from self-dealing unless the fiduciary acts in bad faith. See *O'Hayer v. de St. Aubin*, 293 N.Y.S.2d 147 (App. Div. 1968); *Renz*, 589 F.2d at 745. Such provisions will be strictly applied. See *In re Kemske*, 305 N.W.2d 755 (Minn. 1981); *Jochec v. Clayburne*, 863 S.W.2d 516, 520 (Tex. Ct. App. 1993). See also discussion of "exculpatory provisions" later in this chapter.

c. Court Approval. A fiduciary may petition the court for approval for acts of self-dealing. The court will permit such transactions only after careful scrutiny and determination that the transaction is fair to the beneficiaries. See *Miller v. Miller*, 734 N.E.2d 738 (Mass. Ct. App. 2000) (court approved loan by executor to estate with interest); Comment f to Section 170 of the RESTATEMENT (SECOND) (courts may approve self-dealing transactions). The Uniform Probate Code permits self-dealing if the transaction is approved by the court after notice is provided to all interested parties. Uniform Probate Code Section 3-713. See also Section 5 of the Uniform Trustee's Powers Act (court approval required if conflict of interest exists). The fiduciary may seek approval before or after the transaction. See *Burlington v. Worcester*, 218 N.E.2d 123 (Mass. 1966).

d. Other Exceptions. Certain jurisdictions permit specific acts of "self-dealing" by a fiduciary under principles of common law or by statute. For example, certain jurisdictions allow the trustee to borrow from the trust, or for a corporate trustee to deposit trust funds in its own account during administration. See *Maryland Nat'l Bank v. Cummins*, 588 A.2d 1205 (Md. Ct. App. 1991).

21st Century Estate Planning:
Practical Applications
2005 Edition

©2005 Sonnenschein Nath & Rosenthal LLP
and Cannon Financial Institute, Inc.

- 704 -

4. Liability of the Trustee

a. Disgorgement of Profits. The trustee will be required to reimburse the trust for any loss caused to the trust as a result of the self-dealing and may be required to pay punitive damages in especially egregious situations. See *In re Guardianship and Conservatorship of Jordan*, 616 N.W.2d 553 (Iowa 2000). In addition, some courts also will require the trustee to disgorge any profits made on the transaction even if the trust suffered no financial harm because of the transaction. See *Coster v. Crookham*, 468 N.W.2d 802 (Iowa 1991).

b. Removal of Trustee. A court may remove the trustee if a conflict of interest exists between the trustee and the beneficiaries. See *Hanson v. First State Bank and Trust Co.*, 385 S.E.2d 266 (Ga. 1989) (court approved removing trustee where brother of settlor was beneficiary of trust and major shareholder and chairman of the board of the trustee bank; brother was deemed to be *de facto* trustee).

c. Equitable Remedies. Courts also may exercise any equitable remedy available to them, including enjoining the trustee from completing the transaction (*i.e.*, stop the trustee from purchasing trust property) or compelling the fiduciary to sell the property. See *Matter of Estate of Rolczynski*, 349 N.W.2d 394 (N.D. 1984). If the transaction has already taken place, the court can vacate the transaction. See Section 3-713 of the Uniform Probate Code (transactions involving a "substantial conflict of interest" are voidable).

→ **Planning Point:** A fiduciary always must be aware of his primary duty to the beneficiaries and must put that duty before that of his own self interests. In situations where there is a questionable conflict between the fiduciary's interests and those of the beneficiaries, the fiduciary is well advised to seek the consent of the beneficiaries or the applicable court. This holds true notwithstanding a provision in the governing instrument ostensibly permitting such action.

D. Duty to Deal Fairly With Multiple Beneficiaries

1. General

A fiduciary has a duty to deal fairly and impartially with all beneficiaries and to act with due regard for their respective interests. This rule applies whether the respective interests of the beneficiaries are concurrent (*e.g.*, multiple current beneficiaries) or successive (*e.g.*, current beneficiaries v. remaindermen).

2. Restatement (Third)

Section 183 of the RESTATEMENT (THIRD) provides that "[w]hen there are two or more beneficiaries of a trust, the trustee is under a duty to deal impartially with them."

21st Century Estate Planning:
Practical Applications
2005 Edition

©2005 Sonnenschein Nath & Rosenthal LLP
and Cannon Financial Institute, Inc.

- 705 -

Section 232 of the RESTATEMENT (THIRD) provides that "[i]f a trust is created for beneficiaries in succession, the trustee is under a duty to the successive beneficiaries to act with due regard to their respective interests."

3. Specific Conflicts Among Beneficiaries

The following are a few of the potential areas where the fiduciary's duty to deal impartially with multiple beneficiaries may arise:

a. <u>Concurrent Multiple Discretionary Beneficiaries</u>. Absent specific direction from the settlor in the governing instrument or otherwise, the trustee of a discretionary trust with multiple current beneficiaries is under a duty to deal impartially with respect to all of the beneficiaries, whether they be income and/or principal beneficiaries. A fiduciary's exercise of discretion will not be disturbed unless the fiduciary acts in bad faith or in an unreasonable manner. See *U.S. v. O'Shaughnessy*, 517 N.W.2d 574 (Minn. 1994) (where trust gave trustee complete discretion to distribute all, some or none of the trust assets, the beneficiary had a mere expectancy interest until the trustee elected to make payments and the court will not interfere absent showing of bad faith or failure to act reasonably); *Dunkley v. Peoples Bank & Trust Co.*, 728 F. Supp. 547 (W.D. Ark. 1989) (under Florida law, trustee must exercise discretion reasonably and with proper motives in interest of beneficiaries). Even though there is no clear standard by which to judge reasonableness, courts generally will intervene in such discretionary decisions only where the trustee acts in contravention of his fiduciary duties, *e.g.*, dishonestly, in bad faith or with intentional disregard of the interests of the beneficiaries. See SCOTT ON TRUSTS (4th ed.) Section 187.2. If a trustee acts in an unbiased manner in the exercise of his discretion and applies the same standards to all distribution decisions absent a direction in the trust instrument to the contrary, his actions are likely to be considered reasonable. *McNeil v. Bennett*, 2001 WL 815443 (Del. 2001) (trustees had a duty to consider the interests of beneficiaries, belonging to multiple family generations, impartially and to act reasonably in making allocation decisions). See also U.S. Trust, Practical Drafting, January 2002 at 6699.

b. <u>Successive Beneficiaries</u>. The trustee also may have to make investment and distribution decisions that have an inverse relationship between the current beneficiaries and the remainderman. This is often the case with a marital trust requiring that mandatory income and discretionary principal be paid to the spouse and the remainder to the children. Should the trustee invest in high-income-producing assets (*e.g.*, bonds) or low income but high-appreciating securities? Should the trustee make distributions to the current beneficiaries, thereby leaving less for the remaindeman? The trustee has a dual, and potentially conflicting, duty to the beneficiaries. The trustee has a duty to the income beneficiaries to preserve the trust property and to make it productive. He also has a duty to the remaindermen to preserve the trust principal. As is the case with concurrent beneficiaries, absent specific direction in the governing instrument, the trustee owes a duty of loyalty to all of the beneficiaries and should not adopt a course of conduct that will benefit one class at the expense of the other. See *Dennis v. R.I. Hosp. Trust Nat'l Bank*, 744 F.2d 893 (1st Cir. 1984) (trustee's management of trust assets favored the life tenant to the "very real disadvantage" of the remainder interests in violation of Rhode Island law, which requires the trustee to act impartially in the interests of both the life tenant and the

21st Century Estate Planning:
Practical Applications
2005 Edition

©2005 Sonnenschein Nath & Rosenthal LLP
and Cannon Financial Institute, Inc.

- 706 -

remainderman); *Matter of Maxwell*, 704 A.2d 49 (N.J. Superior Ct. 1997), *cert. denied*, 708 A.2d 65 (1998) (allegations that trustees breached their fiduciary duties by failing to impartially administer assets for the benefit of both the life beneficiaries and the remaindermen were legally sufficient to maintain cause of action); *Matter of Hamill*, 410 A.2d 770 (Pa. 1980) (trustee was not under absolute duty to maximize current trust income for the benefit of the income beneficiaries, but could exercise discretion in preserving balance between successive beneficiaries).

In upholding the duty of impartiality, the trustee should use his discretion and judgment in light of the purposes and terms of the trust. The trust's terms expressly may affect the trustee's duties to the beneficiaries. See *Stevens v. National City Bank*, 544 N.E.2d 612 (Ohio 1989) ("A settlor has the power to make provisions in a trust which alter or even eliminate the trustee's duties to diversify, to make trust property productive, or even the duty to invest as would a prudent man"). For example, the trust may give the trustee the authority to accumulate income or discretion to pay or apply principal for the benefit of an income beneficiary. The trust instrument may also authorize or direct the trustee to purchase or retain property that might otherwise be considered unproductive or wasting and, therefore, an improper investment.

   c. <u>Litigation</u>. Conflict among beneficiaries also may lead to litigation. The fiduciary may not take sides in any conflict between beneficiaries. See *In re Cudahy Family Trust*, 131 N.W.2d 882 (Wis. 1965) (contest between beneficiaries over will construction); *In re James' Estate*, 86 N.Y.S.2d 78 (Surr. Ct. 1948) (conflict over distribution of income). But see *Indian Head Nat'l Bank of Nashua v. Brown*, 455 A.2d 1056 (N.H. 1983) (trustee did not breach its fiduciary duty by suggesting an interpretation of an ambiguous trust instrument that favored one beneficiary over another). It is also improper for the fiduciary to initiate litigation for the purpose of favoring one beneficiary over another. See *Redfield v. Critchley*, 300 N.Y.S. 305 (App. Div. 1937), *aff'd*, 277 N.Y. 336 (1938) (trustees breached duty of impartiality in initiating litigation for judgment declaring that life beneficiary had renounced interest).

   d. <u>Administration</u>. A fiduciary owes a duty of impartiality to all beneficiaries in the administration of the trust and must protect the interests of each beneficiary. In *Estate of Sewell*, 409 A.2d 401 (Pa. 1979), a trustee was deemed to have breached its duty of impartiality by making payments to one beneficiary while having failed to locate and make proper payments to another beneficiary.

  4. **Uniform Prudent Investor Act**

The UPIA attempts to reconcile the needs of the different beneficiaries by adopting a modern portfolio theory whereby investors seek a "total return" of current income and capital appreciation. Section 2(b) of the UPIA provides that "[a] trustee's investment and management decisions respecting individual assets must be evaluated not in isolation but in the context of the trust portfolio as a whole and as a part of an overall investment strategy having risk and return objectives reasonably suited to the trust." Modern portfolio theory's emphasis on total return may be in conflict with the fiduciary's duty of impartiality, which requires a balancing of the interests of the income and remainder beneficiaries. Recognizing this conflict, Section 104 of the Uniform Principal and Income Act was amended in 1997 to enable a trustee, under certain

21st Century Estate Planning:
Practical Applications
2005 Edition

©*2005 Sonnenschein Nath & Rosenthal LLP*
and Cannon Financial Institute, Inc.

- 707 -

circumstances, to adjust between principal and income. The comments to Section 104 provide that the purpose is "to enable a trustee to select investments using the standards of a prudent investor without having to realize a particular portion of the portfolio's total return in the form of traditional trust accounting income such as interest, dividends, and rents." See also New York EPTL Section 11-2.3(b)(5) (trustee has power to adjust between income and principal).

5.   Unitrust Provision

In addition to the power to adjust, New York recently enacted legislation permitting the trustee to elect to make payments of a unitrust amount to the current income beneficiaries in place of the trust's stated distribution. See New York EPTL Section 11-2.4. See also La. Rev. Stat. Ann. Section 2068 (the trust instrument may direct the trustee to distribute a unitrust or annuity amount to the current income beneficiary even if such payments exceed current or accumulated income).

6.   Court Direction

Courts of equity traditionally have permitted a fiduciary to protect himself by applying to the court for direction in certain instances where there is doubt as to whether an action would be a breach of fiduciary duty. See *Messner v. DeMotte*, 82 N.E.2d 900 (Ind. App. Ct. 1948) ("A trustee need not act at his peril. He may under appropriate circumstances apply to the court for advice and instructions."); *Comtrade, Inc. v. First Nat'l Bank of Highland Park*, 497 N.E.2d 527 (Ill. App. Ct. 1986) (the only prudent course of action for the trustee to take when presented with conflicting claims to the trust fund was to apply to the court for direction). This common law principle has been codified by statute in many states. For example, the Ohio Rev. Code Section 2107.46 ("Action by Fiduciary") permits the fiduciary to "ask direction or judgment of the court in any manner respecting the trust, estate, or property to be administered and the rights of the parties in interest." See also Section 259 of the RESTATEMENT (SECOND) which states that "[t]he trustee is entitled to apply to the court for instructions as to the administration of the trust if there is reasonable doubt as to his duties or powers as trustee." The comments to Section 259 provide guidance as to what matters may be the proper subject of such an application. These include the proper construction of the trust instrument, the extent of the trustee's powers and duties, the identity of the beneficiaries of the trust, the character and extent of the beneficiaries' interests, the allocation or apportionment of receipts or expenditures between principal and income, and the persons entitled to the income or to the trust property on the termination of the trust. See also SCOTT ON TRUSTS (4th ed.) Section 259.

➔   **Planning Point:** Absent specific direction to the contrary, a fiduciary must act with impartiality among the various beneficiaries and should not take actions that may benefit one group over another. The best avenues of protection for the trustee to follow are to seek court approval and to periodically account to the beneficiaries, either judicially or by informal receipt and release.

21st Century Estate Planning:
Practical Applications
2005 Edition

©2005 Sonnenschein Nath & Rosenthal LLP
and Cannon Financial Institute, Inc.

- 708 -

E. Payment of Trust Funds to Beneficiary Whose Interest is Terminated or to Non-Beneficiary

1. General

A fiduciary is obligated not only to monitor the needs of a beneficiary to determine if distributions should be made to such beneficiary, but also is obligated to continually monitor whether or not the interest of the beneficiary has terminated under the trust (*e.g.*, beneficiary has died). In addition, it is the trustee's obligation to ascertain if the person to whom a distribution is made is indeed a beneficiary (*e.g.*, does an adopted child inherit under the will). A fiduciary who breaches this duty will be held personally liable to the actual beneficiaries. That the fiduciary may have a cause of action against the person to whom the payment was wrongfully made will not exculpate the fiduciary from his own liability.

2. Restatement (Third)

Section 226 of the RESTATEMENT (THIRD) provides as follows:

> If by the terms of the trust it is the duty of the trustee to pay or convey the trust property or any part thereof to a beneficiary, he is liable if he pays or conveys to a person who is neither a beneficiary nor one to whom the beneficiary or the court has authorized him to make such payment or conveyance.

The comments to the RESTATEMENT (THIRD) provide that the trustee should be held liable even if he makes the payment under a reasonable mistake of law or of fact. See also 106 N.Y. Juris. 2d Trusts, Section 568 ("A trustee who distributes trust property under a mistake of law is nevertheless liable irrespective of his good faith and due care. A trustee who distributes property under a mistake of fact is liable only if he was either in a position to discover the facts or could have taken preventive steps to foreclose the known claimant but failed to do so.") If in doubt, the fiduciary is advised to seek judicial guidance from the court.

> *Query*: A fiduciary under a testamentary trust is directed to pay income to X for life and then to X's "wife" for life and then to X's descendants. At the time the will was signed and the testator died, X was married to Y. Subsequently, X divorces Y and marries Z. At X's death, who is the "wife" and consequentially should receive the income: Y or Z?

3. Specific Situations of Mispayment

The following are a few of the potential scenarios the fiduciary may encounter during administration of an estate or trust:

a. Payment to Deceased Beneficiary. A number of cases have dealt with the situation of a trustee continuing to make payments to a beneficiary who has died. The courts generally have held the trustee liable even if he acted in good faith. See *Darling Stores v.*

21st Century Estate Planning:
Practical Applications
2005 Edition

©2005 Sonnenschein Nath & Rosenthal LLP
and Cannon Financial Institute, Inc.

- 709 -

Fidelity-Bankers Trust Co., 156 S.W.2d 419 (Tenn. 1941) (trustee found negligent for issuing checks to beneficiary after beneficiary's death that were, with the trustee's knowledge, cashed by the beneficiary's wife; trustee had an ongoing duty to inquire as to the authority of the wife to cash the checks). See also *In re Sniffin's Estate*, 36 N.Y.S.2d 527 (Surr. Ct. Westchester Cty. 1942), *rev'd* 39 N.Y.S.2d 1017 (App. Div. 1943) (trustee liable for making payments to dead beneficiary notwithstanding fraud by third party). Cf. *Lanston v. American Sec. & Trust Co.*, 32 A.2d 482 (Mun. Ct. App. D.C. 1943) (trustee held not liable when payments made to deceased beneficiary were deemed an "honest mistake").

b. Payment to Remarried Spouse. Often a clause in a will or a trust conditions the continued payment to a spouse until such time as the spouse remarries or dies. In *National Academy of Sciences v. Cambridge Trust Co.*, 346 N.E.2d 879 (Mass. 1976), the testator's will provided that upon the death or remarriage of his wife, the trust fund was to pass to a charity. The trustee continued to make payments to the wife for over 20 years after she remarried. The court ordered the trustee to repay the trust for payments erroneously made to the wife. The court was especially troubled that the bank had made false representations concerning the marital status of the wife.

c. Adopted Children. The issue of whether adopted children may take under a will or trust agreement has been continually debated in the courts and has taken on many evolutions. The fiduciary is obligated to determine if the terms of the governing instrument or applicable law allow for an adopted child or grandchild to inherit. The fiduciary's liability can arise when wrongfully making payments to an adopted child, see *Old Colony Trust Co. v. Wood*, 74 N.E.2d 141 (Mass. 1947) (payment made by trustee to adopted child not permitted under will); or for failing to make payments to an adopted child, see *Estate of Sewell*, 409 A.2d 401 (Pa. 1979) (trustee held liable for neglecting to make payment to adopted child).

➔ **Planning Point:** The duty of the fiduciary to monitor the entitlement of a beneficiary to receive distributions is an ongoing obligation. The fiduciary must first determine who are the rightful beneficiaries. If in doubt, the fiduciary should make independent inquiries or seek judicial guidance. Finally, the fiduciary must establish a practice of continually monitoring the beneficiary prior to making any distributions to ensure that the beneficiary's interest has not terminated.

F. Use of Exculpatory Provisions

1. General

Often a will or trust instrument will contain an exculpatory provision relieving and insulating the fiduciary from liability for a breach of a fiduciary duty. The effectiveness of such a provision is not always guaranteed and may depend on a number of factors. Courts readily limit the enforceability of such provisions when the particular breach does not fall within the precise scope of the applicable provision; it would be against public policy to relieve the trustee from liability for the particular breach, or if the provision was improperly inserted in the trust instrument. See SCOTT ON TRUSTS (4th ed.) Section 222.

21st Century Estate Planning:
Practical Applications
2005 Edition

©*2005 Sonnenschein Nath & Rosenthal LLP*
and Cannon Financial Institute, Inc.

- 710 -

a. Restatement (Second). Section 222(1) of the RESTATEMENT (SECOND) provides that the trustee generally can be relieved of liability for breach of trust except: (i) for breach of trust committed in bad faith, intentionally or with reckless indifference to the interest of the beneficiary; (ii) for liability for any profit which the trustee derived from a breach of trust; and (iii) where a provision relieving the trustee of liability for breaches of trust is inserted in the trust instrument as the result of an abuse by the trustee of a fiduciary or confidential relationship to the settlor. The comments to Section 222 provide that exculpatory provisions are to be strictly construed and cannot relieve the trustee of liability where to do so would be contrary to public policy.

The Uniform Trust Code ("UTC") was adopted by the Conference of Commissioners on Uniform State Laws in 2000, approved by the American Bar Association in 2000, and introduced in the legislatures of eight states and the District of Columbia as of 2002. Section 1008 of the UTC is almost identical to Section 222 of the RESTATEMENT (SECOND), except that the UTC permits a settlor to exculpate a trustee for a profit that the trustee made from the trust (other than as a result of bad faith or reckless indifference to the purposes of the trust or interests of the beneficiaries).

b. Majority Approach. A majority of states have either adopted the RESTATEMENT (SECOND) approach to enforceability of exoneration provisions or have adopted a similar approach permitting exculpatory clauses within certain set limits. In these jurisdictions, exculpatory clauses may relieve the trustee from liability for errors of judgment, failure to diversify trust investments, or the acts or defaults of co-trustees. See *Hanson v. Minette*, 461 N.W.2d 592 (Iowa 1990) (exculpatory clause valid to relieve trustee from liability for negligent breach of duty); *Estate of McCredy*, 470 A.2d 585 (Pa. Super. 1983) (trustee relieved of liability for purchase of stock in corporation of which he was an officer, director and stockholder). As a general rule, however, such jurisdictions will not permit exculpatory clauses to relieve the fiduciary for liability beyond ordinary negligence. See *Collins v. Storer Broadcasting Co.*, 120 S.E.2d 764 (Ga. 1961) (settlor may relieve trustee of liability for involuntary, inadvertent, negligent, mistaken, careless or accidental default that does not rise to the level of willful default).

c. New York Approach. New York has adopted a statute severely restricting the enforceability of exculpatory clauses. See New York Estates, Powers and Trusts Law Section 11-1.7. The New York statute provides that any provision in a will exonerating a trustee from liability for failure to exercise reasonable care, diligence and prudence is void as against public policy. Therefore, in *Matter of Allister*, 545 N.Y.S.2d 483 (Surr. Ct. 1989), the court held that a provision authorizing the retention of assets by the trustee in his uncontrolled discretion without liability for any decrease in value was void as against public policy as an attempt to exonerate the fiduciary from the duty of exercising reasonable care and prudence. Similarly, in *Matter of Lubin*, 539 N.Y.S.2d 695 (Surr. Ct. 1989), the court held that a will clause attempting to exonerate the fiduciary for any loss or injury to the property except as may result from fraud, misconduct or gross negligence was void as against public policy because it attempted to exonerate the fiduciary from liability for failure to use reasonable care, diligence and prudence. EPTL Section 11-1.7 does not apply to the trustee of an *inter vivos* trust. See *Bauer v.*

21st Century Estate Planning:
Practical Applications
2005 Edition

©2005 Sonnenschein Nath & Rosenthal LLP
and Cannon Financial Institute, Inc.

- 711 -

Bauernschmidt, 589 N.Y.S.2d 582 (App. Div. 1992) (upholding validity of provision in *inter vivos* trust that fiduciary was not to be held liable for any act or failure to act where he acted in good faith).

         d. Texas Approach. Some states, including Texas, have taken a less restrictive approach to exculpatory clauses. Under the Texas statute, the settlor may relieve the trustee of certain duties, liabilities, or restrictions imposed by the Texas Trust Code. V.T.C.A., Property Code §113.059. See *Corpus Christi Nat'l Bank v. Gerdes*, 551 S.W.2d 521 (Tex. Civ. App. 1991) (exculpatory clause enforced even in case of gross negligence); *Burnett v. First Nat'l Bank of Waco*, 567 S.W.2d 873 (Tex. Civ. App. 1978), *writ refuse n.r.e.* (1978) (trustee exonerated of liability for loaning money to companies owned by settlor/beneficiary); *Neuhaus v. Richards*, 846 S.W.2d 70 (Tex. Ct. App. 1992), *reh'g overruled* (1993), *writ granted* (1993), *set aside,* 871 S.W.2d 182 (Tex. 1994) (trustee relieved of duty to comply with prudent person standard).

2. Public Policy

         An exculpatory clause may not relieve a trustee of liability where to do so would violate public policy. Therefore, a trustee is liable if he acts in bad faith or with reckless or intentional disregard of the interests of the beneficiaries. See SCOTT ON TRUSTS (4th ed.) Section 222.3; *Feibelman v. Worthen Nat'l Bank*, 20 F.3d 835 (8th Cir. 1994) (under Arkansas law, trust instrument cannot relieve the trustee of liability for breach of trust committed with reckless indifference of beneficiary's interest); *Mest v. Dugan*, 790 P.2d 38 (Or. Ct. App. 1990) (where trust permitted self-dealing by trustees, they are exonerated for self-dealing in the absence of bad faith).

3. Strict Construction

         Exculpatory clauses are strictly construed by the courts and a fiduciary is relieved from liability only to the extent it is expressly provided in the trust instrument that he is entitled to such relief. See *Perling v. Citizens & Southern Nat'l Bank*, 300 S.E.2d 649 (Ga. 1983) (trustees were relieved from duty of acting as prudent men in clear and unambiguous terms); *Grizzle v. Texas Commerce Bank*, 38 S.W.3d 265 (Tex. Ct. App. 2001) (exculpatory provisions are strictly construed and the trustee is relieved from liability only to the extent clearly provided in the trust instrument).

4. Abuse of Discretion

         An exculpatory provision is not effective to relieve the trustee from liability if it was improperly inserted in the trust instrument, such as where the person named as trustee inserts the provision and in so doing abuses an existing fiduciary or confidential relationship. See SCOTT ON TRUSTS (4th ed.) Section 222.4; *Jothann v. Irving Trust Co.*, 270 N.Y.S. 721 (Sup. Ct. 1934), *aff'd*, 277 N.Y.S. 955 (App. Div. 1935) (reformation permitted where testatrix had little business experience and relied on advice of corporate trustee in preparation and execution of will). The comments to the RESTATEMENT (SECOND) provide the following factors to be considered in determining whether an exculpatory provision was improperly inserted in the trust instrument:

21st Century Estate Planning:
Practical Applications
2005 Edition

©2005 Sonnenschein Nath & Rosenthal LLP
and Cannon Financial Institute, Inc.

- 712 -

- Whether the trustee prior to the creation of the trust had been in a fiduciary relationship to the settlor, as where the trustee had been guardian of the settlor.
- Whether the trust instrument was drawn by the trustee or by a person acting wholly or partially on his behalf.
- Whether the settlor had taken independent advice as to the provisions of the trust instrument.
- Whether the settlor was a person of experience and judgment or was a person unfamiliar with business affairs or was not a person of much judgment or understanding.
- Whether the insertion of the provision was due to undue influence or other improper conduct on the part of the trustee.
- The extent and reasonableness of the provision.

Unlike the RESTATEMENT (SECOND), Section 1008(b) of the UTC establishes a rebuttable presumption that an exculpatory clause drafted by the trustee is invalid. To overcome the presumption of abuse, the trustee must establish that the clause was fair and that its existence and contents were adequately communicated to the settlor. The following factors are suggested for consideration in determining whether the clause was fair:

- The extent of the prior relationship between the settlor and trustee.
- Whether the settlor received independent advice.
- The sophistication of the settlor with respect to business and fiduciary matters.
- The trustee's reasons for inserting the clause.
- The scope of the particular provision inserted.

→ **Planning Point:** The prudent fiduciary will insist that the governing instrument contain an exculpatory provision that affords the fiduciary the greatest protection. The fiduciary, however, must insist that the settlor independently review and approve the scope of the provision, especially where a prior fiduciary or confidential relationship exists between the fiduciary and the settlor.

G. Unauthorized Practice of Law

General

Every state prohibits non-attorneys from engaging in the unauthorized practice of law. The penalty for the unauthorized practice of law can range from the fiduciary being required to disgorge profits, being enjoined from acting, and even criminally prosecuted. See New York Judiciary Law Section 478. What activities constitute the "practice of law" is defined by each state's statutes, case law, and advisory and disciplinary opinions, and must be determined on a case-by-case basis.

21st Century Estate Planning:
Practical Applications
2005 Edition

©2005 Sonnenschein Nath & Rosenthal LLP
and Cannon Financial Institute, Inc.

- 713 -

It is becoming more and more common for banks, trust companies, investment advisors, investment banks, and insurance companies to offer services to their clients that extend beyond their traditional scope. For example, it is rare to find a trust company or investment bank that does not offer estate planning services to their clients. Some companies are even going so far as to prepare estate planning documents for their client (*e.g.*, wills and revocable trusts).

This section will discuss how various jurisdictions treat these activities and what the attorney should be aware of when working with fiduciaries offering such services.

1.   **Estate Planning Kits and "How to" Books**

       a.   <u>Estate Planning Kits</u>. The general view is that the drafting of a will or the supervision of its execution by a non-attorney constitutes the unauthorized practice of law. See 22 A.L.R.3d 1112. In addition, giving advice as to the contents and legal effect of a will was also deemed the unauthorized practice of law. *Indiana State Bar Ass'n v. Osborne*, 172 N.E.2d 434 (Ind. 1961). Frequently, banks, trust companies, and others sell estate planning kits that discuss estate planning techniques and provide forms for the reader to use when implementing these techniques (*e.g.*, blank will and trust agreement forms). The courts are divided as to whether this constitutes the unauthorized practice of law. In *The Florida Bar v. American Senior Citizens Alliance*, 689 So.2d 255 (Florida 1997), the court held that a corporation in the business of creating and selling estate planning documents was engaged in the unauthorized practice of law when non-attorney employees answered specific legal questions, determined appropriateness of different documents for clients, and assembled and drafted documents. See also *Unauthorized Practice of Law Commission v. Parsons*, 1999 WL 47235 (N.D. Tex. 1999), vacated and remanded 179 F.3d 956 (5th Cir. 1999). Others have held that the "mere gathering of information" by the non-attorney so that an attorney may complete the estate planning documents is not prohibited. See *The Florida Bar Re Advisory Opinion--Nonlawyer Preparation Of Living Trust*, 613 So. 2d 426, 428 (Fla. 1992) ("gathering the information ... does not constitute the practice of law, and nonlawyers may properly perform this activity").

       b. <u>"How To" Books.</u> A number of cases have held that the publication of "how to" books that advise the reader on general issues of law and how to represent themselves does not constitute the unauthorized practice of law. See *People v. Landlords Professional Services*, 264 Cal. Rptr. 548 (Cal. 1989); *New York County Lawyer's Ass' v. Dacey*, 234 N.E.2d 457 (N.Y. 1967) (publication of "How to Avoid Probate" book did not constitute the practice of law). A number of the cases addressing the "how to" category of cases stress the fact that there is no direct one-on-one contact between the author and the reader.

       Query: What if the non-attorney author discusses the contents of the book at a seminar? Should it matter if there is a question-and-answer portion to the seminar?

       c. <u>Drafting and Funding Living Trusts.</u> As more and more estate planners are advising their clients to establish and fund living revocable trusts, ostensibly to avoid the difficulties associated with probate, the issue of what services a non-attorney may offer arises in connection with such trusts. See *The Florida Bar Re Advisory Opinion--Nonlawyer Preparation*

21st Century Estate Planning:
Practical Applications
2005 Edition

©2005 Sonnenschein Nath & Rosenthal LLP
and Cannon Financial Institute, Inc.

- 714 -

Of Living (the Supreme Court of Florida held that the assembly, drafting, execution and funding of a living trust document constitutes the practice of law); *People v. Volk*, 805 P.2d 1116 (Colo. 1991) (the creation and sale of trust documents by non-attorneys constitutes the unauthorized practice of law). See also, *Cleveland Bar Ass'n v. Yurich*, 642 N.E.2d 79 (Ohio 1994) (corporation formed to market and sell living trusts to clients engaged in unauthorized practice of law). As discussed above, however, the mere gathering of necessary information for a living trust does not constitute the practice of law, and, thus, non-lawyers may properly perform that activity. See *The Florida Bar Re Advisory Opinion--Nonlawyer Preparation Of Living* at 428.

2. Providing Estate Planning Advice

The trend towards the offering of estate planning advice by non-attorneys brings to the forefront the issue of what are the limits, if any, of the estate planning advice that the non-attorney can provide.

a. Prohibited Activity. In *Green v. Huntington Nat'l Bank*, 212 N.E.2d 585 (Ohio 1965), a bank's repeated practice of giving specific legal information in relation to the specific facts of a client's estate plan for the purpose of obtaining beneficial tax and other legal results was held the unauthorized practice of law. The court did not find it sufficient that the bank advised the client to obtain independent legal counsel. The bank gave the advice with the reasonable expectation that it would receive full compensation in the form of being retained to provide fiduciary services for the client. See also *Trumbull County Bar Ass'n v. Hanna*, 80 Ohio St. 3d 58 (Ohio 1997) (non-attorney financial planner, who reviewed estate planning analysis and advised clients that *inter vivos* trusts would be suitable for their needs, held to have engaged in unauthorized practice of law).

b. Permitted Activity. A fiduciary may discuss estate planning techniques with a client as they are generally applied (*i.e.*, discussion of the structure of the estate and gift tax laws and general use of marital and by-pass trusts in estate planning). In addition, a bank or trust company is permitted to discuss and cooperate with counsel for the client, who is a prospective customer of the bank, any and all of the legal problems involved in the planning and administration of a particular client's estate planning needs. *Green v. Huntington*; see also *Pietz v. Toledo Trust Co.*, 577 N.E.2d 1118 (Ohio Ct. App. 1989) (trust company not engaged in unauthorized practice of law when it advised testator's attorney to make changes to trust agreement). In addition, once a bank is appointed as trustee, it may handle most of the probate and other legal work necessary to administer the trust, including appearing in court. The fiduciary, however, should be careful when undertaking certain tasks associated with the attorney's traditional role, especially if the individual is not a corporate fiduciary. See *In Re Graham*, 30 Pa. D. & C. 531, 534 (Pa. 1935) ("any person not licensed to practice law who prepares and files an inheritance tax return, without the advice and consent of legal counsel for the personal representative, renders legal advice, and, therefore, engaged in unauthorized practice of law").

21st Century Estate Planning:
Practical Applications
2005 Edition

©2005 Sonnenschein Nath & Rosenthal LLP
and Cannon Financial Institute, Inc.

- 715 -

3. Attorney Abetting in Unauthorized Practice of Law

The attorney is ethically and legally prohibited from assisting non-attorneys in the unauthorized practice of law. Accordingly, the attorney must familiarize himself with what constitutes the unauthorized practice of law by the non-attorney.

Model Rule 5.5 provides that an attorney shall not "assist a person who is not a member of the bar in the performance of activity that constitutes the unauthorized practice of law." Model Code DR 3-101(A) ("[a] lawyer shall not aid a nonlawyer in the unauthorized practice of law"). These rules are brought into question each time the attorney assists a fiduciary in any of the activities discussed earlier in this section. See Illinois State Bar Association, Opinion No. 91-10 (October 25, 1991) (attorney held to be aiding unauthorized practice of law when attorney participates in a financial planning company's arrangement whereby the company gathers information necessary to prepare estate planning documents, prepares the documents, and send the documents to the client's selected attorney for review, legal advice, and execution); *People v. Boyls*, 591 P.2d 1315, 1316 (Colo. 1979) (lawyer suspended for one year for aiding non-attorney "educators" in marketing living trusts).

> ➔ **Planning Point:** Any fiduciary contemplating offering services that extend beyond their basic administrative functions should be careful not to offer legal services to the client. Often, the type of services being offered may become secondary to the manner in which the services are being provided. As a general rule, the fiduciary should speak to the general benefits of the estate planning techniques, rather than the application and the benefits to the client's specific facts. Finally, although the fiduciary may gather the information necessary to implement the estate plan, he should not draft or prepare the documents.

21st Century Estate Planning:
Practical Applications
2005 Edition

©2005 Sonnenschein Nath & Rosenthal LLP
and Cannon Financial Institute, Inc.

- 716 -

Chapter XX
Bibliography

Charles Bryan Baron, "Self-Dealing Trustees and the Exoneration Clause: Can Trustees ever Profit from Transactions Involving Trust Property?," 72 *St. John's L. Rev.* 43 (Winter 1998).

George Gleason Bogert, George Taylor Bogert and Amy M. Hess, "Duty of Loyalty to the Beneficiaries," *The Law of Trusts and Trustees*, Sec. 543 (Rev. 2d ed.).

"Duty of Trustee to Diversify Investments, and Liability for Failure to Do So," 24 A.L.R. 3d 730.

William F. Fratcher, *Scott on Trusts* (4th ed.).

William S. Hershberger, "Fiduciary Investing in the 90's-- Restatement Third of Trusts: Panacea or Placebo?," *27th Annual Philip E. Heckerling Inst. on Est. Plan.*, Ch. 5 (1993).

James Lockhart, "Causes of Action Against Trustee for Self-Dealing," 14 *Causes of Action* 411 (1987).

Willam M. McGovern, Jr. and Sheldon F. Kurtz, *Wills, Trusts and Estates, Including Taxation and Future Interests* (2d ed. 2001).

"Propriety of Considering Beneficiary's Other Means Under Trust Provision Authorizing Invasion of Principal for Beneficiary's Support," 41 A.L.R.3d 255.

Restatement (Second) of the Law - Trusts, American Law Institute.

Restatement (Third) of the Law - Trusts, American Law Institute.

Terry L. Stranke, "Self-Dealing by Trustee," 38 *Am. Jur. Proof of Facts* 2d 279 (1996).

"Trustee's Failure to Diversify Investments," 14 *Am. Jur. Proof of Facts 2d* 253 (1977).

"Trustee's Liability for Payment of Trust Fund to One Whose Interest has Terminated," 48 A.L.R.2d 1252 (1956).

Uniform Prudent Investor Act, 1994 Act.

U.S. Trust, Practical Drafting, January 2002.

Robert Whitman, "Exoneration Clauses in Wills and Trust Instruments," 4 *Hofstra Prop. L.J.* 123 (Spring 1992).

21st Century Estate Planning:
Practical Applications
2005 Edition

©2005 Sonnenschein Nath & Rosenthal LLP
and Cannon Financial Institute, Inc.

- 717 -

XXI. COMPREHENSIVE WEALTH MANAGEMENT™

A. Overview of Comprehensive Wealth Management

1.   The Need for A Comprehensive Wealth Advisor

The average high-net-worth client likely involves five or more professionals in their financial life. The venerable attorney, the fastidious accountant, the thought-provoking insurance advisor, and the two or more investment planners all play unique and sometimes ubiquitous roles in the financial management side of the client's life. The positive aspects of involving this array of experts in one's life are numerous and do outweigh the negatives. The positives include access to in-depth knowledge and counsel in the select areas of expertise possessed by the individual advisors; the ability to receive wide-ranging perspectives offered by the unique disciplines; the simple ability to make a choice. The major challenge most super-affluent and many wealthy clients face is simple – with so many advisors, the efforts tend to be uncoordinated and there is little correlation between how one piece of advice impacts other areas of the client's life.

2.   Clients Want Their Issues Addressed. The Techniques Are Secondary

Practitioners often become engrossed in their own world of planning techniques without proper perspective from a client point-of-view. Clients want their problems addressed. While one technique may be more beneficial than another, the particular techniques don't motivate the client to action, the advisor does. More often than not it is the advisor who is the most effective communicator, as opposed to the advisor possessing the greatest legal, accounting or insurance skill, that is most effective in client interaction. These advisors typically do not try to solve just one or two issues for the client, but assume the role of holistic advisor. They practice Comprehensive Wealth Management.

3.   Comprehensive Wealth Management

The world of personal wealth management comprises the gamut from simple debt usage to analyzing proper exercise of compensatory options to appropriate design of a legacy plan. While various tools can be utilized to facilitate planning, but one thing is as certain in personal wealth management as it is in physics – for every action there is an equal and opposite reaction. Therefore it is imperative that practitioners approach any wealth planning opportunity from a Comprehensive Wealth Management process. Comprehensive Wealth Management focuses planning from a client's point of view. There are four simple tasks that wealthy clients seek in an advisory relationship:

- Help and assistance in continuing to create and grow wealth.
- Guidance on protecting and preserving wealth already created and amassed.
- Direction in taking distributions and making distributions of wealth during life.
- Planning for establishing and maintaining a wealth legacy following death.

21st Century Estate Planning:
Practical Applications
2005 Edition

©2005 Sonnenschein Nath & Rosenthal LLP
and Cannon Financial Institute, Inc.

- 718 -

Simple isn't it? Too simple? Hardly! Many wealthy clients would have tremendous difficulty distinguishing between a grantor trust and a charitable trust, but almost all would be able to articulate their wants, needs and desires when it comes to the four phases of Comprehensive Wealth Management. Comprehensive Wealth Management provides a framework for discussions with wealthy clients. It provides a basis of understanding on the part of the client as to why the questions and issues we practitioners raise are important to the client's financial well-being.

➔ **Planning Point**: Give clients a reason to answer your questions and they will tell you anything!

B. Helping Clients Create and Grow Wealth

1. Investments

Building wealth requires not only good planning, but it also requires a good advisor that will help clients execute their plan. The primary responsibility of advisors in the early stage of Comprehensive Wealth Management is helping clients establish an overall investment plan. This planning requires careful analysis not only of the goals and objectives of the client, but also must focus on the client's emotions and feelings towards investments and building wealth. A client with an almost perfectly established plan will still stumble in their attempt to build wealth if their emotions get the best of them. America is the finest country in the world. One reason for this is the ability of anyone to build wealth. But this occurs if, and only if, the client possesses three things:

a. Discipline. A World War II veteran from Georgia began collecting a benefit payment in 1950 for some injuries received in battle. The monthly benefit was modest – the first payment was less than $25. The veteran saw the payments adjusted each year for inflation, but he also watched something else. Every payment received was direct deposited into an investment account. The account was invested in the equity market and has averaged a 10.1% annual return over the last 52 years. Today, the account balance is in excess of $1,100,000.

b. Long-term Time Horizon. Few wealthy individuals got rich quick. In fact, most wealthy individuals took many years to be an "overnight" success. The will to work, the vision to see the end results and the staying power to complete the journey are all traits of the most successful and wealthy entrepreneurs.

c. Lack of Momentary Greed. It is hard – almost impossible – to not jump on any bandwagon that appears to be making billionaires out of ordinary citizens. The dot-com craze of the late nineties is just such an example. Add dot-com to the name of a company and the market value of the firm shot up overnight. Numerous investors rushed to "reap their reward" by investing (often on margin) in these new economy "goldmines." Alas, the gold strike ran dry and many of the paper billionaires are back where they started – poor, but wiser. Yet, many of the seasoned wealthy didn't realize the trials and tribulations experienced by so many investors because they were wise to the proverb "If it appears too good to be true, it probably is!" True

21st Century Estate Planning:
Practical Applications
2005 Edition

©2005 Sonnenschein Nath & Rosenthal LLP
and Cannon Financial Institute, Inc.

- 719 -

investors weathered the dot-com debacle because they never tried to seize riches that didn't exist – they lacked momentary greed!

2. Tax Efficiency

Why does the mood of our nation tend to sour a bit during the first two weeks of February? Some call it the winter doldrums; yet it may be the investment taxation doldrums. Individual investors receive their annual 1099 statements at this time of year. It is often their first indications that something is amiss in their plan for having built wealth in the prior year. Few things are as frustrating to investors to have seen the value of their holding grow at a slower rate (or worse – to have seen them lose value) than the amount of taxable distributions they received from their investment manager. Good wealth advisors help their clients to establish prudent tax-aware investment plans that allow clients to keep a greater portion of their wealth each year by reducing the tax burden.

3. Utilizing Leverage

A regional bank once ran an advertising campaign designed to encourage clients to borrow money for business investment purposes. One tag line that was used was "Even Bill Gates got started using someone else's money!" The use of leverage and its ability to greatly enhance return is not lost on the wealthy. From simple real estate deals to complex monitization strategies, the use of leverage has allowed a significant number of affluent individuals to build significant wealth. Top advisors take this into consideration not only from a use of funds approach, but also from a tax efficiency approach. Using leverage for investment purposes can produce tremendous taxation benefits.

C. Guidance on Protecting and Preserving Wealth Already Created and Amassed

The first interaction many affluent and wealthy-market practitioners have with their clients comes after wealth has been created or amassed. It is at this point that affluent individuals look for guidance on doing the appropriate things necessary to protect their holdings from being negatively impacted by volatile markets and rampant taxation.

The top advisor will work with their clients at this point to identify those issues that would have a negative impact on the created wealth. In analyzing prevalent attitudes among the wealth market, the bias towards having multiple investment advisors is commonplace. While the reasoning behind this trend is often noble, the reality of such strategies often puts affluent clients at risk. Examine the pitfalls:

21st Century Estate Planning:
Practical Applications
2005 Edition

©2005 Sonnenschein Nath & Rosenthal LLP
and Cannon Financial Institute, Inc.

- 720 -

1. Portfolio Management

a. <u>Asset Allocation</u>. The client who works with multiple advisors rarely examines their portfolio in totality. More often, the client simply examines the holdings that are kept with the separate advisors. Upon reviewing the allocation of the totality of their investments, many clients are shocked to discover that the balance of their allocation is not appropriate to their individual objectives.

b. <u>Diversification/Concentrations</u>. The late 90s saw a love affair with the technology sector. Whether it was Sun Microsystems, EMC, Lucent or Dell Computer, a startling number of technology stocks were on the "must own" list of almost all major investment firms. Consider the client who took the advice of each of three advisors, all holding separate assets, to allocate 35% of their portfolio to technology, with the balance allocated among other suggestions of equities and fixed income. Chances are the non-technology recommendations of the separate advisors were diverse in nature – consumer durables, health care, financials, and various debt instruments. However, it would be more than "highly likely" that the recommendations for the technology sector would not only over-lap, but would probably duplicate the efforts of the other advisors. If no one advisor sees the big picture, concentration issues will exist.

c. <u>Tax Efficiency</u>. Investment year 2001 was confusing for many investors. Catastrophic world events, a soft economy and low earnings pushed the markets lower. Most equity investors felt the squeeze as they saw the market value of their investments drop, while many saw the tax consequences of their holdings detrimentally increase. Such occurrences are not uncommon in a weak market. Many money managers are evaluated on simple performance, not after-tax performance. Therefore, turnover within portfolios is a measurement which carries little importance to the majority of portfolio managers. It does have dramatic impacts on the net returns for affluent investors. When one considers that a large percentage of turnover occurring within a portfolio consists of short-term capital gains, the resulting effect is taxation at ordinary income rates for investors who pay the highest rates. The prudent practitioner is quick to not only identify this regrettable circumstance, but they also should advise the client to seek guidance in alleviating this malady.

2. Risk Management Tools

a. <u>Life Insurance</u>. Very few adults relish the opportunity to visit with a life insurance advisor. The requirement that one closely evaluate the financial implications of their own mortality tends to rank very closely in popularity with having gastrointestinal surgery. However, the need to periodically examine both the appropriateness and cost effectiveness of life coverage is essential. Professional practitioners should be mindful that life coverage needs on-going review beyond its initial structure, which will always include analysis of proper ownership.

➔   **<u>Planning Point</u>:** Advisors should ensure that their clients periodically review their life insurance to ensure that the level of protection and policy

---

21st Century Estate Planning:
Practical Applications
2005 Edition

©2005 Sonnenschein Nath & Rosenthal LLP
and Cannon Financial Institute, Inc.

- 721 -

types are still appropriate in light of their level of wealth and station in life.

b. <u>Disability Insurance</u>. Disability always happens to the other person…so the story goes. We live in the real world, however. Real world occurrences are not statistics in an actuarial guide; they impact our clients. Consider the case of the typical entrepreneur/business owner. Having toiled to create wealth by building an enterprise, they begin to see the fruits of their labor. The value of their business grows, their income grows, and their overall wealth grows. However, the single largest asset that most of these individuals hold is that of their business. A large factor in determining the value of the enterprise is that of the owner's ability to work in the business, to be its "rainmaker."

Many individuals who are driven to success as an entrepreneur do so on sheer will. Success in building the business often leads to a feeling of invincibility. This aura leads to heightened risk. Failure to carefully examine the repercussions of not protecting the value of the largest asset in the client's portfolio from the risk of their own disability would not only be imprudent, it could prove catastrophic.

c. <u>Long-term Care Insurance</u>. "I will just self-insure this risk!" Wow, what a comment. Unfortunately, the aforementioned statement wasn't made by someone who simply did not have the monetary means to purchase protection; it was made by an individual who did not understand the impact of the risks involved.

As advances in medicine lead to longer life expectancies, it is a foregone conclusion that chances are very high that a greater percentage of adults will need long-term care services at some point in their life. Whether the service is as complex as in-patient skilled nursing or as basic as in-home assisted care, the likelihood of its necessity is real. Clients must confront this likely eventuality and plan accordingly. While some level of self-retention (self-insurance) is reasonable, it is likely imprudent to retain all the risks.

Top advisors urge clients to consider the impact of failing to address long-term care issues. First are the cash flow considerations for those that would be making decisions on the client's behalf – how will the expenses for care be funded? Second is the possibility of seeing the client's estate depleted to pay the expenses if no other means of support is available. Third is the emotional impact to the loved ones caring for the client of not only seeing a loved one (the client) become feeble, but facing the thought of having to personally provide assistance to them. Fourth involves the labyrinth of governmental program regulations that must be navigated in order to qualify for very basic, Spartan services. When these issues are considered, most prudent individuals make the choice to take appropriate action.

d. <u>Liability Insurance</u>. Affluent and wealth clients face a myriad of challenges in seeking to protect their wealth. One of the more prominent risks is that of a lawsuit seeking damages for personal injuries incurred in relation to contact with the client. This could include automobile, boating, and residential injuries. Obviously, the need for liability protection is great. However, experience shows that a significant number of affluent clients are either unaware of their coverage limits or are grossly underinsured in the area of liability. Simply

21st Century Estate Planning:
Practical Applications
2005 Edition

©2005 Sonnenschein Nath & Rosenthal LLP
and Cannon Financial Institute, Inc.

- 722 -

challenging clients to justify that the level of their protection is commensurate with the level of their wealth will normally be more than enough to motivate a review in the area.

D. Direction in Taking Distributions and Making Distributions of Wealth During Life

It is in the third phase of the affluent/wealthy client's financial life that practitioners really come into play – the planning of wealth distributions both to and from the client. However, all too often the discussions practitioners engage in with their clients are more centric on one or two subjects rather than a more comprehensive approach. When analyzed, there are five major categorical issues that should be discussed in the planning of receiving wealth by clients, while there are two major categorical issues for discussion in planning the gifting of wealth by clients.

1. Distributions and Transitions of Wealth Coming to Our Clients

a. Compensatory Options. A large percentage of today's affluent clients with ties to a publicly traded corporation have some portion of their wealth tied to the value of options granted to them under a corporate compensatory option program. Unfortunately, many of these individuals receive very little advice and counsel on the best overall administration of their option grants. Consideration should obviously be given to the type of option held, be it qualified or non-qualified due to particular tax treatments involved. Additionally, a review of the client's total holdings in their own company stock should take place. Evaluate whether the client has an over-concentration of investment in his or her own firm. This is highly likely to occur for many mid-to-senior level executives, as they will likely own company securities not only received as part of their option grants, but may also have a significant portion of their qualified retirement plan invested in company stock as well.

b. Business Succession Planning. Numerous studies have shown that one of the most common ways to attain a level of wealth is through creating and building a business. Business owners get two levels of wealth opportunity from building a business – high-income flow and equity appreciation. In transitioning a business, the owner will typically seek to secure a plan that either allows some stream of cash flow to continue, or will seek to receive sale proceeds which are sufficient to provide lifetime financial support. The opportunities that surround business succession planning are vast. However, for the client it really comes down to just two key points:

(1) Timing. Is the transition something the owner wants to see begun and possibly completed during their lifetime or do they want the transition completed at their death?

(2) Recipient. There are only three possible recipients – family, company insiders, or company outsiders.

Once the answers to these two questions are determined, the planning process is relatively simple. Advisors work to identify the key issues associated with the timing and recipient choices, including transfer taxation, capital gain taxation, security of the payments, etc., and determine the right transfer vehicle.

21st Century Estate Planning:
Practical Applications
2005 Edition

©2005 Sonnenschein Nath & Rosenthal LLP
and Cannon Financial Institute, Inc.

- 723 -

c. Qualified Property Exchanges. Clients seek growth and appreciation of their holdings. However, in addition to the client, there is another entity that also likes to see the growth and appreciation – the Internal Revenue Service. To the extent the client liquidates their appreciated property, the IRS collects a capital gains tax. Top practitioners will seek to discover any unrealized gains that their clients have in their assets because several sections of the Internal Revenue Code offer potential relief. Such opportunities exist for real estate, property used in a trade or business, qualified securities and life insurance products. Unfortunately, many very affluent individuals do not realize that these strategies exist and therefore bear more than is necessary in tax burden.

d. Distributions Taken from Qualified Retirement Plans and IRAs. There may be no other area of distribution of wealth planning that goes so lacking for the typical affluent client. In 2001, the Service issued new rules governing the distribution of Qualified Retirement Plans and IRAs. One key benefit was the dropping of the requirement under old rules that a designated beneficiary be selected by April 1 of the year following the year that the IRA owner reaches 70½. Therefore, the owner has flexibility in determining and potentially changing beneficiaries. Many pundits have opined that naming a very young beneficiary is the strategy that should "always" be implemented in order to "stretch" the IRA after the owner's death by having the beneficiary take distributions over their own life expectancy.

There are two problems with the "no-brainer" concept of the stretch IRA. First, there will never be any wealth strategy that applies unilaterally across the board to all clients. Second, with the little attention that is paid to the implementation process of ensuring that a stretch IRA will be implemented, there is a very high likelihood that the concept of the "Stretch IRA" will prove to be nothing more than fantasy. Take a common example:

> **EXAMPLE:** John Johnson designates his 25-year old son, Doug to be the beneficiary of his IRA. John dies. John's wealth advisory team meets with Doug to discuss the IRA and all of the benefits surrounding the "stretchability" of Doug taking payments over his own life expectancy. Not being a "savvy," in-the-know investor, Doug asks "Are there any other options I have available?" Not wanting to go down that path, the advisors counsel Doug as to the benefits or stretching and the fact that Doug's father intended for Doug to take the payments over his life expectancy. To this Doug counters with "Answer the question: Are there other options?" After learning of his ability to liquidate the IRA immediately, pay the income tax due, and then be in complete control of the balance, Doug directs the immediate distribution of the IRA. He has the ability to do this, as he is named as the beneficiary.

Ironically, the entire situation that is described above could have been avoided if John had enjoyed a working relationship with advisors who understood the pitfalls and strategies of "no-brainer" concepts like the Stretch IRA, along with tangible solutions such as naming a trust

21st Century Estate Planning:
Practical Applications
2005 Edition

©2005 Sonnenschein Nath & Rosenthal LLP
and Cannon Financial Institute, Inc.

- 724 -

for the benefit of the desired beneficiary as the listed IRA beneficiary. Such as strategy will circumvent the child's ability to cash-out the IRA without the consent of the trustee.

   e. Inheritances and Gifts Received. Internal Revenue Code ("IRC") § 2518 provides for the ability of named recipients to disclaim their rights to the transfer and allow the property to pass to secondary beneficiaries. The ability to disclaim must be proactively sought and is not flexible in its election. Great advisors always query legal heirs as to whether alternative, secondary beneficiaries would make better recipients of the property.

   2.   Distributions of Wealth Made By Our Clients

   a. Gifting to children, descendents and others. Motivations of clients as to the purpose of gifting to children tend to drive the ultimate decision on the type of account that is established. One of the most common account types is the Uniform Transfer to Minors Account (UTMA).

   The UTMA is very simple to establish, but may not offer the best total benefits. UTMAs do create potential Kiddie Tax issues if the child is under the age of 14. They can create estate tax problems if the contributor (presumably the parent) is the custodian. They also grant control of the account to the child once the child reaches the age of majority for their state.

   If education is the driving motivation for gifting, the client should evaluate the §529 Education Savings Accounts. Such accounts offer preferential tax treatment under current law regardless of the income level of the donor.

   If personal planning and/or long-term control is the impetus for gifting, a more complex strategy such as a trust vehicle may prove to be the viable funding vehicle.

   b. Philanthropic Gifting. Wealthy clients are often the first solicited by charitable organizations as part of their fund-raising efforts. With so many requests and commitments, organizing the support strategy may involve little more than writing a check to something as grandiose as the creation of a private foundation for the purpose of funding philanthropic commitments.

   Too many affluent clients are personally tax inefficient in their support strategies. Cash gifts and gifts by check are likely culprits. A step as simple as gifting appreciated securities enhances the personal benefits of charitable gifting. With this technique the client receives a charitable deduction on the full value of the gift, while eliminating the built-in capital gains and its corresponding tax liability.

   More complex strategies for philanthropic transfers such as charitable trusts and family foundations can be found in other sections of this work.

   c. Contingency Planning. The best-laid plans are those that offer effective contingency planning. In the area of planning the distribution of wealth during life in the most tax-advantageous methods, it is important that clients have protected their strategies from the risk

21st Century Estate Planning:
Practical Applications
2005 Edition

©2005 Sonnenschein Nath & Rosenthal LLP
and Cannon Financial Institute, Inc.

- 725 -

of their personal incapacity. Ensuring that a Durable Power of Attorney and/or a Successor Trustee Appointment is appropriately designated helps to ensure the viability and continuation of their lifetime transfer strategies.

E. Planning for Establishing and Maintaining A Wealth Legacy Following Death

When discussing the fourth and final stage of Comprehensive Wealth Management, many practitioners are quick to gloss over the subject because they perceive that the area focuses exclusively on the probate process and transfer process for non-probate property. While it is true that focus is brought to those areas, it is in the communication of ideas, suggestions and alternatives that make the Comprehensive Wealth Management System so effective. There are three areas of interest:

1. Proper Asset Structure or Ownership

One of the strangest twists in the wealth legacy-planning arena is the failure of well-drafted plans due to ineffective asset structure or ownership. The failure to have assets owned in a manner that allows provisions of a will to be effective can prove catastrophic to the intended plan. Clients are usually informed of any changes required in ownership structure when estate plans are created. It is imperative that practitioners ensure the client's completion of such transfers.

2. Distribution Intentions for Spouse, Descendents and Others

More than one client has died leaving his/her estate outright to heirs. In fact, it is the most common form of bequest. However, for many of the clients we deal with on a daily basis outright distributions are not the appropriate answer. But in the minds of the client, they would never want to establish at *trust*! To a great number of clients, the concept of a trust is too foreign to even contemplate. Therefore, these individuals simply direct that all assets be left outright. Perhaps the following framing of questioning will yield a better result:

> **EXAMPLE:** "Ms. Client, based on the various needs of your family, does it make more sense to you to simply distribute the property outright without guidance or control or does the concept of creating a pool of funds to be kept intact for management and distributions based on the unique circumstances of your family carry more appeal?"

Sometimes (most times) it is not so much what is said, as it is how it is said.

Numerous references are noted in other parts of this work addressing the use of marital trusts, exemption trusts and charitable trusts. However, it is in the concept stage that the direction the client will ultimately choose is solidified. Breaking down the complex strategies into simple, digestible concepts is a developed skill.

21st Century Estate Planning:
Practical Applications
2005 Edition

©2005 Sonnenschein Nath & Rosenthal LLP
and Cannon Financial Institute, Inc.

3. Plan Implementation

Procrastination! The human race tends to not address issues of which we are fearful and/or we do not understand. Wealth legacy planning likely falls under both categories for most clients. Clients must have advisors who can explain the complex strategies in simple language. They must have advisors whom they trust. They must have advisors who can motivate and lead them to action. Wealth management is not a reactive practice. In order to be successful, it takes proactive leadership.

F. Summary

Comprehensive Wealth Management is a system that benefits both the client and the practitioner. By focusing on the four stages of the financial life of a client, the system is understandable by the average client. Understanding the role of the advisor and the responsibilities therein lead to a more successful relationship. Secondarily, the system is great for practitioners. It provides a framework for discussing the total landscape of the client's financial situation and provides reference points for identifying the key elements of the client's goals and objectives.

Always remember, no matter the level of technical skill and intelligence, a practitioner who cannot communicate and relate with his/her clients will always struggle. Comprehensive Wealth Management removes that obstacle!

21st Century Estate Planning:
Practical Applications
2005 Edition

©2005 Sonnenschein Nath & Rosenthal LLP
and Cannon Financial Institute, Inc.

- 727 -

Appendix A
Estate Planning Information Form

I. Personal and Family Information

Section A. Client

1. Name: _____   2.   Social Security No.: _____

3. Date of Birth: _____   4. Birthplace: _____

5. Citizen of USA?   ☐ Yes ☐ No   If no, please indicate country of which you are a citizen. _____

6. Business or Profession: _____ (Check ☐ if retired)

    a.   Name of Company or Organization: _____
    b.   Address, Telephone and Fax Number: _____
                           _____

7. Primary Residence: _____

                  Street Address

                  _____   _____   _____ _
                  City   State   Zip Code

                  _____
                  Telephone Number

8.   State or Country (other than that listed in Part I, Section A, Item 7) in which you:

    a.   Maintain a residence or spend more than a nominal amount of time _____
    b.   Are registered to vote _____
    c.   Have one or more automobiles registered _____
    d.   Belong to religious, civic, social or business organizations _____

9. Marital Status: ☐ Single   ☐ Separated

                ☐ Married   Place where marriage occurred: _____

                ☐ Divorced   Name of former spouse and date divorce decree became final: _____
                           _____

                ☐ Widowed   Name and date of death of deceased spouse: _____

10. Do you have any unusual or significant health conditions?   ☐ Yes ☐ No   If yes, please describe: _____

_____

11. Do you have a "Living Will," health care Durable Power of Attorney or other instrument expressing your wishes with regard to the administering or withholding of life support and other health care measures in the event you are unable to participate in decisions regarding your medical treatment?
    ☐ Yes   ☐ No If no, do you desire such a document? ☐ Yes   ☐ No

12. What are your desires relating to your funeral, burial, cremation, etc.? _____

_____

Have you already made any arrangements in this regard? ☐ Yes ☐ No   If yes, please describe: _____

_____

_____

Section B. Spouse

1. Name: _____   2. Social Security No.: _____

3. Date of Birth: _____   4. Birthplace: _____

5. Citizen of USA? ☐ Yes ☐ No   If no, please indicate country of which you are a citizen. _____

6. Business or Profession: _____ (Check ☐ if retired)

    a.   Name of Company or Organization: _____

    b.   Address, Telephone and Fax Number: _____

        _____

7. Primary Residence: _____
              Street Address

              _____   _____   _____
              City   State   Zip Code

              _____
              Telephone Number

8. State or Country (other than that listed in Part I, Section A, Item 7) in which you:

    a.   Maintain a residence or spend more than a nominal amount of time _____

    b.   Are registered to vote _____

    c.   Have one or more automobiles registered _____

    d.   Belong to religious, civic, social or business organizations _____

9. Other states in which you have lived while married to client: _____

10. Name and date of death of any deceased spouse: _____

11. Name of any former spouse and date divorce decree became final: _____

12. Do you have any unusual or significant health conditions? ☐ Yes ☐ No   If yes, please describe: _____

_____

13. Do you have a "Living Will," health care Durable Power of Attorney or other instrument expressing your wishes with regard to the administering or withholding of life support and other health care measures in the event you are unable to participate in decisions regarding your medical treatment?

    ☐ Yes   ☐ No If no, do you desire such a document? ☐ Yes   ☐ No

14. What are your desires relating to your funeral, burial, cremation, etc.? _____

_____

Have you already made any arrangements in this regard? ☐ Yes   ☐ No   If yes, please describe: _____

_____

_____

Section C. Children and More Remote Descendants

Name, Date of Birth and Social Security Number	Residence Address (If not same as client's)	Name of Child's or Descendant's Spouse
1.		
2.		
3.		
4.		
5.		

Name, Date of Birth and Social Security Number	Residence Address (If not same as client's)	Name of Child's or Descendant's Spouse
6. _____ _____ _____	_____ _____ _____	_____
7. _____ _____ _____	_____ _____ _____	_____
8. _____ _____ _____	_____ _____ _____	_____
9. _____ _____ _____	_____ _____ _____	_____

Indicate which of the above are children (c), grandchildren (gc), great grandchildren (ggc), stepchildren (sc), children of a prior marriage (pm), adopted (a) or deceased (d).

Section D. Parents

		Name, Date of Birth and Social Security Number	Residence Address (If not same as client's)
1.	Husband's or Single Client's Father	_____ _____ _____	_____ _____ _____
2.	Husband's or Single Client's Mother	_____ _____ _____	_____ _____ _____
3.	Wife's Father	_____ _____ _____	_____ _____ _____

	Name, Date of Birth and Social Security Number	**Residence Address (If not same as client's)**
4. Wife's Mother	_____	_____
	_____	_____
	_____	_____

Indicate if deceased (de), divorced (di) or remarried (r).

Section E. Other Dependents

Name, Date of Birth and Social Security Number	**Residence Address (If not same as client's)**	**Name of Spouse**
1. _____	_____	_____
_____	_____	
_____	_____	
2. _____	_____	_____
_____	_____	
_____	_____	
3. _____	_____	_____
_____	_____	
_____	_____	
4. _____	_____	_____
_____	_____	
_____	_____	

II.   Financial Information

*As to any property or assets owned jointly, indicate whether as tenants
by the entireties (tbe), joint tenants (jt) or tenants in common (tc).*

Section A. Real Estate
(including residential, farm, vacation and investment property)

	Address, Location and Description	Cost Plus Improvements and Purchase Date	Loans Outstanding	Owner or Owners	Current Value
1.					
2.					

Section B. Tangible Personal Property
(including only unusual or particularly valuable items such as antiques, stamp, coin and art collections, precious and semi-precious stones and metals, jewelry, furs, guns, rare autos, boats, aircraft, etc.)

	Description	Owner or Owners	Current Value
1.			
2.			
3.			
4.			
5.			

Section C. Cash and Cash Equivalents
(including checking and savings accounts, certificates of deposit and money market fund units)

	Type of Account or Instrument	Bank, Savings and Loan or Broker	Owner or Owners	Average Balance or Amount Invested
1.				
2.				
3.				
4.				
5.				

Section D. Securities
(including listed stocks, options, corporate, institutional, municipal and government bonds and mutual fund units)

Number of Shares, Units or Face Value	Description of Security	Cost and Acquisition or Issue Date	Owner and T.O.D. Bene-ficiary (if any)	Current Value
1.				
2.				
3.				
4.				
5.				
6.				
7.				

Section E. Closely-Held Business Interests
(including corporations, partnerships and sole proprietorships)

Name and Address	Type of Business	Cost or Investment and Acquisition or Founding Date	Owner and % of Business Owned	Current Value and Estimated Annual Income or Loss
1.				
2.				
3.				

4._____ _____ _____ _____ _____

_____ _____ _____ _____

Indicate whether corporation (c), subchapter s corporation (sub-s), partnership (p), limited liability company (llc) or sole proprietorship (sp).

Section F. Life Insurance

Company, Policy Number and Owner	Person Insured and Date of Issue	Designated Beneficiary and Annual Premium	Loans Against, Interest Rate and Net Cash Value	Face Amount
1.				
2.				
3.				
4.				
5.				
6.				
7.				

Indicate whether whole life (wl), universal life (ul), variable universal life (vul) or term (t) and whether individual (i) or group (g). Indicate also whether split dollar (sd) and if furnished by employer (fbe).

Section G. Annuities and Employee Benefits
(not including stock options or interest-free loans)

Financial Institution (or Employer) and Account Number	Owner and Amount of Contributions	Death Benefit and Designated Beneficiary	Date Payments Begin and Payment Per Month or Year	Present Value Immediately Obtainable
1._____	_____	_____	_____	_____
_____	_____	_____	_____	
2._____	_____	_____	_____	_____
_____	_____	_____	_____	
3._____	_____	_____	_____	_____
_____	_____	_____	_____	
4._____	_____	_____	_____	_____
_____	_____	_____	_____	
5._____	_____	_____	_____	_____
_____	_____	_____	_____	

Indicate which are private annuities (pa), commercial annuities (ca), pension plan (pp), profit-sharing plans (psp), H.R. 10 plans (HR10), individual retirement accounts (IRA) and miscellaneous deferred compensation arrangements (dca). Indicate also whether payout is in form of annuity for a fixed period (a), annuity for employee's (or owner's) life only (la), joint and survivor annuity for employee (or owner) and spouse (jsa) or lump sum (ls).

Section H. Stock Options

Employer	Number of Shares and Date of Issue	Date of Expiration	Option Price	Current Price	Manner Specified for Paying Option Price
1.					
2.					
3.					

Indicate whether qualified (q) or non-qualified (nq).

Section I. Miscellaneous Property Interests
(including tax shelters, stock options through employer, property subject to power of appointment and other interests in trusts or estates, prospective inheritances, mortgages, notes or other accounts receivable and other significant assets not elsewhere listed in Part II)

Description	Owner or Holder	Current Value
1.		
2.		
3.		

Section J. Liabilities
(including mortgages, liens and significant unsecured debts)

Creditor	Initial Amount	Balance Due	Security	Maturity Date	Interest Rate
1.					
2.					
3.					
4.					

21st Century Estate Planning:
Practical Applications
2005 Edition

©2005 Sonnenschein Nath & Rosenthal LLP
and Cannon Financial Institute, Inc.

A-10

5._____ _____ _____ _____ _____ _____

6._____ _____ _____ _____ _____ _____

7._____ _____ _____ _____ _____ _____

8._____ _____ _____ _____ _____ _____

Indicate if covered by credit life insurance (cl).

Section K. Questions

(each person completing this Section should check appropriate answer and, if appropriate, provide additional information requested)

1.　Are you receiving any income constituting salary, bonuses, commissions or other earnings derived from employment? If yes, what is your approximate annual income from such sources?

Husband or Single Client _____　　　**Wife** _____

____　Yes　$_____　　　　　____　Yes　$_____

____　No　　　　　　　　　　　____　No

2.　Are you receiving any income constituting dividends, interest, royalties or payments from trusts, notes, mortgages, annuities or any employee benefit or deferred compensation plans? If yes, what is your approximate annual income from such sources?

Husband or Single Client _____　　　**Wife** _____

____　Yes　$_____　　　　　____　Yes　$_____

____　No　　　　　　　　　　　____　No

3.　Do you periodically save any of the income you earn or receive? If yes, approximately how much savings do you accumulate annually, and what disposition do you make of such savings?

Husband or Single Client _____　　　**Wife** _____

____　Yes　$_____　　　　　____　Yes　$_____

_____　　　　_____

_____　　　　_____

____　No　　　　　　　　　　　____　No

4.　Have you ever made or received any interest-free loans (whether or not currently outstanding)? If yes, please provide pertinent details.

Husband or Single Client _____　　　**Wife** _____

____　Yes　$_____　　　　　____　Yes　$_____

_____　　　　_____

_____　　　　_____

____　No　　　　　　　　　　　____　No

21st Century Estate Planning:
Practical Applications
2005 Edition

©2005 Sonnenschein Nath & Rosenthal LLP
and Cannon Financial Institute, Inc.

A-11

5.   Have you ever guaranteed a loan made to another person or entity (whether or not such loan is currently outstanding)? If yes, please provide pertinent details.

Husband or Single Client _____   **Wife** _____

____   Yes $_____   ____   Yes $_____

_____   _____

_____   _____

____   No   ____   No

6.   Is any descendant of yours an actual or a potential beneficiary or distributee under any TOD (transfer on death) instrument or account, any trust or estate, or any "Uniform Transfers to Minors Law" custodianship now in existence? If yes, please indicate name of donor, grantor or decedent and initial and current value; please provide other pertinent details.

Husband or Single Client _____   **Wife** _____

____   Yes $_____   ____   Yes $_____

_____   _____

_____   _____

____   No   ____   No

7.   Have you undertaken a program of making annual exclusion gifts in order to reduce the size of your estate at no transfer tax cost? If yes, please provide pertinent details.

Husband or Single Client _____   **Wife** _____

____   Yes $_____   ____   Yes $_____

_____   _____

____   No   If no, are you   ____   No   If no, are you
interested in beginning such a program? interested in beginning such a program?
____   Yes   ____   No   ____   Yes   ____   No

8.   Would you be interested in reallocating ownership of your assets between the two of you in order to minimize or eliminate estate taxes? If yes, are there any assets which either of you would prefer not to transfer to the other?

Husband or Single Client _____   **Wife** _____

____   Yes   (but I prefer not to   ____   Yes   (but I prefer not to
transfer to my wife the following: transfer to my wife the following:

_____   _____

____   No   ____   No

21st Century Estate Planning:
Practical Applications
2005 Edition

©2005 Sonnenschein Nath & Rosenthal LLP
and Cannon Financial Institute, Inc.

A-12

Section L. Attachments

(When submitting this form upon completion, please also submit the documents (or copies of the documents) listed below. Please let us know whether we may retain the actual documents submitted or whether you want us to make photocopies of such documents and then return the submitted documents to you.)

1. Wills, trust instruments, "Living Wills" and Durable Powers of Attorney previously signed.

2. Divorce or separation agreements and related court decrees.

3. Income tax returns for last three years.

4. Gift tax returns (regardless of how long ago prepared).

5. Deeds to real estate listed in Section A.

6. Employment contracts presently in force.

7. Stock purchase agreements, redemption agreements and similar or related documents pertaining to business interests listed in Section E.

8. Balance sheets and profit/loss statements for last five years pertaining to business interests listed in Section E.

9. Policies of Insurance listed in Section F.

10. Contracts, plan documents and recent statements relating to items in Section G.

11. Documents or instruments conferring or relating to stock options listed in Section H.

12. Documents or instruments conferring or relating to property interests listed in Section I.

13. Documents or instruments evidencing or relating to interest-free loans described in the answer to Question 4 under Section K.

14. Documents or instruments conferring or relating to loan guarantees described in the answer to Question 5 under Section K.

15. Documents or instruments conferring or relating to property interests described in the answer to Question 6 under Section K.

21st Century Estate Planning:
Practical Applications
2005 Edition

©2005 Sonnenschein Nath & Rosenthal LLP
and Cannon Financial Institute, Inc.

A-13

Each person completing this Part should check appropriate answer and, if appropriate, provide additional information requested.

1. Do you wish to have the option of disposing of items of your tangible personal property by means of a separate written statement or list outside your Will?

   Husband or Single Client _____   **Wife** _____

   ____ Yes   ____ Yes

   ____ No   ____ No

2. Do you wish to make any gifts at your death to or in trust for any person or charitable organization of any specific item or asset or of a specified amount of money? If yes, please describe.

   Husband or Single Client _____   **Wife** _____

   ____ Yes _____   ____ Yes _____

   _____   _____

   _____   _____

   ____ No   ____ No

3. If you own an interest in a closely-held business, do you wish that interest to be administered or distributed at your death in any manner different from that in which you want your other assets administered or distributed? If yes, please describe.

   Husband or Single Client _____   **Wife** _____

   ____ Yes _____   ____ Yes _____

   _____   _____

   _____   _____

   ____ No   ____ No

21st Century Estate Planning:
Practical Applications
2005 Edition

©2005 Sonnenschein Nath & Rosenthal LLP
and Cannon Financial Institute, Inc.

A-14

4. If you possess one or more powers of appointment, do you wish to exercise any such power? If yes, please describe.

Husband or Single Client   **Wife**

____   Yes   _____   ____   Yes   _____

_____   _____

_____   _____

____   No   ____   No

5. If there were substantial tax advantages to be gained, would you be willing to set aside a substantial amount in a multi-generational trust for the primary benefit of your grandchildren and more remote descendants?

Husband or Single Client   **Wife**

____   Yes   ____   Yes

____   No   ____   No

6. Do you wish to leave all the rest of your property outright to your spouse if he or she survives you (assuming, for purposes of this question, that estate taxes are not a concern)? (If you have no spouse, skip questions 6 through 13; if you have neither a spouse nor any descendants, skip questions 6 through 22.)

Husband   **Wife**

____   Yes   ____   Yes

____   No   ____   No

7. Would you want to leave all the rest of your property in two trusts for the benefit of your spouse (and, perhaps, for the benefit of other persons as well) if that type of disposition could result in substantial minimization or elimination of aggregate estate taxes on your and your spouse's estates? (If your answer is no, skip questions 8 through 13.)

Husband   **Wife**

____   Yes   ____   Yes

____   No   ____   No

8. Should your spouse be entitled to receive the entire net income from each trust that is established at your death for her or his benefit, or should your spouse be entitled to receive the entire net income only from the Marital rust? (If your answer is "each trust," skip questions 9 and 10.)

Husband   **Wife**

____   wife to receive entire net income   ____   husband to receive entire net income
        from each trust   from each trust

____   wife to receive entire net income   ____   husband to receive entire net income
        from Marital Trust only   from Marital Trust only

21st Century Estate Planning:
Practical Applications
2005 Edition

©2005 Sonnenschein Nath & Rosenthal LLP
and Cannon Financial Institute, Inc.

A-15

9. If your spouse is to receive the entire net income only from the Marital Trust, should your spouse be entitled to receive income from the other trust (the Credit Shelter Trust) at the discretion of the Trustee, or should your spouse be excluded as a potential discretionary income beneficiary of the Credit Shelter Trust?

Husband

_____ wife to receive income in Trustee's discretion

_____ wife not to receive income

Wife

_____ husband to receive income in Trustee's discretion

_____ husband not to receive income

10. Should your descendants be entitled to receive discretionary distributions of income (if your spouse is not to be the mandatory income beneficiary) from the Credit Shelter Trust, or (if your spouse is to be excluded as a potential discretionary income beneficiary of the Credit Shelter Trust) should your descendants be entitled to receive all the net income from that trust?

Husband

_____ descendants to receive income in Trustee's discretion

_____ descendants to receive entire net income and wife not to receive income

Wife

_____ descendants to receive income in Trustee's discretion

_____ descendants to receive entire net income and wife not to receive income

11. Should your spouse be entitled to receive discretionary distributions of principal from either the Marital Trust or the Credit Shelter Trust (or both)?

Husband

_____ wife to receive discretionary principal distributions from Marital Trust

_____ wife to receive discretionary principal distributions from Family Trust

_____ wife not to receive discretionary principal distributions

Wife

_____ husband to receive discretionary principal distributions from Marital Trust

_____ husband to receive discretionary principal distributions from Family Trust

_____ husband not to receive discretionary principal distributions

12. Should your descendants be entitled to receive discretionary distributions of principal from the Credit Shelter Trust?

Husband

_____ Yes
_____ No

Wife

_____ Yes
_____ No

21st Century Estate Planning:
Practical Applications
2005 Edition

©2005 Sonnenschein Nath & Rosenthal LLP
and Cannon Financial Institute, Inc.

A-16

13. Should your spouse be given any lifetime powers of withdrawal or appointment of any deathtime powers of appointment with respect to either the Marital Trust or the Credit Shelter Trust (or both)? If yes, when are the powers to be available to be exercised by your spouse, how much do you want your spouse to be able to withdraw or appoint, and, with regard to any power of appointment, to or for whom is your spouse to be permitted to exercise such power?

Husband _____   **Wife** _____

_____ wife to have power(s) of withdrawal or appointment as follows:

_____

_____

_____ wife not to have any such power

_____ husband to have power(s) of withdrawal or appointment as follows:

_____

_____

_____ husband not to have any such power

14. At such time as an actual division of your property into shares is to be made for your descendants, is your property to be divided into such number of equal shares as is needed to provide one share for each then living member of the oldest generation in which there is at least one then living person and one share for each member of that generation who is then deceased but who is then survived by one or more descendants of his or her own (each share for a member of that generation who is then deceased to be divided among his or her descendants in the same manner)? If your answer is no, how do you want division of your property for your descendants to be made? (If you have no descendants, or if you do not wish to provide at your death for any of your descendants, skip questions 14 through 22.)

Husband _____   **Wife** _____

_____ Yes

_____ No _____

_____

_____

_____ Yes

_____ No _____

_____

_____

15. If you have no living spouse, or after your spouse is deceased, should any of your property be retained in trust for young or incapacitated children or young or incapacitated more remote descendants, such as grandchildren? (If your answer is no, skip questions 16 through 22.)

Husband or Single Client _____   **Wife** _____

_____ Yes
_____ No

_____ Yes
_____ No

16. At what age (if at all) should your children become entitled to receive their shares of trust income rather than have it distributed to them or for their benefit at the Trustee's discretion?

Husband or Single Client _____   **Wife** _____

_____ age 21
_____ age _____
_____ never

_____ age 21
_____ age _____
_____ never

21st Century Estate Planning:
Practical Applications
2005 Edition

©2005 Sonnenschein Nath & Rosenthal LLP
and Cannon Financial Institute, Inc.

A-17

17. At what age (if at all) should your grandchildren and more remote descendants become entitled to receive their shares of trust income rather than have it distributed to them or for their benefit at the Trustee's discretion?

Husband or Single Client		**Wife**	
_____	age 21	_____	age 21
_____	age _____	_____	age _____
_____	never	_____	never

18. Should any of your descendants be entitled to receive discretionary distributions of principal from any separate trusts established for their benefit?

Husband or Single Client		**Wife**	
_____	Yes	_____	Yes
_____	No	_____	No

19. Should any descendant of yours be given any lifetime powers of withdrawal or appointment or deathtime powers of appointment with respect to any separate trust created for his or her benefit? If so, when are the powers to be available to be exercised by such descendant, how much do you want such descendant to be able to withdraw or appoint, and, with regard to any power of appointment, to or for whom is such descendant to be permitted to exercise such power?

Husband or Single Client

_____ descendants to have power(s) of

withdrawal or appointment as follows:

_____

_____

_____

_____

_____ descendants not to have any such power

Wife

_____ descendants to have power(s) of

withdrawal or appointment as follows:

_____

_____

_____

_____

_____ descendants not to have any such power

20. At what age or ages should children of yours be entitled to receive outright distribution of their shares of your property? (Note that you can direct distribution to, or allow withdrawals by, your children in a lump sum at one designated age or in fractional shares at designated ages.)

Husband or Single Client

_____ all at age 21
_____ 1/2 at age 25; rest at age 30
_____ 1/3 at age 25; 1/2 of balance at age 30; rest at age 35
_____ other _____

_____

_____ never

Wife

_____ all at age 21
_____ 1/2 at age 25; rest at age 30
_____ 1/3 at age 25; 1/2 of balance at age 30; rest at age 35
_____ other _____

_____

_____ never

21st Century Estate Planning:
Practical Applications
2005 Edition

©2005 Sonnenschein Nath & Rosenthal LLP
and Cannon Financial Institute, Inc.

A-18

21. At what age or ages should grandchildren or more remote descendants of yours be entitled to receive outright distribution of their shares of your property? (Note that you can direct distribution to, or allow withdrawals by, your grandchildren or more remote descendants in a lump sum at one designated age or in fractional shares at designated ages.)

Husband or Single Client   **Wife** _____

_____   all at age 21   _____   all at age 21

_____   other _____   _____   other _____

_____   _____

_____   never   _____   never

22. Are any of your children or more remote descendants in any way disabled or otherwise under special circumstances? (If yes, please describe).

Husband or Single Client   **Wife** _____

_____   Yes   _____   Yes

_____   _____

_____   _____

_____   _____

_____   No _____   _____   No _____

23. Do you wish to make any contingent trust provisions for one or more of your parents, brothers, sisters or other ancestors or collateral relatives or for one or more persons not related to you? (If yes, please describe).

Husband or Single Client   **Wife** _____

_____   Yes   _____   Yes

_____   _____

_____   _____

_____   _____

_____   No _____   _____   No _____

21st Century Estate Planning:
Practical Applications
2005 Edition

©2005 Sonnenschein Nath & Rosenthal LLP
and Cannon Financial Institute, Inc.

A-19

24. To or for whom or to what charitable organization do you wish your property to pass at such time as neither a spouse of yours nor any descendant of yours is living (assuming there is property left that needs to be distributed to some person or entity at that time)?

Husband or Single Client   **Wife**

Husband or Single Client	Wife
_____ to my closest living relative	_____ to my closest living relative
_____ 1/2 to my closest living relatives and 1/2 to my wife's closest living relatives	_____ 1/2 to my closest living relatives and 1/2 to my wife's closest living relatives
_____ to _____	_____ to _____
_____	_____

25. Are you interested in having only a new Will prepared for you or would you be interested in a Durable Power of Attorney or a "pour-over" Will and revocable living trust?

Husband or Single Client   **Wife**

Husband or Single Client	Wife
_____ new Will only	_____ new Will only
_____ new Will and Durable Power of Attorney	_____ new Will and Durable Power of Attorney
_____ "pour-over" Will and revocable trust	_____ "pour-over" Will and revocable trust
_____ "pour-over" Will, revocable trust and Durable Power of Attorney	_____ "pour-over" Will, revocable trust and Durable Power of Attorney

26. If there were substantial tax advantages to be gained, might you be interested in establishing one or more irrevocable trusts (trusts that cannot be changed in any way or terminated)?

Husband or Single Client   **Wife**

Husband or Single Client	Wife
_____ Yes	_____ Yes
_____ No	_____ No

IV. Fiduciaries

Section A. Instructions

1. You may designate as few fiduciaries to serve in a given capacity or as many as you wish. Feel free to attach additional sheets of paper, if necessary, using the same format as is used in the applicable Section of this Part IV.

2. You should designate fiduciaries who are to serve concurrently on the same line in the left-hand column. You should designate successor fiduciaries on different lines in the left-hand column in the order in which you desire them to serve.

3. Unless you designate a bank or a trust company at another point in your chronological listing of Personal Representatives and Trustees, you should designate a "back-up" contingent Personal Representative and successor Trustee on the last line in the left-hand column of the applicable Section.

4. If you wish to establish different successions of Trustees for different trusts, you may do so on additional sheets of paper using the same format as is used in Section D or E of this Part IV.

21st Century Estate Planning:
Practical Applications
2005 Edition

©*2005 Sonnenschein Nath & Rosenthal LLP*
and Cannon Financial Institute, Inc.

A-20

Section B. Personal Representative under Client's Will

Person(s) or Entity	To Assume Office Upon Failure of Whom to Serve	Relationship (if any) to Client
1. _____	_____	_____
2. _____	_____	_____
3. _____	_____	_____
4. _____	_____	_____

Section C. Personal Representative under Spouse's Will

Person(s) or Entity	To Assume Office Upon Failure of Whom to Serve	Relationship (if any) to Client
1. _____	_____	_____
2. _____	_____	_____
3. _____	_____	_____
4. _____	_____	_____
5. _____	_____	_____

Section D. Trustee under Client's Will/Revocable Trust

Person(s) or Entity	To Assume Office Upon Failure of Whom to Serve	Relationship (if any) to Client
1. _____	_____	_____
2. _____	_____	_____
3. _____	_____	_____
4. _____	_____	_____
5. _____	_____	_____

Section E. Trustee under Spouse's Will/Revocable Trust

Person(s) or Entity	To Assume Office Upon Failure of Whom to Serve	Relationship (if any) to Client
1. _____	_____	_____
2. _____	_____	_____
3. _____	_____	_____
4. _____	_____	_____
5. _____	_____	_____

21st Century Estate Planning:
Practical Applications
2005 Edition

©2005 Sonnenschein Nath & Rosenthal LLP
and Cannon Financial Institute, Inc.

A-21

Section F. Guardian for Minor Children

Person(s) or Entity	To Assume Office Upon Failure of Whom to Serve	Relationship (if any) to Client
1. _____	_____	_____
2. _____	_____	_____
3. _____	_____	_____
4. _____	_____	_____

V.   Miscellaneous

Section A. Advisers

(including accountant, attorney, auto and homeowner's (or renter's) insurance agent, banker, investment counselor, life insurance agent, real estate broker, tax return preparer, trust officer).

Name and Occupation	Address	Telephone Number
1. _____	_____	_____
2. _____	_____	_____
3. _____	_____	_____
4. _____	_____	_____
5. _____	_____	_____
6. _____	_____	_____
7. _____	_____	_____
8. _____	_____	_____
9. _____	_____	_____
10. _____	_____	_____

21st Century Estate Planning:
Practical Applications
2005 Edition

©2005 Sonnenschein Nath & Rosenthal LLP
and Cannon Financial Institute, Inc.

A-22

Section B. Location of Documents, Records and Safe Deposit Box

Item	Location
1. Appraisals	_____
2. Auto Insurance Policies	_____
3. Automobile Titles	_____
4. Balance Sheets and Profit/ Loss Statements	_____
5. Bank Statements and Records	_____
6. Birth Certificates	_____
7. Business Agreements (including Stock Purchase Agreements, Partnership Agreements, etc.)	_____
8. Cemetery Plot Deeds	_____
9. Copies of Closely-Held Corporation Articles of Incorporation and By-Laws	_____
10. Deeds	_____
11. Employee Benefit Plan Contracts and Statements	_____
12. Employment Contracts	_____
13. Financial Records	_____
14. Funeral and Burial Instructions	_____
15. Homeowner's (or Renter's) Insurance Policy	_____

21st Century Estate Planning:
Practical Applications
2005 Edition

©*2005 Sonnenschein Nath & Rosenthal LLP*
and Cannon Financial Institute, Inc.

A-23

Item	Location
16. Income Tax Returns	_____
17. Leases	_____
18. Life Insurance Policies	_____
19. Marriage Certificate	_____
20. Medical Insurance Policies	_____
21. Military Service Record	_____
22. Notes, Mortgages, Deeds of Trust	_____
23. Records Relating to Previous Marriages	_____
24. Safe Deposit Box	_____
25. Safe Deposit Box Key	_____
26. Social Security Cards	_____
27. Stock Certificates, Bonds, etc.	_____
28. Trust Instruments	_____
29. Wills	_____

I hereby certify that the information above is accurate and that you may rely on it without independent verification in drafting and assisting me in implementing an estate plan.

Date_____   _____
                                                    Client

Date_____   _____
                                                    Client

21st Century Estate Planning:
Practical Applications
2005 Edition

©2005 Sonnenschein Nath & Rosenthal LLP
and Cannon Financial Institute, Inc.

A-24

Appendix B
Abbreviations/Acronyms Glossary

A/C	Account
ACCT	Account
AFR	Applicable Federal Rate
AGE	Adjusted Gross Estate
AGI	Adjusted Gross Income
AO	Administrative Officer
BDO	Business Development Officer
CFA	Chartered Financial Analyst
CIF	Collective Investment Fund
CLAT	Charitable Lead Annuity Trust
CLU	Chartered Life Underwriter
CLUT	Charitable Lead Uni-Trust
CRAT	Charitable Remainder Annuity Trust
CRUT	Charitable Remainder Uni-Trust
CTF	Common Trust Fund
DNI	Distributable Net Income
DOD	Date of Death
DOL	Department Of Labor
DRD	Deductions In Respect Of A Decedent
DTC	Depository Trust Company
DTD	Dated
ERISA	Employee Retirement Income Security Act
ERTA	Economic Recovery Tax Act
ESOP	Employee Stock Ownership Plan
FAI	Fiduciary Accounting Income
FDIC	Federal Deposit Insurance Corporation
FMV	Fair Market Value
FSLIC	Federal Savings And Loan Insurance Corporation
FTSO	Full Time Sales Officer
GPA	General Power Of Appointment
GRAT	Grantor Retained Annuity Trust
GRIT	Grantor Retained Income Trust

GST	Generation Skipping Transfer
GSTT	Generation Skipping Transfer Tax
I.V.	Inter Vivos
ILIT	Irrevocable Life Insurance Trust
IO	Investment Officer
IRA	Individual Retirement Account
IRC	Internal Revenue Code
IRD	Income In Respect Of A Decedent
IRS	Internal Revenue Service
LTR	Private Letter Ruling
NRA	Non Resident Alien
OCC	Office Of The Comptroller Of The Currency
PLR	Private Letter Ruling
POA	Power of Attorney
QDOT	Qualified Domestic Trust
QDT	Qualified Domestic Trust
QTIP	Qualified Terminable Interest Property
REIT	Real Estate Investment Trust
Rev. Proc.	Revenue Procedure
Rev. Rul.	Revenue Ruling
RLT	Revocable Living Trust
RRA	Revenue Reconciliation Act
SEC	Securities And Exchange Commission
SEP	Simplified Employee Pension
SIPC	Securities Investor Protection Corporation
T/U/W	Trust Under Will
TAI	Trust Accounting Income
TAM	Technical Advice Memorandum
TAMRA	Technical And Miscellaneous Revenue Act
TEST	Testamentary
TIC	Trust Investment Committee

TRA	Tax Reform Act
U.C.	Unified Credit
UCEEA	Unified Credit Effective Exemption Amount
U/A	Under An Agreement
UPC	Uniform Probate Code

RELEVANT IRS FORMS

IRS Form

SS-4:	Application for federal tax identification number
706:	U.S. estate (and generation-skipping transfer) tax return
706-A:	U.S. additional estate tax return
706 CE:	Certificate of payment of foreign in death tax
706 GS(D):	Generation-skipping transfer tax return for distributions
706 GS(D1):	Notification of distribution from a generation-skipping trust
706 GS(T):	Generation-skipping transfer tax for terminations
706 NA:	U.S. estate (and generation-skipping transfer) tax return (for non-resident aliens)
709:	U.S. gift (and generation-skipping transfer) tax return
709-A:	U.S. short form gift tax return
712:	Life insurance valuation statement
1040:	U.S. individual income tax return
1041:	U.S. fiduciary income tax return
2848:	Power of Attorney and declaration of representative
4768:	Application for extension of time to file U.S. estate (and generation-skipping transfer) tax
4808:	Computation of credit for gift tax
4970:	Tax on accumulation distribution of trusts
4972:	Tax on lump-sum distributions
6123:	Verification of fiduciaries federal tax deposit
6166:	Certification of filing a tax return
7990:	U.S. estate tax certificate of discharge from personal liability
7990-A:	U.S. gift tax certificate of discharge from personal liability

GLOSSARY OF TERMS

A–B Trusts: An estate plan for a married couple where the estate is divided into two trusts, with the "A" trust qualifying for the marital deduction and the "B" trust which uses up the decedent's estate tax unified credit.

Abatement: A reduction of a bequest made in a will due to inadequate estate assets to satisfy the bequests in the will after the debts, taxes and other obligations of the estate have been paid. Usually, all bequests are abated on a proportional basis.

Accumulated Distribution: Trust income that has been accumulated in a trust during a previous year and is distributed to the beneficiaries in a later year and is subject to the throwback rules.

Accumulated Income: Trust income that is not paid out and that is retained in the trust.

Active Trust: A trust in which the trustee has some active duty to perform; to be distinguished from a bare, dry, naked, unfunded, or passive trust.

Ademption: A gift of property in a will that fails because the property is not part of the estate at the time of the decedent's death.

Adjusted Gross Estate: The total value of an estate reduced by all allowable debts and expenses, but before Federal Estate Taxes.

Adjusted Taxable Estate: This is the taxable estate (minus $1,500,000); it is the amount used to determine the federal tax credit for state death taxes.

Administration: The management of a decedent's estate including the payment of expenses, debts, and obligations, and the general settling of the estate.

Administrator/Administratrix: An individual or entity, such as a trust department appointed by a court to settle the estate of a person who has died without leaving a valid will. If the individual appointed is a woman, she is known as an administratix. Also See PERSONAL REPRESENTATIVE.

Administrator Ad Litem: An administrator appointed by the court to act as an administrator in some litigation in which the decedent was a party.

Agency: A term used to describe certain types of accounts in trust institutions. The main distinguishing characteristic of an agency is that the title to the property does not pass to the trust institution but remains in the owner of the property, known as the principal.

Agency Account: Account in which someone acts for another but without acquiring title to assets. The agent acts for a principal and agrees to carry out certain duties with respect to the principal's property.

Agent: A person who acts for another person by the other person's written or oral authority. The distinguishing characteristics of an agent are (1) that he acts on behalf and subject to the control of his principal, (2) that he does not have title to the property of his principal, and (3) that he owes the duty of obedience to his principal's orders.

Alien: A person who is not a citizen of the United States. Can be a resident alien (living in the U.S.) or a nonresident alien.

Alternative Minimum Tax (AMT): The Alternative Minimum Tax is an alternative to the regular income tax assessed including certain "items of tax preference." It was enacted to ensure that corporate and non-corporate taxpayers (including estates and trust), who would not otherwise pay income tax because of certain deductions and exemptions, do not escape completely from paying income tax.

Alternate Valuation: For Federal Estate Tax purposes, the value of the Gross Estate six months after the date of death. If property is distributed, sold, exchanged, or otherwise disposed of within those six months, the value of the property is determined as of the date of disposition. The election to use alternate valuation date can only be made if the amount of Federal Estate Taxes will be reduced. The election is to benefit an estate that holds an asset or assets that decline materially in value during the period immediately following the decedent's death.

Ancestor: One from whom a person had descended, whether a mother or father.

Ancillary: Auxiliary or subordinate to something; used in terms such as "ancillary administration" referring to the administration of an estate or property outside of the state of residence of the decedent.

Annual Exclusion: The amount of property (presently $11,000 or $22,000 for a married couple) that may be given annually to a donee free of gift tax consequences.

Annuity: An amount payable annually, or at regular intervals, according to a contract (i.e., insurance or trust) for either a certain or an indefinite term, usually stated as a number of years or based on life expectancy.

Applicable Credit Amount: See UNIFIED CREDIT.

Applicable Exclusion Amount: The amount of taxable transfers that generate the federal estate or gift tax that is exactly equal to the Unified Credit. $1 million in 2002 & 2003 and $1.5 million in 2004 & 2005. Also known as the Credit Shelter Amount, Credit Equivalent, Applicable Exemption Amount, or Unified Credit Effective Exemption Amount.

Applicable Federal Rate (AFR): The statutory rate that must be charged on most loans and installment agreement to avoid income tax consequences. Each month the Treasury Department determines and publishes a short-term, mid-term and long-term AFR.

Asset: Something of value that is owned and hence can be used for the payment of debts.

Assignment: The transfer of title to personal property from one person or entity to another.

Attorney At Law: A person who is legally qualified to represent and act for clients in legal proceedings; a lawyer. To be distinguished from an Attorney In Fact.

Attorney In Fact: A person who acts for another under written authorization usually to transact business; most often designated in a "Power of Attorney" for property. To be distinguished from an Attorney at Law.

Authorized Investment: Investment specifically authorized by a trust account.

Basis Point: Unit used for measuring change in interest rates and the yield of bonds (equivalent to 0.01%).

Beneficiary: Person or entity entitled to receive benefits from a will, insurance policy, trust agreement or employee benefit plan.

Bequest: A gift of personal property by will; the same as a legacy. Bequests are classified as specific or general. A specific bequest is a gift of a designated class or kind of property: for example, a gift of the deceased's heirloom rug to a named individual. A general bequest is one that may be met from the general assets of the estate. An example would be a bequest of a sum of money without reference to any particular fund from which it is to be paid. Since a specific bequest specifies a particular time to be the subject of the gift, if that item does not exist at the time the gift is to occur, the gift fails.

Breach of Trust: When a trustee or other type of fiduciary violates a fiduciary duty owed to a beneficiary.

Broker: Agent handling the buying and selling of property, such as securities, commodities, real estate, for other people in return for a commission.

Bypass Trust: See CREDIT SHELTER TRUST.

Capital Asset: (1) Property held for the purpose of investment, such as securities or real estate. (2) In business, a capital asset is property (machinery, for example) that is costly and expected to last. Also known as a Fixed Asset.

Capital Gain/Loss: Difference between the amount paid for a capital asset and the amount received when it is sold. A CAPITAL GAIN occurs when more is received than was spent. A CAPITAL LOSS occurs when less is received than was spent.

Capital Gains Distributions: Payments of the profits from investments, usually made annually.

Capital Loss: See CAPITAL GAIN/LOSS.

Cash Flow: Amount of disposable income available to a person or corporation over a given period.

Cash Management: Policy of preventing cash balances from going below zero and of placing extra cash into assets that earn income.

Cash Management Report: Reports showing which trust accounts have uninvested cash and which are overdrawn.

Cash Surrender Value: The cash value of a life insurance policy contract if redeemed prior to death.

Cash Value: Fund built up over time from a portion of the premiums paid on a life insurance policy and available as a loan or an outright cash payment.

Caveat: A challenge to a will offered for probate.

Cemetery Trust: A trust created to insure the upkeep of a grave or cemetery.

CERCLA: See SUPERFUND.

Certified Financial Planner (CFP): Title given by the International Bureau of Certified Financial Planners to someone who has passed certain tests indicating that he or she is competent to analyze and develop financial plans for individuals and businesses.

Charitable Bequest: A gift of personal property to a charity by will.

Charitable Deduction: A deduction allowed for income, estate or gift tax purposes and for a gift to a qualified charitable organization. The federal government allows a charitable deduction for gifts made during lifetime and at death if the gift will be used for religious, educational or scientific purposes.

Charitable Devise: A gift of real property by will to a charity.

Charitable Lead Trust: A trust for a fixed term of years in which a charity is the beneficiary of the income and the remainder or principal at the end of the term is given to a non-charitable beneficiary.

Charitable Remainder Annuity Trust (CRAT): An irrevocable trust in which the grantor names a charity as the remainder beneficiary. The grantor also names a different non-charitable beneficiary (usually the grantor, a spouse or other family) to receive annuity payments of a specific dollar amount from the trust for a period of time. These trusts are usually funded with low cost basis assets because there is no capital gain if the trust sells the asset to invest in something that will produce more income.

Charitable Remainder Trust: A trust for a fixed term of the life of an individual in which the income is paid to a non-charitable beneficiary during the term and the remainder or principal passes to a legal charity upon the termination.

Charitable Remainder Unitrust (CRUT): An irrevocable trust in which the grantor names a charity as the remainder beneficiary. The grantor also names a non-charitable beneficiary (usually the grantor, a spouse or other family member) to receive an annual payment from the trust for a specific period of time. The annual payment is stated in an amount equal to a percentage of the value of the trust based on an annual valuation of the trust assets. These trusts are usually funded with low cost basis assets because there is no capital gain if the trust sells the asset to invest in something that will produce more income.

Charitable Trust: A trust created for the benefit of a community, ordinarily without a definite beneficiary; as, a trust for educational purposes. The same as a public trust, to be distinguished from a private trust.

Chartered Financial Analyst (CFA): Title given someone who has passed three examinations requiring knowledge of accounting, economics and finance and competence in investment and securities analysis and management.

Chartered Life Underwriter (CLU): Title given someone who has reached certain standards of education and proficiency in the uses of life insurance; usually an insurance agent.

Chinese Wall: A policy aimed at protecting confidentiality by forbidding the dissemination nonpublic information to others within the same firm or institution; that comes into the possession of other departments from being used by the trust department in making investment decisions.

Claim: Assertion of a right, such as to have a payment made under an insurance policy.

Claim Against Estate: A demand made upon the estate for liabilities of the decedent or to force some act by the estate as a matter of duty. A common example would be the claim submitted by a creditor for a debt owed him by the decedent at the time of his death.

Class Gift: A gift to members of the same class (i.e. – all children from the same parents).

Clifford Trust: An irrevocable trust running for at least 10 years which provides income to a person other than the grantor. At the end of the income period, the trust terminates and the trust property returns to the grantor; a short-term trust used frequently before the 1986 Tax Reform Act.

Closely-Held Corporation: One whose entire stock is held by one or by a few persons, such as the members of a family.

Codicil: An amendment or supplement to a will. It must be executed with all the formalities of a will.

Co-executor: Individual or entity sharing the duties of executor of a will with another or others.

Collective Fund: Investment fund in which the assets of separate trust accounts have been pooled.

Commingled Fund: A common fund in which the funds of several accounts are mixed.

Commission: Fee charged by someone who buys or sells property for another.

Common Trust Fund: A fund maintained by a bank or a trust company exclusively for the collective investment and reinvestment of money contributed to the fund by the bank or trust company in its capacity as trustee, executor, administrator, or guardian and in conformity with the rules and regulations of the Board of Governors of the Federal Reserve System pertaining to the collective investment of trust funds by national banks, as well as with statutes and regulations.

Community Property: Property acquired during marriage in which both husband and wife have an undivided one-half interest. Not more than 1/2 of community property can be disposed of by a will. There are only nine community property states such as: Arizona, California, Idaho, Louisiana, New Mexico, Nevada, Texas, Washington and Wisconsin (called marital property).

Community Trust: Type of trust comprised of gifts from a number of sources to a trustee or trustees (usually trust institutions) and distributed by a committee of selected citizens for benevolent purposes in a particular community.

Complex Trust: A trust in which the trustee is not required to distribute all of the income to the beneficiaries.

Conditioned Gift: A gift that is subject to conditions specified in a will or trust.

Condition Precedent: A condition that must first happen before the estate depending upon it can vest.

Condition Subsequent: A condition annexed to an estate that has already vested where the failure of, or non-performance of, said condition causes the estate to be defeated.

Confidentiality: Legal situation in which an individual entrusted with the private affairs of another is required to keep such matters secret.

Consanguinity: A blood relationship.

Conservator: Generally, an individual or a trust institution appointed by a court to care for property. Specifically, an individual or a trust institution appointed by a court to care for and manage the property of an incompetent, in much the same way that a guardian cares for and manages the property of a ward.

Constructive Trust: A trust imposed by a court of equity as a means of doing justice, without regard to the intention of the parties. To be distinguished from an express trust and a resulting trust.

Contest of a Will: An attempt by legal process to prevent the probate of a will or to prevent the distribution of property according to the will. Also referred to as a caveat.

Contingent Beneficiary: The beneficiary whose interest is conditioned upon a future occurrence which may or may not take place. Unless or until the condition takes place, the interest is only contingent. To be distinguished from a vested beneficiary.

Contingent Executor: An executor who is named in a will, but who will not act unless the principal executor does not act.

Contingent Interest: A future interest in real or personal property that is dependent upon the occurrence or nonoccurrence of a stated event. Thus, the interest may never come into existence. To be distinguished from a vested interest.

Contingent Remainder: A future interest in property that is dependent upon the occurrence or nonoccurrence of some stated event before the termination of an estate. To be distinguished from a vested remainder.

Contingent Trust: A Trustee who is named in a trust but who will not act unless the principal trustee does not act.

Contribution: Money placed in a pension or profit-sharing plan by a company and/or its employees to pay for future benefits for employees.

Convertible Trust: See STANDBY TRUST.

Corporate Fiduciary: A trust institution serving in a fiduciary capacity, such as executor, administrator, trustee, or guardian.

21ˢᵗ Century Estate Planning:
Practical Applications
2005 Edition

©2005 *Sonnenschein Nath & Rosenthal LLP*
and Cannon Financial Institute, Inc.

B-10

Corporate Trust: A trust created by a corporation, usually to secure a bond issue.

Corporate Trustee: A trust institution serving as trustee.

Corpus: The principal or capital of an estate, as distinguished from the income; the body of assets held in a trust or in an estate.

Court Accounting: Report concerning the handling of an estate or certain types of trust that must be made to a court as a matter of course.

Creator: Person or group establishing a trust.

Credit Equivalent Bypass Trust: See CREDIT SHELTER TRUST.

Credit Shelter Amount: See APPLICABLE EXCLUSION AMOUNT.

Credit Shelter Trust: A taxable trust that is funded with the credit shelter amount. Such a trust is often used to provide benefits to a decedent's surviving spouse, while avoiding inclusion in that spouse's gross estate. Assets in the Credit Shelter Trust will pass to descendants with no further estate taxes. Also known as a bypass trust, credit equivalent trust, unified credit trust, family trust, decedent's trust, "B" trust and various other names.

Crummey Power: A limited power of withdrawal from an irrevocable trust that ordinarily lapses within a specified period of time. Because of the limited power of withdrawal, a trust beneficiary has a present interest over property transferred to the trust and the grantor is allowed to secure an annual exclusion allowing trust management of the property for the benefit of the beneficiary. Usually associate with an Irrevocable Life Insurance Trust. (ILIT)

Crummey Trust: A trust where the beneficiaries have a limited power of withdrawal. The withdrawal is typically limited to the amount excludable from gift tax under the annual exclusion.

Curtesy: A common law principal giving a husband a life estate in the property of his deceased wife. To be distinguished from Dower.

Custodian: Individual or entity whose duty is to hold, protect and account for property in its care; a person who holds property for a minor under the Uniform Gifts to Minors Act or Uniform Transfers to Minors Act.

Custody Account: An agency account concerning which the main duties of the custodian (agent) are to safe keep and preserve the property and to perform ministerial acts with respect to the property as directed by the principal. The agent has no investment or management responsibilities. To be distinguished from a managing agency account and a safekeeping account.

21st Century Estate Planning:
Practical Applications
2005 Edition

©*2005 Sonnenschein Nath & Rosenthal LLP*
and Cannon Financial Institute, Inc.

B-11

Cy-pres Doctrine: Cy-pres (pronounced Sigh-prey) means "as nearly as may be." This is a common law doctrine that provides where a testator makes a gift for a charitable purpose that cannot exactly be carried out, the court will directs that the gift be made as nearly as possible in conformity with the intention of the donor.

Death Taxes: A term used to describe estate taxes, inheritance taxes, and other succession or transfer taxes arising at death.

Decedent: A person who has died.

Declaration of Trust: An acknowledgment, usually but not necessarily in writing, by one holding or taking title to property, that he holds the property in trust for himself or for the benefit of someone else, and that he acts as a fiduciary.

Deed of Trust: A writing that transfers property to a trustee.

Deemed Transferor: The parent of the transferee most closely related to the grantor. A parent related to the grantor by blood or adoption is deemed closer than one related by marriage. This relationship is important in understanding the taxation of generation-skipping transfers.

Deferred Annuity: Annuity that begins payment on a specified date in the future; for example, at retirement.

Defined Benefit Plan: Retirement plan provided by an employer that guarantees an employee definite retirement income, usually based on a formula that takes years of service and salary level into account. A pension plan, for example, is a defined benefit plan.

Defined Contribution Plan: Type of retirement plan set up by an employer that does not commit the employer to a set level of contributions but instead ties contributions to the employer's profit levels. Contributions are usually based on a formula, either discretionary or mandatory. A profit-sharing plan is a defined contribution plan.

Depletion: The consumption or wasting away of property (i.e. – oil wells, timberland and other assets than can be exhausted.)

Descendant: All persons who have descended from a common ancestor. Generally includes adopted persons when used in a will or trust.

Descent: Passing of real property by to the heirs of a person who dies intestate.

Devise: A gift of real estate by will. To be distinguished from bequest.

Direct Skip: A generation skipping transfer by gift or at death to a skip person or to a trust where all the beneficiaries are skip persons.

21ˢᵗ Century Estate Planning:
Practical Applications
2005 Edition

©2005 Sonnenschein Nath & Rosenthal LLP
and Cannon Financial Institute, Inc.

B-12

Directed Account: Type of account where the trust institution buys and sells securities only at the discretion of the customer or of a third party designated by the customer.

Disclaimer: A renunciation of a person's right to property.

Discretionary Payment: Payment of income or principal from a trust to a beneficiary that is completely at the discretion of the trustee. Discretionary payments are usually made for special needs, such as medical or educational needs.

Discretionary Powers: Power given to a trustee or executor to base action or inaction on his sole judgment.

Dispositive Provisions: The provisions of a will or trust to the disposition and distribution of property to be distinguished from administrative provisions which relate to the handling of property while it is in the hands of the executor or trustee.

Distribution in Kind: A distribution of specific property from an estate as opposed to a cash distribution equal to the valve of the property.

Distributable Net Income (DNI): Basically, all of the taxable income of a trust or estate.

Distributee: A person to whom something is distributed; frequently applied to the recipient of personal property under intestacy. To be distinguished from heir - a person who inherits real property.

Distribution Committee: Group that determines which organizations will receive money, and how much, from a charitable trust or fund.

Distributive Share: Share an individual receives from the assets of an estate.

Diversification: Purchasing a variety of investments in a way to reduce risk and not be dependent on the "ups and downs" of any one particular kind of investment.

Dividend: (1) Cash, securities or other property that each stockholder of a corporation receives when declared in proportion to the number of shares of stock he or she owns. (2) Return of part of the premium of an insurance policy; paid out of the profits of the insurance company.

Dividend Rate: Amount per share of a dividend

Dividend Reinvestment Plan: Arrangement under which dividends from stocks or investment funds are used to buy more shares of the stock or fund instead of being distributed in cash.

Domicile: An individual's permanent legal and intended home. A person can have multiple residences, but only one domicile.

21st Century Estate Planning:
Practical Applications
2005 Edition

©*2005 Sonnenschein Nath & Rosenthal LLP*
and Cannon Financial Institute, Inc.

B-13

Donee: The recipient of a gift. The term can also refer to the recipient of a Power of Appointment.

Donor: One who makes a gift. The term can also refer to the person who grants a Power of Appointment to another.

Dower: A common law principal giving a wife a life estate in the property of her deceased husband.

Durable Power of Attorney: A power of attorney that will remain valid if the person who grants the power becomes incapacitated.

Dynasty Trust: A trust typically found in states that have done away with the rule against perpetuities that is intended to be in existence for perpetuity. Normally, the trust takes advantage of the GST exemption so the trust property will not be subject to transfer tax. Also known as a Perpetual Trust.

Election: The choice of an alternative right such as the right of a widow to take the share of her deceased husband's estate to which she is entitled under the law, despite a contrary provision in the will.

Eminent Domain: A government's power to take private property for public necessity by paying the property owner reasonable compensation.

Employee Benefit Plan: Plan established or maintained by an employer for the purpose of providing certain benefits to employees, such as medical, insurance or retirement benefits. Assets of such a plan are usually placed in an employee benefit trust account.

Employee Benefit Trust Account: See EMPLOYEE BENEFIT PLAN.

Employee Retirement Income Security Act (ERISA): A federal law passed in 1974 that protects the rights of employees who are in pension or profit-sharing or certain other employee benefit plans of a corporation and that also regulates the conduct of plan trustees.

Employee Stock Ownership Plan (ESOP): Type of employee benefit plan in which the employees can buy shares of the company for which they work.

Equitable Apportionment: A legal doctrine that requires the recipients of probate and non-probate assets to all pay their proportionate share of death taxes. This can be overridden by a tax clause in a will or trust.

21ˢᵗ Century Estate Planning:
Practical Applications
2005 Edition

©2005 Sonnenschein Nath & Rosenthal LLP
and Cannon Financial Institute, Inc.

B-14

Equitable Title: When the rights and responsibilities created by ownership of property are, in appropriate circumstances, separated, one who continues to have the right to benefit of property is said to have equitable title, while one who assumed the responsibilities of managing the property is said to have legal title.

ERISA: An acronym for the Employee Retirement Income Security Act of 1974. See EMPLOYEE RETIREMENT INCOME SECURITY ACT.

Escheat: Assignment of property to the state because there is no verifiable legal owner, such as an heir.

Escrow: Money, securities, instruments, or other property deposited by two or more persons with a third person, to be delivered on a subject matter of the transaction (the money, securities, instruments or other property) is the escrow; the terms upon which it is deposited with the third person constitutes the escrow agreement; and the third person is termed the escrow agent.

Estate: The real and personal property of a decedent; a specific interest in property, i.e. a life estate.

Estate Freeze: An estate planning technique typically used when an owner of a closely held business wants to prevent his interest in the business from increasing for estate tax purposes. Typically, there is a stock recapitalization where the owner exchanges common stock for preferred stock that will not increase in value and the common stock is given to younger members in the family. A gift is the purest form of freeze.

Estate Planning: Process of arranging for the preservation of one's property during one's lifetime and for the transfer of one's property at death. The term is usually associated with tax-saving and investment management strategies. Directions are usually contained in a will or trust agreement.

Estate Settlement: Process of completing all the tasks necessary to the winding up and distribution of an estate by an executor (personal representative).

Estate Tax: A transfer tax imposed on a decedent's estate as such, and not on the distributive shares of the estate or on the right to receive the shares; to be distinguished from an inheritance tax. The tax rate was the same as the tax rate on gift transfers until 2004 when the estate tax went from $1 million to $1.5 million. In 2005 it remains at $1.5 million on the amount over the exemption equivalent.

Estate Trust: A trust that qualifies for the marital deduction since all trust assets pass to the surviving spouse's estate at his or her death.

Ex-Dividend Date: Date on and after which the buyer of a stock will not receive a declared dividend. Instead, that dividend will go to the previous owner (the seller), who was the stockholder of record.

21ˢᵗ Century Estate Planning:
Practical Applications
2005 Edition

©2005 Sonnenschein Nath & Rosenthal LLP
and Cannon Financial Institute, Inc.

B-15

Executor/Executrix: An individual or a trust institution nominated in a will and appointed by a court to settle the estate of the testator. If a woman is nominated and appointed, she is known as an executrix.

Executor De Bonis Non: An individual or entity nominated in a will to take over and settle the estate if the executor originally appointed cannot complete, or has failed to complete, the settlement of the estate.

Exemption Equivalent: See APPLICABLE EXCLUSION AMOUNT.

Express Trust: A trust stated orally or in writing, with the terms of the trust definitely prescribed. To be distinguished from a resulting trust and a constructive trust.

Failure of Issue: Absence of lineal descendants because of death or nonexistence.

Fair Market Value (FMV): The value at which estate property is included in the gross estate for Federal Estate Tax purposes. The price at which property would change hands between a willing seller and a willing buyer, neither being under any compulsion to buy or sell and both having knowledge of all the relevant facts.

Family Trust: See CREDIT SHELTER TRUST.

Federal Estate and Gift Tax: A unified transfer tax levied on the transfer of property or gifts during life or at death.

Fee Simple: The largest or most complete ownership interest or estate in real property a person can have.

Fee Simple Ownership: Property ownership where one person or entity holds the entire property interest.

Fee Tail: Common law principal where an estate is limited to a person and the heirs of his body. Most states have abolished fee tails and convert them to fee simple interests.

Fiduciary: An individual or entity in a position of trust who has accepted the duty of acting for the benefit of another. Some examples of fiduciary relationships are a guardian and his ward, an attorney and his client, one partner and another partner and a trustee and a beneficiary.

Fiduciary Income Tax Return: The IRS Form 1041 that must be filed each year by the executor or administrator of an estate or the trustee of a trust.

"Five by Five" Power: A non-cumulative general power of appointment where the donee can, in each calendar year, appoint or withdraw the greater of $5,000 or 5% of the value of the trust at

21ˢᵗ Century Estate Planning:
Practical Applications
2005 Edition

©2005 Sonnenschein Nath & Rosenthal LLP
and Cannon Financial Institute, Inc.

B-16

the end of the year. The lapse of the power is not a taxable gift and has no estate tax consequences.

Fixed Asset: See CAPITAL ASSET.

Forced Heir: One who cannot be disinherited due to law. Forced heirship is found in some foreign countries and can be a reason why a person will set up an offshore trust.

Formula Clause: A provision in a will or trust which directs that property or assets be first placed in a Credit Shelter Trust up to the remaining Unified Credit Equivalent before the rest is placed in the Marital Trust. The purpose of the clause is to lower federal estate tax.

Foundation: An entity established by donations for a charitable, religious, educational or other benevolent purpose.

Funded Insurance Trust: An insurance trust in which, in addition to life insurance policies, cash and securities have been placed in trust to provide sufficient income for the payment of insurance premiums and other charges.

Future Interest: The postponed right to use or enjoy property in the future after some date or after the happening of some event.

General Power of Appointment: A power to direct the disposition of property. The donee may exercise the power in favor of any person, including himself, his estate, his creditors, or the creditors of his estate. Example: "A" creates a trust in which "B" has the power to dispose of the property in favor of any one he sees fit, including himself, his estate, and his creditors.

Generation-Skipping Transfer Tax (GSTT): A tax imposed on any Generation-Skipping Transfer by gift or otherwise of over $1.5 million to a family member two or more generations below the donor. The tax is at a flat rate equal to the maximum federal estate tax rate applicable at the time of transfer. An example would be the tax applied to a gift made by a grandparent to a grandchild.

Generation-Skipping Transfer (GST): A transfer that is subject to federal generation-skipping tax. There is an exemption that is adjusted for inflation and the tax is imposed at the maximum estate tax rate.

Gift (for Gift Tax purposes): Property, property rights or interests transferred to another for nothing or for less than adequate and full consideration in money or money's worth.

Gift Splitting: A provision allowing a married couple to treat a gift made by one of them to a third party as having been made one-half by each, provided it is consented to by the other on a Gift Tax return. For example, a husband can give $22,000 to each of his children and the gift can be considered to be a gift from both the husband and wife in the amount of $11,000 from each.

21ˢᵗ Century Estate Planning:
Practical Applications
2005 Edition

©2005 Sonnenschein Nath & Rosenthal LLP
and Cannon Financial Institute, Inc.

B-17

Gift Tax: A federal transfer tax assessed on gifts when the total lifetime value of the gifts exceed the lifetime exclusion amount of $1 million. The tax rate was the same as the tax rate on estate transfers until 2004 when the estate tax went to $1.5 million.

Gift Tax Marital Deduction: A deduction allowed for a gift made by one spouse to another. Outright gifts and life estates qualify for the deduction if the donee has the right to the income from the property for life and a general power of appointment over the principal. Certain qualified terminable interest gifts also qualify. The amount of the deduction is unlimited.

Grantee: A person to whom property is transferred. One to whom a grant is made.

Grantor: A person who transfers property. The creator of a trust.

Grantor Retained Annuity Trust (GRAT): An irrevocable trust where the grantor typically puts income producing assets into the trust and retains the right to fixed payments form the trust for a period of years or a lifetime. At the end of the period, the assets pass to the beneficiaries.

Grantor Retained Income Trust (GRIT): An irrevocable trust where a grantor typically puts a residence (or tangible personal property) into a trust and retains the right to live in the residence or use the property for a term of years. At the end of the period, the trust assets will pass to the beneficiaries.

Grantor Retained Unitrust (GRUT): An irrevocable trust where a grantor typically puts income producing assets into the trust and retains the right to a fixed percentage of the trust's value for a term of years. At the end of the period, the assets pass to the beneficiaries.

Grantor Trust: A trust where the grantor retains such control over the income, corpus or both that the grantor is considered the owner of the trust for income tax purposes.

Gross Estate: The total value of all property in which a deceased had an interest at the time of death and which must be included in his or her estate. This is the value of the estate before debts, taxes, expenses and other liabilities have been deducted.

GST Exemption: An exemption from Generation Skipping Transfer Tax that allows all transfers up to the aggregate amount to pass without GST tax. $1,500,000 in 2005.

Guardian: An individual or entity appointed by a court to care for a minor or incompetent person's property or the person or both. In some states the term committee, conservator, curator, or tutor is used to designate one who performs substantially the same duties as a guardian.

Guardian ad Litem: A person appointed by a court to represent and defend a minor or an incompetent in connection with a court proceedings.

21st Century Estate Planning:
Practical Applications
2005 Edition

©2005 Sonnenschein Nath & Rosenthal LLP
and Cannon Financial Institute, Inc.

B-18

Hanging Power: A power of withdrawal that will lapse only when and only to the extent that the lapse will not result in a release of a general power of appointment.

Heir: A person who inherits property when a person dies without a will.

Heir At Law A person entitled by law to inherit all or part of an estate from an ancestor who died without a valid will.

Holographic Will: A will entirely in the handwriting of the testator. Not valid in all states.

Immediate Beneficiary: (also called present beneficiary and primary beneficiary) A beneficiary of a trust who is entitled to receive immediate benefits from the trust property, whether or not limited to income; opposed to ultimate beneficiary.

Implied Trust: A trust created by operation of law or by judicial construction; to be distinguished from an express trust which is created by oral or written language.

Inclusion Ratio: The ratio used to calculate the amount of an asset transferred in a direct skip that is subject to GSTT.

Income: A gain usually measured in money. Examples of income are rent, interest, dividends, profits, and royalties.

Income Beneficiary: The beneficiary of a trust who is entitled to receive the income from it.

Incompetent: A person who is legally incapable of managing his own affairs because of a mental deficiency.

Individual Retirement Account (IRA): An account to which a person can make annual tax deductible contributions up to a specified limit. Withdrawals made from the account before an individual reaches age 59 1/2 are taxed and penalized.

Inheritance Tax: A tax levied by the county of a person who inherits. The tax rate depends on the size of the inheritance and the relationship between the person who inherits and the deceased. To be distinguished from an estate tax.

Institutional Investor: Organization such as a bank, college, insurance company or pension fund that invests assets as a regular and significant part of its activities.

Insurance Trust: A trust that owns or is the beneficiary of life insurance policies.

Intangible Property: Property that has no marketable value itself but merely represents something of value. Examples are stock certificates or a deed to property; to be distinguished from tangible property.

21st Century Estate Planning:
Practical Applications
2005 Edition

©2005 Sonnenschein Nath & Rosenthal LLP
and Cannon Financial Institute, Inc.

B-19

Inter Vivos: Between the living; from one living person to another.

Inter Vivos Trust (Living Trust): A trust created during the grantor's lifetime. It operates during the grantor's lifetime as opposed to a testamentary trust, which does not operate until the grantor dies.

Intergenerational Succession: Property is transferred from one generation to another, usually from an older generation to a younger one.

Intestacy: The condition resulting from a person's dying without leaving a valid will.

Intestacy Laws: State laws that determine how a person's property passes to his heirs if he dies without a valid will.

Intestate (adj.): Not having made and left a valid will. **(noun):** A person who dies without leaving a valid will.

Intestate Succession: Distribution of property to heirs of the deceased according to state law because the deceased did not leave a valid will.

Inventory: An itemized listing or statement of the property, goods or valuables in an estate and their estimated worth made by an executor or administrator.

Investment Adviser: Individual or institution that provides professional advice about investing money and charges a fee or commission for the service.

Investment Advisory Account: An investment account where the financial institution provides specific recommendations, based on the customer's goals and circumstances, but takes action only with the customer's approval.

Investment Management Account: An investment account where the financial institution is authorized to make purchases and sales on a customer's behalf and provides reports of account transactions on a regular basis.

Investment Objectives: Stated needs or goals of an investor, such as long-term growth, immediate income or preservation of purchasing power.

Investment Policies: General guidelines observed by a trust institution when selecting investments for its customers.

Investor (s): Person or group putting money into securities, real estate, commodities or other assets for the purpose of obtaining an income or profit.

Irrevocable: Cannot be terminated or revoked.

21st Century Estate Planning:
Practical Applications
2005 Edition

©2005 Sonnenschein Nath & Rosenthal LLP
and Cannon Financial Institute, Inc.

B-20

Irrevocable Trust: A trust that, by its terms, cannot be revoked by the grantor. To be distinguished from a revocable trust.

Issue: Persons who have descended from a common ancestor. Also referred to as descendants.

Joint Ownership: Shared ownership of property by two or more persons or groups. See also COMMUNITY PROPERTY; JOINT TENANCY; TENANCY BY THE ENTIRETY; TENANCY IN COMMON.

Joint Tenancy: An ownership of property by two or more parties so that when one dies, the survivor or survivors take the entire property (right of survivorship).

Joint Will: A single document that is meant to serve as the will of a husband and wife.

Keogh Plan: Type of retirement plan for self-employed persons and their employees set up under legislation passed in 1962 known as H.R. 10.

Key Person Insurance: A type of insurance for the protection of a business against financial loss stemming from the death or disability of an individual in the business who possesses skills or expertise considered vital (a key employee).

Kiddie Tax: A tax imposed on the unearned income of a minor child under the age of fourteen before the close of the taxable year and who has at least one living parent. All unearned income over the statutory amount will be taxed to the child at the parent's marginal tax rate.

Kin: Persons of the same family; related by blood.

Land Trust: Arrangement for holding real property in which one or more trustees has title to the property and manages it for the benefit of a named beneficiary or beneficiaries. Beneficiary rights are represented by a certificate that is considered personal property akin to a stock certificate.

Lapse: The termination of a right or privilege due to a failure to exercise it.

Last Will and Testament: A formal term referring to a Will. Under Old English law, a "will" was a disposition of real estate and a "testament" was a disposition of personal property. This difference is no longer recognized.

Lateral Succession: Succession in property ownership where property is transferred between members of the same generation.

Laws of Descent: Laws governing the descent of real property from a descendent to his heirs.

Layered Trust: Trusts created to minimize the effect of GSTT where an independent trust is created for the benefit of only one generation.

21ˢᵗ Century Estate Planning:
Practical Applications
2005 Edition

©2005 Sonnenschein Nath & Rosenthal LLP
and Cannon Financial Institute, Inc.

B-21

Legacy: Legally, a gift of personal property by will. Usually referred to as a bequest in today's usage.

Legatee: A person who receives a gift of personal property by will.

Letters of Administration: A certificate of authority issued to an administrator by the probate court to settle a particular estate. To be distinguished from letters testamentary.

Letters Testamentary: A certificate of authority issued to an executor by the probate court; to settle an estate to be distinguished from letter of administration.

Leverage: Using borrowed funds in a financial venture in order to increase the potential for gain.

Liability: 1) Legal responsibility for something. 2) Something owed to someone else; a debt.

Lien: An encumbrance on property for the payment of debt.

Life Beneficiary: Usually refers to the beneficiary of a who will remain a beneficiary only during his or her own life, but can also refer to a person who will remain a beneficiary during the term of another person's life.

Life Insurance Trust: See INSURANCE TRUST.

Life Interest or Life Estate: An interest that a person has in property which is enjoyed only during life, his or her lifetime, or another's lifetime. No possession of such ownership rights may be transferred during life or at death.

Life Tenant: The person who receives the income from a legal life estate or from a trust fund during his own life or that of another person. Often referred to as the income beneficiary.

Limited Liability Company (LLC): A type of business entity that has the liability protection of a corporation, but that is taxed as a partnership for income tax purposes. There are members and managers rather than shareholders and directors.

Limited Partnership: Investment arrangement where general partners, or a professional management team, provides planning and decision-making ability and expertise, and where a group of investors simply invest capital and makes no management decisions. The investors, called limited partners, have no liability risk other than their capital contribution.

Limited Power of Appointment: A special power granted to a donee that is limited in scope. Also called a special power of appointment. To be distinguished from a general power of appointment.

21st Century Estate Planning:
Practical Applications
2005 Edition

©2005 Sonnenschein Nath & Rosenthal LLP
and Cannon Financial Institute, Inc.

B-22

Lineal Descendent: A person in the direct line of descent such as a child or grandchild.

Liquid Assets: Cash or assets that can be readily converted into cash without any serious loss. Examples: cash, money market (FDIC) funds, T-Bills, bank accounts, CDs.

Liquidity: (1) Condition in which assets can be easily and quickly converted to cash, or bought and sold. (2) Condition of having sufficient cash to pay debts or to take an obligation.

Living Trust: A trust that becomes operative during the lifetime of the grantor; opposed to a trust under will or testamentary trust. Also known as an inter vivos trust.

Living Will: A written document that a person uses to declare which death-delaying medical treatments should not be used in the event of a serious injury or terminal illness.

Load: Sales charge added to the price of a share in a mutual fund.

Loss: See CAPITAL GAIN/LOSS.

Lump-Sum Distribution: Payment to an individual from an employee benefit plan that is made all at once rather than in installments.

Marital Deduction: The part of an estate that may be passed to a surviving spouse without becoming subject to the Federal Estate Tax. Under current law, the deduction is unlimited and there is no tax when assets pass to a surviving spouse. However, in no event may the deduction exceed the net value of the property passing to the surviving spouse in a qualifying manner.

Marital Property: Property acquired during a marriage in which each spouse possesses a property interest at death or at some other termination of the marriage, e.g. divorce.

Marital Trust: A trust consisting of property that qualifies for the marital deduction.

Market Value: See FAIR MARKET VALUE.

Merger of Title: When all beneficial interests in and following a trust become owned by one person (or group of persons) by sale, gift or operation of law, equity will cause the ownership interest to merge and the trust will terminate.

Minimum Fee: Lowest amount for which an individual or institution will perform a given service. Trust institutions charge a minimum fee for handling trust accounts.

Minor: A person who is under the legal age to be considered an adult by law. In some states, the legal age is 18 but in most states it is 21.

Minority Discount: A discount allowed when valuing a closely held stock or limited partnership interest due to lack of liquidity or lack of control.

21st Century Estate Planning:
Practical Applications
2005 Edition

©2005 Sonnenschein Nath & Rosenthal LLP
and Cannon Financial Institute, Inc.

B-23

Mortality Table: Tables established by actuaries to determine life expectancies of average people.

Mutual Fund: Investment company that uses the money it raises by selling shares in it to purchase diversified selection of the securities of other companies and/or of governments.

Mutual Wills: Separate wills, usually created by spouses, containing similar provisions in favor of each other.

Natural Guardian: A guardianship that refers to a parent's natural right to guard the person of his or her child.

Net Income with Makeup Charitable Remainder Unitrust (NIMCRUT): A NIMCRUT is a CRUT with a provision that says to pay the noncharitable beneficiary each year the lessor of (1) a percentage of the value of the trust assets for the year or (2) the net income of the trust in the year. A NIMCRUT also provides that if there is a shortfall in the percentage that should be paid out to the beneficiary, the shortfall can be made up in a subsequent year from income earned in excess of the percentage value that should be paid out each year.

Next of Kin: In the law of descent and distribution, the persons in the nearest degree of blood relationship to a decedent who will be entitled by law to personal property when there is no will; to be distinguished from heirs who inherit real property.

NIMCRUT: See NET INCOME WITH MAKEUP CHARITABLE REMAINER UNITRUST.

Nomination: The naming or proposal of a person for an office, position, or duty. To be distinguished from appointment. The testator nominates the executor under a will but the court appoints the executor.

Nominee: A person named for an office, position, or duty; in trust business, usually the person, firm, or corporation in whose name registered securities are held.

Non-Liquid Assets: Assets that are not readily convertible into cash without the possibility of serious loss. Examples: real estate, business interest, art objects, bonds.

Notice to Creditors: Notice to creditors of an estate to make all claims of debt to the executor or administrator and notice to debtors to pay all debts to an estate usually run in the newspaper that is the legal organ (paper) for the county where the decedent was domiciled.

Non-probate Property: Property passing outside the administration of the estate. It passes other than by will or intestacy laws. Examples: jointly held property, life insurance proceeds payable to a named beneficiary, property in an inter vivos trust. (Living Trust)

21st Century Estate Planning:
Practical Applications
2005 Edition

©2005 Sonnenschein Nath & Rosenthal LLP
and Cannon Financial Institute, Inc.

B-24

Nuncupative Will: An oral will made on one's death bed before witnesses and later reduced to writing and offered for probate.

Obligee: The person to whom someone else is obligated under a contract or a bond; a promisee.

Obligor: A person who is obligated to another under a contract or a bond; a promisor.

Option: Right to buy or sell specified property, such as securities or commodities, at a specified price within a specified period of time.

Order of Distribution: An order by a probate court for the estate to distribute the estate's property to those entitled to it.

Over-The-Counter Market (OTC): Buying and selling of securities that are not listed on a stock exchange. In the over-the-counter market, buyers and sellers trade directly with each other or through brokers.

Participant: Employee, or former employee or beneficiaries of same, who are or may become eligible to receive benefits from a given employee benefit plan.

Participant Record Keeping: Figuring out and keeping track of the interests of the various participants in an employee benefit plan.

Partnership: An association of two or more persons to carry on a business for profit. A partnership is not subject to taxation itself and acts as a conduit to the partners as all gains and losses are passed on to the partners.

Partition: A judicial division or separation of the ownership interest of joint property owners or tenants in common so that each may take possession, enjoy and control his or her share of the property.

Passive Trust: A trust where the trustee has no active duties to perform, and acts mainly as a titleholder. It is the same as bare, dry, or naked trust. To be distinguished from an active trust.

Pecuniary Bequest: A bequest of a specific amount of money.

Pecuniary Legacy: A gift of money by will.

Pension Payment: Amount paid regularly to a retired person by a former employee, usually for life.

Pension Plan: Formal arrangement providing for the accumulation of funds from an employer, an employee organization or both to be used for periodic payments to employees after retirement.

21ˢᵗ Century Estate Planning:
Practical Applications
2005 Edition

©2005 *Sonnenschein Nath & Rosenthal LLP*
and Cannon Financial Institute, Inc.

B-25

Pension Trust: Type of trust established by an employer to provide benefits for incapacitated or retired employees.

Per Capita (by the head): A term used in the law of the decent and distribution of property to refer to a distribution of equal amounts to persons as individuals as opposed to persons as members of a family (per stirpes).

Permanent Insurance: Any form of life insurance except term insurance. Permanent insurance develops cash value and includes whole life, endowment, universal life and variable life insurance.

Personal Effects: Personal items of property such as clothes and jewelry.

Personal Property: All property other than real property.

Personal Representative: A general term applicable to the person who is in charge of a decedent's property, usually refers to an executor or an administrator.

Personalty: Personal property.

Per Stirpes (by the root): A term used in the law of the decent and distribution of property to refer to a distribution to persons as members of a family and not as individuals (per capita). If a parent is not living at the time of distribution his or her children take what the parent would have been entitled to.

Pooled Income Fund: A fund of money created by more than one donor where the donors retain an income interest and a charity is given the remainder interest.

Pooled Investment Fund: Collective investment fund used for employee benefit trust accounts.

Portfolio Manager: Person who handles the assets of a managed account, fitting stated investment policy to the needs of the account by deciding what and when to buy and sell.

Posthumous Child: A child born after his or her father's death. To be distinguished from an after born child.

Power of Appointment: Right conferred by one person upon another in a will or deed of trust to determine who will receive the benefit of property owned by the first person.

Pour-over: A term referring to the transfer of property from one estate to another estate or to a trust, which takes place at death or some other event. For example, property that is disposed of by a pour-over will is poured into an existing trust at death.

Power: Authority or right to do or to refrain from doing a particular act, as a trustee's power of sale or a power to withhold income. To be distinguished from trust powers.

21st Century Estate Planning:
Practical Applications
2005 Edition

©2005 Sonnenschein Nath & Rosenthal LLP
and Cannon Financial Institute, Inc.

B-26

Power of Alienation: Power to transfer property as to assign property.

Power of Appointment: A right given to a person to dispose of property which he does not own. A power of appointment may be general or limited. A general power allows the donee to exercise the right to appoint as he or she sees fit. A limited power (also known as a special power) limits the donee's power of appointment to some special group of people. An example of a limited power of appointment is a wife's power to appoint among her children as she sees fit.

Power of Attorney: A document authorizing the person named therein to act as an agent, called an Attorney In Fact, for the person signing the document. If the attorney in fact is authorized to act for his principal in all matters, he has a general power of attorney; if he has authority to do only certain specific things, he has a special or Limited Power of Attorney. If the authority granted in the power of attorney survives the disability of the principal, the attorney in fact has a Durable Power of Attorney. If the authority granted in the power of attorney commences in the future only upon the occurrence of a specific event or contingency, the power of attorney is known as a springing power.

Power of Retention: A power found in a will or trust document allowing the trustee to keep certain investments or assets in a trust even though said investments or assets would not ordinarily be appropriate to be held in a trust.

Precatory Language: Wording in a will requesting some action or inaction, but not demanding it. The language is instructive as to intent, but does not direct a specific action.

Preemptive Right: Right or privilege of a person or group to do or have something before others do or have it.

Premium: (1) Payment for an insurance policy. (2) Amount by which a security sells for or is redeemed for above its par, or face, value. (3) Fee paid to the seller of an option.

Pretermitted Child: A child who is not mentioned in a parent's will without any express statement in the will that the child is being excluded.

Primary Beneficiary: The same as an Immediate Beneficiary. To be distinguished from a secondary beneficiary.

Principal: 1. One who employs an agent to act for him. 2. One who is primarily liable on an obligation. 3. The part of an estate other and apart from the income from the property. Also known as capital or corpus.

Principal Beneficiary: The same as an Ultimate Beneficiary or Remainder Beneficiary.

Private Foundation: In general, this term refers to a charitable foundation that does not derive substantial support from the public.

21st Century Estate Planning:
Practical Applications
2005 Edition

©2005 Sonnenschein Nath & Rosenthal LLP
and Cannon Financial Institute, Inc.

B-27

Private Placement: Selling of securities directly to an investor or a small or private group of investors.

Probate: The process of proving the validity of a will in court and executing its provisions under the guidance of the court. When a person dies, the will may be filed before the proper officer of the proper court, giving the court jurisdiction in the matter of enforcing the document. This is called "filing the will for probate." When the will has been filed, it is said to be "admitted to probate." The process of probating the will involves recognition by the court of the executor named in the will (or appointment of an administrator if none has been named), the filing of proper reports and papers as required by law, determination of validity of the will if it is contested, and distribution and final settlement of the estate under the supervision of the court.

Probate Court: The court that has jurisdiction with respect to wills and intestacies and sometimes guardianships, adoptions, etc. Also called court of probate, surrogate's court, ordinary court, orphan's court and prefect's court.

Probate Estate: See PROBATE PROPERTY.

Probate in Common Form: Probate of a will in an informal proceeding without notice to all interested parties.

Probate in Solemn Form: Probate of a will in a formal proceeding after notice has been given to all interested parties.

Probate Property: Property that passes from a decedent under the terms of a will. If there is no will, the property passes under state intestacy laws.

Probate of Will: Formal proof before the proper officer or court that the instrument offered is the last will of the decedent.

Profit-Sharing Plan: Arrangement in which employees receive a share of the net profits of a business. In a deferred, or retirement, profit-sharing plan, each employee has a share of the net profits set aside for his or her use as a retirement benefit.

Property: Anything of value owned by a person or group.

Prudent Investor Rule: A term applied to a rule laid down by statute or by judicial decision that requires a fiduciary, such as a trustee, to invest and manage all trust funds as would a prudent investor under like circumstances, taking into account risk management and investment diversification. It is a modern adaptation of the Prudent Man Rule.

Prudent Man/Person Rule: A term applied to a rule laid down by statute or by judicial decision that requires a fiduciary, such as a trustee, to invest and manage all trust funds as would a prudent man under like circumstances. A lesser standard than the Prudent Investor Standard.

21ˢᵗ Century Estate Planning:
Practical Applications
2005 Edition

©2005 Sonnenschein Nath & Rosenthal LLP
and Cannon Financial Institute, Inc.

B-28

Public Administrator: A government official whose job is to settle the estate of a person who dies intestate.

Put Option: Contract giving its owner the right to sell specified property, particularly securities and commodities, at a specified price within a specified time.

Qualified Domestic Trust (QDOT): A trust created upon the death of an individual and qualifying for the Federal Estate Tax Marital Deduction where the decedent's surviving spouse is not a United States citizen. A qualified domestic trust is the only form of transfer that will qualify for the marital deduction for a decedent who leaves an alien spouse. In addition to satisfying the normal marital deduction rules, the trust instrument must require that at least one trustee be an individual who is a citizen of the United Sates or a domestic corporation, and that no trust distributions may be made without the consent of that trustee. An appropriate election of the estate tax return is also required.

Qualified Plan or Trust: Employee benefit plan that meets the requirements for favorable federal tax treatment.

Qualified Terminable Interest Property (QTIP): A terminable interest that will qualify for the marital deduction if an appropriate election is made by the donor or executor. In order to be QTI property, the surviving spouse must be entitled to all of the income of the property during the spouse's life and no person, including the spouse, may have the right to appoint the property to anyone other than the spouse during the spouse's life. The major benefit of a QTIP marital trust to a grantor is that, at the surviving spouse's death, the remaining trust property is not subject to a general power of appointment in the spouse, but instead passes to beneficiaries selected by the grantor.

Real Property: Land and/or the buildings and other fixed improvements on the land.

Record Date: Date on which a shareholder or bondholder must still be registered on the books of a corporation or public bond issue in order to receive cash or shares or to be able, among other things, to vote on company affairs.

Remainder Beneficiary: The beneficiary of a trust who is entitled to the principal outright after the prior life beneficiary or other prior beneficiary has died or his interest has been terminated.

Remainder Interest: A future interest that comes into existence after the termination of a prior interest. For example: A creates a testamentary trust under a will in which the principal is to be retained with income paid to B until B's death, at which time the principal (remainder interest) will be given to C.

Remainderman: The person who is entitled to an estate after the prior estate has expired.

21st Century Estate Planning:
Practical Applications
2005 Edition

©2005 Sonnenschein Nath & Rosenthal LLP
and Cannon Financial Institute, Inc.

B-29

Residuary Estate: The property that remains after the testator has made provision out of his net estate for specific and general gifts.

Residue: Property that remains after any bequests have been made and debts and expenses have been paid.

Resulting Trust: A trust which results in law from the acts of the parties, regardless of whether they intend to create a trust, as when a person disposes of property under circumstances which raise an inference that he does not intend that the person taking or holding the property shall have the beneficial interest in it. To be distinguished from an express trust and a constructive trust.

Reversionary Interest: A right to future enjoyment by the transferor of property that is now in the possession or enjoyment of another party. For example: A creates a trust under which a parent, B, is to enjoy income for life, with the principal of the trust to be paid over to A at B's death. A's interest is a reversionary interest.

Reversionary Trust: A trust limited to a specified term of years or for the life of the beneficiary, at the end of which period the trust is automatically terminated and the trust property is returned to the grantor.

Revocable: Capable of being recalled or revoked.

Revocable Trust: A trust that by its terms may be terminated by the settlor or by another person. To be distinguished from an irrevocable trust.

Revocation: The act of annulling, terminating, or making inoperative a will or a trust instrument usually in writing.

Rollover Individual Retirement Account (Rollover IRA): An Individual Retirement Account that is permitted to accept more than the defined annual IRA contribution because the source of the contribution is an employer's qualified retirement plan or another IRA.

Rollover IRA: See ROLLOVER INDIVIDUAL RETIREMENT ACCOUNT.

Royalty: Payment made to the person or organization granting a copyright, patent, lease of land containing natural resources or similar right by the person or organization receiving use of that right.

Securities and Exchange Commission (SEC): Agency of the federal government that regulates the securities business.

Securities Investor Protection Corporation (SIPC): Private insurance corporation created by Congress in 1970 to provide financial protection for the customers of securities brokers and dealers in the event of the bankruptcy or liquidation of the brokers or dealers.

21st Century Estate Planning:
Practical Applications
2005 Edition

©2005 Sonnenschein Nath & Rosenthal LLP
and Cannon Financial Institute, Inc.

B-30

Security: (1) Anything given, deposited or pledged to ensure the fulfillment of an obligation. (2) Evidence of debt or of property, such as a bond or stock certificate.

Self-Employed Retirement Plan: See KEOGH PLAN.

Settle, To: (1) To complete an exchange of money or assets between buyer and seller. (2) To meet all claims on an estate and make all required distributions. (3) To establish certain types of property arrangements, frequently by establishing a trust.

Settlor: A person who creates a trust, such as a living trust, to become operative during his lifetime. Also called donor, grantor, and trustor.

Shareholder: Person or group holding one or more shares of stock in a corporation.

Simplified Employee Pension (SEP): A retirement plan arrangement in which an employer provides retirement benefits by contributing to IRA's set up for each employee. Contributions are made according to a formula and may exceed the usual IRA contribution limit.

Simultaneous Death: The death of two or more people under such circumstances that the order of death cannot be proved.

Single Premium Life Insurance: Life Insurance policy purchased with just one payment.

Special Administrator: An administrator appointed by the court to take over and safeguard an estate pending the appointment of an executor or administrator. Sometimes known as a temporary administrator or as a curator.

Special Guardian: A guardian appointed by the court for a particular purpose connected with the affairs of a minor or an incompetent; sometimes a guardian ad litem is known as a special guardian.

Special Use Valuation: Valuation of family-owned farms or other business operations involving real estate based on actual use rather than highest and best use for estate tax purposes. An executor may elect special valuation if a variety of conditions are met, and they intend to ensure that the qualifying special use of the property continues after the decedent's death.

Specific Bequest: Gift in a will of specific amount(s) of money and/or specific articles(s) of personal property to a certain heir or heirs.

Spendthrift Provision: A provision in a trust instrument which limits the right of the beneficiary to dispose of his interest, as by assignment, and the right of his creditors to reach it, as by attachment.

21st Century Estate Planning:
Practical Applications
2005 Edition

©*2005 Sonnenschein Nath & Rosenthal LLP*
and Cannon Financial Institute, Inc.

B-31

Spendthrift Trust: A trust in which the interest of a beneficiary cannot be assigned or disposed of by him or attached or otherwise reached by his creditors.

Split Gift: A gift made by a husband or wife to a third person may be treated as having been made one-half by each if the other spouse consents to the gift.

Sprinkling or Spray Trust: A trust under which the trustee is given discretionary powers to distribute any of the income or principal among beneficiaries in equal or unequal shares.

Standby Trust: A living trust that allows the creator to continue to manage the trust fund until he or she directs the trustee to take over (usually in the event of illness or disability). Often referred to as a *convertible trust.*

Stock Dividend: Stock a corporation issues instead of paying a cash dividend. Each stockholder receives a certain percentage of the number of shares he or she already owns.

Stock Exchange: Central trading place or national market place in which orders to buy the securities of a list of companies meeting certain financial requirements are matched with orders to sell.

Stockholder: See SHAREHOLDER.

Street Name Securities: Securities held in the name of a broker instead of the name of the actual owner.

Subchapter S Corporation: An election available to a corporation to be treated as a partnership for income tax purposes. To be eligible to make the election, a corporation must meet certain requirements as to kind and number of shareholders, classes of stock, and sources of income.

Superfund: Popular name for the Comprehensive Environmental Response, Compensation, and Liability Act ("CERCLA"), the primary Federal environmental liability law.

Surety Bond: Sum of money put up by one person to guarantee that an act will be carried out or a debt paid by another person. If the act is not carried out, or if the debt is not paid, the bond is forfeited.

Tangible Property: Property that can be touched or realized with the senses, such as a chair. To be distinguished from intangible property.

Tax-Exempt: Not subject to a given tax or taxes.

Tax Return: Form showing the amount of taxes due and the calculations used to derive this amount.

T-Bill: See TREASURY BILL.

21ˢᵗ Century Estate Planning:
Practical Applications
2005 Edition

©2005 Sonnenschein Nath & Rosenthal LLP
and Cannon Financial Institute, Inc.

B-32

T-Bond: See TREASURY BOND.

Temporary Administrator: A fiduciary appointed by the court to administer the decedent's estate for a short period of time until an executor or administrator can be appointed.

Tenancy: Period of a tenant's possession or occupancy of real property.

Tenancy by the Entirety: Ownership of property by a husband and wife so that property may not be disposed of during life by either husband or wife without the other's consent. Upon death, the property goes to the survivor (right of survivorship).

Tenant: A person who possesses or occupies real property.

Tenancy in Common: Ownership of property by two or more persons so that each has an undivided interest which at the death of one is passed by will to the deceased's heirs. (It does not pass automatically to the surviving tenants in common).

Term Insurance: Type of life insurance lasting a specified number of years and providing no money to the insured person if he or she survives the stated period.

Terminable Interest: An interest in property that terminates upon the death of the holder or on the occurrence of some contingencies.

Testamentary: Pertaining to a will.

Testamentary Capacity: Mental capacity to make a valid will.

Testamentary Disposition: The passing of property by will. A testamentary document is one disposing of property at the death of the testator.

Testamentary Trust: A trust established by the terms of a will.

Testate: One who has made and left a valid will. To be distinguished from one who is intestate.

Testator: A man who has made and left a valid will at his death.

Testatrix: A woman who has made and left a valid will at her death.

Thrift Plan: Type of employee benefit plan that matches savings by employees with money from the employer.

Throwback Rule: A rule found at IRC §§ 665-667 that was substantially repealed under Taxpayer Relief Act of 1997 with certain exceptions. Under the rule, a distribution of accumulated trust income was thrown back to be taxed the same way the distribution would have been taxed if it had been made when the income tax was earned.

21ˢᵗ Century Estate Planning:
Practical Applications
2005 Edition

©2005 Sonnenschein Nath & Rosenthal LLP
and Cannon Financial Institute, Inc.

B-33

Title: Legal right to ownership of property.

T-Note: See TREASURY NOTE.

Totten Trust: Trust created by deposit of a person's money in his own name as trustee for another. Title is vested in the trustee owner, who during his life, holds it in a revocable trust for the named beneficiary. At the death of the trustee owner a presumption arises that an absolute trust was created for the beneficiary for the balance of the trust assets at the time of death of the owner. The trust assets are, however, included in the gross estate of the trustee for Federal Estate Tax purposes.

Transaction Fees: Amounts charged for handling different types of transactions; for example, buying or selling securities.

Transfer Tax: A tax imposed on the transfer of property from one to another.

Transferee: The person or entity to which something has been transferred.

Transferor: The person or entity who transfers something to another.

Treasury Bill (T-Bill): Security issued by the U.S. Treasury Department at a discount and redeemed at face value, thus paying a kind of interest; matures in a year or less.

Treasury Bond (T-Bond): Security issued by the U.S. Treasury Department that pays interest every six months and matures in more than seven years.

Treasury Note (T-Note): Security issued by the U.S. Treasury Department that pays interest every six months and matures in one to seven years.

Treasury Securities: Securities issued by the U.S. Treasury Department. Such securities are low-risk investments because they are backed by the U.S. government. Treasury securities include bonds, notes, and savings bonds.

Trust: A fiduciary relationship with respect to property in which one person (the trustee) is the holder of the legal title to property (the trust property) and is subject to an obligation to keep or use the property for the benefit of another (the beneficiary).

Trust Accounting: Record of a trust account, showing its debits, credits to income, credits to principal, asset holdings and asset transactions; may have to be submitted to a court or beneficiaries by the trustee.

Trust Administrator: A person who works for a trust institution who has the responsibility for clients' trust accounts and who handles the direct dealings with grantors and beneficiaries.

Trust Agreement: A written agreement setting forth the terms of a trust.

21st Century Estate Planning:
Practical Applications
2005 Edition

©*2005 Sonnenschein Nath & Rosenthal LLP*
and Cannon Financial Institute, Inc.

B-34

Trust Assets: Things of value owned by a specific trust.

Trustee: A person or entity that holds the legal title to property in the trust for the benefit of someone else.

Trust Fund: Specifically, money in a trust account; more generally, all the income-producing assets in a trust.

Trust Instrument: Any writing under which a trust is created.

Trust Investment Committee: Group of officials of a trust institution responsible for overseeing investments in managed trust accounts and conducting regular reviews of such accounts.

Trustor : Person who creates a trust. See also GRANTOR.

Trust Powers: Authority from the government granted to an institution in its charter that allows it to engage in the trust business.

Trust Under Will: A trust created by a valid will, which will become active only on the death of the testator.

Unfunded Insurance Trust: An insurance trust that is not provided with cash and/or securities to pay the life insurance premium. Premiums are paid by someone other than the trustee, and the proceeds are received by the trust at death of the insured.

Undivided Interest: The interest or right in property owned by each joint tenant or tenant in common. Each tenant has the equal right to use and enjoy the entire property.

Undue Influence: Influence that a person exercises over another to the point that the other person cannot make a decision using his own free will, such as the decision of when to make a will and who to leave property to.

Unified Credit (Against Estate Tax): A credit of up to a specific dollar amount that is applied to reduce the Federal Estate Tax otherwise due. The credit is $555,800 in years 2004 & 2005 and increases until 2009 after which the tax is repealed.

Unified Credit Effective Exemption Amount: The equivalent in gross dollars that the Unified Credit effectively exempts from taxation. The UCEEA is $1,500,000 in 2004 & 2005, increasing until 2009 after which the tax is repealed. Also called, credit equivalent, applicable exclusion amount.

21st Century Estate Planning:
Practical Applications
2005 Edition

©2005 Sonnenschein Nath & Rosenthal LLP
and Cannon Financial Institute, Inc.

B-35

Uniform Gifts to Minors Act (UGMA): A Uniform Act adopted by most states that provides for the transfer of property (usually stocks and bonds) to a minor and where the designated custodian has the right to act for the minor with being appointed a guardian. It is more restrictive than the UTMA.

Uniform Principal and Income Act: State law establishing the rules for determining how transactions by a trustee affect income and principal in an account.

Uniform Simultaneous Death Act: A Uniform Act adopted by many states that provides that each person is presumed to have survived the other for purposes of testamentary distribution of property if both die at the same time.

Uniform Transfer to Minors Act (UTMA): A Uniform Act adopted in many states to replace the UGMA that allows the custodian to have the right to act for the minor with having to be appointed guardian. It is less restrictive than the UGMA.

Unique Asset: Asset, like jewelry or an insurance policy, which is usually held in only one trust or estate.

U.S. Fiduciary Income Tax Return: Income tax return designed specifically for trust accounts.

Valuation: The process of determining the value of property. When a person dies, his or her property must be gathered together and valued (usually at the date of death) in order to determine estate tax liability.

Variable Annuity: An annuity contract whose periodic payment depends upon some uncertain outcome, such as stock market performance.

Vested Interest: Fixed or established right to property when specified conditions have been met. Typically, for example, a participant's interest in an employer-funded retirement plan becomes vested only when certain length-of service requirements have been met.

Vested Interest: A present, fixed right of possession or enjoyment of property. To be distinguished from a contingent interest.

Vested Remainder: A fixed right of possession or enjoyment of property that is postponed or delayed until some future date or event. To be distinguished from a contingent remainder.

Vesting: Conferring upon an employee the right to benefits from an employee benefit plan because he or she has met certain requirements, such as length of service.

Ward: Person under some kind of guardianship because he or she is considered unable to take care of himself or herself, either because of some physical or mental incapacity or because he or she is a minor.

21st Century Estate Planning:
Practical Applications
2005 Edition

©2005 Sonnenschein Nath & Rosenthal LLP
and Cannon Financial Institute, Inc.

B-36

Wasting Asset: An asset that is exhausted or used up, and that loses value over time, such as an oil well.

Will: A legally enforceable declaration of a person's wishes regarding matters to be attended to after his death and inoperative until his death. A will usually, but not always, relates to the testator's property, is revocable (or amendable by means of a codicil) up to the time of his death, and is applicable to the situation that exists at the time of his death.

21st Century Estate Planning:
Practical Applications
2005 Edition

©2005 Sonnenschein Nath & Rosenthal LLP
and Cannon Financial Institute, Inc.

B-37

APPENDIX C
INDEX

C

U

V

W

Workplace Individual Retirement Plans

Z

Zeroed-Out GRAT